P9-COO-915

PROGRAMMING LANGUAGE STRUCTURES

ELLIOTT I. ORGANICK
ALEXANDRA I. FORSYTHE
ROBERT P. PLUMMER

ACADEMIC PRESS
New York
San Francisco
London
A Subsidiary of Harcourt Brace Jovanovich, Publishers

Cover sculpture by Miriam Brofsky

Cover photo by Terry Lennon

ACADEMIC PRESS, INC.
111 Fifth Avenue, New York, New York 10003

United Kingdom Edition published by
ACADEMIC PRESS, INC. (LONDON) LTD.
24/28 Oval Road, London NW1

ISBN: 0-12-528260-5
Library of Congress Catalog Card Number: 78-51655

PRINTED IN THE UNITED STATES OF AMERICA

To

BETTY BLANCHARD ORGANICK

for typing (and retyping) so much of our manuscript with accuracy and enthusiasm, and for her patience and cordiality during the six-year-long pursuit of our goals.

CONTENTS

PART ONE

1 Basic Concepts 2

1-1 Introduction 2
1-2 Flowcharts for structured programming 7
1-3 A computer model 21
1-4 Procedures and environments 26
Executing procedure calls and returns 27
1-5 Global and local variables 40
1-6 The state of the MC 50
Section summary 54
1-7 References and suggestions for further reading 55

2 Interfacing Procedures 56

2-1 Introduction 56
2-2 Reference parameters 62
2-3 Independence and interchangeability of procedures 74
2-4 Automating protection of arguments 77
2-5 Expressions as arguments in a procedure call 89
2-6 Function procedures 93
2-7 Name parameters 101
Name parameters matched to simple arguments 104
2-8 Parameters that stand for procedures or functions 107
Chapter summary 112
2-9 References and suggestions for further reading 121

3 Recursion 122

3-1 Introduction 122
3-2 Additional examples 145

3-3 Tree traversal and recursion 149
3-4 Binary tree traversal 167
3-5 Symbolic differentiation—an application of binary tree traversal 170
3-6 The searching of arbitrary tree structures 173
3-7 References and suggestions for future reading 183

4 Syntax Formalism **184**

4-1 Introduction 184
4-2 The BNF notation 184
4-3 Syntax charts 189
Summary 191
4-4 References and suggestions for further reading 191

PART TWO. SYNTAX AND SEMANTICS OF SEVERAL MAJOR PROGRAMMING LANGUAGES

5 ALGOL **195**

5-1 Introduction 195
5-2 Syntactic structure of Algol-like languages 195
5-3 Syntactic structure of ALGOL 60 202
Summary 206
5-4 Syntax of ALGOL declarations and statements 208
5-5 Semantics of ALGOL blocks 216
Block entry 216
Exit from a block 219
5-6 Semantics of ALGOL procedures 220
Procedure entry 221
Procedure return 223
Name parameters in ALGOL *224*
5-7 Case studies—two elementary examples 226
Discussion 227
5-8 Case studies of recursive functions—two examples 249
5-9 Name parameters matched to expressions 272
5-10 Parameters that are procedures 288
5-11 Own identifiers in ALGOL 305
5-12 References and suggestions for further reading 307

7-5 Avoiding evaluation of arguments: The use of the quote 392
7-6 The Lisp interpreter 394
7-7 Overview of Lisp syntax and semantics 395
7-8 The syntax of LISP and RLISP 398
7-9 Predefined functions of Lisp 412
7-10 Arithmetic operations in Lisp 416
7-11 Case studies 417
7-12 Function arguments and procedure parameters 431
7-13 Case study 4: A program for symbolic differentiation 444
7-14 Achieving the effect of name parameters in Lisp 461
7-15 References and suggestions for further reading 463

8 Snobol **464**

8-1 Introduction 464
8-2 A flowchart language for string processing operations 465
8-3 Snobol syntax 471
1. Assignment 473
2. Pattern match 474
3. Procedure calls 479
8-4 Storage structures for variables 480
8-5 Syntax and semantics of procedure declarations and calls 482
8-6 Snobol case study: Symbolic differentiation 489
8-7 Simulating reference parameters in Snobol 499
8-8 Conversion from one data type to another 502
8-9 Defining and using new data types 504
8-10 Defining the primitive functions of Lisp in Snobol 507
8-11 Tables and arrays in Snobol 512
8-12 A Fortran preprocessor in Snobol 517
8-13 References and suggestions for further reading 518

9 Multisequence Algorithms **519**

9-1 Introduction 519
9-2 Two types of multisequencing: Asynchronous tasks and coroutines 520
9-3 Case study for asynchronous tasking 523
Results using Burroughs ALGOL *533*
9-4 Case studies for coroutine tasks 540
Water-sharing problem 541
Snapshots for coroutine environments 546

6 Fortran 308

6-1 Introduction 308
6-2 Overview of Fortran syntax and semantics 309
Summary 312
6-3 Global variables in Fortran 312
6-4 Syntax of individual Fortran statements and program units 319
6-5 Case study 336
Discussion 337
6-6 New developments in Fortran 340
6-7 Additional case studies 342
Discussion (case 2) 342
Discussion (case 3) 357
6-8 Input/output in Fortran 366
6-9 A brief comparison of ALGOL and Fortran 370
1. Block structure and dynamic storage allocation 370
2. Explicit versus implicit declarations 372
3. Separate compilability of procedures 372
4. Input/output 373
5. Compound and conditional statements 373
6. Algebraic nature of the languages 375
6-10 References and suggestions for further reading 375

7 Lisp

7-1 Introduction 376
7-2 Data objects in Lisp 377
1. Lists 378
2. Binary trees 379
7-3 Storage structures for S-expressions 381
1. Atoms 381
2. S-expressions 381
3. Variables 384
4. Storage management 384
7-4 The five basic Lisp functions 385
1. CONS *385*
2. CAR *387*
3. CDR *387*
4. ATOM *389*
5. EQ *389*

Producer/consumer problem 548
Chapter summary 549
9-5 References and suggestions for further reading 557

10 Pascal **560**

10-1 Introduction 560
10-2 Primitive data types 561
Constant definitions 562
10-3 Structured data types 563
Records 563
Record structure variants 565
Arrays 568
Set structures 568
Pointer types 570
10-4 Program structure 572
10-5 Constructs for structured programming 576
10-6 Parameter specification and treatment 577
10-7 Input/output 580
Sequential Pascal summary 583
10-8 Case study: The four-color problem 597
10-9 References and suggestions for further reading 610

Appendix **612**

Bibliography **618**

Answers to Selected Exercises **621**

Index **649**

PREFACE

In their initial contact with computer programming, many students have been exposed to only one programming language. This book is designed to take such students further into the subject of programming by emphasizing the structures of programming languages. The book introduces the reader to five important programming languages, Algol, Fortran, Lisp, Snobol, and Pascal, and develops an appreciation of fundamental similarities and differences among these languages. A unifying framework is constructed that can be used to study the structure of other languages, such as Cobol, PL/I, and APL.

The book also has other objectives. For instance, it illustrates several of the tools and methodologies needed to construct large programs. Because similar interpreter structures and methods of data structuring and accessing are used to model not only programming languages but also computers, the book indirectly prepares the student to study computer organization. Working programmers whose everyday jobs confine them to a single language can use this book for self-study and gain a better perspective on the tools they now use.

By emphasizing semantics over syntax, this book differs significantly from conventional programming language texts. The *semantics* or meaning of a program can be studied by means of a snapshot sequence produced by an abstract machine-interpreter that executes the program. The semantics of a programming language can be understood (informally) by studying the semantics of a representative set of case study programs. A *snapshot* is a data and control structure that displays the state of a computation. The snapshots, or *contour diagrams*, of this book are drawn in a uniform style, clearly delineating the distinctive control structures and data structures of each language. Other diagramming conventions such as *call trees* and flowcharts are used in the exposition of semantics.

The first three chapters develop the state transition semantic framework and diagramming principles that define an abstract model of a computer. In later chapters the model is applied to describe five specific programming languages. All of these, Algol, Fortran, Lisp, Snobol, and Pascal, were developed between 1955 and 1975.

The same 20-year period saw the development of other important languages such as Cobol, APL, Basic, and PL/I, although space considerations prevent their inclusion in this book. The principles and techniques required to describe those languages, however, are similar to the ones used here for Algol, Fortran, and Lisp. Any serious reader should be able to apply the methods to study other languages and teach them to students. Thus, if an instructor wants to teach the elements of Cobol semantics using the approach of this book, he can use Fortran (Chapter 6) as a guide, since the control structures of Cobol closely match those of Fortran. In the same way, APL semantics can be explained using Lisp (Chapter 7) as a guide, since APL control structures and scoping rules are similar to those of Lisp.

The particular languages in this book were selected for comparative linguistic study because each uses a different set of rules to define the scopes of variables and procedures, and different means to treat procedure parameters. Such rules define the control structure of a language. Other language concepts and features such as pattern matching, concurrent tasks and coroutine structures, data typing, and data structure management are discussed in terms of particular languages or language extensions. These features imply variants of the abstract model of language semantics. The view is taken that one can best comprehend the semantics of a programming language, at least informally, by understanding the abstract model that enforces the control structure of the language.

More recently, other programming languages have come on the scene, such as SIMULA 67, CONCURRENT PASCAL, and Modula, and experimental versions of Alphard and CLU. Not only do these languages allow the programmer to define data types (as Snobol and Pascal do), but they also allow *abstract* data types. This facility makes possible greater clarity and modularity in programs. The snapshot diagramming techniques described in this book will, in all probability, prove as useful in explaining the semantics of the newer languages as they have been in explaining the languages in this book. Another edition or a companion volume may be required later to do justice to this claim.

A Simplifying Theme

"Computations are characterized in terms of the data structures to which they give rise during execution. . . . Programming languages may be syntactically described in terms of the data structures required for their representation and may be semantically described in terms of the data structures which they generate during execution" [Peter Wegner (1971)].

Ten years ago the proliferation of programming languages caused many people to foresee the development of a computer-age Babel where, in total ignorance of every other language, each programmer would learn only his own chosen language. That unhappy situation has not occurred for several reasons. First, effective efforts have been made to standardize particular languages such as Fortran and Cobol. It should be pointed out that pragmatic rather than scientific considerations motivated this standardization movement. However, the second reason that Babel has been averted is that computer scientists have begun to apply the scientific method to organize the classification, comparison, and appreciation of various programming languages.

Due to the efforts of McCarthy (1962), Landin (1964), Strachey (1966), Wegner (1968), and others who provided insight into operational models of computation, we can now evaluate programming languages in terms of a unifying view of *computation structures.* Semantics and the expressive power resulting from modularity can now be studied in terms of the data structures and the accessing paths to them established during the execution of the control statements of the language.

Statements that invoke procedure entry, function entry, coroutine resumption, and block entry are intended to produce a shift of context, that is, to redefine the data structures accessible to the processor. On the other hand, procedure return, function return, and block exit are steps specifying the restoration of an earlier context. The declaration of a variable, a procedure, or a new data type is essentially a rule to allocate or restructure the workspace. These rules are clearly language-dependent, and so is the time at which such allocation and restructuring takes place. Allocation steps cause establishment of access paths and these paths may result in the sharing of data. Another kind of declaration is the specification of a parameter. This, too, can be interpreted as a space allocation rule and may result in the establishment of a new access path for the processor.

In this book we have concentrated on explaining the structures of programming languages in terms of data structures and accessibility concepts. What was previously regarded as a difficult and complex subject is now, we think, becoming a set of simple unifying ideas, concepts, and principles. The pedagogy and display methods used here derive from the pioneering work of John B. Johnston, designer of the Contour Model (1971), and others like Daniel Berry (1971) and Peter Wegner (1971), who were among the first to suggest how to apply the Contour Model to explain the semantics of a variety of programming languages. This book builds on the contributions of these individuals.

The Book in More Detail

The book may be thought of as divided into three parts. Part one, the first four chapters, introduces the basic concepts and models for understanding syntax and semantics. Part one would be a good review if the text were used in an upper division or first-year graduate course for students who come to computer science from other disciplines. Part two (next four chapters) provides the heart of the book, the intimate understanding of the comparative semantics, and secondarily the comparative syntax, of the four "mutually orthogonal" language types: Algol, Fortran, Lisp, and Snobol. Part three, the last two chapters, is intended to illustrate some of the more recent directions in language design—not a complete overview but more of a teaser to convince the student there is much more to learn. Multisequence control structures typified by asynchronous tasks and coroutines are dealt with in Chapter 9. Data structure and data management issues are introduced in Chapter 10.

The first chapter of this text summarizes the relevant concepts and principles about algorithms, flowcharts, and computation that a student is expected to know from the first course. But that is by no means all that the first chapter accomplishes: it carefully introduces flowchart notation used consistently throughout the text (but not regarded as critical to the study) and, more importantly, introduces the abstract machine interpreter and the basic snapshot diagramming conventions. Thus although Chapter 1 might appear to be unnecessary for students whose first course has enabled them to become capable programmers in a particular language, such as Basic or Fortran, we regard the first chapter as important, especially for students not accustomed to top-down decomposition, the design of algorithms with well-documented flowcharts, or the use of an abstract interpreter for understanding the meaning of an algorithm.

Chapter 2 is an in-depth introduction to the semantics of procedure and function call, and to argument–parameter matching with various kinds of parameters. The use of contour diagrams clarifies the subtle distinctions between procedures and functions, and emphasizes the differences between globals and parameters as a means of information sharing among procedure modules.

Recursion was once regarded as a difficult concept in programming semantics, but through the medium of the contour and the call-tree diagram, recursion becomes easy to understand and to treat in some depth. In Chapter 3 recursion is looked at as a process closely related to tree traversal. In later chapters it appears again in terms of the distinctive semantics of Algol, Lisp, and Snobol. In each case *snapshot sequences* and *call trees* are used to trace what happens at key places in the execution of a recursive procedure.

Chapter 4 introduces the essential ideas of syntax formalism (for context-free languages). Backus–Naur Form and Syntax Chart representations are used.

Chapter 5 covers ALGOL 60 but the first part of the chapter deals with the general idea of block structuring. Six case study programs are presented to reinforce the reader's understanding of ALGOL 60 semantics of procedure declaration, block and procedure entry and exit, and parameter treatment.

Fortran, as covered in Chapter 6, includes not only the primary syntactic and semantic structures based on the 1966 ANSI Standard FORTRAN, but also highlights several of the innovations introduced in the new 1977 Standard. Three case study programs reinforce understanding of Fortran semantics of subprograms, parameters, and COMMON blocks. There is also a brief introduction to input–output format. The chapter ends with a general discussion comparing Fortran with ALGOL 60.

Knowing how to describe recursion effectively turns out to be a key to understanding the semantics of an expression-based (functional) language like Lisp. Lisp recursion presents no high hurdle for a student who has already studied recursion in Chapter 3 and ALGOL 60 recursion in Chapter 5. To introduce Lisp in Chapter 7 it is sufficient to emphasize its data structures rather than its control structures. Thus Lisp is presented as a language to manipulate binary tree data rather than a language to process lists.

We deemphasize the unfriendly syntax of McCarthy's LISP 1.5 by first presenting a functional subset of RLISP, A. C. Hearn's (1968) version of Lisp having an Algol-like syntax. (RLISP is available on a variety of computers.) In our threefold attack on the problem of teaching Lisp, control structures are displayed by contour diagrams and call trees; evolving data structures are drawn as binary trees rather than as S-expressions, and the easy-to-learn syntax of RLISP is used. Conventional Lisp syntax is also presented.

Chapter 8 is a survey of SNOBOL 4 emphasizing the pattern matching features, the data management and procedure semantics, and the capability of defining and using new data types. Juxtaposing the chapters on Snobol and Lisp offers the student a good opportunity to compare and contrast the simplicity of Lisp with the expressive power of Snobol. Even without full understanding, one can become aware of some of the trade-offs between these factors.

Chapter 9 is an introduction to the concepts of multitasking and coroutine structures using Burroughs EXTENDED ALGOL as the language vehicle for the case studies. Contour diagrams are again very useful to clarify the semantics of these new features.

Both Chapters 9 and 10 assume the reader has already studied ALGOL 60 (Chapter 5). Chapter 10, therefore, introduces Pascal as a departure from Algol, enabling the reader to quickly encounter Pascal's important (new) data structure definition facilities which are the focus of attention here. A major worked example coded in the dialect SEQUENTIAL PASCAL is discussed and displayed at the end of the chapter.

Place of This Text in the Computer Science and Engineering Curriculum

This text has grown out of our experience in teaching two types of courses at the University of Utah: (1) the second of a four-quarter undergraduate sequence for computer science majors; and (2) a senior/graduate course for nonmajors whose only previous exposure to computer science is a freshman-level course in programming.

The first quarter of the four-quarter sequence emphasizes algorithms, flowcharts, and top-down problem solving, but also includes elementary concepts of procedures such as might be covered in a beginning Fortran, Basic, or Cobol programming course. An elementary but extendable model of computation is used. This model is comparable to the one given in Chapter 1 of this book.

The second quarter, represented by this book, provides the informal introduction to the linguistics of programming. Deferred until later quarters are the formal methods for defining the syntax and semantics of programming languages, syntax analysis, and semantics of abstract machine interpreters.

At Utah most of this text is covered in ten weeks. In addition, students carry out computer laboratory exercises and experiments in two or three languages. We want students to practice with important, unfamiliar languages; at Utah this means Algol and Lisp. At other schools Chapters 6 through 10 could be used as guides to help instructors prepare supplemental class notes in other languages or dialects locally available.

Experience has convinced us that the first set of laboratory exercises should be designed to provide practice with parameter passing and simple recursion. Later exercises can confirm an understanding of specific language features or build more comprehensive programs possibly involving serious use of recursion. Since students need not be encouraged to become expert programmers in any one language, they may be able to complete up to six such exercises in ten weeks.

An instructor who uses this text in a full semester course of fifteen weeks has the pleasant option of treating the subject either in greater depth or greater breadth. For instance, a comprehensive programming project may be assigned to give students in-depth acquaintance with one of the languages covered in this text. Or, one or more other languages may be surveyed. The student may find it a stimulating challenge to apply the structuring concepts of this book to the understanding of a rich but unfamiliar language, such as Cobol, APL, Simula, or Modula.

Acknowledgments

We were unusually fortunate to receive a wide range of valuable and candid criticism from some 15 specialists who read parts or all of our manuscript. Many were anonymous referees, and we thank them sincerely. Others included experts whose help we sought directly. In particular, we gratefully acknowledge the suggestions offered by Allen Ambler, Daniel Berry, Victor Basili, Daniel Friedman, Narain Gehani, Robert Graham, and David Hanson. Daniel Berry's help was invaluable. He offered useful comments on practically every page of two consecutive "final drafts."

We did our best to respond to as many major and minor suggestions as possible. Inevitably, some of the suggestions seemed to us mutually exclusive or implied extending the content of the book or raising its level beyond what we felt was practical. We sincerely hope all the reviewers are pleased with the final product.

We also received considerable help from student assistants at the University of Utah during the years in which the manuscript evolved from crude "handouts" to almost sensible course notes. These helpful and patient people included D. Bourek, M. S. Dye, R. A. Frank, and J. W. Thomas. The support of our other colleagues and students at Utah and the typists, especially Karen Evans and Carol Brown, is gratefully acknowledged as well. We also thank the editorial and production staffs of Academic Press who appreciated our teaching goals and cooperated with us fully to achieve the graphic styling and clarity we believed essential.

E. I. Organick
A. I. Forsythe
R. P. Plummer

PART ONE

1 BASIC CONCEPTS

1-1 INTRODUCTION

Having completed an introductory course in computer science you are probably eager to pursue your programming practice using the language emphasized in that first course. Certainly the desire to improve your programming competence with the tools you started to use makes sense, especially if your job picture includes working full or part time while you continue your education. In this text, however, we deliberately depart from this obvious objective in order to acquire an overview of additional languages. We attempt to explain why this overview of other languages is a good idea.

Initially any high-level language can be understood in terms of the syntactic facilities it provides, such as statement types, data types, operator types, and the rules for forming valid expressions. The more fundamental understanding of a programming language that is required for real expertise in its use, however, can be gained only from a knowledge of its *semantics,* which defines the meaning or effect of executing programs. The semantics of a language is built on concepts and abstractions that can be understood in terms of a machine model executing programs written in that language.

Similarly, several high-level languages can be distinguished only superficially if the comparison is made primarily on syntactic features. For a more fundamental view of the similarities and differences among languages, a comparison of their respective semantics is essential. Since any semantics can be easily understood in terms of a computer model, the study of programming languages should begin with a careful consideration and comparison of the computer models for the respective languages.

The analogy with the appreciation and use of natural language should be clear. We acquire a new perspective regarding our own (native) language (English, say) when we study one or more foreign languages (such as French or German). In studying the underlying structures of other languages we come to notice and appreciate the structures of our own language and begin to make better use of them. The lesson implied here is that to learn even one programming language well, one needs to study it in comparison with several others. Many computer scientists subscribe to this analogy and believe the implied lesson to be sound.

For this reason we propose a study of several programming languages, chosen not for reasons of popularity, but because their respective semantics include distinct features, because together their features embody the semantics of most current programming languages, and because such a study illuminates some of the issues involved in selecting a language for a particular application or systems program. These languages are Algol, Fortran, Lisp, and Snobol, and there is at least one reason to consider each of them important.

Various features in these languages have been simplified, copied, and/or extended in particular dialects and in newer languages. Thus, Basic can be regarded as a simplified Fortran, and PL/I was intended to be a blend of certain features of Fortran, Algol, and Cobol. Algol, in particular the version called ALGOL 60, has perhaps had a stronger influence than any other programming language on the development of computer science up to the present time. Not only is ALGOL 60 presented in this book, but special attention is given to two languages derived from it, Pascal and Burroughs ALGOL. Cobol, although the most widely used language, is not covered in this book mainly because the special features that make it popular in the business community are syntactic in nature. The semantics of Cobol are so simple that they can easily be understood in terms of the principles developed here.

The four languages selected form only an approximate basis to span the spectrum of programming languages, in contrast to, for instance, the three primary colors red, yellow, and blue, which form a true basis for the visible color spectrum. Thus some features of such widely used languages as Cobol and APL are not covered even indirectly in our study.

This book, like any artifact, is a product of design; this implies that trade-offs have been made. In the limited study time available to this subject the first time around, we have opted for a deeper study of a few languages rather than a more sketchy view of many languages. Moreover, the treatment of even the few languages covered is not complete in every respect. For example, do not expect the five chapters on Algol, Fortran, Lisp, Snobol, and Pascal to be equivalent to five complete reference manuals. Our coverage is designed to provide insight so that if subsequent reference manual consultation is required for special facts, forms, and other language details, these manuals can be understood.

Assuming that our study of programming languages is to emphasize a consideration of the underlying models that reflect or define the respective semantics, the next question is how best to approach such a study. To make the study as informal as possible with a minimum loss in rigor, we reasoned that many program examples or *case studies* are needed. A case study begins with a problem statement, followed by an algorithmic solution in the form of a program and then by an explanation of the program execution as a series of steps, each illustrated with the help of our model adapted to the particular programming language. The similarities and differences among languages can be emphasized if we develop some case studies using the same problem statement but with solutions developed in different languages.

These objectives imply the need for a common but neutral medium in which to represent the algorithms before we encode them as programs in the languages to be studied. The choice of such a medium is difficult. We can of course use ordinary English. Another choice is a stylized form of English resembling some well-known programming language like Fortran or Algol, although in this case it is not so easy to ensure "neutrality." A third choice is a flowchart form. In what follows we look more closely at this problem of choosing a common medium.

Consider, for example, the familiar algorithm for finding the first term of the Fibonacci series that is greater than some given number, such as 1000. The Fibonacci series, as you will recall, is often written as

$$0, 1, 1, 2, 3, 5, 8, 13, 21, 34, \ldots$$

where, in general, the jth term is obtained from its two predecessors by the recurrence rule

$$\text{term}_j \leftarrow \text{term}_{j-1} + \text{term}_{j-2}$$

and where the 0th and 1st terms (here 0 and 1, respectively) are regarded as given in advance. In the three algorithms shown in Figure 1-1, the variable SUM represents the value of the most recently generated term (term_j), while the variables LATEST and NEXT_LATEST, respectively, acquire values representing term_{j-1} and term_{j-2} in the above recurrence rule.

A careful study of the alternate representations in Figure 1-1 convinces us they are practically equivalent. There is a marked similarity between (a) the English form and (b) the one designated as English-like. The differences are primarily a matter of wording and punctuation. To deduce the meaning, one proceeds in each case, step by step, from step 1 through step 4. If the steps have substeps, their meanings are also deduced by proceeding in a sequential fashion.

The information in the English-like statement

let NEXT_LATEST, LATEST, and SUM be nonnegative integers

serves to round out the specification of the algorithm. When we later wish to encode it in some particular programming language, such as Fortran or Algol, the information contained in this *let* statement (often called a *declaration*) will be embedded in the program and interpreted by the computer that executes the program. Note that information corresponding to that in the *let* statement can easily be added to a flowchart version of the algorithm by "attaching" an associated legend (Figure 1-1c).

Is the flowchart medium as similar to the English-like medium as the latter is to the English version? Superficially yes, but there is one important but subtle, and perhaps controversial, new aspect introduced by the flowchart.

Note that the control of loop transits is more explicit (more graphic) in the flowchart. A loop step such as step 2 can be regarded as a single indivisible action, or it can be viewed in terms of its major components, which are

(i) the body, box 2b of the flowchart,
(ii) the logic that controls repeated execution of this body, the logic associated with box 2a of the flowchart.

The English and English-like versions have been phrased deliberately to suppress some of the details of this control logic. In particular, the English-like version leaves implicit the detail corresponding to the directed line from box

***Figure 1-1.* Three ways to describe an algorithm. (a) English, (b) English-like, (c) flowchart.**

1. Let NEXT_LATEST, LATEST, and SUM represent nonnegative integers having the initial values 0, 1, and 1, respectively.
2. While SUM ≤ 1000 do the following:
   (i) assign to SUM the value of the expression
   LATEST + NEXT_LATEST.
   (ii) assign to NEXT_LATEST the value of LATEST.
   (iii) assign to LATEST the value of SUM.
3. Display the value of SUM.
4. Stop.

(a)

let NEXT_LATEST, LATEST, and SUM represent nonnegative integers.

```
Step 1: begin NEXT_LATEST ← 0;
              LATEST ← 1;
              SUM ← 1
        end
Step 2: while SUM ≤ 1000 do
          begin SUM ← LATEST + NEXT_LATEST;
            NEXT_LATEST ← LATEST;
            LATEST ← SUM
          end
Step 3: display SUM
Step 4: Stop.
```

(b)

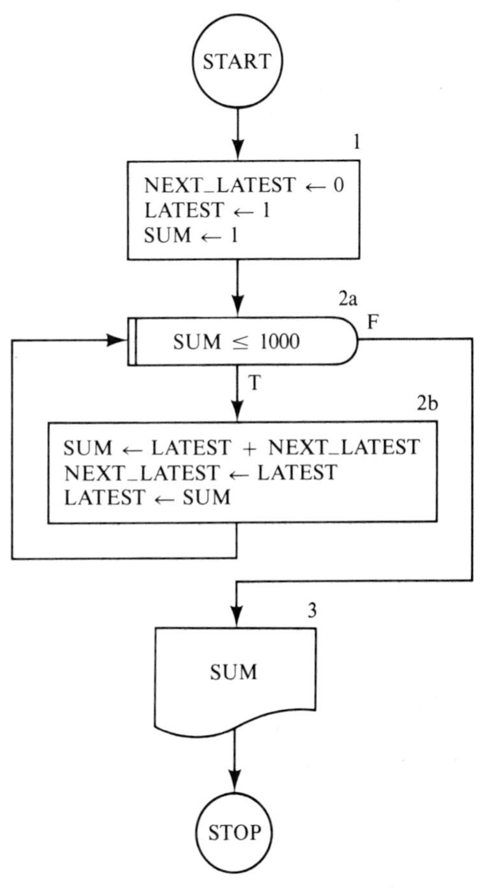

Legend

Identifier	Description
NEXT_LATEST	integer ≥ 0
LATEST	integer ≥ 0
SUM	integer ≥ 0

(c)

2b back to box 2a, and also the false (F) exit from box 2a to box 3. Most computer scientists have grown so accustomed to the logic of loop structures that they prefer to suppress such details, and for this reason they are omitted from the wording of the English and English-like versions of Figure 1-1.

For a precise understanding of an algorithm, however, one must be aware of all the logic left implicit in its description. Would it be desirable to incorporate suppression conventions into the neutral or base language that is to be used to explain other programming languages, each of which may have its own conventions for suppressing detail? Observe also that if the hidden logic of the English or English-like version were restored in explicit form, it would not be so easy to read. (Try it and see for yourself.)

The choice between the flowchart and some textual form of algorithmic description therefore amounts to deciding in favor of or against the explicit display (in two dimensions) of the algorithm's logic structure, and that decision is a matter of *taste.* Our experience is that the explicit display of the logic by means of flow lines causes a visual impact that is helpful even though a flowchart is far less compact than an equivalent textual (linear) representation. We can, however, always *postpone* most detail in flowcharts when we wish to do so using techniques to be reviewed later in this chapter. These techniques make the flowcharts even more space consuming, but allow us to fill in the detail where and when we need it. As you will see, these techniques are quite different from suppression of detail.

To sum up, while we shall use flowcharts most of the time to describe algorithms or to reinforce concepts of algorithmic structure because this is our preference, we shall occasionally use other modes of expression such as the English or English-like notation just discussed. Note that whichever form is used to represent an algorithm, our intention is to show its *essence,* without any details or characteristics peculiar to one particular programming language. The individual details are introduced explicitly when we encode for particular languages.

It requires a manual, but quite routine, *mapping process* to convert from the common medium, for example, the flowchart, to the computer program. Some people find this extra step irksome. However, in a study such as this, when one is becoming acquainted with a number of new programming languages, this final mapping step in producing a correctly encoded program can actually pay a dividend in terms of speed of learning. This bonus comes about because the algorithmic structure one is encoding can be expresssed with precision in the already familiar common medium. Since the mapping step is a relatively mechanical process, students should adopt this approach for themselves if they indeed find that it increases their productivity as programmers.

There are several other reasons why students may wish to practice the "two-step" process of first constructing a flowchart/legend or English-like algorithm, and then mapping it into a computer program. We now discuss one of these reasons, which is related to the criteria for selecting a programming language from all available languages, to encode a particular algorithm. One line of the English-like algorithm, flowchart box, or legend entry cannot always be mapped, one for one, into a target programming language. When this is the case, it may reflect a lack of expressive power of the particular language for that particular application. For example, as we learn later, the legend of the Figure 1-1 flowchart can be mapped into Algol as

integer sum, nextlatest, latest;

and into Fortran as

INTEGER SUM, NEXT, LATEST

Fortran identifiers are limited to a maximum of six characters, so we have encoded NEXT_LATEST as NEXT, thus losing some mnemonic value in the transformation. Also it is not possible in either Algol or Fortran to declare that integers are nonnegative, although in this case the limitation is not serious.

Constraints in the expressive power of programming languages, however, should not discourage us from including detailed specification in our common medium description. Just because we cannot map legend entries precisely into corresponding declarations of a particular target language should not prevent us from using a flowchart/legend as the starting point toward the coded program. On the contrary, the more exactly we can express our intent in the initial representation of an algorithm, the better chance we have to arrive at an equivalent computer program. However, if it is absolutely necessary to express a particular type of specification or phrasing directly in a target programming language, then that fact may lead us to choose some particular target language or even to develop a new language, should such an alternative be available to us. Thus our philosophy is to pay close attention to any mapping problems that arise in translating a flowchart/legend into a program, since this translation step is like implementing a program from its specification. When the use of one language makes this translation process expensive, we have good reason to consider another language for that particular application. Therefore, we should learn about a variety of languages and language types as soon as possible in our professional careers as programmers and computer scientists.

1-2 FLOWCHARTS FOR STRUCTURED PROGRAMMING

Our first case study is designed to achieve a number of objectives, including introducing some flowchart conventions that will be used in this book and reviewing some principles of structured programming.

The problem we want to solve involves printing a series of diagrams, each showing the "scope" of a chess Queen on a chessboard, according to the position of the Queen. Figure 1-2 shows one such diagram where the Queen is positioned at the 3, 2 square. Here the chessboard is regarded as an 8×8 array. Asterisks mark the chessboard squares that are included in the Queen's scope. Dashes represent the other squares.

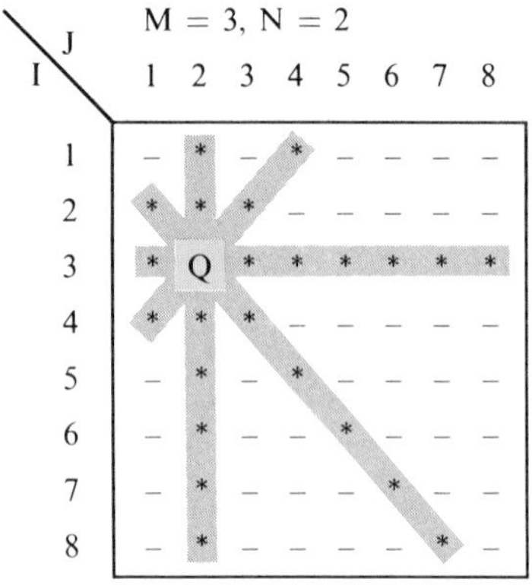

Figure 1-2

The problem can be stated initially in this way:

Given the chess Queen's position represented by a pair of integers M and N, display a chessboard showing the Queen's scope, marking the squares as follows:

Q for the Queen's position,
* for any other square in the scope of the Queen,
– for all other squares.

The scope of the chess Queen includes every square on each row, each column, and each diagonal that contains the Queen's position.

Many algorithmic solutions are possible, depending on how we choose to define and decompose the overall task. At the topmost level we shall assume the job is to make a series of chessboard pictures, one for each given pair M, N. This repetition is to be halted when we encounter the first pair M, N that does *not* represent a valid position on the board, i.e., a pair M, N such that the condition, $1 \leq M \leq 8$ and $1 \leq N \leq 8$ is *false.* To separate a board display from its successor, we print a blank line. Thus, a top-level view of the solution might be as shown in Figure 1-3.

Here Box 1a

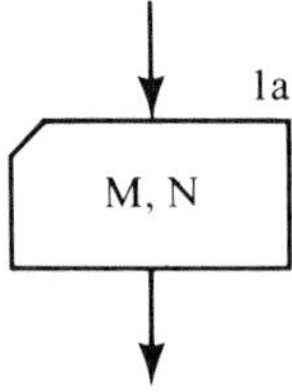

is intended to mean: Read two values from an input data stream and associate the first with M and the second with N.

The details for box 2 in Figure 1-3 depend on what data structures we choose to specify. The most obvious approach is to imagine filling an 8×8 array with the desired characters and then printing that array one line at a time. Realizing

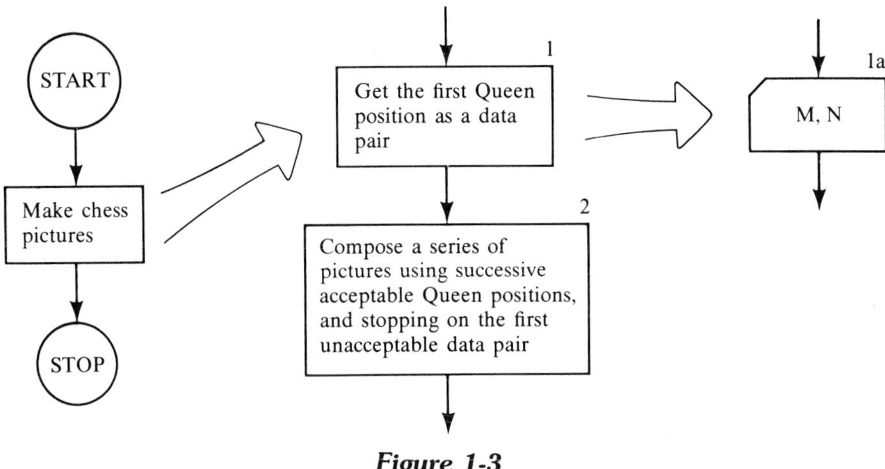

Figure 1-3

that we can print only one line at a time suggests another choice, namely, using a linear array (1 × 8) to represent just one row of the chessboard. For this approach the algorithm must fill and refill the same 1 × 8 array a total of 8 times, printing a copy of the row's contents after each "filling." In what follows, we choose the second approach and call the required 1 × 8 array CHESS.

Now the details for box 2 of Figure 1-3 can be constructed as shown in Figure 1-4. The series of pictures results from the execution of a loop that is controlled by a so-called *while* box (box 2a). The while box controls repetition by forcing execution of the loop body (boxes 2b and 2c) every time the current values of M, N represent an acceptable data pair, that is, while the expression inside box 2a evaluates to *true.* If a pair M, N fails this test, control takes the F exit from box 2a to stop. We call a loop controlled by a while box an *indefinite iteration* because the number of repetitions cannot be specified independently of the data.

Figure 1-4

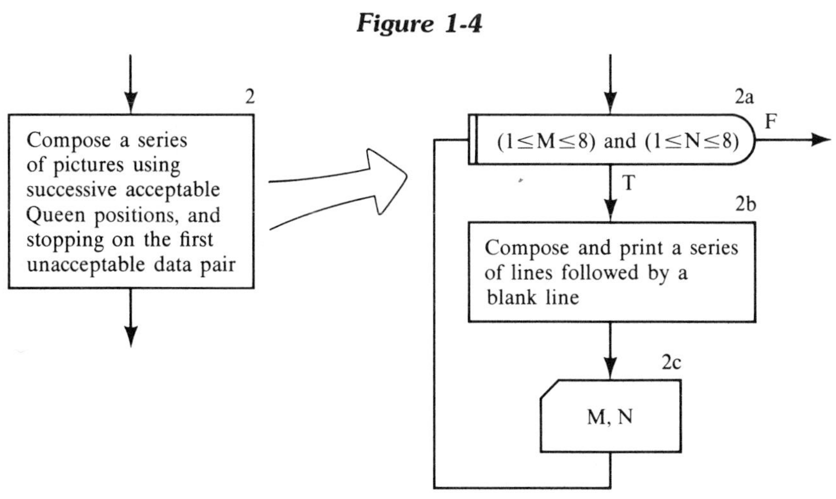

Notice how we have practiced postponing details until we are ready to consider them. Figure 1-5 shows subsequent steps of decomposition until all flowchart boxes represent actions that can easily be expressed in the type of programming languages we will be studying. Such actions may also be regarded as *primitive* with respect to some underlying machine model that can directly interpret, that is, execute, them.

In Figure 1-5 we see that box 2b is detailed as a loop that we call a *definite iteration* because the loop is to be executed a fixed number of times, in this case 8 times. Box 1, called an *iteration box,* controls repeated execution of the

Figure 1-5

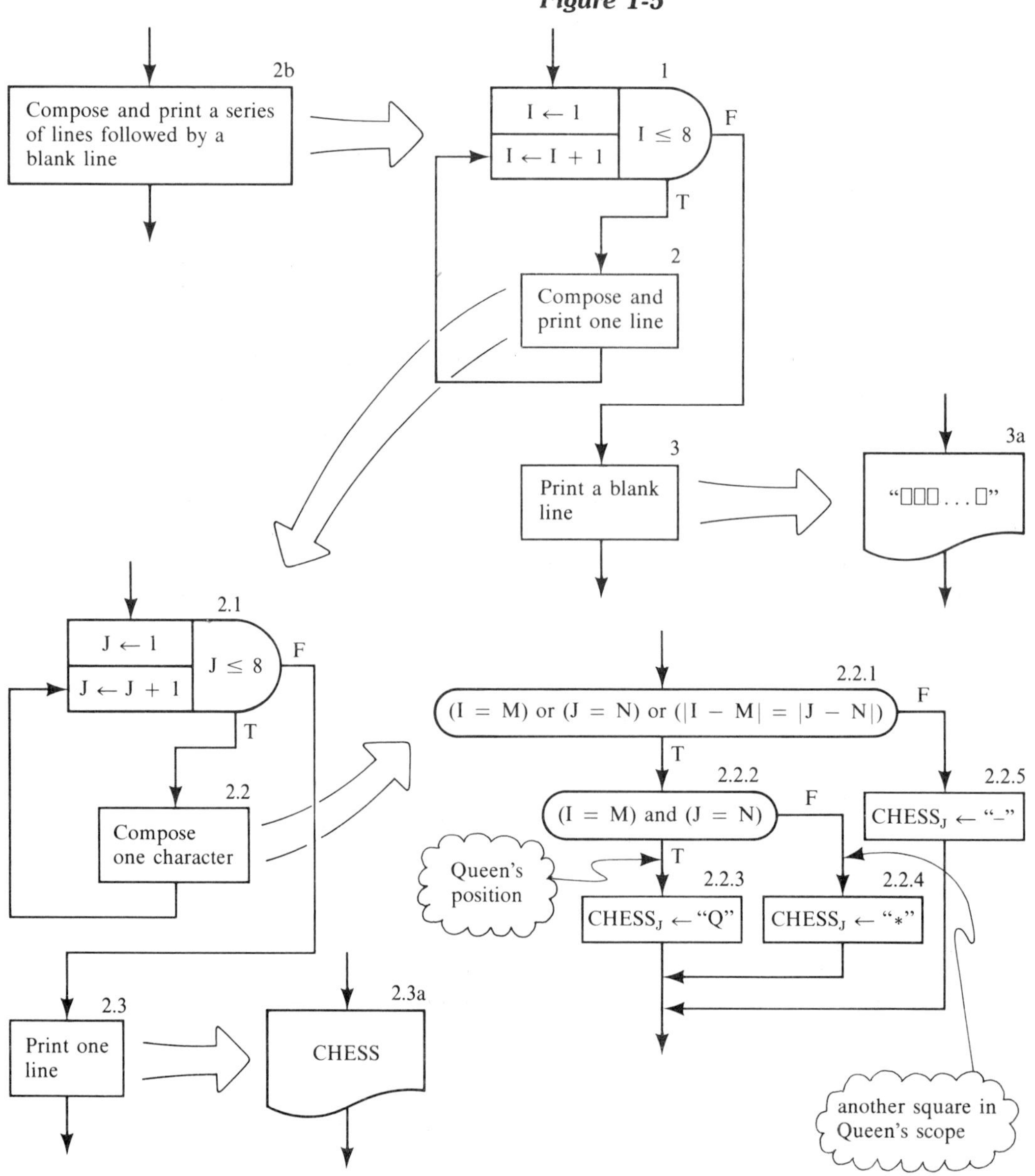

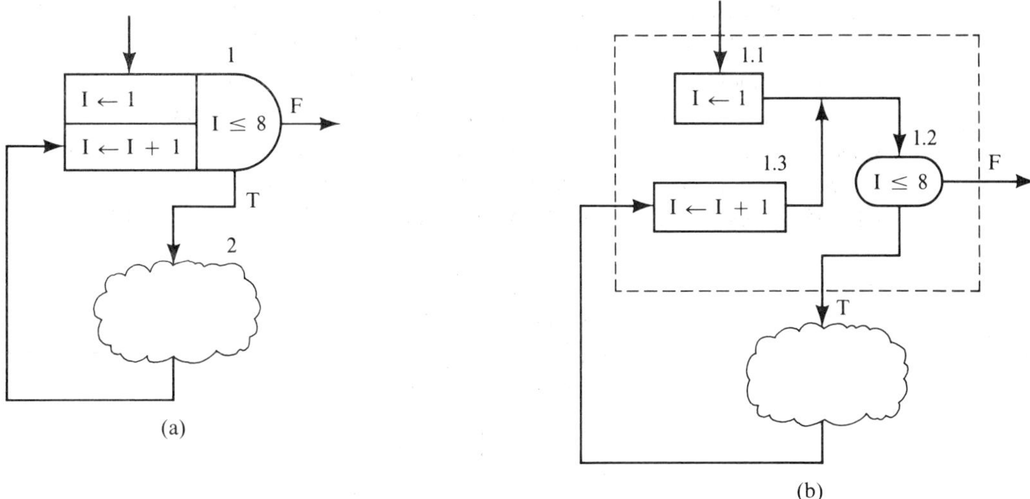

Figure 1-6. **(a) Shorthand version; (b) long version.**

loop body (box 2). Note that an iteration box such as box 1 is actually a shorthand (Figure 1-6a) and is understood to be equivalent to the control sequence shown in Figure 1-6b.

After the iteration variable I is initialized, that is, assigned the value 1 in box 1.1, the value is immediately tested in box 1.2.

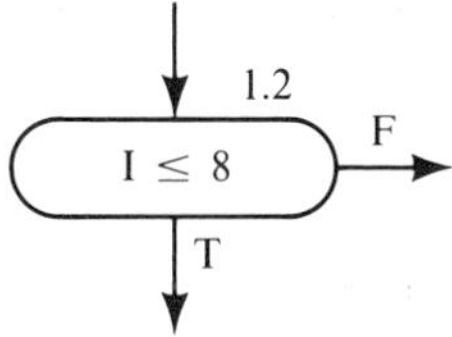

The oval box denotes a decision step. The condition to be tested is written inside the box and the flowlines leaving the box are labeled T for true and F for false to indicate the alternate paths possible. (In much of the computer literature diamond-shaped boxes are used to indicate decision steps.)

After the loop body (represented by the cloud in Figure 1-6) is executed, the iteration variable is incremented in box 1.3 and control flows again to the decision box 1.2. When the condition in box 1.2 is false, the loop body will *not* be executed. Thus box 1 ensures that the controlled loop body will be executed exactly 8 times. It is fairly natural then to identify the successive values of I, the iteration variable, with the 8 rows of the chessboard, that is, when I equals 1, the first row of the chessboard is being processed, etc.

Box 2.1 of Figure 1-5 is another definite iteration, controlling repetition of box 2.2, whose detail is also shown. The body of this loop will also be executed exactly 8 times for each time the loop is entered. If the values of the iteration variable J are associated with the 8 columns of the chessboard, then each pair of values (I, J) represents one of the 64 possible chessboard positions. The two iteration boxes 1 and 2.1 together cause the iteration variables I and J to run successively through these 64 positions rowwise in the order (1, 1), (1, 2), (1, 3), (1, 4), (1, 5), (1, 6), (1, 7), (1, 8) followed by (2, 1), (2, 2), . . . , etc.

To complete the flowchart representation of the algorithm, we include a legend (below) enumerating and describing the program identifiers (variables), which can be thought of as named placeholders. The variables M, N, I, and J are described as integers, meaning they have integer values, while the variable CHESS is described as a list (ordered collection) of (8) single characters:

Legend

Identifier	Description
M, N, I, J CHESS	integer list of eight single characters (the list is a linear array)

CHESS is shorthand for the collection ($CHESS_1$, $CHESS_2$, $CHESS_3$, . . . , $CHESS_8$) and each $CHESS_J$ will hold only a single character. Thus CHESS has the capacity to represent the values in any row of the board; and for example, when I = 3, CHESS will represent row 3. The variable $CHESS_2$ is a placeholder for some value in the second column of the board; exactly *which* position in the second column is determined by the current value of I. When I = 3, $CHESS_2$ is the third element in the second column.

We see how elements of CHESS are assigned appropriate values by examining the details of box 2.2

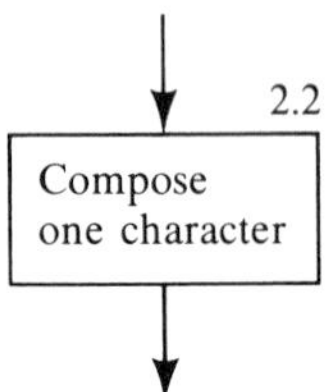

in Figure 1-5. The decision step of box 2.2.1 distinguishes the scope of the Queen (including the Queen's own position) from other squares, while the decision step of box 2.2.2 distinguishes the Queen's own position from other squares within its scope. Boxes 2.2.3, 2.2.4, and 2.2.5 are assignment steps that assign the appropriate value to the list element $CHESS_J$. Notice that we always express the operation of assignment with the left-pointing arrow symbol ←, and we place assignment steps inside rectangular shaped boxes.

The decision rule used in box 2.2.1,

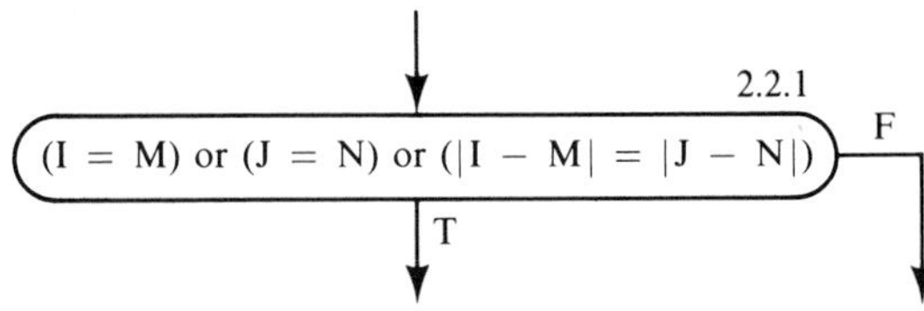

is the technical heart of the algorithm. We explain it here, in case its meaning is not obvious. If I = M is *true*, the row under consideration has the same index as that of the Queen's position. Every position in the row is within the scope of the Queen. If J = N is *true*, $CHESS_J$ is within the scope of the Queen by virtue of being in the same column. If the absolute value of the difference of the row indices I and M is equal to the absolute value of the difference of the column indices J and N, then positions I, J and M, N are on the same diagonal, as in Figure 1-7. If any of these three alternatives is true, $CHESS_J$ is to be assigned either an asterisk or a "Q" as its value; otherwise it is to be assigned a dash. Since the control in the iteration boxes 1 and 2.1 runs successively through all 8 values of I and of J, the assignment steps (boxes 2.2.3, 2.2.4, and 2.2.5) will assign "Q", "*", or "–" as the value of every one of the 64 positions on the board.

After each row list has been completely generated, that is, after the completion of the inner loop action controlled by box 2.1, the false path is taken from box 2.1 to box 2.3a:

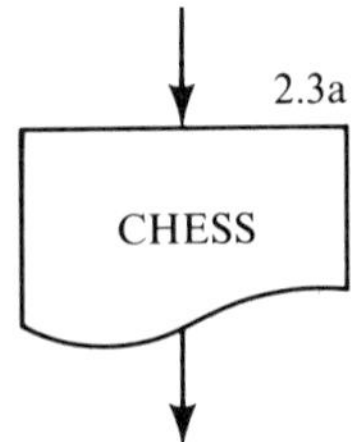

Execution of this *output* box causes a copy of the value of the variable CHESS to be displayed. Thus the first execution of box 2.3a causes the output of the values

– * – * – – – –

Then the iteration variable I is incremented and the whole inner loop is executed again, resulting in the generation and output of line 2,

* * * – – – – –

Figure 1-7

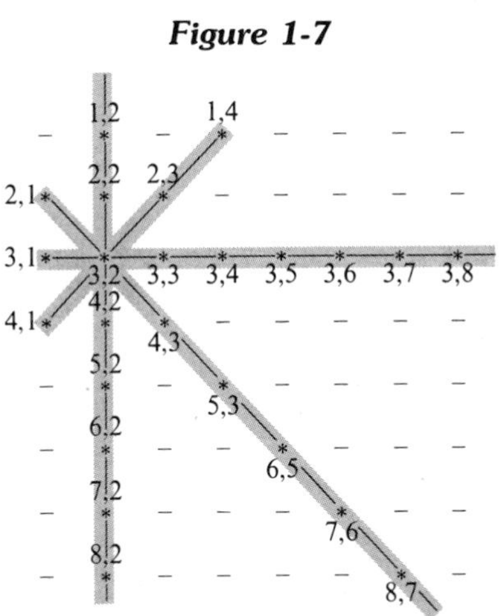

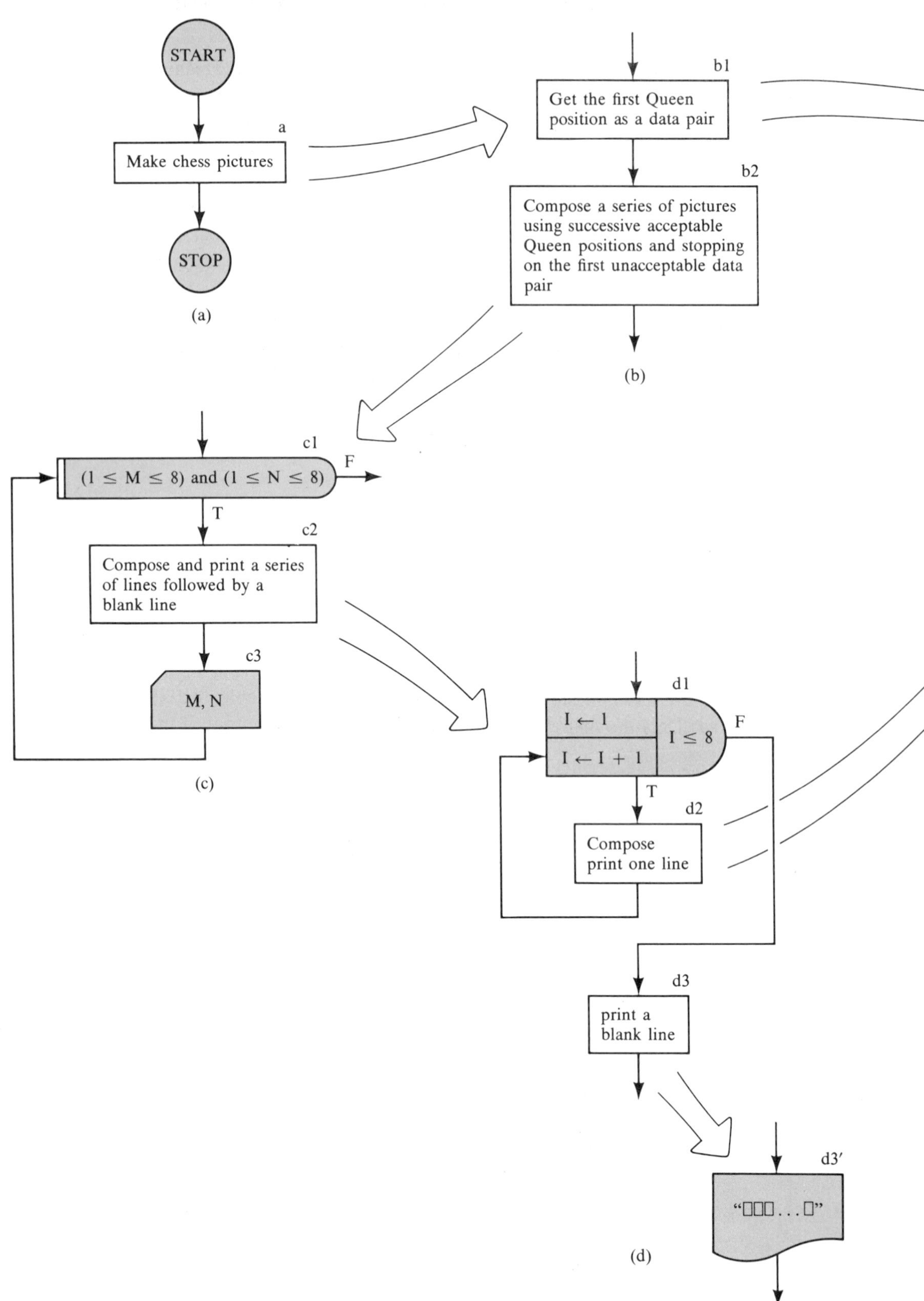

Figure 1-8. **Composite flowchart and legend for printing chessboards, each showing a Queen and its scope.**

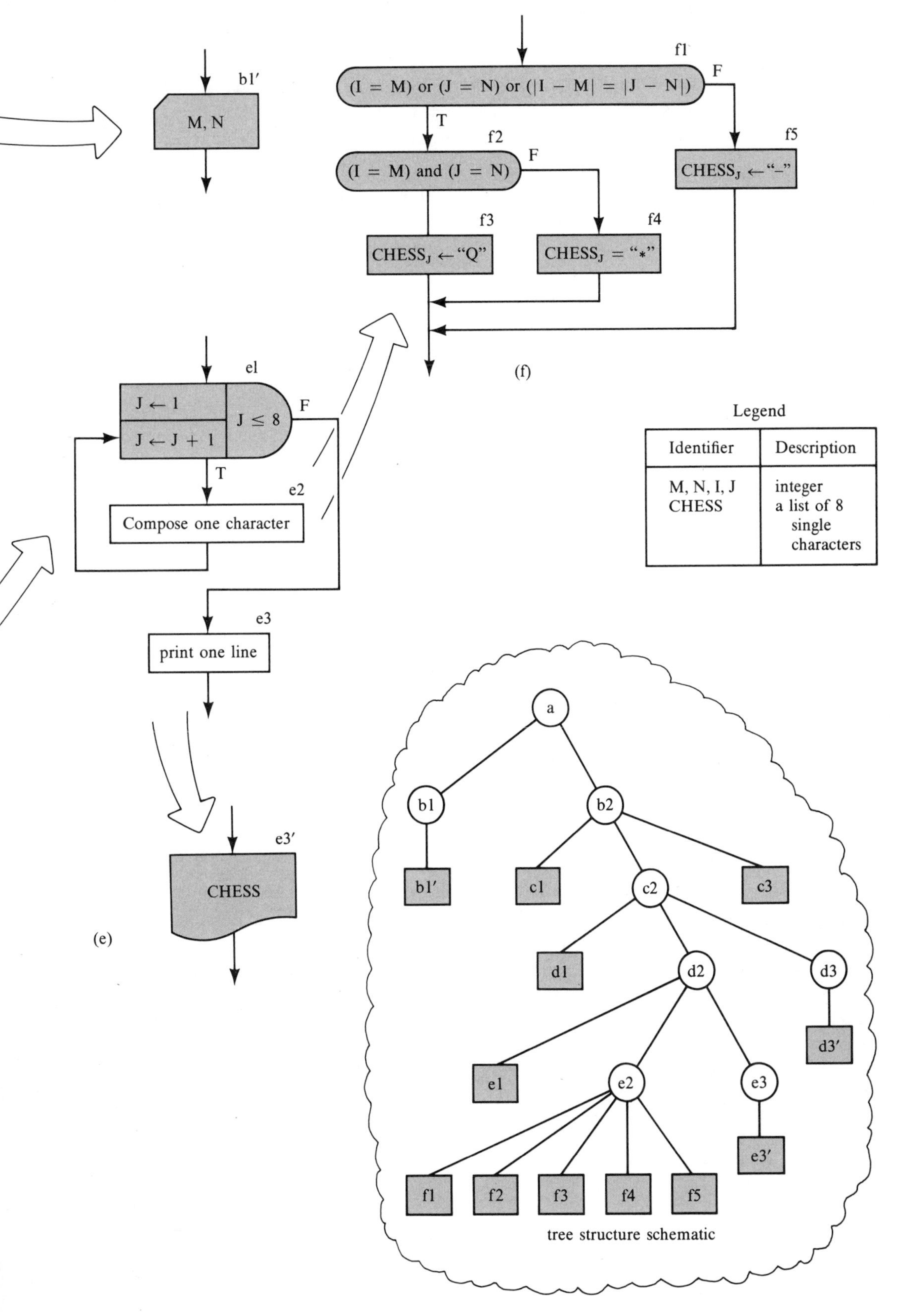
b1′
M, N
f1
(I = M) or (J = N) or (|I − M| = |J − N|)
F
T
f2
(I = M) and (J = N)
F
f5
CHESS_J ← "−"
f3
CHESS_J ← "Q"
f4
CHESS_J = "*"
(f)
e1
J ← 1
J ← J + 1
J ≤ 8
F
T
e2
Compose one character
e3
print one line
e3′
CHESS
(e)
Legend
Identifier
Description
M, N, I, J
CHESS
integer
a list of 8 single characters
a
b1
b2
b1′
c1
c2
c3
d1
d2
d3
d3′
e1
e2
e3
e3′
f1
f2
f3
f4
f5
tree structure schematic

(Our convention is that *each* execution of an output box causes the printing to start on a new line.) When all 8 lines have been output, the action controlled by box 1 takes the false path to output box 3a, whose execution causes a new but blank line to be printed. This completes the action details of box 2b. Control continues to box 2c (in Figure 1-4), where another M, N pair is input. Then the whole cycle repeats: first the test for completion of the while loop, and then possibly the production of another chessboard picture and the reading of another data pair.

To complete the flowchart representation of the algorithm, we need a legend that explains the intended use of the identifiers. This was shown on page 12. For convenience, all the parts are collected and shown as a composite in Figure 1-8. Flowchart boxes have been renumbered to reflect the principal steps of decomposition. Note that a flowchart developed by stepwise decomposition has a *treelike structure** whose root is the top-level statement of the problem and whose *leaves* (terminal nodes) are the primitive action steps (shaded boxes). When mapping the flowchart to a programming language like Fortran, Basic, or Algol, only the primitive actions and the information in the legend are encoded. Information in the other boxes, however, usually appears in the form of descriptive comments. Table 1-1 contains a summary of the flowchart language conventions we use to represent primitive action steps.

This is a good place to summarize the important structuring principles we have been using to design and construct algorithms. Our discussion will relate closely to the use of flowcharts but, in fact, is equally applicable to any equivalent medium for describing algorithms.

Algorithm construction is a creative process in which two diametrically opposing approaches can be taken, namely, *bottom up* and *top down.* Bottom-up development of an algorithm, like that of Figure 1-8 to print a chessboard, would begin by studying an individual position on the board, that is, it would first construct the body of the innermost loop, boxes f1 through f5, and then add the control structure of box e1 followed by box d1, etc.

As we have seen, top-down problem solving takes the opposite view; first, the whole problem or task is studied and subdivided into a small number of nonoverlapping subtasks that accomplish the same net effect as the whole task. Then each subtask is subdivided in the same way, and finally, by this divide-and-conquer strategy (stepwise decomposition), a series of subtasks is arrived at that is not only equivalent to the original task, but also each subtask can be expressed in terms of whatever programming language is available.

When an algorithm is actually created, the problem solver may not have used 100% bottom-up or 100% top-down strategy, but rather some combination of the two, which enabled him to bootstrap his way to a solution. In this book, however, we shall always prefer the top-down method, and we choose to go

*A tree is a hierarchic structure that begins with a *root node.* Each segment that emanates from the root node leads to another node, which may be a *terminal* node (no segments emanating from it) or a *nonterminal* node (one or more segments emanating from it). Each such nonterminal node is the root node of a *subtree.*

TABLE 1-1
Flowchart Language Summary

Typical shape	Name	Meaning (assuming left to right order of evaluation of expressions)
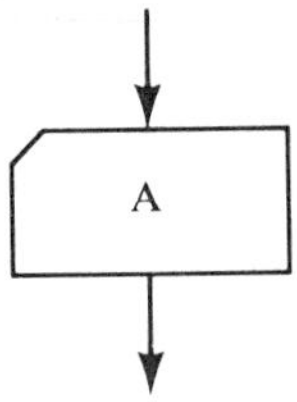 A	Input box	Read a value from the input stream and assign it to the variable A.
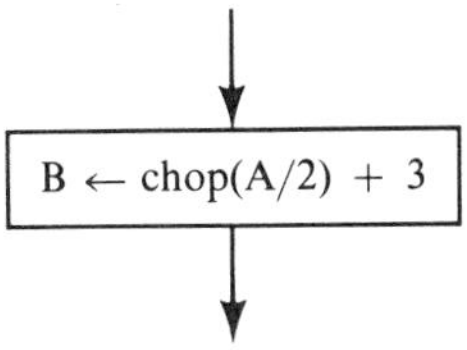 B ← chop(A/2) + 3	Assignment box	Get the value of A from storage. Divide this value by 2 and chop off the fractional part of the quotient. Add 3 to this value and assign the sum as the value of the variable B.
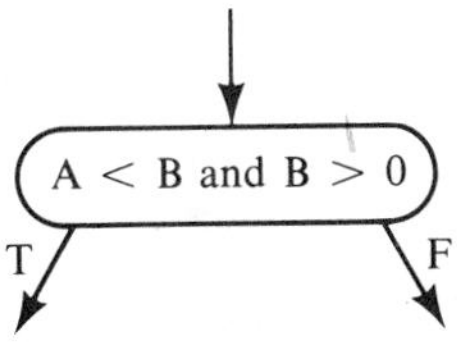 A < B and B > 0 (T, F)	Decision box	Get the values of A and B from storage. Use them to test the condition A < B. If this is false, take the F exit from the box. If A < B is true, then test the condition B > 0. If this is also true, take the T exit from the box. Otherwise take the F exit.
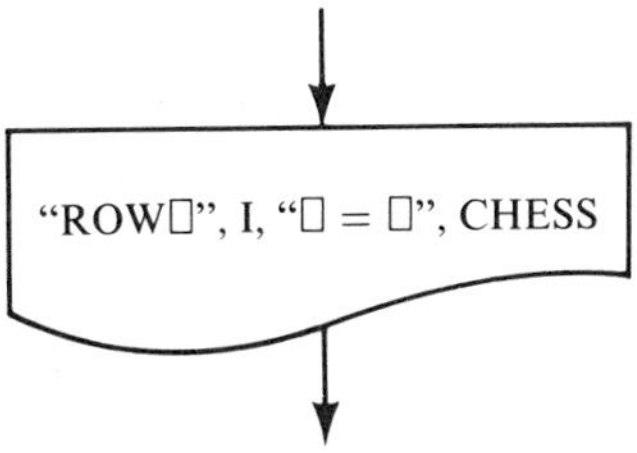 "ROW□", I, "□ = □", CHESS	Output box	Print on one line the characters "ROW□" followed by the value of the variable I. Follow this by the characters "□ = □" and by the value of the variable CHESS. In the context of the environment of Figure 1-16 the box would produce the following line: ROW 1 = −∗−∗−−−−
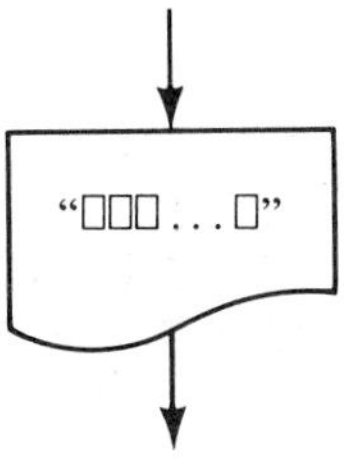 "□□□ . . . □"	Output box	Print a line of blank characters. The symbol "□" is our mark for a blank space.

TABLE 1-1 (*continued*)

Typical shape	Name	Meaning (assuming left to right order of evaluation of expressions)
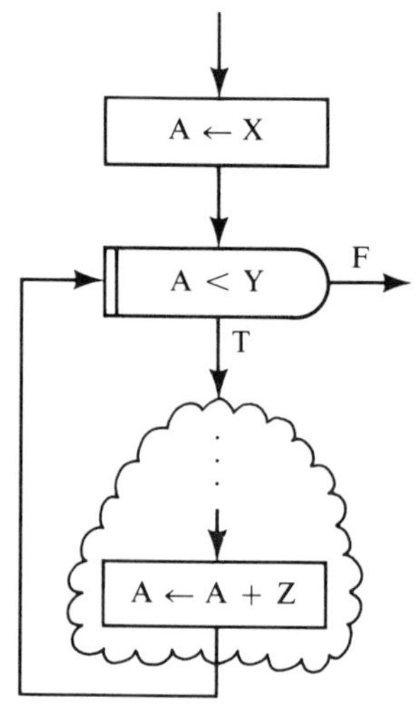	While loop or indefinite iteration	Get the value of X and assign it to the variable A. If A < Y is true, execute the statements in the cloud, which includes a step that adds the value of A and the value of Z and assigns this sum as the new value of A. Then loop back to retest the condition. If A < Y is false, take the false exit from the while box. (If, after looping started, Z < 0 were to become and remain true, the loop would be infinite.)
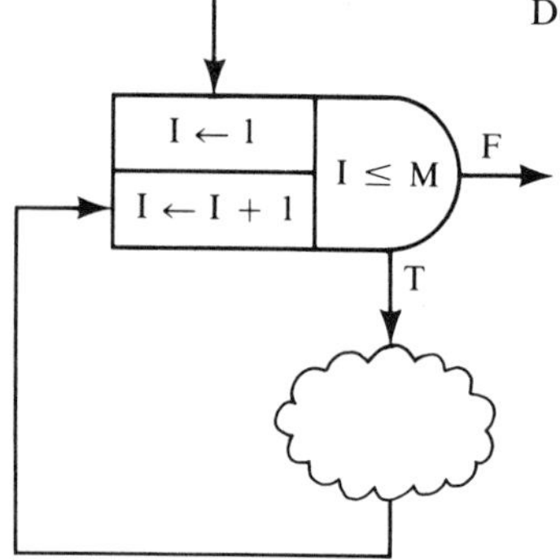	Definite iteration	Initialize the counter variable I to 1. Test the condition I ≤ M. If this condition is true, execute the statements in the cloud. Then increment the counter variable and retest the condition I ≤ M. When the condition is false exit from the loop. Caution: It is possible that statements executed in the cloud may assign a new value to M. If so, the iteration is no longer definite, i.e., the number of transits of the loop cannot be computed in advance.
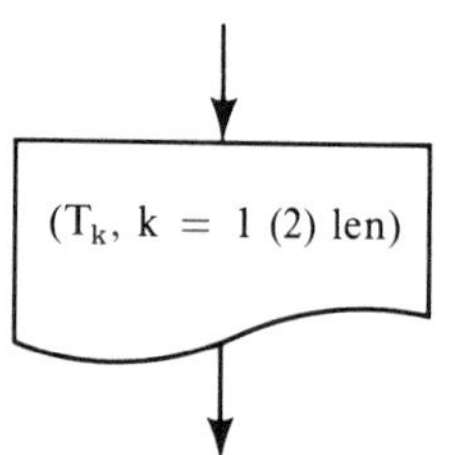	Enumerated list notation for an output box[a]	Same as 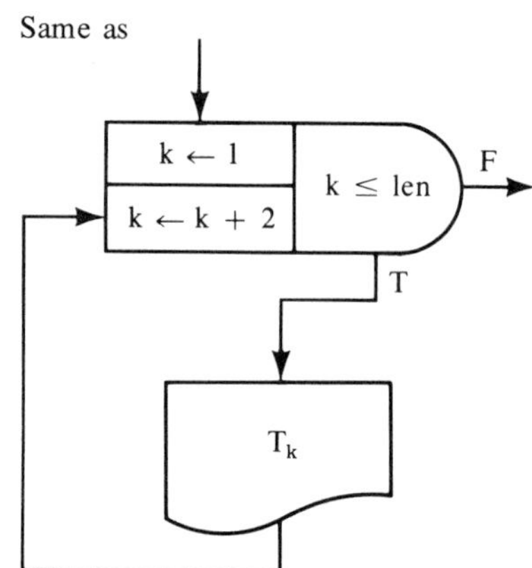 except that, space permitting, printed values of T_k will appear on the same line.

TABLE 1-1 (*continued*)

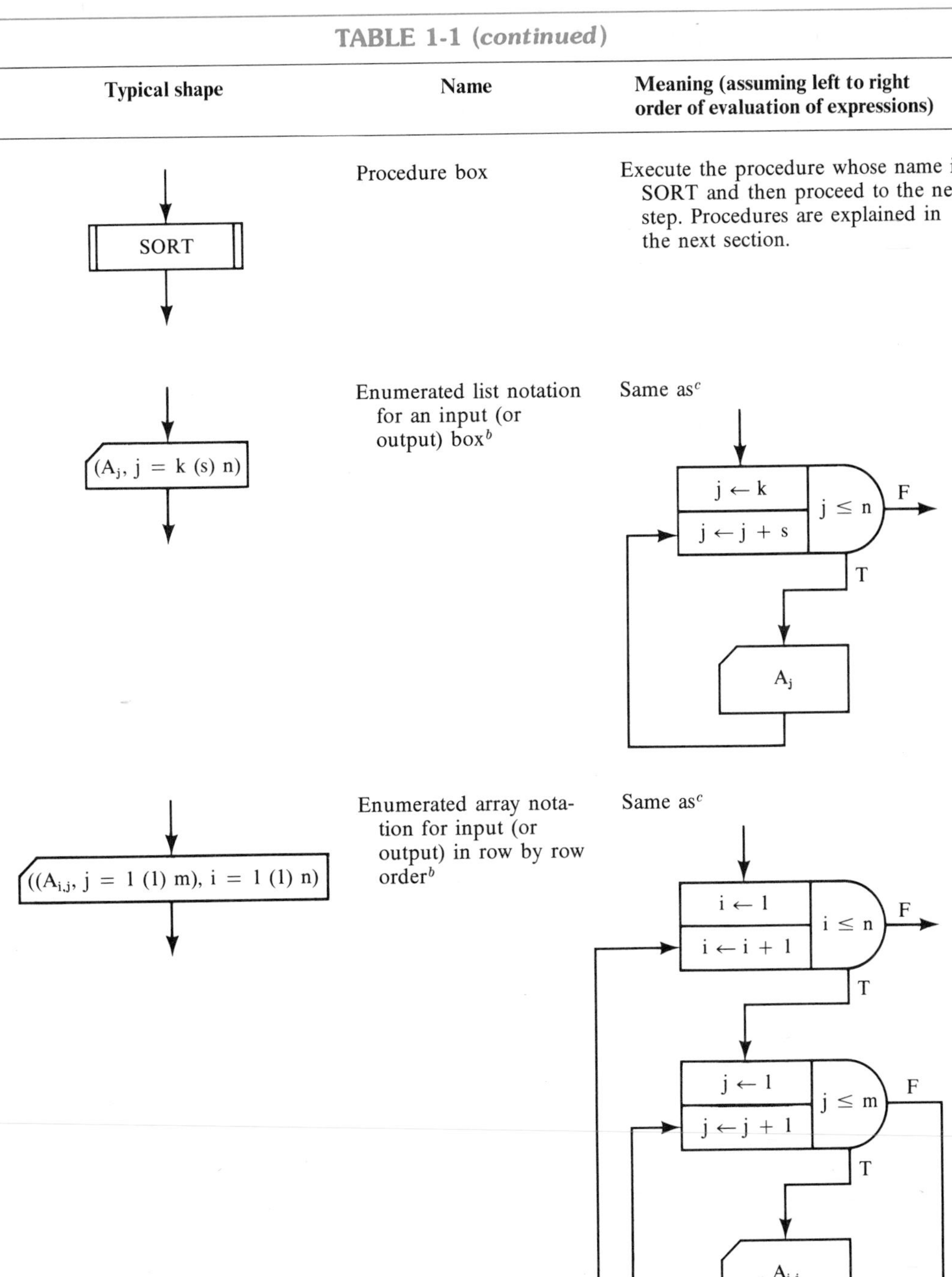

Typical shape	Name	Meaning (assuming left to right order of evaluation of expressions)
SORT	Procedure box	Execute the procedure whose name is SORT and then proceed to the next step. Procedures are explained in the next section.
$(A_j,\ j = k\ (s)\ n)$	Enumerated list notation for an input (or output) box[b]	Same as[c]
$((A_{i,j},\ j = 1\ (1)\ m),\ i = 1\ (1)\ n)$	Enumerated array notation for input (or output) in row by row order[b]	Same as[c]

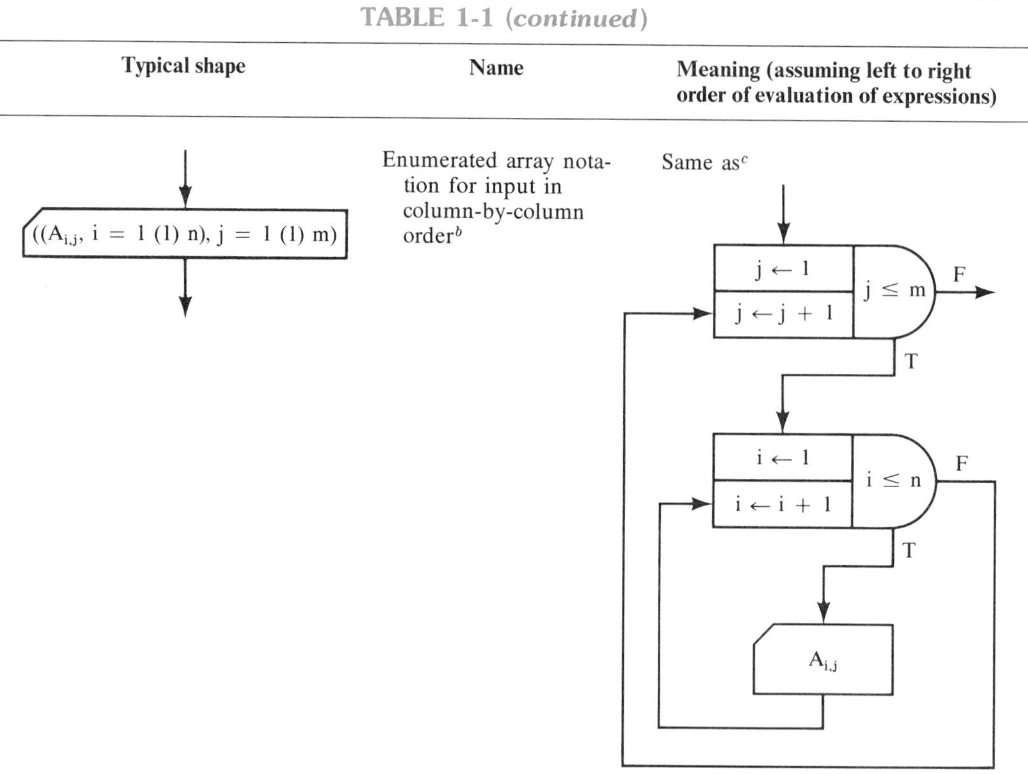

TABLE 1-1 (*continued*)

Typical shape	Name	Meaning (assuming left to right order of evaluation of expressions)
$((A_{i,j}, i = 1\ (1)\ n), j = 1\ (1)\ m)$	Enumerated array notation for input in column-by-column order[b]	Same as[c] (flowchart: $j \leftarrow 1$; $j \leftarrow j + 1$; $j \leq m$ F/T; $i \leftarrow 1$; $i \leftarrow i + 1$; $i \leq n$ F/T; $A_{i,j}$)

[a]The notation "k = 1 (2) len" means that k ranges in value from 1 in steps of 2 until the value of len.
[b]The notation "k (s) n" should be read as "k *by* s *to* n." For example, "i = 1 (1) n" means that i ranges in value from 1 in steps of 1 until n.
[c]The sequence of data values for A_j (or $A_{i,j}$) may appear in left-to-right order on the same input data line or card, as space permits.

even one step further and restrict the *kinds* of flowchart structures that are to be admissible in translating subtasks into flowchart form, as suggested by Dahl *et al* (1972). We want all substructures to be of the "one in and one out" variety. An assignment statement meets this restriction trivially:

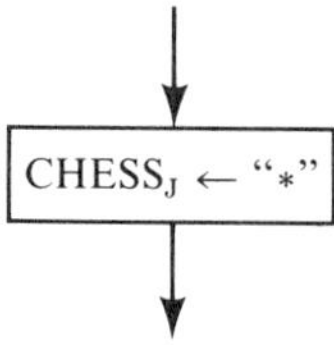

Any assignment box has one entry point and one exit.

For a selection step, the restriction requires that branching flowlines must rejoin *within the same subtask* in which they originally split, as in Figure 1-9.

In an iteration step, "one entry and one exit" requires that there be no premature branching *out* of the loop; the loop must have a structure somewhat similar to that of Figure 1-10.

Experienced computer scientists confirm that adherence to these restrictions leads to algorithms that are easy to understand, and easy to correct. We wholeheartedly agree with this philosophy.

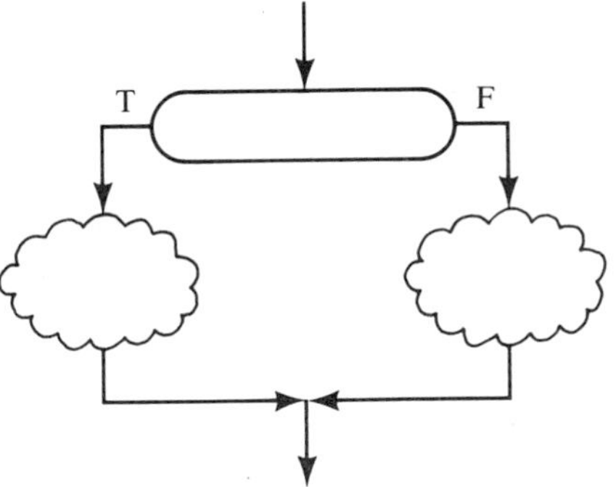

Figure 1-9

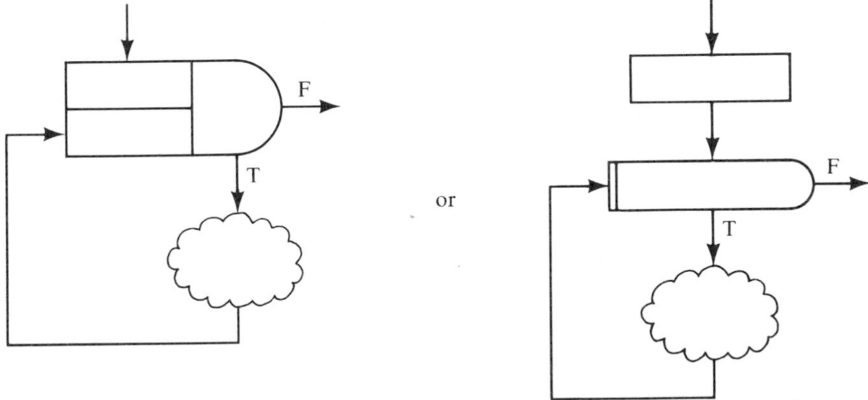

Figure 1-10

1-3 A COMPUTER MODEL

For most of us, the algorithm to print Queen's scope "pictures" is of borderline complexity. Its structure is relatively simple because it exhibits a pure hierarchy, but tracing its execution to be sure it works correctly may not seem quite so easy. (In any case we could find more complex algorithms where the tracing would be difficult for most of us.)

We can make the task of tracing an algorithm straightforward and mechanical with the aid of an appropriate computer model. We said at the outset that the semantics of each programming language is based on some underlying computer model. This should also be true for algorithms expressed in flowchart or English-like languages.

Why not postulate such a model and use it to trace the execution of flowcharts? If we do this, we should be able to acquire an initial, but fairly sophisticated, grasp of the important relationship between a language and its underlying computer model, even before we look at the particulars of any actual programming language. This, in fact, will be our basic learning strategy for the remaining introductory portion of this book.

In this section, therefore, we describe a simple computer model adequate to give meaning to the flowcharts we have looked at so far. As we introduce more flowchart language (syntactic) features, we may have to augment the model so its use can explain the meaning of these new features.

We model our computer *storage* as a collection of *cells.* We choose to use a boxlike style of representation so that each cell looks like a see-through, windowed storage container, as suggested in Figure 1-11. To achieve a proper level of abstraction, we also stylize the *control* and *processing units* of our computer model. These take the form of a robotlike controller called the Master Computer, together with a staff of several assistant robots, one called the Allocator and another called the Reader/Assigner. (In describing how the controller and assistants function, by analogy with human actions, we are sometimes forced to assume that all robots are males. We hope no reader will be offended.)

The Master Computer reads and interprets a primary or *top-level* flowchart on his worktable, delegating what tasks he can to his assistants. There is also available a library of generally useful auxiliary flowcharts, that is, *library procedures,* that can be referred to whenever needed. In addition, auxiliary flowcharts especially prepared as supplements for the top-level flowchart may also be available. For this model of a computer the flowchart used by the Master Computer is a *program.*

When the Master Computer is ready to execute a program, he studies the legend accompanying the flowchart and instructs an assistant (the Allocator) to assemble a collection of storage cells in which to place the values of the variables. In the chessboard example of the preceding section, the assistant might have produced and labeled the containers as shown in Figure 1-11. Notice that the containers for M, N, I, and J are simple cells, while the container for the list CHESS has 8 compartments.

Assigning a value to a variable in this model means placing a copy of the desired value in the storage cell associated with the variable. In the process of placing the new value in the cell, any old value is destroyed or erased. Reading

***Figure 1-11.* Storage cells.**

M

N

I

J

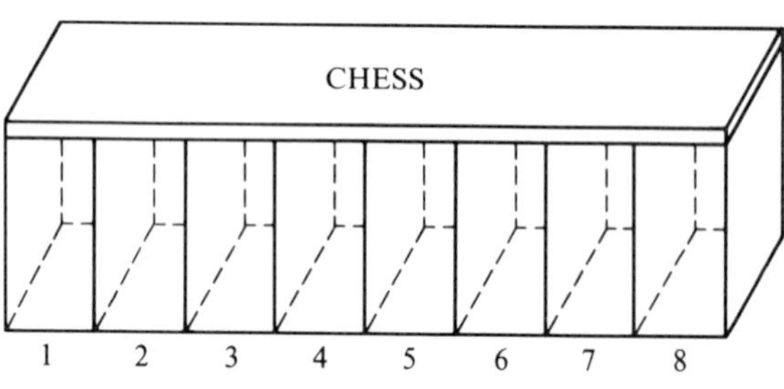

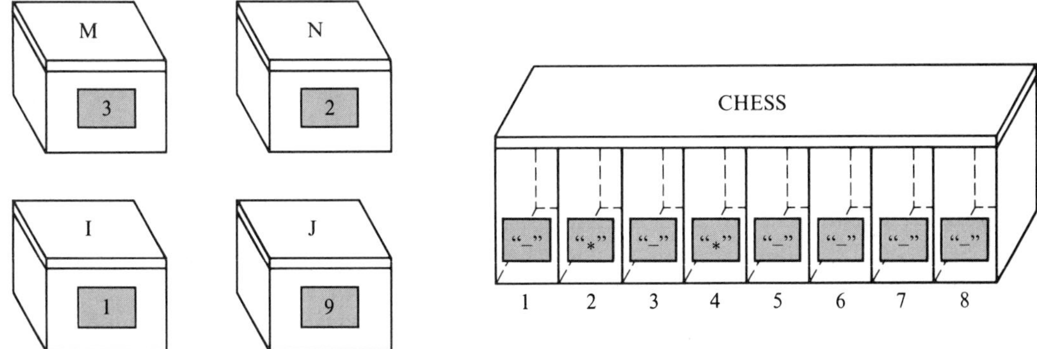

Figure 1-12

or "getting" the value of a variable means making a *copy* of the value found in the container that has the variable on its cover. (Assigning a value to a variable and reading the value of a variable are tasks delegated to the Reader/Assigner.) In our model we assume all containers are built to order and thus are empty in the beginning. Under these circumstances it is clearly incorrect ever to try to get the value of a variable before that variable has received a value, through either input or assignment. Figure 1-12 shows the variables and their values just after box e3′ in Figure 1-8 has been executed for the first time, printing the first row of the chessboard shown in Figure 1-1. Printing the value of a variable does not alter the value in the storage container.

How big is a storage container in the model computer and what kind of information can it store? In this ideal computer model the storage capacity of a container will be assumed to be some finite but unspecified size. Hence a container can store any integer, any real number, or any character string that can be represented in a finite number of bits. A container can store the string ABLE□BAKER or the integer 2 or can be long enough, for example, to hold the decimal representation of $\sqrt{2}$ to whatever precision is desired.

Since a list variable is no more than a collection of similar simple variables, list storage cells have the same definite but unspecified capacity to hold lists. As a matter of fact we can have variables that are arrays of two (or more) dimensions, where each compartment has a definite but unspecified capacity. The reader can easily imagine a single storage cell capable of storing the 8×8 chessboard.

Suppose the Master Computer has placed the chessboard flowchart of Figure 1-8 on his worktable and one of his assistants has already assembled for him the storage containers for the variables shown in Figure 1-11. These five labeled cells constitute the *environment* in which the program will be executed. We shall be studying the execution of many programs in this book and it would be tedious if we always had to draw cells in perspective. Instead let us introduce the shorthand shown in Figure 1-13. Each storage cell in a program will be replaced by a schematic two-part equivalent in which the first part will contain the *name* of the variable and the second part will contain the *value* of the variable. (Of course the value itself may be composite, for example, a list or array.)

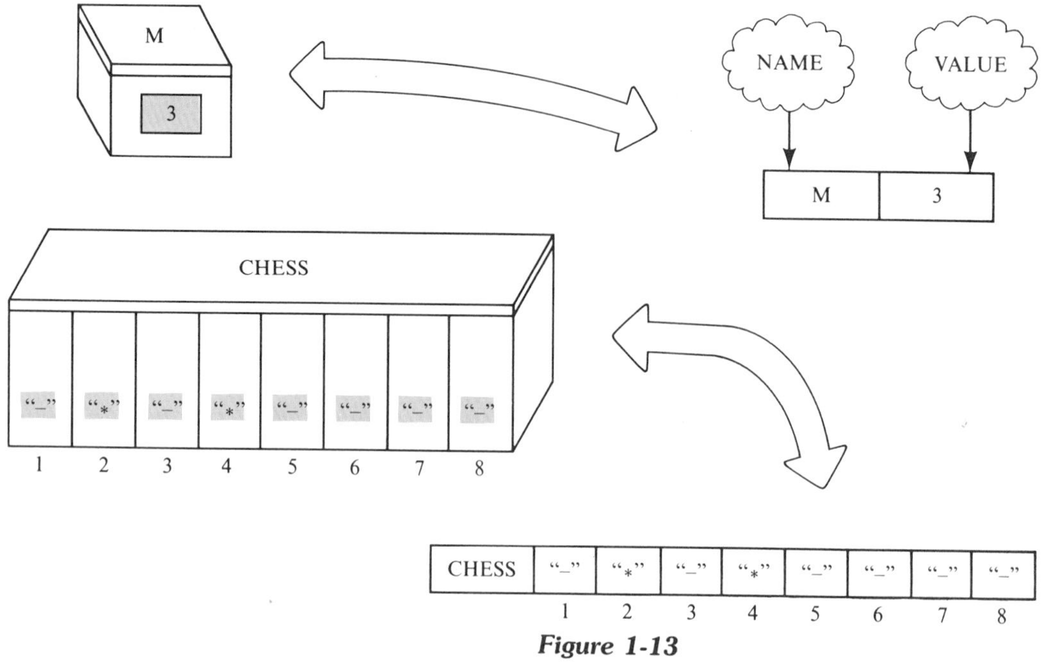

Figure 1-13

Thus Figure 1-11, which shows the *environment* in which the Master Computer is about to execute the flowchart of Figure 1-8, can now be represented more easily as shown in Figure 1-14a. To give it visual unity, we draw an enclosing boundary or *contour* around the environment. To complete a picture of the state of the computation (that is, a *snapshot* of the execution), we also show what the Master Computer is doing by placing the symbol "MC" inside the environment at the bottom, pointing to the name of the flowchart box he is about to execute (see Figure 1-14b).

Suppose the input data for box b1′ of Figure 1-8 is (3, 2), the same data that led to the output shown in Figure 1-2. The second snapshot we may want to take is just after box f5 is executed for the first time, and just prior to incrementing J in box el. The first position on the board, (1, 1), will have been assigned a dash, –, as we can see from Figure 1-2. (The position (1, 2) will get the first asterisk.) Figure 1-15 is otherwise self-explanatory.

What does a snapshot look like just after box e3′ is executed for the first time? That will be our third snapshot, Figure 1-16. When control arrives at box e3′, the inequality $J \leq 8$ in box e1 will have just become false, and since J has been going up by 1 each cycle through the loop, we can deduce that J has the value 9. Since the loop controlled by box e1 has been completed, the correct character values have already been assigned to all the first row elements of CHESS. Notice that after box e3′ the flowchart flowline returns to the *incrementation* part of box d1. Hence Figure 1-16 shows the MC pointing to this very place.

Snapshots such as Figure 1-15 and 1-16 suggest a way to trace the execution of a program. Each snapshot is intended to show all the relevant details about a

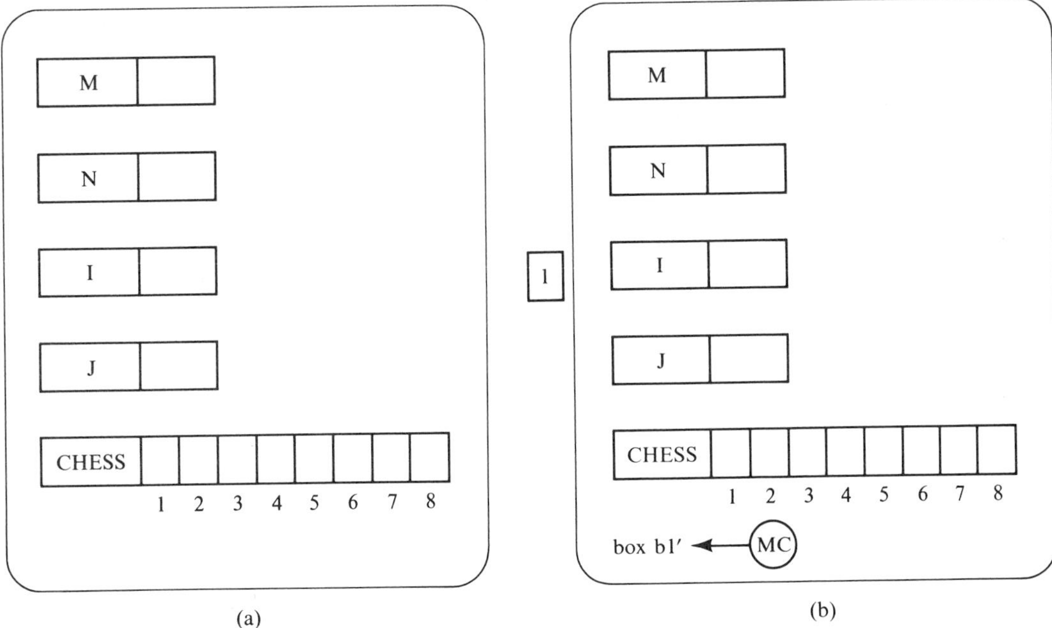

Figure 1-14. **Snapshot 1.**

computation if the action were temporarily frozen at that point. A snapshot not only shows each cell (and its content) that is relevant (that is, accessible) to the MC, but also describes the state of the MC itself, and so we can tell by consulting the flowchart what would happen if the frozen computation were thawed out and resumed.

Figure 1-15. **Snapshot 2.**

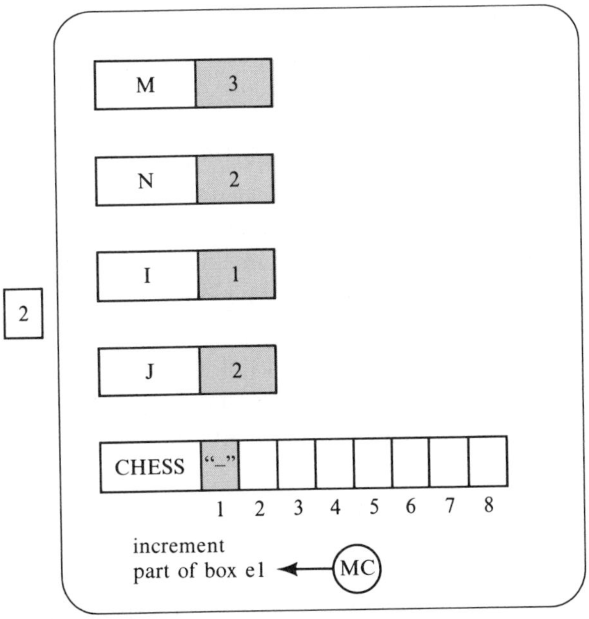

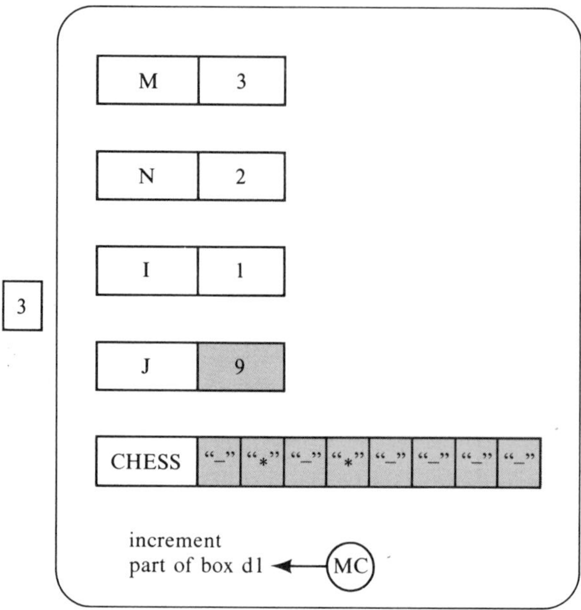

Figure 1-16. **Snapshot 3.**

1-4
PROCEDURES AND ENVIRONMENTS

In composing the Queen's scope algorithm we have utilized the methodology of decomposition, but we have regarded the final result (Figure 1-8) as a single algorithm. We have not yet needed the concept of procedure (some synonyms for procedure are *subroutine, subalgorithm,* and *subprogram*), which if applied to the Queen's scope problem would let us break up the program into a main part and a collection of subsidiary procedures. As soon as we introduce procedures into the structure of a language, its semantics become considerably richer. We explore this step now.

First, observe with regard to the Figure 1-8 flowchart, that any box that is decomposed further can be thought of as an abbreviation for that decomposition. Looked at this way, the English written in the box becomes a name for the flowchart fragment that constitutes the immediate decomposition of that box. As a means of identifying the flowchart fragment, the abbreviation amounts to a *procedure identifier.* Any flowchart step containing a procedure identifier (as a command) may therefore be thought of as a procedure call, that is, as a request for the execution of the subroutine that is spelled out in its immediate decomposition. We shall henceforth use a special striped rectangular box to identify a procedure call (Figure 1-17).

Since many programming languages use names and identifiers that are limited to single words and not phrases or sentences, we convert English phrases into single words by using an underscore as a connector when the description appears in a procedure call box, as shown in Figure 1-17. At the

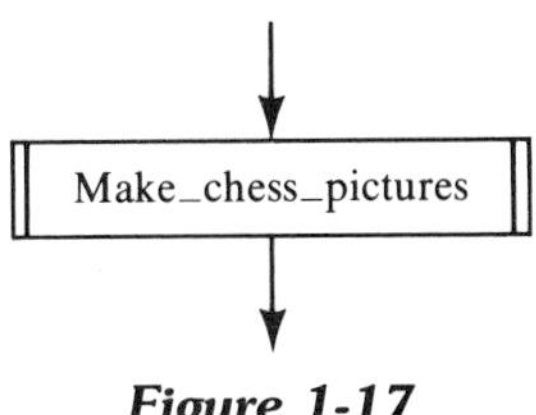

Figure 1-17

same time, we usually shorten the phrase as much as possible without losing all of its English meaning.

Figure 1-18 is a rewrite of Figure 1-8, utilizing the striped procedure call boxes and shortening the phrases as much as possible. There is also one important difference to be noted. Each of the flowchart fragments of Figure 1-8, referred to by a striped call box, has been converted into an independent subflowchart in Figure 1-18. There are five such subflowcharts, each with its own START and RETURN boxes and, at the top, a masthead for the procedure name. These seemingly small changes in notation, from flowchart fragments to *independent subflowcharts,* in fact cause many important repercussions, which we want to explore in some detail.

Executing Procedure Calls and Returns

The executions of the algorithms in Figures 1-8 and 1-18 accomplish the same net effect and therefore, in an important sense, they should be regarded as equivalent. However, to convince ourselves that they really are equivalent in overall effect, we need to understand how the Figure 1-18 flowcharts are executed on our computer model, which must now be augmented to explain how the Master Computer (MC) executes a procedure-call step and a procedure-return step.

To execute a procedure call, the Master Computer must make a record of his place in the calling flowchart and then move to the START box of the subflowchart that has been called, so he can begin executing that subflowchart. Eventually, when he reaches a RETURN box of the subflowchart, the Master Computer will move back to the exit line emerging from the procedure call box whose number he recorded before he transferred to the subflowchart. He will resume execution from that point. However, what about the storage environment for execution of this algorithm? What changes in the environment should or could accompany a procedure call or return?

One point of view we can take is that there is just one legend for an entire ensemble of a flowchart and its subflowcharts, and hence one storage environment holds throughout the computation. When the Master Computer consults such a legend he asks the Allocator to set up storage boxes *in advance* for all the variables that will ever be needed. It is then immaterial in what flowchart or subflowchart a variable first appears. From this viewpoint the legend for Figure 1-18 should be identical with that for Figure 1-8; consequently, the environment that is established and used throughout the computation for the Figure 1-18 algorithm is identical with that for the Figure 1-8 algorithm. (See

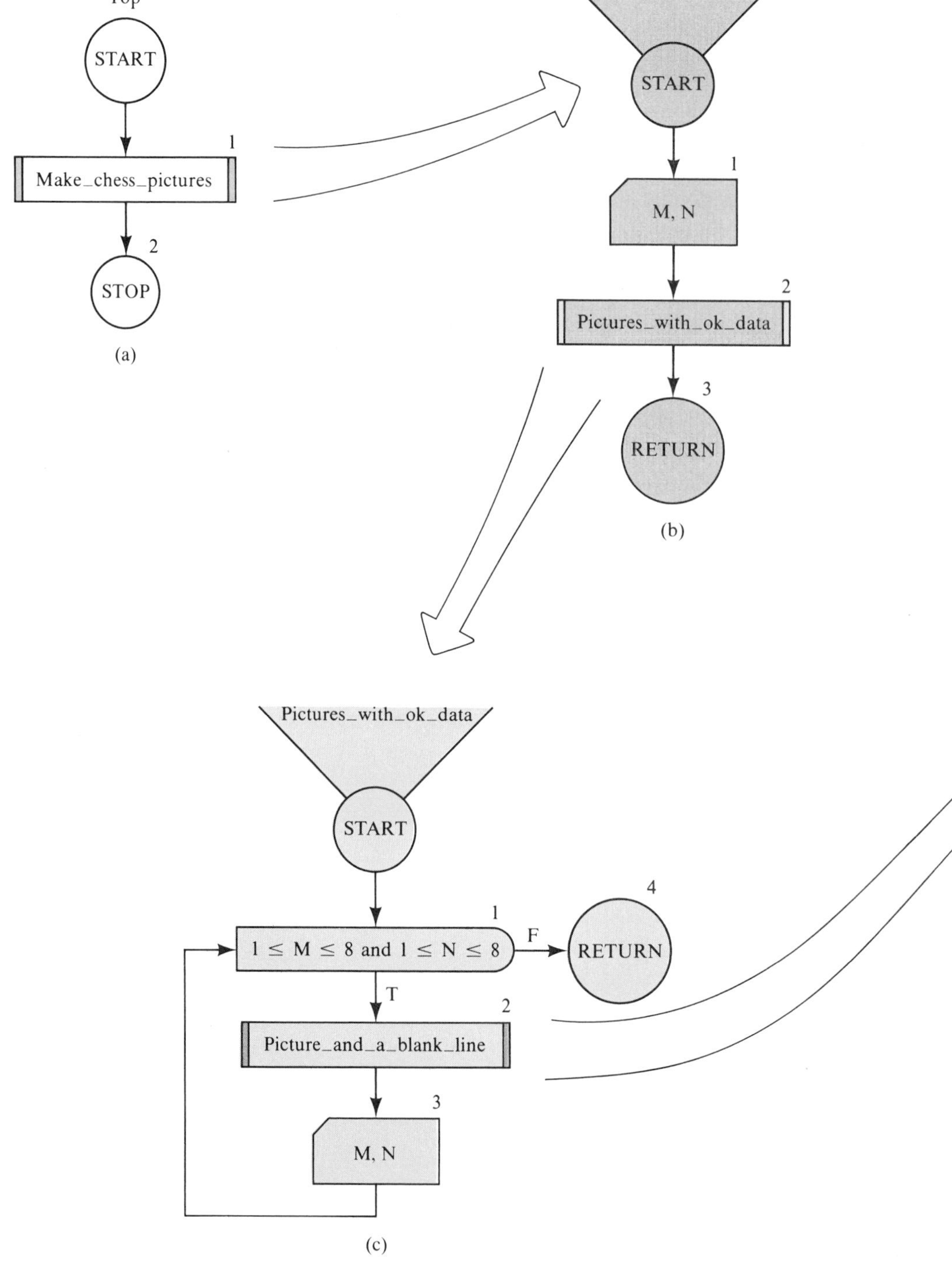

Figure 1-18. **Chessboard flowchart decomposed into procedures. Procedure abbreviations used later: Make_chess_pictures, MCP; Pictures_with_ok_data, PokD; Picture_and_a_blank_line, PBL; One_line, Line; One_character, One_char.**

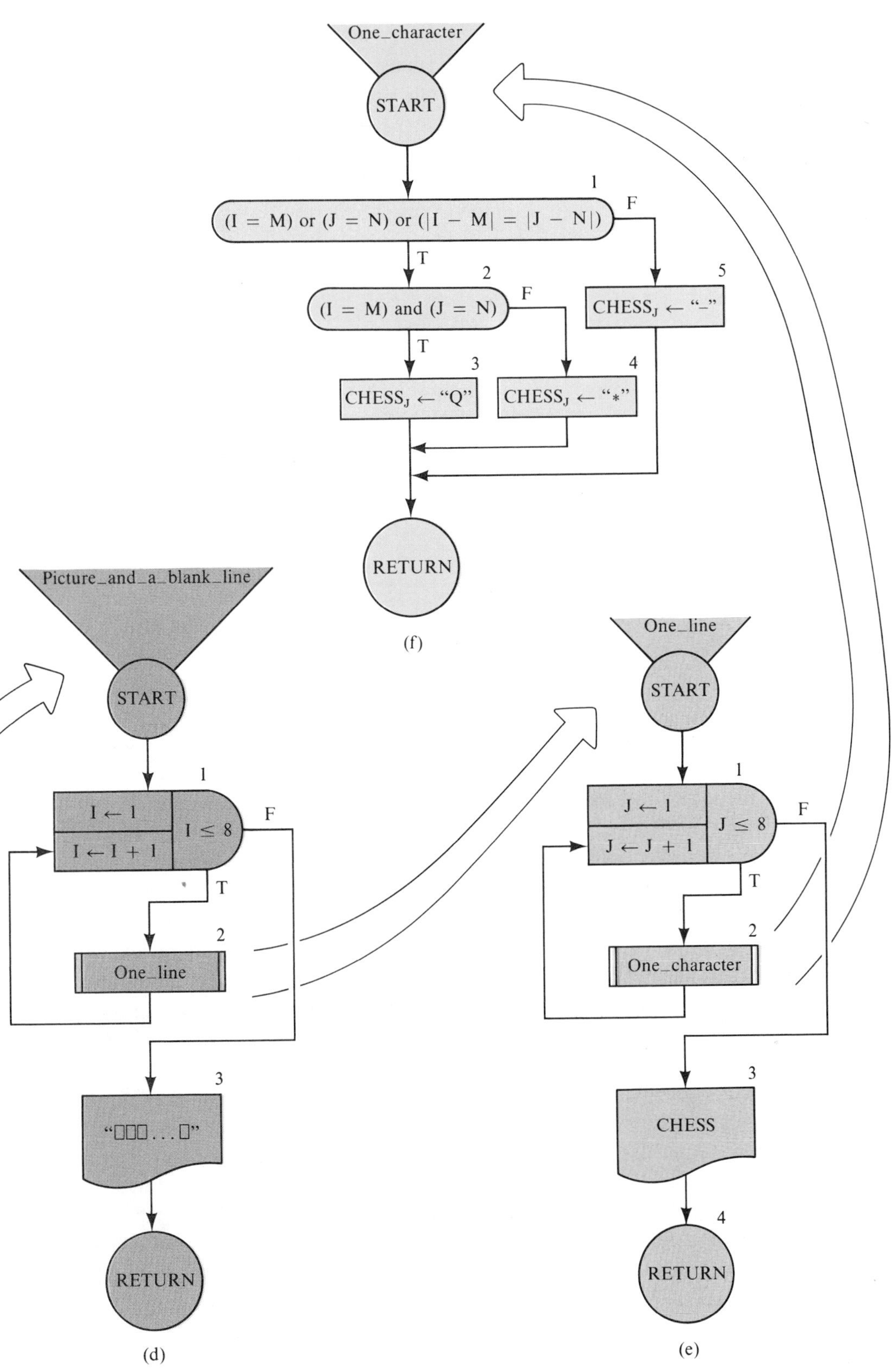
One_character
START
1
(I = M) or (J = N) or (|I − M| = |J − N|)
F
T
2
(I = M) and (J = N)
F
T
5
CHESS_J ← "–"
3
CHESS_J ← "Q"
4
CHESS_J ← "*"
RETURN
Picture_and_a_blank_line
START
1
I ← 1
I ← I + 1
I ≤ 8
F
T
2
One_line
3
"□□□ . . . □"
RETURN
One_line
START
1
J ← 1
J ← J + 1
J ≤ 8
F
T
2
One_character
3
CHESS
4
RETURN

(f)

(d)

(e)

Figure 1-14.) Many actual computer systems are compatible with this viewpoint. The Basic and Cobol language systems are examples.

A second point of view is that a separate storage environment is associated with each subflowchart. This implies that a separate legend is required for each subflowchart and that each procedure call and return is accompanied by a shift from one environment to another. Many actual programming systems follow this point of view, for example, Fortran, Algol, Lisp, APL, and PL/I. Each legend defines the environment to be used with its respective subflowchart. In some systems (for example, Algol) the environment for a subprogram is not actually created until the corresponding subprogram is invoked. In other systems (for example, Fortran) the separate environments for each subprogram are created in advance, along with the environment for the main or top-level program.

Still other variations in the management (for example, creation and deletion) of environments exist in widely used systems. We defer scrutiny of these similarities and differences until Part II of this book. Instead we concentrate here on one possible and consistent view of how to deal with storage environments in our model.

Our approach stems from the second view considered above. *Each procedure subflowchart will have a separate legend. Each time a procedure is called its legend will be consulted and a new storage environment created.* The MC will move into that environment after it has been created, and execute the subflowchart from within the newly created environment. When the MC executes a RETURN step, he will move back into the previous (calling) environment from which the call was made and resume execution of the calling procedure from within that (calling) environment at the box just following the call. Every call on the same procedure will result in the creation of a new storage environment, based each time on the same fixed legend information of the called procedure. Repeated calls on a procedure (P) will therefore result in the creation of identically structured environments, one for each call on P. But the MC will reside only in the environment of the current invocation. We assume that the MC can rely on the Allocator to dispose of environments that are no longer needed. Thus, if the environment created to execute some called procedure (Q) is no longer needed (and it normally will not be), one can assume that after the return is executed the Allocator will eliminate this environment by "recycling" the resources (storage cells) of that environment.

Now let us see how this second view of procedures and their storage environments can be interpreted in the case of the algorithm of Figure 1-18. In the first place, we need a proper set of legends for this ensemble of flowcharts. Figure 1-19 is such a set. Each legend defines the environment needed by the MC to execute the respective flowchart. Thus, when executing in Top, the MC needs no variables, but he does need to know that there exists a procedure named Make_chess_pictures, when he attempts to execute the procedure call step of Figure 1-17.

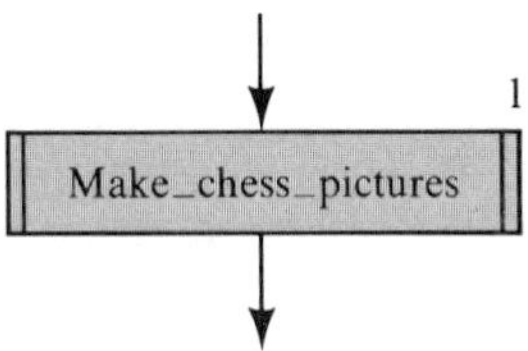

He can deduce that Make_chess_pictures is the identifier of a procedure by the context in which it is used, and he knows that the sub-flowcharts for all called procedures are accessible, that is, they have already been placed on his desk top.

The other legends in Figure 1-19 show entries for the variables that appear explicitly in their respective subflowcharts. Thus entries for integer variables M and N appear in the legend for Make_chess_pictures (MCP). Note that corresponding entries for M and N also appear in two other legends, that of Pictures_with_ok_data (PokD), and that of One_character (One_char). However, the descriptions of M and N in these legends may be surprising, unless one is careful in his thinking. For example, the description for M in the legend for One_character is not that of an integer (cell) named M for the environment of One_character, but is rather a reference or pointer to a storage cell named M in the Make_chess_pictures environment. In other words, there is only one cell to hold the integer value of M (and by similar reasoning only one such cell for N) in this computation. That cell is created for the Make_chess_pictures environment. Any other procedure such as One_character may refer to M, but to be certain that it is the same variable that was first mentioned in Make_chess_pictures, the legend for One_character must make this reference clear and unambiguous. If the description for M in the legend for One_character were simply "integer," confusion would surely result, because a second cell to hold values of M would be created in the environment for One_character.

***Figure 1-19.* Legends for the flowcharts in Figure 1-18 (same procedure abbreviations).**

Legend for Top

Identifier	Description
–	–

Legend for MCP

Identifier	Description
M, N	integer

Legend for PokD

Identifier	Description
M N	M in MCP N in MCP

Legend for PBL

Identifier	Description
I	integer

Legend for Line

Identifier	Description
J CHESS	integer list of 8 characters

Legend for One-Char

Identifier	Description
J M N I CHESS	J in Line M in MCP N in MCP I in PBL CHESS in Line

Then, when executing box 1 in One_character, the Reader/Assigner might be sent to the wrong cell in search of the value of M.

Bearing in mind the foregoing principles for executing procedures, we are ready to consider what execution snapshots for the Figure 1-18 flowcharts will look like. In Figures 1-20, 1-21, and 1-22, we show snapshots corresponding, respectively, to states of execution given in Figures 1-14b, 1-15, and 1-16 for the Figure 1-8 flowchart. Each new snapshot is discussed in turn. Note that we continue to use the abbreviations for the procedure names defined in Figure 1-18.

Snapshot 1 (Figure 1-20) shows the state of affairs after the execution of Top has begun, at a point where the MC is about to make the call on the Make_chess_pictures (MCP) procedure. The MC is operating in an environment empty of variables, that is, no storage cells are yet accessible.

Snapshot 2 (Figure 1-21) shows the situation while the MC is operating in the most detailed level procedure, One_character. This is the second time One_character has been invoked (called). The MC is just about to execute box 2. Each of the five storage cells in the One_char environment is a reference to a cell in an "earlier" environment.

To execute box 2,

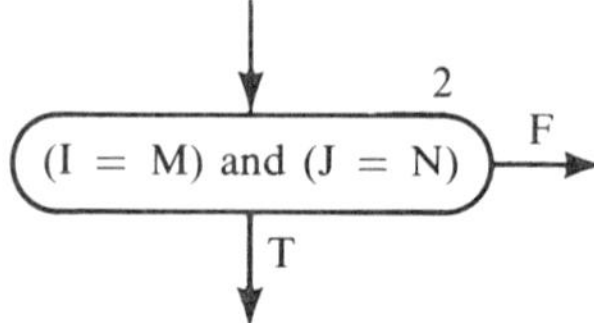

values for I, M, J, and N are to be retrieved. The value of I is obtained by consulting the cell for I that contains a reference to the cell for I in the PBL (Picture_and_a_blank_line) environment. There the value for I is 1. The value of M is obtained by a similar cross-referencing process. The value of M is seen to be *the value of M in the MCP environment,* which is 3. I = M is therefore not true, and so values for J and N are not of interest, since the MC evaluates the expression in box 2 from left to right. However, if values of J and N were required, they would be obtained by a similar cross-referencing process.

Snapshot 3 (Figure 1-22) shows the situation just after the MC has returned to the PBL (Picture_and_a_blank_line) procedure environment and is about to execute the incrementation portion of (iteration) box 1. The first line of the first chess picture has just been printed. The MC has no need for the cells in

Figure 1-20. **The MC is about to execute box 1 of the Top flowchart.**

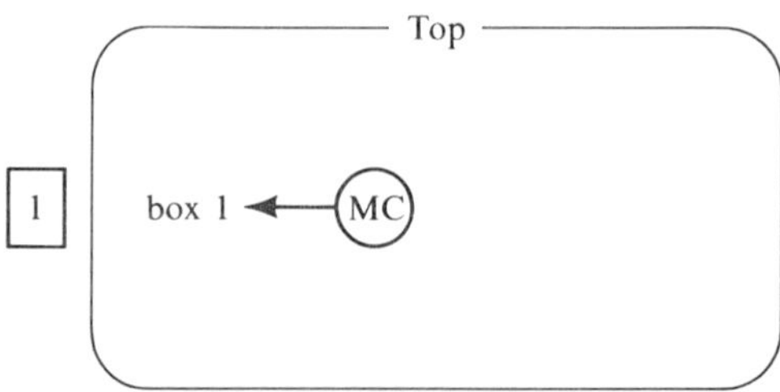

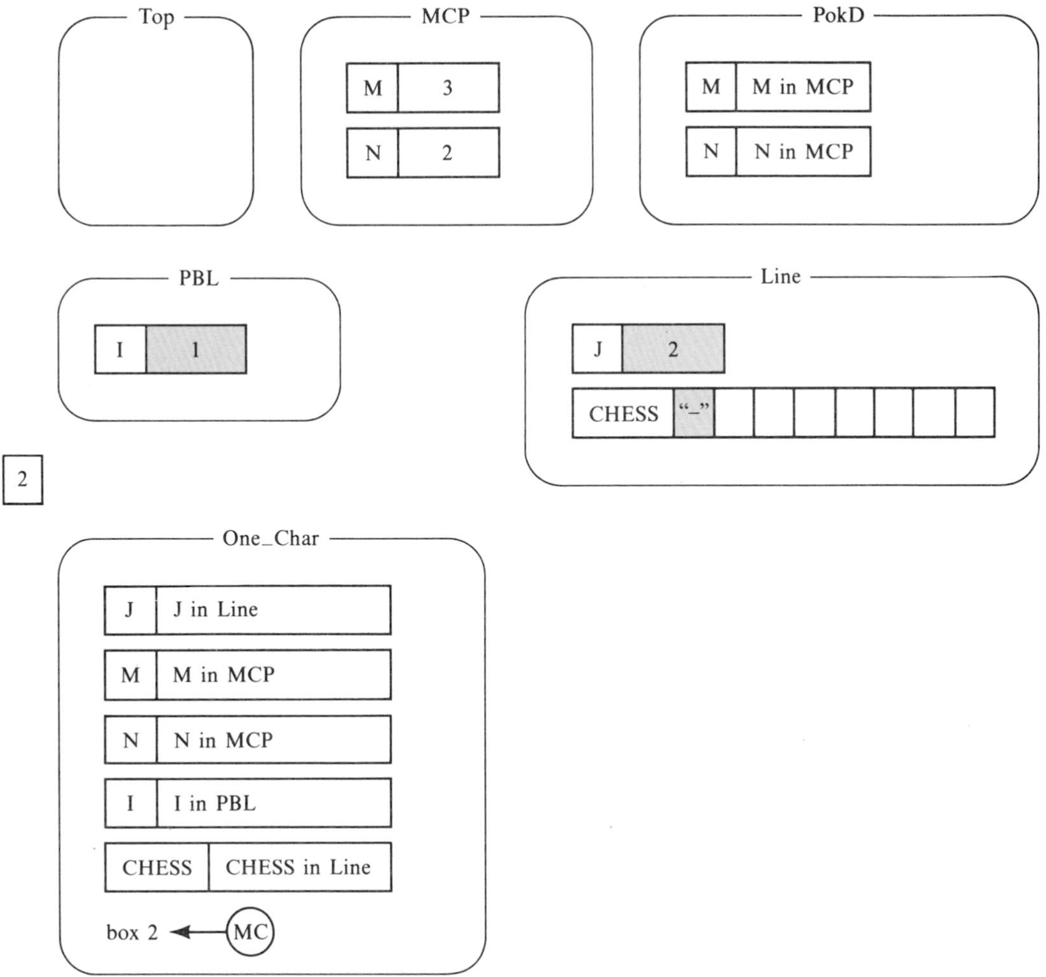

Figure 1-21. **The MC is just about to execute box 2 in the second invocation of the One_character procedure.**

the environments from which he has exited. Therefore, the environments for Line and for One_char are shaded to suggest that they are inaccessible to the MC and may be considered deleted at the instant of snapshot 3. Of course, the One_line and One_character procedures will be called again in this calculation (several times, in fact), and each time this happens, new environments will be created for these called procedures.

Taking stock, we sense that snapshot sequences using diagrams like those just presented can be especially revealing where the underlying model requires creation of a new environment to go with each invocation of a procedure. However, unless we are careful to introduce additional precision in our notation, snapshots will become difficult to interpret. We now extend the notation to address the two following issues:

(1) Since each invocation of the same procedure requires creation of a new contour, we qualify each contour with a superscript to denote the invocation

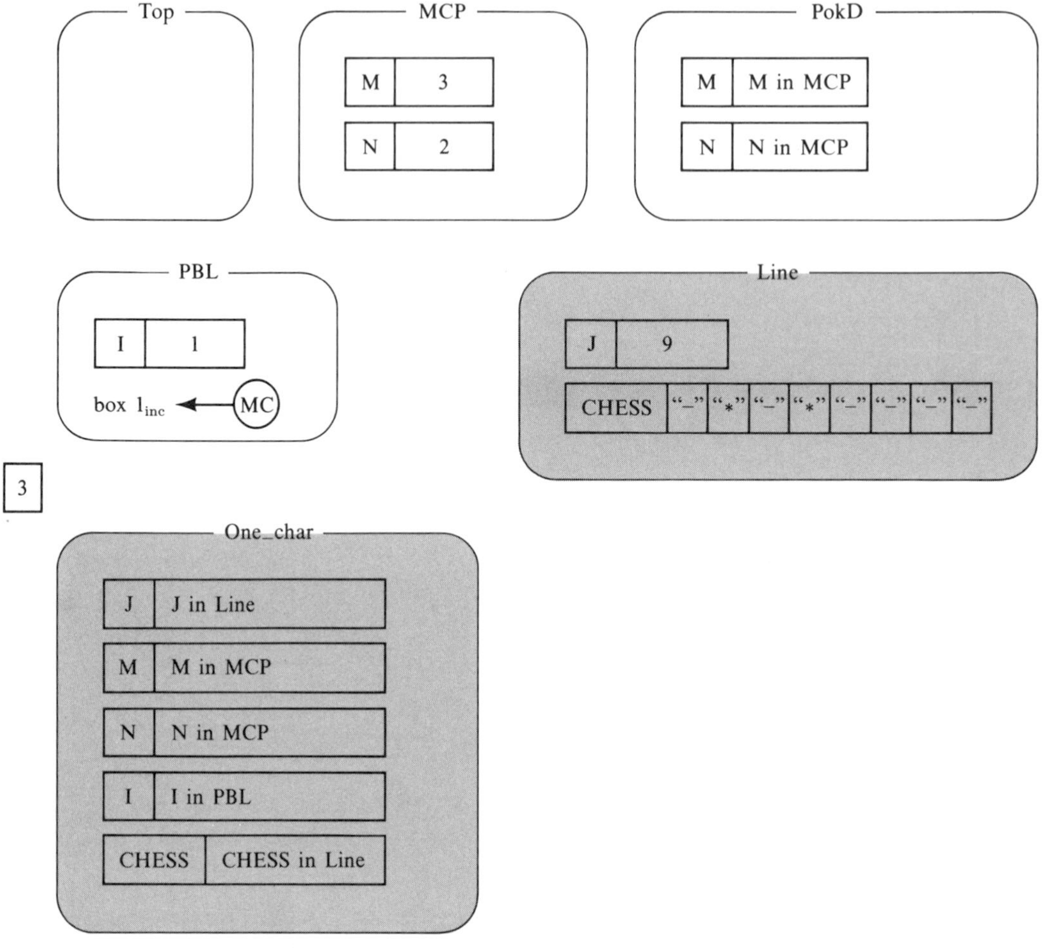

Figure 1-22. **The MC has just returned to Picture_and_a_blank_line from the first call on One_line and is about to execute the incrementation portion of box 1, that is, box 1_{inc}. The environments for Line and One_char have been deallocated.**

to which the contour corresponds. Figure 1-23 is a redrawing of snapshot 2 in Figure 1-21 using this superscripting convention.

A happy by-product results from marking each contour name (and each reference to a particular contour) with an appropriate superscript. The distinction between an environment for a procedure and the procedure itself becomes sharper. For example, when we look at the cell

I	I in PBL^1

in One_char^2, the value in this cell now refers unambiguously to the cell named I in the contour (not the procedure) named PBL^1.

(2) Earlier we said that the MC makes a record of his place in a calling procedure before he transfers to the START box of the called procedure subflowchart. (The purpose of this record, you recall, is to enable execution to resume correctly after control encounters the RETURN box of the subflowchart.)

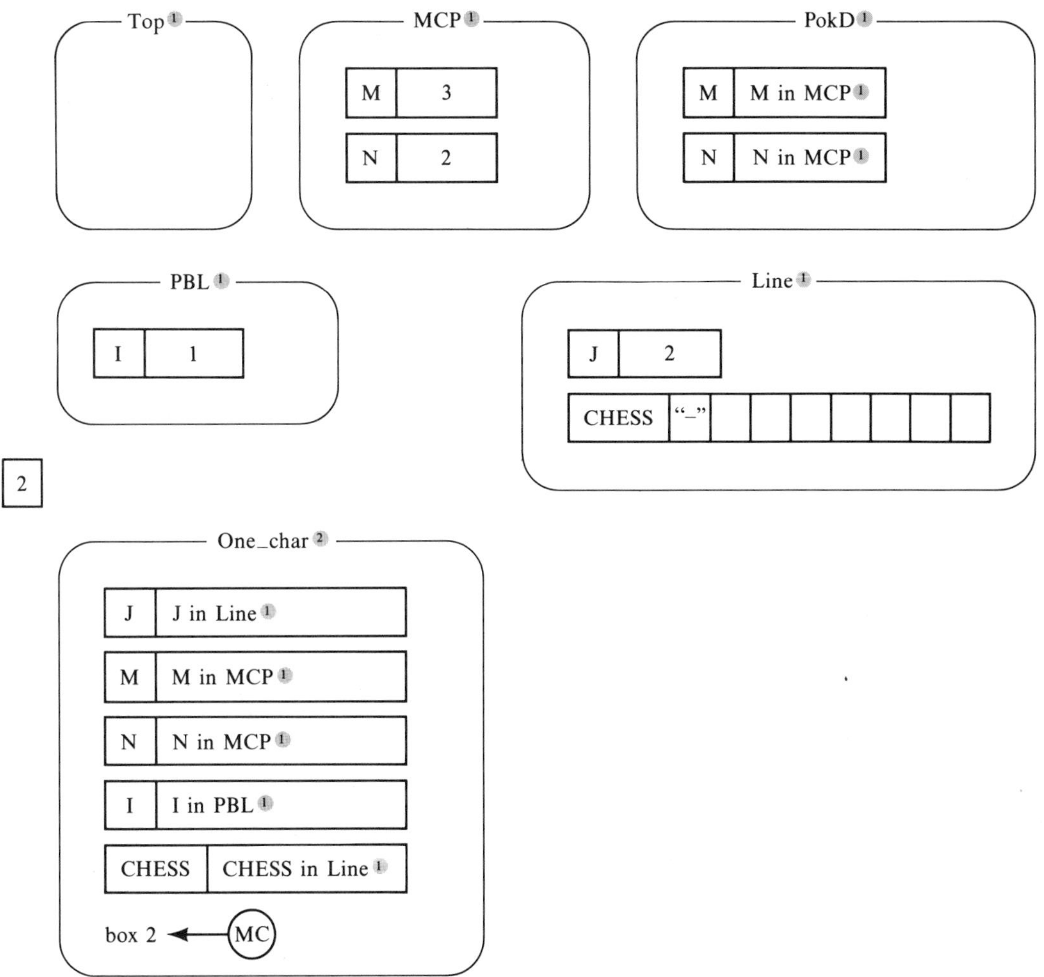

Figure 1-23. **Same as snapshot in Figure 1-21 but using superscripts on contour names.**

Earlier, however, we did not specify how or where this record was to be made. Now we have the tools to make this information much more explicit.

Whenever a new contour is created as part of a procedure invocation, the MC orders a special "return label" cell to be allocated to that contour. This cell is distinguished from the others by having a special name, such as *retlab*. The value inserted in the cell names both (1) the contour that the MC should reenter when executing the RETURN step for this invocation and (2) the instruction that should be executed next. For example,

retlab	box 2 in Top^1

The value in the second compartment is referred to as an (ip, ep) pair,* where ip stands for instruction pointer and ep stands for environment pointer. The (ip, ep) pair is an important concept and will appear often as we proceed.

*Pronounced "eye pee, ee pee pair."

This idea of saving the identity of the caller's environment and the instruction to be executed next in that environment is achieved in analogous ways in actual computer systems. Figure 1-24 shows snapshot 2.5, which follows snapshot 2. Here we illustrate the situation when the MC, executing in the second invocation of One_char, is just about to execute the RETURN step.

***Figure 1-24.* Snapshot showing the use of *retlab* cells in procedure contours.**

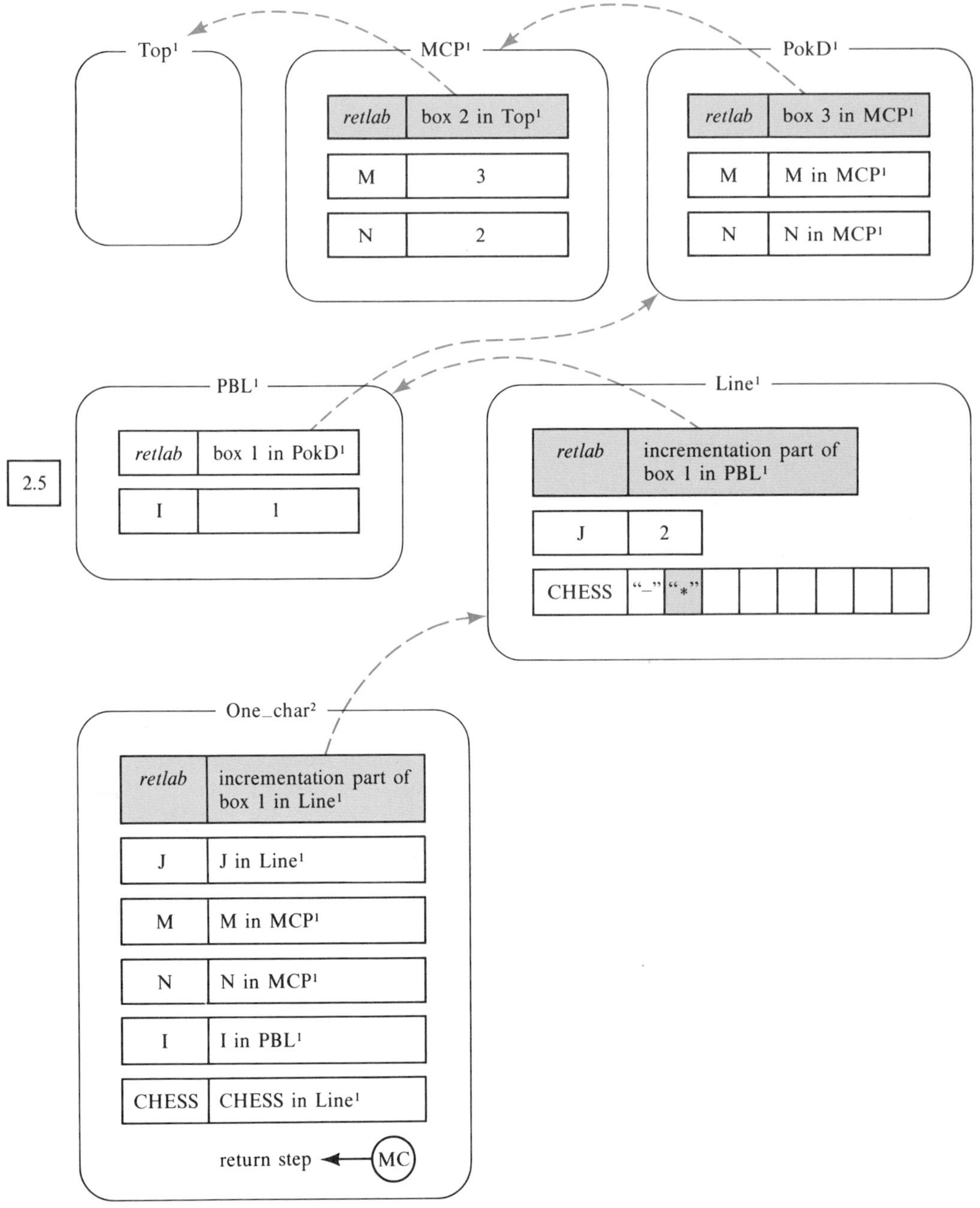

Exercises 1-4

1 The process of integer division consists in starting with two positive integers N and D (called dividend and divisor, respectively) and finding two other nonnegative integers Q and R (quotient and remainder) so that

$$N = Q \times D + R$$

where

$$0 \leq R < D$$

Figure 1-25 shows (a) a top-level flowchart and (b) a procedure flowchart (including legends), which taken together input the dividend and divisor and then calculate and display the quotient and remainder.

Figure 1-25

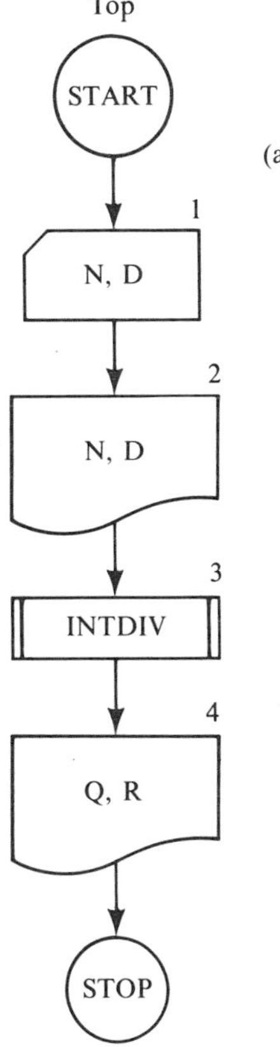

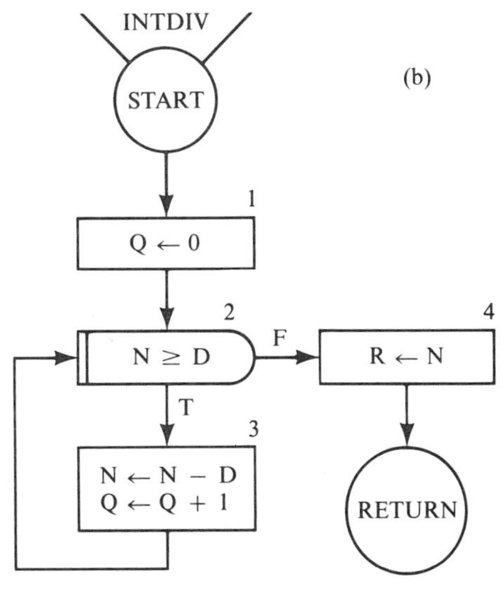

Legend for Top

Identifier	Description
N, D, Q, R	integer

Legend for INTDIV

Identifier	Description
Q R N D	Q in Top R in Top N in Top D in Top

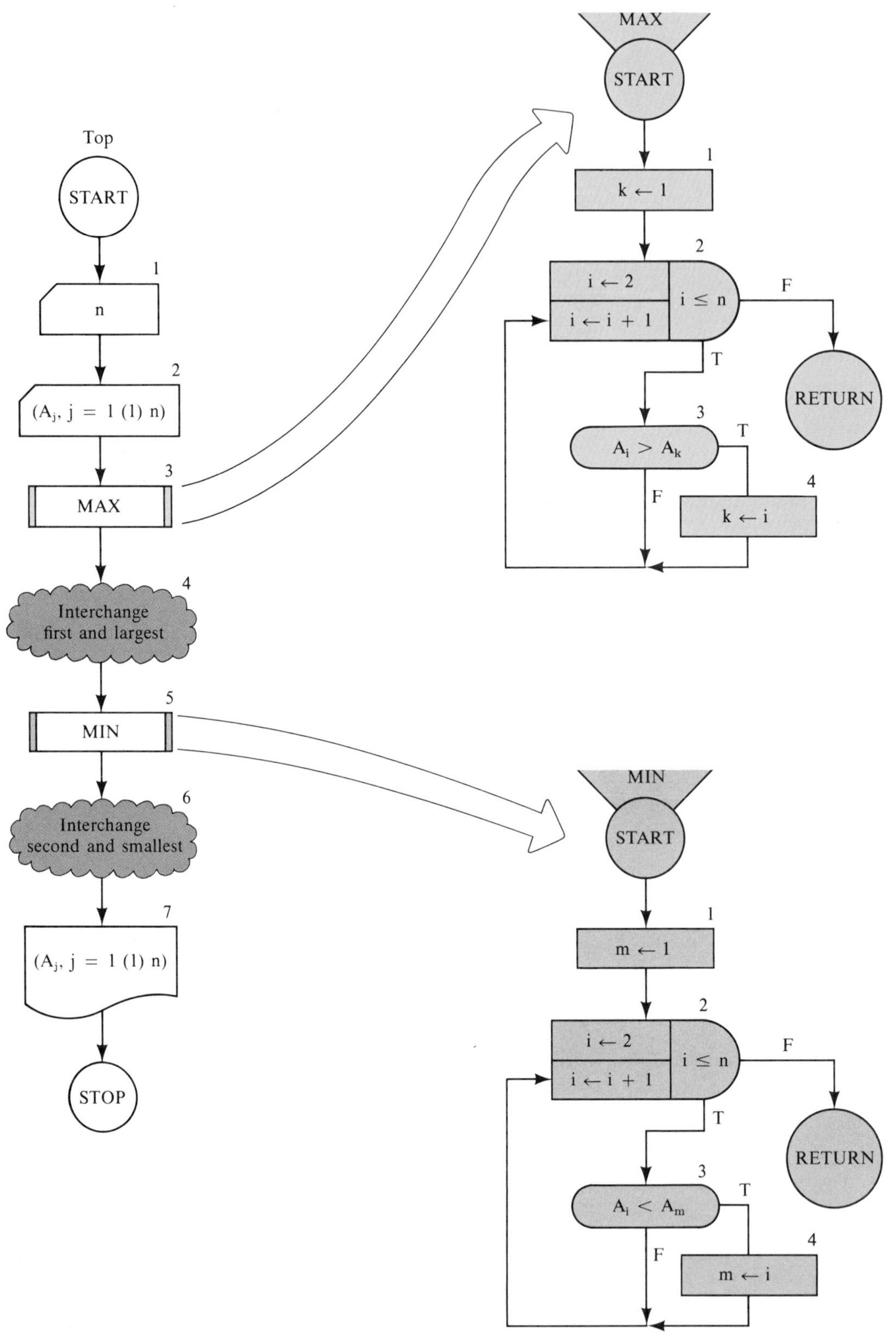
Top
START
1
n
2
(A_j, j = 1 (1) n)
3
MAX
4
Interchange first and largest
5
MIN
6
Interchange second and smallest
7
(A_j, j = 1 (1) n)
STOP
MAX
START
1
k ← 1
2
i ← 2
i ← i + 1
i ≤ n
F
RETURN
T
3
A_i > A_k
T
F
4
k ← i
MIN
START
1
m ← 1
2
i ← 2
i ← i + 1
i ≤ n
F
RETURN
T
3
A_i < A_m
T
F
4
m ← i

Figure 1-26

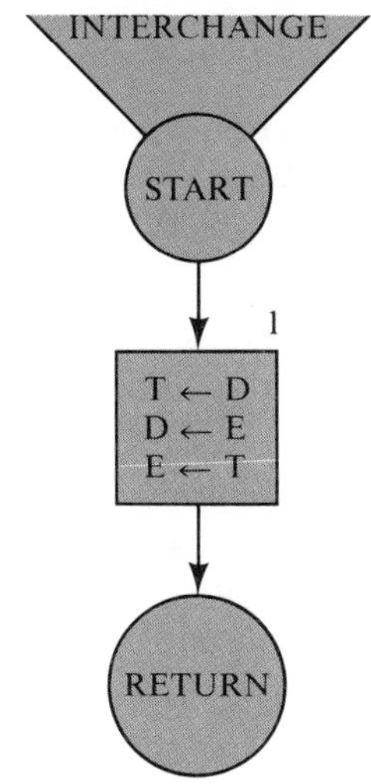

Legend for Top

Identifier	Description
j, n, k, m	integer
A	list of n reals
D, E	real

Legend for MIN

Identifier	Description
n	n in Top
m	m in Top
A	A in Top
i	integer

Legend for MAX

Identifier	Description
n	n in Top
k	k in Top
A	A in Top
i	integer

Legend for INTERCHANGE

Identifier	Description
D	D in Top
E	E in Top
T	real

(a) What is the complete output of Top when input values for N and D are 43 and 12, respectively?

(b) Suppose Top were modified so that box 2 *follows* box 3 rather than preceding it. For the same input values in (a), again give the complete output produced by executing Top.

(c) Draw a snapshot showing the state of the computation just after executing box 3 of INTDIV for the first time. Assume input values are N = 43 and D = 12, and also assume, as in (b), that boxes 2 and 3 of Top have been interchanged.

(d) If you have completed (a), (b), and (c), you should have a clear idea of what causes the change in output resulting from the interchange of boxes 2 and 3 in Top. Show a modification to INTDIV that will make the output of Top independent of the order of boxes 2 and 3 in Top.

2 Assume we are given the set of flowcharts and legends in Figure 1-26. The execution of Top should initiate the following actions:

(1) Input a list A of n real numbers.

(2) Locate the element of A with the largest value and assign to k the index of this location (using the procedure MAX).

(3) Interchange the values of the *first* and the kth elements of A (using INTERCHANGE).
(4) Locate the element of A that has the smallest value and assign to m the index of this location (using the procedure MIN).
(5) Interchange the value of the *second* and the mth elements of A (using INTERCHANGE).
(6) Output the modified list A.

Part I Give two flowchart fragments for the details of clouds 4 and 6 that accomplish the actions specified in (3) and (5) above, respectively. Do this *without* altering INTERCHANGE in any way. This same unaltered version of INTERCHANGE is to be used for both clouds.

Part II Give two flowchart fragments for the details of clouds 4 and 6 as outlined in Part I, using INTERCHANGE′ and the new legend for Top as given in Figure 1-27.

3 Draw a flowchart to do the following:
(a) Input M, N, and two M × N matrices called A and B.
(b) In A replace each row whose elements are in strictly descending order with the corresponding row of B. The nondescending rows of A are not affected.
(c) Output the resulting matrix A.

Use stepwise decomposition to break up the flowchart into an appropriate number of procedures. Be sure your flowchart has good structure and that you choose iteration and while boxes correctly. Provide legends.

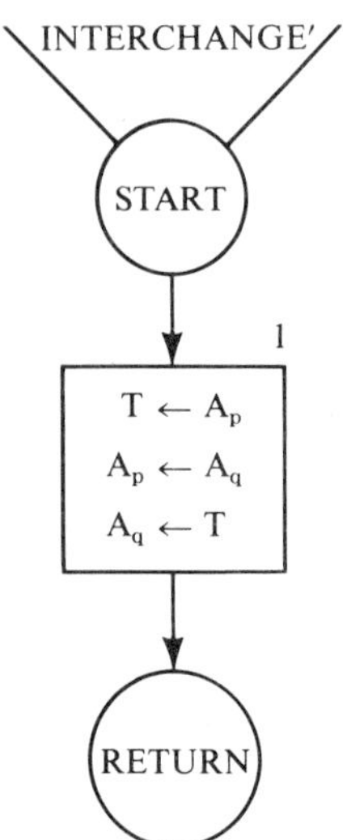

Legend for INTERCHANGE′

Identifier	Description
p	p in Top
q	q in Top
T	real

New Legend for Top

Identifier	Description
j, n, k, m	integer
A	list of n reals
p, q	integer

Figure 1-27

1-5 GLOBAL AND LOCAL VARIABLES

If all the various subflowcharts are truly independent, then it should be perfectly possible to "unplug" any one of them and substitute another, if the substitute has the same name and same purpose or objective, even though perhaps it has a different way of achieving that objective and possibly uses different variables. Nothing "upward" in the flowchart would in any way be disturbed or changed by such a substitution. For example, suppose the subalgorithm under consideration requires an iteration and that one flowchart description names the iteration counter J while a second flowchart names it N. We sense that it is immaterial whether the variable is called J or N, so long as there is not another variable of the same name elsewhere in the program with which it might be confused. But suppose there *is* another variable of the same name. Is it possible to *prevent* interference in this case? For example, Figure 1-28 shows a subflowchart for One_line that is entirely equivalent in action to that of the same name in Figure 1-18; the only difference is that the iteration variable is called N. Can we substitute the subflowchart of Figure 1-28 for One_line in Figure 1-18?

No we cannot, because N already stands for the column index of the Queen. We need to use that column index in the One_character procedure, which is called from within One_line. We want the Queen position to stay fixed while we compose and print the chessboard. In other words, N needs to have the same definition in One_line that it had in the higher level procedure Make_chess_pictures. So we had better not substitute Figure 1-28 as a replacement for

Figure 1-28

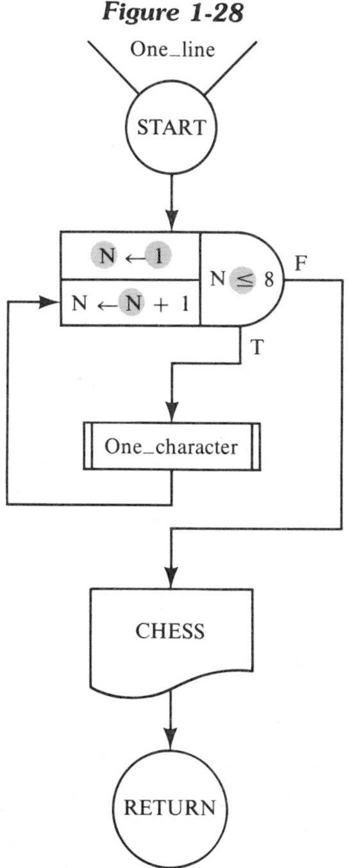

One_line in Figure 1-18. Under the circumstances just described, the variable N is said to be *global* to the procedure One_line.

In the same sense each of the variables listed in the legend for One_character is global to that procedure. They have been created elsewhere (in other environments) but, by the general cross-referencing scheme we have provided, they are accessible to the MC in this environment. We say that a variable A, referred to in a procedure P, *is globally accessible* to P (or *is global to* P) if A has been created during execution of another procedure Q, but A is somehow also made accessible when the MC executes in P. Almost every programming system that allows the programmer to define procedures also provides a means for specifying global accessibility. Various methods for specifying globality are used, and we shall examine some of these in Part II.

With a flowchart language (or an English-like equivalent) a programmer can specify globality of certain variables in a procedure simply by properly identifying them, as in the legend of a subflowchart. This was done in Figure 1-19. When the MC of our model executes such a subflowchart, access to the requested global variables is then ensured, since the MC will consult the legend to determine exactly how to access the global variable, that is, to locate the environment where the cell for that global variable can be found.

At this point we have essentially presented a model that could execute programs written in the well-known computer language Basic. Now let us continue with our development of the model.

How about substituting the One_line procedure shown in Figure 1-29 for the corresponding one in Figure 1-18? This substitution is perfectly all right. However, note that this replacement will also necessitate changing every J to an F in the subflowchart of One_character, since J also denotes the column index of the chess position. Thus now the variable F instead of J must be made *global* to the procedure One_character. Consistent changes are then required in the subflowchart and in the legend for One_character, as well as in the legend for One_line, to complete the "editing" of the Figure 1-18 algorithm.

Every variable in a procedure P, declared in the legend of P to be globally accessible to P, is also *local* to some other procedure. Thus the variable I, which is global to One_char, is *local* to Picture_and_a_blank_line (PBL). Note, too, that not every local variable in a procedure need be globally accessible to any other procedure. To illustrate, consider what is implied should we replace the subflowcharts for Picture_and_a_blank_line and One_character of Figure 1-18 with those in Figure 1-30.

First let us study the role of the new variables MARK, one used in PBL and the other in One_char, in Figure 1-30. In the new version for PBL we use an extra step to assign the blank character "□" to MARK; later in box 3 we cause the value of MARK to be printed. This illustrates another way to create a blank line between printed chessboards.

However, the new PBL in Figure 1-30a calls on One_line and *that* procedure then calls on the procedure of Figure 1-30b. Here we find the variable MARK again. Or *is* it the same variable? This variable MARK is simply a placeholder for the asterisk character, as one can see by comparing Figure 1-30b

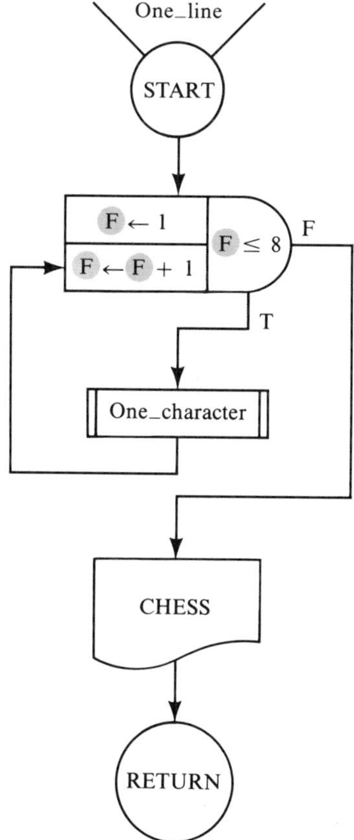

Figure 1-29

with the original version of One_character in Figure 1-18. There should really be two different variables MARK, but they happen to have the same name. In the environment of PBL, MARK should mean the variable whose value is "□", and in the environment of One_character, MARK should mean the variable whose value is "∗". How can we keep these meanings straight?

If we allow the variable MARK in Figure 1-30b to be global to that procedure, then MARK will be the MARK of Figure 1-30a, and its value will be changed from "□" to "∗" when box 0 of Figure 1-30b is executed. When box 3 of Figure 1-30a is executed later, an asterisk "∗" will be printed instead of a blank.

There is a simple solution to this difficulty. MARK should be a local variable of PBL that is *not* global to One_character. This can be accomplished by declaring the variable MARK in One_character *local* to that procedure. Then a new variable MARK will be created in the execution of Figure 1-30b and it will have no connection whatever with any preceding variable MARK in the program. Figure 1-31 shows the appropriate legends for the new PBL and One_char procedures.

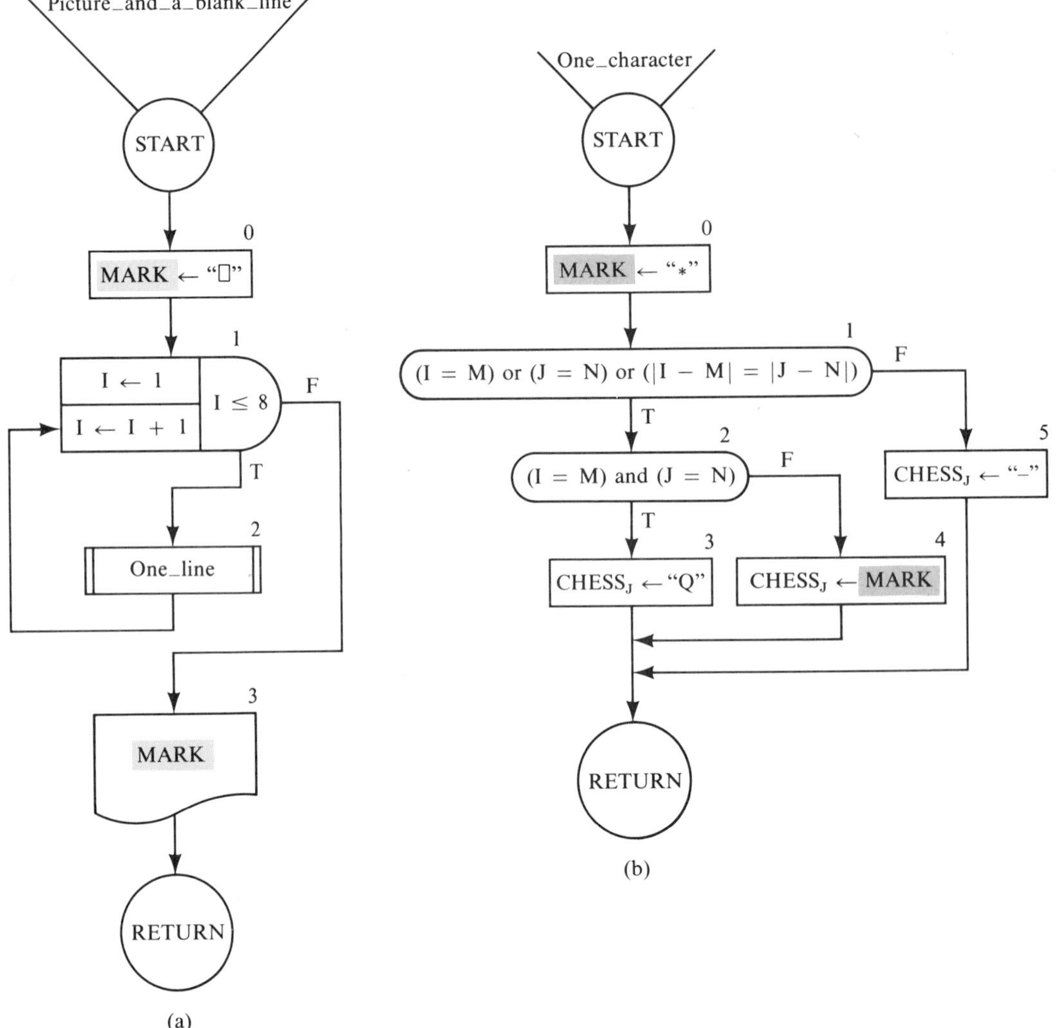

Figure 1-30. **(a) PBL, (b) One_char.**

(a) Legend for PBL (Figure 1-30a)

Identifier	Description
MARK	character
I	integer

(b) Legend for One_char (Figure 1-30b)

Identifier	Description
MARK	character
J	J in Line
M	M in MCP
N	N in MCP
I	I in PBL
CHESS	CHESS in Line

Figure 1-31. **New legends for the new flowcharts of (a) PBL and (b) One_char.**

Legend for P

Identifier	Description
MARK S	character integer

Figure 1-32

Let us summarize our information so far concerning local and global variables. A variable is considered local to a procedure if the variable and the type of value its cell is to hold are listed in the legend of the procedure. For example, in the legend of Figure 1-32, MARK and S are local to P. However, a variable S that is local to a procedure P may or may not be global to another procedure Q, which is called by P or by a "descendant" of P. The globality of S with respect to Q depends on the legend of Q rather than on the legend of P. For example, with the legends of Figure 1-33, the variable S is local with respect to Q. However with the legends of Figure 1-34 the variable S is global with respect to Q. In the next chapter we make such legend entries more explicit by adding an extra column, as in Figure 1-35.

Armed with the concepts of global and local variables in a procedure, we are now able to draw and discuss snapshots showing interesting states of execution of the Figure 1-18 algorithm, modified by the replacements in Figure 1-30. For example, Figure 1-36 is a snapshot of the execution comparable to that in Figure 1-21, where the MC was about to execute box 2 in the second invocation of One_character. Our new diagramming conventions, illustrated in Figure 1-24, are used here.

Legend of P

Identifier	Description
S	integer

Legend of Q

Identifier	Description
S	integer

Figure 1-33

Legend of P

Identifier	Description
S	integer

Legend of Q

Identifier	Description
S	S in P

Figure 1-34

Legend for One_char

Identifier	Treatment	Description
MARK	local	integer
J	global	J in Line
M	global	M in MCP

Figure 1-35

Exercises 1-5

1 Review the flowcharts and legends given in Figure 1-37 for sorting a list of n real elements. Draw a complete execution snapshot of the computation for the following set of conditions.

(a) The data set is $n = 5$, $A = (9, 7, 8, 2, 2)$.

(b) The MC is executing in the third activation (invocation) of Findkay and is about to execute box 2 for the *second time* during this activation.

2 Show a modification to the top-level flowchart given for Exercise 1 that uses without change the procedures SORT, MOVE, and Findkay to sort other lists. In particular, the top-level flowchart should accomplish the following:

(a) Input a list B of m real values.

(b) Input another list C, also having m real values.

(c) Sort the list B, then the list C, each time using the given subflowchart SORT.

(d) Pair off and display corresponding values from the sorted lists B and C, that is, display B_1, C_1, then B_2, C_2, then B_3, C_3, . . . , then B_m, C_m.

3 Figure 1-38 is a flowchart for a procedure MATSUM that sums the elements of a matrix A having M rows and N columns. Assume real elements.

(a) Show a top-level flowchart (Top) that inputs the matrix and outputs the matrix sum computed by means of MATSUM with the help of the sub-flowchart ROWSUM.

(b) Prepare a consistent set of legends for Top [developed in (a)], MATSUM, and ROWSUM. To achieve consistency you may not alter the given flowcharts for MATSUM and ROWSUM, but you may modify Top if necessary.

(c) For the flowcharts and legends you completed in (b), show a snapshot of the state of the computation just after box 3 of ROWSUM is executed for *the first time during* the *second* call (on ROWSUM). Assume the given matrix is

$$\begin{bmatrix} 3 & 4 & 5 & 6 \\ 7 & 8 & 9 & 10 \end{bmatrix}$$

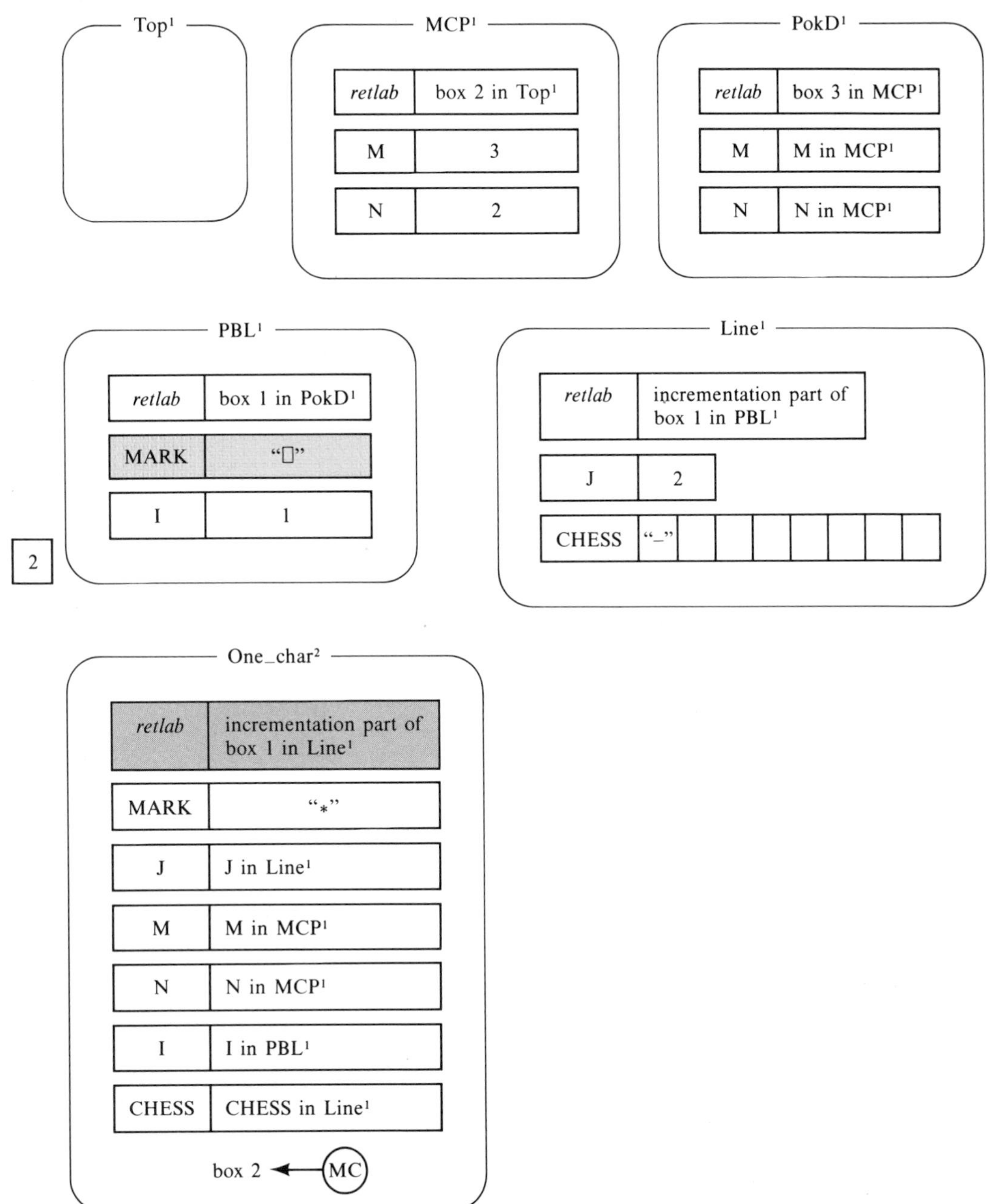

Figure 1-36. **Snapshot for the Figure 1-18 algorithm with new procedures from Figure 1-30 substituted for PBL and One_char. Variable MARK in PBL and variable MARK in One_char are both local variables (see Figure 1-31).**

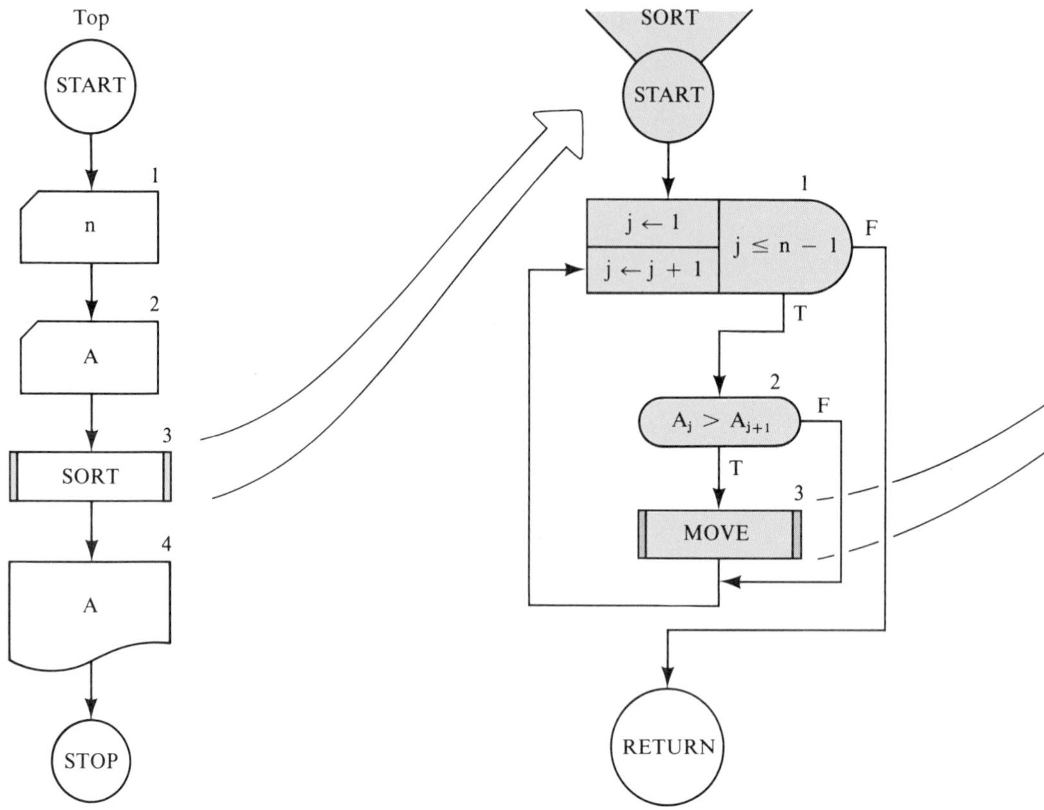

Legend for Top

Identifier	Treatment	Description
n	local	integer
A	local	list of n real elements

Legend for SORT

Identifier	Treatment	Description
j	local	integer
n	global	n in Top
A	global	A in Top

Figure 1-37

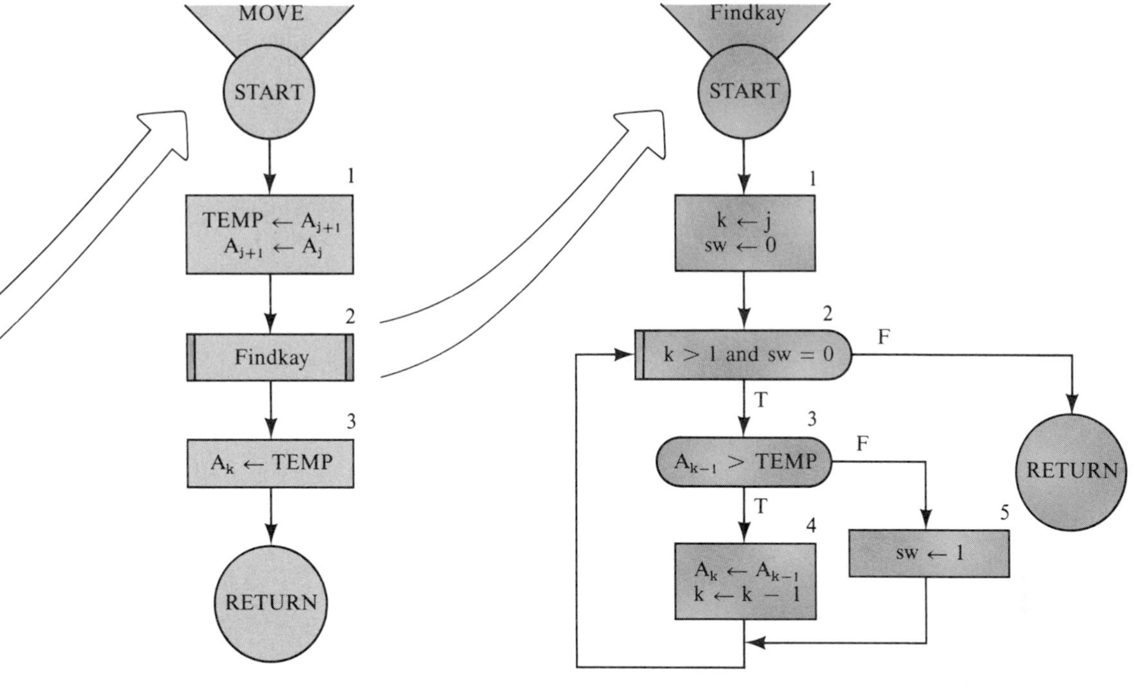

Legend for MOVE

Identifier	Treatment	Description
k	local	integer
TEMP	local	real
j	global	j in SORT
A	global	A in Top

Legend for Findkay

Identifier	Treatment	Description
sw	local	integer
k	global	k in MOVE
j	global	j in SORT
A	global	A in Top
TEMP	global	TEMP in MOVE

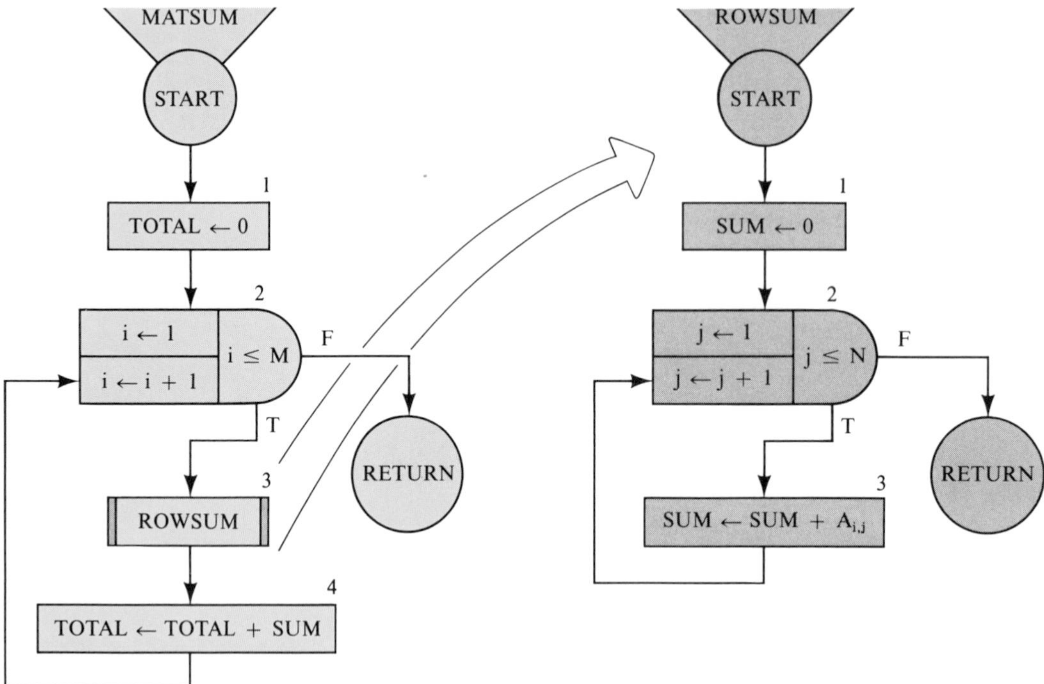

Figure 1-38

1-6 THE STATE OF THE MC

A snapshot gives the state of a computation by combining into one description the state of a computer's data storage (the part that is relevant to the program) and the state of the Master Computer. In the snapshots drawn thus far, the state of the MC could be characterized by two components, but as we shall see shortly, a more detailed study of a computation will require a third component. The first two components, as we have already said, are called the instruction pointer ip and the environment pointer ep. Our snapshot diagramming convention gives the ip value explicitly, but gives the ep value only implicitly. For example,

box 2 ← (MC)

as seen in Figure 1-36, shows that the ip is box 2. Placement of

box 2 ← (MC)

inside the contour for One_char tells us implicitly that the ep value is a pointer to the set of cells in One_char[2] and only those cells of any other contour that can be referenced indirectly via (pointed to from) cells contained within

One_char^2. For the snapshot in Figure 1-36, the cells directly or indirectly accessible to the MC are the *retlab* cell, MARK, J, M, N, I, and CHESS within One_char^2, J in Line^1, M and N in MCP^1, I in PBL^1, and CHESS in Line^1.

The third component of an MC's state specifies some private storage belonging to that MC (the MC's scratch-pad). Let us see why this is necessary. Consider the work required to evaluate the expression in box 2 of One_char:

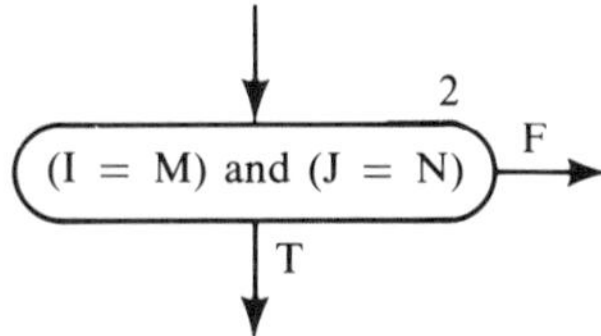

the box about to be executed when the snapshot in Figure 1-21 (or Figure 1-23) is taken. Figure 1-39, a tree for this expression, may help us see the storage problem facing the MC. To evaluate this expression in purely sequential fashion, left to right, the MC must remember the value fetched for I while the value of M is being fetched. Then he performs the operation I = M and gets a value *true* or *false.* Suppose he gets a *true.* Then a similar problem arises in evaluating J = N. After the value of J has been fetched, it will have to be "remembered" while N's value is fetched. We see that the MC needs some type of "scratch-pad" storage to hold intermediate values while working on an expression. A more convincing case for a scratch-pad, if required by the reader, can be made when considering the MC's problem in evaluating, again in left-to-right fashion, an arithmetic expression such as

$$a + (b \times (c + (d \times (e + f)))),$$

whose equivalent tree is given in Figure 1-40.

First the value of a will be fetched and saved, then that of b, then c, then d, and then e. Finally, when f is fetched, the result e + f can be obtained, and that can be combined with d, etc. Notice that a scratch-pad large enough to hold five values (a, b, c, d, e) is needed here, whereas a much smaller pad was needed to handle the simpler expression

$$(I = M) \quad \text{and} \quad (J = N)$$

Yet in each case, the values are placed in the scratch-pad and retrieved from it in *last in-first out* order, suggesting therefore that the MC's private storage should be a *stack.* Whenever we want to take a snapshot at a point where the MC is in the midst of evaluating an expression, we are able to depict the state of the MC by showing the MC's ip, its ep, *and* its stack.

Figure 1-39

and

I = M J = N

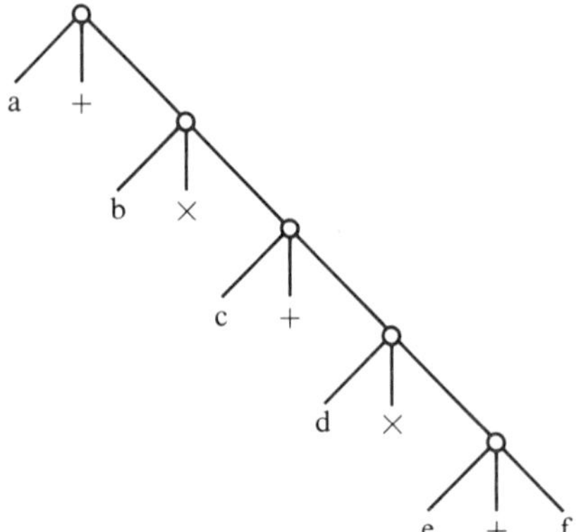

Figure 1-40

Using a stack to evaluate an expression is analogous to using general registers for the same purpose in conventional computers. For readers unfamiliar with stack computers, sometimes called *postfix machines,* it may be instructive to explain briefly how they work.

An expression like

$$(a + b) \times (c + d)$$

is often called an *infix* expression because each operator symbol appears *between* its respective operands. Such an expression can be transformed into an equivalent parenthesis-free form, known as *postfix,* by moving each operator to the right of its right operand and then deleting all parentheses, if any, since they are now superfluous. Thus,

$$(a + b) \times (c + d) \Longrightarrow (a\ b\ +)\ (c\ d\ +)\ \times$$

$$\Longrightarrow a\ b\ +\ c\ d\ +\ \times$$

Now, it is a fact that when a stack is used to hold intermediate results, an expression in postfix form may be regarded as a program to evaluate that expression. To see this, in Table 1-2 let us rewrite elements in the above postfix

TABLE 1-2

Postfix form element	Meaning as an instruction for the postfix machine
a	*push* the value of *a* (onto the stack)
b	*push* the value of *b* (onto the stack)
+	*add*
c	*push* the value of *c* (onto the stack)
d	*push* the value of *d* (onto the stack)
+	*add*
×	*multiply*

expression vertically, instead of horizontally, and next to each element write the *meaning* of that element as an instruction for the postfix machine.

The meaning of each *push* operation is obvious. But what is actually meant by *add* and *multiply?* Well, *add* means: *pop* the top *two elements* off the stack, *form their sum,* and *push* the *sum* onto the stack. Similarly, multiply means: *pop* the top *two* elements off the stack, *form their product,* and *push* the *product* onto the stack. (There are, of course, corresponding stack operations to perform *subtract, divide, change sign,* logical *and, or,* etc.)

We can see how the above "postfix program" would work in detail by following each step in the evaluation of the expression, ab+cd+×, for the case where a = 5, b = 4, c = 6, and d = 7. In Table 1-3 the placement of the cursor ↑ indicates the last instruction executed. In diagramming the MC's stack, we adopt the convention that the top of the stack is always at the left end (nearest the MC). As a reminder, a special button mark indicates the bottom of the stack at the right end.

Next we make the assumption that whenever the MC must evaluate an *infix expression,* in the process of executing a flowchart box, he *automatically converts it to an equivalent postfix form,* and evaluates the postfix form by pushing and popping intermediate results as we have just explained.

For example, in evaluating the statement

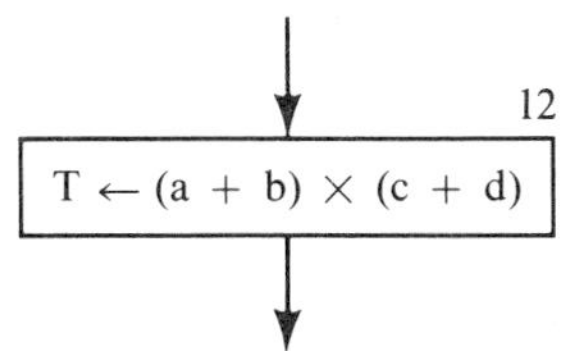

TABLE 1-3
Stack Pictures during Evaluation of a b + c d + ×

Stage	a b + c d + ×	Stack	
Initial stage	a b + c d + ×	MC —•	(stack is empty)
after step 1	↑ (a)	MC — 5 •	
after step 2	↑ (b)	MC — 4 5 •	
after step 3	↑ (+)	MC — 9 •	
after step 4	↑ (c)	MC — 6 9 •	button mark denotes the bottom of the stack
after step 5	↑ (d)	MC — 7 6 9 •	
after step 6	↑ (+)	MC — 13 9 •	
after step 7	↑ (×)	MC — 117 •	stack contains desired value of the expression

let the values for the operands again be a = 5, b = 4, c = 6, d = 7. Suppose a snapshot is to be taken when the MC is just about to fetch a value for d in the left-to-right evaluation of the expression. We could depict the state of the MC as in Figure 1-41, where the MC's stack is shown with two values, the computed value of a + b and the fetched value of c.

When the evaluation of the expression in flowchart box 12 is complete, the MC's stack will hold just the product of (a + b) and (c + d), which is 117 in this case. This value will then be popped off the stack for assignment to T. In general, after one assignment step or other statement has been completed, and before the execution of another statement has begun, the MC's stack is empty, for example,

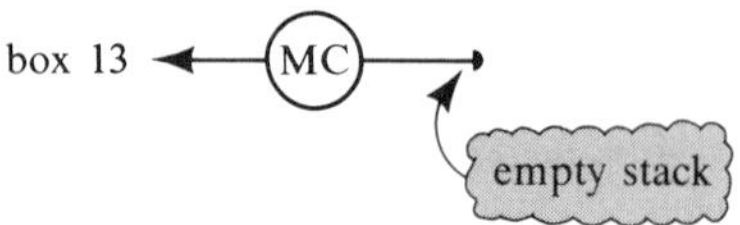

An important idea exploited in subsequent chapers is that the MC's stack *goes with* the MC as it moves from environment to environment in the evaluation of different procedures. Information on the stack is retained, and can be used when the MC returns to an environment where it makes sense to use it.

Section Summary

To summarize what we have said here, the state of a computation may be given by describing the state of the relevant data storage together with the state of the MC, which in turn can be described by a triple of objects: an instruction pointer, an environment pointer (to the relevant data storage), and a stack used by the MC as a private scratch-pad to hold intermediate results used in expression evaluation. Whenever the MC needs to execute a return from a procedure, it consults the return label cell *retlab* and discovers what instruction to execute next and in what environment to execute it. Then the MC reenters the specified environment (the ep) and prepares to execute the specified instruction (the ip). One useful way to trace a computation whose algorithm is given

Figure 1-41

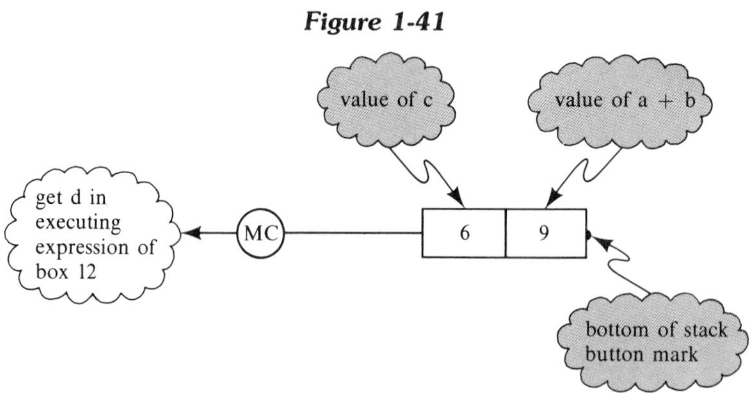

by a set of flowcharts is to construct and study a sequence of snapshots. Selection of the states to display as snapshots is left up to the tracer and his particular objectives and interests.

1-7 REFERENCES AND SUGGESTIONS FOR FURTHER READING

Texts expanding the basic concepts of this chapter range from introductory expositions of computer science principles to treatments written for advanced students and professionals. A good elementary presentation can be found in Forsythe *et al.* (1975a). Indeed, the first sections of Chapter 1 of this book are essentially a condensation of the first five chapters of Forsythe *et al.* Readers who want an introduction to tree structures, expression evaluation, and stacks, as background for Section 1-6, should consult Chapters 6 and 8 of that book.

Four introductory texts that emphasize programming style and the discipline of structured programming are McGowan and Kelly (1975), Wirth (1973), Ledgard (1975), and Kernighan and Plauger (1974). The papers in *Computing Surveys* (1974) and the book by Dahl *et al.* (1972) are written for more experienced programmers.

Elson (1973), Peterson (1974), and Nicholls (1975) all survey programming languages, the first two at a more elementary level than this text and the third at a more advanced. The book by Pratt (1975) is admirable; it parallels our text to a remarkable degree, but at a more advanced level and with a somewhat different emphasis. Wegner (1968) surveys and integrates the subjects of programming languages and information structures. Since it was years ahead of its time, the book is still a valuable reference in this area. Sammet (1969) gives an extensive history of programming languages from the beginning up through 1968.

2 INTERFACING PROCEDURES

2-1 INTRODUCTION

In Chapter 1 we were concerned with global and local variables in the environment of a procedure. To recapitulate, a global variable is one that is identified with, that is, uses the storage container of, another variable *with the same name* occurring at a higher level of the program (such as a calling environment), while a local variable has its own local storage container. Locals are *not* identified with any higher-level variables.

The use of global variables gives rise to the sharing of information among the procedure components of a program. In this chapter we examine other means of interfacing procedures, that is, other means of transmitting or sharing information among related procedures.

The principal method of sharing to be studied is the *parameter* mechanism. When composing a procedure using parameters instead of globals, it is not necessary to know the names of variables used in other parts of the program. A parameter is a dummy or placeholder in a procedure that matches up with information in the program that calls the procedure. The information matching a parameter is called an *argument,* and an argument may take the form of an expression. However, there need be no correlation between the names used for parameters and the names used for arguments (or for parts of arguments). Different ways of achieving the match give rise to different parameter mechanisms, as we shall see. Most programming languages offer the programmer at least some of the parameter facilities that will be described. Procedures that return values to their callers, as function values, are also discussed. To convey a deep understanding of these facilities for information sharing, and their relative merits with regard to the use of globals, we shall continue to rely on the computer model to explain the semantics.

No doubt some readers have already used parameters and functions previously in programming projects. We hope even those readers will not skip this material, since it should considerably increase their understanding of these topics and, at the least, provide a useful review.

Many of the concepts we want to develop can be illustrated using the example problem of printing a chessboard. Before starting our discussion however, let us consider a recomposition of the Figure 1-18 algorithm showing fewer steps of decomposition and hence fewer procedures. Such a version, Figure 2-1, while perhaps less understandable than the more fully decomposed version of Figure 1-18, will prove more convenient for the purposes of diagramming many of the ideas we want to develop in this chapter. A quick glance at the new version in Figure 2-1 shows what has been changed. The first three levels, Top, Make_chess_pictures, and Pictures_with_ok_data, have been "collapsed" or condensed into a new Top level. Also, levels (d) and (e), Picture_and_a_blank_line and One_line, have been condensed into Make_picture_and_line (MPL), while the last level, (f), has been left unchanged. Figure 2-1 also contains a set of legends consistent with these changes.

Now we want to consider how to make our chessboard-printing algorithm more flexible in the choice of characters to represent the scope of the Queen. For this purpose we introduce two new variables, U and V, as placeholders for the character values used to print the positions *in* and *out*, respectively, of the scope of the Queen. Each time we call Make_picture_and_line, the first step we want to take is to input values for U and V. (See box 0 in Figure 2-2a.) Thus, to print Figure 1-2, the value to be read for U is "*" and for V is "–". Corresponding changes must also be made in One_character, as seen in Figure 2-2b. No change is needed in Top. In the environment of One_character, U and V are both global variables referring to the storage cells created in the MPL environment.

This is all very well and in agreement with the ideas so far developed. However, now suppose we want to print two chessboards: not only the chessboard as shown in Figure 1-2 but also that shown in Figure 2-3, that is, with "–" for the scope of the Queen and "*" for the positions outside the scope, instead of vice versa.

At present this second output can be accomplished in the following unsatisfactory way. After control returns to Top from Make_picture_and_line, we can have the input box

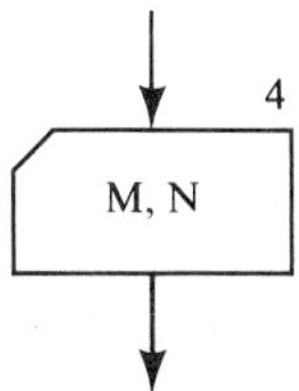

read the same Queen position, (3, 2), again and recheck it in box 2 (needlessly since it must be all right). Now, if the next pair of values for U and V read in box 0 of Figure 2-2a is the reverse of the first pair, that is, if U and V are assigned the values "–" and "*", respectively, then a chessboard similar to that shown in Figure 2-3 will be printed. This solution is devious, however; it does not accomplish its objective directly. There exists a much better way, which we shall now explore.

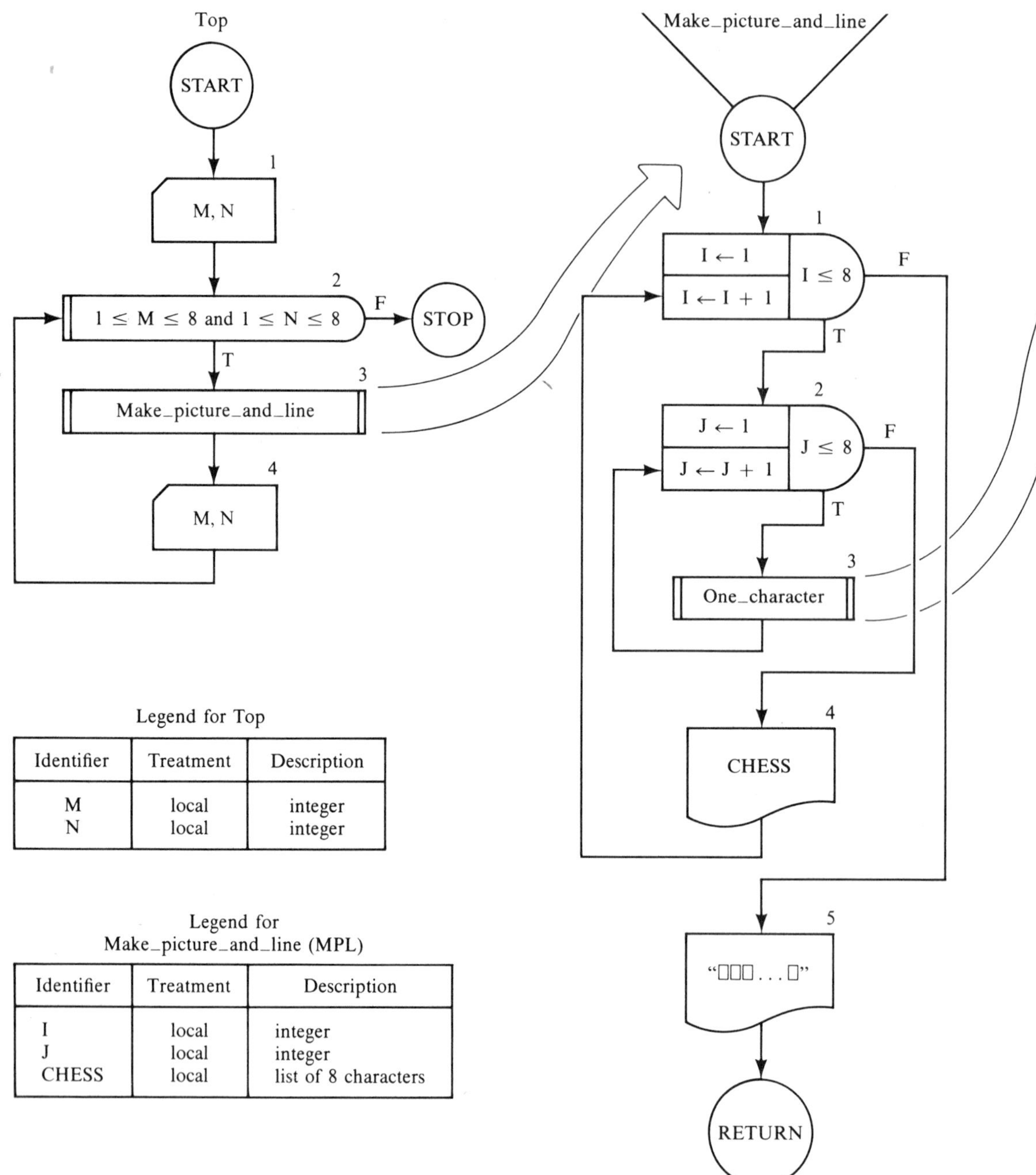

Legend for Top

Identifier	Treatment	Description
M	local	integer
N	local	integer

Legend for
Make_picture_and_line (MPL)

Identifier	Treatment	Description
I	local	integer
J	local	integer
CHESS	local	list of 8 characters

Figure 2-1. **Chessboard solution of Figure 1-18 recomposed with only two procedures.**

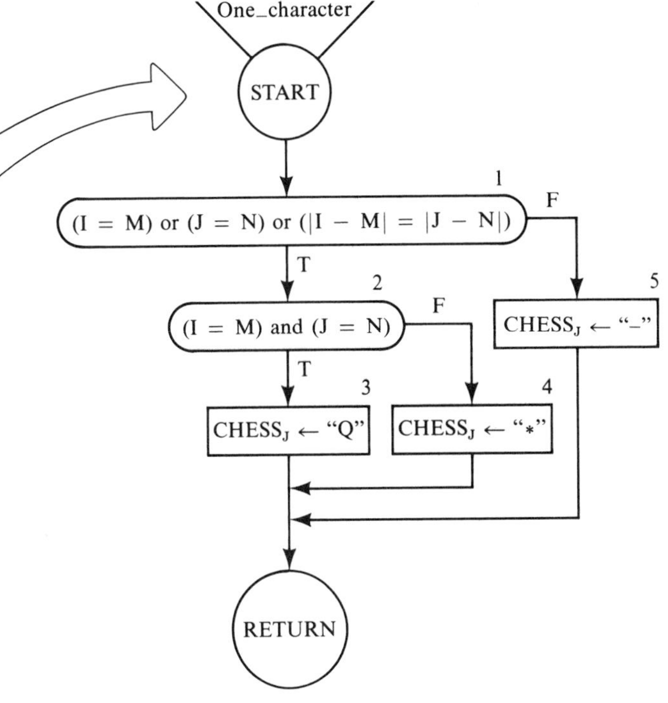

Legend for One_character
(One_char)

Identifier	Treatment	Description
M	global	M in Top
N	global	N in Top
I	global	I in MPL
J	global	J in MPL
CHESS	global	CHESS in MPL

Note that the procedure One_character plays the role of determining for each chess position whether the position *is* or *is not* within the scope of the Queen. If it is, One_character assigns to CHESS the character value used to print the scope, and if not, assigns to CHESS the other character value. The particular choice of character values used in the diagram is really immaterial to the *structure* of the procedure. While we may wish to change this choice from one chessboard to the next, the character values always play the same roles in the procedure. Let us rewrite the One_character procedure using two "dummy" variables or "parameters" as stand-ins for the two character values or variables. (See Figure 2-4.)

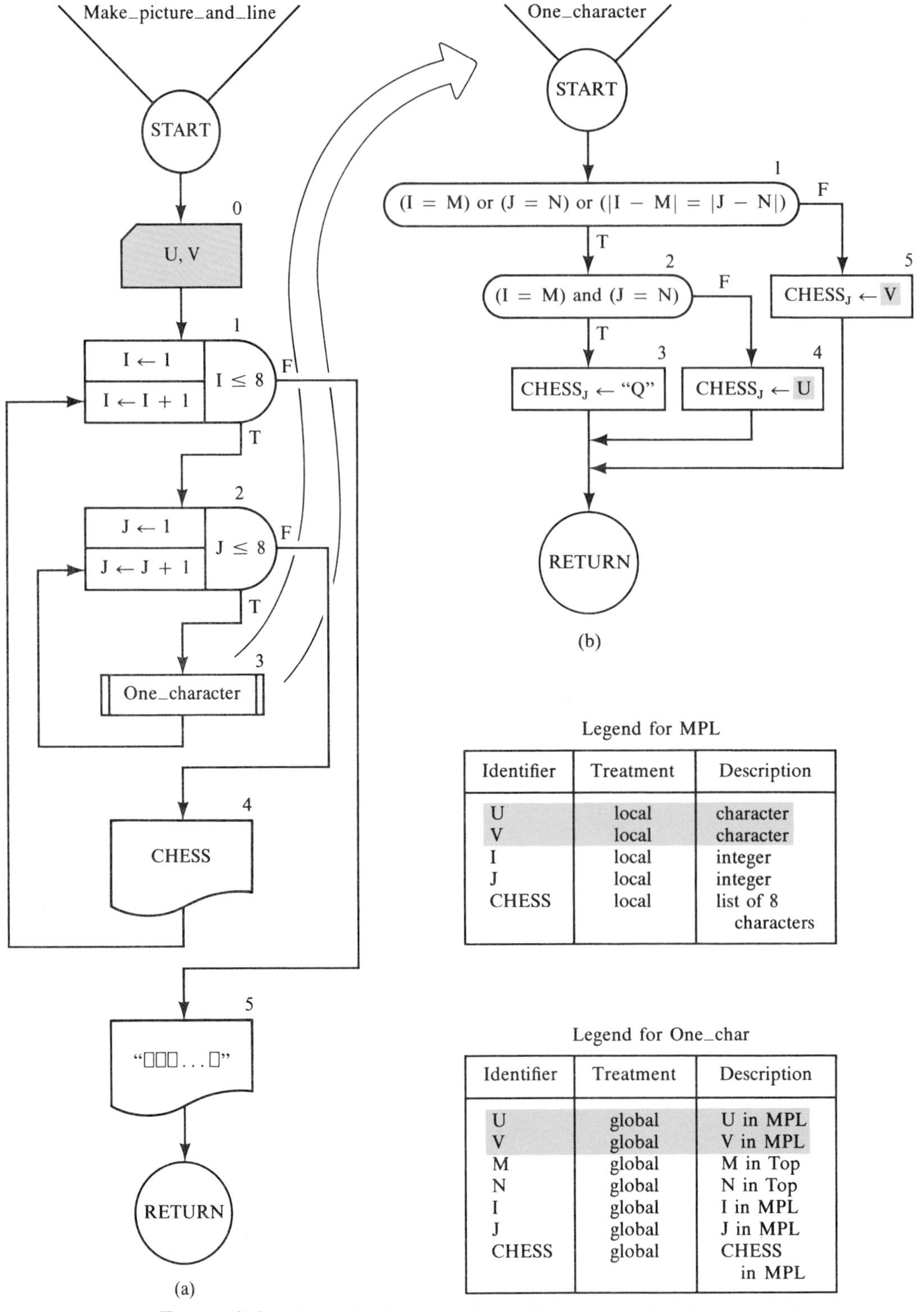

Legend for MPL

Identifier	Treatment	Description
U	local	character
V	local	character
I	local	integer
J	local	integer
CHESS	local	list of 8 characters

Legend for One_char

Identifier	Treatment	Description
U	global	U in MPL
V	global	V in MPL
M	global	M in Top
N	global	N in Top
I	global	I in MPL
J	global	J in MPL
CHESS	global	CHESS in MPL

Figure 2-2. **Introducing variables U and V to hold input values for the characters used to print the scope of the Queen, and the places on the chessboard outside this scope, respectively.**

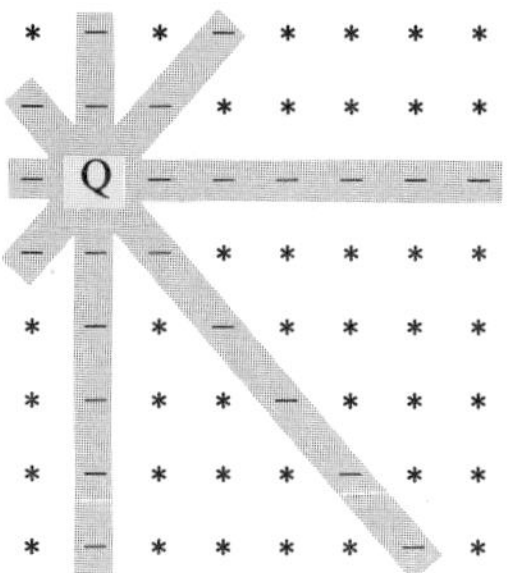

Figure 2-3. **Chessboard with values of U and V interchanged.**

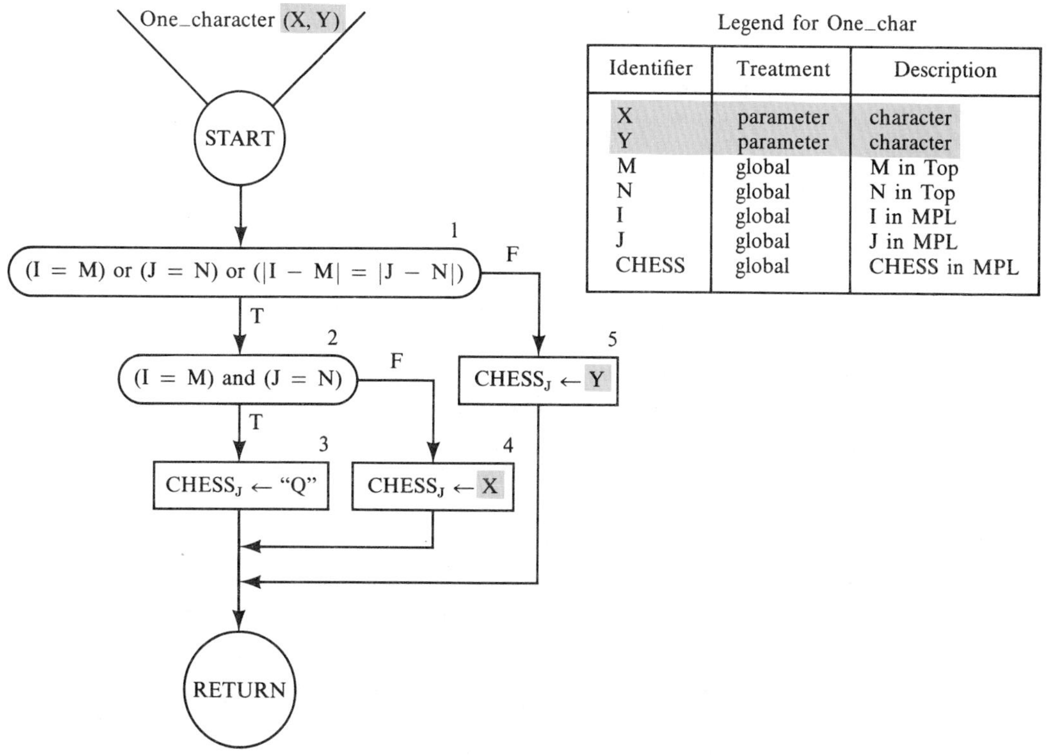

Legend for One_char

Identifier	Treatment	Description
X	parameter	character
Y	parameter	character
M	global	M in Top
N	global	N in Top
I	global	I in MPL
J	global	J in MPL
CHESS	global	CHESS in MPL

Figure 2-4. **Version of One_character with parameters X and Y.**

2-2 REFERENCE PARAMETERS

How will we convey to the MC information concerning the actual variables or values that are to be used in place of X and Y in the execution of One_character? That is, how will we tell the MC which storage cells to make accessible, or which values to match to the parameters X and Y? In the flowchart language this information will be conveyed in the call box. For instance, the procedure call

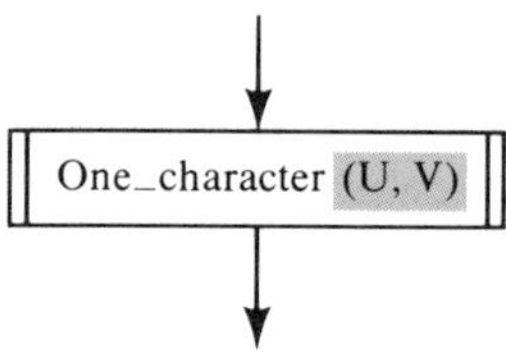

will mean that we want the MC to match the variable U to the parameter X and the variable V to the parameter Y:

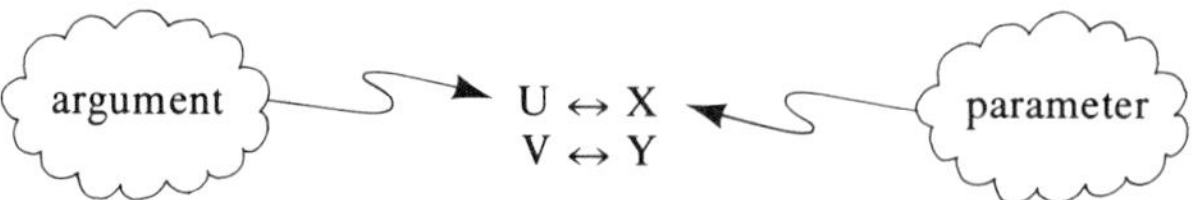

U and V are referred to as "arguments." The arguments of a procedure call must match up, one to one, in order, with the parameters of the procedure heading in the flowchart.

We have certainly achieved new flexibility because, for example, by rewriting the last call as

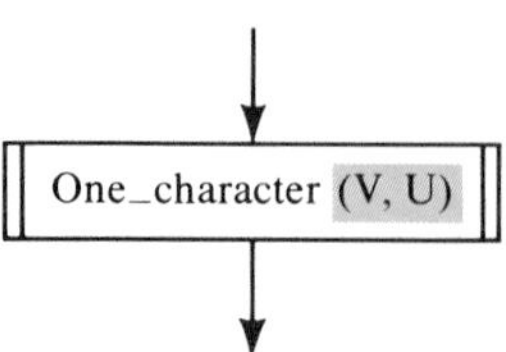

we can bring about the matching of the variable V to the parameter X and the variable U to the parameter Y, if we want to do that. Also, the procedure call in Figure 2-5 certainly means to indicate that the value "*" should be matched to the parameter X, and "–" to Y. We return to this particular procedure call later to discuss its implications.

The point of all this discussion is to suggest that, like the use of globals, parameter–argument matching forms another type of bridge between the environment of the current procedure and the higher environment(s). One way to understand the relationship between parameter and argument is to examine the cell structure of the environments that are bridged, that is, the environment of the called procedure containing the parameters and the envi-

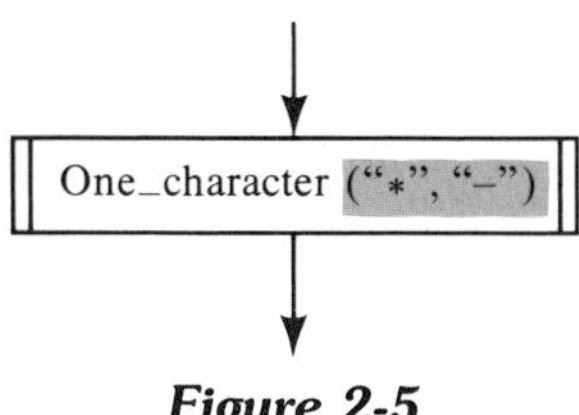

Figure 2-5

ronment(s) that contain the matching argument information. For this purpose let us first bring together, in Figure 2-6, all the changes that Figure 2-4 makes necessary in the Figure 2-1 algorithm. At the same time let us specialize the word "parameter" in the legend for One_char to "reference parameter" since all the parameters described in this section will be reference parameters. Note in Figure 2-6 how box 3 of Make_picture_and_line has been modified to supply arguments U and V in the call on One_character.

Figure 2-7 shows a snapshot of the computation comparable to the snapshot in Figure 1-24. Cells that are relevant to the argument–parameter matching mechanism are highlighted. In keeping with our desire to make attributes of each storage cell as explicit as possible, we henceforth show each storage cell with *three* compartments instead of two, that is, name, *type,* and value. Each return label (*retlab*) cell has the type "ptrs" since its value is an (ip, ep) pair, that is, a pair of pointers.

Looking at the environment for One_char^2 in Figure 2-7, we see that cells for parameters X and Y are indicated to be of type *ref*erence. The value parts for such cells are references to the cells for the matching arguments. Each time the MC needs to fetch or store a value of X or Y the Reader/Assigner, noticing that the cell for X (or Y) is of type reference, consults the cell designated in the value part, for example, "U in MPL^1".

Taking stock, we see that matching a parameter in one procedure to an argument in a "higher-level" environment resembles the matching in the global variable referencing scheme, only in that case the global variable is always matched to a higher-level variable *of the same name.* Matching a parameter of a procedure to a higher-level variable makes the storage cell of the argument, *whatever its name,* accessible to the MC while the procedure is being executed. Achieving access to a referenced storage cell of arbitrary name is the essence of the parameter–argument mechanism that we have been describing so far. A parameter that is given access to its matching argument in this way is termed a *reference* parameter. Actual computer systems use several different methods to effect the access of reference parameters to arguments. Some of these implementation alternatives are discussed later in this section.

A shrewd observer of Figure 2-6 has noticed that, while we have employed parameters in One_character to achieve flexibility in the choice of characters to be printed, we have still not obtained a satisfactory solution to the problem posed earlier to print two chessboards for each input of a Queen's position M, N,

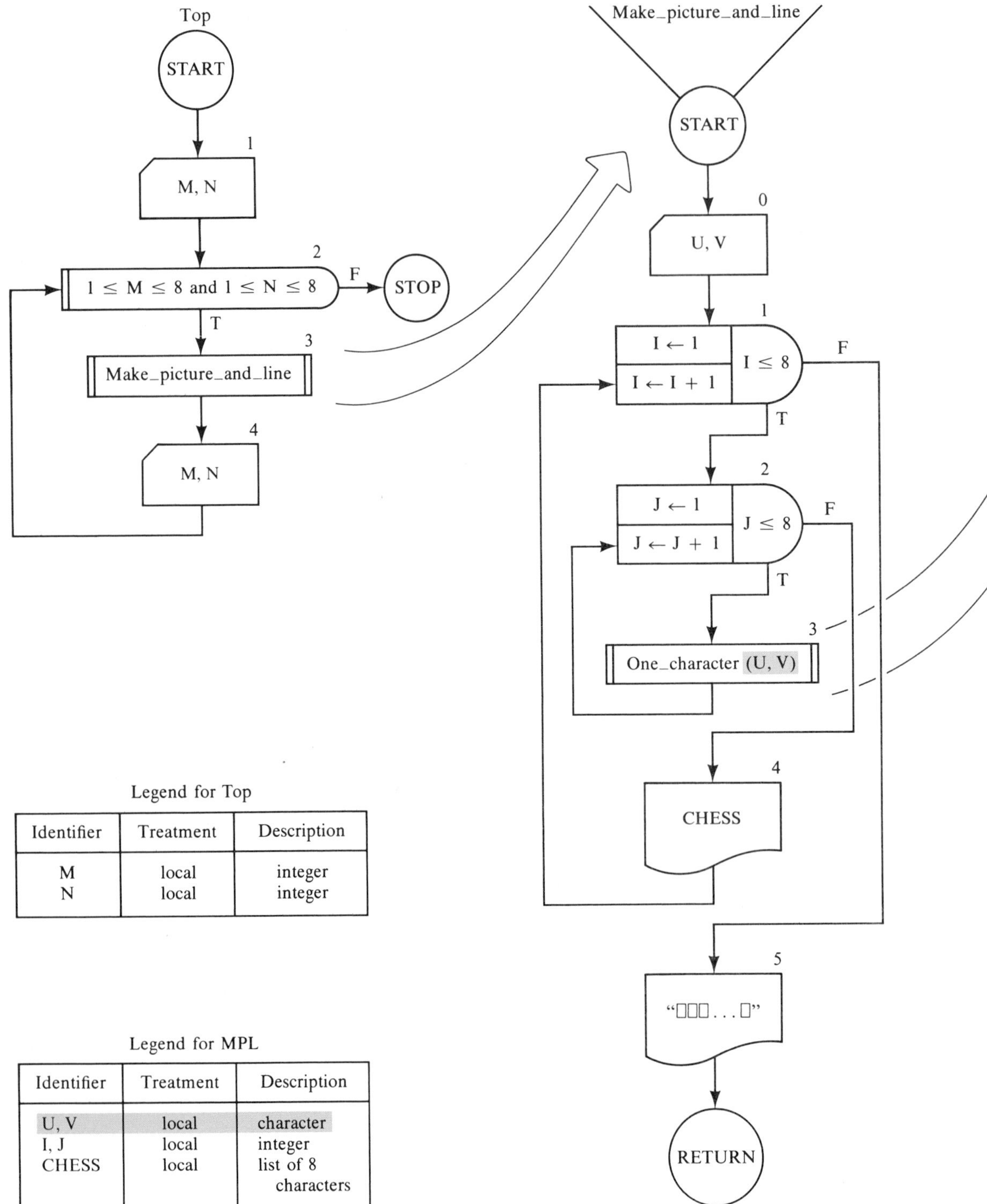

Legend for Top

Identifier	Treatment	Description
M	local	integer
N	local	integer

Legend for MPL

Identifier	Treatment	Description
U, V	local	character
I, J	local	integer
CHESS	local	list of 8 characters

Figure 2-6. **Chessboard solution of Figure 2-1 illustrating use of reference parameters X and Y in One_character.**

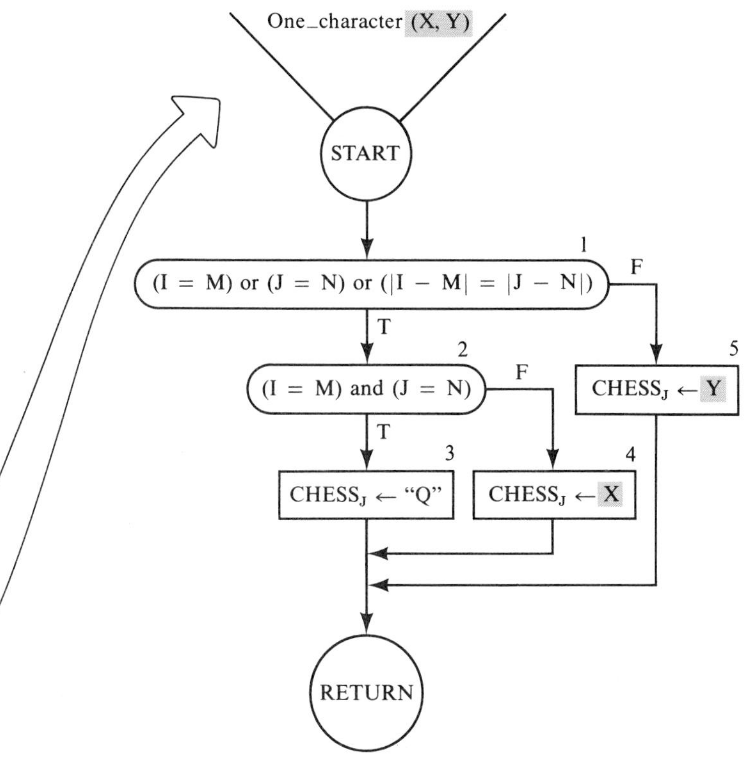

Legend for One_char

Identifier	Treatment	Description
X, Y	ref par	character
M	global	M in Top
N	global	N in Top
I	global	I in MPL
J	global	J in MPL
CHESS	global	CHESS in MPL

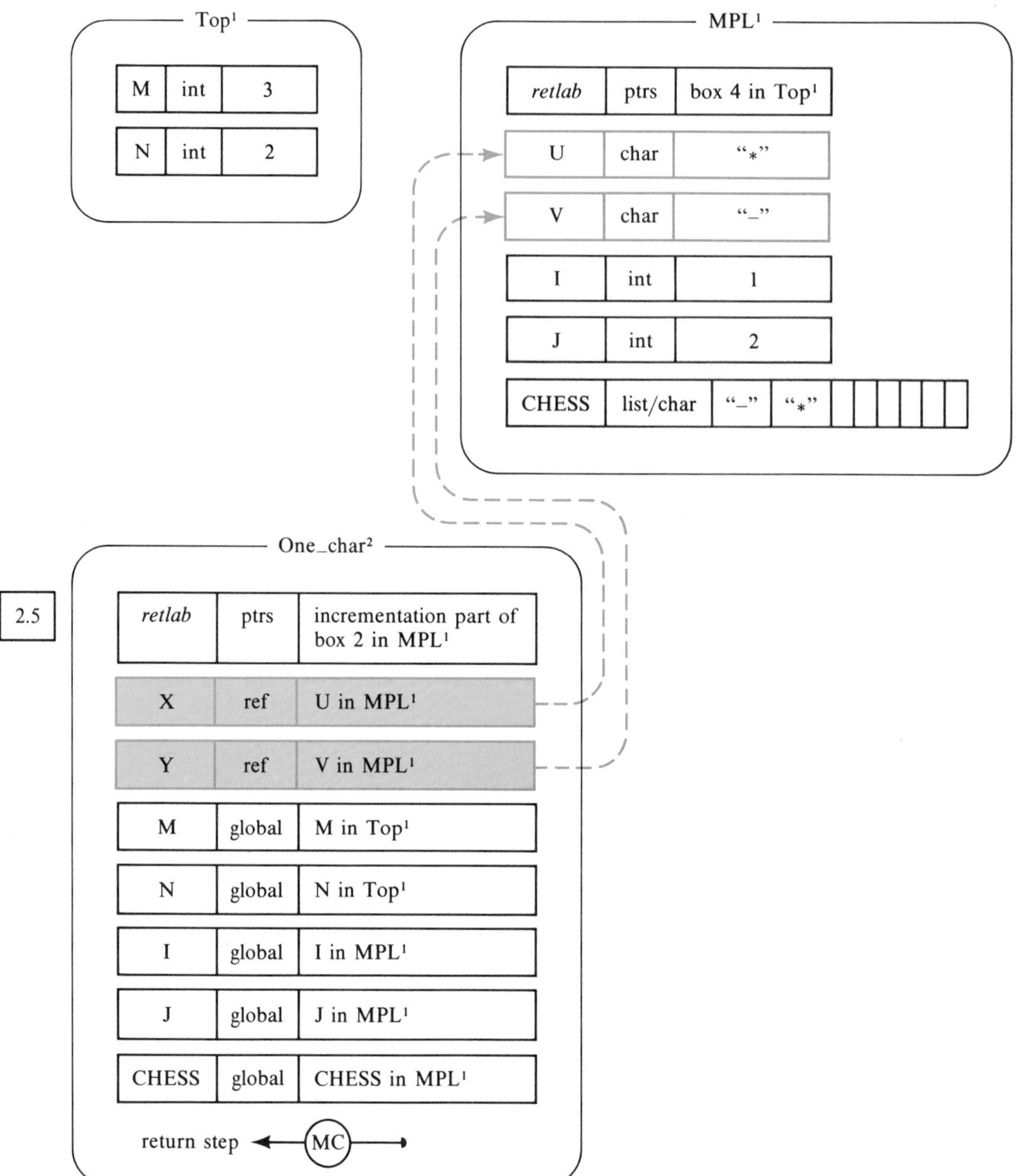

Figure 2-7. **Snapshot to illustrate argument–parameter matching mechanisms.**

one board being the reverse of the other with respect to the character values for U and V. We are now in a position to remedy this shortcoming. Suppose this time we input the values of U, V in Top and let Make_picture_and_line have reference parameters yu, vee, as seen in Figure 2-8. Notice how Top has been altered. Each data set for Top now consists of two pairs of values, the first for M, N and the second for U, V. And there are now two calls on Make_picture_and_line in the body of Top's loop, the second reverses argument pair U, V. The arguments U, V or V, U in each call are made accessible to Make_picture_and_line and also, indirectly, to One_character, and in each case they are matched to parameters X and Y, respectively.

Figure 2-9 shows our favorite snapshot corresponding to that of Figure 2-7. Compare these snapshots. In our latest version of the algorithm, note that if the MC executing within One_character^2 needs the value of X (or Y), the Reader/Assigner will first consult the cell for yu (or vee) in the MPL^1 environment. It will then be noted that this cell is a reference parameter, which refers to the cell U (or V) in Top^1, and so ultimately that cell will be consulted. This is precisely the effect we want. From this last illustration we can see that arguments may be made accessible from one procedure to another either directly or by way of one or more intermediate procedures through a chain of references in the created environments.

Although both globally declared variables and parameters enable two or more procedures to share the same variable, some programmers choose to use parameters in preference to "globals," perhaps to make the identifiers look more local. Notice therefore that it is possible to eliminate all the globals in a program simply by substituting reference parameters. Figure 2-10 shows how our chessboard algorithm appears when all the information is made accessible to procedures via parameter–argument relations. Two more parameters have been added to Make_picture_and_line, and five more to One_character. There is no change in Top from the version in Figure 2-8 except to add M and N in the calls on Make_picture_and_line.

Final remarks in this section have to do with our computer model "machinery" to explain the reference parameter effect. Our objective has been conceptual simplicity, but this may not be synonymous with computational efficiency. As a matter of fact, there is considerable variation in actual computer implementations to achieve the reference parameter effect.

To illustrate, chains of references, as suggested in Figure 2-9, are not essential to match an argument, via a chain of calls, to a corresponding parameter. An alternative approach more like a "bucket brigade" could be used. The idea is to allow an original reference value, for example, "U in Top^1", to be copied from the environment of one intermediate procedure to another, until the copied reference to the argument reaches the final environment where it is used. Thus, when constructing the contour One_char^2, to complete a call on One_char from MPL, the MC could notice that the value of the argument yu is a reference value, rather than a simple datum like an integer or a character

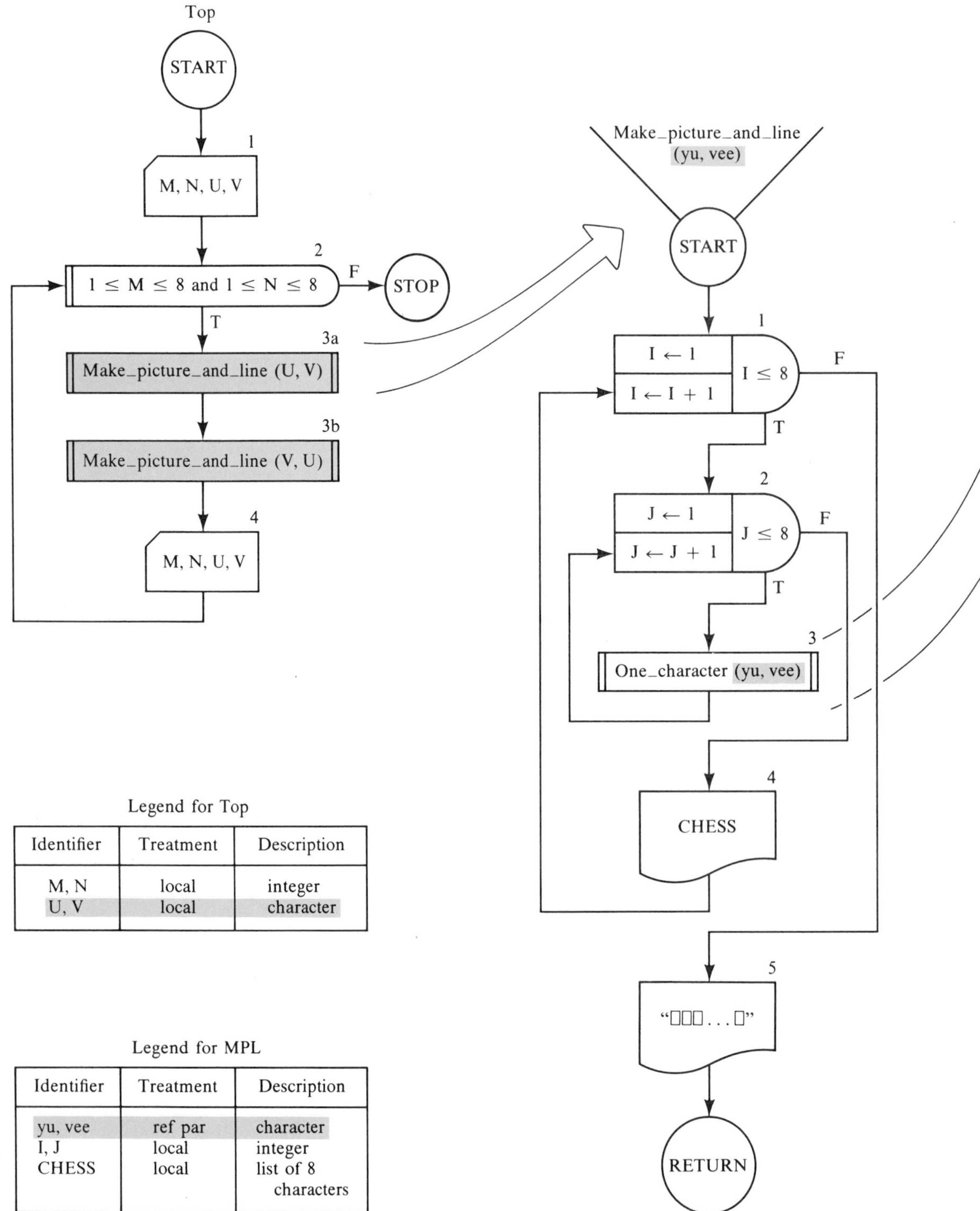

Legend for Top

Identifier	Treatment	Description
M, N	local	integer
U, V	local	character

Legend for MPL

Identifier	Treatment	Description
yu, vee	ref par	character
I, J	local	integer
CHESS	local	list of 8 characters

***Figure 2-8.* Chessboard solution of Figure 2-1 illustrating use of reference parameters X, Y in One_character and *yu*, vee in Make_picture_and_line. There are now *two* calls on Make_picture_and_line in Top.**

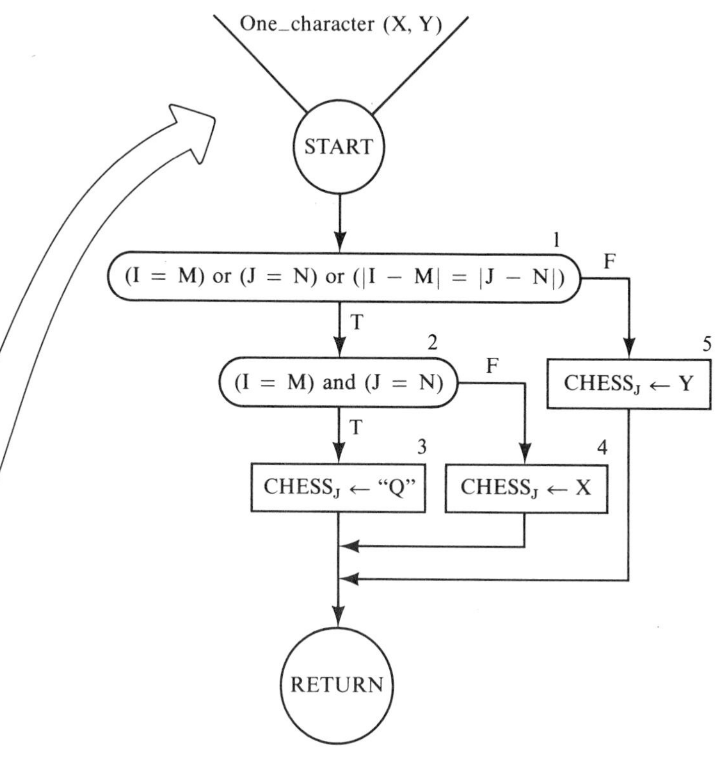

Legend for One_char

Identifier	Treatment	Description
X, Y	ref par	character
M	global	M in Top
N	global	N in Top
I	global	I in MPL
J	global	J in MPL
CHESS	global	CHESS in MPL

value. This reference could be copied into the cell of its corresponding parameter, X, in One_char². Similarly, the reference value of vee in MPL¹ could be copied into the cell for Y, giving a contour that has the following appearance:

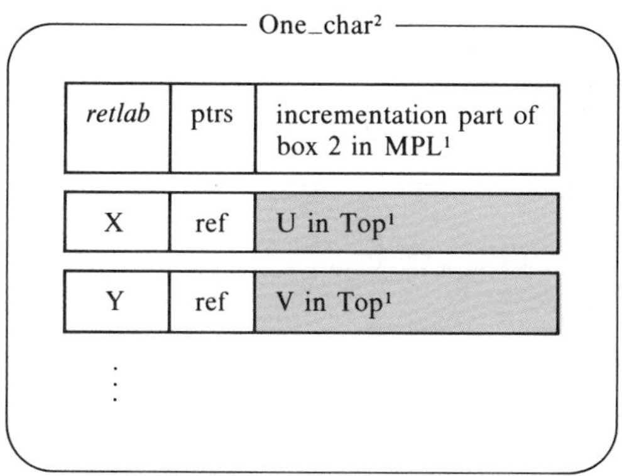

Now, when the parameter X (or Y) is encountered during the execution of One_character, the value in the cell named X (or Y) points directly, rather than indirectly via a cell in MPL¹, to the cell for U in Top¹ (or to V in Top¹) that holds the ultimate argument value.

This alternate way of achieving the reference parameter effect may be more efficient in some applications and on some computers. The main point, however,

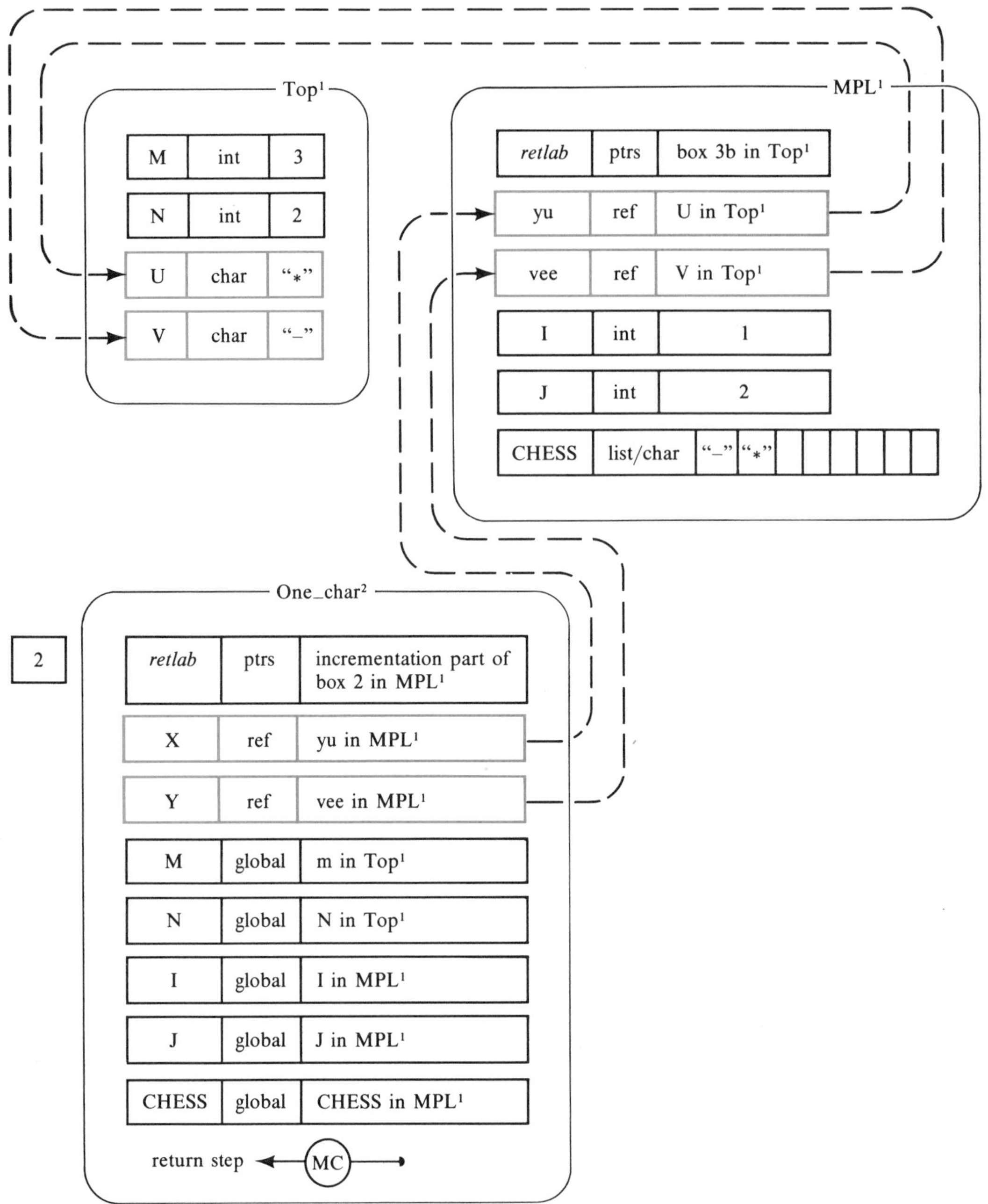

Figure 2-9. **Snapshot illustrating by dashed lines how arguments U and V in Top are matched to parameters yu and vee in MPL, which in turn are matched to X and Y in One_char.**

is that both ways (chaining references and copying references) have the same functional effect (that is, they have the same semantics).

In some computer systems the effect of a reference parameter is achieved using machinery that is even quite different from either of the two methods just described. This third mechanism is sometimes referred to as the *value/result* method to implement a reference parameter.

To understand how the value/result method works conceptually, we have to imagine that the contour cell for a reference parameter has a second value compartment to hold the actual value of the argument, for example,

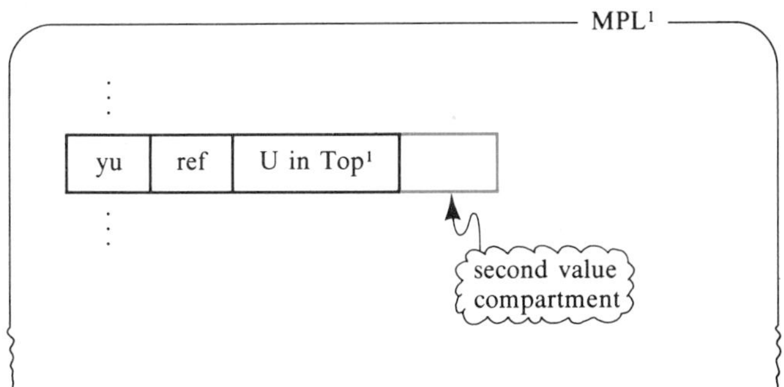

Suppose a procedure has been called, and a contour is being contructed for it. Then for each reference parameter in the procedure, a copy of its matching argument is put into the parameter cell's extra compartment, for example,

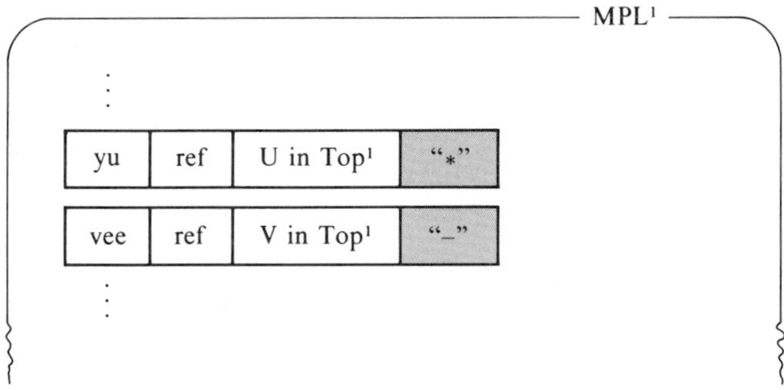

During execution of the called procedure, all references to the parameters are strictly local references, that is, fetches or stores are made to or from these new compartments of the parameter cells. However, when execution of the called procedure has been completed and the MC is executing the return step, the current values of the parameters (in the second value compartments) are *copied back* into the cells of the matching arguments. The MC knows the location of the respective argument cell for each parameter, because the reference to each argument has been saved in the first value compartment of each parameter cell. Thus, the value/result method involves a little more work at the time of procedure entry and exit, but avoids repeated indirect referencing of the arguments *during execution.* Direct referencing of the arguments during execution of the procedure body may, depending on the application and on the

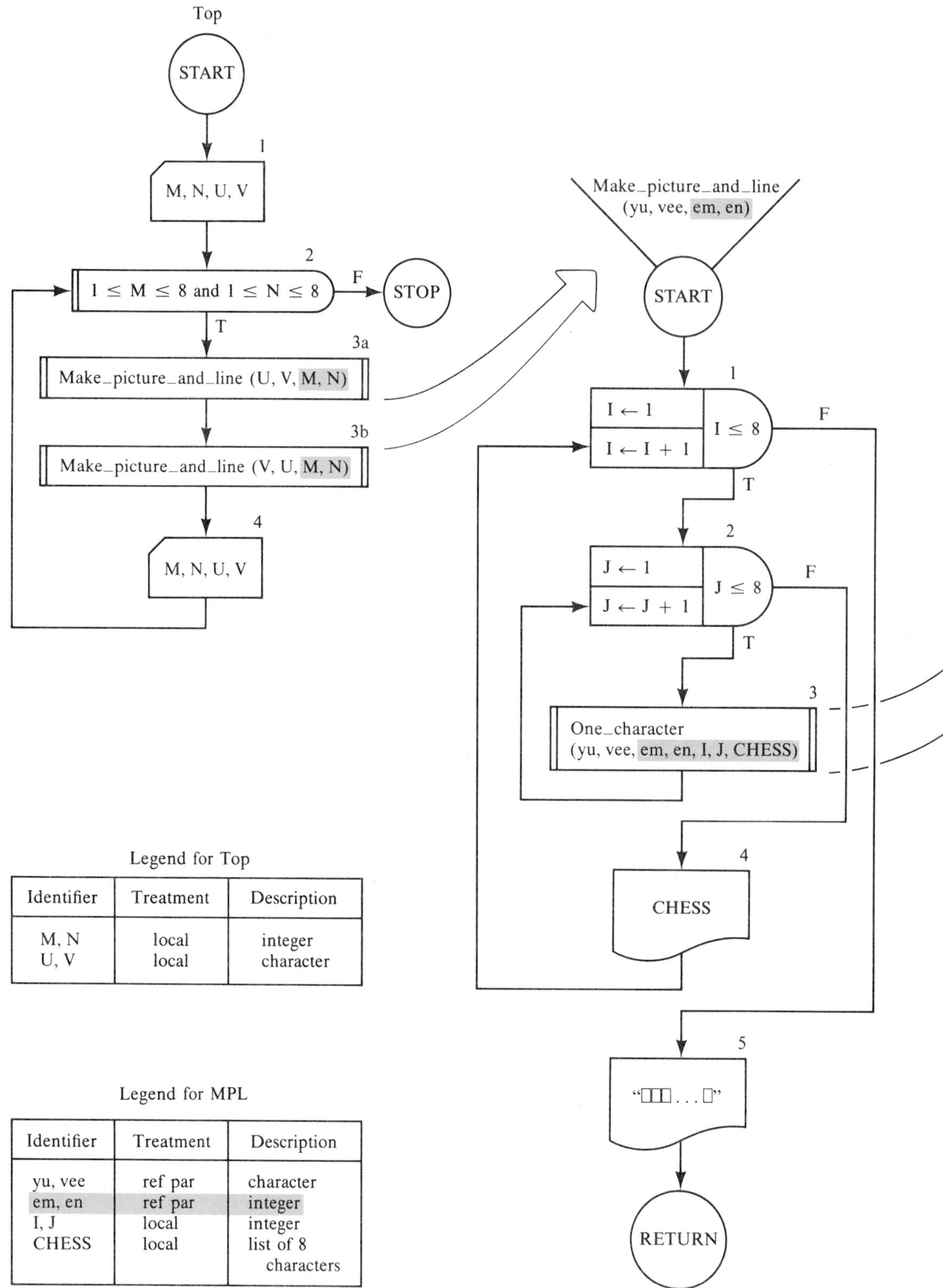

Legend for Top

Identifier	Treatment	Description
M, N	local	integer
U, V	local	character

Legend for MPL

Identifier	Treatment	Description
yu, vee	ref par	character
em, en	ref par	integer
I, J	local	integer
CHESS	local	list of 8 characters

Figure 2-10.* Chessboard solution of Figure 2-1 using parameters and *no globals.

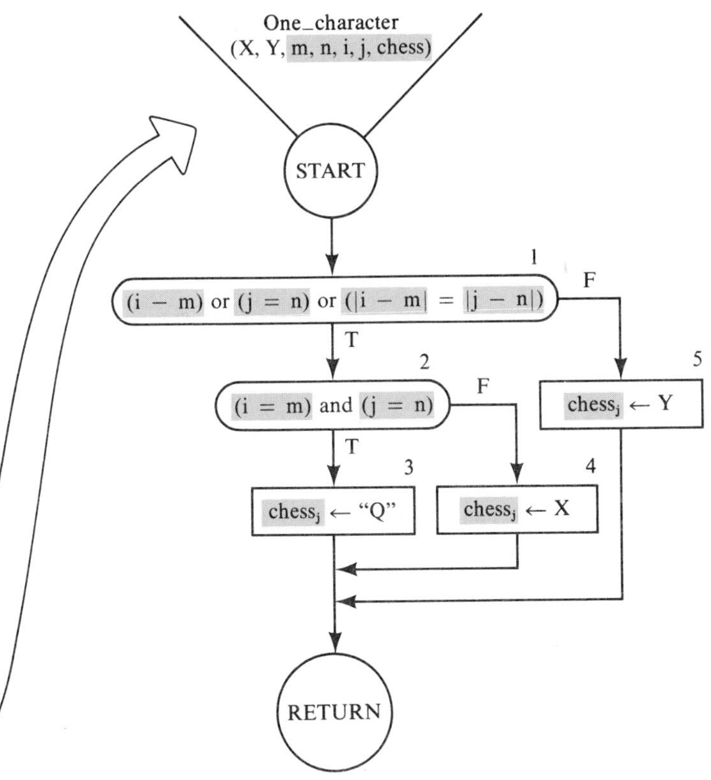

Legend for One_char

Identifier	Treatment	Description
X, Y	ref par	character
m, n i, j	ref par	integer
chess	ref par	list/char

computer system used, save considerable time and more than offset the extra work of copying the argument values (once) into the procedure contours, and copying the final parameter values (once) back into the argument cells.*

Exercises 2-2

1 (a) Review Problem 1 of Exercises 1-5. In that problem we were asked to utilize the subflowchart SORT, which was flowcharted to sort the n elements of the list A, for the purpose of sorting two other lists B and C each having m elements. "Generalize" SORT and its subflowcharts MOVE and Findkay by replacing all globals with parameters. The replacement is to be done without altering the body of any subflowchart except for the trivial change of adding arguments in a procedure call box.

*Potential specialists, however, should take heed: The value/result method gives an effect that is nearly always identical to the reference parameter effect, as described in our model. There can be a disparity, however, if a variable, used as an argument in a procedure, is also globally accessible for reassignment of its value while the called procedure, or any procedure invoked by the called procedure, is being executed. For example, suppose that in Top we have the call P (X) and that in P the variable X is globally accessible. Then, if the value of X is changed by assignment of a new value within procedure P, the change will be lost in the value/result method when control returns to Top, but will be preserved in the simple chaining (copying of references) method. A different net effect can also occur, for example, when the same argument matches two different parameters in a procedure, and both parameters are assigned new values in the body of the procedure. If the order of the assignments to the parameters is the opposite of the order of the parameters in the parameter list for the procedure, the argument may have a different value after the procedure is executed with the value/result method than with the simple chaining method.

(b) When SORT has been redefined as required in (a),

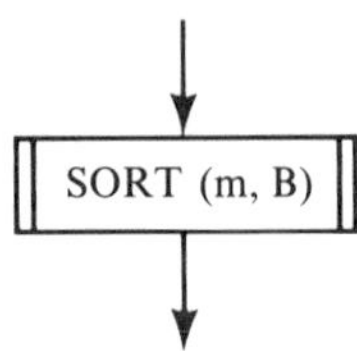

will have, as its net effect, the rearrangement of the m elements of B in nondescending numerical order. Revise the top-level flowchart of Exercise 2, Section 1-5 to take advantage of the generalized version of SORT created in (a). Be sure to show the new legends for Top, SORT, MOVE, and Findkay.

2 (a) Develop a general-purpose procedure MATSUMS, which, given an m row by n element matrix A of real numbers, computes the sums of each of its m rows, and assigns the sum of the row sums to TOTAL. MATSUMS should have no globals and should have as a subflowchart ROWSUM, which sums the elements of a specified row of a specified matrix and assigns it to a specified variable. ROWSUM should have no globals. Naturally, legends are expected to accompany the MATSUMS and ROWSUM flowcharts.

(b) To help test whether you have in mind the appropriate generalizations (abstractions), construct a top-level flowchart and legend that:

(i) inputs two matrixes, C having r rows and s columns, and D having t rows and u columns;

(ii) outputs the row sums of each (first of C, then of D); and

(iii) prints a message to indicate which of the two arrays has the greater sum of row sums, or prints a message to indicate that the sums are equal.

2-3 INDEPENDENCE AND INTERCHANGEABILITY OF PROCEDURES

We would like to use procedures as "black boxes" and be able to plug and unplug them without examining their interiors. If global variables are allowed, one cannot ever blindly replace one procedure by another even though it appears to accomplish the same goal with possibly different variables and a different sequence of computation. Global variables always match higher-level variables, and so storage cells at a higher level are always made accessible. If a global variable appears on the *left* of an assignment in a procedure, then the value of the corresponding higher-level variable will be changed when that statement is executed. This is called a "side effect" of the procedure. In some cases side effects are desirable but they can also be disastrous if the programmer is unaware of the value changes in the higher-level variables.

To prevent important side effects associated with global variables from going unnoticed, one would like a mechanism to alert the reader of a procedure to the presence of globals and to the effects on these globals caused by executing the procedure. In the case of our flowchart language, that mechanism is in part provided in the legend. Scanning down the legend of a procedure, one can easily find the global identifiers.

If the description given for each global were expanded to include an explanation of how that global is affected by the procedure, then all side effects would be explicitly described. Our legends do not provide such detailed descriptions, although in principle they could. Thus it is necessary to study the actual assignment or input statements of the procedure to determine whether a global variable is involved in side effects.

For example, in all our procedurized versions of the chessboard algorithm, except for the most recent one (Figure 2-10), the variable CHESS, viewed by One_character, was a global variable. $CHESS_J$ appears on the left of three assignment statements. Of course, these assignments were needed to assemble the lines of characters for each row of the printout.

Of the most commonly used programming languages that allow globals in procedures, for example, Fortran, PL/I, and Algol, only Fortran requires that globals be listed in the declarative part of the procedure. (The declarative part corresponds to our legend.) Moreover, none of these languages force the programmer to spell out the side effects on globals. Perhaps newer languages will enforce such a discipline.

Is the situation with regard to detecting side effects any better for reference parameters than for globals? Let us take a look.

If the reference parameters of a procedure could be guaranteed to appear only on the *right* sides of assignment statements, the *values* of the argument variables whose storage boxes are made accessible would never be in danger of inadvertent alteration. Of course, it is not reasonable to ask this kind of guarantee because sometimes we really want and need to change these values, for example, in the case of the parameter chess in the Figure 2-10 version of One_character. In One_character, note that when box 4 is executed, that is,

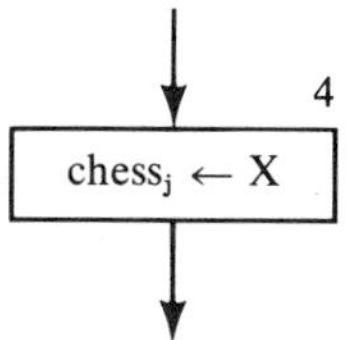

the following correspondences are set up:

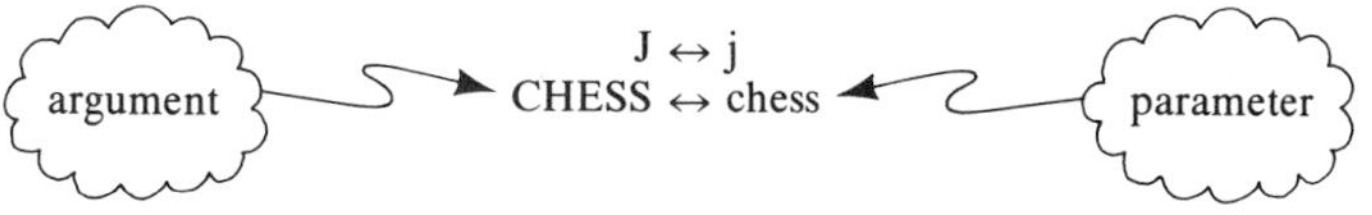

Hence the expression $CHESS_J$ corresponds to the expression $chess_j$. Since $CHESS_J$ represents an element of a local variable, the storage cell in the environment of MPL is used. A reference to $chess_j$ during execution of One_character will use this same storage cell. Boxes 3, 4, and 5 of the procedures all make assignments to $chess_j$. Thus the execution for various values of J will cause corresponding value changes in the MPL storage cell for CHESS. But this is what we want; we are generating values of CHESS to output in box 4 of Make_picture_and_line.

Although it is our intent that, when the MC executes in One_character, he be able to modify values in the MPL storage box for CHESS, we prefer that he *not* change values in storage boxes corresponding to other parameters in One_char. Let us see why.

Suppose by some foolish mistake we inadvertently slipped box 6

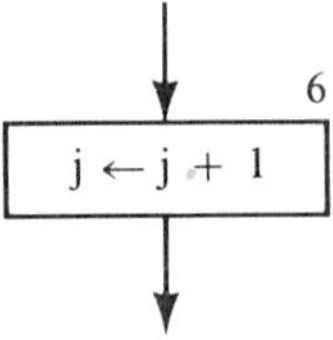

into the Figure 2-10 flowchart for One_character, as seen in Figure 2-11. We have a real disaster on our hands! Every time box 5 of Figure 2-11 is executed, which means every time a chess position (I, J) is *not* in the scope of the Queen, then box 6 will be executed. Box 6 increments the parameter j, which has a parameter–argument relation with the variable J of Make_picture_and_line. That means that every time a position is found outside the scope of the Queen,

***Figure 2-11.* A disastrous change in the One_character procedure.**

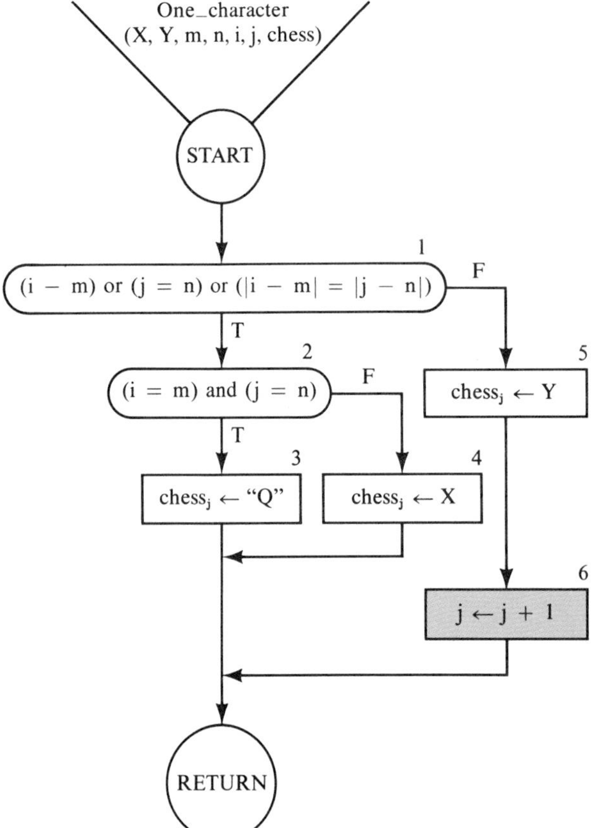

Legend for One_char

Identifier	Treatment	Description
X, Y	ref par	character
m, n, i, j	ref par	integer
chess	ref par	list/char

the *next* position along the same row will be skipped because the value of J is incremented in box 6 and incremented again in box 2 of Make_picture_and_line. The moral of this tale is: Whenever you program the assignment of a new value to a reference parameter in a procedure, be sure you are aware that, when the procedure is executed, the actual change will occur in the value of the corresponding argument in the calling environment. Of course, if the corresponding argument is itself a reference parameter, a similar further chaining will occur.

We see, therefore, that either mechanism, global or reference parameter, can lead to disasters if one is not careful. Each mechanism provides a means for sharing information among two or more modules of a program. As programs grow in complexity and in the number of component modules, the problem of *intellectual manageability* becomes paramount. Well-designed programming languages that encourage careful documentation and detailed specification of program modules will help solve this problem as does a consistent use of legends for flowcharts. In the last analysis, however, too many globals and/or parameters make modules difficult to deal with, no matter how good the documentation. Our ultimate expedient in dealing with complexity of programs is the skill we can develop to decompose programs so that the interface between pairs of modules, that is, the information shared through parameters or globals, is kept to a practical minimum [see Stevens *et al.* (1974)].

Exercises 2-3

1 Exercise 1 of Section 1-4 dealt with the INTDIV procedure. Figure 2-12 is a Top-level flowchart that calls INTDIV, now "equipped" with parameters NUM and DEN.

(a) In general, when box 2 of Top is executed, will the printed values be different if boxes 2 and 3 of Top are interchanged? Explain.

(b) Repeat question (c) in Exercise 1, Section 1-4, namely: Draw a snapshot showing the state of the computation just after box 3 of INTDIV is executed for the first time. (Assume input values are N = 43 and D = 12, and also assume that boxes 2 and 3 of Top have been interchanged.)

2-4 AUTOMATING PROTECTION OF ARGUMENTS

In the problem posed at the end of Section 2-3, the way to correct the foolish mistake in Figure 2-11 is simply to remove box 6 because it is not needed anyway. However, a more convincing example of the underlying difficulty can easily be given.

Consider the procedure ACCUM, which, given the initial and final indexes of a real array A, computes the SUM of the values of the elements A_{begin} through

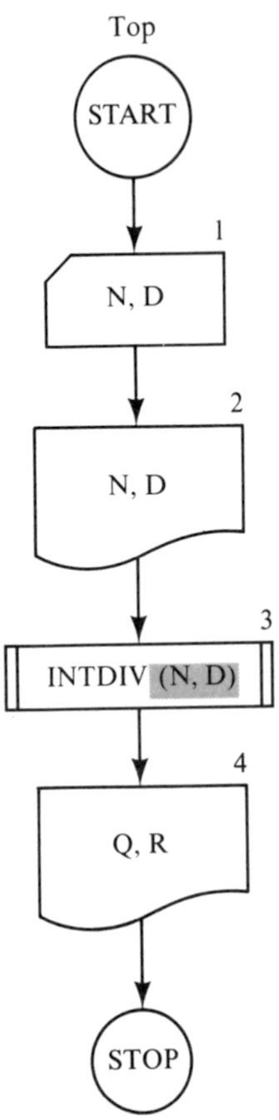

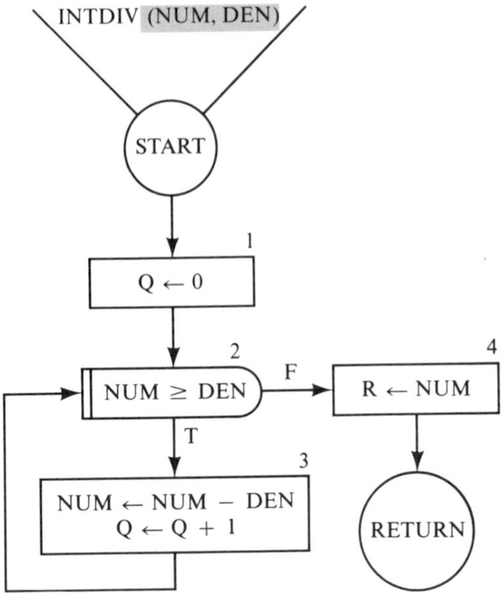

Legend for Top

Identifier	Treatment	Description
N, D, Q, R	local	integer

Legend for INTDIV

Identifier	Treatment	Description
NUM	ref par	integer
DEN	ref par	integer
Q	global	Q in Top
R	global	R in Top

Figure 2-12

A_{end} inclusive. We would like execution of a call such as

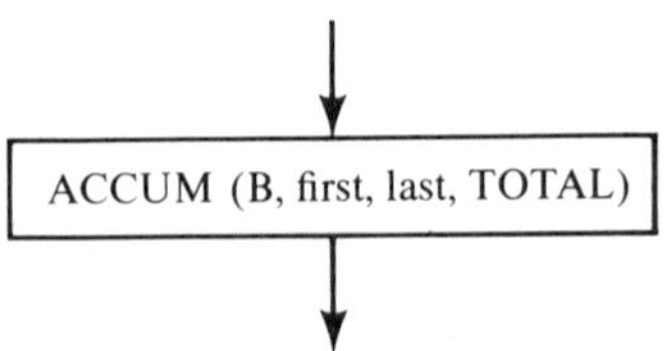

to result in the assignment of the desired sum to TOTAL, *without disturbing values of B, first, or last.* Suppose the procedure flowchart for ACCUM has the structure given in Figure 2-13. To avoid an extra (local) variable, the parameter begin has been used as a loop control counter. If we declare begin as a reference parameter the execution of ACCUM will change the value of its matching argument, first, thus violating our requirement that values of B, first, and last should remain fixed during the execution of ACCUM. There are several ways to solve this difficulty, as will be discussed in this section.

It is possible to define other forms of argument–parameter matching that prevent arguments from being assigned new values by action steps of called procedures. When such forms of information sharing between modules are used, fiascos such as the one described in connection with Figure 2-11 can be avoided. In that situation we wanted the value of J to be read-accessible to the procedure One_character, but we did not want the procedure to be able to *change* the value of J. In other words, we wanted one-way communication, from the argument to the parameter, not the two-way communication offered by a reference parameter.

Computer system designers have invented a variety of mechanisms for automating this constraint, but in essence these mechanisms all fall into only a few categories. We mention two of these here.

(a) The one-way communication is specified in the code of the *called procedure* (that is, it is the responsibility of the person writing the called procedure to specify those parameters, if any, whose arguments are to be protected).

(b) The one-way communication is specified in the code of the *calling procedure* (that is, it is the responsibility of the person writing the calling procedure to specify which arguments, if any, are to be protected).

Figure 2-13

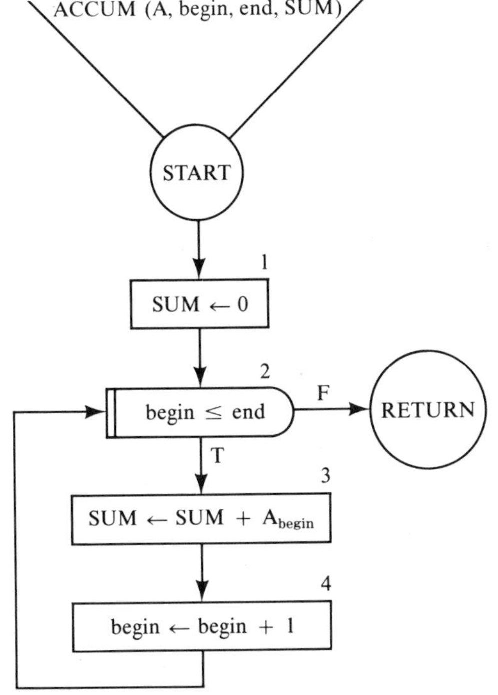

Legend

Identifier	Treatment	Description
SUM	ref par	real
begin	? par	integer
end	ref par	integer
A	ref par	array of reals

We shall discuss examples of both types of protection mechanisms in terms of our model, but discussion of the second type is deferred to Section 2-5.

The first type of protection, namely, that specified in the called procedure, is illustrated by what we call the *value-parameter* treatment. The author of the called procedure specifies in the legend entry (or declaration) that a selected parameter is to be treated as a *value parameter* (the abbreviation "val par" will be used).

For example, suppose we change the legend entry for parameter j in One_character (Figure 2-10) to

Identifier	Treatment	Description
j	val par	integer

Then, when an environment is created for the execution of One_character, it will include a cell of the form

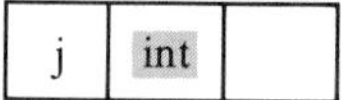

The value portion of this cell will automatically be assigned a copy of the value of the matching integer argument J. Further execution of the procedure One_character will continue as though j is indeed a local variable, that is, the value of J will be protected against changes in j. Now, even if a step like

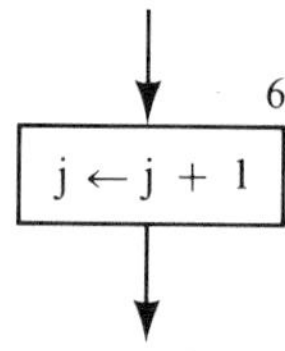

is executed after box 5 in One_character, it will not have any effect on J, since the assignment to the list variable has already been made for the current execution and an assignment to local j can cause no effect beyond the immediate environment.

If we wish to achieve similar protection for the other parameters (i, m, n, X, and Y), it is a simple matter to specify that these parameters should also be treated as value parameters. (The parameter chess of course must *not* be a value parameter.) Figure 2-14 shows a new version of the chessboard solution. (Compare with Figure 2-10.) Now legend entries for all the parameters have been qualified to distinguish *reference* parameters (ref par) from *value* parameters (val par). Figure 2-15 shows us the effect of these legend changes on the resulting computational environments. This figure again shows our favorite snapshot (2.5).

In the absence of a value parameter specification mechanism, it is, of course, still possible for the programmer of a called procedure to "manually" protect matching arguments of parameters or, for that matter, manually protect global variables, which will be referenced in the procedure. The programmer need only set up auxiliary local variables, one for each identifier that is to be protected, and then methodically transfer values of arguments or global variables to auxiliary variables immediately on entrance to the procedure. Then throughout the procedure the local variables are used instead of the parameters or global variables. Incidentally this is the only method of protection available in the unextended BASIC language that has no parameters and hence no possibility of a value parameter specification. In Basic all variables of a procedure are global, including any auxiliary variables selected to protect other global variables. Notice, however, that to apply this method of protection to global variables requires complete familiarity with the legends of every subflowchart. For each global variable to be protected in the procedure, one must set up a local variable. "Black box" interchangeable procedures are not possible in the Basic language, since each procedure must be written with the top-level program in mind.

Even though a computer language has parameters, it may still lack a value specification for parameters. For example, all parameters may have to be of the reference type. Fortran is such a language. In this case, "do it yourself" protection is necessary. Programmers of subflowcharts often routinely set up a local variable for every parameter–argument relation that needs to be protected against the flow of information outward from the environment of the procedure. The first assignments in the procedure then transfer the initial values of parameters to the safety of local variables. Thereafter in the procedure the local variables are used instead of the parameters. Notice that do it yourself protection is not less efficient than the use of value parameters. Essentially the same actions take place in both cases. The important difference lies in convenience; value parameters may be easier for the programmer to use.

Exercises 2-4

1 (a) Construct a top level flowchart and legend for a computation that
(i) inputs a list B of p real elements,
(ii) locates the largest element in B,
(iii) interchanges that element with B_1, and
(iv) displays the modified list.

The top level flowchart should make use of the procedures MAX and INTERCHANGE, whose flowcharts and incomplete legends are given in Figure 2-16. In addition to drawing a top-level flowchart, complete the legends for MAX and INTERCHANGE. (If you have worked Exercise 2, Section 1-4, compare Top of that problem with the one you develop here.)

(b) Answer the following three questions:
(i) Can parameters A and B of INTERCHANGE be value parameters? Justify your answer.
(ii) What would be the disadvantage, if any, of letting the parameter k in MAX be a value parameter?
(iii) Can parameter A of MAX be a value parameter? Justify your answer.

2 Figure 2-17 shows a proposed top-level flowchart for computing the least common multiple (LCM) of two given integers A and B, using the well-known equality

$$\text{LCM (A, B)} = \frac{\text{A} \times \text{B}}{\text{gcd of A and B}}$$

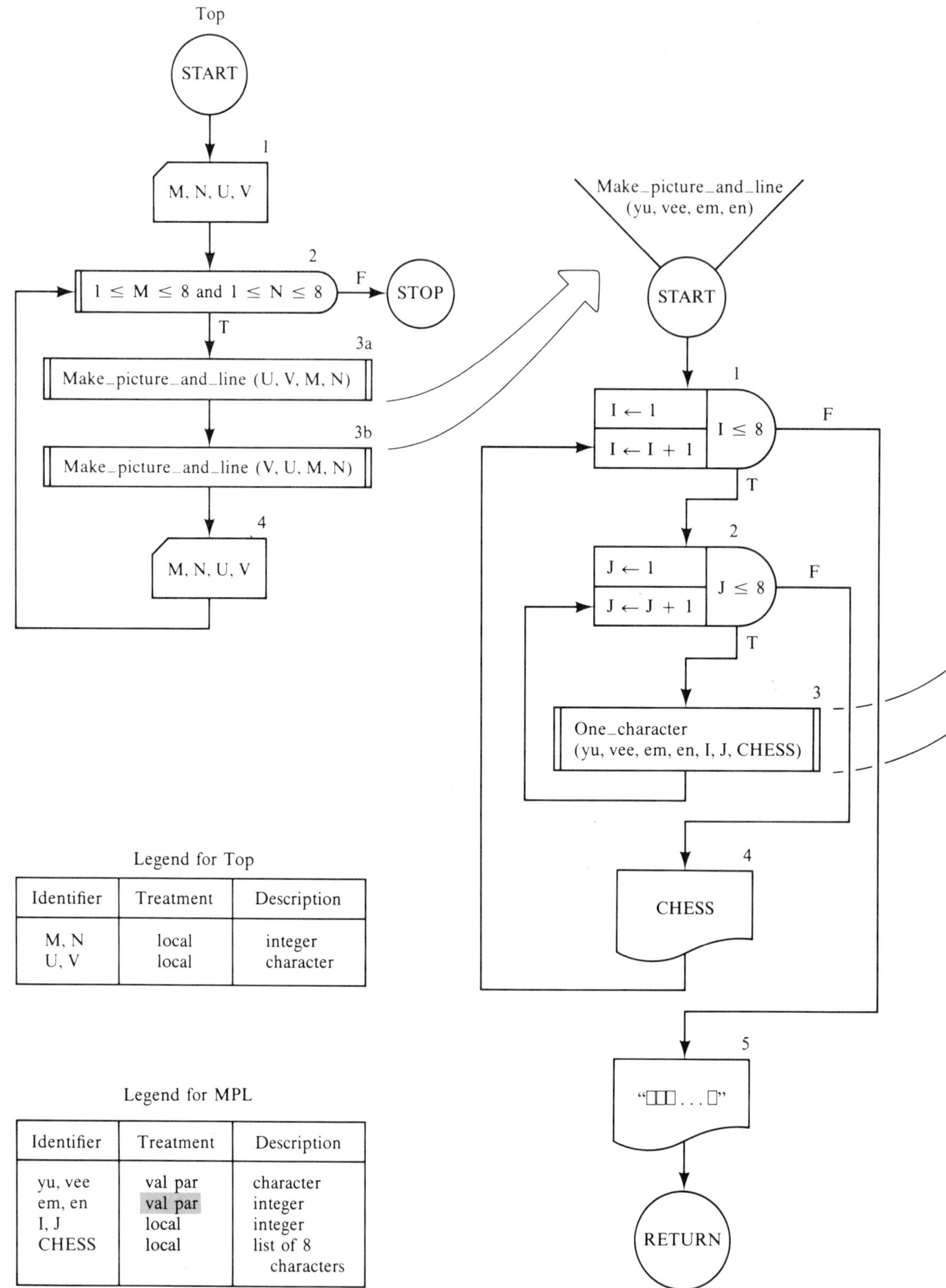

Legend for Top

Identifier	Treatment	Description
M, N	local	integer
U, V	local	character

Legend for MPL

Identifier	Treatment	Description
yu, vee	val par	character
em, en	val par	integer
I, J	local	integer
CHESS	local	list of 8 characters

***Figure 2-14.* Chessboard solution of Figure 2-10 using value parameters as well as reference parameters.**

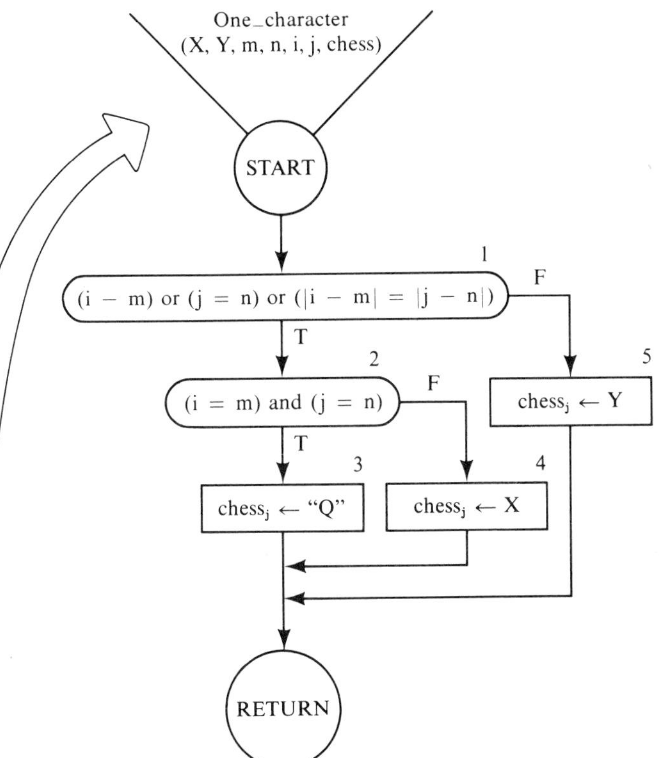

Legend for One_char

Identifier	Treatment	Description
X, Y	val par	character
m, n i, j	val par	integer
chess	ref par	list/char

where gcd is the *g*reatest *c*ommon *d*ivisor. For example,

$$\text{LCM }(15, 10) = \frac{15 \times 10}{\text{gcd of 15 and 10}} = \frac{15 \times 10}{5} = 30$$

The top-level flowchart employs the procedure GCD as a subflowchart. In essence the procedure GCD uses the Euclidean algorithm that is described in elementary programming texts.* Create your own interchange procedure for integers by adapting that shown in Exercise 1.

(a) Trace the execution of the given flowcharts for the case where values of A and B input at box 1 of Top are 15 and 10, respectively, and show what value is printed for the LCM, when box 3 of Top is executed. If you agree that the answer is not 30 as expected, explain what happened.

In (b), (c), and (d), you are asked to show three ways to correct the protection failure in the given flowcharts and legends.

(b) Altering only Top and its legend.

(c) Altering GCD and its legend by adding locals to "protect" parameters that need protection.

(d) Altering only the legend of GCD.

(e) For the solution in (d), construct a snapshot of the computation for the following situation: Input values are A = 15, B = 10. The MC has just executed box 5 of GCD.

*See for example, Forsythe *et al.*, "Computer Science: A First Course," 2nd ed. Wiley, New York, 1975.

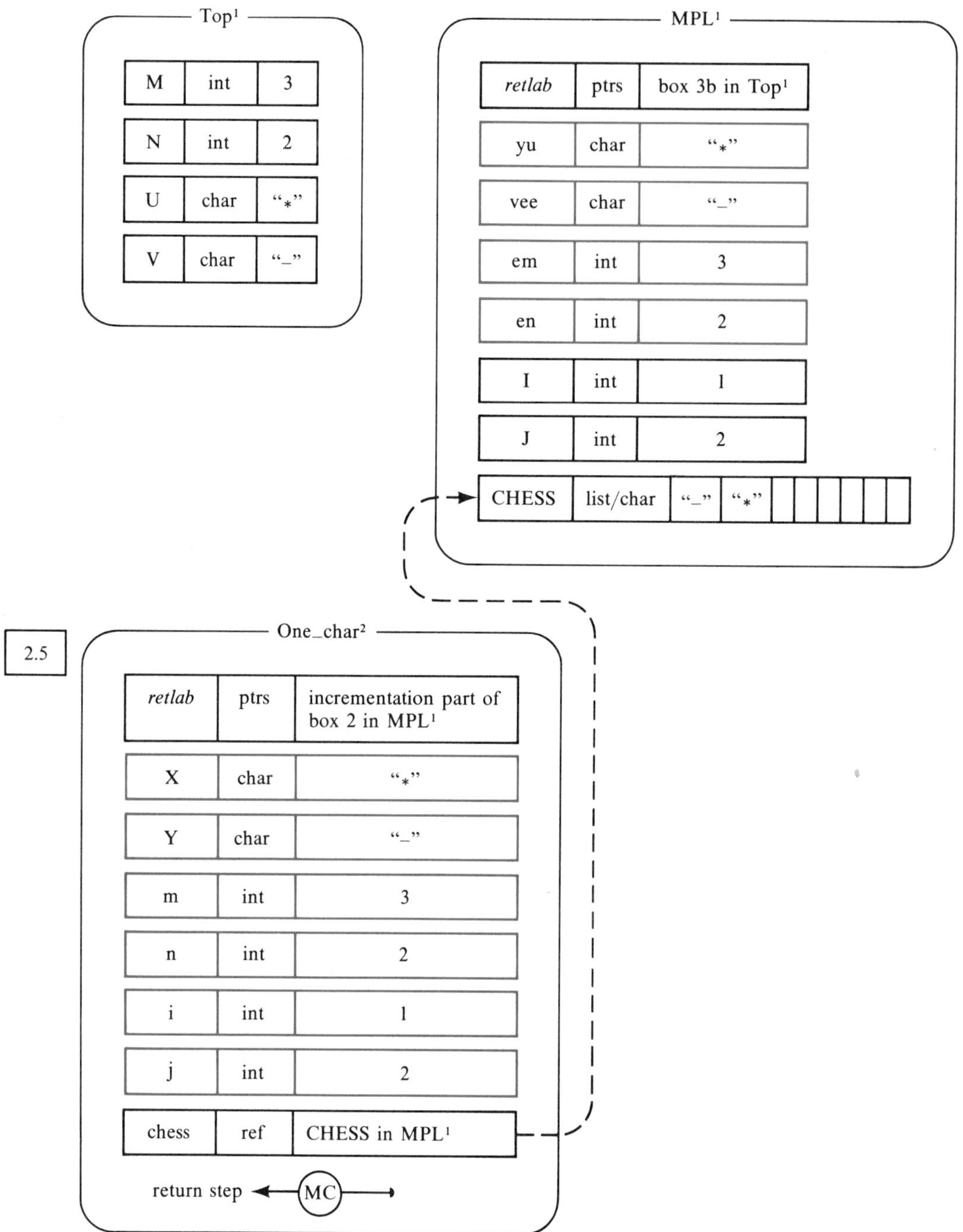

Figure 2-15. **Snapshot to illustrate the mechanism of argument—parameter matching for both value and reference parameters.**

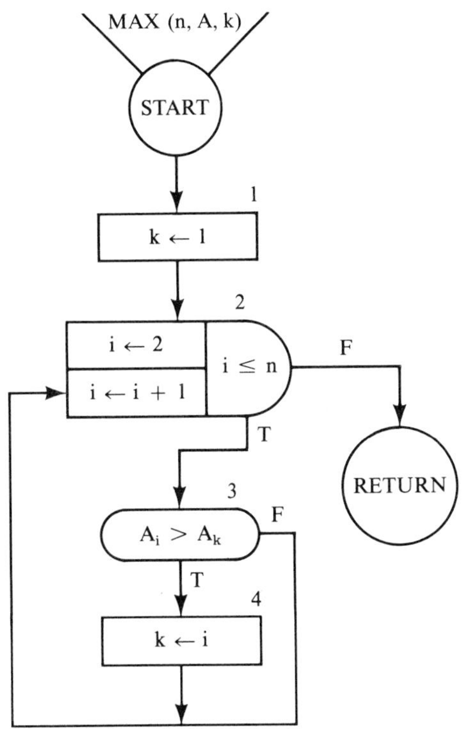

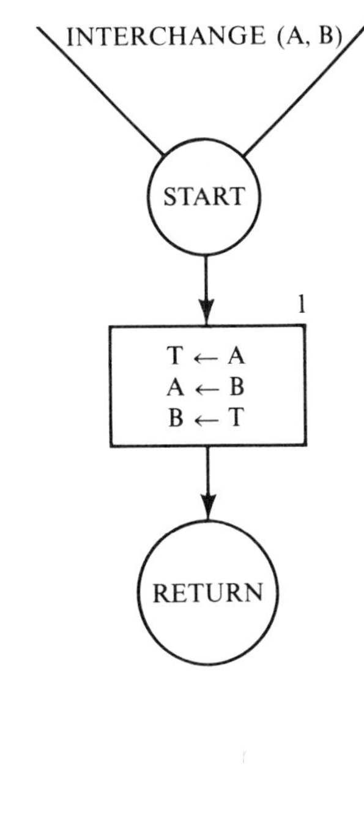

Legend for MAX

Identifier	Treatment	Description
n, k		integer
A		list of reals
i	local	integer

Legend for INTERCHANGE

Identifier	Treatment	Description
A, B		real
T	local	real

Figure 2-16

3 Show a revision to the flowchart and legend for INTDIV given in Exercise 1, Section 1-4, such that there are no globals and such that any parameter needing "protection" gets it.

4 The greatest common factor GCF of several integers can be found by successive use of the GCD of two integers. Thus

$$\text{GCF (A, B, C)} = \text{GCD (GCD (A, B), C)}$$

and

$$\begin{aligned}\text{GCF (A, B, C, D)} &= \text{GCD (GCF (A, B, C), D)}\\ &= \text{GCD (GCD (GCD (A, B), C), D)}.\end{aligned}$$

Accordingly we can construct a flowchart for finding the GCF of the components of a list of integers

$$A_1, A_2, \ldots, A_K.$$

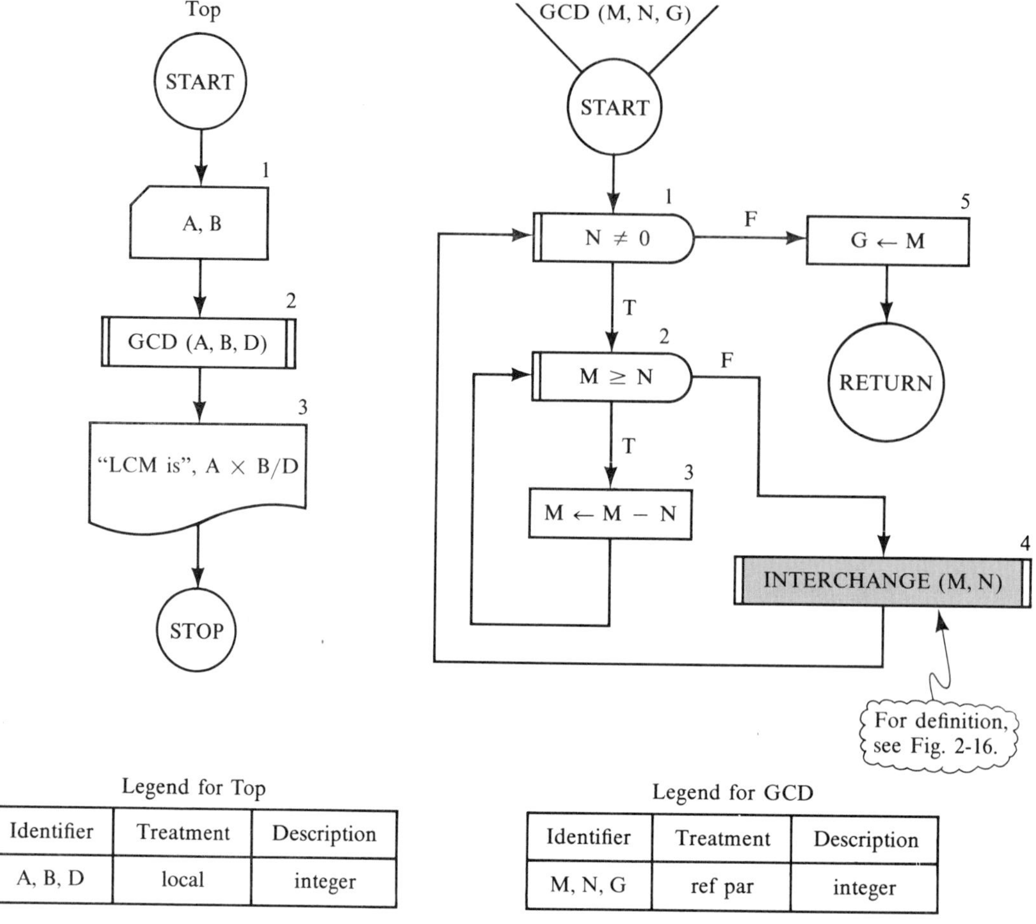

Legend for Top

Identifier	Treatment	Description
A, B, D	local	integer

Legend for GCD

Identifier	Treatment	Description
M, N, G	ref par	integer

Figure 2-17

We present such a flowchart in Figure 2-18, assuming the availability of the GCD procedure shown in Exercise 1.

(a) Your first task is to convert this flowchart into a procedure GCF. Input and output steps will be deleted from GCF and replaced by items in the parameter list. The top-level flowchart that calls GCF will contain the input and output steps. The legend for GCF should include only reference parameters, value parameters, and locals. You need not show the top-level flowchart.

(b) In studying roots of a polynomial equation with integer coefficients of the form

$$a_n \times x^n + a_{n-1} \times x^{n-1} + \cdots + a_2 \times x^2 + a_1 \times x + a_0 = 0$$

it is convenient to simplify by dividing all the coefficients by their greatest common factor. Accordingly, construct a flowchart to input the coefficients, find their greatest common factor using the procedure of (a), divide the coefficients by their GCF, and output the coefficients of the reduced equation. Note: Although we have not yet said so explicitly, it is perfectly permissible for an array subscript to have a zero value in our flowchart language.

5 EQUILAT is a procedure that determines whether a triangle whose sides are A, B, and C is equilateral (has three sides with positive equal lengths) and if so prints

"EQUILATERAL". In addition, the procedure sets k to 0 or 1 to denote failure or success, respectively.

(a) Construct a flowchart and legend for EQUILAT such that the procedure has no locals and no globals.

(b) Choose and justify value or reference parameter treatment for each parameter.

(c) Illustrate the use of EQUILAT by showing a simple main flowchart that calls EQUILAT, then tests to see whether success or failure resulted and, depending on the outcome, chooses between two different action paths. Be sure to provide a legend for the top-level flowchart.

6 ISOSC is a procedure that determines whether a triangle whose sides are A, B, and C is isosceles (two, and only two, sides are equal). If so, it prints "ISOSCELES". In addition, ISOSC sets the global variable k to 0 or to 1 to denote failure or success, respectively.

(a) Construct a flowchart and legend for ISOSC, letting k be the only global variable.

Figure 2-18

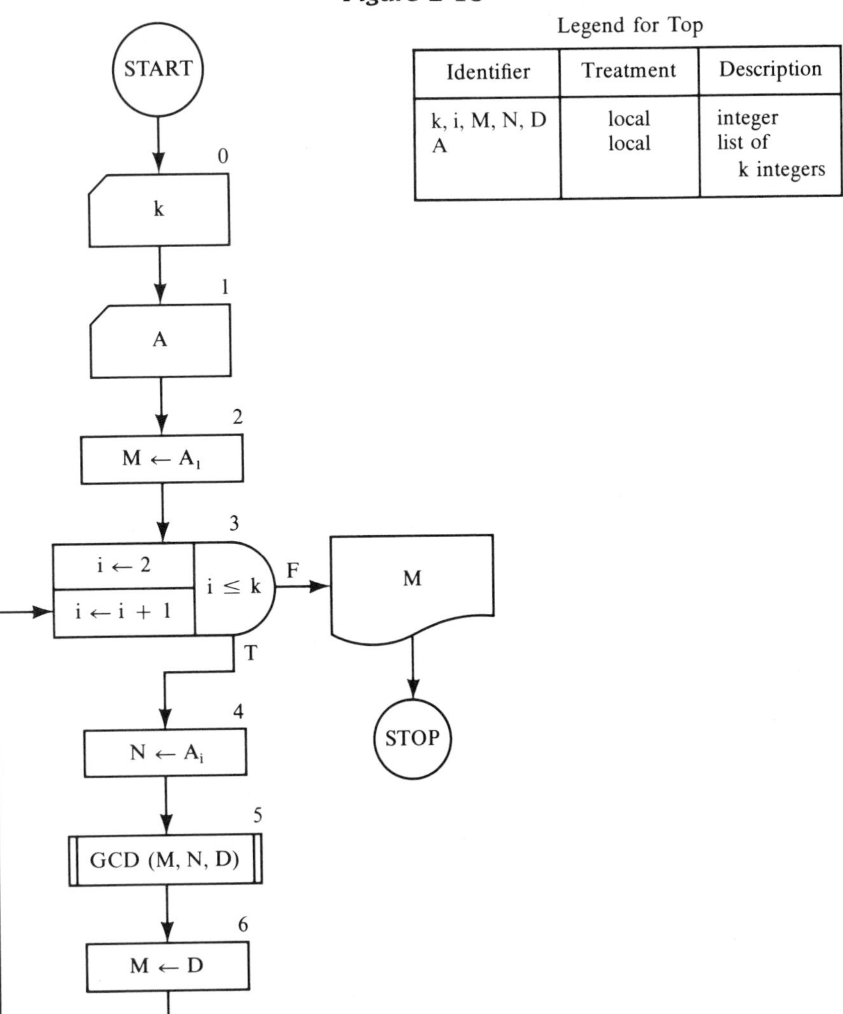

Legend for Top

Identifier	Treatment	Description
k, i, M, N, D	local	integer
A	local	list of k integers

(b) Illustrate the use of ISOSC by constructing a top-level flowchart and legend. Top should call ISOSC and then choose between two action paths depending on the success/fail outcome "reported" by the procedure.

7 Construct and illustrate the use of a procedure called LARGE, which displays the largest value found in the first n elements of the list called A. Use no globals. Show the legend for LARGE and justify the treatment that you select for the parameters.

8 Draw a flowchart and legend for a procedure named printisosc, which, when called, will print the pattern of a right isosceles triangle whose dimension and display character are given as arguments n and C, where n is the height of the triangle (number of printed lines) and C is the character value to be printed. Thus for n = 5 and C = "X", the printed figure would look like

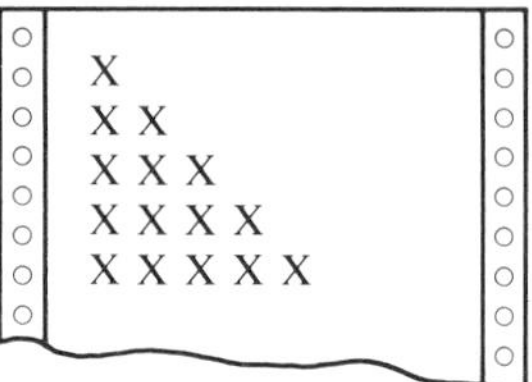

9 Modify the procedure printisosc that you developed in Exercise 8 so that, when called, it will print up to m complete triangles (as many as will fit) from left to right across the page having a width of 120 spaces. Each triangle should be separated horizontally by h characters, with values of m and h given as arguments, for example, for m = 3.

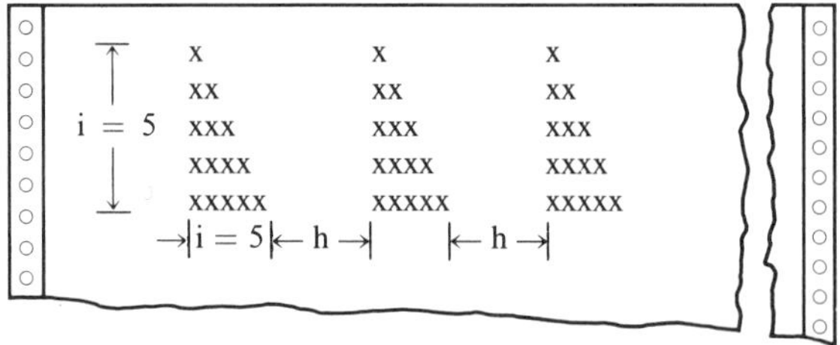

The minimum value for h should be 1.

10 Draw a flowchart and legend for a procedure named printdiamond, which when invoked will print a diamond whose dimensions and display character are given as arguments. For example, when the height R is 7 lines and the display character is the letter K, the output is

```
      K
    K K K
  K K K K K
K K K K K K K
  K K K K K
    K K K
      K
```

The value of R should always be an odd number.

11 Modify the procedure printdiamond developed in Exercise 10 so that a string of up to n diamonds is printed, left to right across the page, with h spaces between each pair of diamonds, for example, for n = 4, the diamonds would line up as

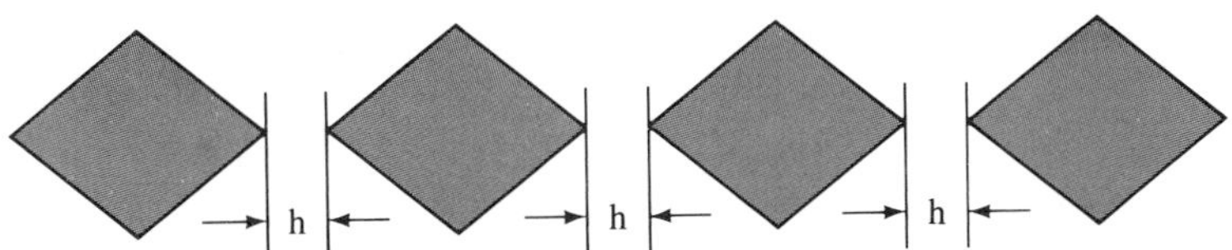

The values for n and h should be supplied as arguments for the modified procedure. The number of diamonds printed should either be n or the maximum number that can be printed across a page having 120 spaces, whichever is the smaller. The minimum value for h should be 1.

2-5 EXPRESSIONS AS ARGUMENTS IN A PROCEDURE CALL

With one exception every illustration of an argument–parameter match in the preceding sections has involved an argument that was either a variable or a parameter that referred to a variable. Now we shall explore how the computer model handles an argument that is an expression other than a simple or list variable. In doing this we shall discover another way to specify protection for arguments, this time in the code of the calling procedure.

While all variables are expressions, the following expressions, for example, are *not* variables:

$$A + 1 \qquad A + 0 \qquad A \times 1 \qquad -A \qquad +A \qquad -15$$

$$-A_j \qquad \text{“Q”} \qquad (A) \qquad A + B$$

An expression can be thought of as a rule for the MC to follow in arriving at a value. Consider the procedure call we saw first in Figure 2-5:

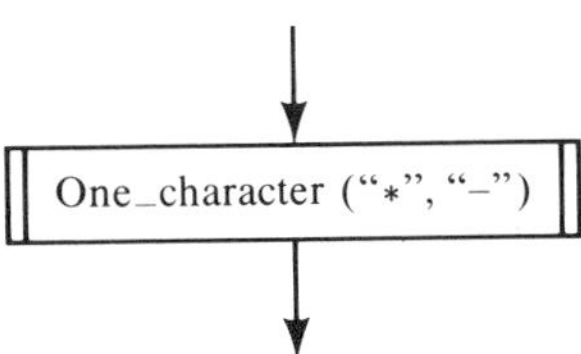

Both arguments are expressions. In the execution of this call, how are the values of these two expressions made available to the MC when he executes in the called procedure? The answer to this question depends on what kind of parameters these arguments are matched to, such as value parameter or reference parameter.

For the value parameter case the answer should be obvious. The MC evaluates the argument and in the case of a literal like "*", 16, or "Q", the evaluation is of course trivial. A copy of this value is transmitted to the new environment, in this example, One_character, and is placed in the value part of the storage cell for the corresponding parameter. No surprises.

In the case of the reference parameter, as we saw in Figure 2-7, the value part of the parameter cell contains a reference to a cell in the caller's environment and that cell contains the value of the argument. But what cell in the caller's environment can the MC use for the value of an expression argument? The cell cannot be that of a variable, since it would lead to confusion if that variable happened to appear in the calling flowchart. Thus the MC invents a new kind of name for the cell that is to hold this value. Then he asks the Allocator to place this name on an empty storage cell and asks the Reader/Assigner to assign the value to it.

The invented name for this box must be such that it cannot be mistaken for one of the variables occurring in the flowchart of the calling procedure. Variables of our flowchart language always begin with a letter of the alphabet, and so the MC makes up a name of some *other* form, for instance one that begins with some special character or digit. We shall assume therefore that the MC makes up distinct names of the form 1temp, 2temp, 3temp, . . . , 987temp, etc., as many as are required. Of course these cell names do not appear in the legend of the flowchart since we regard them as hidden from the programmer. They cannot be referred to explicitly in a flowchart.

Now we see one way that expression arguments can be matched to reference parameters. The argument expression is evaluated, the value is stuffed into a new box with a made-up name, and this name is then assigned to the value part of the corresponding parameter cell in the called procedure's environment.

To illustrate this parameter treatment, we return to Figure 2-14 and modify the top-level flowchart as shown in Figure 2-19. A snapshot taken just before box 3 of Make_picture_and_line is executed for the very first time (Figure 2-20) shows clearly the expression-argument–reference-parameter mechanism that we have just described. Reference parameters yu and vee refer, respectively, to cells 1temp and 2temp in Top^1, which hold values for the matching argument expressions. Cells 1temp and 2temp are "temporary" cells with created names that cannot be confused with variables selected by the programmer.

We can now observe that the very mechanism for matching an argument expression, as opposed to a simple variable argument, to a reference parameter also serves as an important protection mechanism that may be invoked by the calling procedure. When the MC assigns a new value to a reference parameter, and this parameter matches an argument expression, only the special (temporary) cell can have its value changed. No change can occur in the value of any flowchart variable in another environment. Moreover, if and when the temporary cell is reused, a new, although not necessarily different, value will be supplied to it. Thus, referring to the example in Figure 2-19, in reexecuting box 3a of Top, *new evaluations* of "*" and "–" are made, and these new values are reassigned to cells 1temp and 2temp, respectively. Thus, even if the old values of "*" and "–" have been destroyed, by assignment of new values to their corresponding parameters during a previous execution of Make_picture_and_line, no damage will have been done. Therefore, if the author of a calling program wishes to guarantee protection of one or more arguments in a call on

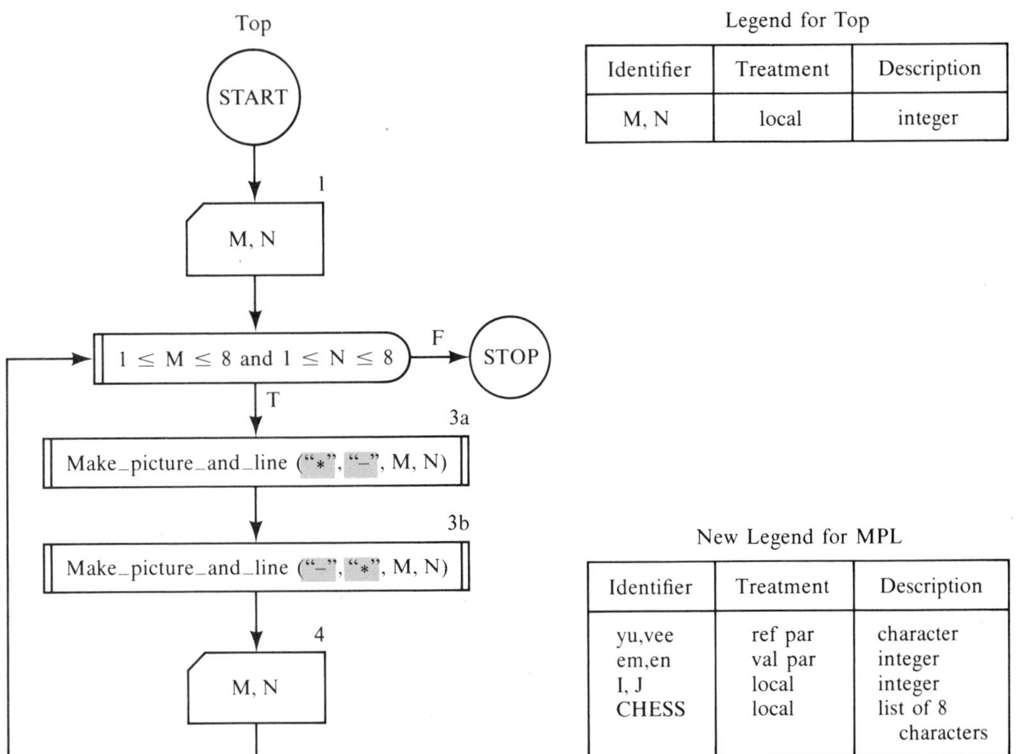

Legend for Top

Identifier	Treatment	Description
M, N	local	integer

New Legend for MPL

Identifier	Treatment	Description
yu,vee	ref par	character
em,en	val par	integer
I, J	local	integer
CHESS	local	list of 8 characters

Figure 2-19. **Modification of Top to illustrate the use of argument expressions.**

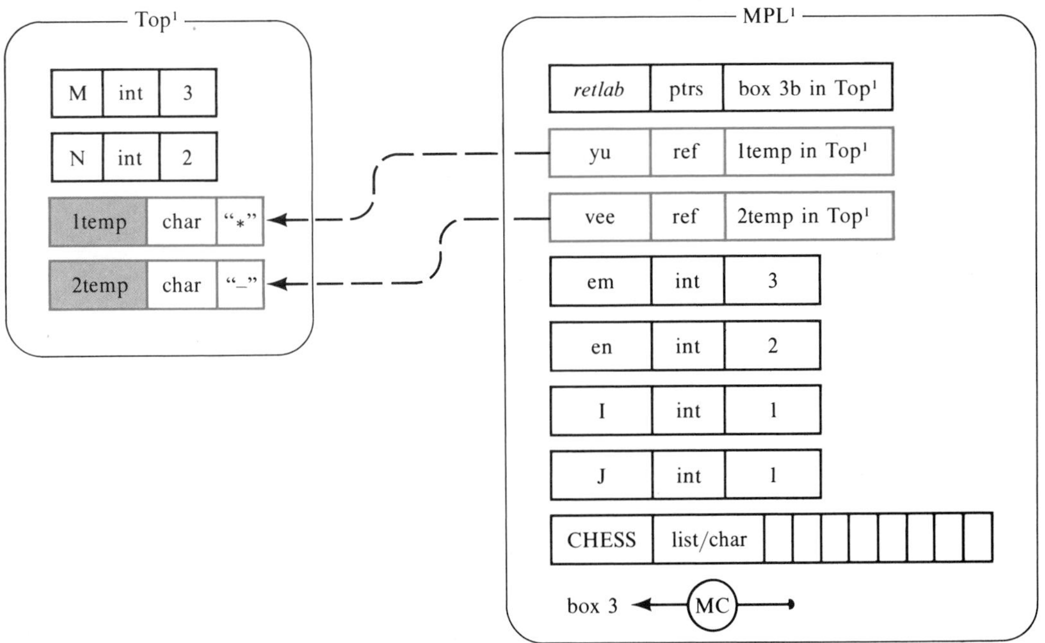

Figure 2-20. **A snapshot taken just before the first execution of box 3 in Make_picture_and_line.**

some procedure, he has merely to reexpress each such argument in the call statement as an expression, rather than as a simple variable. For example, in most programming languages the variable A can be protected if we reexpress it as the expression

$$(A), \quad \text{or } +A, \quad \text{or } A + 0, \quad \text{etc.}$$

(In a language like Fortran, which has no value parameters but does have reference parameters, protection can be easily achieved* for a variable argument matched to a reference parameter simply by converting the variable argument in the call statement to an expression.)

Exercises 2-5

Figure 2-21 is a flowchart to find the prime factorization of a given integer M. The discovered factors are stored in a list FACS and printed out all at once when the computation has been completed. We see that each prime factor of N found in box 201 is divided out of the current value of N in box 202 and stored in the list FACS. After control leaves box 102, N has no factors less than or equal to $\sqrt{N}$, and therefore no factors at all. If in box 104 the current value of N is not equal to 1, then N is prime and therefore a prime factor, and so this value of N is appended to the list of factors (box 105).

Your task is to convert subflowcharts (b) and (c) into procedure flowcharts, and boxes 3 and 103 into procedure call boxes. You are to do this conversion in three different ways, as described in the three exercises. Be sure to include a legend in every case.

1 In this exercise the procedure flowcharts derived from flowcharts (b) and (c) are to be called FACTORIZE1 and REMOVE1, respectively. Use no parameters. All variables are to be global. Has all the necessary protection been provided? How?

2 In this exercise the procedure flowcharts, derived from flowcharts (b) and (c), are to be called FACTORIZE2 and REMOVE2, respectively. Use no globals. Use only locals and reference parameters. Assume the value 30 is read for M in box 1. Draw a sketch of the environment of the computation, just as the MC prepares to execute box 201 for the first time. Show storage cells for all variables: M, N, i, j, FACS, k.
   (a) Which variables appearing in Figure 2-21a will *not* be found in the argument list in the procedure call replacing box 3?
   (b) What are the locals (if any) in FACTORIZE2?
   (c) What is the significance of the fact that the variables FACS and i that appear in Figure 2-21a have never been given values by assignment or input in that flowchart?
   (d) What are the locals of REMOVE2 (if any)?

3 In this exercise the procedure flowcharts derived from the flowcharts of Figure 2-21b and 2-21c are to be called FACTORIZE3 and REMOVE3, respectively. Use locals and value parameters. Use reference parameters only when necessary.

   Explain why the variable M is superfluous in this case and boxes 1 and 2 can be replaced by

*Some compilers, known as *optimizing compilers,* are programmed to simplify expressions, wherever possible, before compiling them. In an optimizing compiler that transforms such expressions as (A) to A, or A + 0 to A, the method of protection described here, of course, would not work.

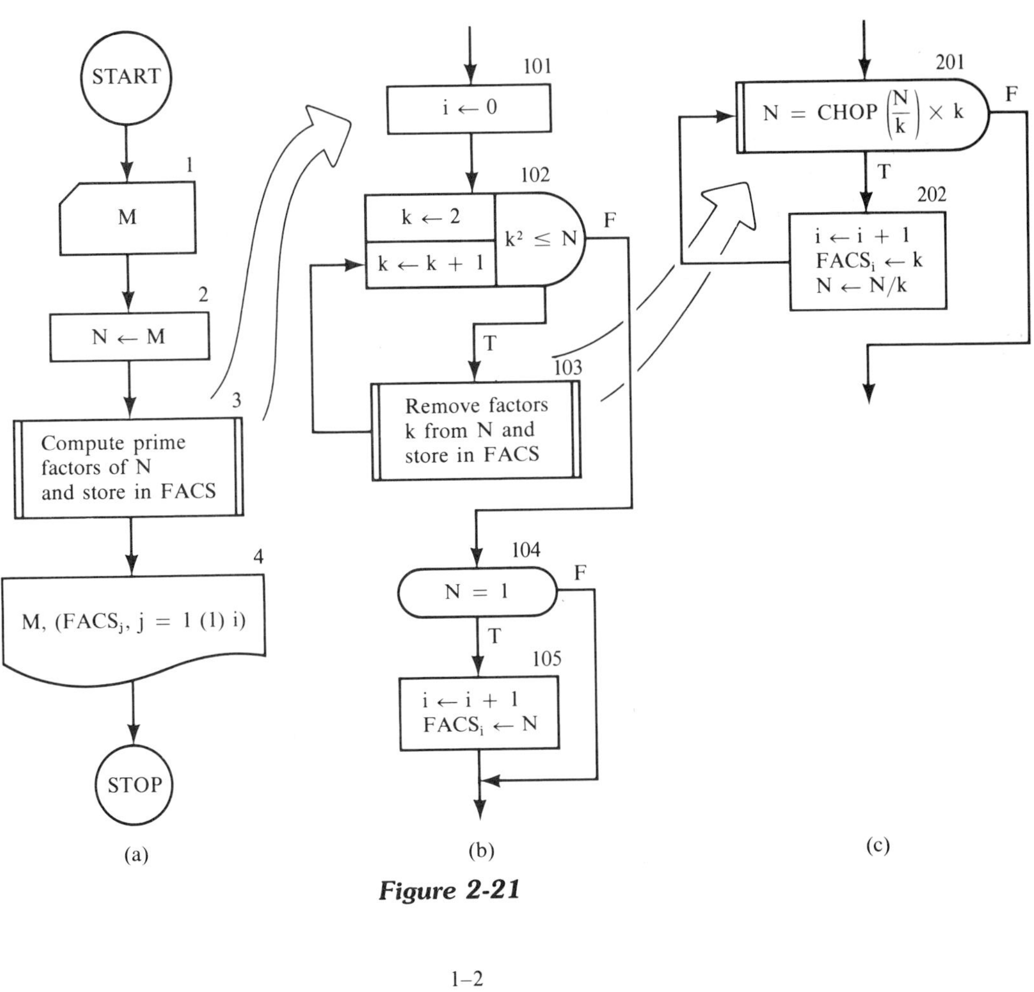

Figure 2-21

1–2

N

The purpose of box 2 was protection. This exercise illustrates that, if values are protected, there is no need for value parameter treatment. Conversely, when value parameter treatment is used, protection of the variable value is unnecessary.

2-6 FUNCTION PROCEDURES

When the main objective of a procedure is to produce *a single value,* simple or composite, it is often convenient to cast the procedure into a special form, called a *function procedure.* The distinguishing features of a function procedure are as follows:

1. (Syntax) The call to execute a function occurs, not when the MC comes to a special striped procedure call box, but rather when he meets the name of the function in some expression.

2. (Semantics) The computed value of a function is not returned to the calling environment through a change in value of either a global variable or a reference parameter. Rather the MC places the "bare" value in his stack and personally carries it back to the calling environment.
3. The execution of a function does not normally change the value of any variable in the calling environment. That type of change, as mentioned earlier, is called a "side effect" and, when introduced, makes the behavior of the function more complex and the program that calls it more difficult to understand. In a function, parameters are usually specified as value-type, in order to prevent side effects.

Function procedures are often referred to as just "functions," and in subsequent sections we shall use this abbreviation when there is no chance of confusion with the term *function* as used in mathematics. In many situations we have a free choice of whether to program an action using the structure of the procedure we are familiar with, or that of the new function procedure. Next we illustrate both ways of flowcharting the action of finding the least common multiple (lcm) of two integers. The lcm you will recall is the product of the integers divided by their greatest common divisor, gcd.

***Figure 2-22.* Least common multiple using a procedure.**

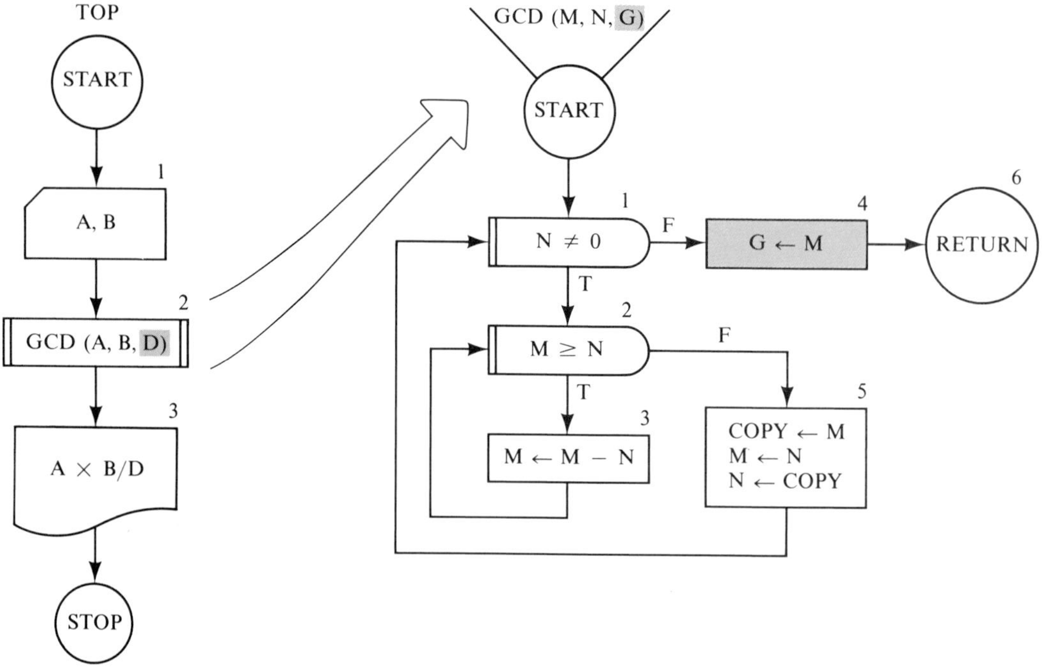

Legend for TOP

Identifier	Treatment	Description
A, B, D	local	integer

Legend for GCD

Identifier	Treatment	Description
M, N	val par	integer
G	ref par	integer
COPY	local	integer

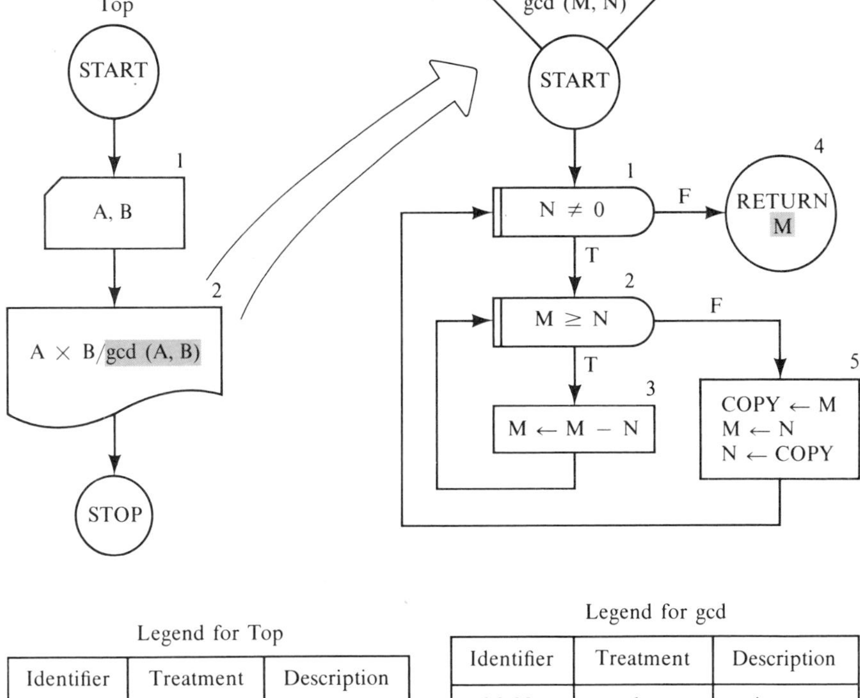

Legend for Top

Identifier	Treatment	Description
A, B	local	integer

Legend for gcd

Identifier	Treatment	Description
M, N COPY	val par local	integer integer

Figure 2-23. **Least common multiple using a function.**

In Figure 2-22 the TOP flowchart reads values for A and B, and then calls on the procedure GCD using as arguments the variables A and B, and a third variable D, which is a place holder for the about-to-be-calculated greatest common divisor of A and B. Box 3 outputs the value of the least common multiple, that is, the value of A × B/D. The procedure GCD has three parameters. The first two, M and N, are value parameters while the third, G, must be a reference parameter in order for the storage box for the corresponding argument D to be made accessible to receive the assignment of the GCD in box 4,

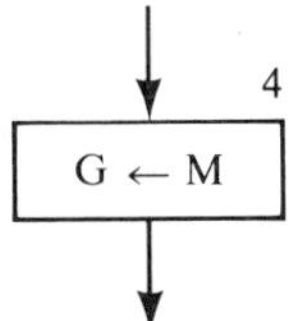

after it has been calculated in the loops of the procedure. The mechanisms so far are all familiar.

Now let us study the comparable action in Figure 2-23, using a function. Again values for A and B are read in box 1 but this time there is no procedure call box! The input box is followed directly by an output box containing the expression A × B/gcd (A, B). When the MC seeks to evaluate this expression, he calculates A × B and saves this product in his stack, since he cannot carry out the division until he has a value for gcd (A, B). Encountering gcd (A, B) in the evaluation of the expression *activates* the gcd function procedure, which has the value parameters M and N specified in the legend. The MC moves to a new environment and carries out the flowchart steps of gcd, finally reaching box 4, but this RETURN box is different from the RETURN box 6 in Figure 2-22. This return box 4 says RETURN M, and so now the MC asks the Reader/Assigner for a copy of the value of M. He puts the copy on the top of his stack (there are now two values on the stack) and returns to the calling environment, "carrying" the stack with him.

Back in the environment of the top program, the MC pops the top value from his stack and uses it as the value for gcd (A, B) in the expression he is evaluating. Then he pops the next, and last, value from the stack, the value of $(A \times B)$, and divides this value by that of gcd (A, B). The quotient value is output as the least common multiple of A and B.

For example, suppose the input values of A and B are 15 and 10, respectively. Figures 2-24 and 2-25 show snapshots of the computation environments of Figures 2-22 and 2-23, just as the return step in each of the procedures is being executed. In the case of Figure 2-25 the MC already has pushed a copy of the value 5 onto his stack, on top of the value 150 for $A \times B$. When the MC returns to Top, these two values will be removed from the stack to compute $150/5 = 30$.

Note the contrasting situation for the return from GCD, as illustrated in Figure 2-24. Here the "result" 5 has already been assigned to the cell for D in TOP[1] at the time the MC executes the return from GCD. Moreover, the MC's stack is empty when the return is executed.

So far this computer interpretation of a function procedure is equivalent to the mathematical concept of a function. The situation changes, however, if the parameters in the function procedure are specified as reference, rather than

***Figure 2-24.* Snapshot of Figure 2-22 when the RETURN box 6 is about to be executed.**

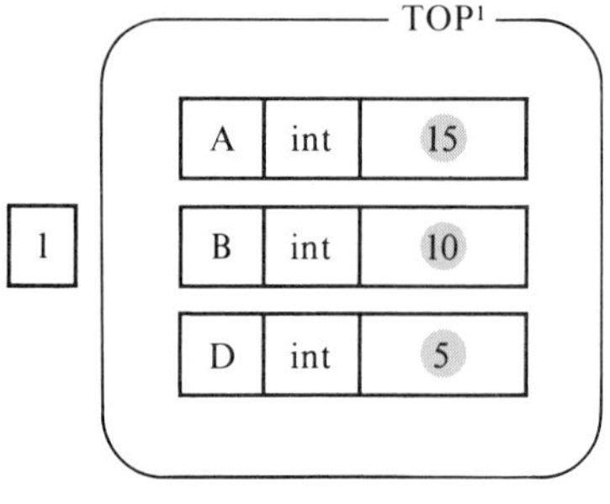

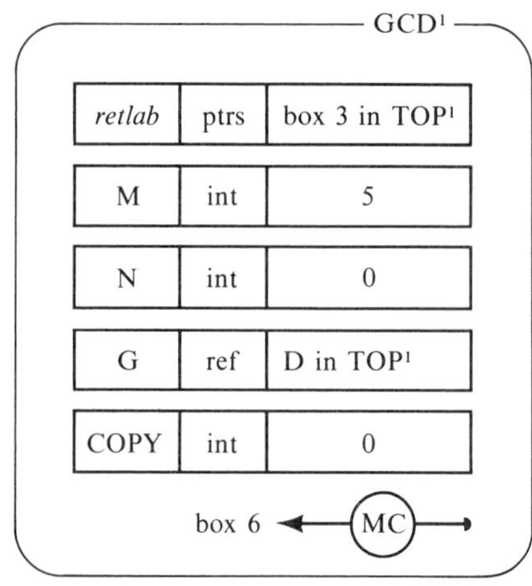

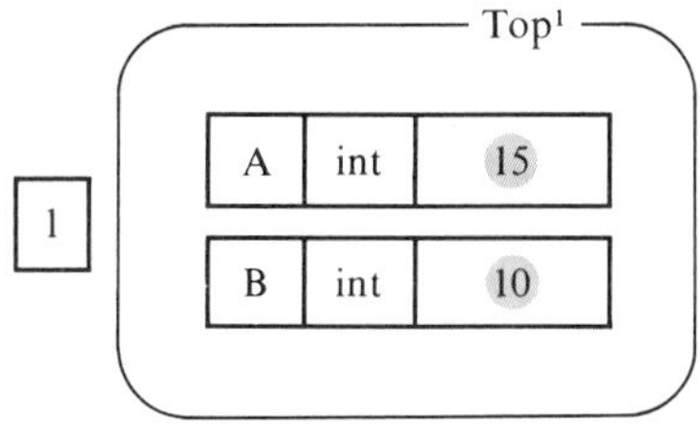

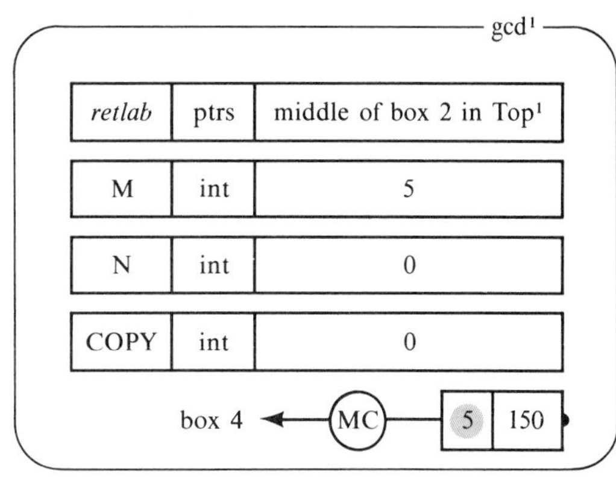

Figure 2-25. **Snapshot of Figure 2-23 when the RETURN box 4 is about to be executed.**

value. Suppose we replace the legend for gcd in Figure 2-23 by the revised legend

Legend for gcd

Identifier	Treatment	Description
M, N	ref par	integer
COPY	local	integer

Now when the gcd function procedure is executed, the actual storage boxes of variables A and B in Top will be made available to hold the values of M and N. Consequently after the "RETURN M" is executed, and control returns to box 2 of Top, the variables A and B will have values 5 and 0, respectively. The least common multiple of 10 and 5 will probably be correctly calculated, however, because in most systems in which left-to-right evaluation is used, the value of $A \times B$ will already have been computed as 150, and saved on the stack, *before* the detour to evaluate the gcd function occurred. The correct value, 30, would be output for the least common multiple.

However, if box 2 in Top were written as shown in Figure 2-26, which is mathematically equivalent to box 2 in Top, then the value of $A \times B$, under the same assumption of left-to-right evaluation, would be calculated *after* the function call rather than before. Thus, with M and N specified as reference

Figure 2-26

4

$$\frac{1}{\text{gcd (A, B)}} \times A \times B$$

parameters in gcd, Figure 2-26 would be evaluated as $\frac{1}{5} \times 5 \times 0$ and the output value would be 0 instead of the correct value, 30.

Compared with an ordinary procedure, a function procedure has the slight disadvantage that the computed value is not automatically placed in a storage cell in the environment of the calling program, and so it is not possible to reuse such a value later. However, a storage cell can always be explicitly created to hold the returned value. For instance, box 2 of Top in Figure 2-23 could be replaced by the steps shown in Figure 2-27.

Exercises 2-6

1 Draw a flowchart and legend for the function f(x, y), where

$$f(x, y) = \frac{(x^3 + y)^2 + 5}{|x| + 2}$$

2 (a) Prepare a function procedure flowchart with legend to evaluate the function

$$\text{RIGHT } (a, b, c) = \begin{cases} 1, & \text{if a, b, c, are lengths (in no particular order) of the sides of a right triangle} \\ 0, & \text{otherwise} \end{cases}$$

(b) Prepare a main flowchart with legend to print out all triples of integers (i, j, k) with $i \leq j < k \leq 100$ such that i, j, k are the sides of a right triangle. Use the function RIGHT developed in (a).

3 Construct a flowchart and legend for the function QUAD, defined as follows: given the values of x and y, the function QUAD (x, y) is to return the value 1, 2, 3, or 4, according to the quadrant of the plane in which the given point (x, y) lies. In cases where x and/or y equals zero, QUAD (x, y) = 0.

4 The Cheerful Finance Company loans money at 1½% per month compound interest. That is, each month 1½% of the balance due is added to the balance, if the borrower makes no payment.

(a) Prepare a flowchart and legend for the function BAL (L, n) that returns the balance due at the end of n months on a loan of L dollars, assuming no payment is made.

(b) Prepare a main flowchart using BAL (L, n) to find the number of months when the balance first exceeds twice the amount of the loan. Use $100 as the

Figure 2-27. **Alternate for box 2 of Top in Figure 2-23.**

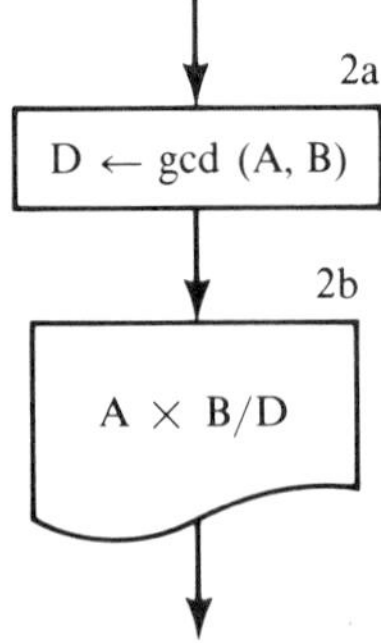

amount of the loan. Would the result be different for a loan of a different amount? Explain.

5 In general, we can convert into a function any procedure whose net effect is to modify one variable in the environment of the main flowchart. Here the procedure GCF from Exercise 4 of Section 2-4 is tentatively revised as a function in Figure 2-28. The value returned is the GCF of the components of the list A. The function GCD called in box 5 is taken from Figure 2-23.

The main flowchart on the left, which calls on the GCF function in box 3, attempts to divide the components of B by the GCF of the components of the original list B. However, this flowchart is very bad on two counts. First, it is highly inefficient, and second, it does not work.

For example, if the input value of B is (18, 24, 30) then the GCF of the components is 6, so that dividing through by 6, the expected output is (3, 4, 5). However, the actual output would be (3, 8, 30).

(a) Explain the above discrepancy.

(b) Make a small modification in the main flowchart to eliminate this discrepancy and greatly increase the efficiency of the program.

***Figure 2-28.* The GCF procedure revised as a function.**

Top

START
1 n, B
2 $i \leftarrow 1$ / $i \leftarrow i + 1$ / $i \leq n$ — F → 4 B → STOP; T →
3 $B_i \leftarrow B_i/GCF(n, B)$

GCF (k, A)

START
2 $M \leftarrow A_1$
3 $i \leftarrow 2$ / $i \leftarrow i + 1$ / $i \leq k$ — F → RETURN M; T →
4 $N \leftarrow A_i$
5 $M \leftarrow GCD(M, N)$

Legend for Top

Identifier	Treatment	Description
i, n	local	integer
B	local	list of n integers

Legend for GCF

Identifier	Treatment	Description
k	val par	integer
A	val par	list
i, M, N	local	integer

6 In Exercise 5 you used the function GCF given in Figure 2-28. Use this GCF to modify the output of Exercise 2b to eliminate similar triangles. Thus, for example, (6, 8, 10) will not be output since this triangle is similar to (3, 4, 5). In general, do not output any right triangle in which the sides have a GCF different from 1.

7 Refer back to the sorting flowcharts and legends given in Exercise 1, Section 1-5. Your job now is to modify the procedure Findkay so it is a value-returning procedure. Make it return the desired value of k, the position in the list A where out-of-order value TEMP should be inserted. Revise the flowchart for MOVE accordingly.

8 Construct a flowchart and legend for the function WHICH as follows: Given a list A of n real elements, WHICH returns a value 0, 1, or 2 according to the following rule. Let S1 be the sum of the elements in the first "half" of the list and let S2 be the sum of the elements in the last half of the list. Then

$$\text{WHICH (n, A)} = \begin{cases} 0 & \text{if} \quad S1 < S2 \\ 1 & \text{if} \quad S1 = S2 \\ 2 & \text{if} \quad S1 > S2 \end{cases}$$

If the value of n is *odd,* then consider the first half of A to be the first CHOP (N/2) elements. You may assume $N \geq 2$. Use no globals.

9 Construct a flowchart and legend for the function RMS (root mean square). Given two real values A and B,

$$\text{RMS (A, B)} = \sqrt{\frac{A^2 + B^2}{2}}$$

Use no globals and no locals.

10 Using no globals, construct a flowchart and legend for the function EXTREM. This function has three parameters, n, A, and CODE. Given a list A of n real elements, EXTREM returns values as follows:

$$\text{EXTREM (n, A, CODE)} = \begin{cases} \text{smallest value in the list A,} & \text{if} \quad \text{CODE} = 0 \\ \text{largest value in the list A,} & \text{if} \quad \text{CODE} = 1 \\ \text{value of CODE,} & \text{if} \quad \text{CODE} \neq 0 \text{ and CODE} \neq 1 \end{cases}$$

11 Construct a main flowchart and legend and select data sets that can be used to test the *correctness* of the function EXTREM that is defined in the preceding exercise. For each data set that you select explain what aspect of the "behavior" of EXTREM you expect to test. A function is considered to be *correct* if it does what it is supposed to do and never does what it is not supposed to do.

2-7
NAME PARAMETERS

Having studied function procedures, we are in an especially good position to understand another kind of parameter treatment that is of some interest, known as the *name parameter.* This treatment occurs in languages like Algol. (We show example uses of name parameters in Chapter 5.) A name parameter is used in preference to a reference or a value parameter when it is desired to postpone, for as long as possible, the evaluation of an argument expression, and/or to reevaluate the argument each time the parameter is encountered.

In value and reference parameter treatment, a matching argument expression is evaluated only once, and that is before execution of the called procedure begins. In name parameter treatment, the argument expression is evaluated on a when-needed basis *during* execution of the called procedure. The advantages of postponing evaluations will become clearer as we proceed. However, since the argument expression makes sense only in the environment of the caller, it is necessary, each time the argument expression is evaluated, to temporarily shift the context back to the environment of the caller. Of course, this back-and-forth shifting of context (i.e., moving the MC to and from environments) raises the cost of using a name parameter, but it may be necessary to pay that price where postponed evaluation of the argument is required in certain applications. We shall now be more specific.

Suppose an argument in the call of a procedure P is an expression such as A + B, but we do not want the MC to evaluate the expression before entering the called procedure. Instead, we want the MC to delay evaluating A + B until the value of its corresponding parameter is needed during execution in P.

Suppose the corresponding parameter is L. How often will the value of L be needed in P? Well, that of course depends on the flowchart structure of P, and so the answer is none, one, or many times. The value of L may never be needed during some invocations of P if the flow of control causes all references to the value of L to be bypassed. Postponing evaluation under such circumstances may actually induce a saving, if the cost of evaluating the argument expression is relatively large. But of more interest is the case where the value of L is needed many times, while P is being executed. Why would one ever wish to evaluate L each time it is needed? Suppose one or more of the components of the argument expression, for example A + B, were accessible to the MC while executing in P. For example, A might be globally accessible to P. Further, suppose that following each reference to L, the value of A is changed. Then the next time L is referenced, it is necessary to reevaluate A + B if the current meaning of A + B is to be matched to L. That is the main reason for considering name parameter treatment. (See Case Study 5 in Chapter 5 for a particular application of this feature.)

How may the delayed evaluation of an argument be achieved in terms of our model? One way is to place in the value portion of the parameter storage cell a *copy of* the argument expression, that is, a *formula,* rather than its value or a pointer to its value, as in the case of value or reference parameters, respectively. Subsequently the copied formula can be evaluated whenever the MC needs an actual value for the parameter. Naturally the formula remains unchanged in the value compartment of the contour cell, ready to be used again. (See Figure 2-29.)

An important fact is that in applying the formula, the evaluation must take place in the same context in which the formula was first supplied. Here are two reasons why this is so:

1. For the argument A + B, B might not be accessible in the environment of the called procedure. Worse yet,
2. There may be some local variable B in P that the caller of P does not even know about. If the formula were evaluated in the environment of P, then the wrong B would be used!

Now our understanding of the function procedure semantics will help us see how to apply the formula in the proper context. When the MC needs to evaluate L, he consults the value compartment of L where he finds a formula *and* the name of the calling environment ($caller^1$). He moves into the environment $caller^1$ and evaluates A + B, just as though *A + B were the body of a function procedure* and A and B were global identifiers whose values were specified as those of A and B in the caller environment. Upon completing the function evaluation, the MC returns to the environment P^1 with the value of A + B in the stack.

Let us work through another simple example here to complete the picture. Suppose the call in Figure 2-30 occurs in the top-level flowchart of some algorithm. Further assume that PROC is defined with name parameter X, and locals N and T as in Figure 2-31. We are interested in how box 22 of PROC is evaluated. The contour in Figure 2-32 shows the state of execution, when the MC has just encountered X^2 in the expression $16 + X^2$. Having put 16 in the stack, the MC's next task is to get the value of X so it can be squared.

Figure 2-29

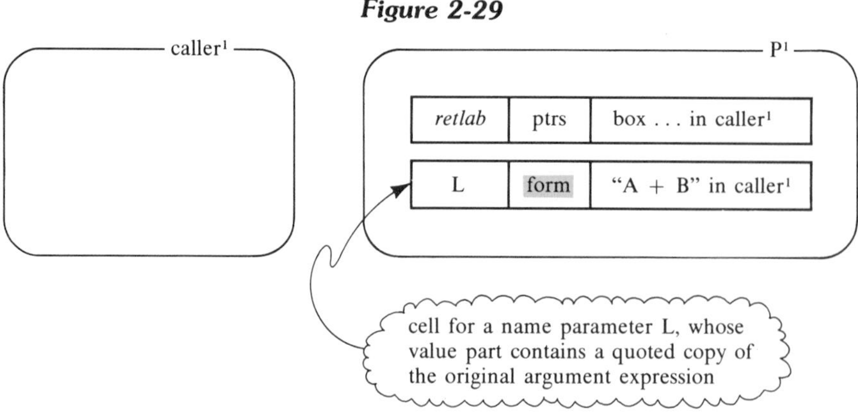

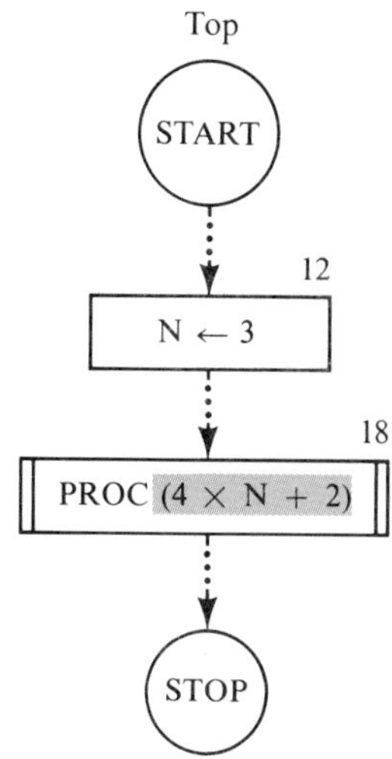

Legend for Top

Identifier	Treatment	Description
N	local	integer

Figure 2-30

The MC notes that X is the formula $4 \times N + 2$ to be evaluated as a function procedure in Top[1]. After moving over into the environment Top[1], the MC computes $4 \times N + 2$ as $4 \times \underline{3} + 2$ or 14 and places this value on top of its stack, which already holds the number 16. Upon return to the environment PROC[1] the MC completes the evaluation of $16 + X^2$ as $16 + \underline{14}^2$ or 212, and this value is assigned to T. Had the MC remained in PROC[1] where N had the value 25, while evaluating $4 \times N + 2$, a completely different value (10420) would have been assigned to T.

Figure 2-31

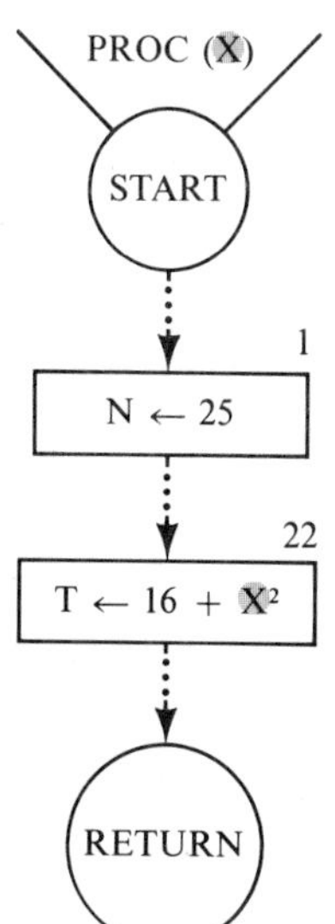

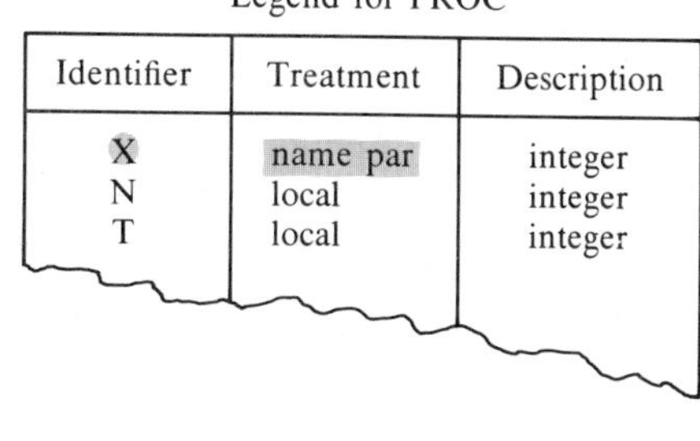

Legend for PROC

Identifier	Treatment	Description
X	name par	integer
N	local	integer
T	local	integer

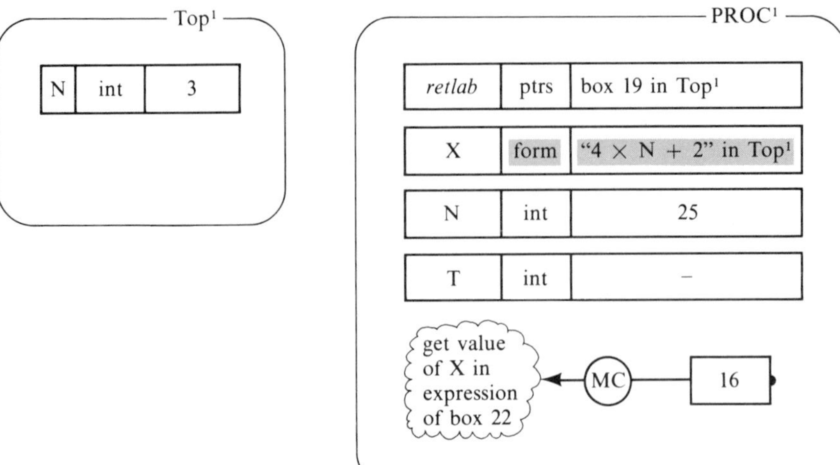

Figure 2-32

Name Parameters Matched to Simple Arguments

In the preceding illustrations, the name parameter appeared on the right-hand side of the assignment step, e.g.,

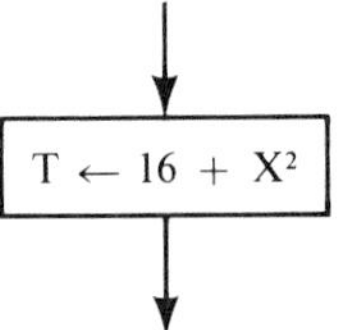

So long as a name parameter like X is matched to an expression argument, it makes sense for X to appear anywhere that an expression is appropriate, e.g.,

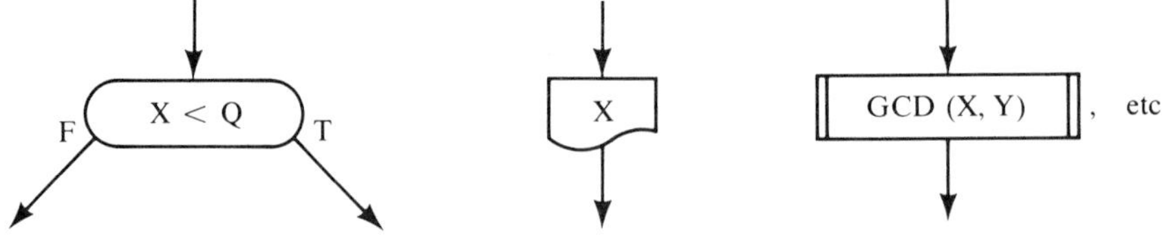

However, if X appears as in

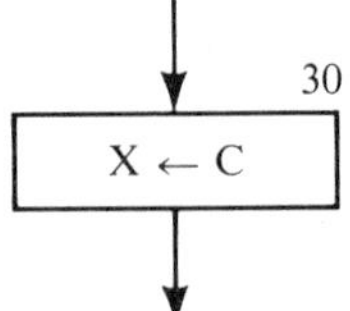

that is, on the left-hand side of an assignment statement, no sense can be made of this, because in this case X represents $4 \times N + 2$. Box 30 would have to be interpreted as assigning a value to an expression, which is nonsense.

Suppose, however, that the argument matching a name parameter X is a simple variable or array element, like R, P_{i+2}, or $A_{i,j}$. In that case statements within the body of the called procedure like either

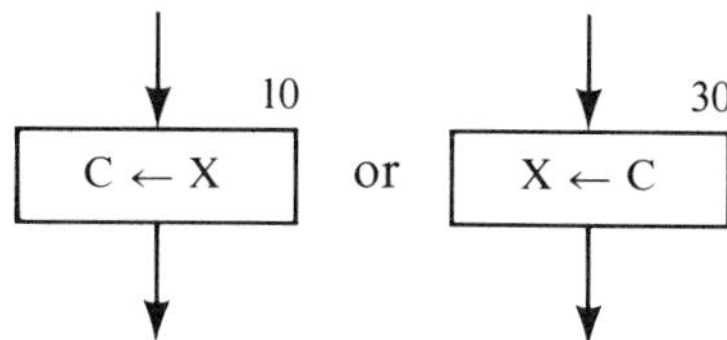

would make sense.

The meaning of box 10 is: assign to C the *value* of R, P_{i+2}, or $A_{i,j}$, as the case may be, while the meaning of box 30 would be: assign the value of C to R, P_{i+2}, or $A_{i,j}$, as the case may be. Is this interpretation consistent with the model we have constructed so far? It is, as can be seen from the following reasoning:

When encountering X in box 10, the MC knows he needs a *value.* So he applies the formula

"R" in caller^1, or "P_{i+2}" in caller^1, or "$A_{i,j}$" in caller^1,

as before, and when the function evaluation of X has been completed, he picks off the value from the stack and asks the Reader/Assigner to place this value in C. By contrast, when encountering X in box 30, the MC knows he needs a *designation for a cell.* The interpretation of X must result in such a designation. A formula in the cell for X such as

X	form	"R" in caller^1

immediately designates the cell R in the caller environment. However, a formula in the cell for X such as

X	form	"P_{i+2}" in caller^1

necessitates the additional work of first evaluating $i + 2$ in the caller environment, using the familiar function procedure mechanism. Suppose, for instance, the value 7 is returned for $i + 2$. Then the formula is interpreted as if it were "P_7" in caller^1.

The reader should, as an exercise, convince himself that a formula in the cell for X such as

X	form	"$A_{i,j}$" in caller^1

can also be interpreted to give the proper cell designation.

The astute reader will no doubt observe that, whenever a name parameter is matched to a simple variable argument or subscripted variable with constant subscripts, the net effect of sharing and transmitting information to and from caller and callee is *identical to that of the reference parameter.* The only significant semantic difference between name parameter and reference parameter treatment occurs when the argument, or a subscript of the argument, is an expression and when the value of that expression can change during execution of the called procedure. It is not surprising, therefore, that most programming languages are designed to offer either reference parameter or name parameter treatment, but not both. Thus Fortran offers reference parameter treatment, while Algol offers name parameter treatment. Finally, one should observe that, whenever a name parameter is matched to a constant argument, the parameter behaves in effect like a value parameter, provided of course that the name parameter does not appear on the left side of an assignment step. (This last observation is also true of a reference parameter matched to a constant argument.)

Exercises 2-7

1 This question refers to the legends and flowchart fragments in Figures 2-33 and 2-34.

Suppose that G has just been invoked in box 2 of Top. Draw a snapshot showing the environment for Top and G just before the first box of G is executed.

Figure 2-33

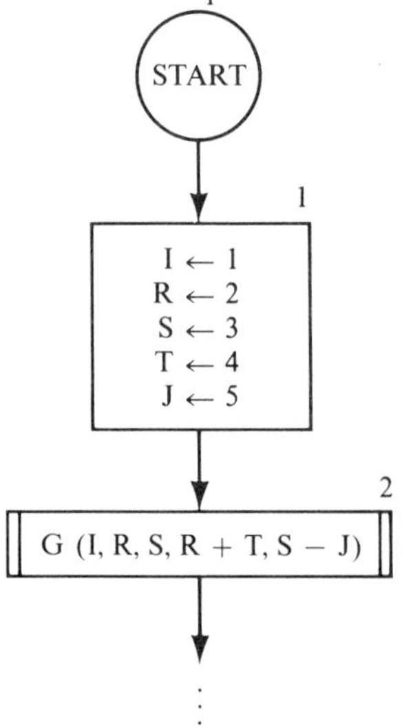

Legend for Top

Identifier	Treatment	Description
I	local	int
R	local	int
S	local	int
T	local	int
J	local	int

Legend for G

Identifier	Treatment	Description
J	val par	int
X	ref par	int
Y	name par	int
Z	ref par	int
W	name par	int

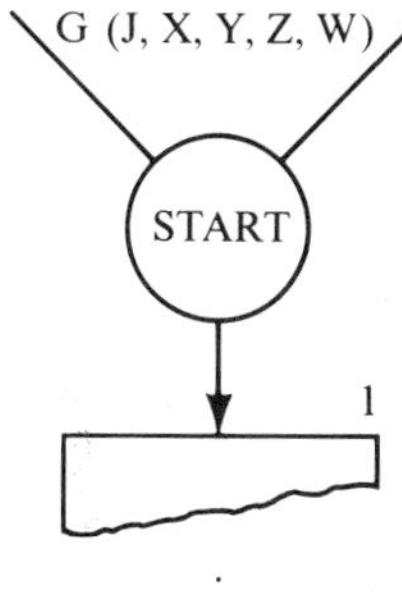

Figure 2-34

2-8 PARAMETERS THAT STAND FOR PROCEDURES OR FUNCTIONS

Sometimes it is convenient to design a procedure P so that, when invoked, P calls on still another procedure f. However at the time P is written, it may not be possible to know the definition of the procedure f that P calls upon.

For example, we could develop a procedure to find the area under the graph of a function f between two lines x = a and x = b, as illustrated in Figure 2-35. The *process* of finding the area is independent of the particular function f and is also independent of the particular interval (a, b). Therefore, we would like to program the computation in such a way that both the interval and the function are parameters of the procedure. Then the particular interval and the particular function could be supplied by the calling program as a list of arguments. It is not difficult to understand how parameters can stand for the endpoints of an interval, but how can we specify that a parameter stands for a function? Clearly a new treatment category for parameters is required in the declarative portion of a program. For example, when they are parameters, legend entries for regular procedures and for function procedures will be treated under the one listing "procedure parameter" or proc par. The distinction between the two will be made clear in the legend entry of the matching argument, in the description column.

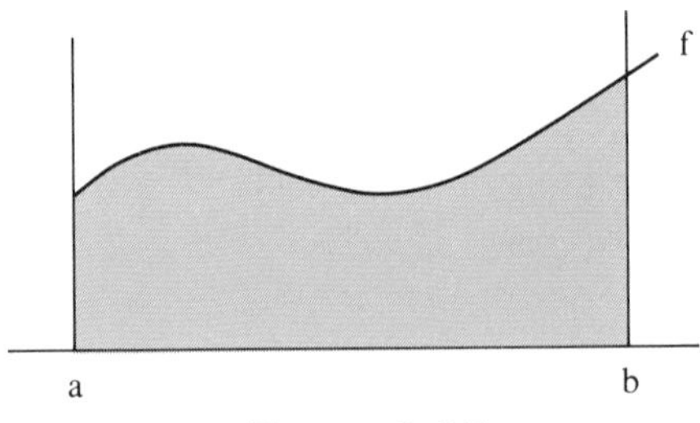

Figure 2-35

To illustrate this idea three schematic flowcharts are shown in Figure 2-36, a top level flowchart, an AREA subflowchart, and a subflowchart defining the particular function of the graph, in this case, the function F. Figure 2-37 shows the legends for Figure 2-36. Clearly there must be considerable interaction among the three flowcharts when they are executed.

When the procedure AREA is called in box 5 of Top, the argument F will be matched to the corresponding parameter func. When the value of func (a + k × h) is called for in box 10 of AREA, h and k will already have been assigned values in AREA and the value of F (L + k × h) will be calculated using the flowchart for the F function. How does the MC handle the mechanics of the function name parameter? To see that we must study further. Figure 2-38 shows a slightly incomplete snapshot just after the AREA procedure has been

***Figure 2-36.* Flowcharts to illustrate procedure parameters.**

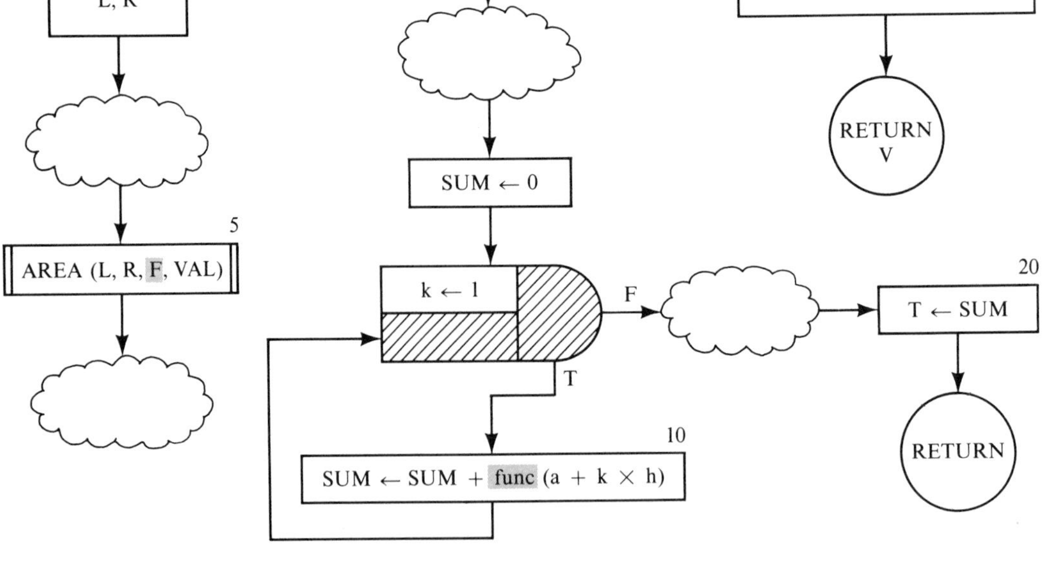

Top
START
1
L, R
5
AREA (L, R, F, VAL)

AREA (a, b, func, T)
START
SUM ← 0
k ← 1
F
T
10
SUM ← SUM + func (a + k × h)
20
T ← SUM
RETURN

F (X)
START
1
$V \leftarrow X^3 + 10X^2 - 3X + 8$
RETURN
V

Legend for Top

Identifier	Treatment	Description
L, R, VAL	local	real
F	proc	returns a real value

Legend for F

Identifier	Treatment	Description
X	val par	real
V	local	real

Legend for AREA

Identifier	Treatment	Description
a, b	val par	real
T	ref par	real
func	proc par	returns a real value
SUM, h	local	real
k	local	integer

***Figure 2-37.* Legends for Figure 2-36.**

entered for the first time, assuming 1 and 2 are the values that were read for L and R in box 1 of Top.

In the contour for Top in Figure 2-38 the variable VAL has no value yet and will not receive a value until box 20 in AREA is executed, because VAL matches the reference parameter T in AREA. But we are especially interested in completing the cell for F in the contour for Top:

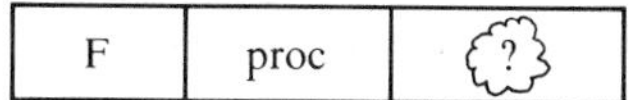

The second or type compartment conveys the information that we are dealing with some sort of procedure that we know from the legend for Top to be a

***Figure 2-38.* Contours for Figure 2-36 just after the AREA procedure has been entered.**

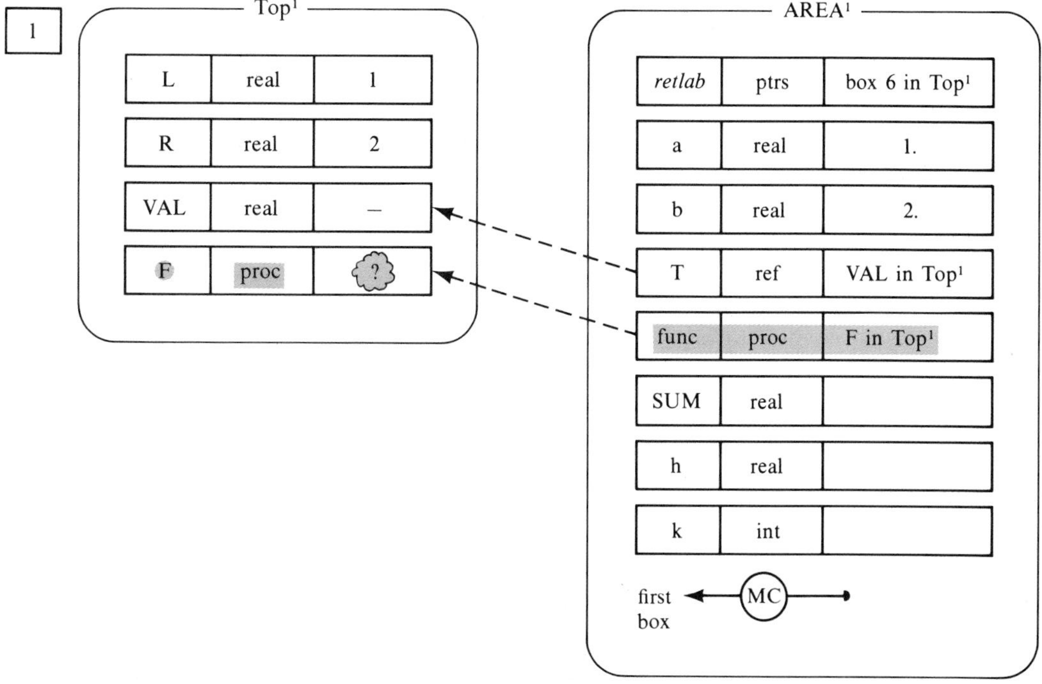

function procedure. What about the third or value compartment? It is supposed to contain a pointer to the flowchart for F. We represent this pointer by the notation "F in packet", since the flowchart for F must be part of the MC's given packet of flowcharts:

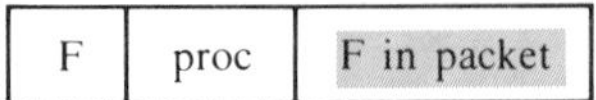

Now suppose the MC is executing box 10 in AREA for the first time and that k = 1 and h = .01.

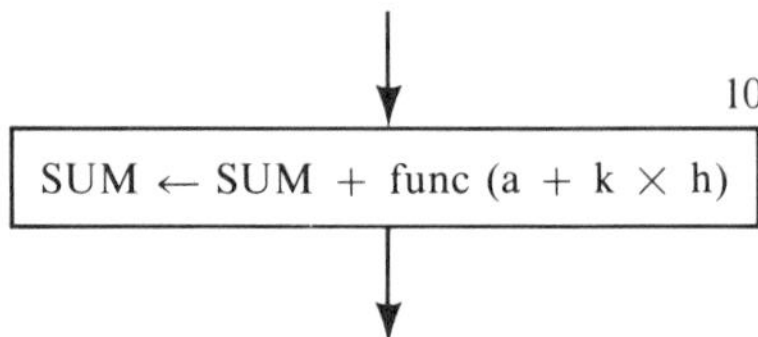

Following a request to the Reader/Assigner, the MC learns that the current value of SUM is 0. This value is put into the MC's stack. Next it needs the value of func (a + k × h). To this end, it evaluates the expression a + k × h in AREA[1], and gets 1.01. Now it needs func (1.01). The legend for AREA says that func is a procedure parameter. The MC has already ascertained that parameter func is matched to the argument F in Top. Consulting the cell F in Top[1], the MC confirms that F is a procedure. The value part of the cell informs the MC that the flowchart for this procedure is in the packet of flowcharts that make up the program. Now the MC knows where to find the F flowchart and prepares to "call" F. After locating the F flowchart in the packet and consulting its legend, the MC directs the Allocator to create an F[1] contour with the appropriate cells. One of these is a return label (*retlab*) cell showing that upon return from F the MC is to reenter the AREA[1] environment and continue with the execution of box 10 of AREA. After creation, the contour appears as:

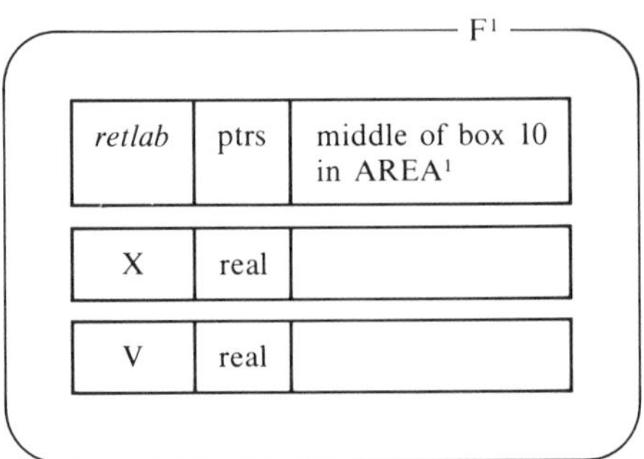

The legend for F shows no globals, one local real variable used for the return of the function value, and one value parameter X of type real. Now the MC has the argument value 1.01 copied into the cell for X and moves over into the F[1] contour to execute F (1.01). Figure 2-39 is a snapshot taken at this instant.

Upon completion of the F function calculation, with the value of the variable V 16.20 copied into the stack, the MC returns to the AREA[1] contour and

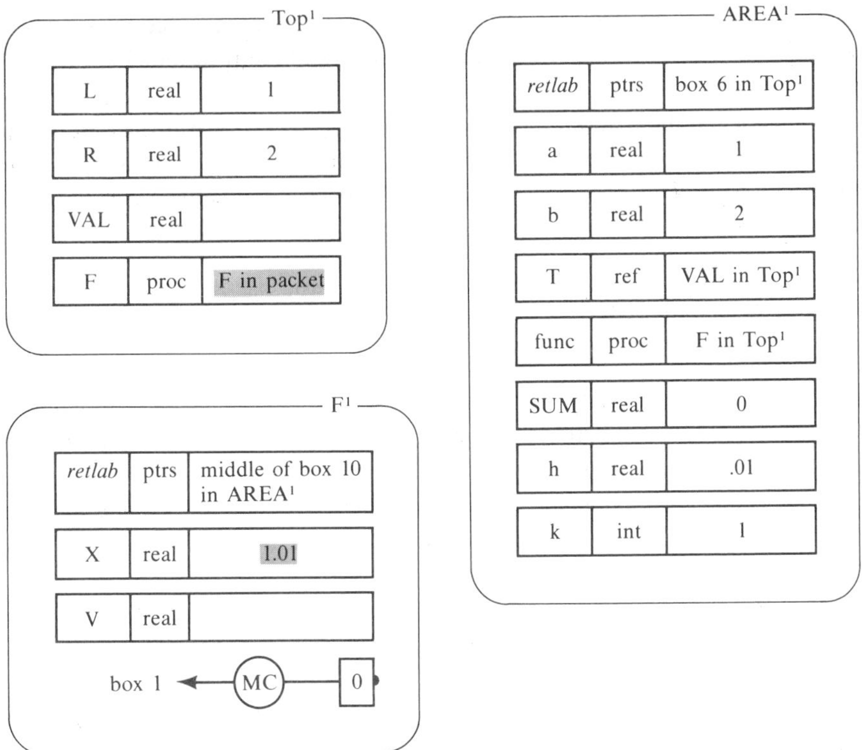

Figure 2-39. **Contours for Figure 2-25 just after the F function procedure has been entered for the first time.**

resumes execution at the proper point in box 10 of the AREA flowchart.

To draw further snapshots of Figure 2-38 would require that we detail the AREA procedure, which would be a digression at this time. However, the general handling of a function procedure parameter should be clear and one can make an analogous explanation to cover procedure parameters.

In studying Figure 2-37 the reader may have wondered why the procedure AREA did not appear in the legend for Top along with the function F. The purpose of a legend entry is to provide necessary information that cannot easily be inferred from the flowchart. Here AREA can be inferred to be a procedure by inspection of Top. AREA appears in a call box; its name is followed by a left parenthesis indicating the beginning of a parameter list. The MC can easily identify AREA as a procedure. However, in Figure 2-36 the function F appears in Top only as an argument of a procedure. It is not obvious that F is a function in Top and so we put that information in the legend. If AREA were a function, either the MC would have to be able to infer its identity easily from its appearance in a flowchart box, or it would have to appear in the legend for Top.

Many programmers argue that no documentation should be left to inference and all program information should be explicit and uniform. To follow that reasoning, every procedure (or function) would appear in the legend of every procedure (or function) in which it is called. ALGOL 68, for example, requires all procedures to be declared explicitly. However, to save space in this book, we shall include procedures or functions in legends only when that information cannot be inferred easily.

One last comment about the legends of Figure 2-37 concerns the description information for the procedure parameter func in AREA and its matching argument F in Top. We might want to replace "returns a real value" with the more explicit description "has a real parameter and returns a real value."

Chapter Summary

The legend and the flowchart together define the computation and its environment. Occasionally we may wish to leave unspecified in the legend those details that are not of interest or that may be inferred. Often such details can be specified in one of several ways, depending on the particular computation. Table 2-1 displays some typical legend entries and their corresponding contour cells. Each of these entries is discussed as a way of summarizing the important concepts of this chapter.

In Table 2-1, M is a *local identifier.* The particular kind of value it takes happens to be integer, but other types, such as real and character, could have been illustrated.

N is a *global identifier,* and so it is essential that the legend spell out the globality relationship by specifying the environment in which to find the cell named N that is to be used to store values of this global N.

TABLE 2-1

Legend Entries			Corresponding Contour Cells		
Identifier	**Treatment**	**Description**	**Name**	**Type**	**Possible Value**
M	local	integer	M	int	5
N	global	N in Top	N	global	N in Top[1]
P	ref par	real	P	ref	L in Job3[2]
Q	val par	real	Q	real	4.6
R	name par	integer	R	form	"A + 5" in Top[1]
S	proc par	returns a character value	S	proc	F in Top[1]
U	proc par	–	U	proc	V in Top[1]
G	proc	returns a real value	G	proc	G in packet
T	proc	–	T	proc	T in packet

If an identifier is a *parameter* of a procedure, it is essential to specify in the treatment column of the legend entry whether it is a *reference* parameter, a *value* parameter, a *name* parameter, or a *procedure name* parameter. Moreover, if the identifier is a function procedure parameter, such as entry S, which returns a value, then it may also be essential to specify, in the description column, the type of value returned, e.g., "returns a character value." It may be necessary also to specify the nature of the parameters of a procedure name parameter. Finally, if we list an identifier for a procedure that does not return a value, such as entry T, no entry in the description column is needed since there is no choice to be made.

Now let us look at the corresponding contour cells:

1. Since M is a local variable, its contour cell contains a type and a value, depending on the problem.
2. Since N is a global identifier, its type is "global" and its value identifies the environment containing the cell that holds the value of global N, i.e., "N in Top^1".
3. Since P's treatment is ref par, its type is abbreviated as "ref", and its value "L in $Job3^2$" identifies the particular cell in the particular environment that holds the value of argument L. If L is itself a reference parameter, then its cell holds a reference to still another cell, which may be the originating argument value. (If L is a global, its cell will also hold a reference to still another cell.)
4. Since Q is a value parameter of type real, its contour cell contains the type "real", and a value, for example, 4.6, of type real.
5. Since R is a name parameter its contour cell's type is "form" and its value is a *formula* together with an environment name that designates the contour in which the formula is to be evaluated, for example, "A + 5" in Top^1.
6. Since S and U are procedure parameters, corresponding contour cells have structures such that the type part is abbreviated as "proc", and the value part is the corresponding function or procedure argument, which is identified by its name and the environment in which the contour cell for that function or procedure may be found, for example, "F in Top^1" for S, and "V in Top^1" for U.
7. The contour cell for a procedure such as G or T is also given a contour cell type abbreviated as "proc", since the MC can locate the appropriate procedure by consulting the value part of the cell, which is a pointer to the appropriate flowchart. Thus, for the identifiers G and T, the flowcharts are designated by "G in packet" and "T in packet", respectively.

Exercises 2-8 Set A

1a Figure 2-40 is a set of flowcharts describing the generation and printing of a simple pattern of integers. Study the flowcharts and then fill out complete legends in a consistent manner. Do not change the flowcharts in any way. For each parameter,

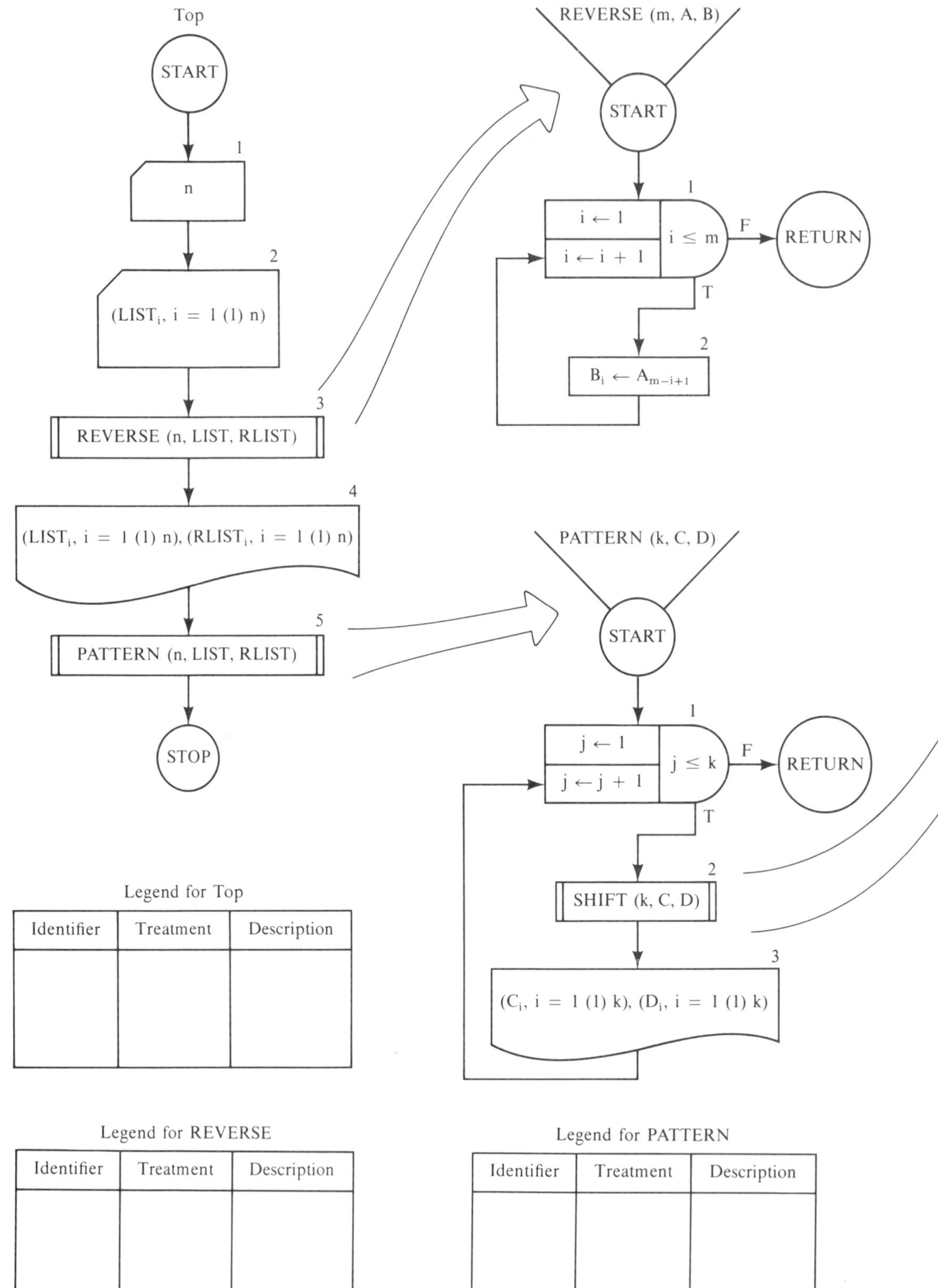

Top
START
1
n
2
(LIST$_i$, i = 1 (1) n)
3
REVERSE (n, LIST, RLIST)
4
(LIST$_i$, i = 1 (1) n), (RLIST$_i$, i = 1 (1) n)
5
PATTERN (n, LIST, RLIST)
STOP
REVERSE (m, A, B)
START
1
i ← 1
i ← i + 1
i ≤ m
F
RETURN
T
2
B$_i$ ← A$_{m-i+1}$
PATTERN (k, C, D)
START
1
j ← 1
j ← j + 1
j ≤ k
F
RETURN
T
2
SHIFT (k, C, D)
3
(C$_i$, i = 1 (1) k), (D$_i$, i = 1 (1) k)
Legend for Top
Identifier
Treatment
Description
Legend for REVERSE
Identifier
Treatment
Description
Legend for PATTERN
Identifier
Treatment
Description

Figure 2-40

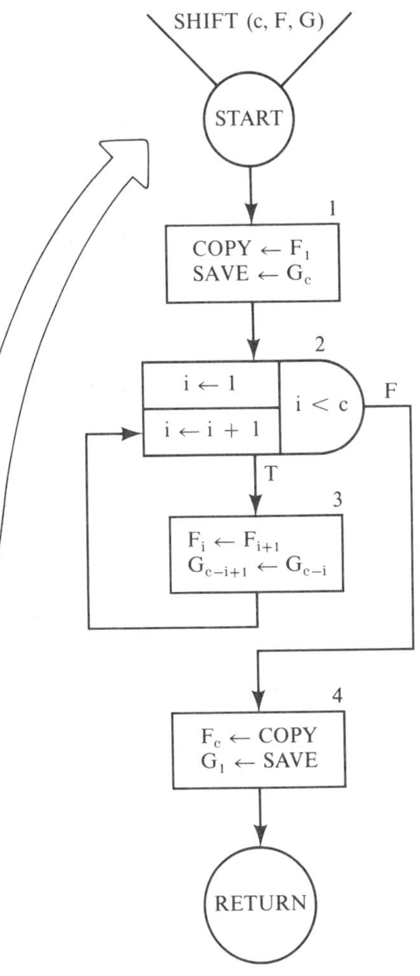

Legend for SHIFT

Identifier	Treatment	Description

specify the type. Choose value type parameters over reference type when there is a choice.

1b If the input data for box 1 in Top is 4, and the data for box 2 is the list (1, 2, 3, 4), show the complete output of the program.

1c For the data set given in part 1b, show a snapshot that depicts the state of the computation just before execution of the RETURN step in SHIFT.

Exercises 2-8 Set B

1 Trace the program given in the flowcharts and legends in Figure 2-41 for the data set

$$r = 7, \qquad A = (4, -5, 7, 9, -4, 8, 6)$$

and show that the printed results should be:

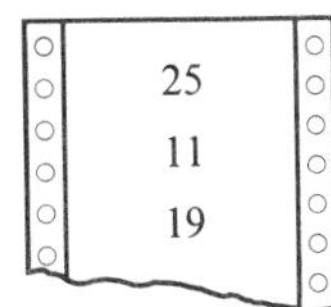

Top

START

1 r

2 $(A_j, j = 1 (1) r)$

3 SUM (F1, r)

4 SUM (F2, CHOP (r/2))

5 SUM (F3, r)

STOP

F1 (i)

START

RETURN i

F2 (i)

START

RETURN $2 \times i - 1$

F3 (i)

START

RETURN $\frac{i \times (i + 1)}{2}$

Legends for F1, F2, and F3

Identifier	Treatment	Description
i	value	integer

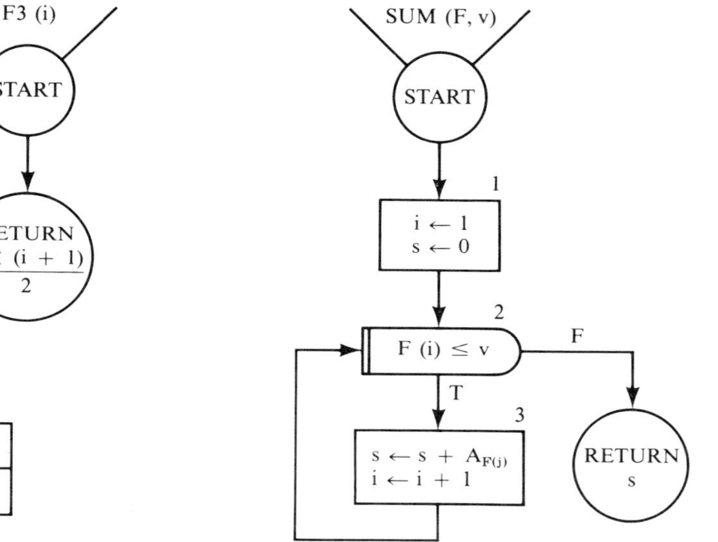

Legend for Top

Identifier	Treatment	Description
r, j	local	integer
SUM	proc	returns integer value
F1, F2, F3	proc	returns integer value
A	local	list of r reals

Legend for SUM

Identifier	Treatment	Description
v	val par	integer
F	proc par	returns integer value
s	local	real
i	local	integer
A	global	A in Top

Figure 2-41

2 In Figure 2-42 is a set of flowcharts and legends for a process that applies a function to a given list, and sums certain of the resulting values. Having done this twice, the algorithm prints the larger sum followed by the smaller one.

(a) Complete a snapshot showing the state of the computation just after box 2.5 has been executed in the first invocation of ADDIF. Show all cells and their contents in all contours on the way to the specified contour. Indicate which contours if any are inaccessible to the MC in this snapshot. If more contours are required, add them. Use the input data n = 5 and C = (3, −4, −3, 0, 2).

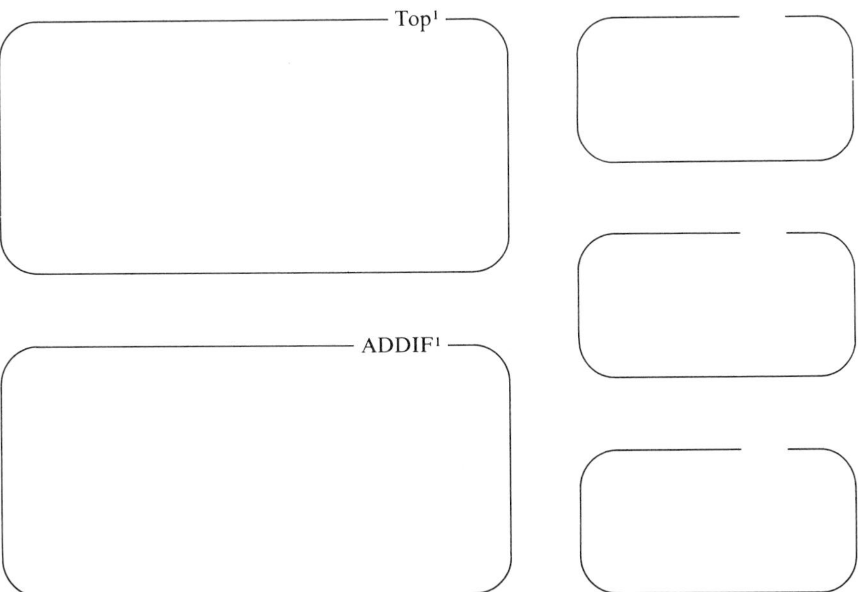

(b) With the above data indicate which output box is used by the program (box 6 or box 7)? What values are output?

(c) What effect, if any, would it have on the program if X in ADDIF were changed from a reference to a value parameter?

3 This question refers to the set of flowcharts and legends in Figure 2-43.

(a) Draw a snapshot showing the state of the computation just *after* box 1 of Top has been executed. Assume the input values are 0.0, 6.0, and 2.0.

(b) Draw a snapshot showing the state of the computation just *after* box 2.5 (in FINDZERO) has been executed for the first time [same input as in (a)].

(c) What is printed in box 3 of Top for the input given in (a)?

(d) What would be the effect of changing Avg in FINDZERO from a reference parameter to a *name* parameter? Explain.

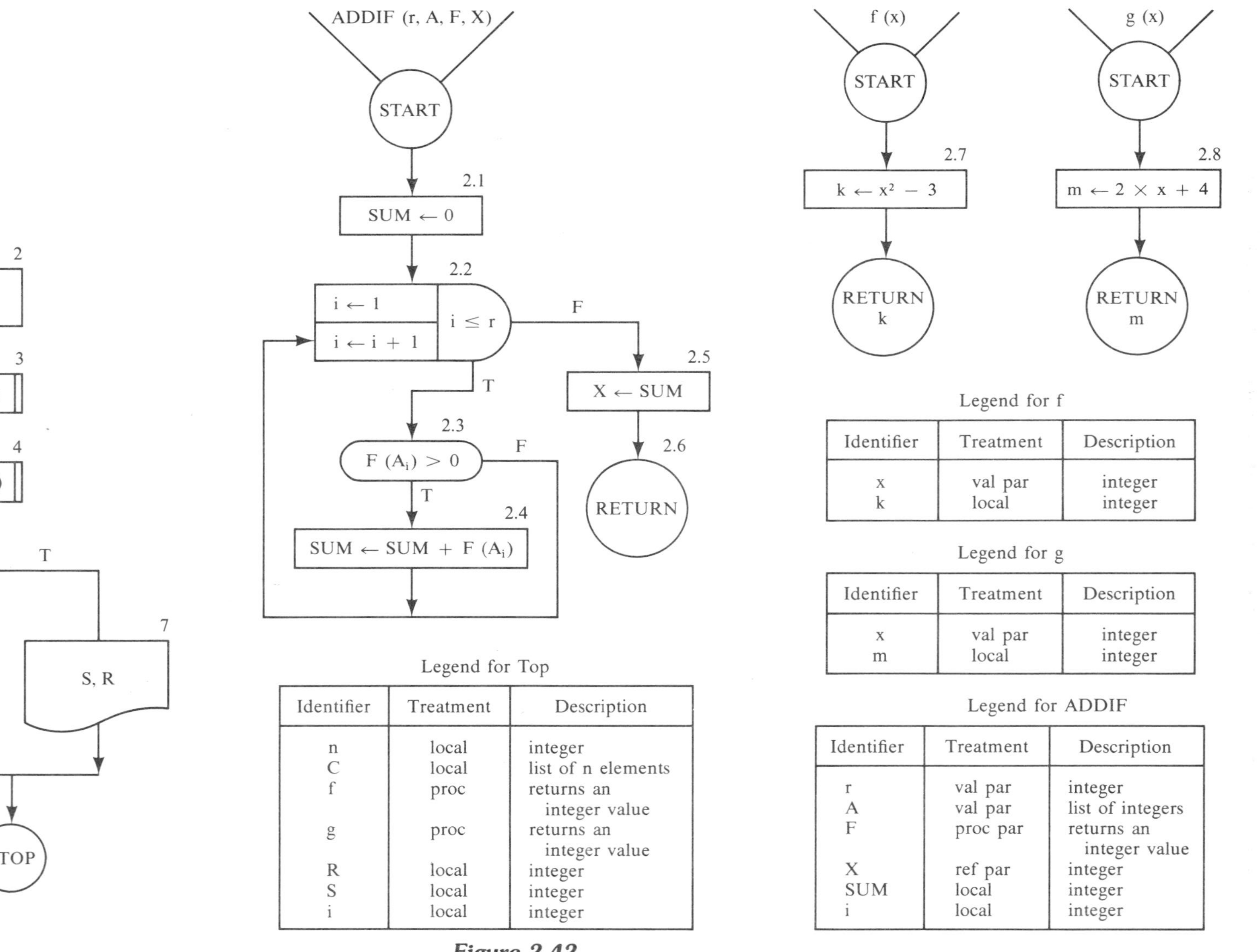

Legend for Top

Identifier	Treatment	Description
n	local	integer
C	local	list of n elements
f	proc	returns an integer value
g	proc	returns an integer value
R	local	integer
S	local	integer
i	local	integer

Legend for f

Identifier	Treatment	Description
x	val par	integer
k	local	integer

Legend for g

Identifier	Treatment	Description
x	val par	integer
m	local	integer

Legend for ADDIF

Identifier	Treatment	Description
r	val par	integer
A	val par	list of integers
F	proc par	returns an integer value
X	ref par	integer
SUM	local	integer
i	local	integer

Figure 2-42

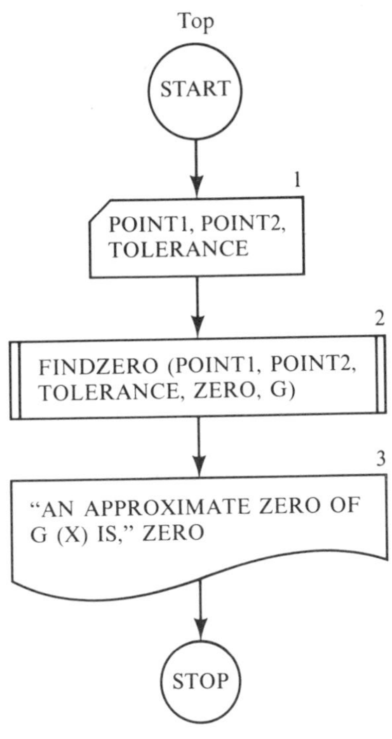

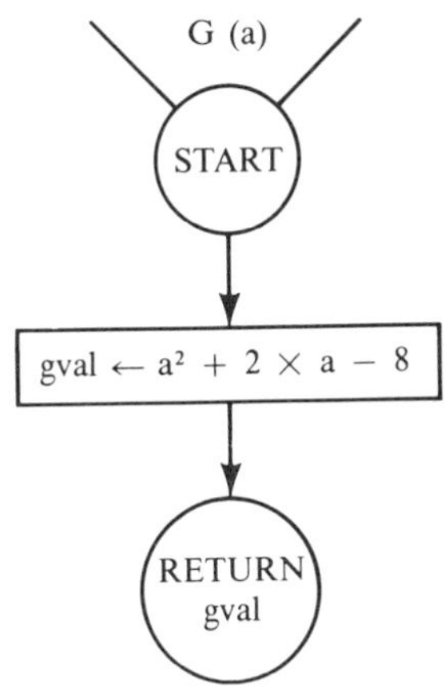

Legend for Top

Identifier	Treatment	Description
POINT1	local	real
POINT2	local	real
TOLERANCE	local	real
ZERO	local	real
G	proc	returns a real value

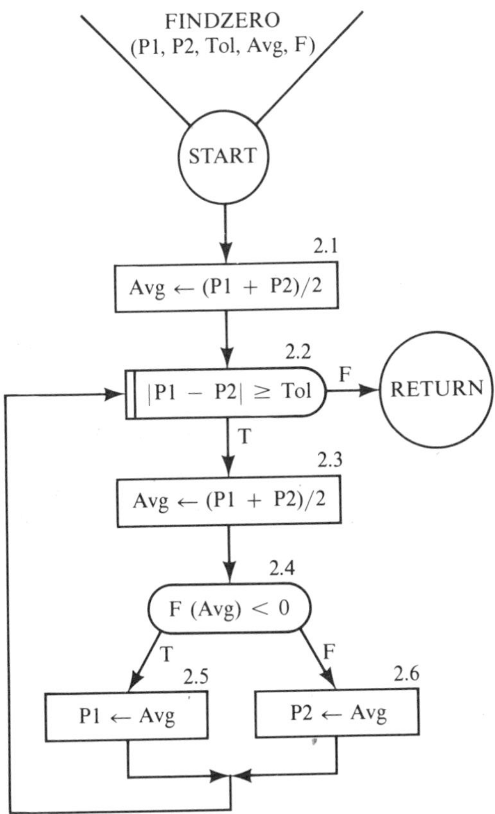

Legend for G

Identifier	Treatment	Description
a	val par	real
gval	local	real

Legend for FINDZERO

Identifier	Treatment	Description
P1, P2, Tol	val par	real
Avg	ref par	integer
F	proc par	returns a real value

FINDZERO is given two points that "bracket" a zero of a function, such that F(P1) is negative and F(P2) is positive. FINDZERO finds, within a given tolerance, an approximate zero of the function, using the well known "method of bisection."

Figure 2-43

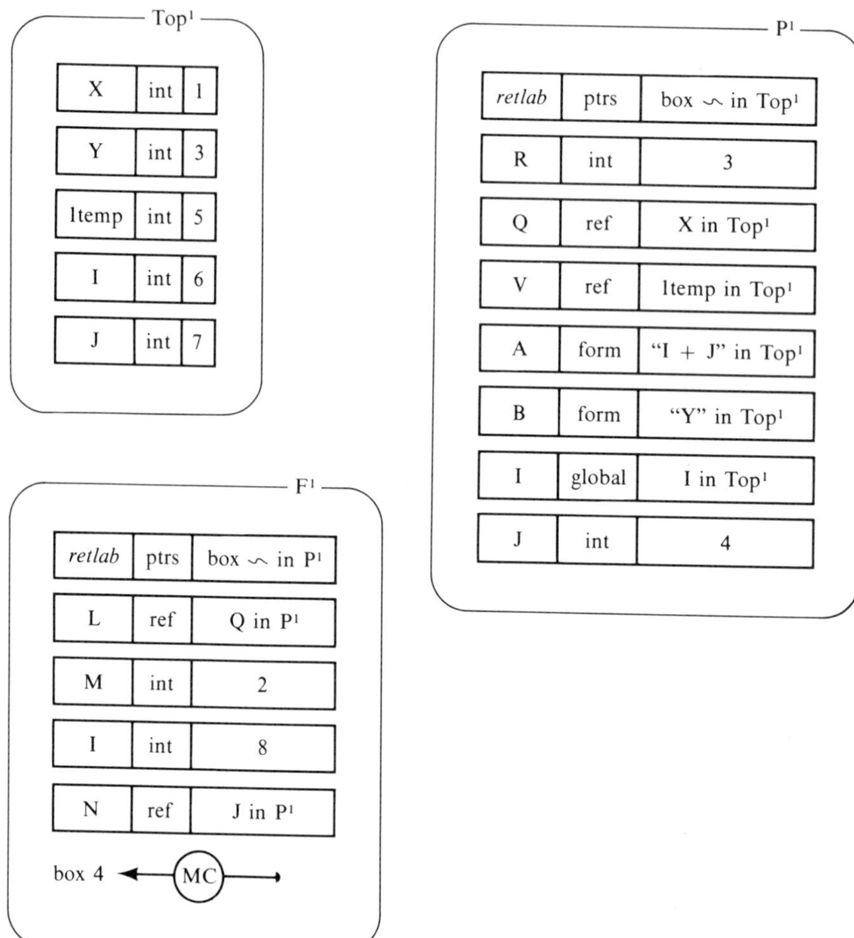

Figure 2-44

4 Answer in sequence parts (a)–(f) below by referring to the above snapshot in Figure 2-44 (flowcharts are not shown and are not needed). The questions below consider various assignment statements executed in procedures F and P. As you figure out what each statement does, update the snapshot so that it always reflects the current values of the variables (since an "updated" variable might appear again).

(a) Given that all three contours shown in the figure exist at the same time and that the MC is executing in F¹, was F called from Top or from P? How do you know?

(b) Suppose that box 4 in F is

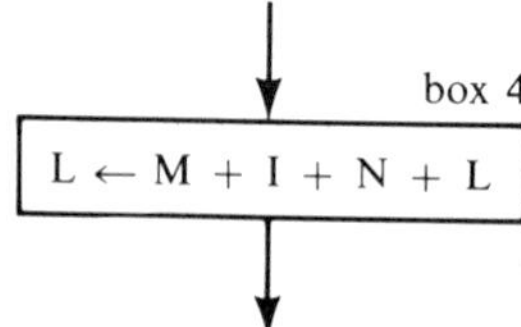

For each variable on the right of the assignment arrow, state the value used in the computation.

(c) With box 4 as in part (b), to what cell is the assignment made? (State here which cell, and indicate the change on the snapshot.)

(d) Suppose the MC moves out of the F^1 environment and into the P^1 environment. Inside P^1, suppose he executes the box

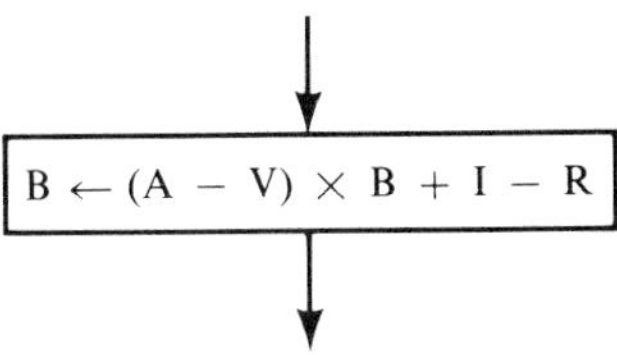

State what value is used in the computation for each of the variables on the right of the assignment arrow.

(e) For the box shown in (d), in what cell is the value stored? (State here which cell, and update the snapshot.)

(f) Suppose the following two boxes are executed, again in the environment for P^1:

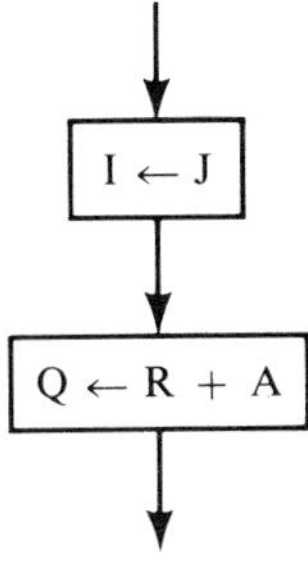

For each box, state what value is assigned to what cell in what environment. (Also, update the snapshot after each box.)

2-9 REFERENCES AND SUGGESTIONS FOR FURTHER READING

This chapter's approach to procedures and parameter treatment is based on Chapter 9 of Forsythe *et al.* (1975a). (In fact, many of the exercises have been borrowed by permission.) Although other elementary texts treat this subject, for example, Gear (1973), Rice and Rice (1969), and Hull and Day (1970), they do not stress the important idea of accessing environments. The exploitation of contour diagrams to achieve graphical display of accessing environments and to trace the execution of a program is relatively new. The contour diagram idea was suggested by J. B. Johnson in the late 1960s and was described fully in papers by Johnston (1971) and Berry (1971). These papers make useful advanced reading for a student who has completed Chapters 5 and 9 in this text.

3 RECURSION

3-1 INTRODUCTION

Like any problem solving activity, the design of computational algorithms requires a set of intellectual tools. General concepts such as stepwise decomposition and structured programming, and more specific ideas such as assignment and interation, enable the problem solver to progress from a problem statement to an algorithm that expresses the desired solution. This set of conceptual tools helps the problem solver understand the problem itself, and without such an understanding, the design of a solution algorithm is impossible.

This chapter explores one such tool—recursion. Like the other concepts mentioned above, the idea of recursion can enable you to see to the heart of many problems and to design algorithms that are straightforward, easy to understand, and correct.

The recursive approach to problem solving substitutes for the given problem another one of the same form, but in such a way that the new problem is *simpler* than the original. If by continuing this process we finally arrive at a problem so simple it can be solved directly (a "primitive" problem), then we have succeeded in solving the original problem.

As an illustration, let us apply this approach in an "everyday" situation. Suppose we wish to formulate a list of instructions to explain how to climb to the top of a stairway. Such a procedure is very easy to describe. Of the many possible algorithms, we propose the following and state it both as an English sentence and in an "English-like" fashion:

English	English-like
To climb a stairway do the following:	*Procedure* Climb_stairs;
if you are already at the top, you are finished;	*if* steps_remaining = 0 *then* stop.
otherwise, take one step up, and then	Move_up_one_step.
follow the instructions for climbing a stairway.	Climb_stairs.

These definitions both have one notable feature: they use the idea of climbing stairs as part of the explanation of how to climb stairs. In the terminology of programming, we have a procedure that calls itself! At first glance, this seems like the kind of "circular" thinking that should be avoided. On closer inspection, however, we see that it is indeed an example of the recursive problem-solving technique described in general above. By taking one step up, we replace the original problem with one of the same form (we still need to climb the stairs), but the new problem is simpler than the original (there is one less step to climb). If we continue to execute this procedure, the problem to be solved ultimately becomes primitive: to climb a stairway when we are already at the top does not require us to do anything.

Consider another example: suppose we require a procedure to produce the "largest possible integer." Using the above approach we are tempted to write the following:

```
procedure make_largest;
    let largest_ever be the largest integer we know
    largest_ever ← largest_ever + 1
    make_largest
```

Something has gone wrong: this algorithm will never terminate! In fact, a crucial ingredient is missing. In the stair-climbing algorithm, step 1 forms an "escape hatch" that ends the recursion. Furthermore, the nature of the process guarantees that the escape hatch will be reached sometime, for every possible stairway. In the make_largest algorithm there is really no escape hatch to propose, and thus the make_largest recursion would be infinite.

These ideas can be illustrated graphically in terms of flowcharts. The second, unsuccessful example has a structure of the type shown in Figure 3-1. Since each call of this procedure P generates *another* call on P, we never reach the

Figure 3-1

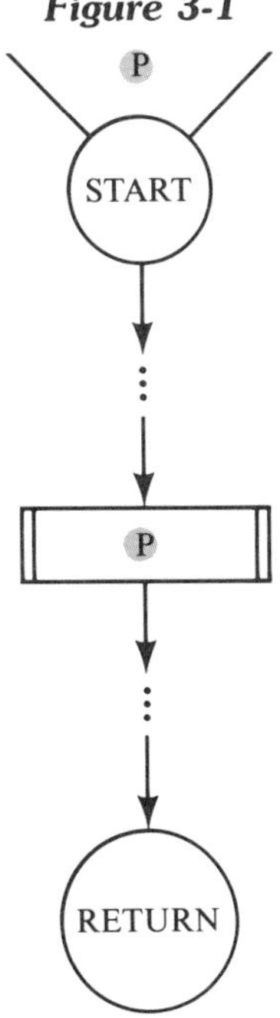

RETURN. The MC will require an infinite set of environments $P^1, P^2, P^3, \ldots,$ clearly impossible in a finite computer.

On the other hand, the first example has the type of flowchart shown in Figure 3-2. The existence of an escape hatch is a *structural requirement* for meaningful recursive algorithms.

We are now ready for some actual examples of recursively defined flowchart procedures and we start with the classic textbook example, the recursive calculation of n factorial, n!. The factorial is defined only for nonnegative integers. But first we review the usual interative way of calculating n factorial, as expressed by the following definition:

$$n! = \begin{cases} 1 & \text{if } n = 0 \\ 1 \times 2 \times 3 \times \cdots \times n & \text{if } n > 0 \end{cases}$$

Figure 3-3 presents a possible function procedure flowchart for the interative calculation. Observe that in IFACT the multiplication instruction in box 3 is repeated (iterated) over and over again until execution emerges from the F exit in box 2. What is important is that each multiplication is completed before the next one is begun. Each time IFACT is called, the proper value for the factorial of n is computed and returned. Only one new environment is created to do the job.

Figure 3-2

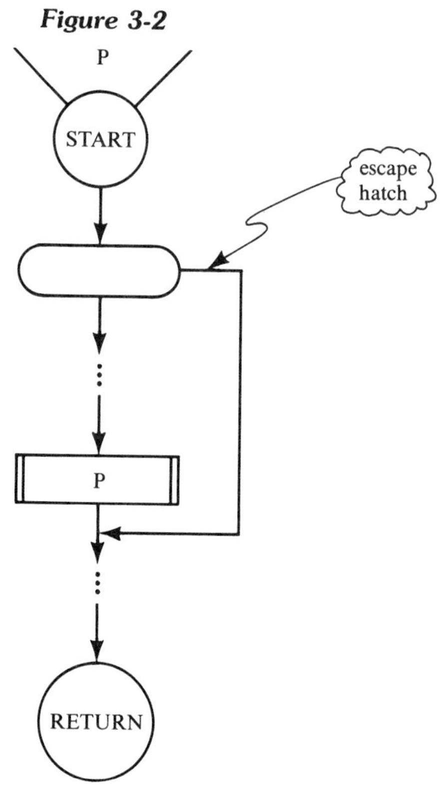

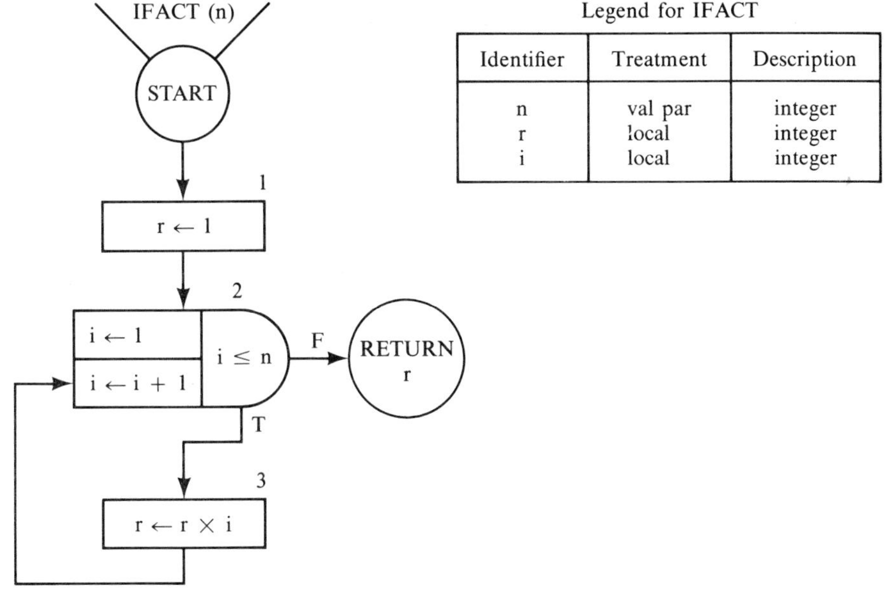

Legend for IFACT

Identifier	Treatment	Description
n	val par	integer
r	local	integer
i	local	integer

Figure 3-3. **Iterative calculation of n factorial.**

Now consider the recursive definition of n factorial:

$$n! = \begin{cases} 1 & \text{if } n = 0 \\ (n-1)! \times n & \text{if } n > 0 \end{cases}$$

Figure 3-4 shows this same definition as a flowchart for function procedure FACT to implement this definition.

Figure 3-4 **Recursive procedure for n factorial.**

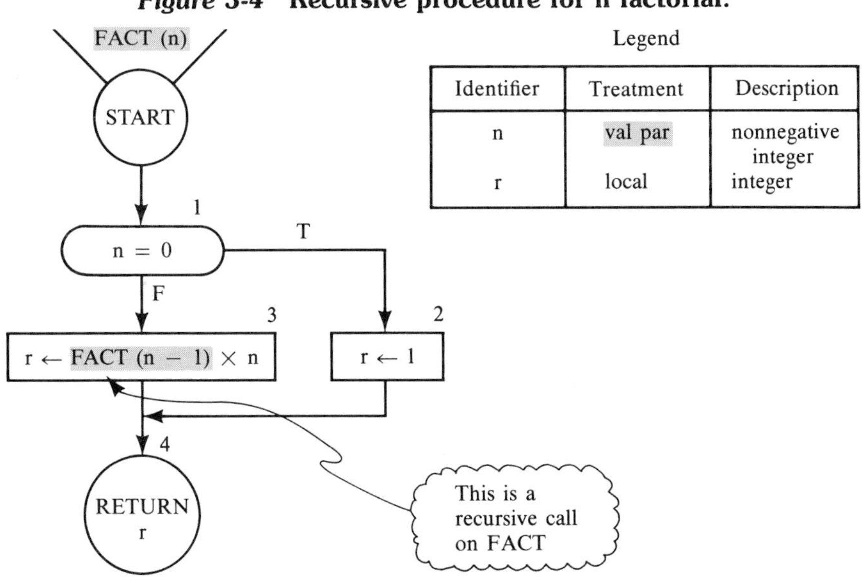

Legend

Identifier	Treatment	Description
n	val par	nonnegative integer
r	local	integer

The structure of this recursive definition meets the escape hatch requirement stated earlier. Box 3 contains a recursive call on FACT. Box 2 lies on the escape hatch path, since whenever box 2 is selected instead of box 3, the chain of calls on FACT terminates. Furthermore, since each call on FACT has a smaller argument than the last, we always reach a call for which n is zero, and the escape hatch is taken.

Let us trace this recursive function procedure, informally, for the case where the initial call has the argument 6. For example, the call might come from the top level flowchart shown in Figure 3-5.

When FACT is entered for the first time, the argument value for n is 6. In box 1, the condition $6 = 0$ is tested; it is false. According to the recursive definition

$$\text{FACT}(6) = \text{FACT}(5) \times 6$$

but the indicated multiplication cannot be carried out until the value of FACT (5) has been determined. Therefore, another call on FACT must be executed, this time with the argument 5. When the condition $5 = 0$ is tested; it is false again and so box 3 is executed:

$$\text{FACT}(5) = \text{FACT}(4) \times 5.$$

Now the whole recursive process can be written as in Figure 3-6. First each of the equations is written in the order shown, from top to bottom, stopping after the function argument is equal to 0. No product can be completely evalu-

Figure 3-5

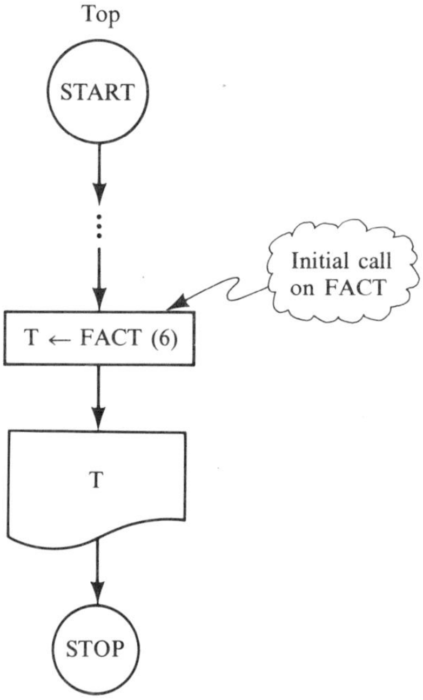

Top

START

Initial call on FACT

T ← FACT (6)

T

STOP

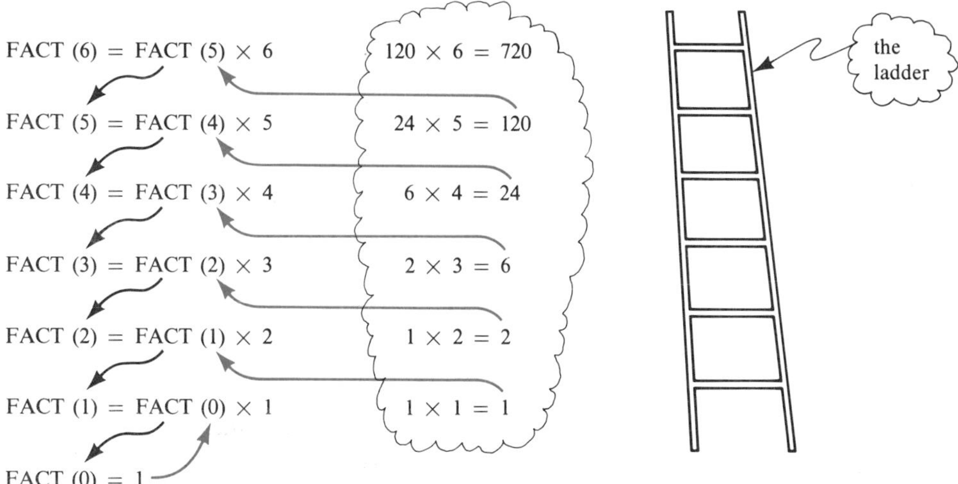

Figure 3-6. **Recursive calculation of FACT (6).**

ated until we reach the case where the function argument is zero. Then the escape hatch of the recursive definition is taken, and box 2 of FACT is executed, as shown in Figure 3-7. The evaluation of FACT (0) is complete when r = 1 is returned.

Now for the climb back up the ladder. First, 1 is substituted for FACT (0) in the next-to-last line, allowing the calculation of FACT (1) to be completed. This corresponds to executing box 3 (Figure 3-8) in the next-to-last call on FACT where n = 1. This in turn allows the calculation of FACT (2) to be completed, etc. The path back up the ladder is represented by the upward arrows in Figure 3-6. The path terminates with the calculation of FACT (6).

Obviously this example does little to illustrate the *need* for recursion since it can be handled just as easily by iteration. And unfortunately, most examples of recursion simple enough to be understood as a first illustration are also trivial in the sense that they can be solved as easily by other means. However, several significant examples of recursion will appear later in this chapter.

Figure 3-7

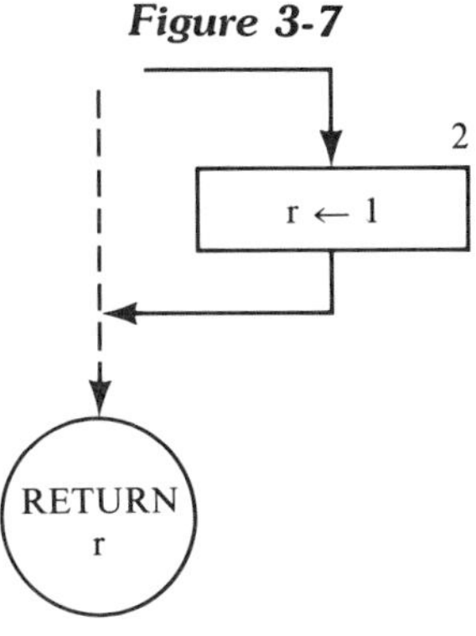

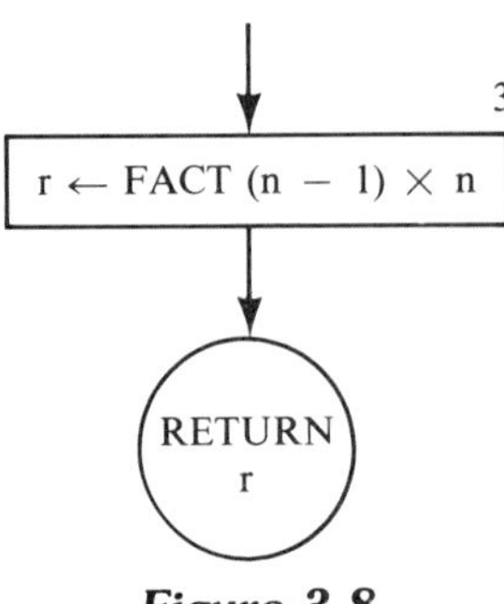

Figure 3-8

Although the flowchart for FACT has a deceptively simple structure, convincing oneself that its execution gives a correct result was not so easy. Let us trace the FACT algorithm again, this time using the snapshot method to gain a better understanding of why the FACT algorithm works correctly. This time let us use the argument 3 instead of 6 in the Top-level program of Figure 3-9.

Figure 3-10 is a snapshot taken when the MC is just about to execute box 10 in Top. There are no storage cells in the Top[1] environment.

Figure 3-11 is a snapshot taken when the MC has just entered FACT for the first time and is about to execute box 1. Since n is not 0 the MC will execute box 3, which results in a call on FACT with the argument n − 1. Since the n of FACT is a value parameter, the expression n − 1 will be evaluated as 3 − 1 or 2, and this value will be copied into a new cell named n in a second environment for FACT. We use superscripts to distinguish these environments. Figure 3-12 is a snapshot taken after the MC has entered FACT for the *second* time but before box 1 is executed. Once again the value of n is not zero, and so another call on (and another environment for) FACT is made in Figure 3-13.

Figure 3-9

Top

START

10

FACT (3)

STOP

Legend for Top

Identifier	Treatment	Description
—	—	—

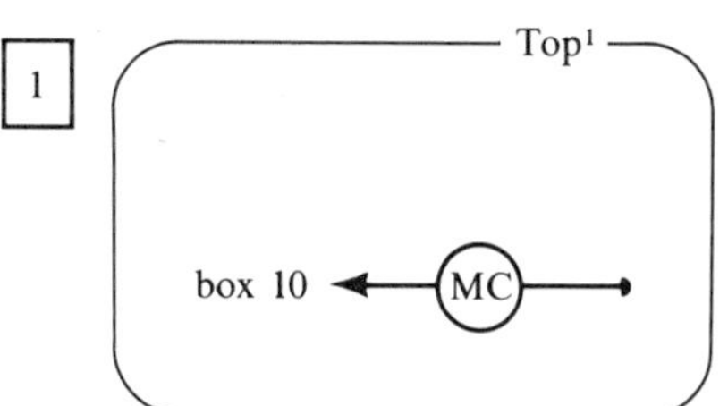

Figure 3-10

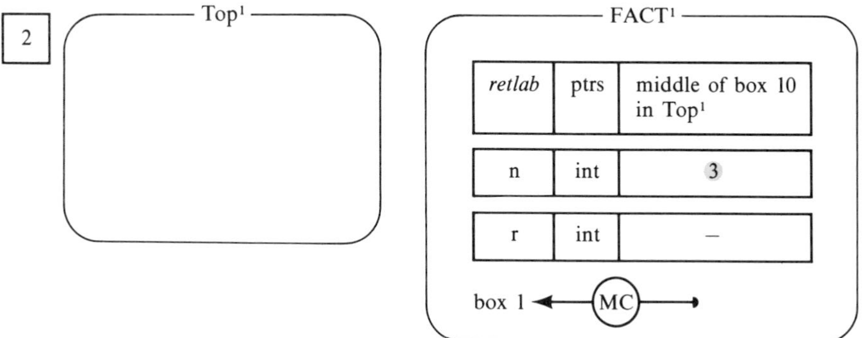

Figure 3-11

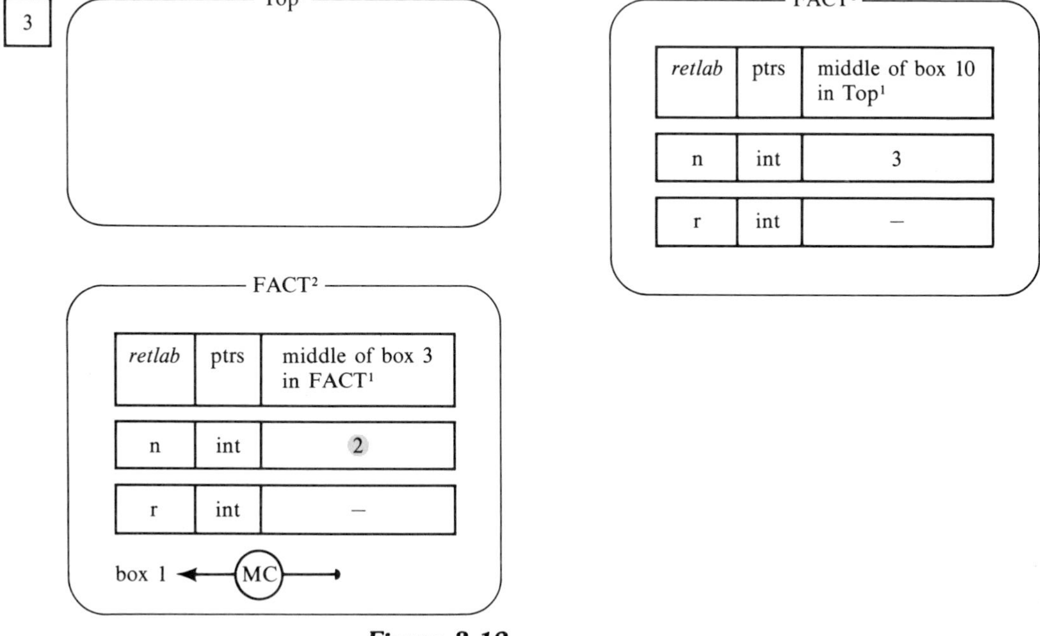

Figure 3-12

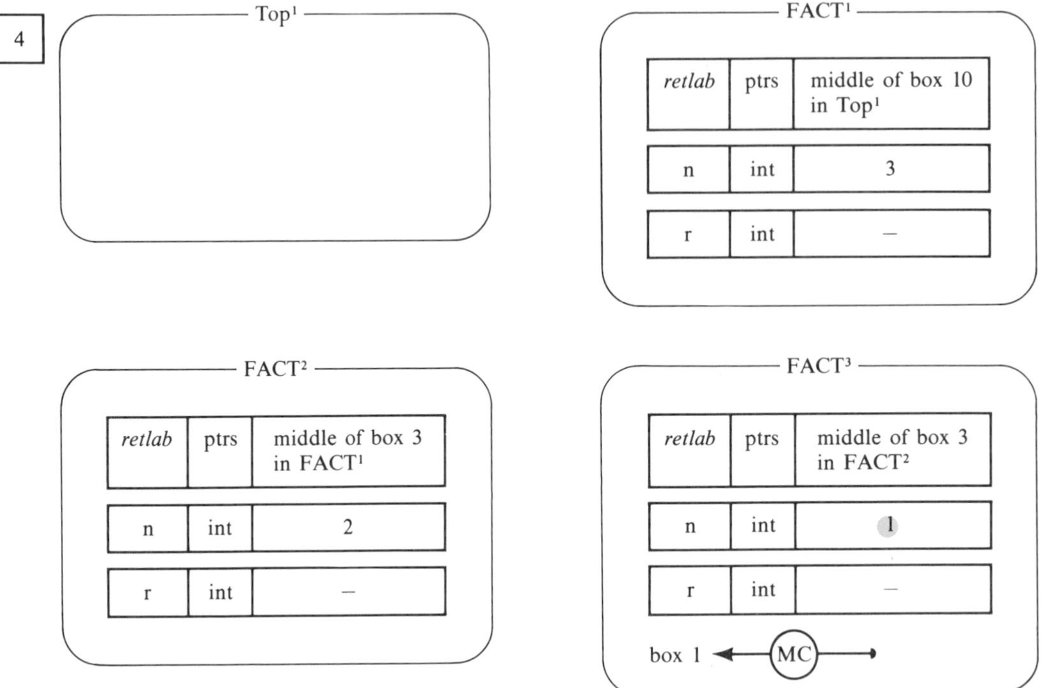

Figure 3-13

Again n is not zero, and so one more call on FACT is made as seen in snapshot 5 (Figure 3-14).

This time the value of n *is* zero, and so the true exit from box 1, the escape hatch, is taken to box 2. Snapshot 6 (Figure 3-15) shows the situation after box 2 has been executed and preparation for the return step has been carried out. Execution of box 2 has resulted in the value 1 being assigned to the cell r in $FACT^4$. In anticipation of the return to the calling procedure, the MC has made a copy of the value of r and placed it in his stack.

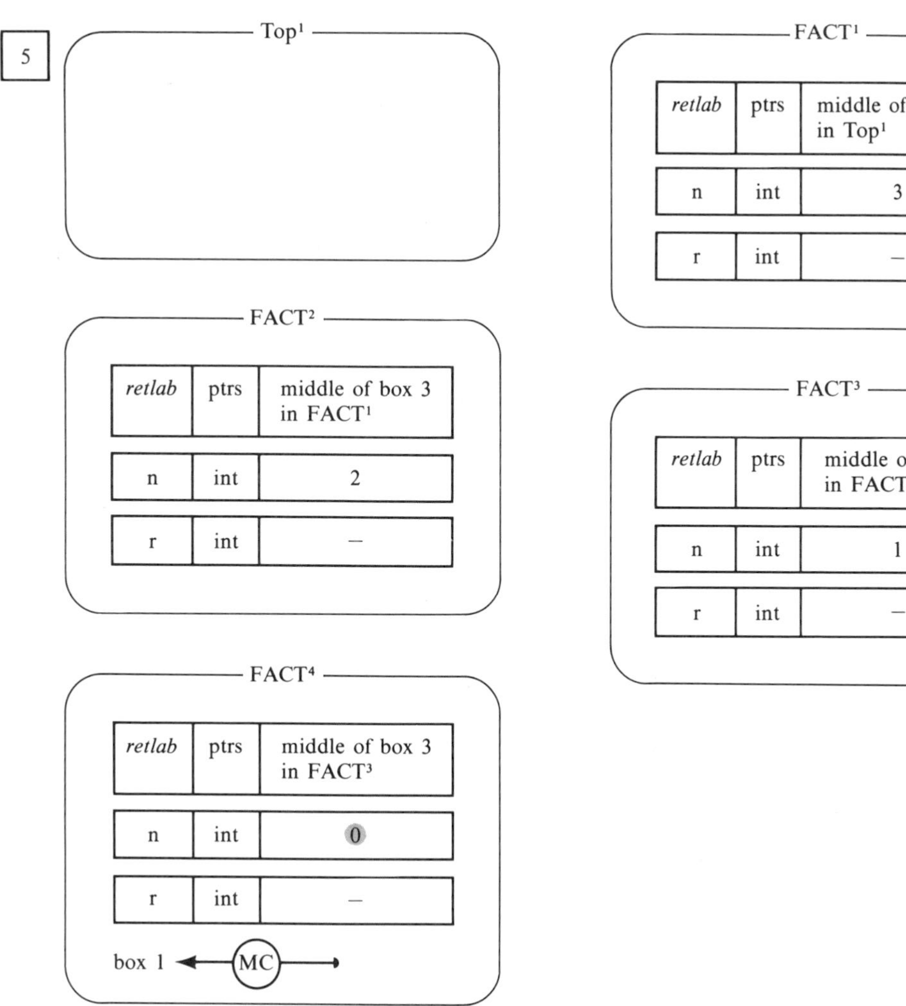
5
Top¹
FACT¹
retlab
ptrs
middle of box 10 in Top¹
n
int
3
r
int
–
FACT²
retlab
ptrs
middle of box 3 in FACT¹
n
int
2
r
int
–
FACT³
retlab
ptrs
middle of box 3 in FACT²
n
int
1
r
int
–
FACT⁴
retlab
ptrs
middle of box 3 in FACT³
n
int
0
r
int
–
box 1
MC

Figure 3-14

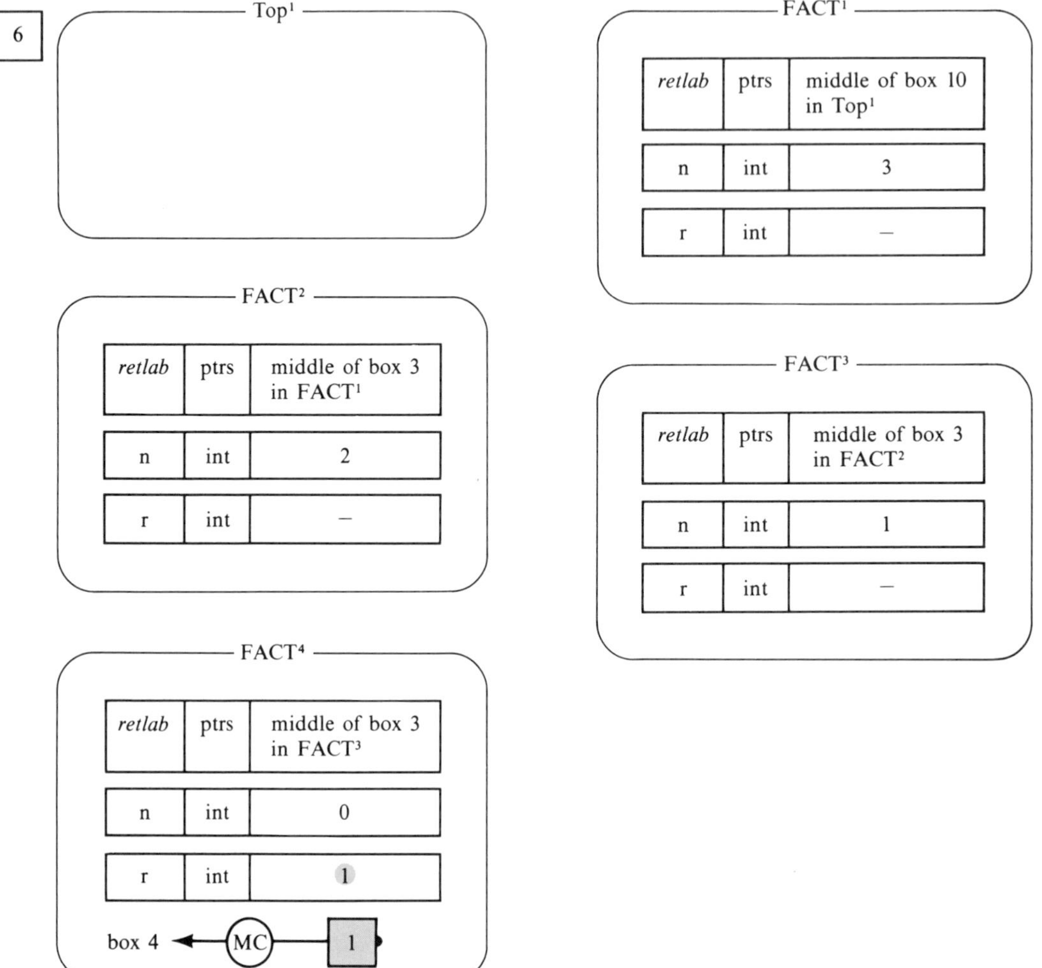

Figure 3-15

As we know, the return label (*retlab*) cell in each contour tells the MC what contour to go to next and what instruction or box to execute next after the RETURN in a procedure has been reached. From the *retlab* cell in the $FACT^4$ contour, the MC knows that the next step to be executed is the continuation of flowchart box 3 *using the $FACT^3$ environment,* because that is the environment of the calling procedure. Of course, the calling procedure is FACT, but what is important is that the MC resumes computing in the $FACT^3$ environment.

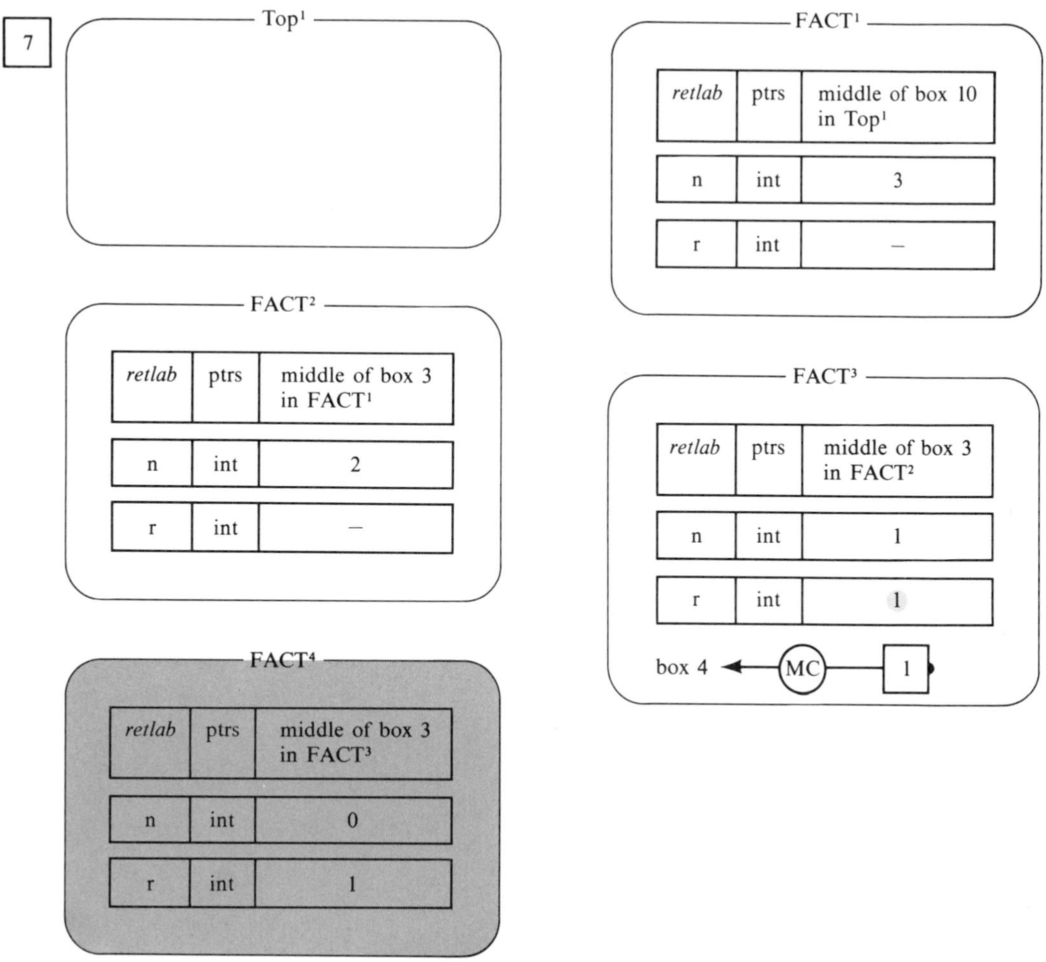

7

Top^1

FACT^1

retlab	ptrs	middle of box 10 in Top^1
n	int	3
r	int	–

FACT^2

retlab	ptrs	middle of box 3 in FACT^1
n	int	2
r	int	–

FACT^3

retlab	ptrs	middle of box 3 in FACT^2
n	int	1
r	int	1

box 4 ← MC — 1

FACT^4

retlab	ptrs	middle of box 3 in FACT^3
n	int	0
r	int	1

Figure 3-16

Snapshot 7 (Figure 3-16) shows the situation after the MC has returned to FACT^3, has completed the execution of box 3, and is preparing to execute the return step. In completing the execution of box 3, the MC has *removed* the value that was held in his stack:

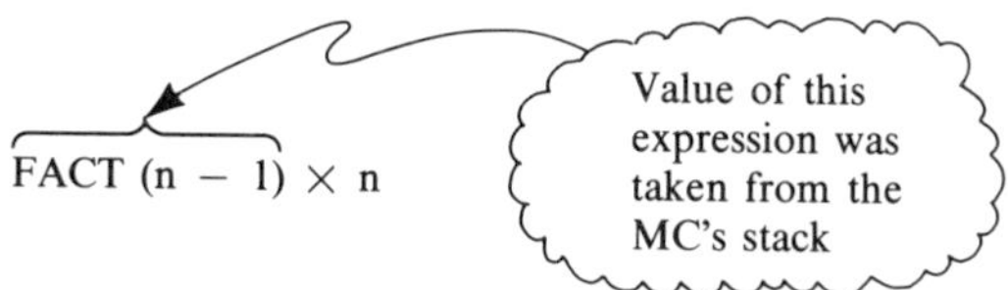

The expression evaluated to $1 \times 1 = 1$. After this value was assigned to r, a copy of that value was placed in the MC's empty stack. Note that the FACT^4

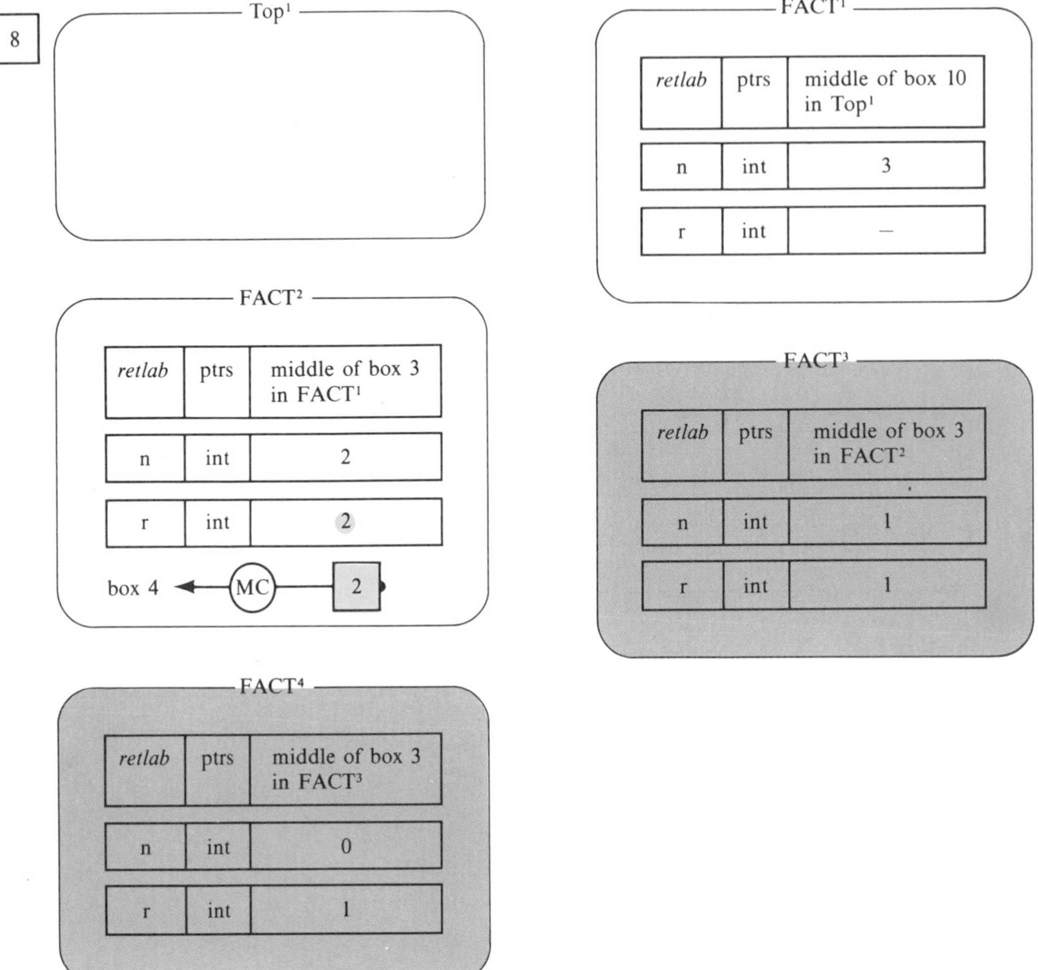

Figure 3-17

environment is shaded over to signify that this environment is no longer accessible to the MC.

The snapshot in Figure 3-17 shows the corresponding situation when the MC is prepared to return from $FACT^2$, and Figure 3-18 shows the similar situation for the return from $FACT^1$.

From the *retlab* cell in $FACT^1$ we see that when the MC returns from FACT while executing in $FACT^1$ the *destination* of his return is the continuation of box 10 in Top^1. The job to be done there is the display of the value of the expression FACT (3), but this is simply the value in the MC's stack. Figure

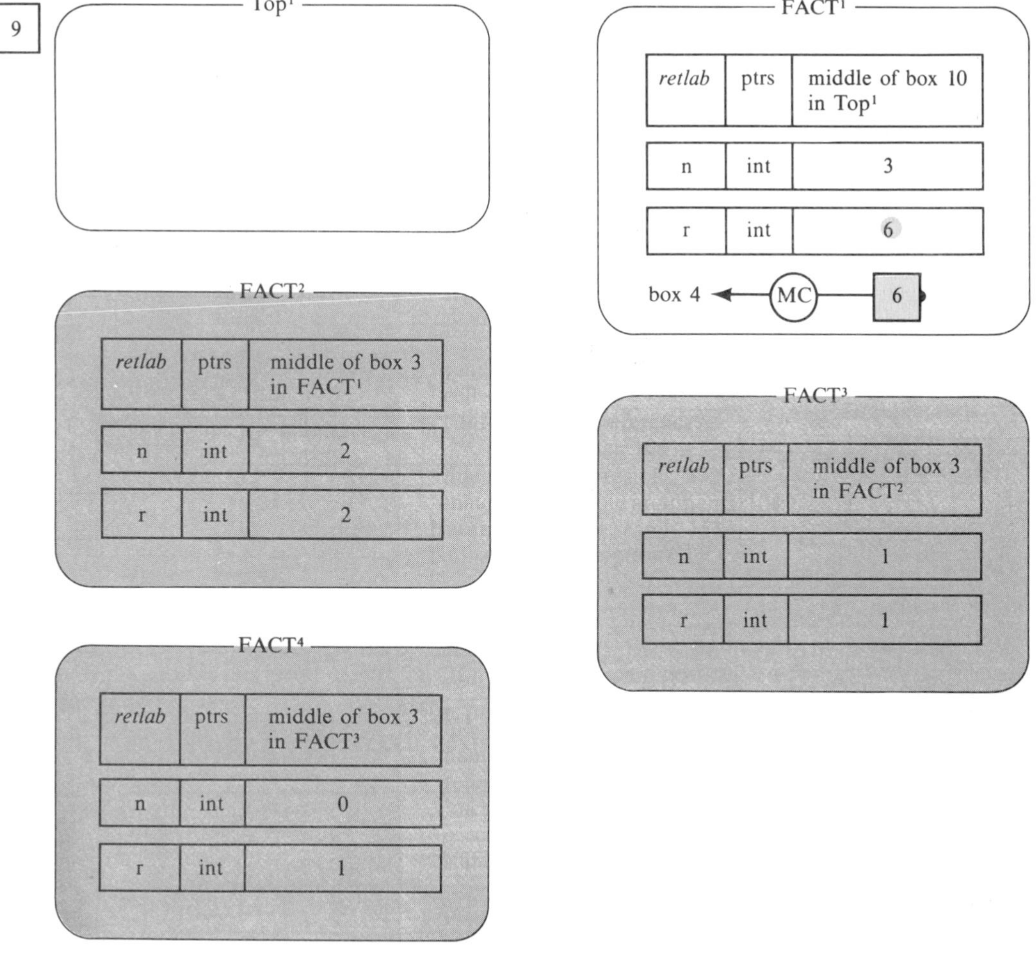

Figure 3-18

3-19 shows the situation upon return to Top[1] just after the MC has emptied the value 6 from his stack and displayed "6".

To sum up, we see that each activation of FACT produces a new environment with new cells n and r, and return information. Since n is a value parameter, this cell always gets a value before execution of FACT begins in any environment. Just before each return step, a value is assigned to the local variable r. This variable r identifies the value to be returned, and so it is the value of r that is copied and placed in the MC's stack.

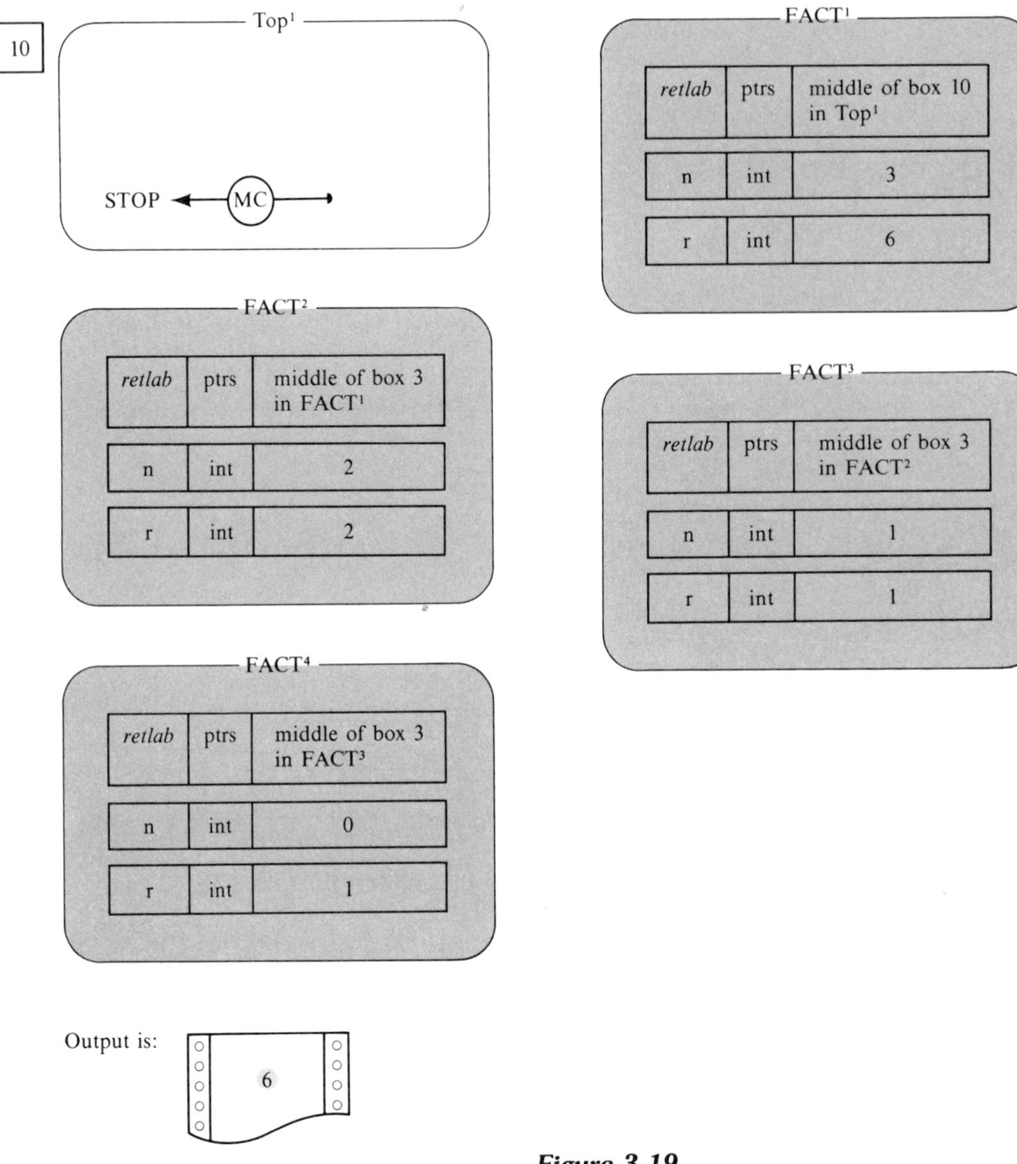

Figure 3-19

Exercises 3-1, Set A

1 Suppose the recursive flowchart and legend for FACT in Figure 3-4 is revised as in Figure 3-20. Show snapshots corresponding to those in Figures 3-15 through 3-19.

2 Assume the legend for FACT in Figure 3-4 is revised as in Figure 3-21. Show execution snapshots corresponding to those in Figures 3-11 through 3-14.

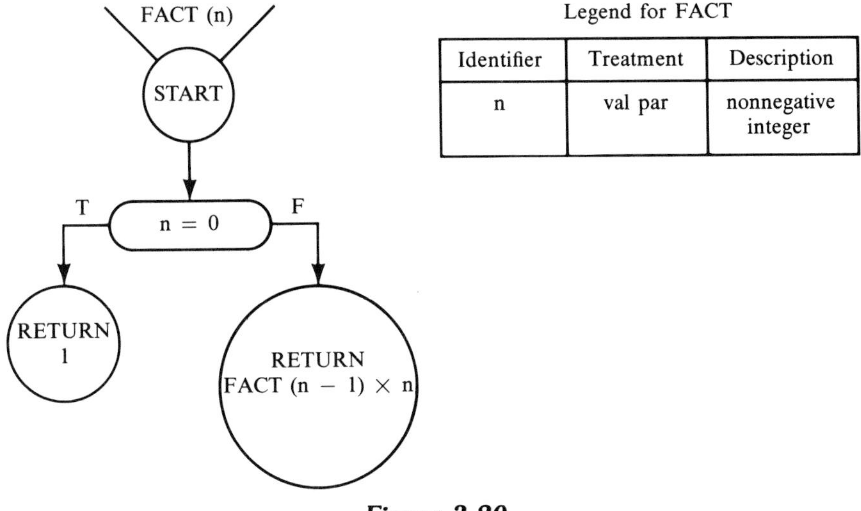

Legend for FACT

Identifier	Treatment	Description
n	val par	nonnegative integer

Figure 3-20

3 Suppose box 3 of Figure 3-4 is revised as follows:

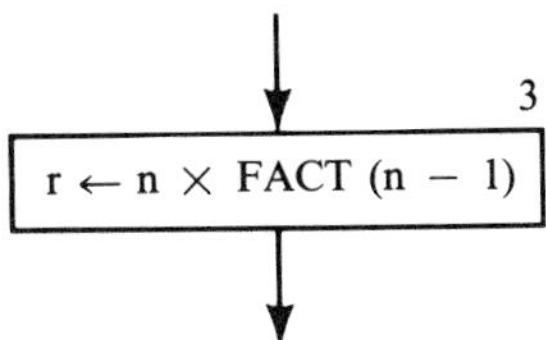

What changes will this cause in the snapshots of Figures 3-10 through 3-19? Explain in detail.

Procedures may be defined recursively, whether or not they return a functional value. For example, we may reexpress FACT as a non-value-returning procedure named FAKT. Compare FAKT in Figure 3-22 with FACT in Figure 3-4.

The "trick" is to use r as a reference parameter rather than as a local variable. Now when FAKT is invoked, the cell for the parameter r receives as its value a reference to the cell x in Top[1], which is to receive the factorial value. For example, Figure 3-23 shows a snapshot taken during the fourth invocation of

Figure 3-21

Legend for FACT

Identifier	Treatment	Description
n	ref par	nonnegative integer
r	local	integer

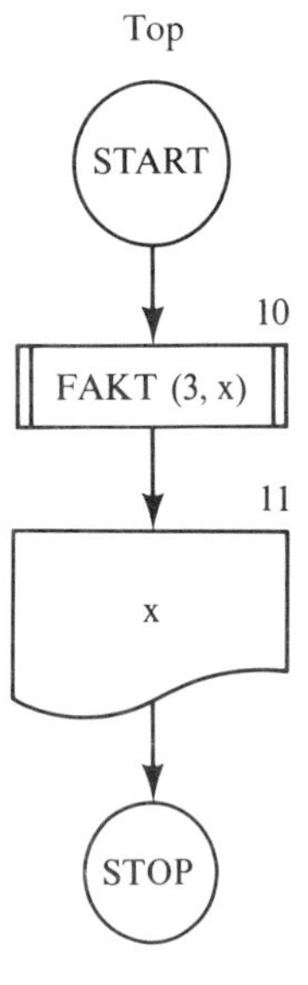

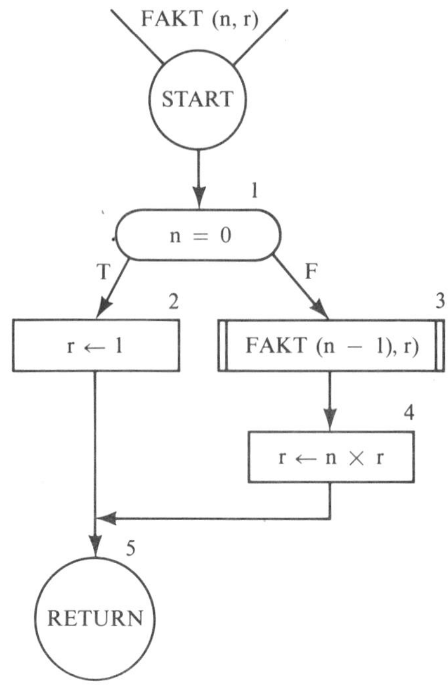

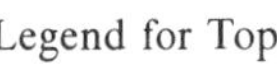

Legend for Top

Identifier	Treatment	Description
x	local	integer

Legend for FAKT

Identifier	Treatment	Description
n	val par	integer
r	ref par	integer

Figure 3-22

FAKT just after box 2 has been executed and the MC is about to execute the return step. (This snapshot should be compared with that shown in Figure 3-15.)

Via the chain of references denoted by the dashed lines, the true meaning of r in

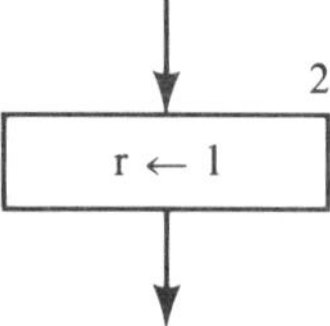

turns out to be the cell named x in Top[1]. As an exercise, draw the snapshot for the execution of FAKT that corresponds to Figure 3-18 where the MC is just about to return to Top.

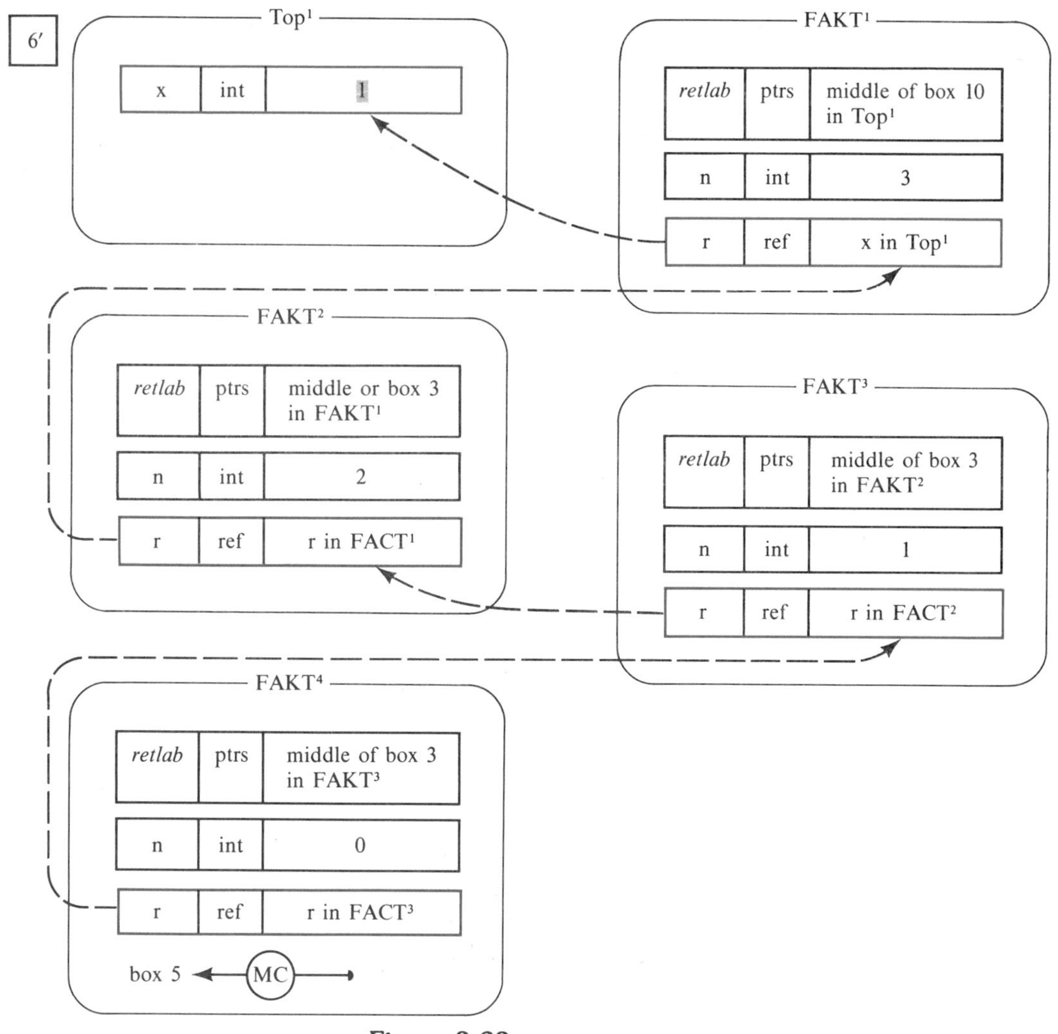

Figure 3-23

Exercises 3-1, Set B

1 The greatest common divisor algorithm can be represented very easily as a recursive function, GCDR, as seen in the flowchart in Figure 3-24.

(a) What is the escape hatch of GCDR?

(b) Which of the two return statements will be the first to be executed and why?

(c) Describe the steps that are taken after the first RETURN is executed.

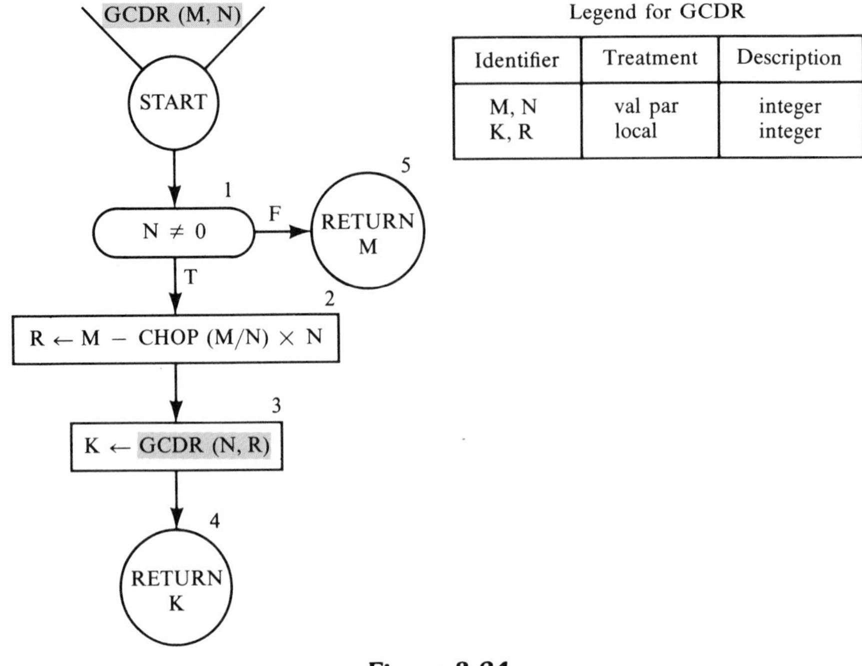

Legend for GCDR

Identifier	Treatment	Description
M, N K, R	val par local	integer integer

Figure 3-24

(d) A student has claimed that the return box

is equivalent to the sequence of boxes 3 and 4 in the above algorithm. Explain why you agree or disagree with this claim.

(e) Assume that the main flowchart given in Figure 3-25 is executed using as data a = 65 and b = 35. Trace the execution of the call on GCDR at box 2 by filling out the table in Figure 3-26.

Note: As the answer to part (c) should show, although these procedures are recursive in structure, the steps taken after the first RETURN are quite trivial in nature. In fact, the value returned in box 5 of Figure 3-24 is returned all the way up the ladder to the calling program.

2 The algorithm for the prime factorization of an integer N can be expressed as a recursive procedure very simply if we are not too concerned with efficiency. For instance, consider Figure 3-27. It is fairly obvious that this process works, by the following reasoning: Once a factor is found and printed (box 3), and then divided out of N (box 4), the whole process starts over (box 5). On emerging from the F exit of box 1, we are sure that the current value of N has no prime factors $\leq \sqrt{N}$ and hence is either a prime or is equal to 1. Boxes 7–9 deal appropriately with this situation.

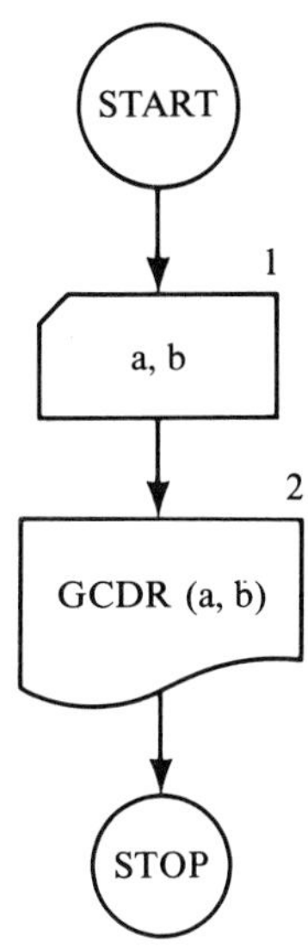

Figure 3-25

call number is	M	N	K	R	value returned
1					
2					
3					
4					
5					
⋮					

Figure 3-26

The flowchart in Figure 3-27 is open to two fundamental objections:

(1) The process is extremely wasteful in that, when FACTOR1 is invoked at box 5, the factorization process again tests 2 as a factor, whereas we know that N has no factors less than the most recent value of k.

(2) The top level program may not be satisfied with having the prime factors output by the procedure but may wish to use these prime factors in a list FACS rather than to output them. (See the Exercises of Section 2-5 for clarification.)

Objection (1) can be eliminated by modifying the procedure so that all factors are removed starting with i, for example,

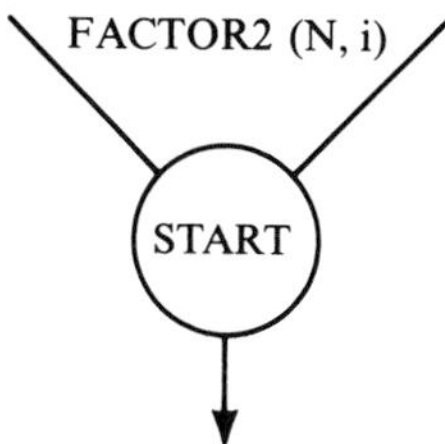

The procedure call in box 5 will then be changed to

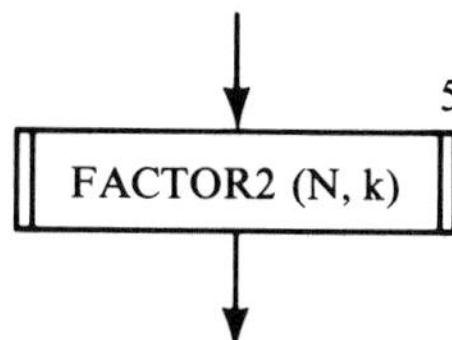

(a) How must box 0 be modified to deal with the change? Explain.

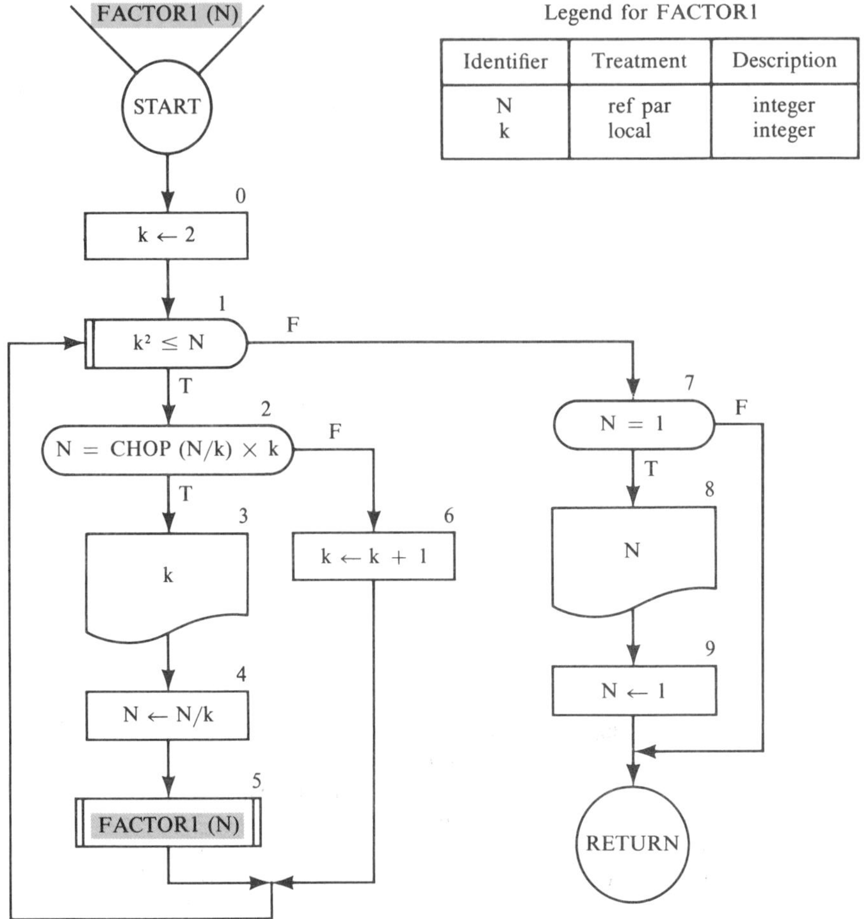

Legend for FACTOR1

Identifier	Treatment	Description
N	ref par	integer
k	local	integer

Figure 3-27

(b) To actually obtain the prime factorization, the main program procedure call must have the form

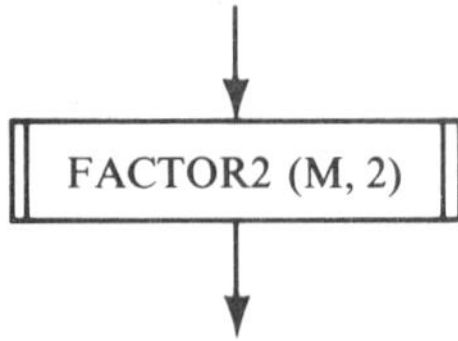

Explain the M and the 2 in the argument list.

(c) Since N is to be a reference parameter, after the first RETURN all further executions of box 7 will emerge from the T exit. Explain. [*Hint:* the key is found in box 9.]

(d) All of the above discussion is geared to the removal of objection (1). If objection (2) is to be dealt with as well, then the parameter list must also be changed, suggesting further modification, for example,

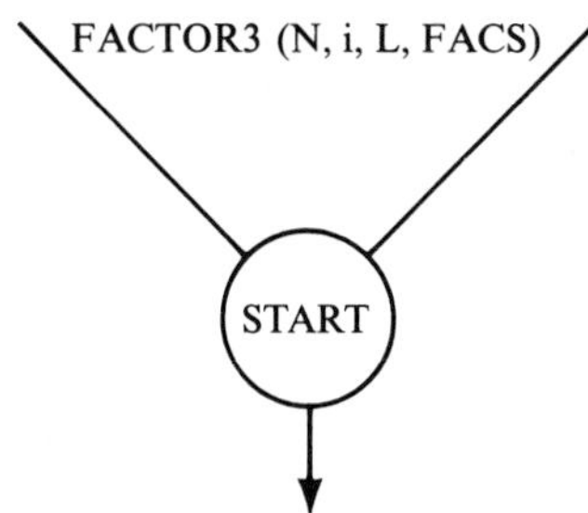

where L is the length (or dimension) of FACS. Must L and FACS be reference parameters or may they be value parameters?

(e) The top level program procedure call must now have the form

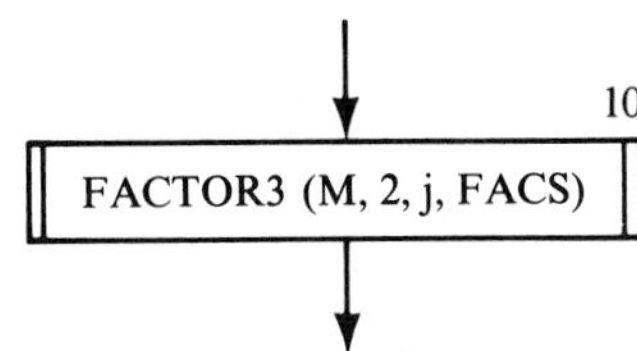

What should be the value of the argument j just before box 10 is executed? Explain.

(f) How must boxes 3 and 8 be modified to accommodate storage of factors rather than output?

(g) What is the escape hatch in this program? How can we be sure that it will eventually be reached?

(h) Show a flowchart and legend for FACTOR3 that satisfactorily eliminates objections (1) and (2).

3 Study the flowcharts and legends given in Figure 3-28. Then

(a) draw a sequence of snapshots for tracing the execution of the computation for the given data set, and show what is displayed as a result of executing box 4 of Top.

(b) revise the flowcharts and legends, eliminating all globals from the procedures, without changing the purpose of procedures Pattern or Filltheline. The given data set is

$$n = 4, \qquad A = (\text{“S”}, \text{“T”}, \text{“O”}, \text{“P”})$$

4 Use the flowcharts of the preceding exercise (Figure 3-28) as a guide for constructing flowcharts (and legends) which, when executed, will accomplish the following:

If the input values are $n = k$, $A = (a_1, a_2, a_3, \ldots, a_n)$, where the a_i are single characters, the algorithm will produce, as output, k “concentric” squares. The outermost square is made up of the letter a_k, the square inside of that is made up of the letter a_{k-1}, etc., with the innermost square consisting simply of the letter a_1. For example, if the data were

$$n = 5, \qquad A = (\text{“Q”}, \text{“U”}, \text{“E”}, \text{“E”}, \text{“N”})$$

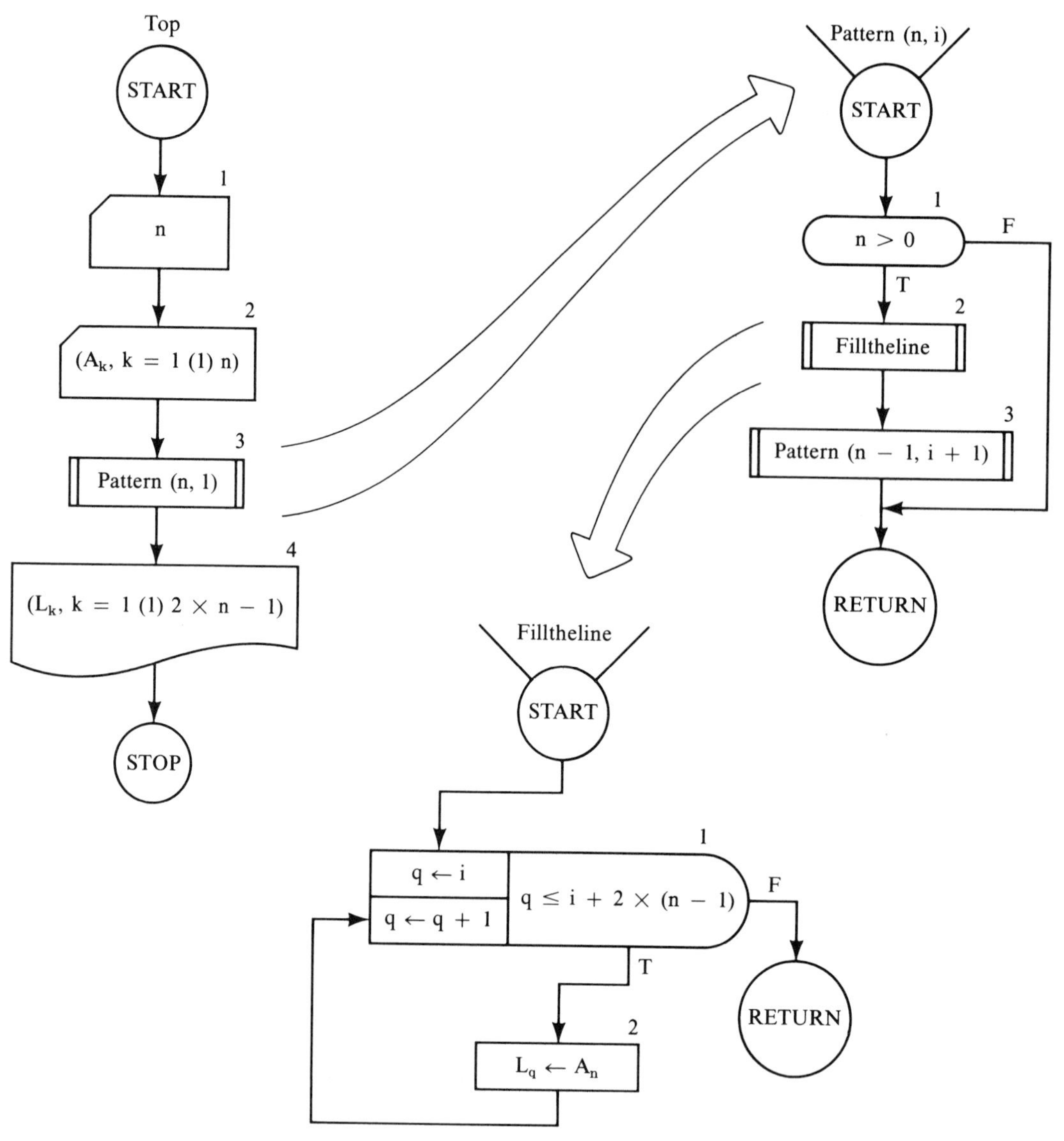

Legend for Pattern

Identifier	Treatment	Description
i, n	val par	integer

Legend for Top

Identifier	Treatment	Description
n, k	local	integer
L	local	list of $2 \times n - 1$ single-character strings
A	local	list of n single-character strings

Legend for Filltheline

Identifier	Treatment	Description
i	global	i in Pattern
n	global	n in Pattern
L	global	L in Top
A	global	A in Top
q	local	integer

Figure 3-28

then the executed program should display

```
N N N N N N N N N
N E E E E E E E N
N E E E E E E E N
N E E U U U E E N
N E E U Q U E E N
N E E U U U E E N
N E E E E E E E N
N E E E E E E E N
N N N N N N N N N
```

5 Design and construct a flowchart and legend for the recursive procedure Evaluate, which converts numbers in a base 4 representation to numbers in base 10 representation. For example, if the parameter list of Evaluate were (n, B, R), then the procedure would assign to R the base 10 value of the list B of n + 1 elements, each element being a digit in base 4. Thus the value assigned to R would be

$$B_n \times 4^n + B_{n-1} \times 4^{n-1} + \cdots + B_1 \times 4^1 + B_0 \times 4^0$$

Evaluate should recognize error conditions, returning a value of 0 for R and printing an appropriate error message as well. Error conditions include

(a) an element of B is negative,
(b) an element of B exceeds 3,
(c) the parameter n is negative.

6 For the preceding exercise show a collection of data sets that might be used by a top level flowchart to test the correctness of Evaluate. Explain what each data set is designed to accomplish and why you feel the collection of such data sets is complete for the purpose intended.

7 Show what changes would be needed in the flowchart and legend of Evaluate (as constructed in Exercise 5) so that this procedure can convert numbers from any base b, $b < 10$, to representation in base 10.

3-2 ADDITIONAL EXAMPLES

After this much exposure to recursive functions, you probably agree that recursive definitions for functions are indeed possible, and their execution in terms of the contour model is probably fairly clear to you. You may even agree that recursive definitions, such as the one for FACT, have a concise and somewhat appealing "style," but you may have little idea of how to go about *designing* a recursive algorithm. In this section we present some additional examples and observations, with the goal of helping you to learn to "think recursively."

The examples we are about to present involve *strings* of *digits,* for example,

"248" (a string of three digits)
"12635" (a string of five digits)
"" (a string of no digits (the empty string))

We shall assume the following three functions, which we will use in defining others. For any digit string l:

1. first (l) is the numerical value of the first digit of l, for example,

   first ("123") = 1

2. rest (l) is l with its first digit removed, for example,

   rest ("123") = "23"
   rest ("3") = ""

3. length (l) is the number of digits in l, for example,

   length ("136") = 3
   length ("") = 0

Now we wish to define a function SUM (l), whose value is the sum of the digits of string l. Our first inclination is to propose the *iterative* definition of Figure 3-29. We can, however, define SUM *recursively* if we notice that to sum a string of digits, we just add the first digit to the sum of the rest. Note also that the sum of the empty string is, of course, 0. Direct translation of this recursive definition leads to the flowchart of Figure 3-30 for a recursive version of SUM. Notice that we test for the escape hatch *first*. The structure and execution of this algorithm are very similar to those of FACT.

The definition for SUM is typical for recursive functions. It says, for example, that we can sum a 10-digit string if we can sum a 9-digit string. But we can do that if we can sum an 8-digit string, . . . , etc. Continuing to apply the rule, we ultimately arrive at the empty string, whose sum is known to be zero.

Figure 3-29. **Iterative definition of SUM.**

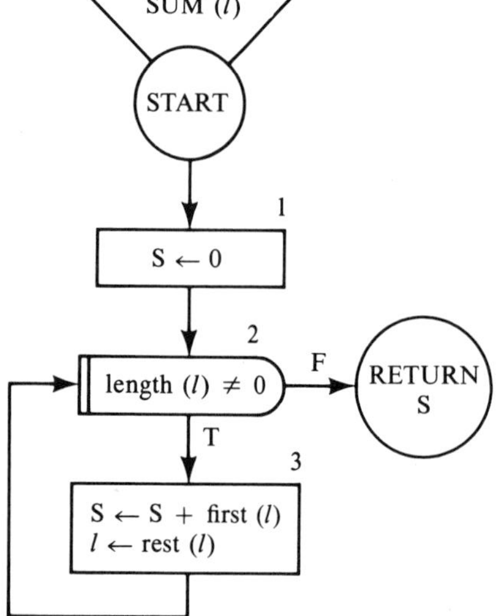

Legend for SUM

Identifier	Treatment	Description
l	val par	string
S	local	integer
length	proc	returns an integer
first	proc	integer
rest	proc	returns a string

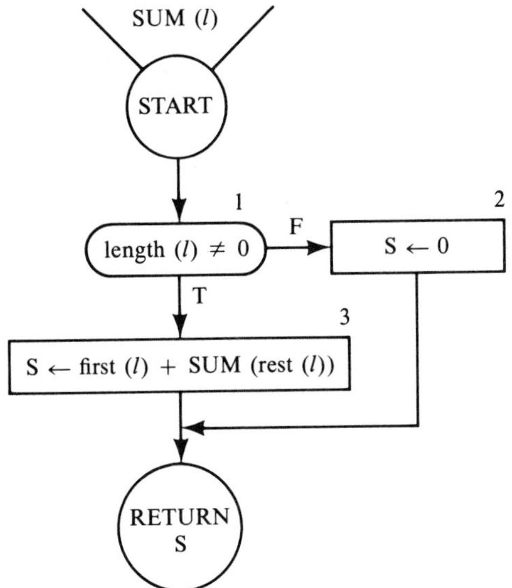

Figure 3-30. **Recursive definition of SUM.**

The process is clearly an example of the "recursive approach to problem solving" discussed in Section 3-1.

As another example, we wish to define the function MEMBER (x, *l*) whose value is "YES", if the digit x *is* in the digit string *l*, and "NO" otherwise. For example

MEMBER (3, "432") = "YES"

This time, we phrase the definition recursively from the start. If *l* is empty, the answer is, of course, "NO". If x is the first character in *l*, then the answer is "YES". If it is not, see if x is a MEMBER of the rest of *l*.

By now, such a recursive definition should seem fairly natural. Figure 3-31 shows the flowchart and legend. We again test the escape hatch first, but this time there are two escapes, one via box 2 and one via box 4. This computation proceeds a little differently from the previous examples of FACT and SUM. There, the value of a recursive call of the function was returned into an arithmetic expression, where it was combined with another value to become the value of a "higher level" call. In MEMBER, when an answer is returned from the recursive call in box 5, nothing is done except assign it to ANS and return it again. Thus the same answer is returned all the way up the ladder.

Notice that recursive definitions such as the one for MEMBER are consistent with the philosophy of stepwise decomposition (top-down programming), which says: "Complicated flowcharts are difficult to understand. In order to avoid them, do *some* of the steps of your solution in the flowchart you are drawing, and let other flowcharts handle the other steps." The only difference in MEMBER is that the "other" flowchart is MEMBER itself!

Before leaving MEMBER, compare the iterative definition of Figure 3-32 with the recursive one given in Figure 3-31.

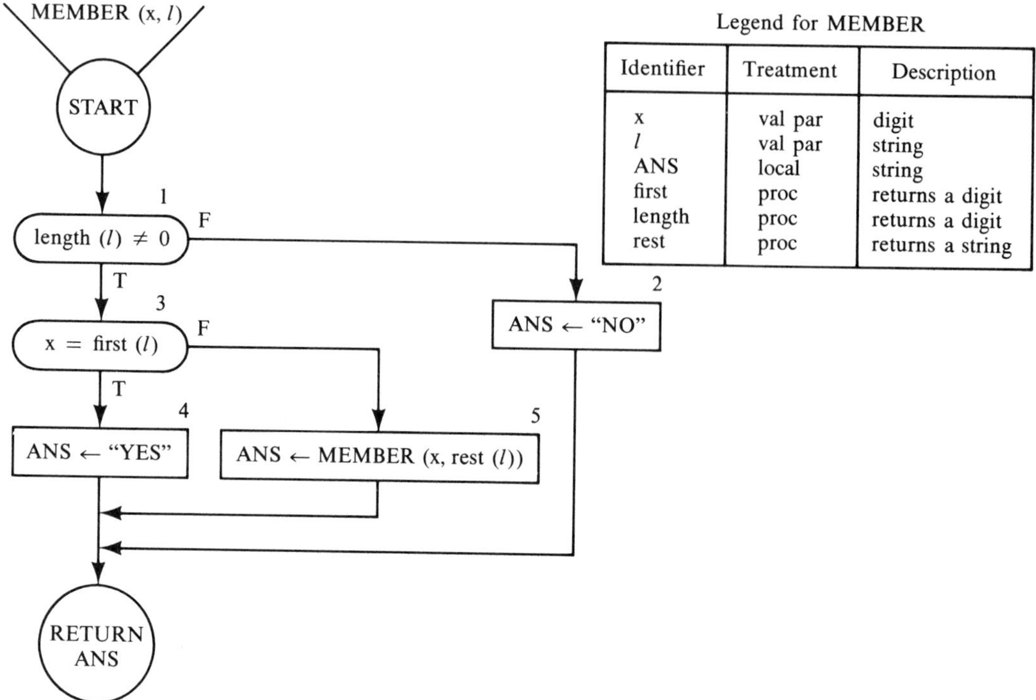

Legend for MEMBER

Identifier	Treatment	Description
x	val par	digit
l	val par	string
ANS	local	string
first	proc	returns a digit
length	proc	returns a digit
rest	proc	returns a string

Figure 3-31

Figure 3-32

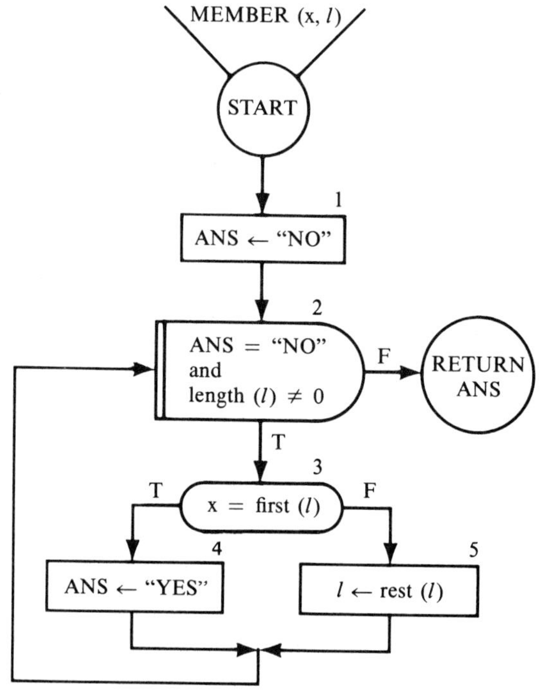

3-3
TREE TRAVERSAL AND RECURSION

So far, in each example of a recursive procedure or function, execution leads to an unbranched chain of recursive calls and returns. Figure 3-33a illustrates this chain for the case when Top calls FACT, with the argument 3. The downward chain links are labeled with the arguments for the successive calls on FACT, and upward links are labeled with the values provided in the successive returns. One can also view such a chain as a tree (Figure 3-33b) that has, at each node, only one offspring. And each node is connected to its single successor by a double link or "double segment." In the figure, the downward-pointing segments represent *calls* and the upward-pointing ones represent *returns.*

When does a recursive procedure or function that calls no procedure or function other than itself lead to a chain of calls that splits into two or more chains like an ordinary tree? For example, can we have a recursive procedure P which, when called, leads to a call chain such as Figure 3-34?

A little thought will lead us to the answer. In order for the call chain to branch, execution of a recursive procedure must in the same activation result in at least two calls on itself. Thus a procedure P which contains at least two

Figure 3-33. **(a) A chain of call, (b) a tree.**

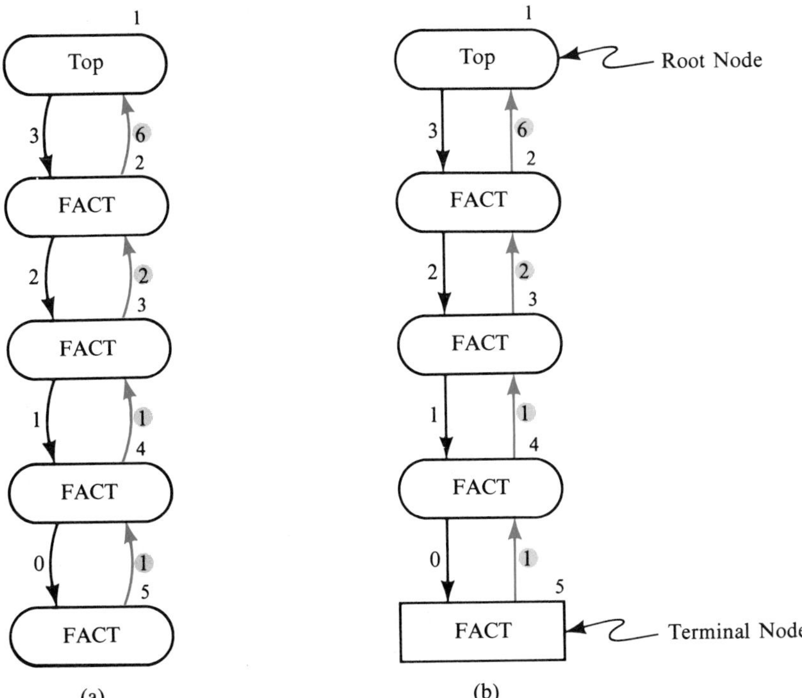

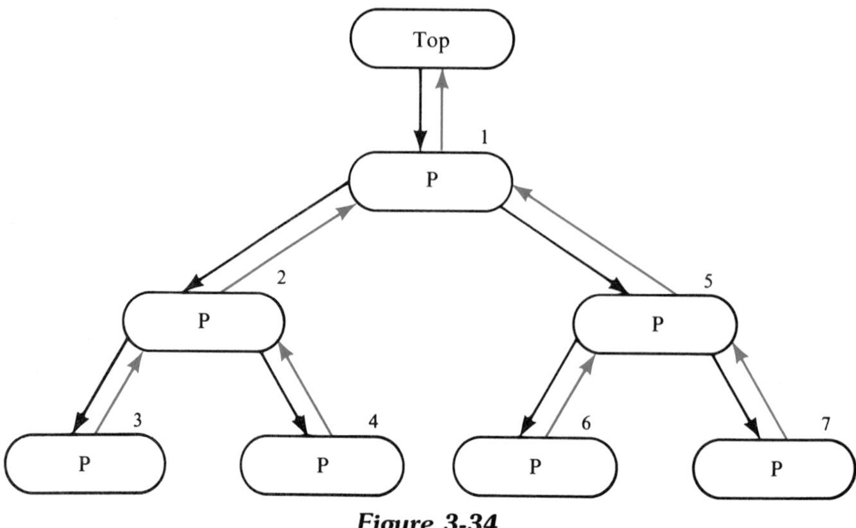

Figure 3-34

distinct references to itself in the body of its flowchart can give rise to a branching call chain.*

Our first illustration of "recursive branching" is a problem familiar to every college algebra student, the calculation of the binomial coefficient BC. Recall

Figure 3-35

BC (n, k)

START

RETURN $\frac{\text{FACT (n)}}{\text{FACT (k)} \times \text{FACT (n − k)}}$

Legend for BC

Identifier	Treatment	Description
n, k FACT	val par proc	integer returns an integer value

*Branching may also occur indirectly through auxiliary procedures. For example, although the body of procedure P does not refer directly to itself, it may call more than once on an auxiliary procedure Q whose body contains a reference to P. One can imagine many similar examples involving auxiliary procedures.

Note that this discussion is not concerned with the kind of branching that results when one procedure calls other procedures. For example, if R calls both S and T, the call chain would be

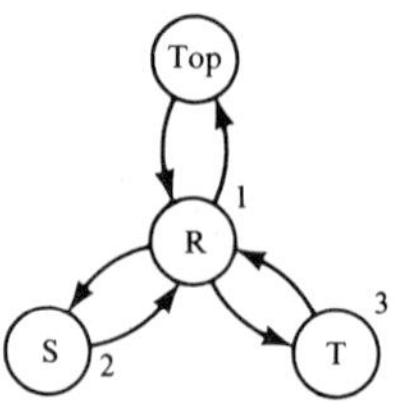

that the binomial coefficient refers to the kth coefficient of the polynomial resulting from the expansion of a binomial of the form $(a + b)^n$:

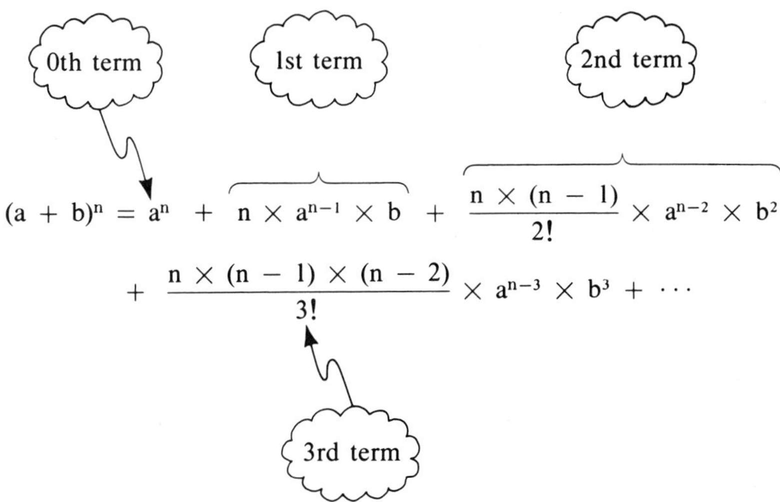

An explicit formula for the kth coefficient of the nth-degree polynomial is

$$\text{BC}(n, k) = \frac{n \times (n-1) \times (n-2) \times \cdots \times (n-k+1)}{k!}$$

which can also be expressed as

$$\text{BC}(n, k) = \frac{n!}{k! \times (n-k)!}$$

Using this formula one could, of course, compute BC (n, k) by making three separate calls on the factorial function, as in Figure 3-35.

Degree \ Term number

n \ k	0	1	2	3	4	5	6	7
0	1							
1	1	1						
2	1	2	1					
3	1	3	3	1				
4	1	4	6	4	1			
5	1	5	10	10	5	1		
6	1	6	15	20	15	6	1	
7	1	7	21	35	35	21	7	1
⋮								

***Figure 3-36.* Pascal's Triangle provides the binomial coefficients for the kth term of the nth-degree polynomial.**

There is another way to compute binomial coefficients, of greater interest to our particular discussion. This second way suggests itself through an examination of Pascal's triangle, which is formed by writing the coefficients for each polynomial, beginning with degree 0 (Figure 3-36). The coefficients on the left edge of the triangle (k = 0) and on the diagonal (n = k) are all 1. Each of the other coefficients is the sum of two of its neighbors, the one immediately above it, and that neighbor's left-hand neighbor.

With these observations in mind, we can now write a recursive definition of BC in mathematical form and its direct analog in flowchart form (Figure 3-37). The mathematical form is

$$\mathrm{BC}\ (n, k) = \begin{cases} 1, & \text{if} \quad k = 0 \quad \text{or} \quad n = k \\ \mathrm{BC}\ (n - 1, k) + \mathrm{BC}\ (n - 1, k - 1), & \text{otherwise} \end{cases}$$

Note that here for the first time we see a recursive procedure exhibiting more than one recursive call within its definition. In this case these calls appear in boxes 2 and 3 of Figure 3-37.

One useful way to trace the execution of BC is to construct a call tree. For example, Figure 3-38 shows the call tree for the computation of BC (4, 2). A call tree shows the entire history of the computation in one figure, and reveals the branching in the chain of calls.

***Figure 3-37.* A recursive definition for the BC procedure.**

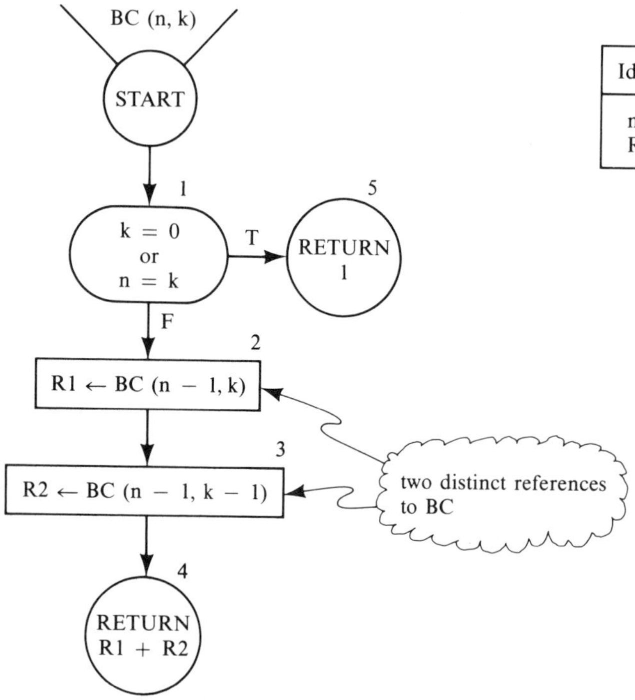

BC (n, k)

START

1

k = 0 or n = k

T → 5 RETURN 1

F

2 R1 ← BC (n − 1, k)

3 R2 ← BC (n − 1, k − 1)

two distinct references to BC

4 RETURN R1 + R2

Legend for BC

Identifier	Treatment	Description
n, k	val par	integer
R1, R2	local	integer

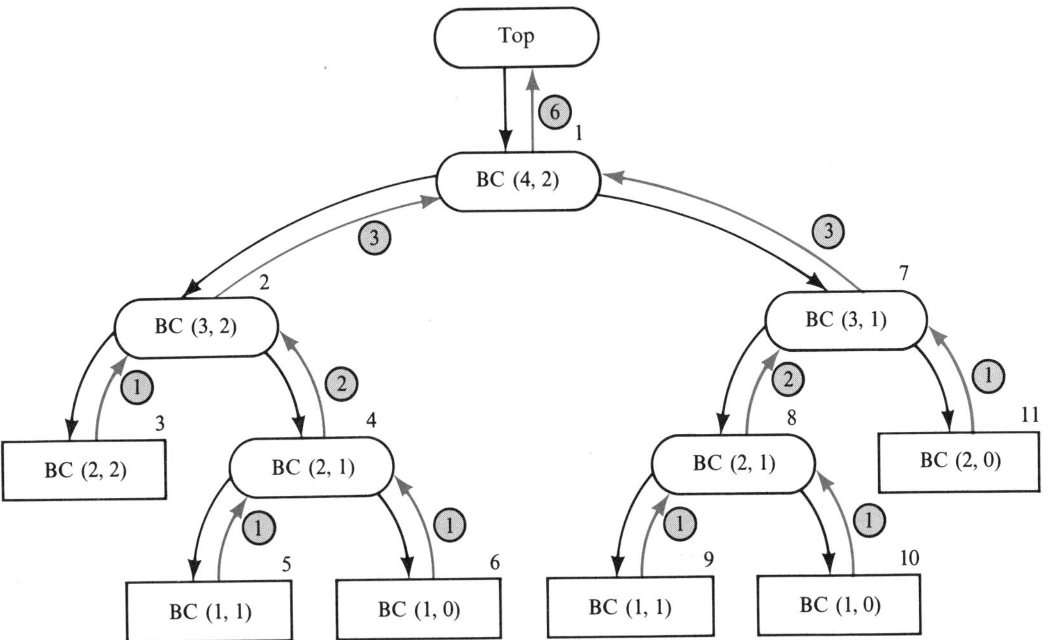

Figure 3-38. **Executing BC (4, 2) results in execution of a tree of calls in the order shown by the small numbers beside each node. Each node represents a call on BC. Circled numbers are the returned values.**

In Figure 3-38, notice that the node numbers, which show the order in which the calls were made, also order the nodes of the tree in depth first or *natural order.** In Figure 3-37, the order in which boxes 2 and 3 are executed is immaterial. If the order were reversed, the same tree of calls would be executed but the order in which the nodes are encountered would be different. [To verify your understanding of this assertion you might trace the execution of say BC (3, 2) two ways: (a) with boxes 2 and 3 in their present order, and (b) with boxes 2 and 3 reversed.]

We can also trace the execution of BC, for Figure 3-39, using a sequence of snapshots. For example, Figures 3-40 through 3-49 show a sequence of 10 snapshots for the execution of BC (3, 2). Study this sequence to satisfy yourself that the two types of tracing mechanisms, call tree and snapshot sequence, are somewhat complementary methods. (Each snapshot includes, as an auxiliary diagram, the partial call tree developed up to the point at which the snapshot was taken.)

*For an introductory discussion of tree structures, notation related to trees, and methods of searching trees, the reader is referred to the elementary treatment given in Chapters 6–9 of Forsythe *et al.* (1975a).

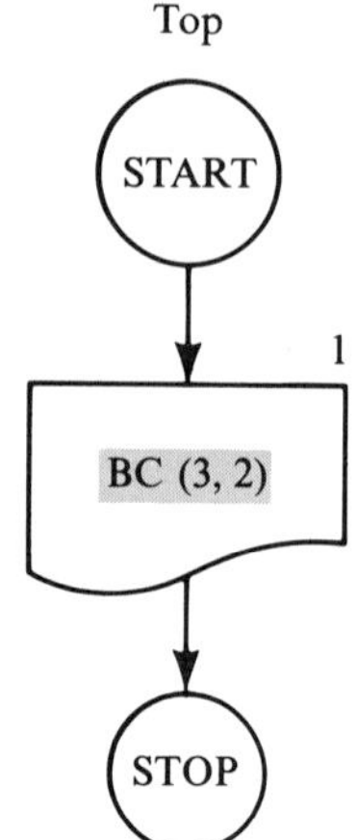

Figure 3-39

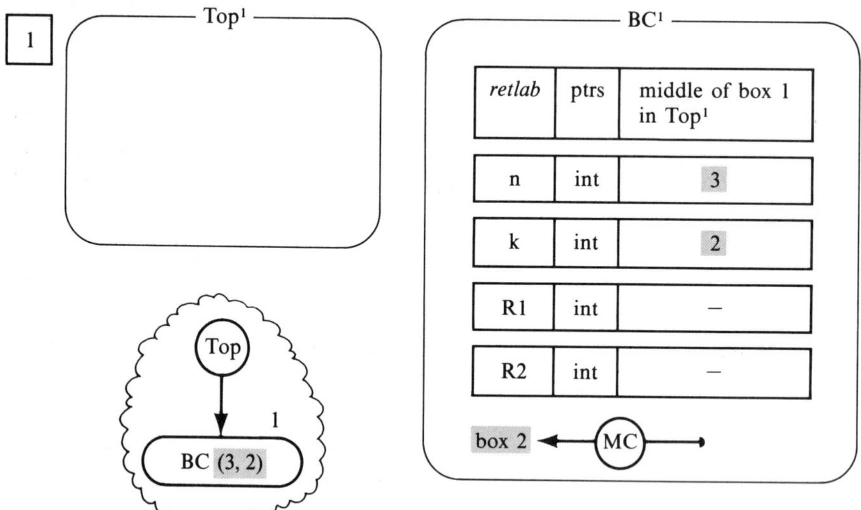

Figure 3-40. **The MC is about to execute the first *recursive* call on BC with the arguments (2, 2).**

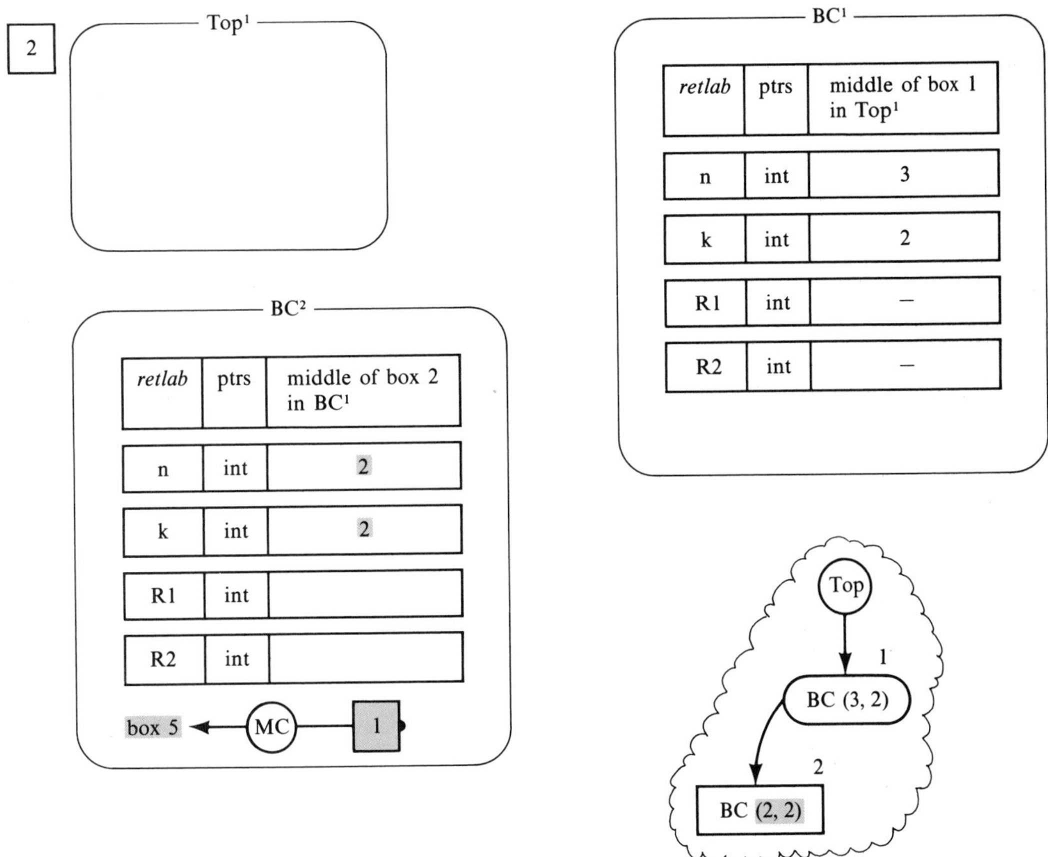

Figure 3-41. **The MC has stacked the value 1 preparatory to *returning* from the T side of box 1. In BC[1] he will complete the assignment step of box 2.**

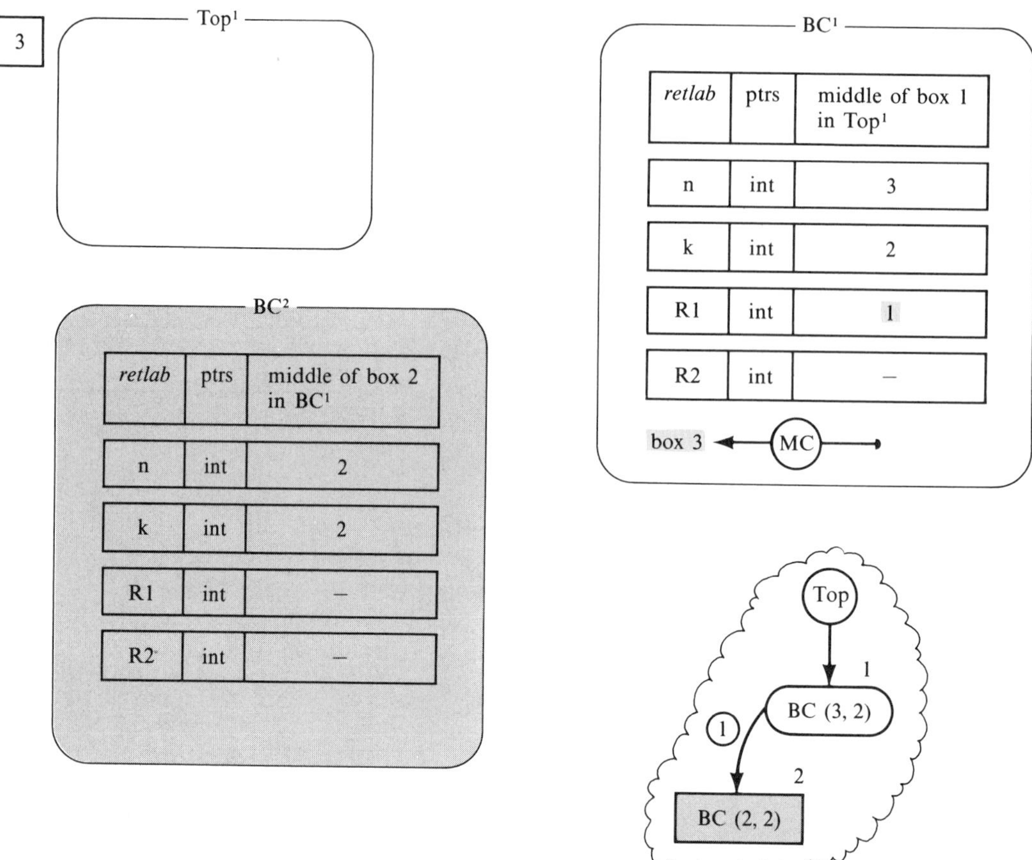

Figure 3-42. **R1 has been assigned the value 1 and the MC is about to execute box 3 involving the second recursive call on BC, with arguments (2, 1).**

4

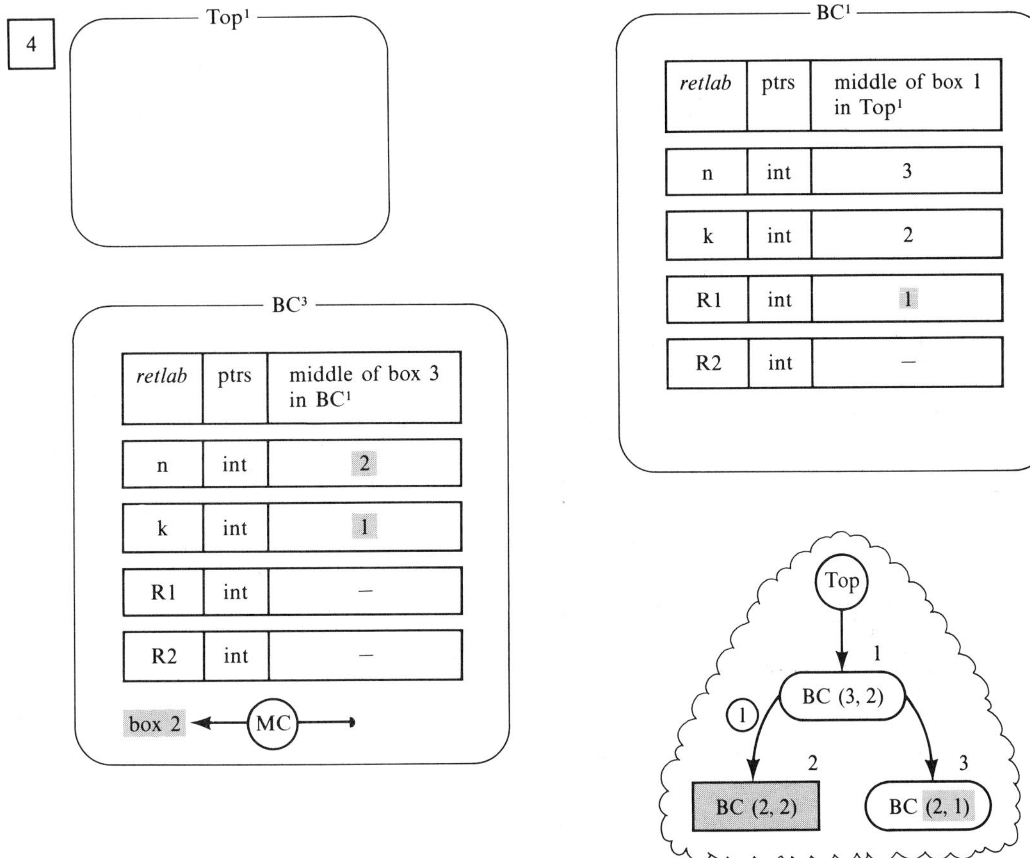

Figure 3-43. **The MC is about to execute box 2 in BC³, which will lead to another call on BC, this time with arguments (1, 1).**

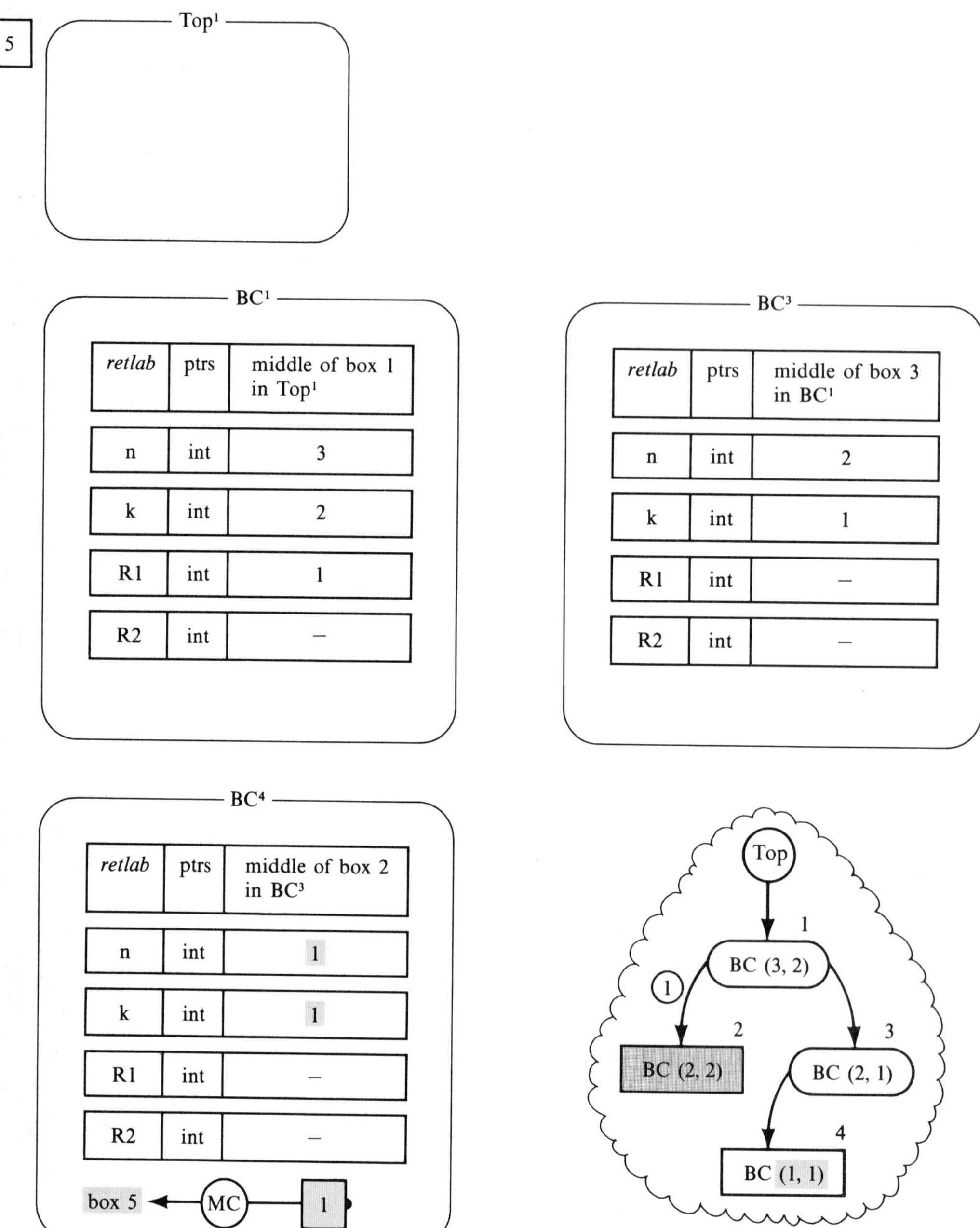

Figure 3-44. **The MC has stacked the value 1 preparatory to returning to complete the assignment step of box 2 in BC³.**

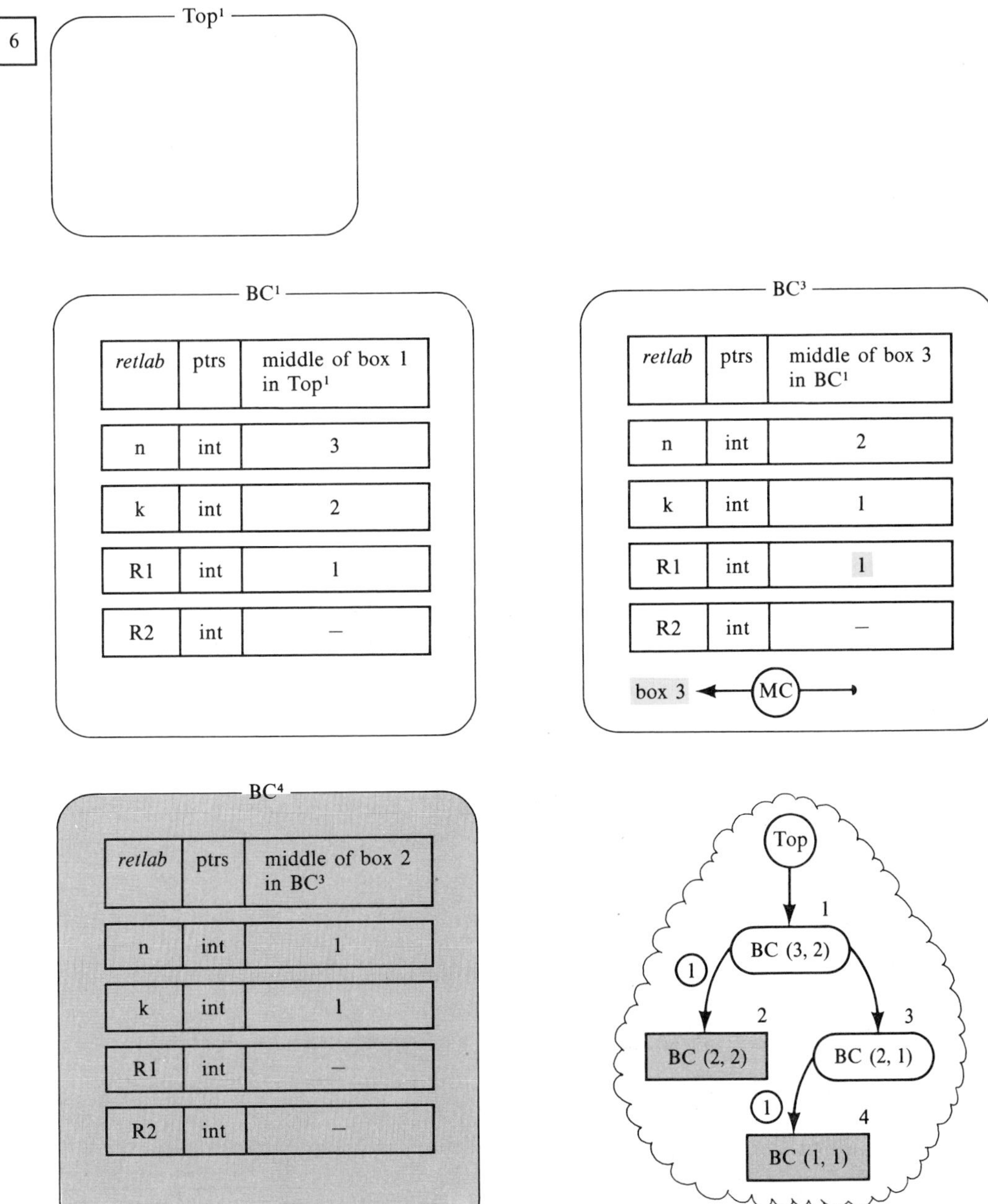

Figure 3-45. **The MC has assigned the value 1 to R1 in BC³ and is about to execute box 3, which will result in the last recursive call on BC, with arguments (1, 0).**

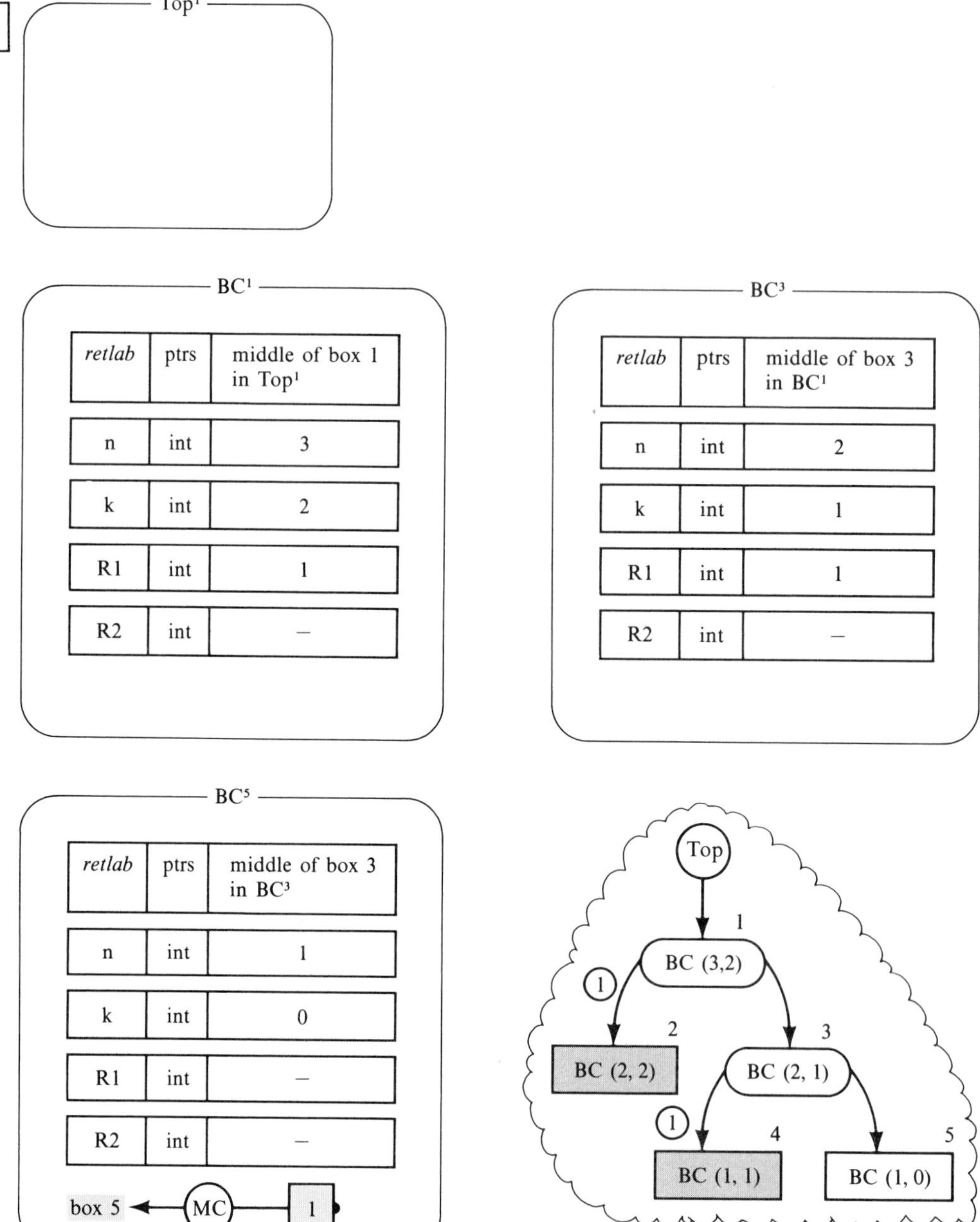

Figure 3-46. **The MC has stacked the value 1 preparatory to returning to complete the assignment step of box 3 in BC³.**

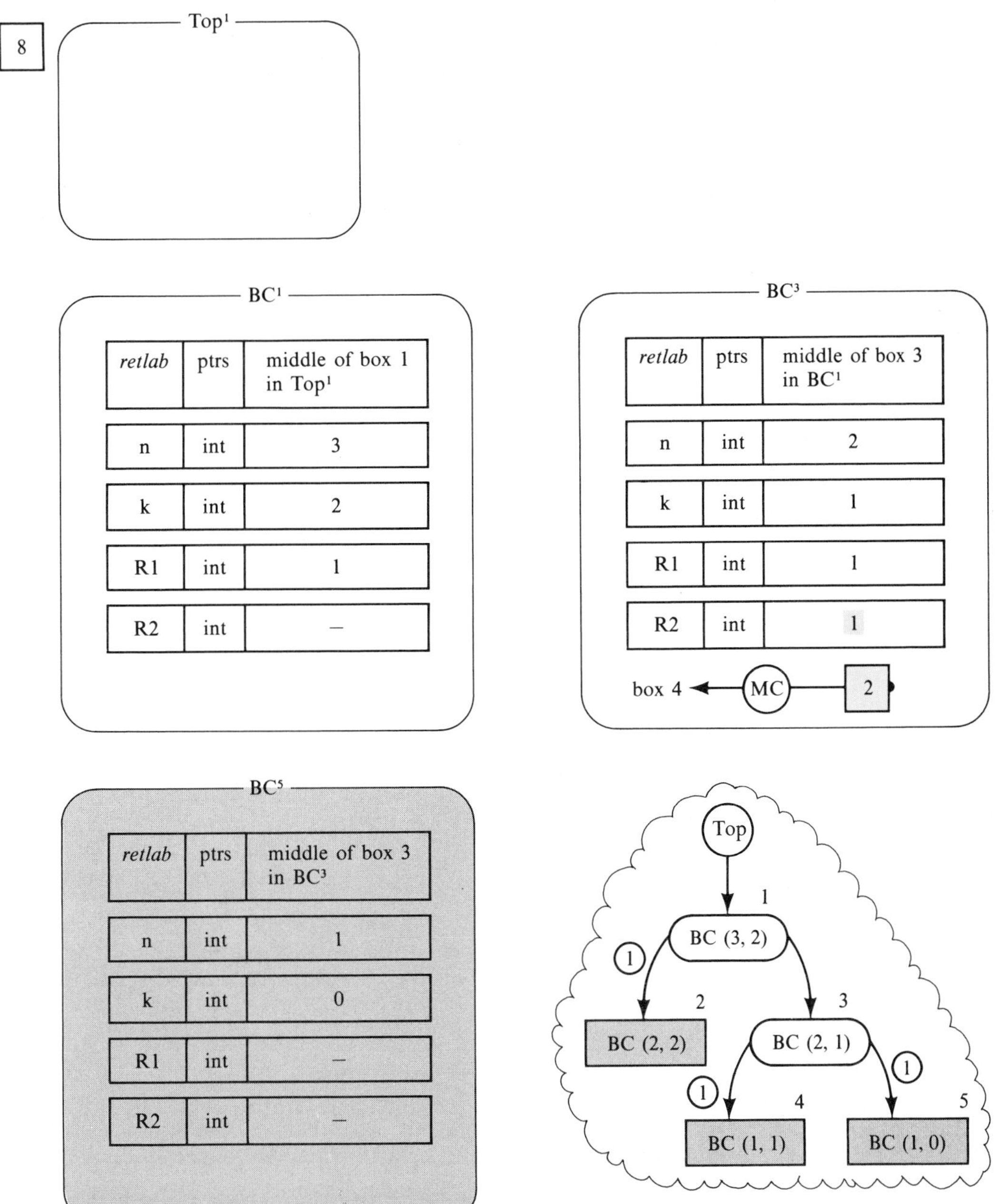

Figure 3-47. **The MC has computed the value of R1 + R2 (=2) and has stacked it, preparatory to returning to complete execution of box 3 in BC[1].**

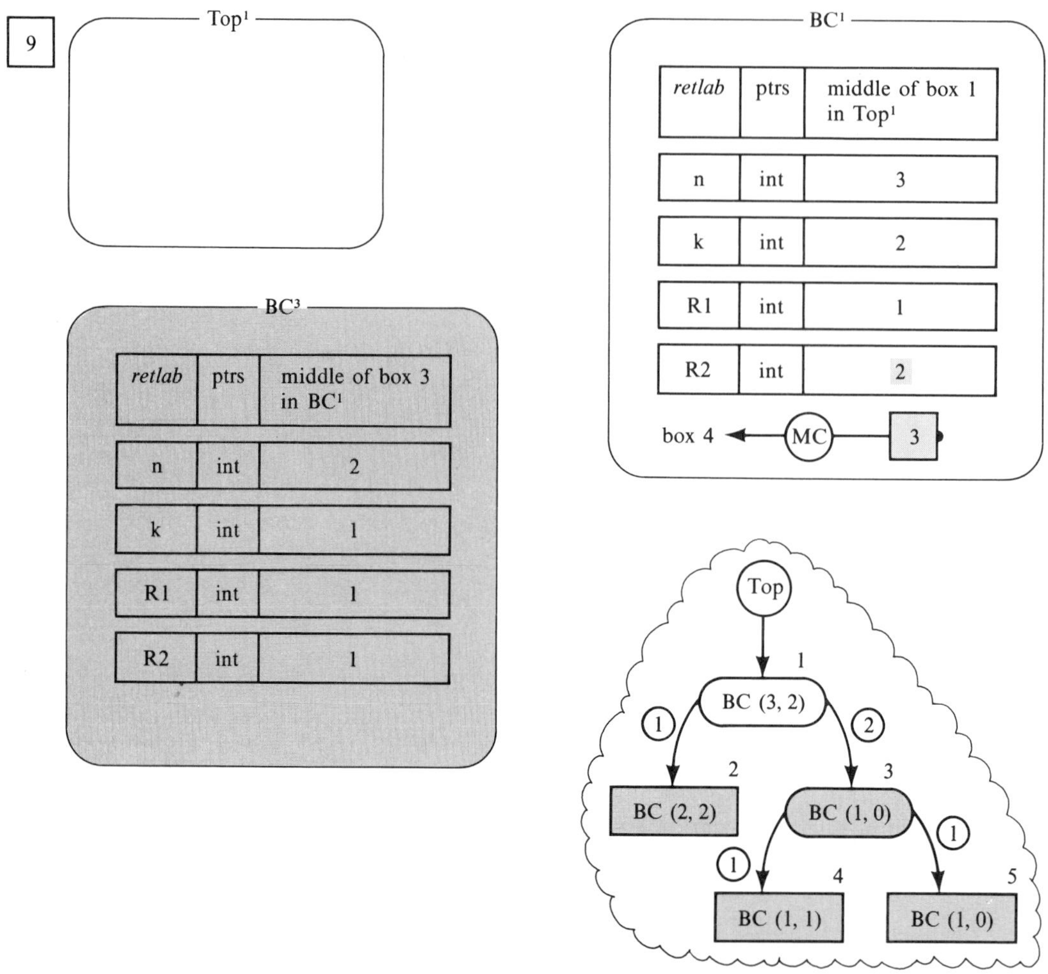

9

Top[1]

BC[1]

retlab	ptrs	middle of box 1 in Top[1]
n	int	3
k	int	2
R1	int	1
R2	int	2

box 4 ← MC — 3

BC[3]

retlab	ptrs	middle of box 3 in BC[1]
n	int	2
k	int	1
R1	int	1
R2	int	1

Top

1

BC (3, 2)

(1) 2 BC (2, 2)

(2) 3 BC (1, 0)

(1) 4 BC (1, 1)

(1) 5 BC (1, 0)

Figure 3-48. **The MC has computed the value of R1 + R2 (= 3) and has stacked it, preparatory to returning to complete execution of box 1 in Top[1].**

The treelike pattern of calls produced by BC might suggest to us that recursive algorithms are appropriate vehicles with which to "traverse" binary trees. They are, indeed, and let us see why this is so. Consider the following definition:

> The rootnode of a binary tree has two offspring, one called the *left subtree* and the other called the *right subtree.* Each is either a terminal node or is itself a binary tree.

Pictorially, a binary tree is

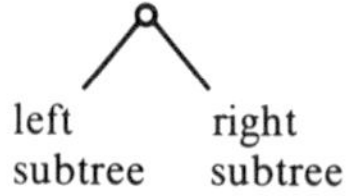

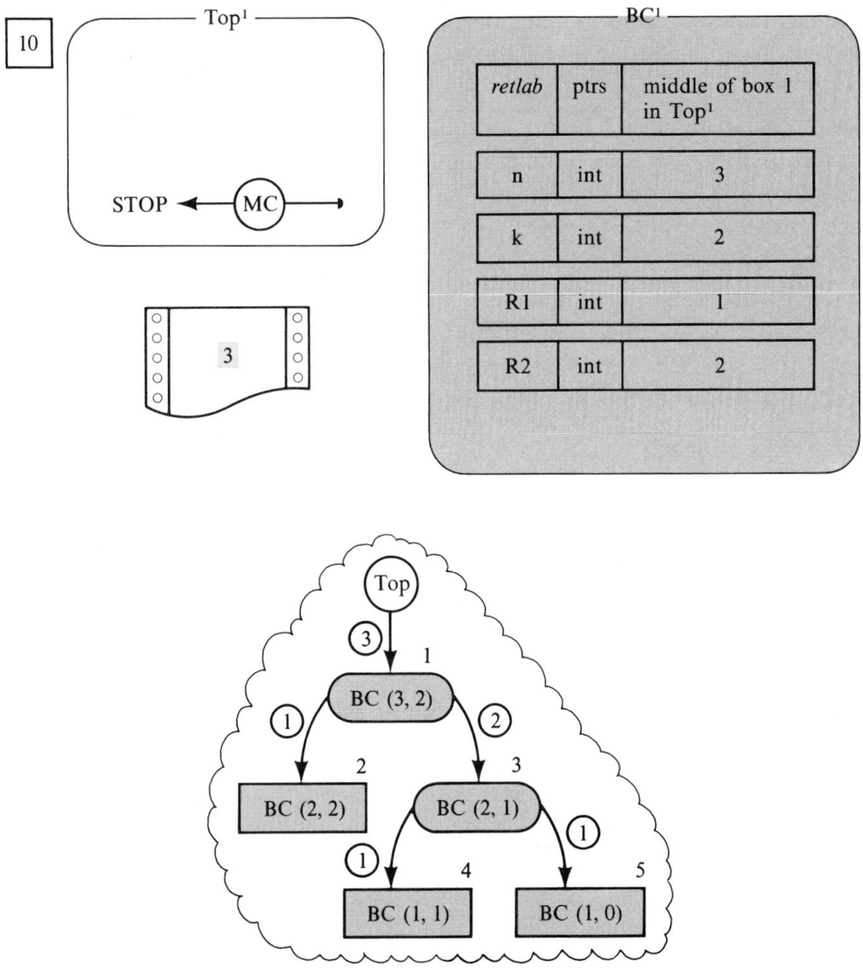

Figure 3-49. **The MC has returned to Top with the value 3 for BC (3, 2), has output the value, and is about to execute STOP.**

Thus we see that *the definition of a binary tree is recursive!* It is not surprising that the natural kind of algorithm for searching such a *recursive data structure* turns out to be a *recursive algorithm.*

Before investigating such algorithms, let us think back for a moment to our earlier examples of recursive functions of strings. Now we can see why the recursive approach worked out so well. It is because even one-dimensional structures, like strings of characters or digits, can be defined recursively: a string is either empty, or it is an element followed by a string, for example,

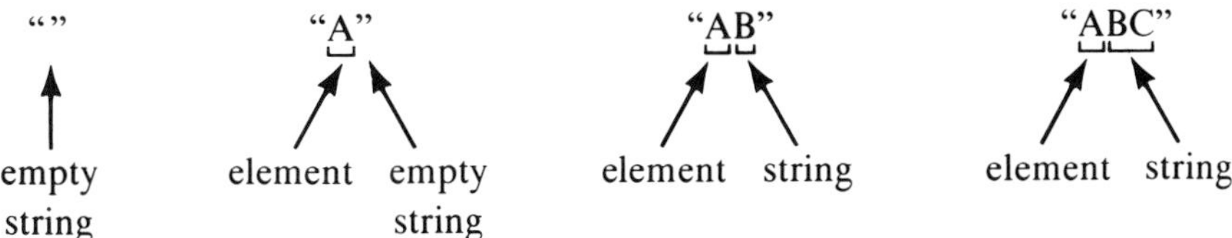

The fact that nonrecursive functions of strings were easy to write follows from the fact that nonrecursive definitions of strings are easy to formulate. The choice between a recursive and a nonrecursive algorithm often depends on which type of definition seems more natural for the data structure involved.

Returning to the idea of binary tree traversal, a little thought produces an algorithm analogous to BC, but *generalized,* as shown in Figure 3-50. The key idea to keep in mind when verifying your understanding of this algorithm is that each time control takes the "No" exit from box 1, that is, each time a nonterminal node is examined, there are two and only two steps to take before the return to the caller: first, the left subtree must be traversed and, second, the right subtree must be traversed. It is as simple as that! This is because, by definition, a nonterminal node of a binary tree can have two and only two subtrees.

Figure 3-50. **Recursive structure for a binary tree traversal algorithm.**

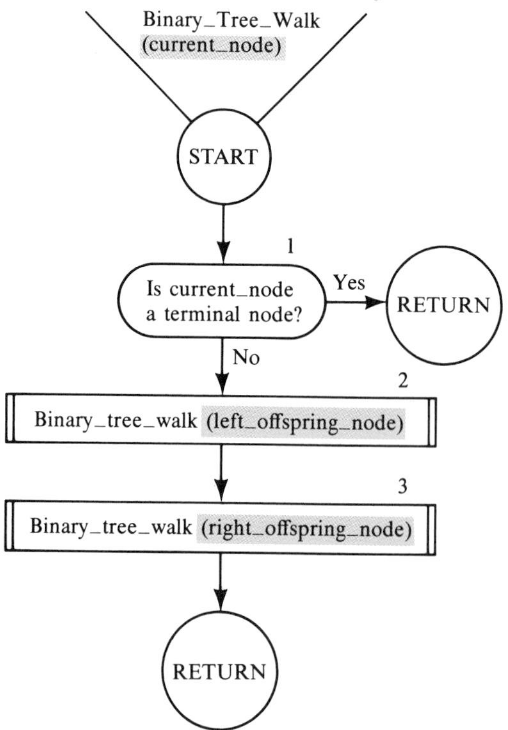

Exercises 3-3

1 It is not always practical to compute a function value using a recursive definition for the function, even when that definition seems simple and natural. For example, the values of the Fibonacci sequence can be computed using a function on the non-negative integers, expressed as follows:

$$\text{FIBR (n)} = \begin{cases} \text{if n} = 0 \text{ then } 0 \\ \text{if n} = 1 \text{ then } 1 \\ \text{else FIBR (n} - 1) + \text{FIBR (n} - 2) \end{cases}$$

(a) Construct a flowchart for the function FIBR based on the above definition.
(b) Draw the tree of calls on FIBR that will be executed when FIBR (4) is evaluated. As a guide for drawing this tree you might consult Figure 3-38. Be sure to indicate arguments and returned values for all calls.
(c) Estimate the number of calls on FIBR required to compute FIBR (10).
(d) Construct a flowchart and legend for the function FIBRWORK, which when executed, will return the number of calls required to compute FIBR (n) for a given value, n.

2 Construct a flowchart and legend for a function FIBI, which, when executed, will compute *iteratively* (and return) the value of the nth term of the Fibonacci sequence for a given value of n. Compare your function FIBI with FIBR produced in the preceding problem.
(a) For what values of n will the computation of FIBI (n) be more efficient than that of FIBR (n)? Explain, stating any assumptions you may have made in arriving at your answer.
(b) For what values of n, if any, might the computation of FIBR (n) be more efficient than that of FIBI (n)? Explain, stating any assumptions you may have made in arriving at your answer.

3 "Utah" numbers U (n) are defined recursively as follows:

$$\text{If n} = 0,\ \text{U (n)} = 2. \quad \text{If n} = 1,\ \text{U (n)} = 1.$$

$$\text{For n} \geq 2,\ \text{U (n)} = 2 \times \text{U (n} - 1) + 4 \times \text{U (n} - 2).$$

Figure 3-51 is a legend and flowchart for the computation of U (n), given a positive integer value of n.
(a) Compute U (4).
(b) Complete the following call tree, numbering the nodes in the order in which the calls are made, and labeling each segment with the (circled) value returned by the call that the segment leads to.

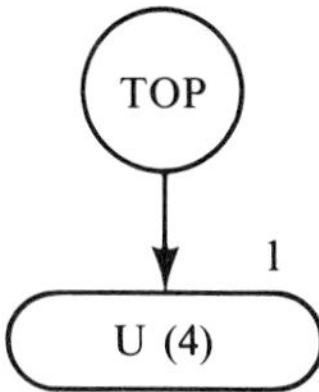

(c) Complete a snapshot (Figure 3-52) to represent the state of execution just before box 2 is executed in the 6th invocation of U. Cross out any contours that are no longer accessible to the MC operating in the U^6 environment.

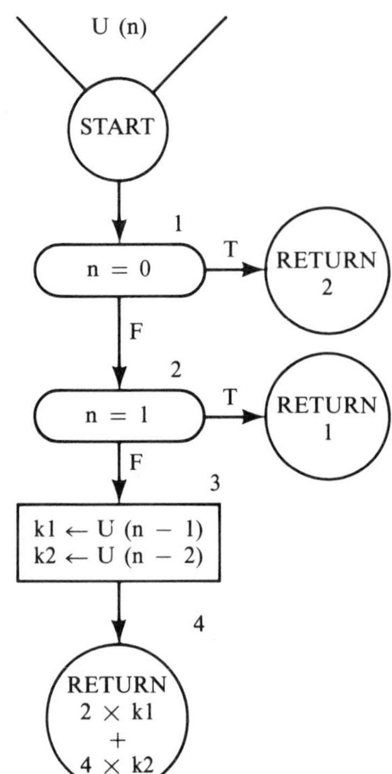

Legend for U

Identifier	Treatment	Description
n	val par	integer
k1	local	integer
k2	local	integer

Figure 3-51

Figure 3-52

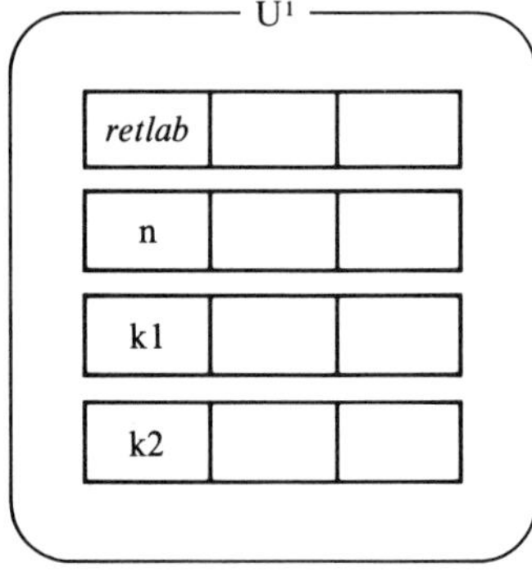

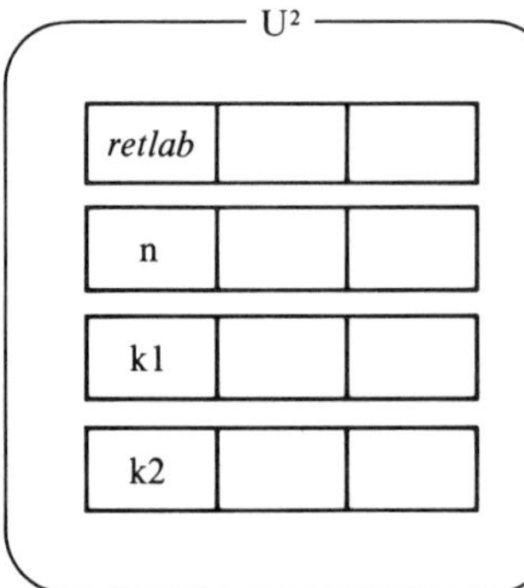

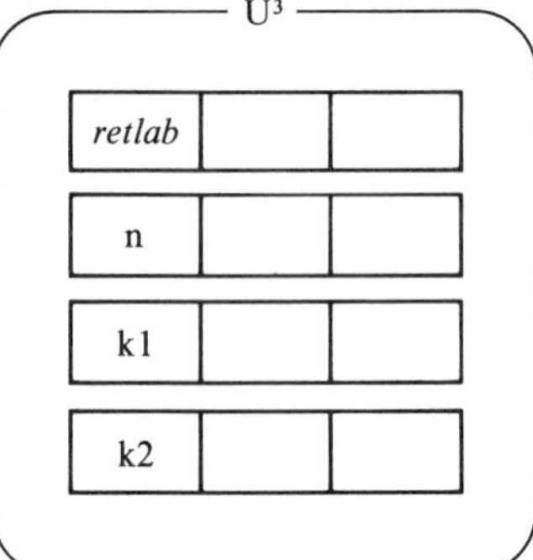

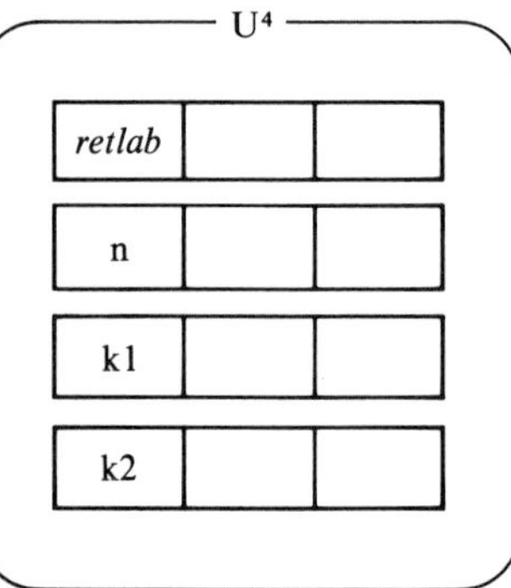

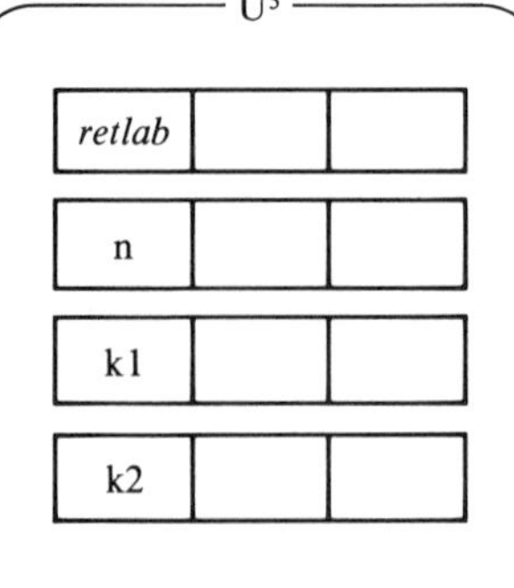

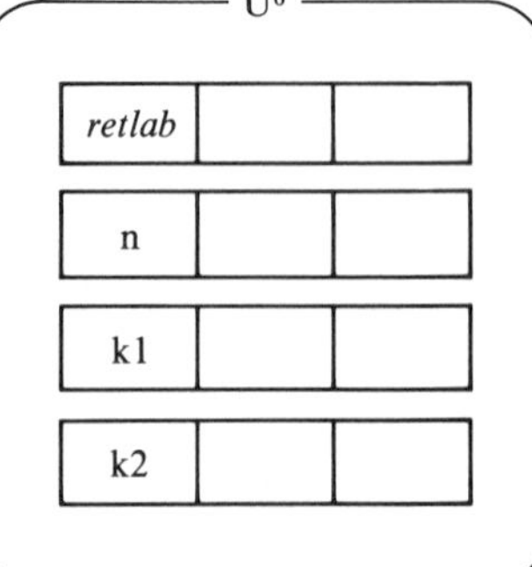

3-4 BINARY TREE TRAVERSAL

Although you understand the semantics of recursive algorithms, you still may not be convinced that recursion is a valuable or useful concept for practical applications. Certainly factorial and binomial coefficient values can be computed in a more straightforward way, using an iterative solution (and perhaps more efficiently as well). In this section we examine several more applications of recursion, each an application of the structure in Figure 3-50, which grew out of the insight we gained from the study of the binomial coefficient example.

First, we expand the structure of Figure 3-50 to that of Figure 3-53. Here we have placed "action clouds" at points marked A, B, C, D, and E to denote the places in the skeletal structure where useful work *appropriate to some particular application* may be specified. We now show applications that illustrate specified actions at each cloud.

Suppose the infix expression

$$(J + K) \times L/(M + N)$$

is currently represented in storage as the binary tree structure given in Figure 3-54a. As our first application, suppose we wish to print out the prefix representation

$$\times \underbrace{\underbrace{+\ J\ K}\ \underbrace{/\ L\ \underbrace{+\ M\ N}}}$$

of the stored expression shown in Figure 3-54a. What special action is needed? Well, a prefix form can be generated if, upon first encountering *any* node, terminal or nonterminal, the symbol associated with that node is typed out. Thus, to convert Figure 3-53 into an algorithm to print the prefix form of a stored binary expression tree, we need specify only one action, in cloud A, namely,

"type out the symbol associated with the current node."

This is because upon each entry to Binary_Tree_Walk, the parameter current_node designates the node being visited (encountered) for the first time during the traversal.

As a second application, suppose we wish to type out the infix representation of the stored expression. Notice that the infix form

$$J + K \times L/M + N$$

will be produced if we follow these two rules:

1. When encountering a terminal node, type out its associated symbol.
2. When encountering a nonterminal node *for the second time,* type out its associated symbol.

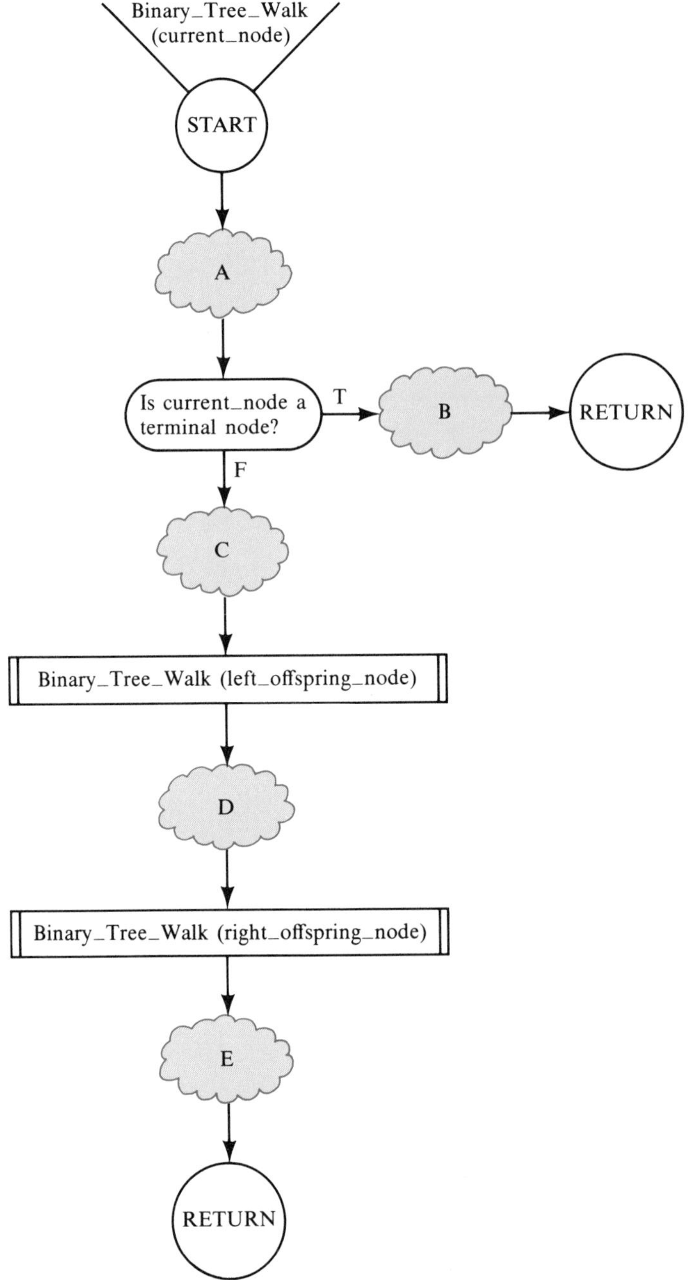

Figure 3-53. **Binary tree traversal algorithm with clouds to indicate where actions relative to the current node may be taken.**

Rule 1 will be followed if cloud B specifies the action

"type out the symbol associated with the current node,"

and rule 2 will be followed if cloud D specifies the same action.

Since the infix expression produced this way is ambiguous, we must put back at least the original parenthesis pairs. The process we use to do this will

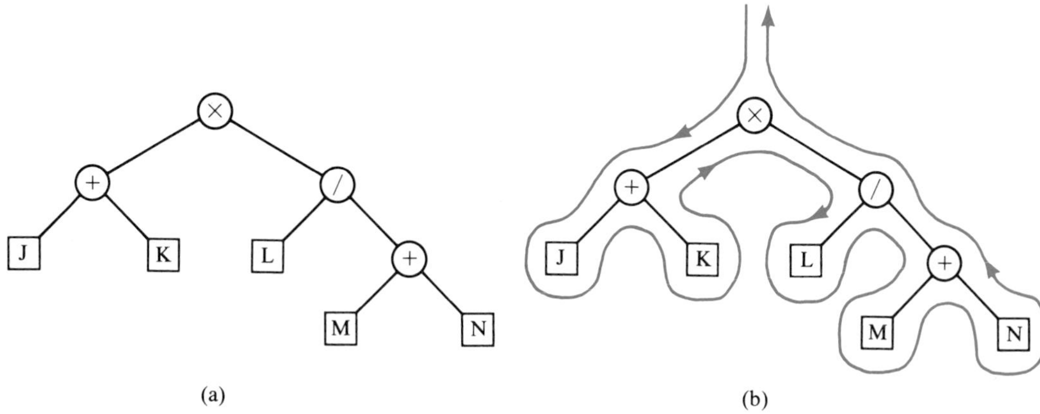

***Figure 3-54.* (a) Binary tree structure representation for (J + K) × L/(M + N). (b) Route of a natural-order tree traversal: note that each terminal node is "visited" once, but each nonterminal node is visited *three* times.**

actually add additional pairs that are, by our normal conventions, superfluous, yielding a fully parenthesized result. Thus to get

$$((J + K) \times (L/(M + N))),$$

we need to add two additional rules:

3. When encountering a nonterminal node for the first time, type out a left parenthesis.
4. When encountering a non-terminal node for the third time, "type out a right parenthesis."

Rule 3 is implemented simply by letting cloud C be the action

"type out a *left* parenthesis"

and rule 4 is implemented simply by letting cloud E be the action

"type out a *right* parenthesis"

To summarize, we see that traversing the binary expression tree to produce a prefix form utilizes action only at cloud A, while traversal to produce a parenthesized infix form uses actions at clouds B, C, D, and E.

Exercises 3-4

What rules are needed to traverse the binary expression tree for the purpose of typing out the *postfix* form, which in the example of Figure 3-54 would be

$$J\ K + L\ M\ N + / \times$$

What are the actions needed (and at what clouds) to implement these rules?

3-5
SYMBOLIC DIFFERENTIATION—AN APPLICATION OF BINARY TREE TRAVERSAL

Another familiar problem whose recursive solution has the structure of a tree traversal is *symbolic differentiation.* It is hard to think of the process of formal differentiation, as taught in Differential Calculus, *except* as a recursive procedure. This is because most of the operations of differentiation are defined recursively, never iteratively. (Moreover, although iterative versions for the differentiation procedure exist, they are much more complex in structure.) For example, consider the set of rules for differentiating with respect to x those algebraic expressions in x that involve the operations of + and ×.

The rules are

1. $\frac{dx}{dx} = 1$

2. $\frac{d\ \text{constant}}{dx} = 0$

3. $\frac{d(f + g)}{dx} = \frac{df}{dx} + \frac{dg}{dx}$

4. $\frac{d(f \times g)}{dx} = f \times \frac{dg}{dx} + g \times \frac{df}{dx}$

(rules 3 and 4:) where f and g are functions of x or constants

Using these rules, we know that, for instance,

$$\frac{d(17 \times x + 32)}{dx} = 17,$$

$$\frac{d((z + 32) \times z)}{dz} = 2z + 32.$$

We use the term *symbolic* differentiation since we are interested in producing formulas for derivatives. Such formulas could be used to produce numerical results, if desired. But how, in the past, did we apply these rules to get the quite plausible results? (We suspect the student who has passed a Differential Calculus course has not thought very much about the recursive algorithm used to solve such problems.) Notice that rules 3 and 4 are recursive in the sense that whenever rule 3 or rule 4 applies, one must make at least *two more* applications of the rules (as with the binomial coefficient algorithm). The "branching" to reapplications of the rules terminates whenever rule 1 or 2 applies. Rules 1 and 2 are nonrecursive and serve as the escape hatches for the procedure.

To be more specific, let us first recast this set of rules into a flowchart function procedure named D, with two parameters: the expression y, and the variable with respect to which we wish to differentiate, x. The flowchart for D is shown in Figure 3-55.

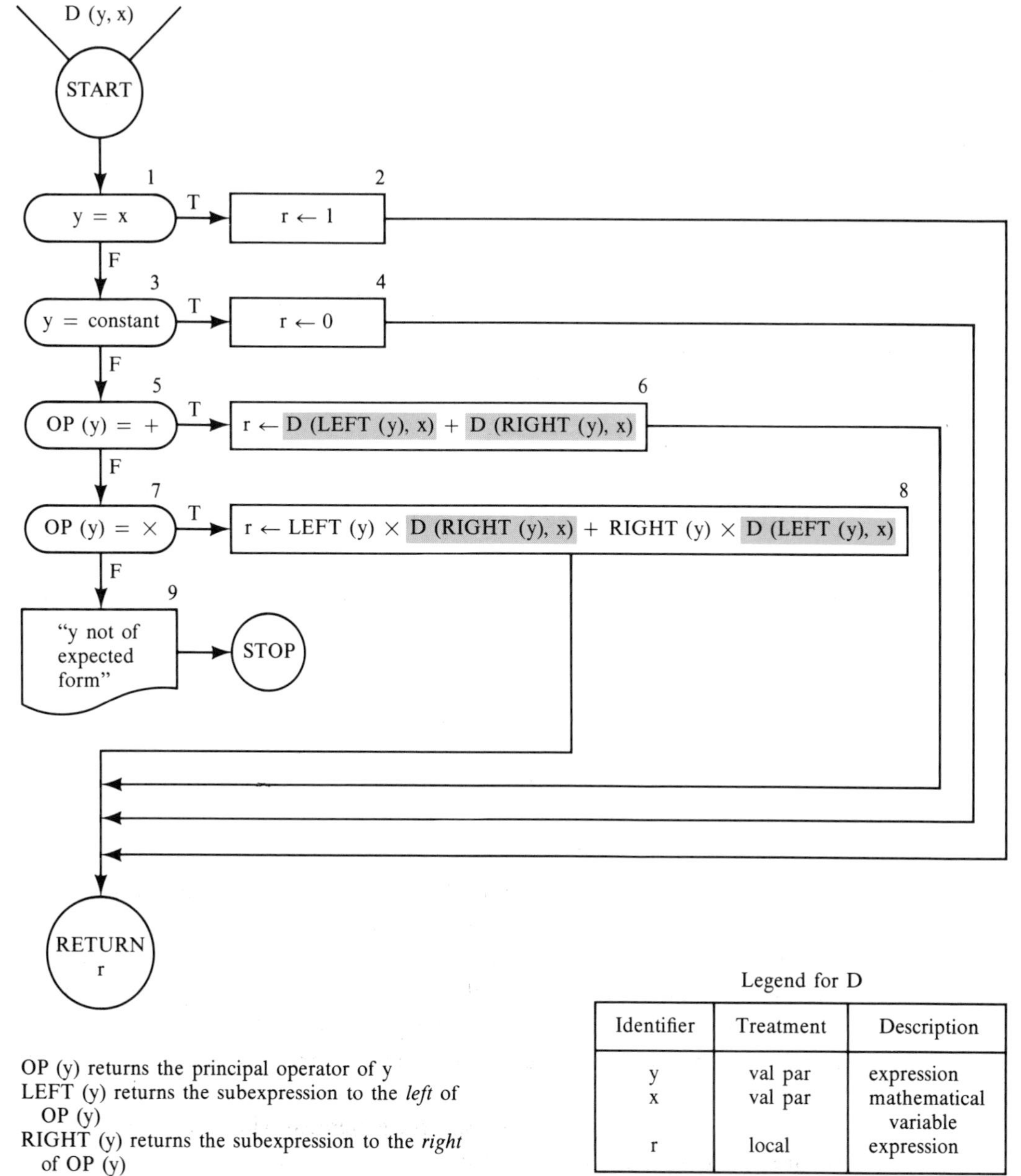

OP (y) returns the principal operator of y
LEFT (y) returns the subexpression to the *left* of OP (y)
RIGHT (y) returns the subexpression to the *right* of OP (y)

Legend for D

Identifier	Treatment	Description
y	val par	expression
x	val par	mathematical variable
r	local	expression

***Figure 3-55.* Conceptual flowchart to differentiate an algebraic expression y with respect to a mathematical variable x. (We deliberately avoid the question as to what internal form is used to represent expressions and variables.)**

In essence, boxes 1 and 2 implement rule 1, boxes 3 and 4 implement rule 2, etc. To make this procedure work on a computer, we need three auxiliary functions, OP, LEFT, and RIGHT. The function OP takes an expression y as an argument and returns the so-called principal operator, that is, the operator that corresponds to the root node of a (binary) tree representation of y. For

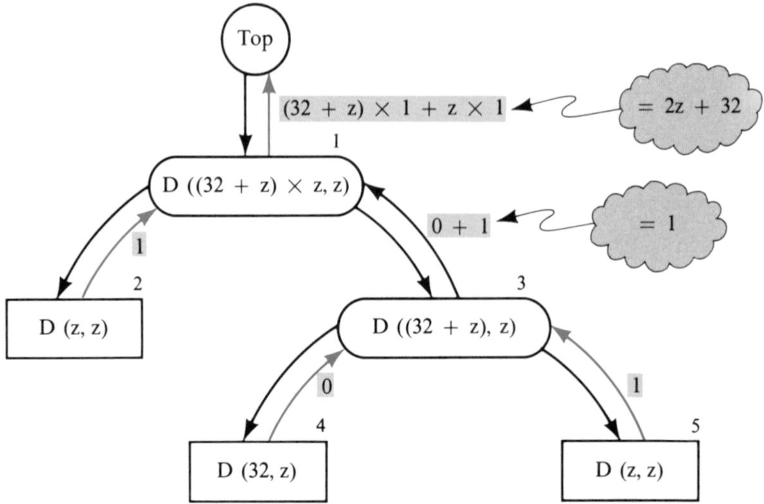

Figure 3-56. **Call tree for the computation D ((32 + z) × z, z).**

example, OP ((z + 32) × z) is ×, because the binary tree equivalent of (z + 32) × z is

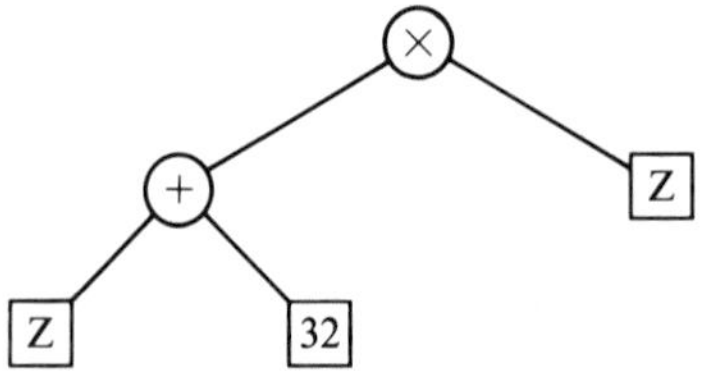

LEFT (y) and RIGHT (y) would return, in this case, z + 32 and z, respectively.

For this discussion we purposely avoid deciding how to represent values of the parameters y and x in computer storage. (The choice of strings, lists, trees, etc., should depend on how the procedures OP, LEFT, and RIGHT are to be implemented, and we prefer to "beg" this question here, since this will become a significant issue later when we implement these procedures in Lisp and Snobol.)

Figure 3-56 reveals the binary call tree generated when we use the D procedure to differentiate the expression

$$(32 + z) \times z.$$

Exercises 3-5

1 Develop the call tree for D (((b × (z × y)) + (c × z)) + a, z).

2 Generalize the flowchart for D in Figure 3-55 to cover cases where y may be an expression that also includes the subtraction and division operators, − and /, respectively.

3 For the generalized flowchart you developed in problem 2, develop a call tree for D ((2 × z)/((b × z) + 3), z).

4 Try to devise a flowchart for a purely iterative version ID of the procedure D given in Figure 3-55. Your procedure ID should neither call itself nor call any other procedure that, in turn, calls ID.

3-6 THE SEARCHING OF ARBITRARY TREE STRUCTURES

Some readers already have probably begun to race ahead with thoughts about how the algorithm of Figure 3-50 can be generalized to trees whose nonterminal nodes have three, four, . . . , or n subtrees. An *n-ary* tree is one whose every nonterminal node has exactly n offspring. One way to modify Figure 3-50 to handle the search of an n-ary tree is to replace boxes 2 and 3 with n such boxes. For example, if n = 4 as in the four-coloring of a map, we might consider the scheme in Figure 3-57.

Figure 3-57. **A recursive approach to the 4-ary tree traversal problem.**

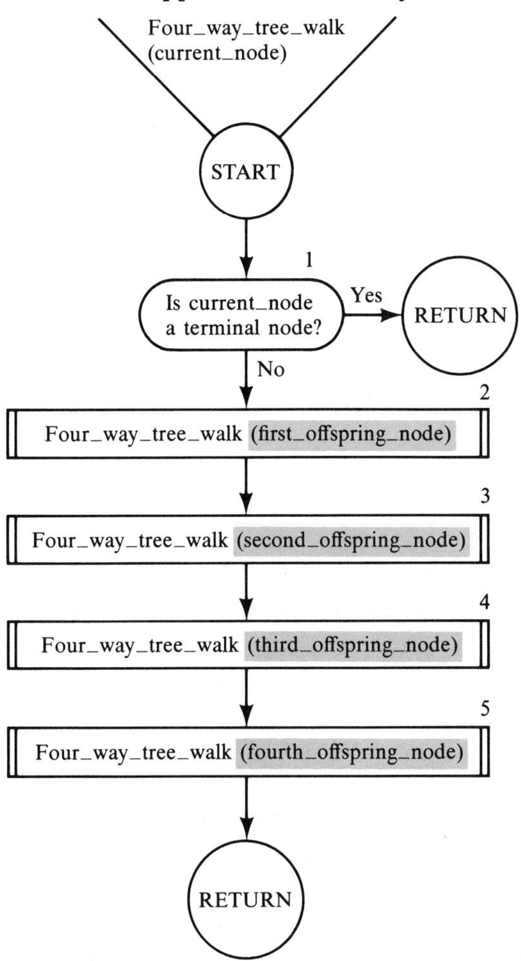

This approach is basically an unsatisfying solution but it does inspire us to see how to go about structuring an algorithm to traverse any tree, even a tree whose nonterminal nodes do not have a fixed number of offspring. Of course, an algorithm to search a general tree structure will also be capable of traversing any special, n-ary tree as well. The approach to be taken is sketched in Figure 3-58. Here we see a while loop controlling a sequence of recursive calls on the Tree_walk procedure, one call for each offspring of the node currently being considered. The structure sketched here is quite general and we attempt to apply it to several problems.

In an actual tree walk, it must be possible for the traversal algorithm to determine certain vital information associated with each node of the tree. In particular, the traversal algorithm must at least be able to determine for each node how many offspring it has. How is this information obtained in actual practice? Sometimes the information is found in a table or other data structure that serves as an explicit representation of the tree and its associated properties. In other cases the tree data are represented implicitly in the form of a set of rules or functions. We will not concern ourselves too much with these details here.

Figure 3-59 sheds considerable light on how an actual recursive tree-traversal procedure can be flowcharted. One detail that we need to consider is the representation of the path to a node in the tree. To illustrate with an example, the path to the node marked "X" in the tree

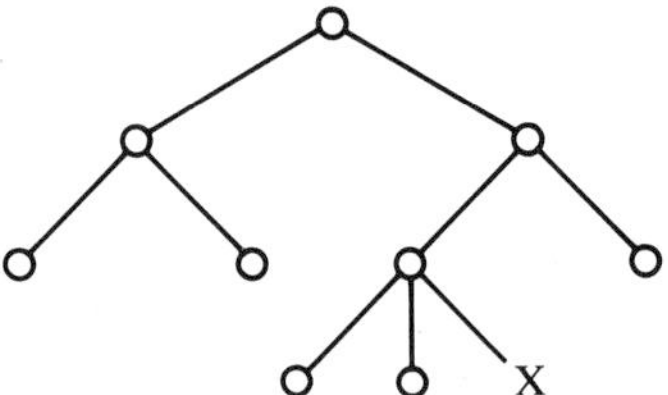

can be represented by the list

$$\text{path} = (2, 1, 3)$$

meaning "to get to X, follow segment 2 (numbered left-to-right) out of the root, then segment 1 out of the next node encountered, then segment 3 out of the next node." [We are using path = (2, 1, 3) as a shorthand for $\text{path}_1 = 2$, $\text{path}_2 = 1$, $\text{path}_3 = 3$.] The variable called length has as its value the number of segments in the path, and so in this case length = 3. The path to the root node is "empty," for which length = 0. We use the notation path = ( ) for the empty path.

When the Treewalk procedure of Figure 3-59 is called, the pair of arguments matching the value parameters path and length, furnished by the top-level program, always represent the root node. To determine whether a node is a terminal node, the algorithm appeals to a function SEGTOTAL, which in turn somehow has access to the representation of the tree. SEGTOTAL returns the number of offspring of the node represented by *path.* If zero, the node is a terminal node; otherwise the value returned by SEGTOTAL is used as the

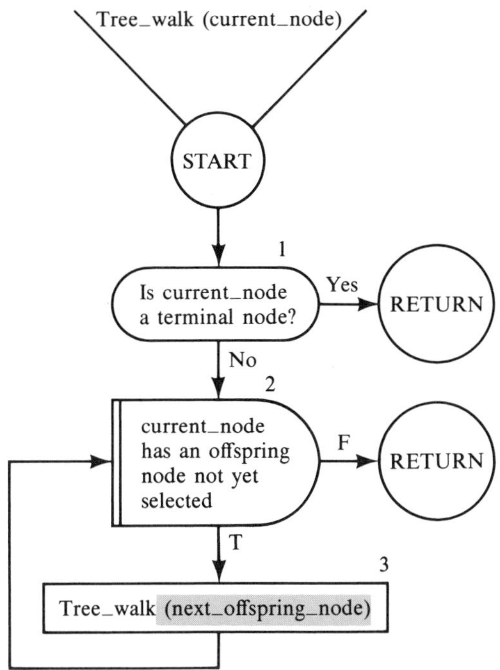

Figure 3-58. **Recursive structure for a generalized tree traversal.**

upper bound in the iteration box that controls the number of recursive calls on Treewalk from the given node. The argument list for each such call requires new values for path and length. Box 4 assigns values to the individual elements of a path list. The function Append (whose details are purposely suppressed) forms a new list called newpath, which represents the offspring node serving as the root of the subtree earmarked for traversal by the call on Treewalk in box 5.

Additional sophistication can, of course, be added to the traversal strategy. For example, we might add an "admissibility check" to avoid searching subtrees that are, for some reason pertinent to a particular application, not to be traversed. The addition of these details is left for the exercises.

Our final concern is to convert the traversal algorithm into a *search* algorithm. While a traversal must "visit" *every* node in the tree, a search should be allowed to halt when some node with a desired attribute is encountered.

Figure 3-60 suggests how a search algorithm can be developed from the structure of the traversal algorithm. There are two important new features in this algorithm:

1. The details of box 1 of Treesearch, were they provided, would have to refer to the representation of the tree, which would be a global data base or function, able to retrieve a recorded property associated with each node. Such details, as those of the function SEGTOTAL, depend on the data representation chosen for the particular problem.

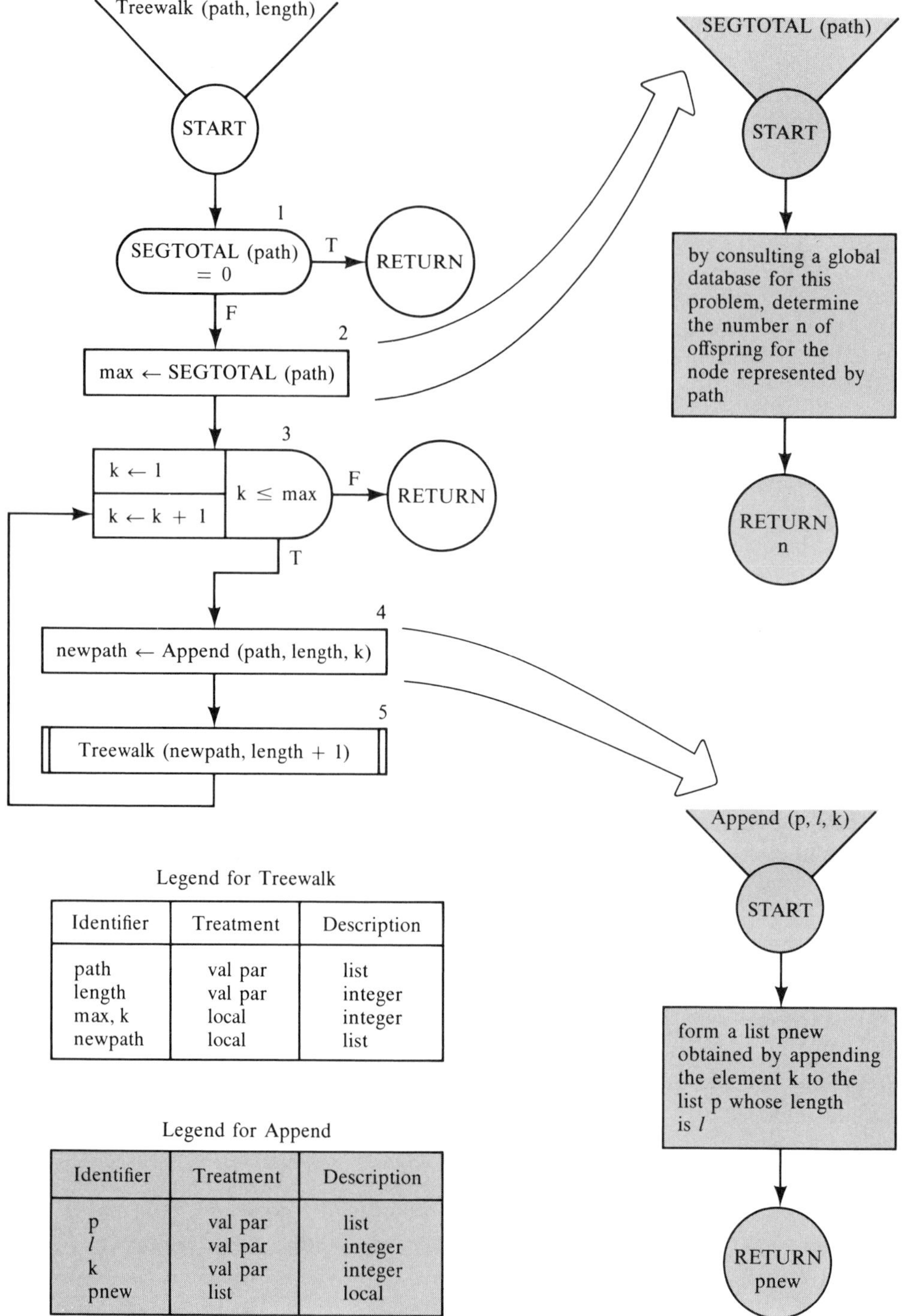

Legend for Treewalk

Identifier	Treatment	Description
path	val par	list
length	val par	integer
max, k	local	integer
newpath	local	list

Legend for Append

Identifier	Treatment	Description
p	val par	list
l	val par	integer
k	val par	integer
pnew	list	local

Figure 3-59. **Partial detail for recursive Treewalk.**

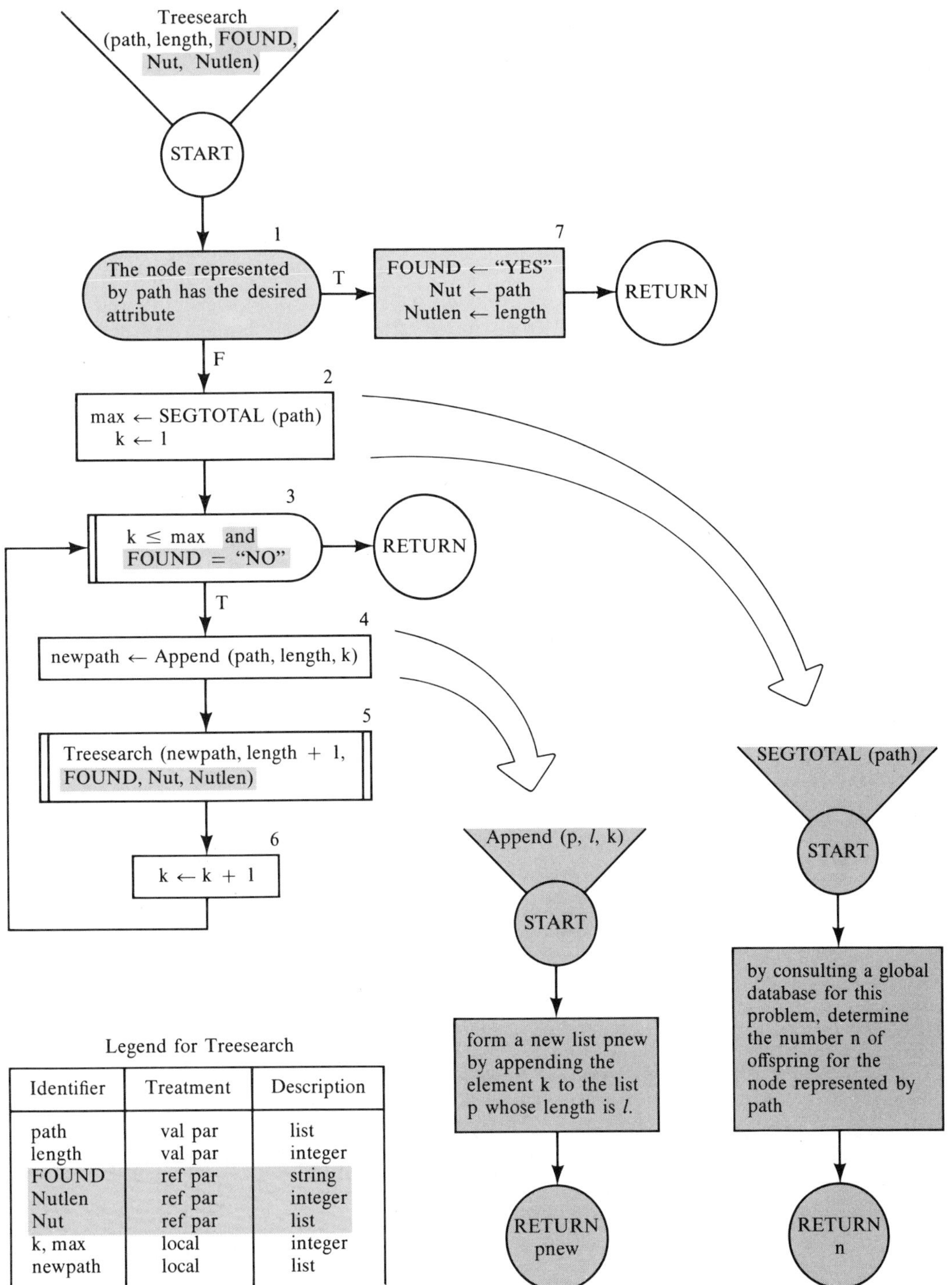

Identifier	Treatment	Description
path	val par	list
length	val par	integer
FOUND	ref par	string
Nutlen	ref par	integer
Nut	ref par	list
k, max	local	integer
newpath	local	list

Figure 3-60. **Partial detail for recursive Treesearch.**

2. At least one more parameter is needed, in this case a reference parameter called FOUND, to force return from each call in the current chain of recursive calls. For clarity we also introduce two other reference parameters. Nut is used to return the description of the path to the (first) node found to have the desired attribute, and Nutlen is used to return the *len*gth of Nut. By setting FOUND to "YES" as soon as the desired node is found, any remaining returns still "pending" will be executed without further search of the tree. At the same time that FOUND is set to "YES", the current value of path and its length are *captured* by assignment to Nut and Nutlen. Notice that if no node is found with the appropriate attribute, the full tree will be traversed and FOUND will never be set to "YES".

A top-level program, including a sequence of the form shown in Figure 3-61, can invoke the search procedure and thereby learn whether the search has been successful. The tree search strategy, like that of Treewalk, can also be improved by introducing steps to determine, for a particular application, whether or not a node is "admissible" as a potentially successful candidate. Again we leave such improvements to the exercises.

***Figure 3-61.* A portion of Top.**

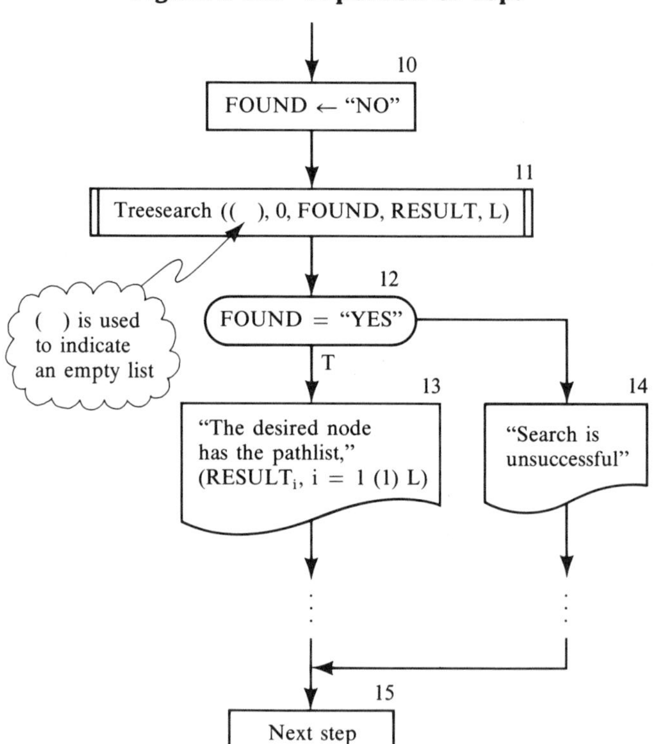

Exercises 3-6

1 Complete a trace table that *audits* the execution of Treewalk (Figure 3-59) for traversal of the following tree. Assume that in the call that invokes Treewalk the arguments for path and length are ( ) and 0, respectively, where ( ) represents the empty list. What is the maximum length of the chain of calls on Treewalk during traversal of this tree?

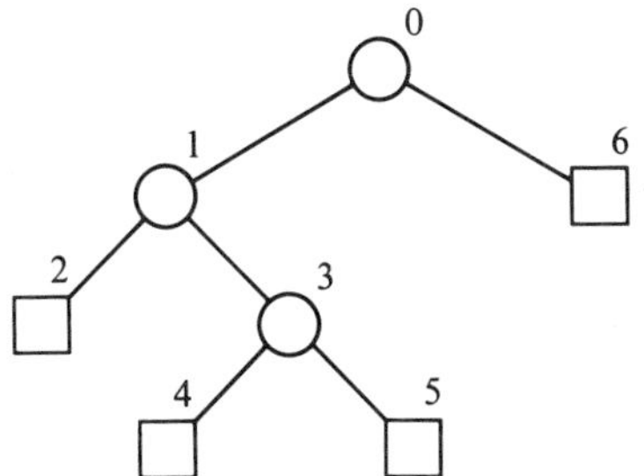

2 Complete a snapshot sequence (begun with Figures 3-62, 3-63, 3-64) that traces the execution of Treesearch (Figure 3-60) in the search for the first nut in the following tree.

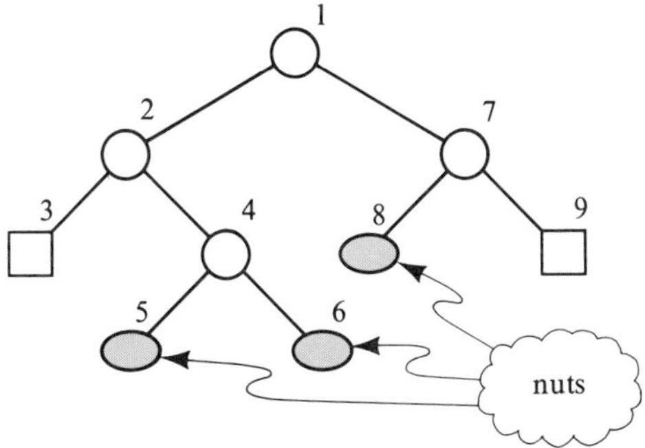

Assume that in the call from Top (in Figure 3-61) that invokes Treesearch, these three "input" arguments are given to match the first three parameters:

path = ( )
Length = 0
FOUND = "NO"

Figure 3-62

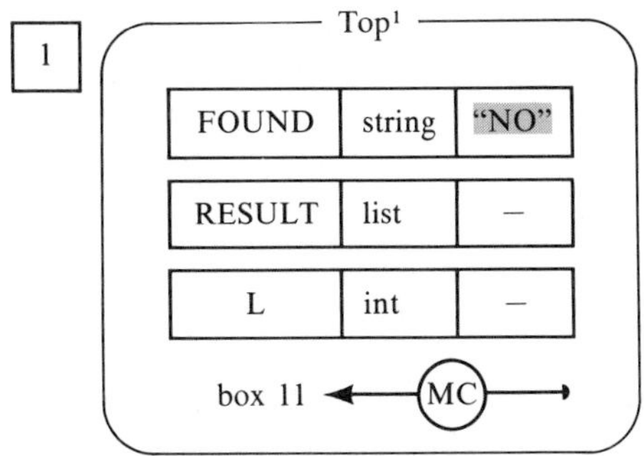

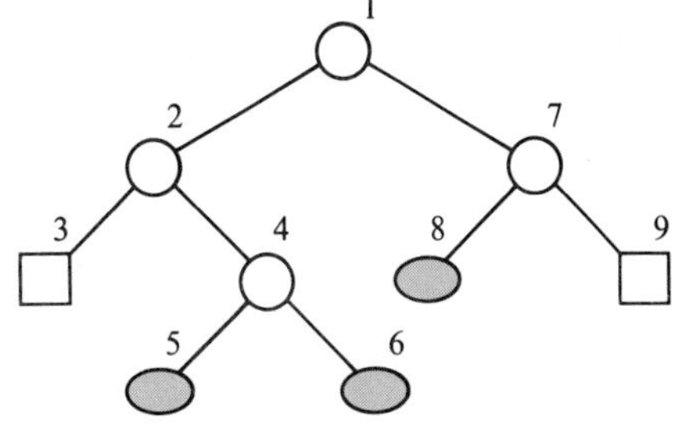

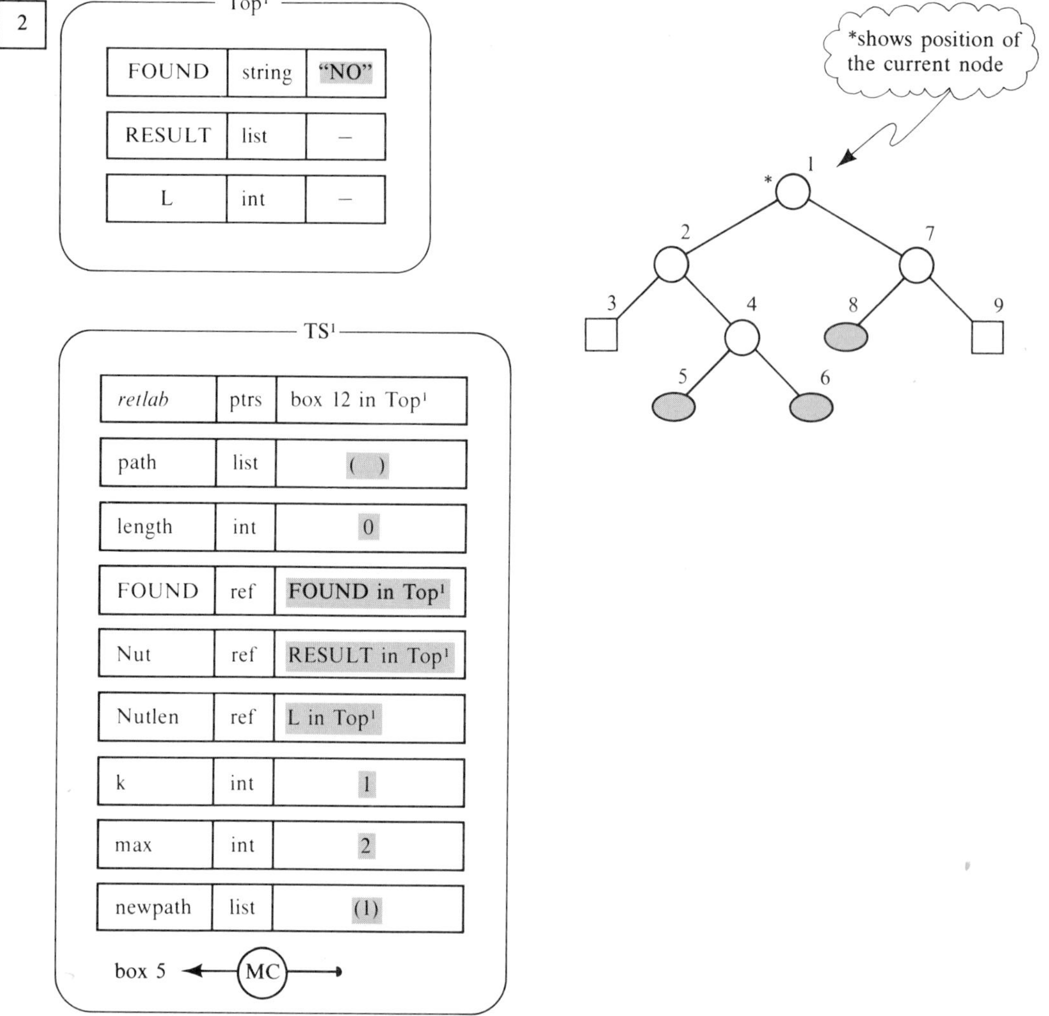

Figure 3-63

where ( ) represents the empty list. Pay special attention during this trace to the steps that ensure returns from the chain of calls when the nut at node 5 is discovered. The value of nut, upon return to the main program, should be (1, 2, 1). Be sure you understand why this is so before you continue.

3 Modify the Treewalk algorithm of Figure 3-59 to include provision for "pruning" as the traversal proceeds. That is, before the subtree defined by each node is "walked," have the algorithm execute steps to test for admissibility of the current node. You do not, however, have to show how information on admissibility is represented.

4 Show what modifications to the Treesearch algorithm are needed to eliminate the need for the reference parameters Nut and Nutlen.

5 Prepare modifications to the Treesearch algorithm (Figure 3-60) similar to those described in Exercise 3.

6 Study the four-coloring algorithm given in Figure 6-24 of *Computer Science: A First Course,* Forsythe *et al.* (1975a) or study the slightly altered version of the algo-

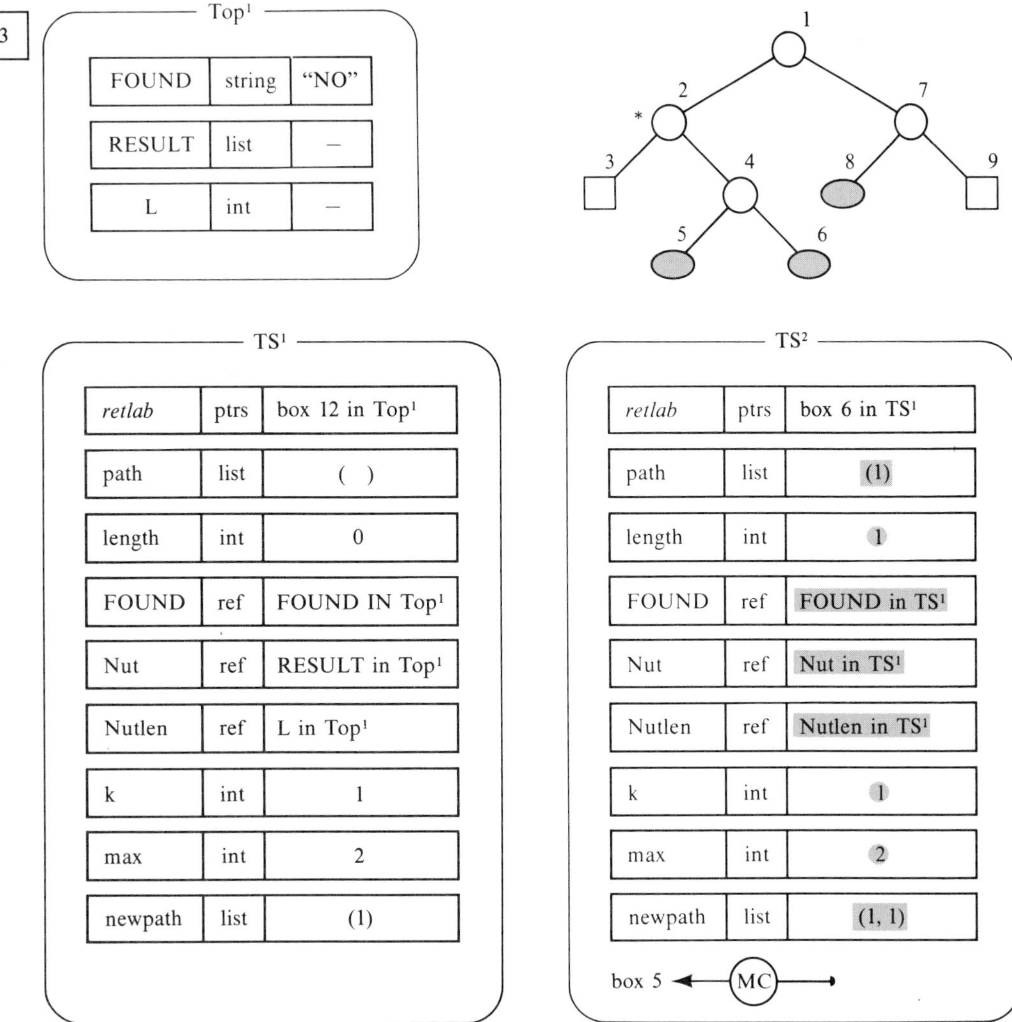

Figure 3-64

rithm given as Figure 10-12 of this book. Adapt the Treesearch algorithm that you prepared in Exercise 5, and substitute it for the nonrecursive version used in Figure 6-24. Comment on the simplifications, if any, that result from this substitution.

7 Study the flowcharts and legends of Figure 3-65 and answer the following questions. *Note:* In answering all parts of this question use the input data

$$n = 4, \quad (Ch_i, i = 1\ (1)\ 4) \quad = \quad (\text{"Y"}, \text{"U"}, \text{"B"}, \text{"A"})$$

(a) What argument value matches the parameter k at the time the F exit is taken from Box 1 in Design?
(b) Draw a snapshot of the state of execution of the algorithm when Box 3 of Design has just been executed for the third time in the second invocation of Design.
(c) At the time control returns to Top from Design show the total output that will have been printed by Box 4 of Design.

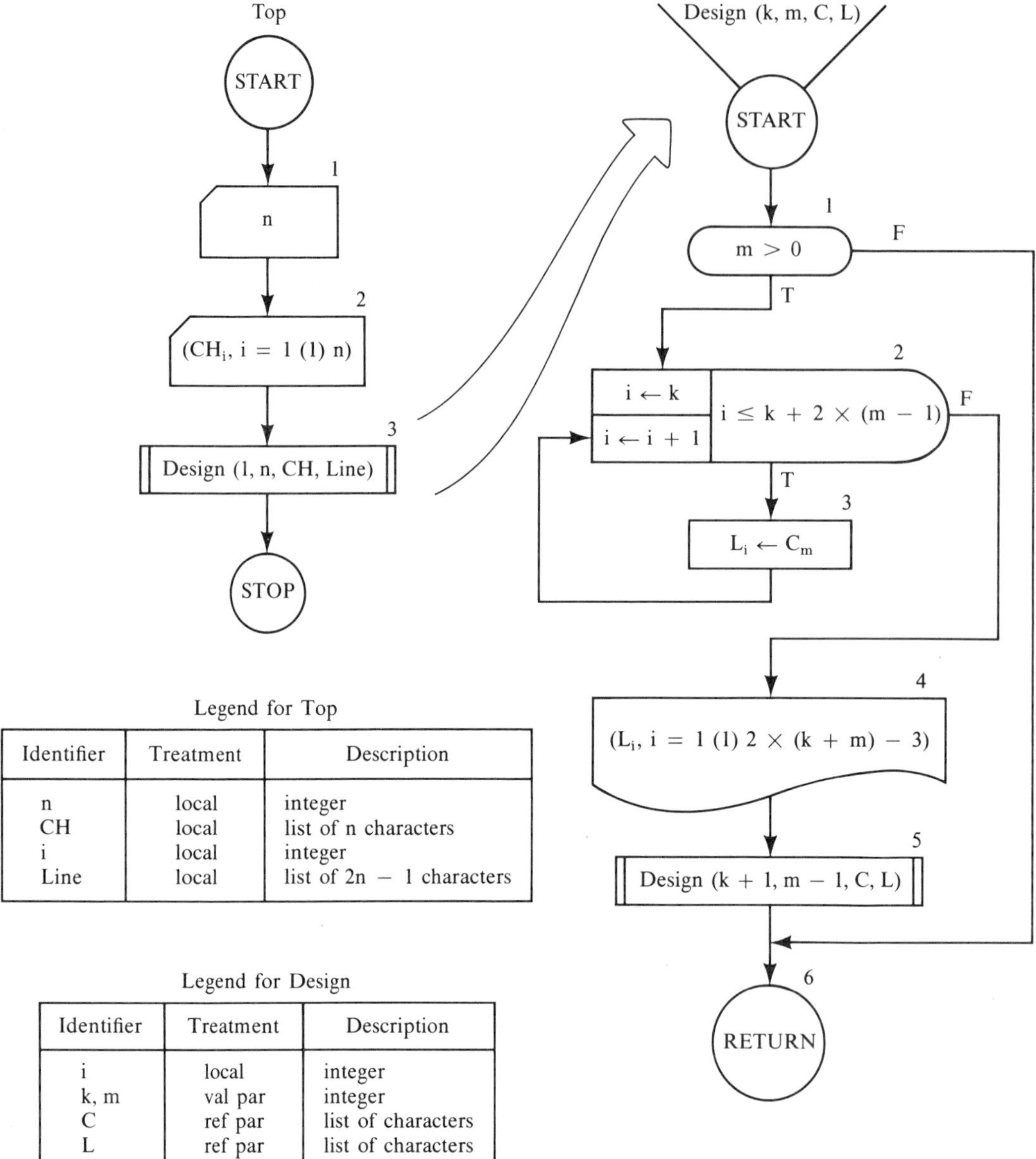

Legend for Top

Identifier	Treatment	Description
n	local	integer
CH	local	list of n characters
i	local	integer
Line	local	list of 2n − 1 characters

Legend for Design

Identifier	Treatment	Description
i	local	integer
k, m	val par	integer
C	ref par	list of characters
L	ref par	list of characters

Figure 3-65

(d) If the parameter L in Design is treated as a value parameter instead of a reference parameter, what change, if any, will result in the outputs of Box 4?

(e) In the interest of declaring storage for lists as late as possible, it is proposed that in the procedure Design we change L from a reference parameter to a local variable. Design will then have only three parameters k, m, and C. Will this change have any effect on the total output? If so, explain the effect.

8 The Towers of Hanoi puzzle is probably familiar to most readers. We are given a board from which three posts project (Figure 3-66). On the left post is a stack of graduated disks such that the bottom one has the largest diameter and no larger disk

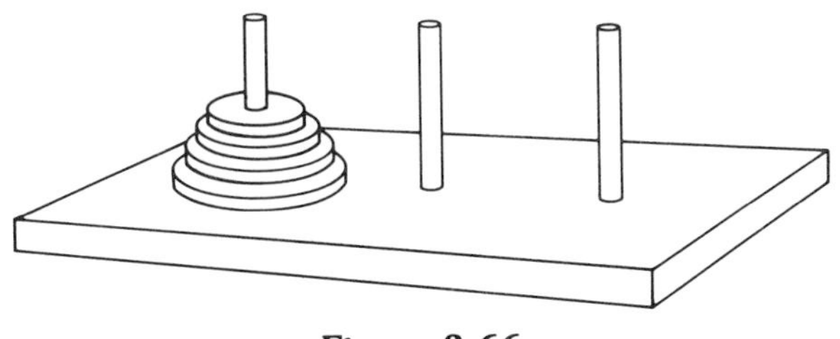

Figure 3-66

rests on a smaller one. The problem is to devise an algorithm for moving n disks from the left post to the right post, observing the two following rules:

1. Only one disk can be moved at a time.
2. No disk is ever to rest on a smaller one.

The algorithm should print a set of instructions that a person can follow to move all the disks to the right post (in a legal way).

A simple recursive solution to this problem is suggested by the following strategy: If $n \geq 2$, we can give general names for the posts involved in the operation and proceed as follows:

(a) Move the *top n − 1 disks* from the *from-post* to the *intermediate post.*
(b) Move the *nth disk* from the *from-post* to the *to-post.*
(c) Move the *n − 1 disks* from the *intermediate post* to the *to-post.*

Notice that this recursive approach guarantees that at each level the largest ("remaining") disk is always moved by itself to an empty post so it is clearly on the bottom. Also notice that steps (a) and (c) amount to recursive calls to reemploy the same method, so the algorithmic solution will give rise, during its execution, to a binary tree of procedure calls.

For $n = 2$ the task requires 3 instructions and for $n = 3$, $3 + 3 + 1 = 7$ instructions are required. In general, it takes $2^n - 1$, which can be a very large number of instructions! Devise a recursive algorithm (flowchart and legend) to solve this puzzle for an arbitrary number of disks but, if you actually try out your algorithm, use $n \leq 7$. Call your procedure Hanoi with parameters FP, TP, and n, where FP and TP are the post names, standing for *f*rom-*p*ost and *t*o-*p*ost, and n is the number of disks in the Tower. Let IP (*i*ntermediate *p*ost) be a local identifier in HANOI. If the posts are identified by 1, 2, and 3 then IP = 6 − (FP + TP). If the posts have no numerical designation then some other simple means must be devised to evaluate IP.

3-7 REFERENCES AND SUGGESTIONS FOR FUTURE READING

Although it is one of the major intellectual tools of programming, the subject of recursion usually receives only minimal treatment in elementary texts on computer science. [An outstanding exception is the introductory text by Perlis (1975).] Our chapter utilizes contour diagramming techniques to expand the treatment of recursion found in Chapter 9 of Forsythe *et al.* (1975a). Indeed, many of the same exercises are used. In contrast, most texts that include recursion or recursive programming techniques, such as Barron (1968), discuss these topics only in the context of particular programming languages. Implementation of recursion is discussed in Pratt (1975).

4 SYNTAX FORMALISM

4-1 INTRODUCTION

Comprehension of the syntax of any programming language is greatly improved when its informal description, conveyed by means of illustrations and case studies, is supplemented by *formal definition.* A formal definition for a language syntax is a set of rules for forming valid programs in the language. These rules are often expressed as formulas (sometimes as flowcharts) that must be strictly applied. Studying a language with the aid of a formal syntax definition ensures that we have an accurate understanding of what can, and cannot, be expressed in that language. Since we intend to look at not one but several languages in quick succession in the second part of this book, there is added incentive for us to use whatever formal methods (formula tools) are available to reinforce our case study approach.

The most widely used scheme to define syntax formally is the so-called Backus–Naur Form (BNF). It was first applied in defining Algol syntax, but is also useful, perhaps with simple amplifications, for many other languages. Other schemes are used to define syntax, and each has certain advantages. However, since our main purpose is not to study syntax, and certainly not to study how to study syntax, this brief chapter examines mainly the Backus–Naur method, illustrating how to use it in several language contexts. The ideas presented here will be applied in the second part of this book.

4-2 THE BNF NOTATION

A BNF definition of a language syntax is a set of syntax rules, formulas, or "equations." With this set of equations, sometimes called "productions," it is theoretically possible to *generate* all legal programs of that language. The same set of rules may be used to *recognize* whether or not a given text is a legal program in that language.

Each syntax rule amounts to a definition. What is being defined appears on the left, and the definition appears on the right. A possible rule might be

⟨declaration⟩ ::= ⟨procedure declaration⟩|⟨variable declaration⟩

This rule is to be read as follows: "A declaration is defined to be a procedure declaration or, alternatively, a variable declaration." The angle brackets around the character sequences "declaration," "procedure declaration," and "variable declaration" make each sequence refer to a *class of objects*. Thus ⟨declaration⟩ means "any member of the class of objects that can be regarded as a declaration," that is, any object that is an instance of a declaration. The special mark ::= means "is defined to be," and the special mark | means "or, alternatively."

Notice that the above definition of a declaration may be regarded as incomplete, in the sense that the reader is assumed to know what a procedure declaration is and what a variable declaration is. Of course there must be accompanying definitions for both ⟨procedure declaration⟩ and ⟨variable declaration⟩, if the definition of ⟨declaration⟩ is to be complete. But the definition of ⟨procedure declaration⟩ may also be expressed in terms of other object classes, for example,

⟨procedure declaration⟩ ::= ⟨function declaration⟩ | ⟨subroutine declaration⟩

These, in turn, may require further definition, in top-down fashion, much as we might progress from the root of a tree to a set of one or more terminal nodes. Ultimately we arrive at object classes defined entirely in terms of the specific symbols of the language, like characters and digits. For example,

⟨arithmetic operator⟩ ::= + | − | × | / | ↑

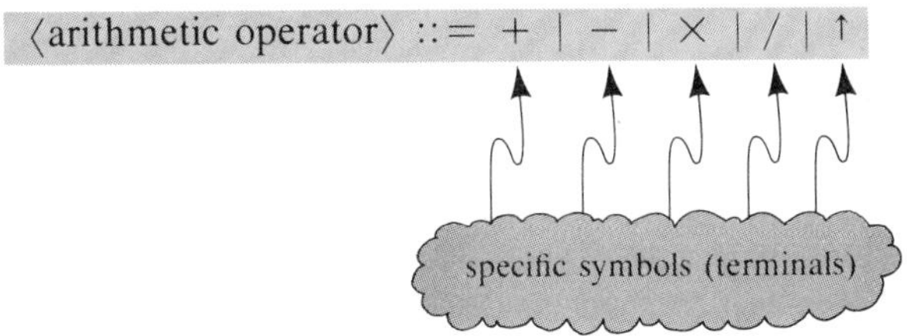

Within any BNF definition a specific object (atom), or terminal, is distinguishable from a nonterminal, or object class, by the absence of angle brackets.

One more notational detail is needed to complete the description of BNF notation. Any particular alternative in the right-hand side of a syntax rule may consist of more than one object or object class, that is, a concatenation of several objects and/or object classes, in sequence. Such concatenation is denoted simply by juxtaposition, placing the things one beside the other, in the intended order. For example:

⟨assignment statement⟩ ::= ⟨arith. variable⟩ = ⟨arith. expression⟩ |
⟨logical variable⟩ = ⟨logical expression⟩

defines the syntax of an assignment statement for a language that uses the equals symbol (=) to represent assignment. The equals symbol is one of the terminals of the language. We read this formula as: "an assignment statement is defined to be an instance of an arithmetic variable, followed by the equal symbol, followed by an instance of an arithmetic expression, or alternatively, an instance of a logical variable, followed by the equals symbol, followed by an instance of a logical expression."

A special one-element class known as ⟨empty⟩ denotes the null or empty string, that is

⟨empty⟩ ::=

For example, we might define the printed form of an integer as an integer prefixed by a sign, but only if negative:

⟨print integer⟩ ::= ⟨print sign⟩⟨unsigned integer⟩
⟨print sign⟩ ::= − | ⟨empty⟩

One reason BNF is a powerful notation is that it permits recursive definition of syntactical forms, allowing us to describe syntactical forms whose structures are inherently recursive. For example, the following is a recursive rule:

⟨unsigned integer⟩ ::= ⟨digit⟩ | ⟨unsigned integer⟩⟨digit⟩

From this definition, and from the additional rule

⟨digit⟩ ::= 0 | 1 | 2 | 3 | 4 | 5 | 6 | 7 | 8 | 9

it is easy to see, for instance, that 3, 31, 317, 3174, etc. are all examples of unsigned integers. The reasoning goes something like this:

Since an unsigned integer may be a digit and since a digit may be 3, it follows that 3 is an unsigned integer. Now, since an unsigned integer may be an unsigned integer (3) followed by a digit, and a digit may be 1, then 31 is an unsigned integer. By repeating this reasoning we can quickly conclude that 3174 is an unsigned integer. An even simpler, recursive definition can be used to define the syntax of sequences. For example, a sequence of one or more integers separated by commas can be defined as

⟨integer sequence⟩ ::= ⟨integer⟩ | ⟨integer⟩,⟨integer sequence⟩

Exercises

1 Explain to what extent the definition

⟨integer sequence⟩ ::= ⟨integer⟩ | ⟨integer sequence⟩,⟨integer⟩

is equivalent and/or different from the one given above.

2 Would the following redefinition of an integer sequence, which allows the sequence to be *empty*, be satisfactory? Explain.

⟨integer sequence⟩ ::= ⟨empty⟩ | ⟨integer⟩ | ⟨integer⟩,⟨integer sequence⟩

One BNF representation of a sequence of objects encloses the sequence element in curly brackets. The right bracket is subscripted to indicate the minimum number of elements, and may be superscripted to indicate the maximum number of sequence elements. Thus, to define an identifier as any sequence of one or more juxtaposed letters, we could write

$$\langle\text{identifier}\rangle ::= \{\text{letter}\}_1$$

as a shorthand in place of

$$\langle\text{identifier}\rangle ::= \langle\text{letter}\rangle | \langle\text{identifier}\rangle \langle\text{letter}\rangle$$

To define an identifier as consisting of a letter followed by a sequence of none, one, or up to five letters or digits, we could write

$$\langle\text{short identifier}\rangle ::= \langle\text{letter}\rangle \{\langle\text{letter}\rangle | \langle\text{digit}\rangle\}_0^5$$

This notation is especially useful for defining the syntax of languages like Fortran.

As a final example, we show two ways to define a parenthesized list of parameters that may be empty, that is, ( ), or contain one or more parameters separated by some defined separator mark, for example, a comma.

(a) ⟨parameter list⟩ ::= (⟨p-list⟩)|(⟨empty⟩)
    ⟨p-list⟩ ::= ⟨parameter⟩|⟨parameter⟩ ⟨separator⟩ ⟨p-list⟩
    ⟨separator⟩ ::= ,

(b) ⟨parameter list⟩ ::= (⟨p-list⟩)
    ⟨p-list⟩ ::= ⟨empty⟩|⟨parameter⟩ {⟨separator⟩ ⟨parameter⟩}$_0$
    ⟨separator⟩ ::= ,

Because most readers are already familiar with at least one programming language, it may be useful to examine some of the more familiar linguistic constructs to see how they can be defined using BNF.

Consider the IF statement as used in Basic, Fortran, and Algol.

Examples

Basic

```
IF    T < El    THEN    490
```

is an instance of the more general form given by

$$\langle\text{if statement}\rangle ::= \text{IF } \langle\text{relation}\rangle \text{ THEN } \langle\text{label}\rangle$$

where ⟨relation⟩ and ⟨label⟩ must be defined further.

Fortran

```
IF    (3 + X) 20, 30, 40
```

and

IF (ABS(Y) .GT. 2.5) Z = T + 4

are instances of the general forms, given by

⟨if statement⟩ ::= ⟨arithmetic if⟩ | ⟨logical if⟩
⟨arithmetic if⟩ ::= IF(⟨arithmetic expression⟩)⟨neglabel⟩,⟨zerolabel⟩,⟨poslabel⟩
⟨neglabel⟩ ::= ⟨label⟩
⟨zerolabel⟩ ::= ⟨label⟩
⟨poslabel⟩ ::= ⟨label⟩
⟨logical if⟩ ::= IF (⟨logical expression⟩)⟨unconditional statement⟩

where again such object classes as ⟨arithmetic expression⟩, ⟨label⟩, and ⟨logical expression⟩ require further definition (in top-down fashion).

Algol

if *c* < *31.4* **then** *a* := *16* **else** *b* := *16*

and

if *c* < *a* + *b* **then** *t* := *time*

are instances of the general form given by

⟨conditional statement⟩ ::= ⟨if statement⟩ | ⟨if statement⟩ **else** ⟨statement⟩
⟨if statement⟩ ::= ⟨if clause⟩⟨unconditional statement⟩
⟨if clause⟩ ::= **if** ⟨Boolean expression⟩ **then**

where object classes such as ⟨statement⟩, ⟨unconditional statement⟩, and ⟨Boolean expression⟩ require further definition.

Given a BNF description of a language or some object class (syntactic category), such as a Fortran IF statement, it is relatively easy to decide on the validity of a candidate member (instance) of that class. Often the analysis consists of attempting to construct a *parse tree* for the candidate class member, based on the relevant BNF definitions. A parse tree of an object is nothing more than a hierarchic structure of syntax subcategories of the object. The hierarchic structure comes directly from the relevant BNF equations. The candidate is proved valid when a one–one correspondence (in left-to-right order) can be established between terminal nodes of the parse tree and the symbols of the candidate. The candidate is proved invalid when it can be shown that no such match (correspondence) can be achieved.

As an elementary example, we can use the parse tree of Figure 4-1 to determine that 1233 is a valid unsigned integer, based on the definitions given earlier. For a more elaborate example, the parse tree will be deeper.

Consider the question, "Is

IF (ABS(Y) .GT. 2.5) Z = T + 4

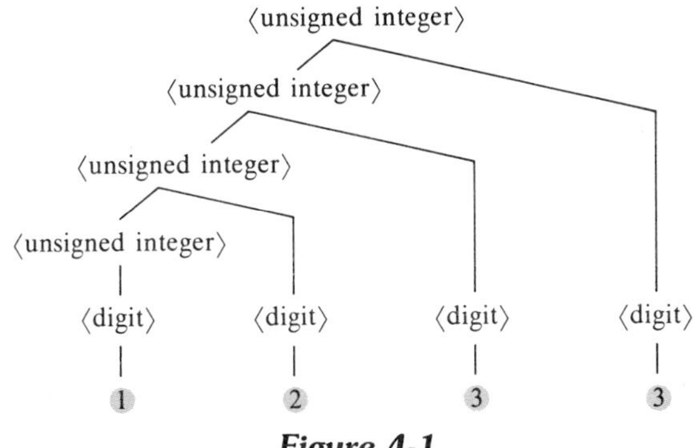

Figure 4-1

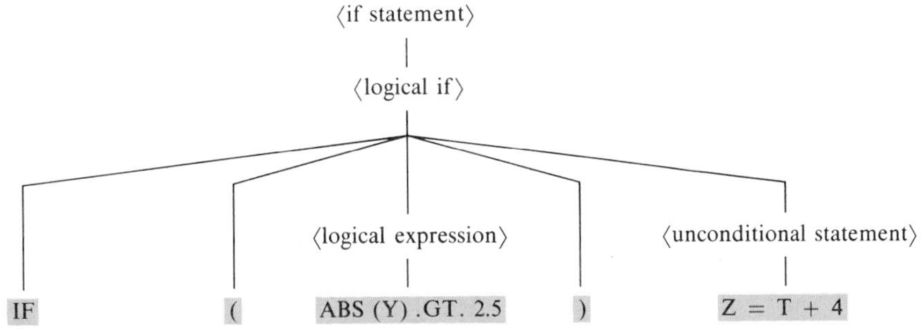

⟨if statement⟩

⟨logical if⟩

⟨logical expression⟩ ⟨unconditional statement⟩

IF (ABS (Y) .GT. 2.5) Z = T + 4

Figure 4-2

a valid Fortran IF statement?" We produce only an incomplete parse tree in Figure 4-2, but for some purposes this may be sufficient. (Again the tree is derived from definitions given earlier.)

We see that the candidate statement is syntactically correct if and only if we can be sure that "ABS(Y) .GT. 2.5" is a valid instance of ⟨logical expression⟩, and if "Z = T + 4" is a valid instance of ⟨unconditional statement⟩. If we are ready to make the "mental leap" and say yes to each of these "conjectures," then the partial parse tree is adequate. If not, we must consult additional BNF definitions and parse the subtrees for ⟨logical expression⟩, and ⟨unconditional statement⟩, as far as necessary, to reach the answer to our original question.

4-3 SYNTAX CHARTS

Instead of the equation format of BNF definitions, one can use a graphical equivalent, known as a *syntax chart*, which is a form of flowchart. A few examples will quickly suggest the concept and the potential value of this form of syntax formalism: Syntax chart equivalents to the previously-given definitions for unsigned integer (Figure 4-3), integer sequence (Figure 4-4), parameter

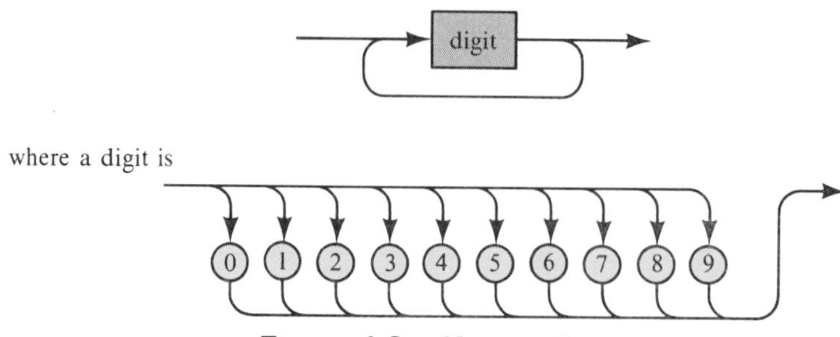

Figure 4-3. **Unsigned integer.**

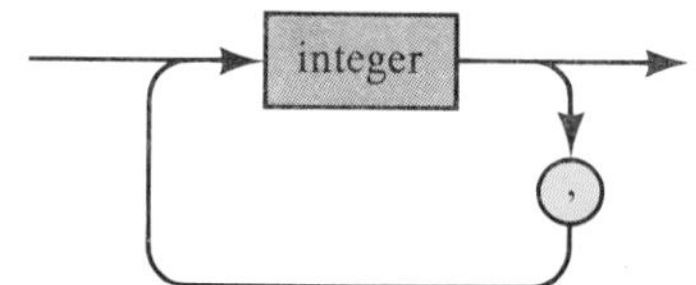

Figure 4-4. **Integer sequence.**

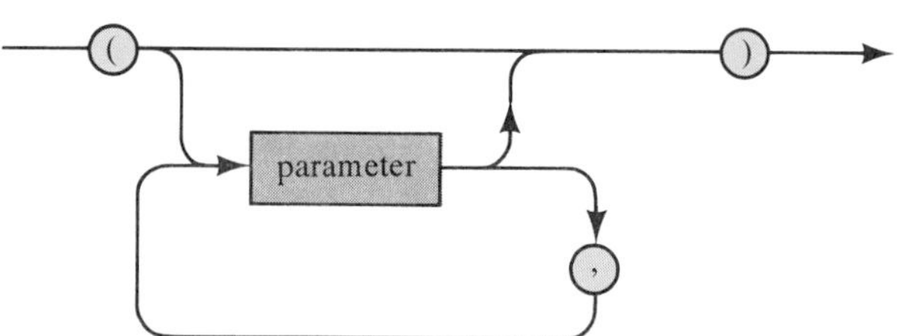

Figure 4-5. **Parameter list.**

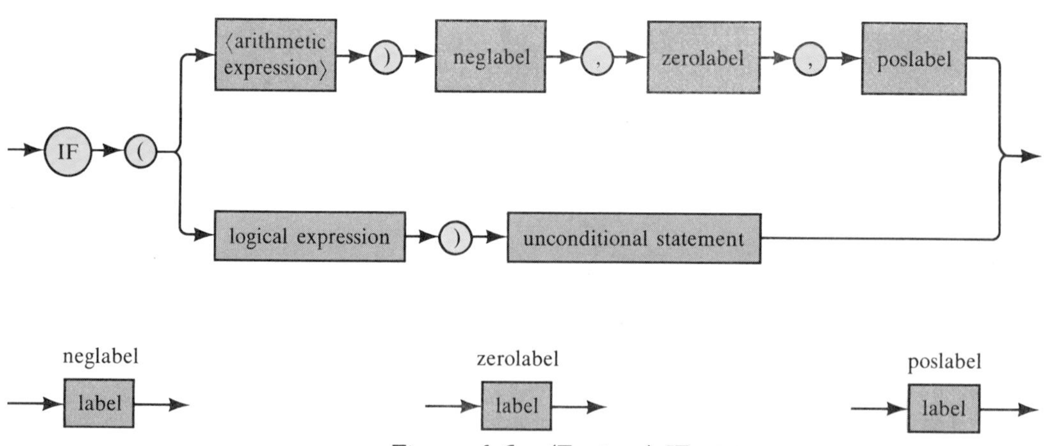

Figure 4-6. **(Fortran) IF statement.**

list (Figure 4-5), and (Fortran) IF statements (Figure 4-6) are illustrated. Each item in a circle or oval represents a terminal symbol or symbol string of the language being defined, and each item in a rectangle represents a nonterminal of the language, which is presumably defined by a companion chart definition. Each chart is to be read by following a path from its beginning on the left to its end on the right. Recursion in a definition is achieved by looping along the path.

SUMMARY

A formal description of a widely used language like Fortran, Basic, or a dialect of Algol usually consists of tables of from 50 to 200 correct and consistent BNF equations or syntax charts. Spread over no more than a few pages, they are easy to use as reference documents. When a question arises on a fine point of a language syntax, one consults the syntax table and in a very few minutes can usually answer a question that might otherwise take hours to answer by checking through relevant texts, examples, or by experimentation with actual computer programs.* In the chapters that follow, BNF definitions are used to make our descriptions of language syntax more concise and precise. The full BNF description of one language (ALGOL 60) is given in the Appendix.

4-4 REFERENCES AND SUGGESTIONS FOR FURTHER READING

A more complete introduction to syntax formalism can be found in Chapter 9 of Pratt (1975), which also contains a useful list of references. Aside from the precise definition of the syntax of particular programming languages, the most important application of syntax formalism has been in the development of compilers and translators [Gries (1971) and Aho and Johnson (1974)].

The introductory texts by Ullman (1976) and Wegner (1968) also include chapters or sections on methods for the formal description of language syntax (grammar) and its application. A rich and useful theory has been developed [Aho and Ullman (1972)].

*A compiler for a language L must somehow contain or have access to a correct formal syntax definition of language L. That is why, when syntax errors occur in a program, a compiler can scan it, and find and mark the errors. Indeed, compilers are often constructed, and sometimes automatically generated, from BNF syntax specifications.

list (Figure 4-5), and (Fortran) IF statements (Figure 4-6) are illustrated. Each item in a circle or oval represents a terminal symbol or symbol string of the language being defined, and each item in a rectangle represents a nonterminal of the language, which is presumably defined by a companion chart definition. Each chart is to be read by following a path from its beginning on the left to its end on the right. Recursion in a definition is achieved by looping along the path.

SUMMARY

A formal description of a widely used language like Fortran, Basic, or a dialect of Algol usually consists of tables of from 50 to 200 correct and consistent BNF equations or syntax charts. Spread over no more than a few pages, they are easy to use as reference documents. When a question arises on a fine point of a language syntax, one consults the syntax table and in a very few minutes can usually answer a question that might otherwise take hours to answer by checking through relevant texts, examples, or by experimentation with actual computer programs.* In the chapters that follow, BNF definitions are used to make our descriptions of language syntax more concise and precise. The full BNF description of one language (ALGOL 60) is given in the Appendix.

4-4 REFERENCES AND SUGGESTIONS FOR FURTHER READING

A more complete introduction to syntax formalism can be found in Chapter 9 of Pratt (1975), which also contains a useful list of references. Aside from the precise definition of the syntax of particular programming languages, the most important application of syntax formalism has been in the development of compilers and translators [Gries (1971) and Aho and Johnson (1974)].

The introductory texts by Ullman (1976) and Wegner (1968) also include chapters or sections on methods for the formal description of language syntax (grammar) and its application. A rich and useful theory has been developed [Aho and Ullman (1972)].

*A compiler for a language L must somehow contain or have access to a correct formal syntax definition of language L. That is why, when syntax errors occur in a program, a compiler can scan it, and find and mark the errors. Indeed, compilers are often constructed, and sometimes automatically generated, from BNF syntax specifications.

Syntax and Semantics of Several Major Programming Languages

PART TWO

To understand any programming language, including our own flowchart language, one must know its *syntax* and its *semantics*. The syntax of a language is the set of rules by which one forms correctly written programs, including statements and expressions. The semantics of a language is the set of rules for interpreting, that is, determining the *meaning* of, a correctly written program. The meaning of a program is the set of actions expected to occur and the set of results, if any, produced when that program is executed.

The rules for determining the meaning of a computer program in a given language are sometimes expressed mathematically. *Mathematical semantics* is especially useful for interpreting the formulas and expressions of mathematics and of some classes of computer algorithms. For computer programs of interest to us it appears best to express operationally the rules for determining meaning. *Operational semantics* are rules based on the behavior of some machine, often an abstract machine, that carries out specific and predictable sequences of actions when directed to execute any command or step of a program. The computer model presented in the first chapters of this book is an example of an abstract machine. Because we know the way this model works, we can state rather precisely what will happen when it executes any step of a flowchart. In fact, the design specifications of this model, that is, how it is to behave in all situations, constitute the semantics of our flowchart language.

The semantics of other languages such as Algol, Lisp, Cobol, Fortran, or Snobol are also of great interest. Each language differs from the others in both syntax and semantics. In this book we are most concerned with the semantic similarities and differences. However, it is not practical to discuss the semantics of a given language divorced entirely from its syntax. Thus we find that some attention to the syntax of each language is necessary.

Fortunately the syntaxes of most programming languages we are interested in have a great deal in common. The differences are largely superficial (cosmetic). In fact, one way we can minimize these differences in syntax is to let our flowchart language serve as a common medium. For example, when we want to compare the same algorithm expressed in different languages, say ALGOL 60 and Fortran, a *flowchart* expression of the algorithm often serves as a useful point of departure.

In this book we take up a series of everyday programming languages, one by one, starting with ALGOL 60. The semantics of each language is explained as a departure from (or modification of) the semantics of the computer model developed earlier.

Computations coded in the languages we study in this part of the book give rise to data structures having some hierarchical ordering, in particular, the data structures evolve in nested environments. To exploit this fact, we will represent hierarchical ordering as diagrams having contours nested one within another. Besides being easy to understand, contour diagrams can be produced relatively easily by a computer, either automatically, or as requested within the program itself. It may be that the now tedious job of producing easy-to-understand traces of program execution will be taken over by the computer. Then the semantics of a programming language can be studied by examining various types of derived contour diagrams for programs written in that language. The comparative semantics of two or more programming languages can, in some sense, be understood by comparing contour diagram snapshots for corresponding states of execution of equivalent computations. To the extent we are successful in seeing similarities and differences in such snapshots we shall have hit upon a unifying theme for discussing the semantics of a wide variety of programming languages.

ALGOL

5

5-1 INTRODUCTION

Scientists all over the world use ALGOL 60 as perhaps *the* principal reference language for communicating, describing, and discussing algorithms. Designed by an international group of scientists, ALGOL 60 derived its name from the terms *algo*rithmic *l*anguage and the fact that the detailed language specification was reported in 1960. There have been many variations and extensions of ALGOL 60: Euler, ALGOL-W, ALGOL 68, BURROUGHS EXTENDED ALGOL, and Pascal, to name a few. These variations typically allow the programmer to handle easily a broader class of data structures than was treated directly in ALGOL 60. ALGOL 60 undoubtedly profited from the experience gained in the design of Fortran, which appeared in 1956. In turn, ALGOL 60 and Fortran have had a strong influence on several later programming languages such as PL/I and PL/C.

Programs in Algol-like languages have a recursive treelike syntactic structure known as *block structure.* In Section 5-2, block structure is introduced with the ideas generalized, here and there, to cover the family of Algol-like languages. After that we focus on ALGOL 60 and specialize the rest of the chapter to this one language, at the same time dropping the 60 and referring to ALGOL 60 as simply ALGOL.

5-2 SYNTACTIC STRUCTURE OF ALGOL-LIKE LANGUAGES

An overview of the syntactic structure of Algol-like languages is necessary to appreciate their semantics, that is, in order to understand how the language designers intended that programs be executed. To discuss programs further we need the concept of a block.

A *block* is an ordered pair of objects consisting of a *head* h and a *body* b. A head, in turn, consists of a sequence of one or more declarations D, and a body, in turn, consists of a sequence of one or more statements S. You will recall that a declaration classifies an identifier, for example, as real or integer if it is a

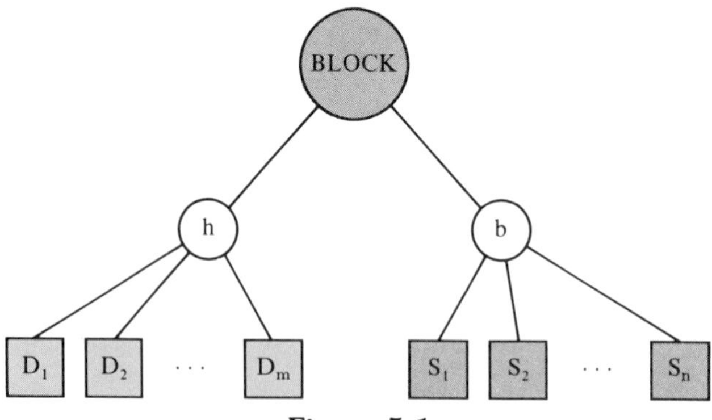

Figure 5-1

number, and that statements are commands to be executed. Thus an Algol-like block has the structure of Figure 5-1.

The general purpose behind block structure is to make apparent what declarations are valid when the statements in the body of any block are carried out. In other words, the statements of the body are executed in an environment determined by the declarations contained in the head of the block.

Now that we know what a block is, we introduce two rules, the second of which is clearly recursive:

1. A *program* is a block.
2. Any statement contained in a block may itself be a block. Thus any statement in the body of a block may be a structure consisting of a head (sequence of declarations) and a body (sequence of statements.)

A program tree structure illustrating this point is shown in Figure 5-2a, where we identify the entire program as the block B_1. In the body of B_1 the second and fourth statements are the blocks B_2 and B_3, respectively, each showing characteristic block structure. B_2 and B_3 are said to be *nested* within block B_1 and block B_3 has the block B_4 nested within it. Thus block B_4 is nested within B_3 which is nested within B_1.

Because block B_2 is nested inside block B_1, the statements in the body of B_2 are to be executed, not only in the environment determined by the declarations in the head of B_2, but also *secondarily,* in the environment determined by the declarations in the head of B_1. The word "secondarily" is used to convey the fact that declarations in B_1 play a supplementary role to those of B_2 and are consulted only when the declarations of B_2 do not supply information required for the execution of the body of B_2. When B_4 is nested within B_3, which is nested within B_1, the same idea is carried one step further. In executing the body of B_4, the declarations in the head of B_4 are consulted first. If a necessary piece of information is missing, the declarations in the head of B_3 are consulted next, and finally those in the head of B_1.

We can illustrate these ideas graphically by looking at them in terms of the MC, executing the program structure of Figure 5-2a, using the model developed in Chapters 1 and 2. First the MC causes a $B_1{}^1$ contour to be constructed in which to execute the program and allots a cell for each identifier described by the

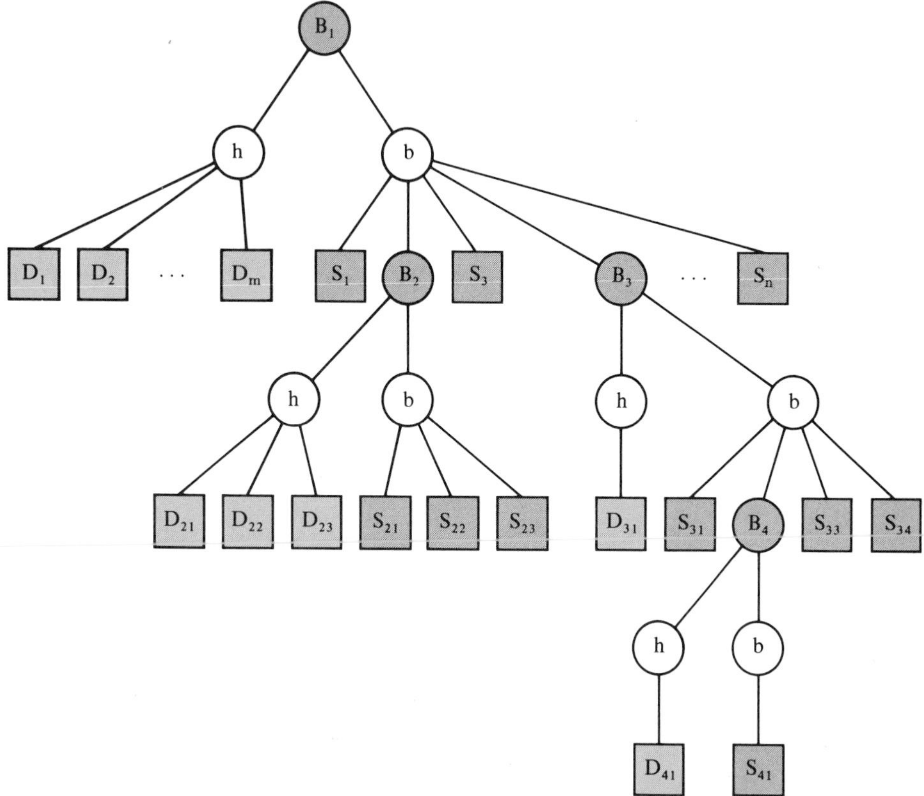

Figure 5-2a. **Program structure with nested program blocks.**

declarations D_1, D_2, . . . , D_m. Then the MC enters that environment and prepares to execute the first statement S_1, as shown in Figure 5-2b. So far all this is familiar.

Now the MC, in contour $B_1{}^1$, prepares to execute the block B_2. To represent the hierarchy of the block structure, he causes the $B_2{}^1$ contour to be constructed *inside* the $B_1{}^1$ contour, allots the cells required by declarations D_{21}, D_{22}, and D_{23}, moves inside, and prepares to execute the statement S_{21}, as shown in Figure 5-2c.

Figure 5-2b. **The MC about to execute the first statement in block B_1 of Figure 5-2a.**

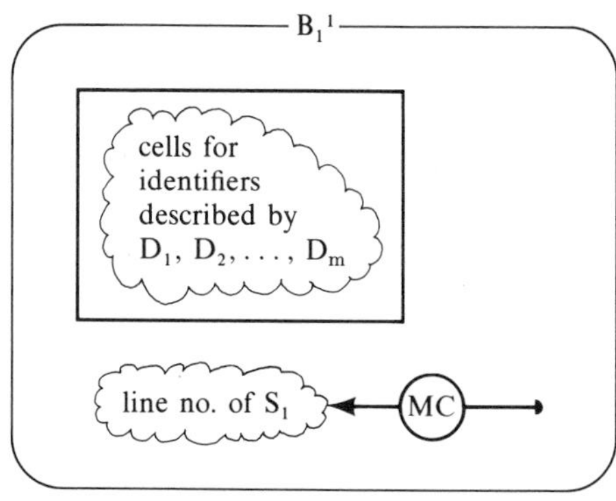

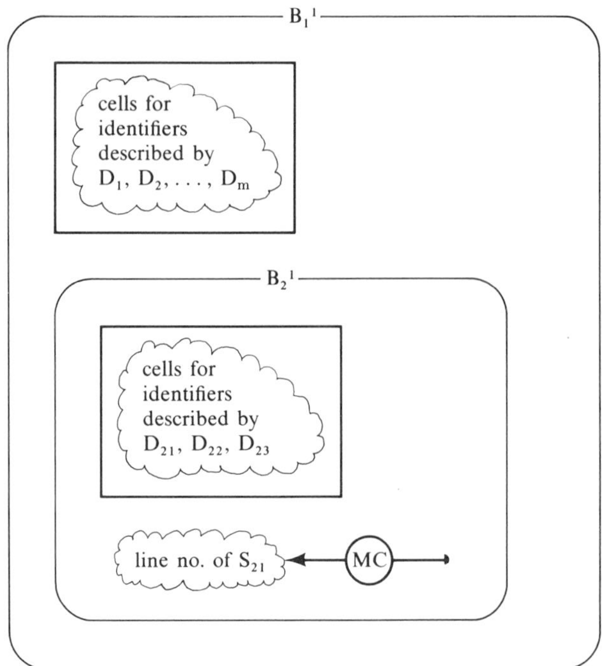

Figure 5-2c. **The MC about to execute the first statement in block B_2 of Figure 5-2a.**

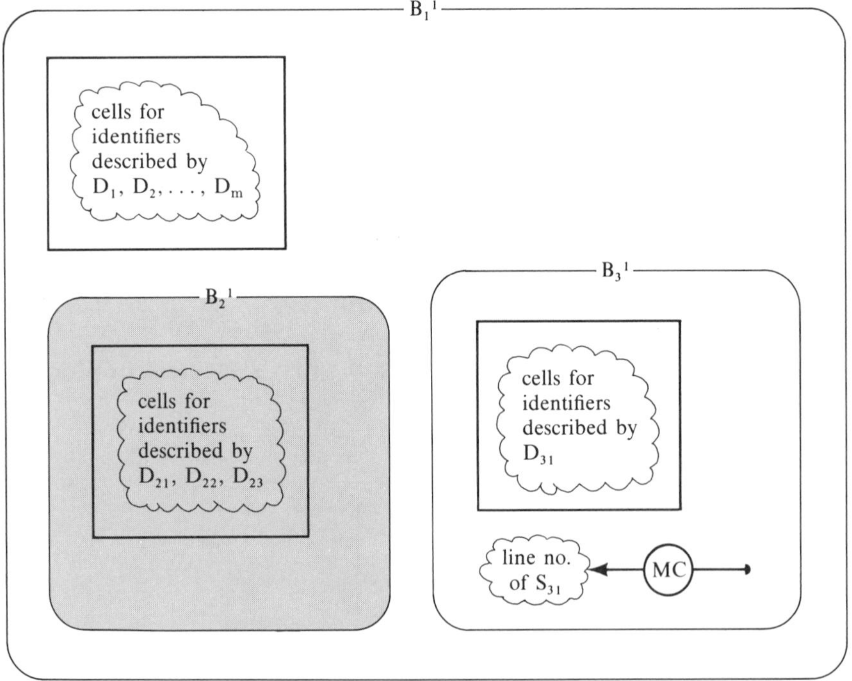

Figure 5-2d. **The MC about to execute the first statement in block B_3 of Fig. 5-2a.**

After the MC has executed S_{21}, S_{22}, and S_{23} from within contour $B_2{}^1$, he steps outside, back into contour $B_1{}^1$ to execute statement S_3. The $B_2{}^1$ contour is no longer accessible. The accessible environment looks like Figure 5-2b again, except that the MC's ip points to the line number of statement S_3.

When the MC, still in contour $B_1{}^1$, is ready to execute block B_3, he causes a contour $B_3{}^1$ to be constructed inside $B_1{}^1$. Figures 5-2d and 5-2e show the environments as the MC prepares to execute the first statements of blocks B_3 and B_4, respectively, of Figure 5-2a. To locate the cell for any identifier at any time, the MC first consults the cells in the contour where he is operating and then, successively, those of the enclosing contours. In Figures 5-2d and 5-2e, the $B_2{}^1$ contour appears shaded, to indicate that it is not accessible. We could have simply omitted drawing it.

In other words the static nesting of the blocks determines what declarations apply in the body of any block: the declarations in the head of the given block are consulted first and then, if necessary, the declarations in the heads of the successively enclosing blocks.

There is a second syntactic structure, very similar to a block, that plays an equally important role in Algol-like languages. This is the *procedure declaration,*

***Figure 5-2e.* The MC about to execute the first statement of block B_4 of Figure 5-2a.**

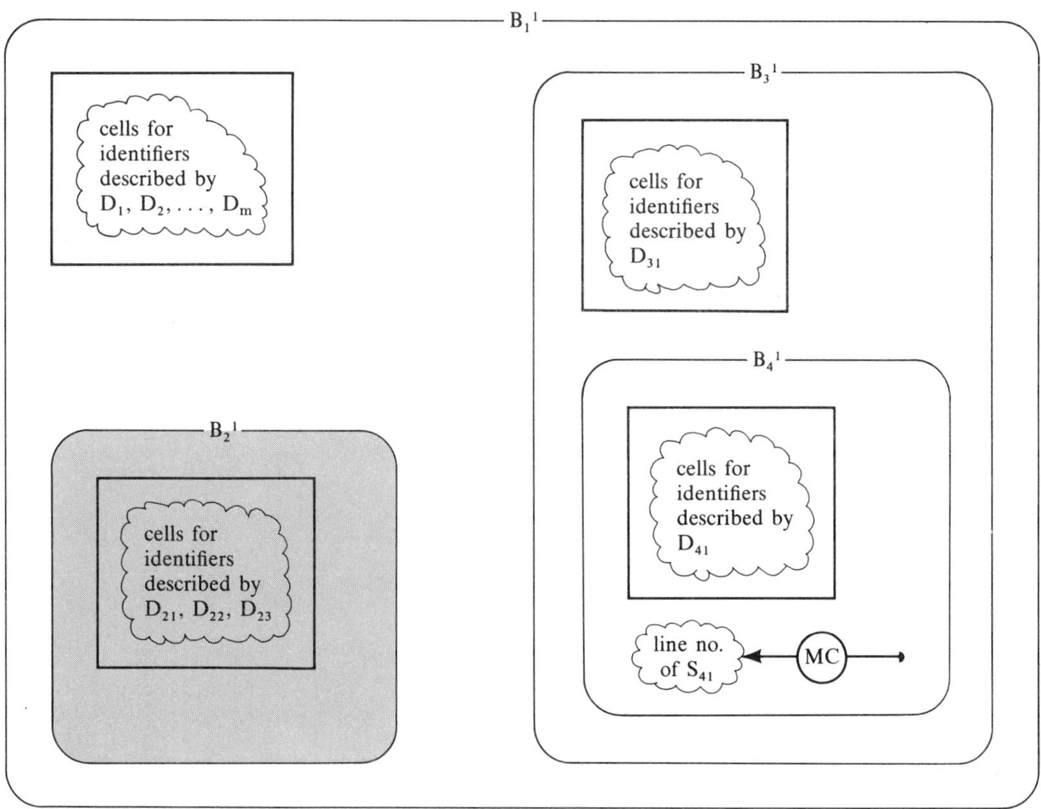

which, like the block, has a head and a body. The head consists of a series of declarations and the body consists of a single statement.

Although it may seem restrictive to allow only one statement in the body of a procedure declaration, actually it is not at all, because that statement may be a block. There also exists a structure called a *compound statement;* a compound statement is a sequence of statements bound together into a unit. The body of a procedure may also be a compound statement, as in Figure 5-3.

We restate the second (recursive) rule to include procedure declarations, and add a third (recursive) rule:

2. Any statement within a block, or within a procedure declaration, may itself be a block.
3. Any declaration in the head of a block may be a procedure declaration.

Now it is clear that a program tree may reach to a great depth. There can be nesting both in the head and in the body of the block that forms the program. Indeed the depth of nesting is limited, practically, only by the size of the storage of the computer on which the algorithm is executed.

Figure 5-3 shows the tree structure of the Algol-like block B_1 whose head contains a procedure declaration P_2. Notice that the body of P_2 is a compound statement C. From what has already been said about blocks, it follows that the

Figure 5-3. **Tree structure of the block B_1 whose head contains a procedure declaration P_2.**

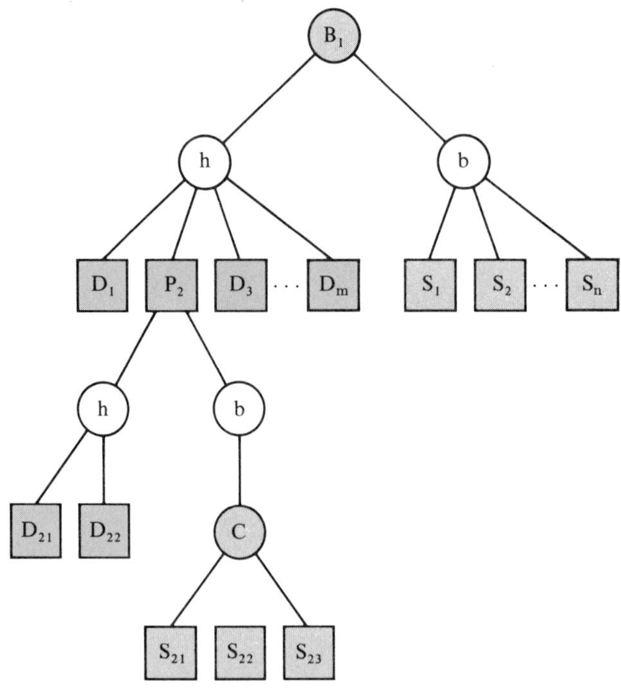

body of block B_1 will be executed in an environment that includes the declaration P_2. In other words, the procedure defined by P_2 is available to all the statements of the body of B_1.

Figure 5-4 shows a more complicated program structure, in which the body of the procedure declaration P_2 is itself block B_3. A second procedure declaration P_5 appears in the head of block B_4. Notice that the procedure defined by P_2, in the head of block B_1, is available to the statements S_{11}, S_{12}, and S_{14} in the body of block B_1. This procedure is also available to statements S_{41} and S_{42} in the body, and to statement S_{51} in the head of block B_4, all nested within B_1. The procedure defined by P_5 in the head of block B_4 is available to statements S_{41} and S_{42} in the body of B_4 but not to statements S_{11}, S_{12}, or S_{14}, which are in an enclosing block.

Because procedure declarations differ slightly among Algol-like languages, we defer showing contour diagrams for procedures until Section 5-6, when we discuss ALGOL 60 procedures. Our initial description of block structure in Algol-like languages is now finished.

***Figure 5-4.* A program structure including both procedure declarations and blocks.**

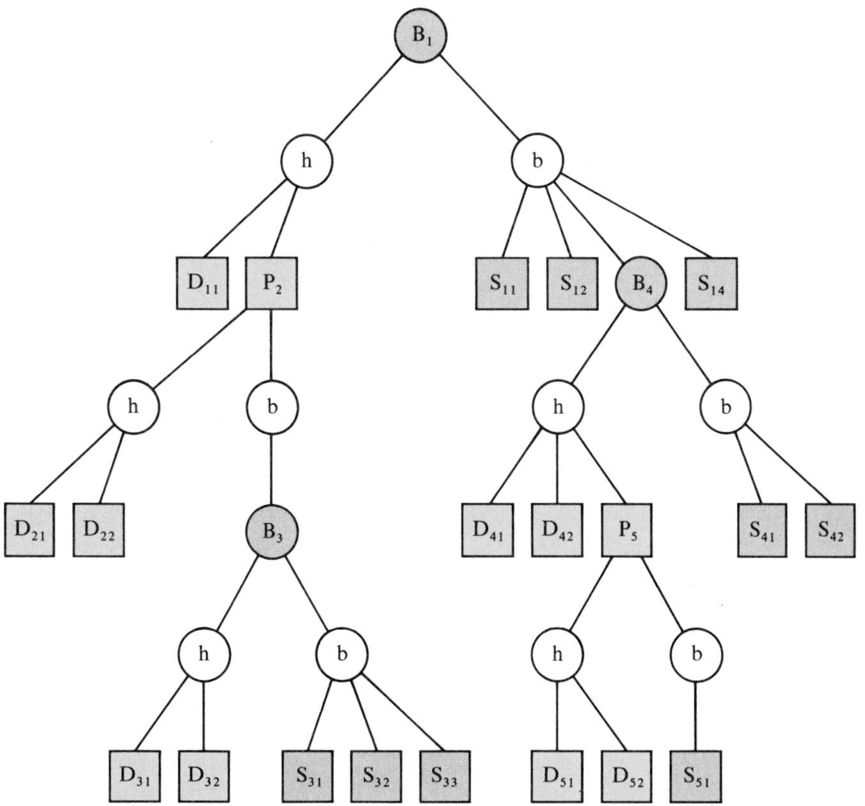

5-3
SYNTACTIC STRUCTURE OF ALGOL 60

We want to specialize the block structure discussion to ALGOL 60 or ALGOL, as we refer to that language in the rest of this chapter. When we translate Figure 5-1 into ALGOL text, the program resembles Figure 5-5. The ALGOL program is a list of declarations followed by a list of statements, and the whole "package" is bracketed by a **begin, end** pair to form a unit. Notice that only the terminal nodes of the corresponding tree structure (Figure 5-1) appear explicitly. The nodes h and b do not appear at all, and the root node BLOCK is represented only by the **begin, end** pair that surrounds the entire block.

ALGOL text is not line-oriented; the end of a line does not indicate the end of a command. Neither is there a fixed position on the line where a new command starts. Therefore, a special indicator is necessary to separate commands. The semicolon acts as this separator in ALGOL.

Figure 5-6 shows how the tree structure of Figure 5-2 might appear on a coding sheet to form an ALGOL program, that is, recast into a line-by-line sequence for input to a computer. Note how every structure and nested substructure can be identified. The entire program is itself a block and is contained within a **begin, end** pair. Notice how the **begin, end** pairs set off the nested blocks of the program. The vertical bracketing lines to the left of the program in Figure 5-6 are called *scoping lines.* They are not part of the program but are added to provide a visual aid to help the reader "see" the nested blocks.

In Figure 5-7 we see an ALGOL schematic for the program structure, including the P_2 procedure declaration shown in Figure 5-3. A procedure definition in ALGOL begins with a procedure title, for example, **procedure** *SORT* (or **real procedure** *SUM* or **integer procedure** *SUM,* if it is a function). If the procedure has parameters, the parameter list follows the name of the procedure, for example, **procedure** *SORT* (*n, A*). The rest of the procedure heading (shown as declarations in the tree discussion) includes a **value** part, which lists any value parameters, and a *specification* part, which lists the "specifier" for each of the parameters. For example, simple parameters are specified as **real, integer,** or **Boolean.** The value and specification parts are analogous to flowchart legend entries for parameters. Many of these details will become clearer when we show an actual ALGOL program.

Figure 5-5. **Schematic ALGOL form of the block shown in Figure 5-1.**

```
begin
   D1 ;
   D2 ;
   .
   .
   .
   Dm;
   S1;
   S2;
   .
   .
   .
   Sn
end
```

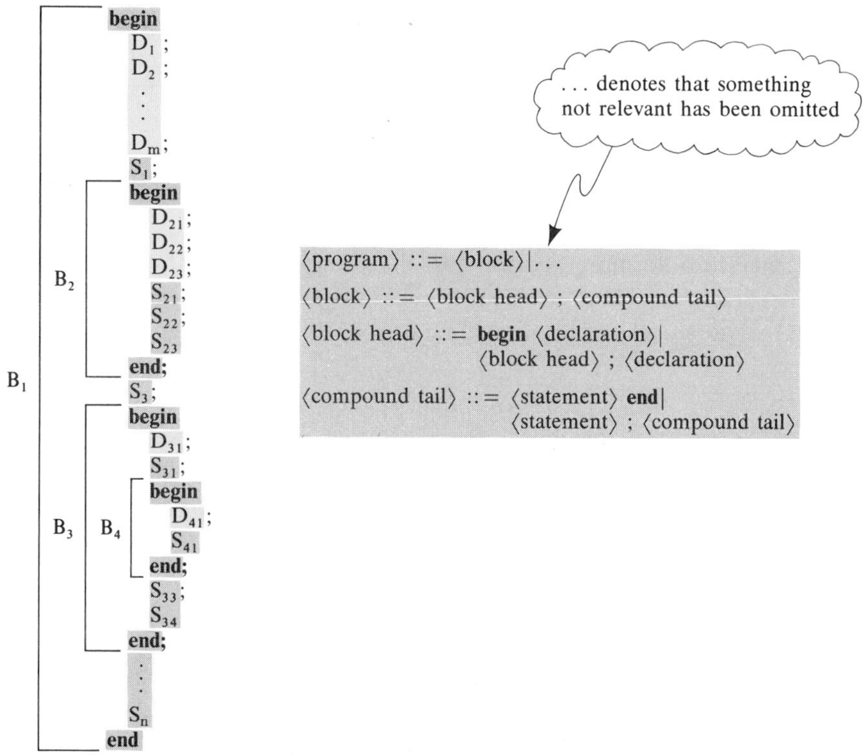

Figure 5-6. **The schematic appearance of ALGOL for the program structure given in Figure 5-2, together with relevant BNF definitions. (See Chapter 4 for an explanation of the notation used in these definitions.)**

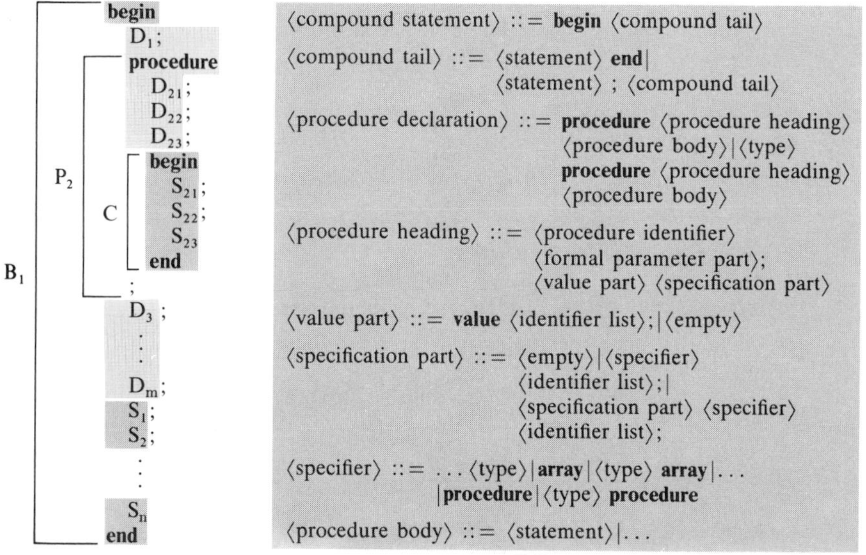

Figure 5-7. **The schematic appearance in ALGOL of the program structure shown in Figure 5-3 together with relevant BNF definitions.**

After the procedure heading comes the procedure body. In Figure 5-7 the procedure body consists of a compound statement indicated by the scoping line labeled C. We have much more to say about this sort of structure when we discuss the semantics of procedure entry and exit. The procedure declaration P_2 is also in a sense contained, or bracketed, by the word **procedure** at the beginning and by the semicolon following the procedure body at the end. Since the declaration of a procedure always occurs in the head of a block, we know that, even if there are no more declarations, the body of that block must follow before the bracketing block **end.** Therefore, a semicolon will *always* be required after a procedure declaration to separate it from the succeeding declaration or statement.

Figure 5-8 shows an ALGOL schema for the program structure shown in Figure 5-4. There are three blocks, B_1, B_3, and B_4, and two procedure declarations P_2 and P_5, shown by the scoping lines. This time we have filled in a name for each procedure and have arbitrarily given each one two parameters. The number of parameters can not be deduced from Figure 5-4; one declaration may cover several parameters and there may be a **value** part identifying value parameters.

Study the ALGOL program structure shown in Figure 5-9. Since declarations in the head of a procedure cover only parameters, one can deduce that the procedure definitions P_2, P_4, and P_6 must each have at least one parameter. Without additional information we cannot say much more about the parameters.

In Table 5-1 you will find BNF syntax definitions for a selected subset of ALGOL. This set includes the definitions already shown in Figures 5-6 and 5-7.

Figure 5-8. **Schematic appearance of the program structure shown in Figure 5-4.**

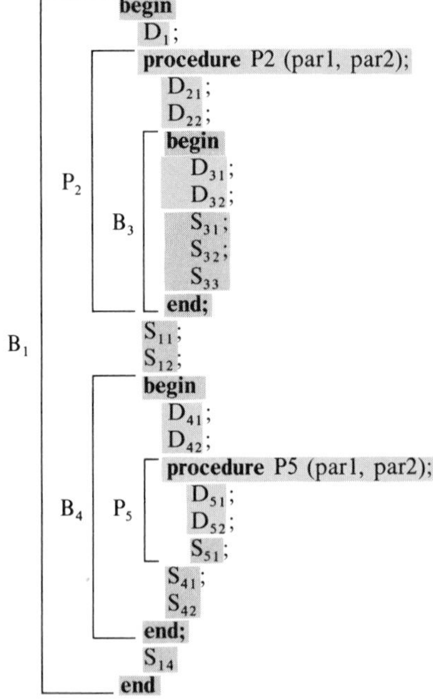

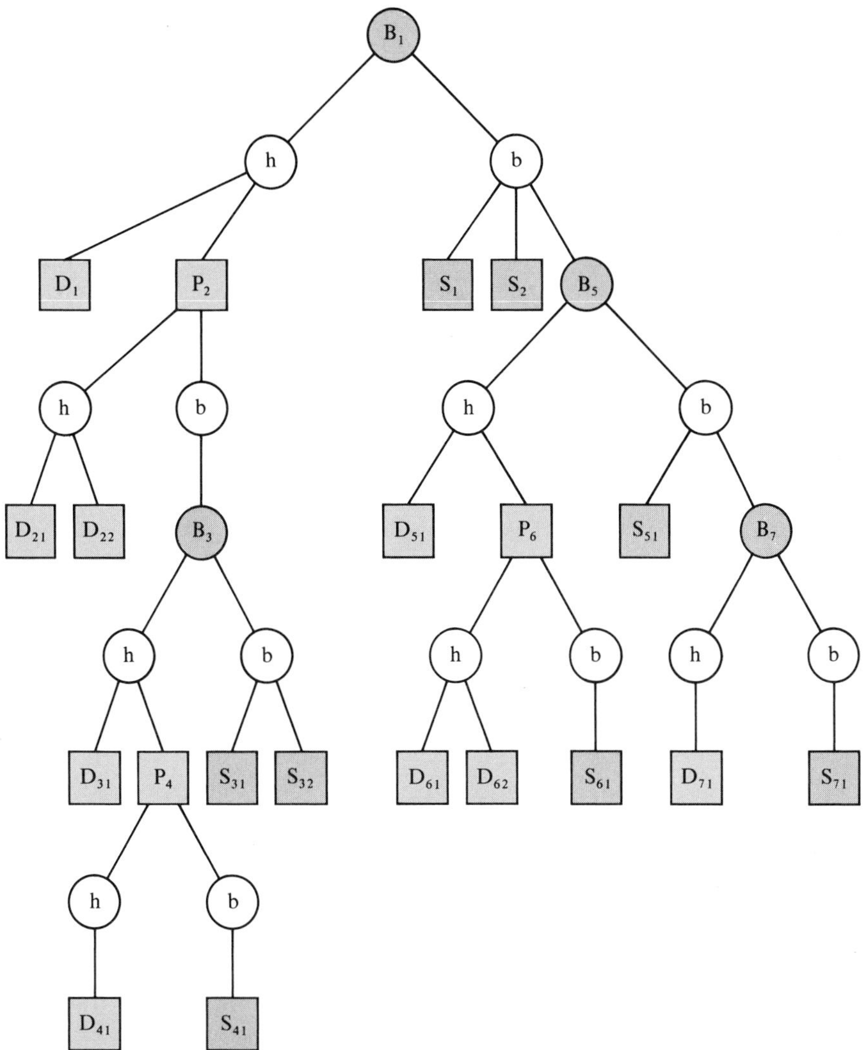

Figure 5-9. **The complex tree structure of an ALGOL program.**

TABLE 5-1
A Partial Set of BNF Syntax Definitions for the ALGOL Language Described in Sections 5-3 and 5-4[a]

1. ⟨program⟩ ::= ⟨block⟩|⟨compound statement⟩
2. ⟨block⟩ ::= ⟨block head⟩;⟨compound tail⟩|. . .
3. ⟨compound statement⟩ ::= **begin** ⟨compound tail⟩|. . .
4. ⟨block head⟩ ::= **begin** ⟨declaration⟩|⟨block head⟩;⟨declaration⟩
5. ⟨compound tail⟩ ::= ⟨statement⟩ **end**|⟨statement⟩;⟨compound tail⟩
6. ⟨declaration⟩ ::= ⟨type declaration⟩|⟨array declaration⟩|. . .|
   ⟨procedure declaration⟩
7. ⟨type declaration⟩ ::= ⟨type⟩⟨type list⟩|. . .
8. ⟨type⟩ ::= **real**|**integer**|**Boolean**
9. ⟨type list⟩ ::= ⟨simple variable⟩|⟨simple variable⟩,⟨type list⟩
10. ⟨simple variable⟩ ::= ⟨identifier⟩
11. ⟨statement⟩ ::= ⟨unconditional statement⟩|⟨conditional statement⟩|⟨for statement⟩
12. ⟨unconditional statement⟩ ::= ⟨basic statement⟩|⟨compound statement⟩|⟨block⟩
13. ⟨basic statement⟩ ::= ⟨assignment statement⟩|⟨go to statement⟩|
    ⟨dummy statement⟩|⟨procedure statement⟩|. . .
14. ⟨procedure declaration⟩ ::= **procedure** ⟨procedure heading⟩⟨procedure body⟩|
    ⟨type⟩ **procedure** ⟨procedure heading⟩⟨procedure body⟩
15. ⟨procedure heading⟩ ::= ⟨procedure identifier⟩⟨formal parameter part⟩;
    ⟨value part⟩⟨specification part⟩
16. ⟨procedure identifier⟩ ::= ⟨identifier⟩
17. ⟨formal parameter part⟩ ::= ⟨empty⟩|(⟨formal parameter list⟩)
18. ⟨formal parameter list⟩ ::= ⟨identifier⟩|⟨formal parameter list⟩
    ⟨parameter delimiter⟩⟨identifier⟩
19. ⟨value part⟩ ::= **value** ⟨identifier list⟩;|⟨empty⟩
20. ⟨specification part⟩ ::= ⟨empty⟩|⟨specifier⟩⟨identifier list⟩;|
    ⟨specification part⟩⟨specifier⟩⟨identifier list⟩;
21. ⟨specifier⟩ ::= . . .|⟨type⟩|**array**|⟨type⟩ **array**|. . .
    |**procedure**|⟨type⟩**procedure**
22. ⟨procedure body⟩ ::= ⟨statement⟩|. . .

[a]In this table a set of three dots (. . .) on the right side of a definition indicates the syntax definition has been abridged. For a full syntax of ALGOL 60 see the Appendix.

SUMMARY

Any ALGOL statement may be a block. A block is a sequence of declarations followed by a sequence of statements, the whole structure being bracketed by **begin, end.** Any ALGOL statement may be a compound statement. A compound statement is a sequence of statements bracketed by **begin, end** with no declarations.

Any ALGOL declaration in the head of a block may be a procedure declaration. If so, it defines a procedure or a function, and the body of either one consists of a statement that may, in turn, be a block. The procedure declaration can be thought of as starting with the word **procedure** and ending with the semicolon following the body of the procedure. [In the special case of a function procedure, the word **procedure** is actually the second word. The first word must be the type of result, for example, **real procedure** *sqrt* (*x*); . . . ;.]

The nested structure of a procedure definition stems from the fact that its body may be a block, while the nested structure of a block, in general, follows from the fact that any declaration in the head of a block may be a procedure definition, and any statement in the body of a block may itself be a block. Figure 5-9 shows a structure illustrating how procedure declarations may be nested within blocks, and blocks may be nested within procedure declarations. Only the size of our computer storage, or our own ability to understand the structure, controls the depth of this recursion.

Exercises 5-3

Verify that the schematic form given in Figure 5-10 corresponds to the structure given in Figure 5-9. To assist yourself in this work, first draw scoping lines around all blocks.

***Figure 5-10.* Schematic appearance of the program structure given in Figure 5-9.**

```
begin
  D1;
  procedure P2 (par1);
    D21;
    D22;
    begin
      D31;
      procedure P4 (par1);
        D41;
        S41;
      S31;
      S32
    end;
  S1;
  S2;
  begin
    D51;
    procedure P6 (par1);
      D61;
      D62;
      S61;
    S51;
    begin
      D71;
      S71
    end
  end
end
```

5-4 SYNTAX OF ALGOL DECLARATIONS AND STATEMENTS

Before we examine actual ALGOL programs and study their execution, we must become familiar with the syntax of commonly used ALGOL statements. It seems natural to begin by setting down in Table 5-2 the BNF syntax definitions for some of the terminal symbols of ALGOL. Then we present some observations about ALGOL and a set of typical examples of ALGOL statements and declarations.

Here are a few observations about ALGOL that may be helpful:

(a) The assignment symbol is :=
(b) Certain symbols, often called keywords, are *always* boldface. Among these are

for	**if**	**Boolean**	**begin**	**true**
step	**then**	**real**	**end**	**false**
until	**else**	**array**	**comment**	
do	**integer**	**value**	**goto**	

TABLE 5-2
A Partial Set of BNF Definitions for ALGOL Terminal Symbols

1. ⟨digit⟩ ::= *0*|*1*|*2*|*3*|*4*|*5*|*6*|*7*|*8*|*9*
2. ⟨letter⟩ ::= *a*|*b*|*c*|*d*|*e*|*f*|*g*|*h*|*i*|*j*|*k*|*l*|*m*|*n*|*o*|*p*|*q*|*r*|*s*|*t*|*u*|*v*|*w*|*x*|*y*|*z*
A|*B*|*C*|*D*|*E*|*F*|*G*|*H*|*I*|*J*|*K*|*L*|*M*|*N*|*O*|*P*|*Q*|*R*|*S*|*T*|*U*|*V*|*W*|*X*|*Y*|*Z*
3. ⟨type⟩ ::= **real**|**integer**|**Boolean**
4. ⟨logical value⟩ ::= **true**|**false**
5. ⟨relational operator⟩ ::= $<|\leqq|=|\geqq|>|\neq$
6. ⟨arithmetic operator⟩ ::= $+|-|\times|/|$. . .$|\uparrow$ ← exponentiation operator
7. ⟨logical operator⟩ ::= . . .$|\vee|\wedge|\neg$

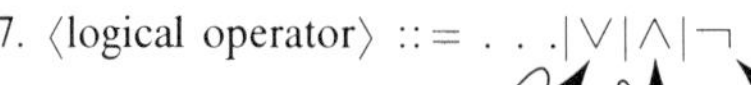

8. ⟨bracket⟩ ::= (|)|[|]|. . .|**begin**|**end**

9. ⟨separator⟩ ::= ,|.|. . .|:|;|:=|. . .|**step**|**until**|. . .|**comment**

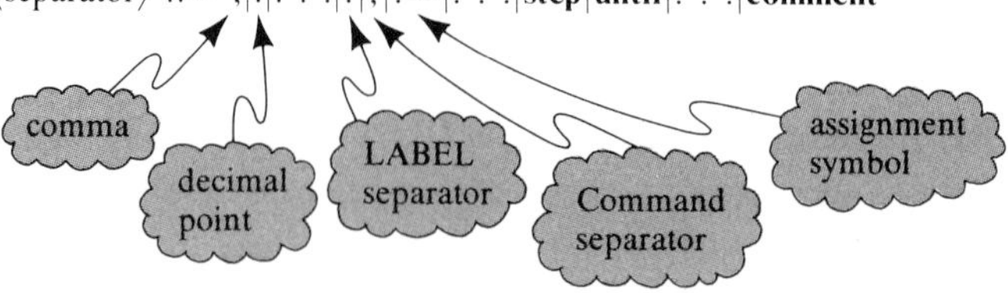

(c) Explanatory information may be interspersed in a program. Such notes begin with the symbol **comment** and conclude with the semicolon symbol, for example,

comment *this is an explanatory note;*

(d) Any statement may be preceded by a label followed by a colon, for example,

LOOP: X := 74

(e) Looping in ALGOL is achieved in one of two ways. For definite iteration, the **for** statement is used, with the understanding that the body of the loop will not alter the initial value, the step value, or the final value of the **for** loop variable. Indefinite iteration can be accomplished using a conditional statement, in conjunction with a jump or **goto** statement leading back to the **if** statement.

(f) To iterate through part or all of the elements of a list (vector) or higher dimensional array, subscripted variables are used in ALGOL as in other languages. The number of subscripts and the (lower and upper) bounds for each subscript position must be declared, for example,

array *X [1:10]*
integer array *Y [−2:5, 1:m]*

Table 5-3 consists of a sequence of typical operations, each with a specific example coded as a flowchart fragment, and recoded as one or more ALGOL statements. In some of the examples we have also included a more general, BNF-like representation of the statement. It will be seen from the examples that ALGOL structures can easily be nested, one within another. Even a reader who has never before seen any ALGOL code will have little difficulty understanding the ALGOL, and the superficial differences between ALGOL syntax and flowchart syntax. A careful study of Table 5-3 is definitely recommended. Many more examples of the mapping from flowchart to ALGOL syntax will appear in the case studies later in this chapter.

TABLE 5-3
Syntactic Summary of ALGOL

Item	Type of Operation	Flowchart Example	ALGOL Example and Possible BNF Form
1	Assignment	$L \leftarrow \sqrt{A^2 + B^2 + C^2}$	*L := sqrt (A ↑ 2 + B ↑ 2 + C ↑ 2)* ⟨variable⟩ := ⟨expression⟩

TABLE 5-3 (*continued*)

Item	Type of Operation	Flowchart Example	ALGOL Example and Possible BNF Form
2	Input[a]	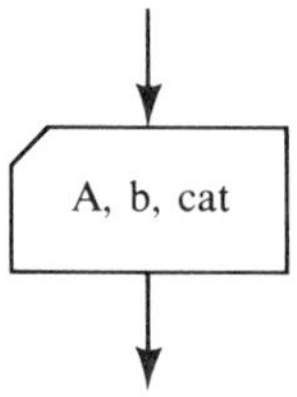 A, b, cat	*read* (*A*, *b*, *cat*) read (⟨variable⟩,⟨variable⟩, . . . , ⟨variable⟩)
3	Input[a]	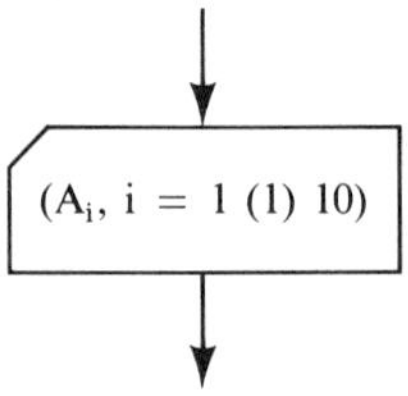 (A_i, i = 1 (1) 10)	**for** *i* := *1* **step** *1* **until** *10* **do** *read* (*A* [*i*]) **for** ⟨variable⟩ := ⟨arith. expr.⟩ **step** ⟨arith. expr.⟩ **until** ⟨arith. expr.⟩ **do** *read* (⟨variable⟩)
4	Input[a]	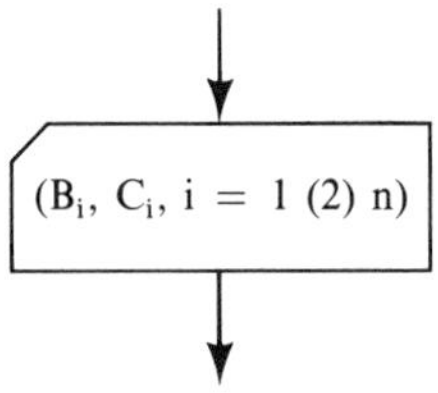 (B_i, C_i, i = 1 (2) n)	**for** *i* := *1* **step** *2* **until** *n* **do** *read* (*B* [*i*], *C* [*i*]) **for** ⟨variable⟩ := ⟨arith. expr.⟩ **step** ⟨arith. expr.⟩ **until** ⟨arith. expr.⟩ **do** *read* (⟨variable⟩,⟨variable⟩, . . . ,⟨variable⟩)
5	Output[b]	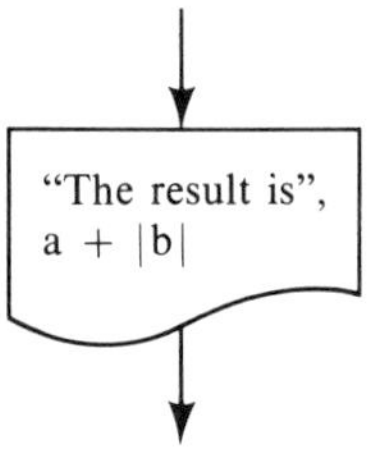 "The result is", a + |b|	*print* ('*The result is*', *a* + *abs* (*b*)) print (⟨expr.⟩,⟨expr.⟩, . . . ,⟨expr.⟩)
6	Output[a]	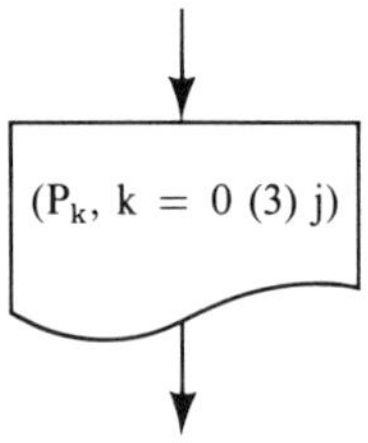 (P_k, k = 0 (3) j)	**for** *k* := *0* **step** *3* **until** *j* **do** *print* (*P* [*k*]) **for** ⟨variable⟩ := ⟨arith. expr.⟩ **step** ⟨arith. expr.⟩ **until** ⟨arith. expr.⟩ **do** *print* (⟨variable⟩)

TABLE 5-3 (*continued*)

Item	Type of Operation	Flowchart Example	ALGOL Example and Possible BNF Form
7a	Path selection[c]	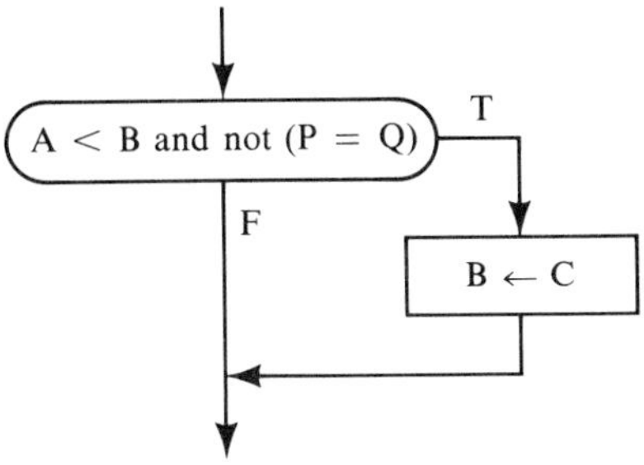 A < B and not (P = Q) → T: B ← C; F	If $A < B \wedge \neg (P = Q)$ then $B := C$ (and, not) **if** ⟨Boolean expr.⟩ **then** ⟨unconditional statement⟩
7b	Path selection[c,d]	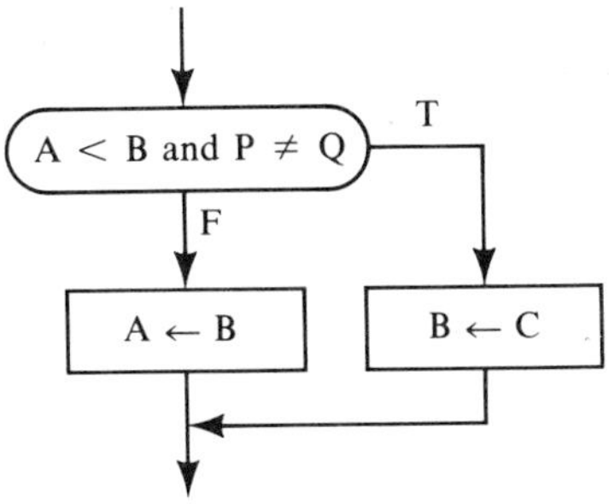 A < B and P ≠ Q → T: B ← C; F: A ← B	**if** $A < B \wedge P \neq Q$ **then** $B := C$ **else** $A := B$ **if** ⟨Boolean expr.⟩ **then** ⟨unconditional statement⟩ **else** ⟨statement⟩
7c	Path selection[c,d]	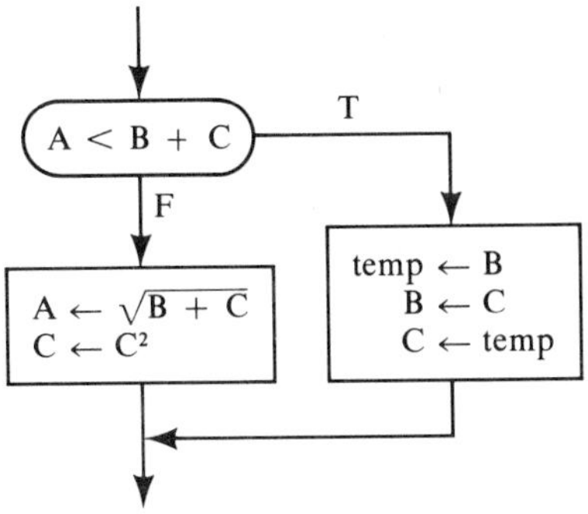 A < B + C → T: temp ← B, B ← C, C ← temp; F: $A \leftarrow \sqrt{B + C}$, $C \leftarrow C^2$	**if** $A < (B + C)$ **then begin** $temp := B$; $B := C$; $C := temp$ **end** **else begin** $A := sqrt\ (B + C)$; $C := C \uparrow 2$ **end** **if** ⟨Boolean expr.⟩ **then** ⟨unconditional statement⟩ **else** ⟨statement⟩
7d	Path selection[c,d]	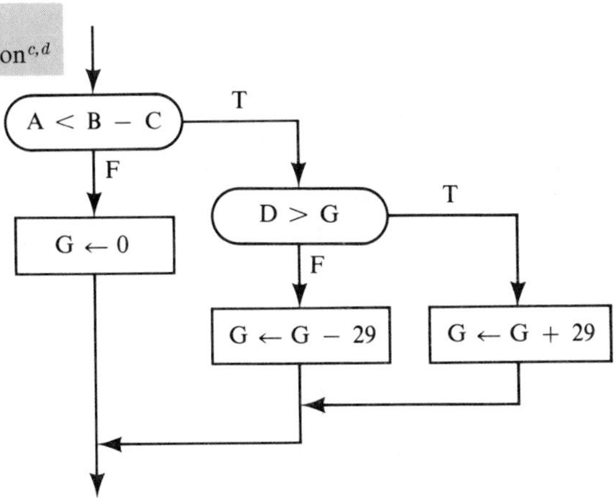 A < B − C → T: (D > G → T: G ← G + 29; F: G ← G − 29); F: G ← 0	**if** $A < (B - C)$ **then** **begin if** $D > G$ **then** $G := G + 29$ **else** $G := G - 29$ **end** **else** $G := 0$ **if** ⟨Boolean expr.⟩ **then** ⟨unconditional statement⟩ **else** ⟨statement⟩

TABLE 5-3 (*continued*)

Item	Type of Operation	Flowchart Example	ALGOL Example and Possible BNF Form

8 Indefinite iteration[e]

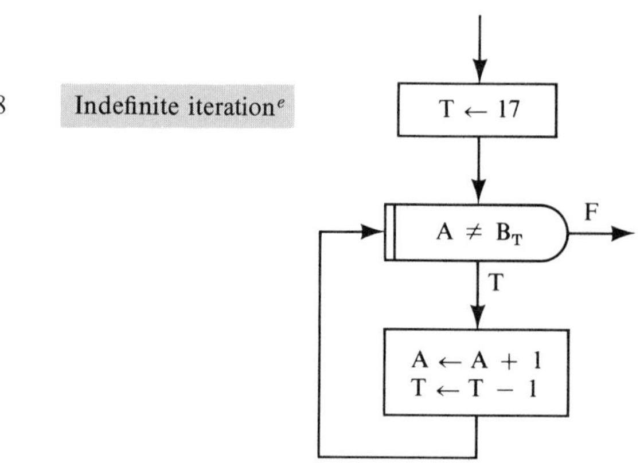

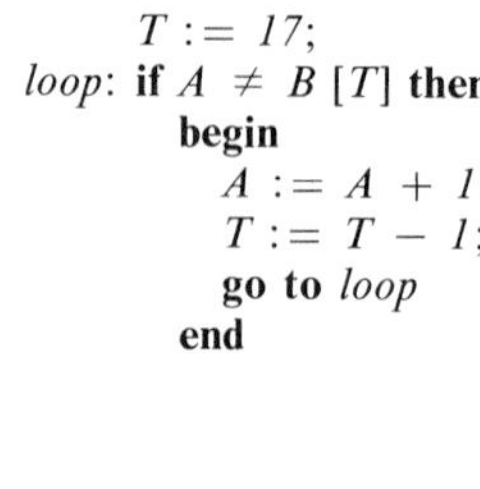

```
      T := 17;
loop: if A ≠ B [T] then
        begin
          A := A + 1;
          T := T − 1;
          go to loop
        end
```

9 Definite iteration

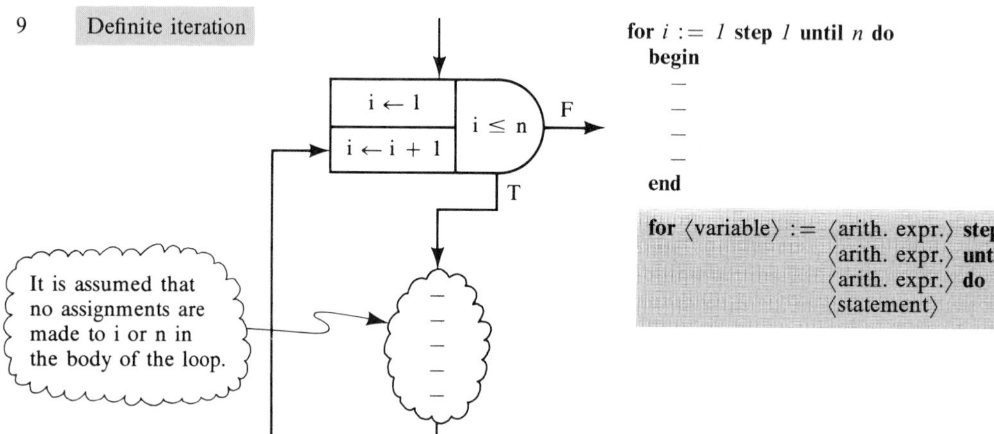


```
for i := 1 step 1 until n do
  begin
    —
    —
    —
    —
  end
```

for ⟨variable⟩ := ⟨arith. expr.⟩ **step** ⟨arith. expr.⟩ **until** ⟨arith. expr.⟩ **do** ⟨statement⟩

10 Type declarations for locals, simple variables and arrays[f]

Legend

Identifier	Treatment	Description
i, J	local	integer
B	local	real
Y	local	list of n real elements
C	local	a two-dimensional real array with rows numbered 3 to 6 inclusive, and with columns numbered 5 to 14 inclusive
test	local	logical

integer *i*, *J*;
real *B*;
real array *Y* [*1*:*n*], *C* [*3*:*6*, *5*:*14*];
Boolean *test*

TABLE 5-3 (*continued*)

Item	Type of Operation	Flowchart Example	ALGOL Example and Possible BNF Form

11 Sharing of globals

Legend for B_1

Identifier	Treatment	Description
A, F	local	int
H	local	real

Legend for B_2

Identifier	Treatment	Description
A, C	local	real
F	global	F in B_1
H	global	H in B_1

Legend for B_3

Identifier	Treatment	Description
D	local	int
G, H	local	real
A	global	A in B_2
C	global	C in B_2
F	global	F in B_1

```
B1  begin
      integer A, F; real H;
        :
    B2  begin
          real A, C;
            :
        B3  begin
              integer D; real G, H;
                :
            end
            :
        end
        :
    end
```

Globals are declared implicitly in ALGOL. To identify a variable, say F, appearing in the body of block B_3, first consult the declarations of block B_3, then those of B_2, and finally those of B_1.

12 Procedure declaration[g]

Legend for Proc

Identifier	Treatment	Description
A	val par	integer
B	ref par	real
i, k	local	integer
C	local	real

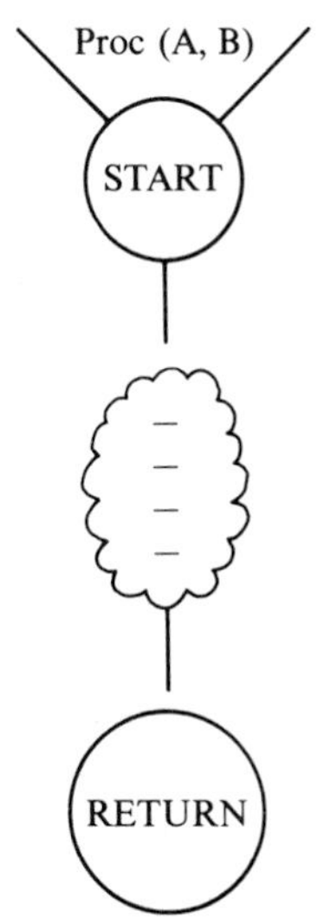


```
procedure Proc (A, B);
  value A; integer A; real B;
  begin
    integer i, k; real C;
    —
    —
    —
  end
```

TABLE 5-3 (*continued*)

Item	Type of Operation	Flowchart Example	ALGOL Example and Possible BNF Form

13a Function declaration[h]

```
real procedure Trace (n, a);
  value n; integer n;
  real array a;
  begin
    integer i; real S;
    S := 0;
    for i := 1 step 1 until n do
      S := S + a [i, i];
    Trace := S
  end
```

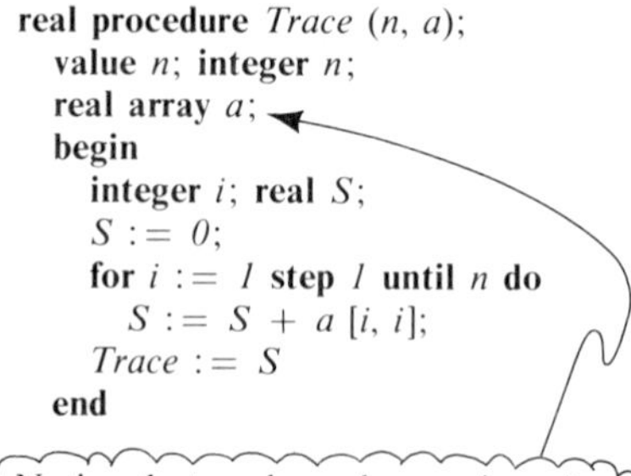

Legend for Trace

Identifier	Treatment	Description
n	val par	integer
a	ref par	list of n reals
S	local	real
i	local	integer

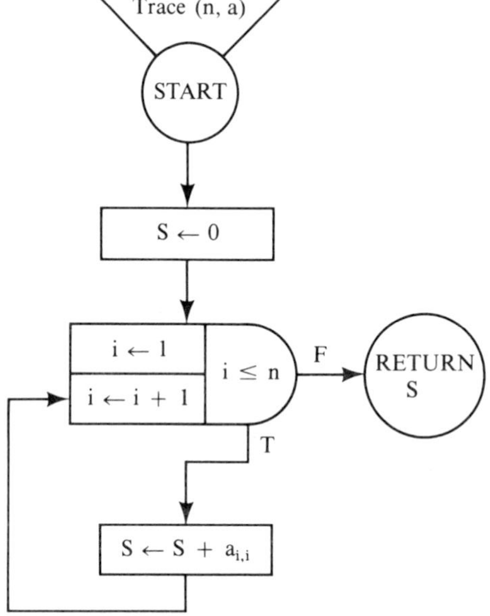

[a]ALGOL input and output are accomplished by procedures that are not themselves a part of the language. However, the actual parameters (arguments) are expected to conform to ALGOL syntax. These procedures are not ordinary procedures, however, since the number of arguments can vary from one call to the next. Several variations of ALGOL allow a **for** statement to appear inside a read or print statement, for example,

read (**for** *i* := *1* **step** *1* **until** *10* **do** *A* [*i*])

[b]Note that a character string enclosed in quote marks is permitted as an argument to a function or procedure. This is the only place in an ALGOL 60 program where a string may appear. Various dialects of ALGOL actually relax this constraint.

[c]The BNF for this item includes the term ⟨Boolean expression⟩. A Boolean expression is an expression that evaluates to either **true** or **false.**

[d]Notice that the word **else** is never preceded by a semicolon.

TABLE 5-3 (*continued*)

Item	Type of Operation	Flowchart Example	ALGOL Example and Possible BNF Form
13b	Function declaration[h]		**integer procedure** *Bigst* (*A*, *n*); **integer** *n*; **integer array** *A*; **begin** **integer** *k*, *CAND*; *CAND* := *A* [*1*]; **for** *k* := *2* **step** *1* **until** *n* **do** **if** *CAND* < *A* [*k*] **then** *CAND* := *A* [*k*]; *Bigst* := *CAND* **end**

```
integer procedure Bigst (A, n);
  integer n; integer array A;
  begin
    integer k, CAND;
    CAND := A [1];
    for k := 2 step 1 until n do
      if CAND < A [k]
        then CAND := A [k];
      Bigst := CAND
  end
```

Legend for Bigst

Identifier	Treatment	Description
A	ref par	list of n integers
n	ref par	integer
k, CAND	local	integer

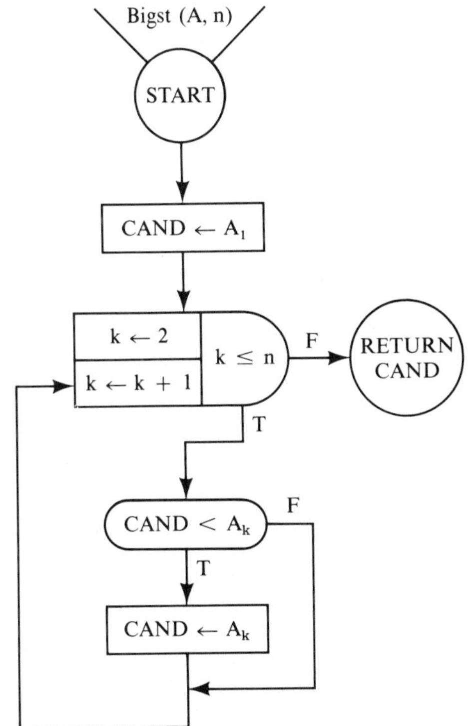

[e]ALGOL has no special indefinite iteration statement. A loop can be constructed from an **if** clause controlling a compound statement, the last statement within the **begin, end** pair being a jump or **goto** statement sending control back to the beginning of the **if** clause. This construction requires the use of a label on the **if** statement. Any statement can be prefixed with a label, and identifiers may be used as labels. The colon is the separator symbol for a label, as shown above. Labels need not be declared in ALGOL. As in all languages, it is the programmer's responsibility to make sure that indefinite loops terminate.

[f]Simple variables or arrays in ALGOL may be of type **real, integer,** or **Boolean.** Boolean variables may assume only the logical values **true** and **false.**

[g]In ALGOL the procedure declaration must, of course, be followed by a separator semicolon when it is embedded in a program.

[h]In ALGOL the function declaration must, of course, be followed by a separator semicolon when it is embedded in a program.

5-5 SEMANTICS OF ALGOL BLOCKS

Execution of an ALGOL block begins with the processing of all the declarations in the head of that block; this activity is called *block entry*. Execution of the body begins with the execution of the first statement in the body. The execution continues according to the control logic inherent in those statements. If the block is well structured, the statements of the block will be executed, in order, from first to last. Each block has exactly one entry point and exactly one exit. (As we have seen from Table 5-3, statements in an ALGOL block bear a close resemblance to boxes of our flowchart language.) The action associated with *block exit* is that of reestablishing the computational environment that existed before the block was entered.

The overall semantics of block execution are as follows,

1. Block entry (enter the block): this means establish a new computational environment based on the declarations in the head of the block entered.
2. Execute the body of the block.
3. Block exit (exit from the block): this means reestablish the computational environment in force just before this block was entered.

Block Entry

Establishing a computational environment is not a new concept. In the computer model of Chapters 1 and 2 this was precisely the action undertaken by the Master Computer (with the help of an assistant) whenever a procedure was to be executed. So now the MC first forms an empty environment and then fills it by processing the declarations of the entered block. Processing a declaration results in the creation and labeling of one cell for each declared identifier.

For example, processing

```
begin
   integer a, b, c;
```

results in the creation of cells a, b, and c in the new contour:

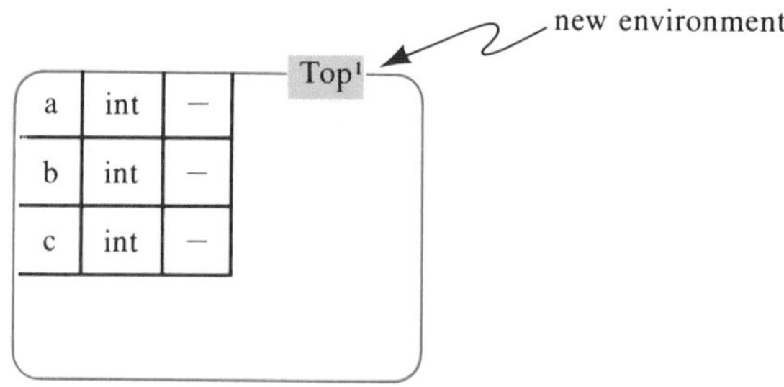

Each created cell in the new environment has three fields: a *name* field to hold a copy of the declared identifier, a *type* field to show the type of identifier being declared, and a *value* field. Since no value has yet been assigned to a declared variable, the value part is initially empty.

Processing a procedure (or function) declaration also results in the creation of a labeled cell having, as its initial value, information telling on what line the code for that procedure begins and in what environment it is to be executed (an ip, ep pair). For example, processing the declaration

line no.	**procedure** *sort* (n, A);
3	—
4	—
⋮	—

after the previous declarations results in the creation of a new cell for the identifier *sort,*

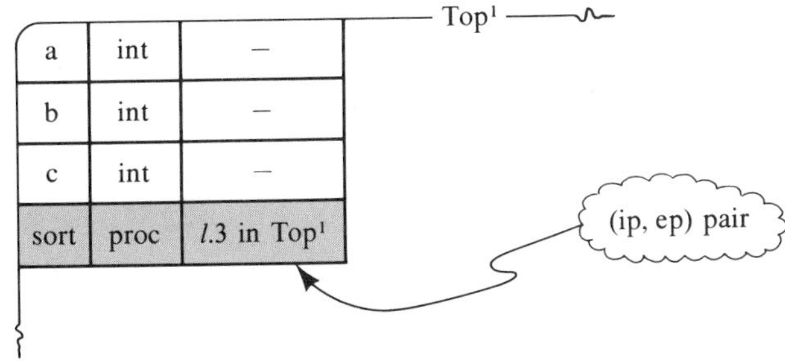

The ep, Top[1], indicates that when sort is called, its local environment, for example, sort[2], should be nested immediately within Top[1]. A general rule for selection of ip values is stated in the next section.

ALGOL environments are nested, with each succeeding one inside another according to the nesting of the blocks, so that variables and procedures declared in outer blocks can serve as globals for inner blocks. For example, suppose block B_2 is nested within another block, say B_1. At the beginning of execution, when B_1 is entered there is no previous environment, and so all of the block B_1 environment (at least in principle) is built during the process of entering B_1. Then, when B_2 is entered, its environment is built inside the environment for B_1.

The program structure outlined in Figure 5-11 serves as a more concrete example. The environment created upon entry to B_1 consists of the integer variables D and F, and the real variable E. The third statement in B_1 is the block B_2. When B_2 is entered, new variables E, F, and G are created. Environments constructed thus far are shown in Figure 5-12a. Note that we use the same contour labeling conventions as in earlier chapters.

While execution proceeds within block B_2, *four* variables are accessible: E, F, and G, created on entry to B_2 and local to B_2, and D, previously created upon entry to the enclosing environment B_1 and global to B_2. There can be no confusion as to which E and which F belong in B_2's environment, because *locals always take precedence over globals.*

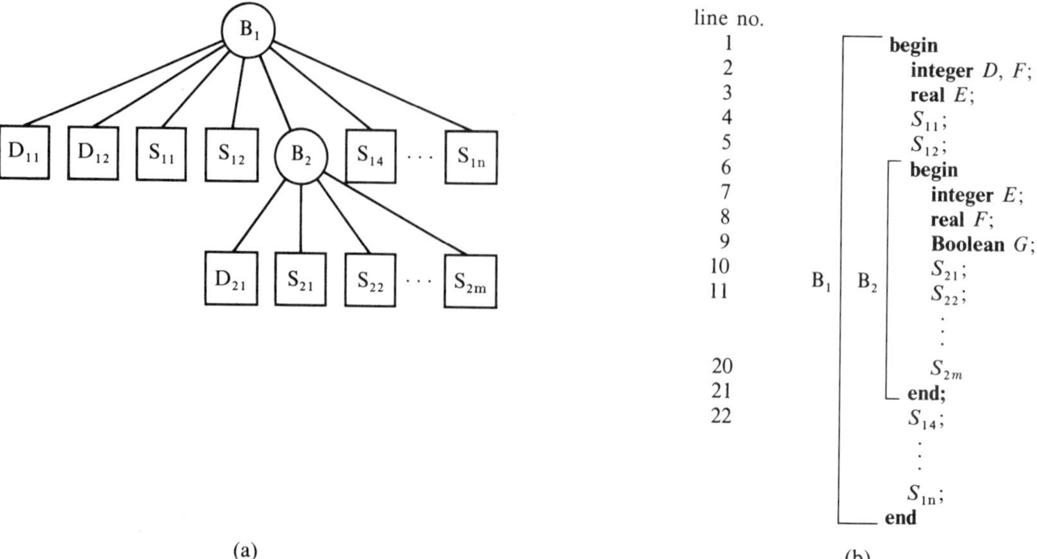

Figure 5-11. **(a) Structure of block B_1. (b) Skeleton of the code for block B_1.**

The *locals-take-precedence-over-globals* rule is easily followed if we picture the action in the following way. Entry into block B_2 amounts to the MC creating the environment contour $B_2{}^1$ and ordering the Allocator to create storage boxes in that contour for the new variables E, F, and G. Once execution of the body of B_2 has begun, if the MC asks the Reader/Assigner to fetch or store a value, the latter always *searches for the required storage cell, starting the search in the current contour and proceeding from a smaller contour to the next larger en-*

Figure 5-12. **Contour diagram of the environments for Figure 5-11b.**

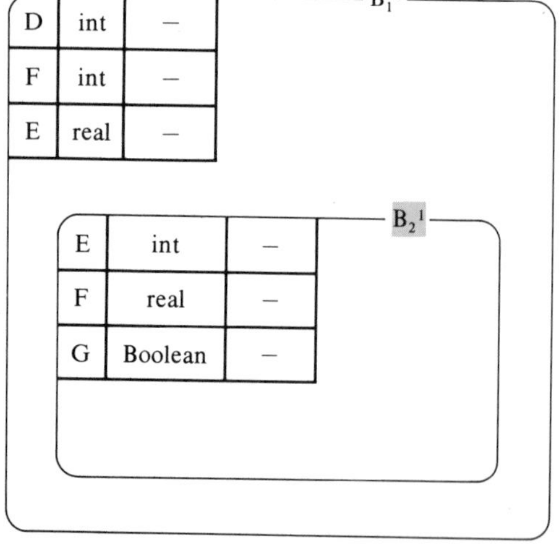

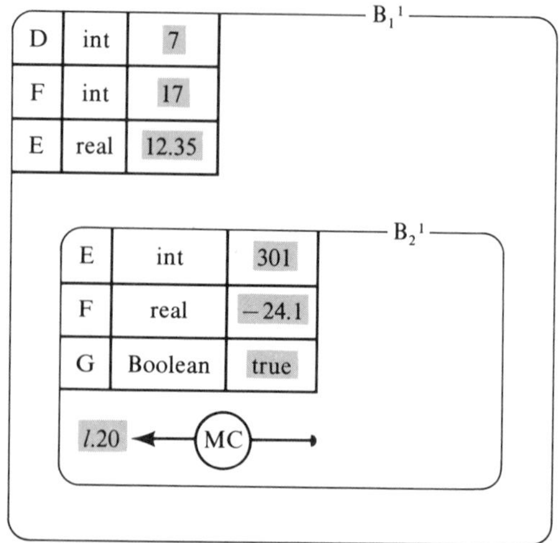

closing contour. The first storage cell that he encounters with the correct identifier is the right cell. The variables E and F in the enclosing contour can never be encountered while the MC executes in block B_2 because cells E and F can be found in the local environment of B_2. Cells E and F of $B_1{}^1$ are temporarily invisible! The only visible variable of the $B_1{}^1$ contour is D, because there is no D in the contour $B_2{}^1$ to *mask* the cell with that name in $B_1{}^1$. Absence of a local variable D makes the variable D declared in B_1 accessible to B_2. D is then said to be *global* to B_2.

Figure 5-12b shows the environment of the computation after the MC has executed first in $B_1{}^1$ and then in $B_2{}^1$, and after values have been assigned to the variables as indicated, and assuming that line 20 of the program contains the next statement to be executed.

Observe that in Chapter 2 we modeled each program segment as a separate flowchart and specified every global variable explicitly in a flowchart legend. In ALGOL, however, global variables are specified implicitly by the nesting of blocks and the following rules apply: (1) local variables always take precedence over other variables with the same name, and (2) the search for a given variable proceeds from a given block outward to the next enclosing block.

Exit from a Block

When execution of block B_2 of Figure 5-11 has been completed, an exit from the block takes place, accompanied by a reinstatement of the environment that prevailed before block B_2 was entered. The snapshot in Figure 5-13a shows the state of the computation in the first stage of block exit. The MC has already stepped out of the contour $B_2{}^1$ and back into $B_1{}^1$. From $B_1{}^1$ the MC can no longer access (or even see) cells E, F, and G within contour $B_2{}^1$, and can now access

***Figure 5-13.* Snapshots showing the substeps of block exit. (a) Before deallocation of $B_2{}^1$. (b) After deallocation of $B_2{}^1$ and the cells within it.**

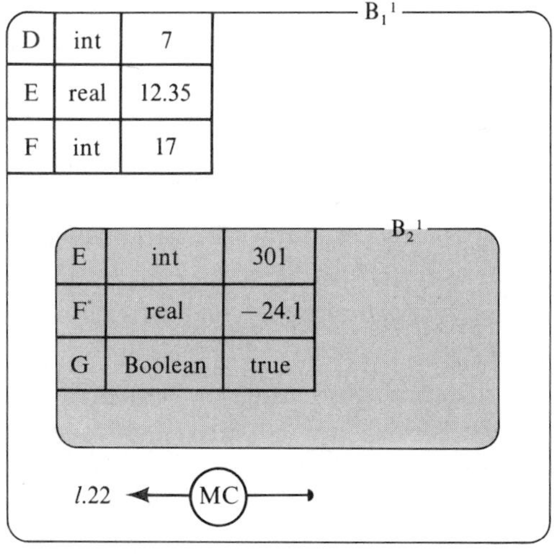

(a)

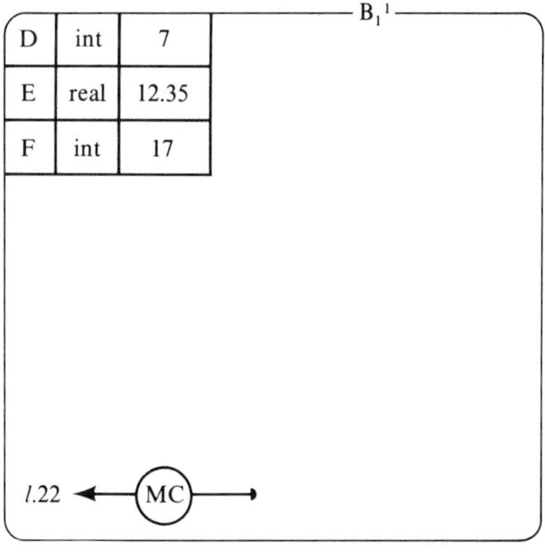

(b)

only D, E, and F of $B_1{}^1$. Moreover, if execution later reenters block B_2 by looping back, a new environment $B_2{}^2$ will have to be created and new cells will have to be allocated for E, F, and G. Never again can cells E, F, and G of $B_2{}^1$ be accessed. Therefore in an ALGOL program, during block exit, the MC discards or *deallocates* the contour of the block from which the exit takes place.

After deallocation, the situation resembles that shown in Figure 5-13b. Notice that this environment is precisely the one that existed prior to the entry into block B_2. Notice also that there has been no net change in the environment $B_1{}^1$ as a result of the execution of block B_2. Changes could have occurred, however, in the *values* of the cells within $B_1{}^1$ and the environment would still have been constant. Thus, the environment is to be distinguished from its contents since the environment is a structure of cells, while the contents are the values in those cells.

5-6 SEMANTICS OF ALGOL PROCEDURES

In our study of ALGOL procedures we want to distinquish carefully between two related ideas:

1. procedure declaration (the ALGOL translation of the procedure flowchart and legend) and
2. procedure invocation (the ALGOL translation of the flowchart procedure call)

An ALGOL procedure must be declared in the head of some ALGOL block. Thus when that block is entered, a cell is created for the identifier of the procedure, and the initial value in that cell is an (ip, ep) pair giving the program line number where the code for the procedure begins and the environment in which it is to be executed. A procedure can therefore be invoked or called only if the (ip, ep) pair for the procedure already exists and is accessible to the MC from the point of call.

A procedure is always executed in the environment of the block in which it is *declared* (which is not necessarily the block in which it is called). If P is declared within an immediately enclosing block B, then to execute P, its contour must be constructed and nested within the corresponding contour for B. This placement rule for procedure contours is referred to as *static binding* because each contour position (binding) relates exactly to the static nesting of the corresponding procedures and blocks within the program.

The semantics of executing an ALGOL procedure are very similar to the semantics of ALGOL blocks. Procedures have exactly one entry point and exactly one exit. A procedure is executed by first *entering* it, then *executing* its body, and then *exiting* from it.

While a block is encountered directly when control reaches a block **begin,** a procedure is reached through a procedure call. The procedure call sets in motion the semantic action of procedure entry. The MC first forms an empty contour in which to execute the procedure, and then creates a return cell to hold information necessary to reestablish the calling computational environment when control exits from this procedure. Then, for each parameter specified in the heading of the procedure, the MC creates a cell in the new environment and inserts an initial value, reflecting the matching argument.

In short the semantics of procedure execution are as follows:

1. Enter the procedure: this means establish a new computational environment, saving information required for the return.
2. Execute the body of the procedure.
3. Exit from the procedure: this means reestablish the computational environment in effect just before this procedure was called.

The rest of this section pursues some of the semantic details of procedure entry, procedure body execution, and procedure exit. As an example for discussion, consider the program structure shown in Figure 5-14.

Procedure Entry

We picture the effect of processing all the declarations in the head of the outer block B of Figure 5-14 as creating the situation shown in Figure 5-15a. The MC has already moved inside B[1] and is ready to execute line 8 (Figure 5-14b) as the next step.

***Figure 5-14.* Program structure containing a declaration for the procedure P in the outermost block B.**

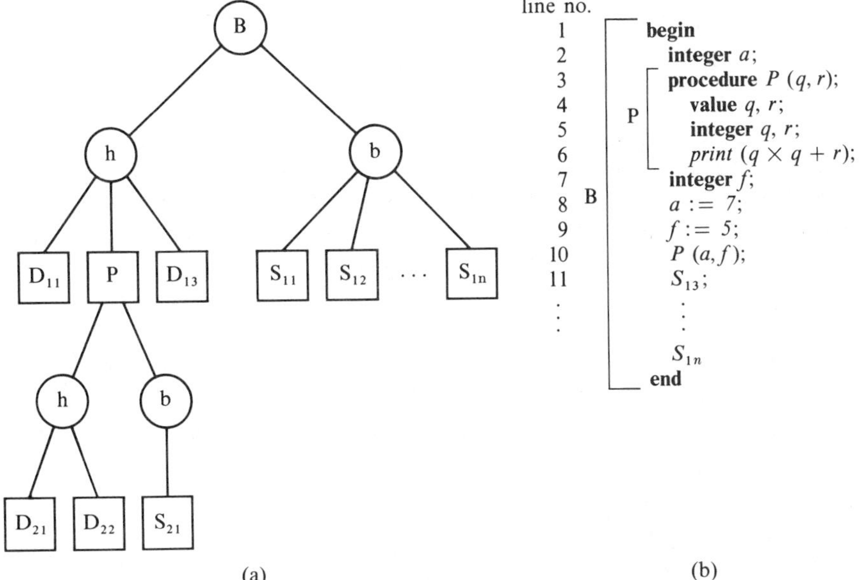

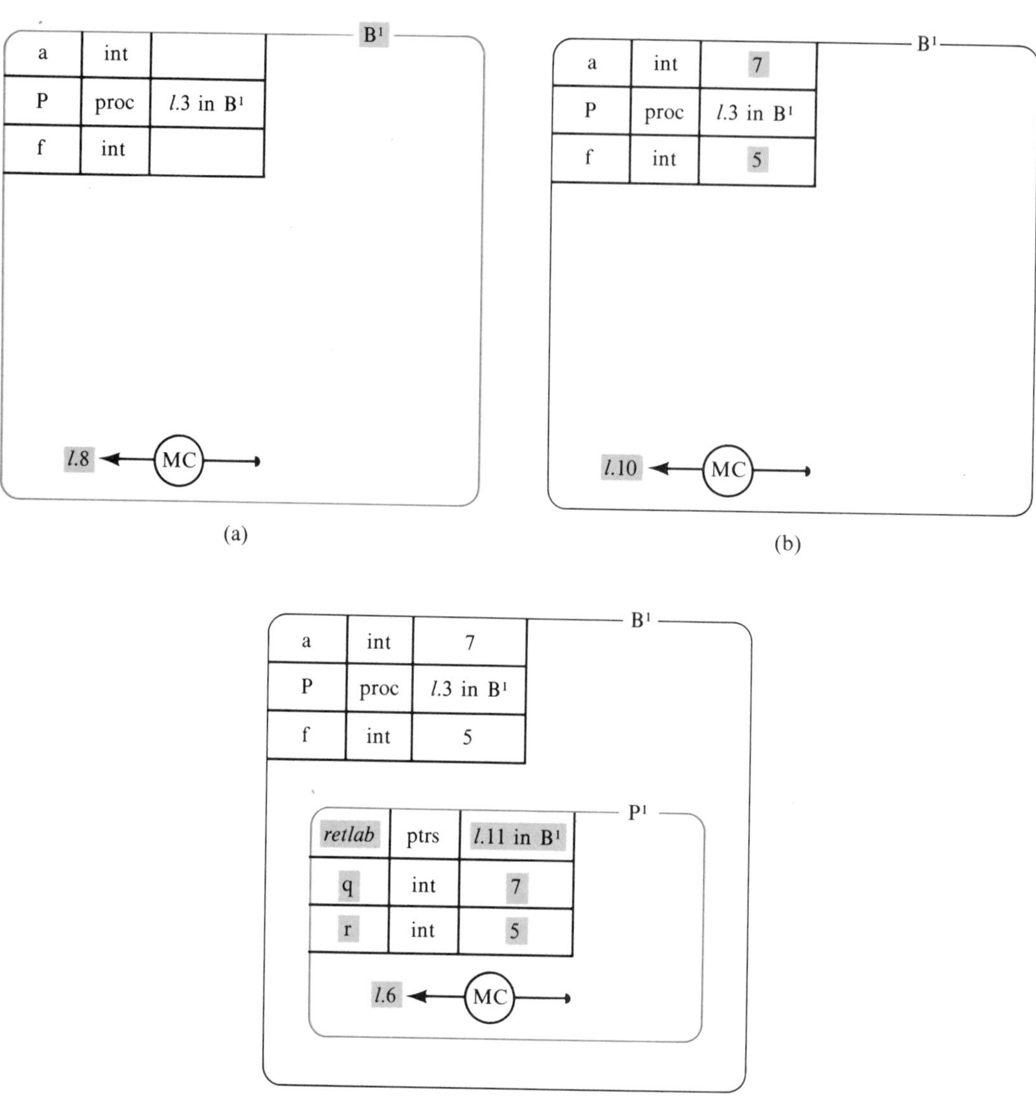

Figure 5-15. **Snapshots showing the entry into the contour P¹ for procedure P. (a) The environmental situation after the three declarations of block B have been processed. (b) Snapshot just before a call on the procedure P with arguments a and f. (c) Snapshot of the newly created contour P¹ showing a return cell, and parameter cells, q and r.**

Figure 5-15b shows the environment of the computation just before the procedure call on line 10. When executed, the procedure call, P(a, f), activates the semantics of procedure entry. The MC locates and consults the cell for P to find out what code to execute and in what environment. As a result of the ep in the (ip, ep) pair of the P cell, he creates a new environment P¹ inside B¹. This nesting reflects the fact that in the ALGOL program, the procedure declaration for P lies within the block B, i.e., is *statically bound* to B.

In Figure 5-15c the first cell in contour P^1 is labeled *retlab* and holds *return information* identifying the statement to be executed and the environment to be reestablished when execution of the procedure has been completed. (This information, line 11 in contour B^1, is a pair of pointers, that is, an (ip, ep) pair, and is abbreviated as *ptrs.*) Figure 5-15c shows that the MC has moved inside P^1 and is about to execute the body of the procedure.

Procedure Return

The steps involved in executing a return from a procedure are comparable to exit from an ALGOL block. To see how procedure returns are executed, use Figure 5-16 to follow the execution of the example procedure P in Figure 5-14 and the return following its completion.

Figure 5-16. **Substeps in the return from procedure P. (a) The return point is looked up in the *retlab* cell and found to be line 11 in B^1. (b) The MC steps out of the P^1 environment. The next instruction to be executed is line 11. (c) The P^1 environment is no longer needed, and so it has been deallocated.**

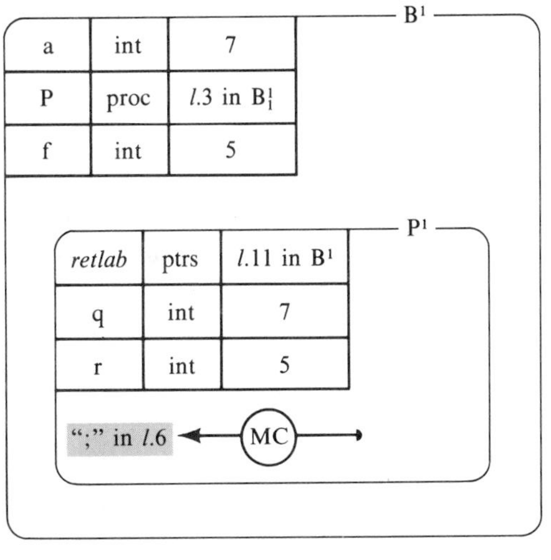

(a)

(b)

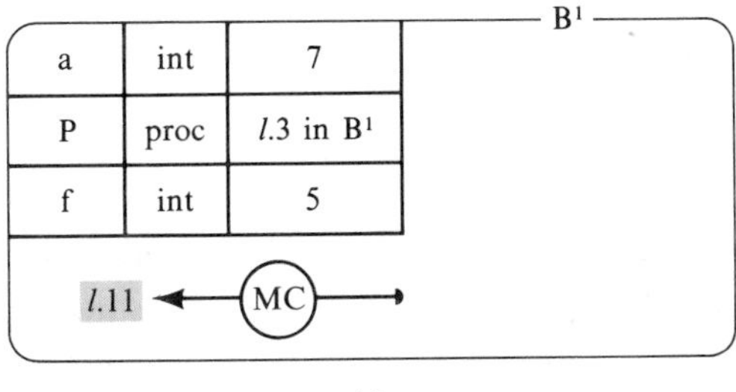

(c)

When line 6 of procedure P is executed, the value $7 \times 7 + 5 = 54$ is computed and printed out. Then the MC encounters the semicolon at the end of line 6. This separator symbol signals the end of the body of the procedure declaration P. (Had there been more than one statement in the body of P, the body would have been enclosed in a **begin, end** pair.) Consulting the return cell, the MC determines that the next statement to be executed is line 11 in the environment B^1, and moves out of the environment P^1 into B^1. Figure 5-16 shows the substeps required to return control from P to line 11 in B.

The procedure P in Figure 5-14 had, as its body, a single print statement. While the body of any procedure is a single statement, that statement may be considerably more complicated than that shown in Figure 5-14. If the body of the procedure is a compound statement, the MC sets up the procedure contour and cells for the parameters, as before, and executes the sequence of statements. The semicolon following the "end" of the **begin, end** pair of the compound statement signals the end of the body of the procedure, and thus activates the return mechanism.

If the body of the procedure is a block, then there is at least one declaration in the head of the block, and one might expect that a new contour would be set up within the procedure contour, in which to place the local cells and execute the body of the block. But then the MC would execute nothing whatever within the procedure contour, using it only as a base from which to set up the contour for the inner block. Instead, when the body of the procedure is a block, we show cells for the local variables, declared in the head of the block, added to the set of parameter cells already present in the procedure contour, and we picture execution of the block body taking place directly in the procedure contour. No new environment needs to be constructed. Hence the only contour exit that is required is from the procedure contour. This exit is part of the return mechanism triggered by the semicolon following the block "end". The action of the return is exactly as described for the example case shown in Figure 5-16.

Name Parameters in ALGOL

The sample program in Figure 5-14 used only value parameters. In ALGOL, parameters are treated in either of two ways, by *value* or by *name.* In the value case, the matching argument is evaluated at the time of the call, in the calling environment, and a copy of this value is placed in the correspoinding parameter cell in the proper environment of the called procedure. Thus, in Figure 5-16a we showed the cell for the value parameter q matching the integer argument a as having a type *int* and a value *7.* This was a copy of the value of a in B^1. In a similar way the value parameter r received a copy of the value 5 of the integer argument f.

All parameters in ALGOL not specified by value are treated as name parameters. For name parameters, as discussed in Section 2-7, evaluation of the matching argument is *postponed* until its evaluation is needed. Postponement is made possible by copying information *about the matching argument* into the parameter cell in the called environment. This information consists of a literal copy of the argument paired with the name of the environment of the caller. This is the environment in which that argument should be evaluated whenever it is needed.

To illustrate the name parameter, suppose that line 4 of Figure 5-14b is changed from

value *q*, *r*;

to

value *q*;

This change makes r a name parameter by default. In the execution of the resulting program, the snapshots of Figures 5-15a and 5-15b remain unchanged. In Figure 5-15c the cell for r in P^1 becomes

And when the MC executes line 6, the body of the procedure, the same value as before, 54, is printed.

Now suppose that q is a value parameter, r a name parameter, and that the body of the procedure P is replaced by the following compound statement:

line 6a **begin**
line 6b $\quad$ *print* $(q \times q + r)$;
line 6c $\quad$ $r: = 2 \times q$;
line 6d $\quad$ *print* $(q \times q + r)$
line 6e **end**;

When line 6b is executed, we have already seen that the value 54 is printed. When line 6c is executed the MC has to know into what cell to put the value of $2 \times$ q. The parameter cell for r contains the formula ' "f" in B^1'. When the name parameter appears on the left of an assignment symbol the formula is interpreted to mean assign the value to *the cell f in* B^1. Thus after line 6c has been executed we have the snapshot situation shown in Figure 5-17. The value of f in B^1 has been changed from 5 to 14. When line 6d is executed the value printed will be $7 \times 7 + 14$ or 63.

We see then that the information in the value part of a name parameter cell is used either (1) to obtain the value of an expression or (2) to locate a specific cell, depending on the *context* in which the parameter occurs in the procedure body (for example, in an expression or on the left-hand side of an assignment statement). If the argument for a name parameter is an expression other than a simple variable, a subscripted variable, or an array name, the corresponding name parameter cannot meaningfully appear on the left-hand side of an assignment statement. For, suppose the call on P is

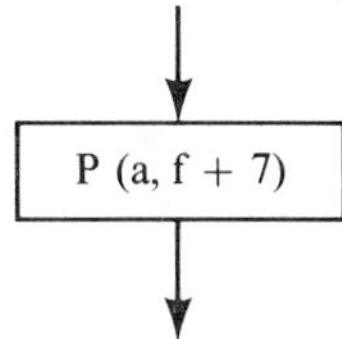

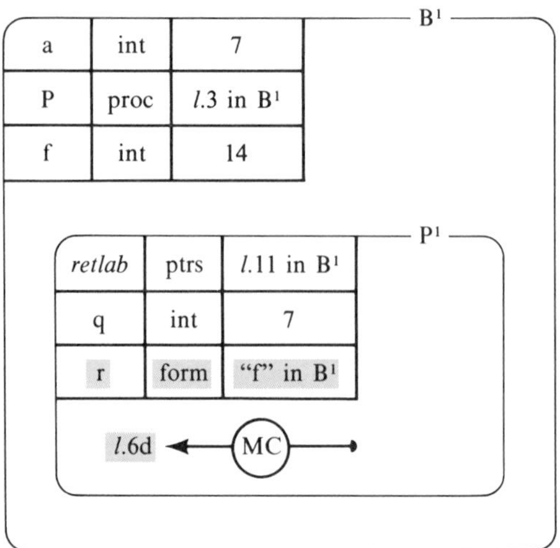

Figure 5-17. **Snapshot of computation just after line 6c has been executed.**

In that case the cell for r appears as

r	form	"f + 7" in B^1

Thus it would still make sense to have a statement in P like

$$a := r$$

but it would make no sense at all to have the statement

$$r := a$$

in P, since there cannot be a cell named "f + 7" in B^1 to which to assign the value of *a*.

5-7 CASE STUDIES—TWO ELEMENTARY EXAMPLES

This section contains two simple illustrations, each of which is presented as a case study beginning with a short description of the situation, followed by flowcharts and legends that are self-explanatory. The question of how to select an appropriate block structure for the corresponding ALGOL program is discussed at length only in Case 1, and therefore the discussion for Case 1 should be read carefully. In both cases the ALGOL program is displayed, together with a series of contour diagram snapshots showing the execution of the program for a given data set. Where the reader might need help, the snapshots are annotated.

Case 1 This case study utilizes a procedure called SQUEEZE whose purpose is to remove all zero elements from a list, counting the number of zeros eliminated, and reducing the index of each remaining element by the number of zeros removed up to that point. In other words the zeros of the list are squeezed out. The procedure SQUEEZE has three parameters and one local identifier, but no global identifiers. The parameters may be either reference or name parameters, according to what treatment is available in the "target" language. In this chapter, where the target language is ALGOL, we will use name parameters, but in the next chapter on FORTRAN, this same case study will use reference parameters.

The parameter n represents the length of the list to be compressed. The parameter A represents the list itself, as an ordered set of n elements. The parameter k is initially set to zero and then is incremented every time a zero element is found in the list A.

Squeezing is accomplished as follows: Each nonzero element of the list, as it is encountered, has its subscript decreased by the current value of k. When all the elements of the list have been tested, the value of the parameter n is corrected by subtracting the final value of k. This makes n now represent the length of the list of nonzero elements.

The top-level flowchart reads in values for m, the length of the list, and the elements of the list, $(B_i, i = 1\ (1)\ m)$. Then the procedure SQUEEZE is called with the arguments m, B, and a local identifier t, denoting the number of elements squeezed out of the list B. After SQUEEZE has been executed, the value of t is tested. If t equals zero, no elements have been eliminated, and this information is printed. If t is not equal to zero, its value and an appropriate message are printed. See Figure 5-18.

Discussion

Translating a set of flowcharts into an ALGOL program usually requires some preliminary study to understand the block structure required. The types of questions usually considered are

(a) Should we code the Top flowchart as a single block, or should we embed part of it as a subblock? In most cases, a single block will do, unless there are arrays involved whose bounds may be determined *dynamically*. For example, suppose the input step

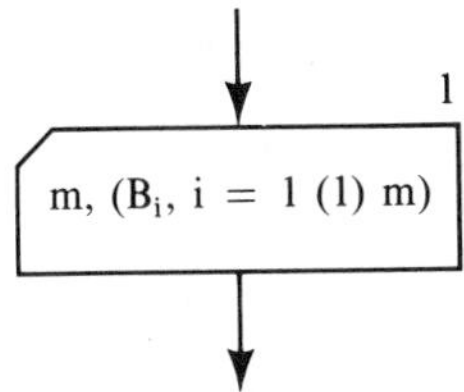

is redrawn as

outer block
1a
m
inner block
1b
(B_i, i = 1 (1) m)

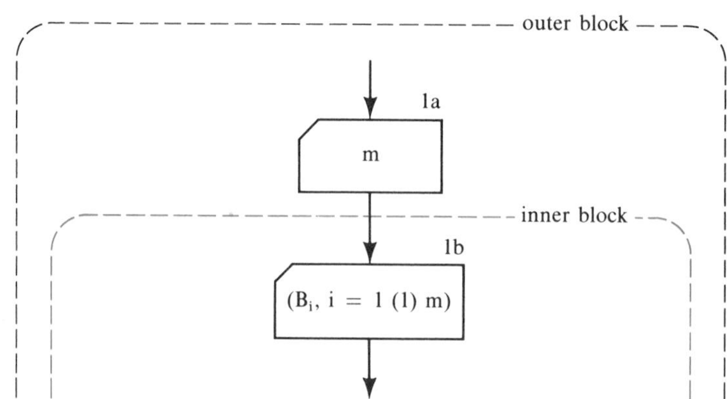

***Figure 5-18.* Flowcharts and legends for Case 1. The procedure SQUEEZE compresses a given list A of n elements.**

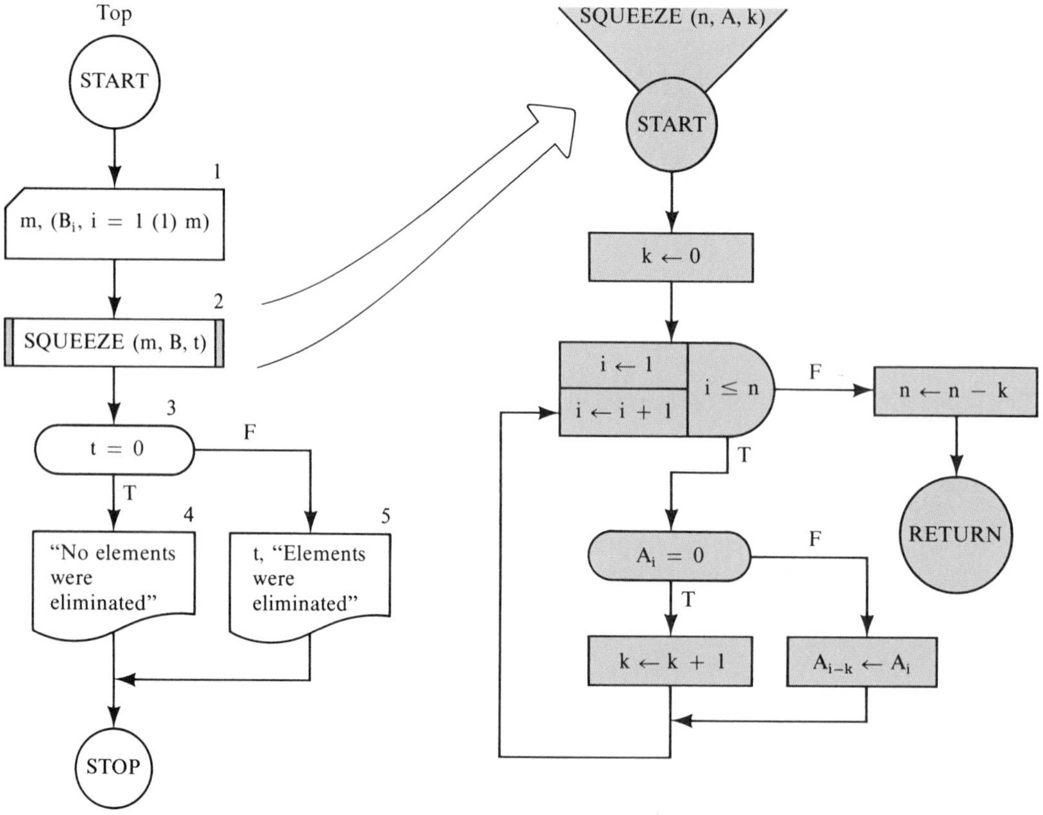

Top
START
1
m, (B_i, i = 1 (1) m)
2
SQUEEZE (m, B, t)
3
t = 0
F
T
4
5
"No elements were eliminated"
t, "Elements were eliminated"
STOP
SQUEEZE (n, A, k)
START
k ← 0
i ← 1
i ← i + 1
i ≤ n
F
n ← n − k
RETURN
T
A_i = 0
F
T
k ← k + 1
A_{i−k} ← A_i

Legend for Top

Identifier	Treatment	Description
i, m, t	local	integer
B	local	list of m reals

Legend for SQUEEZE

Identifier	Treatment	Description
n, k	name par	integer
A	name par	list of n reals
i	local	integer

Then box 1b can be coded in the ALGOL program as the first statement of an *inner* block. This inner block can begin with a declaration for the array B having an upper bound that is the value of m, for example,

real array *B* [*1* : *m*];

Since the variable m is global to the inner block, its value will already have been obtained by execution in the outer block. An important aspect of ALGOL dynamic storage allocation is that it permits us to write code (for example, for the above flowchart boxes) without knowing exactly how much storage will be required for the arrays. Furthermore, this approach to the structuring of Top allows the allocation of just the right amount of storage. The allocation can generally be postponed until it is actually needed, that is, until control enters the block where references to cells of array B are actually executed.

(b) In which program block should we embed the various procedures and functions? We can usually answer this question by ascertaining where each procedure is referenced. For example, if a procedure P is referenced only in the inner block Inner, then P should probably be declared in Inner rather than Outer. If P is declared in Inner, then some of the resources, needed when P is executed, need not be allocated until after the MC enters Inner. Among these are the cell for the procedure P itself, for example,

P	proc	*l*.— in Outer[1]

and cells for globals, which are required in the execution of P but can be made local to Inner. It is better to postpone specification and allocation of environment components until they are actually needed. Avoiding this so-called premature binding keeps a program more flexible.

A program should certainly work correctly, however, with a procedure P declared in Outer, a block outside the one in which the actual reference to P is made. In fact, if several parallel inner blocks all use procedure P, then clearly it would not be desirable to have P declared in any one, or all, of them. The general rule is that a procedure declaration must be placed where it is visible (accessible) to all of its callers, and where all the globals it needs are visible (accessible) to it.

Figure 5-19 shows an ALGOL program for Case 1 and Figure 5-20 shows its tree structure schematic. As an aid in reading and discussing this program, and all similar programs in the case studies, each line is numbered and each program block or procedure block is outlined and given a name that can be referred to in the contoured snapshots of execution. The Top flowchart of Figure 5-18 has been coded as two blocks, Outer and Inner. Block Inner includes the declaration (allocation) of the m-element array B. Note, however that the procedure block for SQUEEZE, which is referred to only in Inner, could have been de-

```
                                                        Outer
 1  begin
 2    integer m;
                                                     SQUEEZE
 3    procedure SQUEEZE (n, A, k);
 4      integer n, k;
 5      real array A;
 6      begin
 7        integer i;
 8        k := 0;
 9        for i := 1 step 1 until n do
10          if A [i] = 0 then k := k + 1 else a [i - k] := A [i];
11        n := n - k
12      end
13    ;
14    read (m);
                                                       Inner
15    begin
16      real array B [1:m];
17      integer i, t;
18      for i := 1 step 1 until m do read (B [i]);
19      SQUEEZE (m, B, t);
20      if t = 0 then print ("No elements were eliminated")
21               else print (t, "Elements were eliminated")
22    end
23  end
```

Figure 5-19. **ALGOL Program to match the flowcharts and legends of Figure 5-18. The print statements in lines 20 and 21 are not standard ALGOL 60.**

clared local to block Inner. The recoding of Case 1, with this change and the verification of its correctness, is left to the reader as an exercise.

The following is a series of eight snapshots tracing the execution of the ALGOL program for Case 1 where the data set is m = 4, B = (3, 0, 0, 5). A brief discussion follows each snapshot.

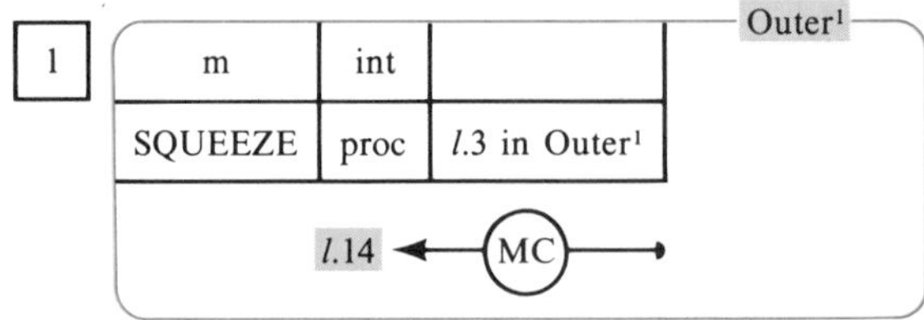

The outermost block of the program has been entered (Snapshot 1). Contour Outer¹ has been created. The cells for the variable m and for the procedure SQUEEZE have been allocated in this contour. The MC is ready to execute

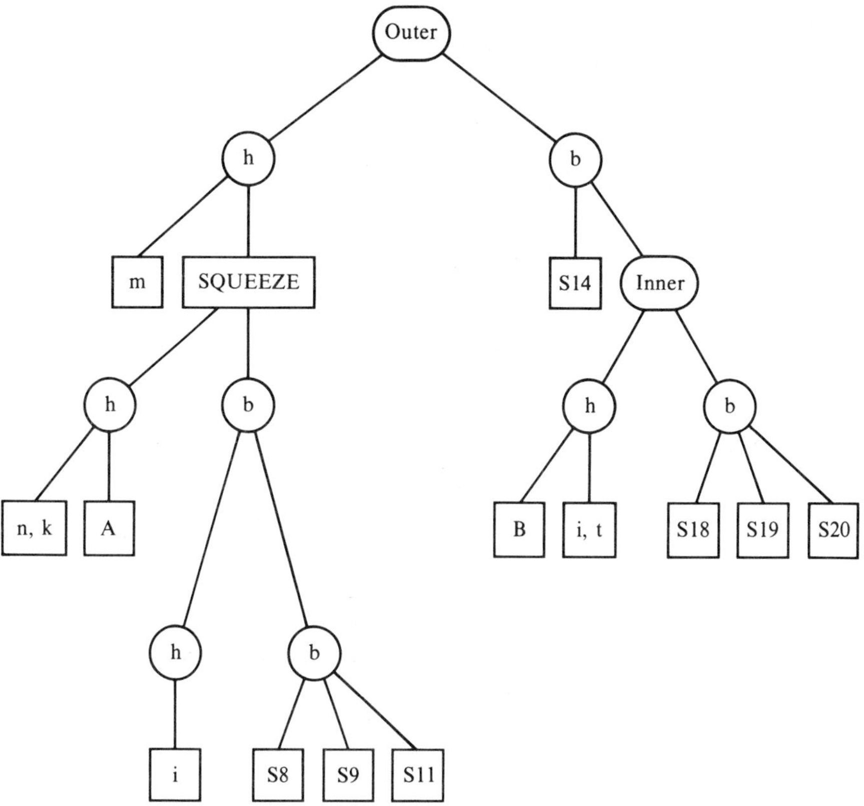

Figure 5-20. **Tree structure schematic for the ALGOL program of Figure 5-19. Declarations are represented by the identifiers they declare and statements are represented by the line on which they begin, for example, the assignment statement on line 8 is represented as the terminal node S8; the *if* statement on lines 20 and 21 is represented by the terminal node S20.**

line 14, the first statement in Outer. Note that the value part of the SQUEEZE cell, *l*.3 in Outer[1], is an (ip, ep) pair.

2 — Outer[1]

m	int	4
SQUEEZE	proc	*l*.3 in Outer[1]

l.15 ← MC →

The input step in line 14 has now been executed (Shapshot 2), giving m the value 4, and the MC is ready to execute line 15, that is, to enter the block Inner.

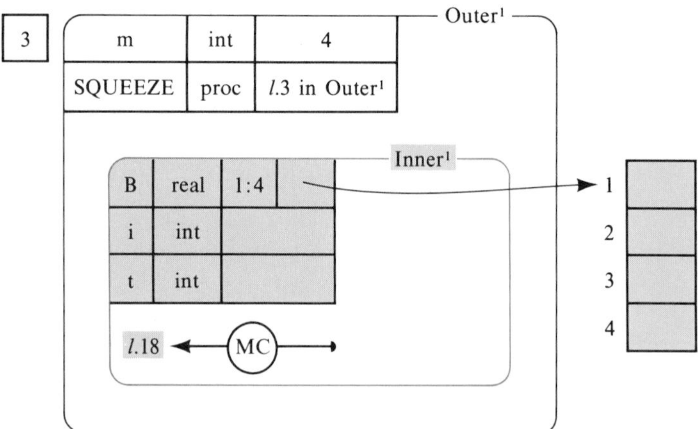

In snapshot 3 the contour for Inner¹ has been created and nested within Outer¹. Inner¹ includes a cell for the list B. The bounds of B are 1:4, since m has the value 4. These bounds are placed in the value part of the cell for B. A four-compartment cell, which we shall call a *list cell,* has been allocated. The arrow from the cell for B to the list cell indicates that the "value" assigned to B includes a *pointer* or reference to that list cell. The list cell itself could have been drawn *inside* the contour Inner¹, as we drew the cell for CHESS in Section 1-3. The reasons for placing the list cell outside the contour are largely visual.*

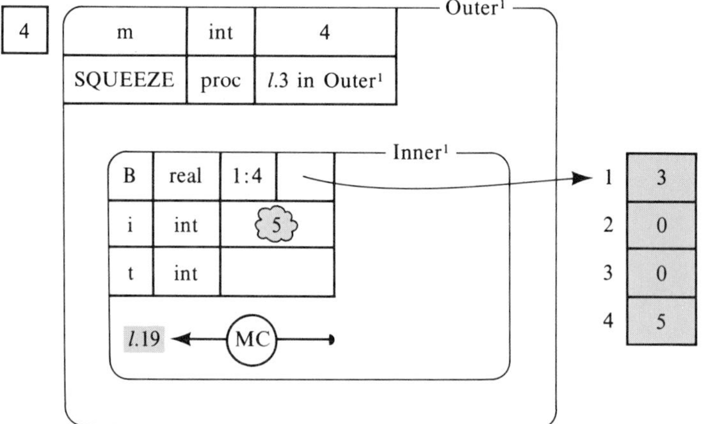

Snapshot 4 shows the state of the computation after line 18, the second input step, has been executed with the net effect of assigning values to the list cell. (The value of the loop counter i now exceeds m. In ALGOL the value of a loop counter is not *defined* once the upper limit of the loop has been exceeded and a

*We would like to be able to make comparisons of snapshots, like snapshot 3 for Figure 5-19, for several different data sets. We can compare snapshots more easily if the comparable contours (for example Inner¹) are the same size. However, especially with dynamic storage allocation, it is impossible to standardize the size for a contour like Inner¹, if it has to accommodate the list cell for array B. Furthermore, too many values tend to clutter the contour. Thus we represent the list cell in the right-hand margin and put a pointer to that list cell inside the contour.

normal exit from the loop has been executed. To remind us that i is no longer defined we place the value in a cloud, i.e., (5). But, this causes no problem, because it is never essential to know the value of a control variable after a normal exit from an iteration.) The MC is about to execute the call on SQUEEZE at line 19.

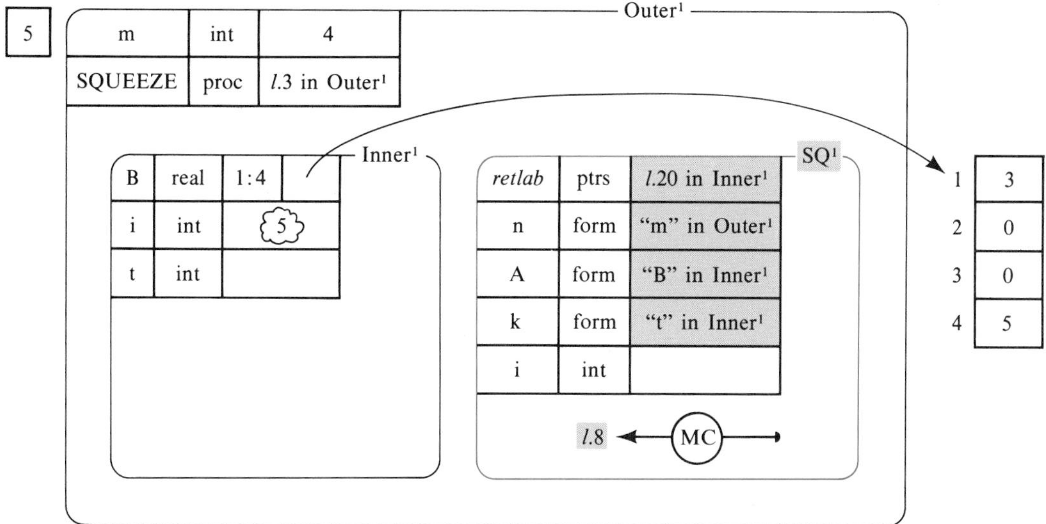

In calling SQUEEZE, the MC first notes the ip and ep values for SQUEEZE in the global SQUEEZE cell located in Outer[1]. A contour SQ[1] is constructed and nested inside Outer[1], since this is designated as the ep part of SQUEEZE. The cells to be allocated for the new contour are determined by executing the procedure entry beginning at line 3 (see snapshot 5). These cells are designated partly in the head of SQUEEZE (lines 4 and 5 tell about the formal parameters, and in this case, all are name parameters) and partly in the head of the body of SQUEEZE (line 7 tells about the one local of SQUEEZE). The value part of the cell for each name parameter is assigned a quoted copy of the matching argument expression and the name of the environment within which to "evaluate" that argument when the time comes.

The cell for the local i is allocated in SQ[1] and, of course, also a *return* cell, *retlab.* The value of *retlab* is set to *l.*20 in Inner[1]. This constitutes the ip, ep pair that identifies the resumption point in the program and the environment for that resumption.

Snapshot 5 shows the MC ready to execute the first statement in the body of SQUEEZE, line 8. Note that the MC has moved inside SQ[1] to execute SQUEEZE. Thus the *addressing environment,* the set of cells accessible to the MC during the execution of SQUEEZE, is as follows:

locals:	the variable i in SQ[1]
parameters:	the identifiers n, A, and k
globals:	the variable m and the procedure SQUEEZE in Outer[1]

In fact, SQUEEZE is coded so it never refers directly either to m or to SQUEEZE, although the MC would be able to access (can see) these cells while executing in SQ[1].

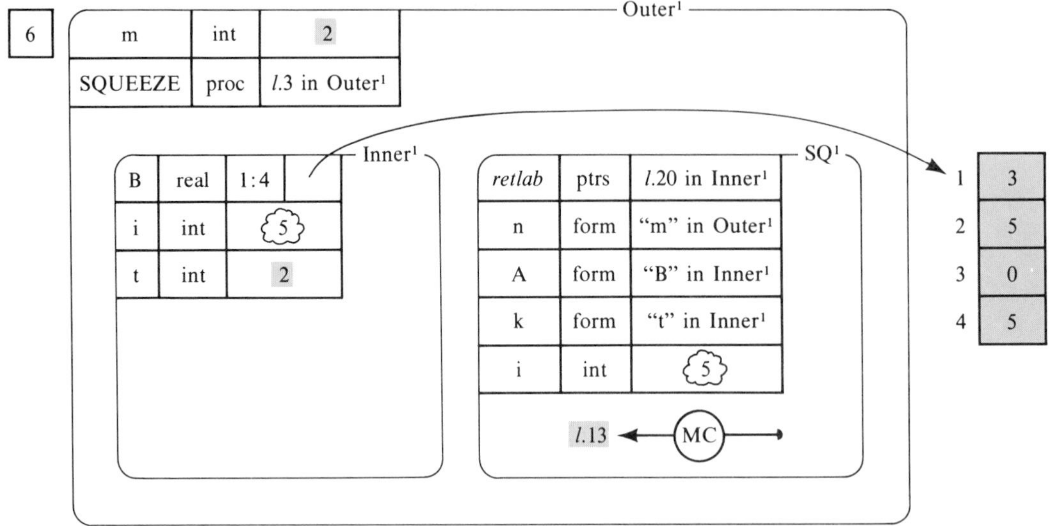

Snapshot 6 shows the state of the computation after the MC has executed the body of SQUEEZE and is about to return from the procedure (the ip points to line 13). Values of the arguments m, B, and t have all been changed by SQUEEZE.

When the MC returns to Inner[1] and executes lines 20 and 21, the output is

2 elements were eliminated

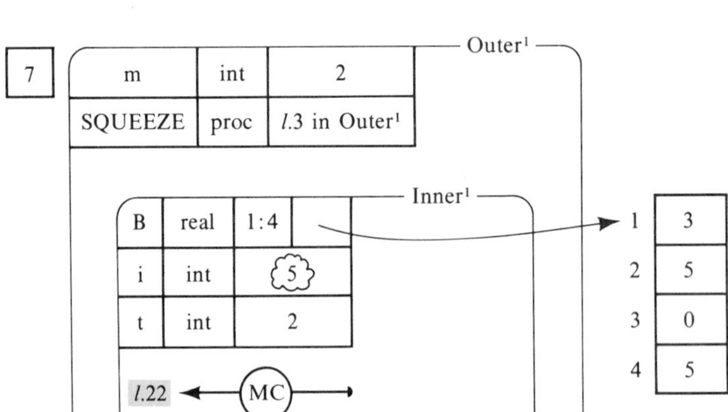

Snapshot 7 is taken after the MC has exited from SQUEEZE and returned to the calling environment, determined by consulting the value in the return cell

of SQ^1. The consequence of returning from SQUEEZE is that the contour SQ^1 is no longer accessible to the MC and has therefore been deallocated (and made to disappear from the snapshot). The MC is now ready to exit from Inner, that is, ready to execute line 22.

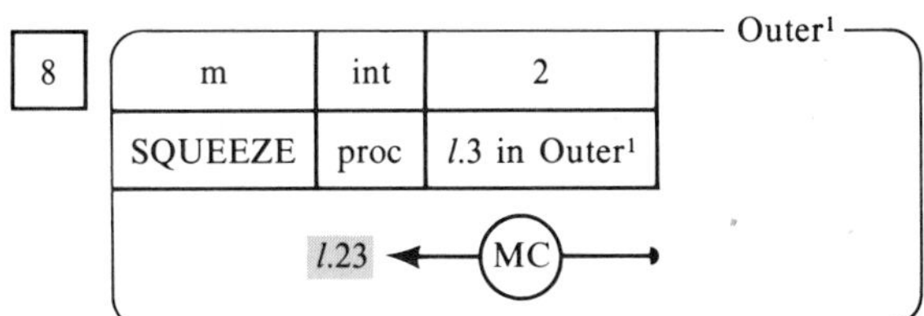

Upon exit from Inner, the contour $Inner^1$ is no longer accessible, and so in Snapshot 8 contour $Inner^1$, and the list cell pointed to from cell B in $Inner^1$, have been deallocated. Deallocation results from the fact that none of these cells is accessible after the MC moves out of $Inner^1$ into $Outer^1$. The MC is now ready to execute line 23 and exit from $Outer^1$, completing the program.

This is the end of Case 1. The discussion in each subsequent case assumes you are becoming increasingly familiar with the mechanics of snapshot construction that has been illustrated here.

Case 2 This second case study (see Figure 5-21) contains both a procedure and a function, each of which has parameters and locals. The procedure EVENLIST has two parameters: m, the length of a list, and C, the ordered set of m elements in the list. The primary action of EVENLIST is to copy the even-valued elements of C into a new list E of length k, and when this action has been completed, to print the word "None" if k has the value zero, and otherwise to print the new list E of even-valued elements selected from C. To determine the evenness of a given element of C, EVENLIST calls on the function EVEN, which returns the value 1 if the argument passed to it is even, and 0 if it is odd.

The purpose of this case study is to examine the semantics of value-returning ALGOL procedures (functions). The syntax of such a procedure, call it PROC, requires that an assignment statement of the form

$$\text{PROC} := \text{expression}$$

be executed at least once during the invocation of PROC. The return from the function occurs when the end of the procedure body is reached, and the expression value last assigned to PROC is the value returned. The mechanism for returning the value to the caller (that is, the semantics) suggests that we visualize the MC carrying that value back from the environment of the function to that of the caller.

Figure 5-22 displays an ALGOL program equivalent to the given flowcharts and legends of Figure 5-21. The block structure has been selected with an eye to efficient storage allocation; the procedure EVEN is declared within the procedure EVENLIST since EVEN is called only from EVENLIST. Also, the upper limit of the array B is determined dynamically, as explained in Case 1. To allow

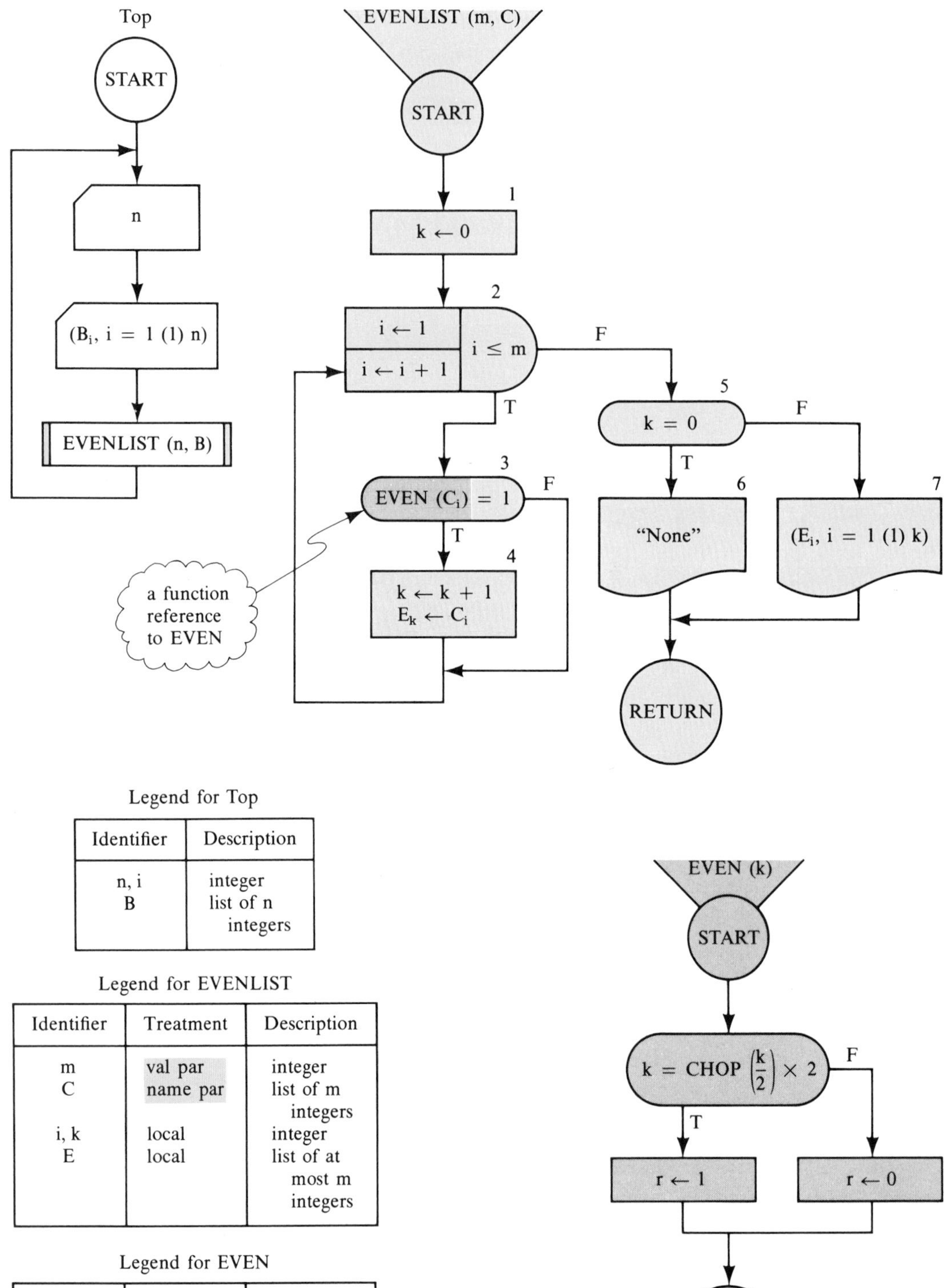

Legend for Top

Identifier	Description
n, i B	integer list of n integers

Legend for EVENLIST

Identifier	Treatment	Description
m	val par	integer
C	name par	list of m integers
i, k	local	integer
E	local	list of at most m integers

Legend for EVEN

Identifier	Treatment	Description
k	val par	integer
r	local	integer

Figure 5-21. **Flowcharts and legends for Case 2.**

```
     0   1   2   3   4   5   6   7   8   9
                                              Outer
 1  begin
 2    integer n;
 3    start: read (n);
                                              Inner
 4    begin
 5      integer i; integer array B [1:n];
                                              EVENLIST
 6      procedure EVENLIST (m, C);
 7        value m; integer m; integer array C;
 8        begin
                                              EVEN
 9          integer procedure EVEN (k);
10            value k; integer k;
11            begin
12              integer r;
13              if k = (k ÷ 2) × 2 then r := 1 else r := 0;
14              EVEN := r
15            end
16          ;
17          integer i, k; integer array E [1:m];
18          k := 0;
19          for i := 1 step 1 until m do
20            if EVEN (C [i]) = 1 then begin k := k + 1; E [k] := C [i] end;
21          if k := 0 then print ("None")
22                  else for i := 1 step 1 until k do print (E [i])
23        end
24      ;
25      for i := 1 step 1 until n do read (B [i]);
26      EVENLIST (n, B)
27    end;
28    go to start
29  end
```

Figure 5-22. **ALGOL program for Case 2.**

more accurate place identification of the ip, especially in the return cells of the EVEN contours, we have put column numbers across the top of the ALGOL program. Thus, for example, the assignment operator in line 14 can be identified by *l*.14.3.

Two remarks are in order about Figures 5-21 and 5-22. The first remark concerns the apparently infinite loop shown in the top-level flowchart of Figure 5-21. There is an underlying assumption here that if no more data are available, the looping will stop. Figure 5-23 shows an alternate top-level flowchart that has a more acceptable structure, together with its related function procedure more_data.

In this top-level flowchart we have made more_data a logical or Boolean procedure; it returns the value *true* or *false*. We give to the function more_data the task of deciding whether there are indeed more data to be read. In more_data

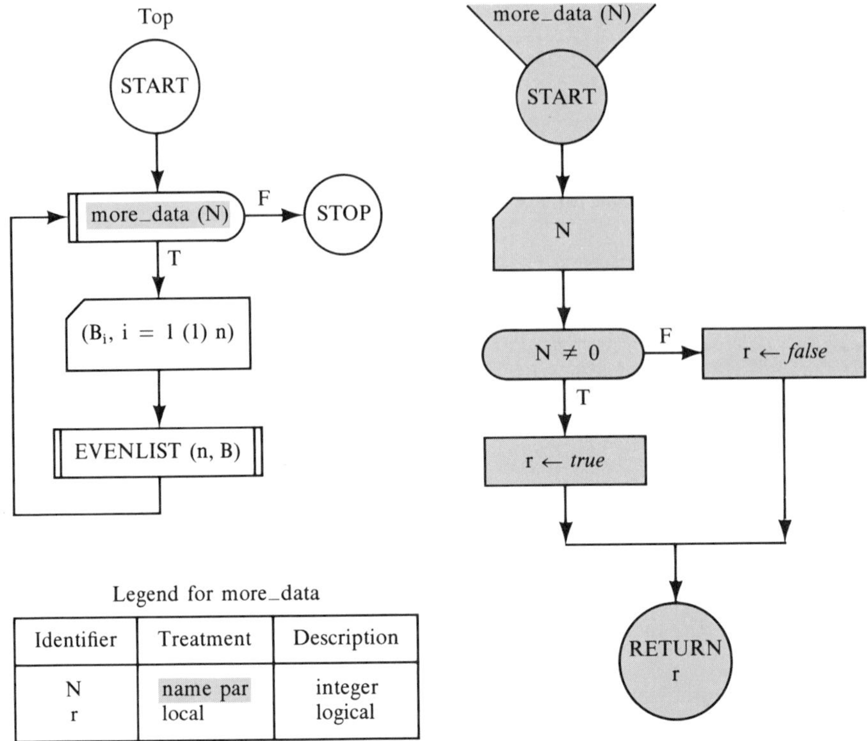

Legend for more_data

Identifier	Treatment	Description
N	name par	integer
r	local	logical

Figure 5-23

a zero value of N acts as a sentinel to indicate that all the data have been processed. Now, knowing we *could* correct the top-level structure by adding the complication of another function, let us proceed to study the execution of Case 2 with Figures 5-21 and 5-22, as shown. (See the end of this section for an exercise incorporating Figure 5-23 with Figure 5-21.)

The second remark concerns the procedure EVEN. Now that we are aware of the possibility of defining a function to be of type logical, it seems natural to define EVEN to return a logical value, *true* if its argument is even and *false* otherwise. In the corresponding ALGOL program, EVEN would be declared as a **Boolean** procedure and the local identifier r would also be declared of type **Boolean.** Then the **if** clause

if *EVEN* (*C*[*i*]) = *1*

in the EVENLIST procedure would be replaced by

if *EVEN* (*C*[*i*])

Semantically, the execution of the function procedure EVEN is the same whether its type is **integer** or **Boolean,** but the latter makes the program simpler and clearer.

We present next a series of ten snapshots tracing the execution of the ALGOL program for Case 2 with the data set n = 7, B = (3, −6, 2, 18, 13, 931, 10). A brief discussion follows each snapshot.

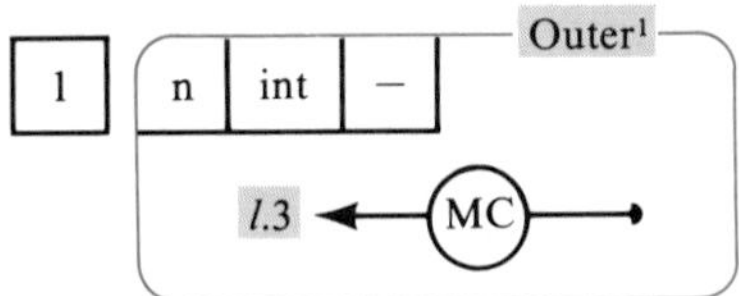

The outer block has been entered and the contour Outer[1] has been constructed. The MC is ready to execute the statement on line 3.

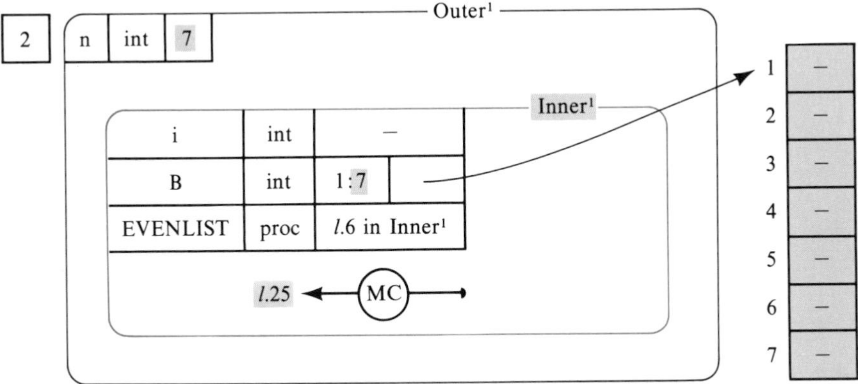

After the statement on line 3 has been executed and the value 7 has been assigned to n, block Inner is entered, resulting in the creation of contour Inner[1] nested within Outer[1]. Cells for the identifiers i, B, and EVENLIST are allocated. Since B is a one-dimensional array, its cell gets an initial value consisting of the bound pair 1 : 7 and a pointer to a newly allocated list cell containing storage for 7 elements. Since EVENLIST is a procedure, its cell also acquires an initial value, the instruction pointer, environment pointer pair, "line 6 in Inner[1]". Snapshot 2 shows the state of the computation just before the MC executes the first statement in Inner (at line 25).

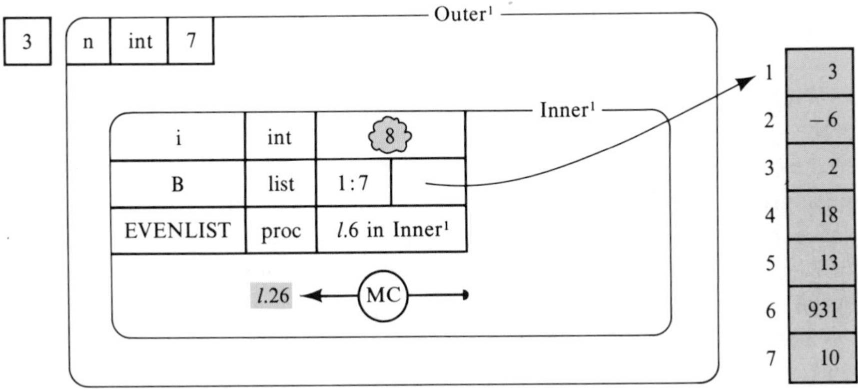

Snapshot 3 shows the result of executing line 25. Values are assigned to the seven elements of the array B.

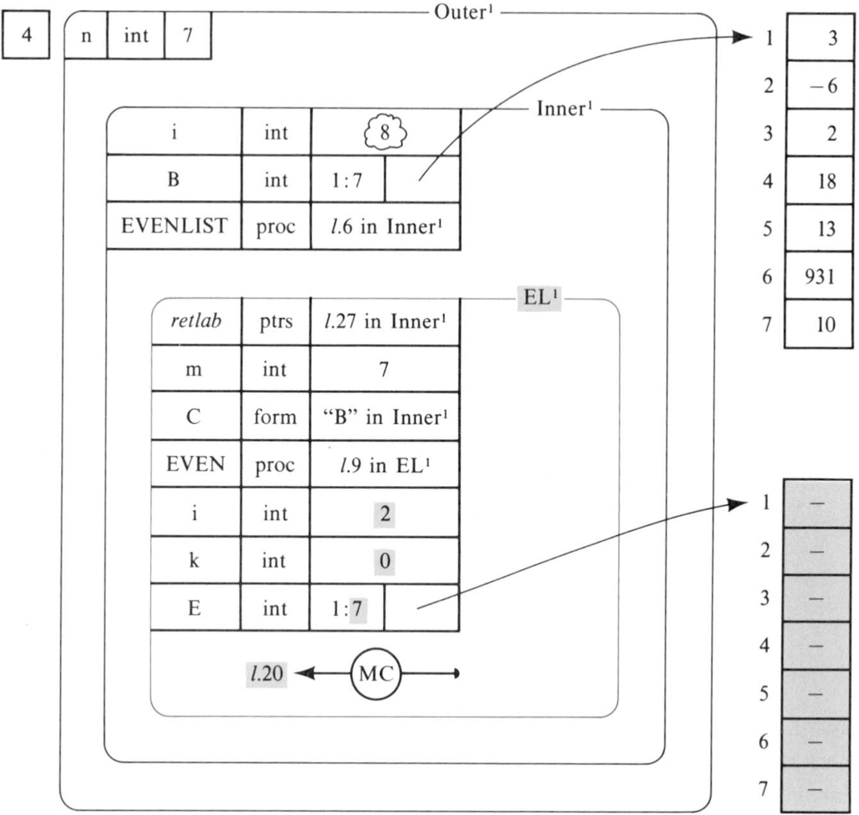

Snapshot 4 pictures the computation after EVENLIST has been entered, the statement on line 18 has been executed, and execution is now partway through the loop described by lines 19 and 20. The value of cell i in EL^1 is 2, and the value of k in EL^1 is 0, confirming that line 20 is about to be executed for the second time in this invocation of EVENLIST. In other words, EVENLIST is about to examine the second element in the list B and as yet has found no even-valued elements.

Note the construction of the contour EL^1. Among the locals of EVENLIST is the array E, with bounds 1 : m. Upon entry to EVENLIST the value assigned to the cell for E consists of the bound pair 1 : 7 (since the value parameter m has been given the value 7), and a pointer to a newly allocated list cell, which has space for 7 elements. This list cell must have seven "slots" in case every element of B is even, since EVENLIST copies every even-valued element from B to E. As of snapshot 4, however, the list cell for E is still empty.

Snapshot 5 is taken after EVEN has been called the second time to decide on the evenness of B[2]. A second, entirely new contour for EVEN has been allocated. Note that $EVEN^2$ contains a special return value cell, *retval.* Execution of the statement

$$\text{EVEN} := r$$

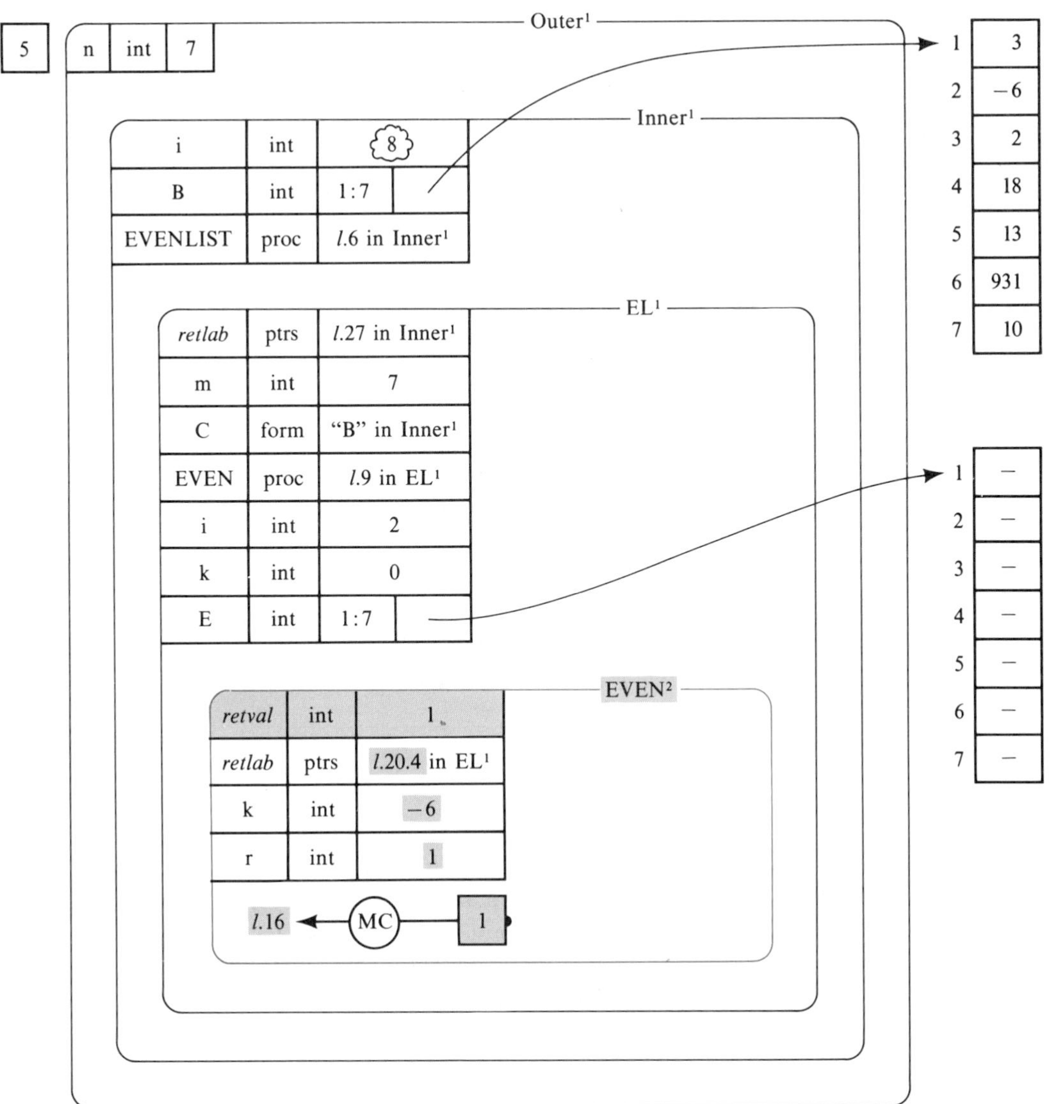

on line 14 causes the value of r to be assigned to the retval cell. When about to return to EL¹, the MC copies into the stack the value held in the retval cell. [We choose the name *retval* rather than "EVEN" for this special cell to prevent confusion with the cell used to hold the (ip, ep) value of EVEN as shown in EL¹. We regard the identifier *EVEN* in line 14 as only a pseudovariable.]

In regard to snapshot 5, notice that value parameter k in EVEN matches the argument C [i], which in this case represents B_i or B_2 in Inner¹, and the copied value is −6. Since this value is even, the local variable r has been set to 1. The MC has already executed the statement on line 14 that defines the value to be returned and that value has been copied into the MC's stack for transport back to EVEN's caller. The MC is about to step out of the EVEN² contour. Notice that in the *retlab* cell of the EVEN² contour, the ip is *l*.20.4, indicating that control will return to the "=" on line 20.

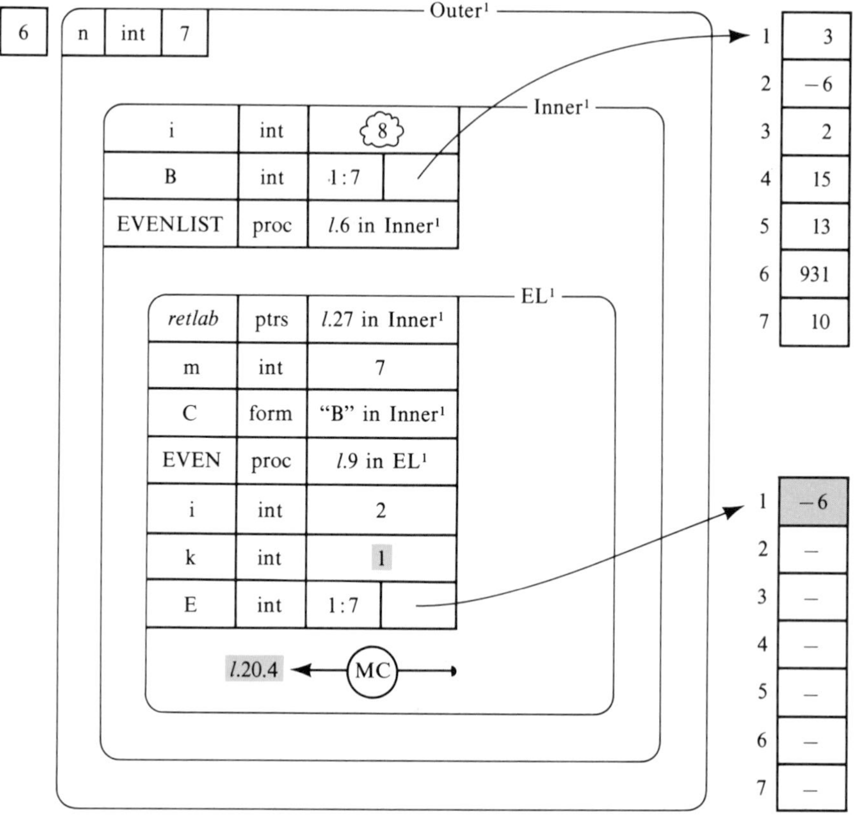

Snapshot 6 shows the condition of the computation soon after the MC has returned from EVEN with the value 1. The compound statement after the "then" on line 20 has just been completed for the first time. k has been increased to 1 and E_1 has been assigned the value of C_2. The MC is ready to increment i once again in executing the **for** statement on line 19.

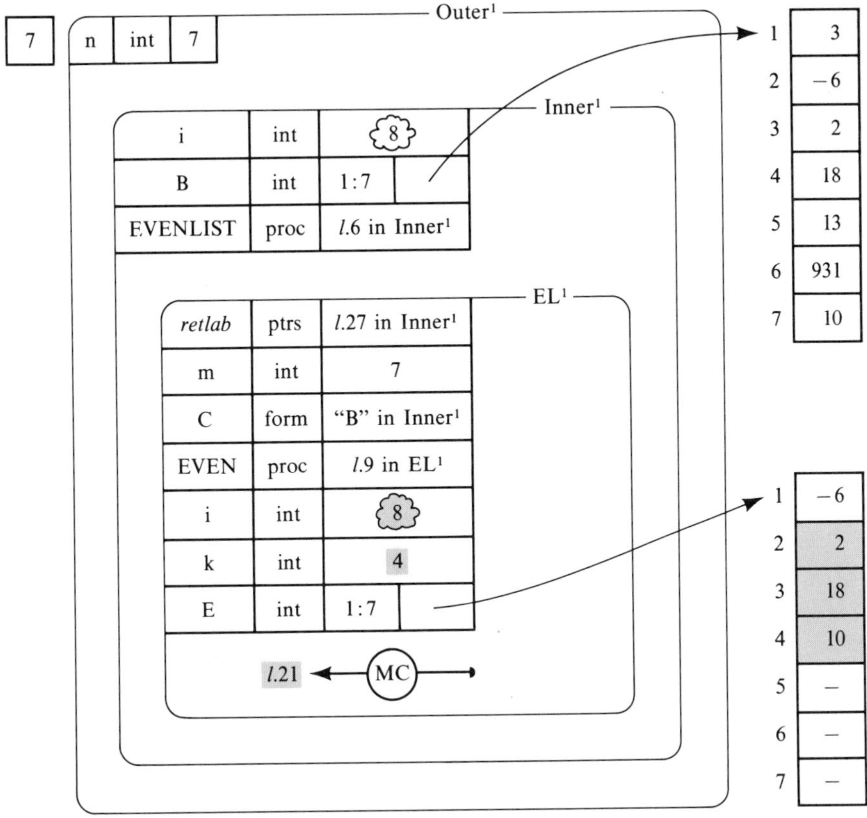

Snapshot 7 shows the situation after the **for** loop has been completed. The list E contains all the even-valued elements that were found in the list B. The count k of such values is 4. The MC is ready to execute the **if** statement that begins on line 21.

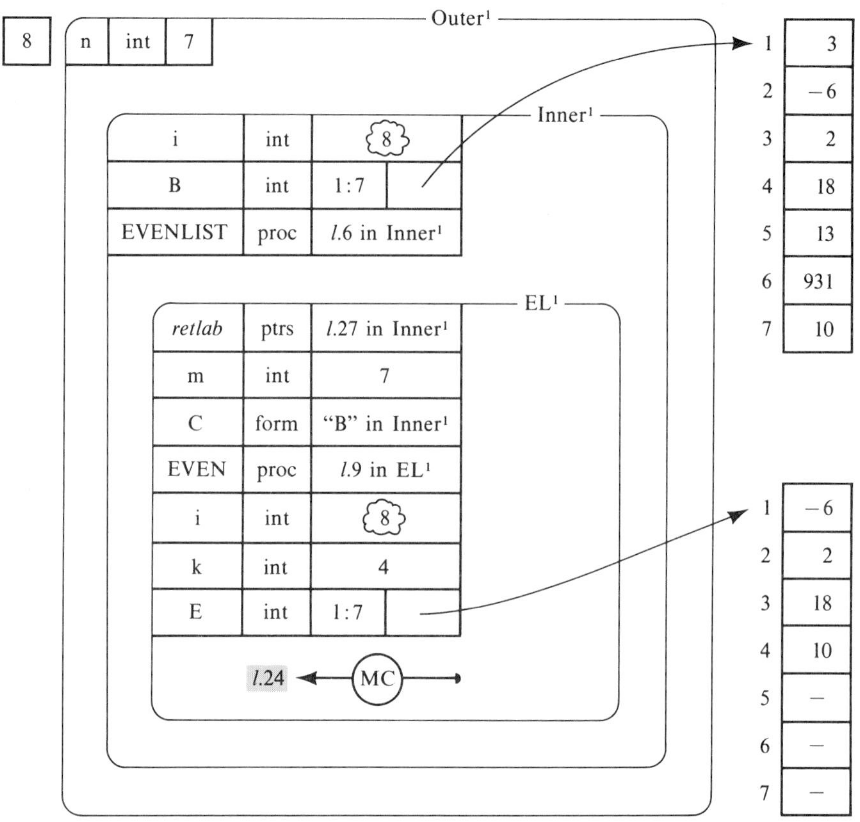

Output is: 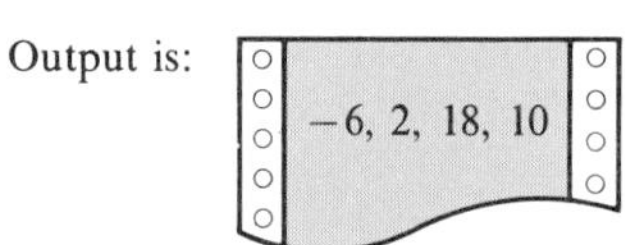

The false consequence (line 22) of the **if** statement has been executed, resulting in the output shown. The MC is now ready to execute the return from EVENLIST, that is, to step from the EL¹ contour back into Inner¹.

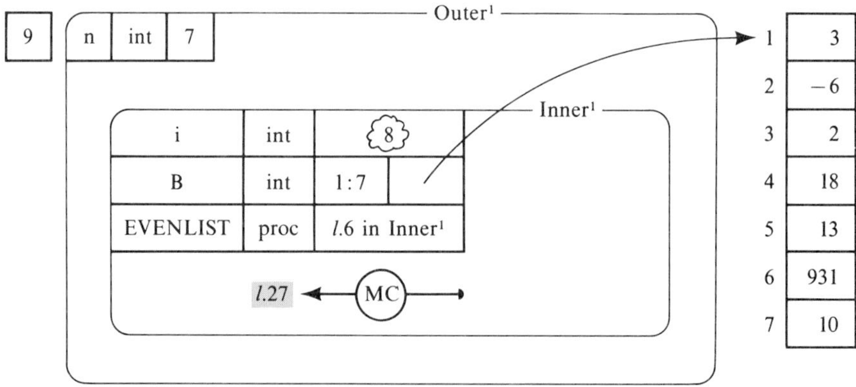

The return from EVENLIST is complete. Contour EL[1] is gone, and so is the list cell for E. The MC is now ready to exit from block Inner (line 27).

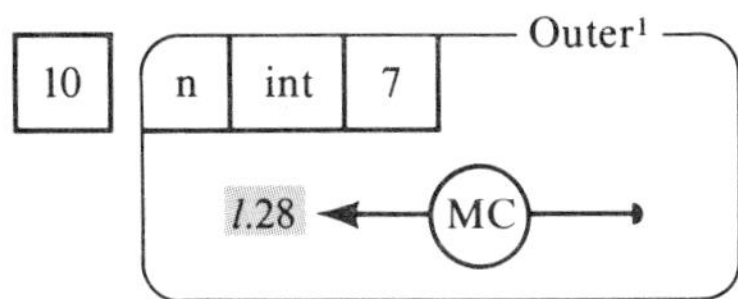

The exit from Inner has been completed. All that remains is the contour Outer[1] with its single cell for n. The MC is about to execute the **goto** statement on line 28. Notice that this is our first **goto** statement in ALGOL. The **goto** is used sparingly in ALGOL, but in this type of situation there is no alternative. Every **goto** requires a labeled statement as destination. Labels can be any identifiers and a colon is used to separate a label from the statement that follows it. Labels need not be (are not) declared in ALGOL.

Exercises 5-7

1 (a) Suppose the top-level flowchart of Figure 5-21 is replaced by the top-level flowchart of Figure 5-23, and that the flowchart and legend for the function more_data are added to those for EVENLIST and EVEN.

Revise the ALGOL program of Figure 5-22 so it is a translation of these revised flowcharts.

(b) Draw a snapshot of the execution of your ALGOL program just before the MC returns from the function more_date for the first time to the top-level program. Use the data that appear in the text. The type compartment for a contour cell representing a Boolean value can be drawn, for example, as

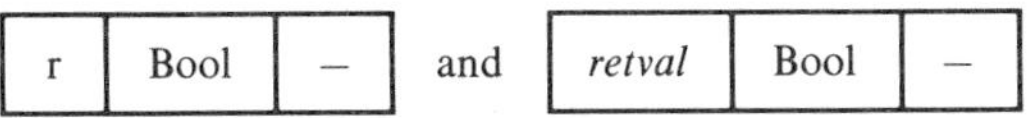

(c) Draw a snapshot of the execution of your ALGOL program just before the MC returns from the procedure EVENLIST. How does your snapshot compare with snapshot 8 of the text sequence?

2 Figure 5-24 shows flowcharts and legends for the two related procedures NORMALIZE and LRGST, together with a top level flowchart to use them.

NORMALIZE replaces each element C_i of the list C by C_i divided by a value supplied by the procedure LRGST.

LRGST finds the nonzero element in C, if any, of largest absolute value, and returns the value of this designated element. LRGST sets the global variable k to 1 if the search is successful and to 0 if unsuccessful.

These related procedures have parameters and both local and global identifiers. Figures 5-25 and 5-26 display two possible ALGOL translations of the Figure 5-24 flowcharts and legends. In Figure 5-25, the procedures NORMALIZE and LARGST are "on a par" or in parallel with each other. Neither is nested within the other, but both are nested within the top program, which is written as a single block. The second program nests LRGST, which is used by NORMALIZE, directly within NORMALIZE, which in turn is nested within Inner, the inner block of Outer, the top-level program. The second program thus exhibits a maximum of hierarchic structure.

(a) Study the flowcharts and ALGOL programs. Think about and compare the execution of the programs for the data set m = 5, B = (−12, 4, 0, 60, −72).

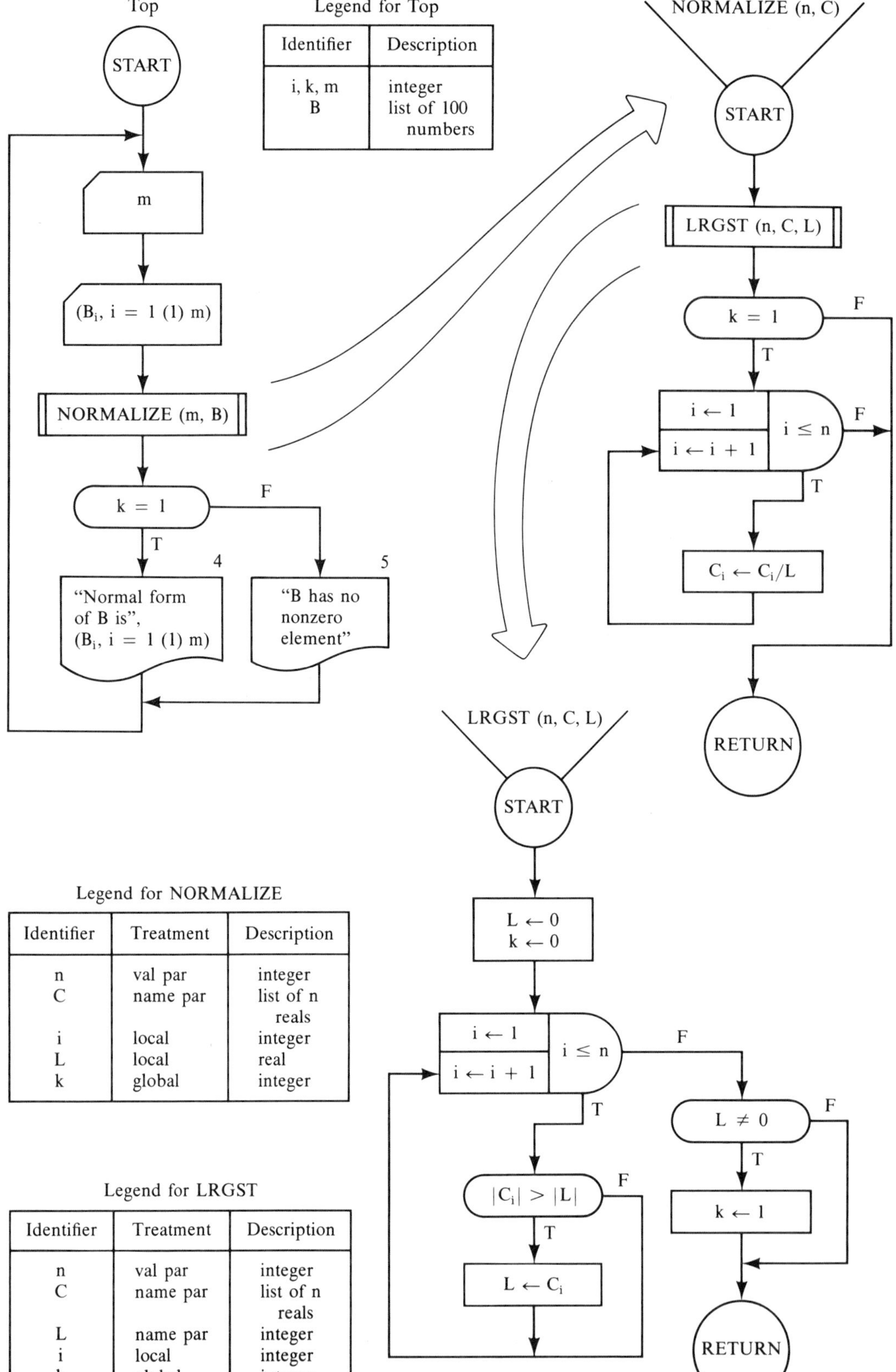

Legend for Top

Identifier	Description
i, k, m	integer
B	list of 100 numbers

Legend for NORMALIZE

Identifier	Treatment	Description
n	val par	integer
C	name par	list of n reals
i	local	integer
L	local	real
k	global	integer

Legend for LRGST

Identifier	Treatment	Description
n	val par	integer
C	name par	list of n reals
L	name par	integer
i	local	integer
k	global	integer

Figure 5-24

```
                                                   Outer
begin
  integer i, k, m;
  real array B [1:100];
                                          Norm
  procedure normalize (n, C);
    value n;
    integer n;
    real array C;
    begin
      integer i;
      real L;
      lrgst (n, C, L);
      if k = 1 then
        for i := 1 step 1 until n do C [i] := C [i]/L
    end
  ;
                                                   Lrg
  procedure lrgst (n, C, L);
    value n;
    integer n; real L;
    real array C;
    begin
      integer i;
      L := 0; k := 0;
      for i := 1 step 1 until n do
        if abs (C [i]) > abs (L) then L := C [i];
      if L ≠ 0 then k := 1
    end
  ;

  start: read (m);
  for i := 1 step 1 until m do read (B [i]);
  normalize (m, B);
  if k = 1 then begin print ("Normal form of B is");
                  for i := 1 step 1 until m do print (B [i])
                end
              else print ("B is empty");
  go to start
end
```

Figure 5-25. **First ALGOL Program for Figure 5-24**

Then for comparison draw several of the following snapshots for *each* program.

1. After entry into the Outer block, just before the first statement is executed.
2. Just before the NORMALIZE procedure is called for the first time.
3. Just before the LRGST procedure is called for the first time.
4. After entry into LRGST, before the first statement is executed.
5. Just before the return from LRGST.
6. Just before the return from NORMALIZE.
7. Just before the output statement is executed. Show that the output will be

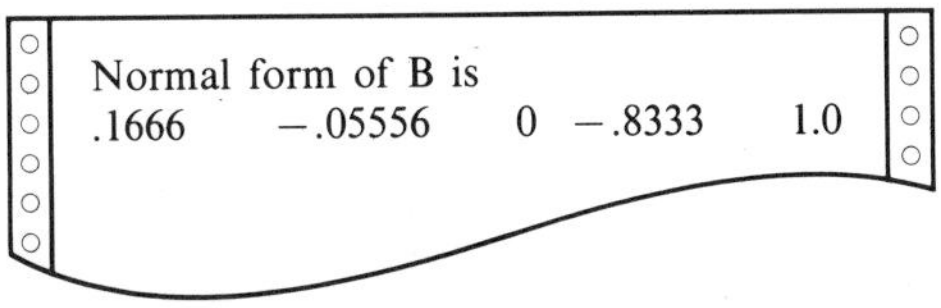

```
Normal form of B is
.1666    -.05556    0  -.8333    1.0
```

```
                                                Outer
begin
  integer m;
  start: read (m);
                                                Inner
  begin
    integer i, k;
    real array B [1:m];
                                                Norm
    procedure normalize (n, C);
      value n;
      integer n;
      real array C;
      begin
                                                Lrg
      procedure lrgst (n, C, L);
        value n;
        integer n; real L;
        real array C;
        begin
          integer i;
          L := 0; k := 0;
          for i := 1 step 1 until n do
            if abs (C [i]) > abs (L) then L := C [i];
          if L ≠ 0 then k := 1
        end
      ;
        integer i;
        real L;
        lrgst (n, C, L);
        if k = 1 then
          for i := 1 step 1 until n do C [i] := C [i]/L
      end
    ;
    for i := 1 step 1 until m do read (B [i]);
    normalize (m, B);
    if k = 1 then begin print ("Normal form of B is");
                        for i := 1 step 1 until m do print (B [i])
                  end
             else print ("B is empty")
  end;
  go to start
end
```

Figure 5-26. Second ALGOL Program for Figure 5-24.

(b) Reconstruct the top-level flowchart in Figure 5-24 so that it does not contain an infinite loop. If you use a procedure in the process, include a flowchart and legend for it.

5-8 CASE STUDIES OF RECURSIVE FUNCTIONS—TWO EXAMPLES

Here we present two simple illustrations to show how useful contour diagrams are in following the execution of recursive functions. Case 3 gets us started by looking at the contour diagrams of the familiar factorial function (see Section 3-3). Case 4, which describes the binomial coefficient function, shows us how snapshots help in tracing the tree of recursive calls that develop when this function is executed.

Case 3 This example uses the recursive factorial function, fact, defined by

$$\text{fact (n)} = \begin{cases} \text{if} \quad n = 0 \quad \text{then } 1 \\ \text{else} \quad \text{fact } (n - 1) \times n \end{cases}$$

The flowcharts and legends are displayed in Figure 5-27 and an equivalent ALGOL program is shown in Figure 5-28.

The following are snapshots of the execution of Figure 5-28 for the data set n = 3.

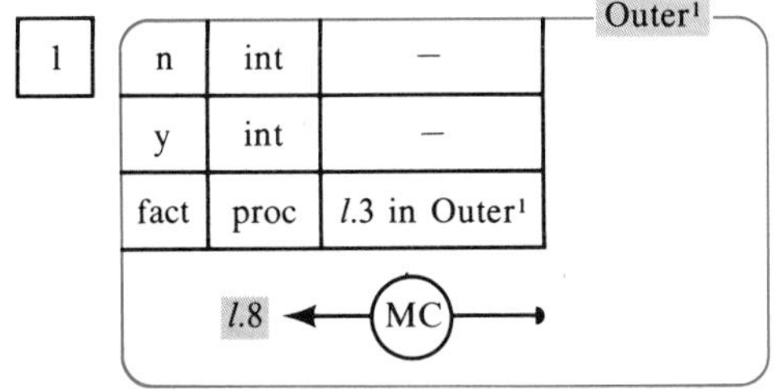

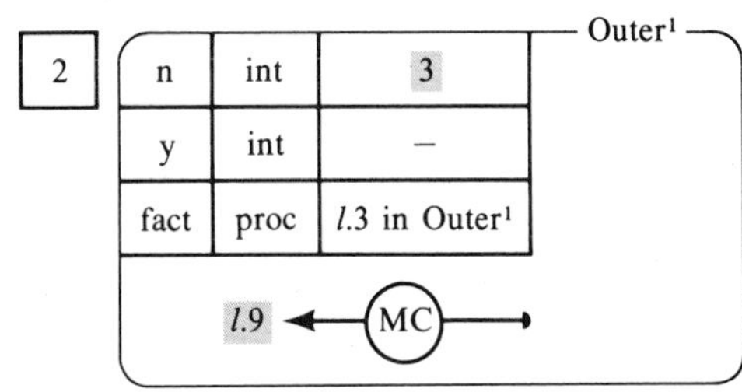

Snapshot 1 shows the environment Outer¹ created when the Outer program block is entered. Snapshot 2 shows the situation just after the input step at line 8 has been executed and just before the MC executes line 9, which includes the call on fact.

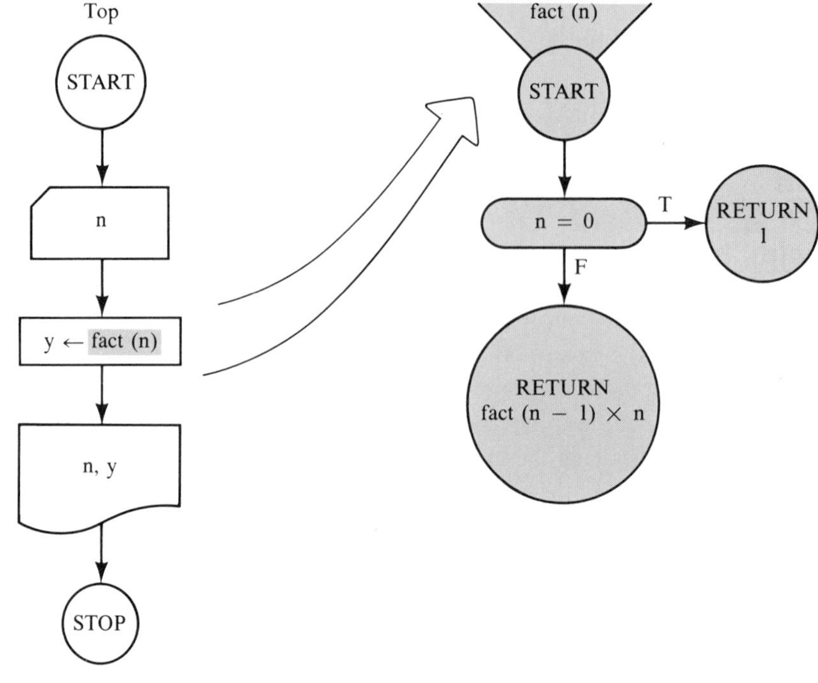

Legend for Top

Identifier	Description
n, y	integer

Legend for fact

Identifier	Treatment	Description
n	val par	integer

Figure 5-27

```
0   1   2   3   4   5   6   7   8   9
                                    Outer
begin
  integer n, y
                                    fact
  integer procedure fact (n);
    value n; integer n;
    if n = 0 then fact := 1
             else fact := fact (n − 1) × n
  ;

  read (n);
  y := fact (n);
  print (n, y)
end
```

Figure 5-28. **ALGOL Program for case 3.**

3

Outer^1

n	int	3
y	int	—
fact	proc	*l*.3 in Outer^1

fact^1

retval	int	—
retlab	ptrs	*l*.9.1 in Outer^1
n	int	3

l.5 ← MC →

A contour, fact^1, is created and nested in Outer^1 as directed by the ep value of the cell, fact, in Outer^1. After assigning values to the cells n and *retlab*, the MC is ready to execute the fact procedure's first statement, which is at line 5.

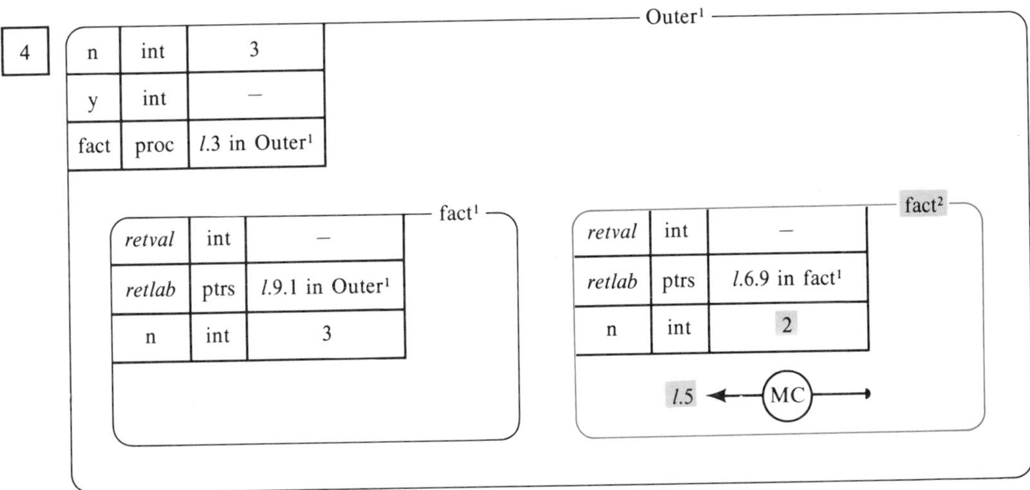

Since n was not 0, the MC executed the **else** clause on line 6, which resulted in another call on fact, this time with an argument whose value is 2. Snapshot 4 shows the situation after the second entry into fact. Another contour for fact has been created. Since each such contour must be placed in Outer^1, as prescribed by the environment pointer, ep, in the cell value for fact, the second contour, called fact^2, is shown side-by-side with (and *not* nested within) fact^1. The MC has moved into the new environment of fact^2. As one would expect, the structure of fact^2 is identical with that of fact^1 and only the cell values differ. Values in the return cells form a dynamic chain back to the original calling site in line 9 of Outer and to the original calling environment, Outer^1. The MC is again ready to execute the first statement in the fact procedure (line 5).

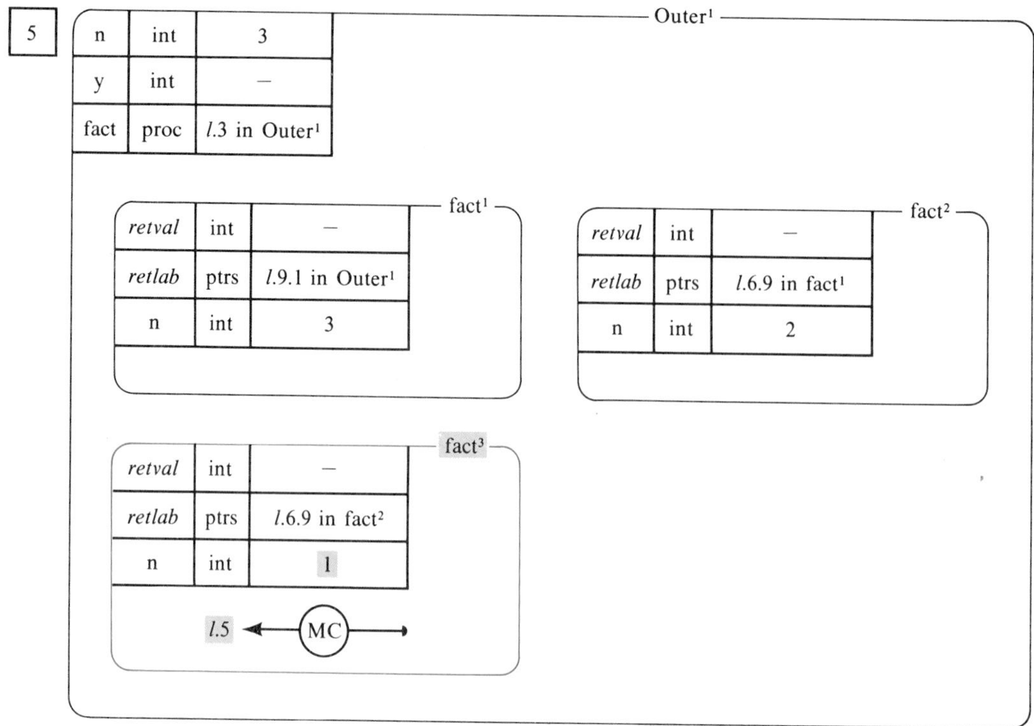

Snapshot 5 shows a state of affairs similar to that of the preceding snapshot, only one call later. The third entry to fact has now been completed, this time generating the contour fact^3. The value parameter n has the value 1 and the dynamic chain (of returns) has been extended by one link.

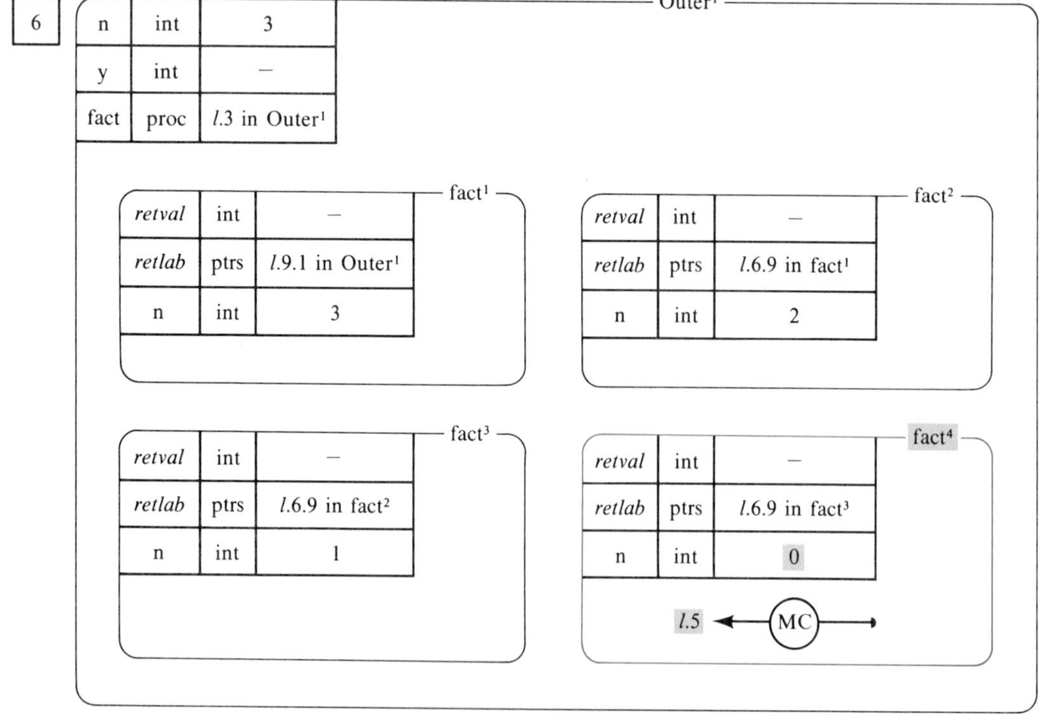

Snapshot 6 is taken after the fourth and final call on fact. This time the value of n is 0, so when the MC, now inside fact^4, executes the **if** statement on line 5, the assignment *fact := 1* is carried out, storing 1 in *retval.* Then when the end of the body of fact is reached, the 1 in *retval* is pushed onto the MC's stack and the MC returns to (line 6.9 in) fact^3.

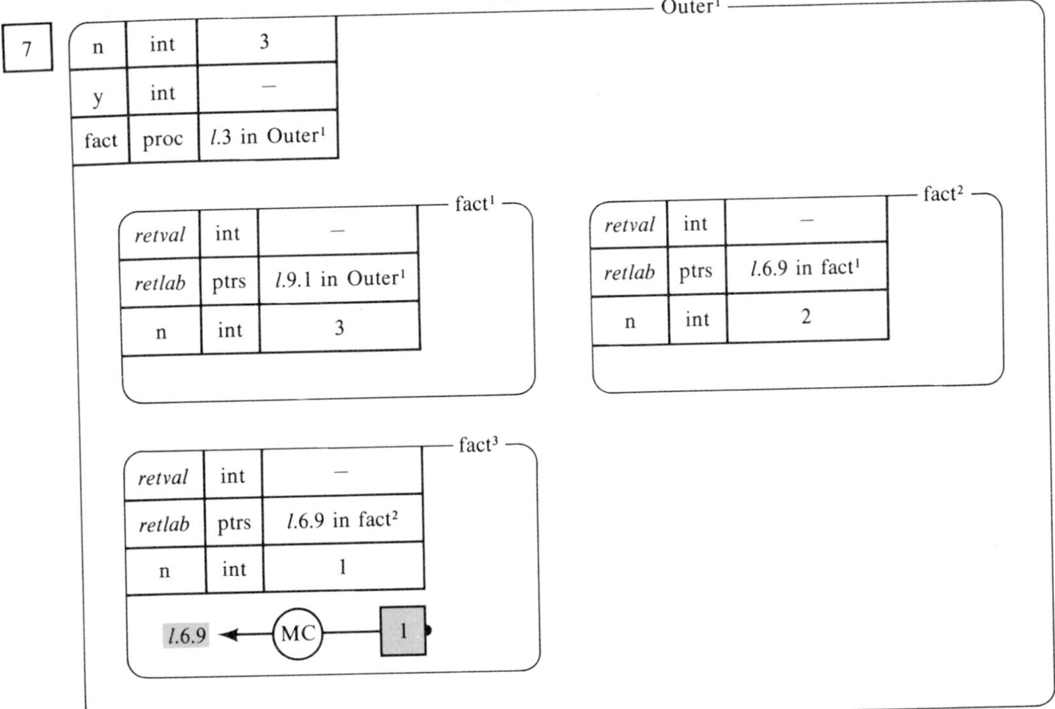

The "windup" process has begun. In snapshot 7, the MC is back in the fact^3 environment with the value 1 in his stack, ready to execute the multiply operation in line 6, which was the ip of the return cell in fact^4. Using the value 1 from the stack, the MC computes the value of the expression *fact* $(n - 1) \times n$, as 1×1, or 1. This new return value is stored in the *retval* cell in fact^3 to be carried back later to the fact^2 environment on top of the MC's stack.

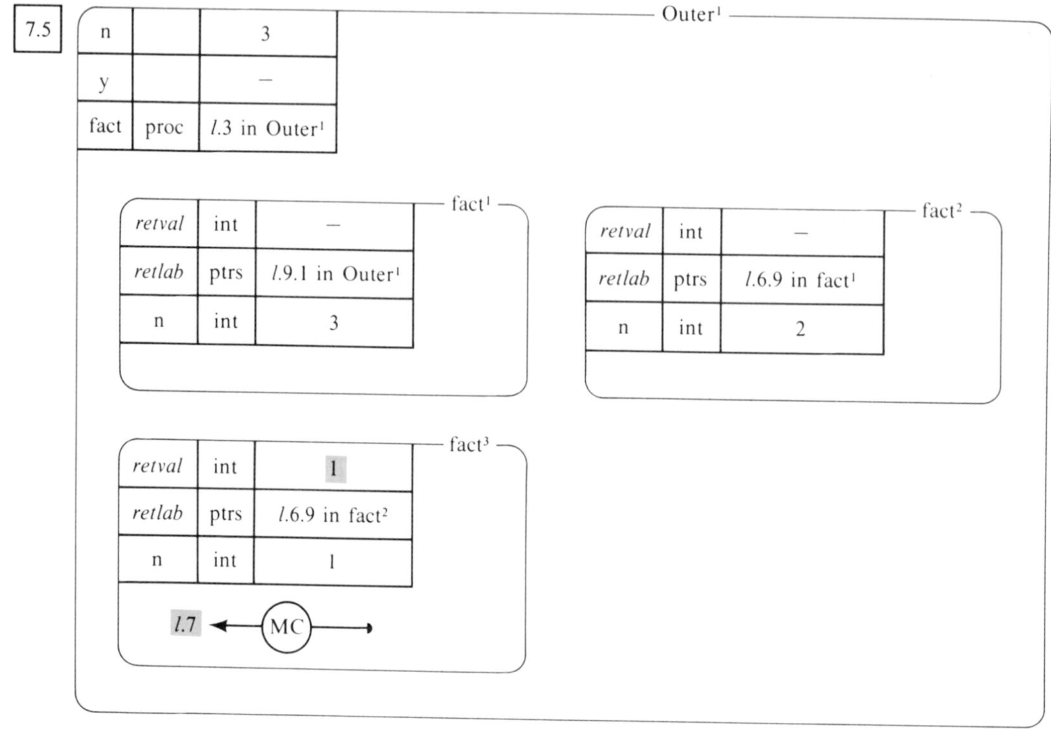

Snapshot 7.5 shows the situation after the assignment of the value 1 to the *retval* cell in fact³, but just before the return to fact² is initiated. At the moment the stack is empty, but again at the beginning of the return mechanism, the value in *retval* will be copied and pushed onto the stack to be carried back to fact².

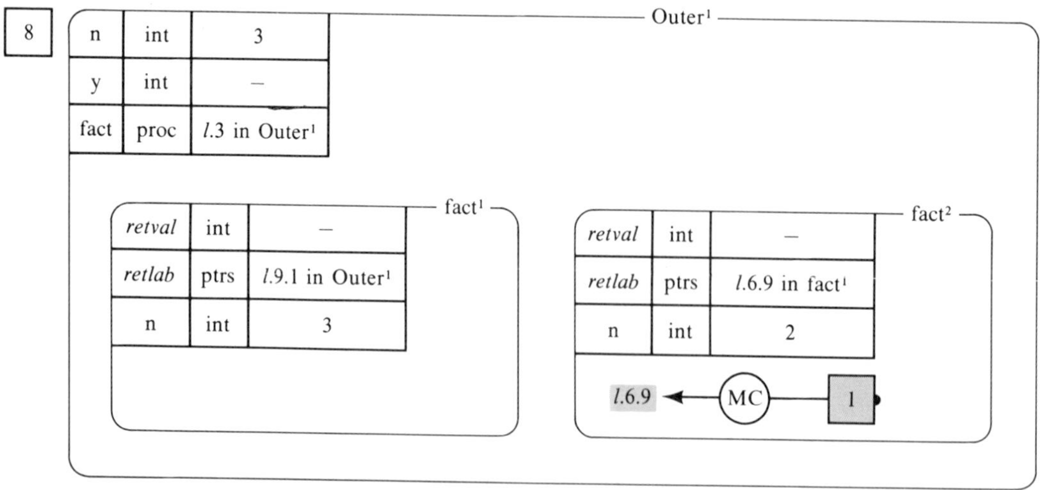

Snapshot 8 shows the MC in fact² again ready to execute the multiplication in line 6. This time the computed expression in line 6 has the value 2, which is returned in the MC's stack to the fact¹ environment, as shown in snapshot 9.

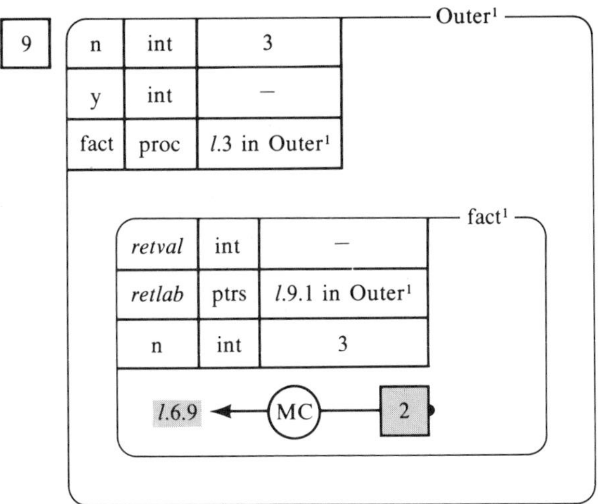

Again the expression in line 6 is evaluated, this time yielding the value 6, which is returned to the Outer[1] environment as shown in snapshot 10. Now the MC is ready to execute the assignment part of line 9, as specified by the ip in the return cell of fact[1].

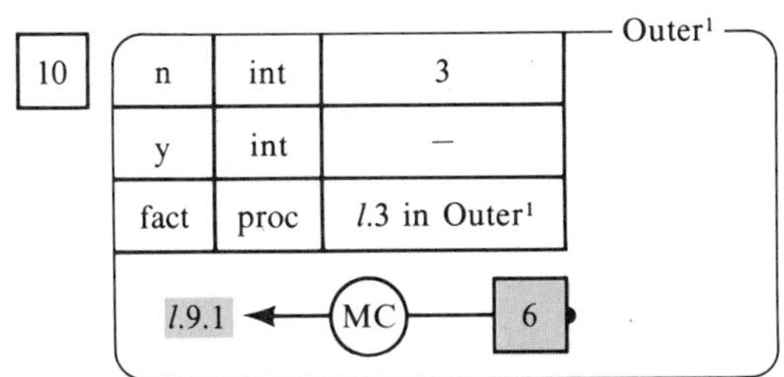

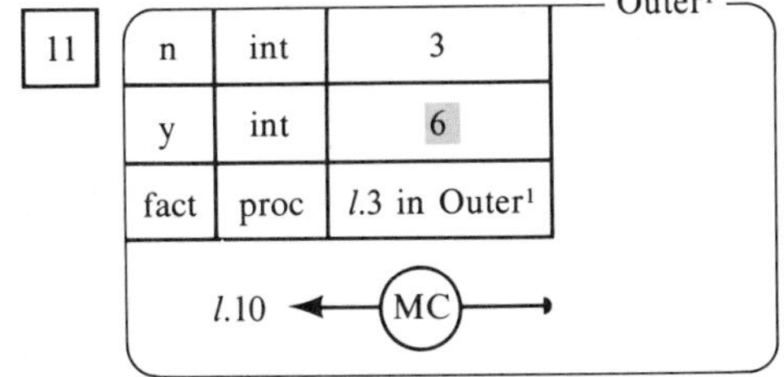

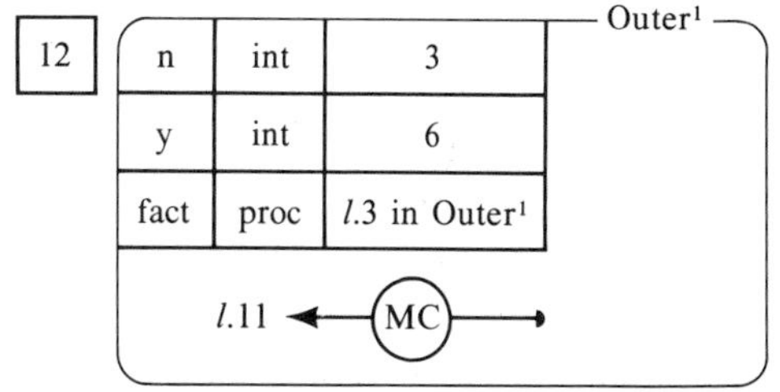

Output is:

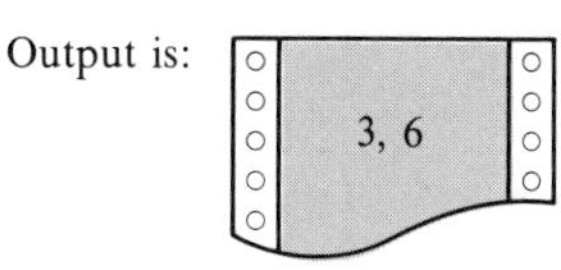

Snapshots 11 and 12 show the effects of executing lines 9 and 10 in the main program block, resulting in the output shown with snapshot 12.

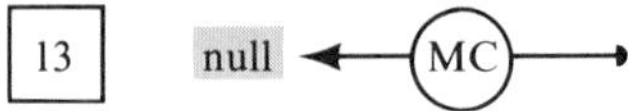

When line 11, the block exit, is executed, the MC moves out of the Outer[1] environment and stands ready to execute the next statement, but there isn't any next statement and there isn't any remaining environment. The ip and ep of the MC are both null and the stack is empty too! So the computation halts.

Exercises 5-8

1 Suppose we replace the definition of fact (n) in case 3 by the following:

$$\text{fact (n)} = \begin{cases} \text{if} \quad n = 0 \quad \text{then } 1 \\ \text{else} \quad n \times \text{fact (n} - 1) \end{cases}$$

Discuss what effect this change will have on the snapshots for case 3.

Case 4 This example utilizes a recursive function with locals. The function called BC is the binomial coefficient function discussed in Section 3-3 and defined by

$$\text{BC (n, k)} = \begin{cases} \text{if} \quad k = 0 \text{ or } n = k \quad \text{then } 1 \\ \text{else} \quad \text{BC (n} - 1, k) + \text{BC (n} - 1, k - 1) \end{cases}$$

The flowcharts and legends, including a top-level program that calls on BC, are given in Figure 5-29. The corresponding ALGOL program is found in Figure 5-30. A second version (Figure 5-32) is discussed later.

The sequence of snapshots that follows depicts execution of the program of Figure 5-30, where the data set is n = 3, k = 2. Executing the call on line 14 for BC (3, 2) causes a tree of calls to be generated (Figure 5-31). This tree has five nodes, counting the root node, and each node is numbered to correspond with its respective contour that appears in the snapshots. Each upward arrow is labeled with the value returned by the corresponding call. Frequent reference to this tree will help you to follow the execution sequence shown in the snapshots. In fact, for very simple recursive functions, like fact and BC, such call trees can serve as useful alternatives to the snapshots themselves. In any case, each type of representation of the execution sequence tends to confirm the value and validity of the other.

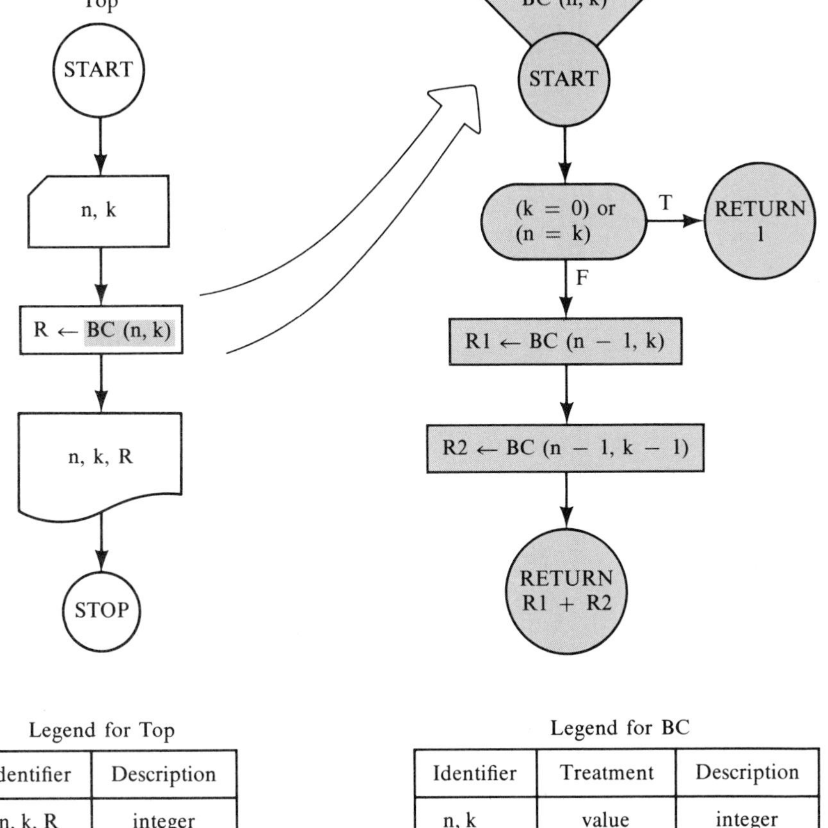

Legend for Top

Identifier	Description
n, k, R	integer

Legend for BC

Identifier	Treatment	Description
n, k R1, R2	value local	integer integer

Figure 5-29

```
0  1  2  3  4  5  6  7  8  9
                                          Outer
begin
  integer n, k, R;
                                          BC
  integer procedure BC (n, k);
  value n, k; integer n, k;
  begin
    integer R1, R2;
    if (k = 0) ∨ (n = k) then BC := 1
      else begin  R1 := BC (n − 1, k);
                  R2 := BC (n − 1, k − 1);
                  BC := R1 + R2
             end
  end;
  read (n, k);
  R := BC (n, K);
  print (n, k, R)
end
```

Figure 5-30. **ALGOL program for case 4, version 1.**

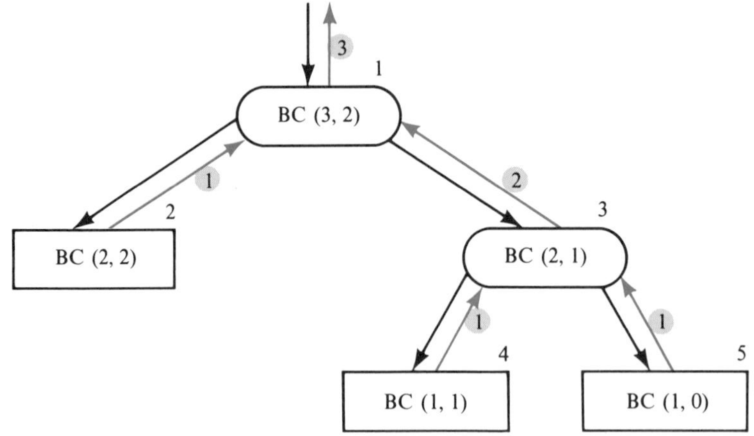

Figure 5-31. **Tree of calls on BC generated by the call BC (3, 2).**

1

Outer[1]

n	int	–
k	int	–
R	int	–
BC	proc	*l*.3 in Outer[1]

l.13 ← MC →

2

Outer[1]

n	int	3
k	int	2
R	int	–
BC	proc	*l*.3 in Outer[1]

l.14.2 ← MC →

Snapshot 1 shows the environment created for execution of the outer block. Snapshot 2 shows the state of the computation after the input step at line 13 has been executed. The MC is about to execute the procedure call on line 14 (about two-tenths of the way toward the end of that line).

Snapshot 3 shows the state after the first entry to BC has been executed. Value parameters n and k have received values 3 and 2, respectively. The MC has moved into the new environment BC[1]. Upon return from this call, execution is to resume at the assignment operation on line 14. (This point is shown in the *retlab* cell as *l*.14.1 to suggest that the ip is at a distance of about one-tenth of a line from the beginning of line 14.) The MC has already executed the **if** test on line 7 and found it false, and so execution is about to continue on line 8 with the execution of the second call on BC.

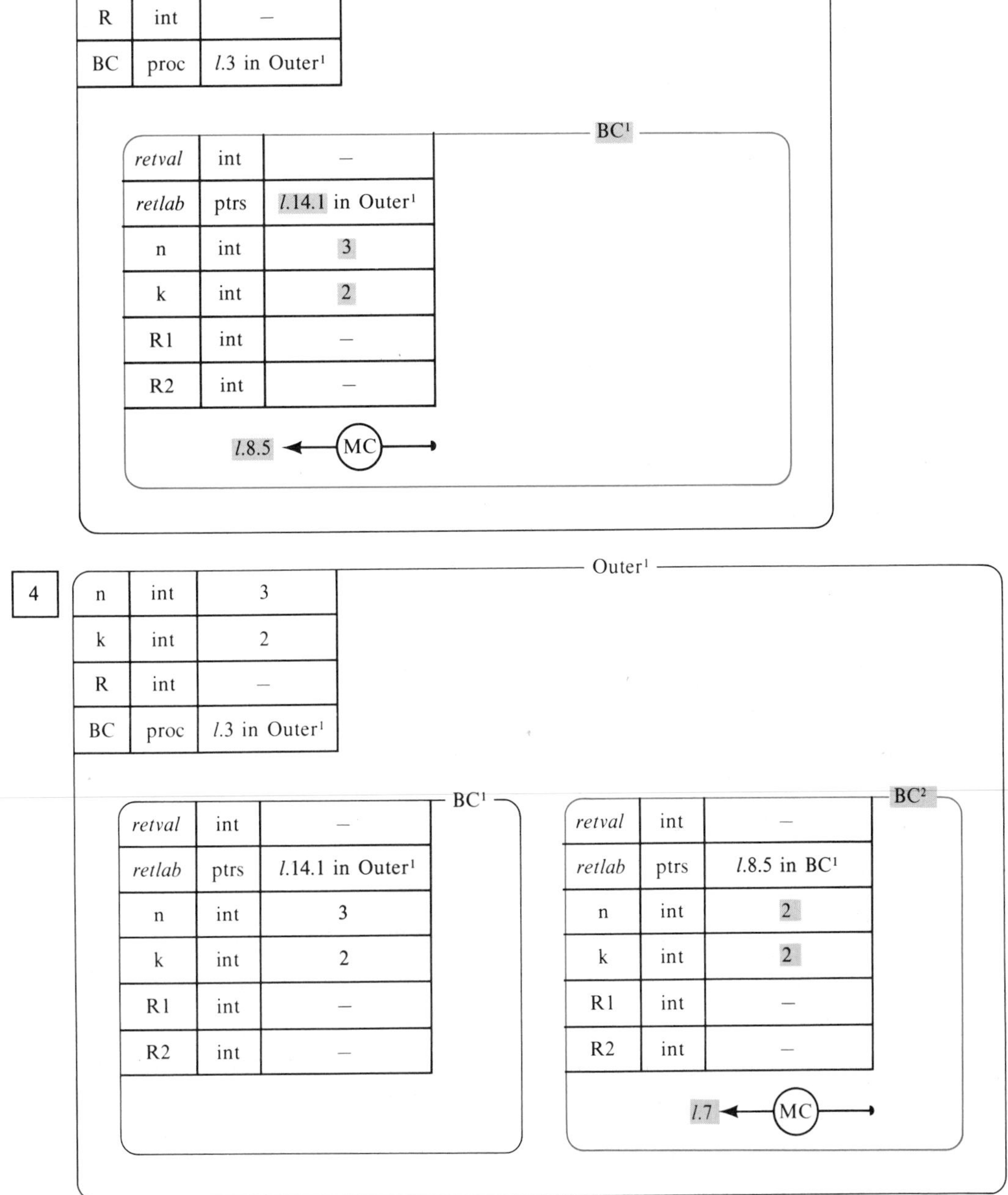

The second entry to BC creates the contour BC^2, as shown in snapshot 4. The return ip is *l*.8.5; this represents a return to the part of line 8 that indicates the assignment of the returned value to R1. The MC is now ready to execute the **if** statement at line 7.

5

Outer¹

n	int	3
k	int	2
R	int	–
BC	proc	*l*.3 in Outer¹

BC¹

retval	int	–
retlab	ptrs	*l*.14.1 in Outer¹
n	int	3
k	int	2
R1	int	1
R2	int	–

l.9.5 ← MC →

Since the **if** test at line 7 was **true,** the MC has executed a return to the BC¹ environment with the value 1. Snapshot 5 shows the situation after that value has been assigned to R1. The MC is now ready to execute the call on BC that appears on line 9.

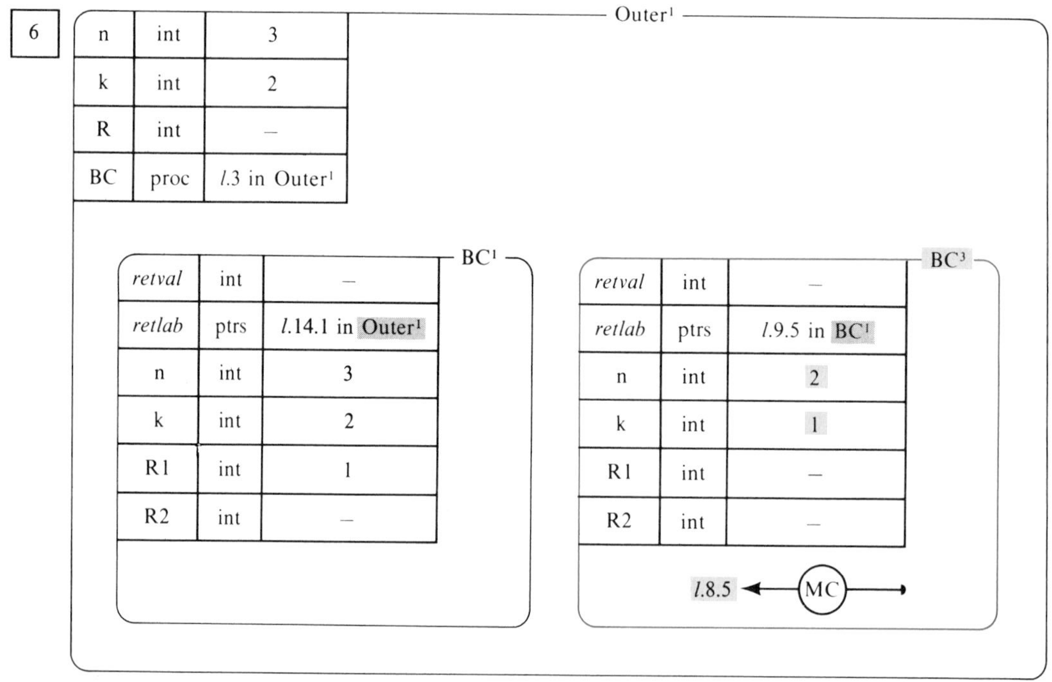

Snapshot 6 shows the situation after the third entry to BC has been executed with argument values 2 and 1. The **if** test on line 7 has been found to be **false** so the MC is again ready to make the call on BC that is indicated on line 8. Notice that the contour BC^2 has disappeared, and so the dynamic return chain links backward from BC^3 to BC^1 to $Outer^1$.

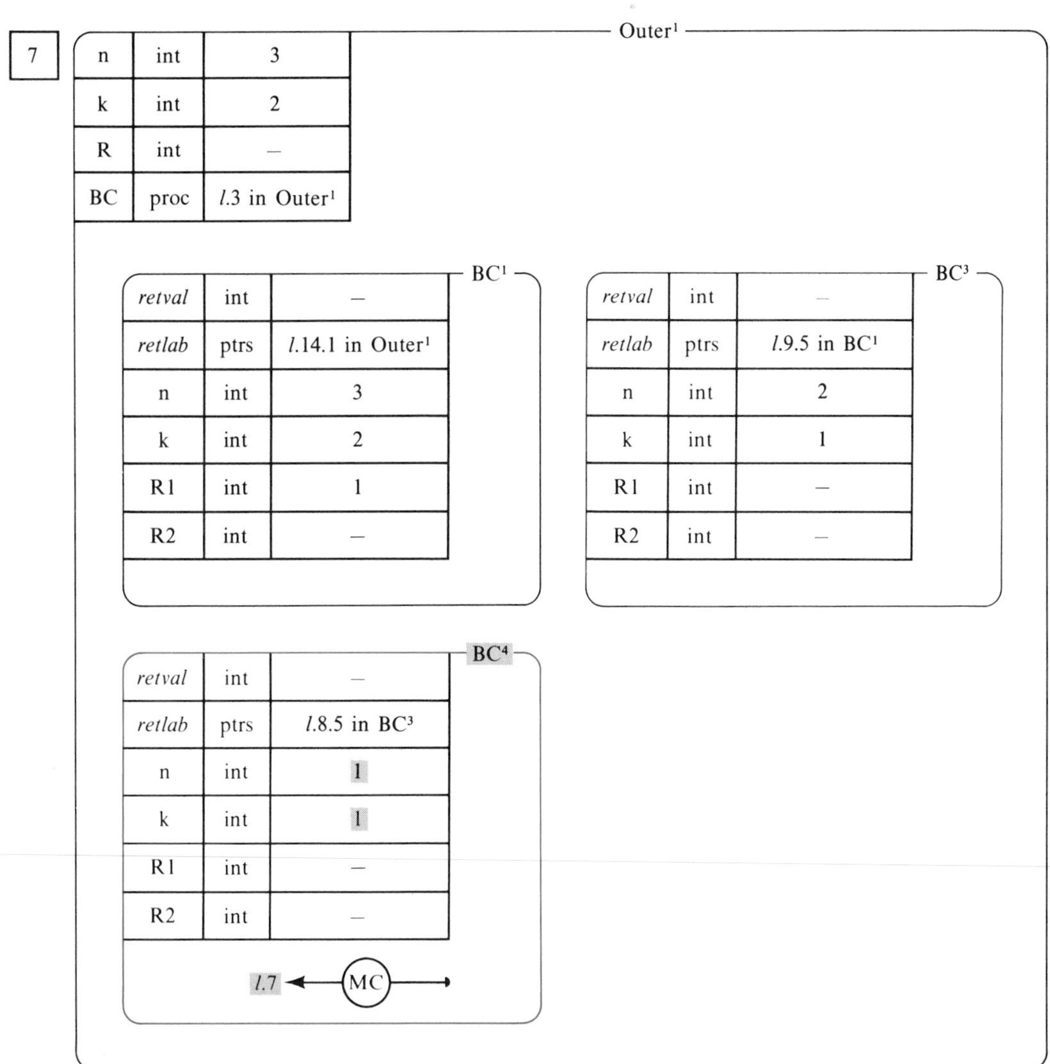

Snapshot 7 illustrates the state after the fourth call on BC has been made with arguments 1 and 1. The contour BC^4 has been created, extending the dynamic chain by one more return link. The MC is about to execute the **if** test again. The **if** test will indicate that the value 1 should be returned to BC^3. Notice that so far the only *recorded* return value appears in the cell for R1 in BC^1. The values of all other cells for R1 and R2 are as yet undefined. The computation of BC cannot be completed until cell R2 in BC^1 has also received a value.

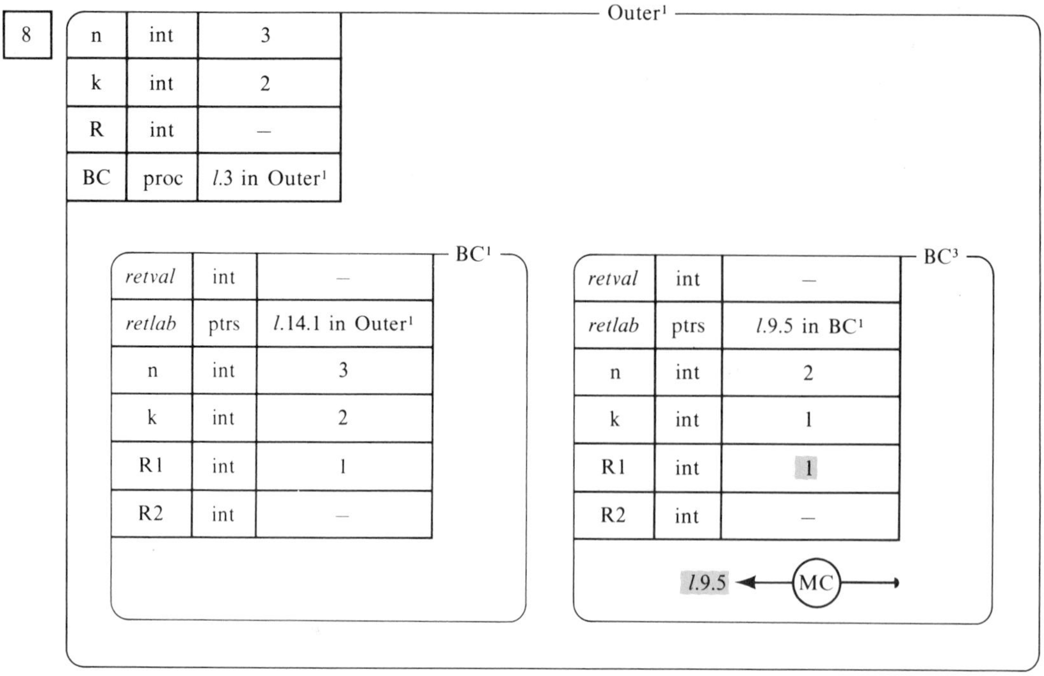

8

Outer[1]

n	int	3
k	int	2
R	int	–
BC	proc	*l*.3 in Outer[1]

BC[1]

retval	int	–
retlab	ptrs	*l*.14.1 in Outer[1]
n	int	3
k	int	2
R1	int	1
R2	int	–

BC[3]

retval	int	–
retlab	ptrs	*l*.9.5 in BC[1]
n	int	2
k	int	1
R1	int	1
R2	int	–

l.9.5 ← MC →

Snapshot 8 shows the situation after the MC has returned from the fourth call on BC with the value 1 and has assigned that value to the cell R1 in BC[3], the environment from which that fourth call was made. The MC is now ready to execute the call on BC that is indicated on line 9.

9

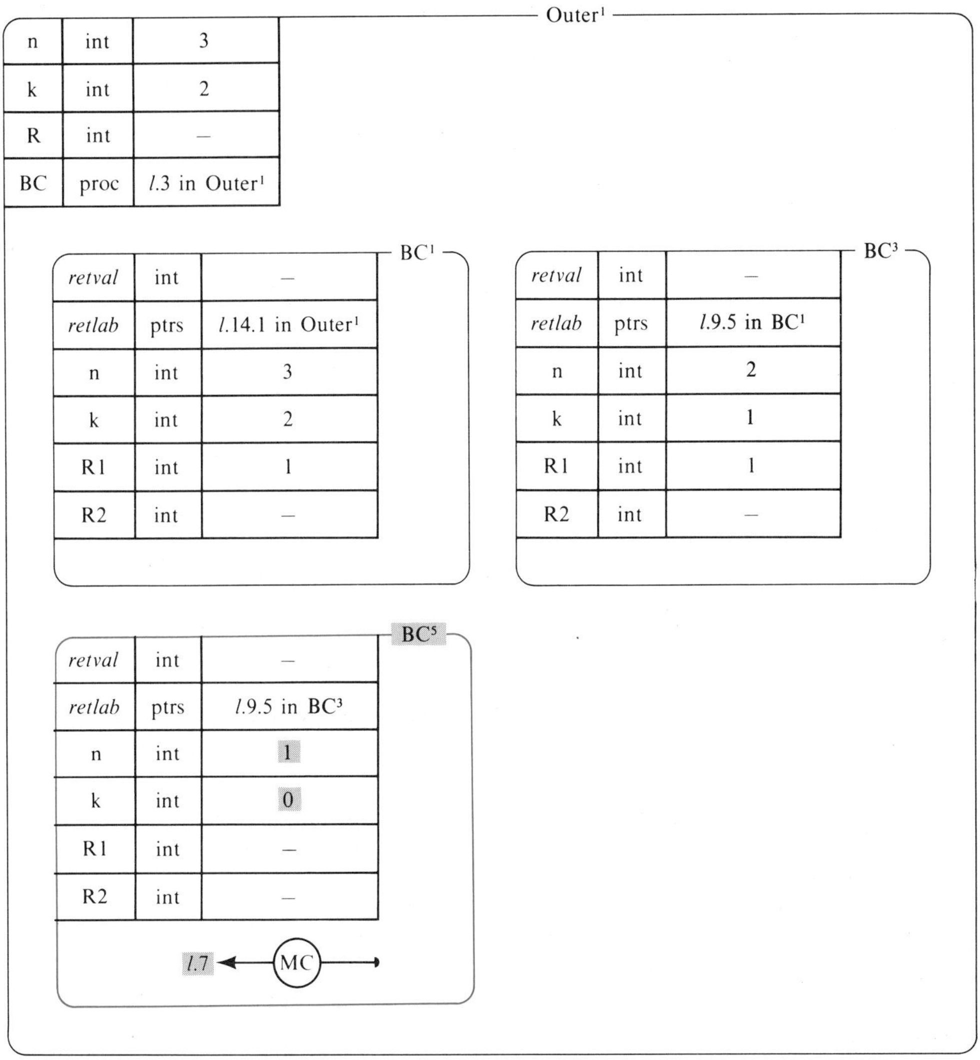

Outer[1]

n	int	3
k	int	2
R	int	—
BC	proc	*l*.3 in Outer[1]

BC[1]

retval	int	—
retlab	ptrs	*l*.14.1 in Outer[1]
n	int	3
k	int	2
R1	int	1
R2	int	—

BC[3]

retval	int	—
retlab	ptrs	*l*.9.5 in BC[1]
n	int	2
k	int	1
R1	int	1
R2	int	—

BC[5]

retval	int	—
retlab	ptrs	*l*.9.5 in BC[3]
n	int	1
k	int	0
R1	int	—
R2	int	—

l.7 ← MC →

Snapshot 9 shows the situation after this last (fifth) call on BC has been executed with arguments 1 and 0. The **if** test on line 7 is about to be executed by the MC from within the contour BC[5].

10

Outer[1]

n	int	3
k	int	2
R	int	—
BC	proc	*l*.3 in Outer[1]

BC[1]

retval	int	—
retlab	ptrs	*l*.14.1 in Outer[1]
n	int	3
k	int	2
R1	int	1
R2	int	—

BC[3]

retval	int	2
retlab	ptrs	*l*.9.5 in BC[1]
n	int	2
k	int	1
R1	int	1
R2	int	1

l.11 ← MC →

Since the **if** test in the fifth call was **true,** the MC again has returned to BC[3] with the value 1. However, this time the assignment operation on line 9 was executed, assigning the returned value to R2. The MC has just executed the summing operation on line 10 causing the value 2 to be assigned to the *retval* cell in BC[3].

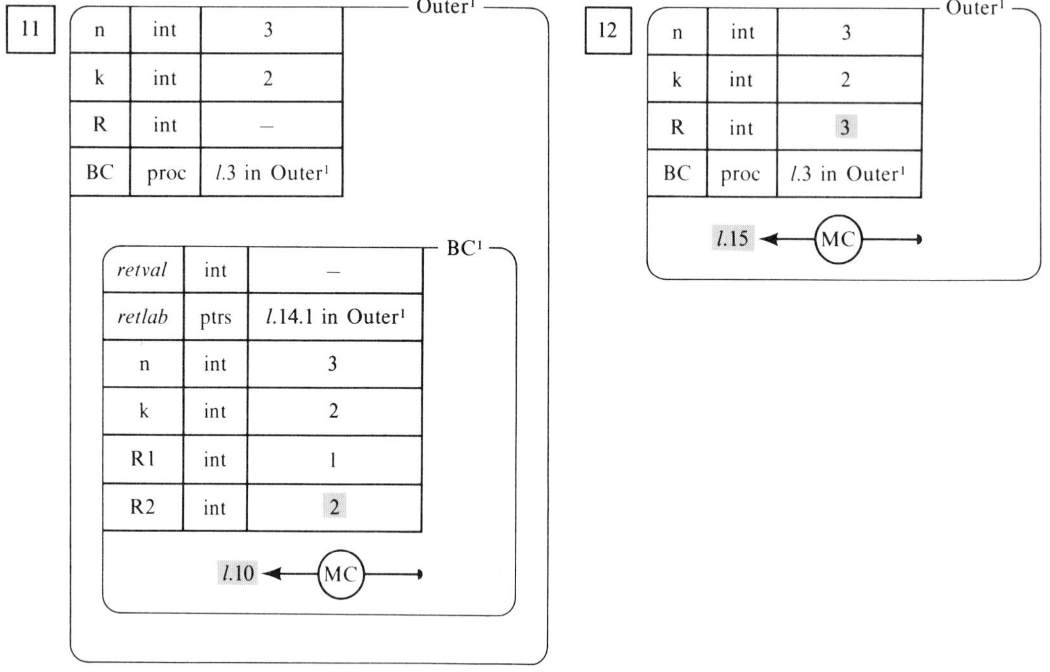

The sum of R1 and R2, the value 2, is then returned to the BC[1] environment and assigned to R2 in that environment. This is the situation in snapshot 11, where the MC is again ready to execute the summing operation on line 10. Snapshot 12 shows the situation upon return with the new sum 3 to the Outer[1] environment where the returned value has been assigned to R, and the MC is now ready to execute the print statement on line 15. The output produced by execution of line 15 is

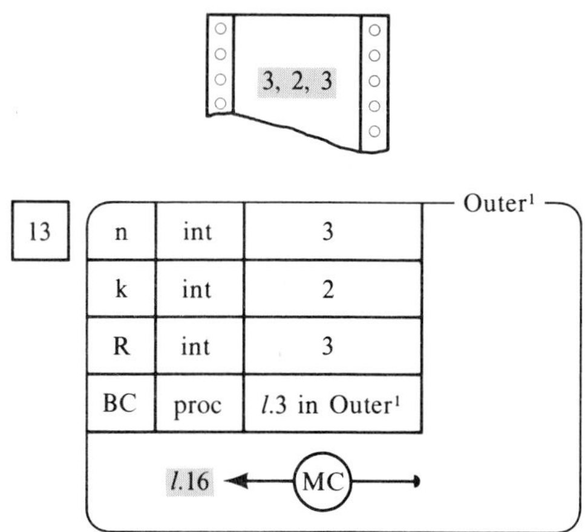

Snapshot 13 shows the situation when the MC is about to execute the **end** statement.

Snapshot 14 shows the "naked" MC after executing line 16. One by one the contours have been discarded after they have become inaccessible.

Figure 5-32 illustrates a slightly different version of the previous ALGOL program. The local variables R1 and R2 have been deliberately removed from

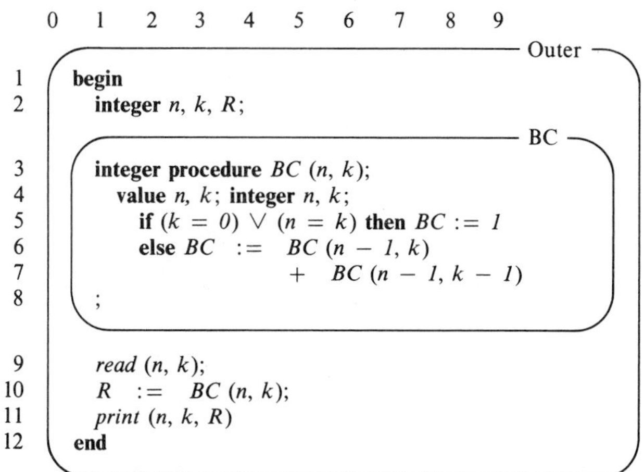


```
begin
  integer n, k, R;
  integer procedure BC (n, k);
    value n, k; integer n, k;
      if (k = 0) ∨ (n = k) then BC := 1
      else BC  :=  BC (n − 1, k)
                 +  BC (n − 1, k − 1)
  ;
  read (n, k);
  R  :=  BC (n, k);
  print (n, k, R)
end
```

Figure 5-32. **Version 2 ALGOL program for case 4.**

BC to show what effect this has on the behavior of the MC. Now the MC must maintain a stack of return results.

The sequence of snapshots that follows is intended to correspond to those of version 1 of the same number. Thus, snapshot 2 of version 1 matches snapshot 2 of version 2, etc. Of necessity, line numbers have been changed in the version 2 snapshots because of the renumbering of the version 2 program. In the new sequence the stack is more fully utilized as a resource of the MC.

To assist in understanding the following snapshots, let us recall our stack notation. When the stack is empty, as it will be in snapshot 1, the state of the MC looks like

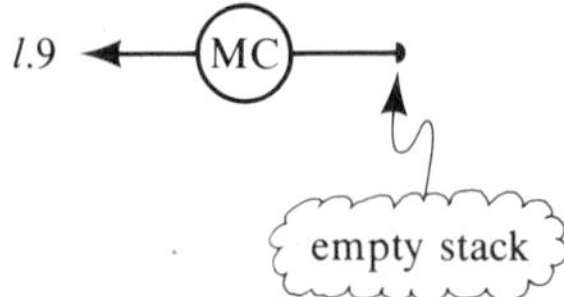

When a value is returned, it is pushed onto the stack, as will be seen in snapshot 5. Then the state of the MC looks like

When still another value is returned before the first one has been "used up," the new value is pushed onto the left end of the stack, as will be seen in snapshot 8. Then we have this state of the MC:

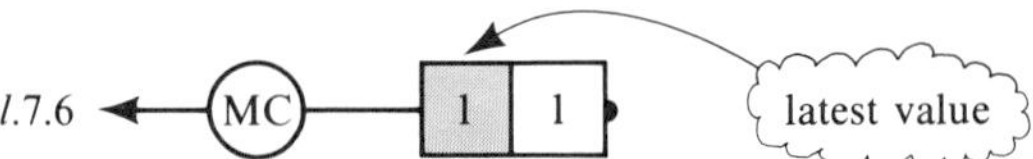

With another value pushed onto the stack, this is the state of the MC:

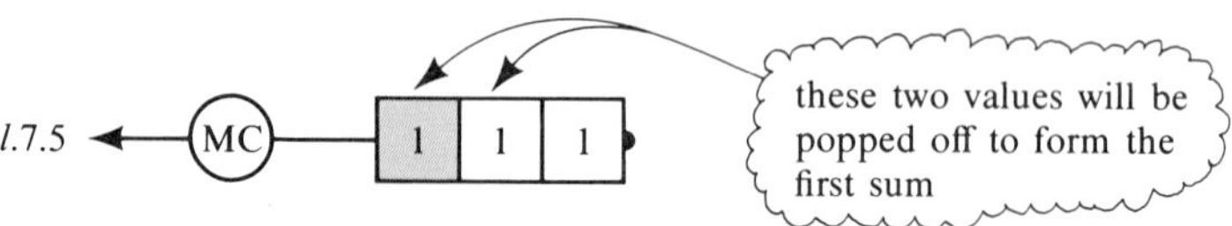

In the Figure 5-32 program, returned values are used up two at a time from the left end by the summing operation at line 7.5. Since that sum is actually returned, its value is pushed back onto the stack from which the leftmost two values were popped off to form the sum. This operation leaves the stack in the following condition, as shown in snapshot 11. The state of the MC is

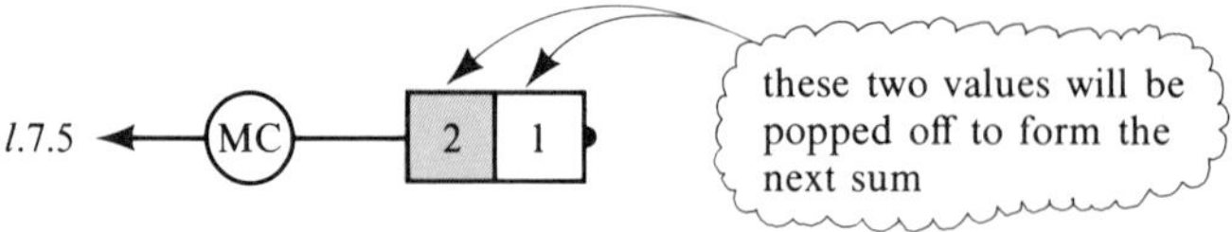

Snapshot 11.5, for which there is no comparable snapshot in version 1, shows the stack in its final form, just before the last value is used up in the execution of the line 10 assignment operation. The state of the MC is

Snapshots for execution of the version 2 program of case 4, Figure 5-32, again with the data set n = 3, k = 2, are as follows:

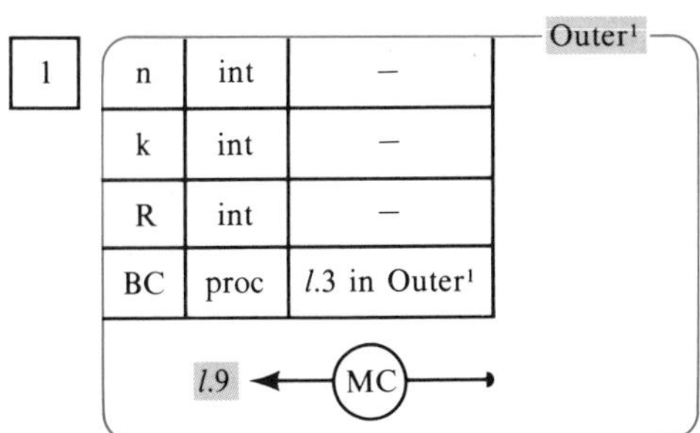

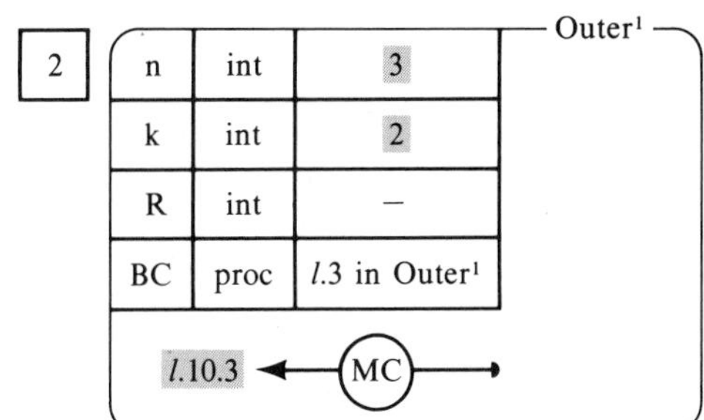

3

Outer[1]

n	int	3
k	int	2
R	int	—
BC	proc	*l*.3 in Outer[1]

BC[1]

retval	int	—
retlab	ptrs	*l*.10.2 in Outer[1]
n	int	3
k	int	2

l.6 ← MC →

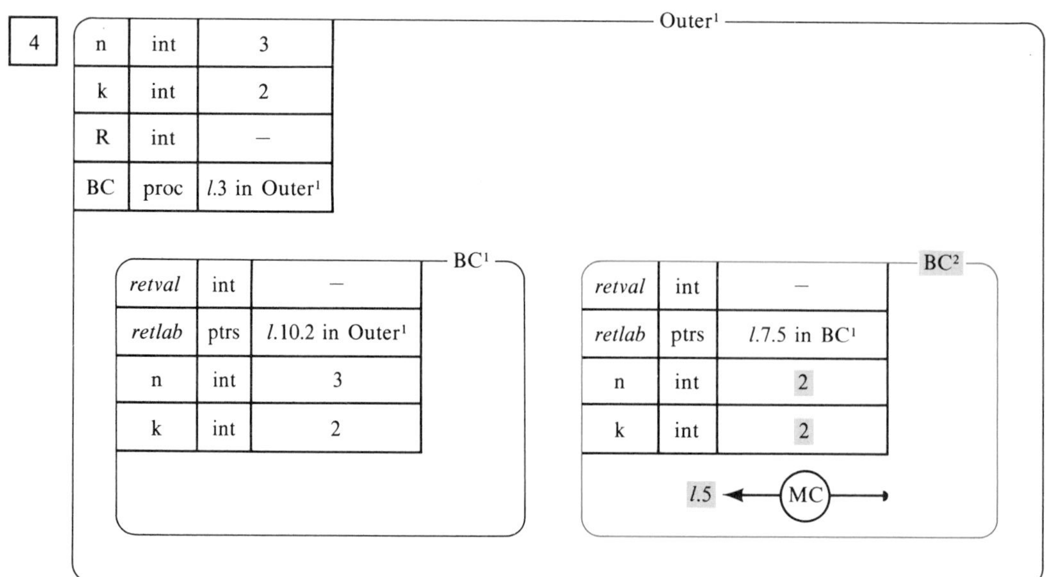
4
Outer1
n int 3
k int 2
R int –
BC proc l.3 in Outer1
BC1
retval int –
retlab ptrs l.10.2 in Outer1
n int 3
k int 2
BC2
retval int –
retlab ptrs l.7.5 in BC1
n int 2
k int 2
l.5
MC

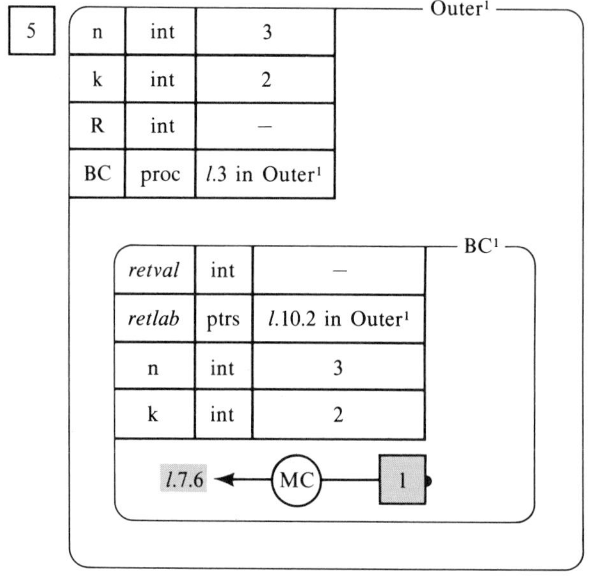
5
Outer1
n int 3
k int 2
R int –
BC proc l.3 in Outer1
BC1
retval int –
retlab ptrs l.10.2 in Outer1
n int 3
k int 2
l.7.6
MC
1

6

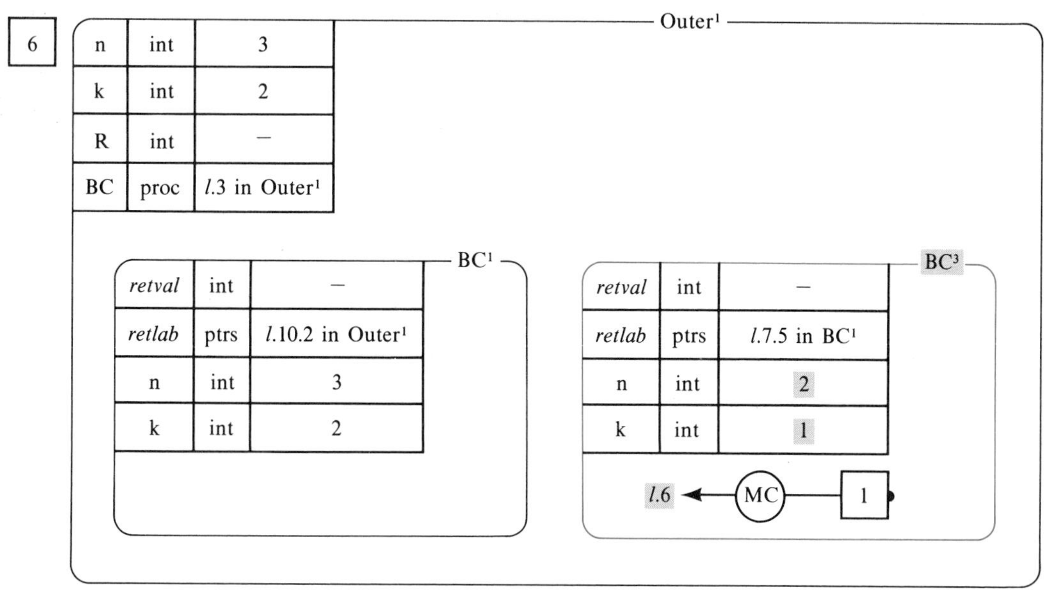

7

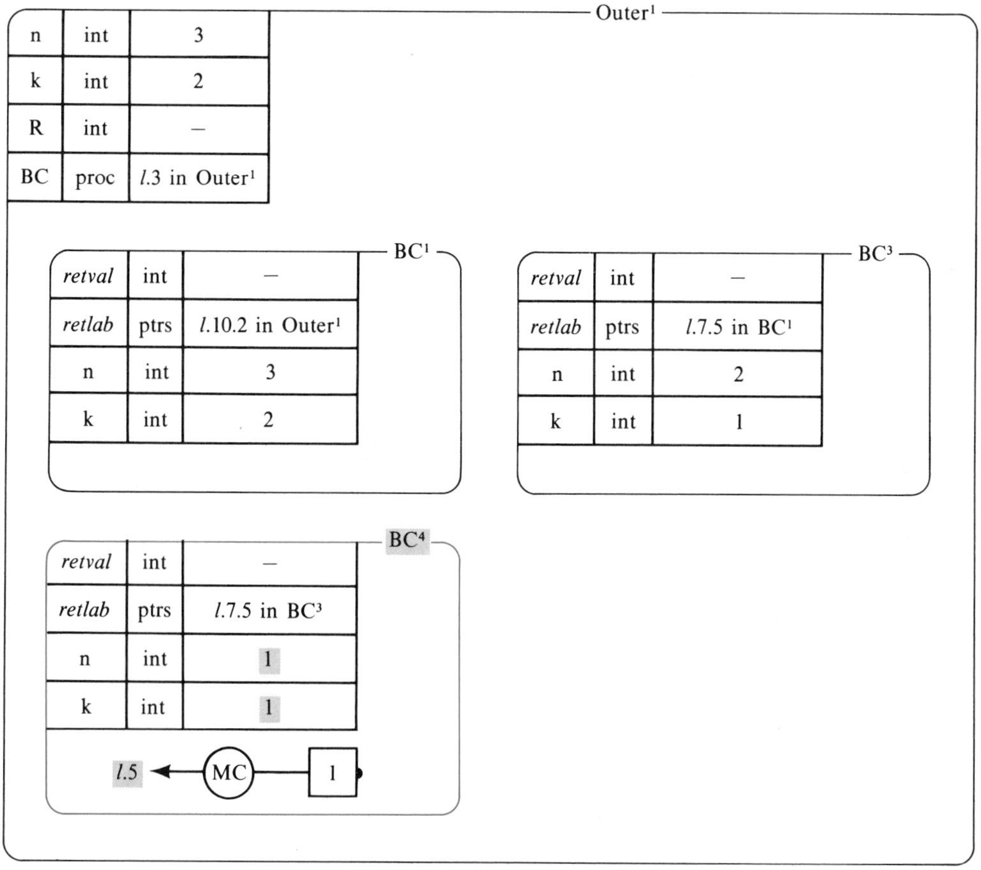

Outer[1]

n	int	3
k	int	2
R	int	—
BC	proc	*l*.3 in Outer[1]

BC[1]

retval	int	—
retlab	ptrs	*l*.10.2 in Outer[1]
n	int	3
k	int	2

BC[3]

retval	int	—
retlab	ptrs	*l*.7.5 in BC[1]
n	int	2
k	int	1

BC[4]

retval	int	—
retlab	ptrs	*l*.7.5 in BC[3]
n	int	1
k	int	1

l.5 ← MC — 1

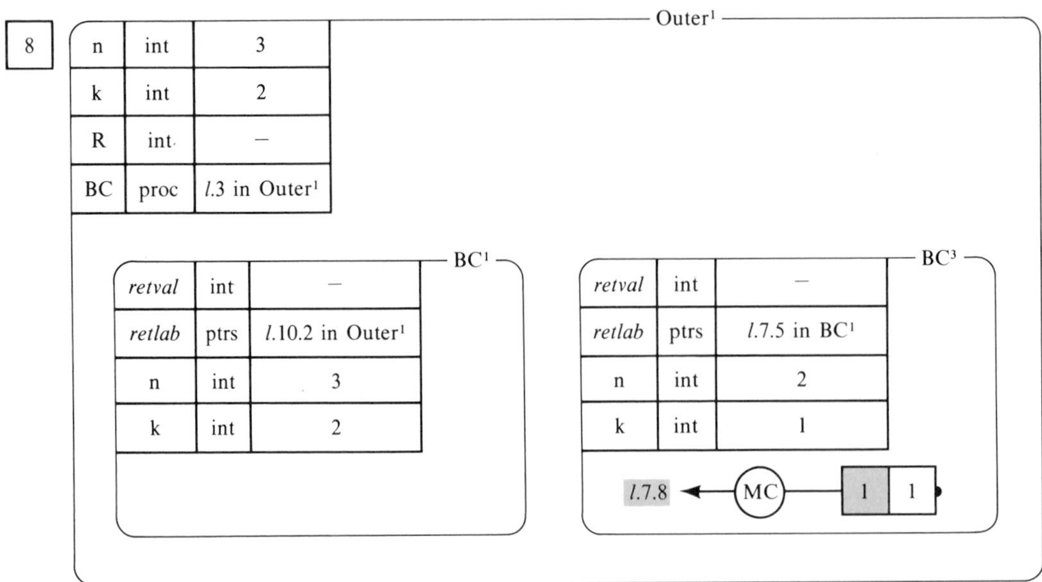

9

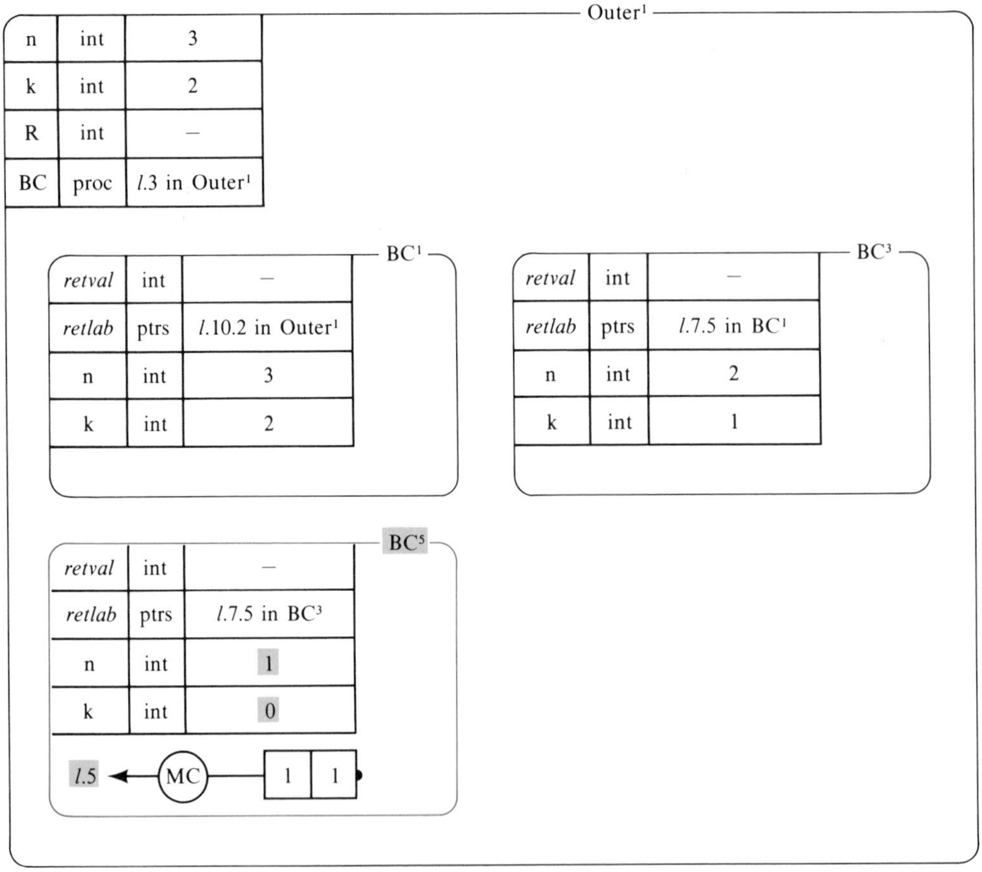

Outer¹

n	int	3
k	int	2
R	int	–
BC	proc	*l*.3 in Outer¹

BC¹

retval	int	–
retlab	ptrs	*l*.10.2 in Outer¹
n	int	3
k	int	2

BC³

retval	int	–
retlab	ptrs	*l*.7.5 in BC¹
n	int	2
k	int	1

BC⁵

retval	int	–
retlab	ptrs	*l*.7.5 in BC³
n	int	1
k	int	0

l.5 ← MC — 1 1

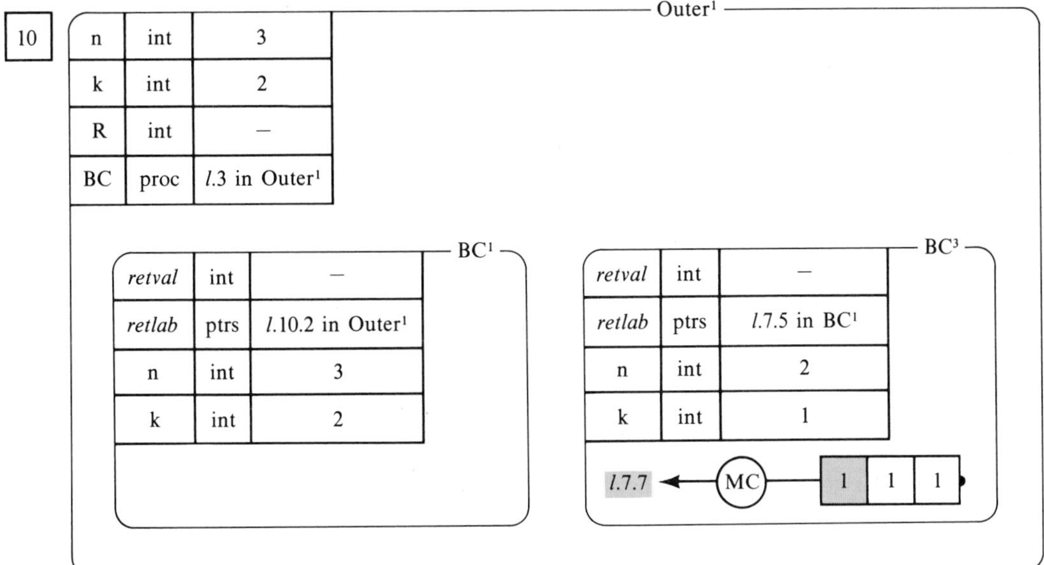

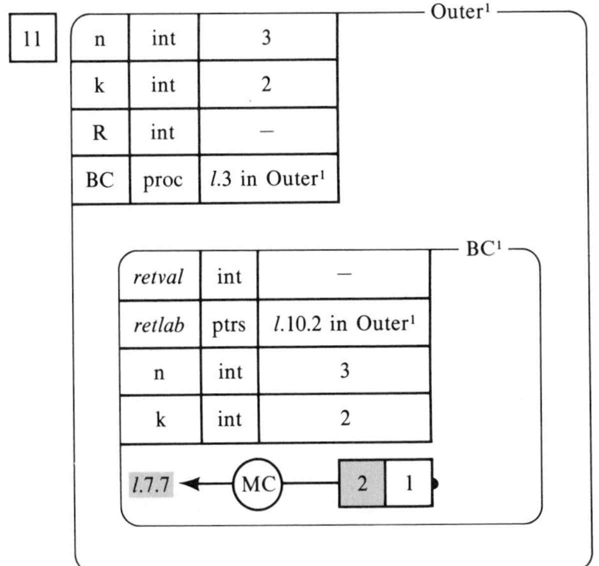

11.5 — Outer¹

n	int	3
k	int	2
R	int	–
BC	proc	l.3 in Outer¹

l.10.2 ← MC — 3

12

n	int	3
k	int	2
R	int	3
BC	proc	l.3 in Outer¹

l.11 ← MC

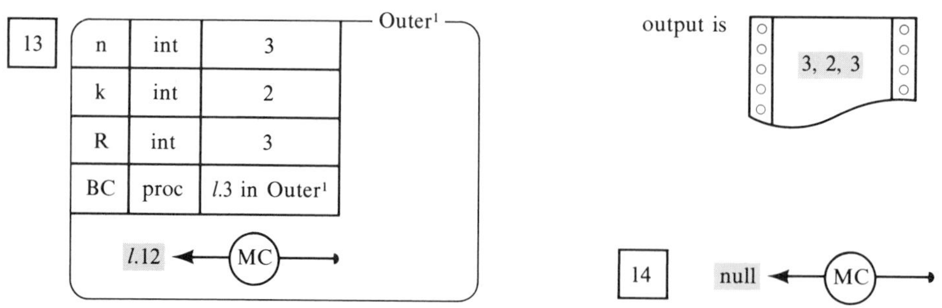

Exercises 5-8 (continued from page 256)

2 Compare corresponding snapshots from version 1 and version 2 of the binomial coefficient algorithm and convince yourself of their equivalence.

5-9 NAME PARAMETERS MATCHED TO EXPRESSIONS

In ALGOL any parameter not specified to be a value parameter is necessarily treated as a name parameter. In previous case studies name parameters were always matched to arguments that were simple variables, subscripted variables, or array names. In the next case study, a name parameter is matched to several arguments, each a different *expression.* Recall that in name parameter treatment, the argument is not evaluated at the time of the call, but later, whenever its value is needed during execution of the called procedure. The ability to make an expression argument accessible to the called procedure amounts to an ability to transmit a *computation rule* or formula to another procedure, which can invoke that rule when and if necessary. However, since the formula must be evaluated in the context of the caller, rather than in the context of the callee, the *intent* (or meaning) of the formula, as issued by the caller, is preserved. Before starting our case study, we first show a simple example. The reader who is statisfied he has understood name parameter treatment through his study of Chapter 2 may wish to go directly to case 5.

Let PROC be a function procedure with a parameter y. Let the argument expression that matches y be $(x + 1)^2$. When the value of y is needed in PROC, the formula $(x + 1)^2$ will be evaluated using the value of variable x that is found in the environment of the calling program, and not the value of some other variable x that may, for instance, be found in the environment of PROC. Thus, suppose inside PROC there is a local variable x whose cell-value is 2, while in the calling program the variable x is represented by a cell whose value is 4. For the purpose of evaluating the formula that y stands for, the cell containing the 4 would be accessed rather than the cell containing the 2.

The flowchart fragments in Figure 5-33a illustrate the situation. When box 12 in PROC is executed, the value assigned to t is $(4 + 1)^2 + 2$, or 27. To see how the evaluation of y can be postponed in this manner, we show, in Figure 5-33b, a skeleton ALGOL program and then describe, with the aid of a series of snapshots, how the postponement mechanism might work.

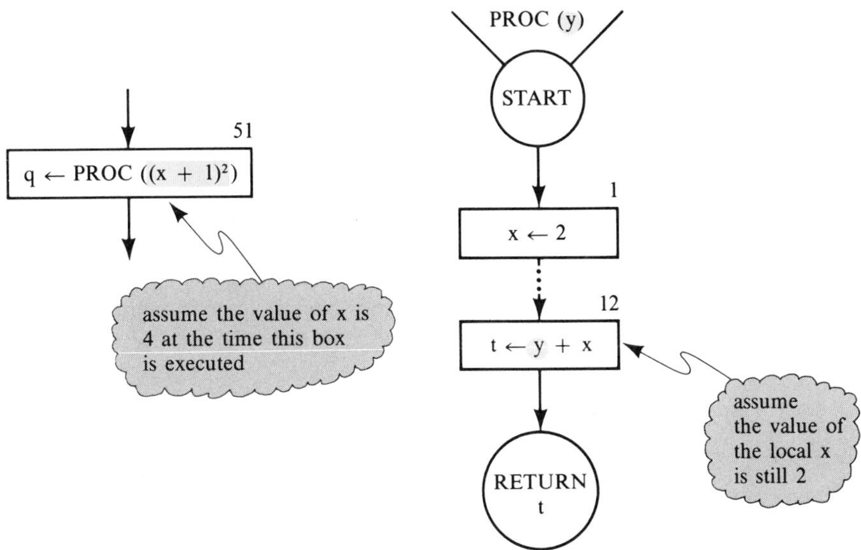

Legend for Top

Identifier	Treatment	Description
x	local	real
q	local	real
⋮	⋮	⋮

Legend for PROC

Identifier	Treatment	Description
y	name par	real
x, t	local	real

```
0 1 2 3 4 5 6 7 8 9
                                   Outer
begin
   real q, x;
                                   PROC
   real procedure PROC (y);
      real y;
      begin real x;
         x := 2;
             :
         PROC := y + x;
      end
   ;
   x := 4;
       :
   q := PROC ((x + 1) ↑ 2);
     :
end
```

Figure 5-33. **(a) Flowchart fragments to illustrate use of a name parameter. (b) ALGOL program skeleton.**

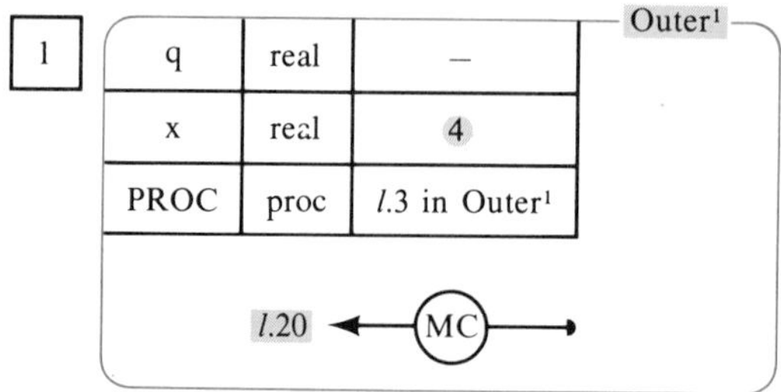

The Outer program block has been entered and the statements on lines 13 to (but not including) 20 have been executed. The MC is about to execute the call on PROC.

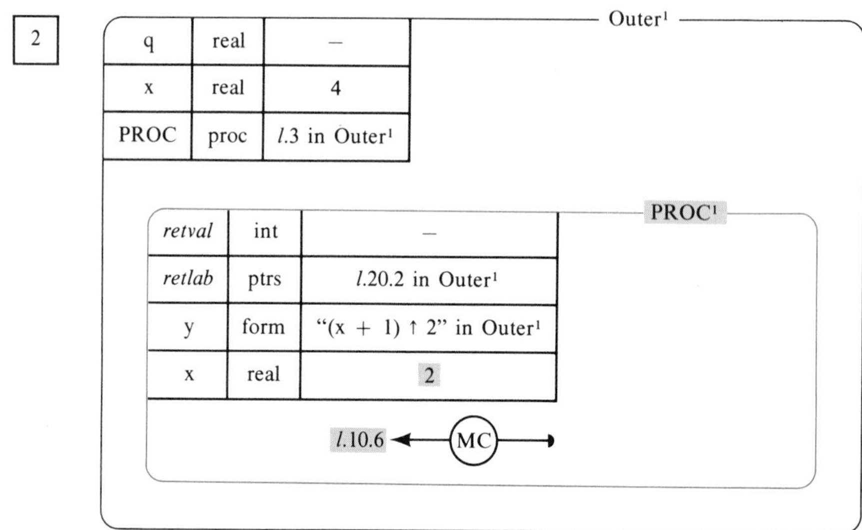

The procedure PROC has been entered, setting up the contour PROC¹ in which a cell has been created for the name parameter y. This parameter is recorded as of type *form*ula. The purpose of the formula, which is similar to a procedure body, is to compute a value for the expression represented by the matching argument. The MC, as seen in snapshot 2, has executed the statements beginning on line 6 and is about to evaluate the expression y + x on line 10.

There are several equally acceptable ways to denote the value of a formula like y. Because the whole formula is such a short expression, we picture a quoted copy of the argument expression copied into the name parameter cell. We could also represent the value part of a name parameter using an ip, ep pair.*

*Alternate ways to represent the ip for this procedure are suggested below. Take your choice, but be consistent in its use.

y	form	*l*.20.6 in Outer¹

or

y	form	*l*.20.6 thru 20.9 in Outer¹

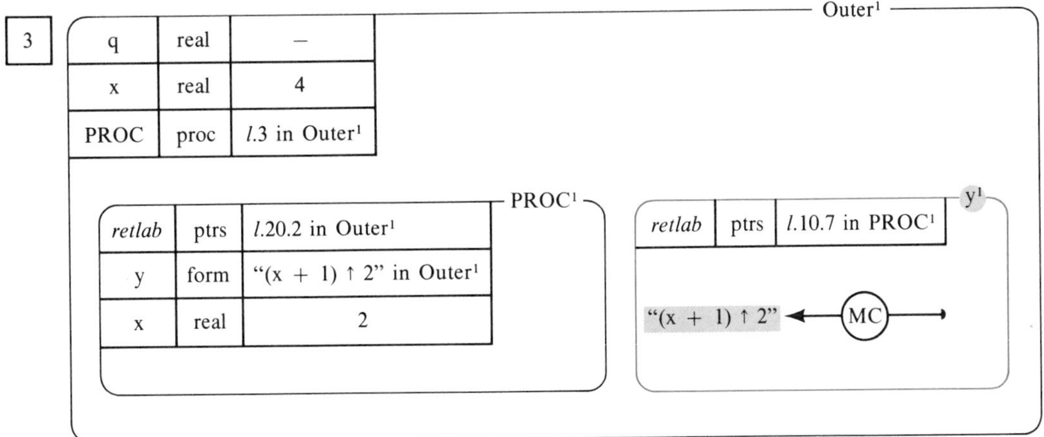

Snapshot 3, the key snapshot in this series, shows how name parameter y is evaluated. A contour y^1 is created nested immediately within $Outer^1$ as the proper environment for evaluating y, as suggested (but never actually shown) in Section 2-7. The only cell within y^1 is a return label, in this case to the place where the remainder of the expression in which y has been encountered is to be evaluated. The MC with its private stack moves inside y^1 to evaluate the expression (x + 1) ↑ 2. Note that from within y^1 there can be no doubt which cell named x is accessible. It is the one in $Outer^1$. Accordingly, the expression is evaluated as (4 + 1) ↑ 2. The value 25 is pushed onto the MC's stack and a return is executed to the calling site as shown in snapshot 4.

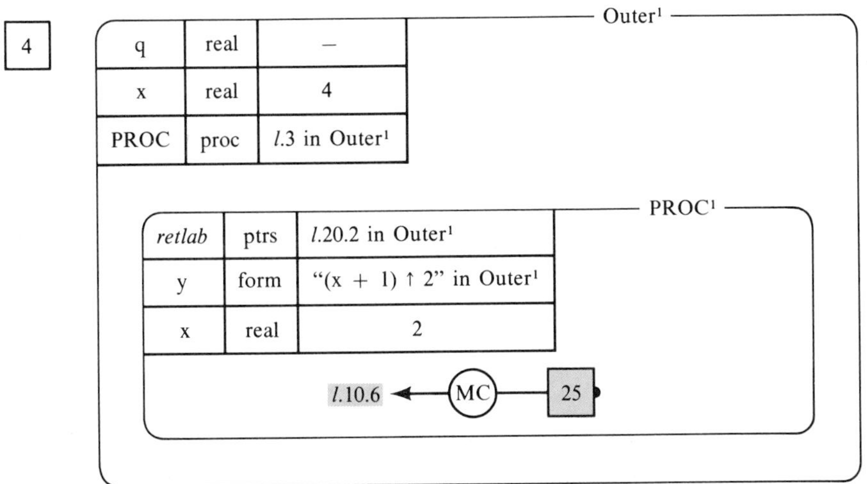

Back in $PROC^1$ the MC is about to pop the returned value from the stack and add to it the value of x. Again, there can be no question as to what cell named x is referred to in this context. It must be the (only) one that is visible, namely, the one in $PROC^1$ whose value is 2.

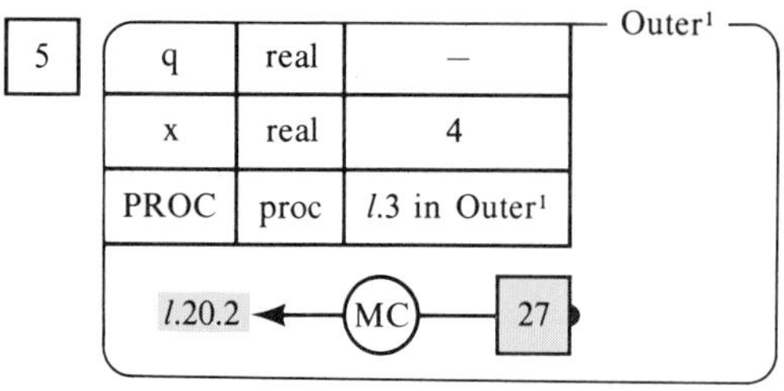

5

Outer[1]

q	real	–
x	real	4
PROC	proc	*l*.3 in Outer[1]

l.20.2 ← MC — 27

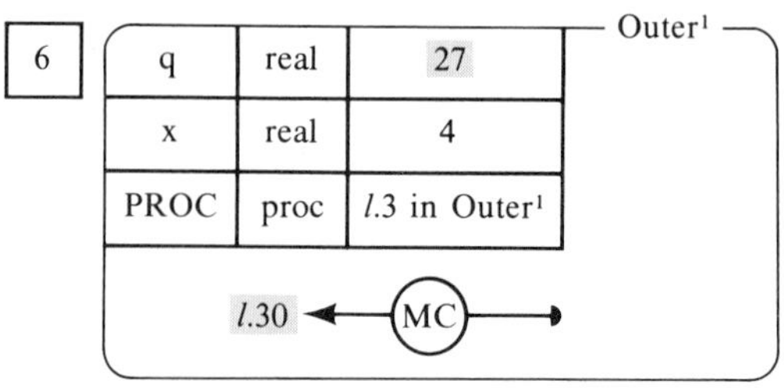

6

Outer[1]

q	real	27
x	real	4
PROC	proc	*l*.3 in Outer[1]

l.30 ← MC →

Snapshot 5 shows the condition of the computation just after return from PROC with the value 27. The MC is about to complete execution of line 20 by popping the returned value from the stack and assigning it to q, yielding the situation shown in snapshot 6.

Case 5 offers a somewhat more realistic and complete example to illustrate the semantics of the name parameter. In general, this type of parameter is used whenever it is desired to transmit a formula as an argument to a procedure. Although not every programming language offers name parameter treatment (they usually offer reference parameter treatment instead), most "procedural" languages like Fortran and PL/I do offer an alternative and equally useful means of accomplishing the same objective. This alternative approach, *procedure parameter* treatment, is illustrated in case 6. In this approach, rather than transmitting the formula as an argument, one transmits the name (procedure or function name) of that formula.

Case 5 This example* illustrates the name parameter. After inputting a list A of r real numbers, Top calls three times on the function SUM, each time obtaining the sum of a different subset of A. The flowcharts and legends for this case are given in Figure 5-34, and some explanatory remarks follow.

The name parameter u in SUM represents an indexing formula whose evaluation is dependent on the global variable i. Each time u is referenced, in boxes 7 and 8, it evaluates to a different value since i changes each time control passes through box 8.

The three calls on SUM, in boxes 3, 4, and 5 of Top, result in different accumulations:

The box 3 call produces $A_1 + A_2 + A_3 + \cdots + A_r$.
The box 4 call produces $A_1 + A_3 + A_5 + \cdots + A_z$, where $z \leq$ CHOP (r/2).
The box 5 call produces $A_1 + A_3 + A_6 + A_{10} + A_{15} + \cdots + A_z$, where $z \leq r$.

*For a more complete discussion of this particular example, see Baumann *et al.* (1964).

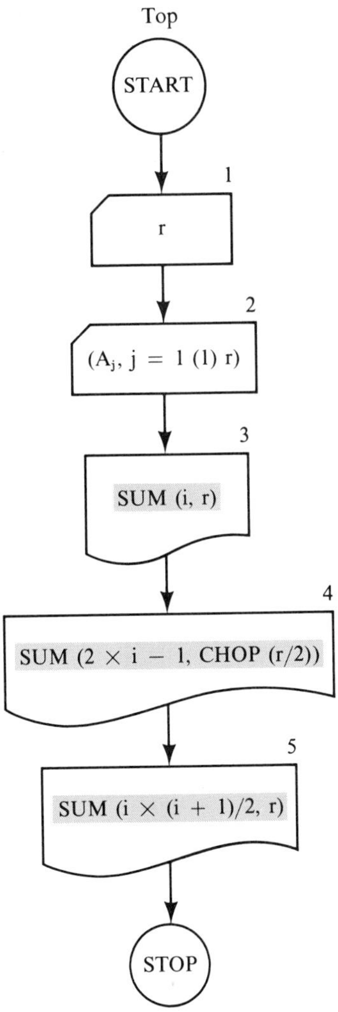

Top

START

1 r

2 $(A_j, j = 1\ (1)\ r)$

3 SUM (i, r)

4 SUM (2 × i − 1, CHOP (r/2))

5 SUM (i × (i + 1)/2, r)

STOP

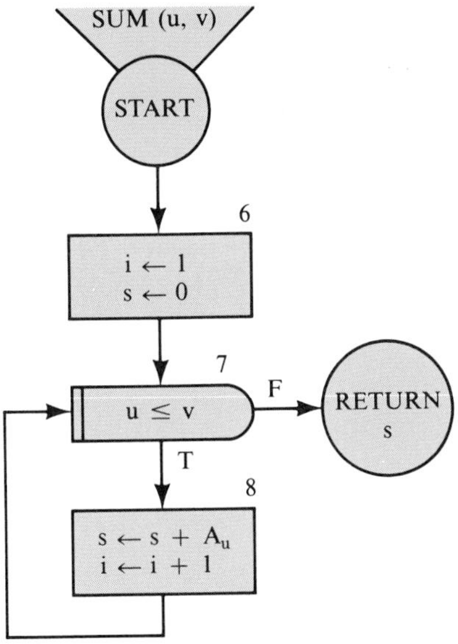

SUM (u, v)

START

6 $i \leftarrow 1$, $s \leftarrow 0$

7 $u \leq v$ — F → RETURN s; T ↓

8 $s \leftarrow s + A_u$, $i \leftarrow i + 1$

Legend for Top

Identifier	Description
r, i, j	integer
A	list of r reals

Legend for SUM

Identifier	Treatment	Description
v	val par	integer
u	name par	integer
s	local	real
i	global	integer
A	global	list of v reals

Figure 5-34

Figure 5-35 is an ALGOL program equivalent to the flowcharts and legends of Figure 5-34. In line 20 of the ALGOL program, the symbol for integer division, ÷, appears. This means, of course, that the result of the division is also to be an integer, the chopped value of the quotient. Since $i \times (i + 1)$ is sure to be an even integer, $i \times (i + 1)/2$ will certainly be an integer even without prescribing integer division. Therefore, integer division is not required in line 21.

The sequence of snapshots that follows assumes the following data set: $r = 7$, $(A_j, j = 1(1)7) = (4, -5, 7, 9, -4, 8, 6)$. Printed results should be

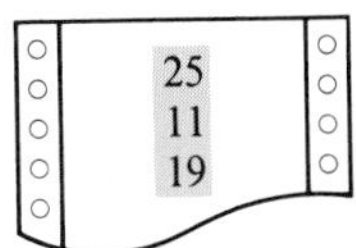

```
       0 1 2 3 4 5 6 7 8 9
                                         Outer
1   begin
2     integer r;
3     read (r);
                                         Inner
4     begin
5       integer i, j; real array A (1:r);
                                         SUM
6       real procedure SUM (u, v);
7         value v; integer u, v;
8         begin real s;
9           i := 1; s := 0;
10          loop:  if u ≦ v then
11            begin s := s + A [u];
12                  i := i + 1;
13                  go to loop
14            end;
15            SUM := s
16        end
17      ;
18      for j := 1 step 1 until r do read (A [j]);
19      print(SUM(i, r));
20      print(SUM(2 × i − 1, r ÷ 2));
21      print(SUM(i × (i + 1) ÷ 2, r))
22    end
23  end
```

***Figure 5-35.* ALGOL program for case 5.**

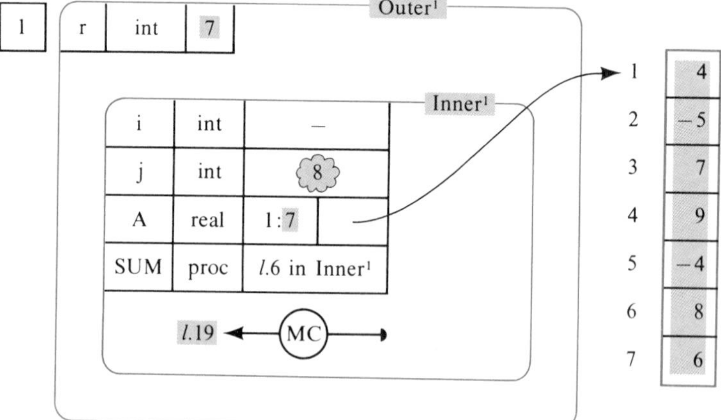

Snapshot 1 shows the state of the computation after completion of the preliminaries of block entry into the outer and inner blocks, and after the input step on line 18 has been executed.

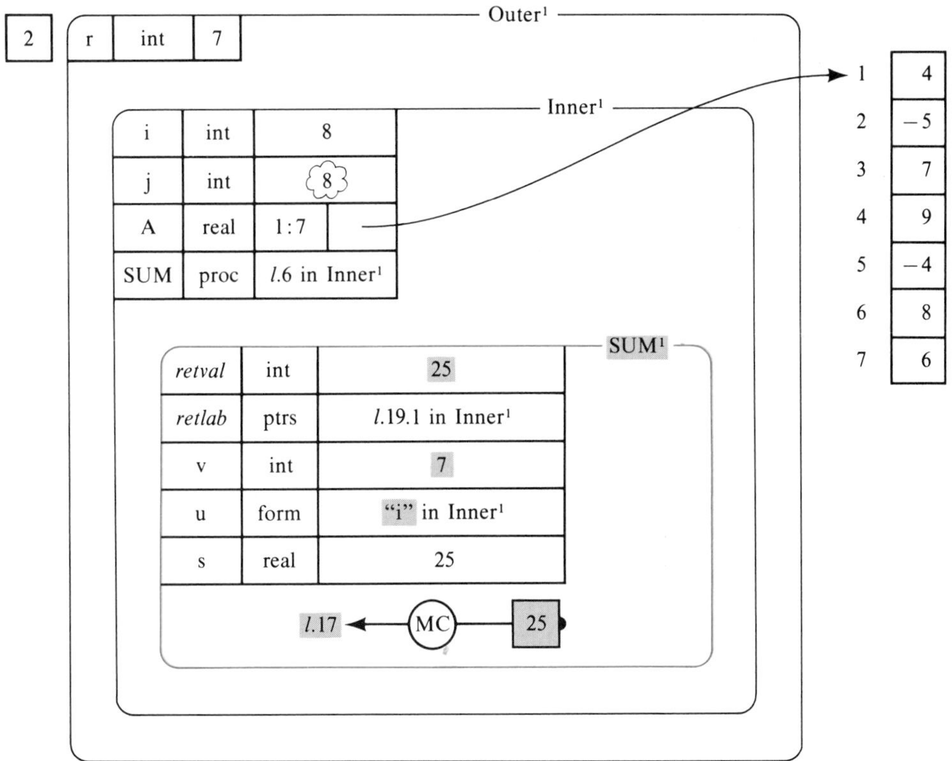

Snapshot 2 shows the situation after SUM has been called on line 19. The contour SUM[1] has been created and the MC has completed the work of summing the r elements of the array A. The contour SUM[1] has a cell for the name parameter u. The value in this parameter cell,

"i" in Inner[1] or, alternatively, *l*.19.4 in Inner[1]

could be read

Eval ("i") in Inner[1] or, alternatively, Eval (*l*.19.4) in Inner[1]

In other words, evaluate the expression i in the contour Inner[1]. The sum of the elements assigned to s is 25 and the MC, with the value 25 in his stack, is about to return to environment Inner[1], from which a call will be made on the print subroutine using the returned value as the argument.

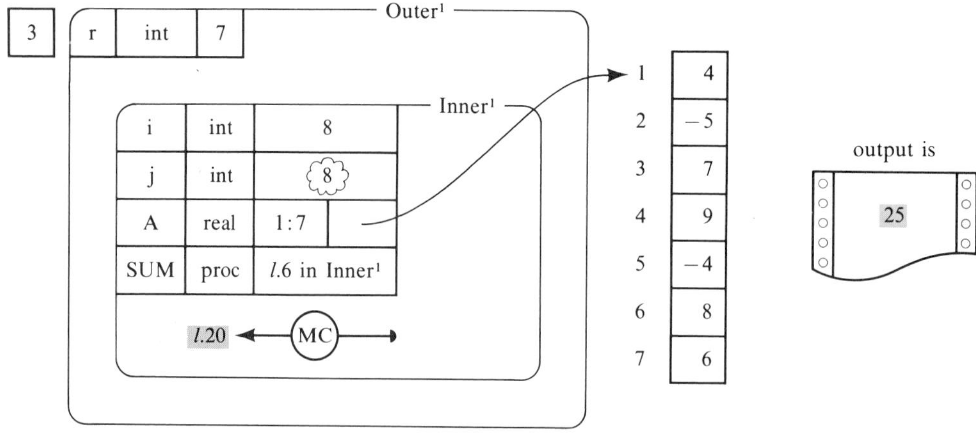

The result of executing the print statement on line 19 is shown in snapshot 3. Execution of the second print statement, line 20, will be illustrated next, using extra snapshots to emphasize the details of the name parameter evaluation. In the second call on SUM, the matching argument expression is not trivially the identity formula "i" but something slightly more elaborate, "2 × i − 1".

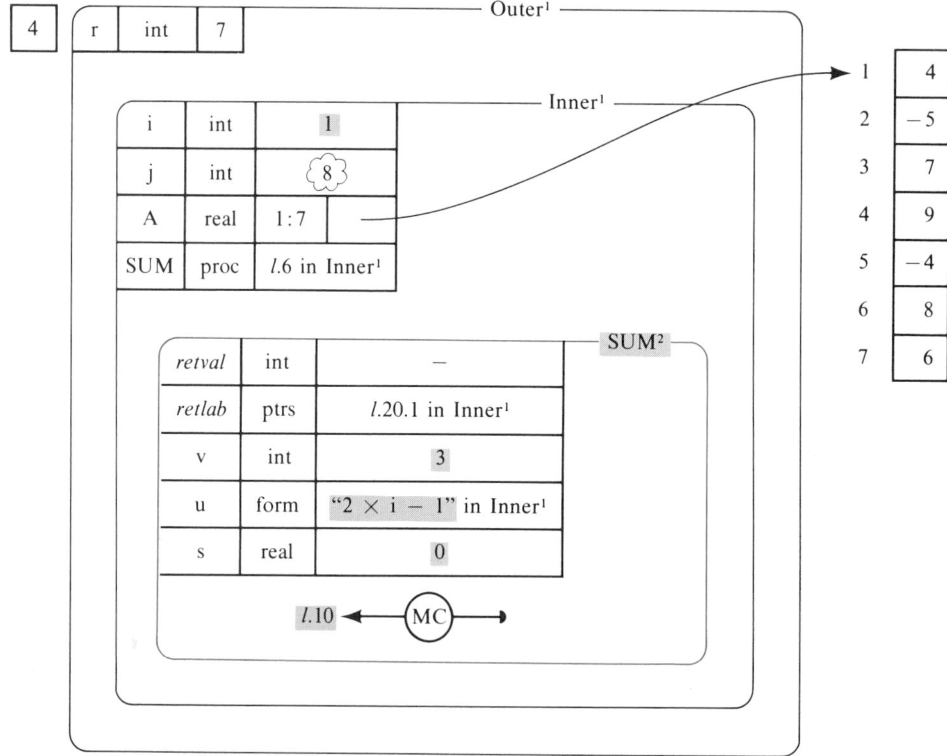

Snapshot 4 shows the situation after the execution of the second call on SUM on line 20. The value parameter v has received the value 3 in its cell in SUM[2], because the argument expression r ÷ 2 in ALGOL means CHOP ($\frac{r}{2}$), or CHOP

$(\frac{7}{2}) = 3$. The cell for the name parameter u has received the value "2 × i − 1" in Inner¹. The MC has just initialized the value of the global i to 1, and the local s to zero (line 9), and is about to execute the **if** test on line 10, requiring an evaluation of u.

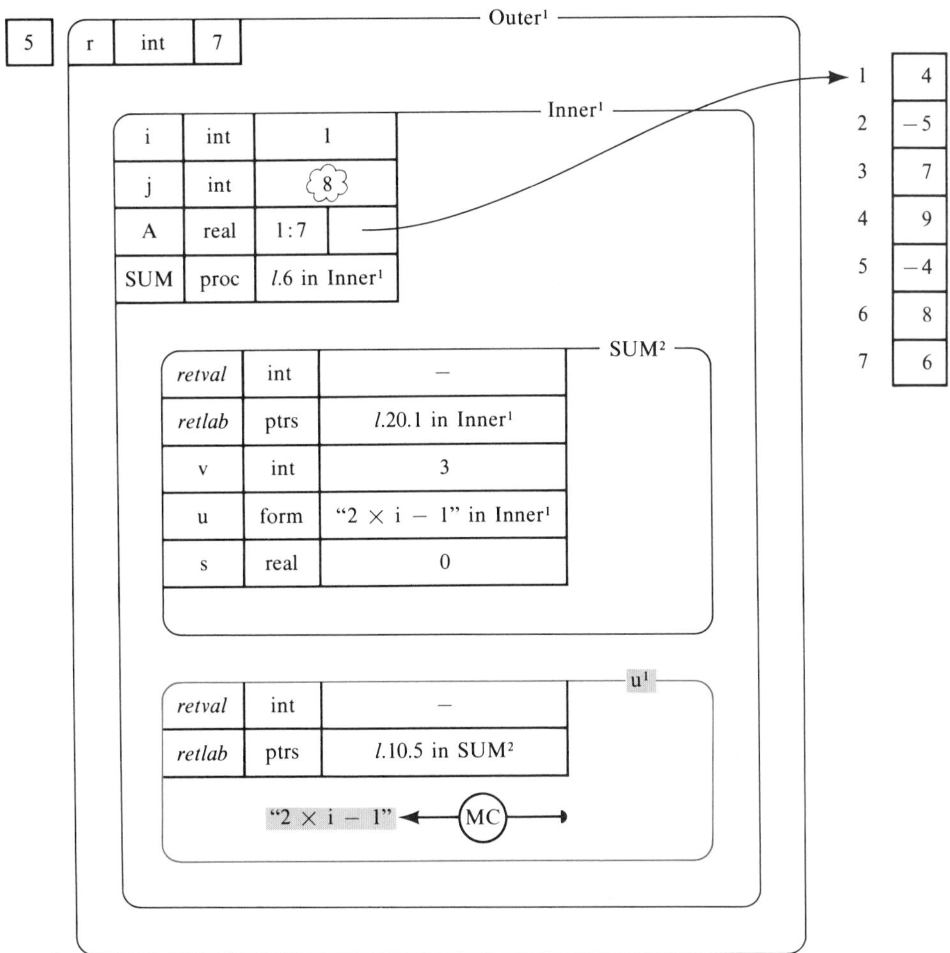

Snapshot 5 reveals the mechanism of postponing evaluation of the name parameter. The parameterless formula u is evaluated by creating and entering a new environment u¹ nested directly within Inner¹, as prescribed by the ep of the cell u. The MC moves into u¹ to evaluate the expression "2 × i − 1". From u¹ the value of i can be accessed globally in contour Inner¹. In this case the value of i is 1, and 2 × 1 − 1, or 1, will be pushed on to the MC's stack before a return to SUM is executed.

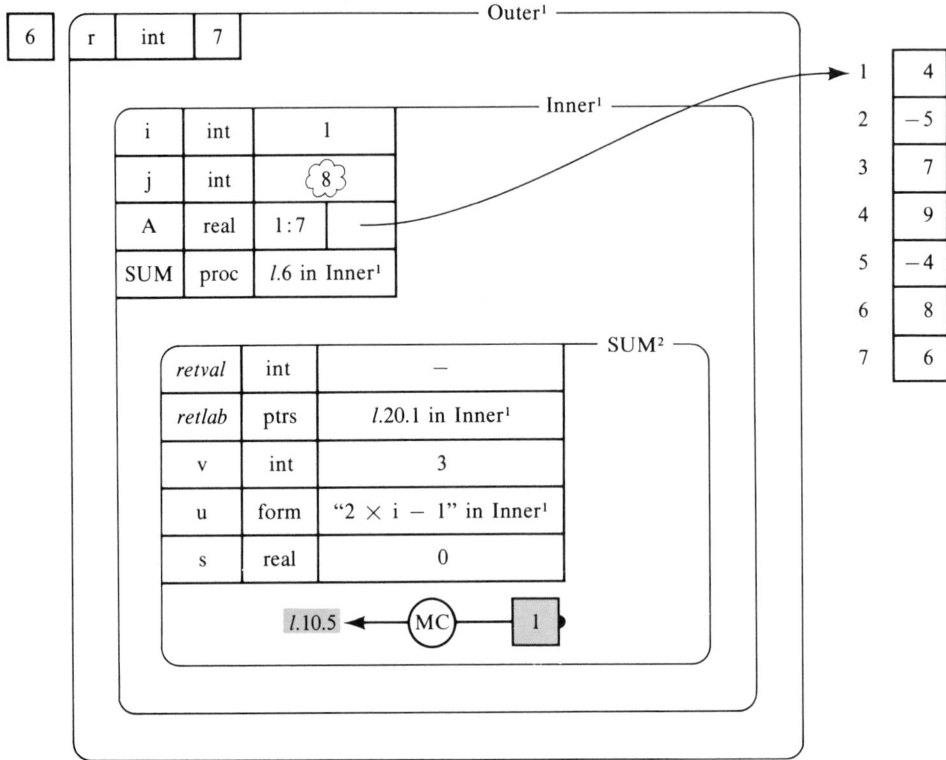

Snapshot 6 shows the MC back in SUM² after the "excursion" to u¹. Notice that the value of u is present in the MC's stack. Now the **if** test, $u \leq v$, on line 10 can be completed. Since the outcome of this test is **true,** the compound statement beginning on line 11 will be evaluated next. This will require another evaluation of u by the mechanism just described. We could recode the loop on lines 10 through 14 using an auxiliary variable, say t, and then only one evaluation of u per cycle would be required. If we did that, we could use the ALGOL **for-while*** statement and write

*The semantics of the execution of the **for-while** statement can be understood by examining the following flowchart equivalent of the statement given next:

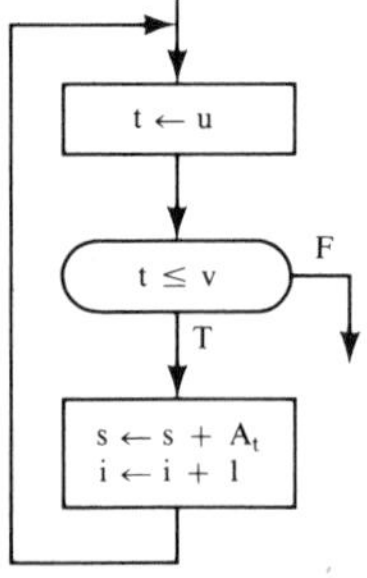

A peculiarity of the **for-while** statement is that the "initialization" portion (t ← u above) is repeated on every transit through the loop. For this reason the **for-while** statement is not often used.

```
for t := u
    while t ≤ v do
        begin s := s + A [t];
                 i := i + 1
        end;
```

On each successive transit of the loop in Figure 5-35 or of the **for** loop above, u must be reevaluated to obtain the index of the next element in A whose value is to be added to the summing variable s.

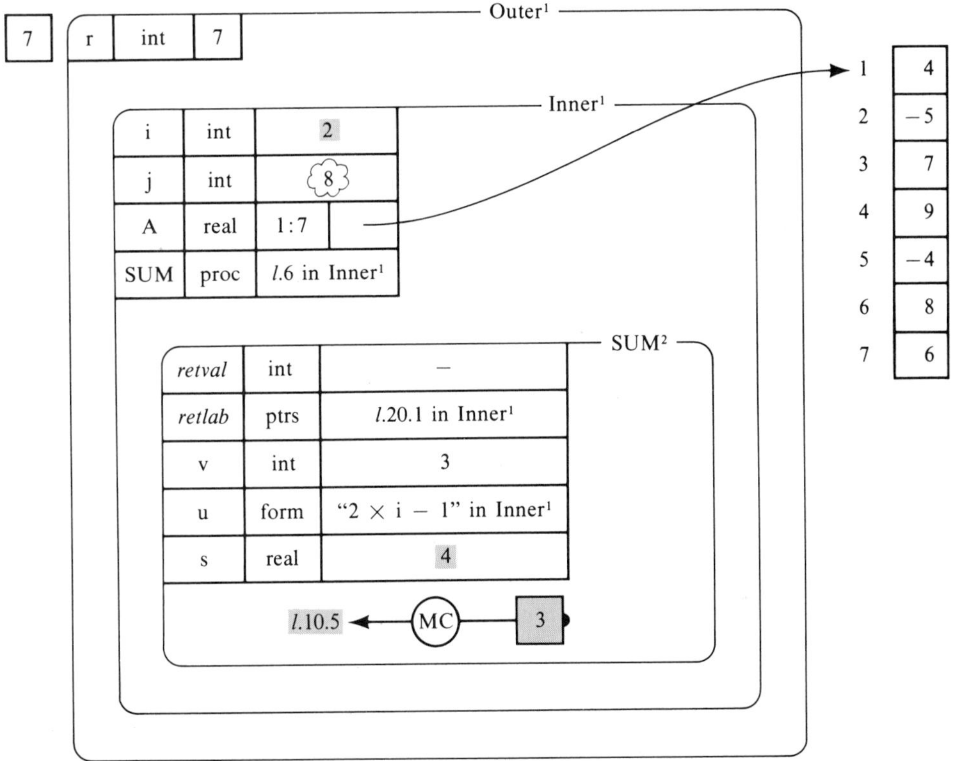

Thus, snapshot 7 shows the MC after having returned to SUM² with the next value of u (for i = 2).

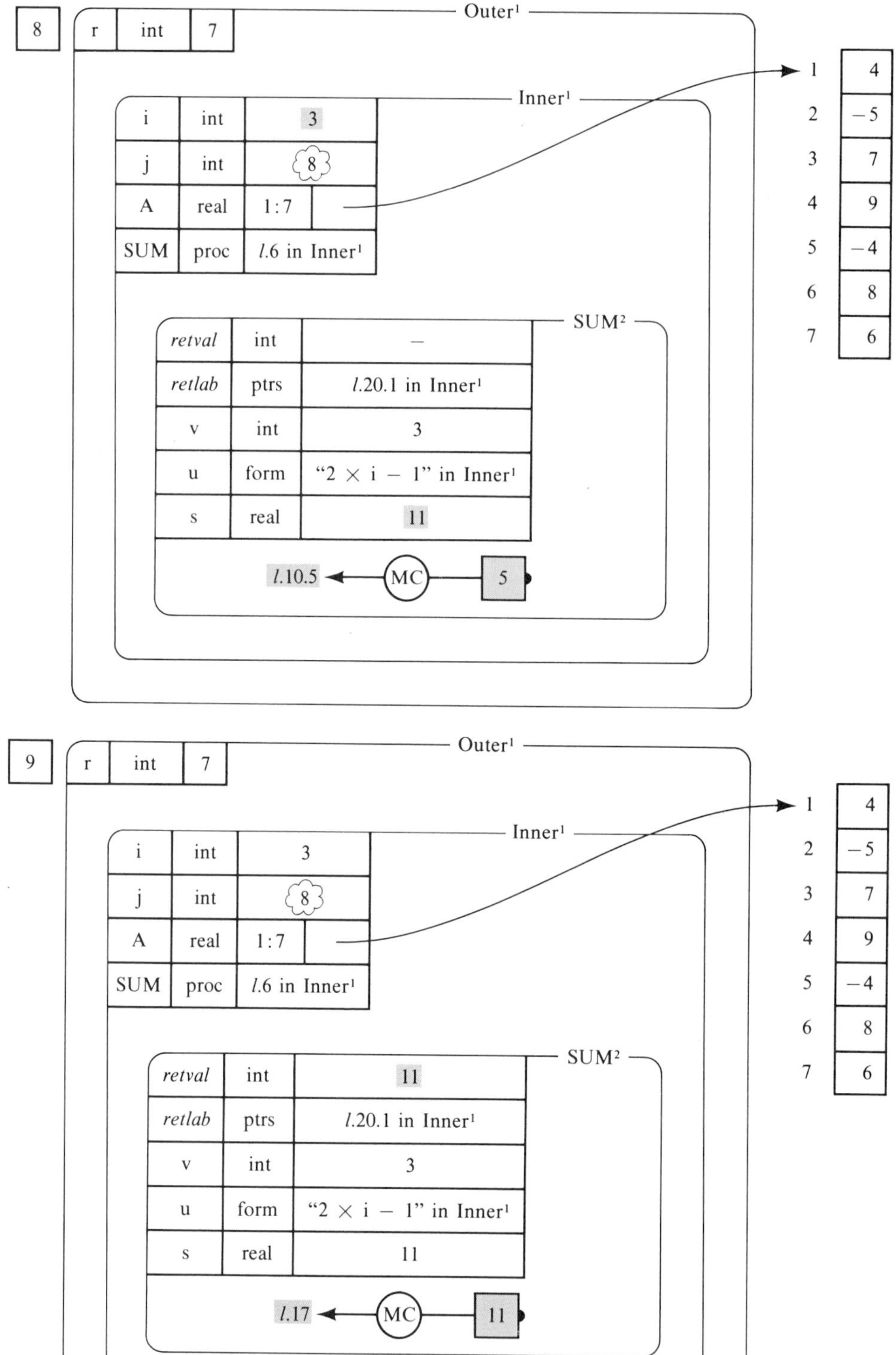
8
r int 7
Outer¹
Inner¹
i int 3
j int 8
A real 1:7
SUM proc l.6 in Inner¹
SUM²
retval int –
retlab ptrs l.20.1 in Inner¹
v int 3
u form "2 × i – 1" in Inner¹
s real 11
l.10.5
MC
5
1 4
2 –5
3 7
4 9
5 –4
6 8
7 6
9
r int 7
Outer¹
Inner¹
i int 3
j int 8
A real 1:7
SUM proc l.6 in Inner¹
SUM²
retval int 11
retlab ptrs l.20.1 in Inner¹
v int 3
u form "2 × i – 1" in Inner¹
s real 11
l.17
MC
11
1 4
2 –5
3 7
4 9
5 –4
6 8
7 6

Snapshot 8 shows the MC after having returned to SUM[2] with the third and last value of u (for i = 3). This value, 5, exceeds 3, the upper bound value of v. Thus only the values of A_1 and A_3, that is, 4 and 7, are actually summed, giving s the value 11.

Snapshot 9 shows the situation after the MC in SUM[2] is about to execute a return. The value of s has been pushed onto the MC's stack, ready for the return to the contour Inner[1] where the print routine will be called with the returned value as the argument.

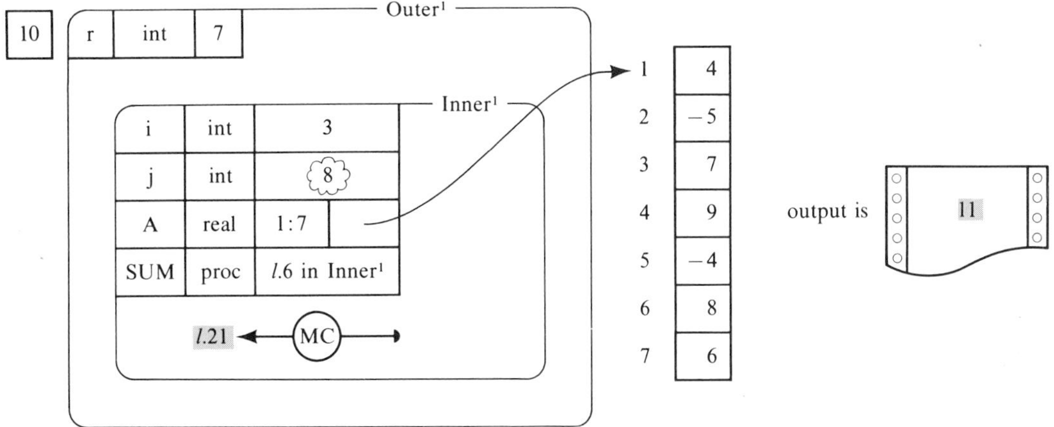

Snapshot 10 shows the state of the computation after execution of the print statement on line 20 has been completed. Snapshots showing details of the next call on SUM are not presented here, but would be similar to snapshots 4–9, leading to another printout. The construction of these snapshots is left as an exercise for the reader.

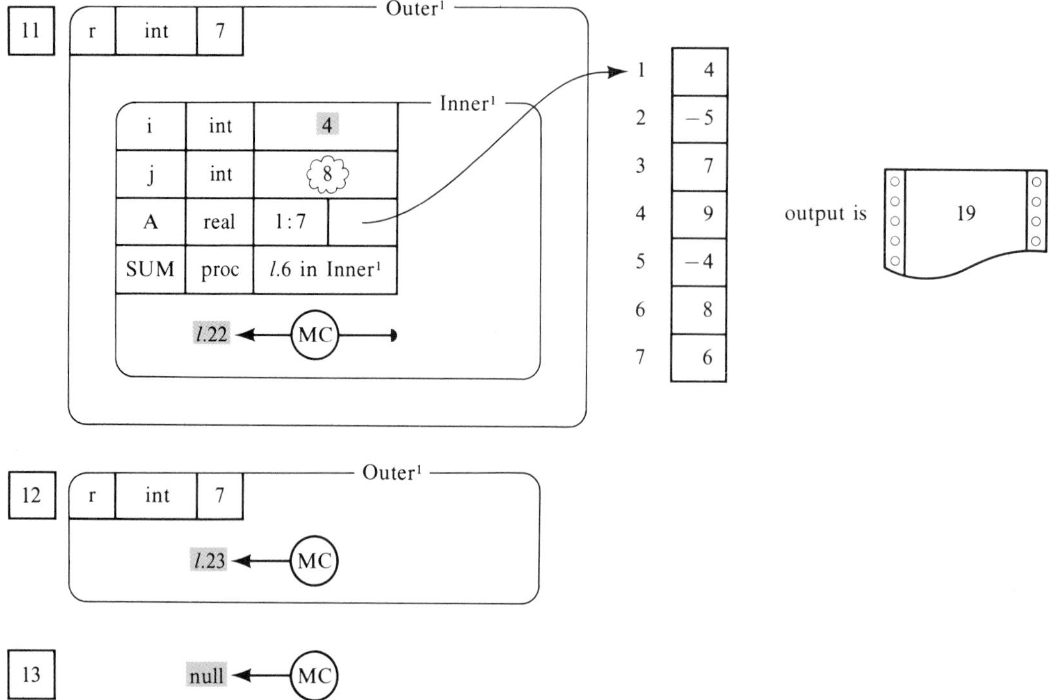

Snapshot 11 shows the state of the computation after the third and last printout. Snapshots 12 and 13 show the "windup" resulting from successive block exits, first from Inner, then from Outer.

This case illustrates the subtle effects that can be achieved by matching expressions to name parameters in ALGOL. The benefits gained seem to be offset by the complexity of the resulting program.

Exercises 5-9

1 Suppose the flowchart and legend for the procedure SUM of Figure 5-34 are appropriately revised so that i is no longer a global integer variable defined in Top, but a name parameter. Thus, suppose the masthead for SUM is now

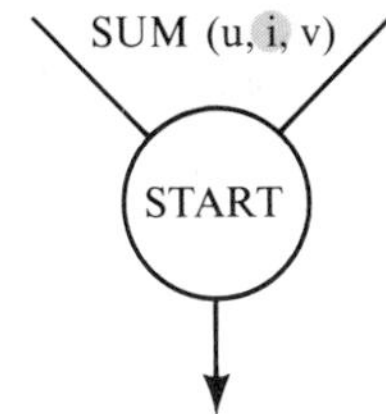

and calls on SUM from Top are also modified appropriately, e.g., box 4 is now

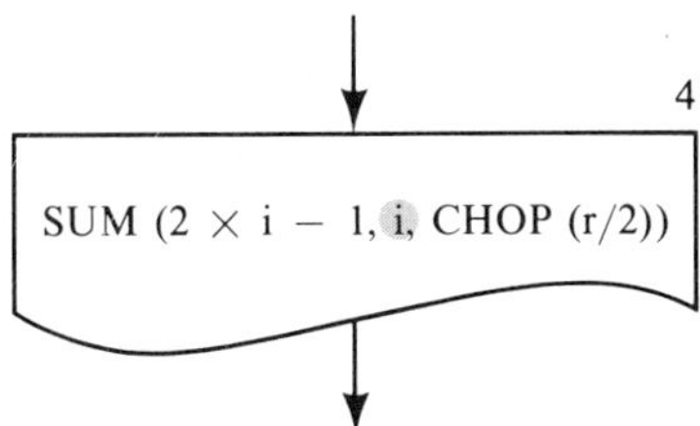

What will be the functional effect of such changes? In particular, what changes, if any, will occur in the printed results for the snapshot sequence of the correspondingly modified ALGOL program of case study 5? Explain.

2 Consider the procedure SUMR defined by a flowchart as follows:

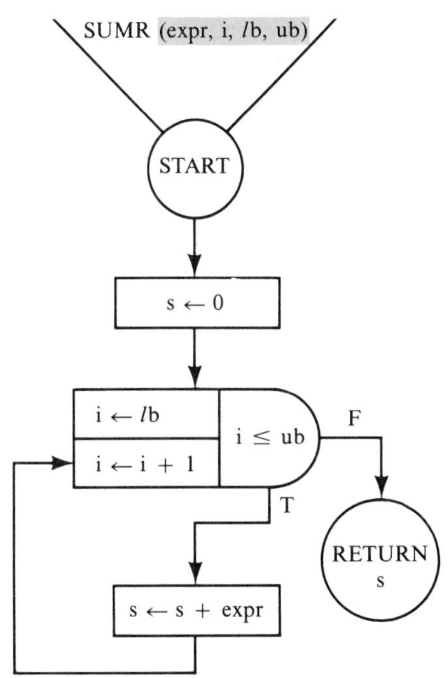

Legend for SUMR

Identifier	Treatment	Description
expr	name par	real
i	name par	integer
*l*b	val par	integer
ub	val par	integer
s	local	real

Write an ALGOL program that uses SUMR as follows:

Given input sequences of real numbers A, B, and matrices E and F, the program prints out values for r, s, t, and G, where

$$r = \sum_{i=1}^{25} A_i$$

$$s = \sum_{i=5}^{35} A_i \times B_i$$

$$t = \sum_{i=1}^{10} \left(A_i \times \sum_{j=1}^{10} B_j \right)$$

and G is a 10 × 20 array such that

$$G_{i,j} = \sum_{k=-5}^{20} E_{i,k} \times F_{k,j}$$

and where the arrays are declared as:

```
real array  A[1:35], B[1:35],
            E[1:10, -5:20],
            F[-5:20, 1:20],
            G[1:10, 1:20];
```

3 A function such as SUMR in Exercise 2 uses a programming trick sometimes referred to as *Jensen's device.* This trick takes the form of a procedure that evaluates an expression argument for various values of its variables. The given expression and one or more of its variables are arguments that match *name parameters* of the procedure.

Using this concept, construct a flowchart and legend and a corresponding ALGOL procedure MIN, which returns the minimum value of a two-variable expression of the form g(m, n). The variables m and n are integers and the domain of the argument g in which the minimum of g(m, n) is to be found is defined by the integer intervals

$$lb1 \leq m < ub1 \qquad \text{and} \qquad lb2 \leq n < ub2,$$

respectively.

5-10 PARAMETERS THAT ARE PROCEDURES

An alternative mechanism to a name-parameter-matched-to-an-expression-argument is a *procedure-parameter*-matched-to-a-*procedure-argument.* The procedure argument is the *name* of a procedure and not a reference to a procedure, i.e., not an expression that happens to involve a procedure name, and not an invocation of a procedure.

Case 6 In this example the indexing formulas, used in case 5, are redefined as distinct procedures P1, P2, and P3, respectively. Figure 5-36 presents the flowcharts and legends for case 6 and Figure 5-37 shows an equivalent ALGOL program. Notice that i must be included in the Top legend so that it can be global to P1, P2, P3, and SUM.

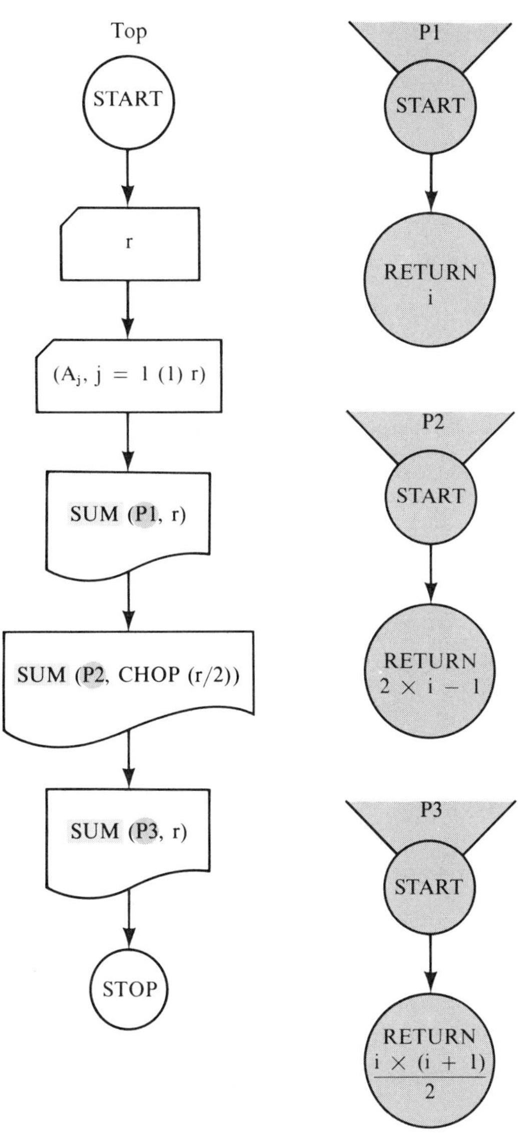

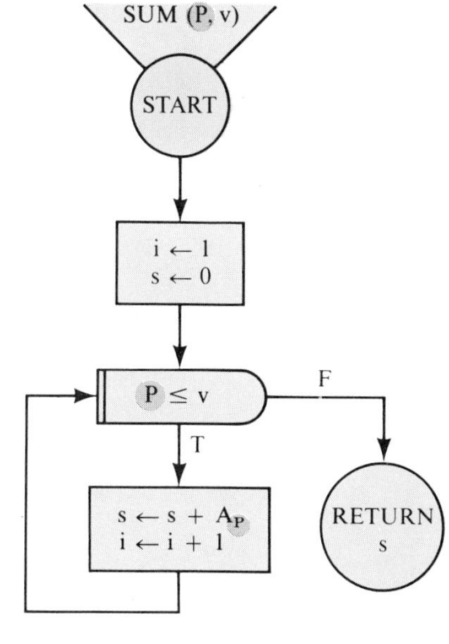

Legend for SUM

Identifier	Treatment	Description
v	val par	integer
P	proc par	integer procedure
s	local	real
i	global	i in Top
A	global	A in Top

Legends for P1, P2, and P3

Identifier	Treatment	Description
i	global	i in Top

Legend for Top

Identifier	Treatment	Description
i, r, j	local	integer
SUM	local	real procedure
P1, P2, P3	local	integer procedure
A	local	list of r reals

Figure 5-36

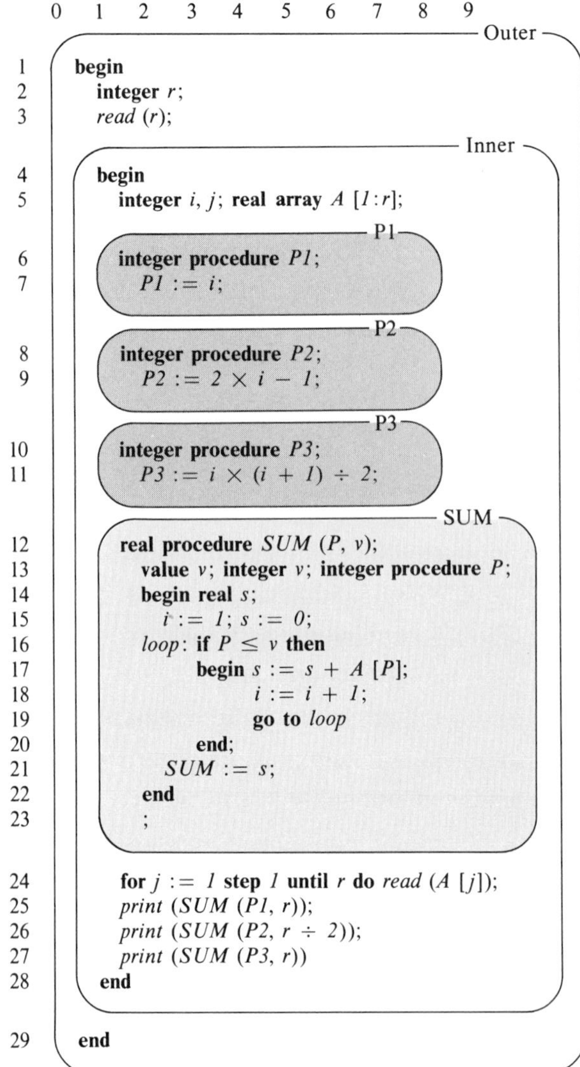

Figure 5-37. **ALGOL program for case 6.**

To understand how procedure parameters work, let us examine the procedure declaration for SUM whose first parameter P is a place holder for a procedure argument. Consider, say, the second call on SUM at line 26. The procedure name P2 is the matching argument for P. When the parameter P is referenced, as on line 16, it is intended that P2 should be called and executed in its proper environment. Notice that the variable i is global to both SUM and procedure P2. It is declared in Inner, just as it was in case 5. The snapshot sequence in this case study shows that it all works out as we would like it to. We use the same data set as in case 5.

Comparing Figures 5-34 and 5-36, or Figures 5-35 and 5-37, it is evident that the name parameter and the procedure parameter accomplish the same objective. In the case 6 version of Inner, the procedure P2, for example, replaces the formula 2 × i − 1. In the case 6 version of SUM, there are two explicit procedure references, P and A_P, using the "dummy" procedure name P in place of the dummy expression u. Whereas u is evaluated as the value of 2 × i − 1 in case 5, P is interpreted as P2 in case 6. This call then produces the value of 2 × i − 1 because of the particular declaration of P2 as an integer procedure on lines 8 and 9.

Although the net effect is the same, the case 6 mechanism appears to have greater generality in ALGOL. The argument matching a name parameter is limited to a single expression, whereas the argument matching a procedure parameter is the name of a procedure, whose body may have the greater complexity of a program block. In practice, the main advantage of the procedure parameter mechanism is stylistic. Some people consider it better style to simplify a program step by substituting a name for an expression and then specifying that expression elsewhere as the body of a procedure declaration.

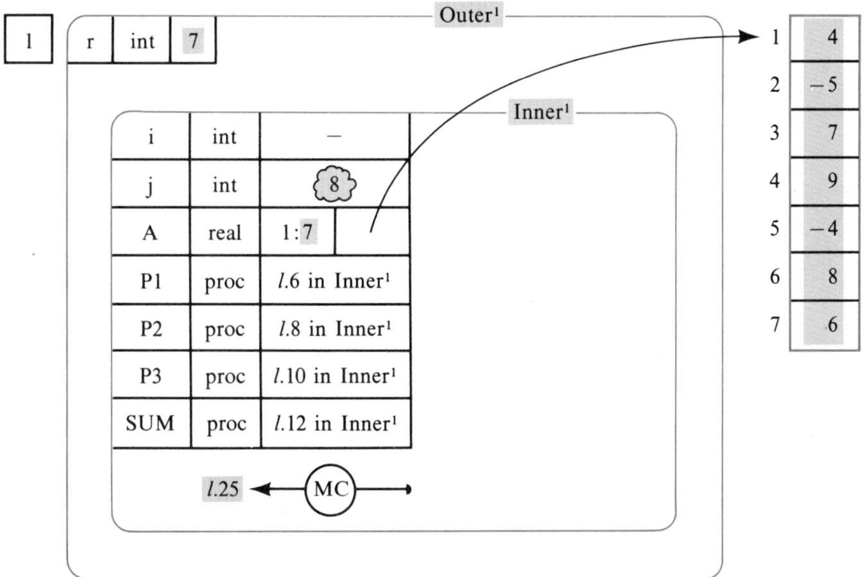

Snapshot 1 shows the state of the computation after the preliminaries of block entry into the outer and inner blocks have been completed and the input step on line 24 has been executed. Notice that all four procedures P1, P2, P3, and SUM are local to Inner, and so cells for each appear in Inner¹, each with ip, ep value pairs.

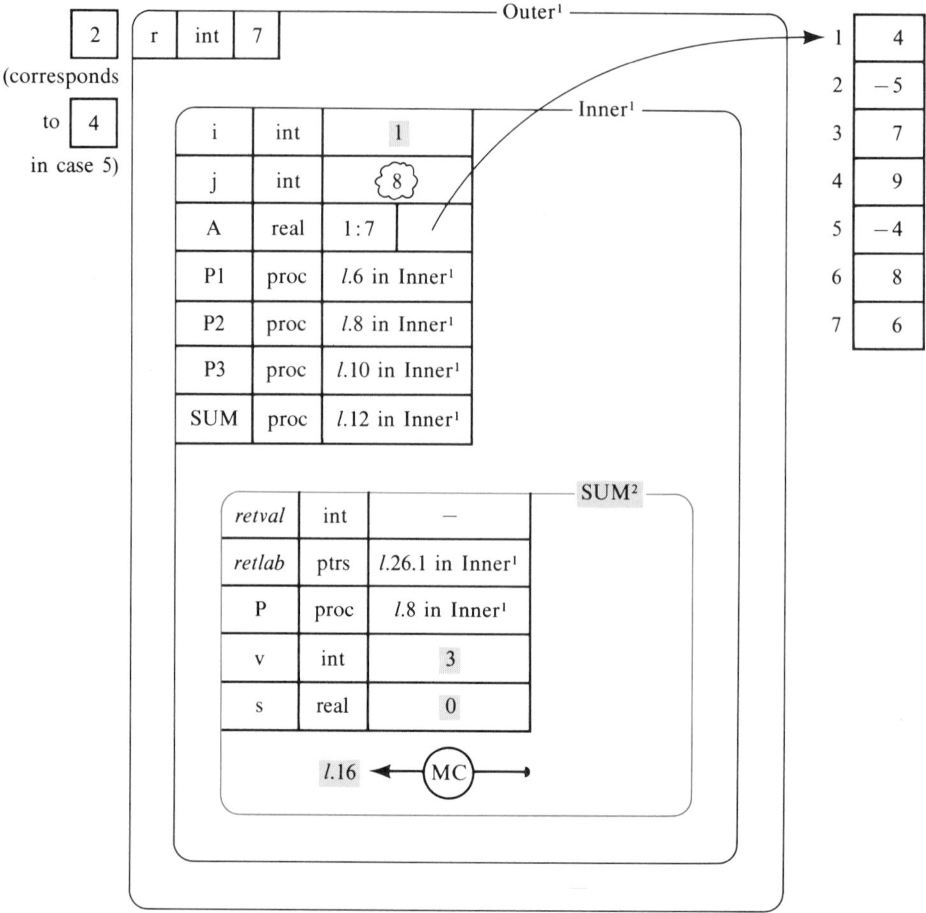

Snapshot 2 corresponds roughly to snapshot 4 in case 5. The second call on SUM has been executed on line 26. The procedure parameter P is treated as though it were a value parameter. As such, a cell for P is allocated in SUM^2 and given a value that is a copy of the ip, ep pair of the matching argument P2. The value parameter v has been assigned the value 3 as it was in case 5. The MC has just set the local s to zero and is about the execute the **if** test on line 16. The global i has value 1.

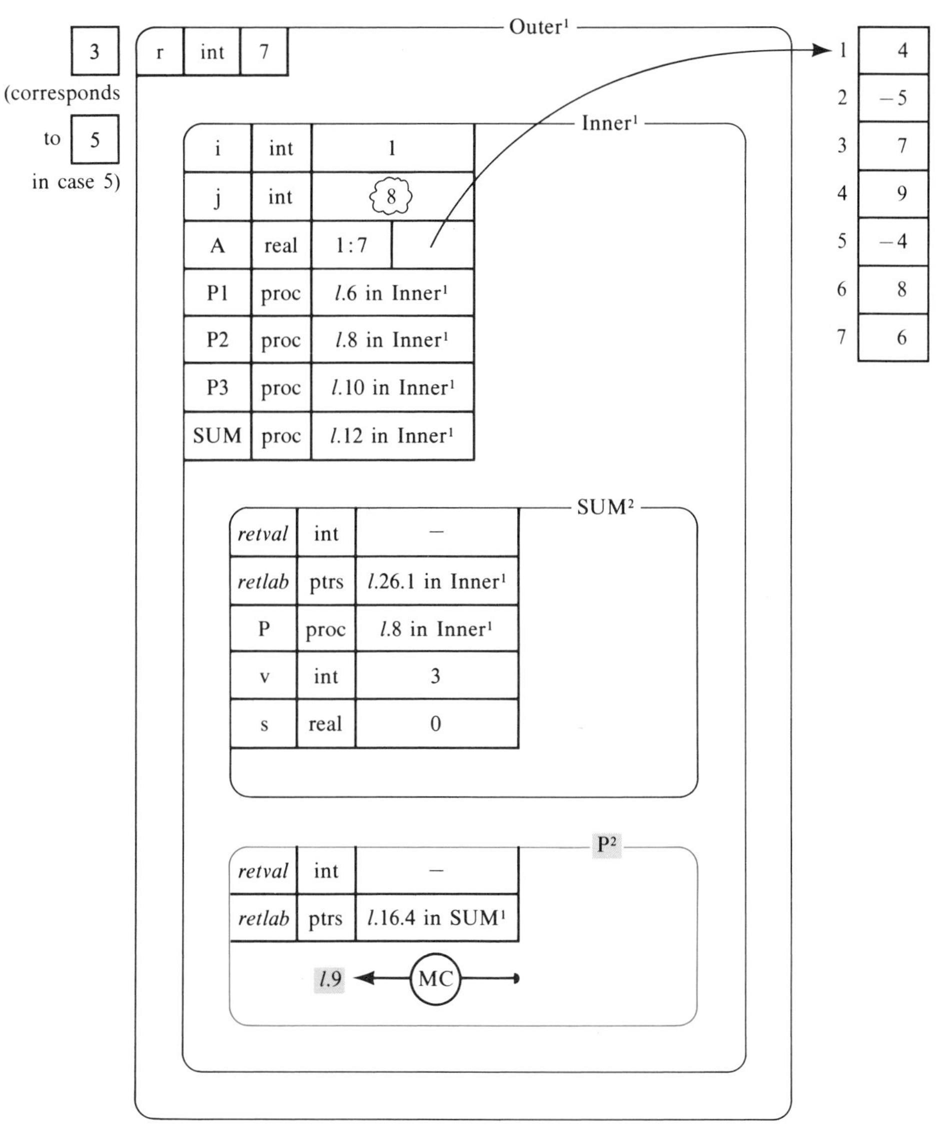

Snapshot 3 corresponds to snapshot 5 in case 5. Here we see that the parameter P has been called as a procedure. Since the value of P is *l*.8 in Inner^1, it is clear that to enter the procedure, a contour P^2 must be created and nested in Inner^1. The contour itself must look exactly like one for P^2 would look if that procedure had been called directly. Since all the necessary information, the (ip, ep) value pair of P, is available and accessible to the MC at the time of the call, there is no problem in creating the new environment P^2. The cell for the global i has already been assigned a value. Also, the return cell in P^2 has been properly initialized, so that control can return to the correct place in the calling procedure, SUM. In the snapshot we see that the MC has entered the P^2 environment and is ready to execute the evaluation of the expression $2 \times i - 1$, found on line 9.

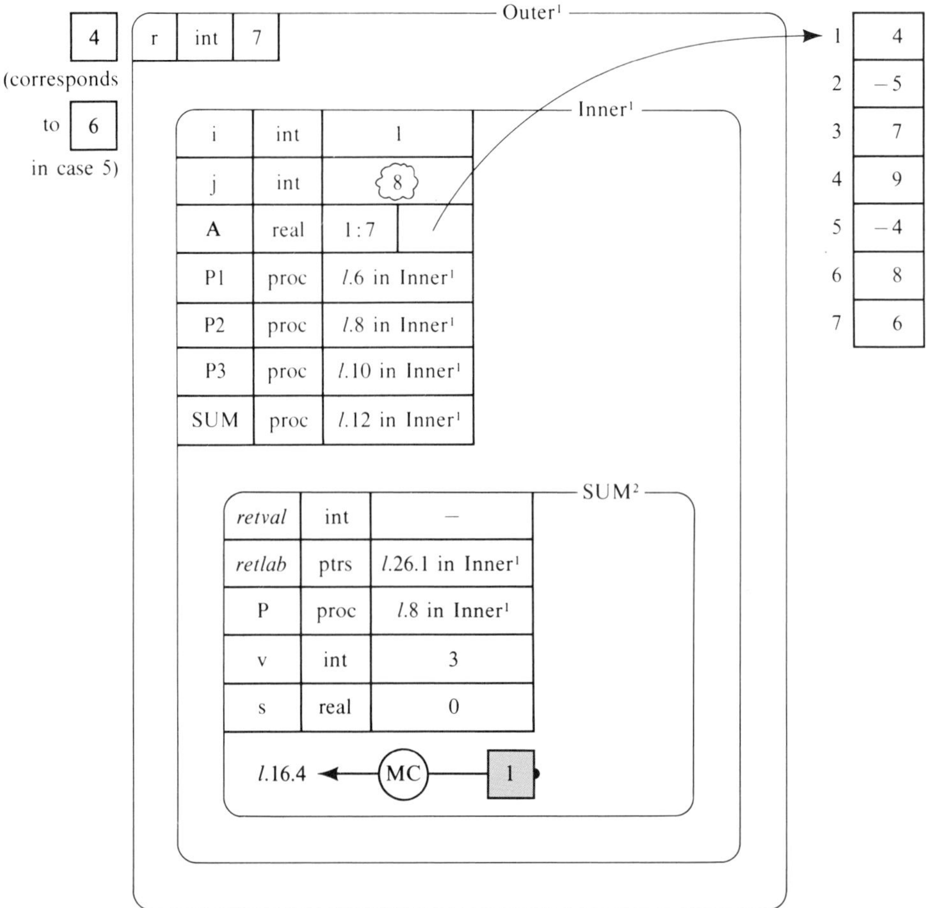

Snapshot 4, similar to snapshot 6 in case 5, shows the MC back in SUM² after having returned from P with the computed index value of 1 stored in the portable stack. The MC can now complete the **if** test on line 16. The value of s has not yet been augmented by the value of A_1.

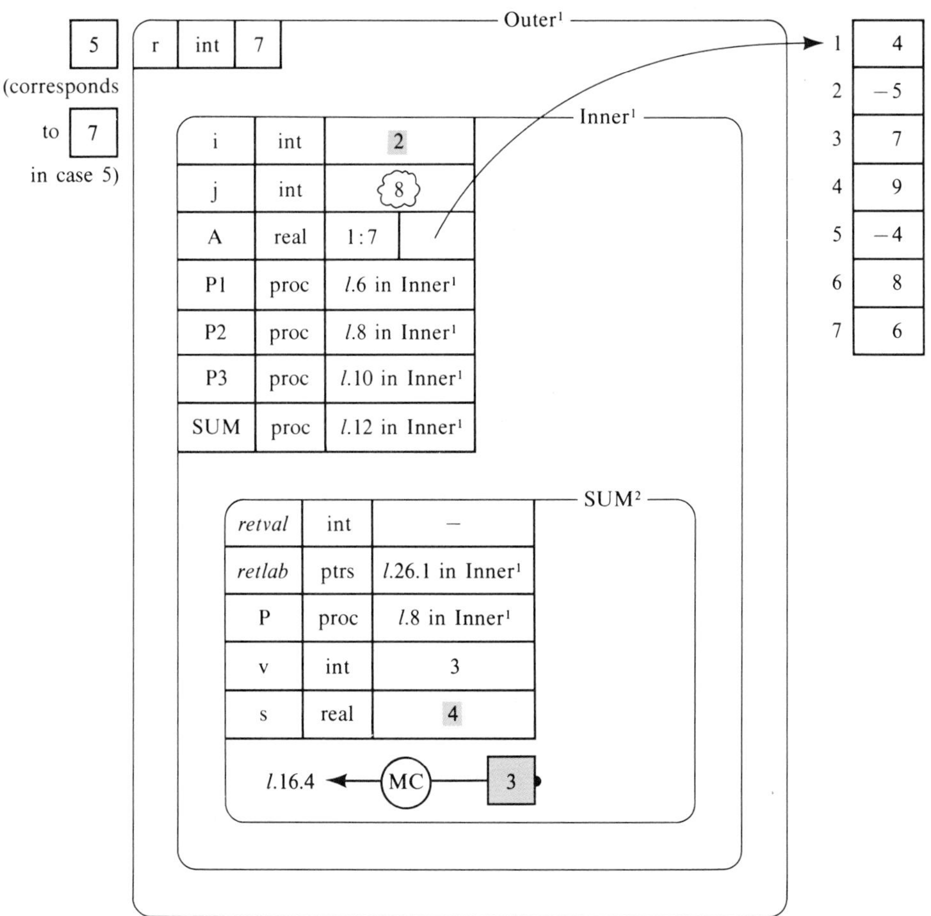

On each successive transit of the loop described by lines 16–20, P is evaluated for a new value of i. The returned value of P gives the index of the next element in A whose value is to be added to the summing variable s. In snapshot 5 we see the situation just after the MC has returned with the value of P in the portable stack. The value of s has been previously augmented by the value of A_1, and so it is currently 4, but will soon be increased by the value of A_3.

Many more snapshots for case 6 could be presented here, and explained in detail. However, instead, the reader is challenged to produce some of these snapshots as exercises, and to verify them by computer experiment.

Exercises 5-10, Set A: ALGOL Block Structure and Recursion

(Solutions are given for Exercises 1 and 2)

1 Below is an ALGOL program containing two parameterless procedures, each of which has a print statement. Each procedure also contains a call on the other procedure. Your task is the following:

(a) List every pair of values output by this program together with the (ip, ep) pair of the corresponding print statement.
(b) Justify your answer by drawing a snapshot just after each print statement has been executed.
(c) Check your snapshots with those that follow and your complete output with that given.

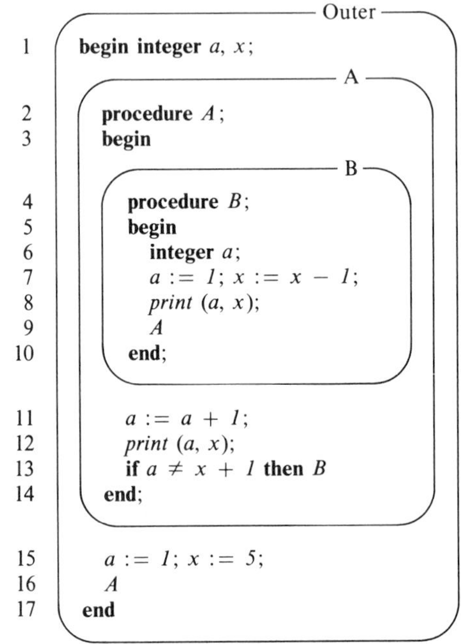

1 — Outer[1]

a	int	1
x	int	5
A	proc	*l*.2 in Outer[1]

l.16 ← MC →

2

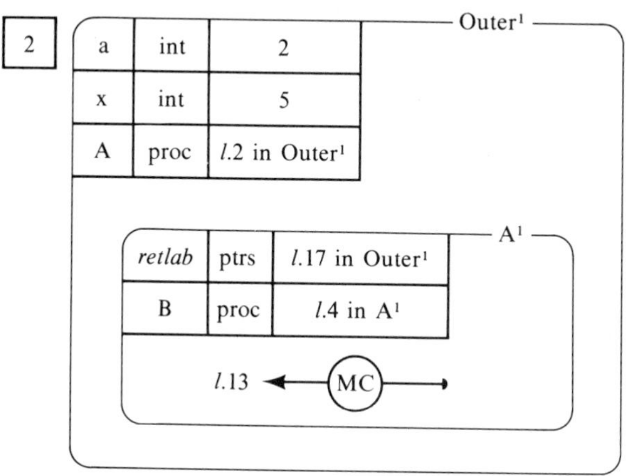
Outer[1]
a
int
2
x
int
5
A
proc
l.2 in Outer[1]
A[1]
retlab
ptrs
l.17 in Outer[1]
B
proc
l.4 in A[1]
l.13
MC

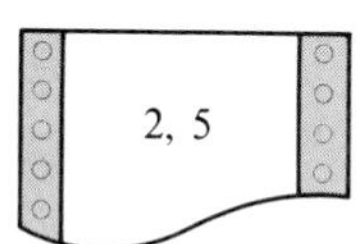
2, 5

3

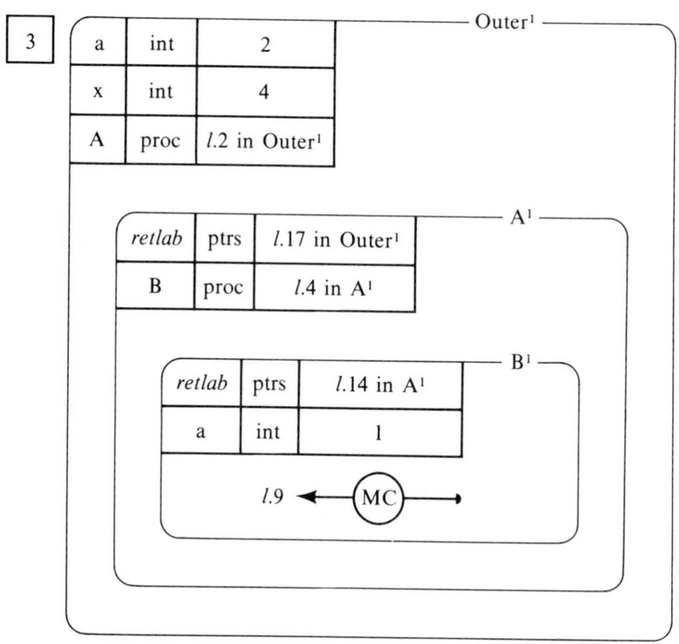
Outer[1]
a
int
2
x
int
4
A
proc
l.2 in Outer[1]
A[1]
retlab
ptrs
l.17 in Outer[1]
B
proc
l.4 in A[1]
B[1]
retlab
ptrs
l.14 in A[1]
a
int
1
l.9
MC

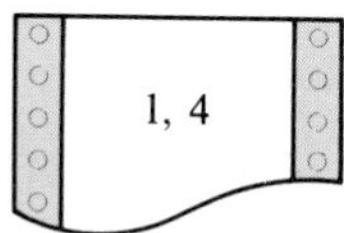
1, 4

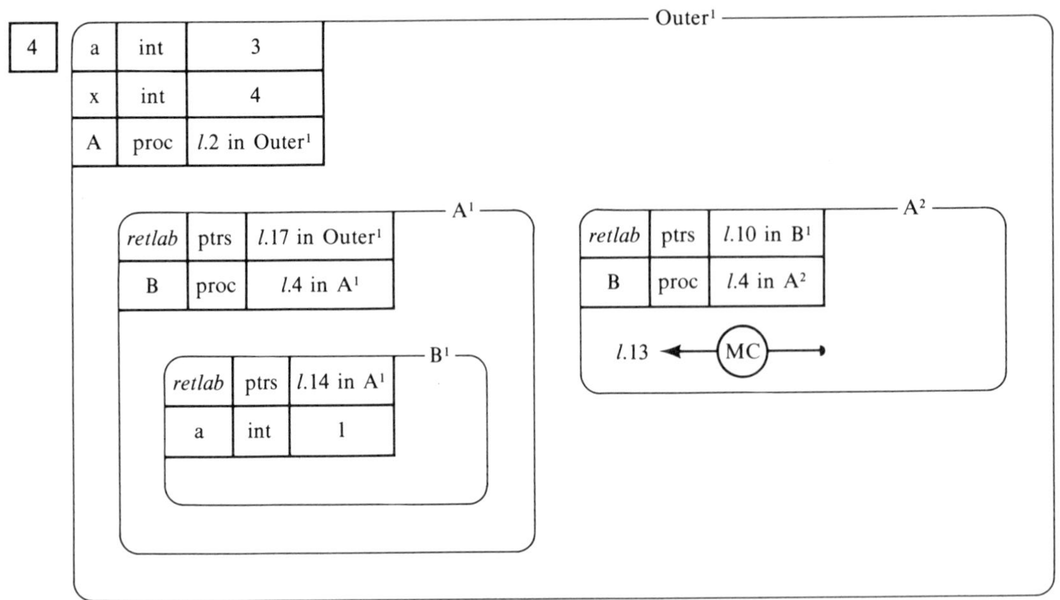
4
Outer1
a int 3
x int 4
A proc l.2 in Outer1
A1
retlab ptrs l.17 in Outer1
B proc l.4 in A1
B1
retlab ptrs l.14 in A1
a int 1
A2
retlab ptrs l.10 in B1
B proc l.4 in A2
l.13
MC

3, 4

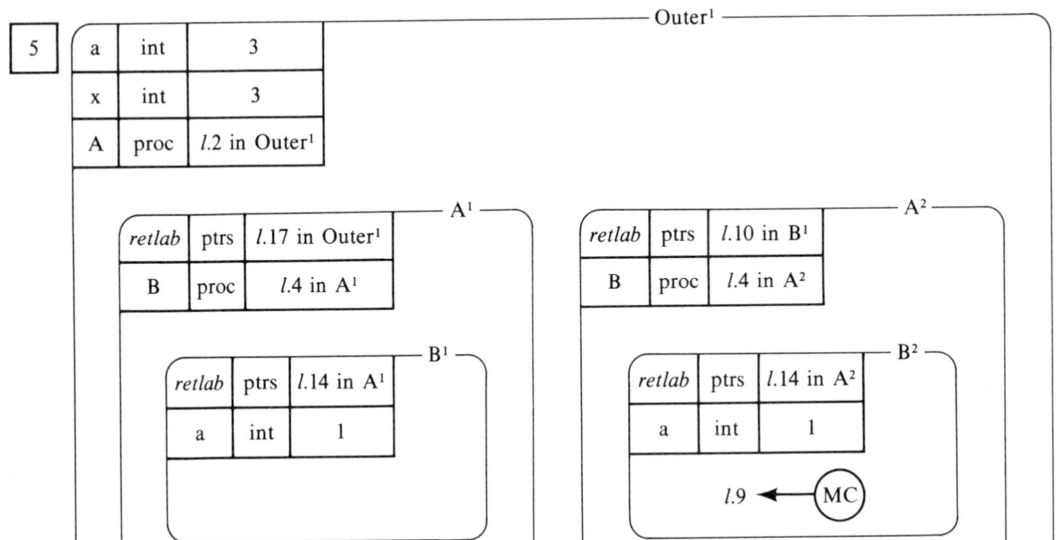
5
Outer1
a int 3
x int 3
A proc l.2 in Outer1
A1
retlab ptrs l.17 in Outer1
B proc l.4 in A1
B1
retlab ptrs l.14 in A1
a int 1
A2
retlab ptrs l.10 in B1
B proc l.4 in A2
B2
retlab ptrs l.14 in A2
a int 1
l.9
MC

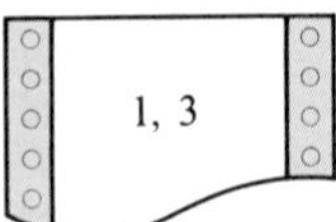
1, 3

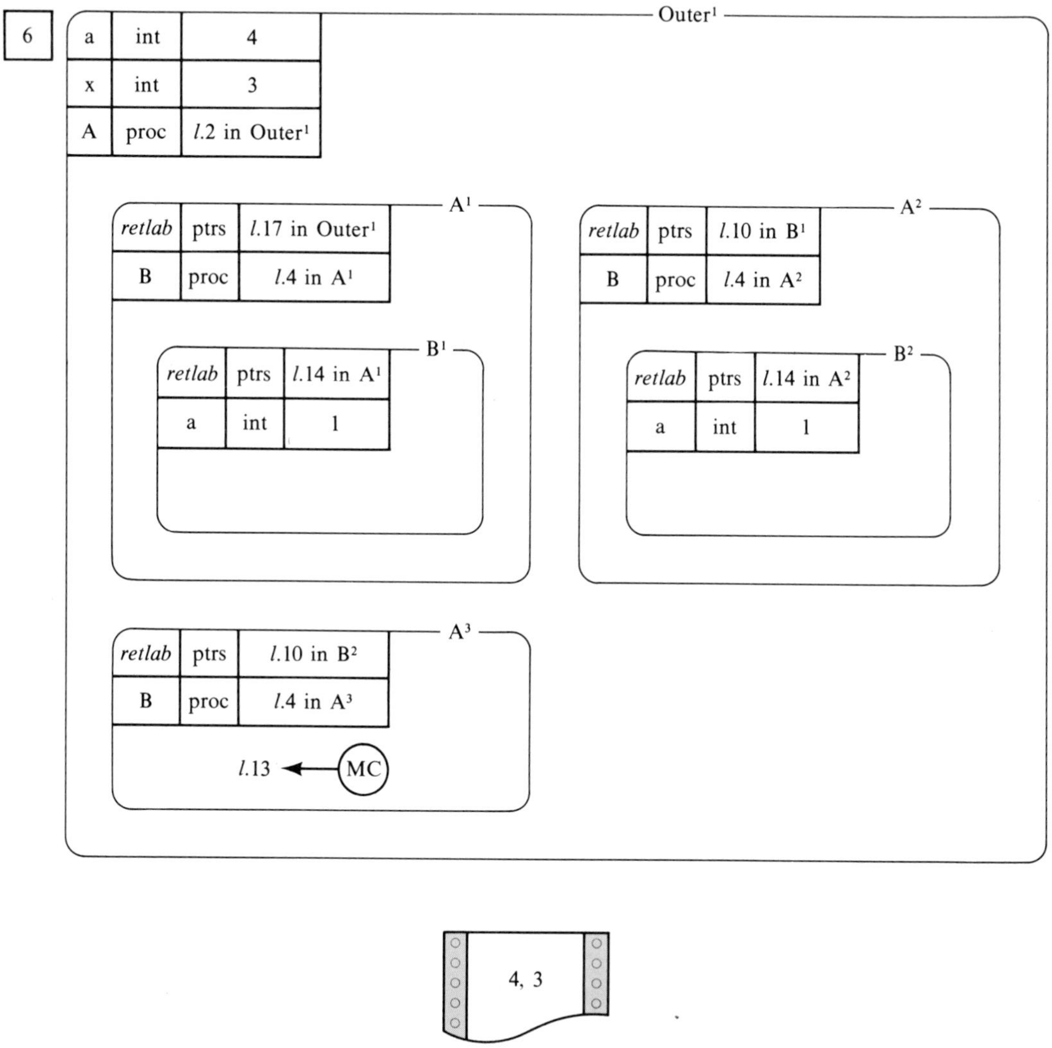

6

Outer^1

a	int	4
x	int	3
A	proc	*l*.2 in Outer^1

A^1

retlab	ptrs	*l*.17 in Outer^1
B	proc	*l*.4 in A^1

B^1

retlab	ptrs	*l*.14 in A^1
a	int	1

A^2

retlab	ptrs	*l*.10 in B^1
B	proc	*l*.4 in A^2

B^2

retlab	ptrs	*l*.14 in A^2
a	int	1

A^3

retlab	ptrs	*l*.10 in B^2
B	proc	*l*.4 in A^3

l.13 ← MC

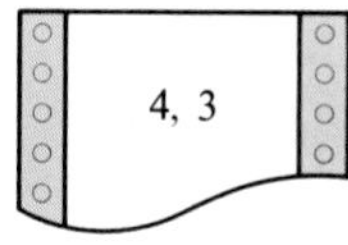

Each return is to an **end** statement; the end of A, the end of B, or the end of the program. Thus the return chain goes back rapidly to line 17, the end of the program.

The contour for procedure B is constructed *inside* the contour for procedure A because the declaration for procedure B was made inside the declaration for procedure A. The reverse is not true. Thus the contour A^2 for the second call on procedure A should not be drawn inside the contour B^1. If this were done it would lead to the incorrect output sequence shown on the right below:

Correct output sequence

from *l*.12 in A^1	2, 5
from *l*.8 in B^1	1, 4
from *l*.12 in A^2	3, 4
from *l*.8 in B^2	1, 3
from *l*.12 in A^3	4, 3

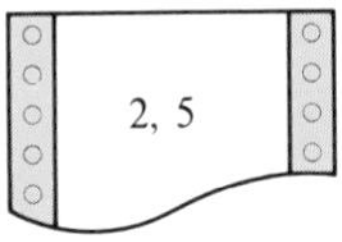

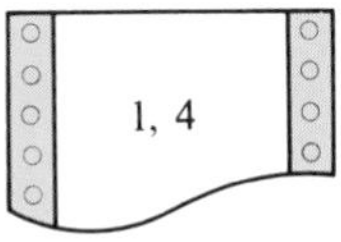

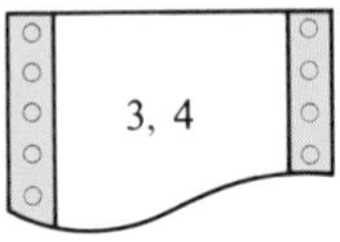

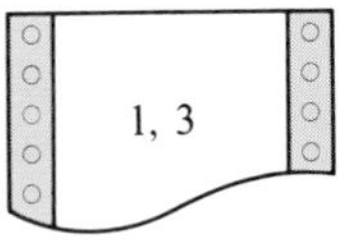

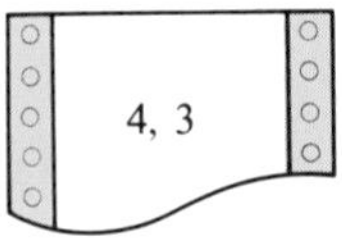

Incorrect output sequence

from *l*.12 in A^1	2, 5
from *l*.8 in B^1	1, 4
from *l*.12 in A^2	2, 4
from *l*.8 in B^2	1, 3
from *l*.12 in A^3	2, 3
from *l*.8 in B^3	1, 2
from *l*.12 in A^4	2, 2
from *l*.8 in B^4	1, 1
from *l*.12 in A^5	2, 1

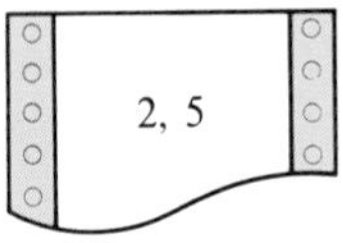

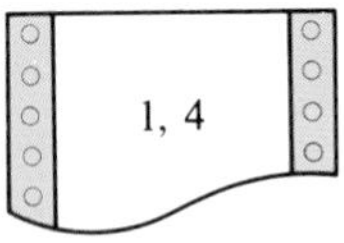

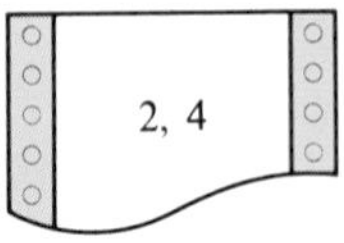

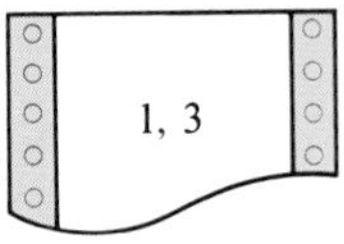

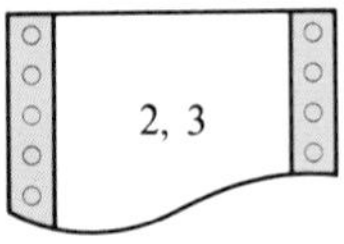

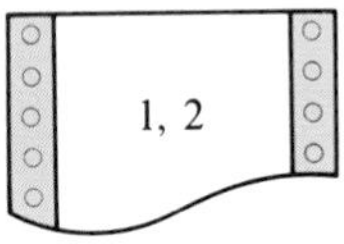

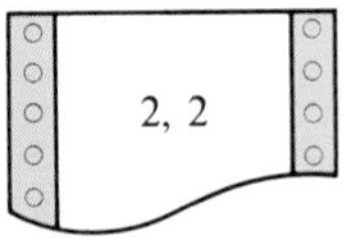

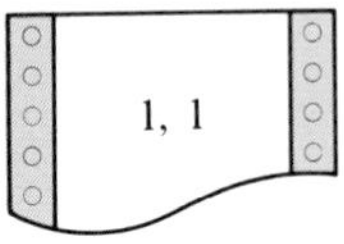

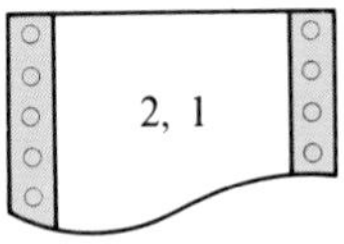

2 The following ALGOL program also contains two procedures A and B, but this time the procedures have parameters and, in line 14, procedure A is called with expression arguments. Each procedure calls recursively on the other. Your task is to list each line of output produced by the program, together with its line number and environment (ip, ep). To arrive at the output, trace the program constructing all the necessary contours as you go. When you have finished check your results with the output sequences and contour diagram that follow.

```
                                                   Outer
1   begin integer a, x;
                                                 A
2     procedure A (a, x); integer a, x;
3     begin
                                               B
4       procedure B (z); integer z;
5       begin integer a, x;
6         a := 1; x := z + 2;
7         print (a, x);
8         A (a + 1, x)
9       end;

10      print (a, x);
11      if a + x ≠ 9 then B (x)
12    end;

13    a := 5; x := 5;
14    A (a − 1, x − 2)
15  end
```

Output sequences

ip	ep	a	x
l.10	A¹	4	3
l.7	B¹	1	5
l.10	A²	2	5
l.7	B²	1	7
l.10	A³	2	7

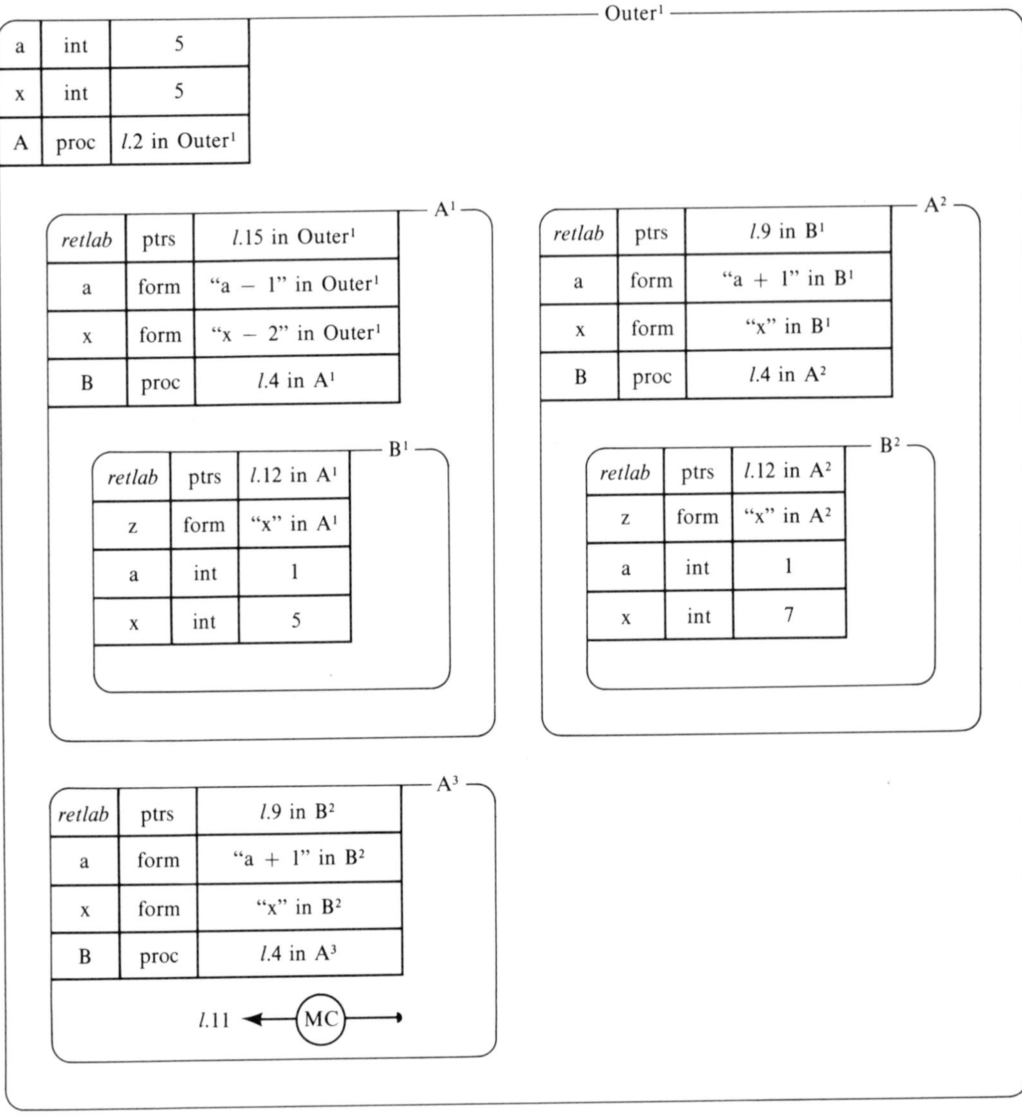

3 Figure 5-38 is another ALGOL program on which to test your understanding of block structure. This time no solution is included.

(a) Draw a snapshot of the environments just after the MC has executed the print statement at line 14 in the second call on procedure Z. Show inactive environ-

```
                                              Outer
1   begin comment test program;
2     integer a, b, c;
                                              X
3     procedure X (y);
4     integer y;
5     begin
                                              Z
6       procedure Z;
7       begin
8         integer a, b;
9         a := c; b := y;
10        if b > a then
11        begin
12          c := c + y;
13          b := b + a;
14          print (a, b, c)
15        end
16      end;

17      integer a, c;
18      a := 4; b := b + 2; c := 6;
19      Z;
20      print (a, b, c)
21    end;

22    a := 5; b := 3; c := 1;
23    print (a, b, c);
24    X (a + b);
25    print (a, b, c);
                                              Inner
26    begin
27      integer c;
28      c := 10;
29      X (a + c);
30      print (a, b, c)
31    end;

32    print (a, b, c)
33  end
```

Figure 5-38

ments with a slanted line (diagonal) across them. If values of variables change, show the old values with a slash through them, and show the new values, e.g.,

a	int	~~1~~ ~~2~~ 3

(b) Complete the table below to show *all* the output of the test ALGOL program. Give the MC's line number (ip) and the environment (ep) associated with each line of output.

MC's line # ip	environment ep	a	b	c

Exercises 5-10, Set B
ALGOL Review Exercise

1 You are given the NUALGOL program* in Figure 5-39 together with the following data:

"grape"	1	5
"banana"	2	4
"artichoke"	3	−1
"apple"	−1	−1
"carrot"	−1	−1
"potato"	6	7
"orange"	−1	−1
"zucchini"	8	−1
"rutabaga"	−1	−1

These data represent a tree. Each triple gives three pieces of information about node i. The first is the value of data (i), the second and third are the node numbers (assume natural treesearch order) of the leftoffspring node and the rightoffspring node of the node i. We have used the convention that −1 indicates the absence of an offspring. Thus the root node 0 has a data value "grape", and its left offspring is node 1 and right offspring is node 5. Node 3 has a data value "apple" and no left or right offspring. Thus node 3 is a terminal node.

Figure 5-39

```
begin
  integer array leftoffspring, rightoffspring [0:8];
  string array data [10:0:8];
  integer i;

  procedure printout [currentnode];
    value currentnode; integer currentnode;

    if currentnode ≠ −1 then
    begin
      printout (leftoffspring [currentnode]);
      print (data [currentnode]);
      printout (rightoffspring [currentnode])
    end;

  for i := 0 step 1 until 8 do
    read (data [i], leftoffspring [i], rightoffspring [i]);
  printout (0)
end
```

*NUALGOL is a dialect of ALGOL that allows the use of simple and array character string variables. In this dialect, for example,

string array *data* [*10*:*0*:*8*]

declares data to be a nine-element array of elements (with subscript range 0–8), each a 10-character string.

(a) Draw the tree structure represented by the *data* in storage. Label each node with its index and place its data value inside the node.

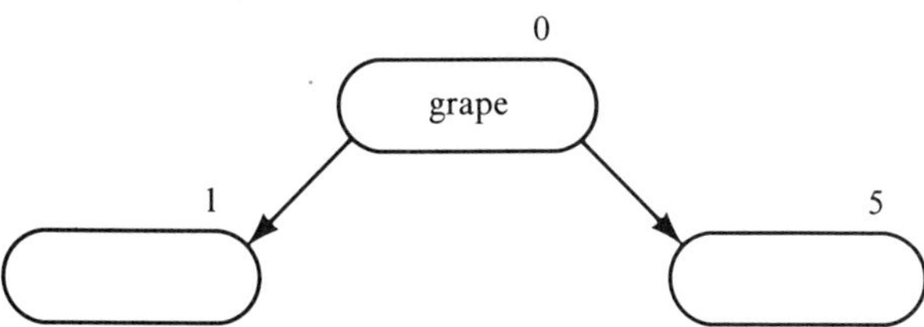

(b) Show the complete output of the program when it is executed.
(c) Draw a snapshot of the execution of the ALGOL program when the MC has just executed the print statement (line 11) in the second call on printout. Show all contours (active or inactive) that have ever been active. Use a light diagonal line across a contour to indicate it is inaccessible. Show any output that has already occurred and for each output indicate in which contour the MC was operating when it occurred.
(d) We are not satisfied with a data list of nine items (and their left and right pointers). We want the program and its storage structures to be able to accommodate n data items and their pointers, where the value of n is read in the first (executable) statement of the program. Describe what changes to the program are required to accomplish this.

5-11 OWN IDENTIFIERS IN ALGOL

ALGOL has a number of syntactic structures we have not mentioned, but our point of view has been to describe a minimum ALGOL, including only those features required to understand the case studies presented in this chapter. We now touch briefly on one other feature of the language, the **own** declarator.

According to our model of Algol semantics, when an ALGOL block is entered, the MC causes an environment to be established and this environment contains a cell for each identifier declared in the head of that block. Correspondingly, when an exit from that block takes place, the MC causes the environment to be deallocated, in effect making all the local cells available for recycling. If that block is reentered at a later time, the whole allocation process is reinitiated. This means, of course, that values of local variables or identifiers can not be "held over" from one activation of a block to another.

The ALGOL designers, however, wished to make it possible to hold over values in the case of selected local identifiers and they indicated these particular identifiers by inserting the word "own" into their declarations. For example, suppose the head of block A contains the declarations

own integer *x*, *y*, *z*;
integer *p*, *q*

Then when the MC establishes the environment for block A, cells are created, as before, for the identifiers x, y, z, p, and q. There is a slight difference now in the type compartment of the cell, suggested by a lowercase o to indicate an **own** identifier, as seen in Figure 5-40a.

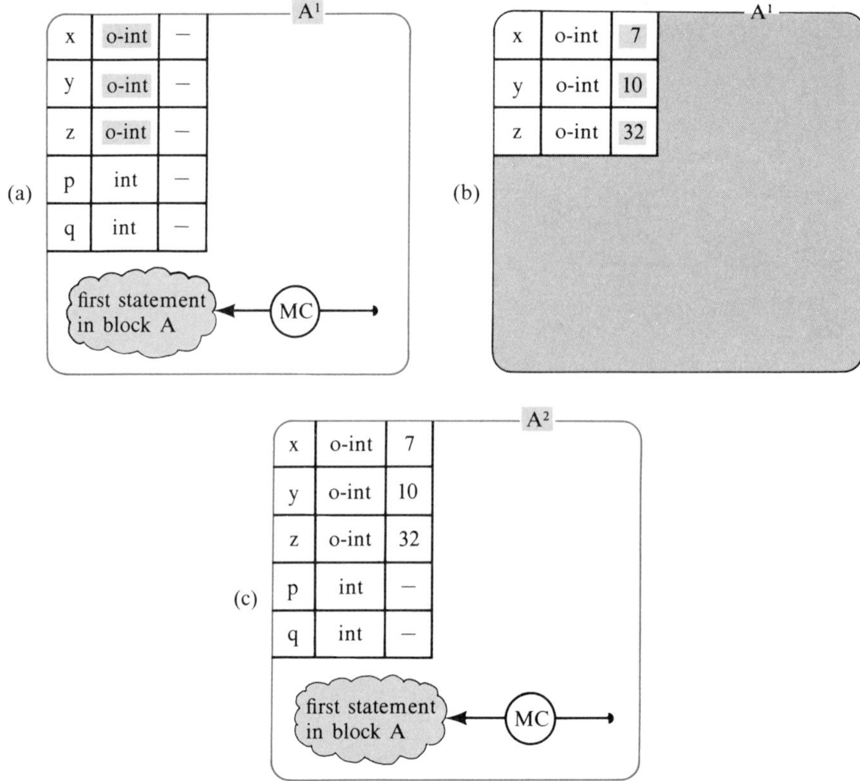

Figure 5-40. **(a) Environment just after block A has been entered for the *first* time. (b) Environment just after the first exit from block A. (c) Environment just after block A has been entered for the *second* time.**

The real effect of the "own" declarator becomes evident when the block exit is executed. Then the cells for p and q become available for recycling, as expected, but the cells covered by the "own" declarations remain in existence and, as suggested in Figure 5-40b, their values are preserved. (We assume these values are x = 7, y = 10, and z = 32 at the time of the first exit from block A.) If block A is reentered at a later time, the environment A^2 is constructed, reusing the "own" cells with their preserved values, but all other local cells are recreated, as shown in Figure 5-40c.

The feature of **own** variables has not been found to be especially helpful in promoting program clarity. One has to trace quite carefully to be sure a program with **own** variables is operating correctly. On the other hand, the effect of **own** variables can easily be achieved by simply making the variables in question global to the block in which they had been declared "own". Since this is the case,

own variables are not used a great deal and have not been implemented fully in many Algol dialects.*

5-12 REFERENCES AND SUGGESTIONS FOR FURTHER READING

Considerable literature is available on ALGOL 60 and languages derived from it. Chapter 11 of Pratt (1975) is an overview of ALGOL 60 useful for review. The official report defining ALGOL 60 syntax and semantics can be found in Naur (ed.) *et al.* (1963); part of that syntax is reproduced as Appendix A of our book. Other texts such as Baumann *et al.* (1964) and Rosen (1967) reproduce the entire report.

Techniques to implement Algol compilers have been widely discussed in the literature. One valuable text is Randell and Russell (1964). Organick (1973) describes the structure of a computer system modeled on ALGOL 60 semantics.

There are numerous interesting extensions of ALGOL 60: EULER, described by Wirth and Weber (1966), ALGOL-W first described by Wirth and Hoare (1966), Burroughs ALGOL, ALGOL 68, and Pascal. A lucid introduction to ALGOL 68 is given by Tannenbaum (1976). Burroughs ALGOL and Pascal are treated in Chapters 9 and 10 of this book and appropriate references for these languages appear at the ends of those chapters. The foregoing recommendations are good starting points to the rest of the Algol literature.

*A practical difficulty arises in implementing an ALGOL system that permits **own** variables to be arrays. In particular, suppose an **own** array is declared in an inner block B to have variable dimensions (a "dynamic array"), e.g.,

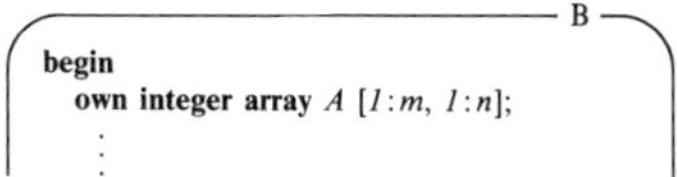

In principle, the array A should be accessible during any execution of block B. However, each time block B is entered, values of m and n may have changed and therefore space for such a dynamic array cannot be preallocated (before execution time) as can space for simple **own** variables or **own array** variables of fixed dimensions. For this reason many ALGOL systems permitting **own arrays** require that they have fixed dimensions, thus limiting the relative advantage they have over ordinary arrays declared in the outermost block.

In addition, there is another difficulty even when dynamic **own arrays** are permitted. This is to decide whether or not the elements of an array, like A in block B above, whose dimensions decrease and then increase on successive reentries to block B, should be *undefined* in the reexpanded portion or "recover" old values assigned in a prior "invocation" of B.

6 FORTRAN

6-1 INTRODUCTION

Fortran was one of the world's first "high-level" programming languages, coming into operation in the late 1950s. Today, it is probably the most widely used language for the programming of scientific and engineering computations. This chapter examines Fortran in terms of the same semantic and syntactic concepts applied to the study of Algol in Chapter 5.

Historically, Algol came on the scene after Fortran and, as a result, many people have tried to understand Algol as an extension or enrichment of Fortran. This approach has usually been unsuccessful. By reversing the historical order in our presentation of Algol and Fortran, we hope to delineate the important and unique properties of each, and enable the reader to understand the advantages and shortcomings of these two languages quickly and easily.

The early development of Fortran was quite different from that of ALGOL 60. From its very beginning, ALGOL 60 was defined precisely by the syntax (and associated discussion of semantics) published in the "Revised Report of the Algorithmic Language ALGOL 60" (Naur *et al.,* 1963). The implementers of ALGOL 60 actually used this definition to produce operating versions of the language on various machines. As new ideas and techniques have developed in the area of programming languages, other Algol-like languages have been defined and implemented, but the original ALGOL 60 language has remained available.

Initially Fortran did not have a precise definition. The first versions were developed for particular IBM machines, and subsequently other implementors produced versions of Fortran for other machines. In the process, variations were introduced and, although most of these were minor, a few were significant. To describe the language, the user was given a reference manual discussing the language and giving examples.

In contrast with Algol, new developments were continually amalgamated into Fortran, appearing in augmented or amplified versions, rather than generated as new languages. Although one's first reaction to the idea of an "evolving" language might be negative, the resulting continuity has no doubt greatly contributed to the popularity of Fortran. In 1966, the American National Standards Institute published what was regarded as *the* (machine-independent) definition of the language* but even that effort remains within the evolutionary framework, since revised "standards" are to be issued from time to time. The emphasis in this chapter is consistent with 1966 ANSI Fortran but in later sections we also discuss the newer 1977 ANSI Fortran.

The designers of Fortran aimed at the highest possible execution speed for compiled programs on the currently available computers. To achieve this goal a number of constraints were imposed on the syntax of the language (for example, on iteration statements and array declarations), and on the language semantics (for example, in loop control, procedure calls, and the treatment of parameters). Some of these design tradeoffs are discussed later in this chapter.

6-2 OVERVIEW OF THE SYNTAX AND SEMANTICS OF FORTRAN PROGRAMS AND SUBPROGRAMS

A Fortran program is a collection of *program units* (translations of the flowchart for Top, and any accompanying procedure flowcharts). The program units matching the procedure flowcharts are called subprograms. These subprograms are not nested hierarchically within the main program (Top) or within one another. Therefore, a Fortran program may be viewed as a two-level tree, as suggested in Figure 6-1. Figure 6-1a shows the structure of a program with only one component, Top, while Figure 6-1b shows the structure of another with n subprograms in addition to Top.

Figure 6-2 shows (a) a Fortran program broken down into its component declarations and statements, along with (b) a schematic representation of the program as it would be prepared for input to a computer, and (c) relevant BNF definitions.† Fortran allows only one declaration or statement to appear on each line, although the displayed syntax does not enforce this rule. In Section 6-4 we return to rules for preparing Fortran programs.

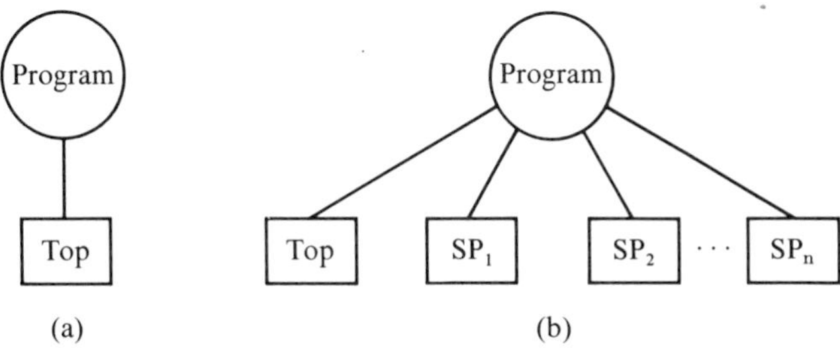

Figure 6-1. **Structure of Fortran programs.**

*See ANSI (1966).

†A partial Fortran syntax is given in this chapter; for a complete definition see Nolan (1971) or Burkhardt (1968).

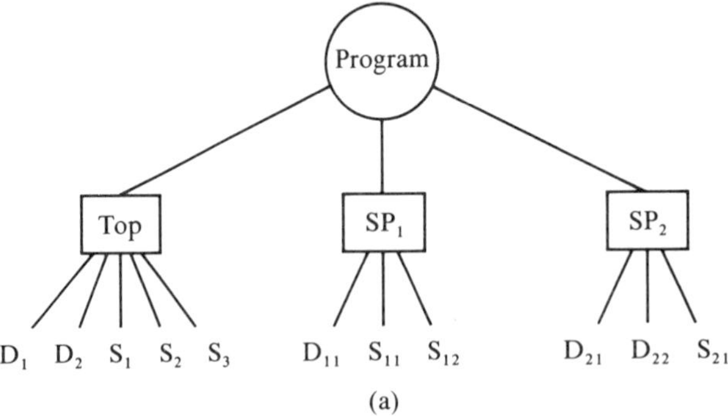

(a)

Top
D_1
D_2
S_1
S_2
S_3
END

SP_1
SUBROUTINE . . .
D_{11}
S_{11}
S_{12}
END

SP_2
FUNCTION . . .
D_{21}
D_{22}
S_{21}
END

(b)

⟨program⟩ ::= ⟨top level⟩{⟨procedure⟩}$_0$
⟨top level⟩ ::= ⟨head⟩⟨body⟩
⟨head⟩ ::= {⟨declaration⟩}$_0$
⟨body⟩ ::= {⟨statement⟩}$_1$ END

⟨procedure⟩ ::= ⟨procedure heading⟩⟨head⟩⟨body⟩
⟨procedure heading⟩ ::= SUBROUTINE⟨subroutine heading⟩|
{⟨type⟩}$_0^1$ FUNCTION⟨function heading⟩

⟨subroutine heading⟩ ::= ⟨identifier⟩{⟨formal parameter part⟩}$_0^1$
⟨function heading⟩ ::= ⟨identifier⟩⟨formal parameter part⟩

⟨type⟩ ::= INTEGER|REAL|. . .

(c)

***Figure 6-2.* Tree structure and schematic appearance of a Fortran program, along with relevant BNF syntax.**

It can be deduced from the syntax of Figure 6-2c that individual Fortran program units do not have the recursive structure of Algol. Thus any Fortran program can be represented by a three-level tree similar to that in Figure 6-2a.

In our study of Fortran semantics, we use contour diagrams to model the environment of an executing program. However, first an essential characteristic of Fortran semantics must be understood: all contours and cells are allocated at the very beginning of the execution of a program and remain allocated until the program halts. That is, the declarations in Top *and* in all subprograms are processed before any other statements. In terms of our model, the MC tells the Allocator at the start of the computation to allot a cell for every procedure identifier and for every global variable, and to build an outer contour that we call $Prog^1$ in which to place these cells. Then the MC tells the Allocator to build an additional contour within $Prog^1$ for each program unit (that is, one for Top and one for each subprogram) and then to allot cells for these contours. The cells allotted for Top^1 constitute the locals for Top, and the cells allotted for subprogram contour $SP_j{}^1$ are the locals for subprogram j. (In the next section we discuss some other cells that can appear in these contours.) The placement of the program unit contours, as shown in Figure 6-3, reflects the nonnested structure of the language.

When the allocation process has been finished, the MC moves into Top^1 and begins to execute the first "action step" (that is, nondeclarative statement) in the top level of the Fortran program. When a subprogram is invoked, or "called," the MC moves over into the appropriate contour and executes the action steps of the subprogram. To exit from a subprogram, the MC just returns to the contour of the caller. As mentioned above, there is no *deallocation* of resources until the program as a whole terminates. If a subprogram is called more than once, the MC reenters the same preestablished contour each time, although all local variables are considered to have lost any leftover values.* Superscripts on Fortran contour names are therefore unnecessary; "1" is the only superscript that is ever used, but we retain that notation to distinguish the program Top from the contour Top^1, etc.

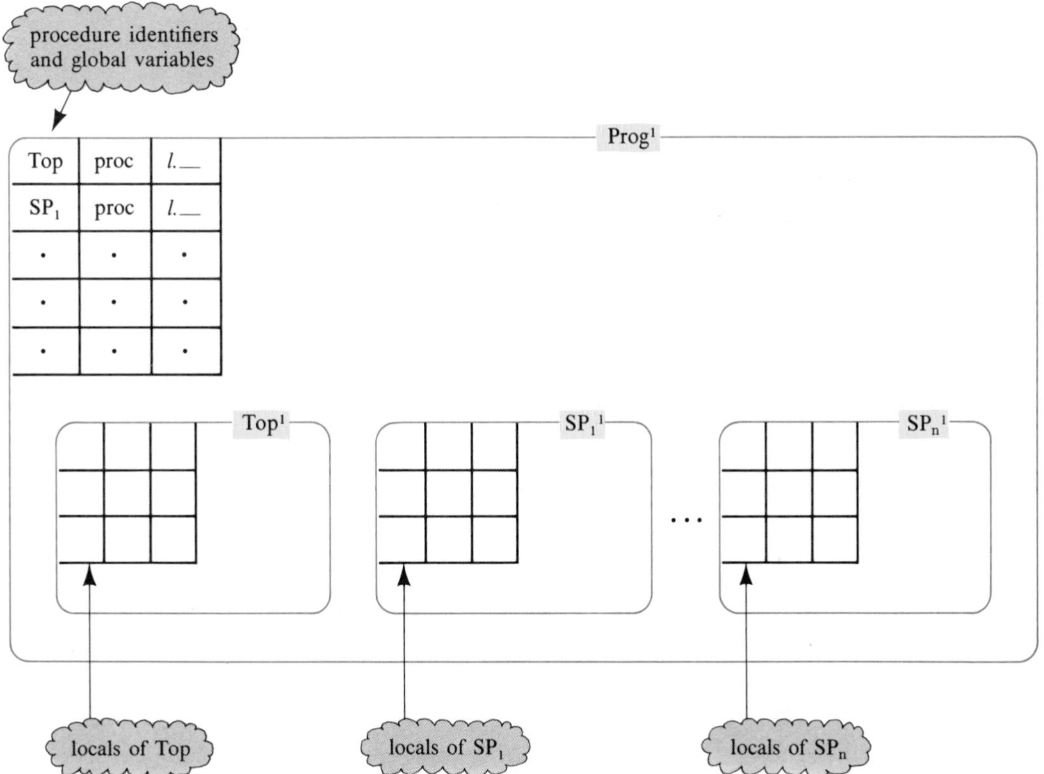

Figure 6-3. **Environment for a Fortran program with n subprograms.**

*In many actual Fortran systems in common use, such leftover values are in fact accessible to the MC when the contour is reentered. This fact is exploited in applications where it is desired to have a subprogram "remember" effects of prior calls. The **own** variable of ALGOL 60, as mentioned in Section 5-11, is a comparable feature.

It is also important to point out that Fortran procedures may *not* be called recursively. This conclusion follows from the fact that all contours are established (allocated) at the outset. If procedures could be called recursively, it would be necessary either to break this rule or to provide, in advance, a contour for every potential activation of every procedure in the program, and this is clearly impractical. Even though procedures cannot be called recursively, it is always possible to compose Fortran programs and subprograms that achieve the *same semantic effect* as recursive programs in other languages. To accomplish this effect, data that would have been placed in the separate environments of successive activations of a recursive procedure can instead be explicitly stored and retrieved in last-in-first-out fashion from successive elements of a globally accessible list or array. (See the exercises at the end of Section 6-7.)

A further characteristic of Fortran subprograms (procedures and functions) is that all parameters are of the reference type; there is no value or name treatment. The reference parameter effect is implemented using one of the techniques discussed in Section 2-2, that is, chaining of references, copying of references, or the value/result method. (As pointed out in the earlier discussion, these methods are not strictly equivalent—see the footnote on p. 73.) In the case studies that appear later in this chapter, we use the copy method for the reference parameter mechanism.

Summary

A Fortran program is a collection of nonnested components matching flowcharts for a top level and for procedures. Contours and cells for each program unit are allocated in advance and surrounded by an outer contour Prog[1], which contains cells for procedure identifiers and for globals. Cells for contours remain allocated until the program as a whole terminates. Procedures may not be called recursively, and all parameters are of the reference type.

By preallocating the workspace for every contour and storage cell (static allocation), the compiler can compute the location associated with every program identifier. Thus, to access stored data or to enter a subprogram, the Fortran compiler can generate an instruction sequence that maximizes speed of execution. Preallocation of workspace was especially advantageous in executing programs on the type of computer generally available through the 1960s.* The designers of the Cobol language chose static allocation for the same reason.

6-3 GLOBAL VARIABLES IN FORTRAN

In Fortran, as in Algol, global variables provide a means of communication between program units. The rules for determining the scope of globals in Fortran differ significantly, however, from those of Algol. An important syn-

*Since then some computer systems have been designed with the stacklike characteristics required for Algol dynamic storage allocation. The availability of such systems encourages the execution of Algol programs in preference to equivalent Fortran programs. See Organick (1973).

tactic characteristic of Fortran globals is that they *must be explictly declared* in every program unit that references them. Hence, a program unit can reference only those globals that are declared within the program unit to be global. (Compare this rule with Algol, where every variable local to a given block is *implicitly* global to all blocks nested within.) However, no matter where the globals are declared and used, cells for Fortran globals are regarded as belonging to the outer contour $Prog^1$. Declarations of globals are called COMMON declarations, for example,

```
COMMON X, Y, Z (100)
```

and have the following syntax:

$$\begin{aligned}\langle\text{common declaration}\rangle &::= \text{COMMON } \langle\text{variable list}\rangle\\ \langle\text{variable list}\rangle &::= \langle\text{variable}\rangle \{,\langle\text{variable}\rangle\}_0\\ \langle\text{variable}\rangle &::= \langle\text{unsubscripted variable identifier}\rangle \mid\\ &\quad\ \langle\text{array identifier}\rangle \{ \langle\text{upper bounds}\rangle\}_0^1\end{aligned}$$

Suppose, for example, that the declarations

```
INTEGER X, Y
REAL Z
COMMON X, Y, Z (100)
```

all appear in both Top and SP_1.* The accessing structure set up by the Allocator is shown in Figure 6-4.

A block of storage containing 102 cells is allocated in $Prog^1$ and given the name Blank (we explain this particular choice of name later). In Top^1 and SP^1 there are cells X and Y of type integer and array cell Z of type real. All six cells contain references to the cells of Blank. Note that the association of list Z with cells $Blank_3$, $Blank_4$, . . . , $Blank_{102}$ is established by placing a reference to the first of those cells in the value compartment of Z.

The variable names used in the COMMON declarations of different program units need not all be the same. For example, Fortran allows us to have in Top the declarations

```
INTEGER X, Y
REAL Z
COMMON X, Y, Z (100)
```

and in SP_1 the declarations

```
INTEGER A, B
REAL C
COMMON A, B, C (100)
```

*An equivalent set of declarations is

```
INTEGER X, Y
REAL Z (100)
COMMON X, Y, Z
```

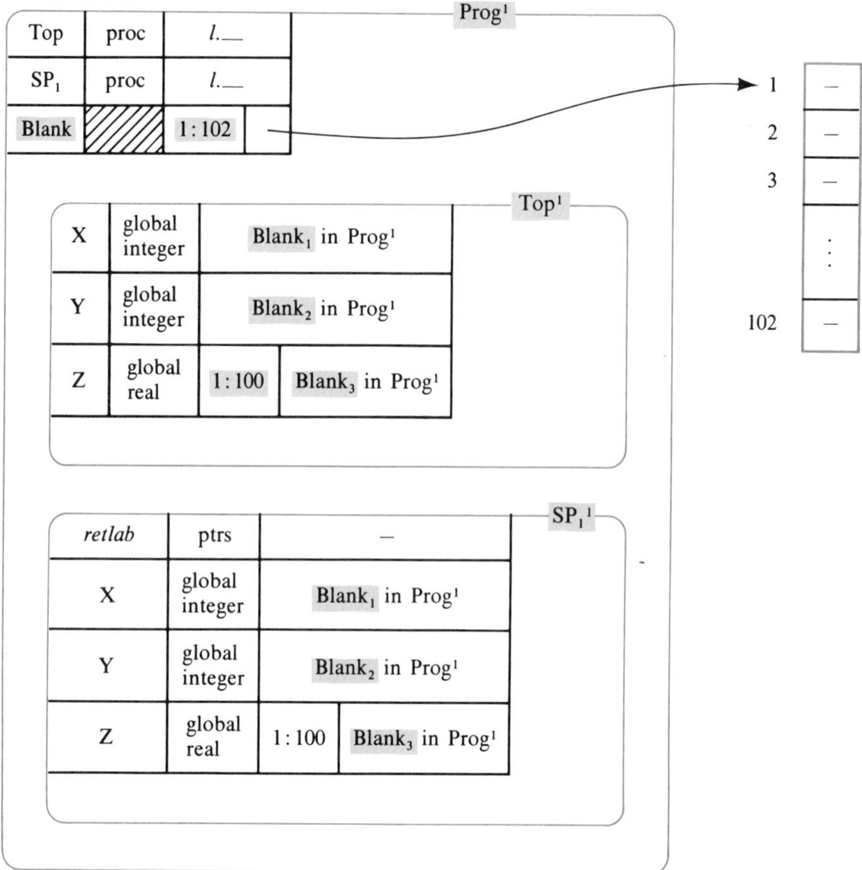

Figure 6-4. **Allocation of cells for globals.**

and in SP_2 the declarations

```
INTEGER P, Q
REAL R
COMMON P, Q, R (100)
```

The resulting environment, shown in Figure 6-5, explains conceptually how this flexibility is achieved. The block of storage known as "Blank" is globally accessible. However, the individual names declared for the elements of this block are purely local to each program unit.

The renaming of variables can occasionally be useful. For example, in the main program we may wish to refer to a set of COMMON *weight* variables as WEIGH1, WEIGH2, and WEIGH3, whereas in a subprogram the names COEFF1, COEFF2, and COEFF3 might be more meaningful. Balanced against this convenience is the extra mental load required to keep track of an additional set of names.

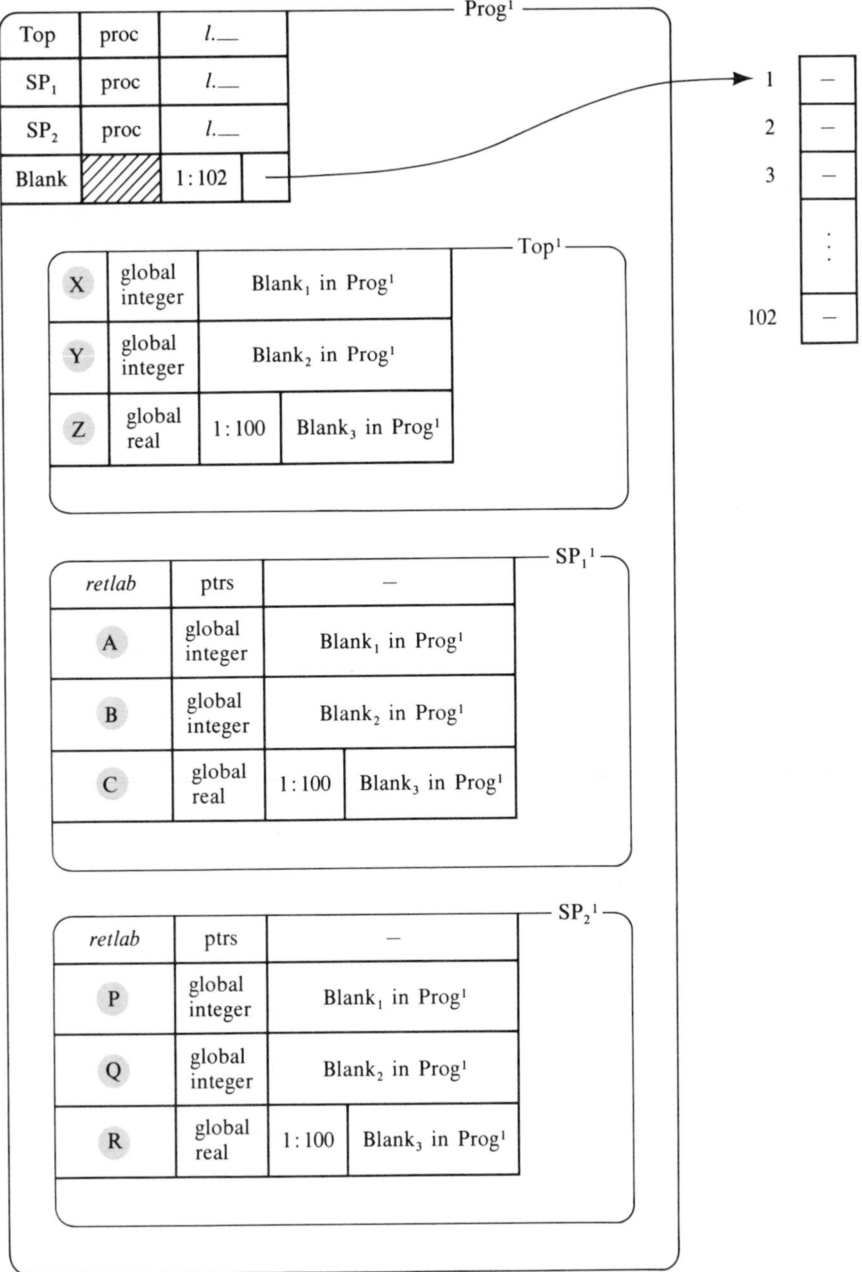
Prog¹
Top proc l.__
SP₁ proc l.__
SP₂ proc l.__
Blank 1:102
1 2 3 102
Top¹
X global integer Blank₁ in Prog¹
Y global integer Blank₂ in Prog¹
Z global real 1:100 Blank₃ in Prog¹
SP₁¹
retlab ptrs
A global integer Blank₁ in Prog¹
B global integer Blank₂ in Prog¹
C global real 1:100 Blank₃ in Prog¹
SP₂¹
retlab ptrs
P global integer Blank₁ in Prog¹
Q global integer Blank₂ in Prog¹
R global real 1:100 Blank₃ in Prog¹

Figure 6-5

More details concerning COMMON declarations will be found in the examples of the next section. There are, however, two more concepts that should be mentioned here:

1. The global cells of the Blank array in $Prog^1$ are matched up one by one, in order, with the variables appearing in COMMON declarations.* Given this rule, suppose that there is another subprogram SP_3 that needs global access to the cell referred to as Y in Top^1 in Figure 6-5. This access could not be achieved by including the declarations

```
INTEGER Y
COMMON Y
```

   in SP_3, because these declarations associate Y with the *first* global cell in $Prog^1$, $Blank_1$, rather than the second cell, $Blank_2$. This particular problem can be solved by supplying the declarations

```
INTEGER DUMMY, Y
COMMON DUMMY, Y
```

   in SP_3, so the otherwise unused name DUMMY is associated with $Blank_1$, and Y is then associated with $Blank_2$.
2. The last "wrinkle" in the Fortran handling of globals attaches names, or "labels" as they are called in Fortran, to "blocks" of global cells. For example, the declaration

```
COMMON /SET1/ A, B, C, D
```

   states that the global variables A, B, C, and D belong to a block of shared storage known as SET1.

We revise the BNF rule for COMMON declaration to the following:

$$\langle\text{common declaration}\rangle ::= \text{COMMON } \{/\langle\text{label}\rangle/\}_0^1 \ \langle\text{variable list}\rangle$$
$$\langle\text{label}\rangle ::= \langle\text{identifier}\rangle$$

Now consider the following declarations:

```
In Top:    INTEGER EMPNUM
           REAL R1, R2, HRS
           COMMON EMPNUM
           COMMON /RATES/ R1, R2
           COMMON /HOURS/ HRS
```

*Two or more COMMON declarations in the same program unit function as a single declaration with the variable lists concatenated into one list. For example,

```
COMMON X
COMMON Y, Z
```

is treated the same as COMMON X, Y, Z.

In subprogram 1:
```
REAL HRS, X, Y
COMMON /HOURS/ HRS
COMMON /RATES/ X, Y
```

In subprogram 2:
```
INTEGER NUMEMP
REAL R
COMMON NUMEMP
COMMON /RATES/ R(2)
```

(Note that the order in which these declarations appear is unimportant, although the order *within* each declaration remains very important. Note also that a program unit need not refer to all of the COMMON areas used by other program units.)

The environment that would result from these declarations is shown in Figure 6-6. COMMON blocks such as RATES and HOURS are called *named COMMON* or *labeled COMMON*. An *unlabeled* COMMON block is often called *blank COMMON;* hence our choice of the name Blank for the single global cell in this example.

Exercises 6-3

1 Shown below are the declarations for the various parts of a Fortran program. Draw a contour diagram showing the environment after all storage has been allocated.

```
INTEGER I, J, A(100), C(100), V(10)
REAL B(100), L, M, W, Z
COMMON C, L, M
COMMON /X/ I, J, A
COMMON /Y/ B
   .
   .
   .
END

SUBROUTINE R
INTEGER K, N, H, C(100)
REAL E(100), L, M
COMMON /Y/ E
COMMON C, L, M
   .
   .
   .
END

SUBROUTINE S
REAL P(100)
INTEGER G(100), I, J
COMMON /X/ I, J, G
COMMON /Y/ P
   .
   .
   .
END
```

2 Is the following statement true or false?

In Fortran, it is not possible for a cell that is local to one procedure to be global to another procedure; in Algol, such a situation can occur. Explain your answer.

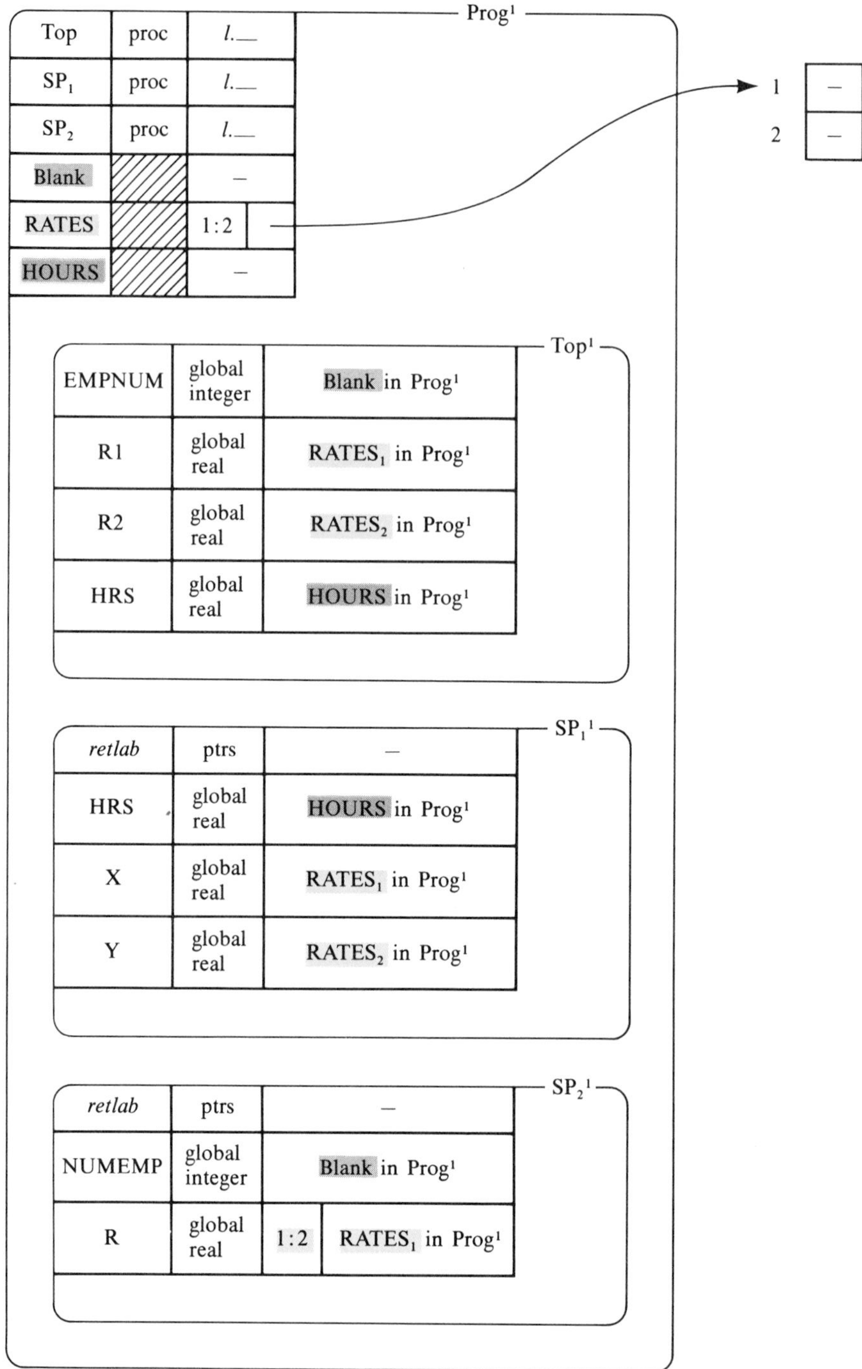

Prog1
Top
proc
l.__
SP1
proc
l.__
SP2
proc
l.__
Blank
–
RATES
1:2
HOURS
–
1
–
2
–
Top1
EMPNUM
global integer
Blank in Prog1
R1
global real
RATES1 in Prog1
R2
global real
RATES2 in Prog1
HRS
global real
HOURS in Prog1
SP11
retlab
ptrs
–
HRS
global real
HOURS in Prog1
X
global real
RATES1 in Prog1
Y
global real
RATES2 in Prog1
SP21
retlab
ptrs
–
NUMEMP
global integer
Blank in Prog1
R
global real
1:2
RATES1 in Prog1

Figure 6-6

6-4 SYNTAX OF INDIVIDUAL FORTRAN STATEMENTS AND PROGRAM UNITS

Before we examine actual Fortran programs and study their execution, we should become familiar with the syntax of several usual types of Fortran statements and declarations. We shall use the same informal approach we used for Algol. Table 6-1 collects together the BNF syntax definitions given earlier in the chapter, along with a few additional rules, and Table 6-2 contains definitions for some of the terminal symbols of Fortran. Note that the assignment operator is =, and that the relational operator for equality is .EQ..

TABLE 6-1
A Partial Set of BNF Syntax Definitions for Fortran[a]

1. ⟨program⟩ ::= ⟨top level⟩{⟨procedure⟩}$_0$
2. ⟨top level⟩ ::= ⟨head⟩⟨body⟩
3. ⟨head⟩ ::= {⟨declaration⟩}$_0$
4. ⟨body⟩ ::= {⟨statement⟩}$_1$ END
5. ⟨declaration⟩ ::= ⟨type declaration⟩|⟨array declaration⟩|
   ⟨common declaration⟩|⟨equivalence declaration⟩|
   ⟨data declaration⟩|. . .
6. ⟨type declaration⟩ ::= ⟨type⟩⟨variable list⟩
7. ⟨type⟩ ::= INTEGER|REAL|LOGICAL|. . .
8. ⟨variable list⟩ ::= ⟨variable⟩{,⟨variable⟩}$_0$
9. ⟨variable⟩ ::= ⟨unsubscripted variable identifier⟩|
   ⟨array identifier⟩{⟨upper bounds⟩}$^1_0$
10. ⟨unsubscripted variable identifier⟩ ::= ⟨identifier⟩
11. ⟨array identifier⟩ ::= ⟨identifier⟩
12. ⟨upper bounds⟩ ::= (⟨integer⟩{,⟨integer⟩}$^2_0$)
13. ⟨array declaration⟩ ::= DIMENSION⟨array identifier⟩⟨upper bounds⟩
    {,⟨array identifier⟩⟨upper bounds⟩}$_0$
14. ⟨common declaration⟩ ::= COMMON{/⟨label⟩/}$^1_0$ ⟨variable list⟩
15. ⟨label⟩ ::= ⟨identifier⟩
16. ⟨statement⟩ ::= ⟨assignment statement⟩|⟨conditional statement⟩|
    ⟨do statement⟩|⟨goto statement⟩|⟨procedure call⟩|
    ⟨input statement⟩|⟨output statement⟩|. . .
17. ⟨conditional statement⟩ ::= ⟨logical if statement⟩|⟨arithmetic if statement⟩|
    ⟨computed goto statement⟩.
18. ⟨procedure⟩ ::= ⟨procedure heading⟩⟨head⟩⟨body⟩
19. ⟨procedure heading⟩ ::= SUBROUTINE⟨subroutine heading⟩|
    FUNCTION⟨function heading⟩
20. ⟨subroutine heading⟩ ::= ⟨identifier⟩{⟨formal parameter part⟩}$^1_0$
21. ⟨function heading⟩ ::= ⟨identifier⟩⟨formal parameter part⟩
22. ⟨formal parameter part⟩ ::= (⟨identifier⟩{,⟨identifier⟩}$_0$)
23. ⟨identifier⟩ ::= ⟨letter⟩{⟨letter⟩|⟨digit⟩}$^5_0$

[a] In this table a set of three dots (· · ·) on the right side of a definition indicates the syntax definition has been abridged.

TABLE 6-2
A Partial Set of BNF Definitions for Fortran Terminal Symbols

1. ⟨digit⟩ ::= 0|1|2|3|4|5|6|7|8|9
2. ⟨letter⟩ ::= A|B|C|D|E|F|G|H|I|J|K|L|M|N|O|P|Q|R|S|T|U|V|W|X|Y|Z
3. ⟨type⟩ ::= REAL|INTEGER|LOGICAL|. . .
4. ⟨logical value⟩ ::= .TRUE.|.FALSE.
5. ⟨relational operator⟩ ::= .LT.|.LE.|.EQ.|.NE.|.GE.|.GT.

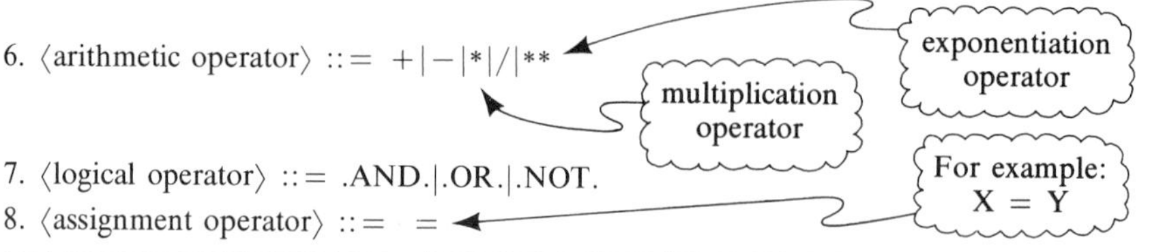

Fortran is a line-oriented language: each statement of a program must begin on a new line. Furthermore, each line is subdivided into sections or "fields," which contain the various parts of the statement on the line. We illustrate these concepts in Figure 6-7, which shows how the familiar Fibonacci sequence problem maps from flowchart to Fortran code. The body of each Fortran statement may be preceded by a statement number that *labels* the statement for purposes of cross reference. For instance, the exit from box 4 of the flowchart is coded as "GO TO 2" in the Fortran program, where 2 means the statement numbered 2 several lines above. Labels must be integers, and the statement number must be contained within columns 1–5 of the line.

Fortran statements appear in columns 7–72. A statement may run over onto another line if some character other than a blank or zero is placed in column 6, of the "spillover" lines. For example, the IF statement in Figure 6-7b appears in Figure 6-8 spread out over two lines, showing how the second line can be designated as a continuation of the preceding one. Alternate positioning of various other statement components is also illustrated. Lines with the letter "C" in column 1 are treated as *comments,* meaning they have no effect on the execution of the program.

Every Fortran program unit (i.e., Top and each procedure) must conclude with the symbol END, which can be thought of as a form of punctuation. Specifying a *type* for a variable is optional in Fortran programs because every Fortran interpreter or compiler applies default rules to decide on the type of a program variable. In particular, in the absence of explicit declarations to the contrary, identifiers that begin with the letter I, J, K, L, M, or N are treated as type *integer,* and all other identifiers are treated as type *real.* It is considered good practice always to give explicit declarations, and so in our case studies, as in Figures 6-7 and 6-8, we declare explicitly the type information that might otherwise be assumed implicitly. A group of such declarations at the beginning of each program unit documents the program in the same way that a legend documents its respective flowchart.

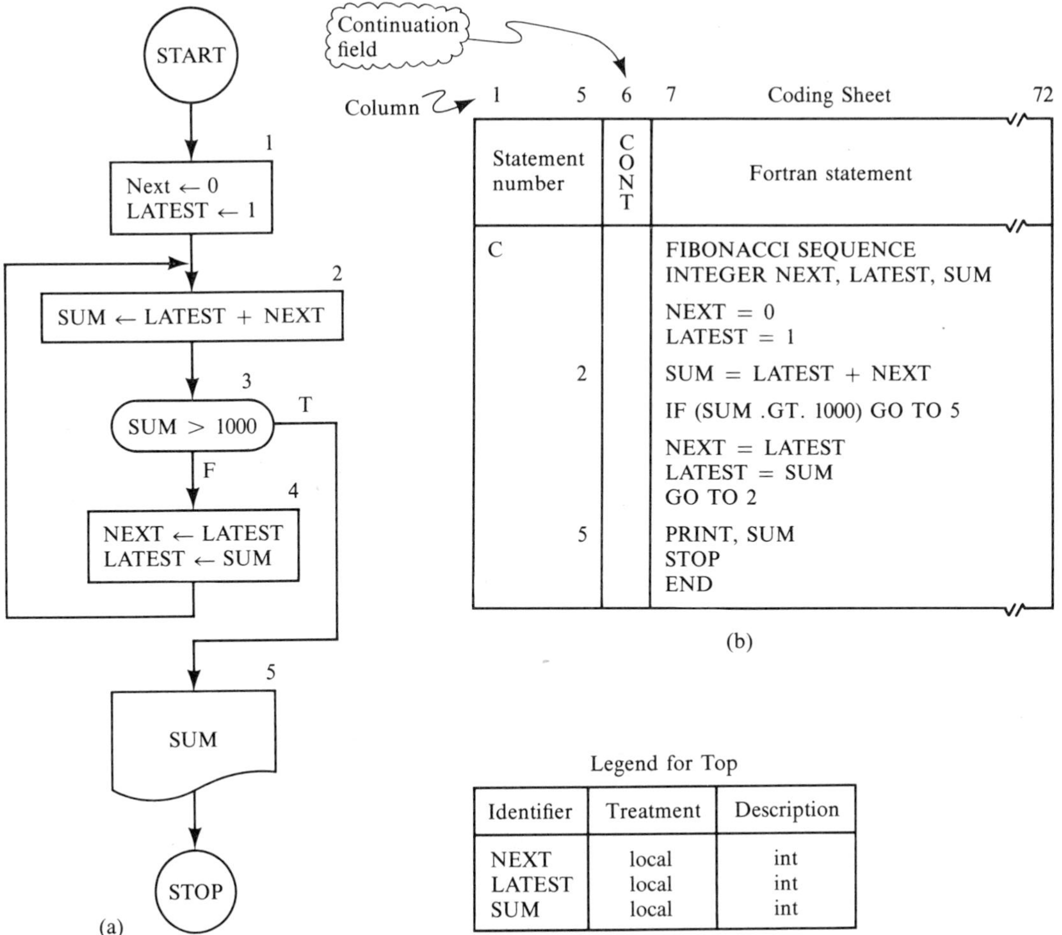

Legend for Top

Identifier	Treatment	Description
NEXT	local	int
LATEST	local	int
SUM	local	int

Figure 6-7. **Fortran statements corresponding to a flowchart. (a) Flowchart. (b) Corresponding Fortran program. Note that the statement labeled 5 is not standard. For an explanation, see the footnote to Item 3, Table 6-3.**

Coding Sheet

Column 1 5 6 7 72

```
C     FIBONACCI SEQUENCE
      INTEGER NEXT, LATEST, SUM
      NEXT = 0
      LATEST = 1
2     SUM = LATEST + NEXT
      IF (SUM .GT. 1000)
     1                              GO TO 5
        NEXT = LATEST
        LATEST = SUM
        GO TO 2
5     PRINT, SUM
      STOP
      END
```

Figure 6-8. **Program of Fig. 6-7 using a continuation line.**

Table 6-3 displays a set of typical operations, each with a specific example coded as a flowchart fragment, and then recoded as one or more Fortran statements (and possibly the necessary declarations). A BNF form covering the example is included in each case. The superficial differences that exist between the Fortran syntax and the flowchart syntax should introduce little, if any, difficulty. More examples of the mapping from flowchart to Fortran syntax will appear in the case studies presented in the remaining sections of this chapter.

Here are a few points to notice about 1966 Fortran as you study Table 6-3:

(a) Fortran uses only uppercase letters; keywords are not marked in any special manner. Names (identifiers) are limited to six letters or digit, the first being a letter.

(b) Definite iteration is achieved with a DO statement (item 6), the counterpart of the **for** statement in Algol. Indefinite iteration (item 7) is most naturally coded as an IF statement, in conjunction with a GOTO statement leading back to the IF.

(c) The allowable range for subscripts of a list or array is 1, 2, 3, . . . up to the declared maximum; for example, INTEGER A(10) declares an integer array named A having ten elements $A_1, A_2, \ldots, A_{10}$. Thus, it is not possible to have a subscript range from say, −3 to 3. This 1966 Fortran restriction simplifies the declaration of lists and arrays; only the upper limit must be given for each subscript since the lower limit is always 1. Subscripts are enclosed in parentheses; for example, in Fortran we write A(2, 4) and not $A_{2,4}$ or A[2, 4].

(d) There is no punctuation mark between statements, since each statement begins on a new line.

(e) The "computed GOTO" statement, illustrated in item 4 of the table, is a convenient and compact way to express a multiway decision step. (The *case* statement of Pascal (see Table 10-2) and other recent languages derives indirectly from the computed GOTO of Fortran, but exhibits better structure.)

(f) The data initialization declaration (item 10) is useful, and has no counterpart in ALGOL 60. It allows the programmer to preset the values of specified variables prior to actual program execution. These variables may be part of the top-level program or may be local variables of subprograms.* Such initial values may, of course, be superceded by other values via assignment statements encountered during execution of the program. The effect of data initialization declarations can also be achieved by assignment statements placed at the beginning of the program (or subprograms).

(g) The special significance of the EQUIVALENCE declaration illustrated as item 20 is discussed in Section 6-8.

*Variables of labeled COMMON blocks may also have their values preset via DATA declarations, but it is not legal to preset a variable declared in blank COMMON. Attempting to do so interferes with the process by which programs and data are loaded into computer storage prior to execution.

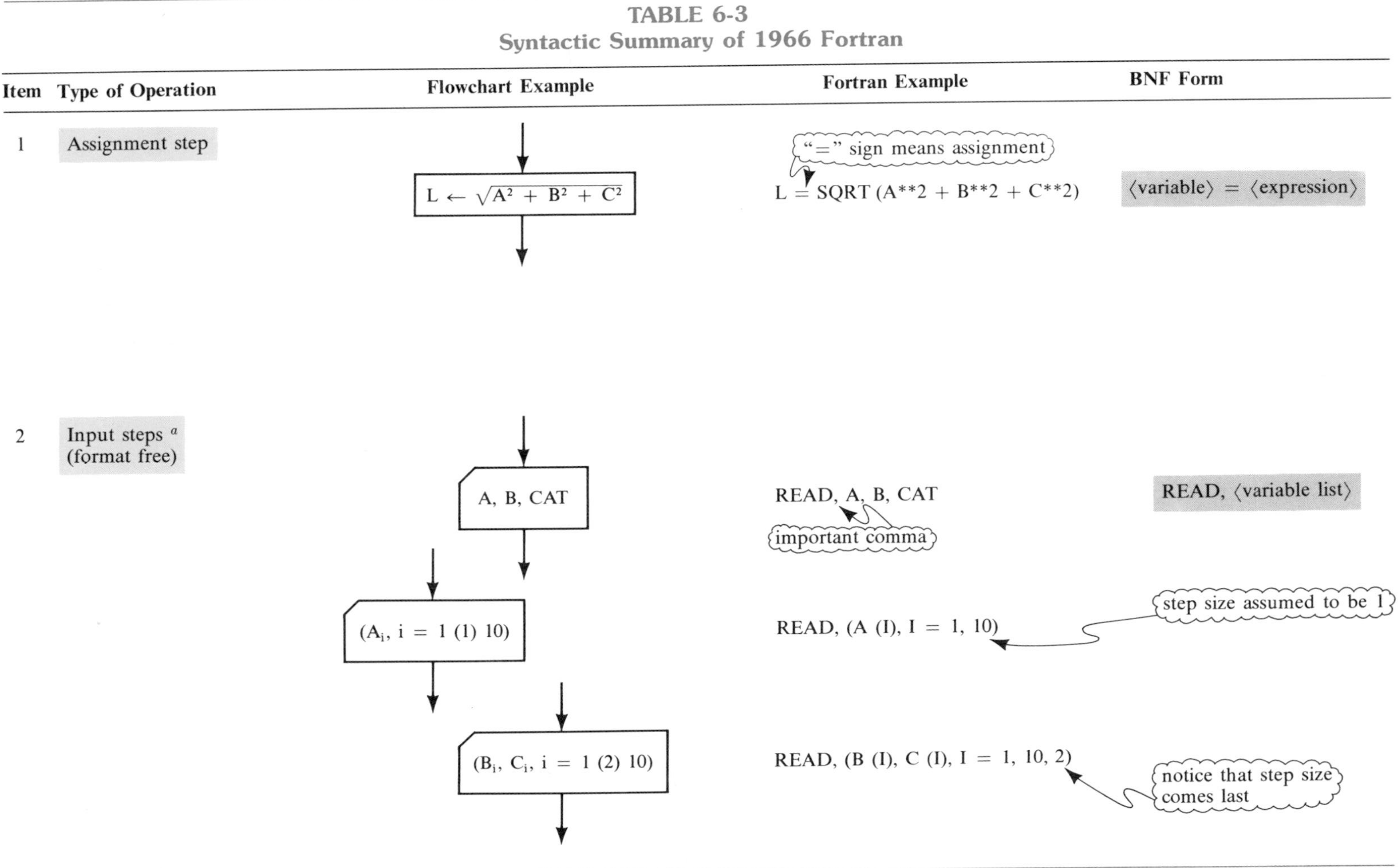

TABLE 6-3
Syntactic Summary of 1966 Fortran

Item	Type of Operation	Flowchart Example	Fortran Example	BNF Form
1	Assignment step	$L \leftarrow \sqrt{A^2 + B^2 + C^2}$	L = SQRT (A**2 + B**2 + C**2) ("=" sign means assignment)	⟨variable⟩ = ⟨expression⟩
2	Input steps [a] (format free)	A, B, CAT	READ, A, B, CAT (important comma)	READ, ⟨variable list⟩
		(A_i, i = 1 (1) 10)	READ, (A (I), I = 1, 10) (step size assumed to be 1)	
		(B_i, C_i, i = 1 (2) 10)	READ, (B (I), C (I), I = 1, 10, 2) (notice that step size comes last)	

[a]The FORTRAN READ and PRINT statements shown in this table are of the form used in WATFOR and similar student-oriented simplified (but nonstandard) dialects of FORTRAN. More information on FORTRAN input/output is given in Section 6-6. For a complete description of the standard forms, see for instance Organick and Meissner (1974).

TABLE 6-3 (*continued*)

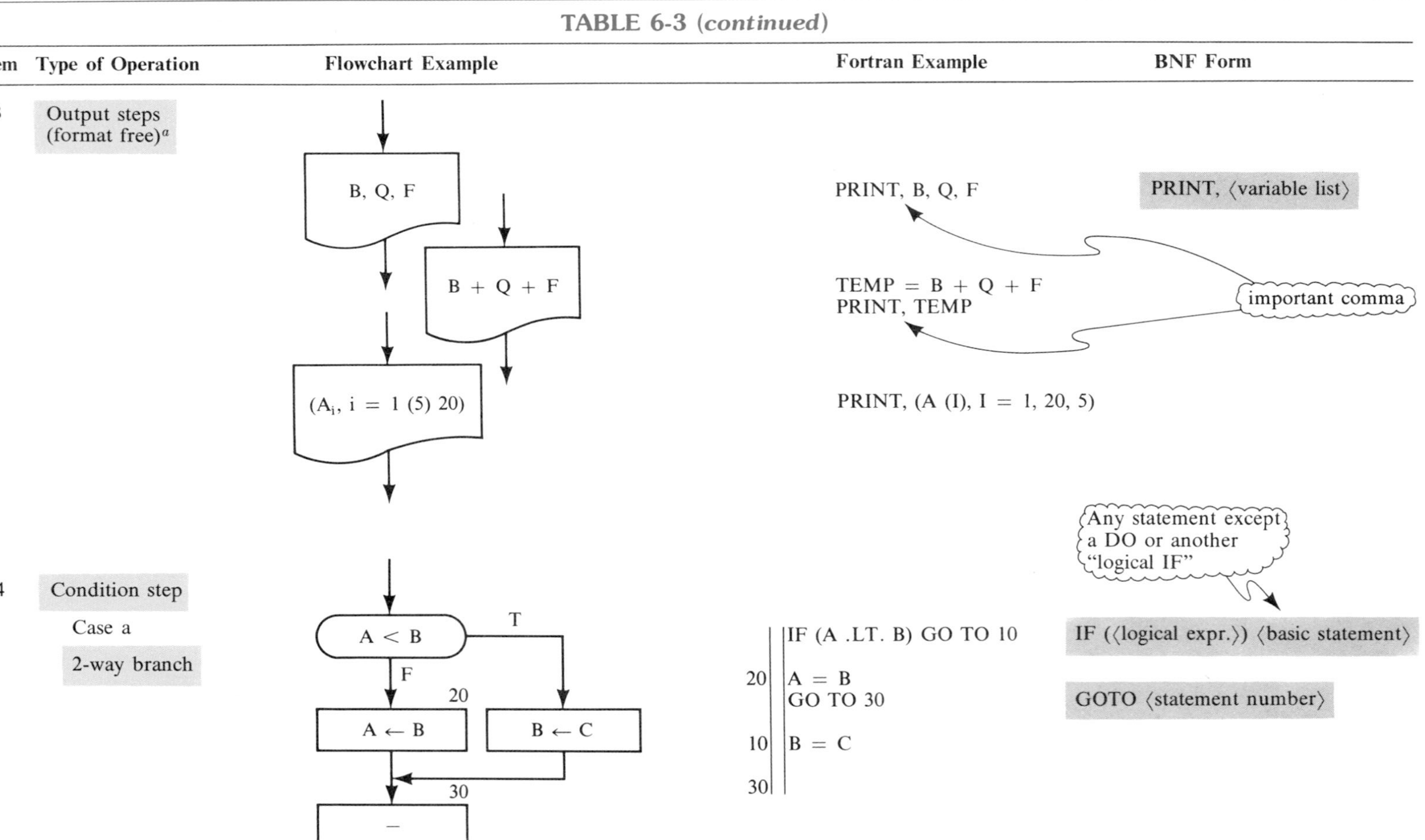

Item	Type of Operation	Flowchart Example	Fortran Example	BNF Form
3	Output steps (format free)[a]	B, Q, F	PRINT, B, Q, F	PRINT, ⟨variable list⟩
		B + Q + F	TEMP = B + Q + F PRINT, TEMP	(important comma)
		(A_i, i = 1 (5) 20)	PRINT, (A (I), I = 1, 20, 5)	
4	Condition step Case a 2-way branch	A < B (T: 10 B ← C; F: 20 A ← B; 30 —)	IF (A .LT. B) GO TO 10 20 A = B GO TO 30 10 B = C 30	IF (⟨logical expr.⟩) ⟨basic statement⟩ (Any statement except a DO or another "logical IF") GOTO ⟨statement number⟩

Case b
n-way branch

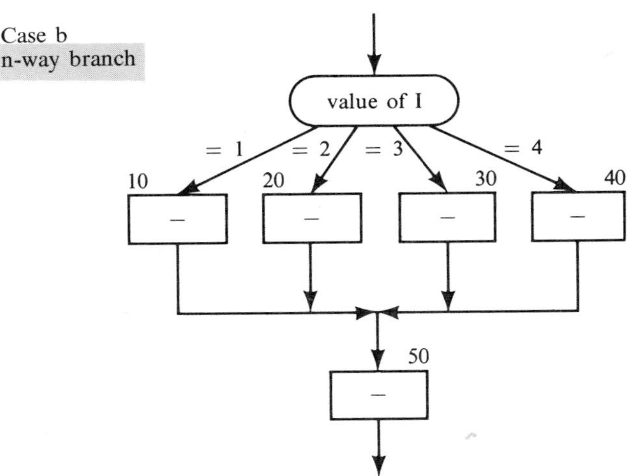

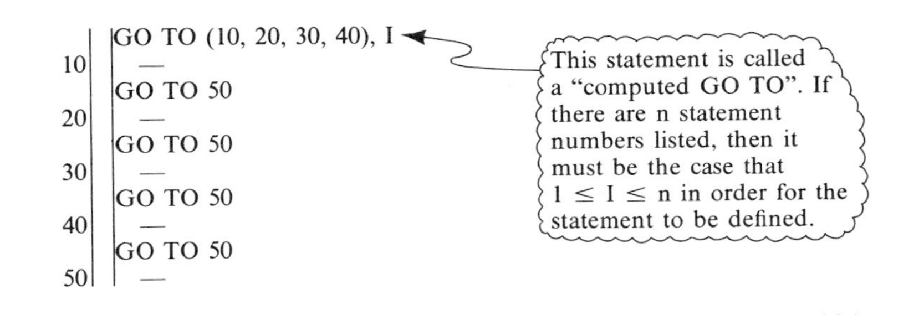

GO TO (⟨statement number⟩{,⟨statement number⟩}$_0$),⟨integer variable⟩

5 Indefinite iteration
(While loop)

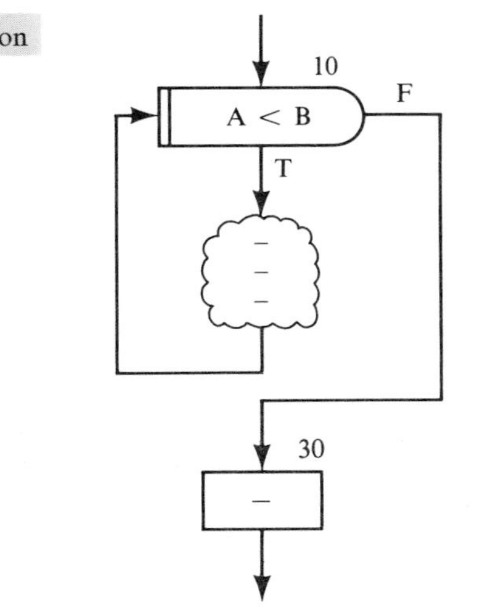

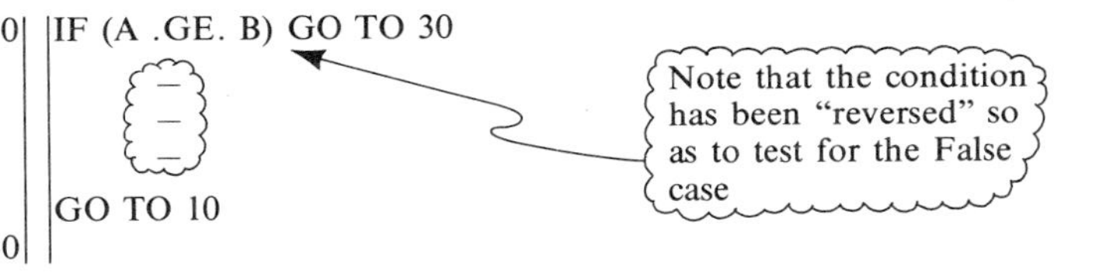

TABLE 6-3 (*continued*)

Item	Type of Operation	Flowchart Example	Fortran Example	BNF Form

6	Definite iteration
	Case a
	(when initial value of i is known to be ≤ upper limit n)
		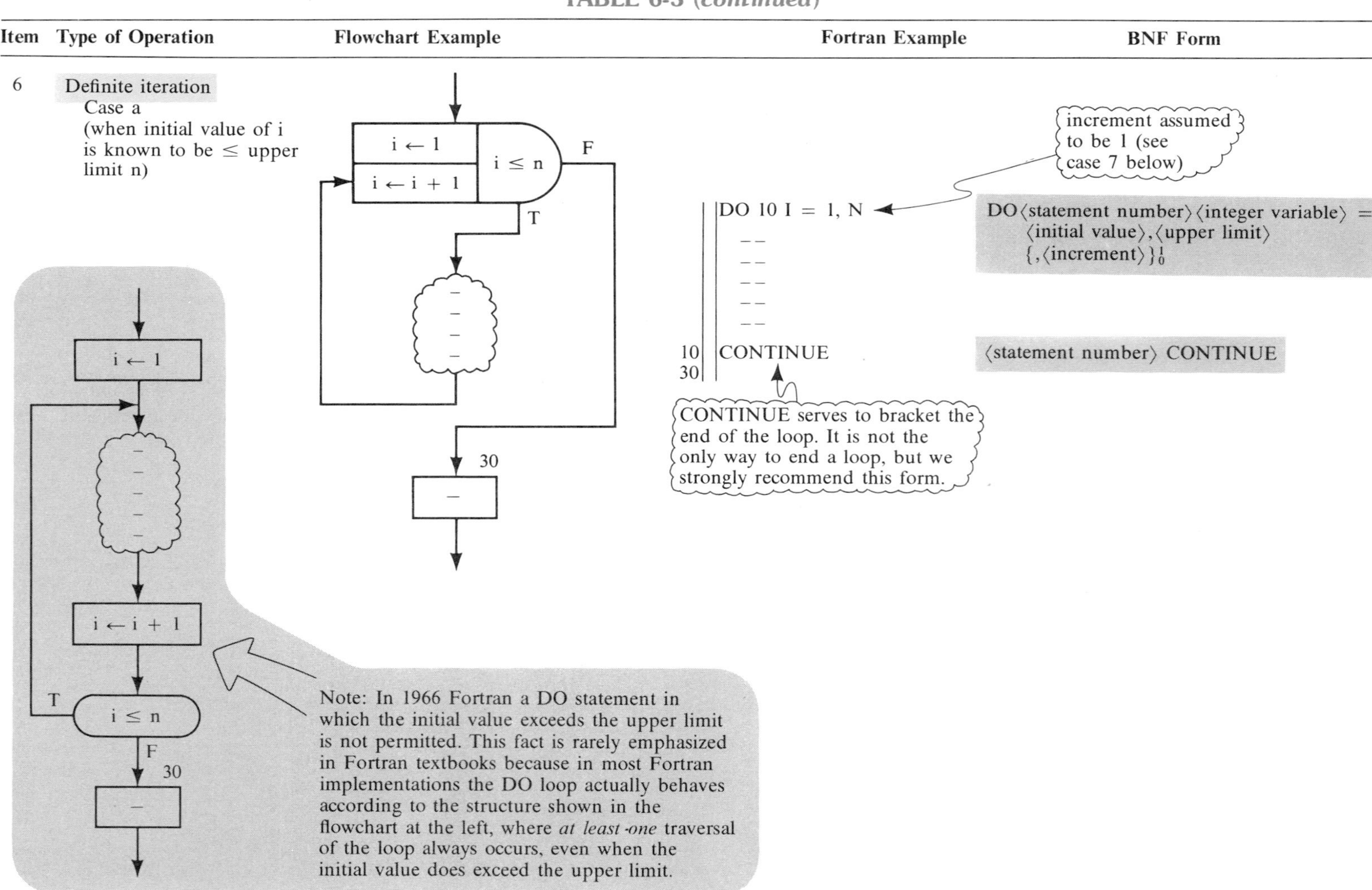	`DO 10 I = 1, N`
			`--`
			`--`
			`--`
			`--`
			`--`
			`10 CONTINUE`
			`30`
				DO⟨statement number⟩⟨integer variable⟩ = ⟨initial value⟩,⟨upper limit⟩ $\{,\langle\text{increment}\rangle\}_0^1$
				
				⟨statement number⟩ CONTINUE

7 Definite iteration
Case b
(when initial value of i possibly exceeds upper bound n)

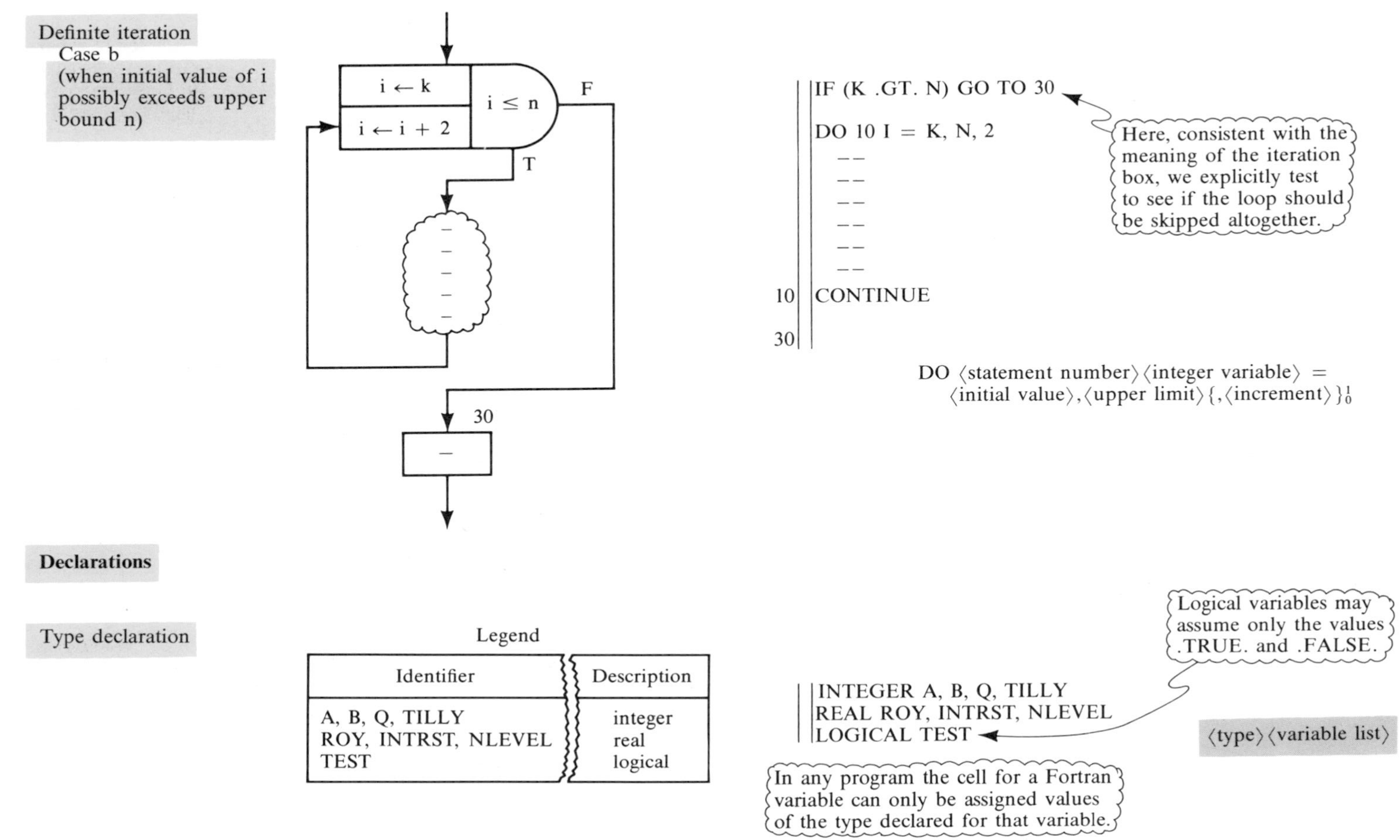


```
   IF (K .GT. N) GO TO 30
   DO 10 I = K, N, 2
     --
     --
     --
     --
     --
     --
10 CONTINUE
30
```

Here, consistent with the meaning of the iteration box, we explicitly test to see if the loop should be skipped altogether.

DO ⟨statement number⟩⟨integer variable⟩ = ⟨initial value⟩,⟨upper limit⟩$\{,\langle\text{increment}\rangle\}_0^1$

Declarations

8 Type declaration

Legend

Identifier	Description
A, B, Q, TILLY	integer
ROY, INTRST, NLEVEL	real
TEST	logical

```
INTEGER A, B, Q, TILLY
REAL ROY, INTRST, NLEVEL
LOGICAL TEST
```

Logical variables may assume only the values .TRUE. and .FALSE.

In any program the cell for a Fortran variable can only be assigned values of the type declared for that variable.

⟨type⟩⟨variable list⟩

TABLE 6-3 (*continued*)

Item	Type of Operation	Flowchart Example	Fortran Example	BNF Form
9	Dimension declaration	Legend Identifier | Description A | List of 50 integers B | Matrix of integers 10 by 12	INTEGER A, B DIMENSION A (50), B (10, 12) or equivalently: INTEGER A (50), B (10, 12)	DIMENSION ⟨variable list⟩
10	Data initialization declaration	Legend Identifier | Description C | integer with initial value 5 D | list of 5 reals with initial values 1.0, 3.0, 5.0, 7.0, and 9.0, respectively	INTEGER C REAL D (5) DATA C, D/3, 1., 3., 5., 7., 9./	DATA ⟨variable list⟩/⟨constant list⟩ where ⟨constant list⟩ ::= ⟨constant⟩{,⟨constant⟩} ⟨constant⟩ ::= ⟨integer value⟩| ⟨real value⟩| ⟨logical value⟩| . . .
11(a)	Sharing of global variables using the unlabeled COMMON declaration	in Top → in subprogram number 1 → in subprogram number 2 → These declarations cause M, M1, and MATER to reference to the same global cell. Likewise, N, N1, and NATER, etc.	INTEGER M, N, A, L COMMON M, N, A (300), L INTEGER M1, N1, A1, L1 COMMON M1, N1, A1 (300), L1 INTEGER MATER, NATER, APE, LEMON COMMON MATER, NATER, APE (300), LEMON	COMMON ⟨variable list⟩
11(b)	Sharing of global variables using the labeled COMMON declaration	in Top → in subprogram 1 → in subprogram 2 →	REAL X, Y, Z COMMON /B1/ X, Y, Z REAL R, S, T COMMON /B1/ R, S, T REAL I, J, K COMMON /B1/ I, J, K	COMMON /⟨label⟩/⟨variable list⟩

12 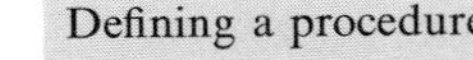

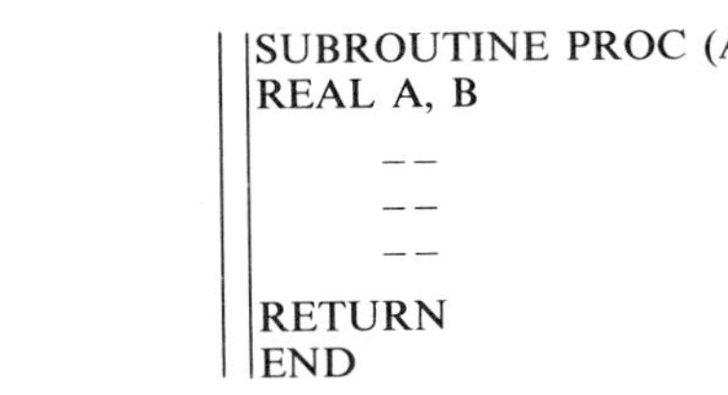


```
SUBROUTINE PROC (A, B)
REAL A, B
      --
      --
      --
RETURN
END
```

```
SUBROUTINE ⟨identifier⟩⟨formal parameter part⟩
  --
  --
  --
  --
RETURN
END
```

Legend for Proc

Identifier	Treatment	Description
A, B	ref par	real

TABLE 6-3 (continued)

Item	Type of Operation	Flowchart Example	Fortran Example	BNF Form
13	Defining a *real* function	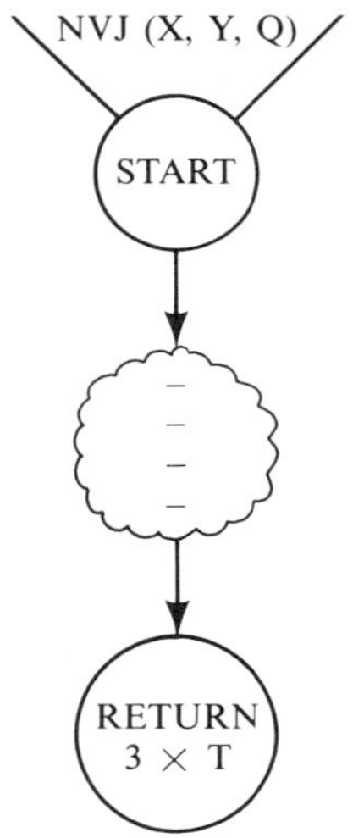 NVJ (X, Y, Q) → START → – – – – → RETURN 3 × T	REAL FUNCTION NVJ (X, Y, Q) REAL X, Y, Q, T – – NVJ = 3. * T RETURN END	⟨type⟩ FUNCTION ⟨identifier⟩⟨formal parameter part⟩

Value to be returned is assigned to the function name

Note: The type of the value that a function is to return is declared explicitly by assigning the type with the function's name in the opening declaration of the function subprogram. The name NVJ must also be declared to be of type REAL in the calling program.

Note that there is no separation of legend information for parameters from legend information for locals.

A function subprogram must have at least one parameter.

Legend for NVJ

Identifier	Treatment	Description
X, Y, Q	ref par	real
T	local	real

14 Defining an *integer* function

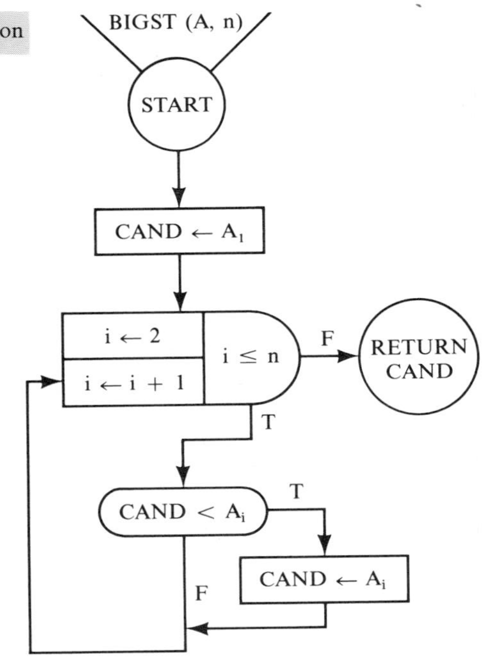

Legend for BIGST

Identifier	Treatment	Description
A	ref par	list of 100 integers
n	ref par	integer
i, CAND	local	integer

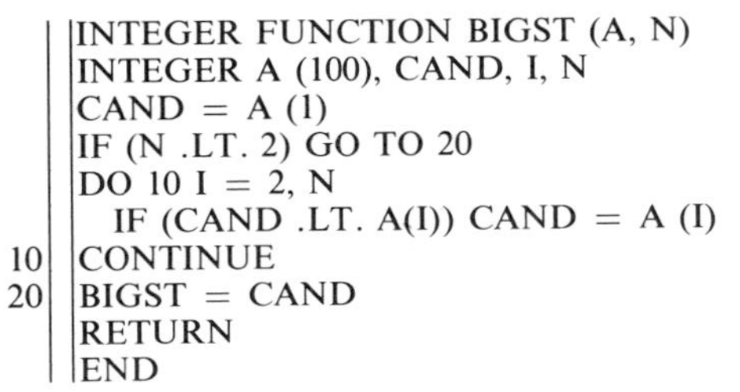

```
   INTEGER FUNCTION BIGST (A, N)
   INTEGER A (100), CAND, I, N
   CAND = A (1)
   IF (N .LT. 2) GO TO 20
   DO 10 I = 2, N
     IF (CAND .LT. A(I)) CAND = A (I)
10 CONTINUE
20 BIGST = CAND
   RETURN
   END
```

TABLE 6-3 (*continued*)

Item	Type of Operation	Flowchart Example	Fortran Example	BNF Form
15	Calling a procedure	PROC (P1, A, F7)	| |CALL PROC (P1, A, F7)	CALL ⟨identifier⟩⟨argument list⟩
16	Referencing a function	A ← FUN (3, 4, T) × COS (X)	| |A = FUN (3, 4, T)*COS (X)	⟨variable⟩ = ⟨expression⟩
17	Array subscripting	A_i, $B_{i,j+1}$	A (I), B (I, J + 1)	

18	Special rounding rule for Fortran: If Y is declared to be of type integer, and B of type real, then assigning the real value of B to the integer variable Y causes the fractional part of the real value to be chopped off. The function INT causes chopping to be done explicitly	Y ← CHOP (B)	 ||Y = B
		Y ← CHOP (B/D)	||Y = B/D ||Y = INT (B/D)
19	Converting values from type real to type integer and vice versa	Not applicable in flowchart language	||R = FLOAT (I + 2) + 7.4 ||I = 7 + IFIX (COS (.4))

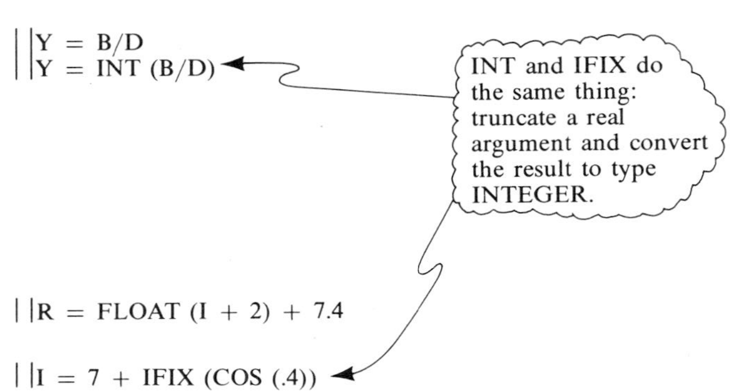

TABLE 6-3 (*continued*)

Item	Type of Operation	Flowchart Example	Fortran Example	BNF Form
20	Alternate name for a cell within a single program unit	Not applicable in the flowchart language.	INTEGER EMPDAT (20), EMPNUM, X (1000), Y (1000) EQUIVALENCE (EMPDAT (1), EMPNUM), (X (1), Y (1)) EMPDAT (1) and EMPNUM refer to the same cell, and by virtue of the alignment of their first cells, the arrays X and Y both use the same storage area. In the corresponding contour diagram we would simply place more than one name in the first cell component. Convenience and/or efficiency of storage utilization can sometimes be achieved with EQUIVALENCE statements, but these advantages may be offset by the increased complexity of the program.	
21	How to write variable names	A flowchart identifier can be composed of any number of characters but the first character must be a letter. Either capital or lowercase letters, digits, and the underscore character are acceptable, e.g., Admissibility, Function_71, Able, Baker, P1	Identifier is a maximum of *six* characters. Capital letters and digits only. First character must be a letter. Blank spaces are permitted between the characters of an identifier. Sometimes the use of spaces can enhance readability. For example, FUNC 71 in place of FUNC71. ADMISS, FUNC 71, ABLE, BAKER, P1	$\langle \text{letter} \rangle \{ \langle \text{letter} \rangle \mid \langle \text{digit} \rangle \}_0^5$

Exercises 6-4

(a) Shown below are flowcharts for Top and a procedure DIV. Explain in a sentence or two what is accomplished by the flowcharts.

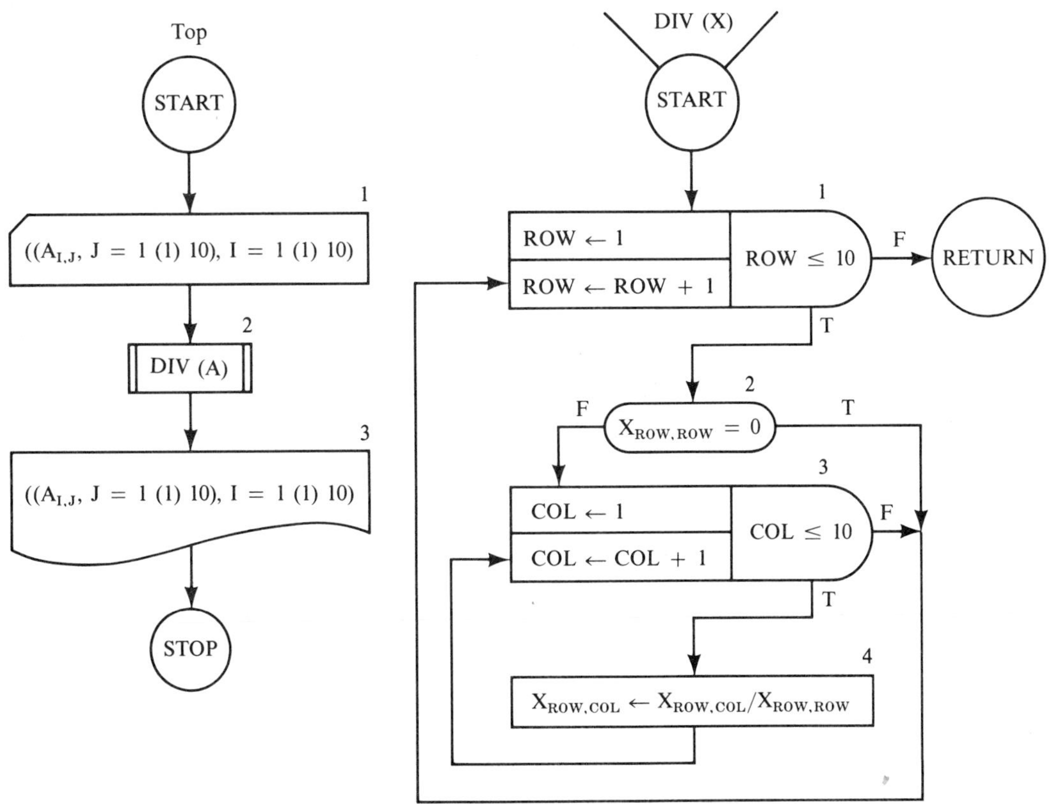

Legend for Top

Identifier	Treatment	Description
I	local	integer
J	local	integer
A	local	10 × 10 matrix of reals

Legend for DIV

Identifier	Treatment	Description
ROW	local	integer
COL	local	integer
X	ref par	10 × 10 matrix of reals

(b) Translate the above flowcharts into Fortran (refer to Table 6-3 and Figure 6-7).

(c) Draw a snapshot taken just before the input step of your Fortran program is executed.

(d) Draw a snapshot taken just before the statement corresponding to box 4 is executed. You need not show the input values for the matrix A.

6-5 CASE STUDY

Case 1 Our first Fortran case study is the same as case 1, Chapter 5. It concerns a procedure SQUEEZE whose purpose is to remove all zero elements from a list, count the number of zeros eliminated, and reduce the index of each remaining element by the number of zeros removed up to that point.

Figure 6-9 presents flowcharts for Top and SQUEEZE, a procedure having locals and reference parameters only (the ALGOL version, of course, used name parameters). The parameter n represents the length of the list to be compressed; the parameter A represents the list itself; and the parameter k is used to count

***Figure 6-9.* Flowcharts and legends for case 1.**

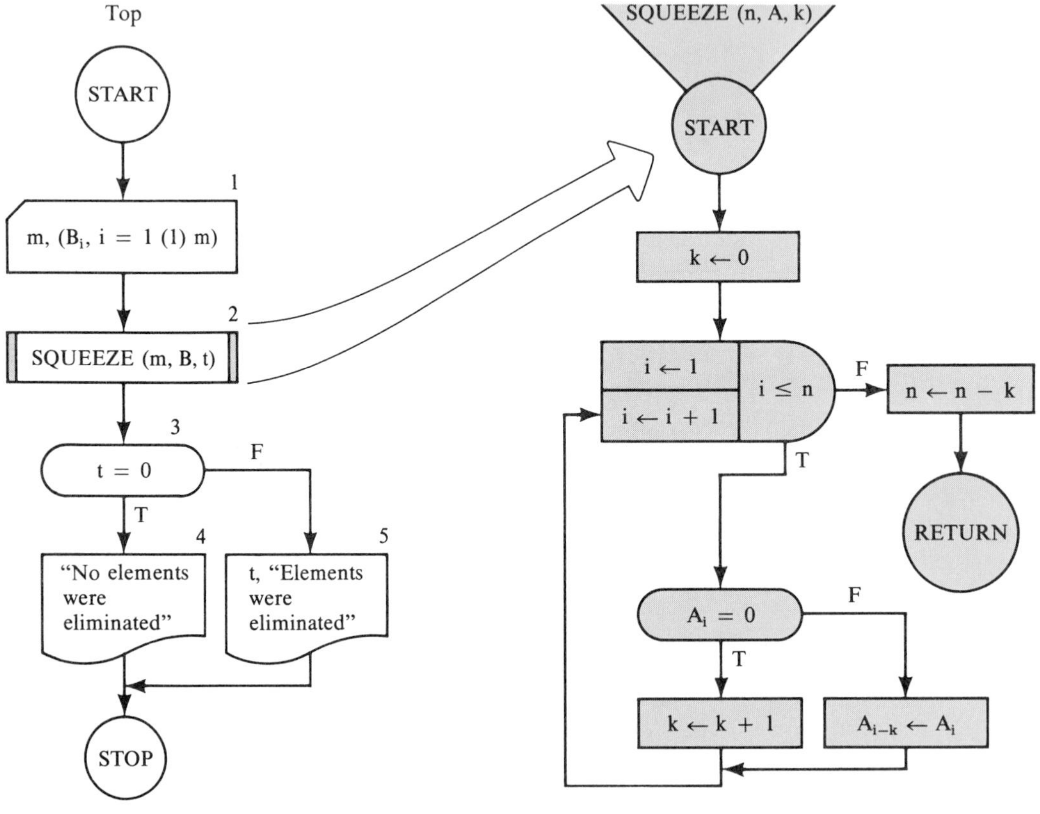

Legend for Top

Identifier	Treatment	Description
m, i, t	local	integer
B	local	list of m reals

Legend for SQUEEZE

Identifier	Treatment	Description
n, k	ref par	integer
A	ref par	list of n reals
i	local	integer

the number of zeros encountered. Every nonzero list element, as it is encountered, has its subscript decreased by the current value of k. When all the elements of the list have been tested, n is made to represent the length of the list of nonzero elements by subtracting the value of k from it. Figure 6-10 shows a Fortran program for Top and SQUEEZE (whose name must be shortened to six characters in Fortran).

Note that the DO-loop in SQUEEZ will be executed at least once, even if the value of N is less than zero, because M, the argument matching N, has already been found to be greater than zero in Top (line 5), and so we know that at least one traversal of the loop will always be required when SQUEEZ is invoked.

Discussion

The initial environment constructed for execution of this program is shown in snapshot 1. The outermost contour, $prog^1$, contains a cell for each program unit; values in these cells are starting line numbers. Contours for each of these program units are constructed within $prog^1$. Since the declaration of B in Top

Figure 6-10. **Fortran program for case 1.**

```
Line No.
 1   C          TOP. LEGEND INFO ON NEXT TWO LINES
 2              REAL B(1000)
 3              INTEGER M, I, T
 4              READ, M
 5              IF (M . LE . 0) STOP
 6              READ, (B(I), I=1, M)
 7              CALL SQUEEZ (M, B, T)
 8              IF (T .EQ. 0) GO TO 4
 9              PRINT, T, 'NO ELEMENTS WERE ELIMINATED'
10              GO TO 10
11         4    PRINT, 'NO ELEMENTS WERE ELIMINATED'
12        10    STOP
13              END

14   C          PROCEDURE STARTS HERE. LEGEND INFO ON LINES 15 AND 16
15              SUBROUTINE SQUEEZ (N, A, K)
16              REAL A (1000)
17              INTEGER N, K, I
18              K = 0
19              DO 100 I = 1, N
20                 IF (A(I) .EQ. 0) GO TO 30
21                 A(I-K) = A(I)
22                 GO TO 100
23        30       K = K + 1
24       100    CONTINUE
25              N = N-K
26              RETURN
27              END
```

must state exactly how many cells are to be allocated, in Fortran we must employ a *worst case allocation* strategy for array space. Line 2 declares that real array B is to have a fixed-in-advance size of 1000. Hence, a list cell containing 1000 compartments is allocated for B in Top^1, even though a shorter list might often be sufficient. Notice that the return cell in sq^1 is not given an initial value. A value is assigned only as a result of invoking SQUEEZ. The MC in snapshot 1 is ready to begin executing the program, starting on line 4.

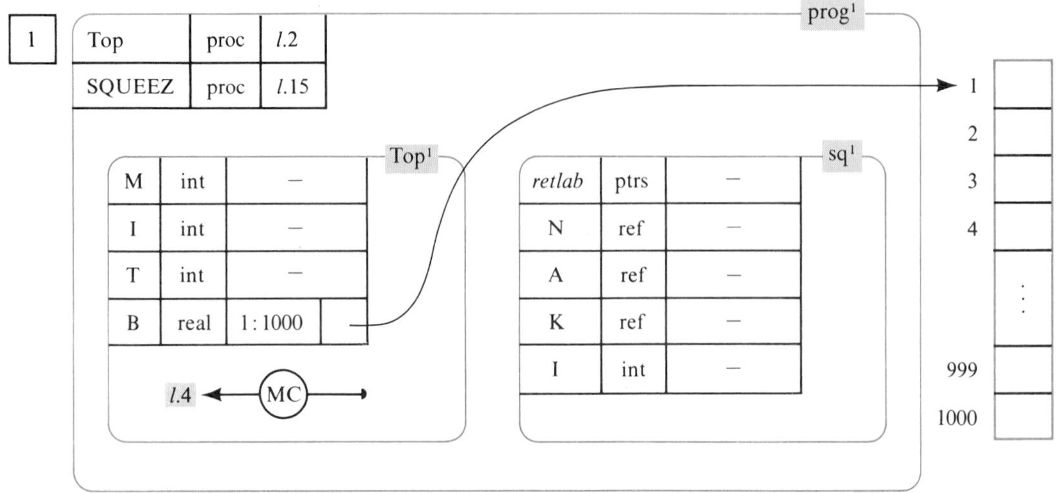

Snapshot 2 shows the state of affairs just after control has been passed to SQUEEZ for the first time. The return cell has been assigned the value "*l*.8 in Top^1". Cells for M, I, and B in Top^1 have been assigned values as a result of inputting the given data set, M = 4 and B = (3, 0, 0, 5).

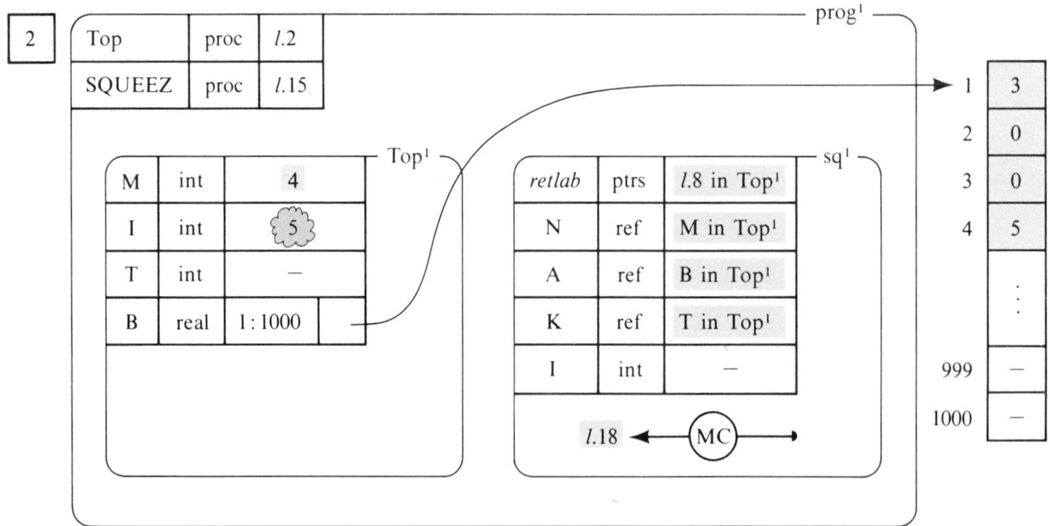

The local loop-counter variable I of Top^1 has been incremented from 1 until it exceeds 4. In 1966 but not 1977 Fortran the loop counter variable is considered to be undefined after a normal exit is taken from a regular or "implied"

DO loop (line 6 is an example of the latter). To remind us that such loop variables are no longer defined we place the value in a cloud, i.e., (5). (However, in many implementations of Fortran and in 1977 Fortran the value of I in Top^1 would indeed *be* 5.)

Snapshot 3 shows the state of the computation when the RETURN statement on line 26 of SQUEEZ is about to be executed.

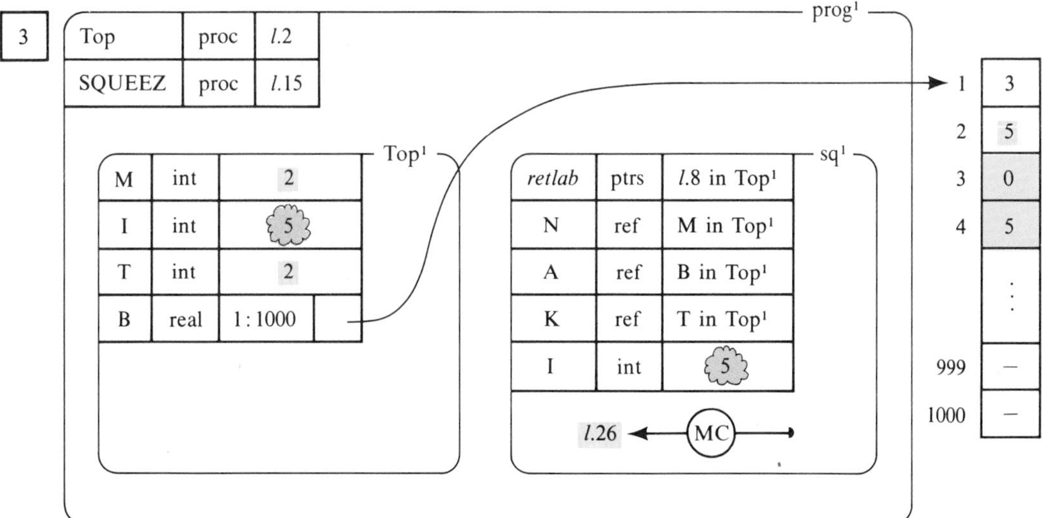

Two zero-valued elements were found in the course of executing SQUEEZ, and so the cell referred to by K has been incremented from an initial value of 0 to 2 and the value in the cell referred to by N has been decremented from 4 to 2. The values in the list cell for A have been adjusted so the first two elements are the two nonzero elements of the original list, that is, 3, 5.

Snapshot 4 shows the state of the computation upon return to Top just before the MC executes the IF statement on line 8. Notice that the contour sq^1 is retained, and its cells, although they are ready for reuse in any subsequent invocation of SQUEEZ, currently have no accessible values, as suggested by the cloud in sq^1.

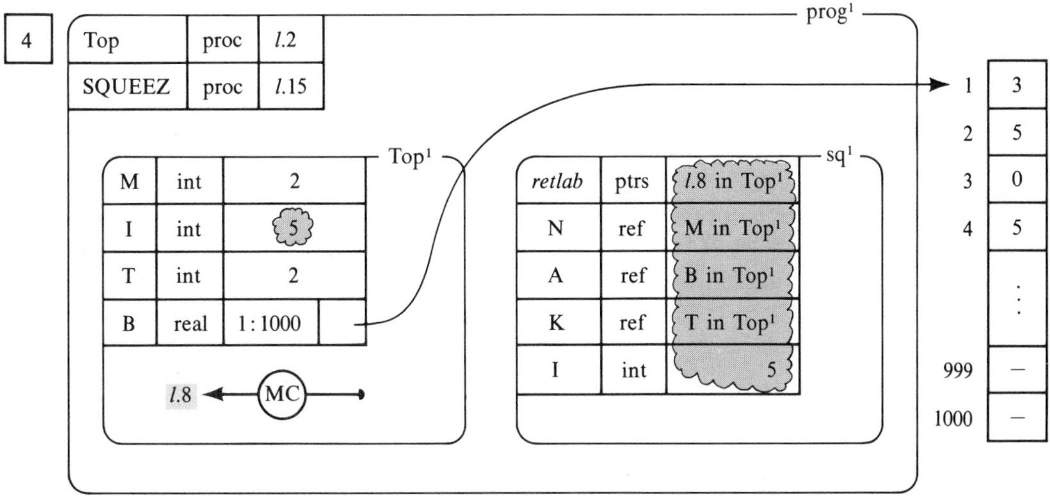

Snapshot 5 shows the state of the computation after lines 8, 9, and 10 have been executed. The displayed output is generated by executing line 9; the MC has also executed the statement GOTO 10. The program will terminate when the STOP statement on line 12 is encountered.

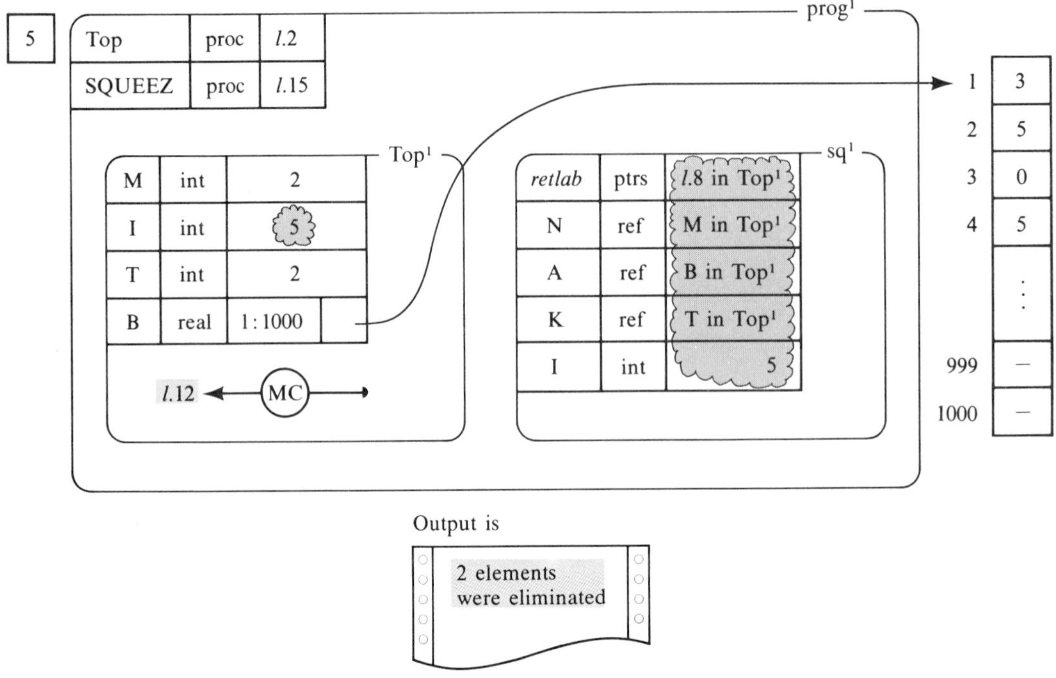

Again notice that the structure of the environment has remained *static* throughout this computation loop. Subsequent reexecutions (for additional data sets) will not change this structure.

6-6 NEW DEVELOPMENTS IN FORTRAN

It was pointed out earlier that Fortran is an *evolving* language. We list below several features included in the new 1977 Fortran standard; some of these features already exist in particular implementations.

1. A CHARACTER data type for variables whose values are strings, with a concatenation operation (//) and the ability to refer to substrings.
2. A SAVE statement that causes the definition of locals to a procedure to be maintained when the procedure returns (similar to the **own** declaration in ALGOL).
3. DO-loops which, like our flowchart iteration box, test the initial value of the control variable against the bound value *before* the loop body is

executed, and hence result in *zero* or more traversals of the loop. Moreover, when given negative increments, the control variable counts *down;* for example

DO 4 I = 10, 1, −1

will cause 10 traversals of the loop.

4. Conditional statements of the form

$$\begin{array}{l} \text{IF } \langle\text{logical expression}\rangle \text{ THEN} \\ \qquad \langle\text{statement block}\rangle \\ \quad \{\text{ELSE IF } \langle\text{logical expression}\rangle \text{ THEN} \\ \qquad \langle\text{statement block}\rangle\}_0 \\ \quad \{\text{ELSE} \\ \qquad \langle\text{statement block}\rangle\}_0^1 \\ \text{END IF} \end{array}$$

A statement block is a sequence of statements and may include conditional statements and DO-loops.

5. Removal of the requirement that functions must have at least one argument.
6. Simplified (formatless) input and output similar to that shown earlier in this chapter.
7. Arrays may have as many as seven dimensions and hence an array element may have up to seven subscripts (up from 3 in 1966 Fortran). Moreover, as in Algol, subscripts may have zero or negative values. Lower and upper bounds for subscripts may also be explicitly given when declaring an array. For example

   REAL C(−5:6), D(0:14, 4)

   declares C to be a linear array of 12 real elements and D to be a two-dimensional real array having 15 rows (0 through 14) and 4 columns (1 through 4).

In almost all cases, these changes are in the form of *additions* to the language, so that existing programs need not be modified. The fact that changes such as these are periodically issued as new standards helps to maintain uniformity among the various implementations of Fortran. Figure 6-11 shows the program of case study 1 (Figure 6-10) recoded using the 1977 standard. In the rest of this chapter the case studies and examples are shown in both the 1966 and 1977 versions of Fortran.

```
C..TOP
      INTEGER M, I, T
      REAL B(100)
      READ *, M, (B(I), I = 1, M)
      CALL SQUEEZ(M, B, T)
      IF (T .EQ. 0) THEN
                      PRINT *, 'NO ELEMENTS WERE ELIMINATED'
                    ELSE
                      PRINT *, T, 'ELEMENTS WERE ELIMINATED'
                    END IF
      END
C..PROCEDURE SQUEEZ STARTS HERE
      SUBROUTINE SQUEEZ (N, A, K)
      INTEGER N, K, I
      REAL A(100)
      K = 0
      DO 10 I = 1, N
         IF (A(I) .EQ. 0) THEN
                            K = K + 1
                          ELSE
                            A(I-K) = A(I)
                          END IF
   10 CONTINUE
      N = N - K
      RETURN
      END
```

Figure 6-11. **Case study 1 program using 1977 Fortran standard.**

6-7 ADDITIONAL CASE STUDIES

Case 2 Our second Fortran case study is the same as case 2 in Chapter 5. The procedure EVENLIST has two parameters : m, an integer, and C, a list of m reals. The primary action of EVENLIST is to copy the *even-valued* elements of C into a new list E, of length k. When this action has been completed, EVENLIST prints "None" if k has the value zero, and otherwise prints the new list E of even-valued elements from C. To determine the evenness of a given element of C, EVENLIST calls on the function EVEN, which returns the value 1 if its argument is even and 0 if it is odd. (See Exercises 6-7, Set A, Exericse 2.)

Flowcharts and legends are displayed in Figure 6-12 and an equivalent Fortran program is shown in Figure 6-13. Figure 6-14 shows the same program recoded using the 1977 standard.

Discussion

In the Fortran program the procedure name EVENLIST is abbreviated as EVLIST due to the Fortran language restriction that identifiers may not be longer than six characters. In all other respects the program in Figure 6-13 is a straightforward mapping of the flowcharts and legends in Figure 6-12. The snapshots below use the following data: n = 7, B = (3, −6, 2, 18, 13, 931, 10).

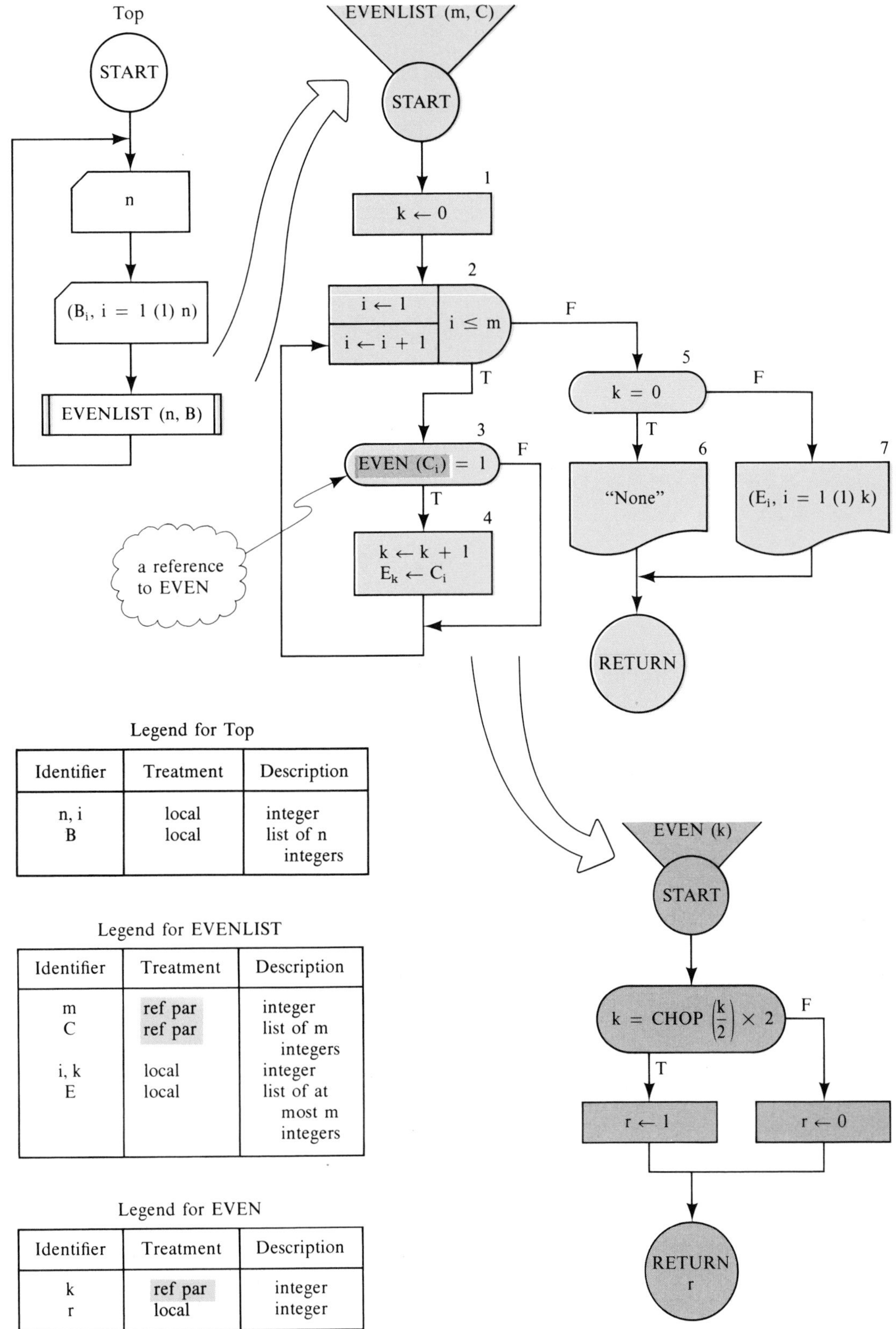

Legend for Top

Identifier	Treatment	Description
n, i	local	integer
B	local	list of n integers

Legend for EVENLIST

Identifier	Treatment	Description
m	ref par	integer
C	ref par	list of m integers
i, k	local	integer
E	local	list of at most m integers

Legend for EVEN

Identifier	Treatment	Description
k	ref par	integer
r	local	integer

Figure 6-12. **Flowcharts and legends for case 2.**

```
C        TOP STARTS HERE ***
         INTEGER B(50), N, I
   20    READ, N
         READ, (B(I), I = 1, N)
         CALL EVLIST (N, B)
         GO TO 20
         END

C        * EVENLIST STARTS HERE ***
         SUBROUTINE EVLIST (M, C)
         INTEGER C(50), M, K, E(50), I, EVEN
         K = 0
         DO 45 I = 1, M
              IF (EVEN (C(I)) .NE. 1) GO TO 45
                 K = K + 1
                 E (K) = C(I)
   45    CONTINUE
         IF (K .EQ. 0) GO TO 6
           PRINT, (E(I), I = 1, K)
           GO TO 8
    6      PRINT, 'NONE'
    8    RETURN
         END

C        * EVEN STARTS HERE ***
         INTEGER FUNCTION EVEN (K)
         INTEGER K, R
         IF (K .EQ. INT (K/2) * 2) GO TO 2
         R = 0
         GO TO 4
    2    R = 1
    4    EVEN = R
           RETURN
           END
```

Note:
There are often more compact and still legal ways of coding most of these programs in Fortran. For example, the code on the right is also correct for the function EVEN.

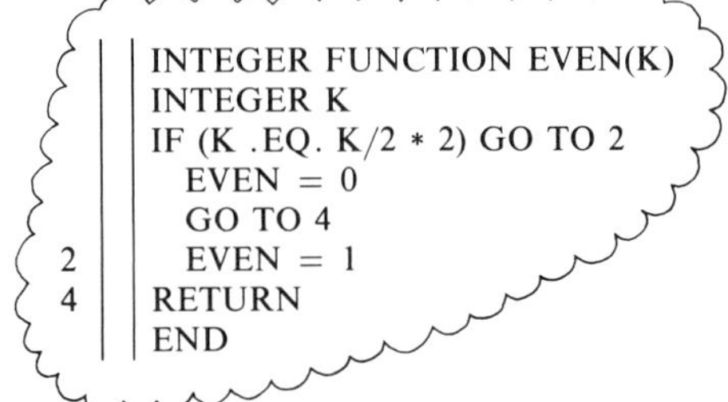

Figure 6-13

```
C      TOP STARTS HERE ***
         INTEGER B(50), I
   20  READ *, N
       READ *, (B(I), I=1, N)
       CALL EVLIST(N, B)
       GO TO 20
       END

C      EVENLIST STARTS HERE ***
       SUBROUTINE EVLIST(M, C)
         INTEGER C(50), M, K, E(50), I, EVEN
       K = 0
       DO 45 I = 1, M
         IF (EVEN(C(I)) .EQ. 1) THEN
                                    K = K + 1
                                    E(K) = C(I)
                                  END IF
   45  CONTINUE
       IF(K .EQ. 0) THEN
                      PRINT *, 'NONE'
                    ELSE
                      PRINT *, I, (E(I), I=1, K)
                    END IF
       RETURN
       END

C      EVEN STARTS HERE ***
       INTEGER FUNCTION EVEN(K)
         INTEGER K, R
       IF (K .EQ. INT(K/2)*2) THEN
                                R = 1
                              ELSE
                                R = 0
                              END IF
       EVEN = R
       RETURN
       END
```

Figure 6-14. **Case study 2 program using the 1977 Fortran standard.**

Snapshot 1 shows the initial data structure with the MC about to execute line 3. Because an auxiliary list is required as a local variable in EVLIST, two list cells, each with a capacity of 50 elements, have been preallocated.

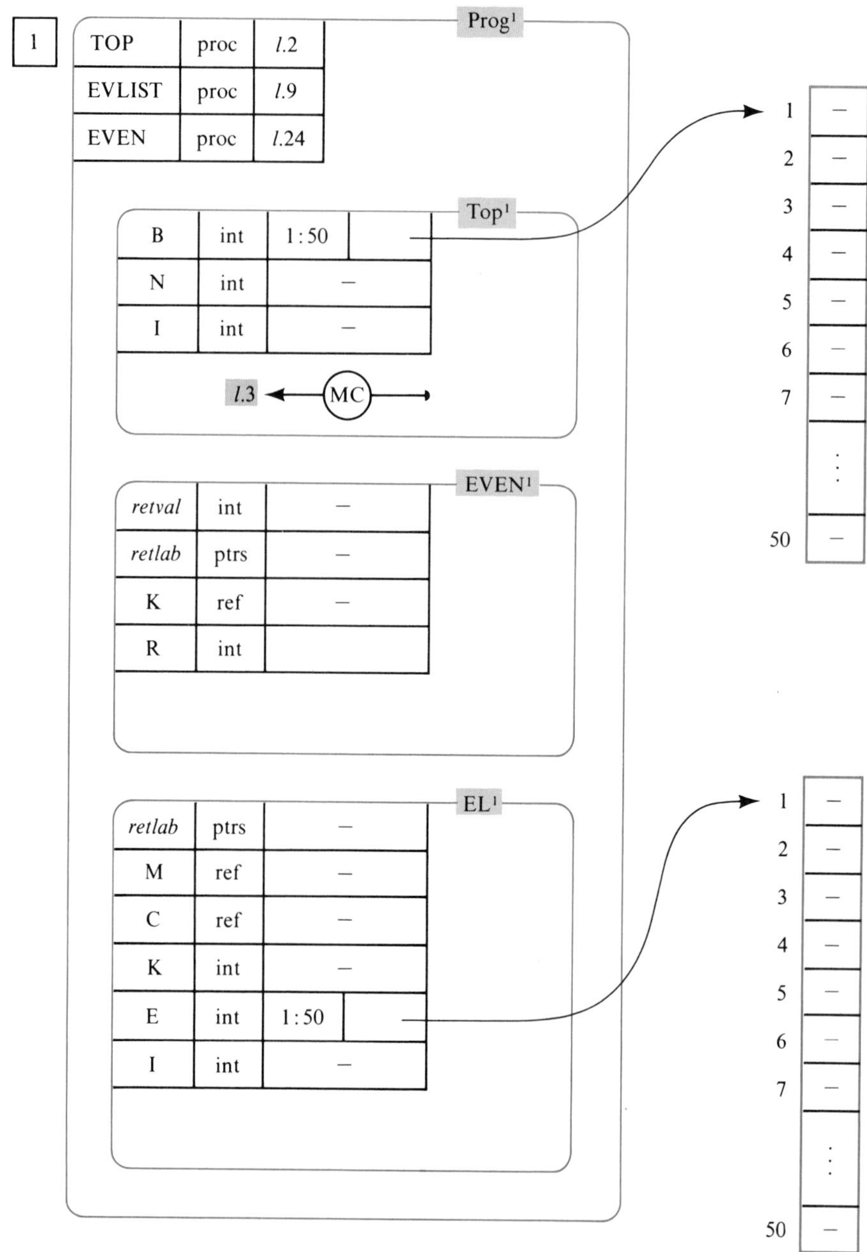

Snapshot 2 is taken at a point where the MC is about to execute a return from EVEN to EVLIST. This was the first time EVEN has been called. At this point all the data have been entered (see cells B, N, and I in Top¹). Also, upon entry to EVLIST, values were assigned to the parameter cells M and C in EL¹. The local variable K of EVLIST was set to zero (as a result of executing line 11). The return cells in EL¹ and EVEN¹ were assigned return values when each was entered. As part of the task of the first call on EVEN, the MC set the local variable R to zero (in EVEN[1]) because the argument was found not to be EVEN. Execution of line 30 causes a copy of the value of R to be placed in the *retval* cell. From there it is copied into the MC's stack as part of the return mechanism.

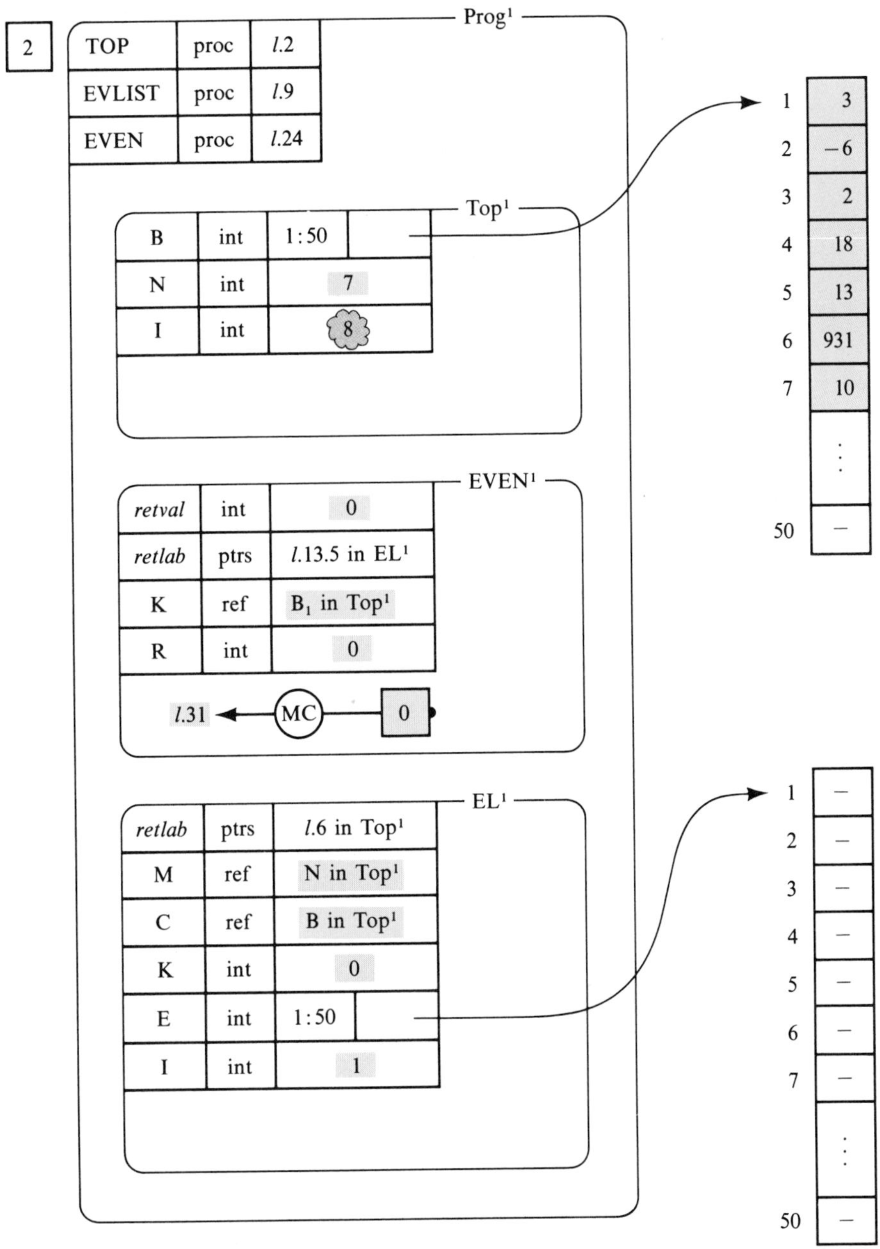

The handling of the argument of EVEN illustrates the *copying of references* technique. The argument was C_i, which might have been expected to produce, in the cell for K in EVEN[1], a reference to C_1 in EL[1]. But since C itself is a reference parameter, K receives instead a reference to B_1 in Top[1], thus avoiding a chain of references from K to C to B.

Snapshot 3 shows the MC about to execute the return from the second call on EVEN. This time, the value of the argument, C_2, *was* even (that is, B_2 in $Top^1 = -6$), and so the local variable R has been assigned the value 1, as a result of executing line 29. Execution of line 30 has placed a copy of this value on the MC's stack.

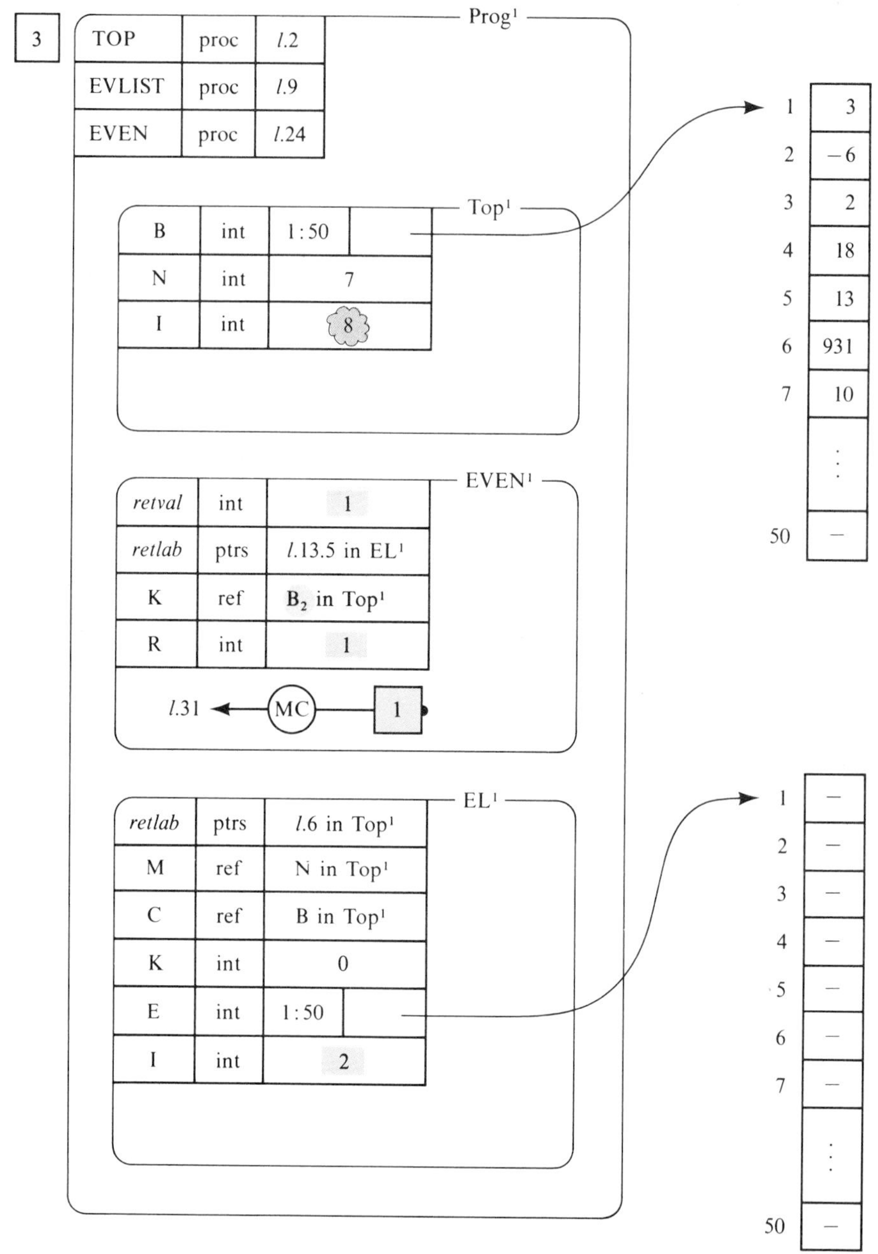

Snapshot 4 shows the computation state after the second return from EVEN with the MC about to execute the CONTINUE statement on line 16. The MC has just executed lines 14 and 15 because the value returned by EVEN was 1. We can see that the first of the even numbers has been copied from list B to list E. The cell in EL[1] for the local variable K has been incremented to 1.

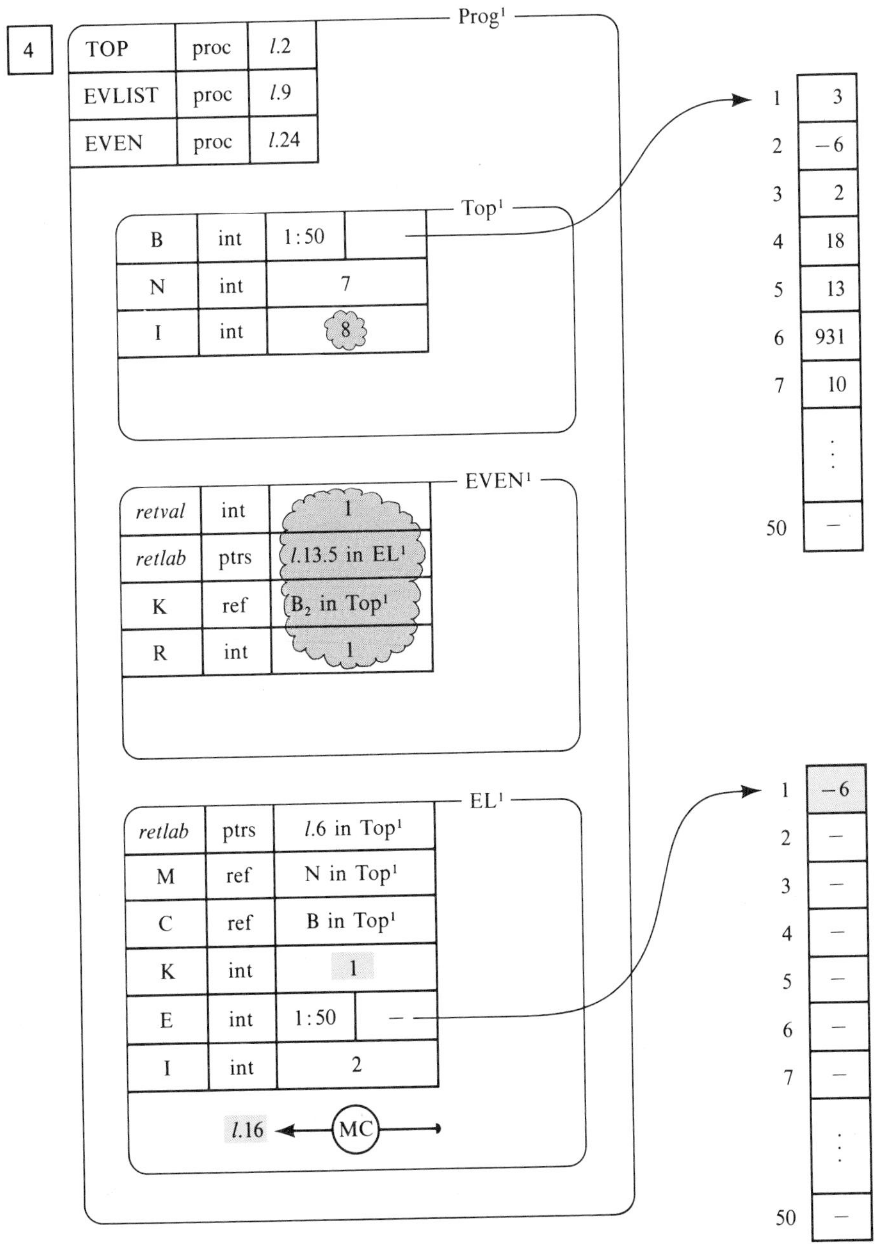

Snapshot 5 shows the computation state when EVLIST is about to execute its return to Top. The DO loop has been completed and the print statement on line 18 has produced the output shown. In all, four even values were discovered in B and copied into E. The value K = 4 in EL[1] has served as the upper bound in the "implied DO loop" in the print statement on line 18 and indicates that four even values were found. All four even values are printed out as shown.

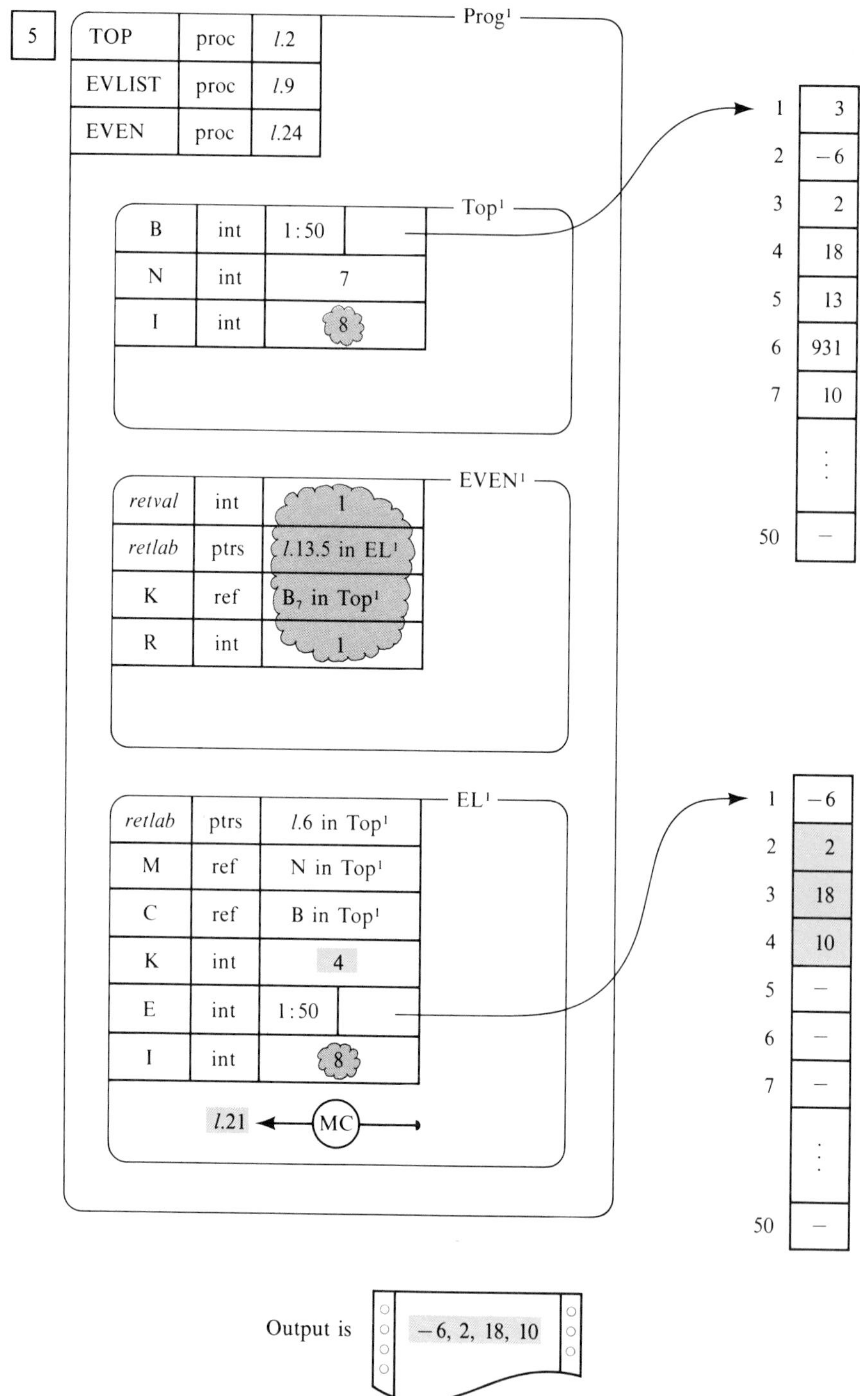

Snapshot 6 shows the state of the computation when the processing of the given data set has been completed. The MC is about to execute the GOTO statement on line 6 for a return to input another data set. Once again we see that the data structure environment, that is, all allocated storage, is preserved for the "life" of the computation, even though the cells in EVEN[1] and EL[1] are now considered to be undefined.

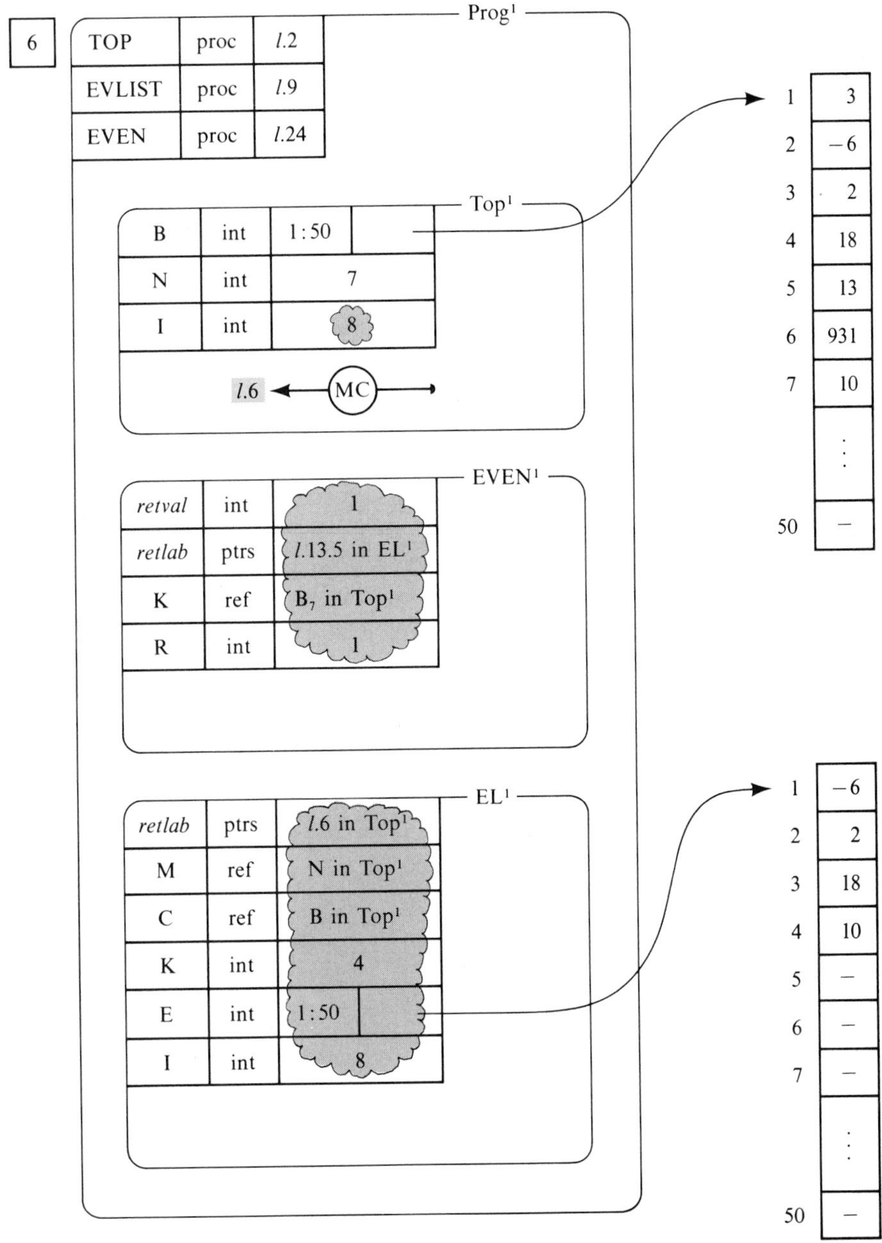

Exercises 6-7, Set A

1 By using labeled and unlabeled COMMON blocks, modify the program of case 2 (see Figures 6-12 and 6-13) so that EVENLIST and EVEN have no parameters. Draw a snapshot taken just after EVEN is entered for the first time. Use the following data: n = 7, B = (3, −6, 2, 18, 13, 931, 10).

2 In the flowcharts for case 2, Figure 6-12, the function EVEN is defined to return an integer r.

(a) Your first task is to redefine EVEN as a logical function. Draw a flowchart and legend for this function, naming it LEVEN, that returns the logical value *true* if k is even and *false* otherwise.

(b) Redraw box 3 of the flowchart EVENLIST in Figure 6-12 to reflect the replacement of the function EVEN by your newly defined function LEVEN.

(c) Using the original top-level flowchart of Figure 6-12, your function LEVEN defined in (a), and the procedure EVENLIST as modified in (b), construct an equivalent Fortran program.

(d) Assuming the same data used in the case 2 study, draw a snapshot for the execution of your Fortran program showing the computation state just after box 4 of EVENLIST has been executed for the first time. Compare your snapshot with snapshot 4 of case 2. Explain any differences.

3 Figure 6-15 shows a Fortran translation of flowcharts and legends already displayed in Figure 5-24. This Fortran program has a top-level segment (lines 1–14), a subroutine subprogram NORMAL (lines 15–27), and a subroutine subprogram LRGST (lines 28–41). NORMAL replaces each element C_i of the list C, by C_i divided by a value supplied by the procedure LRGST. LRGST finds the nonzero element in C, if any, of largest absolute value, and returns the value of this designated element. LRGST sets the global variable k to 1 if the search is successful and 0 if unsuccessful. These related procedures have parameters and both local and global (COMMON) variables.

Study the Fortran program and consider its execution for the data set m = 5, B = (−12, 4, 0, 60, −72). Then draw some, or possibly all, of the following snapshots:

(a) Just before the statement on line 5 is executed for the first time.

(b) Just before line 7 is executed and NORMAL is called for the first time.

(c) Just before line 21 is executed and LRGST is called for the first time.

(d) Just before line 33, the first statement in LRGST, is executed for the first time.

(e) Just before line 40, the RETURN from LRGST, is executed for the first time.

(f) Just before line 26, the RETURN from NORMAL, is executed for the first time.

(g) Just before output lines 11 and 12 are executed for the first time.

Finally, show that the output will be

Case 3 This example, shown in Figure 6-16, illustrates the use of procedure parameters and is similar to case 6 of Chapter 5. After inputting a list A of r reals, Top calls three times on the function SUM, each time obtaining the sum of a different subset of A. Each sum is obtained by supplying as arguments in the call of SUM the name of a procedure P1, P2, or P3, which designates a particular

```
C     TOP PROGRAM STARTS HERE ***
        COMMON K
        REAL B(500)
        INTEGER M, K, I
    1 READ, M
      READ, (B(I), I = 1, M)
      CALL NORMAL(M, B)
      IF (K .EQ. 1) GO TO 4
      PRINT, 'B IS EMPTY'
      GO TO 1
    4 PRINT, 'NORMAL FORM OF B IS'
      PRINT, (B(I), I = 1, M)
      GO TO 1
      END

C     NORMALIZE STARTS HERE ***
      SUBROUTINE NORMAL(N, C)
        COMMON K
        REAL C(500), L
        INTEGER I, K, N, NN
      NN = N
      CALL LRGST (NN, C, L)
      IF (K .NE. 1) GO TO 50
      DO 40 I = 1, NN
        C(I) = C(I)/L
   40 CONTINUE
   50 RETURN
      END

C     LRGST STARTS HERE ***
      SUBROUTINE LRGST (N, C, L)
        COMMON K
        REAL C(500), L
        INTEGER K, I, N, NN
      NN = N
      L = 0
      K = 0
      DO 20 I = 1, NN
        IF(ABS(C(I)) .GT. ABS(L)) L = C(I)
      CONTINUE
      IF (L .NE. 0) K = 1
      RETURN
      END
```

Figure 6-15. **Fortran program.**

rule of summation ("marching" rule), and an upper bound for the index in the summation. It is necessary to transmit the rules of summation via procedure parameters, since name parameters, the alternate way to transmit such rules in Algol, are not available in Fortran.

Figure 6-16 differs from Figure 5-36 primarily in the handling of i, which here is local to SUM and is an argument of the procedures P1, P2, and P3 (in 1966 Fortran, function procedures *must* have at least one argument). A Fortran program is shown in Figure 6-17. (The 1977 version is shown in Figure 6-18.)

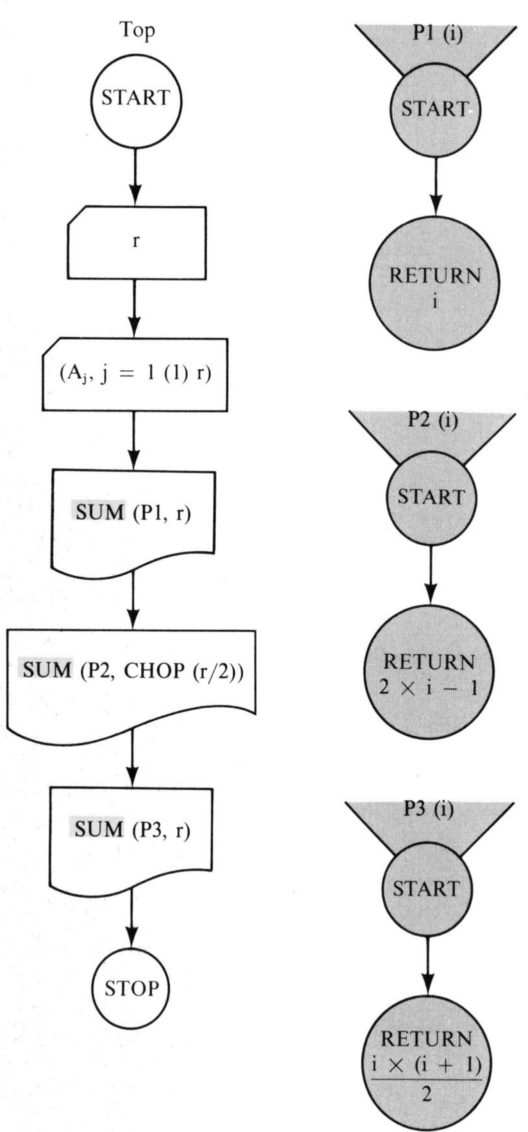

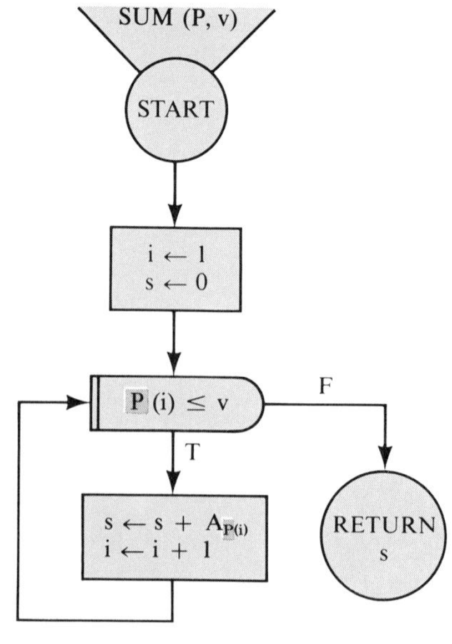

Legend for SUM

Identifier	Treatment	Description
v	ref par	integer
P	proc par	integer procedure
s	local	real
i	local	integer
A	global	A in Top

Legends for P1, P2, and P3

Identifier	Treatment	Description
i	ref par	integer

Legend for Top

Identifier	Treatment	Description
r, j	local	integer
SUM	local	real procedure
P1, P2, P3	local	integer procedure
A	local	list of r reals

Figure 6-16

Line No. Case 3 (same as case 6 in Algol)

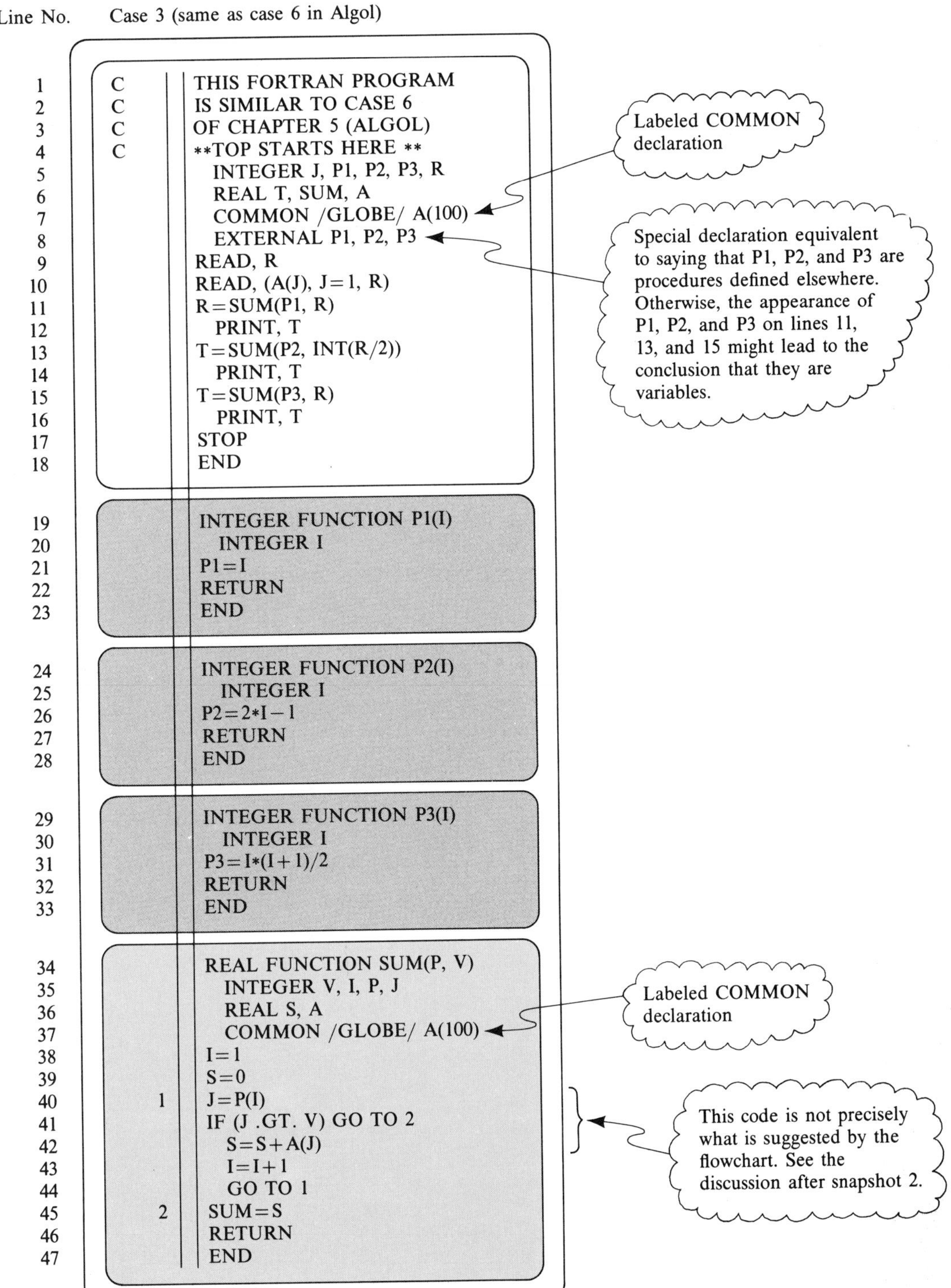

```
1   C      THIS FORTRAN PROGRAM
2   C      IS SIMILAR TO CASE 6
3   C      OF CHAPTER 5 (ALGOL)
4   C      **TOP STARTS HERE **
5            INTEGER J, P1, P2, P3, R
6            REAL T, SUM, A
7            COMMON /GLOBE/ A(100)
8            EXTERNAL P1, P2, P3
9          READ, R
10         READ, (A(J), J=1, R)
11         R=SUM(P1, R)
12           PRINT, T
13         T=SUM(P2, INT(R/2))
14           PRINT, T
15         T=SUM(P3, R)
16           PRINT, T
17         STOP
18         END

19         INTEGER FUNCTION P1(I)
20           INTEGER I
21         P1=I
22         RETURN
23         END

24         INTEGER FUNCTION P2(I)
25           INTEGER I
26         P2=2*I-1
27         RETURN
28         END

29         INTEGER FUNCTION P3(I)
30           INTEGER I
31         P3=I*(I+1)/2
32         RETURN
33         END

34         REAL FUNCTION SUM(P, V)
35           INTEGER V, I, P, J
36           REAL S, A
37           COMMON /GLOBE/ A(100)
38         I=1
39         S=0
40       1 J=P(I)
41         IF (J .GT. V) GO TO 2
42           S=S+A(J)
43           I=I+1
44           GO TO 1
45       2 SUM=S
46         RETURN
47         END
```


Figure 6-17

```
C     CASE 3 USING 1977 STANDARD
C     **TOP STARTS HERE**
        INTEGER J, P1, P2, P3, R
        REAL T, SUM, A
        COMMON /GLOBE/ A(100)
        EXTERNAL P1, P2, P3
      READ *, R
      READ *, (A(J), J = 1, R)
      T = SUM(P1, R)
        PRINT *, T
      T = SUM(P2, INT(R/2))
        PRINT *, T
      T = SUM(P3, R)
        PRINT *, T
      STOP
      END

      INTEGER FUNCTION P1 (I)
        INTEGER I
      P1 = I
      RETURN
      END

      INTEGER FUNCTION P2 (I)
        INTEGER I
      P2 = 2*I - 1
      RETURN
      END

      INTEGER FUNCTION P3 (I)
        INTEGER I
      P3 = I*(I+1)/2
      RETURN
      END

      REAL FUNCTION SUM(P,V)
        INTEGER V, I, P, J
        REAL S, A
        COMMON /GLOBE/ A(100)
      I = 1
      S = 0
      J = P(I)
    1 IF J .LE. V THEN
                    S = S + A(J)
                    I = I + 1
                    GO TO 1
                 ELSE
                    SUM = S
                    RETURN
                 END IF
      END
```

Figure 6-18

Discussion

The initial structure of the execution environment for this program is displayed in snapshot 1, where we see a global cell in Prog[1] with the name GLOBE. Top and SUM are the only program units that contain labeled COMMON declarations naming GLOBE. These declarations make the list A accessible to Top and SUM but to no other unit of the program. The outermost contour lists all program units that are referenced including the library function INT, which is the equivalent of the flowchart CHOP.

Snapshot 2 shows the situation after the first call on SUM. That procedure is getting ready to make a function reference of the form P (I) on line 40. When SUM is entered, values are assigned to the return cell and to the two parameter cells P and V in Sum[1]. Variables I and S local to SUM have already been given their initial values.

The code on lines 40–44 of the program reflects a modification of the flowchart so that, for efficiency, only one call is made on P for each transit of the loop. The value returned from P is assigned to a local auxiliary variable, here the variable J.

The first reference, P (I), is interpreted as P1 (1) since the value of P is P1 in Prog[1], and I = 1. This is seen in snapshot 3, where the MC is now found inside P1[1] about to execute a return with the value P1 (1) = 1 placed in the stack. (Note that upon entry to P1, the return cell in P1[1] has been set for a return to the Sum[1] environment.)

Snapshot 4 shows the condition of the computation after the first return from P1. Execution of lines 41–43 has resulted in the value of A_1 being used to increment the value of S, and the loop counter I has been incremented.

Snapshot 5 shows the situation after control has returned to Top from the call on P1. SUM has returned the value 25, which has been assigned to T, and a copy of T has been printed.

Snapshot 6 shows the MC about to execute the return step from the *second* call on SUM. The value to be returned is 11 (that is, $A_1 + A_3$). SUM has used P2 as an argument, as indicated by the value in the cell for P in Sum[1]. It can be seen that the return cell in P2[1] has been set as has the *retval* cell for P2[1]. Note that the loop counter I has reached 3. It can also be seen, by inspecting the cell for J, that its last value is 5, and this value exceeds the value 3 referred to by V.

We can now explain the previously unused cell labeled 1TEMP in Top[1]. For the second call on SUM, the second argument is the expression INT (R/2). This expression was evaluated as 3 and stored in the "temporary" 1TEMP, which is a name that cannot conflict with a programmer-written identifier. A reference to this cell was then assigned to V in SUM[1].

Finally, snapshot 7 shows the state of things after the given data set has been fully processed and the computation is about to halt on line 17. The third and last sum has been printed. Inspection of the values in cells I, J, and S in Sum[1] tells what happened in the last "round."

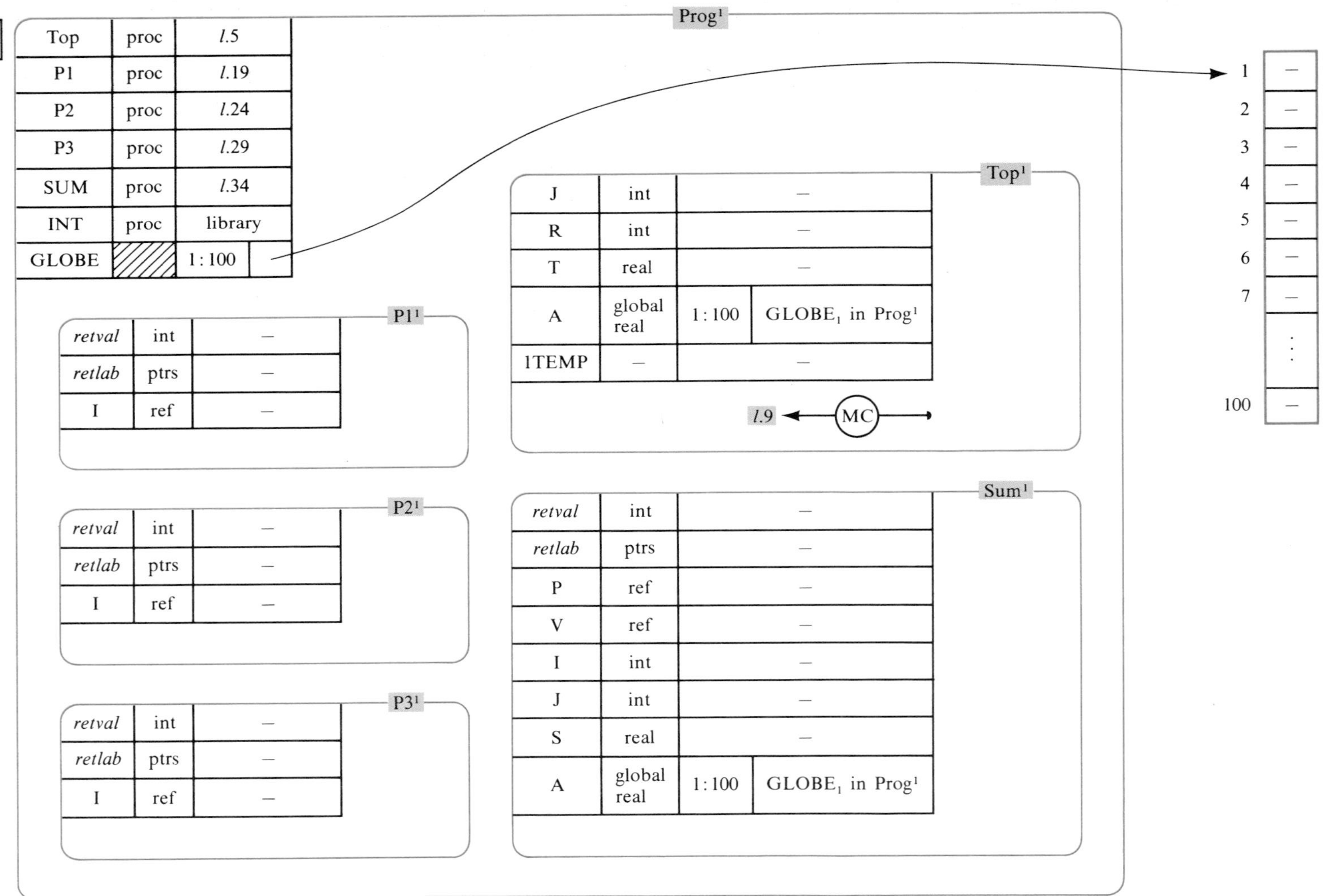
1
Prog¹
Top proc l.5
P1 proc l.19
P2 proc l.24
P3 proc l.29
SUM proc l.34
INT proc library
GLOBE 1:100
Top¹
J int –
R int –
T real –
A global real 1:100 GLOBE₁ in Prog¹
ITEMP – –
l.9 MC
P1¹
retval int –
retlab ptrs –
I ref –
P2¹
retval int –
retlab ptrs –
I ref –
P3¹
retval int –
retlab ptrs –
I ref –
Sum¹
retval int –
retlab ptrs –
P ref –
V ref –
I int –
J int –
S real –
A global real 1:100 GLOBE₁ in Prog¹
1
2
3
4
5
6
7
100

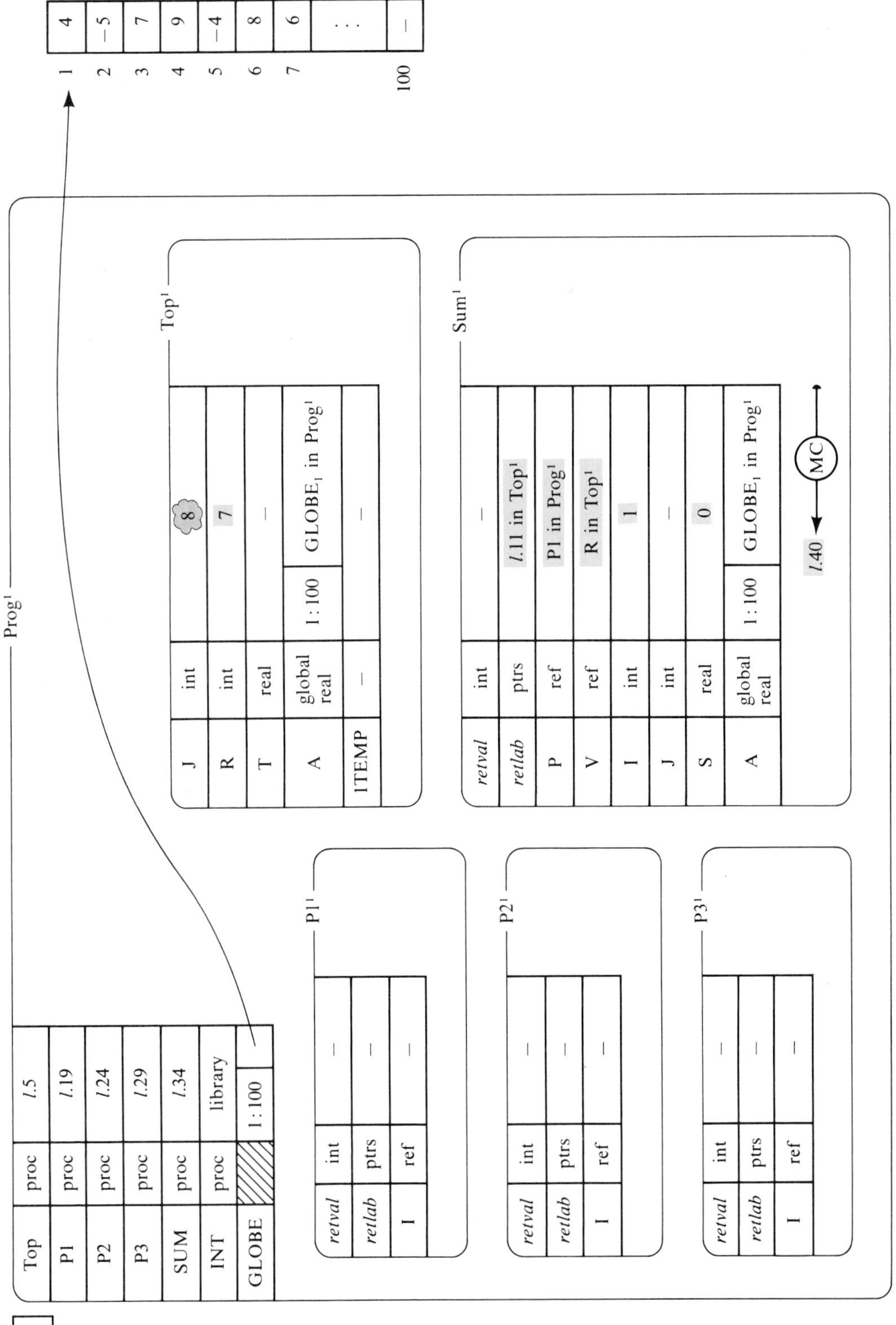

2
Prog¹
Top | proc | l.5
P1 | proc | l.19
P2 | proc | l.24
P3 | proc | l.29
SUM | proc | l.34
INT | proc | library
GLOBE | 1:100
P1¹
retval | int | —
retlab | ptrs | —
I | ref | —
P2¹
retval | int | —
retlab | ptrs | —
I | ref | —
P3¹
retval | int | —
retlab | ptrs | —
I | ref | —
Top¹
J | int | 8
R | int | 7
T | real | —
A | global real | 1:100 | GLOBE₁ in Prog¹
ITEMP | — | —
Sum¹
retval | int | —
retlab | ptrs | l.11 in Top¹
P | ref | P1 in Prog¹
V | ref | R in Top¹
I | int | 1
J | int | —
S | real | 0
A | global real | 1:100 | GLOBE₁ in Prog¹
l.40
MC
1 2 3 4 5 6 7 100
4 −5 7 9 −4 8 6 . . . —

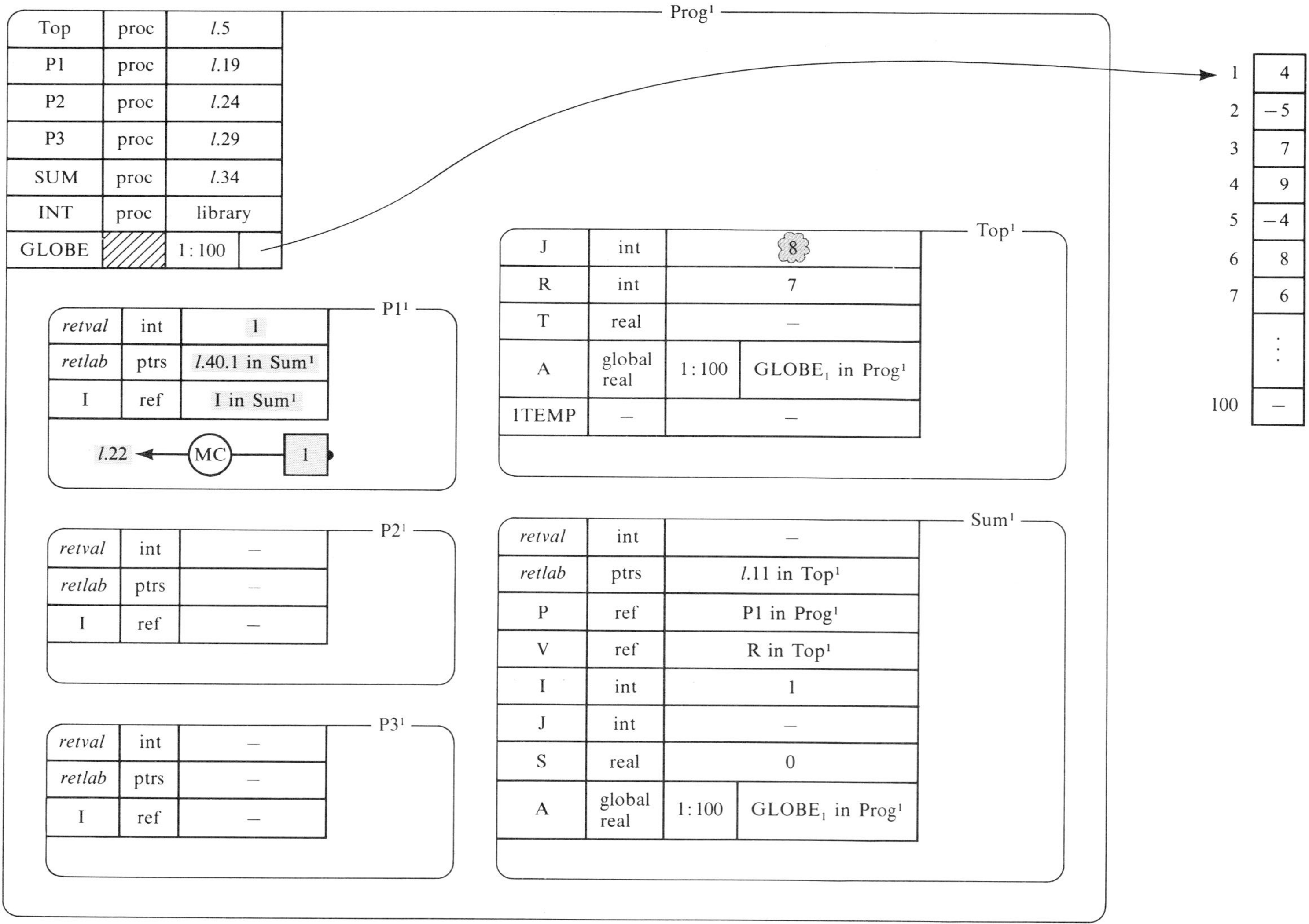
3
Prog¹
Top proc l.5
P1 proc l.19
P2 proc l.24
P3 proc l.29
SUM proc l.34
INT proc library
GLOBE 1:100
P1¹
retval int 1
retlab ptrs l.40.1 in Sum¹
I ref I in Sum¹
l.22
MC
1
P2¹
retval int —
retlab ptrs —
I ref —
P3¹
retval int —
retlab ptrs —
I ref —
Top¹
J int 8
R int 7
T real —
A global real 1:100 GLOBE₁ in Prog¹
ITEMP — —
Sum¹
retval int —
retlab ptrs l.11 in Top¹
P ref P1 in Prog¹
V ref R in Top¹
I int 1
J int —
S real 0
A global real 1:100 GLOBE₁ in Prog¹
1 4
2 −5
3 7
4 9
5 −4
6 8
7 6
. . .
100 —

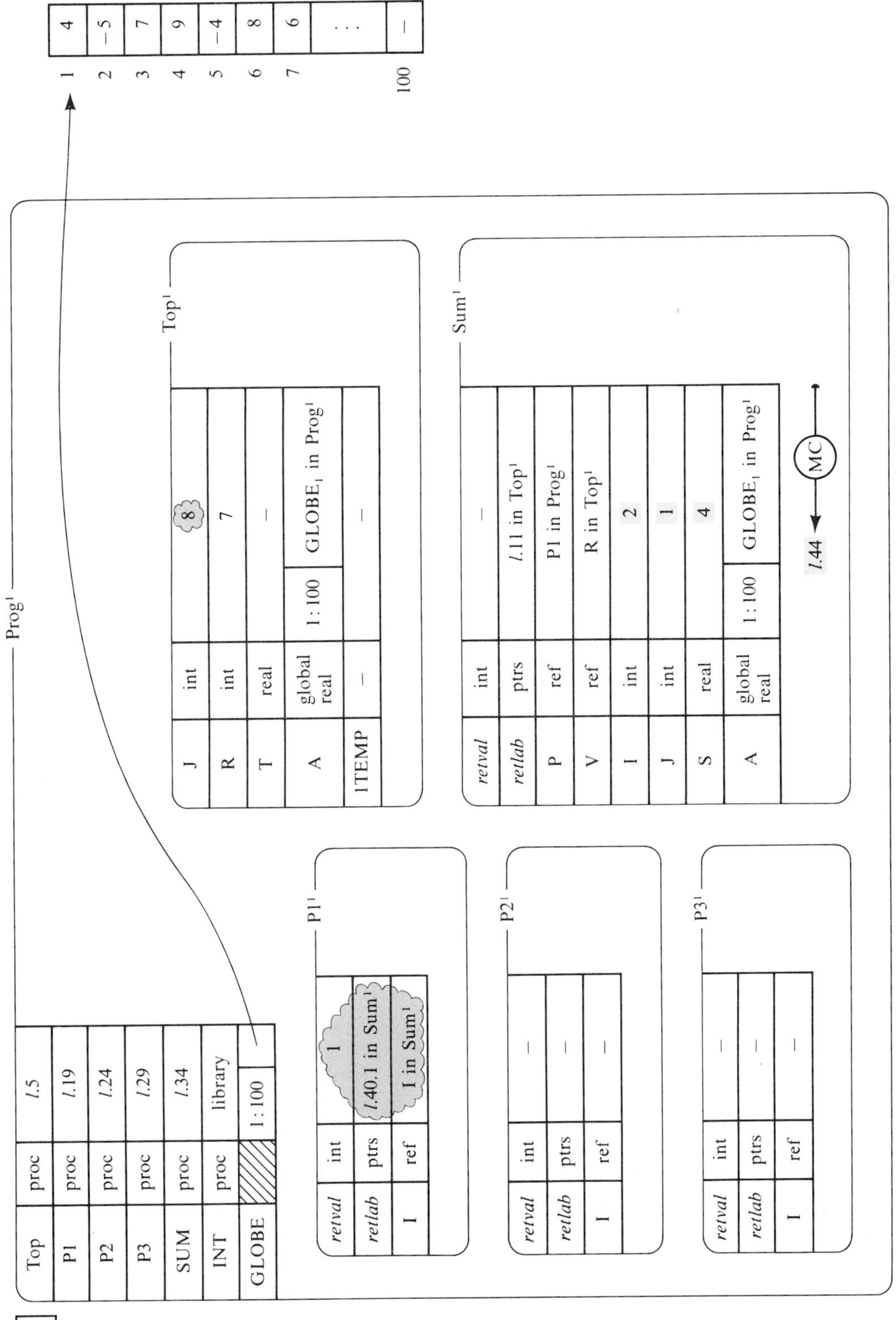
4
Prog¹
Top proc l.5
P1 proc l.19
P2 proc l.24
P3 proc l.29
SUM proc l.34
INT proc library
GLOBE 1:100
Top¹
J int 8
R int 7
T real —
A global real 1:100 GLOBE₁ in Prog¹
ITEMP — —
Sum¹
retval int —
retlab ptrs l.11 in Top¹
P ref P1 in Prog¹
V ref R in Top¹
I int 2
J int 1
S real 4
A global real 1:100 GLOBE₁ in Prog¹
MC
l.44
P1¹
retval int 1
retlab ptrs l.40.1 in Sum¹
I ref I in Sum¹
P2¹
retval int —
retlab ptrs —
I ref —
P3¹
retval int —
retlab ptrs —
I ref —
1 4
2 −5
3 7
4 9
5 −4
6 8
7 6
100 —

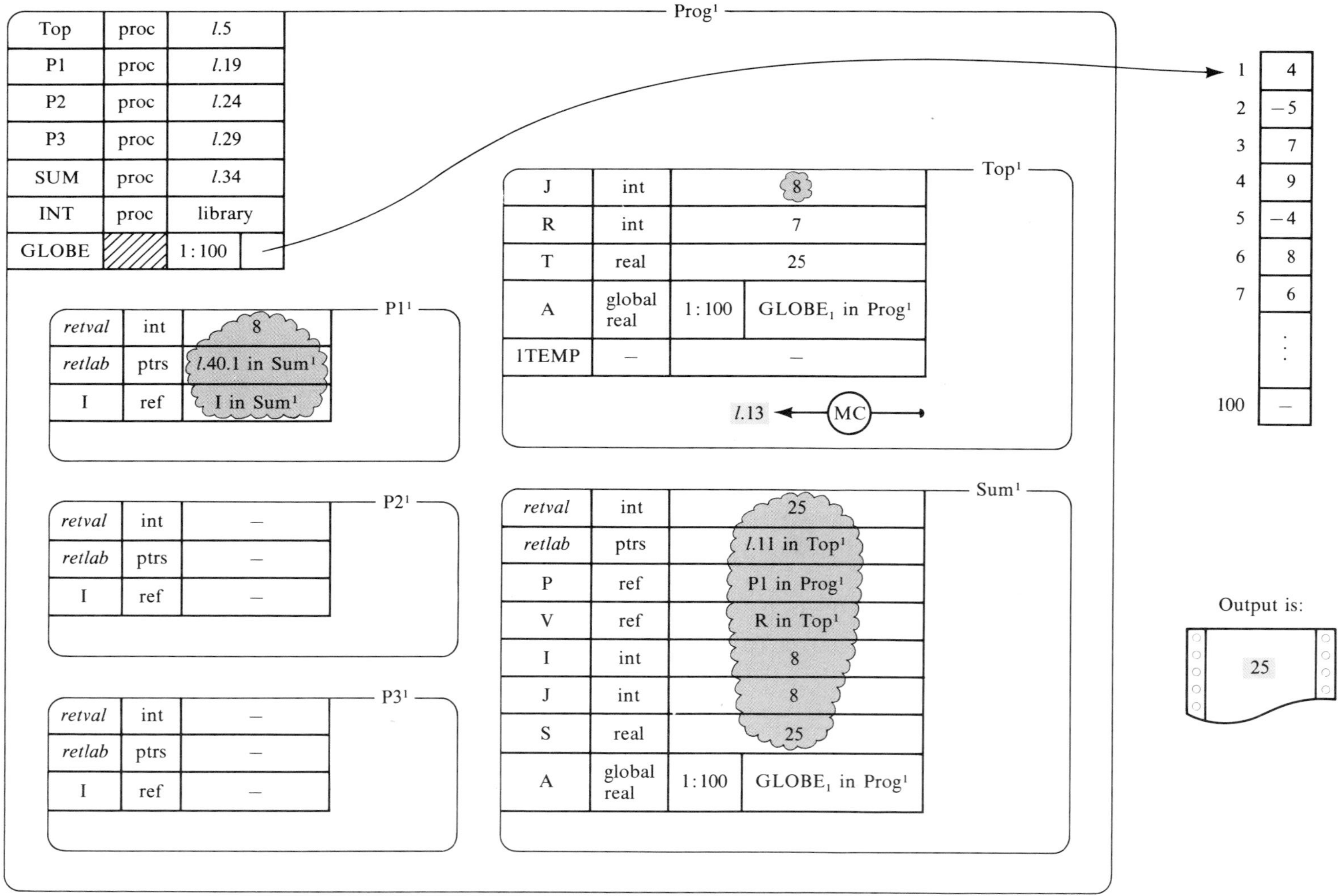

5
Prog¹
Top
proc
l.5
P1
proc
l.19
P2
proc
l.24
P3
proc
l.29
SUM
proc
l.34
INT
proc
library
GLOBE
1:100
Top¹
J
int
8
R
int
7
T
real
25
A
global real
1:100
GLOBE₁ in Prog¹
ITEMP
—
—
l.13
MC
P1¹
retval
int
8
retlab
ptrs
l.40.1 in Sum¹
I
ref
I in Sum¹
P2¹
retval
int
—
retlab
ptrs
—
I
ref
—
P3¹
retval
int
—
retlab
ptrs
—
I
ref
—
Sum¹
retval
int
25
retlab
ptrs
l.11 in Top¹
P
ref
P1 in Prog¹
V
ref
R in Top¹
I
int
8
J
int
8
S
real
25
A
global real
1:100
GLOBE₁ in Prog¹
1
4
2
−5
3
7
4
9
5
−4
6
8
7
6
. . .
100
—
Output is:
25

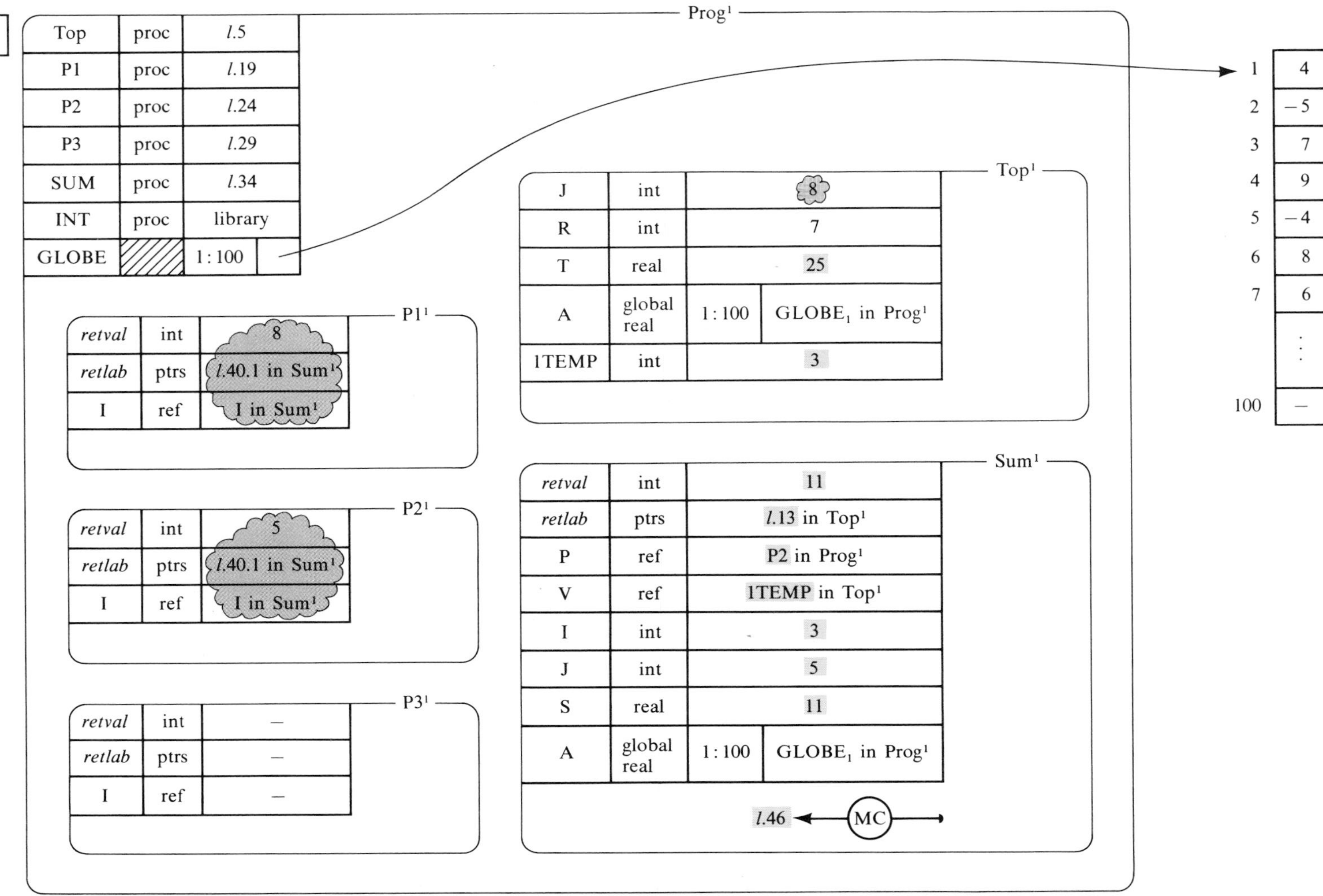
6
Prog¹
Top proc l.5
P1 proc l.19
P2 proc l.24
P3 proc l.29
SUM proc l.34
INT proc library
GLOBE 1 : 100
P1¹
retval int 8
retlab ptrs l.40.1 in Sum¹
I ref I in Sum¹
P2¹
retval int 5
retlab ptrs l.40.1 in Sum¹
I ref I in Sum¹
P3¹
retval int —
retlab ptrs —
I ref —
Top¹
J int 8
R int 7
T real 25
A global real 1 : 100 GLOBE₁ in Prog¹
ITEMP int 3
Sum¹
retval int 11
retlab ptrs l.13 in Top¹
P ref P2 in Prog¹
V ref ITEMP in Top¹
I int 3
J int 5
S real 11
A global real 1 : 100 GLOBE₁ in Prog¹
l.46
MC
1 4
2 −5
3 7
4 9
5 −4
6 8
7 6
100 —

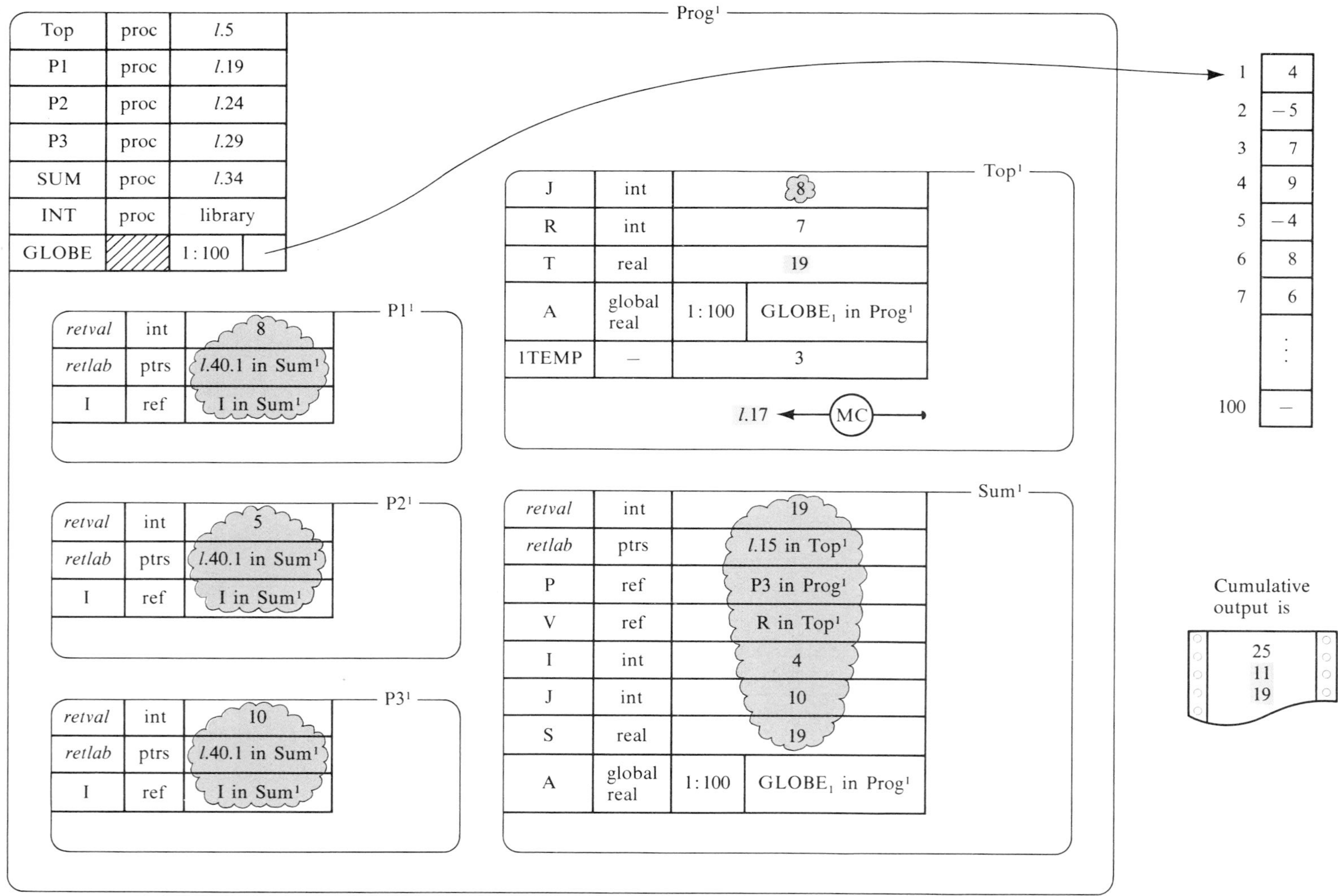

7
Prog¹
Top proc l.5
P1 proc l.19
P2 proc l.24
P3 proc l.29
SUM proc l.34
INT proc library
GLOBE 1:100
P1¹
retval int 8
retlab ptrs l.40.1 in Sum¹
I ref I in Sum¹
P2¹
retval int 5
retlab ptrs l.40.1 in Sum¹
I ref I in Sum¹
P3¹
retval int 10
retlab ptrs l.40.1 in Sum¹
I ref I in Sum¹
Top¹
J int 8
R int 7
T real 19
A global real 1:100 GLOBE₁ in Prog¹
ITEMP — 3
l.17
MC
Sum¹
retval int 19
retlab ptrs l.15 in Top¹
P ref P3 in Prog¹
V ref R in Top¹
I int 4
J int 10
S real 19
A global real 1:100 GLOBE₁ in Prog¹
1 4
2 −5
3 7
4 9
5 −4
6 8
7 6
100 —
Cumulative output is
25
11
19

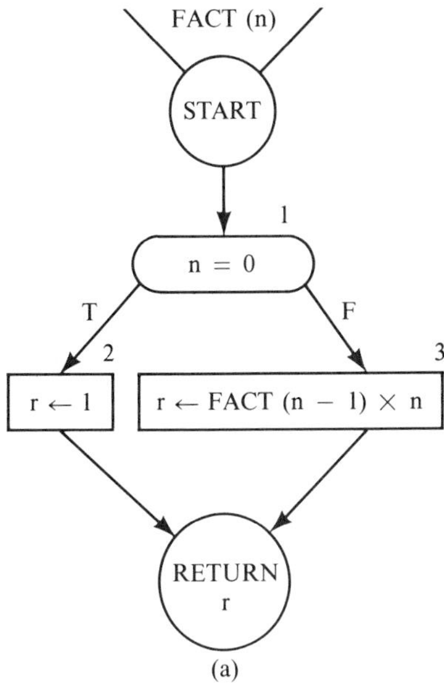

(a)

Legend for FACT

Identifier	Treatment	Description
n	val par	nonnegative integer
r	local	integer

Legend for SFACT

Identifier	Treatment	Description
n	val par	nonnegative integer
r	local	integer
LEVEL	local	integer
NLIST	local	list of n integers

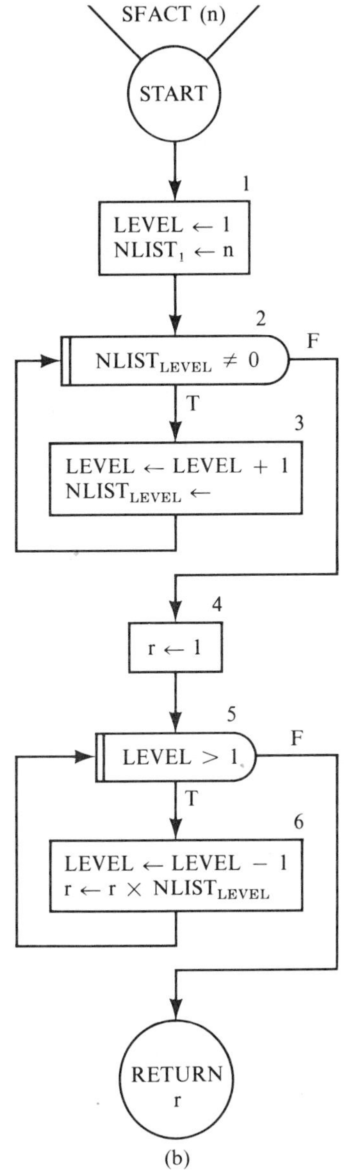

(b)

Figure 6-19. **Flowcharts for N factorial for (a) true recursion and (b) simulated recursion.**

Exercises 6–7, Set B*

Although Fortran subprograms cannot be called recursively, we can *simulate* recursive calls. It has been shown that every recursive algorithm can be translated into an equivalent nonrecursive (iterative) form, which simulates the recursion. The general idea involved consists of replacing each local variable and each parameter with a list in

*This exercise is based on material in Forsythe *et al.* (1975b).

which the first element contains the value of the identifier in the first activation of the subprogram, the second element contains the value in the (simulated) second activation, and so forth. In addition, a new local variable LEVEL can be defined to keep track of the number of simulated activations. The value of LEVEL is the number of the current simulated activation.

Figure 6-19a repeats the recursive factorial flowchart first seen in Figure 3-4. Figure 6-19b is an incomplete nonrecursive translation that simulates the recursive calls of Figure 6-19a.

Your task is to complete the second assignment statement in box 3 of Figure 6-19b and to translate the program into FORTRAN. (Since there are no assignments to the parameter n, this value parameter can safely be coded as a reference parameter.)

Lest one think that Figure 6-19b is a *good* way to compute n factorial in Fortran, look back at Figure 3-3. There is a straightforward iterative computation of n factorial that is undoubtedly simpler!

6-8 INPUT / OUTPUT IN FORTRAN

In Table 6-3 and in the case studies, we have dealt only with "simplified forms" of input and output. Statements such as

PRINT, A, B, C

allow the programmer to state what values are to be output, but give him little control over *how* they are to be displayed (that is, where the values will appear on the page, how many significant digits will be shown, etc.).

Simplified input/output statements are provided in most Fortran systems. They are most useful when one wants to concentrate on making a good translation from flowchart to Fortran, without the burden of producing a "pretty" printout. At a later stage of program development, one may want to display the results in some special form so that they are easy to read and understand. Such a refinement will involve more complicated output statements. Similar considerations apply to input. In the initial testing of a program, the data might be set up with simplified input statements, whereas reading the actual data might require more sophisticated techniques.

Consider the following example: suppose a program produces as its final results a 4 × 5 matrix A of real numbers and two lists of real numbers ROWSUM and COLSUM, whose values are the sums of the individual rows and columns of A. Figure 6-20a shows simplified output statements for these results, and Figure 6-20b shows the display that they might produce. The exact form of the output depends on the particular implementation of Fortran. Although the display in Figure 6-20b is sufficient for many purposes, in some cases we might prefer to use more powerful output techniques to produce the display shown in Figure 6-21.

It is not our intention to discuss all input/output techniques available in Fortran (see the reference manual for the machine you are using or a Fortran text). However, we can provide a feeling for what is required to produce a display such as Figure 6-21 by showing how the lines containing the rows of the

```
         ⋮
         PRINT, 'MATRIX A'
         DO 10 I=1, 4
             PRINT, 'ROW', I, (A(I, J), J=1, 5), 'ROWSUM = ', ROWSUM(I)
10       CONTINUE
         PRINT, 'COLSUMS = ', (COLSUM(J), J=1, 5)
         ⋮
```

(a)

```
MATRIX A
ROW                        1 1.2830,+01 1.4600,+01 1.0923,+01 2.2000,+01
  8.5120,+00ROWSUM           6.8865,+01
ROW                        2 8.6400,+00 9.7585,+00 6.6666,+00 3.8521,+00
 1.5620,+01ROWSUM            4.4537,+01
ROW                        3 4.2210,+01 7.3900,+01 8.0000,+01 1.2000,+00
  3.2190,+00ROWSUM           2.0053,+02
ROW                        4 5.1200,+01          0 3.9000,+00 7.6420,+01
  4.1440,+01ROWSUM           1.7296,+02
COLSUMS          1.1488,+02 9.8258,+01 1.2149,+02 1.0347,+02 6.8791,+01
```

Note that each execution of PRINT (except the last) produces 2 lines of output due to the wide fields of the simplified output and the narrow page of the printer used for this run.

Real numbers are output in a form of scientific notation. Thus this number is 1.0347×10^2

(b)

Figure 6-20. **"Simplified" output in Fortran. (a) Simplified output statements; (b) output produced by the statements in (a).**

matrix are output. Figure 6-22 shows one of these lines "dissected" into its component *fields.* To produce the desired line of output, we associate a *format statement* with the output statement. The format will contain, for each field on the line, a *field descriptor* stating exactly how the value in the field is to be displayed, or, if there is no value for a field, the descriptor states what is to occupy the corresponding space (blanks, special characters, etc.).

The set of field descriptors available in Fortran and the form in which they are written constitute a "language within the language." Figure 6-23 explains the descriptors needed for our example.

Figure 6-21. **Alternate display of the information shown in Figure 6-20b.**

```
                           MATRIX A
                           ********

               1         2         3         4         5           ROWSUM
        *********************************************           ******
   1    *    12.83     14.60     10.92     22.00      8.51   *     68.87
   2    *     8.64      9.76      6.67      3.85     15.62   *     44.54
   3    *    42.21     73.90     80.00      1.20      3.22   *    200.53
   4    *    51.20      0.00      3.90     76.42     41.44   *    172.96
        *********************************************

COLSUM      114.88     98.26    101.49    103.47     68.79
```

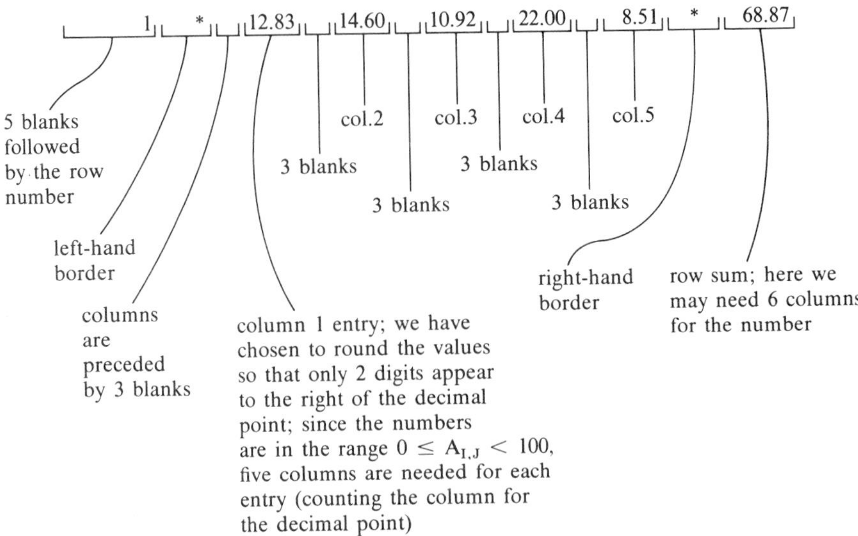

Figure 6-22. **Dividing an output line into "fields."**

Type of value in field	Example: Value	Example: Field descriptor	General form	Meaning
Integer	235	I3	Iw	An integer value is displayed in a field w columns wide (counting the minus sign for negative numbers)
Real	728.3	F5.1	Fw.d	A real value is displayed in a field w columns wide (counting the decimal point and the minus sign for negative numbers). The value is rounded to have d digits to the right of the decimal.
Blanks	□□□□	4X	wX	A blank field w columns wide appears in the line.
Character string	**□XY□**	8H**□XY□**	$wHc_1c_2 \ldots c_w$	w characters are displayed in the field, known as a "Hollerith" field. Note that the characters themselves are part of the format when this technique is used.
		'** XY **'	$'c_1c_2 \ldots c_w'$	This alternate form is allowed in many Fortran implementations.

Figure 6-23. **Fortran field descriptors. Note: if the value to be printed, according to an I or F descriptor, requires fewer than the specified number of columns, leading blanks will be inserted in the field to give the correct number of columns. If the value is too large for the field, a loss of information results.**

In Figure 6-24 we show how the format for our sample line is composed, along with the Fortran statements needed to display the matrix.

FORMAT statements are also used with input statements. For example, if unit 5 is a card reader, the statements

```
   |  |READ (5, 53) I, J
53 |  |FORMAT (2X, I3, 10X, I4)
```

mean: Skip the first 2 columns of the next data card, then read an integer value for I from the next 3 columns, then skip 10 columns, then read an integer value for J from the next four columns of the same card. It is necessary, of course, that there be a proper match between the format specification and the actual data cards.

Although we shall not discuss input/output techniques further, we hope that the reader who is programming in Fortran will be encouraged to pursue the subject.

Figure 6-24. **Use of a FORMAT statement. (a) Field descriptors for a line of the matrix. (b) Fortran statements to output the matrix.**

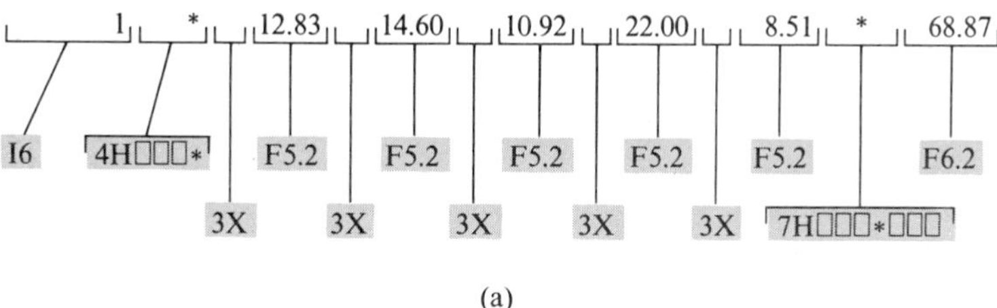

(a)

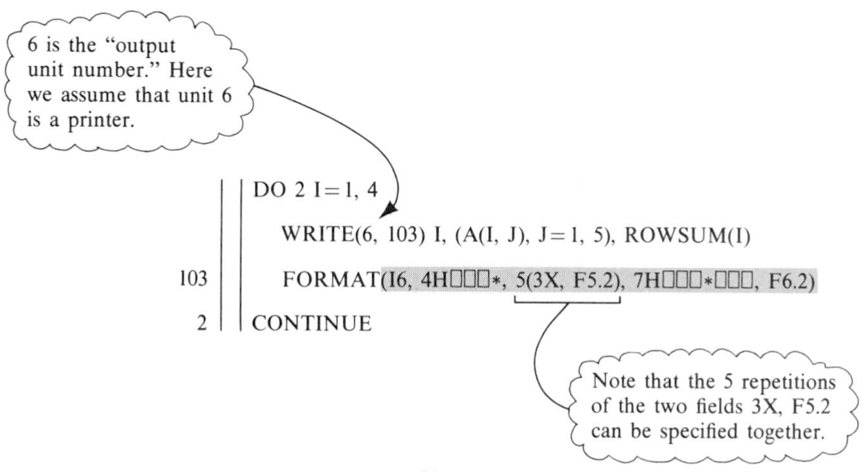

(b)

Exercises 6-8

Suppose that 20 three-digit integers have been punched on a data card, beginning in column 1 and with a space following each integer. Write a Fortran program, complete with FORMAT statements, that inputs the 20 integers, finds the largest, and produces output similar to the following:

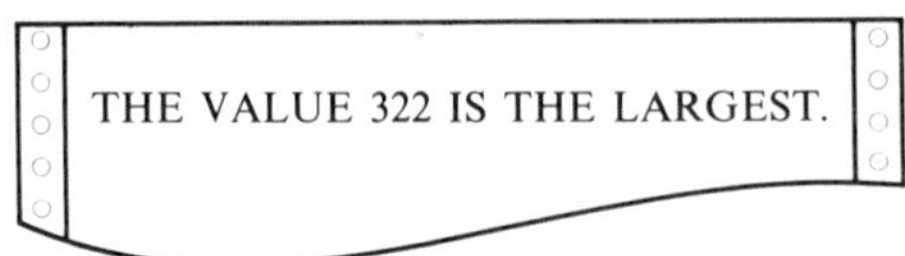

6-9 A BRIEF COMPARISON OF ALGOL AND FORTRAN

Now that we have examined two rather similar "algebraic" languages, we wish to compare them. Our purpose in doing so is not to provide a basis for choosing one language or the other in a particular application, but simply to explore the implications for the programmer of some of the decisions made by the language designers. Our discussion touches on six aspects of the languages.

1. Block Structure and Dynamic Storage Allocation

A clear difference in the languages is that Algol is block structured and Fortran is not. Thus Algol programs can possess a nested, hierarchic structure of any complexity, whereas Fortran allows only a nonnested structure. The obvious question is: How can the Algol programmer *exploit* block structure?

Our case studies have provided some answers. Algol programs such as the one in Figure 6-25 have been typical.

This program using dynamic declaration of arrays X and Y is efficient in its utilization of storage. The programmer may code the inner blocks without having to specify in advance how large the arrays X and Y will be. This approach is not possible in Fortran, where some sort of worst case guess must always be made.

Can block structure ever be a disadvantage? Yes, if the programmer creates a structure that is *too* complicated, then the resulting program will be difficult to understand and prone to error. Block structure, like most tools, must be used judiciously.

Because Fortran uses static allocation of workspace, a Fortran programmer must simulate any dynamic allocation of storage. This can be done by inserting statements and subprograms that accomplish the management of the allotted workspace.

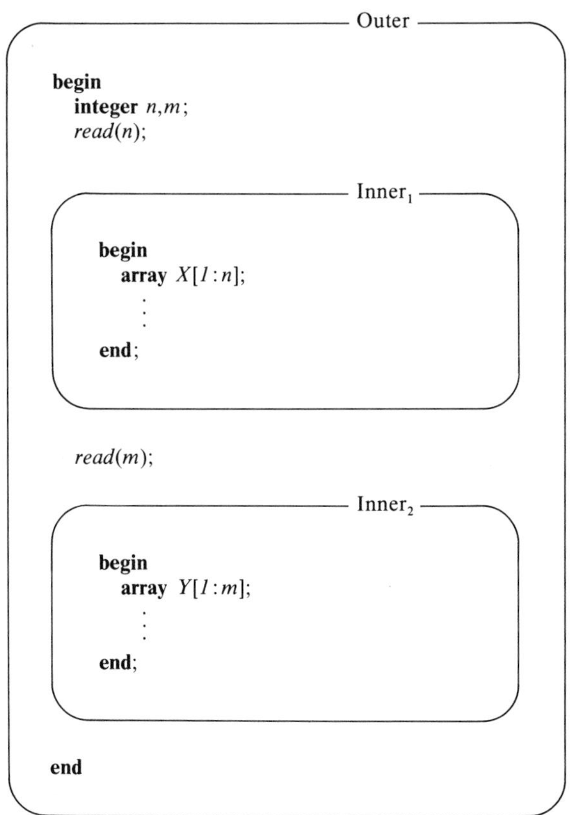

Figure 6-25

The Fortran EQUIVALENCE declaration (see item 20 of Table 6-3) helps programmers to describe the use and reuse of storage space. In many programs not every variable has a "lifetime" extending from the very beginning to the very end of the computation. If, as in Figure 6-26, variables A, B, and C are arrays of comparable size, say 100 elements, each with a distinct (nonoverlapping) lifetime, then only one block of storage cells (for 100 elements) need be allocated. The declarations

```
DIMENSION A (100), B (100), C (100)
EQUIVALENCE (A (1), B (1)), (A (1), C (1))
```

ensure that only one block will be preallocated.

Figure 6-26

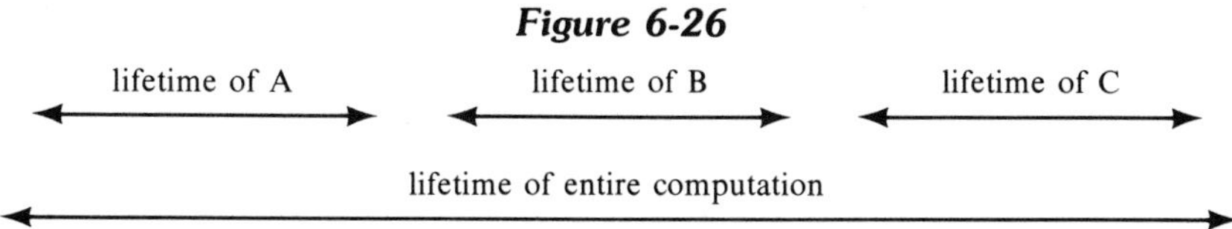

If a Fortran block is used to store data first of one type and then another, it is necessary to refer to this block by different names. For instance, the additional type declarations

```
INTEGER A
REAL    B
LOGICAL C
```

allow the same storage space to hold INTEGER, REAL, and LOGICAL data successively. Thus, during the lifetime of A, when A (5) has an integer value, the statement

```
IF (6 .LE. A(5)) GOTO 100
```

will give a meaningful comparison of 6 with the integer valued represented by A_5. And, during the lifetime of B, if B(5) and B(6) have previously been assigned values of type REAL, the statement

```
IF (SQRT (B(5)) .LE. SQRT (B(6))) GOTO 200
```

will provide meaningful calls on the library SQRT function, which accepts only type REAL arguments. Appropriate use of the EQUIVALENCE declaration allows reuse of the same storage by local variables or shared COMMON variables of different data types. In practice, however, the explicit programming of such dynamic multiple use of storage can greatly increase the complexity of Fortran programs and complicate the task of verifying their correctness.

2. Explicit versus Implicit Declarations

In Fortran, type declarations are not necessary if the default rules for variable types are followed. Thus, for example, I and J may be used as integer variables without being declared as such. In this chapter, we have encouraged the use of type declarations for *all* variables, functions, and parameters in Fortran, whereas explicit declarations are required in Algol. Explicit declarations make a program more readable by providing some documentation (essentially a legend) as part of the program itself. Furthermore, use of default types in Fortran tends to conflict with the selection of clear and "revealing" names for variables and functions. Some programmers disagree with this viewpoint and argue that implicit (default) declarations make programming less tedious and the resulting programs shorter.

It is interesting that with respect to the declaration of global variables, the Fortran and Algol positions are reversed. In Fortran, a variable must be explicitly declared to be global, whereas in Algol an outer block variable is global to an inner block unless there is a declaration to the contrary.

3. Separate Compilability of Procedures

An ALGOL program is a single block that, in principle, must be compiled (translated into machine language) as a unit. If, for example, a procedure is replaced with a "new improved model," then the replacement must take place in every program that includes the procedure, and *every* program must be recompiled.

In Fortran, the situation is very different. Since program units (the top level and procedures) are *not* nested, each program unit may be compiled *separately.* If a procedure is rewritten, only that procedure needs to be recompiled. Of course, each program using the procedure must then be *relinked* to the procedure, but this usually involves less computer work than a complete recompilation. Thus we see that deciding to make a computer language block structured, like most design decisions, may involve significant tradeoffs.

In practice, many professional programmers choose Fortran over Algol because of the critical importance of the separate compilability feature, especially for the construction of very large programs involving hundreds, or even thousands, of subprograms and requiring teams of programmers. Only a few commercial Algol systems offer separate compilability, and so this feature, although possible to engineer even in Algol, is not widely available. Ironically, a very good Algol compiler can entirely recompile a large Algol program in less time than it takes to relink the compiled parts of an equivalent Fortran program using a poorly implemented linking program. (The opposite, of course, is also true.)

4. Input/Output

Fortran was one of the first languages to provide formatted input and output. The Fortran system of field descriptors, etc., described in Section 6-8 is powerful enough to handle almost any eventuality, is easy to learn and use, and is standard across all implementations of the language (at least down to certain machine-dependent details).

The designers of ALGOL, on the other hand, did not provide *any* details on input/output. They felt that input/output techniques invariably *are* machine dependent, and that their inclusion would counteract the goal of machine-*independent* language definition. The unfortunate result is that each implementation of ALGOL has its own conventions for input/output, making it more rather than less difficult to transport programs from one machine to another. Proposals for standardization have been made [Knuth *et al.* (1964)] but the issue is far from settled. The most successful ALGOL input/output systems today are probably those patterned after Fortran. The more recent descendent of ALGOL 60, known as ALGOL 68 [see Tanenbaum (1976)] does indeed define input/output operations in detail, including a formatting feature.

5. Compound and Conditional Statements

Figure 6-27 shows a flowchart fragment and its translation into Fortran and ALGOL. 1966 Fortran requires statement numbers and GOTOs because it lacks (1) compound statements and (2) the if–then–else form of conditional statement. Most programmers feel that these are among the most useful features in

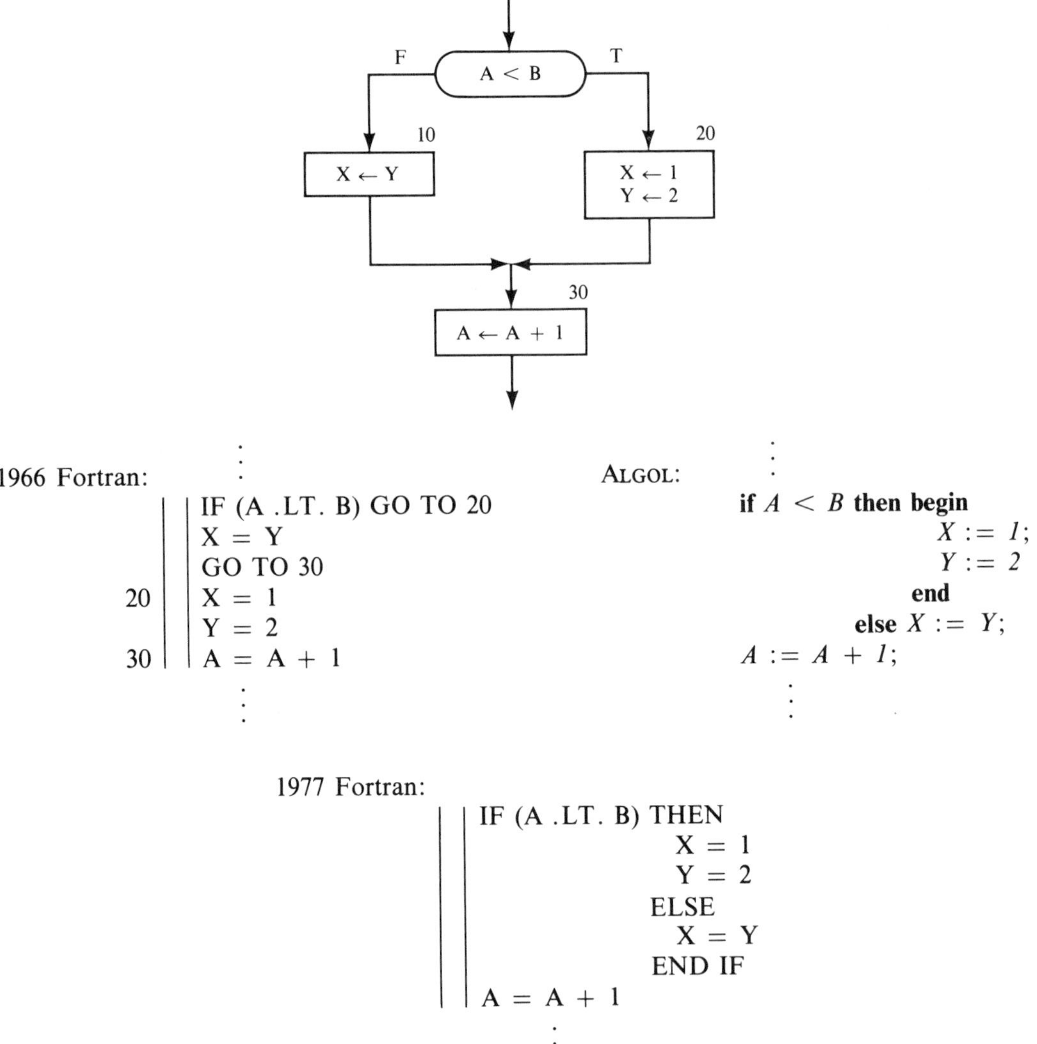

***Figure 6-27.* Conditional statements in Fortran and ALGOL.**

ALGOL, and that they are particularly helpful in maintaining good structure. The 1977 standard removes this "deficiency" from Fortran, but implementations of the new standard may not be available everywhere.

Must we wait for new implementations before we can take advantage of the new features of Fortran? An interesting approach is the following. We first design a "super-Fortran" language that includes compound statements, an if–then–else statement, etc. Then we develop a *preprocessor* program that inputs super-Fortran programs and outputs Fortran programs, achieving the same effect but using only 1966 standard Fortran statements. A flowchart containing such steps as in Figure 6-27 could then be coded in super-Fortran and the resulting program presented to the preprocessor. The output would be ordinary Fortran that could then be compiled and executed. We consider the design of a Fortran preprocessor in our chapter on Snobol (see Exercises 8-11).

6. Algebraic Nature of the Languages

Both ALGOL and Fortran are "algebraic" languages: they are well suited to computations that can be described by algebraic formulas (for example, a formula for computing the product of two matrices, $A_{i,k} = \Sigma_{j=1}^{n} (B_{i,j} \times C_{j,k})$). *Neither* language is particularly good for the processing of nonnumeric, *symbolic* data. For example, implementation of the symbolic differentiation algorithm discussed in Chapter 3 would be difficult in either language. This comment serves as a point of departure for the next two chapters, where we discuss languages whose primary data types *are* nonnumeric and which are especially designed to process symbol strings such as formulas and lines of texts.

Exercises 6-9

Compare Algol and Fortran with regard to the following:
- (a) Parameter treatment
- (b) Implementation of globals
- (c) Recursion
- (d) Storage allocation

6-10 REFERENCES AND SUGGESTIONS FOR FURTHER READING

There is an abundant supply of textbooks, reference manuals, and periodicals on Fortran, its dialects, its evolution to standard form, and its broad range of application. Chapter 10 of Pratt (1975) provides a useful supplement and review of Fortran. The text by Organick and Meissner (1974) describes the full language [see also ANSI (1966), ACM (1964), and ACM (1971) as well as various important Fortran dialects]. Many universities and colleges prefer the dialects WATFOR and WATFIV [Cress *et al.* (1970)] because they require no format statements and because fast compilers have been developed for these dialects. Computer manufacturers offer reference manuals describing the dialects supported on their systems. When the 1977 Standard Fortran, known as ANS FORTRAN, is adopted by the American National Standards Institute, another new set of books and reports will no doubt follow. The first, but preliminary, description of ANS FORTRAN is given in SIGPLAN (1976). A new periodical, FOR-WORD, a Fortran Development Newsletter (1975–), has chronicled the development of the new standard. Finally, Brainerd *et al.* give a comprehensive review critically comparing the features of the 1977 and 1976 Standard Fortrans.

The early development of Fortran is well documented in Sammet (1969). Rosen (1967) reproduces the earliest full report on Fortran, co-authored by J. W. Backus, who led the design team that produced the first Fortran system.

7 LISP

7-1 INTRODUCTION

Lisp was invented in the late 1950s by Professor John McCarthy, then at MIT and now at Stanford University. Unlike Algol and Fortran, which are designed almost exclusively for the manipulation of numeric values, Lisp is used to process nonnumeric, *symbolic* data. Emphasis in Lisp is on the application of functions to arguments rather than on the assignment of values to variables. Hence, Lisp programs are in essence just expressions which are to be evaluated, based on previously defined functions. The unique syntax and semantics of Lisp, and the fact that it may be used *interactively*, provide a contrast to the algebraic languages we have seen so far.

What are symbolic data? There are endless possibilities. We might, for example, wish to manipulate a set of "facts" such as

Canada is north of Mexico.
Mexico is north of Guatemala.

with a program that could "deduce" from them that Canada is north of Guatemala (since "north of" is a transitive relation). Such a program could form the basis for a *question-answering* system.

As another example, consider the manipulation of algebraic formulas, such as $x^2 + 2xy + y^2$. In Algol or Fortran, this formula might appear on the right of an assignment operator, indicating a calculation to be performed using the values of x and y. In Lisp, the formula might be an item of *data*, to be manipulated by a program that could determine that it is equivalent to $(x + y)(x + y)$ and to $(x + y)^2$.

Given that Lisp can process symbolic data, we would expect it to be used for algorithms very different from those commonly programmed in Algol and Fortran, and this is indeed the case. Lisp and its various dialects are the primary languages in at least two areas of computer science: *symbolic computation*, which involves algorithms such as the one for differentiation discussed in Chapter 3, and *artificial intelligence*, which is concerned with programs to perform tasks we usually say require intelligence. With such areas of investigation in mind, we begin our study of the language that hastened their development.

7-2 DATA OBJECTS IN LISP

Lisp data are called S-expressions (*s*ymbolic expressions). The simplest S-expression is an *atomic symbol* or *atom,* which may be defined syntactically as follows:

⟨atomic symbol⟩ ::= ⟨literal atom⟩|⟨numeric atom⟩

⟨literal atom⟩ ::= ⟨letter⟩|⟨letter⟩⟨atom part⟩

⟨atom part⟩ ::= ⟨empty⟩|⟨letter⟩⟨atom part⟩|⟨digit⟩⟨atom part⟩

⟨letter⟩ ::= A|B|C|D|. . .|Z

⟨digit⟩ ::= 0|1|2|. . .|9

Thus the following are examples of atomic symbols (we shall show the forms for numeric atoms in a later section):

X

ABC23

LONGATOMNAME

We can now give a complete definition for any data object in Lisp:

⟨S-expression⟩ ::= ⟨atomic symbol⟩|(⟨S-expression⟩.⟨S-expression⟩)

The recursive part of this rule tells us that S-expressions can be built out of other S-expressions by using enclosing parentheses and a separating dot (period).* Here are some examples of "dotted pairs:"

(A . B)

((A . B) . C)

(A . (B . C))

((A . B) . (B . C))

(A . (X . (R . (S . H))))

((((K . L) . C) . W) . V)

((((R . S) . V) . (W . (L . M))) . Z)

(ONE . (TWO . THREE))

((ME . YOU) . (YOU . ME))

S-expressions are the *only* data type in Lisp. A question that comes naturally to mind is the following: If Lisp is intended to be a general purpose symbol manipulation language, is one data type sufficient to represent all possible symbolic data structures? The answer is yes. In Lisp what is provided is a basic building block, the atomic symbol, and a simple construction, the dotted pair, and by virtue of their simplicity these are sufficient to build essentially any desired structure. We illustrate this idea by considering two important data structures:

*Spaces before and after the dot improve readability but are not required unless the dotted pair contains a number (see Section 7-10). Spaces before and after left and right parentheses are also optional.

1. Lists

A convenient arrangement of data in many applications is an ordered list. For example, simple algebraic expressions can be represented by lists of atoms such as

(PLUS X Y)
(TIMES B Z)

Here we have used a "prefix" notation that places operators ahead of their operands.

Allowing the elements of lists also to be lists provides the opportunity for more complicated structures. An algebraic expression such as $X^2 + 2XY + Y^2$ can be represented by the list structure

(PLUS (EXP X 2)(TIMES 2 X Y)(EXP Y 2)),

or, if we wish to restrict ourselves to only binary operators, the representation becomes

(PLUS (EXP X 2)(PLUS (TIMES 2 (TIMES X Y))(EXP Y 2)))

To represent lists in Lisp, we need only establish a convention for mapping them into S-expressions. Lists are in fact so common that such a convention already exists in the language:

1. The S-expression for a list of one element is that element dotted with the atom NIL. Thus the S-expression for the list (A) is (A . NIL).
2. The S-expression for a list of two elements such as (A B) is the first element dotted with the S-expression for the list (B). In general, the S-expression for a list of n elements (m_1 m_2 . . . m_n) is m_1 dotted with the S-expression for the list (m_2 . . . m_n). (Note that rule (1) is an "escape hatch" for the recursion of rule (2)). The atom NIL plays a special role as "list terminator," as seen in the examples in Figure 7-1.
3. An element of a list can be a list. Thus the list of the two elements (A) and (C D), which we would write as ((A) (C D)), corresponds to the S-expression ((A . NIL) . ((C . (D . NIL)) . NIL)).
4. The *empty list* (the list of no elements, written as ( ) in list notation) corresponds to the S-expression NIL. This second special role for the atom NIL is derivable from the first. Consider the action necessary to reduce a list of two elements to a list of one element:

   (A . (B . NIL)) $\Rightarrow$ (B . NIL).

   Applying the same kind of "stripping away" to a list of *one* element should produce a list of *no* elements:

   (B . NIL) $\Rightarrow$ NIL.

5. While these rules insure that there is an S-expression corresponding to every list, the reverse is not true. For example, the S-expression (A . B)

List	S-expression
(A B)	(A.(B.NIL))
(D K H)	(D.(K.(H.NIL)))
(X Y Z W)	(X.(Y.(Z.(W.NIL))))

***Figure 7-1.* Correspondence between list and dotted pair notation.**

does not correspond to a list since the terminator NIL does not appear. The S-expression (A . (NIL . B)) also does not correspond to a list, due to the placement of the B. (An interesting question is: How can we characterize those S-expressions that *do* correspond to lists? We shall provide the answer shortly.) Lisp will accept lists as input and produce the corresponding S-expressions internally. When an S-expression is output, it is printed as a list, if possible, and in dotted form if not.

2. Binary Trees

We have seen enough examples of trees in Chapters 2 and 3 to be convinced of their importance. There is a simple correspondance between S-expressions and *binary* trees, as shown in Figure 7-2.

The last two examples involve S-expressions that correspond to the *lists* (R V Z B) and ((A)(C D)). A little thought leads us to the following answer to the question asked earlier:

> An S-expression corresponds to a *list* if and only if the binary tree for the S-expression has NIL for every *terminal* right subtree.

For example, the S-expression for

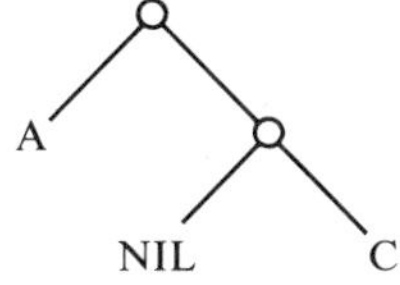

is *not* a list since the atom C is a terminal node that is a right subtree. The rule could, of course, be rephrased to refer to atomic right members of dotted pairs: (A.(NIL.C)) is not a list since there is a dotted pair whose right part is an atom other than NIL.

Exercises 7-2

1 Give S-expressions in dotted pair form for the following Lisp lists:
   a. (A (B))
   b. (X Y Z (A B) W)
   c. (((X)))

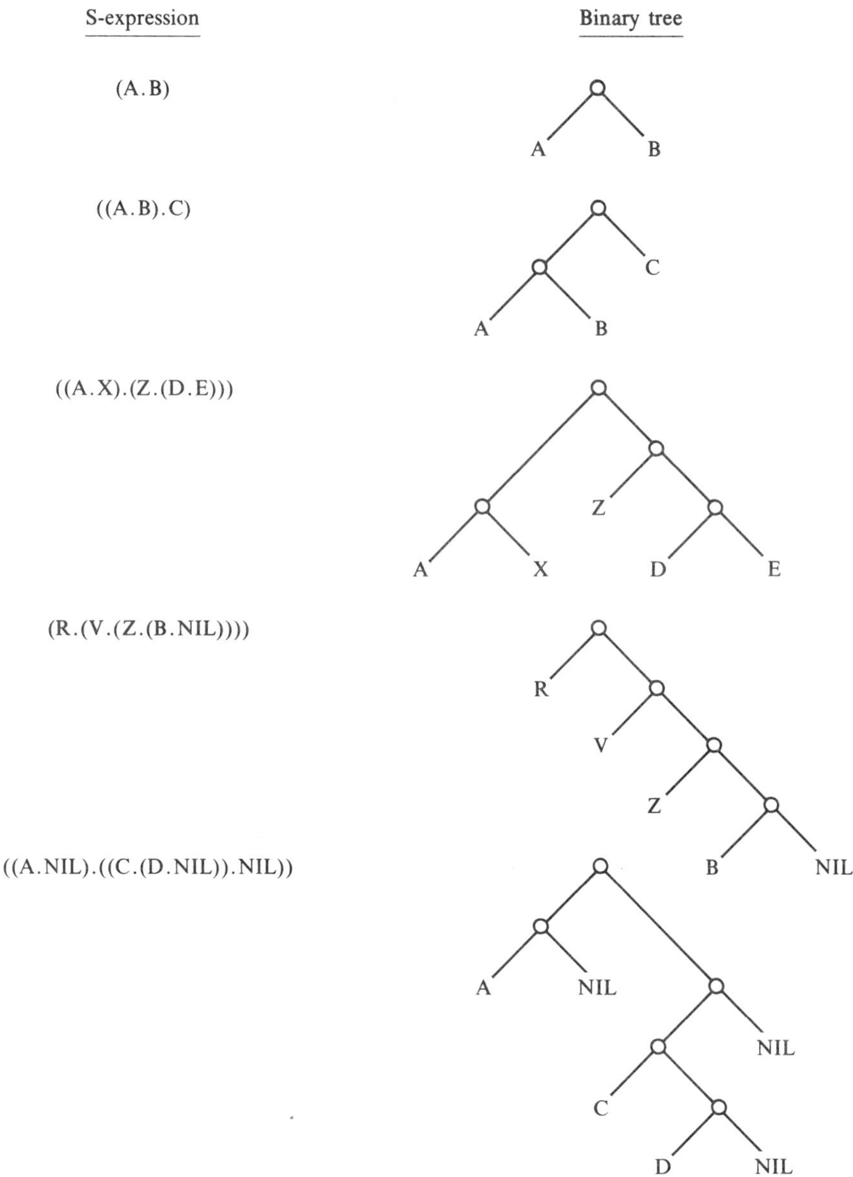

Figure 7-2. **Correspondence between S-expressions and binary trees.**

2 Draw binary trees for the following S-expressions:

a. (A.(B.(C.NIL)))
b. (A.((B.C).NIL))
c. ((A B) C)
d. (A B (C D))
e. ((A) (B) (C))
f. ((B.(C.NIL)).(A.(B.NIL)))
g. ((((A B))))
h. (((A) B) (C) D)

3 For each S-expression below, give the corresponding *list* or explain why no list can be given.

a. ((A.NIL).NIL)
b. ((A.(B.C)).NIL)
c. (((A.(B.NIL)).NIL).(G.NIL))
d. (A.(NIL.((C.NIL).D)))
e. (NIL.NIL)

7-3 STORAGE STRUCTURES FOR S-EXPRESSIONS

In order to understand Lisp, it is useful to examine the way S-expressions (and thus their list and tree equivalents) are stored in typical Lisp systems. We discuss these storage structures in the context of contour diagrams.

1. Atoms

The first cell in Top[1] points to a table of atoms, as shown in Figure 7-3. The atom table contains the actual character strings that make up the names of all the literal atoms currently in use. Each literal atom appears in the table *only once.* The atom table also contains numeric atoms, and in most Lisp systems it is possible for the same numeric atom to appear more than once in the table.

2. S-expressions

In almost all Lisp systems, nonatomic S-expressions are stored in two-compartment cells located in a special storage area we call the HEAP. Figure 7-4 illustrates the basic principle of storage in Lisp: a dotted pair is represented as a two-compartment storage cell whose left and right parts hold pointers to the left and right parts of the dotted pair. Thus a dotted pair of atoms is stored by placing pointers to the appropriate atom table entries in a two-compartment HEAP cell.

Suppose the right part of the dotted pair we wish to store is not an atom, as in (A.(B.C)). Our storage principle tells us we need a cell with a pointer to A in its left compartment and a pointer to (B.C) in its right compartment. This presents no difficulty if we simply store (B.C) in another cell in the HEAP, as shown in Figure 7-5. Figure 7-6 shows the storage structure for the list (X Y Z W). For S-expressions that are lists, we notice that the right part of a cell links an element of the list to the *next* element (if there is one). For this reason such a storage structure is often called a *linked list.*

***Figure 7-3.* The atom table.**

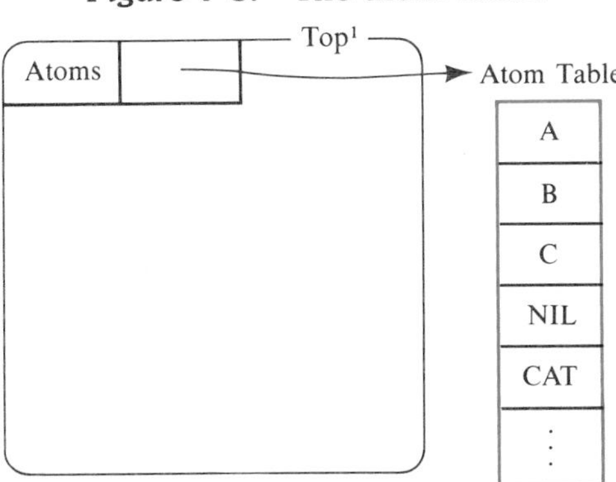

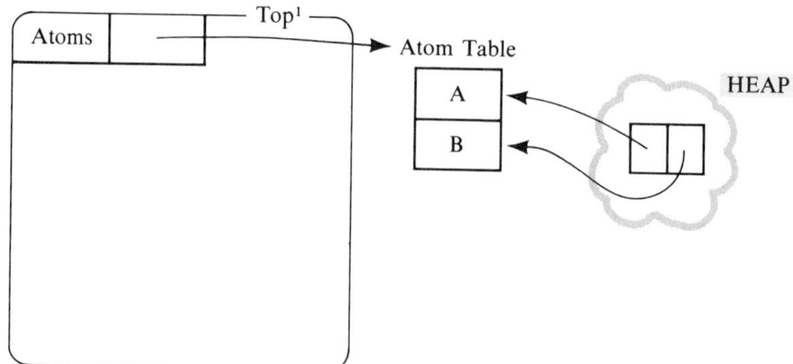

Figure 7-4. **HEAP containing a storage cell for (A.B).**

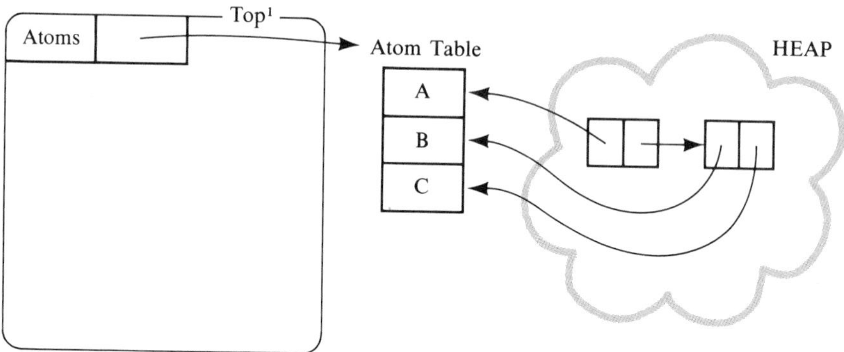

Figure 7-5. **Storage structure for (A.(B.C)).**

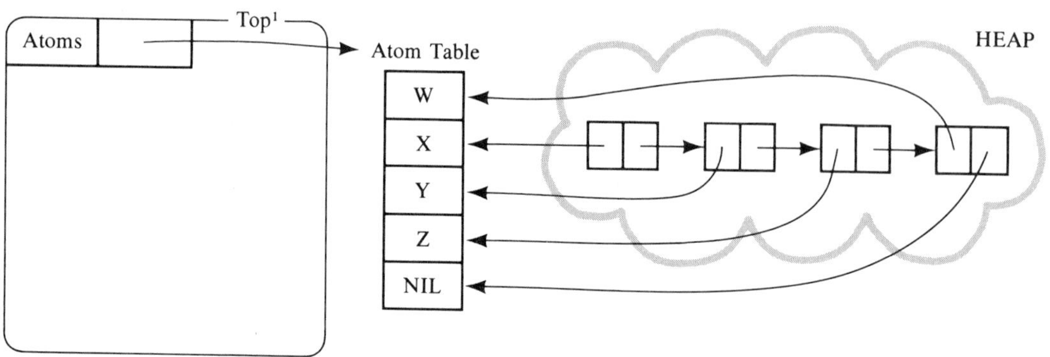

Figure 7-6. **Storage structure for (X Y Z W).**

Figure 7-7a shows a treelike arrangement of HEAP cells, suggesting the correspondence between S-expressions and binary trees. The HEAP cells are somewhat cumbersome even though they may reflect Lisp storage accurately. In Figure 7-7b we show a streamlined version of the HEAP.

Figure 7-8 uses the streamlined HEAP for an S-expression that is a list. Notice that in the case illustrated there is more than one pointer to some atoms, and recall the special role of NIL as list terminator.

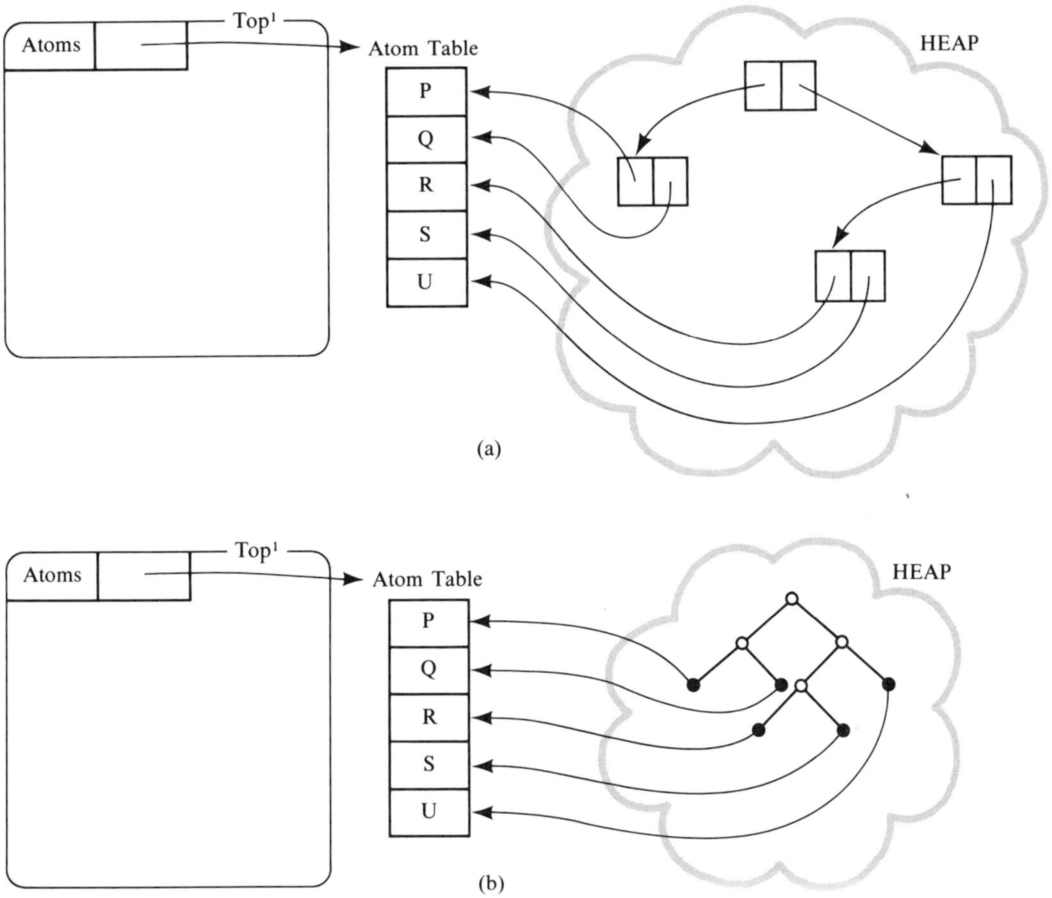

Atoms
Top¹
Atom Table
P
Q
R
S
U
HEAP
(a)
Atoms
Top¹
Atom Table
P
Q
R
S
U
HEAP
(b)

Figure 7-7. **Storage structure for ((P.Q).((R.S).U)). (a) Storage structure using two-compartment HEAP cells. (b) Streamlined version of the HEAP.**

Atoms
Top¹
Atom Table
A
B
NIL
X
Y
HEAP

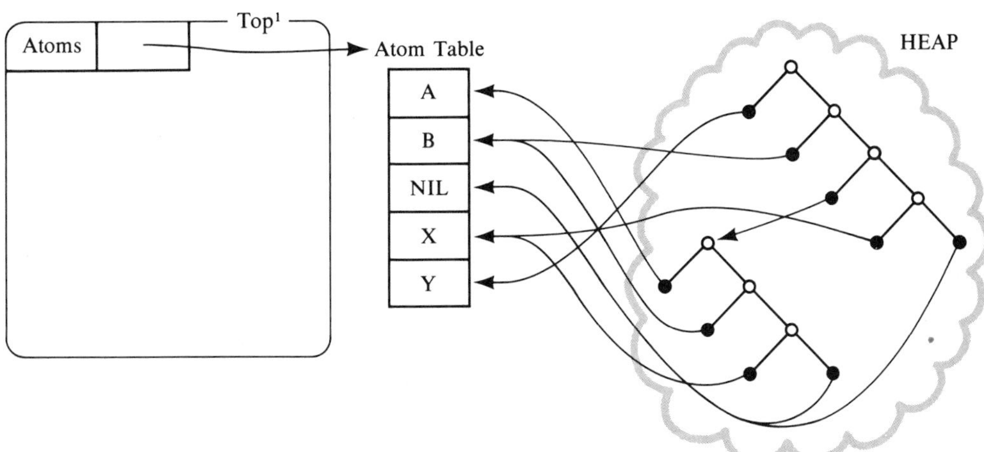

Figure 7-8. **Storage structure for (Y B (A B X) X).**

3. Variables

In the next section, we begin our discussion of the basic operations in Lisp. To do so, we must add variables to our diagrams. The values of variables are, of course, S-expressions—either atoms or dotted pairs. Figure 7-9 shows that in the value portion of the cell for a variable we store a *pointer* to the S-expression that is its value. The values of the variables shown in Figure 7-9 are as follows:

C = B	K = (A.X)
Y = (A.X)	R = (X)
Z = (B X)	

We postpone until a later section deciding how to fill in the type compartment of the cell for a variable.

Notice that it is possible for variables to *share* all or part of structures in the HEAP. Variables Y and K share the cells for (A.X), and variables Z and R share cells for (X).

As a matter of terminology, we must decide whether to say that the value of a variable such as Y in Figure 7-9 *is* (A.X) or *is a pointer to* (A.X). We shall choose the simpler approach and say that the value of Y is (A.X).

4. Storage Management

An important feature of Lisp is that the programmer need not concern himself with the allocation of storage for S-expressions. HEAP cells are provided when needed during the execution of a Lisp program. Furthermore, should the supply of cells be exhausted, all cells no longer needed by the program are reclaimed through a process known as *garbage collection.** The reclaimed cells may then be reused in new data structures.

Figure 7-9. Variables and their values.

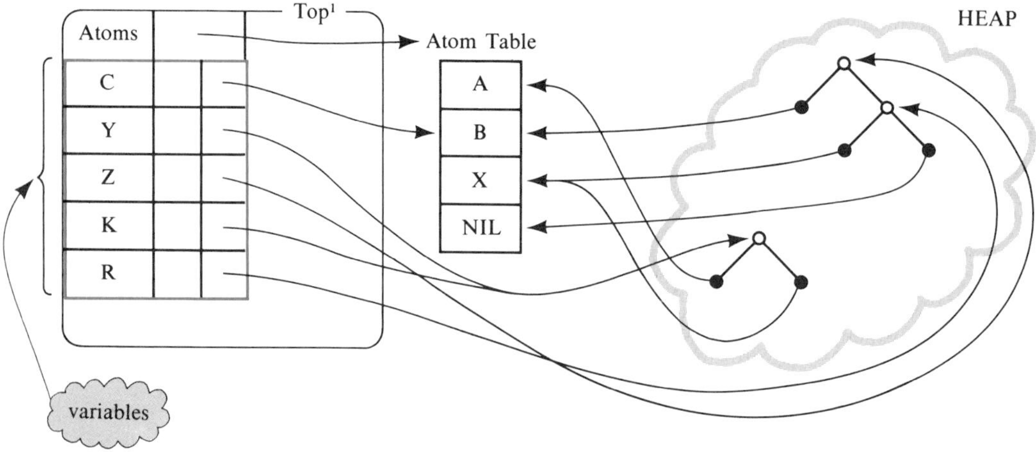

*An excellent introduction to garbage collection techniques is given in Chapter 7 of Pratt (1975).

7-4 THE FIVE BASIC LISP FUNCTIONS

Every computer language provides a set of basic or "primitive" operations that can be applied to data objects. For example, in Fortran the primitive operations denoted by +, −, *, etc., can be applied to data objects (numeric values) to produce new data objects, and the operations denoted by .EQ., .LT., .LE., etc., can be used to compare data objects. In terms of our computer model, these operations are basic in the sense that the MC can execute them directly—they do not have to be defined by the programmer, and they are used by the programmer in the definition of higher level procedures.

In Lisp there are five basic functions of S-expressions:

1. CONS

If X and Y are variables, then CONS (X, Y) *cons*tructs a dotted pair whose left part is the value of X and whose right part is the value of Y. For example, if the value of X is the atom A and the value of Y is the atom B, then CONS (X, Y) = (A . B). The storage structure resulting from this CONS operation is shown in Figure 7-10. To execute CONS (X, Y) the MC (1) obtains a new HEAP cell, (2) copies the values of its first and second arguments into the left and right compartments of the HEAP cell, respectively, and (3) returns a pointer to the HEAP cell as the value of the CONS operation.

Figure 7-10. **The basic function CONS.**

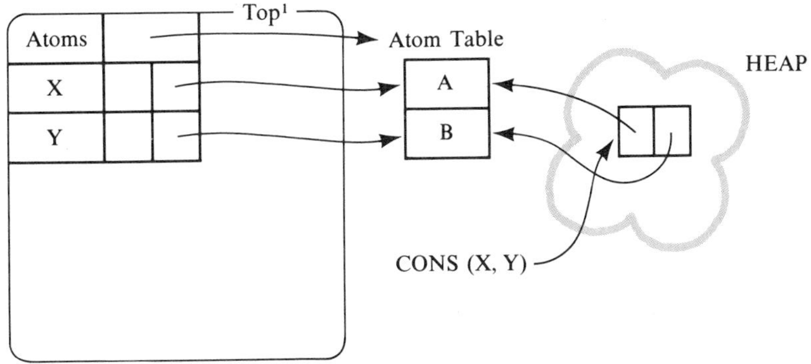

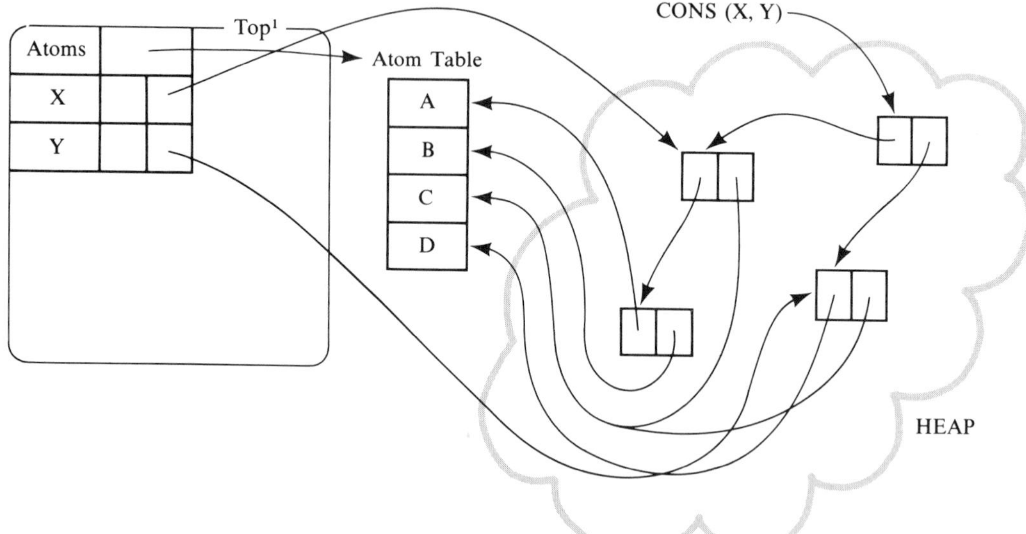

Figure 7-11. **CONS applied to nonatomic S-expressions.**

In the example of Figure 7-10, the values of X and Y are atoms. The MC takes exactly the same action if the values of X and Y are more complicated S-expressions, such as ((A.B).C) and (D.C), as shown in Figures 7-11 and 7-12.

Note that CONS (X, Y), as shown in these examples, means CONS the *values* of the variables X and Y. This is, of course, directly analogous to Algol and Fortran, where X + Y means add the *values* of X and Y.

Figure 7-12. **Same situation as Figure 7-11, using the tree representation of HEAP storage.**

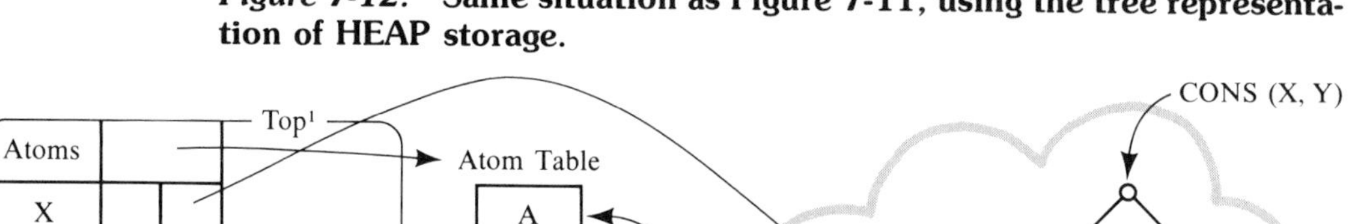

2. CAR

If the value of X is a dotted pair, then the value of CAR (X) is the *left* part of the dotted pair. For example, if X = (A.B), then CAR (X) = A; if X = ((A.B).C), then CAR (X) = (A.B). The expression CAR (X) is *undefined* if the value of X is an atom.

In terms of storage structures, CAR (X) returns a copy of the pointer in the left compartment of the structure pointed to by X, that is, the left subtree of X. An example is shown in Figure 7-13.

3. CDR

If the value of the variable X is a dotted pair, then the value of CDR (X) is the *right* part of the dotted pair. For example, if X = (A.B), then CDR (X) = B; if X = (A.(B.C)), then CDR (X) = (B.C). Thus, as shown in Figure 7-14, CDR (X) returns the right subtree of the structure that is the value of X. The expression CDR (X) is undefined if the value of X is an atom.*

It is common in Lisp to chain together CAR and CDR operations. For example, if X = ((A.NIL) . (B.(C.(D.NIL)))), then

CAR(CDR(X)) = B   [CAR is applied to the value of CDR(X)]
CDR(CAR(X)) = NIL
CAR(CDR(CDR(CDR(X)))) = D

To simplify the writing of such expressions, the following notation is allowed: a chain of CARs and CDRs may be abbreviated by writing a function name con-

***Figure 7-13.* The basic function CAR.**

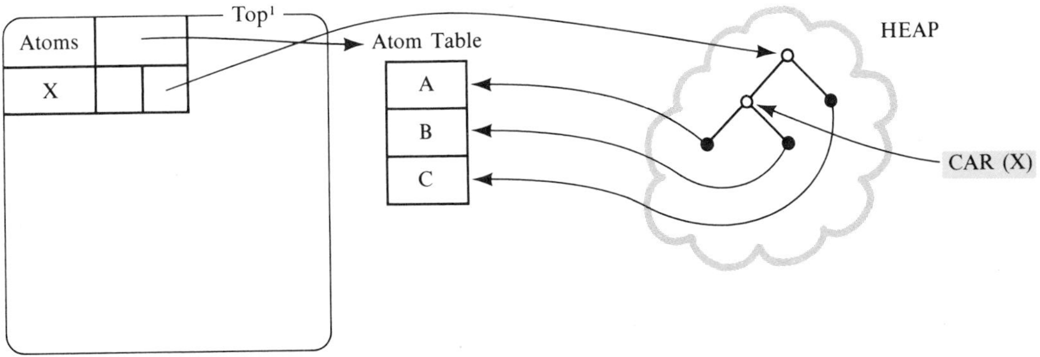

*The names CAR and CDR were originally abbreviations for "contents of the address register" and "contents of the decrement register," terms relevant to the machine on which Lisp was first implemented. CDR is pronounced 'kŭd-ər. In many programming systems derived from the original Lisp system, the keywords CAR and CDR have been replaced by HEAD and TAIL (or FIRST and REST), which reveal more clearly the purpose of these functions.

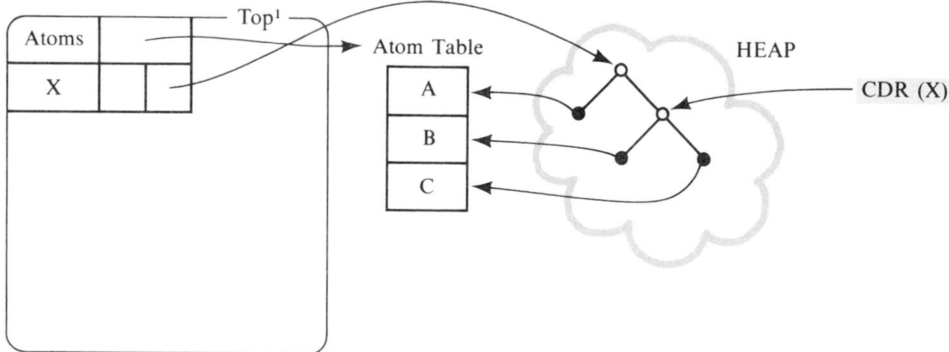

Figure 7-14. **The basic function CDR.**

sisting of C, followed by A or D for each CAR or CDR in the chain, followed by R. Thus

CADR(X)	is the same as	CAR(CDR(X))
CDAR(X)	is the same as	CDR(CAR(X))
CADDDR(X)	is the same as	CAR(CDR(CDR(CDR(X))))

The order of application of the CARs and CDRs is obtained by reading the As and Ds from *right* to *left;* CADR (X) means apply CDR to X, then apply CAR to CDR(X).

Special notice should be taken of the effect of applying CAR and CDR to S-expressions that are lists. Figure 7-15 shows the variable X having as its value the list (A B C D). We observe that

CAR(X) = A
CDR(X) = (B C D).

Thus CAR and CDR are analogous to the functions *first* and *rest* used in Section 3-2. Furthermore, the following expressions "pick out" the individual items of the list:

CAR(X) = A
CADR(X) = B
CADDR(X) = C
CADDDR(X) = D

In general, we may obtain the nth item on a list (if it has that many) by writing one A and (n − 1) Ds in the function name. Care must be exercised; note that in the above case

CDDDDR(X) = NIL

and CADDDDR(X) is undefined (it is not possible to apply CAR to NIL).

The two remaining basic functions belong to the class of functions known as *predicates.* A predicate is a function whose value is either true or false. In Lisp, true is represented by the atom T, and false by the atom NIL (another special use for NIL).

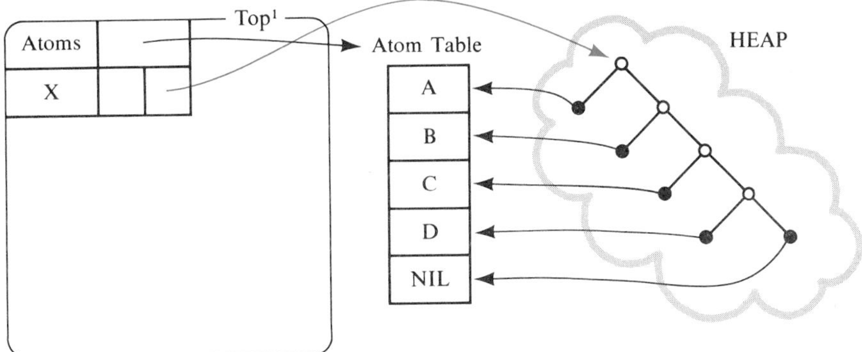

Figure 7-15. **Storage for a variable with a list value.**

4. ATOM

ATOM (X) returns T if the value of the variable X is an atom and returns NIL otherwise.

5. EQ

The predicate EQ performs an equality test. In explaining the meaning of EQ(X, Y), we must recall that if X and Y are variables, the value compartment of the cell for X (or Y) holds a pointer to a cell in either the atom table or the HEAP. EQ (X, Y) returns T if these pointers are the *same* (that is, point to the same cell), and NIL if they are different.* Note the following implications of this definition:

1. If the values of both X and Y are literal atoms, then EQ (X, Y) is T if they are the same atom and NIL otherwise, since each literal atom appears in the atom table only once. Because numeric atoms *may* appear more than once, EQ cannot be used to test numeric atoms for equality.
2. If the value of X is an atom but the value of Y is not (or vice versa), then EQ (X, Y) is NIL, since one pointer is to a cell of the atom table and the other is to a cell in the HEAP.
3. If neither X nor Y has an atom as its value, then EQ (X, Y) returns T only if the values of X and Y are pointers to the same cell of the HEAP, that is, if X and Y are the *same copy* of the same S-expression. Consider the situation shown in Figure 7-16. Here we have a case where each of X, Y, and Z has the value (A.B), but EQ (X, Y) = T and EQ (X, Z) = NIL.

*The original documentation for Lisp defined EQ in a more restricted way, stating that the result is undefined unless both arguments are atoms. The less restricted definition given above, however, has been adopted in virtually all implementations of the language. See McCarthy *et al.* (1962).

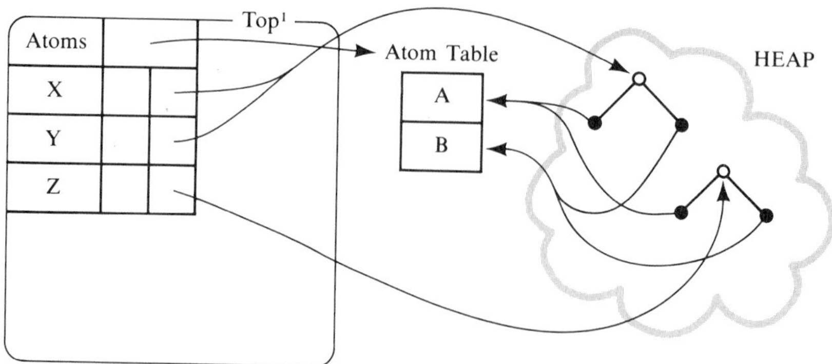

Figure 7-16

Multiple occurrences of the same S-expression in the HEAP are perfectly allowable and even quite common in Lisp. For this reason, EQ is normally used only when it is certain that the value of at least one of the arguments is an atom. In a later section we discuss an equality test that would return T for X and Z (as well as X and Y) in Figure 7-16.

Exercises 7-4, Set A

1 Convert the following trees to Lisp S-expressions. Where possible use list notation in preference to dotted pair notation but do not mix both in one expression. (Ignore asterisks for now.)

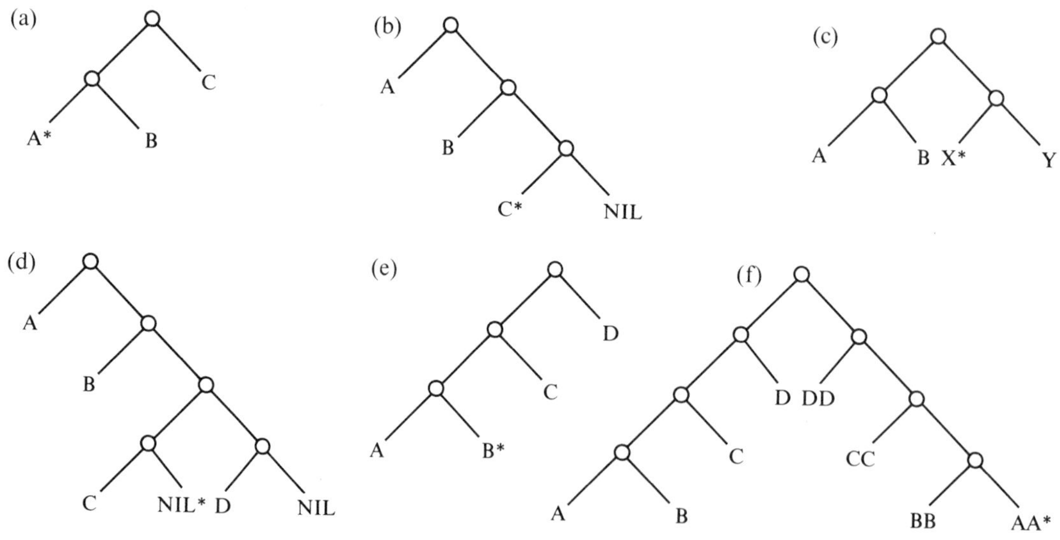

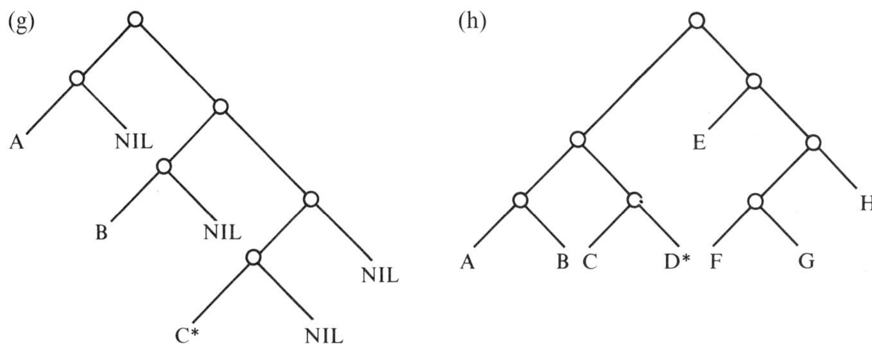

2 For each tree in exercise 1, write an expression consisting of CARs and CDRs that will return a pointer to the node marked by an asterisk. Assume that the tree shown is the value of the variable Z. For example, for the tree

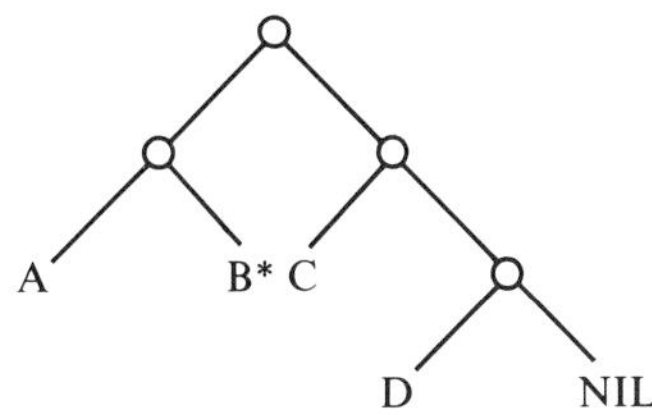

the desired expression would be CDR (CAR (Z)), or CDAR (Z).

Exercises 7-4, Set B

1 What is the effect of CONS (X, Y) when the value of Y is a *list?* Show some examples and provide a general answer. Does your answer hold when Y is the empty list?

2 Consider the storage structures shown in Figure 7-17.

(a) Write S-expressions for the values of X, Y, and Z.

(b) Give the value of each of the following expressions:

(1) CADR (X)	(5) EQ (CADR (Y), CADR (Z))
(2) CDDR (Z)	(6) EQ (CADDDR (X), CAR (Z))
(3) CAR (Y)	(7) EQ (CADR (X), Y)
(4) ATOM (CADDR (X))	(8) EQ (Y, Z)

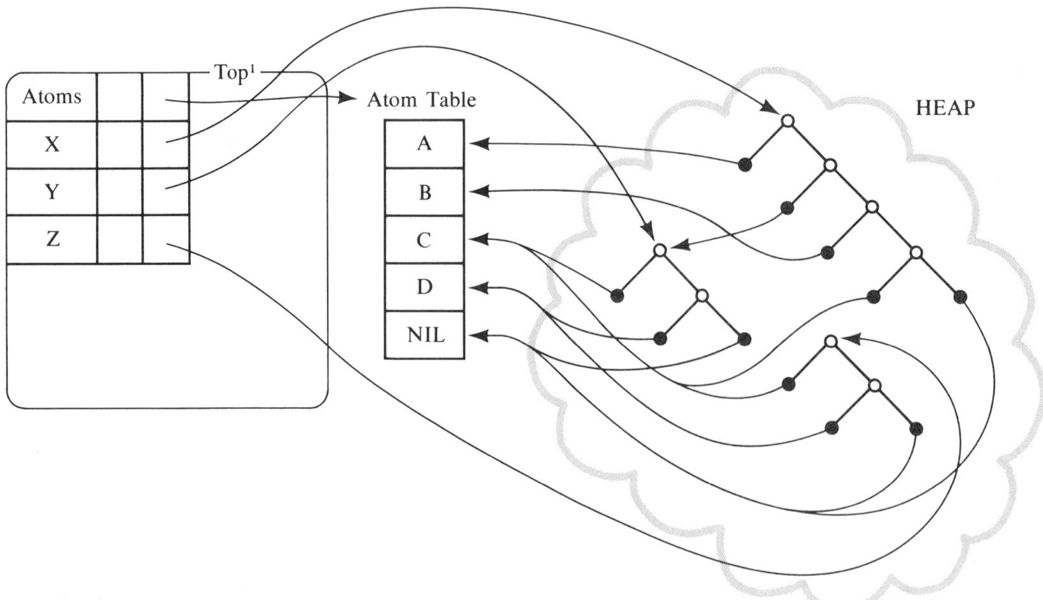

Figure 7-17

7-5 AVOIDING EVALUATION OF ARGUMENTS: THE USE OF THE QUOTE

In all of the examples in Section 7-4, the function arguments are either variables or expressions. The guiding principle in determining the value of a function applied to arguments is: First *evaluate* the arguments, and then apply the function to those values.

Suppose, however, that we want to devise a CONS expression to produce, say, (C.D). The principle just stated tells us that CONS (C, D) will not produce (C.D) because C and D will be treated as variables and their values will be CONSed. Moreover, if C and D have no values, CONS (C, D) will be undefined. To get the desired result in Lisp, we quote the arguments of CONS, which *prevents* the evaluation that would otherwise take place. Quoting is indicated by placing a single quote mark (apostrophe) in front of the argument. This causes the item quoted, instead of its value, to be used by the function. Thus, if we write CONS ('C, 'D), then it is the atoms C and D that are CONSed, producing the desired result (C.D) as shown in Figure 7-18.

Notice in this figure that the value of CONS (C, 'D) would be ((A.B).D), and the value of CONS ('C, D) would be undefined since D does not appear among the variables of Top^1. Notice also that C appears both as a variable and in the atom table. Although we have omitted this detail from earlier figures, there is indeed an atom table entry for each variable, since variable names are

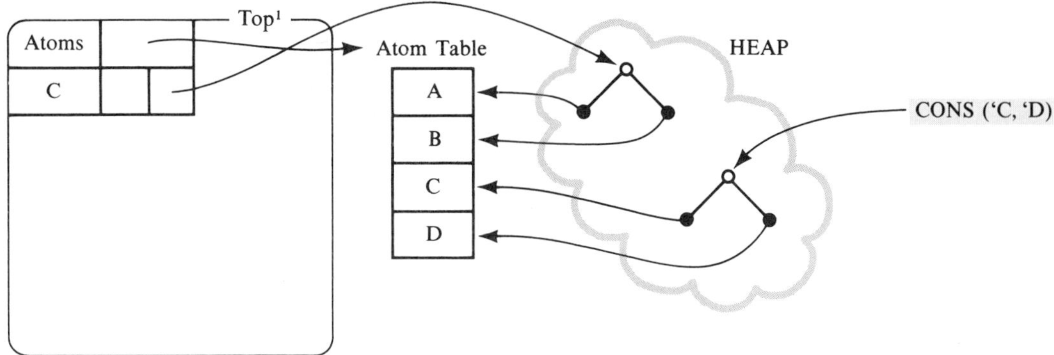

Figure 7-18. **CONS applied to quoted atoms.**

also atomic symbols. To keep our diagrams simple, we show variable names in the atom table only if they are referred to, directly or indirectly, from other components of the snapshot.

The final topic in our discussion of the quoting of atoms is a special property of the atoms T and NIL. Each of these atoms is always present as a *variable* in Top¹, and each has as its value a pointer to its own entry in the atom table, as shown in Figure 7-19.

Thus we see that the values of the *variables* NIL and T are the *atoms* NIL and T, respectively. This arrangement makes it unnecessary to quote NIL and T in expressions such as EQ (X, NIL), which produces the same result as EQ (X, 'NIL). To avoid clutter in our diagrams, we do not show T and NIL as variables. We simply consider them to be a special case, that is, two atoms that *never* need to be quoted.

It is possible to quote not only atoms, but any S-expression. Suppose that X has the value ((B) (C)), and we wish to produce the value ((A) (B) (C)). The

Figure 7-19. **Values of NIL and T.**

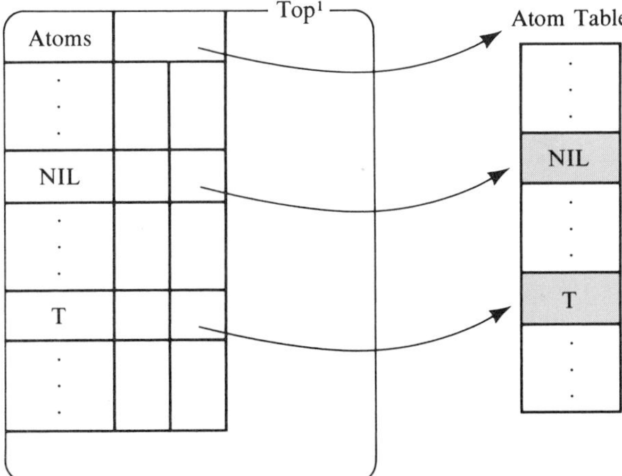

expression CONS ((A), X) would not work, since the first argument of CONS is neither a variable nor a function invocation (and thus cannot be evaluated). We do get the desired value, however, from CONS ('(A), X); the quote *prevents* an evaluation of (A) and provides (A) itself as the first argument of CONS. We can summarize the action the MC takes upon encountering a quoted expression as follows:

1. If an atom follows the quote, then a pointer to that atom is the value of the quoted expression.
2. If a left parenthesis follows the quote, then the MC *builds* in the HEAP the structure corresponding to the S-expression being quoted, and a pointer to this structure is the value of the quoted expression.

7-6 THE LISP INTERPRETER

Algol and Fortran are generally implemented as *compiled* languages. That is, a program in one of these languages is read by a *compiler,* which translates it into the *machine language* (low-level instructions) of the machine being used. This machine language program is then executed in order to produce results.

By contrast, Lisp is usually implemented as an *interpreted* language. A flowchart for the Lisp interpreter is shown in Figure 7-20.

A Lisp program consists of a sequence of commands that are to be evaluated. Typically, a command is a procedure call or a procedure definition. The interpreter is a program that inputs a command, evaluates it, outputs the results, and then repeats these steps until it runs out of inputs. The interpreter does not

Figure 7-20. **The Lisp interpreter.**

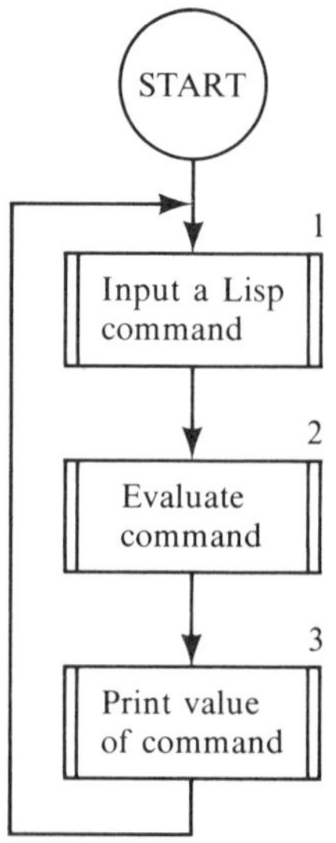

START

1

Input a Lisp command

2

Evaluate command

3

Print value of command

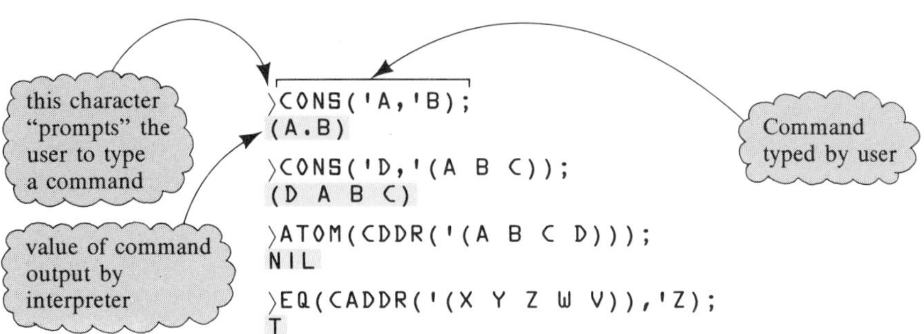

Figure 7-21. **Interaction with the Lisp interpreter.**

translate the entire program into machine language before execution begins. Instead each command is read and acted upon (evaluated) before the next command is input.

When Lisp is implemented by an interpreter it is easy to use as an *interactive* language. The user may present a command to the interpreter by, say, typing it on a keyboard terminal, and he receives back from the interpreter the value of the command. He then types the next command, etc. This interaction enables the user to determine each step of the "session" on the basis of the results up to that point.

Figure 7-21 shows the printout from a brief interactive run. This simple example contains only commands that are calls on basic functions, but it is sufficient to show the nature of the interaction with the interpreter.

Lisp was one of the first computer languages to operate interactively, but it can also be used for "batch" runs. These typically require a card deck containing the commands to be evaluated. However, the action taken by the Lisp system is still the read–evaluate–output loop suggested by Figure 7-20. Lisp compilers also exist; they translate commands into machine code that can usually be executed much faster than the interpreter can evaluate the corresponding commands.

7-7 OVERVIEW OF LISP SYNTAX AND SEMANTICS

The interpretive nature of the language means that the "top level" of a Lisp program plays a slightly different role than in other languages. We are accustomed to a top level that declares variables, inputs data, does some processing, calls on the procedures of the program for additional processing, and outputs results. We are accustomed to procedure declarations nested within the top level (as in Algol) or essentially in parallel with it (as in Fortran).

In Lisp, the top level involves direct interaction with the interpreter, and usually consists only of procedure declarations and calls on those procedures. Explicit input and output statements are not needed, since "data" are provided in the form of arguments in procedure calls and since the value produced by a procedure called at the top level is automatically displayed (output) by the interpreter. At the top level there is also no need for variable declarations, assignments, loops, tests, etc., since usually the first environment where such things are meaningful is the environment established by a procedure called from the top level.* Figure 7-22 shows a schematic version of a typical Lisp program, along with relevant BNF syntax rules.

As suggested by the syntax, a procedure definition is a command that has the effect of a declaration; the value returned after the execution of the command is simply the name of the procedure declared. The purpose of evaluating a procedure definition is not, of course, to obtain this value. What is of interest is the *effect* of the declaration, which is to make the procedure available for use. Figure 7-23 shows that the result of the procedure declarations is the creation of a cell in Top[1] for each procedure so declared.

***Figure 7-22.* Schematic form of a typical Lisp program, with BNF syntax.**

LISP PROCEDURE P1
. . . } Definition of procedure P1

LISP PROCEDURE P2
. . } Definition of procedure P2

P1 (. . .)
P2 (. . .) } calls on P1 and P2
. . . } more procedure definitions and/or calls

⟨program⟩ ::= ⟨command sequence⟩
⟨command sequence⟩ ::= ⟨command⟩; | ⟨command⟩; ⟨command sequence⟩

⟨command⟩ ::= ⟨procedure definition⟩ | ⟨procedure call⟩

***Figure 7-23.* Environment for the program of Figure 7-22 just after the evaluation of the procedure definitions.**

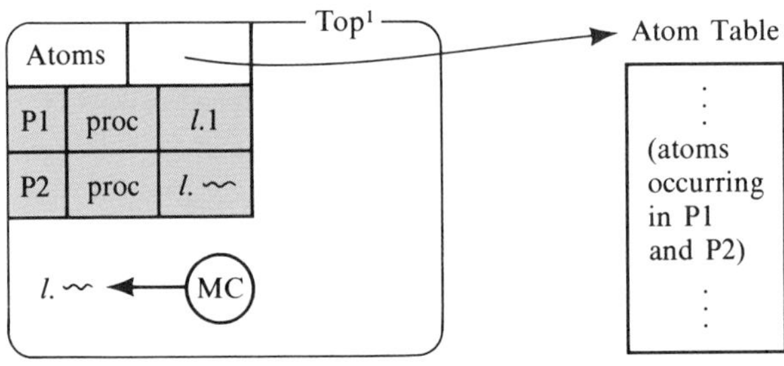

*The contour diagrams of the preceding sections of this chapter, while expedient for the discussion they accompanied, were thus somewhat atypical in that they showed variables occurring in Top[1]. Such occurrences *are* possible in Lisp, but the need for them will not arise in this chapter.

In Lisp, any procedure may be called from any other one, because procedures are all defined at one level. Furthermore, the placement of procedure contours upon invocation is not a *static* property of the program. Rather, the contour for a procedure is placed *inside the contour from which the procedure is called.* (This is why we show an ip but no ep inside proc cells. The ep cannot be determined in advance.) For example, procedure P1 is called from the top level in Figure 7-22. If the evaluation of P1 produces a call on P2, which then calls P1, the situation shown in Figure 7-24 will result. The cells in the procedure contours include parameters, locals, and a return cell. Only *value* parameters are used in Lisp.*

***Figure 7-24.* Nesting of contours of Lisp.**

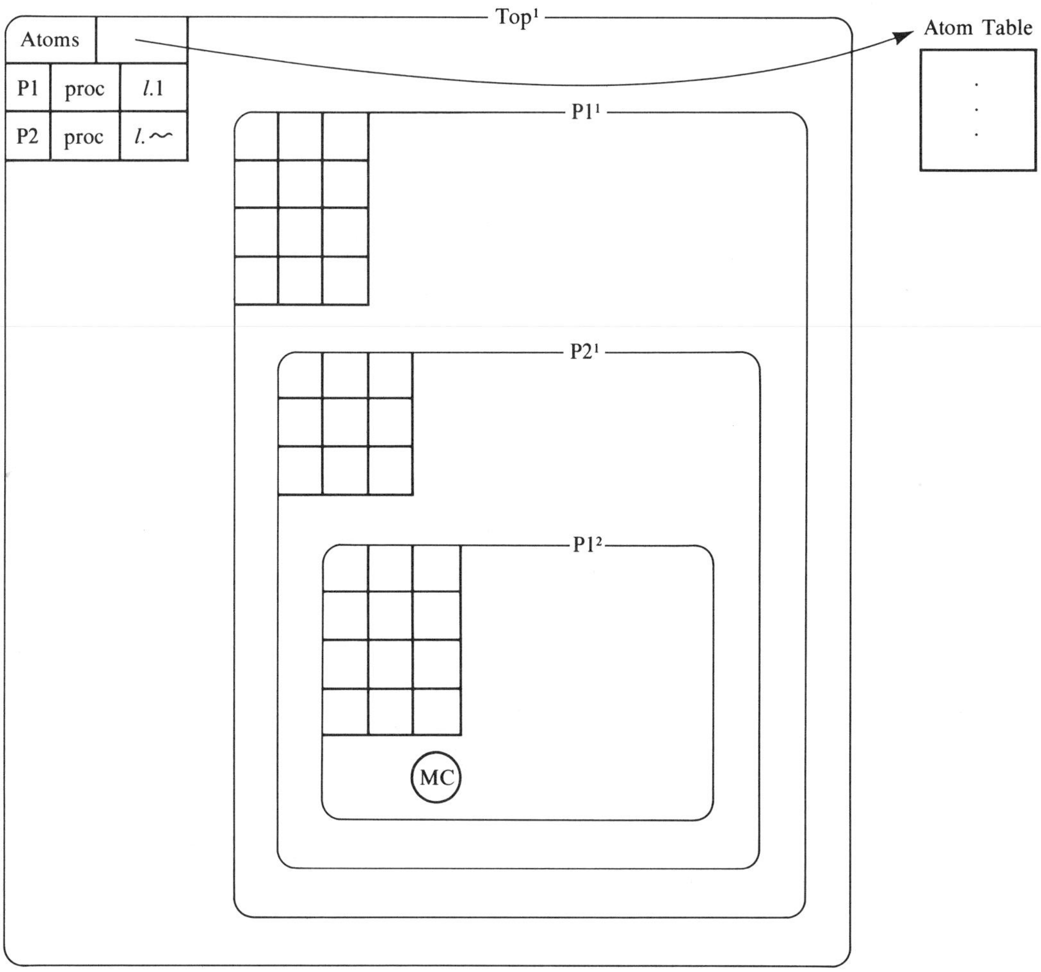

*Mechanisms exist, however, for passing arguments to a procedure in *unevaluated* form, thereby achieving the effect of Algol name parameters. We defer the discussion of these techniques until Section 7-14.

Every procedure in Lisp must return a value, that is, all Lisp procedures are *function procedures.* When the MC returns with the value in his stack, from a procedure contour to the calling contour, the contour he left (exited from) is deallocated.

7-8 THE SYNTAX OF LISP AND RLISP

In this section we present the syntax of two versions of Lisp: the language as it was originally proposed (and is most often implemented) and RLISP, a version with Algol-like syntax developed by A. C. Hearn of the University of Utah. Its apparent resemblance to Algol makes RLISP somewhat easier to present, and we thus consider that version of the language first. The examples shown so far have in fact been RLISP.

Table 7-1 provides a partial BNF syntax for RLISP. Note that rules 18 and 19 generalize the notion of a list, allowing any sequence of S-expressions enclosed in parentheses, even if those S-expressions are dotted pairs. For example,

TABLE 7-1
Partial BNF Syntax for RLISP

<table>
<tr><td>1. ⟨program⟩</td><td>::=</td><td>⟨command sequence⟩</td></tr>
<tr><td>2. ⟨command sequence⟩</td><td>::=</td><td>⟨command⟩;|⟨command⟩;⟨command sequence⟩</td></tr>
<tr><td>3. ⟨command⟩</td><td>::=</td><td>⟨procedure definition⟩|⟨procedure call⟩|⟨quoted expression⟩|. . .</td></tr>
<tr><td>4. ⟨procedure definition⟩</td><td>::=</td><td>LISP PROCEDURE ⟨procedure identifier⟩
⟨formal parameter part⟩;⟨body⟩</td></tr>
<tr><td>5. ⟨formal parameter part⟩</td><td>::=</td><td>⟨empty⟩|(⟨formal parameter list⟩)</td></tr>
<tr><td>6. ⟨formal parameter list⟩</td><td>::=</td><td>⟨variable⟩|⟨formal parameter list⟩,⟨variable⟩</td></tr>
<tr><td>7. ⟨variable⟩</td><td>::=</td><td>⟨identifier⟩</td></tr>
<tr><td>8. ⟨body⟩</td><td>::=</td><td>⟨expression⟩|. . .</td></tr>
<tr><td>9. ⟨expression⟩</td><td>::=</td><td>⟨procedure call⟩|⟨conditional expression⟩|⟨quoted expression⟩|⟨variable⟩</td></tr>
<tr><td>10. ⟨procedure call⟩</td><td>::=</td><td>⟨procedure identifier⟩⟨actual parameter part⟩</td></tr>
<tr><td>11. ⟨actual parameter part⟩</td><td>::=</td><td>⟨empty⟩|(⟨actual parameter list⟩)</td></tr>
<tr><td>12. ⟨actual parameter list⟩</td><td>::=</td><td>⟨expression⟩|⟨actual parameter list⟩,⟨expression⟩</td></tr>
<tr><td>13. ⟨conditional expression⟩</td><td>::=</td><td>⟨if expression⟩|⟨if expression⟩ ELSE ⟨expression⟩</td></tr>
<tr><td>14. ⟨if expression⟩</td><td>::=</td><td>IF ⟨predicate expression⟩ THEN ⟨expression⟩</td></tr>
<tr><td>15. ⟨quoted expression⟩</td><td>::=</td><td>'⟨S-expression⟩</td></tr>
<tr><td>16. ⟨S-expression⟩</td><td>::=</td><td>⟨dotted pair⟩|⟨list⟩|⟨atomic symbol⟩</td></tr>
<tr><td>17. ⟨dotted pair⟩</td><td>::=</td><td>(⟨S-expression⟩.⟨S-expression⟩)</td></tr>
<tr><td>18. ⟨list⟩</td><td>::=</td><td>(⟨S-list⟩)</td></tr>
<tr><td>19. ⟨S-list⟩</td><td>::=</td><td>⟨S-expression⟩|⟨S-list⟩⟨S-expression⟩</td></tr>
<tr><td>20. ⟨atomic symbol⟩</td><td>::=</td><td>⟨literal atom⟩|⟨numeric atom⟩</td></tr>
<tr><td>21. ⟨predicate expression⟩</td><td>::=</td><td>⟨expression⟩</td></tr>
</table>

((A.B) (C.D)) is now considered to be a list whose first element is (A.B) and whose second element is (C.D). An equivalent S-expression is

((A.B).((C.D).NIL)).

The storage structure of a list always has the appearance

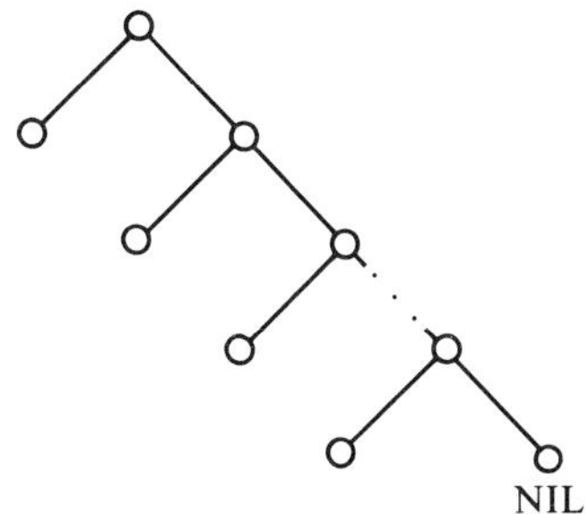

In the generalized list a left subtree can be any S-expression.

We now consider a sample program in RLISP. Figure 7-25 shows a flowchart for a procedure LOOK, whose arguments are a list of dotted pairs and an atomic symbol. If the list is not null and the given atomic symbol is the same as the left part of one of the dotted pairs of the given list, the value of LOOK is the right part of the (first such) dotted pair. Otherwise the value of LOOK is NIL. For example, LOOK('((A.B) (C.D)), 'C) = D. Thus LOOK performs a kind of *table look-up:* it searches a "table" of dotted pairs for an entry beginning with a specified atom. If such an entry is found, its right part is returned. LOOK uses the procedure NULL to determine whether the list L is empty. NULL is a "predicate" function that is true if its argument is the atom NIL:*

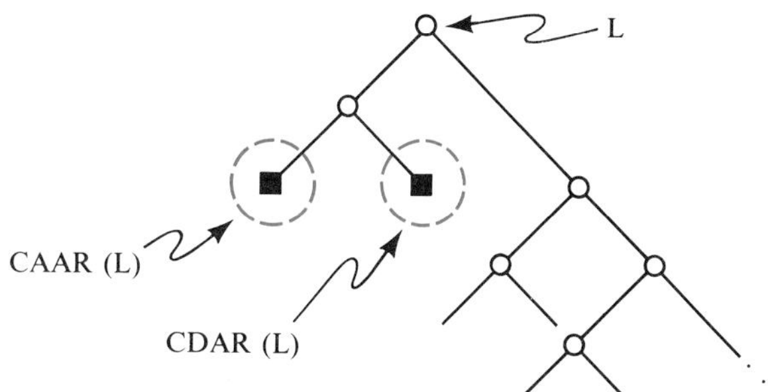

If NULL is false, the left part of the first pair in the list is tested for equality with the parameter A. If they are equal, the right part of the pair is returned; if not, LOOK is called recursively with the list remaining when the first pair is removed from L.

*NULL is actually a *predefined* function in Lisp. A list of predefined functions is given in Table 7-3; for now we include a definition of NULL in our program.

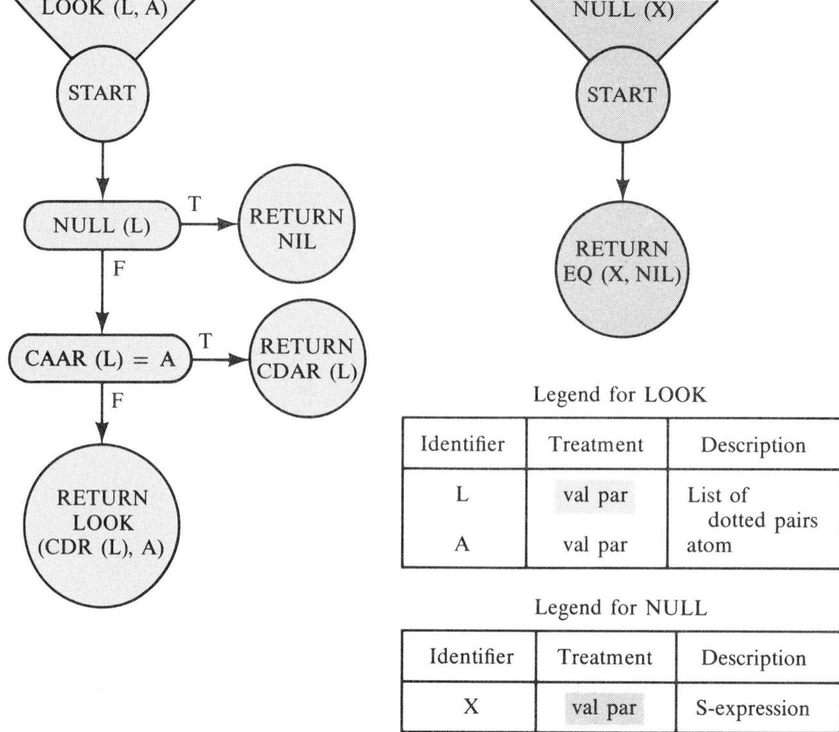

Legend for LOOK

Identifier	Treatment	Description
L	val par	List of dotted pairs
A	val par	atom

Legend for NULL

Identifier	Treatment	Description
X	val par	S-expression

Figure 7-25

An RLISP program that declares and tests LOOK and NULL is shown in Figure 7-26. Notice the following features of the program:

1. The program consists of three commands: the definition of LOOK (lines 1–4), the definition of NULL (lines 5 and 6), and a call on LOOK (line 7). Each command is followed by a semicolon, as required by rule 2, Table 7-1.
2. The semicolons on lines 1 and 5 are required by the syntax of procedure definitions (rule 4, Table 7-1).
3. The body of each procedure is an expression: a *conditional expression* in the case of LOOK, and a *procedure call* in the case of NULL (rules 8 and 9, Table 7-1).
4. The arguments of LOOK on line 7 are quoted so that they will not be *evaluated.* The arguments given to LOOK will thus be the list of dotted pairs and the atom R. The former will be constructed in the HEAP by the interpreter.
5. The value returned by LOOK is the value of the *conditional expression* that is its body. The value returned by NULL is the value of the call of EQ.

```
LISP PROCEDURE LOOK (L, A);
  IF NULL (L)   THEN NIL
    ELSE IF EQ (CAAR (L), A) THEN CDAR (L)
    ELSE LOOK (CDR (L), A);

LISP PROCEDURE NULL (X);
  EQ (X, NIL)   ;

LOOK ('((A.X)(Z.K)(R.D)(U.V)), 'R);
```

Figure 7-26. **An RLISP program.**

Figure 7-27 is a copy of an actual computer run of this program.

Figure 7-27

```
)LISP PROCEDURE LOOK(L, A);
  IF NULL(L) THEN NIL
   ELSE IF EQ(CAAR(L), A) THEN CDAR(L)
   ELSE LOOK(CDR(L), A);

 LOOK

)LISP PROCEDURE NULL(X);
  EQ(X, NIL);

 NULL

)LOOK('((A.X)(Z.K)(R.D)(U.V)),'R);

 D
```

We now present snapshots for the execution of the program of Figure 7-26 to confirm an understanding of the important intermediate steps. For the rest of the chapter we adopt the snapshot convention that instead of showing pointers from the HEAP to the atom table, we simply write the atomic symbols at the appropriate place in the HEAP diagram. That is, instead of

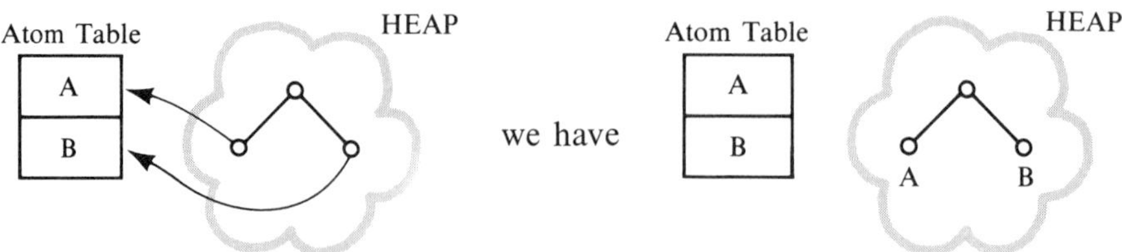

This convention will reduce clutter in snapshots.

Snapshot 1 shows the MC ready to execute the call on LOOK. Procedures LOOK and NULL have been declared, and the atom table is currently empty.

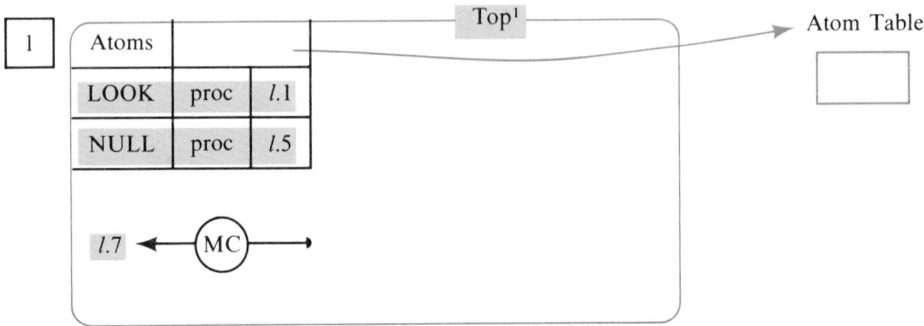

When the procedure LOOK is called, a new contour LOOK[1] is created and, as discussed earlier, nested inside Top[1] (since LOOK was called from the top or command level). As in Algol, the new contour must contain a cell for each parameter and also a return cell. We also include a *retval* cell, but as shown below, it is not really required in Lisp snapshots.

Snapshot 2 shows the state of affairs after LOOK has been entered but before line 2 is executed. Since Lisp uses value parameters, the cells for L and A in LOOK[1] have received the appropriate values. In order to provide these values a structure has been constructed in the HEAP and entries have been made in the atom table.

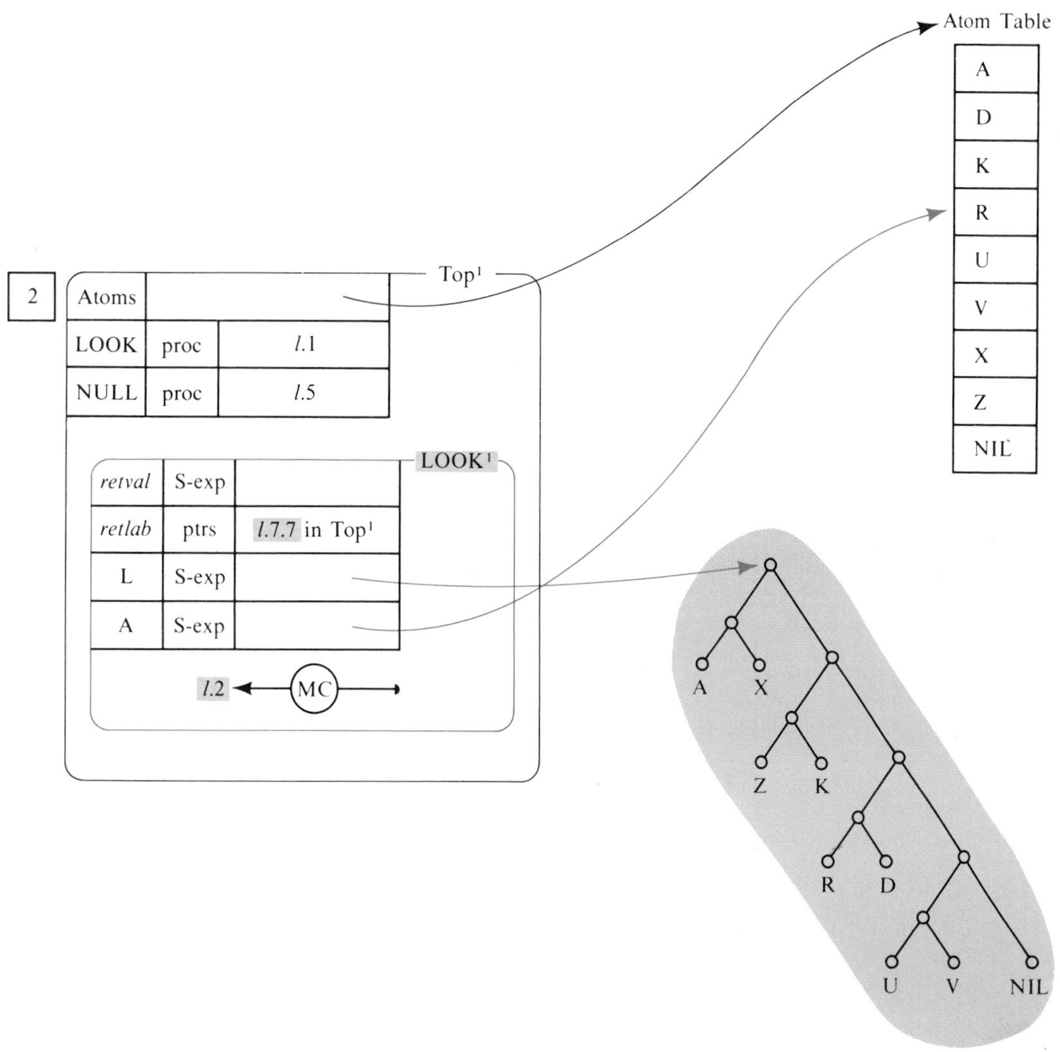

Execution of line 2 begins with a call on procedure NULL. Snapshot 3 shows the MC about to return to LOOK[1] with the value NIL.

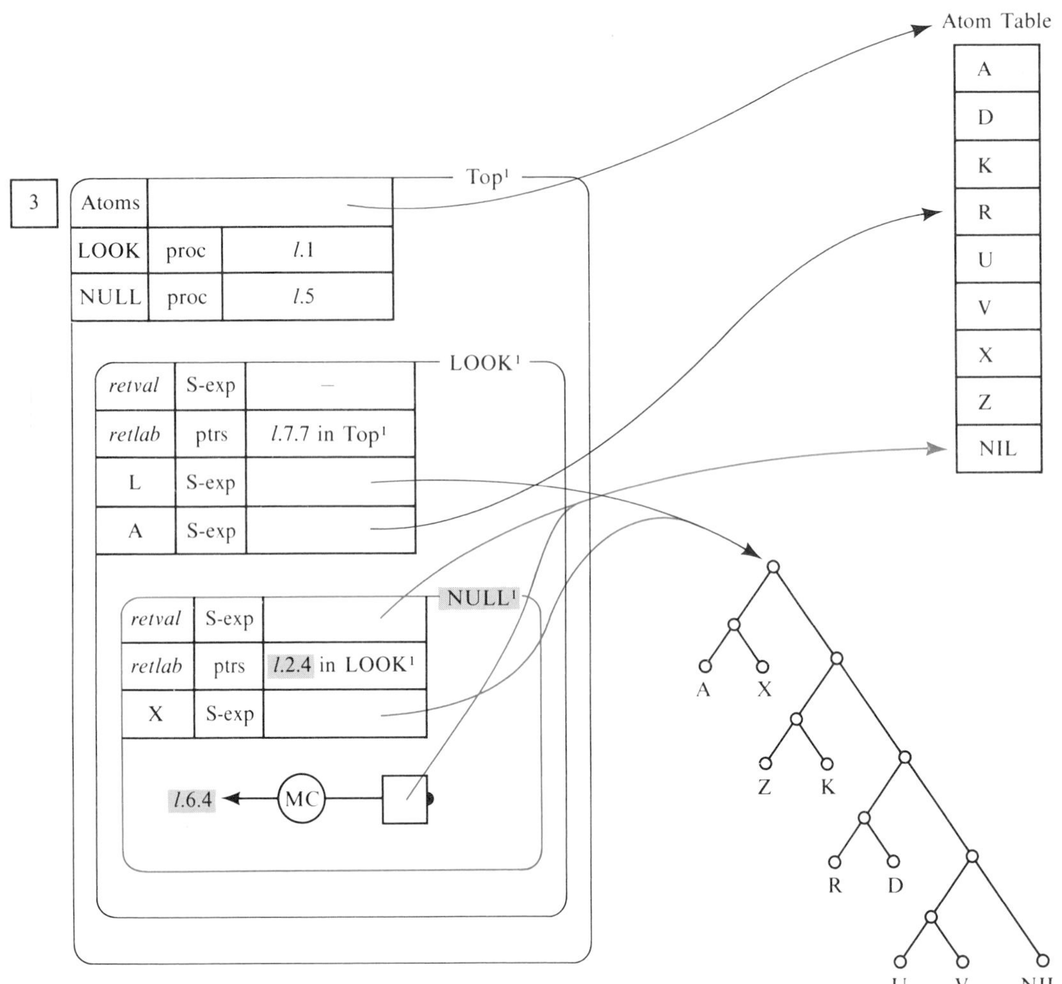

After the return from NULL, the MC evaluates EQ (CAAR (L), A) on line 3. Since the value of CAAR (L) is the atom A and the value of the *variable* A is the atom R, EQ has the value NIL. This in turn leads to a recursive call of LOOK on line 4. Snapshot 4 shows the MC just after he has entered LOOK².

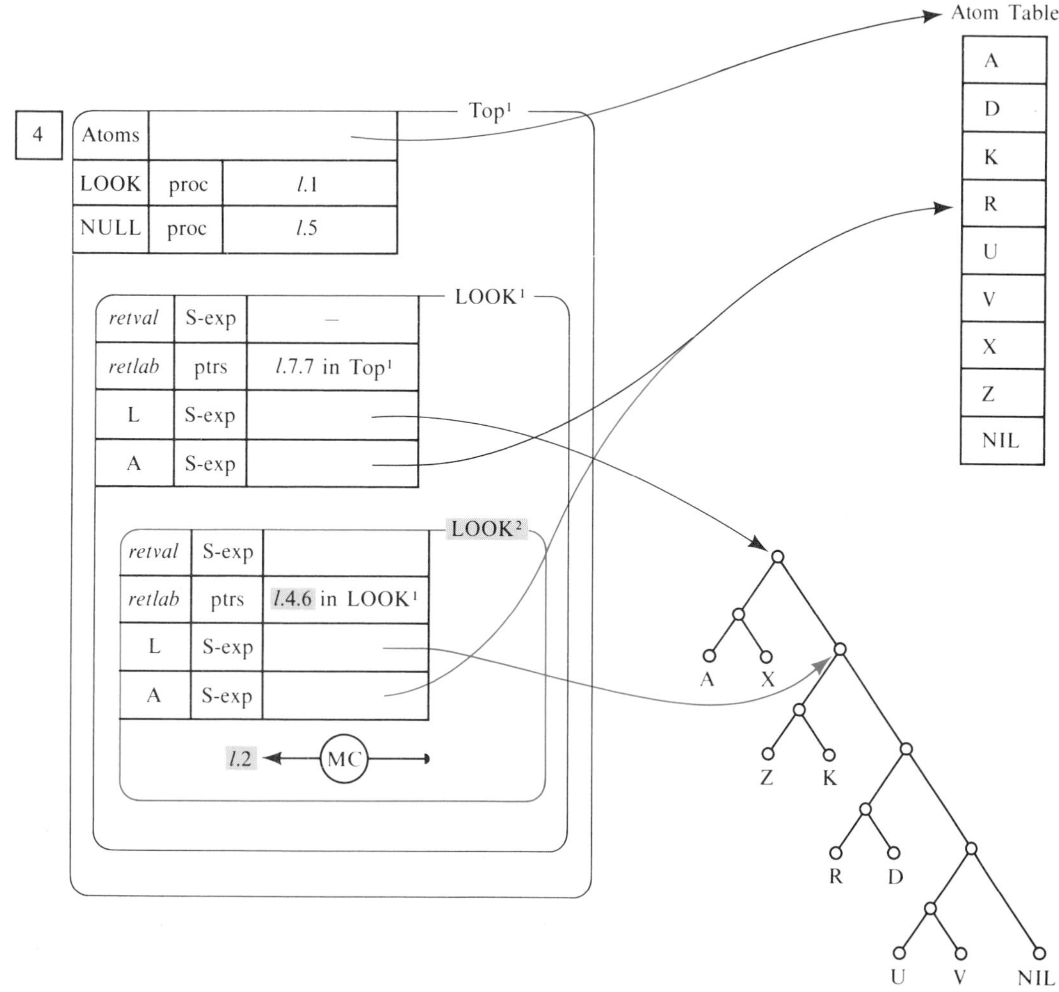

The call of NULL (which involves a contour NULL² nested inside LOOK²) again produces the result NIL, as does the subsequent evaluation of EQ (CAAR (L), A) [this is because CAAR (L) now evaluates to the atom Z]. A third call on LOOK therefore occurs, and this time the search process succeeds, as can be seen by examining snapshot 5. CAAR (L) now has the atom R as its value, and the snapshot shows the MC having placed D, which is CDAR (L), on his stack just before returning to LOOK².

Particular attention should be paid to the value of the parameter L in the contours LOOK¹, LOOK², and LOOK³. This is a very typical situation in Lisp: an argument of a recursive function is a list, and in each recursive call the parameter matching the list argument points one step further down the list. If the search fails, the recursive chain of calls will ultimately end when the value of L becomes NIL, causing the "escape hatch" NULL (L) to return T.

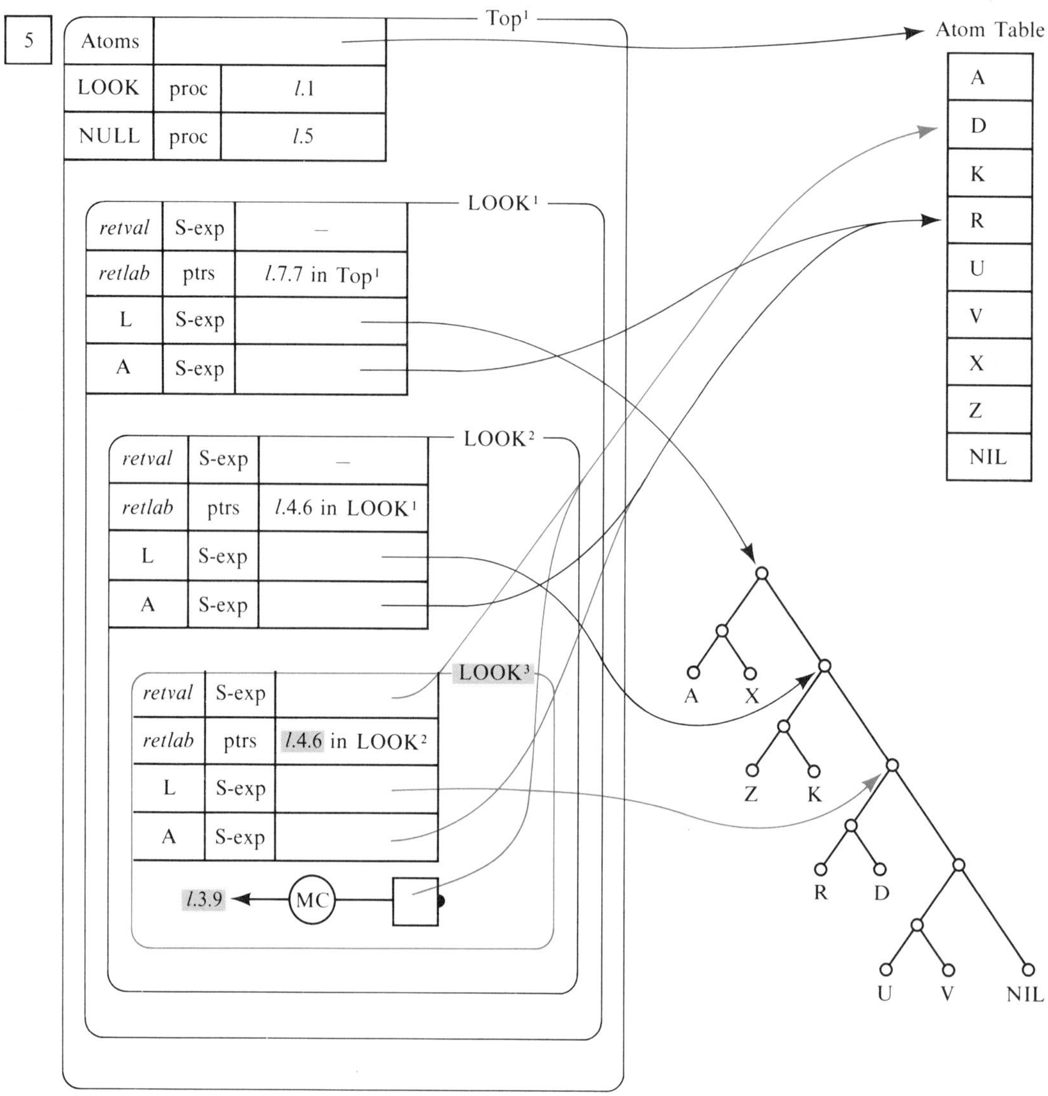

5

Top^1

Atoms		
LOOK	proc	*l*.1
NULL	proc	*l*.5

LOOK^1

retval	S-exp	–
retlab	ptrs	*l*.7.7 in Top^1
L	S-exp	
A	S-exp	

LOOK^2

retval	S-exp	–
retlab	ptrs	*l*.4.6 in LOOK^1
L	S-exp	
A	S-exp	

LOOK^3

retval	S-exp	
retlab	ptrs	*l*.4.6 in LOOK^2
L	S-exp	
A	S-exp	

l.3.9 ← MC

Atom Table: A, D, K, R, U, V, X, Z, NIL

A X Z K R D U V NIL

Upon returning to LOOK^2, the MC finds no more work to be done in the second call on LOOK, and so he carries D on his stack into environment LOOK^1. Once again there is nothing to do but return, this time to Top^1.

Recall that the Top level in Lisp is the level of direct communication with the interpreter, and as each expression presented is evaluated, its value is automatically output. Thus the output in this case is

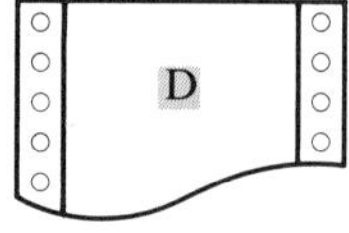

Lisp, in contrast to Algol and Fortran, closely resembles our flowchart language with respect to RETURN semantics. In the flowchart language and in

Lisp the designation of an expression whose value is to be returned, and the act of returning that value, are coupled, that is,

(although the word RETURN does not appear in Lisp). For this reason a *retval* cell in the contour for a Lisp procedure is not really needed. As soon as the value to be returned has been computed, it can safely be placed on top of the MC's evaluation stack because the very next step the MC takes is to move back into the environment of the caller, where the returned value can be picked off the stack when needed. Hence, there is no need to hold the returned value temporarily in a *retval* cell of the called procedure. We can therefore do away with *retval* cells in our Lisp contour diagrams.

While the previous snapshots have given a detailed picture of the storage structures involved in Lisp, they approach the limit of complexity that can reasonably be drawn in this way. To simplify the appearance of the diagrams, we propose the following shorthand notation: in the value compartment of the cell for each variable, rather than show a pointer to the value in the atom table or HEAP, we simply write the *S-expression* that is the value of the variable. For example, the cell for L in LOOK^3 in Snapshot 5 above would appear as

L	S-exp	((R.D)(U.V))

This notation eliminates the need for the HEAP and the atom table as well, but places more burden on the reader to understand the nature and extent of the sharing of cells in the Lisp environment. For example, suppose in some contour the cells X and Y have values as follows:

⋮

X	S-exp	(A.B)
Y	S-exp	(A.B)

From this diagram we cannot tell whether X and Y point to *different* copies of (A.B) or share the *same* copy, and thus we cannot tell whether the value of EQ (X, Y) is T or NIL. Where such considerations are important, we resort to the previous style and explicitly show the HEAP.

We present below a second set of snapshots for LOOK (beginning with snapshot 2), this time using the shorthand notation. Study the two methods and satisfy yourself that they are equivalent, at least for this problem. Notice that we have eliminated *retval* cells in these snapshots.

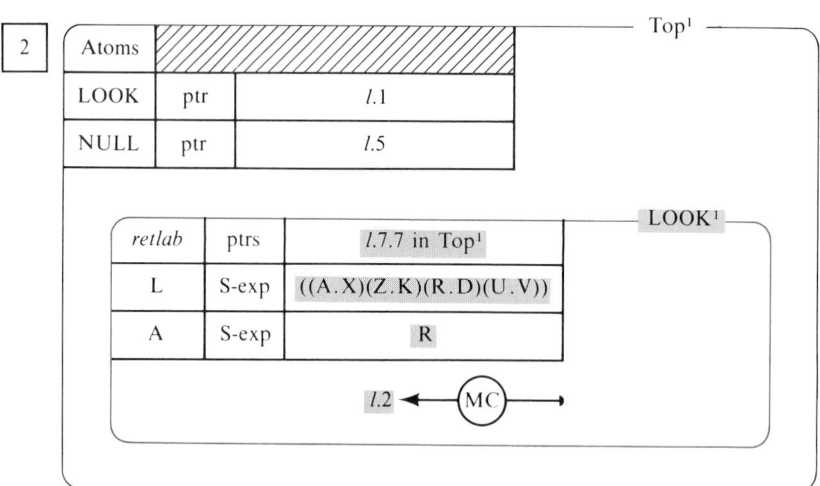
2
Top¹
Atoms
LOOK
ptr
l.1
NULL
ptr
l.5
LOOK¹
retlab
ptrs
l.7.7 in Top¹
L
S-exp
((A.X)(Z.K)(R.D)(U.V))
A
S-exp
R
l.2
MC

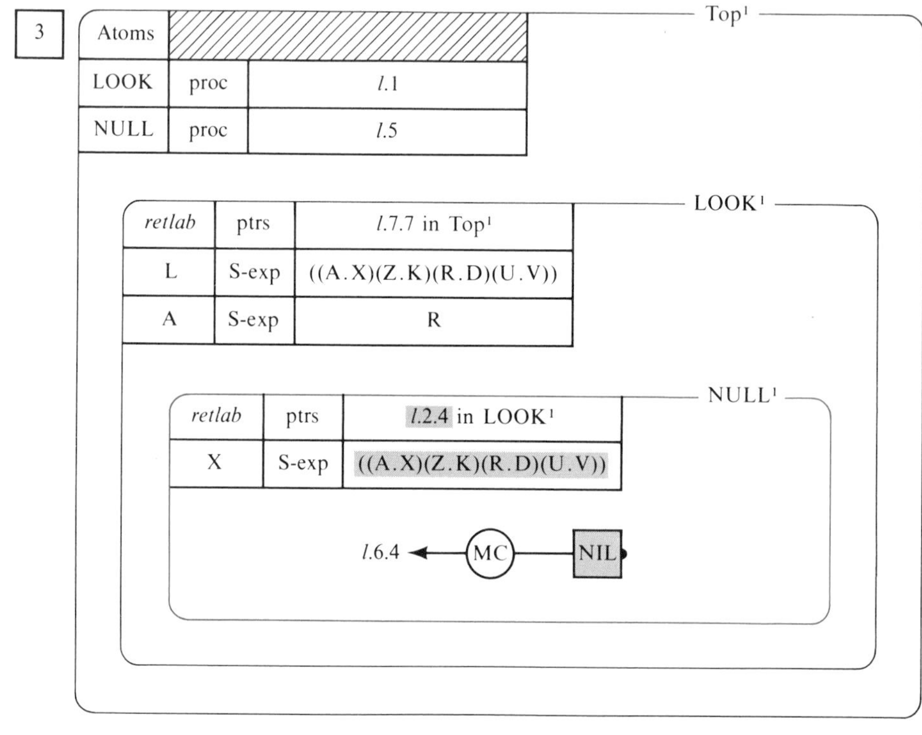
3
Top¹
Atoms
LOOK
proc
l.1
NULL
proc
l.5
LOOK¹
retlab
ptrs
l.7.7 in Top¹
L
S-exp
((A.X)(Z.K)(R.D)(U.V))
A
S-exp
R
NULL¹
retlab
ptrs
l.2.4 in LOOK¹
X
S-exp
((A.X)(Z.K)(R.D)(U.V))
l.6.4
MC
NIL

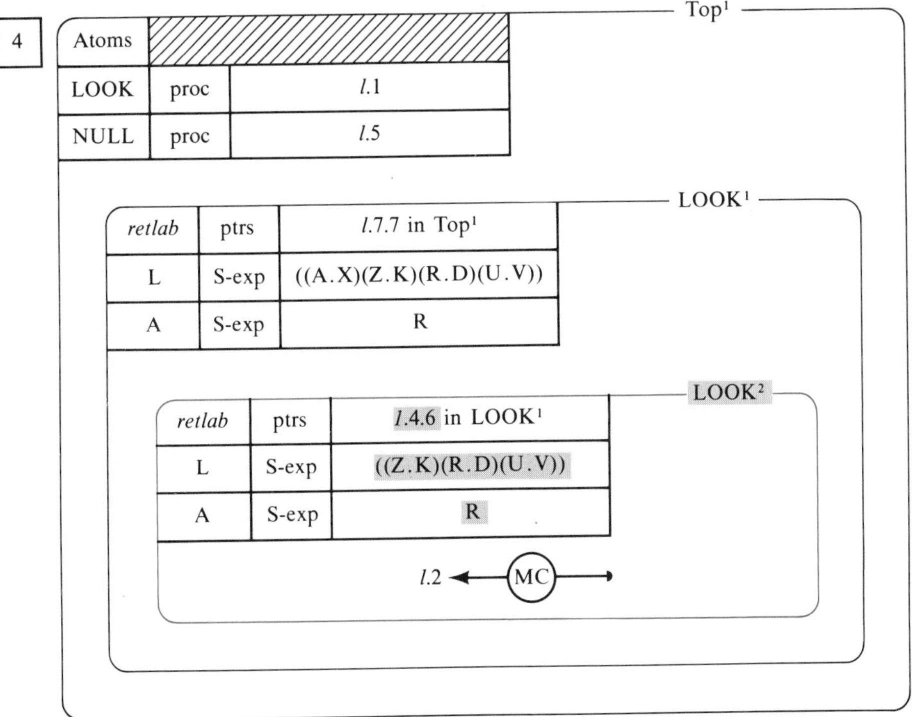
4
Top1
Atoms
LOOK proc l.1
NULL proc l.5
LOOK1
retlab ptrs l.7.7 in Top1
L S-exp ((A.X)(Z.K)(R.D)(U.V))
A S-exp R
LOOK2
retlab ptrs l.4.6 in LOOK1
L S-exp ((Z.K)(R.D)(U.V))
A S-exp R
l.2
MC

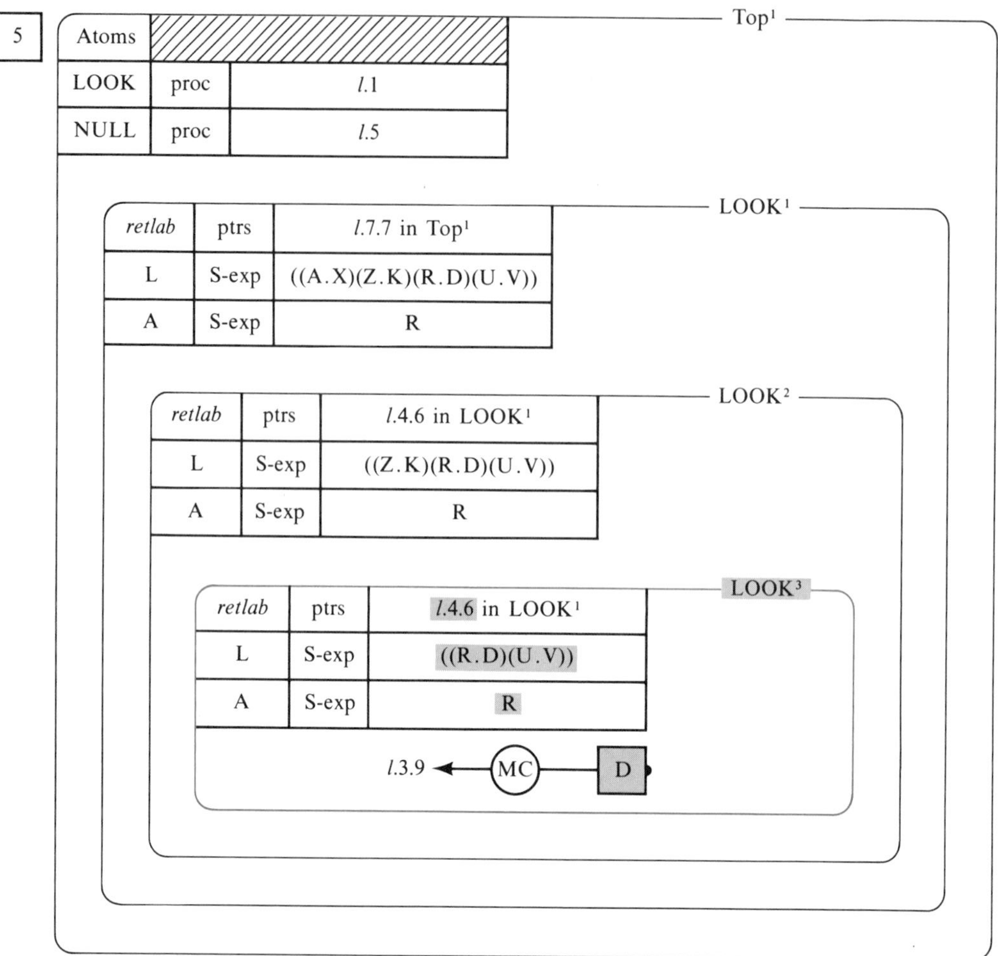

We now turn our attention to a second version of Lisp, which is actually the original version of the language. The "official" name for this version is LISP 1.5; we shall refer to it [McCarthy *et al.* (1962)] as just LISP (and retain Lisp as the generic term). The difference between the two dialects is purely syntactic—the operations, data structures, etc., are exactly the same. In fact, RLISP has been implemented through a preprocessor program that translates RLISP programs into LISP. The remainder of this section can be skipped without loss of continuity if you are content to know the syntax of RLISP only. A partial BNF syntax for LISP is given in Table 7-2.

The first important feature of LISP syntax has to do with procedure calls. Instead of writing EQ (X, Y) or CAR (L), in LISP we write (EQ X Y) and (CAR L). This is, of course, simply a prefix notation as opposed to the more "mathematical" style of RLISP, but one feature stands out immediately: these expressions, which are part of LISP *programs,* are in fact written as *S-expressions.* This approach carries through the entire LISP syntax, and in Section 7-13 we shall investigate some of the implications of the fact that LISP programs are written as LISP data objects.

```
        ⟨define call⟩ ::= (DEFINE '(⟨procedure list⟩))
     ⟨procedure list⟩ ::= ⟨procedure definition⟩|⟨procedure list⟩
                                                ⟨procedure definition⟩
⟨procedure definition⟩ ::= (⟨procedure identifier⟩
                              (LAMBDA (⟨parameter list⟩)⟨body⟩))
```

Figure 7-28. **BNF description of a call on DEFINE.**

Conditional expressions in LISP also differ from their RLISP counterparts. The RLISP expression

IF p_1 THEN e_1 ELSE IF p_2 THEN e_2 . . . ELSE IF p_n THEN e_n ELSE e_{n+1}

is written as follows in LISP:

$$(\text{COND } (p_1\ e_1)\ (p_2\ e_2)\ \ldots\ (p_n\ e_n)\ (\text{T } e_{n+1})).$$

Thus a conditional expression is written as a call on a function COND. COND is actually what is called a "special form" both in LISP and RLISP, since the number of arguments is not fixed. Moreover, the arguments are *not evaluated* before the body of COND is entered but are evaluated only as required while the body is executed. The ith argument is a list of two items: a predicate expression p_i and an expression e_i that is the value of the COND if the predicate returns T. Notice that the final ELSE clause is handled by simply writing a predicate that is always true, the atom T itself.

The final major difference between the two versions occurs in the definition of procedures. LISP uses a notation based on the "lambda" notation of the mathematician Alonzo Church. In that system, if e is an expression containing the variables x_1 . . . x_n, then $\lambda\ [(x_1\ \ldots\ x_n);\ e]$ represents a function of n variables (i.e., parameters) whose body is e.

The list $(x_1\ \ldots\ x_n)$ establishes the order in which the parameters of the function are matched to the arguments given when the function is invoked. Procedure definitions in LISP are accomplished by giving a list of such lambda expressions (each preceded by a name) as the argument to the function DEFINE. Figure 7-28 shows a BNF description of a call on DEFINE. The syntax rules given in Figure 7-28 are not included in Table 7-2 since what is described in the figure is simply the form of a call on one of the predefined functions of LISP.

Snapshots for the execution of the Figure 7-29 program would be exactly the same as for the RLISP version and thus will not be shown. A partial syntax for LISP is shown in Table 7-2. The rules that differ from RLISP syntax are marked with arrows.

Figure 7-29. **Program of Figure 7-26 written in LISP.**

```
(DEFINE '(
   (LOOK (LAMBDA (L A) (COND ((NULL L) NIL)
                             ((EQ (CAAR L) A) (CDAR L))
                             (T (LOOK (CDR L) A)))))
   (NULL (LAMBDA (X) (EQ X NIL)))
   ))
(LOOK '((A.X) (Z.K) (R.D) (U.V)) 'R)
```

TABLE 7-2
Partial BNF Syntax for LISP

	1. ⟨program⟩	::=	⟨command sequence⟩
→	2. ⟨command sequence⟩	::=	⟨command⟩|⟨command⟩⟨command sequence⟩
→	3. ⟨command⟩	::=	⟨procedure call⟩|⟨quoted expression⟩|. . .
→	4. ⟨procedure call⟩	::=	(⟨procedure identifier⟩⟨actual parameter list⟩)
→	5. ⟨actual parameter list⟩	::=	⟨empty⟩|⟨expression⟩|⟨actual parameter list⟩⟨expression⟩
→	6. ⟨expression⟩	::=	⟨procedure call⟩|⟨conditional expression⟩| ⟨quoted expression⟩|⟨variable⟩
→	7. ⟨conditional expression⟩	::=	(COND ⟨if pairs⟩)
→	8. ⟨if pairs⟩	::=	(⟨predicate expression⟩⟨expression⟩)| ⟨if pairs⟩(⟨predicate expression⟩⟨expression⟩)
	9. ⟨predicate expression⟩	::=	⟨expression⟩
	10. ⟨quoted expression⟩	::=	'⟨S-expression⟩
	11. ⟨variable⟩	::=	⟨identifier⟩
	12. ⟨S-expression⟩	::=	⟨dotted pair⟩|⟨list⟩|⟨atomic symbol⟩
	13. ⟨dotted pair⟩	::=	(⟨S-expression⟩.⟨S-expression⟩)
	14. ⟨list⟩	::=	(⟨S-list⟩)
	15. ⟨S-list⟩	::=	⟨S-expression⟩|⟨S-list⟩⟨S-expression⟩
	16. ⟨atomic symbol⟩	::=	⟨literal atom⟩|⟨numeric atom⟩

Exercises 7-8

Define the following recursive functions in RLISP or LISP:

1 COPATOMLIST (X). X is a list of atoms; COPATOMLIST (X) produces a *copy* of X.

2 PAIR (X, Y). If X is the list $(x_1\ x_2\ \ldots\ x_n)$ and Y is the list $(y_1\ y_2\ \ldots\ y_n)$, then PAIR (X, Y) = $((x_1 \cdot y_1)\ (x_2 \cdot y_2)\ \ldots\ (x_n \cdot y_n))$. X and Y may be assumed to be of the same length, that is, to have the same number of components.

7-9
PREDEFINED FUNCTIONS OF LISP

Every function definable in Lisp can be defined using the five basic functions (CONS, CAR, CDR, ATOM, EQ), conditional expressions, and procedure declarations. For convenience to the programmer, however, many often-used functions are *predefined;* that is, they are included in the system "library" and may be used without declaration. Table 7-3 lists many of these functions (the exact set defined varies from implementation to implementation). One function worth special attention is EQUAL, which is discussed further in Exercise 5, Section 7-9.

Exercises 7-9

1 Give a definition in LISP or RLISP for a function EQATLISTS (X, Y). X and Y are lists of *atoms;* the length of X may be assumed to be the same as the length of Y. EQATLISTS is a predicate that returns T only if X and Y contain the same atoms in the same order. *Hint:* It is not sufficient just to check the value of EQ (X, Y), since X and Y might be different copies of the same list. X and Y must be examined atom by atom.

2 Give a definition in LISP or RLISP for a function MEMB (A, L). A is an atom and L is a list. MEMB is a predicate that returns T only if the atom A is a member of list L.

3 Give a definition in LISP or RLISP for a function REMOVE (A, L). A is an atom and L is a list. The value of REMOVE is a list that is the same as L except the atom A has been deleted. If A does not occur on L, the value is L. If A occurs twice, the first occurrence is deleted, for example,

REMOVE ('X, '(A X B X)) = (A B X)

This is one of the first functions we have met that constructs a list as its result. *Hint:* A study of Exercise 1, Section 7-8, may be helpful.

4 Give a definition in LISP or RLISP for a function EQ2 (X, Y), whose arguments X and Y are lists of atoms. EQ2 is a predicate that is true only if Y is a rearrangement of X or is the same list as X. For example,

EQ2 ('(A B C), '(C B A)) = T
EQ2 ('(X Z), '(Y X Z)) = NIL
EQ2 ('(X Z), '(X A)) = NIL

Hint: Use REMOVE.

5 Table 7-3 lists a predicate EQUAL (X, Y) with the following description: T if X and Y are the same S-expression (even if they are *not* the same copy) else NIL. Another way of phrasing this definition is: EQUAL (X, Y) returns T if the storage structures for X and Y have the same shape and have the same atoms at the terminals. Thus

EQUAL (CONS ('A, 'B), CONS ('A, 'B)) = T

whereas EQ applied to the same arguments would be NIL.

Provide an RLISP or LISP definition for a predicate EQUAL that tests two S-expressions for equality in the above sense. Consider only S-expressions containing literal atoms.

TABLE 7-3
Predefined Functions in Lisp

Function	Parameters	Description	RLISP definition
CONS (X, Y)	X: S-exp Y: S-exp	Forms the dotted pair (X.Y)	
CAR (X)	X: nonatomic S-exp	Left subtree of X	
CDR (X)	X: nonatomic S-exp	Right subtree of X	
ATOM (X)	X: S-exp	T if X is an atom, else NIL	
EQ (X, Y)	X: S-exp Y: S-exp	T if X and Y are the same atom or the same copy of the same structure, else NIL	
NULL (K)	X: S-exp	T if X is the atom NIL, else NIL	LISP PROCEDURE NULL (X); EQ (X, NIL);
LIST (X_1, . . . , X_n)	X_1, . . . , X_n: S-exp (indefinite number of arguments)	Forms a list with elements X_1, . . . , X_n	
EQUAL (X, Y)	X: S-exp Y: S-exp	T if X and Y are the same S-expression (even if they are not the same copy) else NIL; note: EQUAL is also the equality test for numbers in Lisp	See Exercise 5, Section 7-9.
AND (X_1, . . . , X_n)	X_1, . . . , X_n: predicates	Logical "AND" of arguments	LISP PROCEDURE AND (X, Y); IF X THEN Y ELSE NIL;
			definition for 2 argument case
OR (X_1, . . . , X_n)	X_1, . . . , X_n: predicates	Logical "OR" of arguments	LISP PROCEDURE OR (X, Y); IF X THEN T ELSE Y;
NOT (X)	X: predicate	Logical "NOT" (negation) of argument	LISP PROCEDURE NOT (X); IF X THEN NIL ELSE T;

DEFINE (L)	L: List of procedures to be declared	Declares procedures (used only in LISP)	
SUBST (X, Y, Z)	X: S-exp Y: S-exp Z: S-exp	Produces S-exp obtained by substituting X for all occurrences of Y in Z	LISP PROCEDURE SUBST (X, Y, Z); IF EQUAL (Y, Z) THEN X ELSE IF ATOM (Z) THEN Z ELSE CONS (SUBST (X, Y, CAR (Z)), SUBST (X, Y, CDR (Z)));
APPEND (X, Y)	X: List Y: List	Combines X and Y into one new list	LISP PROCEDURE APPEND (X, Y); IF NULL (X) THEN Y ELSE CONS (CAR (X), APPEND (CDR (X), Y));
REVERSE (X)	X: List	Reverses list X	LISP PROCEDURE REVERSE (X); R1 (X, NIL); LISP PROCEDURE R1 (X, Y); IF NULL (X) THEN Y ELSE R1 (CDR (X), CONS (CAR (X), Y));
MEMBER (X, Y)	X: S-exp Y: List	T if X is a member of Y else NIL	LISP PROCEDURE MEMBER (X, Y); IF NULL (Y) THEN NIL ELSE IF EQUAL (X, CAR (Y)) THEN T ELSE MEMBER (X, CDR (Y));

7-10
ARITHMETIC OPERATIONS IN LISP

Even though Lisp is a language for manipulating symbolic data structures, it also has some arithmetic capabilities that are useful. For example, we might want to compute the length of a list, or the sum of a list of numbers.

Numbers are a type of atomic symbol in Lisp. Real and integer values are allowed and, although there is some variation from implementation to implementation, the forms shown in Figure 7-30 are allowable in most systems.

Because real numbers are included in Lisp, care must be taken to prevent confusion between a decimal point and the dot in a dotted pair. Here are two rules for writing dotted pairs containing numbers:

1. A real number should not begin or end with a decimal point. For example, write 32.0 and 0.4 instead of 32. and .4.
2. In a dotted pair containing numbers (real *or* integer), surround the dot of the pair with blanks. For example, (3.4 . 4) has 3.4 as left part and the integer 4 as right part of the dotted pair.

Numbers, even though they are atomic symbols, are treated slightly differently from literal atoms. Most Lisp systems do not store numbers uniquely in the atom table (that is, there may be more than one entry for the same number), so that EQ can not be used to test numbers for equality. The function EQUAL gives correct results. Furthermore, it is not necessary to quote numbers. They are constants that evaluate to themselves, like T and NIL.

TABLE 7-4
Arithmetic Functions and Predicates in Lisp

Function	Parameters	Description	Example application	Result
PLUS ($X_1, \ldots, X_n$)	Numbers[a]	$X_1 + X_2 + \cdots + X_n$	PLUS (1, 2, 3, 4.8)	10.8
DIFFERENCE (X, Y)	Numbers	$X - Y$	DIFFERENCE (2, 4)	−2
MINUS (X)	Number	$-X$	MINUS (3)	−3
TIMES ($X_1, \ldots, X_n$)	Numbers	$X_1 * X_2 * \ldots * X_n$	TIMES (2, 4, 3)	24
ADD1 (X)	Number	$X + 1$	ADD1 (3)	4
SUB1 (X)	Number	$X - 1$	SUB1 (3)	2
QUOTIENT (X, Y)	Numbers	$\frac{X}{Y}$ (integer division, if both are integer)	QUOTIENT (5, 2)	2
LESSP (X, Y)	Numbers	T if $X < Y$ else NIL	LESSP (2, 1)	NIL
GREATERP (X, Y)	Numbers	T if $X > Y$ else NIL	GREATERP (2, 1)	T
ZEROP (X)	Number	T if $X = 0$ else NIL	ZEROP (2)	NIL
NUMBERP (X)	S-exp	T if X is a number else NIL	NUMBERP ('A)	NIL
LENGTH (X)	List	Length of list X	LENGTH ('(A B C))	3

[a] To say the parameters must be numbers means they can be any expressions that evaluate to numbers, for example, CAR of a list whose first element is a number or a variable whose value is a number.

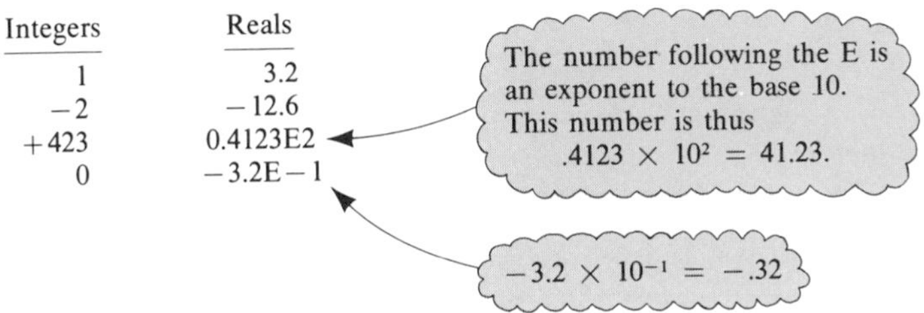

Figure 7-30. **Numbers in Lisp.**

Table 7-4 shows some of the numeric functions and predicates that are predefined in Lisp. All of the functions producing numeric results return integer values if all their arguments are integers, and return real values otherwise.

As a simple example involving numbers, let us define LENGTH, whose value is the length of the list that is its argument, as follows (LENGTH is actually a predefined function)*:

```
LISP PROCEDURE LENGTH (L);
  IF NULL (L) THEN 0 ELSE PLUS (LENGTH (CDR (L)), 1);
```

7-11 CASE STUDIES

Case Study 1 A recursive procedure to append a list Y to a list X.

Our first case study involves the function APPEND (X, Y), which is shown in flowchart and RLISP form in Figure 7-31† (APPEND is actually a predefined function in Lisp).

APPEND creates a list containing the elements of list X followed by the elements of list Y. For example, APPEND ('(A B), '(C D)) = (A B C D). We now trace the execution of the program shown in Figure 7-31, using the more explicit trace style that shows the HEAP. The atom table is omitted to reduce clutter, and we show contours only for APPEND (and not for the predefined functions NULL, CAR, CDR, and CONS called by APPEND).

*For the remainder of the chapter, we shall show RLISP definitions in the text, and the equivalent LISP in footnotes.
In LISP:

```
(DEFINE '(
  (LENGTH (LAMBDA (L) (COND ((NULL L) 0) (T (PLUS (LENGTH (CDR L)) 1)))))
))
```

†The LISP equivalent of the RLISP procedure APPEND in Figure 7-31 is given as a footnote on page 418.

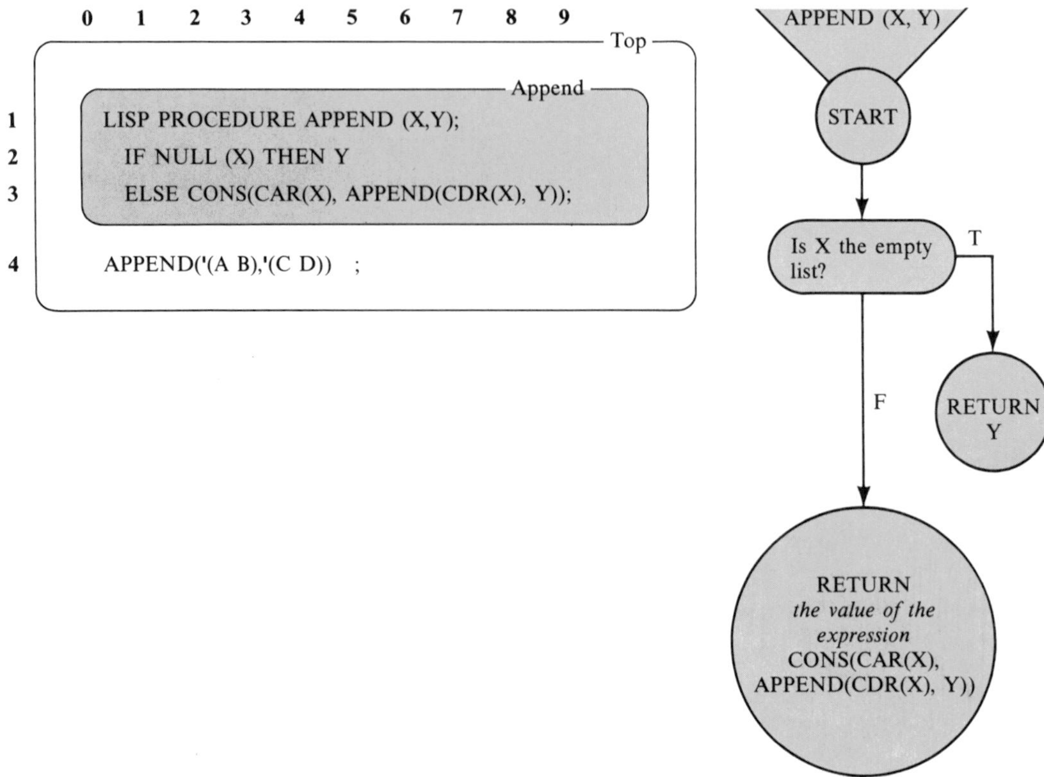

Figure 7-31. **Flowchart and RLISP for APPEND.***

*The LISP equivalent of the RLISP procedure APPEND in Figure 7-31 is:

```
(DEFINE '(
  (APPEND (LAMBDA (X Y) (COND ((NULL X) Y) (T (CONS (CAR X)
    (APPEND (CDR X) Y))))))
  ))
(APPEND '(A B) '(C D))
```

Snapshot 1 shows the situation after APPEND has been called and the MC is about to execute line 2.

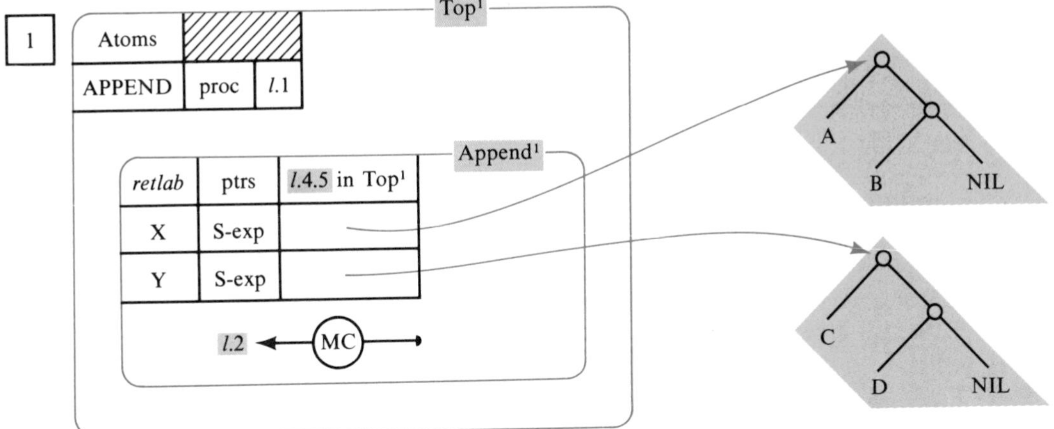

New cells are created for Append¹. Cells for the value parameters X and Y receive copies of the pointers to the list structures of their respective arguments '(A B) and '(C D).

Since NULL (X) returns NIL (that is, *false*) when called in line 2 of Append¹, the MC executes the ELSE clause on line 3. This requires a recursive call on APPEND with arguments CDR (X) and Y, whose values are (B) and (C D), respectively. Snapshot 2 shows the situation when the MC is again about to execute line 2, this time inside Append².

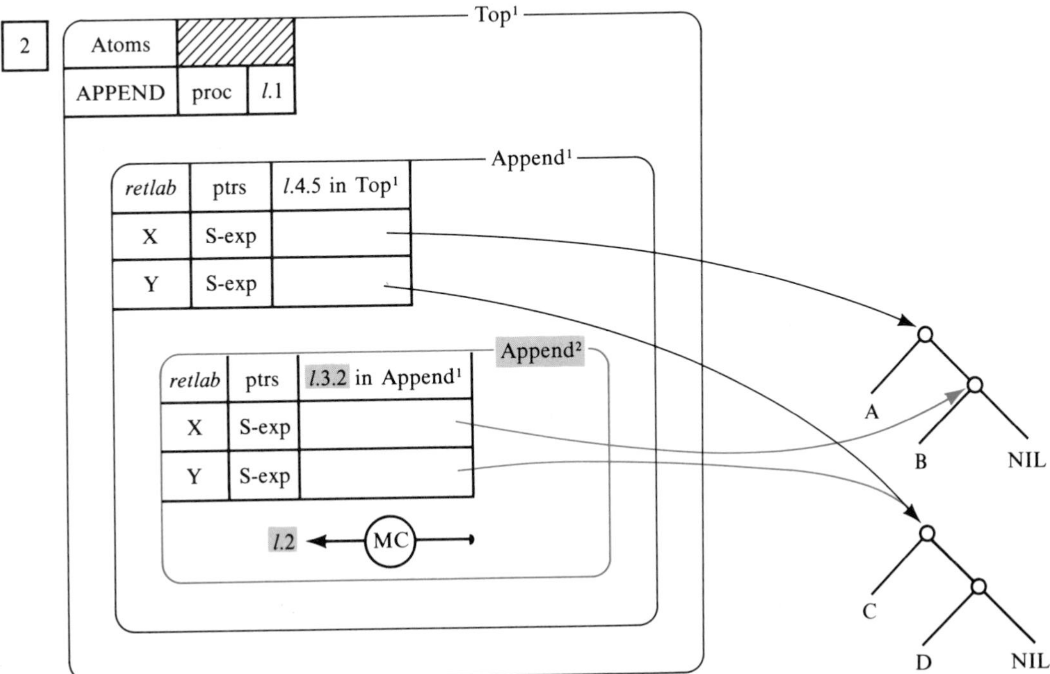

Snapshot 3 shows the situation just after the MC has made a third call on APPEND because the value of X in Append² was not NIL.

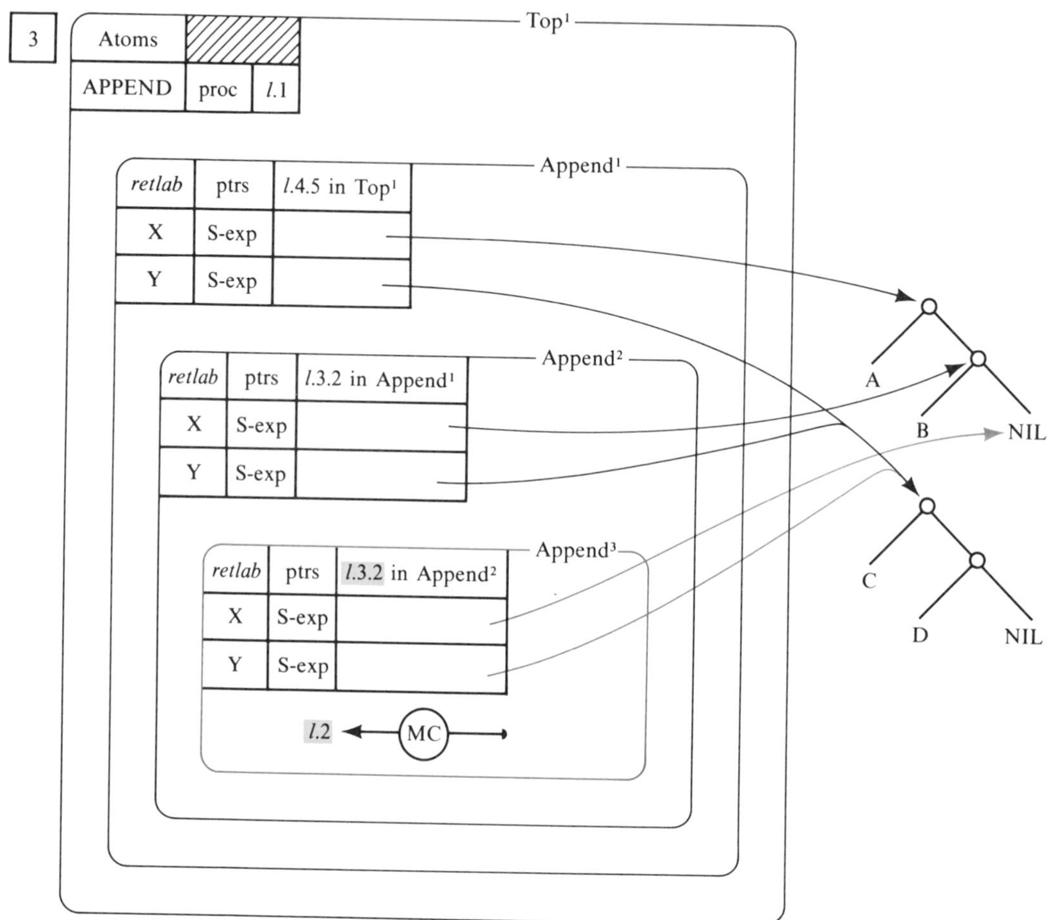

In Append[3] the value of X *is* NIL (the empty list), and so NULL (X) will be *true,* and APPEND will return the value of Y, which is the list (C D).

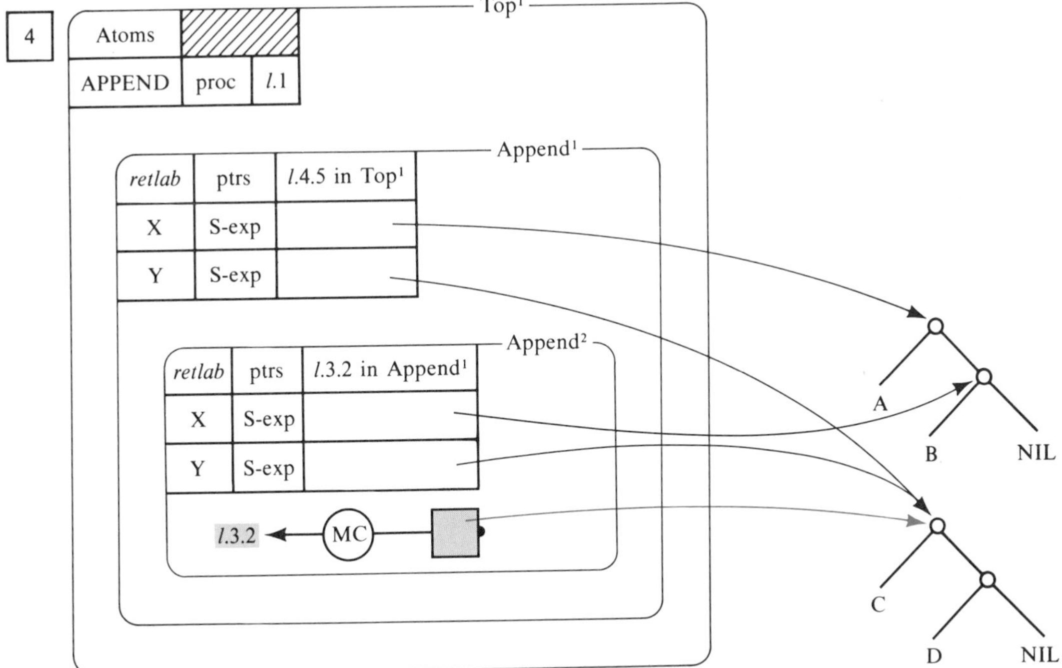

In Snapshot 4 the MC, having stacked the return value, a copy of the value of Y, has already returned to the previous invocation of APPEND. There he will execute the CONS function using as arguments the CAR of (B) and (C D), the value returned by the MC from Append[3]. The CAR of (B) is simply B, and so the CONS of B and (C D) is (B C D), as seen in Snapshot 5, which shows the MC having returned to Append[1] with this value.

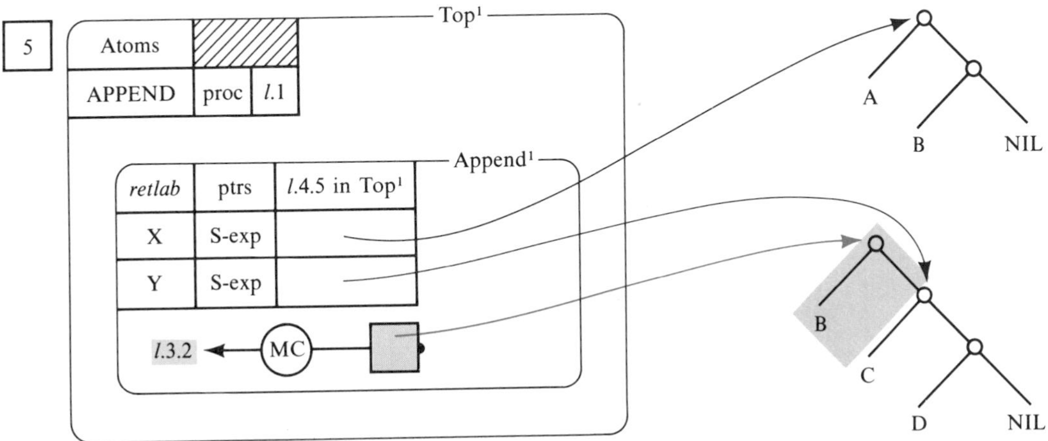

Snapshot 6 shows the result of the next CONS operation. This time the arguments are CAR (X), where X is (A B), and the value in the stack, which is

(B C D). The CONS operation produces (A B C D), since CAR (X) is simply A. Snapshot 6 shows this value returned in Top[1] just before it is printed. Snapshot 7 shows the printed result.

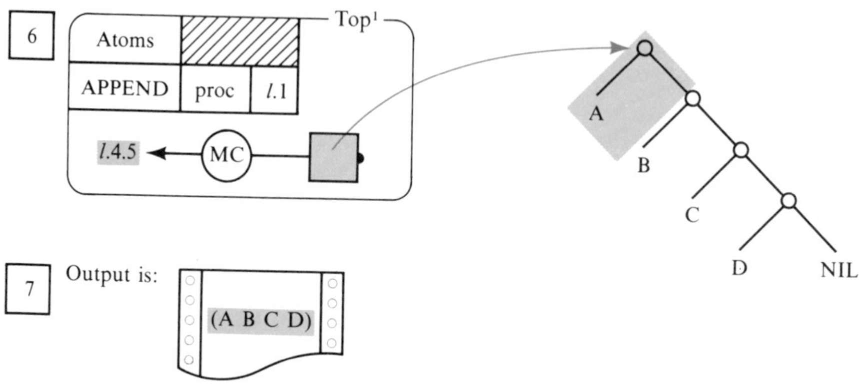

Before we leave this series of snapshots, look again at snapshot 5 and observe that the subtree

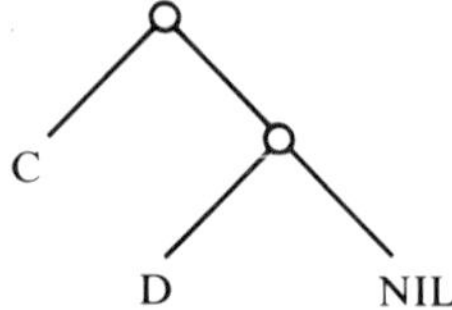

is shared; not only is it the value of the variable Y but it is also a subtree of the tree value the MC is returning to Top[1]. The value of Y is, of course, still (C D), but this situation leads us to question the safety of sharing values. Suppose for the moment that there are additional function calls in APPEND, and that in these function contours the cells pointed to by Y in Append[1] are used in various ways. Is it possible that when the MC returns to Append[1], the value of Y could have been changed? The answer is no, and the reason is that none of the five fundamental operations CAR, CDR, CONS, ATOM, and EQ alter or change any previous tree structure. CAR identifies a left subtree while CDR identifies a right subtree. CONS builds a new root node using its two parameters as left and right subtrees. ATOM and EQ only answer questions. Thus even though the cells of Y may be shared with other variables in the same or other contours, none of the fundamental operations applied to these variables can change Y since no operation actually changes the contents of any cell already in the HEAP.

Case Study 2 A Recursive Procedure to Reverse a List

In this case we consider the function REVERSE, which is given a list as its argument, and which returns a list whose elements are the same as in the given list *but in reverse order.* For example,

REVERSE ('(A B C)) will return (C B A).
REVERSE ('((A B) C)) will return (C (A B)).
REVERSE ('((A B) (C D))) will return ((C D) (A B)).

Note that only the "top level" of the argument list is reversed.

We explain the idea behind the definition of REVERSE in terms of the list (A B C D) as follows:

We first break the list to be reversed into two pieces: (A B C D)
If we then reverse the second piece: (D C B)
and append to it a list made out of the first piece: (A)
then we have reversed the original list: (D C B A)

To reverse the second piece, we simply call REVERSE recursively.

The definition of REVERSE uses the predefined function LIST (see Table 7-3) that takes one or more arguments and returns a list whose elements are the given arguments. For example,

LIST ('B) returns (B).
LIST ('B, 'C) returns (B C).
LIST ('(B C)) returns ((B C)).

That is,

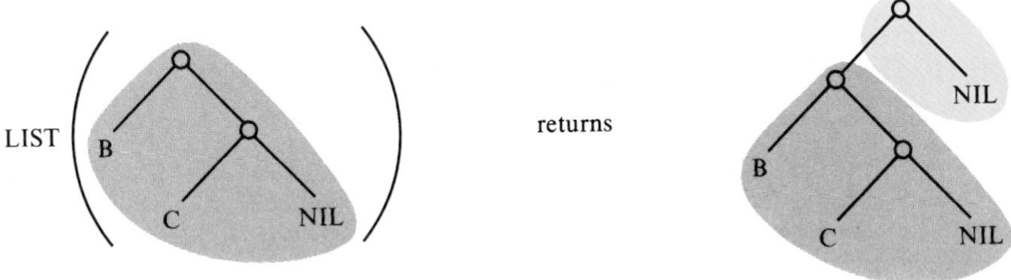

In general, LIST applied to n arguments $x_1, \ldots, x_n$ returns the list $(x_1 \ldots x_n)$.

The RLISP definition of REVERSE (a predefined function in Table 7-3) and a program using it are given in Figure 7-32.*

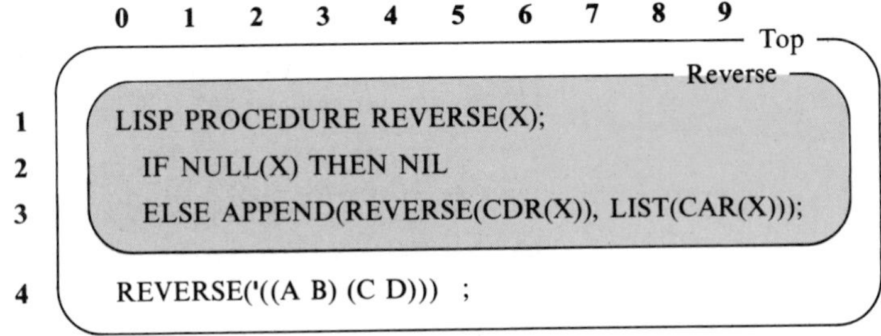


```
LISP PROCEDURE REVERSE(X);
  IF NULL(X) THEN NIL
  ELSE APPEND(REVERSE(CDR(X)), LIST(CAR(X)));

REVERSE('((A B) (C D))) ;
```

Figure 7-32

*In LISP:

```
(DEFINE '(
  (REVERSE (LAMBDA (X) (COND ((NULL X) NIL)
    (T (APPEND (REVERSE (CDR X)) (LIST (CAR X)))))))
  ))
(REVERSE '((A B) (C D)))
```

We present the snapshot sequence to trace execution of the REVERSE program using the shorthand method to represent values. To follow this sequence you must be able to answer questions such as: What is the CDR of ((C D))? The answer is NIL—be sure you see why!

And now the snapshot sequence for REVERSE. In snapshot 1, the MC is about to execute a second call on REVERSE because X in Reverse[1] is not NIL. The argument of this second call, CDR (X), is ((C D)).

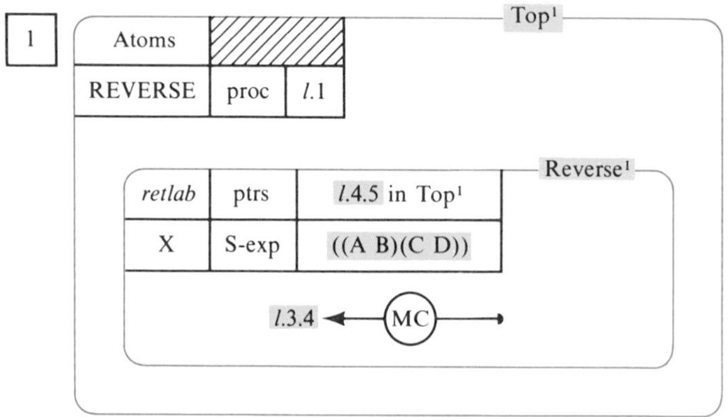

In shapshot 2, a call on REVERSE is again needed because X in Reverse[2] is not NIL. The argument will be CDR (X), which in this case will be NIL, and NULL(NIL) is T.

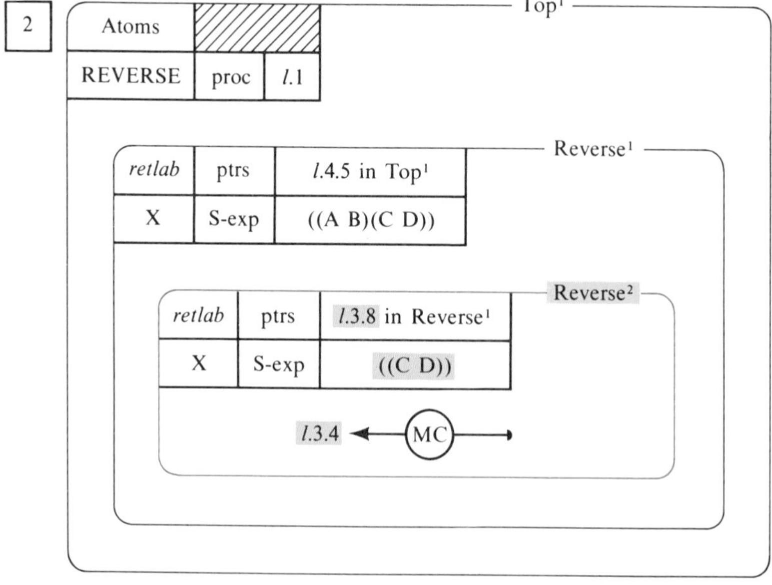

In snapshot 3, the MC has just stacked NIL in preparation for a return to Reverse[2].

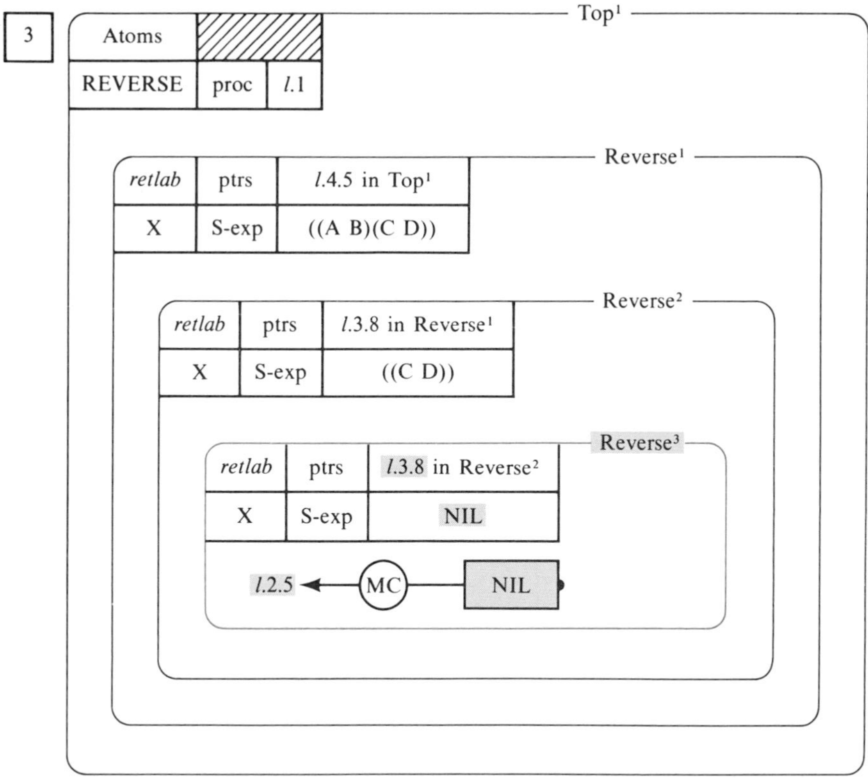

In snapshot 4, the MC is back in Reverse² and is about to evaluate LIST (CAR (X)).

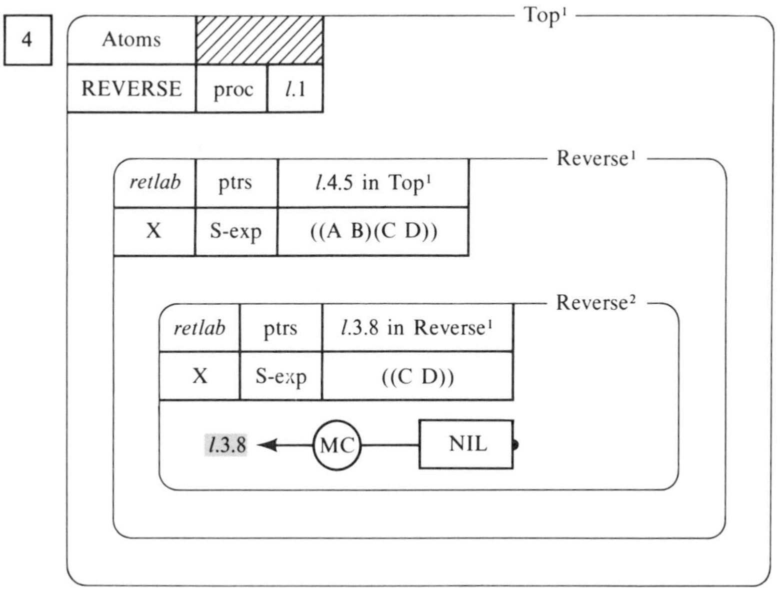

In snapshot 5, the MC has just evaluated LIST and stacked the result ((C D)). The MC is now ready to evaluate APPEND. The top-of-stack element becomes the second argument while the next-to-top-of-stack element becomes the first argument of APPEND.

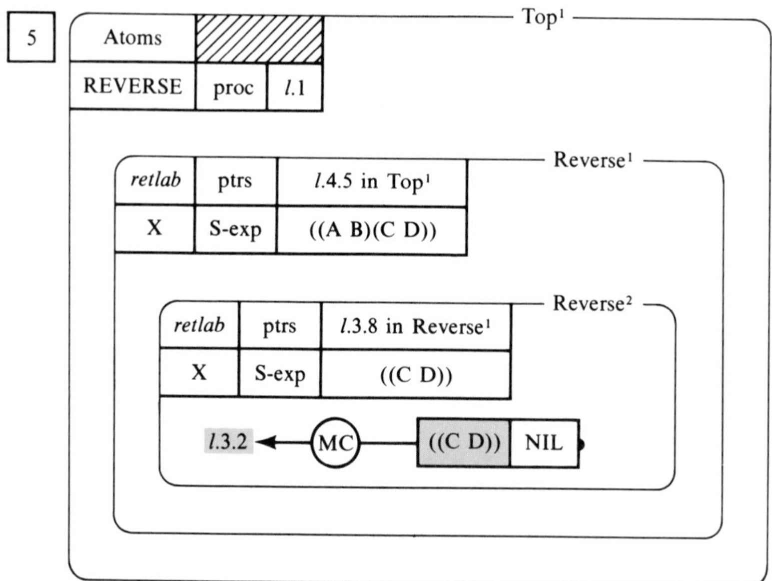

In snapshot 6, the MC is about to return from Append¹ after stacking the return value ((C D)). (We do not normally show contours for predefined functions called by the function being traced, but contours for APPEND will be shown for comparison with the computer run that follows the snapshots.)

6

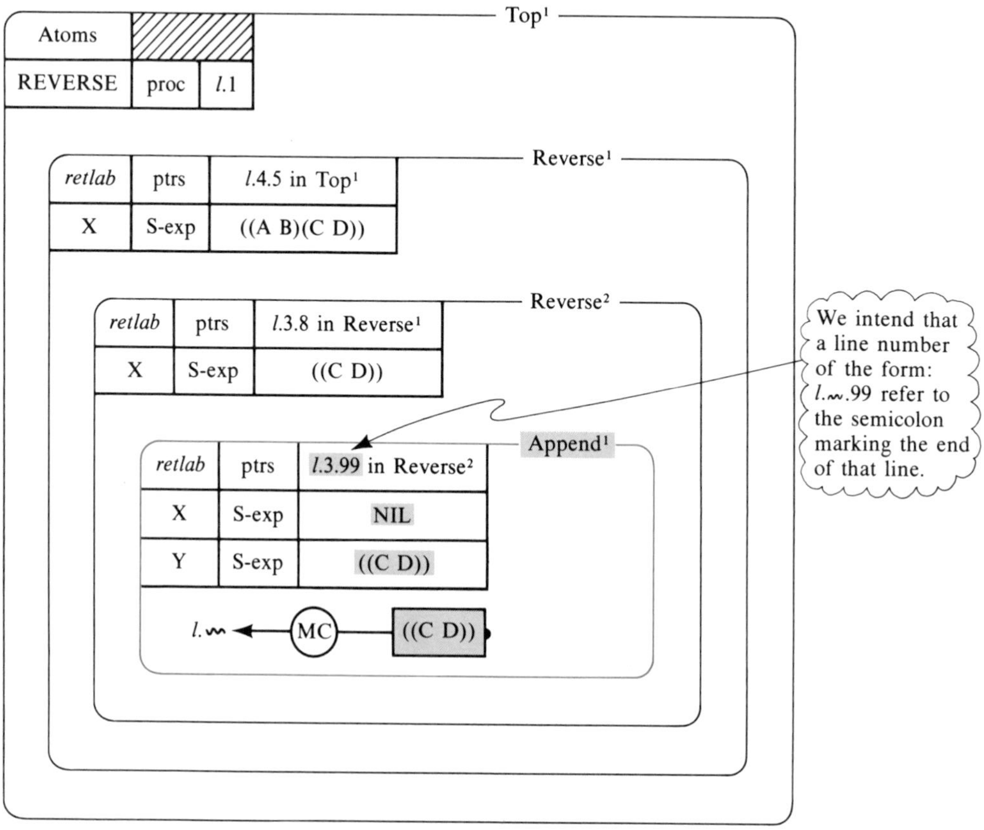

Top¹

Atoms		
REVERSE	proc	*l*.1

Reverse¹

retlab	ptrs	*l*.4.5 in Top¹
X	S-exp	((A B)(C D))

Reverse²

retlab	ptrs	*l*.3.8 in Reverse¹
X	S-exp	((C D))

Append¹

retlab	ptrs	*l*.3.99 in Reverse²
X	S-exp	NIL
Y	S-exp	((C D))

l.~ ← MC — ((C D))

We intend that a line number of the form: *l*.~.99 refer to the semicolon marking the end of that line.

In snapshot 7, the MC has returned to Reverse² with the value ((C D)). This same value can now be returned to Reverse¹ as seen in snapshot 8.

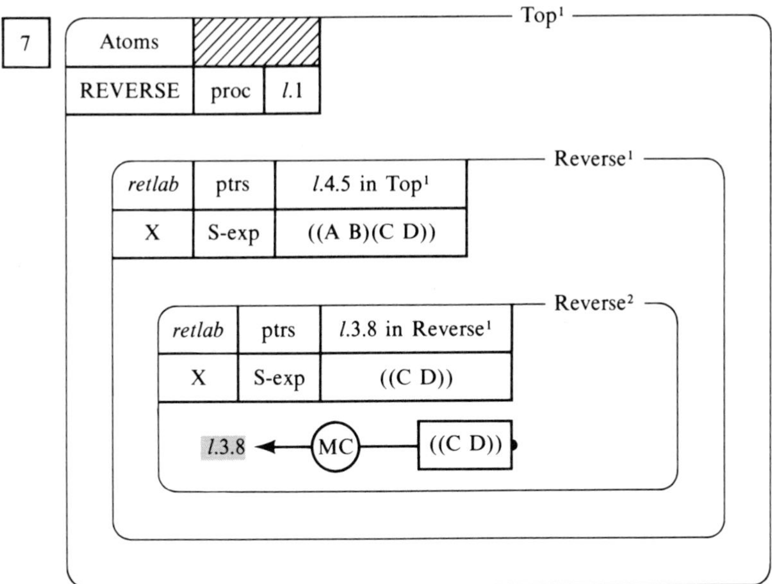

In snapshot 8, the MC is again ready to evaluate LIST (CAR (X)), where CAR (X) now is (A B).

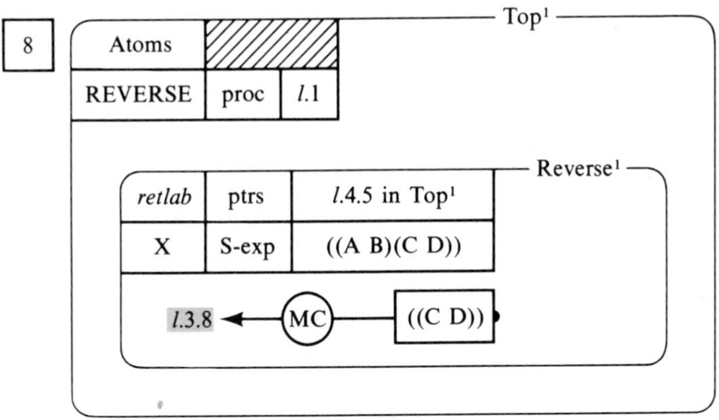

In snapshot 9, the value returned from LIST has been stacked, and the MC is now ready to call APPEND. Note that the next-to-top stack element becomes the *first* argument for APPEND.

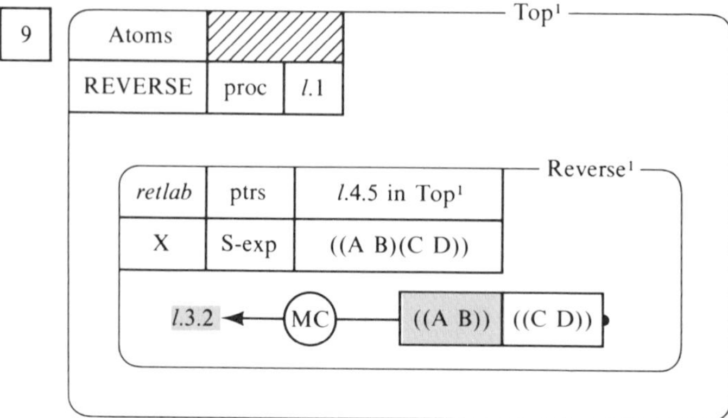

In snapshot 10, the MC is about to return from Append[2] with a new value in the stack. (Previous values in the stack were "popped off" to provide arguments for this invocation of APPEND.)

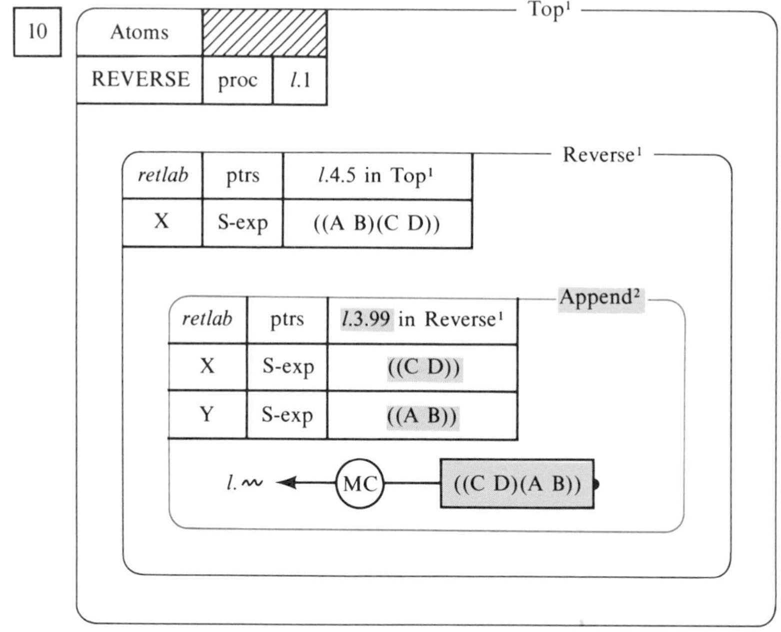

In snapshot 11, the MC is about to return from the original call on REVERSE and display the value in the stack (snapshot 12).

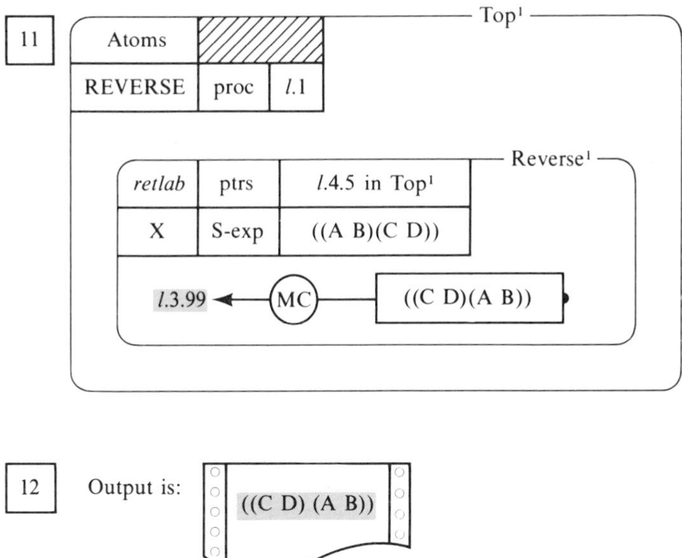

Figure 7-33 is a copy of an actual computer run of the RLISP program for REVERSE ('((A B) (C D))). This run demonstrates the use of the *trace* feature of Lisp. When a function is traced, its arguments are printed each time it is called, and its value is printed each time it returns. The trace shown exactly parallels the series of snapshots given on the previous pages.

Exercises 7-11

1 Table 7-3 shows a definition for REVERSE that uses an auxiliary function R1. Using this definition, draw snapshots that trace the execution of REVERSE ('(A B)). Include contours for each call of REVERSE and R1.

2 We noted above that REVERSE reverses only the top level of a list. Thus

REVERSE ('((A B) C (D E) F)) = (F (D E) C (A B)).

Define a procedure SUPERREVERSE that reverses *all* levels of a list. That is,

SUPERREVERSE ('((A B) C (D E) F)) = (F (E D) C (B A)).

```
 >@REDUCE*LISPLIB.RLISP

 REDUCE 2 (SEP-19-76) ...

  LISP PROCEDURE REV(X);
 >   IF NULL(X) THEN NIL
 >   ELSE AP(REV(CDR(X)),LIST(CAR(X)));

 REV

  LISP PROCEDURE AP(L1,L2);
 >   IF NULL(L1) THEN L2
 >   ELSE CONS(CAR(L1),AP(CDR(L1),L2));

 AP

 >TR REV,AP;

 T

 >REV('((A B)(C D)));

1  >ENTERING REV [0]
    X: ((A B) (C D))

2      >ENTERING REV [1]
        X: ((C D))

3          >ENTERING REV [2]
            X: NIL

4          <LEAVING REV [2]
            $VAL: NIL

6          >ENTERING AP [2]
            L1: NIL
            L2: ((C D))

6          <LEAVING AP [2]
            $VAL: ((C D))

8      <LEAVING REV [1]
        $VAL: ((C D))

10     >ENTERING AP [1]
        L1: ((C D))
        L2: ((A B))

           >ENTERING AP [2]
            L1: NIL
            L2: ((A B))

           <LEAVING AP [2]
            $VAL: ((A B))

10     <LEAVING AP [1]
        $VAL: ((C D) (A B))

11 <LEAVING REV [0]
    $VAL: ((C D) (A B))

12  ((C D) (A B))
```

The names REV and AP are used to prevent confusion with the predefined functions REVERSE and APPEND.

RLISP command to trace REV and AP

Numbers in square brackets indicate the current depth of the call tree.

Numbers in boxes to the left of the trace show (as closely as possible) the correspondence between the trace and the snapshots given earlier.

Final Result

Figure 7-33

7-12 FUNCTION ARGUMENTS AND PROCEDURE PARAMETERS

In Lisp, a procedure may have a parameter whose matching argument is itself a procedure. The contour cell for a procedure parameter of type *proc* has as its value an ip,ep pair. For example, if procedure PROC has a procedure parameter P, then when PROC is called, the cell for P appears as shown in Figure 7-34.

As in Algol, the ip part of the value serves to locate the body of the procedure argument, and the ep specifies the environment (contour) in which a contour for that procedure is placed when and if it is invoked in PROC. Lisp *differs* from Algol in the way the ep is determined, and in this section we examine the Lisp technique.

To make our example a bit more concrete,

1. Suppose that procedure PROC has two parameters: P, a procedure parameter, and X, whose matching argument is an S-expression, that is, PROC (P, X).
2. Suppose also that PROC is to be called from inside procedure CALLER, and that the arguments provided for PROC are FN, a function, and Y, a parameter of CALLER.

The call of PROC appears in the body of CALLER as follows:

```
LISP PROCEDURE CALLER (. . . Y . . .);
  . . . PROC (FUNCTION (FN), Y) . . . ;
```

Notice that the first argument in the call on PROC is not simply the procedure name FN, but rather is FUNCTION (FN). FUNCTION is a special function in Lisp whose job is to establish the ep for arguments that are procedures. Since all procedures in Lisp are functions, such an argument is referred to as a *function argument* and is nicknamed a *funarg*. Now for the important point: the value of FUNCTION (FN) is an ip,ep pair that becomes the value of the procedure parameter P of PROC. The intended ep of this pair is the *environment in which FUNCTION is called,* and this is the same as the environment in which PROC is called. Thus Figure 7-35 shows the state of affairs after entry into PROC.

Figure 7-34. Cell for procedure parameter P.

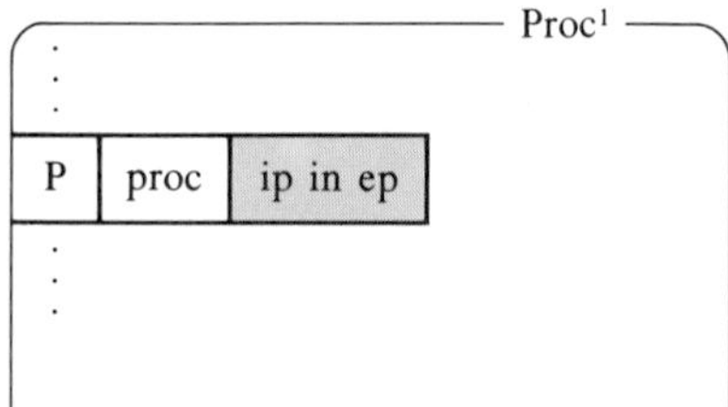

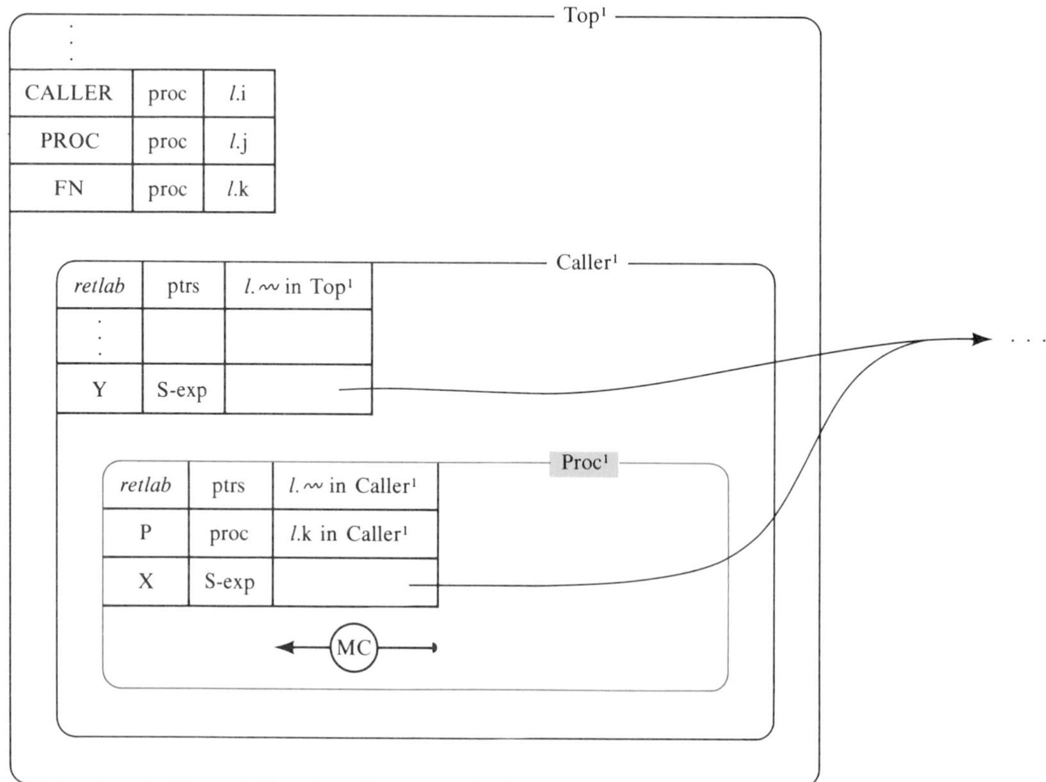

Figure 7-35. **The situation after the call on PROC.**

Since the funarg was supplied to PROC inside the first invocation of CALLER, the ep of P in PROC¹ is CALLER¹. Assuming P is called inside PROC, a possible call might be P (X). Then the effect is as shown in Figure 7-36. The function executed inside P¹ is, of course, FN, the argument matching P in PROC.

What is distinctive about the Lisp scheme for funargs becomes clearer when we recall that in Algol the placement of a contour like P¹ is a *static* property of the program. That is, P¹ would be placed *in the environment where FN is declared,* since *every* execution of FN must take place in that environment. In Lisp, however, the funarg mechanism* makes the placement of the contour P¹ a *dynamic* property of the program that depends on where FN was used as a function argument.†

*Readers should be aware that some actual Lisp systems are "deficient" in that they fail to implement funargs according to this rule. Such systems usually cause the funarg to execute inside the environment of its caller, which in this case is PROC¹. After you finish reading this section you should be able to construct a program to test whether your Lisp system implements funargs correctly.

†There is yet another possibility for the handling of functional arguments in Lisp. If in CALLER we *quote* the functional argument, rather than apply FUNCTION to it [that is, we write PROC ('FN, Y) in CALLER], then the contour for FN will be placed inside the contour from which it is invoked. In the example above, this would result in P¹, the contour in which FN is executed, being placed inside PROC¹.

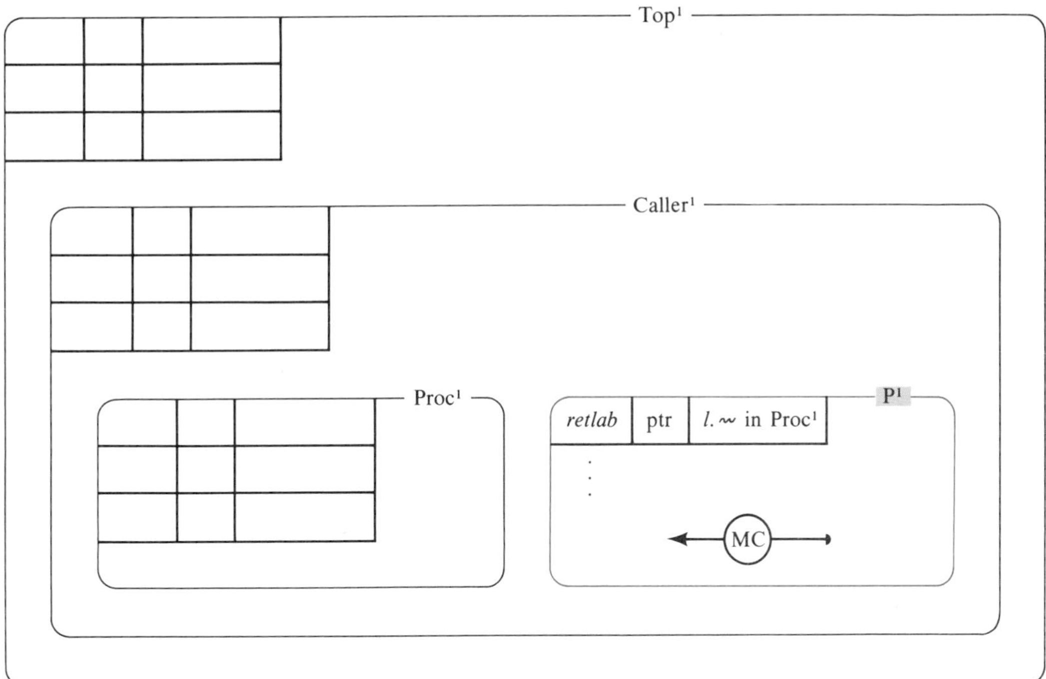

Figure 7-36. **The situation after PROC calls P.**

Before we look at an example, there is one additional point to be made. Inside the procedure PROC, there are *two* possible ways to use the parameter P:

1. PROC can invoke P as a procedure, as described above.
2. PROC can pass P as an argument to still another procedure (or possibly to itself in a recursive call), thus enabling a "descendant" procedure to invoke the original funarg. In this case, the argument provided is just P. (It is not necessary to express this argument as FUNCTION (P).) The ip,ep pair that is the value of P in PROC^1 becomes the value of the appropriate parameter in the descendant procedure contour, with the result that FN will still be executed in the environment where it was first passed as a funarg.*

Both of these uses of P will be illustrated in the next case study.

Case Study 3 *Use of Funargs.* This case study is in two parts. The first part illustrates a simple and plausible use of a funarg. The second part, which some

*It is interesting to speculate about what would happen if we did provide FUNCTION (P) as an argument in a procedure call inside PROC. Would the ep of the funarg be changed? The answer is no. Although this "extra" use of FUNCTION would not produce an error, it would have no effect. The ep of the funarg in any descendant of PROC will always be the same as it is in PROC itself.

readers may choose to skip on first reading, illustrates an important subtlety of function argument treatment in Lisp.

Part 1. The MAPCAR Procedure. This procedure has two parameters—a list X and a procedure P—whose matching argument is a funarg that is a procedure of one argument. MAPCAR returns a new list whose successive elements are values obtained by applying P to the respective elements of X. The RLISP program in Figure 7-37 serves as our illustration. (See Exercise 2, Section 7-11 for a specification of SUPPERREVERSE.) Note the use of the word FUNCTION in the calls on MAPCAR, for example, FUNCTION (LENGTH).

A series of snapshots will explain the semantics of procedure calls that involve procedure parameters. We show execution of line 5 of the preceding program in some detail (snapshots 1–10). Here the procedure parameter P represents the funarg REVERSE. The environment in which the funarg originates is Top^1, and so whenever P is called, the corresponding argument REVERSE must (and does) execute in a contour nested immediately within Top^1, as can be seen in snapshots 2 and 5.

If we inspect the body of MAPCAR, line 3 in particular, we see the two possible uses of procedure parameter P (which represents the funarg). The first use invokes P in the expression P (CAR (X)), where P's argument is CAR (X). The second use passes P along as an ordinary argument to a procedure, in this case to MAPCAR itself, in the expression MAPCAR (CDR (X), P). Notice that FUNCTION is not used here even though P serves as an argument that represents a function. This is because the value of the argument P in the MAPCAR^1 environment is already the desired ip,ep pair. We use FUNCTION only when we want to create such a pair.

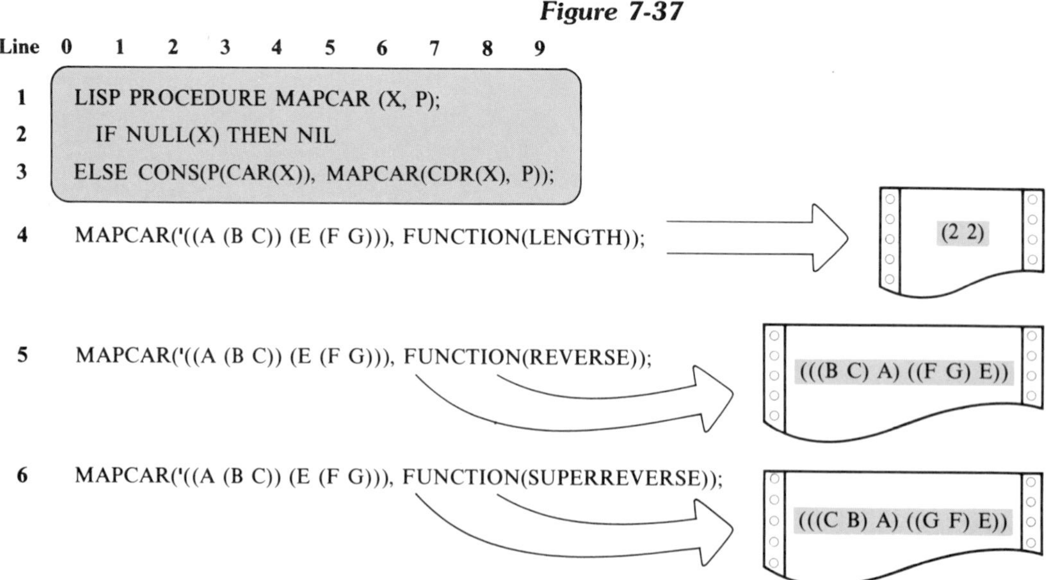

Figure 7-37

To save space in these snapshots, MAPCAR and REVERSE are abbreviated as MPC and REV, respectively. In snapshot 1, the MC has called MAPCAR. The contour MPC¹ has been formed. The parameter P's matching argument is the funarg REVERSE, and so P is assigned an ip,ep pair. The ip is a pointer to the predefined function REVERSE; the ep is Top¹.

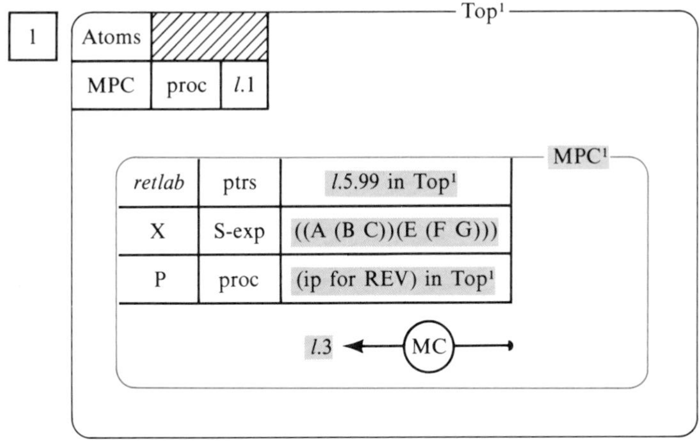

Since the argument X in MPC¹ is not NIL, the arguments for the CONS operation on line 3 must be evaluated. The first one, P (CAR (X)), requires calling P with an argument CAR (X), which is (A (B C)) in this case. But P is specified as the REVERSE function. P is called by establishing a contour P¹ in Top¹ as specified by the ep for P. Inside P¹ the cell for parameter X gets the value (A (B C)). When P has been executed to completion, the MC places on his stack the value P (X), which is really REVERSE (X), which is ((B C) A). This is the situation shown in snapshot 2 just prior to the MC's return to MPC¹.

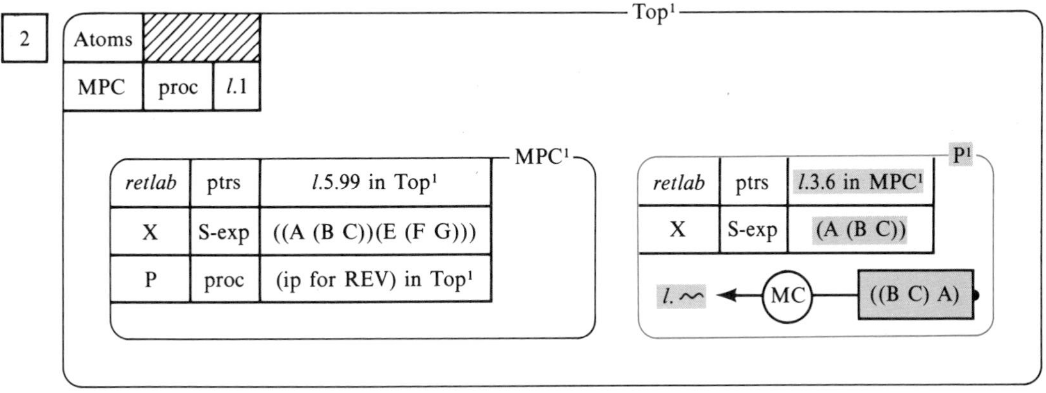

Snapshot 3 shows the MC about to execute a recursive call on MAPCAR to get the second value for the CONS operation on line 3.

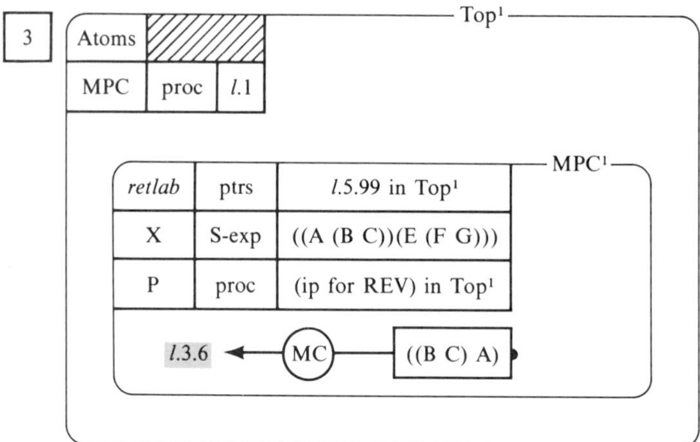

The second call on MAPCAR produces the contour MPC². The parameter value for X in this contour is the CDR of the previous X, or ((E (F G))). The parameter value for P is an exact copy of the value of P in MPC¹. In snapshot 4, the MC is about to execute the ELSE clause, requiring first a call on the parameter P and then another recursive call on MAPCAR. The value on the MC's stack came with him from MPC¹.

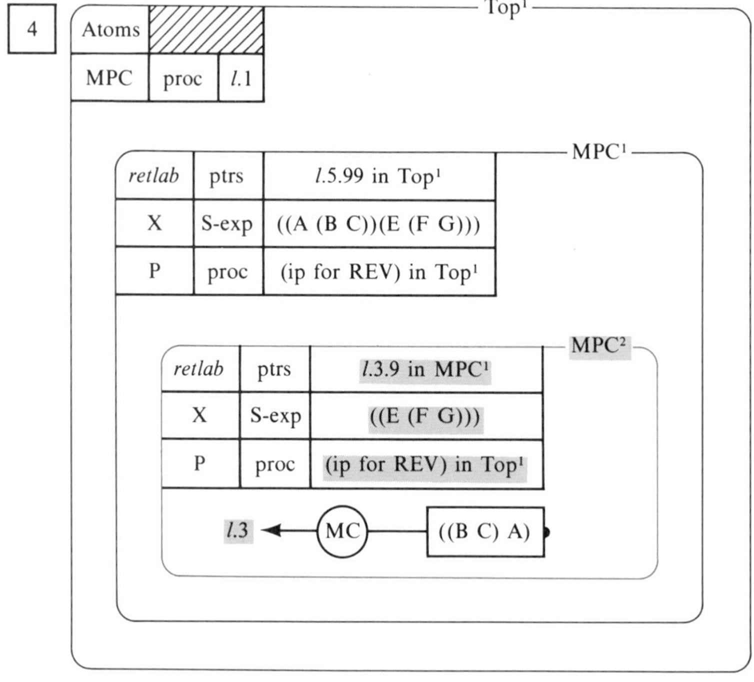

Snapshot 5 shows the MC about to return from the second call on P (that is, REVERSE), after REVERSE (X), which is ((F G) E) in this case, has been stacked. Upon return to MPC², a third call must be made on MAPCAR as seen in snapshot 6. [Note again that the parameter P is and must be executed in Top¹ as required by its ep value. In this particular simple example the same result would have been obtained had P^2 been mistakenly nested inside MPC^2 (and P^1 inside MPC^1). However, more complex examples can easily be devised where the proper placement of the contour for the called procedure is of critical importance. One such example contrived for the purpose is given in part 2 of this case study.]

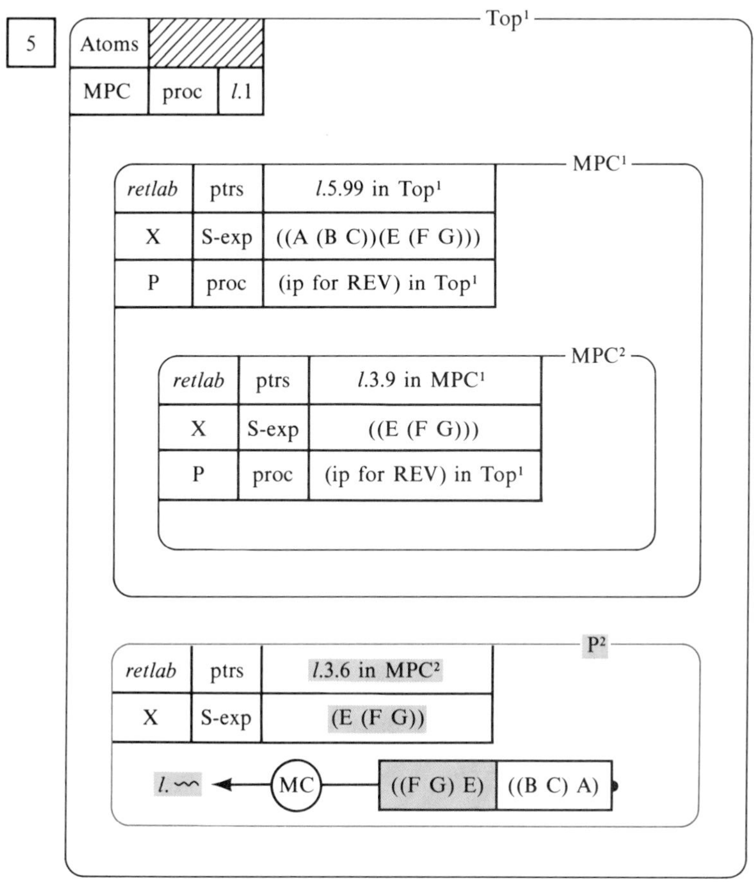

In snapshot 6, the MC is about to return from the third invocation of MAPCAR. Since X is NIL, the value NIL has been stacked. Upon return to MPC², the CONS function will be called. Values for the arguments of CONS will be taken from the top of the stack. For completeness we will show explicitly the calls on the basic function CONS, using X and Y as the names of its parameters.

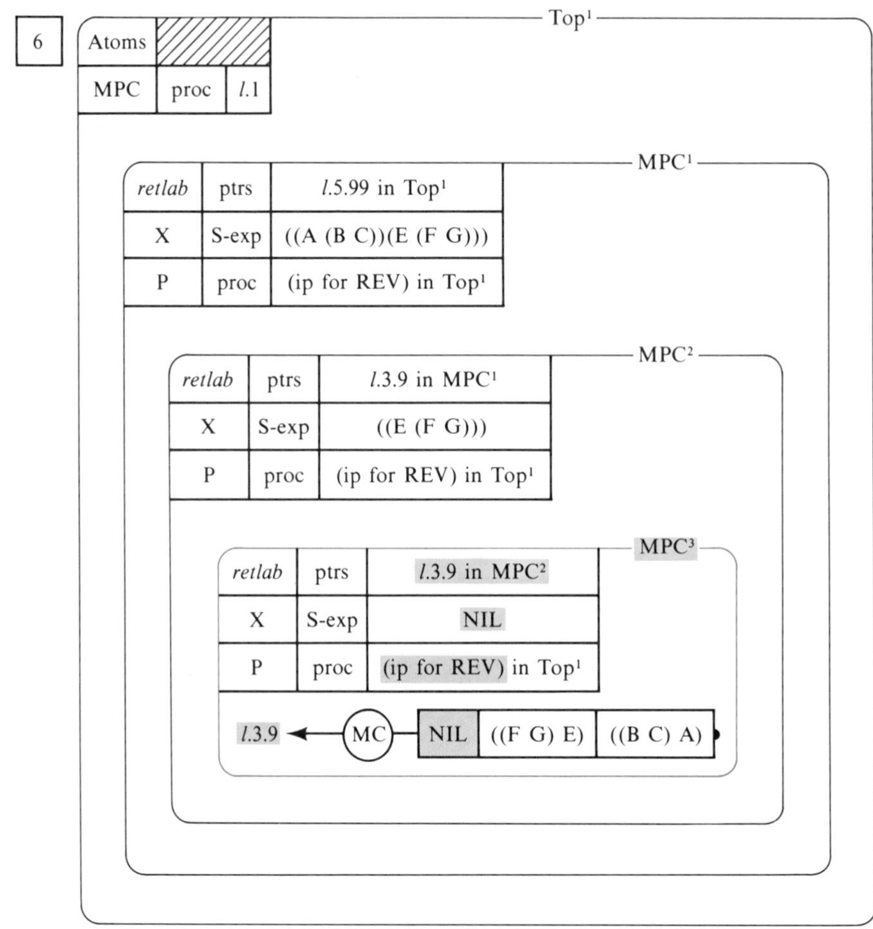

Snapshot 7 shows the MC about to return from the call on CONS. The arguments ((F G) E) and NIL were taken from the top of the stack, the top-most going to the parameter Y and the next-to-top going to X. The value to be returned from CONS is the list (((F G) E)), which has already been pushed onto the stack, preparatory to the return to MPC².

7

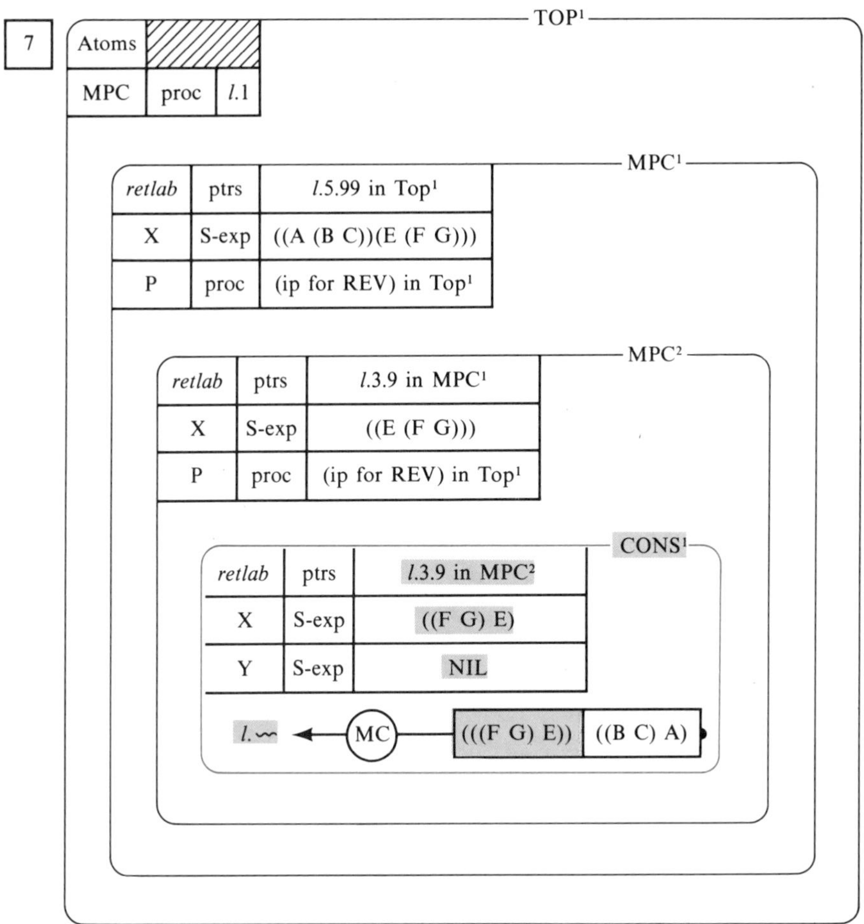

Snapshot 8 shows the situation just after the second call on CONS has been made, this time within MPC¹. The arguments for this call were obtained from the stack, as was the case in the first call on CONS. At this point the stack is empty.

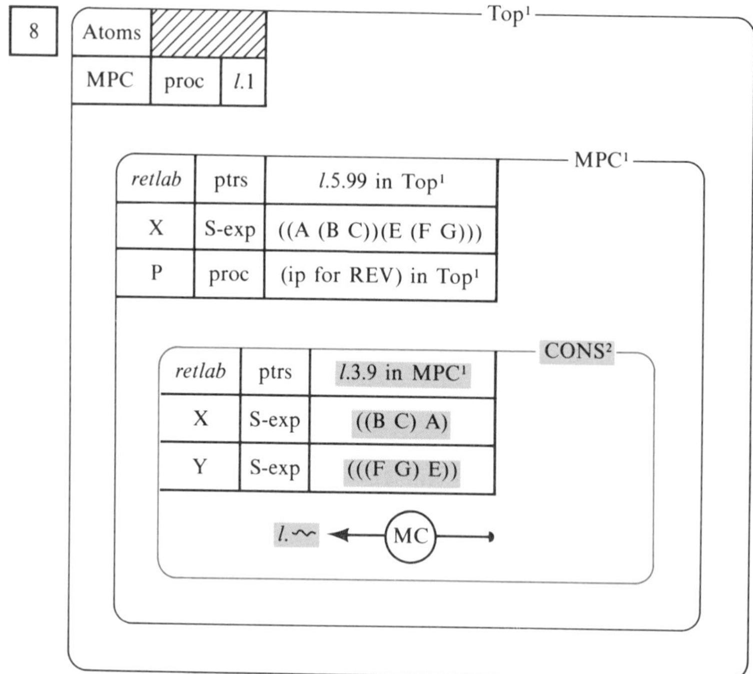

Snapshot 9 shows the situation on return from CONS² to MPC¹ with the stacked value, (((B C) A) ((F G) E)). The MC is about to return to Top¹. The value to be displayed is on the top of the stack. Snapshot 10 shows the final results.

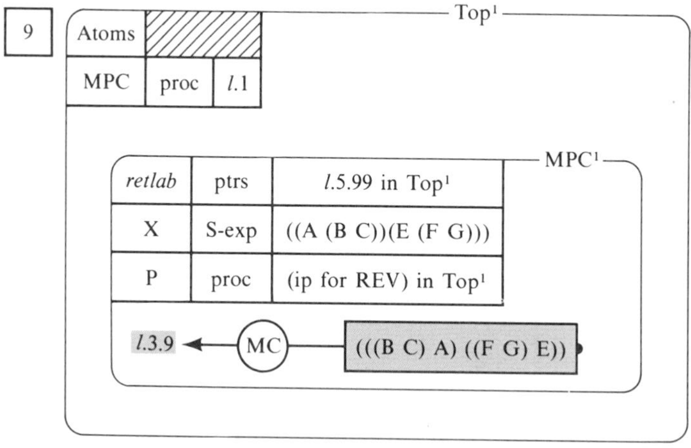

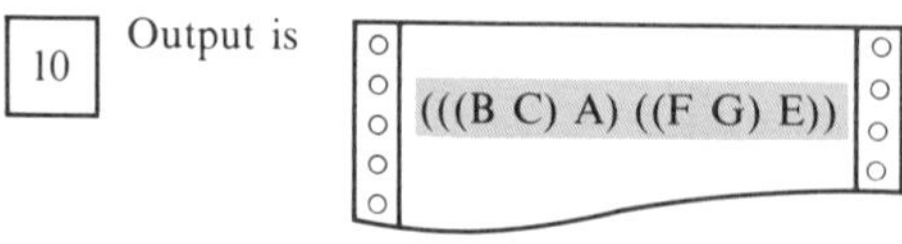

Part 2. A Case Where the Placement of the Contour for the Funarg Is Critical. In the funarg examples given in part 1 of this case study, the body of each function argument, when executed, refers only to its own parameter(s) and/or to itself, but never to a value in a cell that is global to the contour for the given function. Critical cases arise when the funarg procedure does refer to such a global value, that is, to a cell in any contour enclosing the contour of the funarg procedure. For such a funarg, proper placement of its contour is necessary so that the required global value is "visible."

The program given in Figure 7-38 and the snapshots of its execution represent such a case. Function USEY uses the variable Y globally (line 2), and is a funarg to function TEST (line 4). Notice that the declaration of procedure USEY does not, by itself, contain on line 2 enough information to determine *which* cell Y will be accessed. Since USEY is invoked via the funarg mechanism, it is the action of FUNCTION (line 4) that determines the placement of the contour for USEY, and thus what cell for Y will be visible during USEY's execution.

Now study the following snapshot sequence, which traces the execution of the command on line 7. Snapshot 1 shows the state of affairs after CALLER has been invoked with arguments 'A and 'B and when the call on TEST at line 4 is about to be executed. This call will supply a funarg, USEY, and an ordinary argument, X.

Figure 7-38

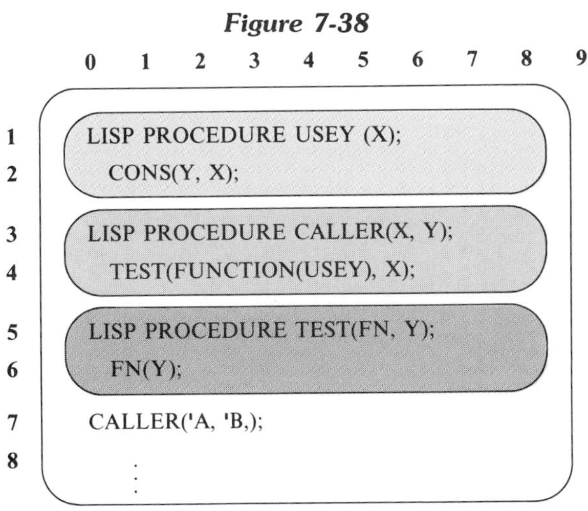

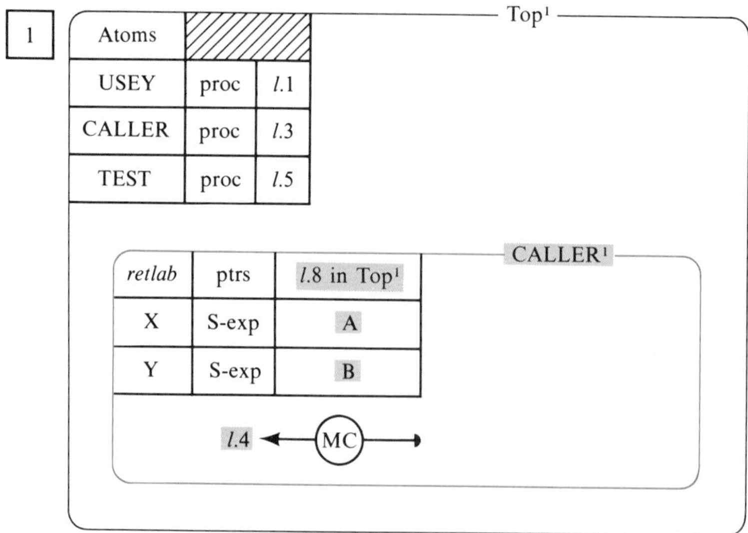

In snapshot 2, the procedure TEST has been invoked. The value of the funarg is an ip,ep pair, where ip is the line number for USEY and ep is CALLER¹, the environment supplying the funarg. This ip,ep pair is assigned to the cell of parameter FN. CALLER also passes the value of X, which is the atom A, to parameter Y in TEST. At this point the MC is about to execute the call on FN on line 6. This will result in a call on the funarg USEY.

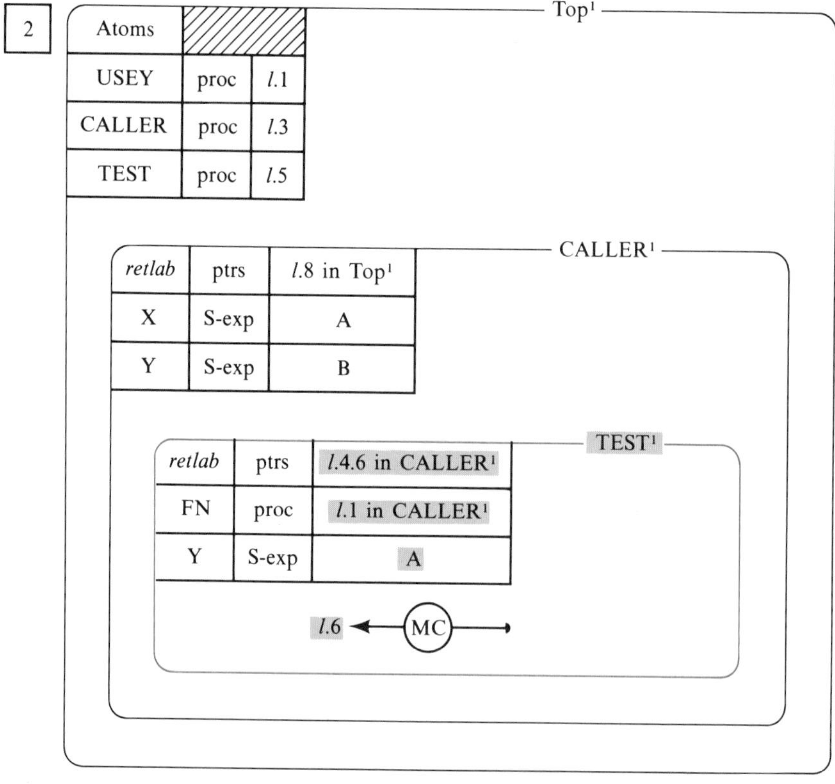

Snapshot 3 shows what happens when the funarg USEY is invoked. A contour FN¹ is created nested immediately within the environment specified by the ep (namely, CALLER¹). Executing within FN¹ the MC computes the line 2 expression, CONS (Y, X), which in this case evaluates to the dotted pair (B.A). The global Y is accessed in CALLER¹ and X in FN¹.

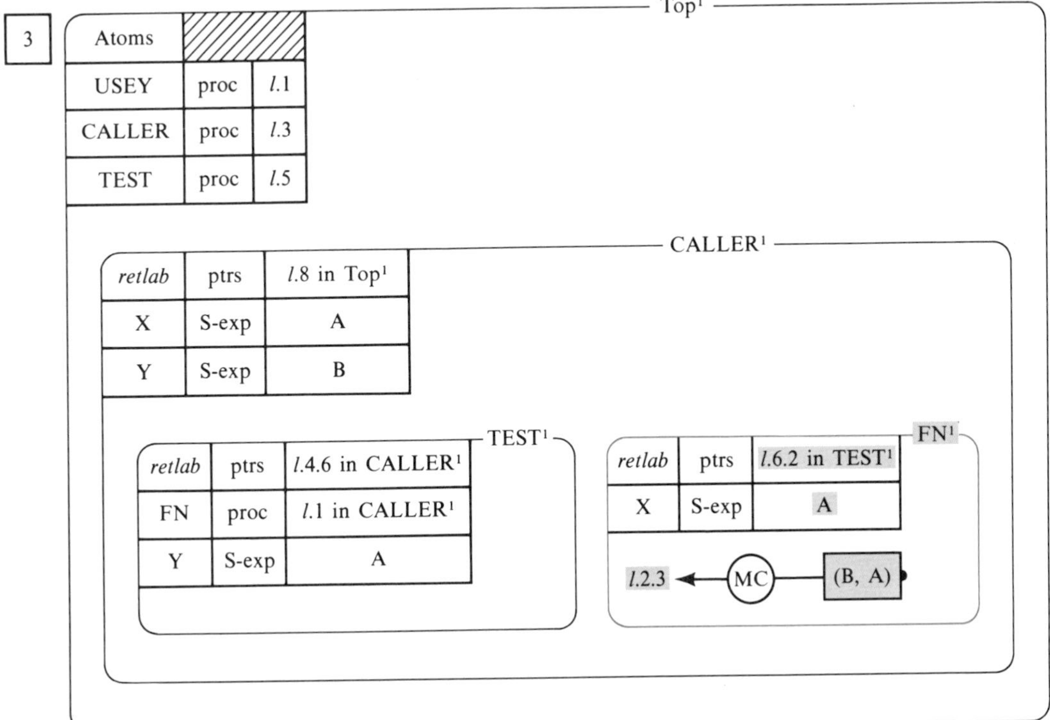

We can now see how critical it is that FN¹ be nested within CALLER¹. Had it been nested either within TEST¹, the environment of the funarg's caller, or within Top¹, the environment in which the funarg was defined, the outcome would have been quite different. If FN¹ were nested within TEST¹, the result returned would have been (A.A) instead of (B.A). If FN¹ were nested within Top¹, the value of Y in the expression CONS (Y, X) would have been undefined and an error message would have been produced.

This example was, of course, contrived to present the "critical" case: a funarg containing a global reference. Although rare, such situations can and do occur in Lisp. The funarg mechanism represents an interesting alternative to the methods used in other languages for determining the environment in which a function argument is executed. The paper by Moses (1970) pursues this subject further.

7-13
CASE STUDY 4: A PROGRAM FOR SYMBOLIC DIFFERENTIATION*

The recursive process of differentiation as taught in elementary differential calculus courses is one that can easily be carried out manually on simple algebraic expressions, but not so easily on more complex expressions. However, as explained in Section 3-4, this process can be expressed in algorithmic form with very little difficulty, provided we use a language in which the algebraic expression can be represented as a simple data structure and provided that this data structure can be manipulated by relatively simple-to-express operations. This case study shows how we can program *symbolic differentiation* in Lisp, a language ideally suited to this task because:

1. Algebraic expressions are directly mappable into binary tree structures, which Lisp is designed to handle.
2. Many of the operations we need to execute on such mapped expressions are primitive in Lisp.
3. The process of differentiation can be seen from the rules to be recursive and the mechanism to support recursion is built into Lisp.

For this case study we shall confine our differentiation to algebraic expressions involving constants, variables, and the binary operations of + and ×. Extensions to expressions involving other operators are left as exercises.

The rules of differentiation are repeated in Figure 7-39. Note again that the third and fourth are "doubly" recursive, leading to binary call trees.

We shall represent algebraic expressions in Lisp in *prefix* form, where the operator precedes its two operands. Well-formed infix expressions may easily

Figure 7-39

1. $\dfrac{dx}{dx} = 1$

2. $\dfrac{d\ \text{constant}}{dx} = 0$

3. $\dfrac{d(f + g)}{dx} = \dfrac{df}{dx} + \dfrac{dg}{dx}$

4. $\dfrac{d(f \times g)}{dx} = f \times \dfrac{dg}{dx} + g \times \dfrac{df}{dx}$

(rules 3 and 4: where f and g are functions of x or constants)

*This case study is drawn from "Introduction to LISP" by D. Lurie, Department of Physics, Technion-Israel Institute of Technology. The lecture was given at a seminar course on Computing as a Language of Physics, Trieste, August 1971.

be converted to prefix form: if FIRST and SECOND refer to the two operands of an operator OP, then FIRST OP SECOND translates into OP FIRST SECOND. There is a Lisp S-expression representation that is practically the same as the prefix form of an algebraic expression, as can be seen from the examples given in Figure 7-40.

Figure 7-41 is a flowchart for a differentiation procedure D. This flowchart is very closely related to the one in Figure 3-51, with the main difference being the switch from infix to prefix notation in Figure 7-41.

Given the Lisp form for prefix expressions shown in Figure 7-40, it is easy to see how the functions OP, FIRST, and SECOND used in Figure 7-41 may be implemented.

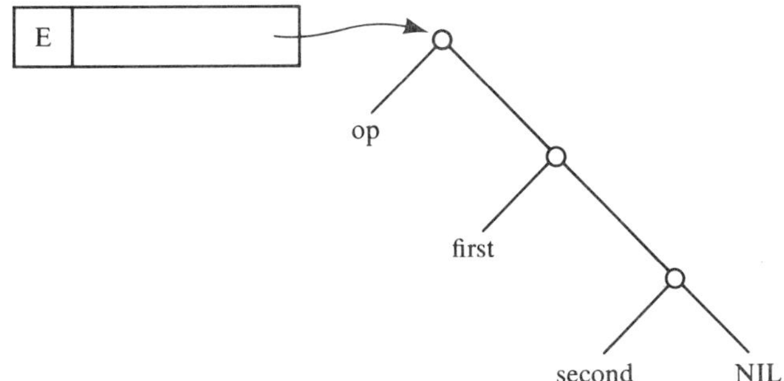

If, as indicated above, E is the structure (op first second), then

op is CAR(E)
first is CAR(CDR(E))
second is CAR(CDR(CDR(E)))

These relationships are formalized in Figure 7-42. Notice how easily one can refer to components of interest within an S-expression, using these definitions. For example, if E is (PLUS X (PLUS Y Z)) then the Y may be referred to as FIRST (SECOND (E)).

Figure 7-43 shows the RLISP equivalent* of the Figure 7-41 flowchart for D incorporating the definitions of Figure 7-42. The correspondence between flowchart and RLISP procedure is so direct as to require no further comment.

Figure 7-40

Infix Form	Prefix Form	Lisp Form
x + y	+ x y	(PLUS X Y)
x × y	× x y	(TIMES X Y)
x × (y + z)	× x + y z	(TIMES X (PLUS Y Z))
$3y^2 + 2y$	+ × 3 × y y × 2 y	(PLUS (TIMES 3 (TIMES Y Y)) (TIMES 2 Y))

*The LISP equivalent of the Figure 7-43 program is given as a footnote on page 446.

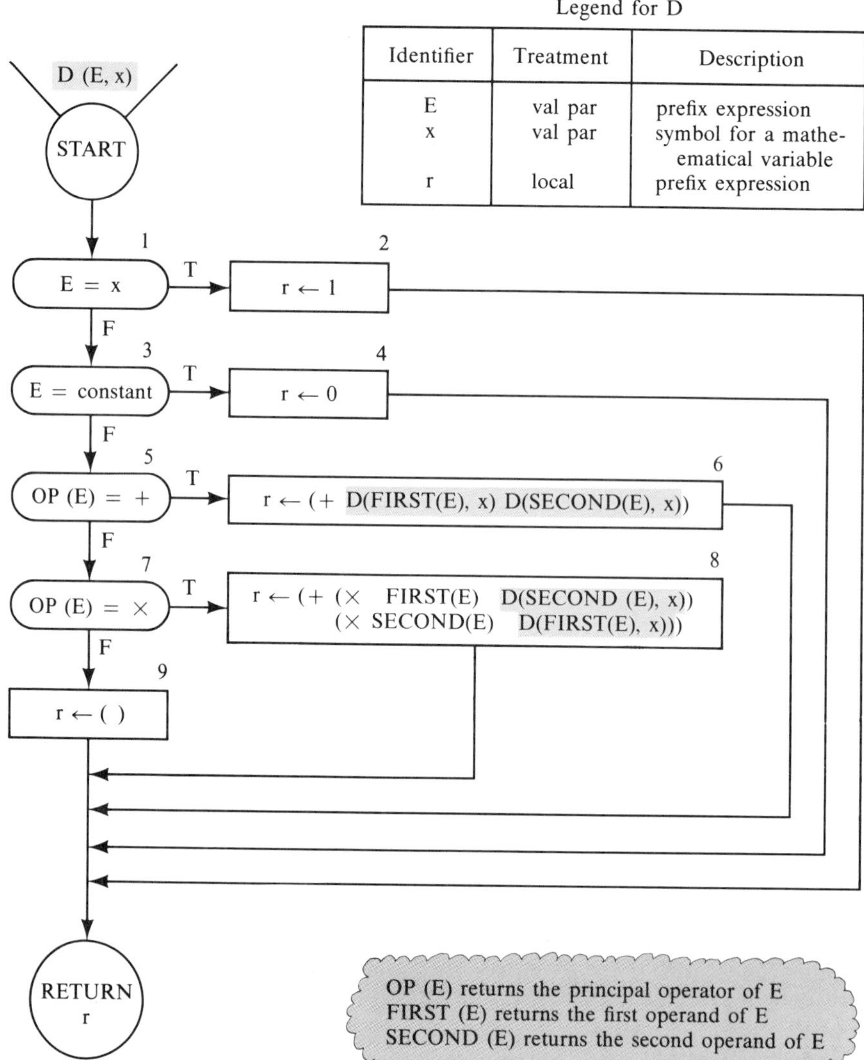

Figure 7-41. **Conceptual flowchart to differentiate, with respect to x, a prefix expression E that can involve constants, the variable x, and binary addition and multiplication. The notation in box 6 means that the value assigned to r is a list of three items: the addition operator, the derivative of the first operand of E, and the derivative of the second operand. A similar notation is used in box 8, where the value of r is a list containing two sublists.**

*The LISP equivalent of the RLISP procedure D in Figure 7-43 is:

```
(DEFINE (
  (D LAMBDA (E X)
    (COND ((ATOM E) (COND ((EQ E X) 1) (T 0)))
      ((EQ (OP E) 'PLUS) (LIST 'PLUS (D (FIRST E) X) (D (SECOND E) X)))
      (( EQ (OP E) 'TIMES) (LIST 'PLUS
        (LIST 'TIMES (FIRST E) (D (SECOND E) X))
        (LIST 'TIMES (SECOND E) (D (FIRST E) X))))
      (T NIL))))
))
```

Note: In some LISP systems, one must write (QUOTE PLUS) instead of 'PLUS, etc.

OP

```
LISP PROCEDURE OP(E);
  CAR(E);
```

FIRST

```
LISP PROCEDURE FIRST(E);
  CAR(CDR(E));
```

SECOND

```
LISP PROCEDURE SECOND(E);
  CAR(CDR(CDR(E)));
```

Figure 7-42. **Procedure definitions for OP, FIRST, and SECOND.**

Example 1 D can be invoked by a command like

D('(TIMES X X), 'X);

and will yield as output

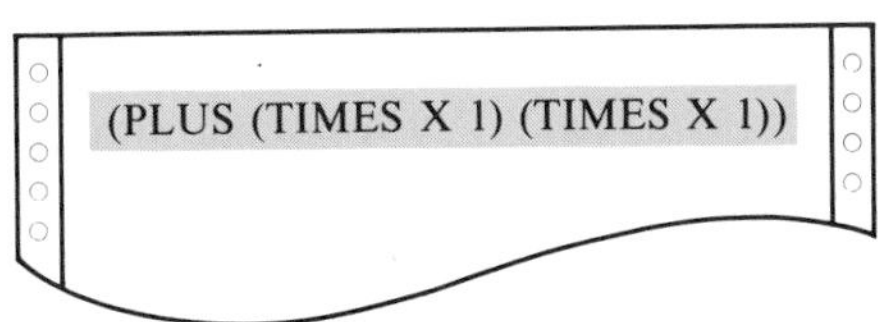

which is, of course, mathematically equivalent to 2X.

Example 2 The derivative of $3y^2 + 2y$ with respect to y can be evaluated by executing the command

D('(PLUS (TIMES 3 (TIMES Y Y)) (TIMES 2 Y)), 'Y);

Figure 7-43. **The differentiation procedure D coded in RLISP.**

D

```
LISP PROCEDURE D(E, X);
  IF ATOM(E) THEN
    IF EQ(E, X) THEN 1
    ELSE 0
  ELSE IF EQ(OP(E), 'PLUS) THEN
    LIST('PLUS, D(FIRST(E), X), D(SECOND(E), X))
  ELSE IF EQ(OP(E), 'TIMES) THEN
    LIST('PLUS,
      LIST('TIMES, FIRST(E), D(SECOND(E), X)),
      LIST('TIMES, SECOND(E), D(FIRST(E), X)) )
  ELSE NIL;
```

and will yield as output

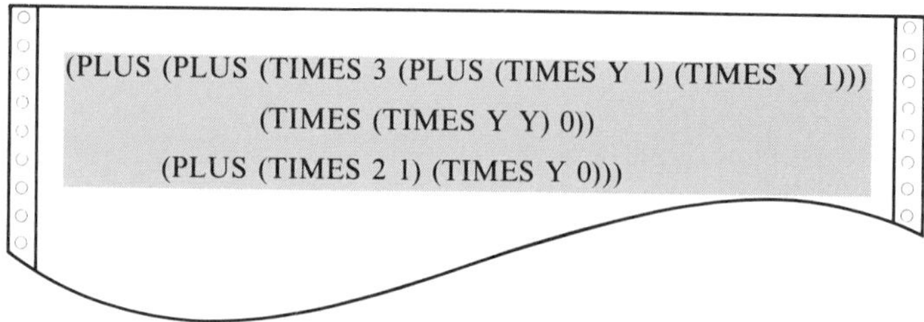

But how complicated this list looks! We need to develop an algorithm to simplify the resulting expression above so it looks more like 6y + 2, the "correct" answer. Results like

(PLUS (TIMES 6 Y) 2) or (PLUS 2 (TIMES 6 Y))

would be far more appealing!

To gain some insight into how a satisfactory simplification algorithm can be developed, it is helpful to look at the binary tree representation of the *unsimplified* result expression for Example 2. First verify that the tree given in Figure 7-44 *is* equivalent to the result expression.

A program to simplify this tree can be similar in structure to one that *evaluates* the tree. That is, we search for a nonatomic subtree that can be replaced with an atom by applying an *appropriate simplification rule.* We continue this process until no more simplifications can be done.

Rule 1. If the operator terminal node is ×, a subtree of the form

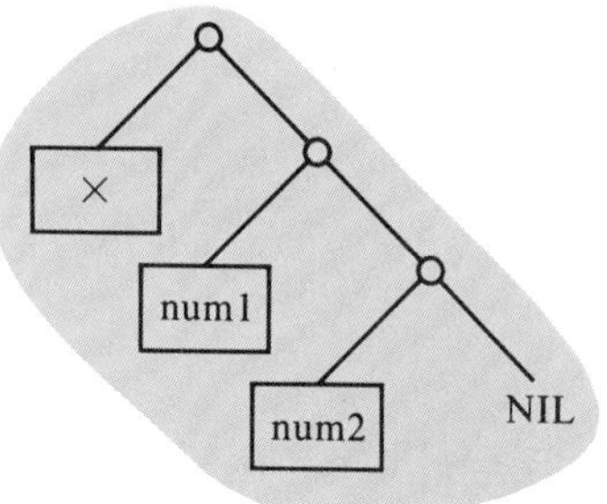

can be replaced by

value of num1 × num2

Thus,

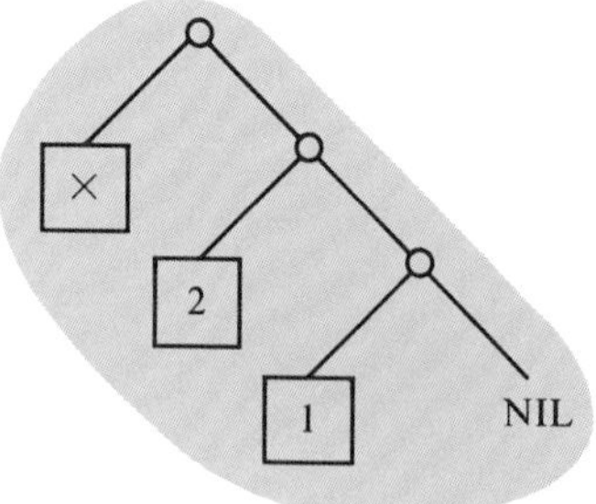

can be replaced by [2].

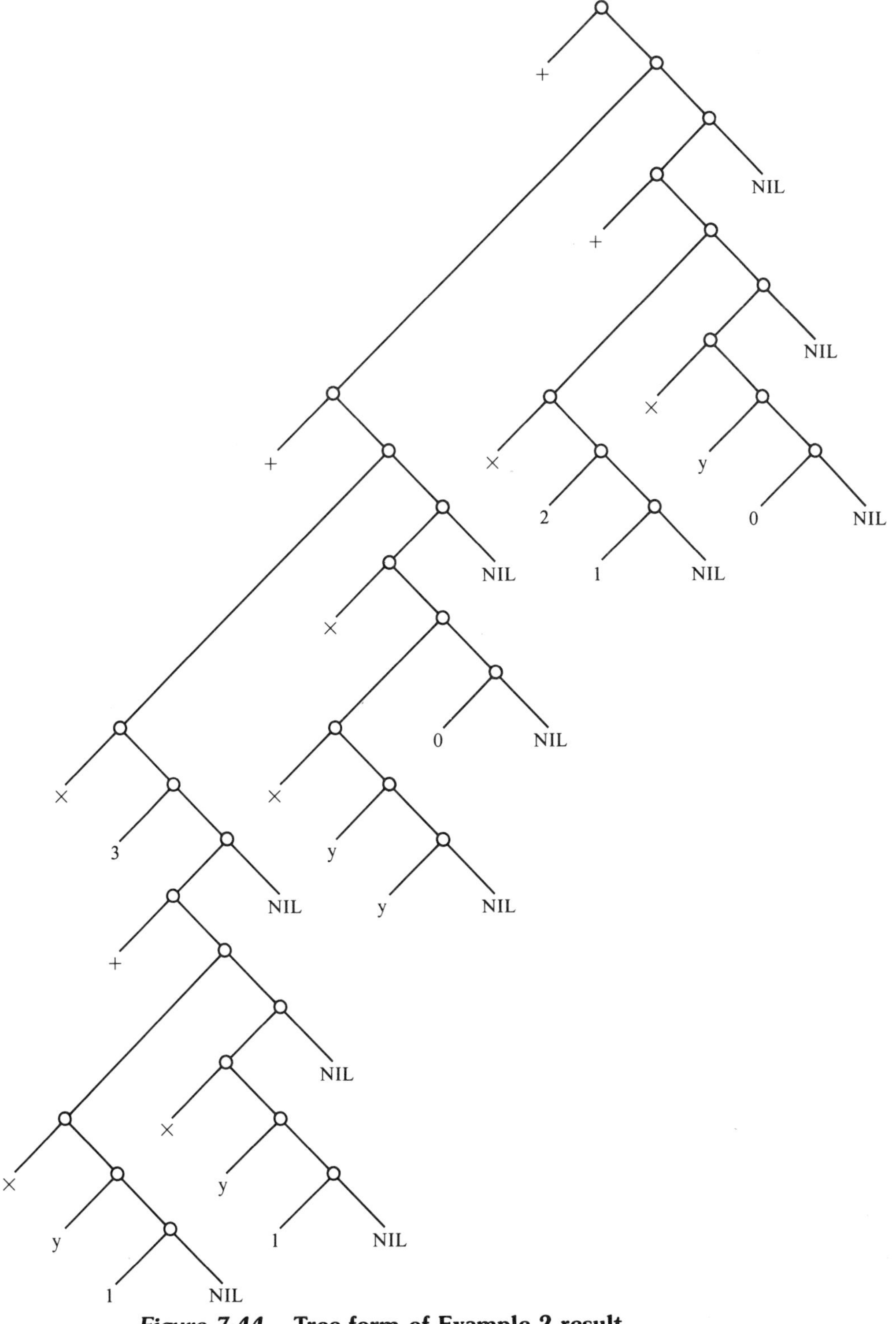

Figure 7-44. **Tree form of Example 2 result.**

Rule 2. Subtrees of the form

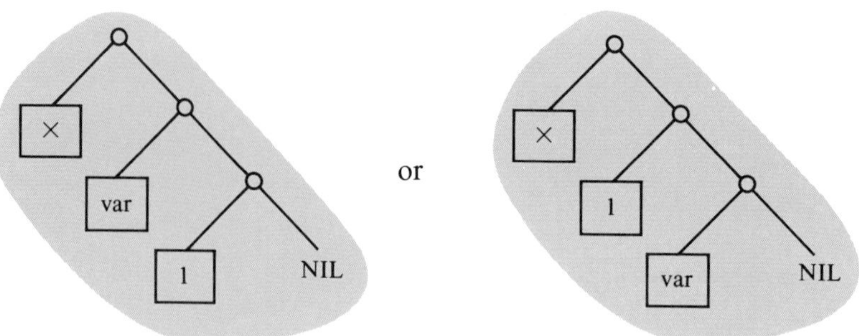

can be replaced by var.

By making changes of these types and other comparable simplifications involving + and × operators, the tree in Figure 7-44 can be successively reduced to the one given in Figure 7-45. Check that this is so.

Pattern match simplification Even more simplification can be achieved if we use pattern matching to identify subtrees containing certain nonatomic components. For example,

Rule 3 A subtree of the form

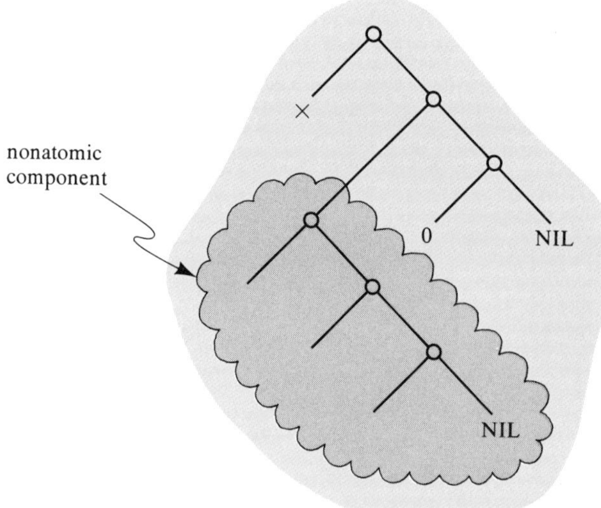

can be reduced to 0 regardless of the details of the nonatomic component.

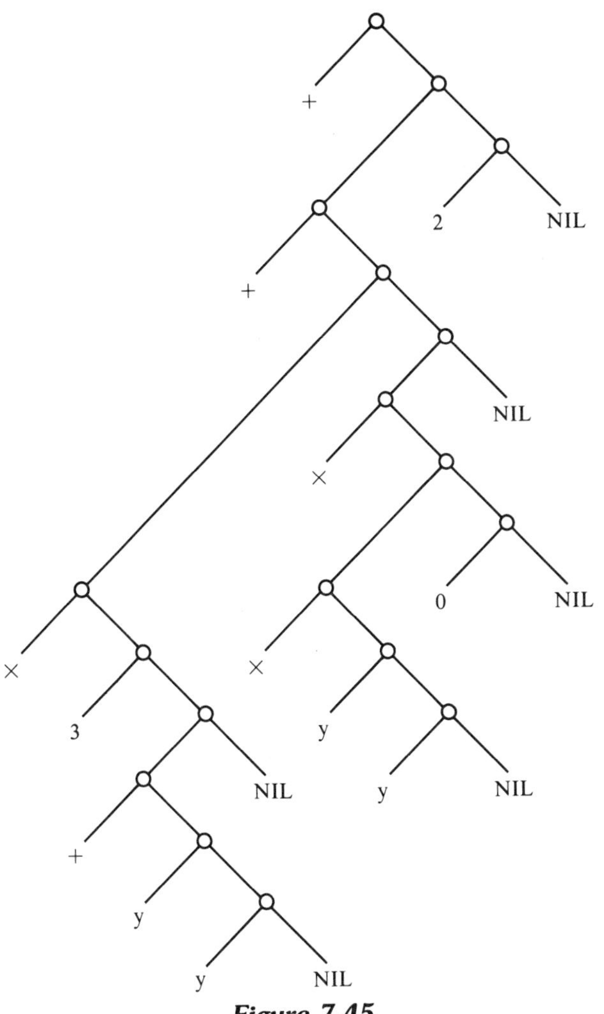

Figure 7-45

Rule 4. A subtree of the form

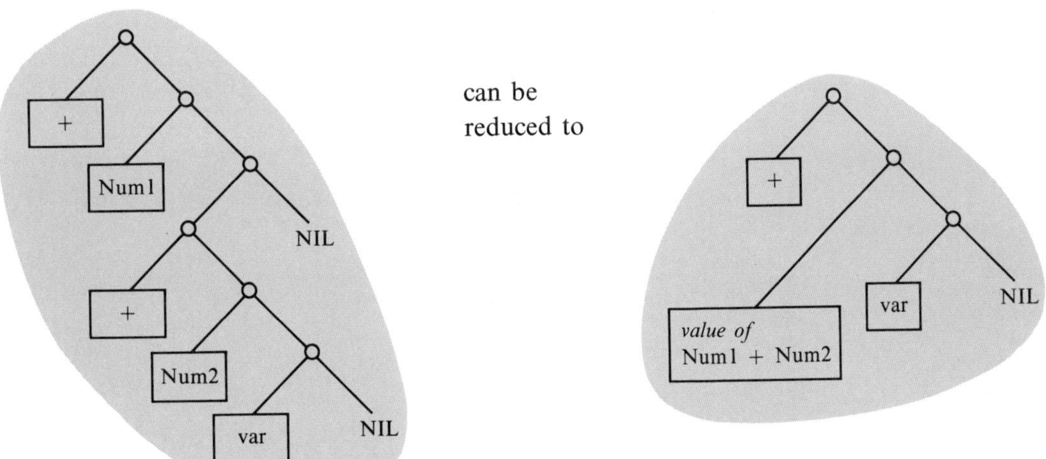

Figure 7-46 shows a flowchart and RLISP definition for the procedure SIMPLIFY that searches an expression tree for terminal subtrees, that is, subtrees of the form

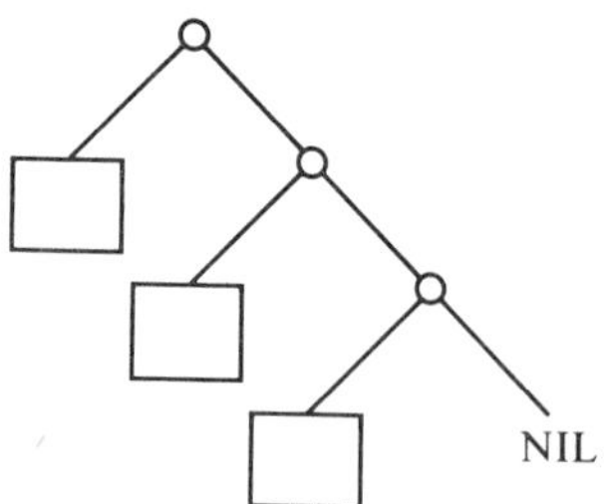

where all the components are terminals and rules like 1 and 2 may be applicable. We omit LISP definitions for this and the remaining procedures.

For each appropriate subtree, SIMPLIFY calls on the procedure STIMES (*simplify times*) or SPLUS (*simplify plus*) to try to simplify that subtree. Along the way, additional simplification may be achieved by application of pattern match rules, like rules 3 and 4. Such simplification is handled by the procedure COLLECT, which is called by STIMES and SPLUS. (See Figure 7-47.)

The SIMPLIFY algorithm is purely recursive, performing a natural order traversal of the given tree (argument).

If E is an atom then the value of SIMPLIFY (E) is E itself, whereas if E is a list, that is, an algebraic expression of the form (op first second), then, depending on whether the operator is PLUS or TIMES, the value of SIMPLIFY (E) is respectively the value returned by SPLUS when applied to the list:

('PLUS SIMPLIFY(first) SIMPLIFY(second))

or the value of STIMES applied to

('TIMES SIMPLIFY(first) SIMPLIFY(second))

SPLUS and STIMES are called only after their arguments have been reduced to their simplest form by virtue of the earlier application of SIMPLIFY to the subexpressions. The implementation of the actual simplification rules, as was

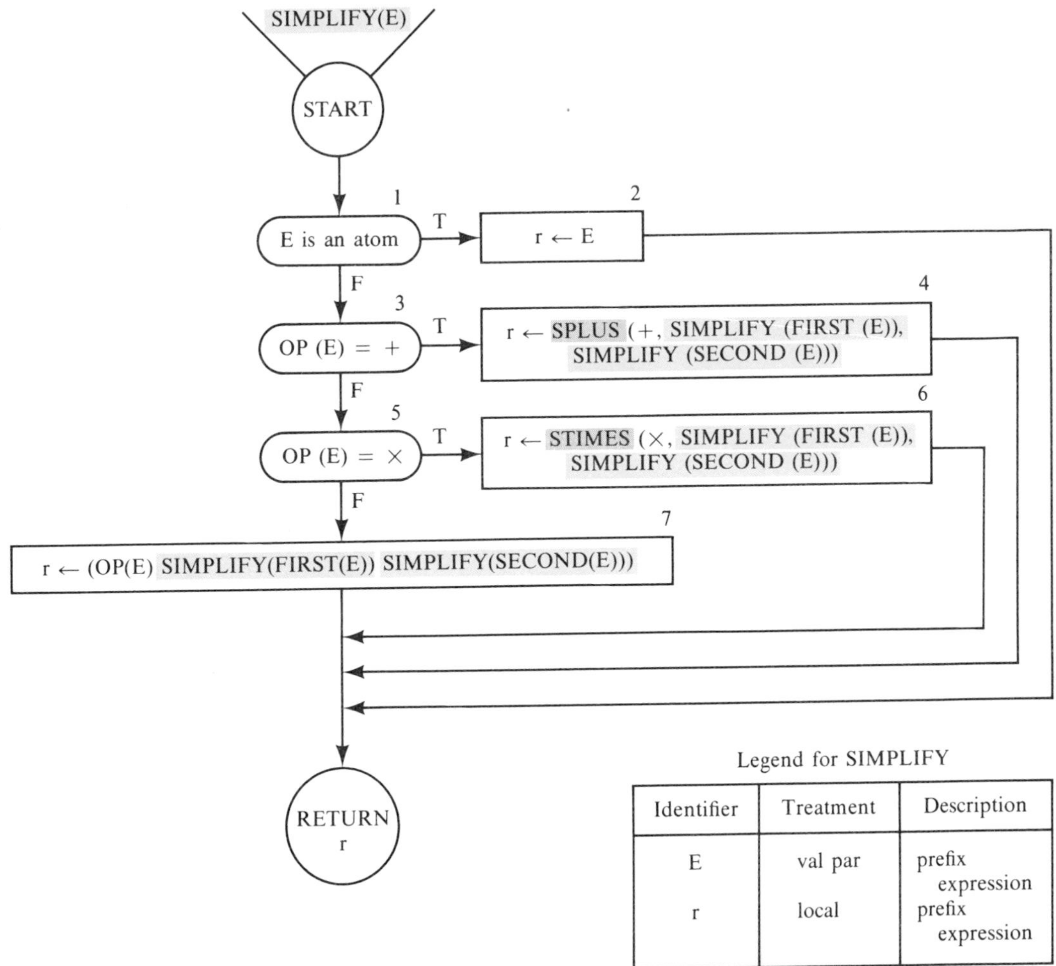

Legend for SIMPLIFY

Identifier	Treatment	Description
E	val par	prefix expression
r	local	prefix expression

Figure 7-46a. **If the operator is not + or ×, the default action in box 7 makes no simplification at this node but proceeds recursively to try to simplify the first and second operands of E.**

indicated above, is delegated by SIMPLIFY to SPLUS and STIMES (and to COLLECT, a procedure called by SPLUS and STIMES to achieve such simplifications as rules 3 and 4).

The two functions SPLUS and STIMES are fairly similar in structure and we shall discuss only SPLUS. We first observe that the program calls on the predefined predicates NUMBERP, AND, and EQUAL. Definitions for these predicates may be found in Tables 7-3 and 7-4; note in particular that EQUAL (X, Y) returns T if X and Y are structurally equal and contain the same atoms, and NIL if they are different. Thus EQUAL tests the contents of the S-expressions as opposed to the elementary predicate EQ, which tests the pointers to atoms or S-expressions.

```
                                    SIMPLIFY
LISP PROCEDURE SIMPLIFY (E);
  IF ATOM(E) THEN E
    ELSE IF EQ(OP(E), 'PLUS) THEN
      SPLUS(LIST('PLUS,
        SIMPLIFY(FIRST(E)),
        SIMPLIFY(SECOND(E))))
    ELSE IF EQ(OP(E), 'TIMES) THEN
      STIMES(LIST('TIMES,
        SIMPLIFY(FIRST(E)),
        SIMPLIFY(SECOND(E))))
    ELSE LIST(OP(E),
        SIMPLIFY(FIRST(E)),
        SIMPLIFY(SECOND(E)));
```

Figure 7-46b

Armed with these definitions we now turn to the actual operation of the function SPLUS (Figure 7-47b). The input to SPLUS is always a list of the form

(PLUS a b)

where a and b are either atoms or lists (algebraic expressions in prefix form) that are already assumed to be in their simplest form. The function first checks to see if both a and b are numeric atoms. If so then (line 33) SPLUS returns as its value PLUS (a, b). Now PLUS is in fact a LISP system function that takes two or more *numeric* atoms as its arguments and returns their sum. Thus SPLUS will return the *value* of a + b. As an example, if SPLUS is given the argument (PLUS 2 1) it will return 3 as the value.

Assuming now that b is a number but a is not, the algorithm goes on (line 34) to check if b is zero; if so, the value returned is a. If b is not zero SPLUS forms the list (PLUS b a) and passes it to COLLECT (line 35) for further possible simplifications.

If b is *not* a number then line 36 checks to see if a is zero; if so then b is returned as the value of SPLUS. If this fails, the algorithm proceeds to check if a and b are the same S-expression. If they are, SPLUS forms the list (TIMES 2 a) and calls COLLECT with this argument (line 39). If all these steps fail, the original list is passed on to COLLECT (line 40).

The input from SPLUS to COLLECT, defined in Figure 7-48, is therefore a list of the form (PLUS a b) in which the first argument a is always the numeric atom *if there is one;* the second argument is either a literal atom or a list. COLLECT attempts to carry out some further simplifications by means of elementary pattern matching such as rules 3 and 4. If COLLECT receives a list (PLUS a b), where a is a list but where b is an (nonnumeric) atom, it calls itself recursively

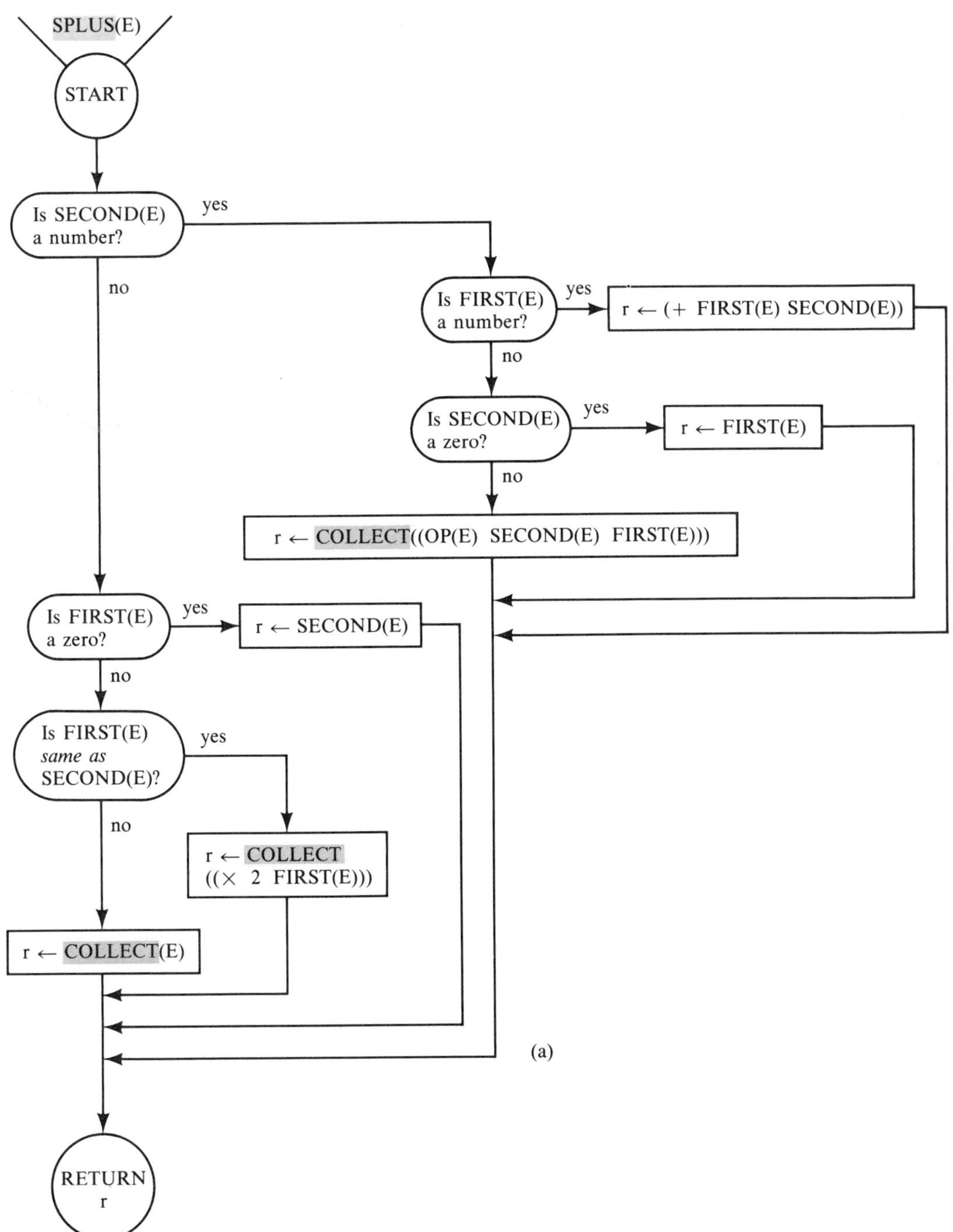
SPLUS(E)
START
Is SECOND(E) a number?
yes
no
Is FIRST(E) a number?
yes
r ← (+ FIRST(E) SECOND(E))
no
Is SECOND(E) a zero?
yes
r ← FIRST(E)
no
r ← COLLECT((OP(E) SECOND(E) FIRST(E)))
Is FIRST(E) a zero?
yes
r ← SECOND(E)
no
Is FIRST(E) same as SECOND(E)?
yes
r ← COLLECT ((× 2 FIRST(E)))
no
r ← COLLECT(E)
(a)
RETURN r

Figure 7-47

SPLUS

```
LISP PROCEDURE SPLUS(E);
  IF NUMBERP(SECOND(E)) THEN
    IF NUMBERP(FIRST(E)) THEN PLUS(FIRST(E), SECOND(E))
    ELSE IF EQUAL(SECOND(E), 0) THEN FIRST(E)
    ELSE COLLECT(LIST(OP(E), SECOND(E), FIRST(E)))
  ELSE IF AND(NUMBERP(FIRST(E)), EQUAL(FIRST(E), 0)) THEN
    SECOND(E)
  ELSE IF EQUAL(FIRST(E), SECOND(E)) THEN
    COLLECT(LIST('TIMES, 2, FIRST(E)))
  ELSE COLLECT(E);
```

(b)

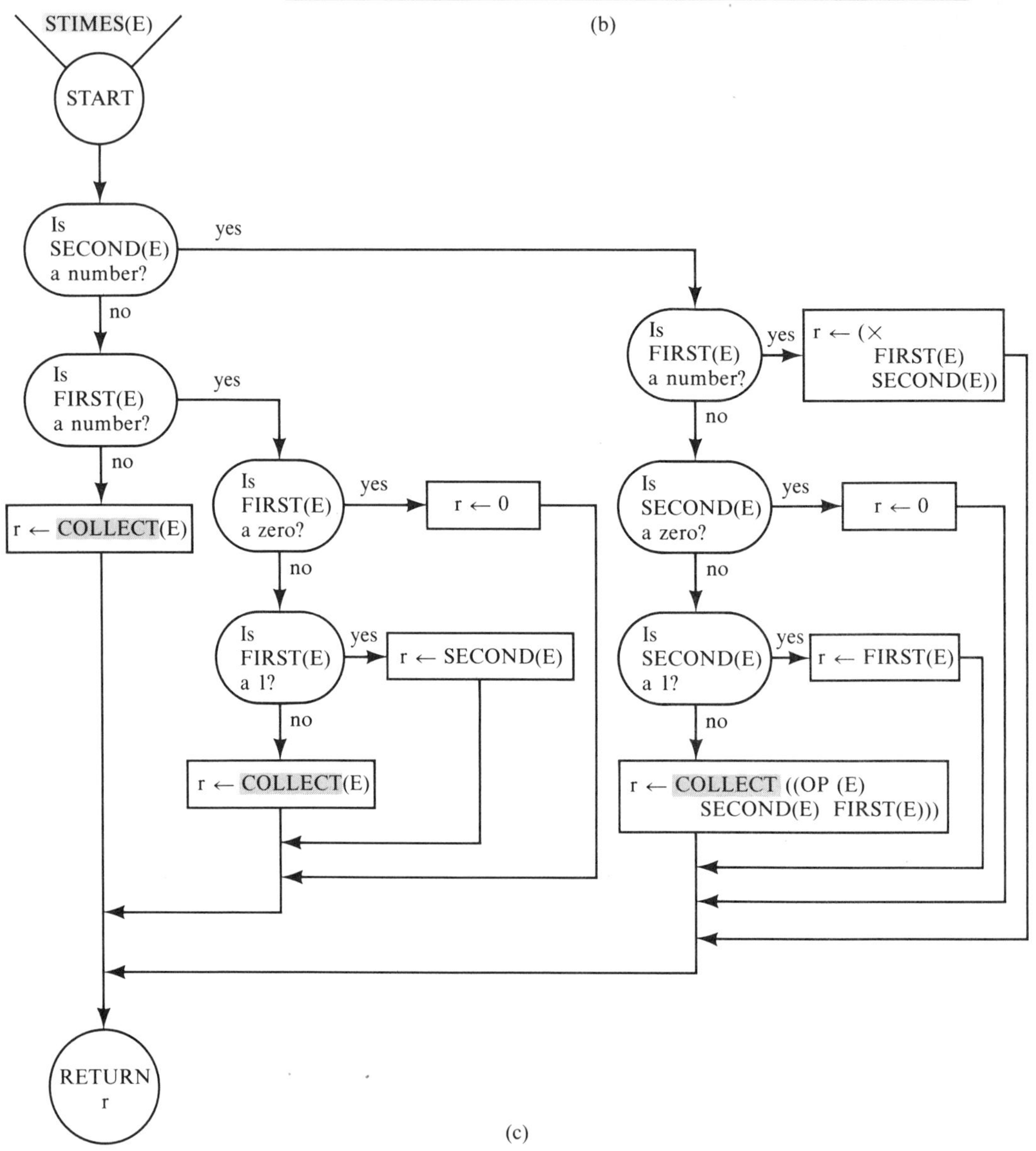

(c)

Figure 7-47 ***(continued)***

STIMES

```
LISP PROCEDURE STIMES(E);
  IF NUMBERP(SECOND(E)) THEN
    IF NUMBERP(FIRST(E)) THEN TIMES(FIRST(E), SECOND(E))
    ELSE IF EQUAL(SECOND(E), 0) THEN 0
    ELSE IF EQUAL(SECOND(E), 1) THEN FIRST(E)
    ELSE COLLECT(LIST(OP(E), SECOND(E), FIRST(E)))
  ELSE IF NUMBERP(FIRST(E)) THEN
    IF EQUAL(FIRST(E), 0) THEN 0
    ELSE IF EQUAL(FIRST(E), 1) THEN SECOND(E)
    ELSE COLLECT(E)
  ELSE COLLECT(E);
```

(d)

Figure 7-47 (*continued*)

with the list (PLUS b a) as its argument (line 56). This ensures that the first argument is always an atom if there is one. It then carries out the following simplifications:

1. If a and b are numbers then (lines 60–62) any occurrence of (PLUS a (PLUS b c)) is reduced to (PLUS a+b c) and any occurrence of (TIMES a (TIMES b c)) is reduced to (TIMES a×b c).
2. If a and c are numbers then (lines 66–68) any occurrence of (PLUS (PLUS a b) (PLUS c d)) becomes (PLUS a+c (PLUS b d)) and any occurrence of (TIMES (TIMES a b) (TIMES c d)) becomes (TIMES a×c (TIMES b d)).

If none of these simplifications can be applied, COLLECT returns the list unchanged.

The Lisp function EVAL, used in the code for COLLECT seen in Figure 7-48b, plays a key role in the workings of the Lisp interpreter. When applied to a list of the form

$$(\mathrm{fn}\ \mathrm{arg}_1\ \mathrm{arg}_2\ \ldots\ \mathrm{arg}_n)$$

where fn is some predefined or user-defined function of n arguments, EVAL returns as its value the value of the function fn applied to the *values* of the n arguments, that is,

$$\mathrm{fn}(\mathrm{arg}_1, \mathrm{arg}_2, \ldots, \mathrm{arg}_n)$$

This concludes our discussion of the program that has been displayed *piecemeal* in Figures 7-43, 7-46b, 7-47b, 7-47d, and 7-48b.

Note that the last line of the program (line 71 in Figure 7-48b) asks for the simplified form of the derivative of X^2 with respect to X. The call is to SIMPLIFY whose argument is the value to be returned from a call on D.

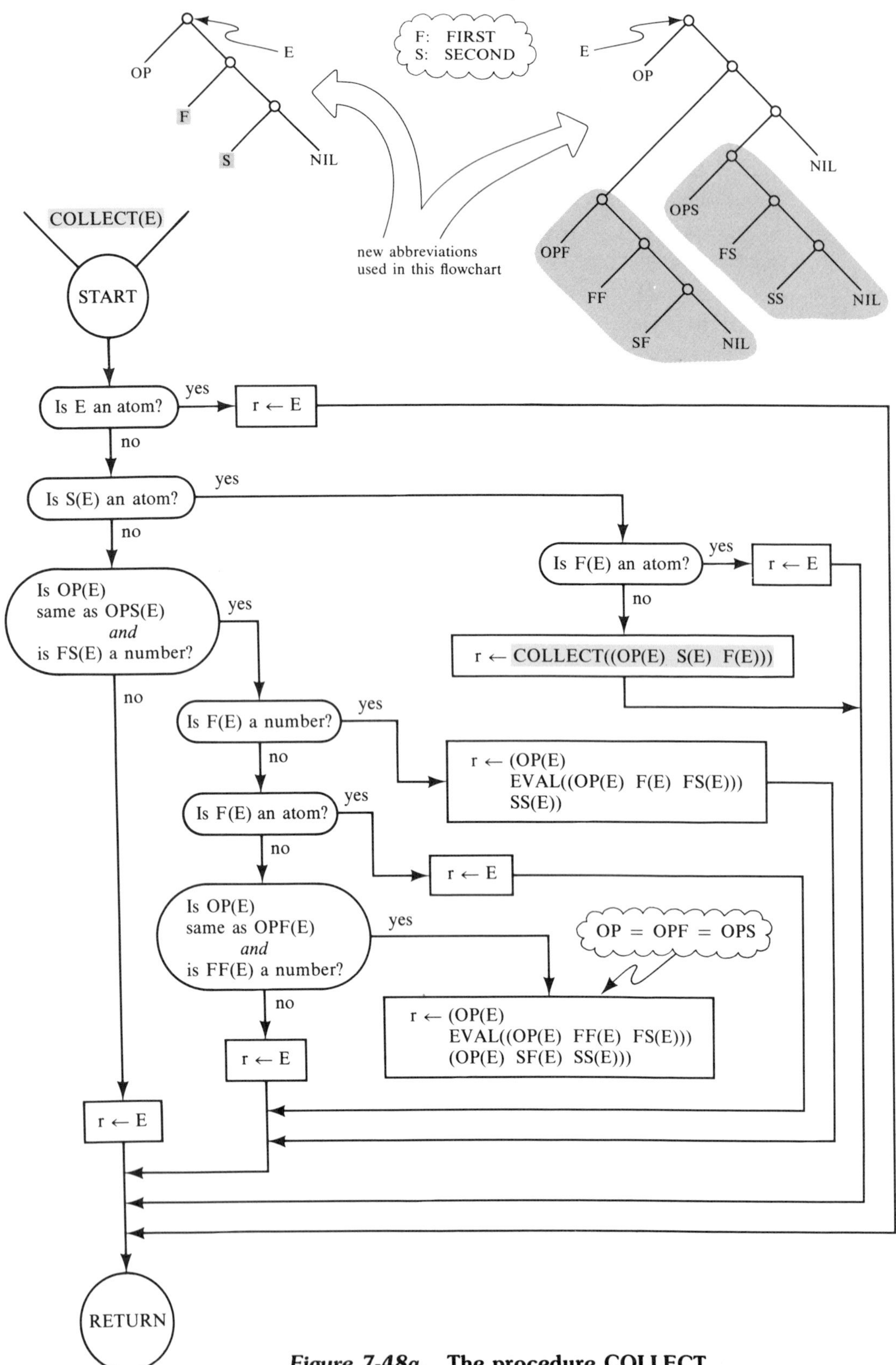

Figure 7-48a. **The procedure COLLECT.**

COLLECT

```
LISP PROCEDURE COLLECT(E);
  IF ATOM(E) THEN E
  ELSE IF ATOM(SECOND(E)) THEN
    IF ATOM(FIRST(E)) THEN E
    ELSE COLLECT(LIST(OP(E), SECOND(E), FIRST(E)))
  ELSE IF AND(EQ(OP(E), OP(SECOND(E))),
      NUMBERP(FIRST(SECOND(E)))) THEN
    IF NUMBERP(FIRST(E)) THEN
      LIST(OP(E),
        EVAL(LIST(OP(E), FIRST(E), FIRST(SECOND(E)))),
        SECOND(SECOND(E)))
    ELSE IF ATOM(FIRST(E)) THEN E
    ELSE IF AND(EQ(OP(E), FIRST(E)),
        NUMBERP(FIRST(FIRST(E)))) THEN
      LIST(OP(E),
        EVAL(LIST(OP(E), FIRST(FIRST(E), FIRST(SECOND(E)))),
        LIST(OP(E), SECOND(FIRST(E)), SECOND(SECOND(E))) )
    ELSE E
  ELSE E;

SIMPLIFY(D( '(TIMES X X), 'X));
```

This is the command that invokes the code on the preceding 70 lines.

Figure 7-48b

The names PLUS and TIMES were chosen to indicate addition and multiplication in our expressions precisely because they *are* names of predefined Lisp functions, and so each may be used as the first argument of EVAL. Notice that a list such as

$$(\text{fn arg}_1 \; . \; . \; . \; \text{arg}_n) \qquad \text{or} \qquad (\text{PLUS } 1 \; 2)$$

may be viewed as either

1. an S-expression, that is, a data object (possibly part of a larger data object), or
2. an *expression* in LISP (not RLISP), that is, a fragment of LISP code. By supplying such an S-expression as an argument for EVAL, we obtain the value that would have been produced by executing the S-expression.

It was pointed out in Section 7-8 that LISP programs are written as S-expressions, and this is indirectly true of RLISP as well, since RLISP is implemented via a translator into LISP. In either version the argument of EVAL must be an S-expression.

Exercises 7-13, Set A

1 What will be the output produced upon execution of the command on line 71 of Figure 7-48b?

2 Trace the execution of SIMPLIFY assuming its argument is an expression corresponding to the tree in Figure 7-45.

3 Trace the execution of SIMPLIFY assuming its argument is an expression corresponding to the tree in Figure 7-44. Show the series of *simpler* trees produced, leading to the final one:

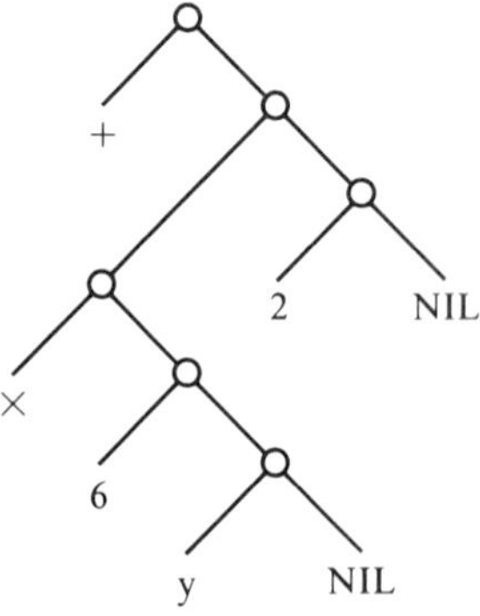

Exercises 7-13, Set B

This problem is concerned with the processing of *character strings*, and in particular, the operation known as *pattern matching with replacement.*

We introduce the following flowchart notation (which will be used again in Chapter 8):

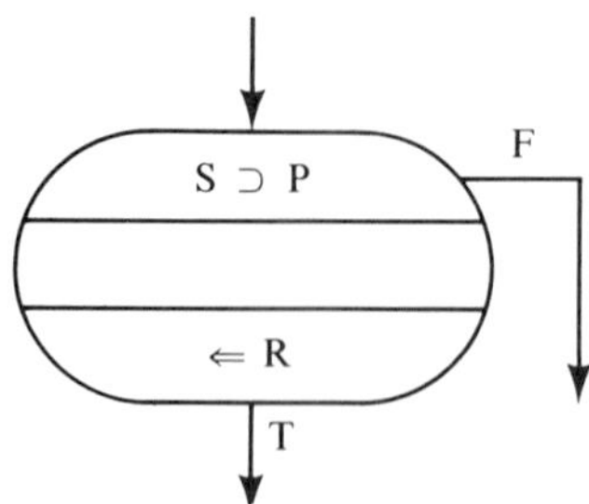

The meaning of this box is as follows: S, P, and R are character strings. This conditional box represents a test to see if the *subject* S contains the *pattern* P as a substring (that is, if some part of S is exactly the same as P). If so, the leftmost occurrence of P in S is *replaced* with R, and the T exit is taken. If not, no change is made to S and the F exit is taken.

Examples:

1 If X = "ABCD", Y = "BC", Z = "K", then

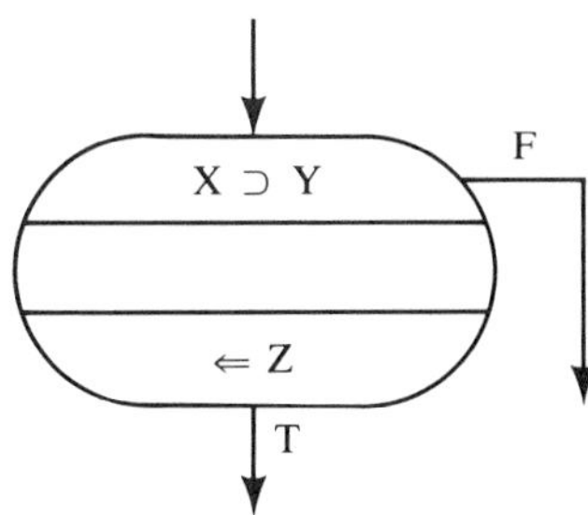

changes X to "AKD" and takes the T exit.

2 If Y had been "ABCD", X would have been changed to "K" and the T exit taken.

3 If Y had been "ABD", X would not have been changed and the F exit taken.

We may represent character strings in Lisp as *lists* of atoms whose names are single letters. For example, "ABCD" may be represented as (A B C D).

Your job is to define in RLISP or LISP a function PATMATCH (S, P, R) whose arguments are list representations of strings and whose value is the result of replacing pattern P in subject S with R. If P does not occur, the value is just S. Note that you cannot really *change* S—just build a new list that is the same as S except R has taken the place of P. For example,

PATMATCH('(A H O U S E), '(U S), '(M)) = (A H O M E)

Be sure to decompose: several functions will no doubt be needed!

7-14 ACHIEVING THE EFFECT OF NAME PARAMETERS IN LISP

The name parameter treatment of ALGOL allows an argument to be passed to a function in *unevaluated* form. Only when the value of the matching parameter is needed does an evaluation take place. An example is shown in Figure 7-49. When the value of Z is needed in P^1, the MC moves into $Outer^1$ and evaluates the formula "X + Y".

In Lisp it is easy to prevent the evaluation of arguments: we simply quote them. We have been doing this for some time, but always because we *never* wanted the argument evaluated. The question we must now ask is: If a parameter matches an argument that was quoted, how can we get that argument evaluated when necessary? The answer, as we hope you have guessed, is: Apply EVAL. Consider the example given in Figure 7-50. After the call on P, the situation exists as shown in Figure 7-51. The value of Z in P^1 is (PLUS X Y), but the value of EVAL (Z) is 7.

We are thus able to achieve *nearly* the effect of name parameters in Lisp. The important difference is that in Lisp, the evaluation takes place in the environment of the *called* procedure P, whereas in ALGOL, evaluation takes place

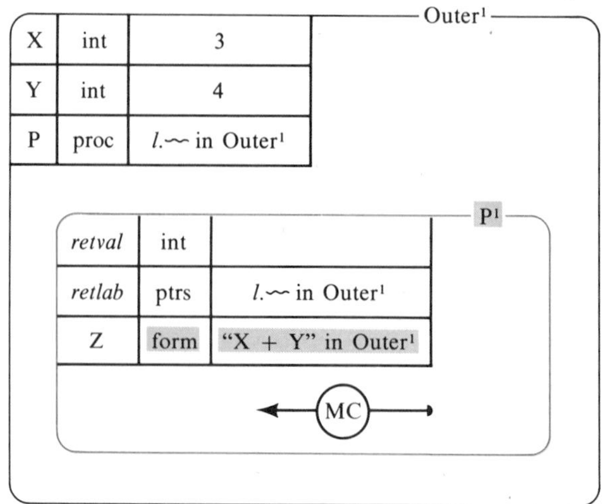

Figure 7-49. **Use of a name parameter in ALGOL.**

```
LISP PROCEDURE P(X, Y, Z):
  IF ZEROP(X) THEN 0 ELSE EVAL(Z);

P(3,  4,  '(PLUS X Y));
```

Figure 7-50

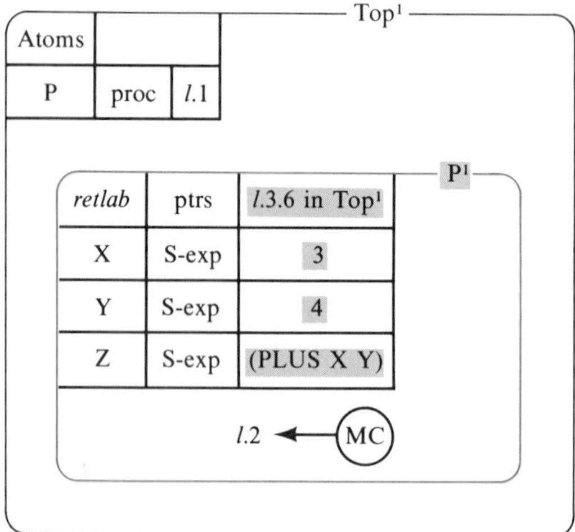

Figure 7-51

in the environment of the *caller,* Outer. In many Lisp systems EVAL has a second argument that is an *environment.* This does, in fact, allow us to specify the environment in which the EVAL will take place.

7-15 REFERENCES AND SUGGESTIONS FOR FURTHER READING

Most of the literature on Lisp is based on McCarthy *et al.* (1962). [See also Berkeley and Bobrow, Eds. (1964).] Useful primers and texts, such as Weissman (1967) and Friedman (1974), came along later. Chapter 14 of Pratt (1975) contains a helpful supplement and review of Lisp. The dialect RLISP is now available on many computers accessible to universities. RLISP was developed by Hearn (1971, 1974), and forms the basis of a mathematical symbol processing language known as REDUCE. [See also Hearn (1968, 1973).]

8 SNOBOL

8-1 INTRODUCTION

The Snobol language was especially designed for the easy manipulation of character strings. Created at Bell Telephone Laboratories in the early 1960s, today Snobol is the most widely used string processing language. The powerful version known as SNOBOL4 is the culmination of the Snobol development. At the end of this chapter some SNOBOL4 references are discussed. In the body of the chapter the generic name Snobol is used for convenience although actually the SNOBOL4 language is discussed.

Among the distinctive features of Snobol are the following:

1. A powerful set of string manipulation primitives, centered around the concept of *pattern matching.*
2. A unique and very compact syntax.
3. Provision for *user-defined data types,* allowing the programmer to extend the language in significant ways, in particular, to list processing.
4. Automatic data type conversion.
5. A TABLE data type with associative lookup for access.

In this chapter we present only an introduction to Snobol. There are many features of the language, some of them quite powerful, that are not covered here. What does appear here is an overview illustrating the "mainstream" of string processing as it is done in Snobol. In this chapter we apply Snobol of two areas mentioned earlier in this book: symbolic differentiation and language preprocessors (such as an RLISP to LISP translator). In both cases the problems yield to string processing techniques.

8-2 A FLOWCHART LANGUAGE FOR STRING PROCESSING OPERATIONS

For reasons cited in Chapter 1, we have presented algorithms both as flowcharts and as programs in particular languages. To continue that practice here, we must extend our flowchart language to include common operations performed on and with character strings.

The fundamental operation on strings is *concatenation,* which produces a string containing the characters of both its operands. Figure 8-1 shows a simple example as a reminder of the notation used in Chapter 3. Recall that in flowcharts we enclose strings in double quotes.

The symbol "□" stands for the character *blank;* we use it to show explicitly the presence of a blank in a string. The *empty* or *null string* (the string of no characters) we denote by " " (consecutive double quote marks) or, when assigned to a variable, by an empty space. Thus

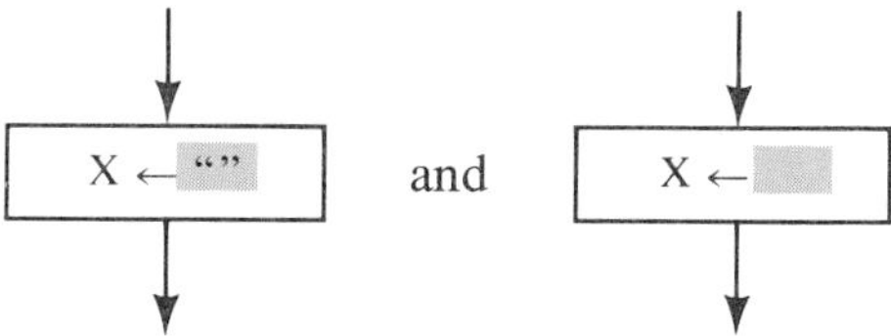

are equivalent flowchart steps.

Figure 8-1. A simple flowchart using strings.

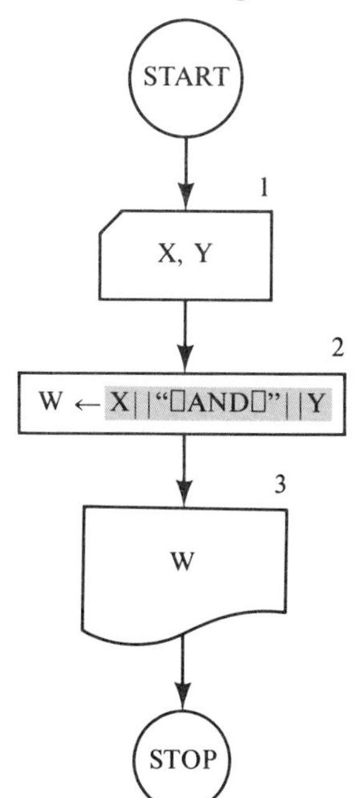

Legend

Identifier	Treatment	Description
X	local	string
Y	local	string
W	local	string

Inputs: "JACK", "JILL"

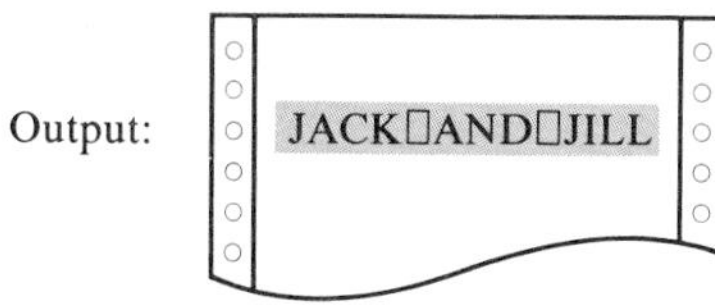

Our primary tool to manipulate character strings is the *pattern match:* a test to see whether a string designated as the *pattern* occurs as a substring of a string designated as the *subject.* In the flowchart language it occupies the top part of a three-compartment *pattern match box,* as illustrated in Figure 8-2. (The reader who studied Exercise 7-13, Set 2, received a preview of this notation, as well as an understanding of the processing involved in pattern matches.)

The bottom compartment of a pattern match box enables us to combine a *replacement* with a pattern match, so that the subject can be modified as well as searched. That is, if (and only if) the pattern match is successful, the *leftmost occurrence* of the pattern *in the subject* is replaced with the string given to the right of the replacement arrow ⇐ in the bottom compartment. Replacement is meaningful only if the subject is a single variable; it is the value of that variable that is modified. Examples are shown in Figure 8-3.

***Figure 8-2.* The pattern match operation.**

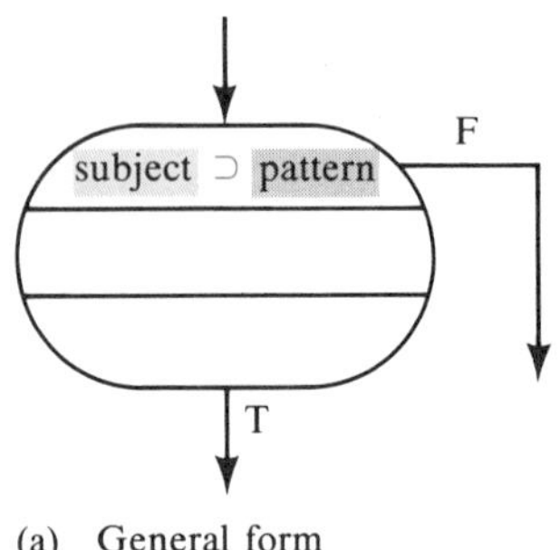

(a) General form

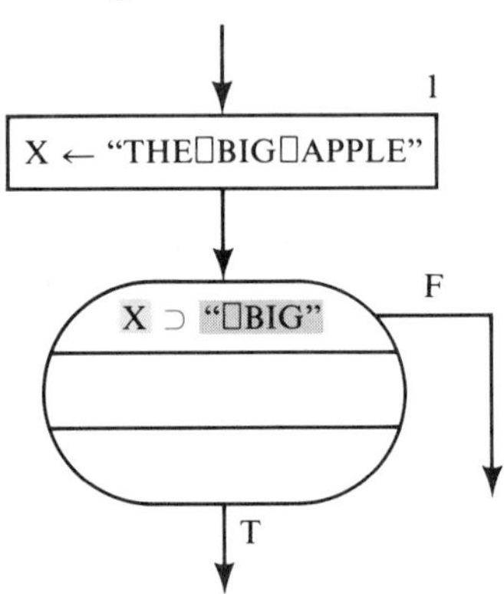

(b) T branch would be taken.

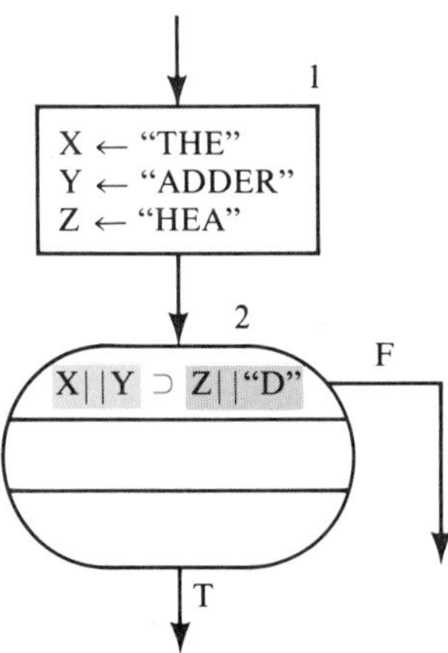

(c) T branch would be taken. Concatenation may be used in both subject and pattern.

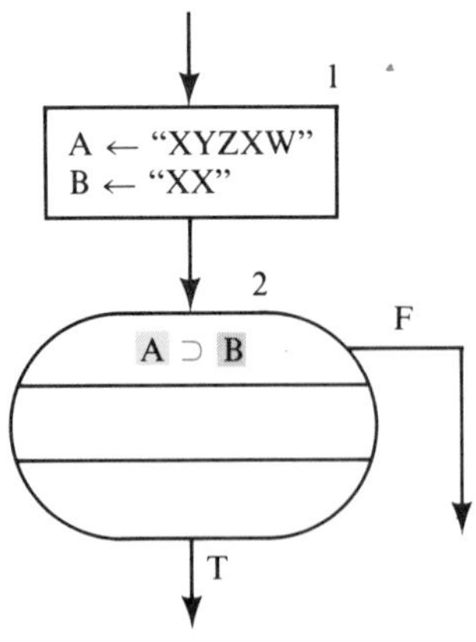

(d) F branch would be taken. The characters of the pattern must occur consecutively in the subject for the match to be successful.

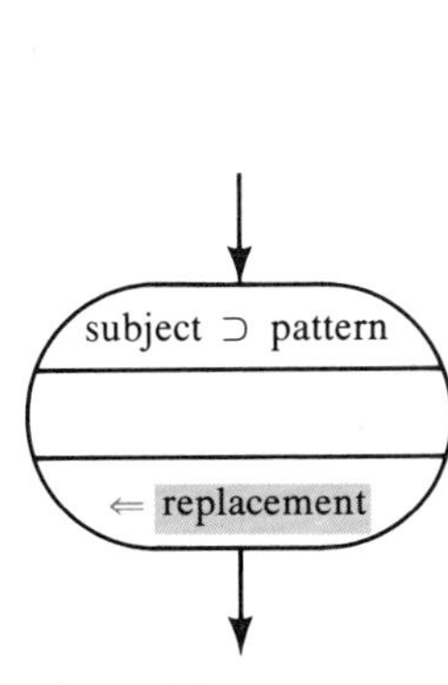

(a) General form

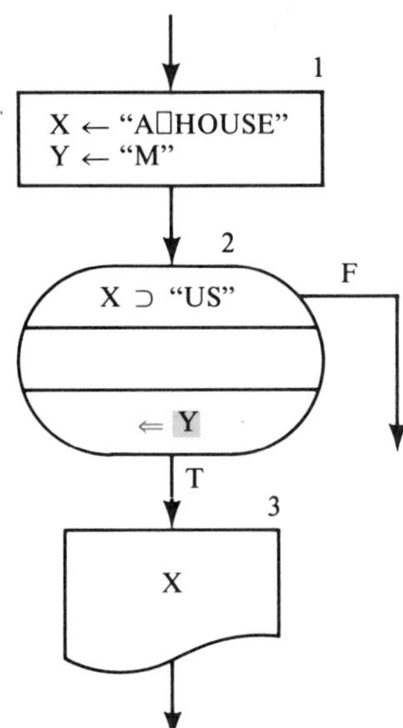

(b) Replacement of pattern. The T branch is taken and the string "A HOME" is output.

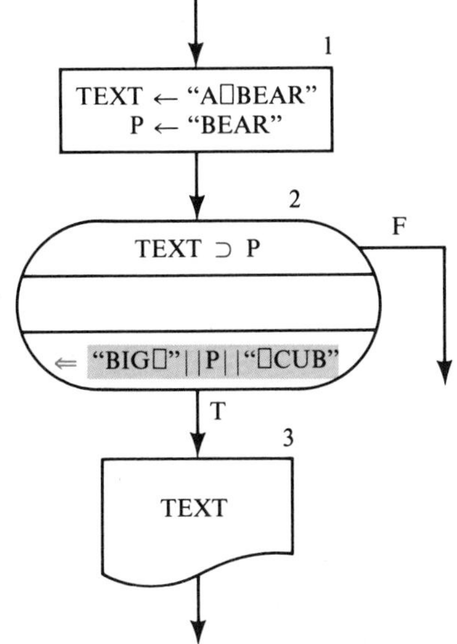

(c) Insertion. The T branch is taken and "A□BIG□BEAR□CUB" is output.

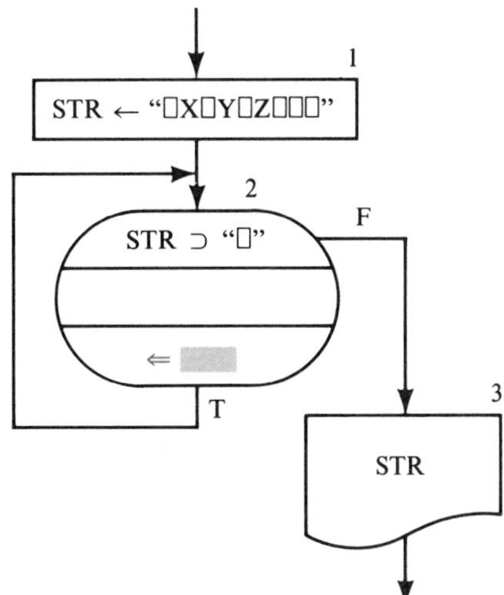

(d) Deletion (pattern is replaced by the empty string). The leftmost blank is matched, and the T branch is taken until there are no more blanks in STR. Then the F branch is taken and "XYZ" is output.

Figure 8-3. **Pattern match with replacement.**

It is often desirable to search for a pattern that has one or more *unknown* components. For example, we might wish to search a line of text for the occurrence of any single character enclosed in parentheses. To do so, we need to be able to specify a pattern component that will match *any* character. The use of unknowns in pattern matches is illustrated in Figure 8-4.

Pattern matches involving unknowns of arbitrary length (**) are executed by successively substituting *0*, *1*, *2*, . . . for ** until either a match occurs or no match is possible because the length of the pattern exceeds that of the subject. In other words, ** always matches the *shortest possible string.* This rule eliminates the possibility for ambiguity in a pattern match such as the one shown in Figure 8-5. The initial pattern match succeeds with ** matching the null string, and the output produced is "ABXCYDXE". The second attempt for a match succeeds with ** matching "C", leading to the output "ABDXE". The third matching attempt fails.

A final type of pattern component, the *list element unknown,* allows us to search for any member of a prespecified set of strings. Figure 8-6 shows an example that counts the number of occurrences of a digit followed by a decimal point in an input string. In box 1 the data string "1.4□OR□12.3□OR□2" is input. In box 2, a *list* of strings is assigned to V, and in box 4, we use $*\{V\}*$ to denote a pattern that matches any one of the strings in the list V. On the first entry to box 4, a pattern match occurs with $*\{V\}*$ matching "1", and "." matching the first decimal point in ZCOPY. The matched substring "1." is deleted, leaving "4 OR 12.3 OR 2" as the value of ZCOPY when the T exit of Box 4 is taken. After N is incremented in box 5, a second pattern match takes place, with $*\{V\}*$ matching "2". The third execution of box 4 fails to produce a match, leading to the output of 2 in box 6.

Often the purpose of a pattern match involving unknowns is to discover (for later use) just what characters occur in the unknown position. The middle compartment of the pattern match box allows us to specify a *capture variable* for each unknown in the pattern. If the pattern match is successful, then the string matching the first unknown in the pattern is assigned to the first capture variable, the string matching the second unknown is assigned to the second capture variable, etc. (There can be fewer capture variables than unknowns if desired.) An example is presented in Figure 8-7. Here the match is successful: "241" is assigned to DOL, the first capture variable, and "06" is assigned to CTS, the second capture variable, respectively. The new values of DOL and CTS are then used to form the string in the replacement step in the bottom compartment of the pattern match box.

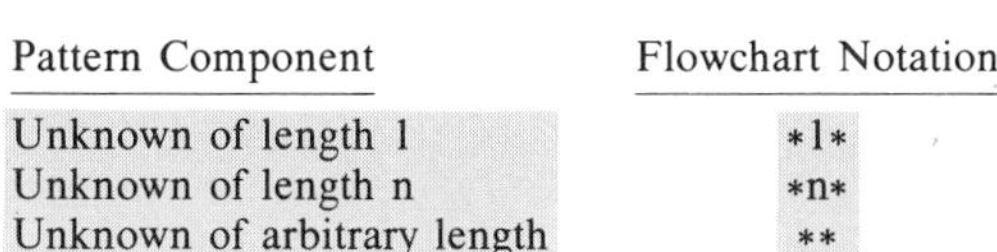

Pattern Component	Flowchart Notation
Unknown of length 1	*1*
Unknown of length n	*n*
Unknown of arbitrary length	**

(a) Flowchart notation for unknown pattern components.

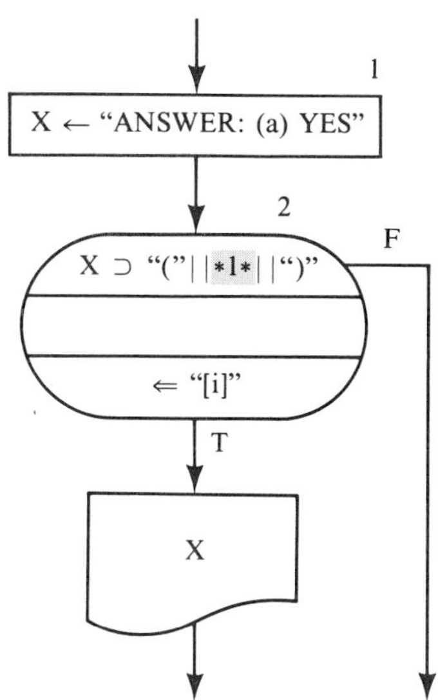

(b) T branch is taken and "ANSWER: [i] YES" is output.

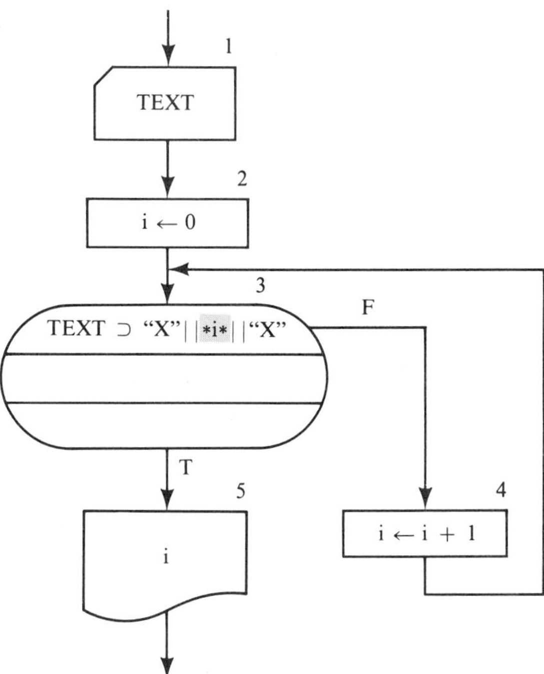

(c) If it is known that "X" appears twice in TEXT, then this flowchart will output the number of characters between the occurrences of "X". For example, if TEXT = "HEXAGONAL□FLEX", the output would be 10. Note that *0* matches the empty string, so that if TEXT = "AXXA", the output would be 0.

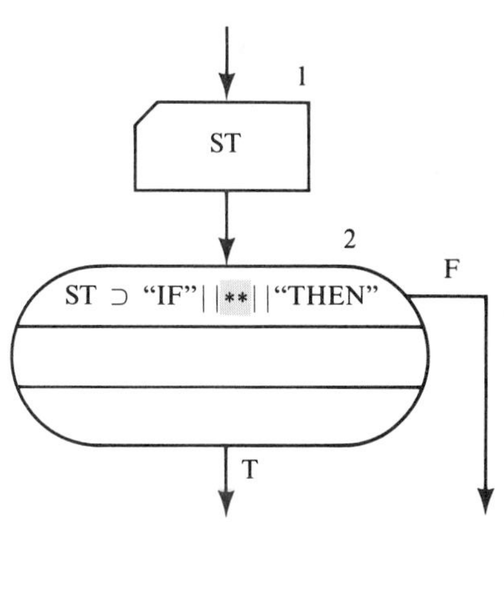

(d) The T branch is taken if ST contains "IF" and "THEN" separated by any number of characters (including none). For example, the T branch would be taken if ST = "IF (X.GT.0) THEN Y = 1" or if ST = "X = IFTHEN".

Figure 8-4. **Patterns with unknown components.**

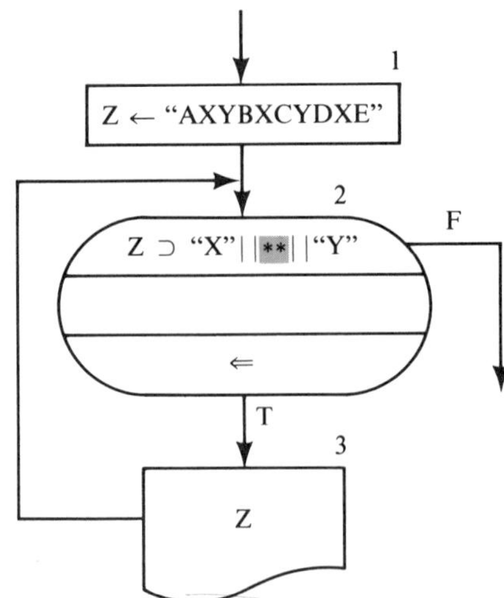

Figure 8-5. **Pattern match with an unknown of arbitrary length.**

Figure 8-6. **The list element unknown *{V}* matches any string that is an element of list V, in this case, any digit.**

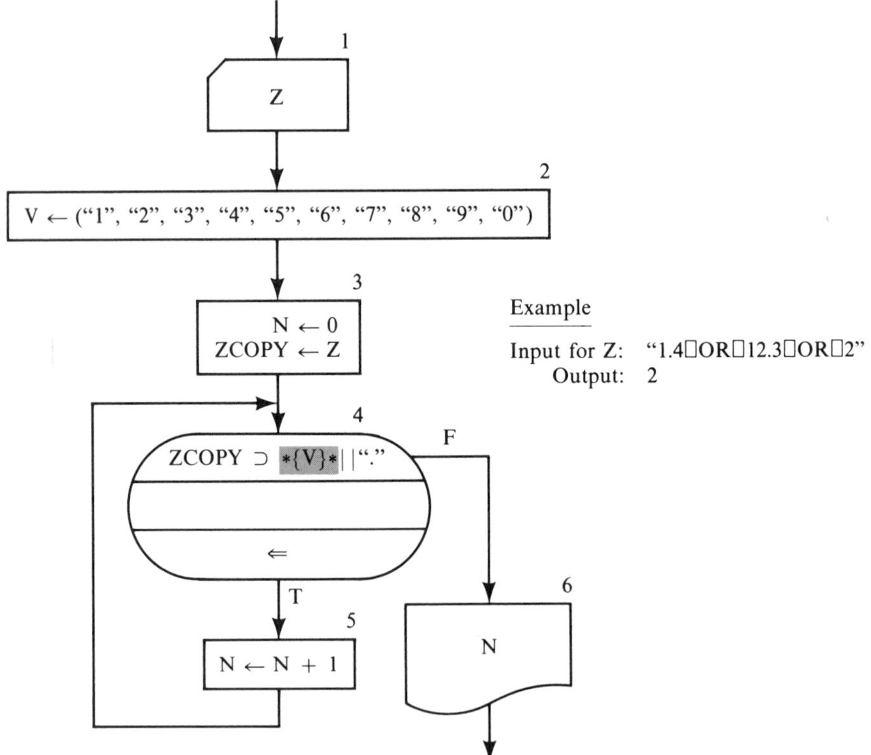

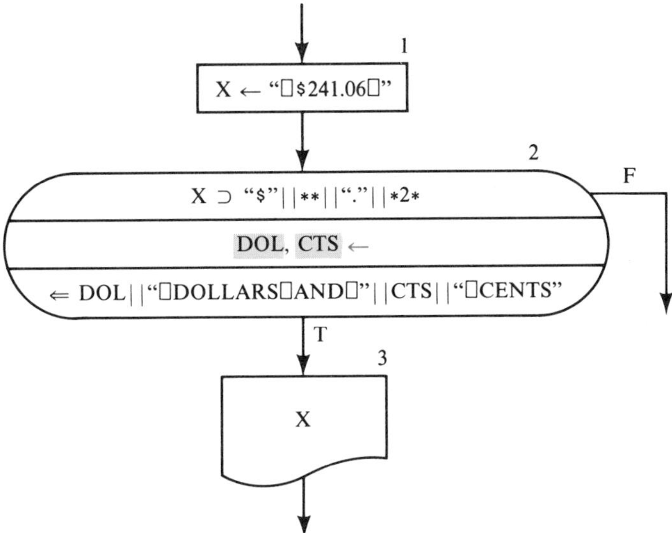

Figure 8-7. **Capture of two unknowns. The output is "□241□DOLLARS□AND□06□CENTS."**

8-3 SNOBOL SYNTAX

Our discussion of Snobol syntax begins with Table 8-1, which shows the correspondence between constants and expressions in the flowchart language and in Snobol. The examples of constants illustrate three data types in Snobol: string, integer, and real. Additional discussion of data types is given in Sections 8-8 and 8-9.

Table 8-2 presents a partial BNF syntax for Snobol that will prove a useful reference when we discuss examples of Snobol statements and programs.

A Snobol program is a sequence of statements followed by an end (the label END). One feature discernible from the syntax is that there are no declarations for variables. As we shall see below, cells for variables are allocated as they are needed during execution, not on the basis of explicit or implicit declaration.

Each Snobol statement begins on a different line. A period in column 1 indicates a continuation of the statement on the previous line. There is only *one* type of statement in Snobol; it consists of a *label field,* a *statement field,* and a *control field* (rule 3 of Table 8-2). Each of the fields may be empty.

A *label,* if present, must begin in column 1. Any sequence of characters beginning with a letter or digit may be used as a label (rules 5 and 6). Labels also appear as the destinations of branching instructions given in the *control field* (discussed below).

TABLE 8-1
Constants and Expressions in Snobol

<table>
<tr><th rowspan="2">Item</th><th colspan="2">Examples</th><th rowspan="2">Remarks</th></tr>
<tr><th>Flowchart</th><th>Snobol</th></tr>
<tr><td>Constants</td><td></td><td></td><td></td></tr>
<tr><td>Strings</td><td>"X"
"123"
"ZA4624"
" "<br>" "</td><td>'X'
'123'
'ZA4624'
''
NULL</td><td>Strings in Snobol are enclosed in single quotes. (Double quotes may also be used.) The null string is represented in Snobol by consecutive quotes or by the variable NULL (which has the null string as its preassigned value).</td></tr>
<tr><td>Integers</td><td>4
123</td><td>4
123</td><td></td></tr>
<tr><td>Reals</td><td>−6.29
3.2
.15</td><td>−6.29
3.2
0.15</td><td>Real constants must have at least one digit preceding the decimal point.</td></tr>
<tr><td>Expressions</td><td></td><td></td><td></td></tr>
<tr><td>Concatenation</td><td>"BIG"||"BIRD"</td><td>'BIG'□'BIRD'</td><td>There is no explicit concatenation operator in Snobol. Concatenation is implied between strings (or string-valued variables or expressions) written next to each other and separated by one or more blanks.</td></tr>
<tr><td></td><td>"("||X||")"</td><td>'(□X□')'</td><td>X is a string-valued variable.</td></tr>
<tr><td>Arithmetic operations</td><td>Z + 2
2.3 × Y
A↑2/(C − D)</td><td>Z□+□2
2.3□*□Y
A□**□2□/□(C□−□D)</td><td>Arithmetic operators in Snobol must be preceded and followed by at least one blank.</td></tr>
<tr><td>Conversion between strings and numbers</td><td>2 + stoi ("2")
itos(2)||"2"</td><td>2□+□'2'
2□'2'</td><td>In our flowchart language, we use functions stoi and itos to explicitly indicate string-to-integer and integer-to-string conversion. Snobol converts between numbers and numerical strings automatically. Thus 2□+□'2' has the value 4, and 2□'2' has the value '22'. Numerical strings are strings of digits, optionally preceded by a sign. A decimal point may be included if it is preceded by at least one digit. In an arithmetic expression, the empty string is equivalent to the integer zero.</td></tr>
</table>

The *statement field* and *control field,* if present, must begin with a blank (rules 7 and 15). Thus any two fields present are separated by a blank, and a statement with no label *has a blank in column 1.** There are three types of *statement field:* assignment, pattern match, and procedure call (rule 7).

*Anywhere a blank is required, more than one blank is permissible. Failure to begin an unlabeled statement with at least one blank is a common error in Snobol! While this rigid rule of blanks is painful to get used to, the pain is usually quickly replaced by enthusiasm for Snobol's expressive power.

TABLE 8-2
Partial BNF Syntax for Snobol

<table>
<tr><td>1.</td><td>⟨program⟩</td><td>::=</td><td>⟨statement sequence⟩⟨end⟩</td></tr>
<tr><td>2.</td><td>⟨statement sequence⟩</td><td>::=</td><td>⟨statement⟩|⟨statement⟩⟨statement sequence⟩</td></tr>
<tr><td>3.</td><td>⟨statement⟩</td><td>::=</td><td>⟨label field⟩⟨statement field⟩⟨control field⟩</td></tr>
<tr><td>4.</td><td>⟨label field⟩</td><td>::=</td><td>⟨empty⟩|⟨label⟩</td></tr>
<tr><td>5.</td><td>⟨label⟩</td><td>::=</td><td>⟨letter⟩|⟨digit⟩|⟨letter⟩⟨label part⟩|⟨digit⟩⟨label part⟩</td></tr>
<tr><td>6.</td><td>⟨label part⟩</td><td>::=</td><td>⟨any character⟩|⟨label part⟩⟨any character⟩</td></tr>
<tr><td>7.</td><td>⟨statement field⟩</td><td>::=</td><td>⟨empty⟩|□⟨assignment⟩|□⟨pattern match⟩|□⟨procedure call⟩</td></tr>
<tr><td>8.</td><td>⟨assignment⟩</td><td>::=</td><td>⟨variable⟩□=□⟨expression⟩</td></tr>
<tr><td>9.</td><td>⟨procedure call⟩</td><td>::=</td><td>⟨procedure identifier⟩(⟨argument list⟩)</td></tr>
<tr><td>10.</td><td>⟨argument list⟩</td><td>::=</td><td>⟨expression⟩|⟨expression⟩,⟨argument list⟩|⟨empty⟩</td></tr>
<tr><td>11.</td><td>⟨pattern match⟩</td><td>::=</td><td>⟨subject⟩□⟨pattern⟩□⟨replacement⟩</td></tr>
<tr><td>12.</td><td>⟨subject⟩</td><td>::=</td><td>⟨string expression⟩</td></tr>
<tr><td>13.</td><td>⟨pattern⟩</td><td>::=</td><td>⟨pattern expression⟩</td></tr>
<tr><td>14.</td><td>⟨replacement⟩</td><td>::=</td><td>⟨empty⟩|□=□⟨string expression⟩</td></tr>
<tr><td>15.</td><td>⟨control field⟩</td><td>::=</td><td>⟨empty⟩|□:⟨unconditional branch⟩|□:⟨conditional branch⟩</td></tr>
<tr><td>16.</td><td>⟨unconditional branch⟩</td><td>::=</td><td>(⟨label⟩)</td></tr>
<tr><td>17.</td><td>⟨conditional branch⟩</td><td>::=</td><td>S(⟨label⟩)|F(⟨label⟩)|S(⟨label⟩)F(⟨label⟩)|F(⟨label⟩)S(⟨label⟩)</td></tr>
<tr><td>18.</td><td>⟨end⟩</td><td>::=</td><td>END</td></tr>
</table>

1. Assignment

Assignments are straightforward translations of their flowchart equivalents. The assignment operator is =, which, like all binary operators in Snobol, must be preceded and followed by at least one blank. Some examples are shown in Figure 8-8. For the moment, necessary blanks are shown explicitly using the □ symbol.

***Figure 8-8.* Assignment steps.**

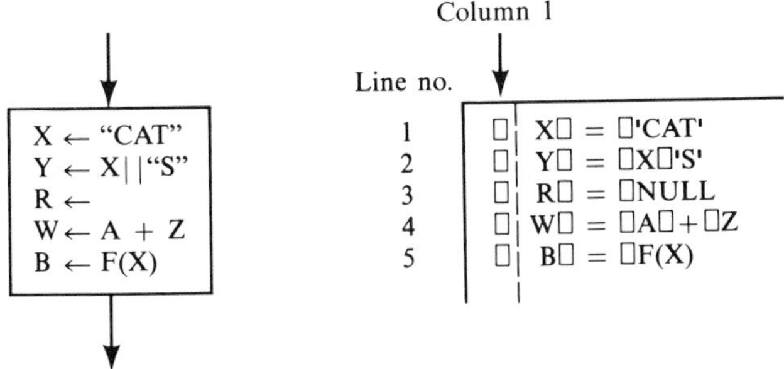

Input and output operations are written as assignment statements in Snobol by treating the names INPUT and OUTPUT as if they were variables. The statement

□X□=□INPUT

causes a data card or card image to be read and the resulting record (usually an 80-character string) to be assigned to X. The statement

□OUTPUT□=□X

causes the value of X to be displayed.

2. Pattern Match

Simple pattern matches are illustrated in Figure 8-9. The upper compartment of the pattern match box is translated into Snobol by writing the subject, then at least one blank, and then the pattern; there is no special operator to denote pattern match. The lack of an explicit operator for either pattern match or concatenation creates a potential ambiguity in a pattern match expression such as

STR□X□Y

(Is the subject STR or STR concatenated with X?) Figure 8-9b shows that the default rule in such cases is to consider the subject to be the first item only. Parentheses are used to indicate concatenation in the subject, as shown in Figure 8-9c.

Pattern matches in Snobol are said to *succeed* or *fail* (we have used T and F in our flowcharts for consistency with other decision boxes). What statement to execute next is determined by the result of the match and the contents of the control field.

The replacement operator in Snobol is the equal sign = (rule 14, Table 8-2). Examples of pattern match with replacement are shown in Figure 8-10.

Pattern match with capture of unknowns is illustrated in Figure 8-11. Note the following features of Snobol:

1. An unknown of length N is written LEN(N).
2. An unknown of arbitrary length is written ARB.
3. Capture is indicated by placing the capture operator (which is a period) between the unknown and the capture variable, with at least one blank space on each side of the period.

The Snobol statements of Figure 8-11a are rewritten in Figure 8-11b without the explicit symbol for blank. We shall adopt this style for the remainder of the chapter.

Figure 8-12 illustrates a list element unknown and provides an example of a complete Snobol program. The program inputs a string called TEXT and outputs a string consisting of all the vowels in TEXT, followed by all the consonants, followed by all the punctuation marks and blanks. On lines 2 and 3 we see that

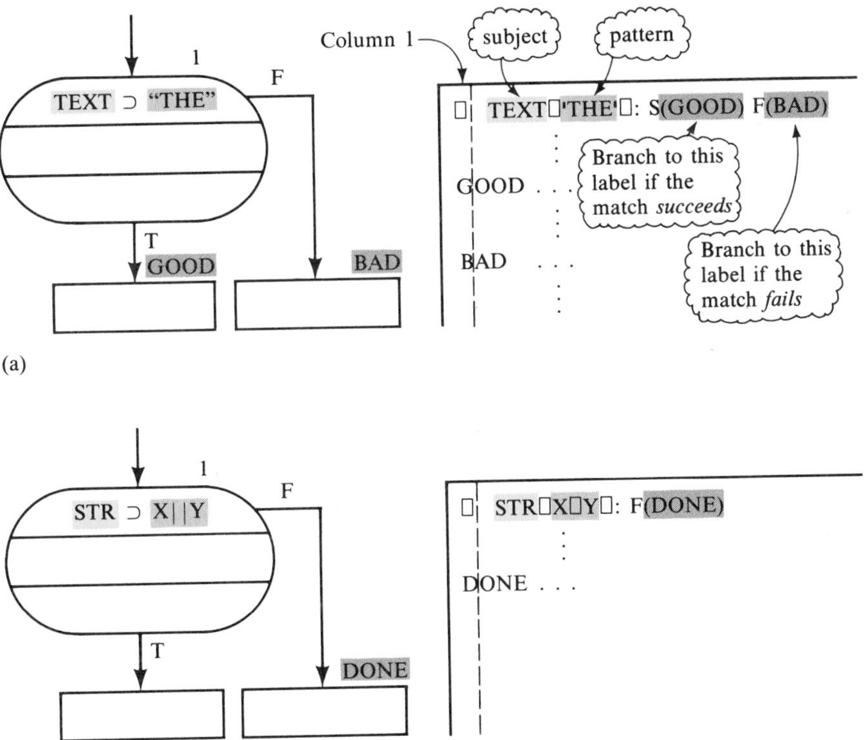

(b) The pattern consists of X concatenated with Y. Failure causes a branch to DONE; success causes execution to continue with the next statement.

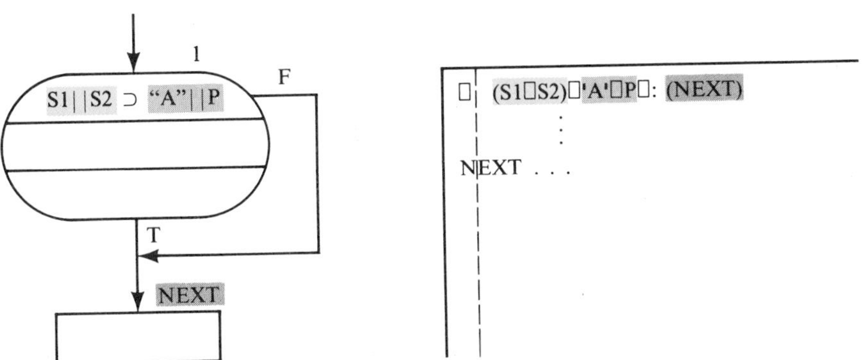

(c) Concatenation in the subject is indicated by parentheses. The control field contains an *unconditional* branch to NEXT.

***Figure 8-9.* Pattern matching in Snobol.**

a list element unknown is formed in Snobol by use of the *alternation operator*, | (vertical bar). As with the other operators in Snobol, a blank must occur on both sides of |. The program contains no translation of box 2 of the flowchart, since in Snobol all variables receive the null string as their initial value. Lines 5 and 6 search the input text for vowels, concatenate those found with the string

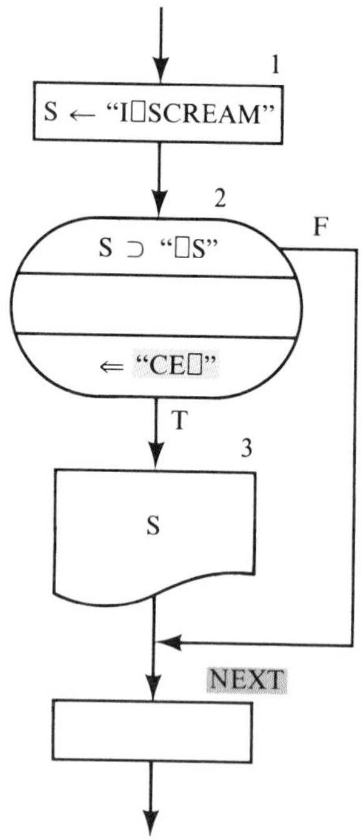

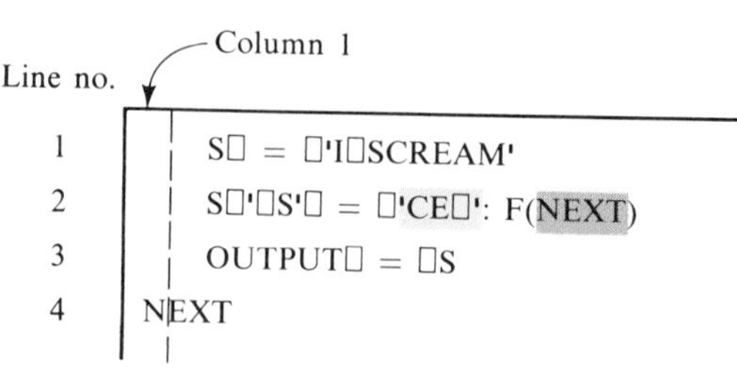

(a) The string displayed is "ICE CREAM".

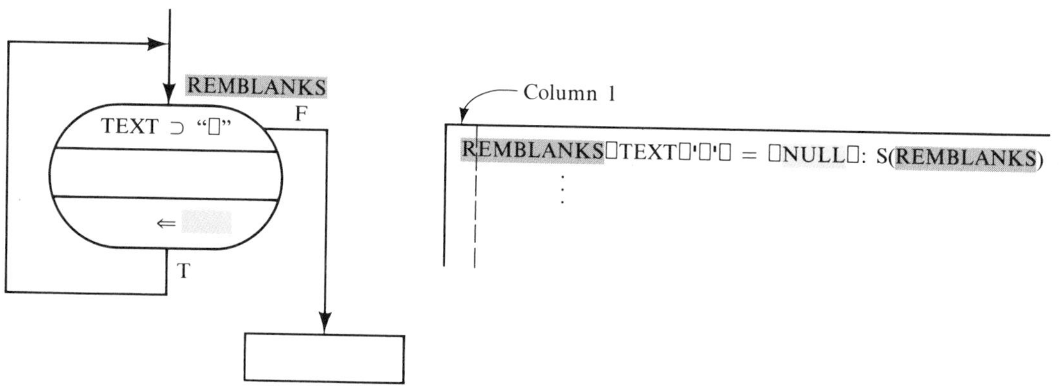

(b) When all blanks have been removed from TEXT, execution continues with the next statement.

Figure 8-10. **Pattern match with replacement.**

V (initially null), and delete them from TEXT. Lines 7 and 8 repeat the process for punctuation symbols, and line 9 produces the revised output. Note that no declarations for variables appear in the Snobol program, and that the final statement is simply the label END. Also note that a comment line may be placed anywhere in the program. A comment line is one that begins with an asterisk (*) in column 1.

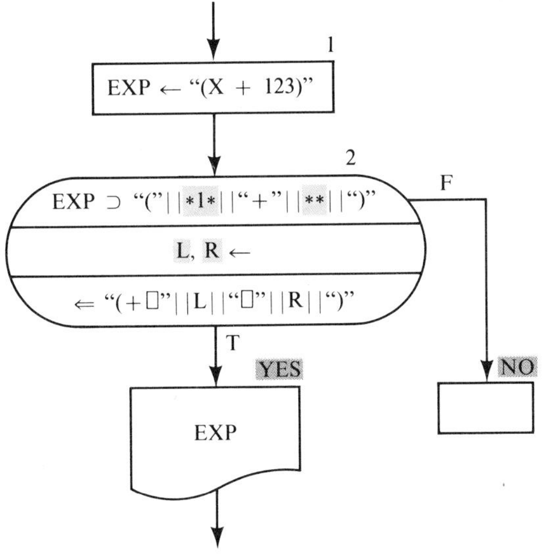

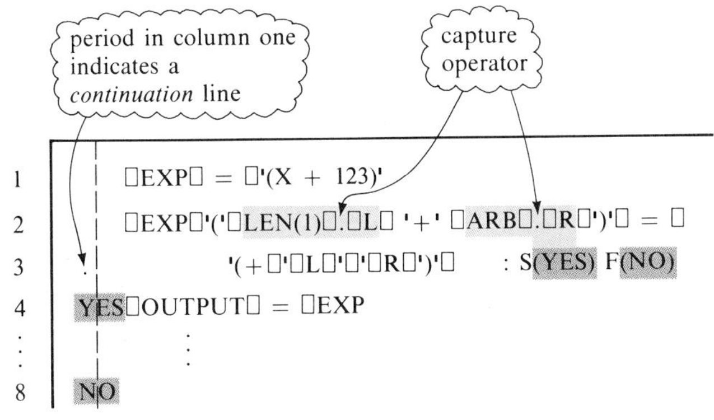

(a) The value output is '(+□X□123)'.

```
      EXP = '(X + 123)'
      EXP '(' (LEN(1) . L) '+' (ARB . R) ')' =
            '(+ ' L ' ' R ')'      : S(YES) F(NO)
YES   OUTPUT = EXP

NO
```

(b) Restatement of (a) without the explicit symbol for blank. Note that parentheses have been added around the two "capture clauses;" these are optional in Snobol.

***Figure 8-11.* Pattern match with capture of unknowns.**

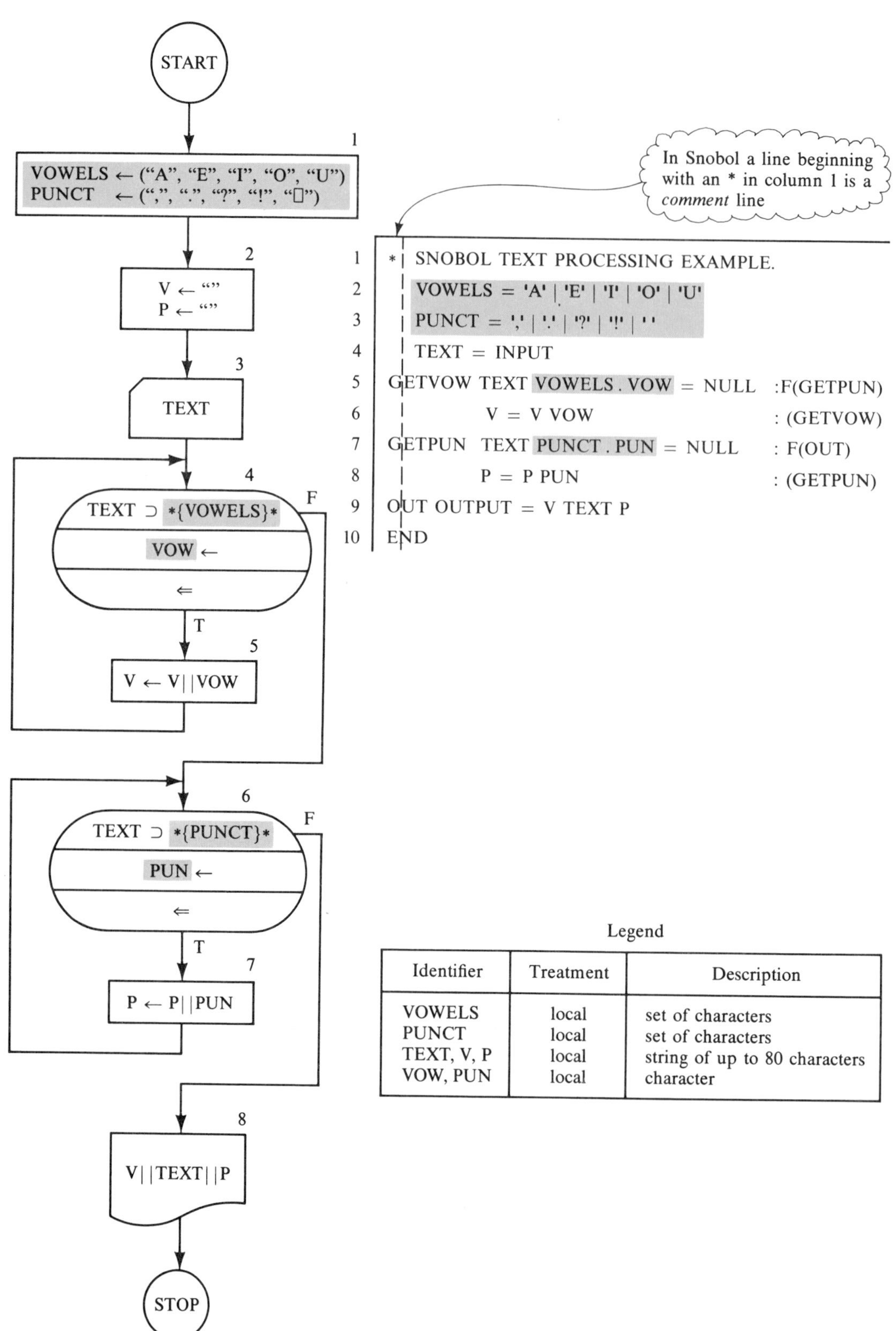


```
* SNOBOL TEXT PROCESSING EXAMPLE.
  VOWELS = 'A' | 'E' | 'I' | 'O' | 'U'
  PUNCT = ',' | '.' | '?' | '!' | ' '
  TEXT = INPUT
GETVOW TEXT VOWELS . VOW = NULL    :F(GETPUN)
           V = V VOW               :(GETVOW)
GETPUN TEXT PUNCT . PUN = NULL     :F(OUT)
           P = P PUN               :(GETPUN)
OUT OUTPUT = V TEXT P
END
```

Legend

Identifier	Treatment	Description
VOWELS	local	set of characters
PUNCT	local	set of characters
TEXT, V, P	local	string of up to 80 characters
VOW, PUN	local	character

Figure 8-12

3. Procedure Calls

A statement field may consist of a call on a predefined or user-defined procedure. Arguments of procedures are enclosed in parentheses and separated by commas. The parentheses must appear even if there are no arguments, and no space may separate the function name from the left parenthesis that follows.*

Table 8-3 lists the most commonly used predefined functions in Snobol.

TABLE 8-3
Predefined Functions in Snobol

Function	Arguments	Result
IDENT(X,Y)	Any data objects	Succeeds and returns the null string if X and Y have identical types and identical values, else fails.
DIFFER(X,Y)	Any data objects	Fails if X and Y have identical types and identical values, else succeeds and returns the null string.
LT(X,Y) LE(X,Y) EQ(X,Y) NE(X,Y) GE(X,Y) GT(X,Y)	Numbers or numeric strings	Succeeds and returns the null string if $\left\{\begin{matrix} X < Y, \\ X \leq Y, \\ X = Y, \\ X \neq Y, \\ X \geq Y, \\ X > Y, \end{matrix}\right\}$ else fails.
TRIM(X)	String	Returns the string X with any trailing blanks removed. For example, TRIM('A□□') returns 'A'.
SIZE(X)	String	Returns the length of X. For example, SIZE('A□□') returns 3.

Procedure calls, like pattern matches, either *succeed* or *fail.* For example, the predefined function IDENT(X,Y) succeeds if and only if its arguments are identical, that is, if they are of the same data type and are the same object. IDENT may be used to control conditional branching in a statement such as

```
 IDENT(X,'ABC') : S (NEXT) F (DONE)
```

Note that IDENT(5,'5') would fail because the first argument is an integer and the second a string; thus the arguments are of different data types.

Snobol provides six predefined functions LT, LE, EQ, NE, GE, and GT, which mean $<, \leq, =, \neq, \geq$, and $>$, respectively. They may be used to compare any two numbers or numeric strings. For example, EQ('4',4.0) succeeds.

A procedure call that succeeds must return a value. Thus, in Snobol all procedures are functions (as they are in Lisp) and procedure calls may appear in expressions. For example, if COUNT(C,S) has been defined to be a function

*Spaces are optional before or after a comma separator of a Snobol argument list. However, spaces are not allowed on either side of a separating comma in the parameter list of a procedure definition or other declarative form. To avoid confusion, we simply adopt the convention of not putting a space before or after a comma.

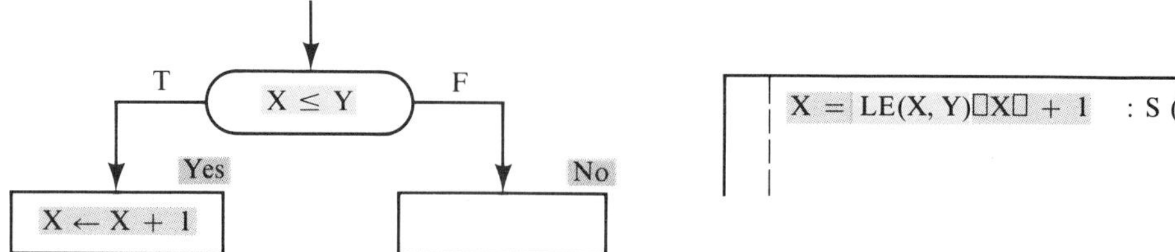

(a) Flowchart fragment

(b) Snobol. If X ≤ Y is true, the null string is concatenated with X, the result (which is just X) is added to 1, the sum is assigned to X, and a branch to label YES occurs. If X ≤ Y is false, X is unchanged, and the branch is to label NO.

***Figure 8-13.* Conditional assignment.**

that returns the number of occurrences of character C in string S, then the statement below assigns the value 2 to X.

```
X = COUNT('A', 'A BEAR')
```

The two roles of a function call, returning a value and controlling a branch, may be combined in a single statement. If a function call on the right side of an assignment operator fails, then the *assignment* is said to fail. This means that the variable on the left of the assignment operator is *unchanged.* This feature of the language, along with the fact that the functions IDENT, LT, LE, etc., return the *null string* when they do succeed, allows compact coding of conditional assignments, but tends to make the code more difficult to read and comprehend. An example is shown in Figure 8-13.

Another example of success or failure in an assignment is the statement

X = INPUT

which fails if there are no data to be read.

8-4 STORAGE STRUCTURES FOR VARIABLES

In preparation for the study of the semantics of Snobol procedures in Section 8-5, we now consider storage structures for variables. The main Snobol feature to be accounted for is the fact that strings are stored *uniquely.* That is, each string in use by a program appears in storage only once; every variable with a given string as its value holds a *pointer* to a HEAP cell containing that string. These ideas are illustrated in Figure 8-14.*

*Some implementations of Snobol do not store strings uniquely, but by other means these implementations remain semantically equivalent to the language as described here.

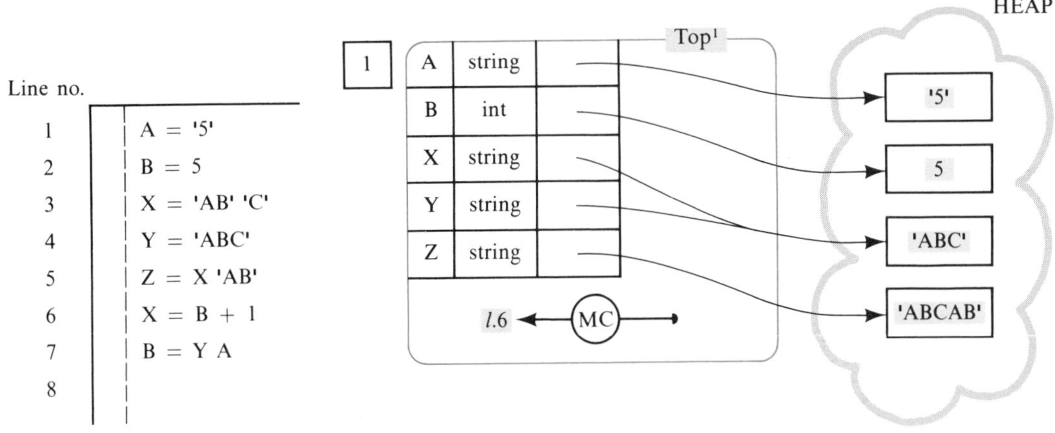

(a) Snobol program.

(b) Snapshot taken after the first five lines of the program in part (a) have been executed.

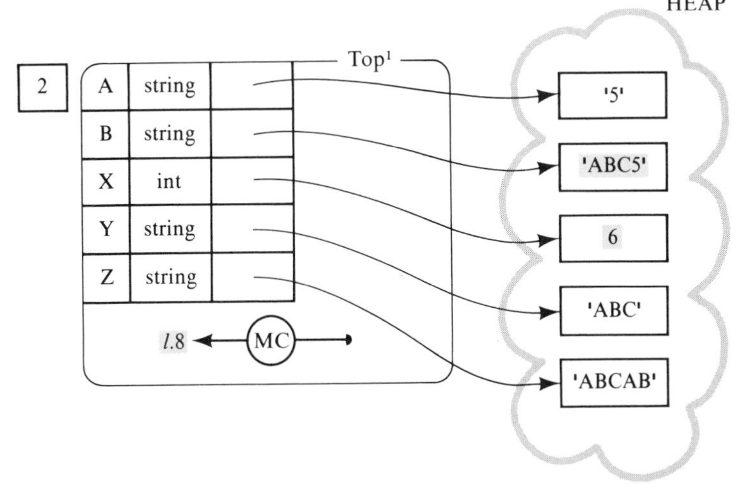

(c) Snapshot taken just after line 7 is executed.

Figure 8-14

In Figure 8-14b, we see that X and Y both point to a HEAP cell holding the string 'ABC', even though the values of X and Y resulted from different expressions (lines 3 and 4 of the program in Figure 8-14a). The uniqueness of storage of strings does *not* extend to the level of *substring*, however. Thus the variable Z holds a pointer to a cell containing 'ABCAB'; it is immaterial that the first three characters of this string appear in another cell.*

*The data representations in actual implementations of Snobol may differ somewhat from those suggested by our contour modeling method. Our model is, however, functionally equivalent to the implementations of the language; that is, it achieves the same net effect for all data accessing operations. Consult the references for more information on implementations.

As mentioned earlier, no *declarations* for variables appear in the top level of a Snobol program. Cells are allocated as variables are encountered, and the type associated with a variable is *dynamic;* that is, a variable assumes the type of the value most recently assigned to it. In Figure 8-14c, the execution of lines 6 and 7 of the program has caused the types of variables X and B to change.

8-5 SYNTAX AND SEMANTICS OF PROCEDURE DECLARATIONS AND CALLS

Snobol procedures are declared in two parts:

1. a *head* consisting of a call on the special function DEFINE, and
2. a *body* comprising one or more statements.

Figure 8-15 shows a "skeleton" declaration of a procedure FN. The head specifies the name of the procedure, its parameters and local variables, and the *label* that appears on the first line of the procedure body. Notice that the head of a procedure declaration can be separate from the body. The label may be omitted from the head, but then the first line of the body must contain the procedure name as a label. (See line 2 of Figure 8-16.)

As stated earlier, procedure calls in Snobol are said either to *succeed* or *fail.* Return from the procedure is indicated by a statement that branches to the pseudolabel RETURN if the execution is successful and to the pseudolabel FRETURN if the procedure fails. The actual return is, of course, to the point of

Figure 8-15. **Procedure declaration in Snobol.**

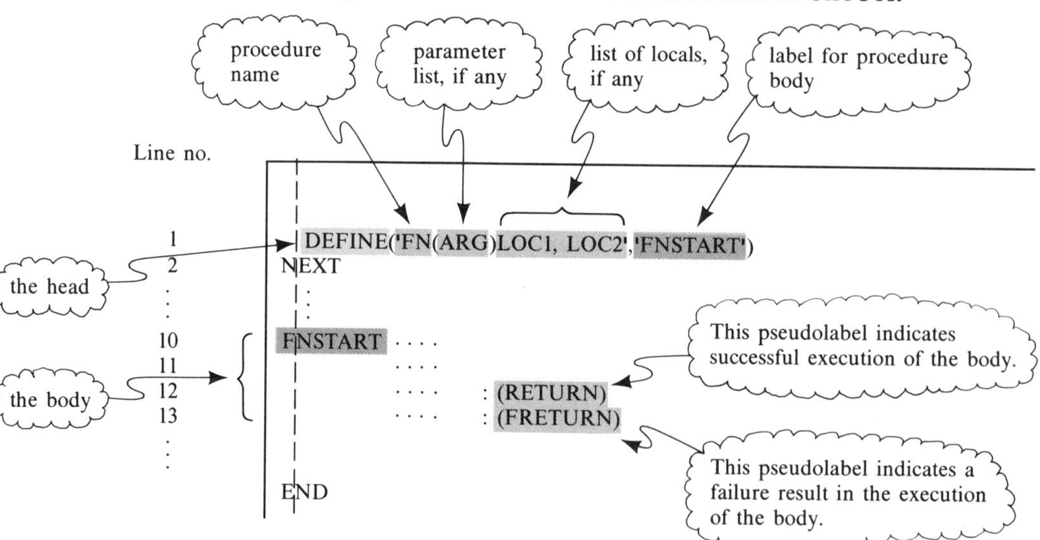

the call. The pseudolabels RETURN and FRETURN never actually appear as label fields in the program.

The result of executing the call on DEFINE (line 1) is the creation of a procedure cell in Top[1]. The value in the third compartment in that cell is a pointer to the call on DEFINE. For the program of Figure 8-15 we have the procedure cell

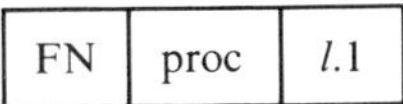

The procedure body may be placed anywhere in the program except in the "flow" of execution of the Top level or within another procedure. Figure 8-16 shows an alternative placement for the body of Figure 8-15: immediately after the call on DEFINE. Since the call on DEFINE is the first statement of Top, its control field contains an unconditional branch around the body, so that execution will not flow into the body. The statements of the body will be executed when the procedure FN is *called.* As we shall see, the contour for a procedure is placed, as in Lisp, inside the contour of its caller.

Note in Figure 8-16 that since a starting label is not specified in the call on DEFINE, the procedure name is used to label the first line of the body. This practice may be followed regardless of where the body is placed.

Example 1 Consider a function PD that determines whether its argument string is a palindrome (reads the same backward as forward). For example, the strings 'MADAM', 'RADAR', 'TOOT', and 'X + Y + Z + Y + X' are all palindromes. A program declaring and using PD is shown in Figure 8-17.

The technique used in PD to identify palindromes is a simple one: a second string, STR2, is constructed such that it is the reverse of the given string, WORD. If the two strings are identical, then the given string is a palindrome.

Line 1 is the head of the definition of the function PD. Line 2 reads a line of input, trims the trailing blanks, and branches to the END statement on line 9 if no more input is forthcoming. Line 3 calls the function PD with the value of IN as the argument. A successful return, meaning that the input was indeed a palindrome, leads to the output statement of line 4. After success or failure, control returns to line 2 to input another string, if any.

Figure 8-16. **Placement of a procedure body immediately after its head.**

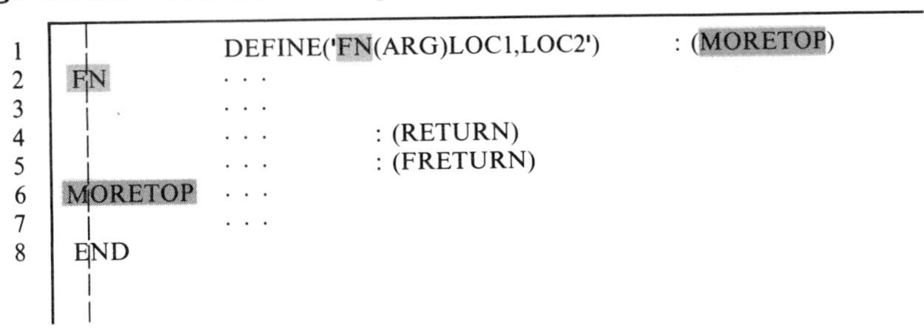

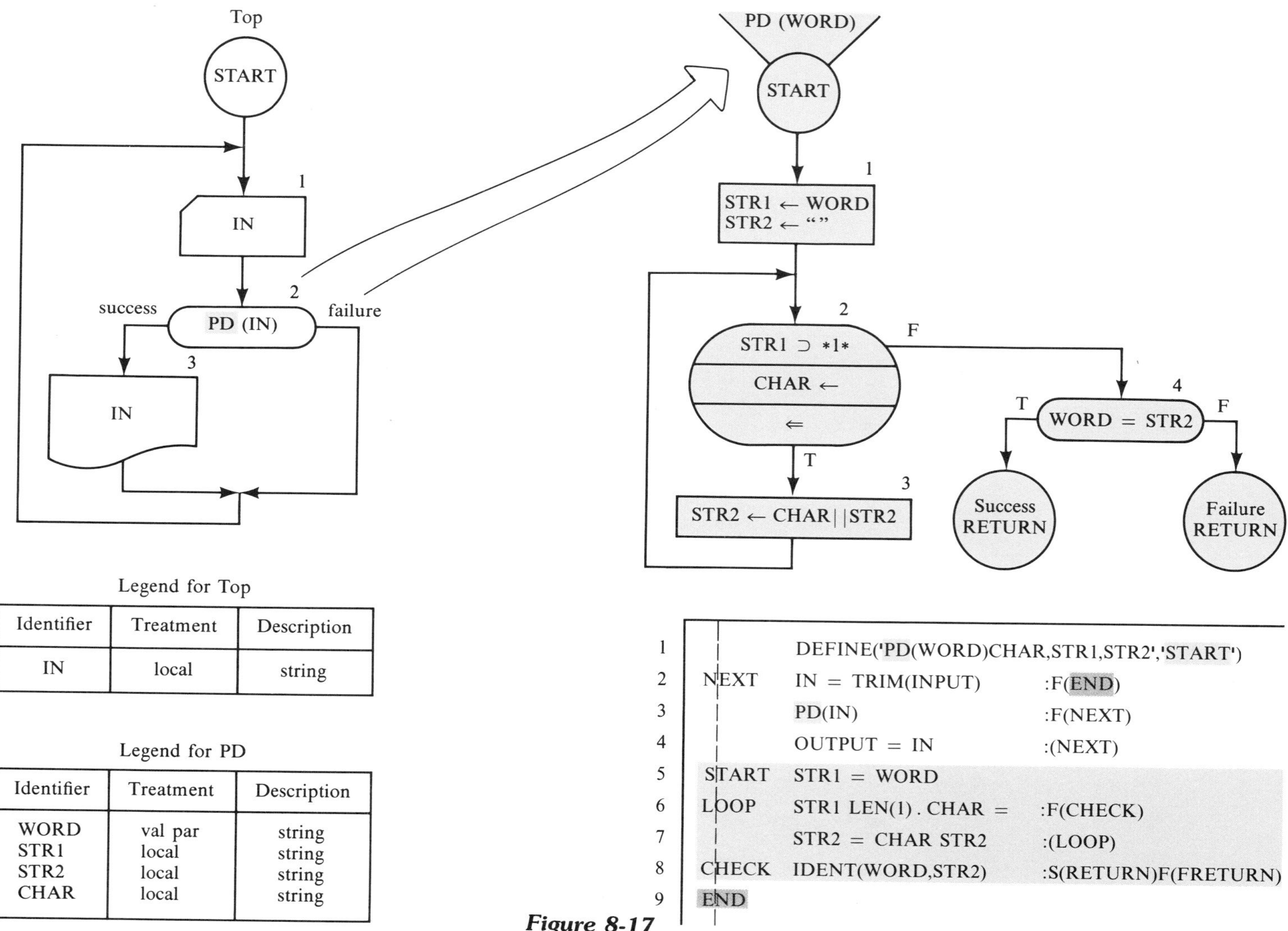

Legend for Top

Identifier	Treatment	Description
IN	local	string

Legend for PD

Identifier	Treatment	Description
WORD	val par	string
STR1	local	string
STR2	local	string
CHAR	local	string

Figure 8-17

The body for function PD begins with the statement labeled "START" (line 5). This line copies the value of the parameter WORD into a local variable, STR1. The next line, labeled LOOP, begins the action. Here the first character of STR1 is captured in CHAR and deleted from STR1. The captured character is then concatenated on the front of STR2 (which is initially NULL) and control returns to LOOP, to pick off another character. If no character remains in STR1 the match on line 6 fails, and a transfer to CHECK results.

When the label CHECK is reached, the value of WORD is compared with its reverse in STR2; if the two strings are identical, then WORD is a palindrome. The success or failure of the comparison determines whether the "RETURN" or "FRETURN" is executed.

Assuming that the first input value is 'MADAM', Figure 8-18 shows the situation just after line 2 has been executed. Cells for PD and IN have been allocated as a result of executing lines 1 and 2, respectively, and the input value has been assigned to IN. Note that no declaration for IN was necessary; a cell was allocated automatically when it was needed.

The procedure PD is called by the statement on line 3. The steps taken in invoking PD are described below, and lead to the state shown in Figure 8-19.

1. The MC follows the ip in the value compartment of cell PD in Top^1, leading to the DEFINE statement. He instructs the Allocator to use the information given in the DEFINE statement to construct a new contour PD^1 immediately inside Top^1, the environment from which PD was called. This contour PD^1 has cells for the parameters and locals of PD, as well as *retval* and *retlab* cells.
2. The proper ip and ep values are assigned to the *retlab* cell; that is, to represent the current state of the MC, a line number or statement label and a contour name are assigned to the return cell. Thus, in the example of Figure 8-19 the return cell is given the values

retlab	ptrs	*l*.3 in Top^1

3. Values and types for all matching arguments are assigned to the PD^1 cells for the corresponding parameters. In Snobol all *parameters are value parameters;* a pointer to the value is placed in the parameter cell and the type of the argument becomes the type of the parameter. Cells for the

Figure 8-18

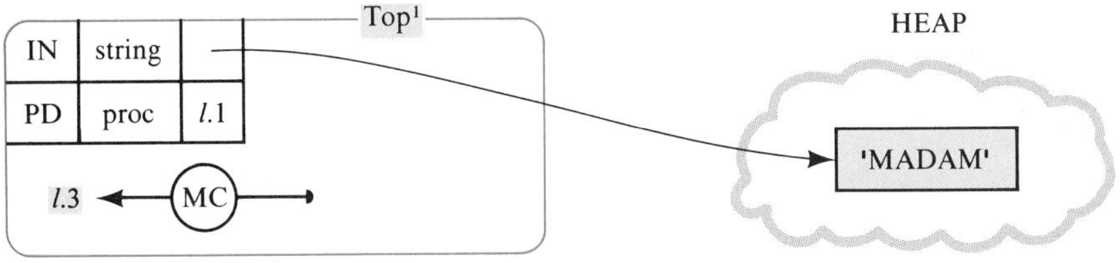

IN	string	→ 'MADAM'
PD	proc	*l*.1

locals and the *retval* are assigned the null string as initial values. In our example the value of the argument IN is 'MADAM', and so a pointer to that value is assigned to the parameter WORD, which is therefore of type string.

4. The MC sets his ip to the label of the first line of the body for PD and moves inside the PD[1] contour. Snobol uses the name of the procedure, in this case PD, as a pseudovariable to which a value may be assigned. This value has to have a storage cell and in our model the *retval* (return value) cell fulfills this function. Figure 8-19 shows the situation just before the first statement of the body is executed. Note that the locals and *retval* cell of PD[1] have been given the null string as their initial values.

When the execution of PD is finished the MC must return to the caller, Top. The following steps are carried out:

1. If the function call is successful (that is, if a branch to RETURN is to be executed), then as the final action in the procedure contour PD[1], the MC pushes *two* values on to the portable stack. The first is the final value assigned to the pseudovariable PD, if any was assigned, and otherwise the null string. The second value is the signal s, for SUCCESS. If the function call is not successful (that is, if a branch to FRETURN is to be executed), then only the signal "f" is entered in the portable stack. In the example shown, the MC first enters the null value ' ', and then the signal s into the stack:

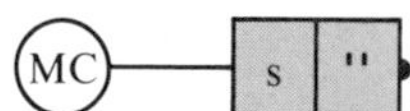

***Figure 8-19.* Snapshot just after the MC enters PD[1].**

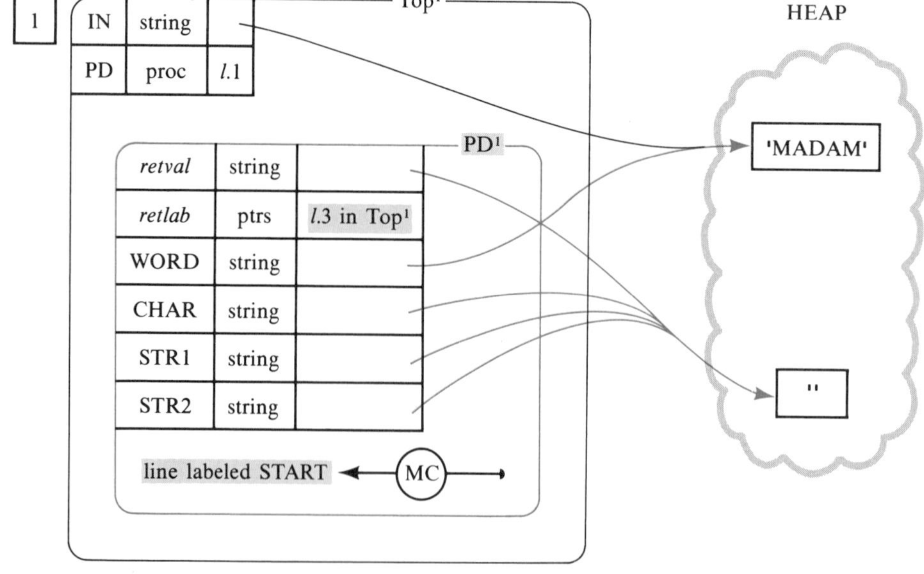

2. Now the MC, along with this stack, reenters the calling environment, in this case Top^1. His instruction pointer has already been set to line 3, as specified by the return cell in PD^1. The contour PD^1 is deleted.
3. In line 3 the MC returns precisely to the point at which the PD procedure call was made, and pops a value from the stack. This value, the signal s or f, determines what happens next. If it is an f, the MC immediately pursues the fail path in the control part of line 3. If the popped value is an s, the second value is then popped and entered as the value of the procedure call in the expression undergoing evaluation. In this example there is no explicit assignment of the value of this expression (on line 3) and so it is lost, but watch for this assignment in Example 2. When execution of the statement portion is complete, the MC pursues the true path (or in some cases the only path) in the control portion. In the example, because the returned signal was s, control is transferred to the succeeding OUTPUT statement and the palindrome 'MADAM' is printed.

Example 2 By slightly revising the palindrome program of Example 1 a value can be returned to the calling program, as seen in Figure 8-20.

If we were to draw a snapshot of the execution of this program just after control returns from the procedure PLD, it would be almost identical to Figure 8-19. The only difference would be in the MC's portable stack, assuming as before the input string "MADAM". This time the stack looks like this:

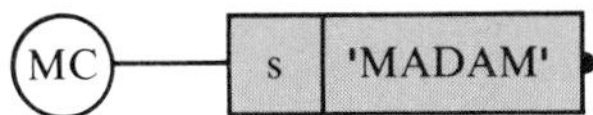

Upon return from the procedure PLD, the MC pops a value from the stack. Since it is an "s", he pops the second value and substitutes it for the expression "PLD(IN)" on line 3 of the Figure 8-20 program. Execution of the output assignment statement is complete when the value 'MADAM' has been printed. Now the MC moves on to the statement labeled NEXT.

The above examples involve only a single procedure. If a procedure P calls another procedure Q, the contour for Q is nested *within the contour for the*

Figure 8-20. **Revised palindrome program.**

Line no.

```
1           DEFINE('PLD(WORD) CHAR,STR1,STR2','START')
2   NEXT    IN = TRIM(INPUT)                      :F(END)
3           OUTPUT = PLD(IN)                      :(NEXT)
4   START   STR1 = WORD
5   LOOP    STR1 LEN(1) . CHAR =                  :F(CHECK)
6           STR1 = CHAR STR2                      :(LOOP)
7   CHECK   PLD =
8           PLD = IDENT(WORD,STR2) WORD           :(RETURN)
9   END
```

caller, P, as shown in Figure 8-21a. Snobol procedures can be recursive, and in this case the same rule for contour nesting is followed. Figure 8-21b shows the situation that results if procedure Q in Figure 8-21a calls itself recursively.

Access to global variables is as suggested in Figure 8-21. The significance of this type of nesting is that a reference to an identifier selects the *most recently allocated cell* for that identifier, a rule similar to that used in Lisp.

Figure 8-21. **Placement of procedure contours in Snobol.**

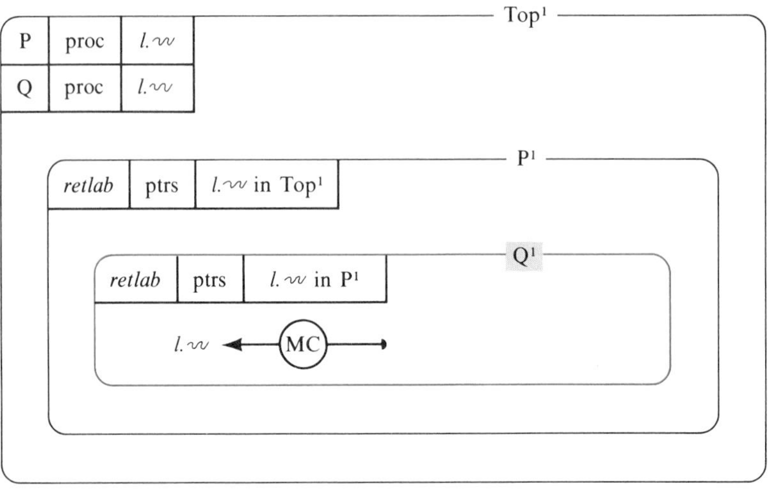

(a)

Top¹
P proc l.~
Q proc l.~
P¹
retlab ptrs l.~ in Top¹
Q¹
retlab ptrs l.~ in P¹
Q²
retlab ptrs l.~ in Q¹
l.~ MC

(b)

One syntactic feature of the language not yet mentioned is that all labels must be distinct. For example, a label used in Top may not also label a statement in a procedure.

Snobol and Lisp are somewhat similar in the semantics of procedure call and return, and both differ substantially from Algol. In Algol, enclosing contours represent statically enclosing blocks of code. In Snobol and Lisp, enclosing contours represent dynamic antecedents, that is, procedures within which the procedure in question was called (with the lone exception of funargs in Lisp, as discussed in Section 7-12).

8-6 SNOBOL CASE STUDY: SYMBOLIC DIFFERENTIATION

The example we have chosen as a case study is closely related to the final case study in Lisp, *symbolic differentiation,* and to the earlier discussion of the same problem in Section 3-5. Our procedure D in this section is also recursive and symbolically differentiates a fully parenthesized string expression S with respect to the symbol X. While division was excluded as an operator in the Lisp case study, it is included here along with exponentiation.

The differentiation procedure does not require that the expression supplied as data have the form of an expression in a Snobol *program.* But if it does, both it and its derivative can be *evaluated* later by the Snobol program, if that is desirable. For this reason we have assumed that our input expression S is a fully parenthesized Snobol expression. A particular expression to keep in mind as an example to differentiate is

$$S = (((X + 1) \uparrow 2)/(5 \times X))$$

where $\uparrow$ is the exponentiation operator. Since any fully parenthesized expression is directly translatable into a binary tree, we can also write S as

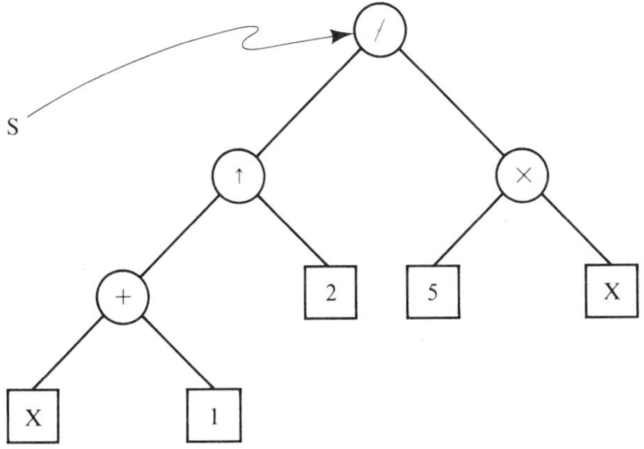

The procedure D, flowcharted in Figure 8-22, makes calls on four auxiliary procedures ADDOP, MULT, DIV, and EXP, which perform the differentiation

Differentiation rules

$$\frac{dx}{dx} = 1$$

$$\frac{d}{dx}\text{const} = 0$$

$$\frac{d}{dx}(u \pm v) = \frac{d}{dx}u \pm \frac{d}{dx}v$$

$$\frac{d}{dx}(u \times v) = u \times \frac{d}{dx}v + v \times \frac{d}{dx}u$$

$$\frac{d}{dx}(u/v) = \frac{v \times \frac{d}{dx}u - u \times \frac{d}{dx}v}{v^2}$$

$$\frac{d}{dx}u^n = n \times u^{n-1} \times \frac{d}{dx}u$$

Legend for D

Identifier	Treatment	Description
S	val par	string of characters representing a fully parenthesized arithmetic expression
X	val par	string
OP	local	character
A	local	string
B	local	string

(a)

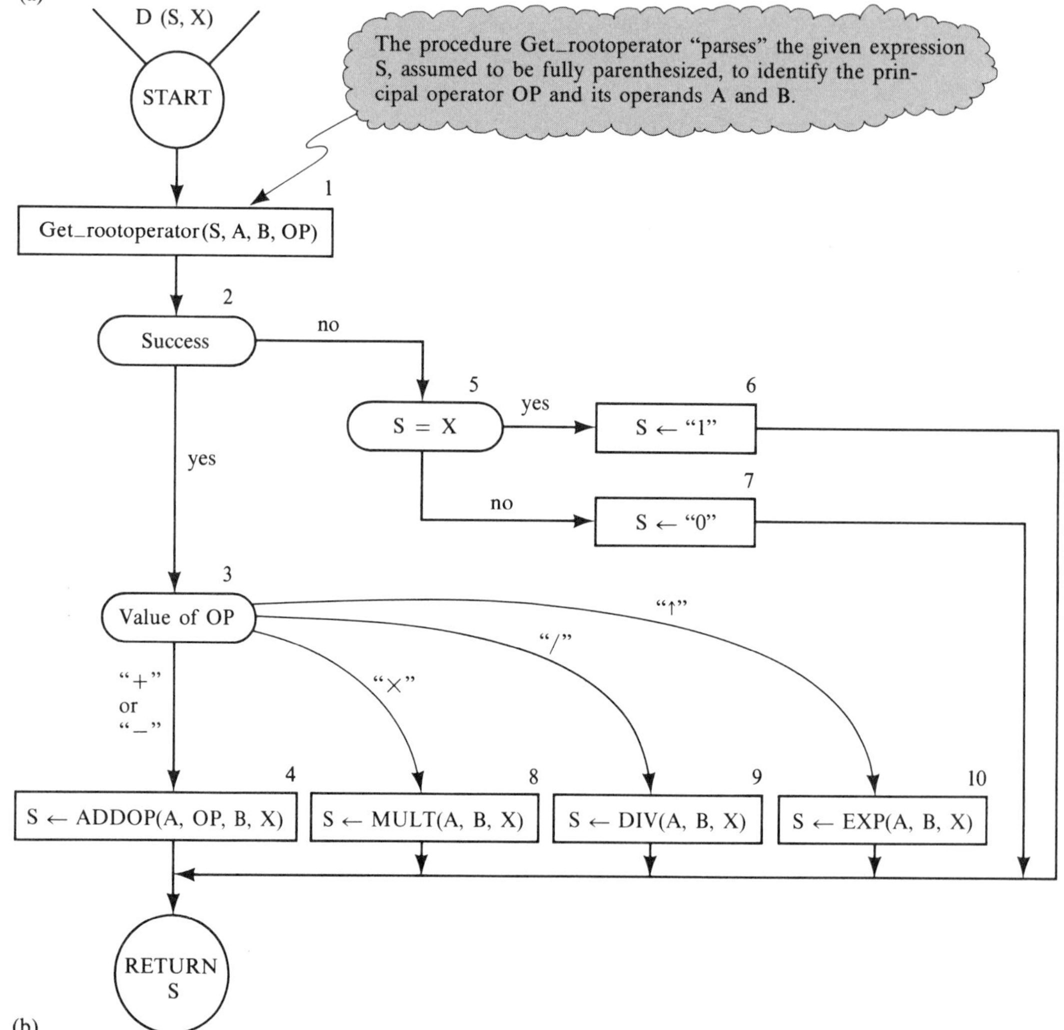

(b)

Figure 8-22 **The differentiation procedure D(S,X). Compare this structure with Figures 3-53 and 7-35.**

of the four basic forms: (u ± v), (u × v), (u/v), and (u ↑ n), respectively. When the differentiated expression is finally returned by D, it is correct, but may be in a very complicated form. As in the Lisp case study, a SIMPLIFY procedure is now activated. SIMPLIFY uses a preselected set of rules to recognize subexpressions that can be replaced by simpler ones. Thus, what we want to execute is

SIMPLIFY(D(S,X))

The rules for differentiation are given in Figure 8-22a. The flowchart shown in Figure 8-22b may be regarded as fairly high-level.

Figure 8-23 is a revised version of Figure 8-22 using string variables and pattern match operations. The new auxiliary procedures DADDOP, DMULT, etc., defined in Figure 8-24, are intended to operate on forms similar to those for ADDOP, MULT, etc., of Figure 8-22, except for enclosing parentheses. Notice that in box 2 of Figure 8-23, the outermost set of parentheses of the expression S are stripped off, and so DADDOP, DMULT, etc., work on forms like u ± v without enclosing parentheses. It is conceptually simpler to leave them off until we are ready to assign a value to S in box 4, 6, 8, or 9. A flowchart for the procedure SIMPLIFY that acts on the string expression returned by D(S,X) is given in Figure 8-25.

Finally, a top-level flowchart is required to call the procedure SIMPLIFY which calls the procedure D. Figure 8-26 is a possibility. Snobol code corresponding to the preceding flowcharts is shown in Figure 8-27. The statements shaded in gray cause certain steps in the execution of the program to be *traced.* Setting the "keyword" &TRACE to 1000 allows up to 1000 lines of trace output to be produced. The remaining statements in the shaded section are calls on the predefined function TRACE, and specify the procedures that are to be traced. Each time a traced procedure is called, its argument(s) are output, and when it returns, its value is also output.

Note in Figure 8-27 that "*" means multiplication in Snobol, and "**" means exponentiation. In our discussion we shall continue to use "×" and "↑", respectively.

Before we exhibit the computer output for this Snobol program using as data the expression

$$S = (((X + 1) \uparrow 2)/(5 \times X))$$

it is helpful to draw the call tree for the procedure D, using Figures 8-26, 8-25, 8-24 and 8-23. Because the call tree shown in Figure 8-28 bears a resemblance to the binary tree structure of the expression to be differentiated, we repeat the tree with the principal operator and its left and right subtrees identified, to help get us started.

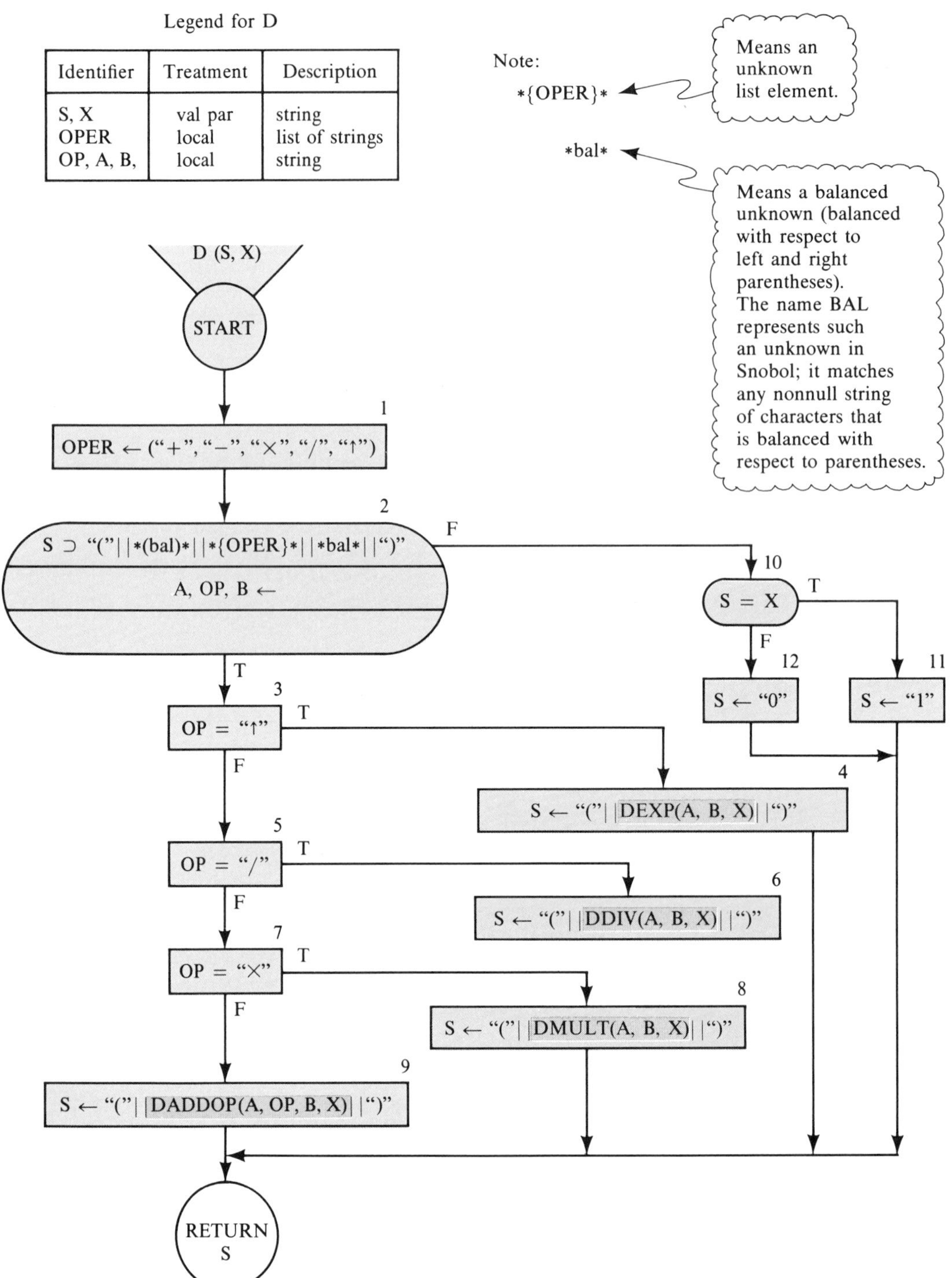

Figure 8-23. **Flowchart for derivative procedure using string variables and string pattern match.**

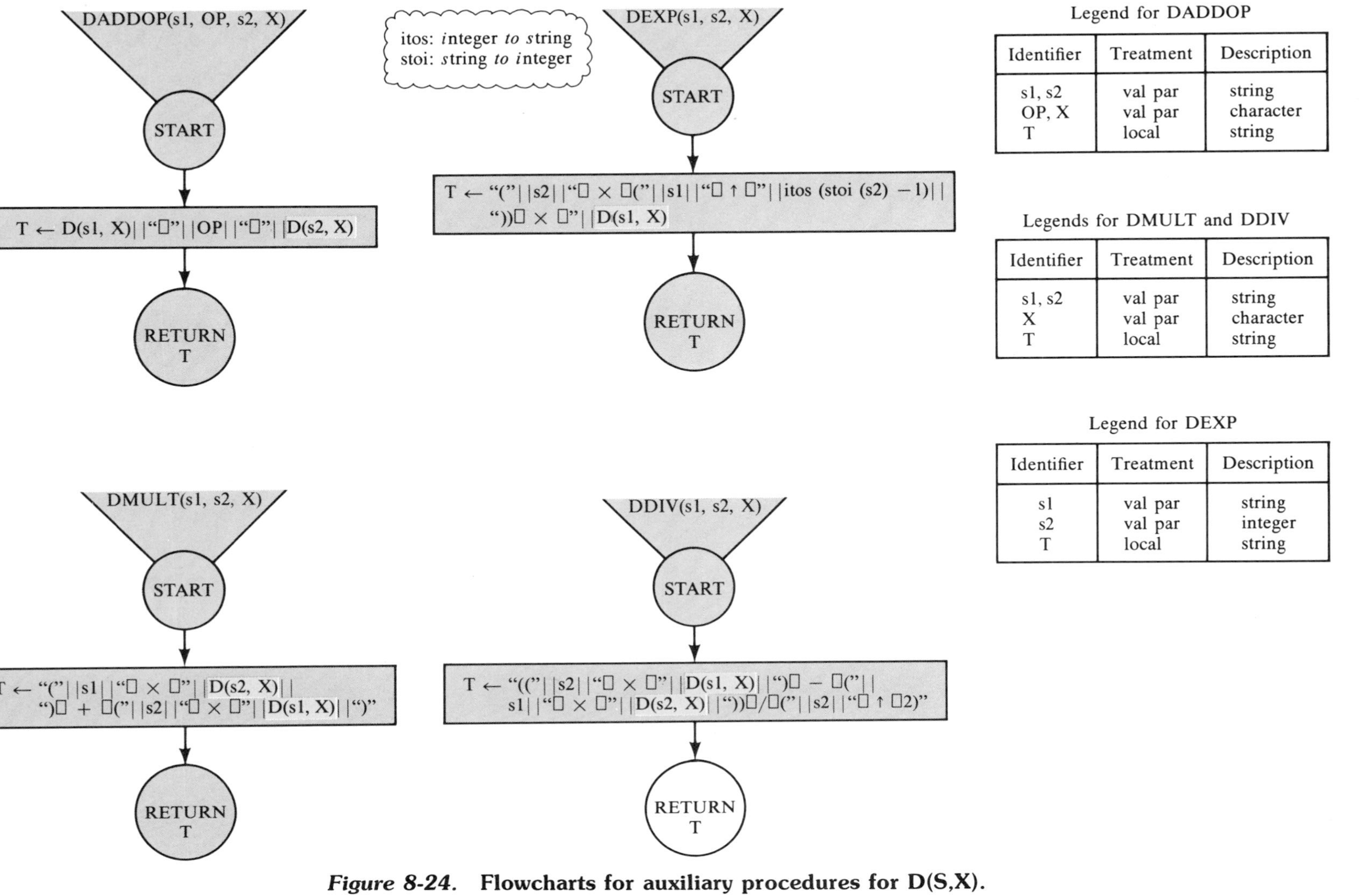

Legend for DADDOP

Identifier	Treatment	Description
s1, s2 OP, X T	val par val par local	string character string

Legends for DMULT and DDIV

Identifier	Treatment	Description
s1, s2 X T	val par val par local	string character string

Legend for DEXP

Identifier	Treatment	Description
s1 s2 T	val par val par local	string integer string

Figure 8-24. **Flowcharts for auxiliary procedures for D(S,X).**

Legend for Simplify

Identifier	Treatment	Description
S	ref par	string
U	local	any subexpression (string) *balanced* with respect to parentheses

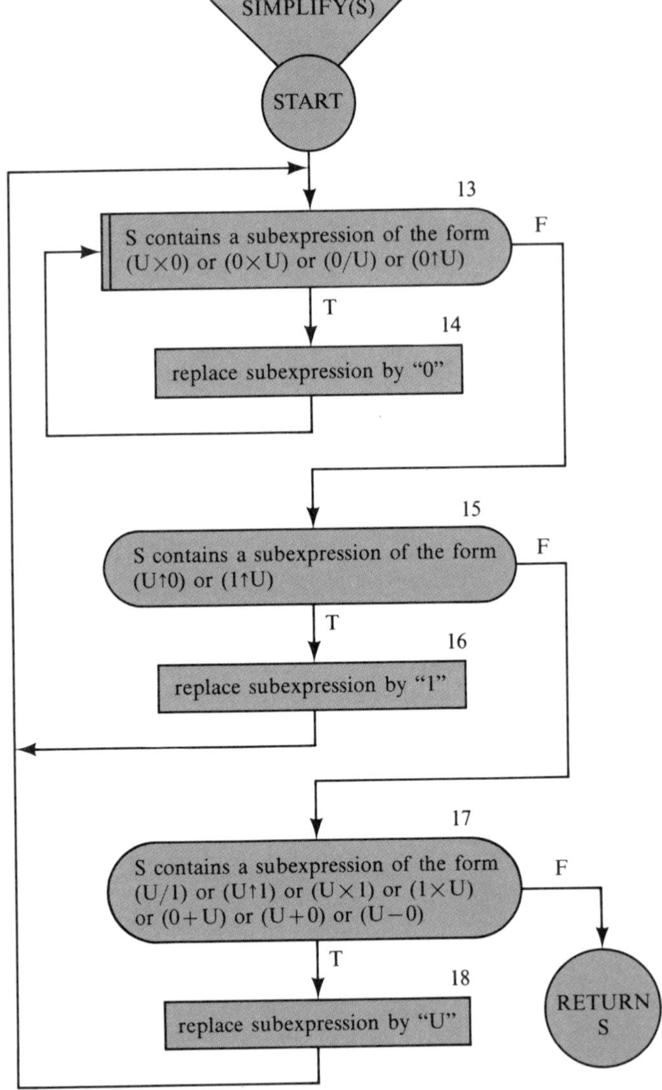

Figure 8-25. **Flowchart for SIMPLIFY procedure.**

Legend for Top

Identifier	Description
S	string of characters representing a fully parenthesized arithmetic expression
X	character

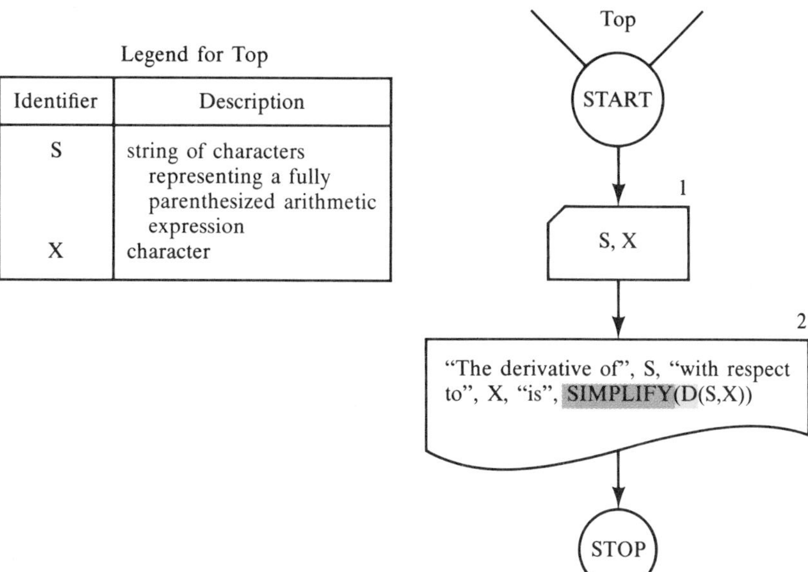

***Figure 8-26.* A top-level flowchart for the derivative procedure.**

```
*     SNOBOL PROGRAM TO DIFFERENTIATE A FULLY PARENTHESIZED
*     EXPRESSION S WITH RESPECT TO A VARIABLE X.
*
*****DEFINE STATEMENTS FOR PROCEDURES
*
        DEFINE('D(S,X)OP,A,B','DIFFBEGIN')
        DEFINE('DADDOP(S1,OP,S2,X)T','DADDOPBEGIN')
        DEFINE('DMULT(S1,S2,X)T','DMULTBEGIN')
        DEFINE('DDIV(S1,S2,X)T','DDIVBEGIN')
        DEFINE('DEXP(S1,S2,X)T','DEXPBEGIN')
        DEFINE('SIMPLIFY(S)U','SIMPBEGIN')
*
*****STATEMENTS TO INVOKE TRACE
*
        &TRACE = 1000
        TRACE('D','FUNCTION')
        TRACE('DADDOP','FUNCTION')
        TRACE('DMULT','FUNCTION')
        TRACE('DDIV','FUNCTION')
        TRACE('DEXP','FUNCTION')
        TRACE('SIMPLIFY','FUNCTION')
*
*****TOP LEVEL PROGRAM
*
        S = TRIM(INPUT)           :F(END)
        X = TRIM(INPUT)           :F(END)
        OUTPUT = 'DERIVATIVE OF ' S ' WITH RESPECT TO ' X ' IS '
                 SIMPLIFY(D(S,X))     :(END)
*
```

Figure 8-27

```
*****PROCEDURE BODIES
*
DIFFBEGIN OPER = ' + ' ! ' - ' ! ' * ' ! ' / ' ! ' ** '
         S '(' (BAL . A) (OPER . OP) (BAL . B) ')'    :F(BOX10)
         IDENT(OP,' ** ')                           :S(BOX4)
         IDENT(OP,' / ')                            :S(BOX6)
         IDENT(OP,' * ')                            :S(BOX8)
         S = '(' DADDOP(A,OP,B,X) ')'               :(RET)
BOX4     S = '(' DEXP(A,B,X) ')'                    :(RET)
BOX6     S = '(' DDIV(A,B,X) ')'                    :(RET)
BOX8     S = '(' DMULT(A,B,X) ')'                   :(RET)
BOX10    IDENT(S,X)                                 :F(BOX12)
         S = '1'                                    :(RET)
BOX12    S = '0'
RET      D = S                                      :(RETURN)
DADDOPBEGIN T = D(S1,X) OP D(S2,X)
             DADDOP = T                             :(RETURN)
DMULTBEGIN   T = '(' S1 ' * ' D(S2,X) ') + (' S2 ' * ' D(S1,X) ')'
             DMULT = T                              :(RETURN)
DDIVBEGIN    T = '((' S2 ' * ' D(S1,X) ') - (' S1 ' * ' D(S2,X)
                 ')) / (' S2 ' ** 2)'
             DDIV = T                               :(RETURN)
DEXPBEGIN    T = '(' S2 ' * (' S1 ' ** ' S2 - 1 ')) * ' D(S1,X)
             DEXP = T                               :(RETURN)
SIMPBEGIN
S1       S '(' BAL ' * 0)' = '0'                    :S(S1)
         S '(0 * ' BAL ')' = '0'                    :S(S1)
         S '(0 / ' BAL ')' = '0'                    :S(S1)
         S '(0 ** ' BAL ')' = '0'                   :S(S1)
         S '(' BAL ' ** 0)' = '1'                   :S(S1)
         S '(1 ** ' BAL ')' = '1'                   :S(S1)
         S '(' (BAL . U) ' / 1)' = U                :S(S1)
         S '(' (BAL . U) ' ** 1)' = U               :S(S1)
         S '(' (BAL . U) ' * 1)' = U                :S(S1)
         S '(1 * ' (BAL . U) ')' = U                :S(S1)
         S '(0 + ' (BAL . U) ')' = U                :S(S1)
         S '(' (BAL . U) ' + 0)' = U                :S(S1)
         S '(' (BAL . U) ' - 0)' = U                :S(S1)
         SIMPLIFY = S                               :(RETURN)
END
```

Figure 8-27 (*continued*)

The final result returned by D(S,X) is

$$((((5 + X) \times ((2 \times ((X + 1) \uparrow 1)) \times (1 \times 0)))$$
$$- (((X + 1) \uparrow 2) \times ((5 \times 1) + (X \times 0)))) / ((5 + X) \uparrow 2))$$

It is the same as the result returned to level zero by procedure DDIV except that one outer pair of parentheses has been added to completely parenthesize the expression.

If the procedure SIMPLIFY is called with the above output from D as the argument, the printed result of SIMPLIFY(D(S,X)) is

THE DERIVATIVE OF (((X + 1) ↑ 2) / (5 × X)) WITH RESPECT TO X IS
((((5 × X) × (2 × (X + 1))) − (((X + 1) ↑ 2) × 5)) / ((5 × X) ↑ 2))

Now study the computer output of this program in Figure 8-29.

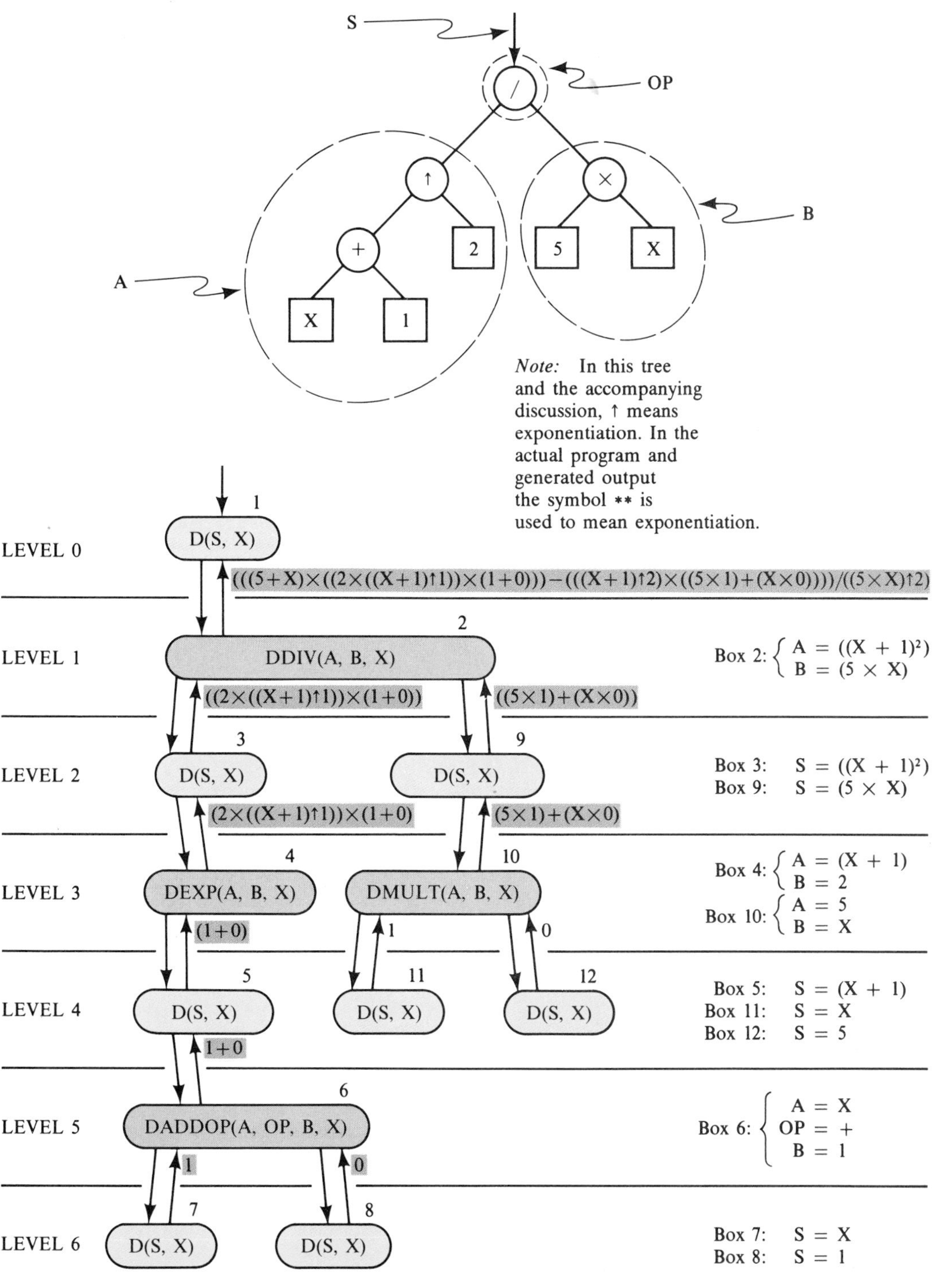

Figure 8-28. **Call tree for the derivative of $(((X + 1)^2)/(5 \times X))$. Shaded values are the returned results of calls on the procedure D.**

```
STATEMENT 16: LEVEL 0 CALL OF D('(((X + 1) ** 2) / (5 * X))','X')
STATEMENT 24: LEVEL 1 CALL OF DDIV('((X + 1) ** 2)','(5 * X)','X')
STATEMENT 34: LEVEL 2 CALL OF D('((X + 1) ** 2)','X')
STATEMENT 23: LEVEL 3 CALL OF DEXP('(X + 1)','2','X')
STATEMENT 36: LEVEL 4 CALL OF D('(X + 1)','X')
STATEMENT 22: LEVEL 5 CALL OF DADDOP('X',' + ','1','X')
STATEMENT 30: LEVEL 6 CALL OF D('X','X')
STATEMENT 29: LEVEL 6 RETURN OF D = '1'
STATEMENT 30: LEVEL 6 CALL OF D('1','X')
STATEMENT 29: LEVEL 6 RETURN OF D = '0'
STATEMENT 31: LEVEL 5 RETURN OF DADDOP = '1 + 0'
STATEMENT 29: LEVEL 4 RETURN OF D = '(1 + 0)'
STATEMENT 37: LEVEL 3 RETURN OF DEXP = '(2 * ((X + 1) ** 1)) * (1 + 0)'
STATEMENT 29: LEVEL 2 RETURN OF D = '((2 * ((X + 1) ** 1)) * (1 + 0))'
STATEMENT 34: LEVEL 2 CALL OF D('(5 * X)','X')
STATEMENT 25: LEVEL 3 CALL OF DMULT('5','X','X')
STATEMENT 32: LEVEL 4 CALL OF D('X','X')
STATEMENT 29: LEVEL 4 RETURN OF D = '1'
STATEMENT 32: LEVEL 4 CALL OF D('5','X')
STATEMENT 29: LEVEL 4 RETURN OF D = '0'
STATEMENT 33: LEVEL 3 RETURN OF DMULT = '(5 * 1) + (X * 0)'
STATEMENT 29: LEVEL 2 RETURN OF D = '((5 * 1) + (X * 0))'
STATEMENT 35: LEVEL 1 RETURN OF DDIV = '(((5 * X) * ((2 * (
(X + 1) ** 1)) * (1 + 0))) - (((X + 1) ** 2) * ((5 * 1) + (X * 0
)))) / ((5 * X) ** 2)'
STATEMENT 29: LEVEL 0 RETURN OF D = '((((5 * X) * ((2 * ((X
 + 1) ** 1)) * (1 + 0))) - (((X + 1) ** 2) * ((5 * 1) + (X * 0))
)) / ((5 * X) ** 2))'
STATEMENT 16: LEVEL 0 CALL OF SIMPLIFY('((((5 * X) * ((2 *
((X + 1) ** 1)) * (1 + 0))) - (((X + 1) ** 2) * ((5 * 1) + (X *
0)))) / ((5 * X) ** 2))')
STATEMENT 52: LEVEL 0 RETURN OF SIMPLIFY = '((((5 * X) * (2
 * (X + 1))) - (((X + 1) ** 2) * 5)) / ((5 * X) ** 2))'
 DERIVATIVE OF (((X + 1) ** 2) / (5 * X)) WITH RESPECT TO X IS (
(((5 * X) * (2 * (X + 1))) - (((X + 1) ** 2) * 5)) / ((5 * X) **
 2))
```

Figure 8-29. **Computer output for the program in Figure 8-27.**

Exercises 8-6, Set A

Identify the six simplifications made by procedure SIMPLIFY in reducing the result returned by D(S,X) to the final output value.

If we study the call tree in Figure 8-28 it is apparent that procedure D calls procedure DDIV, which again calls D. Within this second procedure call on D, DEXP is called and DEXP calls procedure D again. This time D calls DADDOP, which makes a fourth and terminal call on D at level 6. The call tree provides concise information about the order of calls on various procedures. We can follow through all the calls and subsequent returns until the MC returns to level zero. Each return arrow in Figure 8-28 is labeled with the value returned (color shaded).

Exercises 8-6, Set B

Select a node of the call tree in Figure 8-28. Then select a line in the procedure named by the selected node. Draw a snapshot of the computation of Figure 8-29 just after the MC has executed your chosen line in your chosen activation of your procedure.

8-7 SIMULATING REFERENCE PARAMETERS IN SNOBOL

The unary operator $ in Snobol is called the *indirect reference operator.* If the value of X is a string, then $X stands for the variable whose name is the value of X.

For example, consider the statements shown in Figure 8-30. Execution of line 1 requires (1) allocation of a cell X in Top¹, (2) creaction of a HEAP cell to contain the value 'Y', and (3) storing of a pointer to 'Y' in the value compartment of X, as shown in snapshot 1.

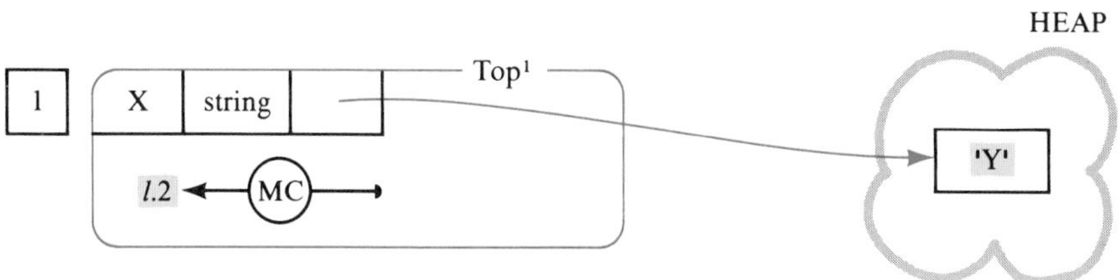

The meaning of line 2 is "assign 'VAL' to the variable whose name is the string that is the value of X." That is, "assign 'VAL' to Y." Once again cells must be created in both the HEAP and Top¹; the resulting situation is shown in snapshot 2.

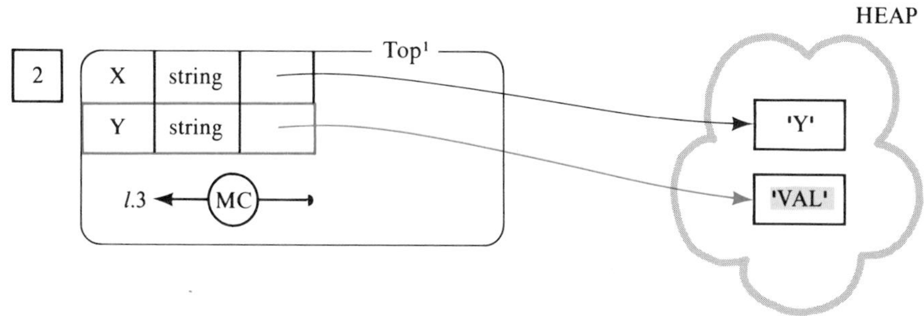

Figure 8-30

Line no.

```
1    X = 'Y'
2   $X = 'VAL'
3    Z = $Y
```

Line 3 now means that the value of the variable VAL is to be assigned to Z. Since no such variable exists, a cell named VAL is allocated in Top[1]. The assignment then takes place, with the result shown in snapshot 3.

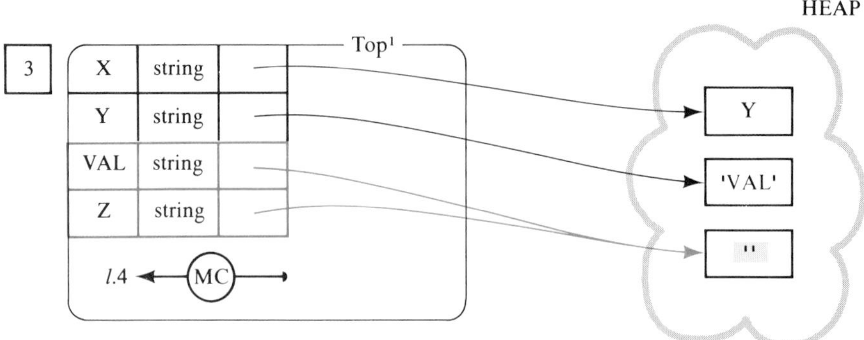

Note that since the initial value of the variable VAL is the null string, this value (the null string) is also assigned to Z.

This example illustrates not only the use of $, but the fact that in Snobol, cells are not allocated until they are needed. Thus, the number of cells in a contour (in Snobol) may increase as execution proceeds.

The $ symbol may be used to achieve the effect of reference parameters. Suppose we wish to define a procedure ASSINE that assigns the value of its second parameter to its first parameter, as shown in the flowchart of Figure 8-31a. A corresponding Snobol procedure ASSIGN is given in Figure 8-31b. The procedure ASSIGN would be called primarily for its *effect,* but since all Snobol procedures must return values (when successful), ASSIGN returns the value it assigns (that is, the value of its second parameter, RIGHT). Thus a call on the Snobol procedure, such as ASSIGN('Z','A'), will assign to the variable Z the value 'A', and return 'A' as the value of the call on ASSIGN (but see Exercises 8-7). The call ASSIGN('Z',ASSIGN('X',3)) assigns 3 to both X and Z.

As another example of indirect reference, we consider a variation of the symbolic differentiation program of Section 8-6. Recall that the result returned to

SIMPLIFY(D(S,X))

is a symbolic expression (that is, a string). For example, if the following three Snobol statements are executed,

```
S = '((Y ** 2) + (Y ** 3))'
X = 'Y'
OUTPUT = SIMPLIFY(D(S,X))
```

the value output is

((2 * Y) + (3 * (Y ** 2)))

We could *evaluate* this derivative for a particular value of Y by using the Snobol function EVAL, which requires as its argument a string expression in

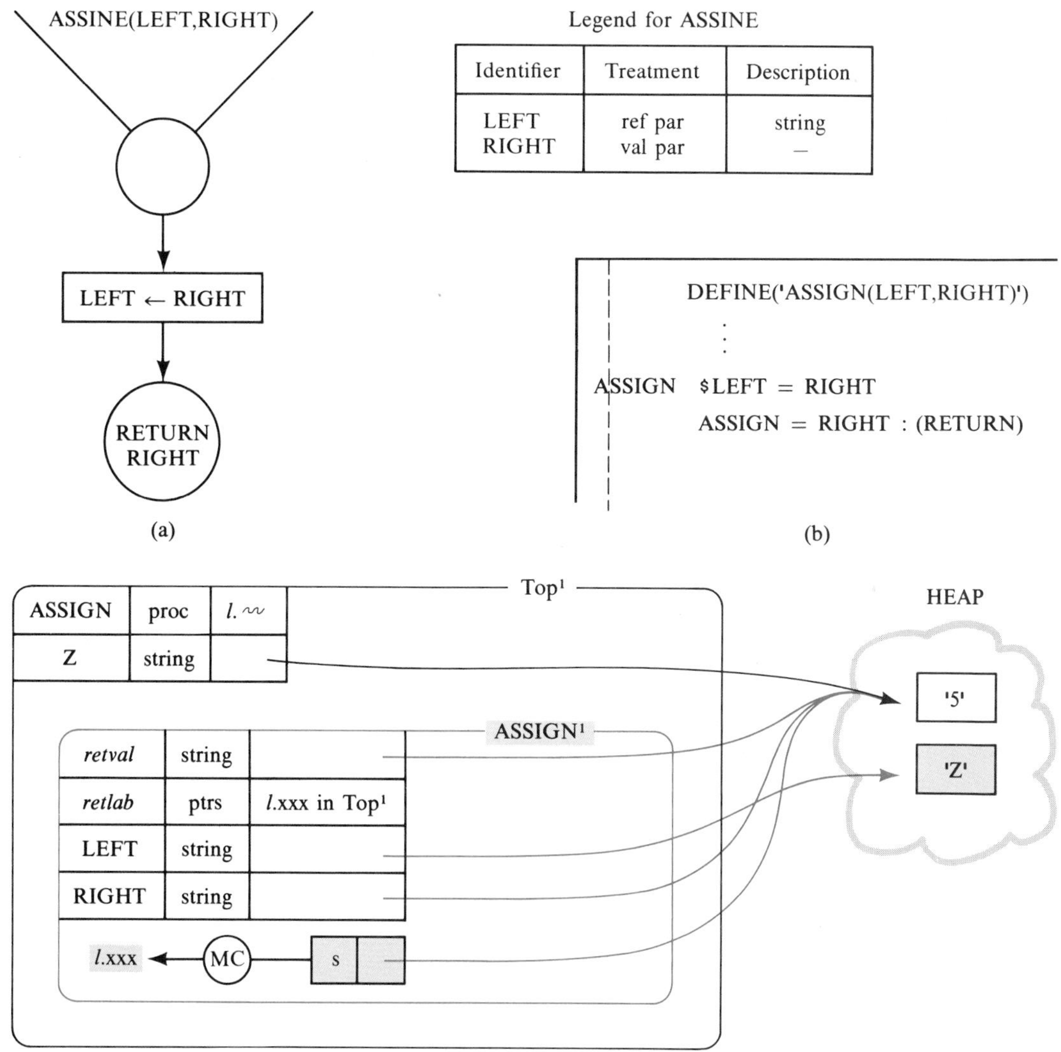

(c) Snapshot taken just before successful return from ASSIGN¹. The call in Top was ASSIGN('Z','5').

Figure 8-31. **Achieving the effect of reference parameters.**

Snobol, and whose value is the result of evaluating that expression. (Thus EVAL in Snobol does exactly the same job as EVAL in our description of Lisp.) For example, we could obtain the value of the derivative of S at Y = 3 by executing the following sequence of Snobol statements:

```
S = '((Y ** 2) + (Y ** 3))'
X = 'Y'
$X=3
VAL = EVAL(SIMPLIFY(D(S,X)))
OUTPUT = 'THE VALUE OF THE DERIVATIVE AT ' X ' = 3 IS ' VAL
```

For the values of S and X shown, the resulting printout would be

THE VALUE OF THE DERIVATIVE AT Y = 3 IS 33

Notice the use of indirect reference. The expression that is the argument of EVAL involves whatever variable was input as the value of X. We may assign 3 to that variable, which is Y in this example, by using the indirect reference $X. Then when EVAL evaluates the derivative, Y has the desired value.

Exercises 8-7

What happens if we execute in Top the Snobol statement sequence

```
LEFT = '0'
ASSIGN('LEFT','S')
OUTPUT = LEFT
```

Is there a good way to get around the problem that occurs? Explain. Can this difficulty also arise in the scheme given above for evaluating derivatives? How?

8-8 CONVERSION FROM ONE DATA TYPE TO ANOTHER

In the examples shown so far in this chapter, we have seen that conversion from one data type to another often takes place automatically in Snobol. For example, execution of the statements

```
Line no.
1          X = '2'
2          Y = 3
3          P = X * Y
4     OUTPUT = Y 'X IS ' P
```

involves the conversion of a copy of the value of X from type string to type integer on line 3, and the conversion of copies of values of Y and P from type integer to type string on line 4. The output produced is '3X IS 6'.

The automatic conversion of data types is usually all that is necessary, but if desired the predefined function CONVERT may be used to convert the value of an expression to a compatible data type. The call is of the form CONVERT(expression, data type), as shown in the following example:

R = CONVERT(41,'REAL')	assigns the real number 41.0 to R
T = CONVERT(R,'STRING')	assigns the string '41.0' to T
I = CONVERT(2.8,'INTEGER')	chops the real number 2.8 to the integer 2 and assigns it to I

If the specified conversion is not possible, for example,

CONVERT('ABC','INTEGER')

then the call on CONVERT *fails.*

The predefined function DATATYPE can be used to determine the current type associated with a variable or expression. For example, if the value of R is 41.0, then DATATYPE(R) returns the value 'REAL'.

A Snobol data type that we have not yet mentioned is type CODE. A variable of type CODE has as its value compiled Snobol code. This can come about in the following way: A Snobol program can include a statement assigning a string of Snobol commands as the value of a variable. A later statement can convert this sequence from type STRING to type CODE, and a still later command can cause this code to be executed.

The command

T = CONVERT(STRING1,'CODE')

assigns to T the value of STRING1 converted, that is, *compiled,* into type CODE. The code assigned as the value of T can then be executed as part of the Snobol program.

For example, suppose the sequence of Snobol statements given in Figure 8-32 is executed. Execution of line 1 assigns to STRING1 a string that looks like a valid sequence of Snobol statements, that is, a "block of program." Notice that each substring representing a statement terminates with a semicolon. Execution of line 2 converts, that is, compiles, that string value into SNOBOL code and assigns it to the variable T. Execution of line 3 causes the block of code assigned to T to be executed after the string of Snobol "source" statements, assigned to STRING1, has been printed. The syntax :⟨T⟩ is a special "go to" rule that causes a transfer to the first line of Snobol code assigned to T. The code assigned to T is, in this case, a loop and eventually this loop will terminate. At that point control will transfer to OUT, the label on line 4.

Exercises 8-8

Explain the effect of executing the code value of the Snobol variable T in Figure 8-32.

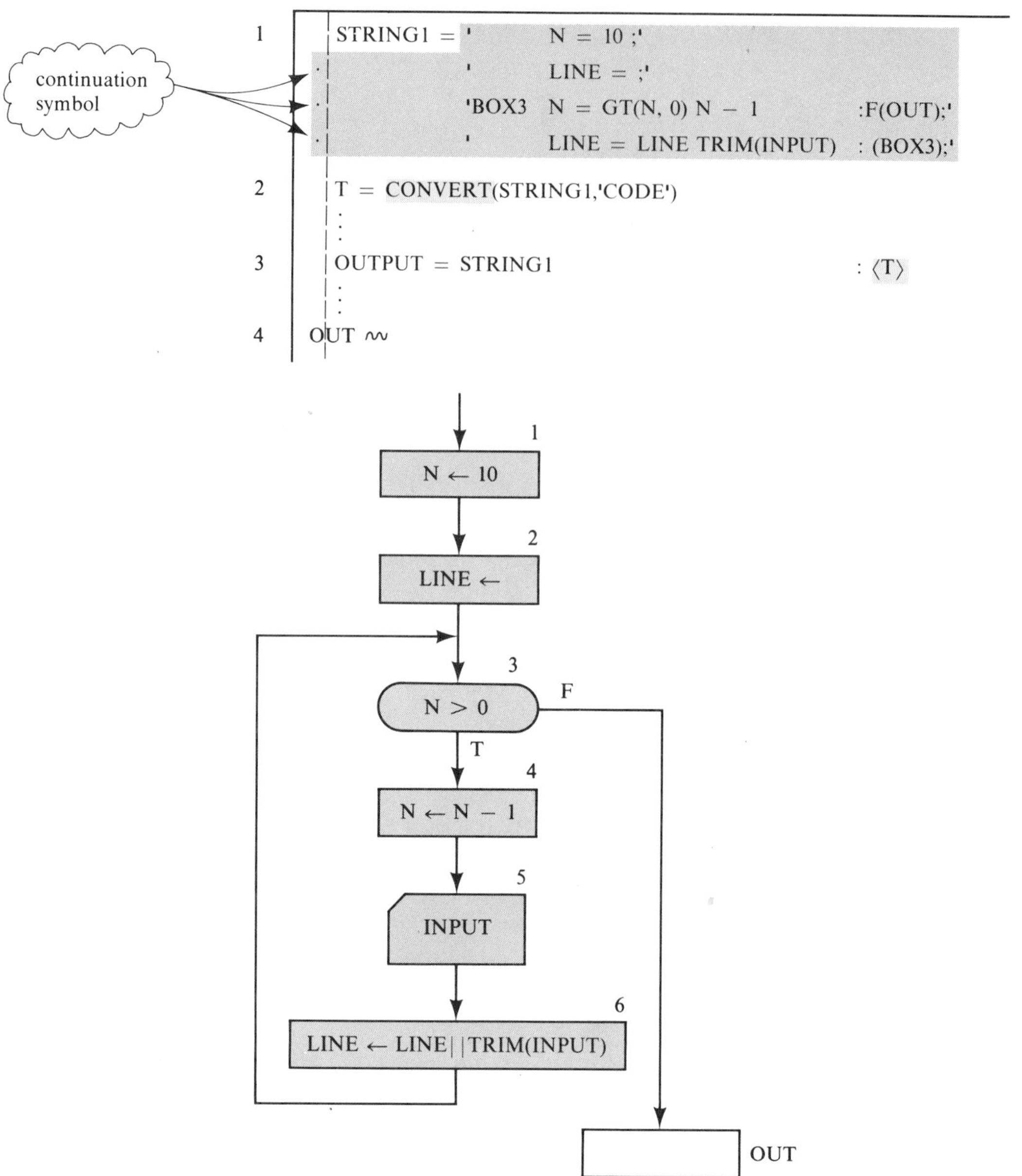

Figure 8-32

8-9 DEFINING AND USING NEW DATA TYPES

Among the languages we have studied, Snobol is unique in that the range of its data types is *extendable.* That is, the programmer may define and use data objects with whatever structure is appropriate for the task at hand, thus adapting and extending the language.

The predefined function DATA is used to name and describe the structure of a new data type. For example, consider the following call on DATA:

DATA('TYPEA(S1,S2,S3)')

When this function call, which may be thought of as a declaration, is executed, a new data class called TYPEA is defined. Each member of this class is a *composite object* that has a tree structure consisting of three fields or elements named S1, S2, and S3, respectively:

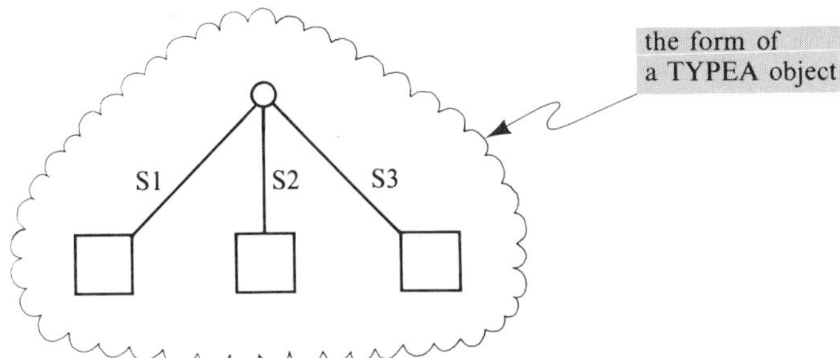

To create *an instance* of this data type we execute assignments such as the following:

```
V1 = 'PIG'
T1 = 79.5
Z = TYPEA(V1,T1,'BOY')
```

These commands assign to Z a tree-structured data object of type TYPEA, drawn from the HEAP:

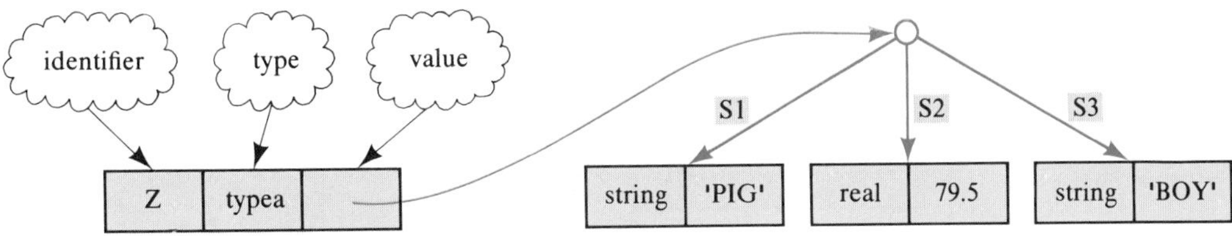

To refer to an individual component of Z later, one uses the name of this component as a selecting function. For example, executing the command

OUTPUT = S2(Z)

causes the printing of the value of the S2 component of Z (that is, 79.5). Individual components may also be *changed;* the statement

S3(Z) = 'GIRL'

alters only the S3 component of Z.

The function DATATYPE may be applied to data objects of newly defined types. In the above example, DATATYPE(Z) would have the value 'TYPEA'.

As a second example of defined data types, suppose the DATA declaration and statements appear in a Snobol program as shown in Figure 8-33. Executing

Line no.

```
1   DATA('CONS(CAR,CDR)')
2   Z = CONS('X',CONS('Y','NIL'))
        :
3   P = CAR(Z)
4   Q = CAR(CDR(Z))
5   OUTPUT = P Q
```

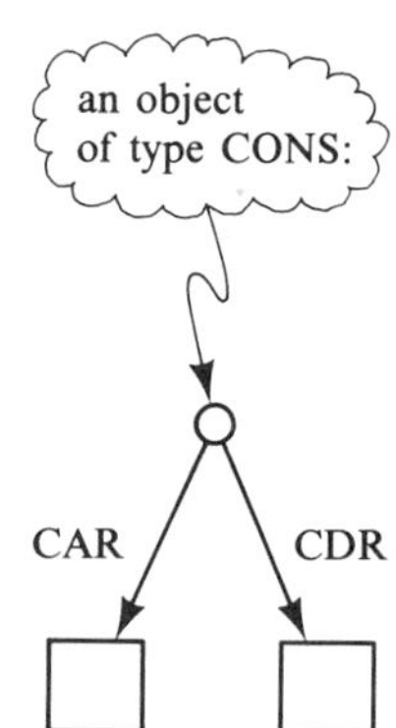

Figure 8-33

line 1 causes a data type called CONS to be defined. As a result of executing line 2, an instance of CONS is created and assigned to Z, as shown below:

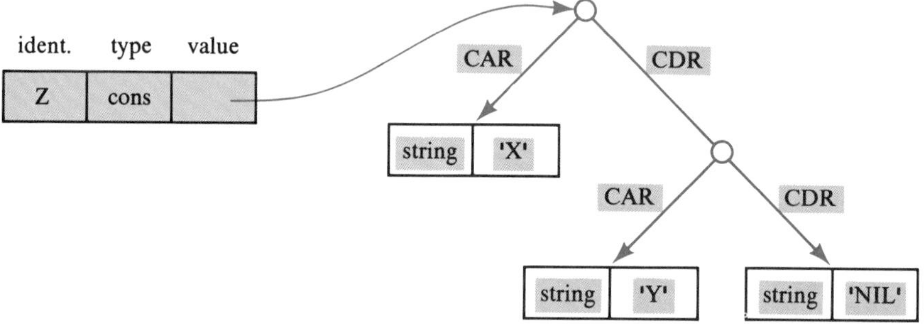

At some time later, we execute lines 3 and 4, assigning to P and Q the values "extracted" from Z:

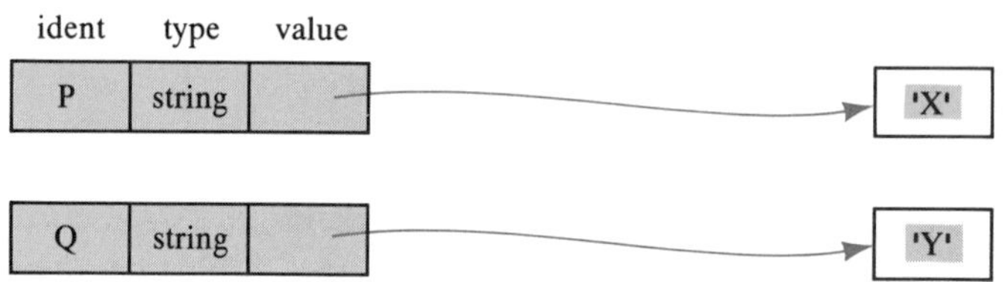

Then executing line 5, we print the concatenated values of P and Q:

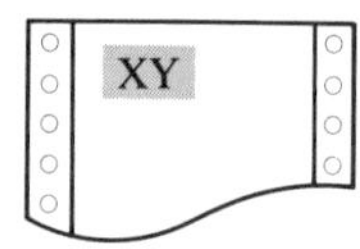

8-10 DEFINING THE PRIMITIVE FUNCTIONS OF LISP IN SNOBOL

In this section we bring together the concepts of the preceding sections by discussing the development of a Lisp simulator expressed in Snobol.* We can start as in Section 8-9 by declaring CONS as a data type with components CAR and CDR. Then we can write Snobol code to define the primitives ATOM(X) and EQL(X). These few declarations are almost sufficient to support a simple Lisp simulator.

ATOM(X) is to be a function that returns 'T' if X is an atom and 'NIL' otherwise. To keep things simple we assume that an atom is any object of type string. Later this definition can be expanded to include numbers.

The procedure ATOM can be formulated as shown in Figure 8-34. Notice that the procedure ATOM has no locals. When control returns to the calling program, the MC will have the correct predicate value of ATOM in the portable stack.

The procedure EQL(X,Y) is to return 'T' if X and Y are both atoms and if their string values are identical. If both are atoms but the values are not identical, EQL is to return 'NIL'.

This procedure EQL should not be confused with the Snobol procedure EQ, which deals with numerical values. ERROR is presumed to be a label for a statement that prints an error message or attempts corrective action. The definition of EQL is shown in Figure 8-35.

Now suppose we want to define a Snobol procedure APPEND(X,Y) similar to the Lisp procedure of the same name. Figure 8-36 is a possible definition. To test this procedure we could conceivably use the driver program given in Figure 8-37. The call tree for Figure 8-37 should resemble Figure 8-38. We wish the output of APPEND(X,Y) to appear as

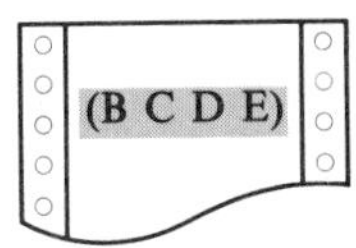

Figure 8-34

```
              DEFINE('ATOM(X)','ATOMSTART')
                 :
ATOMSTART     ATOM = 'NIL'
              ATOM = IDENT(DATATYPE(X),'STRING') 'T'   : (RETURN)
```

*This follows a suggestion by Wegner (1971).

```
          DEFINE('EQL(X,Y)','EQLSTART')
              :
EQLSTART  IDENT(ATOM(X),'T')        :F(ERROR)
          IDENT(ATOM(Y),'T')        :F(ERROR)
          EQL = 'NIL'
          EQL = IDENT(X,Y) 'T'      : (RETURN)
```

Figure 8-35

```
          DEFINE('APPEND(X,Y)','APSTART')
              :
APSTART   IDENT(X,'NIL')                                :F(NEXT)
          APPEND = Y                                    : (RETURN)
NEXT      IDENT(DATATYPE(X),'CONS')                     :F(APERR)
          APPEND = CONS(CAR(X),APPEND(CDR(X),Y))        : (RETURN)
```

If X is neither 'NIL' nor an object of type CONS, then X is not a list and an error has occurred.

Figure 8-36

```
        DATA('CONS(CAR,CDR)')
        X = CONS('B',CONS('C','NIL'))
        Y = CONS('D',CONS('E','NIL'))
        OUTPUT = APPEND(X, Y)                         : (END)
APERR   OUTPUT = 'ARGUMENT OF APPEND NOT A LIST'
END
```

Figure 8-37

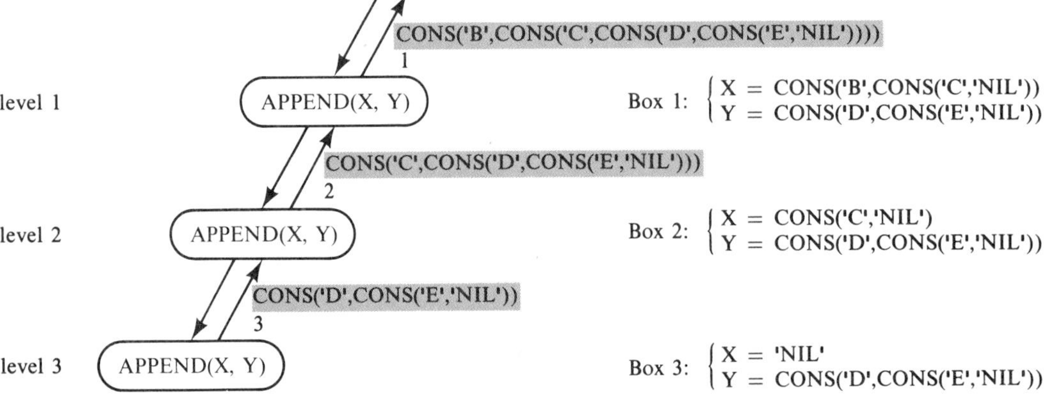

Figure 8-38

However, Snobol can only output a data value of type 'STRING', and so in this case what is actually printed is simply

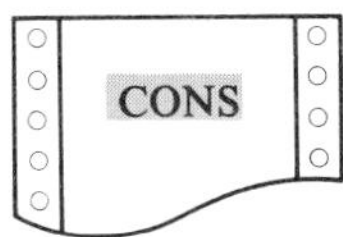

indicating that the data are of type CONS and therefore cannot be printed. The following exercises discuss ways of solving this problem.

Exercises 8-10

1 In Snobol write a procedure equivalent to the REVERSE procedure in RLISP (see Case Study 2, Chapter 7) using at most the ATOM, EQL, and APPEND procedures, together with the data declarations for CONS.

2 Write a Snobol procedure PDOTTED, which takes as an argument a value of type CONS, not necessarily a list, and converts it into an equivalent string in Lisp dotted pair notation. Thus, if

OUTPUT = PDOTTED(APPEND(X,Y))

is used in place of

OUTPUT = APPEND(X,Y)

in the driver program above, then the output should appear as

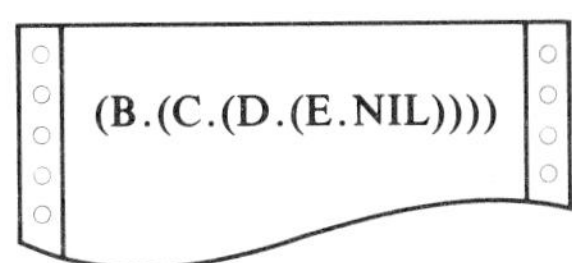

3 Write a Snobol procedure BUILD, which takes as an argument a string that is in Lisp dotted pair notation, for example, '(X.Y)' or '(X.(Y.NIL))', then builds and returns a corresponding object of type CONS.
Hint: Any string that represents a legal Lisp S-expression in dotted pair notation must be of the form

(*bal*||"."||*bal*)

where *bal* is the flowchart notation for a string that is balanced with respect to parentheses. This form is a necessary but not sufficient condition. In Snobol the predefined pattern BAL plays the role of the flowchart *bal*.

4 Using the procedures that you developed in exercises 1, 2, and 3, write a Snobol driver program to accept as input a series of strings in dotted pair notation, *build* a corresponding object of type CONS, then perform some Lisp-like operation on it, for example, CAR, CDR, ATOM, EQL, APPEND, and/or possibly REVERSE, and then print out the result in dotted pair notation, as appropriate.

5 Write a Snobol procedure PLIST whose argument is an object of type CONS, which is a *list*. PLIST returns an equivalent string in Lisp list notation. For example, if

OUTPUT = PLIST(APPEND(X,Y))

is used in place of

OUTPUT = APPEND(X,Y)

in the driver program of Figure 8-37, then the output should appear as

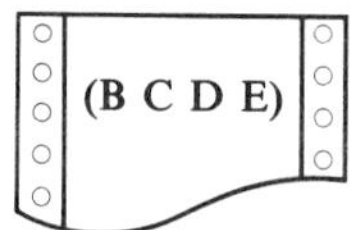

Discussion: The strategy for forming a "printform" of a list from its binary tree structure involves a subtle point. Basically we need to traverse the tree and produce a printform as the traversal proceeds. As a zeroth approximation the strategy might be flowcharted as in Figure 8-39.

The problem with this flowchart definition begins to come to light in the call tree for PLIST(X) shown in Figure 8-40. The zeroth approximation mishandles the termination of the list. For example, call 3 returns '(B NIL)' when we want it to return 'B'. As a result, unwanted extra parentheses are inserted, producing '(A (B NIL))' as the result of call 1 rather than '(A B)'. Be sure your solution does not suffer from this deficiency.

6 If you have worked all the preceding exercises in this set, it will be a simple matter to undertake the next step and write a program that behaves like an RLISP interpreter. Recall (from Section 7-6) that the flowchart for a Lisp interpreter is the simple loop shown in Figure 8-41. Writing a Snobol program to achieve this effect is not difficult. Note the following:

1. The inputs to your interpreter will be strings that are (approximately) RLISP commands.
2. Since the input command is also a Snobol expression (for example, CONS('A', 'B')), it may be evaluated by the Snobol function EVAL.
3. The resulting data value may be output by the function PDOTTED (see Exercise 2). Be sure your version of PDOTTED will work even if the value to be printed is an atom and therefore not of type CONS.

A refinement of your interpreter would be to use the function PLIST instead of PDOTTED when the value to be printed is a list.

Figure 8-39

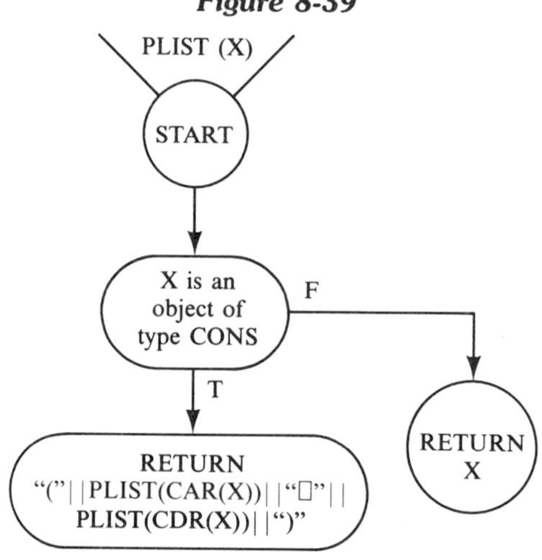

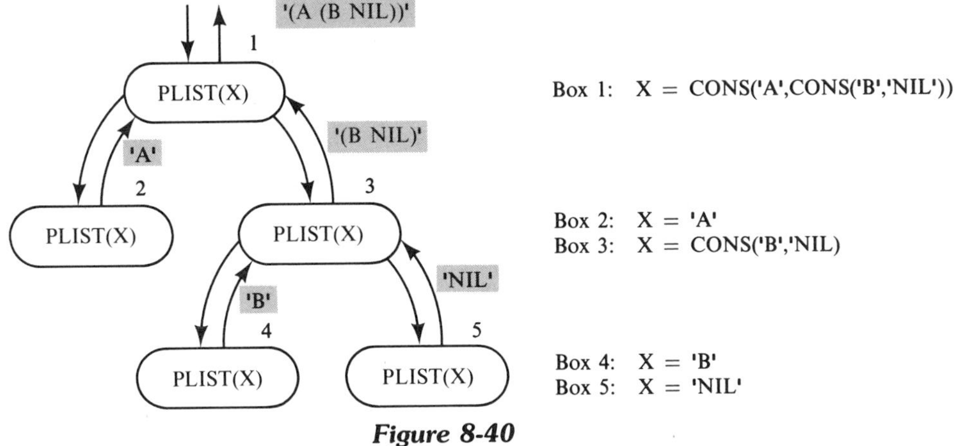

Figure 8-40

Table 8-4 gives a possible sequence of Snobol expressions to input for interpretation as Lisp commands. In order to use the same expression in more than one command, use an ASSIGN procedure such as the one shown in Section 8-7 (but be sure to read Exercises 8-7) to produce the effect of assignment statements at the top level in Lisp. (Such statements *do* exist in impure versions of Lisp. A cell is allocated in Top[1] for each variable to which a value is assigned.)

Figure 8-41

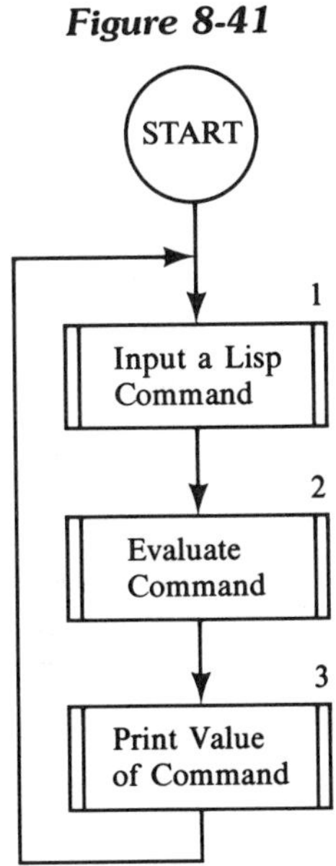

Table 8-4

Snobol expression	RLISP expression	Desired printout
ASSIGN('X',CONS('A', 'NIL'))	X := '(A);	(A.NIL)
ASSIGN('S',BUILD('(X.(Y.(Z.NIL)))'))	S := '(X Y Z);	(X.(Y.(Z.NIL)))
APPEND(X,X)	APPEND(X,X)	(A.(A.NIL))
APPEND(REVERSE(S),X)	APPEND(REVERSE(S),X)	(Z.(Y.(X.(A.NIL))))

8-11 TABLES AND ARRAYS IN SNOBOL

A common programming task is the manipulation of a table of information. For example, a program to interpret (evaluate) an arithmetic expression such as "X * Y + Z/W" would have to maintain and access a table of values such as that shown in Figure 8-42. This section illustrates three ways to manipulate a table in Snobol.

The first method uses pattern matching. We store the table as a string of variable names and values, as suggested in Figure 8-43. The separating character, in this case "#", cannot appear in either a variable name or in a value.

Adding a row to a table becomes simply a matter of concatenating a variable–value pair (with separators) to the string representation of the table. To access the value of a variable, we use pattern matching to search for the variable name and to capture the corresponding value. Figure 8-44 shows an example where the name of the variable to be evaluated is assumed to have been assigned to VAR, and the table itself is assumed to have been assigned to VALUETABLE.

A second method to represent a table in Snobol uses an array data type. Although we have not yet discussed Snobol array structures, we can view the table of Figure 8-42 as an array of four rows and two columns. Such a structure can be created in Snobol by applying the function ARRAY. For example,

```
VALUETABLE = ARRAY('4,2')
```

Variable	Value
W	2.0
X	3.5
Y	−1.6
Z	4.2

Figure 8-42. **A table associating values with variables.**

causes a 4 × 2 array structure to be allocated and assigned to VALUETABLE:

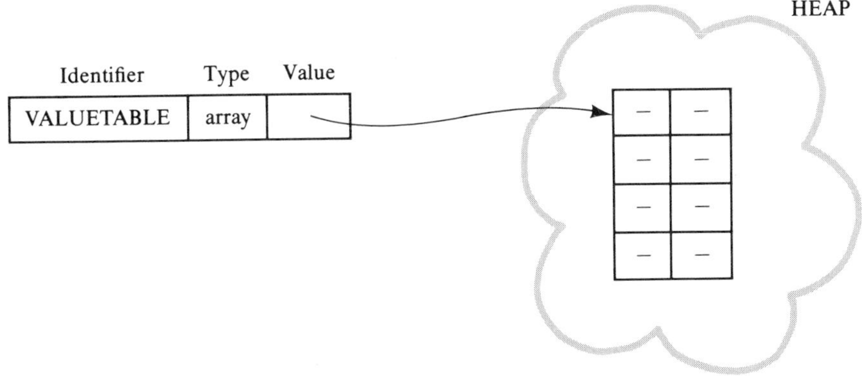

Elements of the resulting array may be referenced by expressions of the form

VALUETABLE⟨ROW,COL⟩

where ROW and COL have values in the range from 1 to 4 and from 1 to 2, respectively. Note the use of angled brackets.

Assume that input steps have already assigned 'W' to VALUETABLE⟨1,1⟩, 2.0 to VALUETABLE⟨1,2⟩, etc., as suggested in Figure 8-42. A value in the table is accessed by searching the first column for the variable in question, and then retrieving the value from the second column of the appropriate row. See Figure 8-45.

When an array is created, each element is given the null string as its initial value. Should a different initial value be desired, it can be achieved through the value of the second argument of the function ARRAY. For example, the statement

VECTOR = ARRAY('100',0.0)

creates a one-dimensional array VECTOR of 100 elements, each having the initial value 0.0.

Figure 8-43. **Representing tables as strings.**

(a) String representation of the table shown in Figure 8-42.

"W # 2.0 # X # 3.5 # Y # −1.6 # Z # 4.2 #"

(b) String representation of a table (general form).

"⟨variable 1⟩ # ⟨value 1⟩ # . . . # ⟨variable n⟩ # ⟨value n⟩ #"

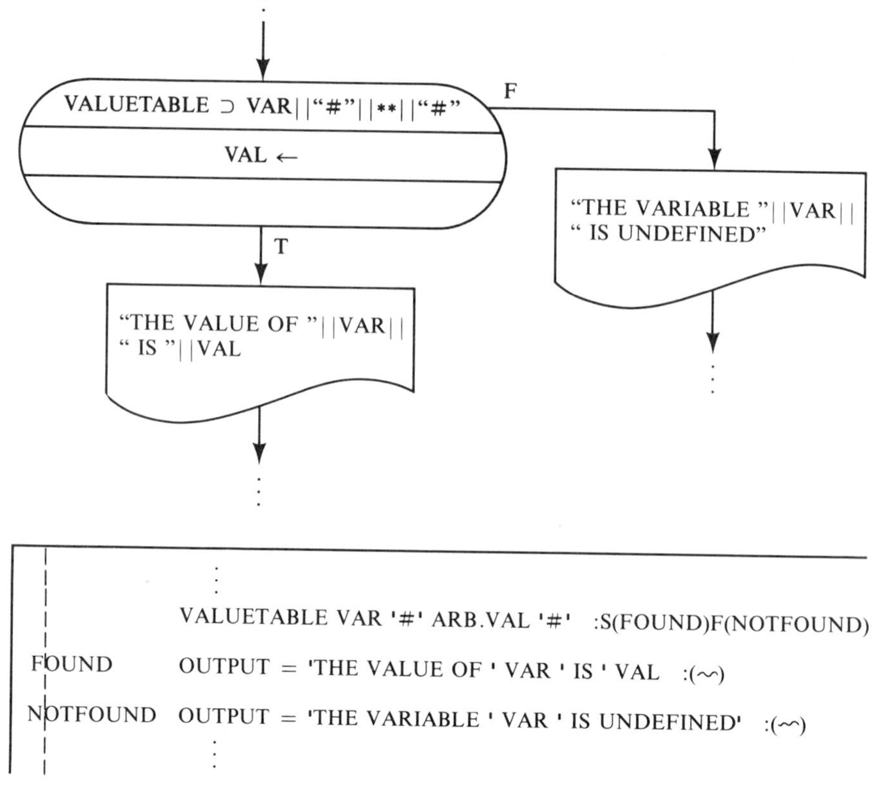


```
                 ⋮
           VALUETABLE VAR '#' ARB.VAL '#'   :S(FOUND)F(NOTFOUND)
FOUND      OUTPUT = 'THE VALUE OF ' VAR ' IS ' VAL   :(~)
NOTFOUND   OUTPUT = 'THE VARIABLE ' VAR ' IS UNDEFINED'   :(~)
                 ⋮
```

***Figure 8-44.* Retrieving a value from a table stored as a string.**

Although the two techniques already illustrated are sufficient to manipulate tables, Snobol designers also provided a special data type TABLE, which is even more appropriate for this purpose. The table of Figure 8-42 can also be created by executing the statements shown in Figure 8-46.

Line 1 creates the table, VALUETABLE, and allocates storage for up to four table entries. After line 1 has been executed, Top[1] contains the following cell:

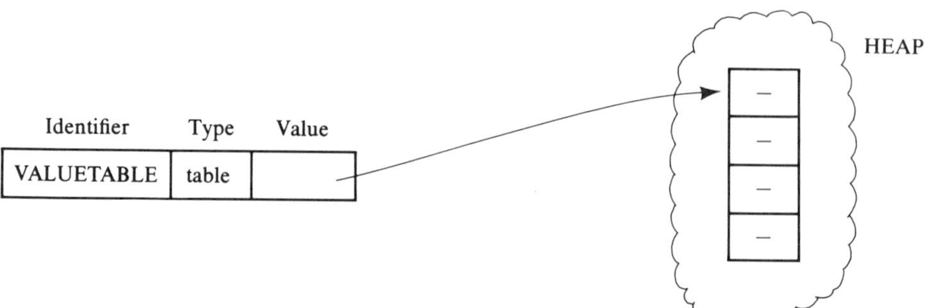

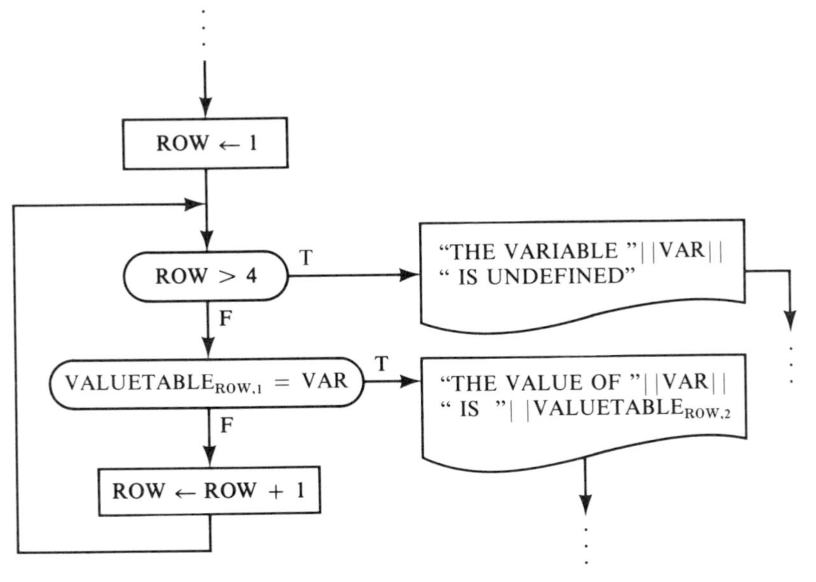


```
            ROW = 1
LOOP        GT(ROW, 4)                          :S(NOTFOUND)
            IDENT(VALUETABLE⟨ROW,1⟩,VAR)        :S(FOUND)
            ROW = ROW + 1                       :(LOOP)
FOUND       OUTPUT = 'THE VALUE OF ' VAR ' IS '
                     VALUETABLE⟨ROW,2⟩
                .
                .
                .
NOTFOUND    OUTPUT = 'THE VARIABLE ' VAR
                     ' IS UNDEFINED'
                .
                .
                .
```

Figure 8-45. **Retrieving a value from a table stored as an array.**

Lines 2–5 store appropriate values in the table. After line 2 has been executed we have

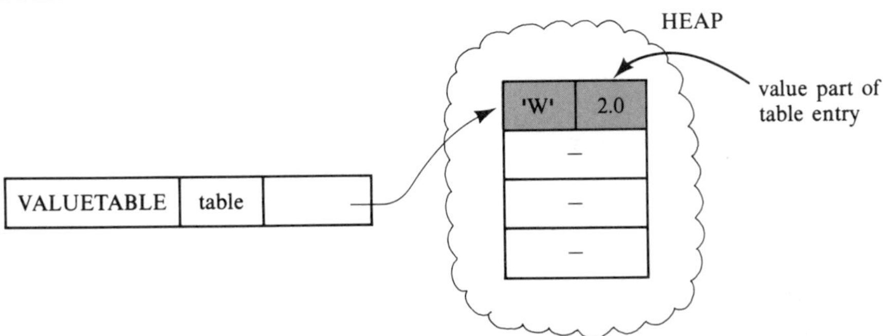

```
Line
1    VALUETABLE = TABLE(4)
2    VALUETABLE⟨'W'⟩ = 2.0
3    VALUETABLE⟨'X'⟩ = 3.5
4    VALUETABLE⟨'Y'⟩ = –1.6
5    VALUETABLE⟨'Z'⟩ = 4.2
⋮         ⋮
```

Figure 8-46. **TABLE data type example.**

and after line 3 has been executed, we have

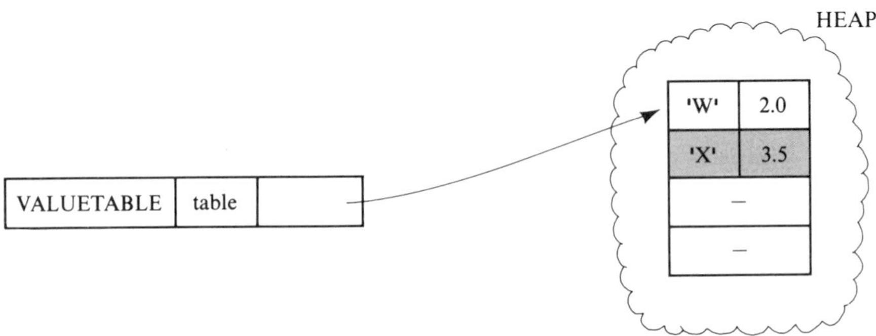

The important idea here is that the identifiers, 'W', and 'X' are used as keys or "indices" to the table values. Suppose the variable VAR has the value 'W'. If a table entry for 'W' already exists, then evaluating the expression VALUE-TABLE⟨VAR⟩ amounts to a search for the value part of the table entry whose key or index is 'W'. If there is no table entry for 'W', then one is created with a NULL initial value. This type of table access is often referred to as *associative lookup,* in contrast to array access methods where the location of a table value is *computed* from one or more indices.

Some additional details on the use of TABLE are the following:

1. It is often convenient to read values for a table as data. In our example, if the data available are 'W', 2.0, 'X', 3.5, etc., as before, and if no more input follows the table, then we can achieve the effect of Figure 8-46 with the statements shown in Figure 8-47.
2. The guides or indices of a table (or the values) need not all have the same data type. If V is a table, then V⟨'2'⟩ and V⟨2⟩ refer to *different* table entries.
3. The function TABLE may have two arguments, for example,

   T = TABLE(10,5)

   This statement creates a table T and allocates space for 10 table entries. If additional entries are required, they are allocated in groups of 5. Thus the assignment of the eleventh value to T automatically increases the

```
            VALUETABLE = TABLE(4)
BUILD       VALUETABLE⟨INPUT⟩ = INPUT     :S(BUILD)
```

Figure 8-47

allocation to 15 elements, the assignment of the sixteenth value automatically increases the allocation to 20 elements, etc. Arguments of TABLE that are zero or omitted are given default values that may vary from implementation to implementation.

8-12 A FORTRAN PREPROCESSOR IN SNOBOL

In Section 6-9, we remarked that a "do-it-yourself" extension of a language such as Fortran can include creating a preprocessor to translate an extended version into ordinary Fortran. Snobol is an ideal language in which to write such a preprocessor, since the task is one of manipulating text (Fortran statements). This exercise suggests some of the possibilities.

Your job is to write a Snobol program that translates programs in "Super-Fortran" comparable to the new 1977 Standard Fortran into 1966 Standard Fortran. Table 8-5 lists the distinctive Super-Fortran statements and possible

TABLE 8-5

Extension	Super-Fortran example	Fortran translation
Mathematical symbols for relational operators	IF (J < NWD) NEXT = NEXT + 1	IF (J .LT. NWD) NEXT = NEXT + 1
IF-THEN-ELSE statements	IF (X < 7) THEN X = 0 ELSE X = 1	IF (X .LT. Y) GO TO 9000 X = 1 GO TO 9001 9000 X = 0 9001 ⋮
Compound statements	IF (I = N) THEN BEGIN X = SUM I = 0 END ELSE BEGIN SUM = SUM + Z I = I + 1 END	IF (I .EQ. N) GO TO 9002 SUM = SUM + Z I = I + 1 GO TO 9003 9002 X = SUM I = 0 9003 ⋮
Symbolic labels	LOOP IF (X (I) > 100) GO TO DONE CALL PROC1 I = I + 1 GO TO LOOP DONE ⋮	9005 IF (X (I) .GT. 100) GO TO 9004 CALL PROC1 I = I + 1 GO TO 9005 9004 ⋮

translations. Note that most of the translations require new statement numbers and these numbers must not, of course, appear elsewhere in the program. You may choose to adopt a convention such as limiting the programmer to statement numbers less than 9000. You may also choose a convention to divide a Super-Fortran statement into more than one line.

Feel free to add other extensions to the list, such as nested IF THEN ELSE and DO WHILE constructs. You are almost certain to find tables helpful. For example, a table might be used to associate symbolic labels in Super-Fortran with statement numbers in Fortran.

If you can make the output of your Snobol program available to a Fortran compiler (for example, by having it directed to a disk or tape, as well as printed), then you will have implemented a new language!

8-13 REFERENCES AND SUGGESTIONS FOR FURTHER READING

To supplement this chapter on Snobol an excellent summary of the SNOBOL4 language can be found in Chapter 15 of Pratt (1975). The most complete and authoritative Snobol literature, however, is found in the books produced by Griswold and his co-workers. This literature includes a reference manual [Griswold *et al.* (1971)], a description of the implementation of a Snobol system [Griswold (1972)], a primer [Griswold and Griswold (1973)], and a book [Griswold (1975)] covering a variety of applications. Recently Griswold has incorporated the pattern matching features of Snobol into a new language called SL5. See Griswold and Hanson (1977).

MULTISEQUENCE ALGORITHMS 9

9-1 INTRODUCTION

Every algorithm and program in this text has been based on the premise that a *single sequence* of instructions is to be executed. That is, we have assumed there is only one controller (the MC) responsible for controlling and keeping track of the sequence of action steps. It is easy to think up algorithms whose actions are performed by two or more controllers, such as any team effort involving humans, where each person controls his own action steps, and where, collectively, the actions of the team achieve a common practical purpose. In some such algorithms the desire for speed is a motivating factor. Two persons can usually do a job, like summing a series of numbers, in less time than one if each person sums half the sequence, and then one person adds the subtotals. A speedup is achieved if, indeed, concurrent (parallel) action sequences can be realized. In many cases, however, the goal of clarity of structure and implementation also motivates the design of multisequence algorithms. A simple example is a program to print out a series of computed values. The actions of the algorithm may be divided, for clarity, into two sequences. One sequence (producer) produces the stream of numbers, and the other sequence (consumer) takes the values from the stream, formats them, and prints them.

Producer and consumer cannot be thought of as separate algorithms. They are mutually dependent because each depends on the other to receive or to provide information in a consistent manner. If, for example, a storage cell, regarded as a *buffer* and capable of holding only one value, is shared between producer and consumer, then the consumer can proceed ("take" a value from the buffer) only after one has been put there by the producer. If there is no new value in the buffer, the consumer must wait. The producer must also pace his actions. He may not put a second number into the buffer until the consumer has "taken" the previous one. In the event that part of the consumer's actions, for example, transferring data from storage to the printer device and the actual printing, can be done concurrently with the actions of the producer, then some actual speedup can be realized. Modern computers are designed to achieve such overlap in cases where the printing device is controlled by an independent sequence controller. In fact, in the special case where, on the average, it takes about as much time to produce a number in the sequence as to print it, full overlap of the producer and consumer activities can achieve a speedup of 2 to 1 over a corresponding single sequence algorithm that accomplishes the same overall action.

Given that we may want to program a multisequence algorithm for a computer, what prevents us? The answer is quite simple. None of the languages we have studied thus far, including our flowchart language, provides linguistic features to express or specify multisequencing. All we can do is specify where to start, possibly where to stop, and give a single sequence, albeit with looping, branching, and procedure calls, of intermediate steps. The requisite syntactic features are missing, and even more importantly, there is no *semantic basis* for multisequencing in these languages. There is only one MC!

A language designer, wishing to extend a language such as Algol to provide facilities for multisequencing, must decide what new commands (and expressions) are needed to indicate initiation, termination, and coordination of separate action sequences. He must state how information is to be shared among them, and at the same time must augment the underlying computer model (provide the additional semantic basis) so the new types of commands can be executed properly.

Some languages have, in fact, been extended to include multisequencing features. Burroughs EXTENDED ALGOL has a comparatively rich capability. PL/I and SIMULA 67 also include some multisequencing features. A few newer languages having these capabilities are also coming on the scene (for example, ALGOL 68, CONCURRENT PASCAL, and SL5). This chapter provides a brief introduction to the semantic structures and syntactic features of multisequencing, using Burroughs EXTENDED ALGOL as the example language, hereafter referred to simply as Burroughs ALGOL.*

We develop several case studies to explain the semantics of multisequence algorithms with the aid of simple amplifications of our computer model. Contour diagrams again make easier the explanation of state-to-state transitions involved in execution of special multisequencing commands. We hope this chapter will convince our readers that a deep understanding of programming language structures can be obtained through use of the models developed in this text.

9-2 TWO TYPES OF MULTISEQUENCING: ASYNCHRONOUS TASKS AND COROUTINES

For a multisequence algorithm to be interesting to us, the separate sequences must be coordinated at some points during their execution. Such coordination can be guaranteed if the algorithm begins as a single sequence of steps. Additional (concurrent) sequences may then be created by steps within the starting

*This innovative language has the advantage that it is well tested (it has been in use for ten years) and exhibits many of the properties necessary for multisequence programming. However, because the language is available only on Burroughs B6700-type computers, it is not well known or widely used. See, however, Organick (1973).

or subsidiary sequences. By symmetry, for an algorithm to be interesting, if the algorithm is to have a stopping point, each sequence must stop. That is, the true stopping point occurs when all but one sequence has stopped, and then the last sequence stops.

Although not essential, it is convenient to regard the initiation and termination of sequences as part of a hierarchical structure of sequences. That is, steps within the originating sequence "spawn" other sequences. Steps within these may spawn still others. A spawned sequence is terminated (stops or "dies") before its "spawner" dies, and that spawner dies before its spawner dies, etc., until only the original sequence remains in execution. In practice and in principle, the spawning and dying of sequences could be repeated indefinitely, as required to accomplish the goal of the program. When the single remaining sequence (the original one) reaches its stopping point, the algorithm as a whole will be said to have terminated.

We can express such structures graphically as suggested in Figure 9-1. In Figure 9-1a we see a simple case of one sequence (1) starting a second (1.1). The latter terminates first, as we have prescribed. In Figure 9-1b sequence 1 initiates two others (1.1 and 1.2). Sequence 1.1 in turn spawns two others (1.1.1 and 1.1.2). The former has the offspring 1.1.1.1. Figure 9-1c, d shows tree structures corresponding to the spawning in Figure 9-1a, b, respectively.

The spawning of a new action sequence involves an act of *resource allocation.* Each new sequence may be thought of as requiring a new MC, and more than likely some new storage (a new contour) may be allocated as well. We can look at the meaning of "allocating a new MC" in one of two ways, *literally* (that is, in actuality) or figuratively (that is, in a *virtual* sense). Literally speaking, allocating a new MC is possible only if there is indeed another physical device that can perform the required functions, and that is either idle or can be freed up or preempted in some way, so it can be used for this computation. In actual computer systems that have two or more physical MC resources (that is, processors), it is *possible* for the system's operating system to allocate an actual MC in this way. Typically, an actual MC is considered such a scarce resource that in practice only executive-level operating system algorithms have the jurisdiction and authority to perform such allocation functions. An ordinary program can appeal for such a resource, but never is assured of getting it.

For these reasons, it is more practical to treat the phrase "allocate a new MC" in the figurative or virtual sense. By that we mean that a new *virtual processor* is allocated. A virtual processor may be thought of as storage for a data structure that can capture the state of an MC, for example, the ip, ep, and stack needed to describe an MC state.

When each sequence is spawned, including the original one at START, a virtual MC (virtual processor) is allocated. Eventually the operating system supervisor will allocate an actual processor so the sequence of actions can actually start up. The startup involves copying the data held by the virtual MC into corresponding registers and storage of the actual MC.

During actual execution the corresponding virtual MC may be regarded as a backup copy of the actual MC. When, for purposes such as "time-sharing," the actual MC is temporarily needed for some other purpose, the current state

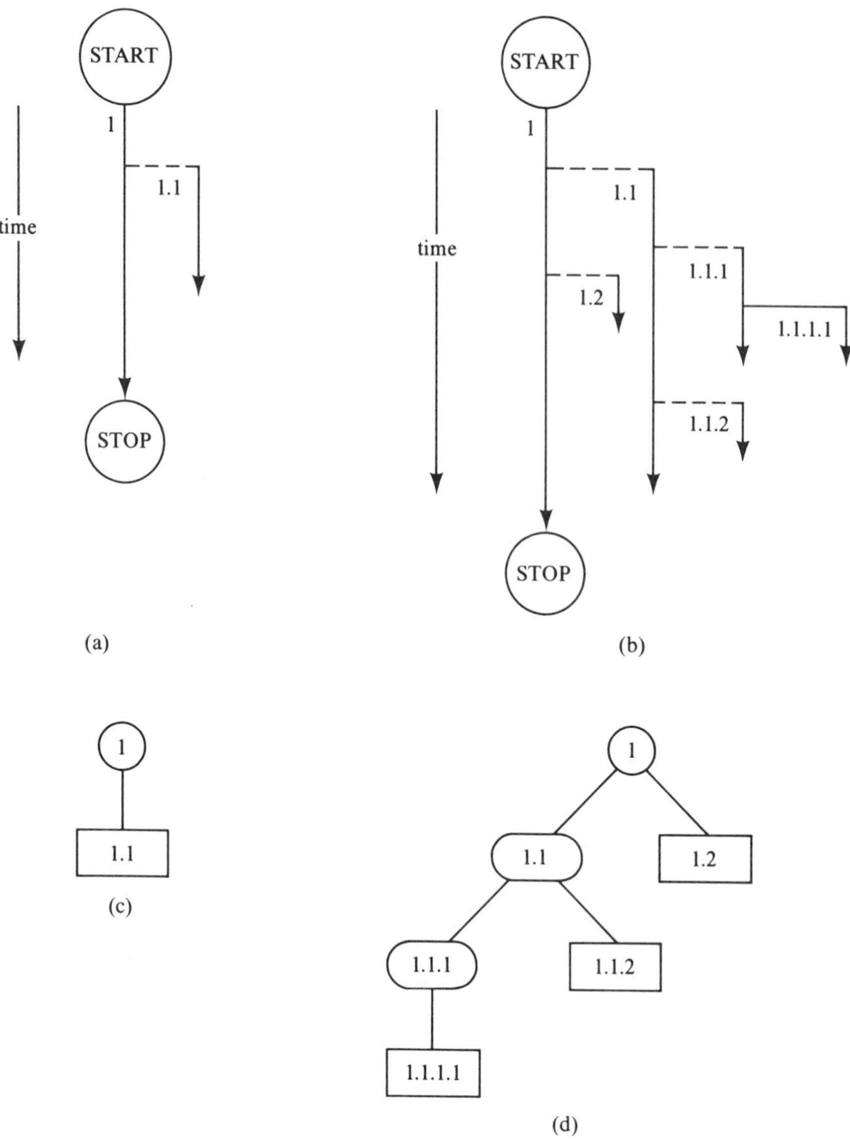

Figure 9-1

of the action sequence is automatically copied back into the virtual MC, thereby updating the latter. Later the action can be resumed by the same startup mechanism used earlier to award an actual MC. When an action sequence actually reaches its stopping point, not only can the actual MC be used for another purpose but, since the virtual MC is no longer needed, it can be deallocated.

We are now ready to consider the types of relationships that spawned and spawner sequences may have to one another. Only two such relationships are of interest: (a) an *asynchronous* relationship and (b) a *coroutine* relationship. In discussing both relationships, we shall now use the term *task,* instead of *sequence,* since this term is more commonly used for the purpose.

In an asynchronous relationship the spawned task (sequence) begins executing when it is spawned, *and the spawner task* (sequence) *continues to execute also.* The relative speeds with which the tasks execute *are not predetermined,* since each executes at a speed defined by the resources that happen to be at its disposal. Tasks that execute asynchronously can be coordinated (synchronized) only by action steps they individually execute. To achieve proper coordination, each task needs to be able to execute a step that has the effect of *waiting* for an event to occur, an occurrence *caused* by the other task, or by some "third party" such as an external signal.

In a coroutine relationship the spawned task begins executing when spawned, but the spawner *suspends execution.* The spawner task remains suspended, its state preserved, until the spawned task calls for the former's resumption. Calling for the other coroutine task's resumption is often referred to as *continuing* the other task. When one coroutine continues another, the first becomes suspended, with its state preserved, while the continued task resumes executing from the point defined by its (previously) preserved state. One coroutine may continue the other, in ping-pong fashion, until the spawner coroutine task chooses to *delete* the spawned task, thus doing away with it and deallocating its resources.

The above scheme is often generalized to allow the original task to spawn two or more coroutines. In this case any coroutine may *continue* any other "sibling" coroutine or *continue* the spawner. Likewise, whenever the spawner has been resumed, it may *continue* any of the already spawned coroutines. The decision as to what task to *continue* next may be entirely data dependent.

In most systems that offer the coroutine relationship, a spawned coroutine task cannot terminate itself directly, since its spawner task is suspended and cannot then be reactivated. By contrast, however, a spawned asynchronous task may terminate itself either directly (by executing a stop step) or indirectly, by having its spawner execute a command to terminate its offspring.

In the sections that follow we consider simple case studies, illustrating both asynchronous task and coroutine task relationships. Each study is cast in the form of a Burroughs ALGOL program, and a sequence of contour diagrams is presented to explain the key steps of task allocation and coordination. The case studies are not intended to be realistic applications, but elements of their structures are typical. More elaborate (and typical) applications may be found in the literature on computer operating systems.

9-3 CASE STUDY FOR ASYNCHRONOUS TASKING

The program in Figure 9-2 illustrates asynchronous tasking using Burroughs-like ALGOL. Spawning an asynchronous task is doen by invoking a procedure in such a way that a new MC is allocated to execute the called procedure, and so that the MC of the caller is not forced to pause until that invocation has been

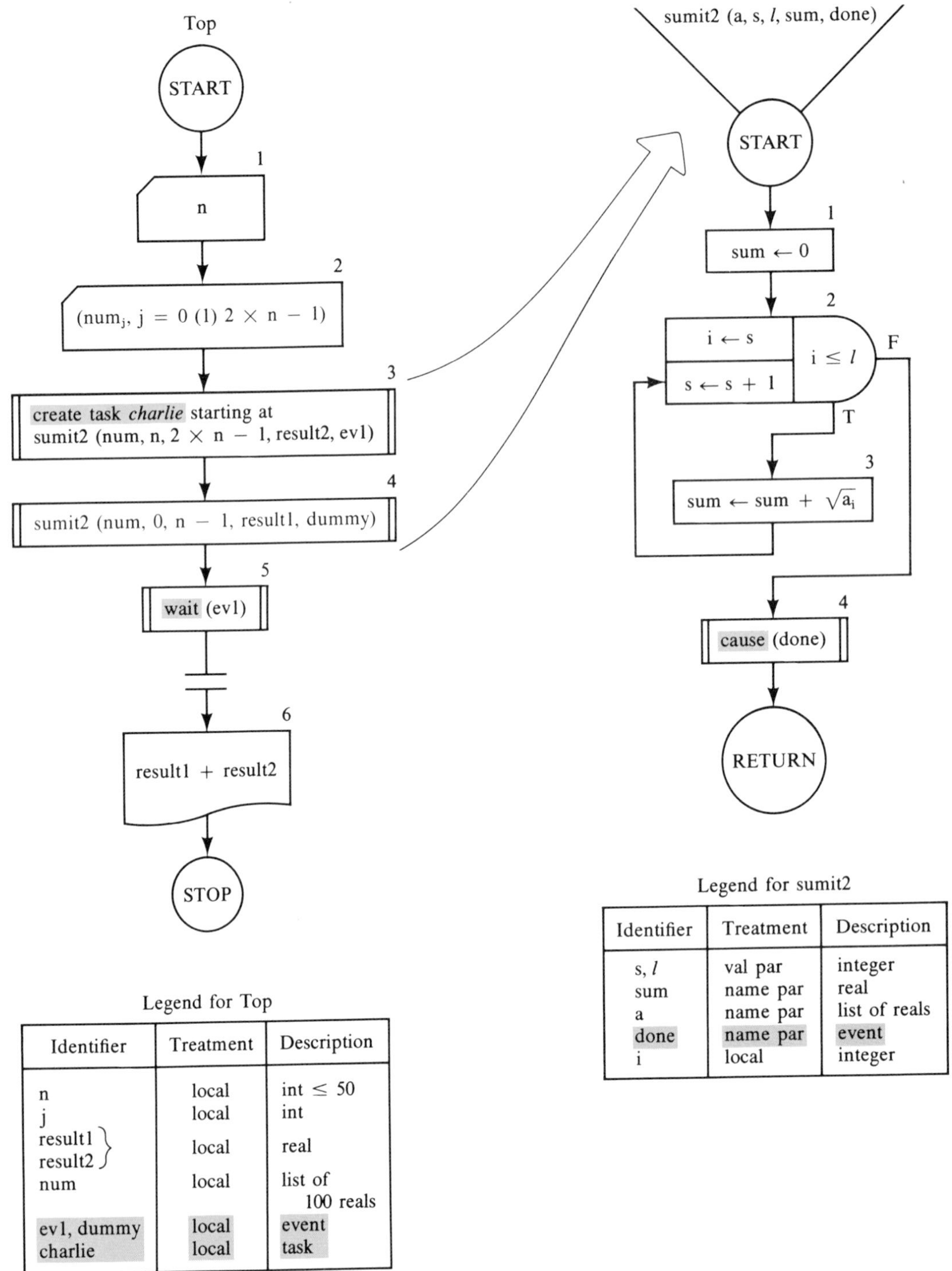

Legend for Top

Identifier	Treatment	Description
n	local	int ≤ 50
j	local	int
result1 } result2	local	real
num	local	list of 100 reals
ev1, dummy	local	event
charlie	local	task

Legend for sumit2

Identifier	Treatment	Description
s, *l*	val par	integer
sum	name par	real
a	name par	list of reals
done	name par	event
i	local	integer

(a) Flowcharts and legends.

***Figure 9-2.* Asynchronous tasking example.**

```
Line No.  0   1   2   3   4   5   6   7   8   9
                                              Top
 0   begin
 1     integer j, n; real result1, result2;
 2     real array num [0:99];
 3     event ev1, dummy; task charlie;
                                              Sumit2
 4     procedure sumit2 (a, s, l, sum, done);
 5       value s, l; integer s, l; real sum; array a [*]; event done;
 6       begin
 7         integer i;
 8         sum := 0;
 9         for i := s step 1 until l do sum := sum + sqrt (a[i]);
10         cause (done);
11       end sumit2
12     ;
13     [input value for n ≤ 50 and values for num_j, for j := 0 step 1 until
       2 × n − 1]
14     process sumit2 (num, n, 2 × n − 1, result2, ev1) [charlie];
15     sumit2 (num, 0, n − 1, result1, dummy);
16     wait (ev1);
17     [print (result1 + result2)]
18   end
```

(b) Burroughs-like ALGOL program.

Figure 9-2 (continued)

completed. In principle, any number of tasks may be invoked (spawned), and executed, in this quasi-concurrent fashion.

Tasks that proceed in this manner may, and usually do, need to synchronize their actions with one another. One task may wait for a message from another task to tell of some event that has happened. For example, in this case study the total job is to sum up square roots of the elements of an array. The top-level program invokes the task called charlie (see line 14), whose job is to execute the procedure named sumit2 to sum up square roots of elements of half the array. Having invoked task charlie, the main program continues its work, and itself calls the procedure sumit2 (on line 15) to sum up square roots of elements of the other half of the array. Since both the main program and the subsidiary task named charlie are proceeding asynchronously, it is not clear which will complete the execution of sumit2 first. Hence, two steps are taken to guarantee coordination of the two tasks:

1. The procedure sumit2 is coded so that one of its jobs is to "send a message," when its action is nearing completion (at line 10), to the effect that its summing operation has been completed.
2. When the main program reaches line 16, it will wait for a message from charlie, by executing a call to the library routine *wait.* This call forces a pause if charlie's message has not yet arrived. As soon as the message is received, the MC for the main program is free to resume its action by executing line 17. In the meantime, the task charlie simply *dies* when it

has completed the procedure sumit2, because, like all invoked tasks, sumit2 was given a NIL return pointer. If charlie's message is sent before line 16 has been executed by the main program, then no pause occurs. Instead the call on *wait* results in an immediate return to the caller.

To achieve tasking and coordination of tasks, several new constructs are added to the programming language:

1. Two new data types are needed: *event* values and *task* values. For example, in our case study the variables evl and dummy are declared to be of type *event* and the variable charlie is declared to be of type *task*. Any event variable can have one of two possible values, *happened*, H, and *not happened*, N. The initial value of a declared event is *not happened*. A task variable is used to name (point to) a created (spawned) task.
2. To invoke a designated task, the syntax of the procedure call must be modified. Line 14 illustrates one way this can be done, that is, by prefixing the call with the key word *process* and by appending to the call, in a pair of square brackets, the name given to the task being spawned.

The mechanism for sending and receiving messages uses the library routines *wait* and *cause*, each of which has a parameter of type *event*. Any task or the top-level program (which may also be regarded as a task) can wait for a message by calling *wait* and by giving an event variable as the argument. Whenever the value of this named event variable changes to *happened*, it means the message has arrived. The waiting task can then return from *wait* and continue execution. Another task can signal a waiting task by executing a call on the *cause* procedure, supplying the proper named event variable as the argument (or a parameter whose matching argument is that variable). The *cause* procedure sets the value of the event argument to *happened*. The waiting task is thereby alerted, since the value of the event variable in question changes from *not happened* to *happened*. The effect of this change permits the waiting task to resume.

When a task pauses, waiting for a message, we picture that its state changes from *awake* to *asleep*. When it is allowed to resume, the state of the task is changed back from asleep to awake. This state of the task is pictured on our contour snapshots in the way we show the MC for the task (a different MC for each task). An asleep MC is shown as [MC], while an awake MC is shown as (MC).

The following annotated snapshots explain the semantics of the program of Figure 9-2. In snapshot 1, the MC has entered Outer[1] and has executed the input steps of line 13. One hundred data values have been input for the array num. The next step is to execute line 14, whose purpose is to invoke a task to be referred to as "charlie". Each new task requires its own MC. Since there are two MC's to keep track of in this program, a number 1 or 2 is written above to serve as an identifier.

Note that in the sytem described here, declared event variables such as evl and dummy, are given *not happened* initial values of the form

N	–

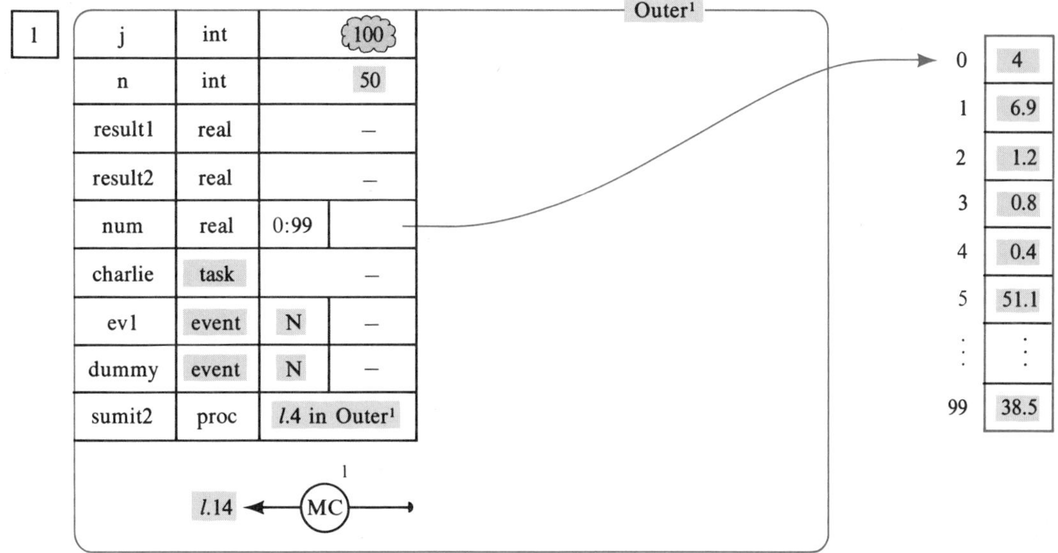

The task charlie begins (snapshot 2) when the first MC creates a contour, named $sumit2^1$ and also a new MC, named MC^2. A pointer to this MC is assigned as the value of charlie. Then, MC^2 enters $sumit2^1$ and begins to execute the body of sumit2 at line 8. In the meantime the original MC is now ready to execute line 15, which is a call on the procedure sumit2. During execution in sumit2, each task will have the job of summing the square roots of (in this case) 50 numbers. Charlie will work on elements indexed 50–99 and "main" will work on elements indexed 0–49. Note that the principal or main task has no explicit name, although in this type of system each subtask that works asynchronously with the main task must be given an explicit name, for example, *charlie.*

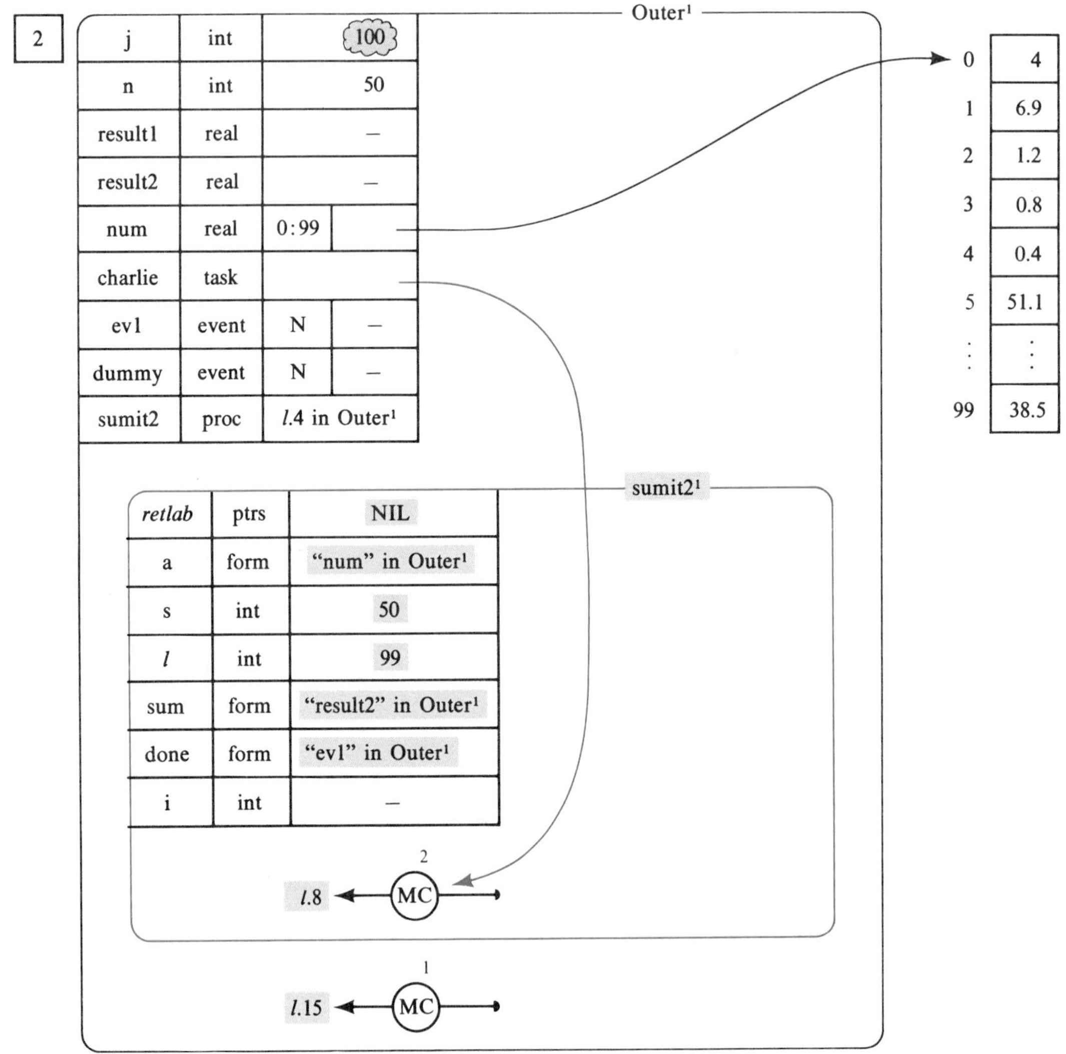

Snapshot 3 shows the state of the computation after the main task, executing in the Outer block of the program, has called sumit2 in a normal procedure call at line 15.

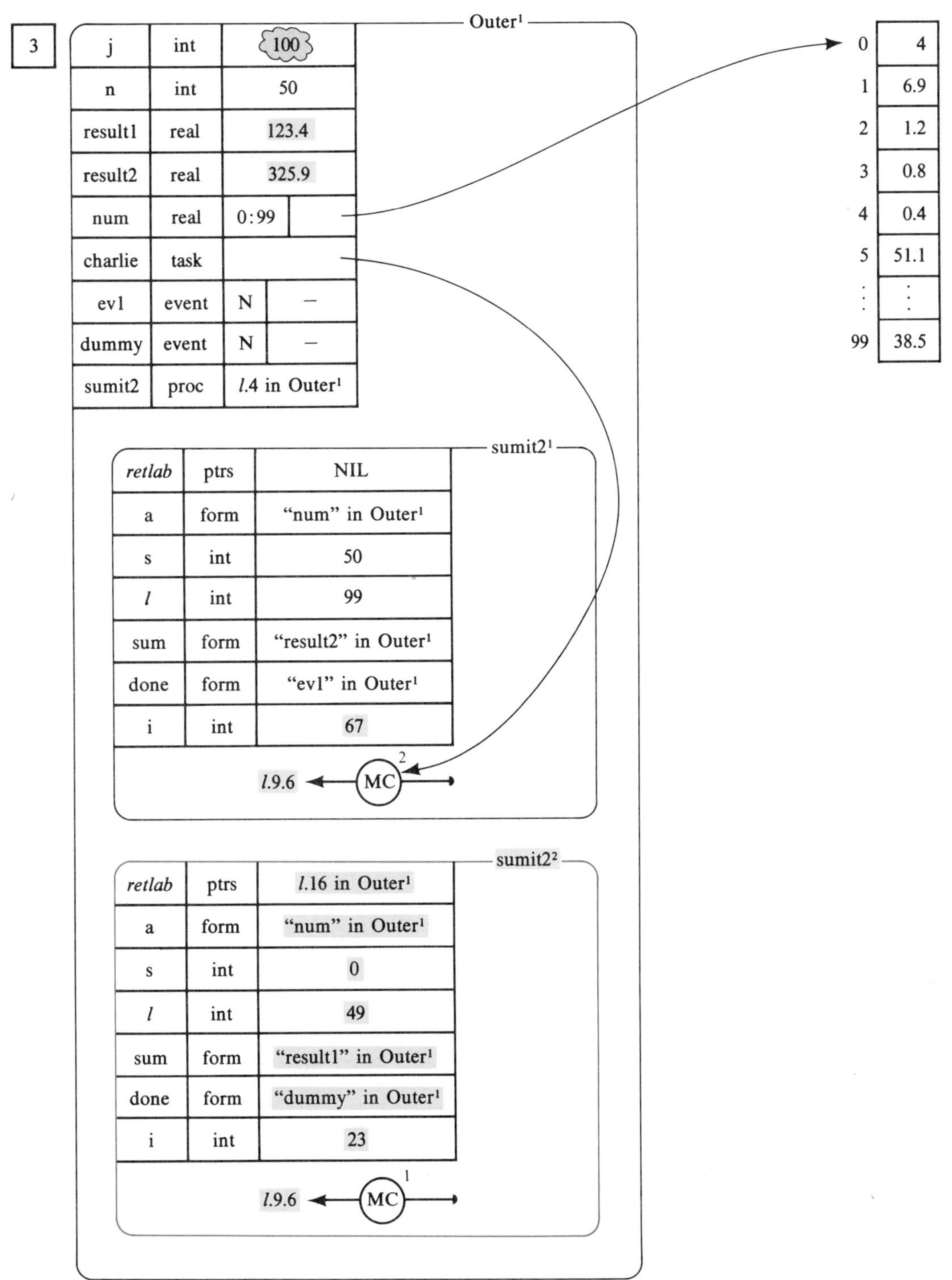

A new contour, sumit2^2, has been created. The main MC is now executing inside this contour, and is busy accumulating a total in the global variable result1. The local loop counter i = 23 shows that this MC is approximately halfway through its work (the range of i is 0–49). Meanwhile the MC for task charlie is also busy and has progressed partway toward its objective. The local loop counter in sumit2^1 is now pictured as having the value 67. The individual rates of progress of the two MCs are of no special significance. Each has a *speed of execution* independent of the other. Eventually, each MC will complete the work of the sumit2 procedure, but we cannot say which MC will finish first for at least two reasons:

1. On some actual computers there may be two or more processing units (processors) that can be allocated to this computation, as needed, but these units need not be equally fast.
2. On some actual computers having only *one* processing unit, a supervisor program is responsible for allocating the one processing unit among the several asynchronous tasks of a computation. The supervisor's rules for awarding the processing unit may lead to "random" rates of progress. For example, suppose that each time the computer is *interrupted* for any reason (for example, as a result of having received a signal from a high-speed input/output device indicating an urgent need for service), the supervisor awards the processor to a task that *did not* have a processor prior to that interrupt. Then, depending on the frequency of these external interrupts, which may be totally unpredictable, each task will progress at a different speed because it will have more or less opportunity than other tasks to run on the processor.

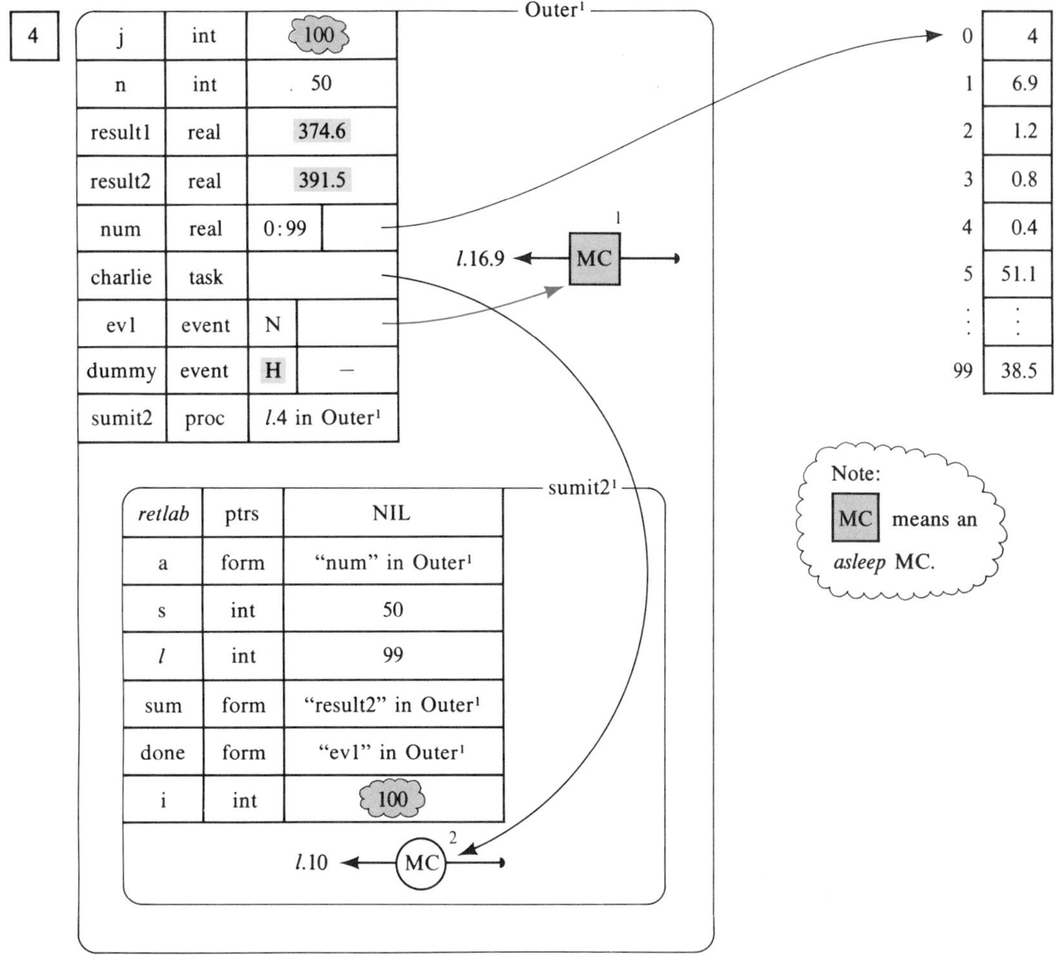

For the purpose of drawing the next snapshot, we assume the MC in sumit2[2] completed the task first. Thus in snapshot 4 the first MC has returned from sumit2 and is back in Outer[1]. It has executed the call on *wait* at line 16. Since the event argument ev1 still has the value *not happened* (N), the MC goes to sleep (square MC) but is now *linked* to the event variable, so that when ev1 has its state changed to *happened* (H), the MC will be awakened by virtue of the link that exists between ev1 and MC[1]. Meanwhile, the second MC has completed the summing loop in sumit2 and is about to execute line 10, the call on the *cause* procedure. The parameter done in sumit2 refers to its matching argument, in this case ev1, and when line 10 of Figure 9-2b

cause (*done*);

is executed, the effect is to awaken the first MC. This is seen in snapshot 5. (Note that when the first MC executed line 10, as it was about to return from sumit2, the matching argument for *done* was the event variable *dummy,* which was never linked to any MC. Hence no MC was awakened.)

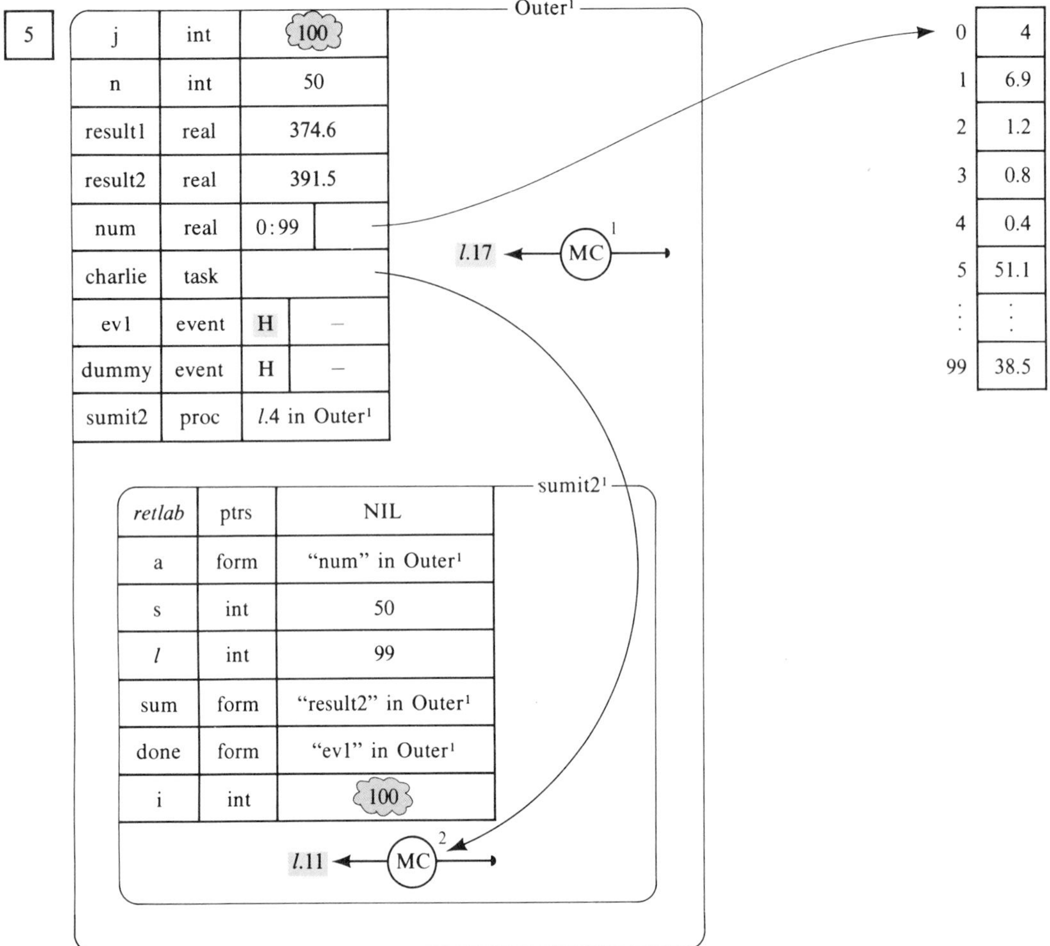

In snapshot 5 the first MC has been awakened. The second MC is attempting to execute a return to sumit2's caller, but the return pointer is NIL, so this MC will be *deallocated.* Once MC^2 is deallocated, $sumit2^1$ will no longer be accessible, and so it, too, will be deallocated, as seen in snapshot 6. Of course, when line 18 is executed, the remaining MC and its environment $Outer^1$ will also be deallocated.

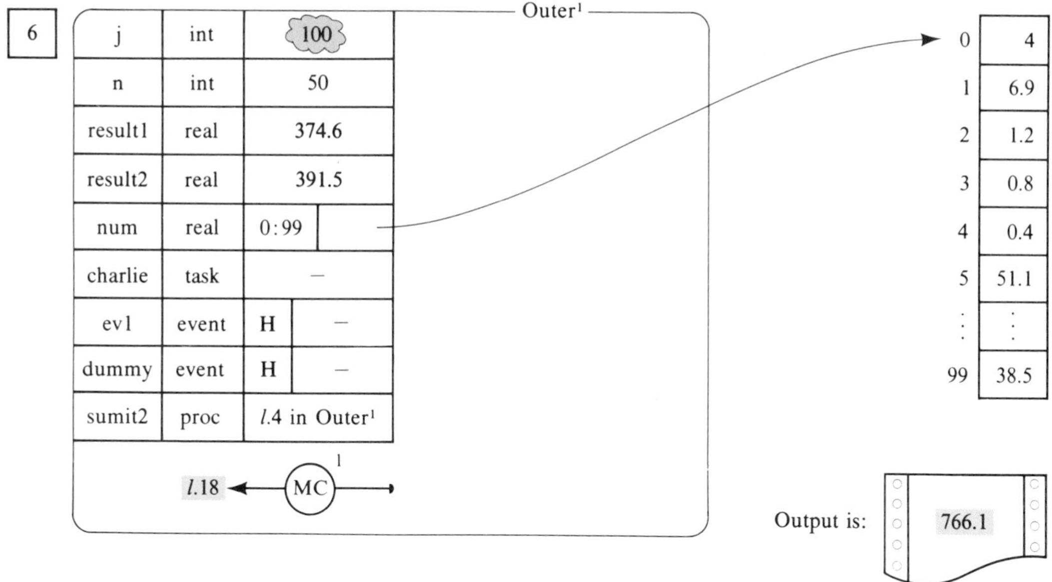

Let us see how the system would have behaved had task charlie finished first. It would have *caused* the value in ev1 to switch from N to H *before* the main task was ready to execute the call on *wait.* Eventually the main task would have executed this call. Note that when charlie had been completed, sumit2¹ would have been deallocated. When the value of the argument of procedure *wait* is H (happened), the semantics of a call on *wait* is like a "no op," that is, the procedure *wait* returns to its caller immediately, without doing anything. Thus, the main task would have proceeded to line 17, printed the same result 766.1, and then reached the end of the computation on line 18. At this point all resources still held by the computation would have been deallocated.

In short, no matter how fast or slow a task progresses, we get the same overall net effect. This is, in fact, what we were hoping for. Of course, to make it all happen properly, we had to learn how to use the *synchronizing* procedures *wait* and *cause,* the *event* variables, etc., provided in this extended Algol language.

Results Using Burroughs ALGOL

Algol extensions such as those just discussed are available on some computers, such as the Burroughs B6700-type computer. The program of Figure 9-2 was coded for this computer as shown in Figure 9-3, and actual experiments were run with this program using several different data sets. The program in Figure 9-3 differs in only one major respect from that of Figure 9-2. (Other purely superficial differences are noted in Figure 9-3.)

The main difference is that in the Burroughs program (line 2000), we print out values for the index i and SUM after each new addition to SUM. This print step was inserted so that we can monitor the relative rates of progress of the two tasks. Three experiments were run to confirm that the relative speeds of the two tasks are not fixed (and not predictable). For each experiment the same computation was run several times using the same data set. These experiments are discussed below.

Table 9-1a shows the results of experiment 1. Four terms are summed by each task (charlie sums terms 4, 5, 6, and 7). Five runs were made. The main task finished first in all five runs. In fact, in four of the five runs the main task finished its summing work even before charlie began! (The exception is the run numbered 13.)

Table 9-1b shows the results of experiment 2. Ten terms were summed and five runs were made. Charlie finished first in one of the five runs, even though the main task started first in all five cases.

Table 9-1c shows the results for experiment 3, where 18 terms were summed. Charlie finished first in one out of the four runs made. In one case (the run numbered 7) charlie actually got started ahead of the main task but finished last.

Figure 9-4 shows the printouts for the third and fourth runs of experiment 1 (runs 12 and 13), revealing a difference in the order in which the computation was carried out, although in both runs the main task finished first and waited for charlie to be completed.

Figures 9-5, 9-6, and 9-7 shows the results of runs 7, 8, and 9 in experiment 3. Larger variations in the order of events are revealed here, even though the final outcome is (of course) the same.

TABLE 9-1
Summary of Experimental Results[a]

Run	Order of Terms Summed																	
(a) Experiment 1: N = 4, number of runs = 5																		
1	0	1	2	3	**4**	**5**	**6**	**7**										
2	0	1	2	3	**4**	**5**	**6**	**7**										
12	0	1	2	3	**4**	**5**	**6**	**7**										
13	0	1	2	**4**	**5**	**6**	3	**7**										
14	0	1	2	3	**4**	**5**	**6**	**7**										
(b) Experiment 2: N = 5, number of runs = 5																		
3	0	1	2	3	4	**5**	**6**	**7**	**8**	**9**								
4	0	1	2	3	4	**5**	**6**	**7**	**8**	**9**								
5	0	1	2	3	4	**5**	**6**	**7**	**8**	**9**								
10	0	1	**5**	**6**	**7**	**8**	**9**	2	3	4								
11	0	1	2	3	4	**5**	**6**	**7**	**8**	**9**								
(c) Experiment 3: N = 9, number of runs = 4																		
6	0	1	2	3	4	5	6	7	8	**9**	**10**	**11**	**12**	**13**	**14**	**15**	**16**	**17**
7	**9**	0	1	2	3	4	5	6	7	8	**10**	**11**	**12**	**13**	**14**	**15**	**16**	**17**
8	0	1	2	3	4	5	6	7	8	**9**	**10**	**11**	**12**	**13**	**14**	**15**	**16**	**17**
9	0	**9**	**10**	**11**	**12**	**13**	**14**	**15**	**16**	**17**	1	2	3	4	5	6	7	8

[a]A digit enclosed in a box indicates a term summed by charlie.

```
100  BEGIN
200   FILE LINE(KIND=REMOTE),CARD(KIND=REMOTE);
300   INTEGER J,N,K;
400   REAL RESULT1,RESULT2;
500   ARRAY NUM[0:99];
600   EVENT EV1,DUMMY;
700   TASK CHARLIE;
800   PROCEDURE SUMIT2(A,S,L,SUM,DONE);
900    VALUE S,L;
1000   INTEGER S,L;
1100   REAL SUM;
1200   ARRAY A[*];
1300   EVENT DONE;
1400   BEGIN
1500    INTEGER I;
1600    SUM:=0;
1700    FOR I:=S STEP 1 UNTIL L DO
1800     BEGIN
1900      SUM:=SUM+SQRT(A[I]);
2000      WRITE(LINE,⟨16,F9.5⟩,I,SUM);
2100     END;
2200   CAUSE(DONE);
2300  END SUMIT2;
2400 READ(CARD,/,N);
2500 FOR K:=0 STEP 1 UNTIL 2*N-1 DO
2600   BEGIN
2700    READ(CARD,/,J);
2800    NUM[K]:=J;
2900   END;
3000  PROCESS SUMIT2(NUM,N,2*N-1,RESULT2,EV1)[CHARLIE];
3100  SUMIT2(NUM,0,N-1,RESULT1,DUMMY);
3200  WAIT(EV1);
3300  WRITE(LINE,⟨3F9.5⟩,RESULT1,RESULT2,RESULT1+RESULT2);
3400 END.
▽
```

Figure 9-3. Burroughs ALGOL version of the program in Figure 9-2. The following superficial differences are noted: (a) The input and output devices were declared on line 200 so we could operate from the teletype. (b) Certain lines in Figure 9-2 were coded on two or more lines here. For example, line 3 of Figure 9-2 is shown on lines 600 and 700 here. (c) The input step on line 13 is coded here on lines 2400–2900. Lines 2700 and 2800 could have been coded as the single line: READ (CARD,/,NUM [k]). (d) The output step on line 17 was recoded to print the individual sums RESULT1 and RESULT2, as well as their sum. Format code was inserted into the write statements.

RUN #12

```
E
*TASK ASSIGNED AS NON-SWAPPED
*RUNNING 6252
*?
4

1
2
3
4
5
6
7
8
      0  1.00000
      1  2.41421
      2  4.14626
      3  6.14626
      4  2.23607
      5  4.68556
      6  7.33131
      7 10.15974
   6.14626 10.15974 16.30600
*CPU = 0.00,  ELAPSED = 0.31 MINUTES
```

data input by user

output generated by program—note that real values are sums of square roots

RUN #13

```
E
*TASK ASSIGNED AS NON-SWAPPED
*RUNNING 8257
*?
4

1
2
3
4
5
6
7
8
      0  1.00000
      1  2.41421
      2  4.14626
      4  2.23607
      5  4.68556
      6  7.33131
      3  6.14626
      7 10.15974
   6.14626 10.15974 16.30600
*CPU = 0.00,  ELAPSED = 0.30 MINUTES
```

Figure 9-4

RUN #7

```
E
*TASK ASSIGNED AS NON-SWAPPED
*RUNNING 8235
*?
9

1
2
3
4
5
6
7
8
9
10
11
12
13
14
15
16
17
18
          9   3.16228
          0   1.00000
          1   2.41421
          2   4.14626
          3   6.14626
          4   8.38233
          5  10.83182
          6  13.47757
          7  16.30600
          8  19.30600
         10   6.47890
         11   9.94300
         12  13.54856
         13  17.29021
         14  21.16320
         15  25.16320
         16  29.28630
         17  33.52894
   19.30600 33.52894 52.83494
 *CPU = 0.00,  ELAPSED = 0.63 MINUTES
```

Figure 9-5

RUN #8

```
E
*TASK ASSIGNED AS NON-SWAPPED
*RUNNING 8237
*?
9

1
2
3
4
5
6
7
8
9
10
11
12
13
14
15
16
17
18
       0   1.00000
       1   2.41421
       2   4.14626
       3   6.14626
       4   8.38233
       5  10.83192
       6  13.47757
       7  16.30600
       8  19.30600
       9   3.16223
      10   6.47890
      11   9.94300
      12  13.54856
      13  17.29021
      14  21.16320
      15  25.16320
      16  29.28630
      17  33.52894
 19.30600 33.52894 52.33494
*CPU = 0.00,  ELAPSED = 0.60 MINUTES
```

Figure 9-6

RUN #9

```
E
*TASK ASSIGNED AS NON-SWAPPED
*RUNNING 8239
*?
9

1
2
3
4
5
6
7
8
9
10
11
12
13
14
15
16
17
18
          0   1.00000
          9   3.16228
         10   6.47890
         11   9.94300
         12  13.54856
         13  17.29021
         14  21.16320
         15  25.16320
         16  29.28630
         17  33.52894
          1   2.41421
          2   4.14626
          3   6.14626
          4   8.38233
          5  10.83182
          6  13.47757
          7  16.30600
          8  19.30600
  19.30600 33.52894 52.83494
 *CPU = 0.00,  ELAPSED = 0.62 MINUTES
```

Figure 9-7

9-4 CASE STUDIES FOR COROUTINE TASKS

We have just seen that an asynchronous task has the characteristics of a mini-computation in the sense that during its lifetime a task has code to be executed, a distinct structured environment in which to execute, and an MC or processor of its own. Communication between tasks is achieved by reading or writing messages in storage cells that are *common* to, that is, shared between, the environments of the two tasks.

Now we consider computation structures that occur with the use of coroutine tasks. Like the asynchronous task, a coroutine has code to be executed, a distinct structured environment in which to execute, and an MC. Unlike asynchronous tasks, which may execute concurrently, coroutines execute by *taking turns.*

Once *created,* coroutines can be pictured as structures between which activity shifts back and forth. Each coroutine retains the same distinct initial environment throughout its lifetime, independent of the number of times it gets a chance to execute. Coroutine A causes coroutine B to resume execution by executing a *continue* command. After executing some section of its code, B can then cause A to resume its computation, by issuing a *continue* command, etc. Some type of command is required to set up the distinct environment structure of a coroutine and get it started, and some method may also be needed to terminate the action of a coroutine.

If you picture that two high school students share one trigonometry table in doing their respective mathematics homework assignments, you get a good analogy to a pair of coroutines. You have to image that while A is using the trig tables, B can't do anything but wait. After A voluntarily gives the trig tables to B at some point, A must now wait until B voluntarily returns the tables to A, etc. The two students may share books, tables, and even some of their computed results during the computation, and thereby increase the value of their cooperative effort. In a like manner, each cooperating coroutine has its own workspace held intact, and reused each time the coroutine gets a chance to execute. If coroutine A is at step i when it *continues* coroutine B, then A will resume its computation at step i + 1 when and if B lets A continue with its work.

A comparison between the coroutine model of sharing resources and an analogous model using asynchronous tasks should now be instructive. In the coroutine model, the student holding the table is free to decide who is to "run" next and gives the table to that person. In an asynchronous task model, sharing is coordinated by the teacher (spawner task) who always intervenes by taking the table away from one student and giving it to the next. The teacher decides who the recipient should be by one means or another, possibly by flipping a coin.

Coroutine structures have been used and understood in the sense discussed above for over ten years, but only by a small number of programmers. This is explained partly by the fact that only a few of the available procedural languages have the coroutine mechanism built into their semantics.* Another reason is that few of us have learned to exploit the mechanism.

To find a nontrivial example beyond the producer/consumer type of application suggested in the chapter introduction, one needs, as for recursion, to go to a fairly complex application. To illustrate cases where coroutine structures offer significant benefits, we might discuss compiling, a complex searching process, the simulation of a multiperson game such as Bridge, or a data management application. We shall not try to develop such an example here. Instead we give two much simpler ones. The first one is purely fiction but we hope illustrative of the key principles. The second one is a variant of the producer/consumer problem.

Water-Sharing Problem

When a homesteader in central Utah died, his farm was divided among his three sons. Each heir was also to receive one-third of the water from a central well on the property. One of the sons was a chemical engineer, another was a control engineer, and the third was a computer scientist. Together they developed a plan to pipe water from the well to their three separate homesites on the property, and to install metering stream controllers at each of three collecting tanks. The purpose of the controllers was to ensure that, during any given month, each of the three new homesites would be apportioned approximately one-third of the total well effluent, but in aggregate not exceeding the maximum water allotment set by the county.

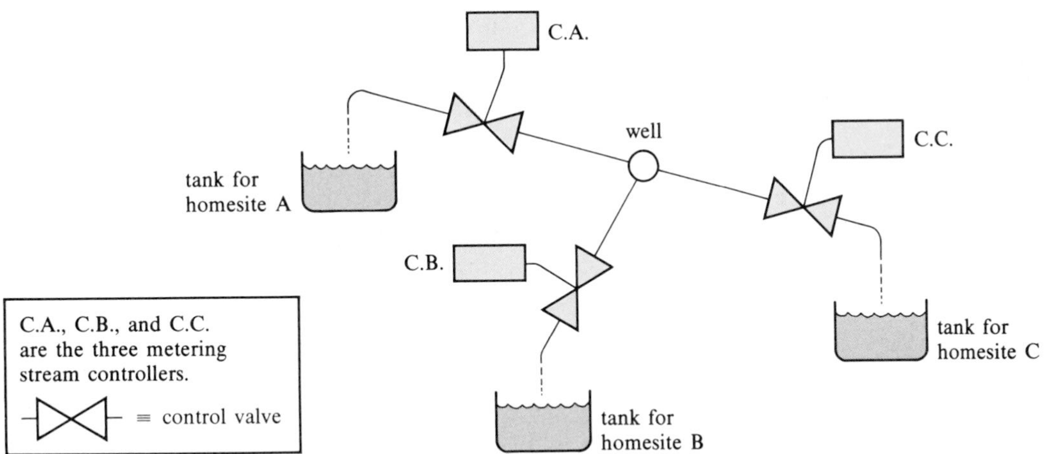

*Only two well-established languages and a scattering of still experimental languages support coroutine mechanisms. The former are Burroughs ALGOL and SIMULA 67 [see Birtwistle *et al.* (1973)]. An example of the latter is SL5 [see Griswold and Hanson (1977)]. Of course, it is possible to simulate coroutines in other languages using procedures and arrays.

A metering stream controller is built with certain digital logic. A controller governs the flow through a pipe by opening and closing a "control valve" in the pipeline. An accumulator register is periodically updated to show the total amount of fluid metered through the control valve, measured from some start-up moment when the registers have zero values. Each controller can be wired to receive data from the other controllers and also to send commands to each of the other controllers. During normal operation a controller can go out of action by shutting its control valve, and by either sending a command to one of the other controllers (now inactive) to *resume* its operation, that is, to open up its control valve and resume its metering function, or by sending a command to shut down the whole operation, such as by shutting down the pump at the well itself.

Each controller is to be "wired" to behave in a "cooperative manner" so as to maintain an input flow that is kept in balance with the flows governed by the other controllers. Each tries to admit no more water to its collecting tank than the other controllers have admitted to their respective collecting tanks.

One way to model the behavior of the controllers specified above is to picture that only one controller is active at any given time. While it is in operation, it makes periodic checks to see if it should shut off the flow on its line and start up the flow through another line by activating one of the other controllers. For example, let C.A, C.B, and C.C be names for the three controllers, and let Acc.A, Acc.B, and Acc.C be names of their respective accumulator registers. Then, while controller C.A is running, it can periodically test to see if the condition

$$\text{Acc.A} > \text{Acc.B} \qquad \text{and} \qquad \text{Acc.A} > \text{Acc.C}$$

is *true*. If so, it could shut itself down (close off the valve) and start up the controller whose accumulator register has the smaller value, as suggested by the logic in Figure 9-8.

The coroutine task structure is ideally suited to represent a stream controller, since the information environment of the controller (like that of a coroutine) should be *preserved* during shutdown periods so that, when a controller's operation is resumed, all the information needed to continue is accessible.

To force a controller out of its otherwise endless loop, one could use any of a number of control criteria. For example, ask that all controllers shut down if any one collecting tank were in danger of overflowing, or shut down all controllers when and if, for one of the controllers, the total amount of water metered for the month exceeds the prorated share of water, that is, one-third the county allotment, etc. In the algorithmic model, the corresponding coroutine could be structured in a similar way, as seen in Figure 9-9.

Our objective is to use coroutines to develop an Algol-type computer program, which closely models the water distribution planned for "down on the farm." Observe that the logic for all the controllers should be identical except for the names each uses to refer to itself and the other controllers, and except for the names each uses to refer to its own accumulator and those of the other controllers. Therefore, adding appropriate parameters to the definition of the

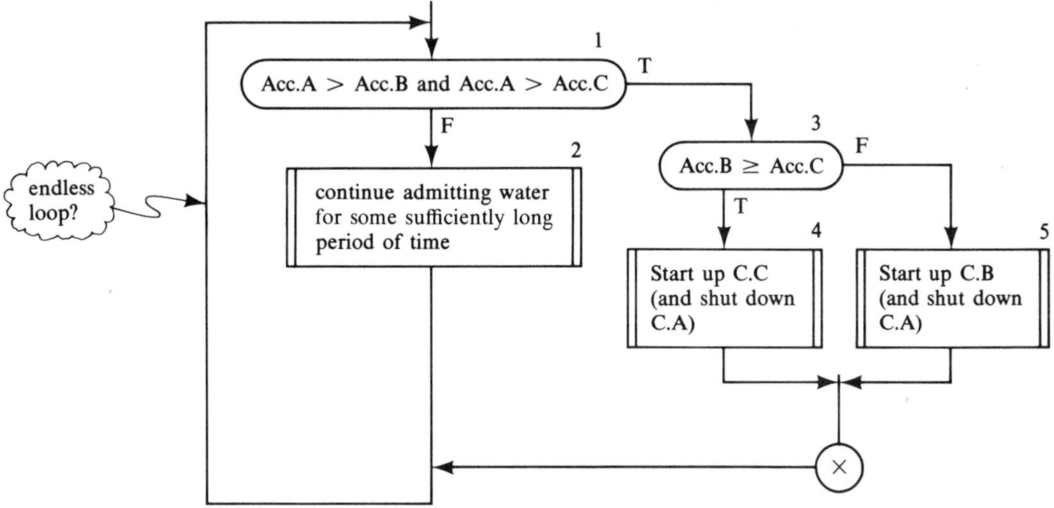

Figure 9-8. **Logic for controller C.A. The spot marked × is where controller C.A would *resume* its operation if it were restarted by either C.B or C.C.**

procedure (such as described in Figure 9-9) should make it possible to use one procedure declaration to define the action of any of the three controllers.

What is required now is an outer-block program that will *supervise* the startup (and later the shutdown) of the three controllers. This outer block itself behaves as a coroutine in the sense that it should do nothing while the three controllers are operating properly, but must itself be restarted (that is, resumed) when a condition arises that demands its attention (for example, to decide what to do next).

Figure 9-10 shows an Algol-type program (very similar to what can be coded in Burroughs ALGOL for the B6700 computer) that implements essentially all the ideas discussed so far. The outer block declares the three controllers as *tasks* C.A, C.B, and C.C, and their respective accumulator registers Acc.A, Acc.B, and Acc.C (line 2). It then declares the procedure *controller* (line 3), which has five parameters. These are the name parameters s1, s2, and s3, representing the respective accumulators (s1 for *this* controller and s2, and s3 for each of the *other* controllers). There are also two name parameters t2 and t3, which stand for the names of the other two controllers (that is, coroutine task names).

This completes the explanation of the head of the outer block. The beginning of the body initializes all the accumulators to zero and then inputs the monthly water allotment, which is assumed to be the same for each controller (lines 23 and 24). Next, the outer block supervisor starts up each of the controller coroutines (lines 25, 26, and 27).

When each **call** statement is executed, the environment necessary for the coroutine is created and control is passed to it to start execution. For example,

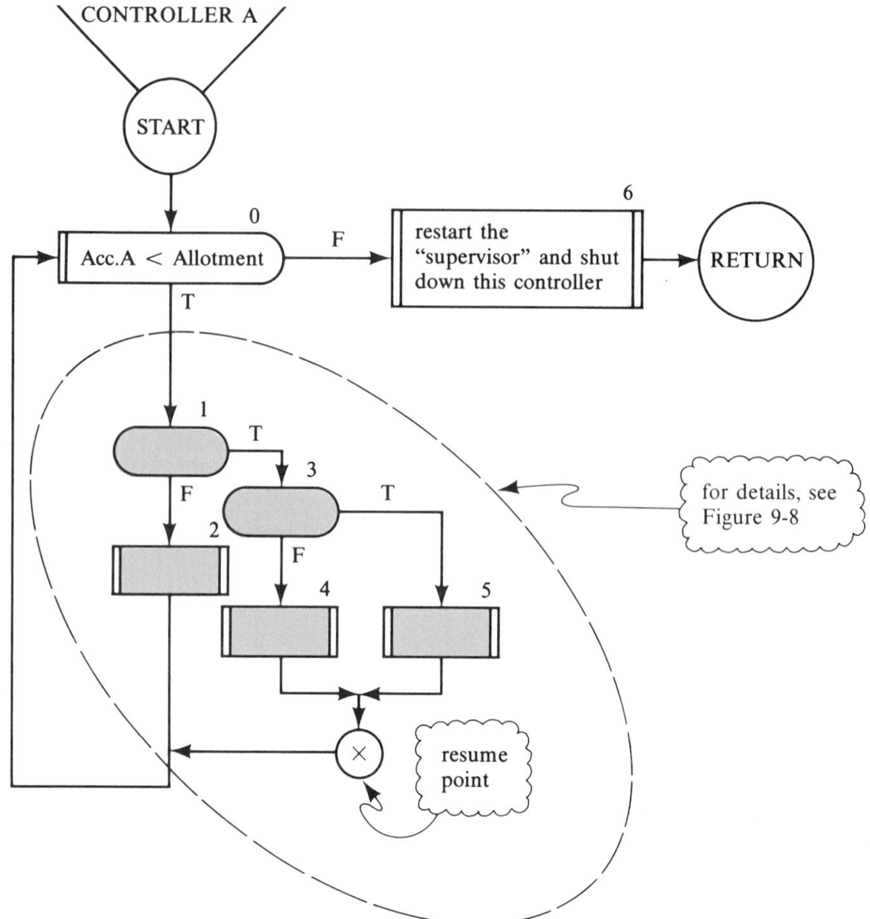

Figure 9-9. **Complete logic for a coroutine for controller A. It is assumed that before box 0 is executed, Acc.A is set to zero and Allotment has been set to one-third the county allotment. (It is also assumed that there are three controllers in all.)**

line 25 starts up controller C.A, but note that the very first step executed by the coroutine, as seen on line 7, is

continue;

This is deliberately placed in the logic to force a temporary shut-down, so that control can return to the supervisor for the purpose of starting up the other controllers, one by one, in a similar fashion. After all three controllers have been started up (and then temporarily suspended in this way), the supervisor selects one of the three controllers to be restarted, in this case controller C.A. This is done by executing a *specified continue* command (see line 28),

continue *C.A;*

A specified continue command is one that designates by name (or by a parameter standing for that name) a particular coroutine task, now dormant, that is to

```
Line   0   1   2   3   4   5   6   7   8   9
                                              OUTER
1    begin
2      task C.A, C.B, C.C; integer Acc.A, Acc.B, Acc.C, Allotment;
                                              CONTROLLER
3      procedure controller (s1, s2, s3, t2, t3);
4        integer s1, s2, s3; task t2, t3;
5        begin
6          integer VAL;
7          continue;
8            comment Resume computation in OUTER to let
9                    another controller, if any, be started up;
10         while s1 ≤ Allotment do
11           if s1 > s2 and s1 > s3 then
12             if s2 < s3 then continue t2
13                        else continue t3
14           else begin
15             [input a value of VAL from the input data file, values
16               of which represent the next "slug" of water that has
17               been metered by the currently active controller];
18             s1 := s1 + VAL
19               end flow period; comment end of loop;
20         continue; comment control is now resumed in OUTER;
21       end
22     ;
23     Acc.A := Acc.B := Acc.C := 0;
24     [input the value for Allotment];
25     call controller (Acc.A, Acc.B, Acc.C, C.B, C.C) [C.A];
26     call controller (Acc.B, Acc.A, Acc.C, C.A, C.C) [C.B];
27     call controller (Acc.C, Acc.A, Acc.B, C.A, C.B) [C.C];
28     continue C.A;
29     [print out ("Let's have a family conference")]
30   end
```

Figure 9-10. **Algol-type program to model water distribution plan for "down on the farm."**

be restarted at its resumption point. When, in this case, controller C.A is restarted, it will resume at line 10, since it last executed the continue command on line 7 (and lines 8 and 9 are only comments).

The semantics of an *unspecified continue* statement is to cause the *initiator* to resume its computation. (The initiator of a coroutine task t is the task that created t.) In this case the outer block supervisor is the initiator of each of the three controller coroutines, and so whenever a controller executes an unspecified continue (as on lines 7 and 20), the supervisor will resume operation. We see then that any time a controller escapes from its **while** loop to execute the **continue** on line 20, control will resume at line 29 in the supervisor where the message "Let's have a family conference" will be printed out. This step marks the end of the entire computation. When the MC exits from the outer block, the three coroutine environments are no longer needed, and so they are deallocated along with the outer block environment.

Snapshots for Coroutine Environments

Greater understanding of the coroutine structure, and how it is used, can be gained by studying some execution snapshots. Figure 9-11 is one snapshot taken from the Figure 9-10 computation at a point where all three controller coroutine environments have been created and where controller C.B is about to execute the **if** statement on line 11.

The water allotment in this case is 323,000 units. The MC for coroutine C.B is executing in the controller² environment. The MCs for the coroutines C.A and C.C are dormant.

Each coroutine environment, except that of the outer block supervisor, must have a special *initiator* cell to indicate which MC created the given coroutine. It is this MC that is awakened by the created MC as a result of the execution of an unspecified *continue.*

Each coroutine, *including* the outer block "supervisor", has its own MC. When any MC is awakened as a result of a *continue,* the resumption point of that MC is the ip associated with it. (Thus, an awakened MC knows immediately what to do next.)

Since each coroutine environment created by a **call** statement also has the structure of a procedure environment, we show each environment for a controller as having a *return cell,* but note that under ordinary circumstances this cell will never be consulted by the MC since a coroutine should never *return* to its caller. Hence, the value of each *retlab* cell is NIL. Should a coroutine execute a return, possibly by an error in the logic, the NIL-valued return label could, when sensed, trigger deallocation of the coroutine's environment and the resumption of the initiator task.

Armed with this general understanding, we can now take a closer look at the snapshot in Figure 9-11, and predict in detail what will happen next. Since, at this point, controller C.B's accumulator value exceeds those of the other two controllers, the MC for C.B will relinquish control to the MC for C.A by executing

continue (*t2*)

on line 12, because it will be discovered that s2 < s3 is *true,* and t2 stands for C.A. The new MC can be found by consulting the contents of the cell that t2 points to, which is the contents of the cell C.A in outer¹, which designates MC². The dormant MC² starts up at line 10.2, as indicated by its ip, and MC³ will at the same time become dormant. (Line 10.2 refers to the test in the **while** statement.) The construction of other snapshots for this computation, at states occurring both before and after that depicted in Figure 9-11, is left as an exercise for the interested reader.

The coroutine example we have just studied is interesting mainly because we have been able to describe a computation whose control flow, even through deterministic, is highly data dependent. The various paths that may be taken in a coroutine control structure may be concisely diagrammed as a state transition

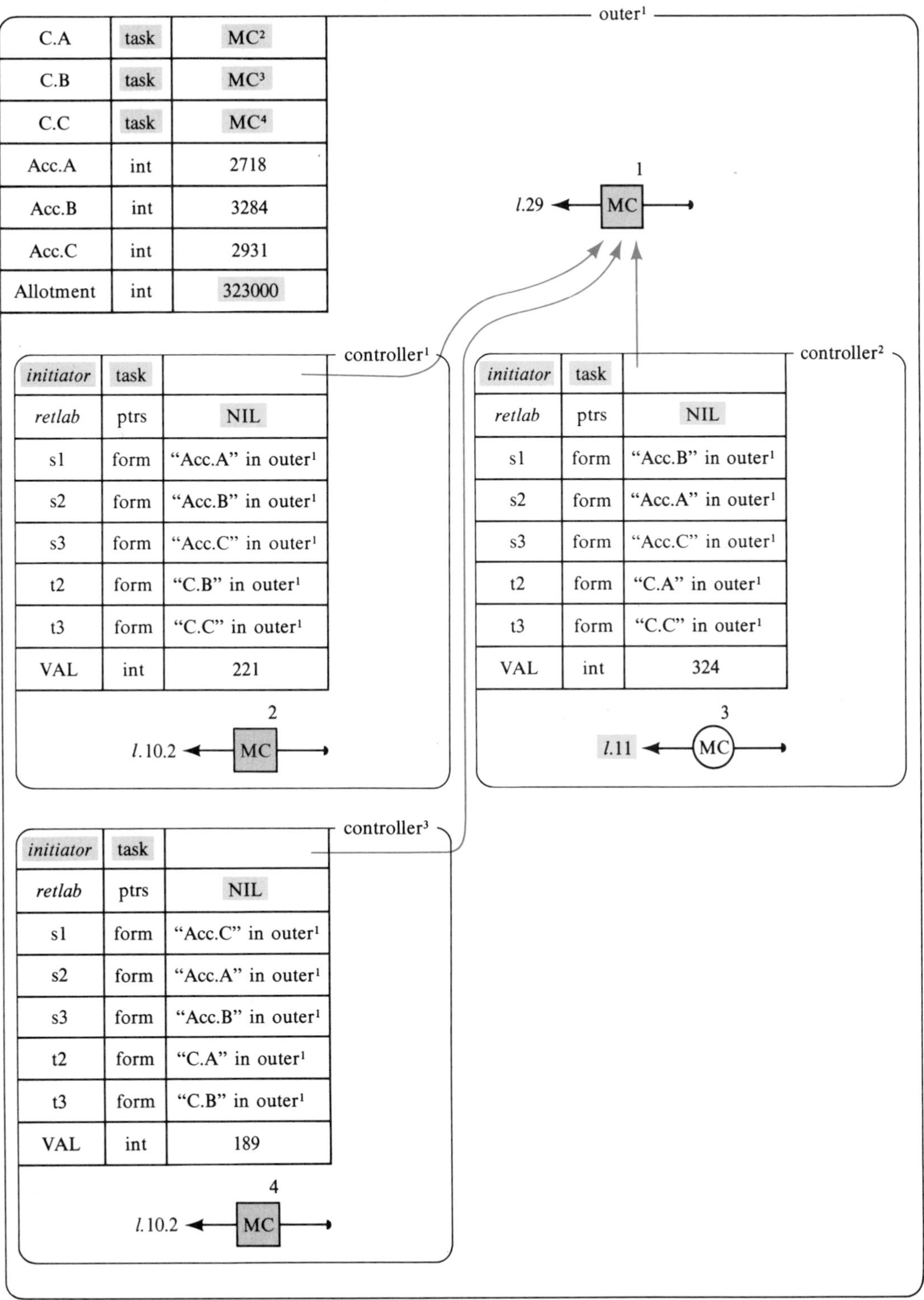

Figure 9-11. **Snapshot of coroutine computation of Figure 9-10.**

graph (Figure 9-12.). Such graphs represent a useful abstraction of the coroutine program. Their value in understanding the execution of coroutine programs is equivalent to that of call-trees for recursive program structures. Readers who pursue their study of coroutine structures may wish to keep this in mind.

Producer/Consumer Problem

This case study discusses another problem whose solution program uses *coroutine modules* to simplify the logic of the algorithm and to make its correctness more easily verified. The problem is to convert a file from one containing m characters per record to one that contains n characters per record. Thus, if m is 5 and n is 4, the input file

ABCDE	FGHIJ	KLM#□

would be converted to the output file

ABCD	EFGH	IJKL	M#□□

where # is the end-of-file sentinel character and the last record is padded with blanks to the right of #, as required.

The approach used here is to set up two coroutines, one the "reader" and the other the "writer." The reader module repeatedly fills and empties a private input buffer, m characters in length, with values obtained by reading from the input file. After filling the input buffer, the reader module copies characters from the input buffer, one character at a time, into a special cell (or mailbox) C, which is shared with the writer module. After each transfer to C, the reader module lets the writer resume execution.

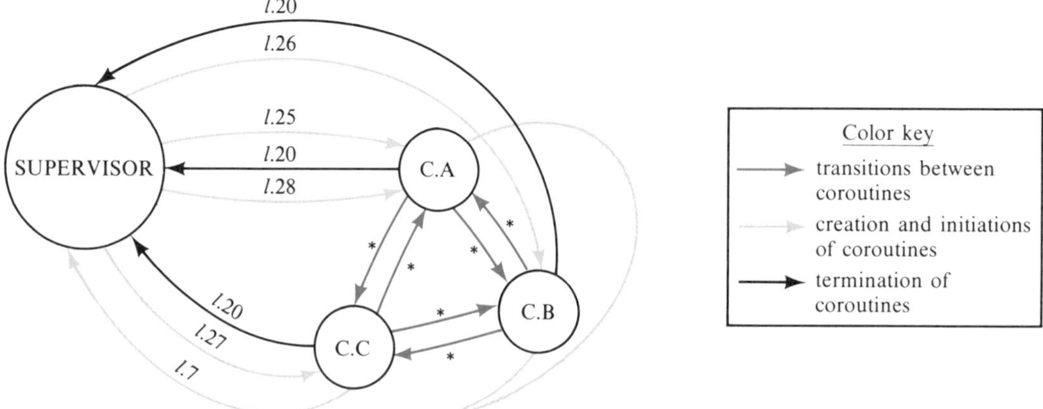

Figure 9-12. **State transition diagram representing the water-sharing problem. Line numbers refer to *call* and *continue* commands in the program of Figure 9-10. (An asterisk means line 12 or 13.)**

The writer module repeatedly fills and then "empties" a private output buffer that is n characters long. Each time the writer gets control, it loads a copy of the character that the reader placed in C into the next available slot of the output buffer. In the special case where the transferred character is the sentinel #, the output buffer is padded with blanks, if necessary, and then "emptied," that is, printed out. Then control is resumed in the top-level program, since the job of copying the file has been completed. In the usual case, however, after the value is copied from C into a slot of the output buffer, the writer module lets the reader module resume execution. After each complete filling of the output buffer, it is emptied.

Flowcharts and legends are given in Figure 9-13 for the top-level program and for two procedures, input and output. When created, the reader coroutine executes input and the writer coroutine executes output. An Algol program following the plan of these flowcharts is given in Figure 9-14. Multisequencing commands following Burroughs ALGOL are used here.*

Chapter Summary

Three case studies have been presented that use multisequencing commands (one case for asynchronous tasks and two cases for coroutines). We have only scratched the surface of this important subject. Further study of this topic will be excellent preparation for understanding operating systems and large applications programs. Operating systems are sometimes structured as collections of coroutines. More often, however, especially in systems having two or more processors (including input/output device controllers), operating systems are structured as collections of asynchronous tasks. In such structures the tasks must use their shared resources in consistent fashion. Not only must one task be in a position to claim exclusive use of a data structure while it consults or updates it, but at the same time other tasks must not be prevented indefinitely from using such shared but currently "captive" resources.

Resources must be reclaimed when no longer needed. Hence some supervisor program must be able to learn about tasks that die to reclaim ("garbage collect") their storage and device resources. To solve this type of problem special help has been required from language designers who have also had experience in implementing operating systems and from language theorists who struggle with problems of verifying and proving the correctness of large programs. A follow-on course that addresses programming and programming language design at a more formal level, as well as laboratory practice in the construction of large programs, would undoubtedly help the reader to progress further in this field.

*In the version of Algol used in Figure 9-14, an array of type string is declared with the syntax
⟨string array declaration⟩ ::= **string array** ⟨identifier⟩ [⟨string length⟩ : ⟨*lb*⟩:⟨ub⟩]
where ⟨string length⟩ is an integer that denotes the maximum length (in characters) of each string element.

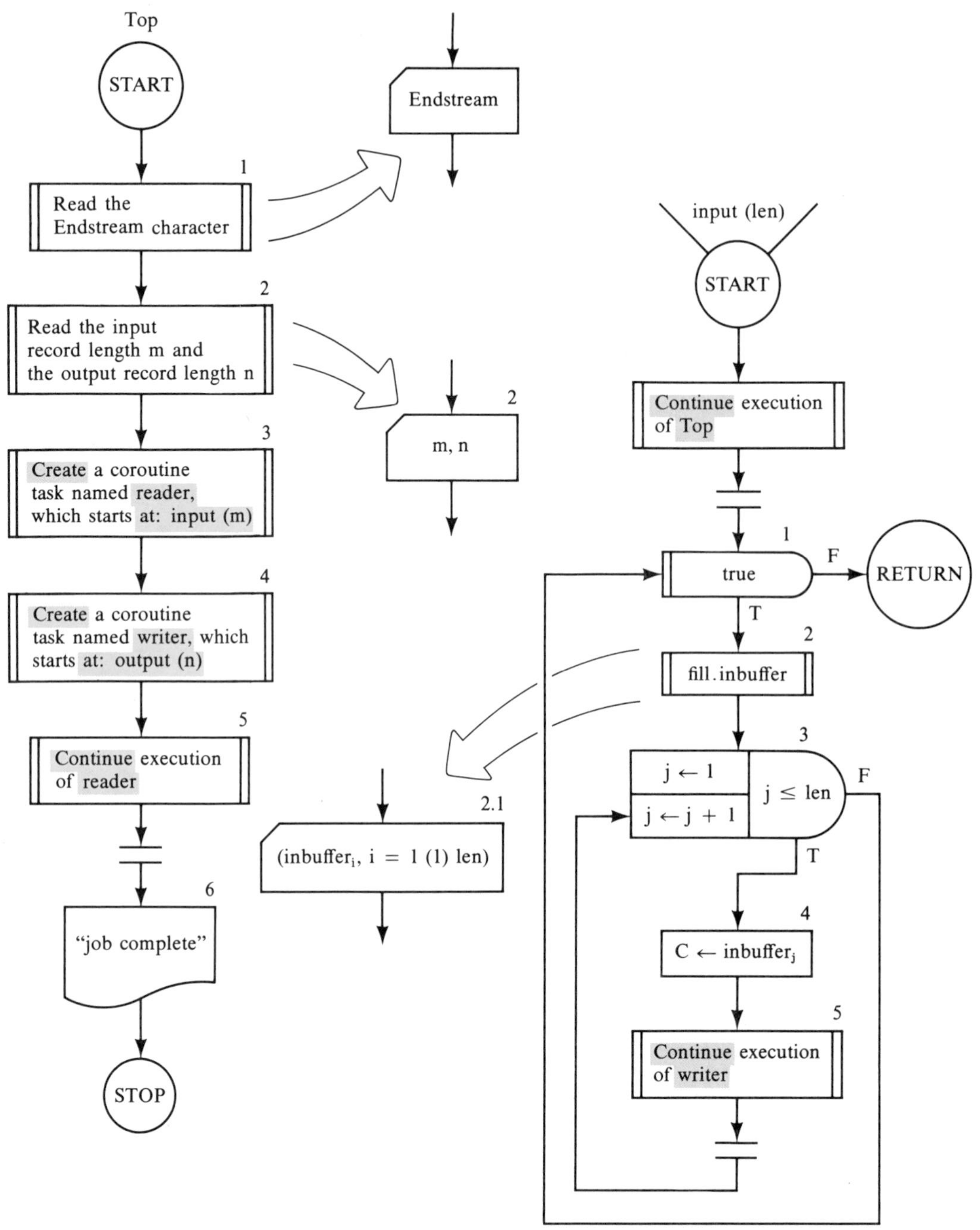

Legend for Top

Identifier	Treatment	Description
Endstream, C	local	character
m, n	local	integer
reader, writer	local	coroutine task

Legend for Input

Identifier	Treatment	Description
len	val par	integer
i, j	local	integer
inbuffer	local	list of len characters
C	global	C in Top
writer	global	writer in Top

Figure 9-13

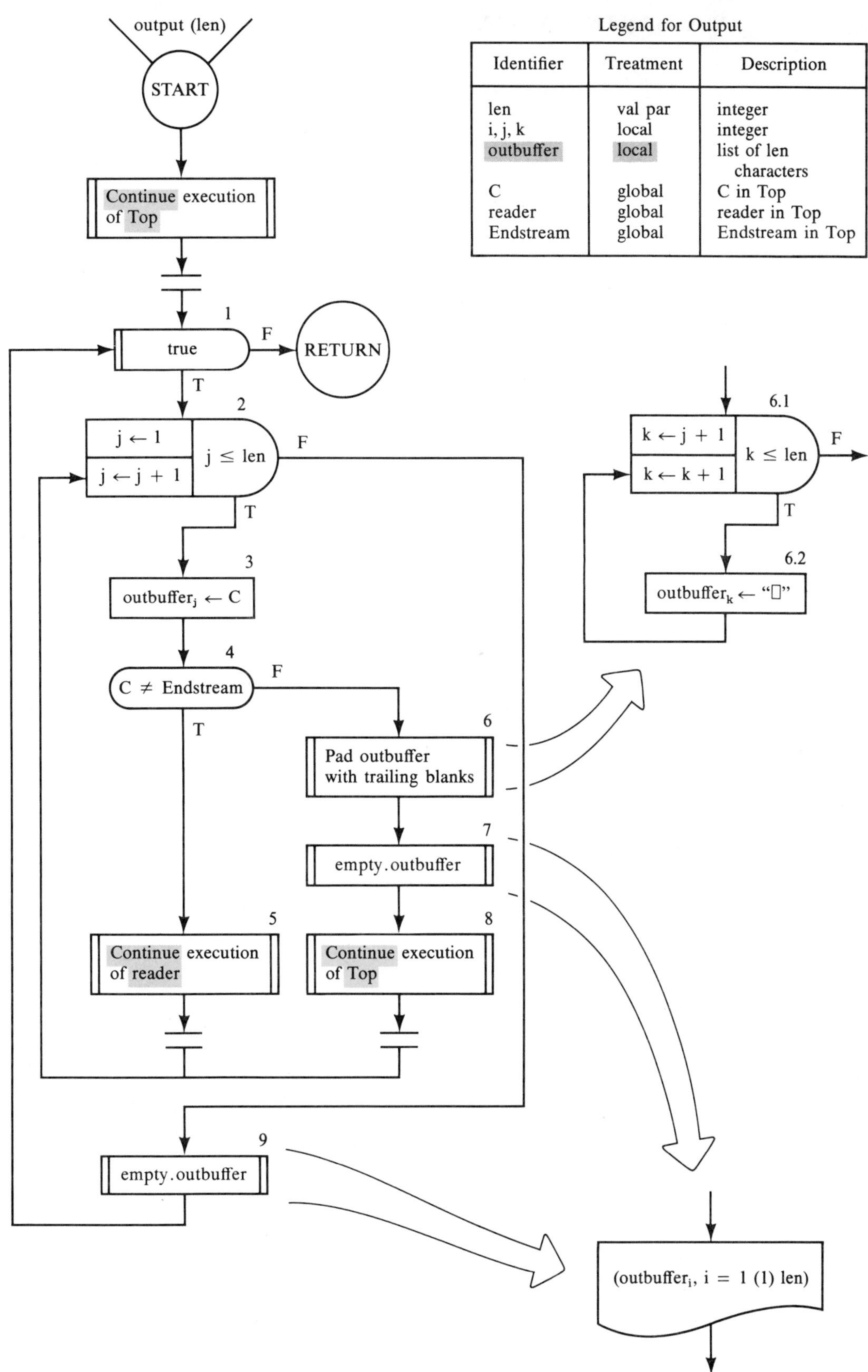

Legend for Output

Identifier	Treatment	Description
len	val par	integer
i, j, k	local	integer
outbuffer	local	list of len characters
C	global	C in Top
reader	global	reader in Top
Endstream	global	Endstream in Top

Figure 9-13 (continued)

```
Top
begin
  task reader, writer; integer m, n;
  string C [1], Endstream [1];

  input
  procedure input (len);
    value len; integer len;
    begin string array inbuffer [1:1:len];
      integer j;
      procedure fill.inbuffer;
      begin integer i;
        read (for i := 1 step 1 until len do inbuffer [i])
      end fill.inbuffer;
      continue;
      while true do
         begin fill.inbuffer;
           for j := 1 step 1 until len do
             begin C := inbuffer [j];
               continue (writer)
             end;
         end forever loop;
    end input
  ;

  output
  procedure output (len);
    value len; integer len;
    begin string array outbuffer [1:1:len];
      integer j, k;
      procedure empty.outbuffer;
      begin integer i;
        write (for i := 1 step 1 until len do outbuffer [i])
      end empty.outbuffer;
      continue;
      while true do
        begin for j := 1 step 1 until len do
          begin outbuffer [j] := C;
            if C ≠ Endstream then continue (reader)
            else begin for k := j + 1 step 1 until len do
                    outbuffer [k] := '□';
                    empty.outbuffer;
                    continue
                 end
          end
          empty.outbuffer;
        end forever loop;
    end output
    ;

  read (Endstream);
  read (m, n);
  call input (m) [reader];
  call output (n) [writer];
  continue (reader);
  write ("job complete")
end
```

Figure 9-14

Exercises 9-4

1 (a) Consider the following incomplete flowcharts. Legends are not shown—all you need to know is that eventA and eventB are "event" variables local to Top and used globally by procedures A and B.

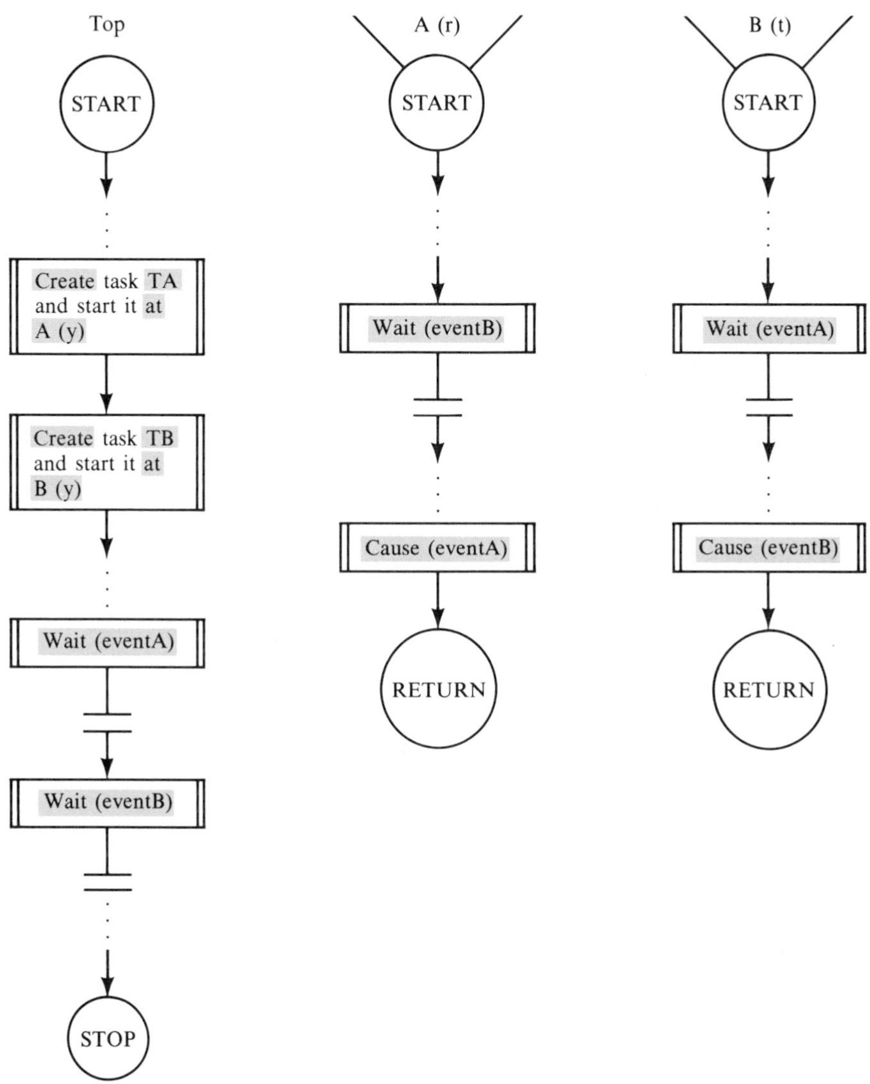

What happens when this program is executed? Draw a snapshot showing the "final" state. Be sure to show any event-variable-to-MC links that exist at the time of your snapshot, and use (MC) to indicate an MC that is awake, and [MC] for an MC that is asleep.

(b) The final situation in (a) is called a *deadlock*. Consider the procedures on the next page, which do disk and tape input and output. They communicate via global variables DISK and TAPE, which will be initialized to "FREE" by Top (not shown), and are set to "P" or "Q" to show which procedure is using which resource.

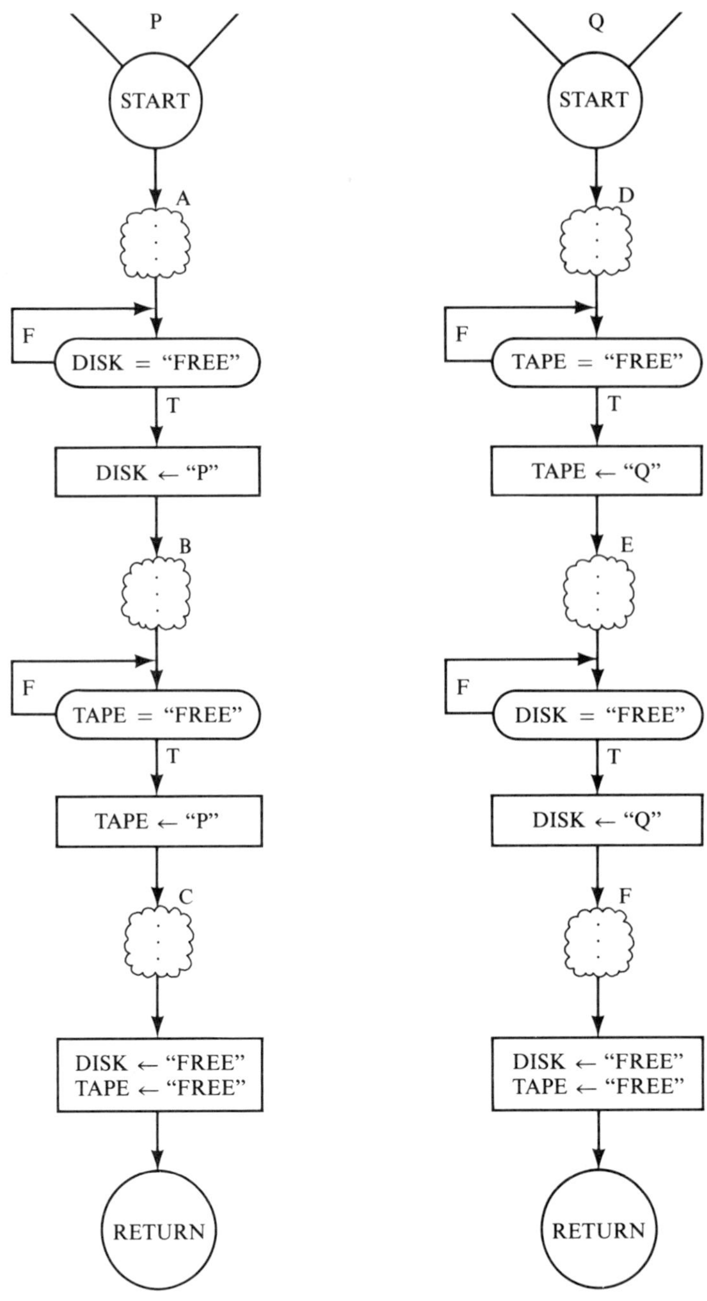

Assume P and Q are started as asynchronous, concurrent tasks, that no section changes the value of DISK or TAPE, and that the final section of each flowchart contains an I/O operation that uses both disk and tape.

(i) Describe a "lucky" sequence of events that would allow both tasks to finish.
(ii) Describe an "unlucky" sequence of events that would cause P and Q to deadlock.

(iii) Redraw the flowcharts so that each will ultimately accomplish its job and deadlock is not possible. If you can, do this in a way that does not impose a fixed order of completion of the two tasks.
Hints: (1) More tests for "who has what" may be needed. (2) A task may, under certain circumstances, have to "give up" a resource. (3) You may want to impose some rules concerning the order in which resources have to be obtained or some other useful rules. (4) *All* of these hints may not be needed, but then again . . .

2 Draw a state diagram (in the style of Figure 9-12) for the program given in Figure 9-14, showing all possible transitions. Draw a second diagram showing only the transitions possible after each coroutine has proceeded beyond its first step, that is, beyond lines 12 and 30, respectively.

3 The *eight Queens problem* is a classic in computer science and mathematics. The object is to place eight chess Queens on an empty chessboard so that no Queen can capture any of the others. A Queen can capture another piece encountered on the same row, column, or diagonal. If a solution exists, then each Queen must be positioned on a different row, column and diagonal. Figure 9-15a shows two Queens positioned so that neither one can capture the other. Figure 9-15b shows a complete solution. There are in fact 92 distinct solutions, but no formula for them is known. The problem has been solved by trial and error. A sequence of trials must be selected which can guarantee that all 92 solutions will be found. The most familiar successful approach is to place the Queens on the board one at a time. The first Queen is placed in column 1 and the object is to place each remaining Queen successfully in a succeeding column.

In placing the first Queen in column 1 there are eight row positions to choose from. Whichever position (i, 1) is selected, the choice of positions for the Queen in the second column is reduced. Whichever position (i, 2) is chosen in the second column further reduces the choices for placing a Queen at a position (i, 3) in the third column, etc. Thus, there is a tree of choices, beginning at the root node with eight choices (offspring nodes) but with a decreasing number of choices (offspring nodes) for nodes at succeeding levels. Only paths that extend from the root node (at level 0) to nodes at level 8 represent solutions.

Figure 9-15

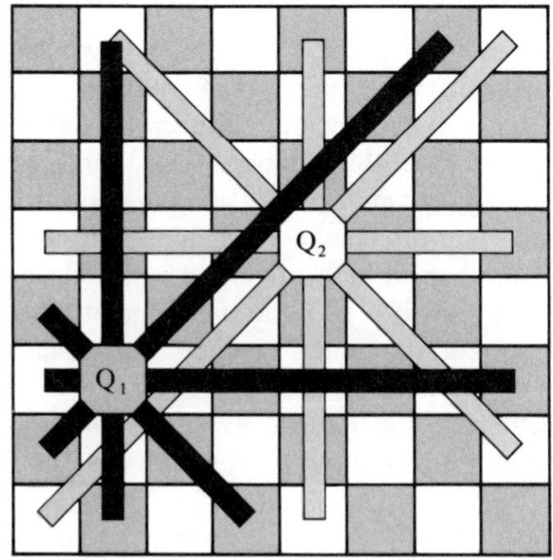

(a) heart of the matter

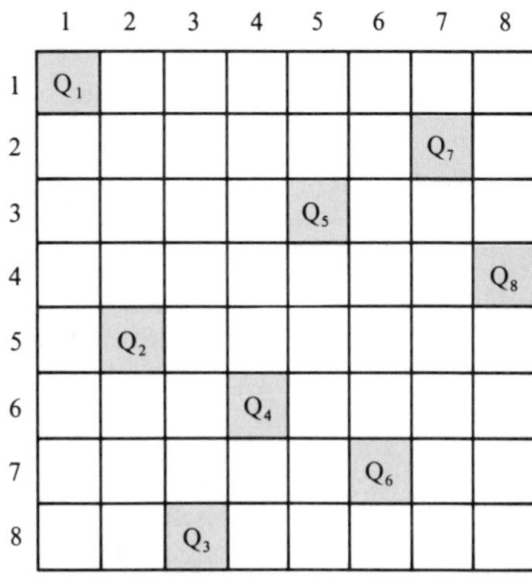

(b) a solution

It is possible to construct algorithms that find one or all 92 solutions using either iterative or recursive solutions. In fact, many textbooks that introduce recursion use the eight Queens problem as an illustrative example of the elegance of recursion. See, for instance, Wirth (1976).

Another elegant, but less well known solution, uses coroutines, one coroutine for each column of the Chessboard (Hanson [1976]). Let us call these coroutines Queen_1, Queen_2, etc. Note that Burroughs ALGOL allows us to declare an array of tasks such as

task array *QUEEN* [*1*:*8*];

The job of the jth coroutine task, that is, QUEEN [j], is to select a row i such that [i, j] becomes the position of the jth Queen. If coroutine QUEEN [j] succeeds, it must *continue* QUEEN [j + 1] to try to place the [j + 1]st Queen, while if QUEEN [j] fails, it must *continue* QUEEN [j − 1] to try to find another possible row for the Queen in column [j − 1].

For the coroutine solution described here, the top-level program must create eight nearly identical coroutines. They differ only in that each has a different (column) value j placed in the corresponding environment at the time it is created.

Figure 9-16a shows a top-level flowchart and Figure 9-16b shows a procedure flowchart q, used as the starting procedure for each of the eight coroutines in the array QUEEN. A top-level loop of calls creates the array of coroutine environments. The top level then *continues* coroutine QUEEN_1, which in turn *continues* its successor QUEEN_2, etc. While executing in QUEEN_j, control may *continue* "forward" to QUEEN_{j+1}, or *continue* "backward" to QUEEN_{j-1}. A solution is reached when QUEEN_8 has found a valid position (i, 8).

a. Complete a Burroughs ALGOL program corresponding to the flowcharts and legends of Figure 9-16. You are free to invent the details needed for coding boxes 1 of Top and 4, 6, and 9 of procedure q. These details depend on how you decide to keep the records on the positions selected for the Queens and on other information representing the condition of the chessboard at a given point in the computation.

   Wirth (1976) suggests that there be four arrays to keep track of the progress toward a solution and to promote efficiency of execution. In Algol terms, these arrays might be declared as follows:

   integer array *rowofcol* [*1*:*8*];
   Boolean array *onrow* [*1*:*8*];
   Boolean array *onSWdiag* [*2*:*16*];
   Boolean array *onSEdiag* [−*7*:*7*];

   The solution array rowofcol need not be initialized. The element rowofcol_j is assigned the value i to represent a Queen placed in row i of column j. The array element onrow_i denotes the absence or presence of a Queen on the ith row. The array elements onSWdiag_k and onSEdiag_l denote the absence or presence of a Queen on the kth ↙ − diagonal and *l*th ↘ − diagonal, respectively. There are fifteen ↙ − diagonals and fifteen ↘ − diagonals, and they are indexed 2 through 16, and −7 through 7, respectively. These indexes correspond to the range of row–column sums i + j, and to the range of row–column differences i − j, respectively. These sums and differences are constant for each respective ↙ − and ↘ − diagonal.

b. Produce an execution snapshot that depicts the state of execution the first time box 12 of q is executed. The snapshot in Figure 9-11 should serve as a useful guide.

c. Modify the flowcharts in Figure 9-16 so that all possible solutions (not necessarily distinct from the point of view of symmetry) will be printed out when the new algorithm is executed.

9-5 REFERENCES AND SUGGESTIONS FOR FURTHER READING

A valuable general discussion of tasking appears in Berry (1971). Unfortunately, the literature on Burroughs ALGOL, the language vehicle for this chapter, is quite limited, although the language itself is available on Burroughs B6700-type computers at many universities and other organizations. Burroughs (1971) is a full reference manual for Burroughs ALGOL. Organick (1973) illustrates the language and describes the organization of the B6700 computer system designed to support both asynchronous and coroutine tasks such as those coded in Burroughs ALGOL. Both asynchronous *and* coroutine task features were incorporated into SAIL, an Algol-based language for artificial intelligence applications, by Feldman *et al.* (1972), who in turn had been influenced by the powerful tasking features of Burroughs ALGOL.

The language PL/I [see Beech (1970), Wegner (1968), and Pratt (1975)] is a block-structured language partly derived from Algol. PL/I is the only other general-purpose, widely used language that offers a full set of asynchronous tasking constructs but it does not contain primitives for coroutines.

The language SIMULA 67 [see Birtwistle *et al.* (1973)] was probably the first Algol-based language to support coroutines, although it does not support asynchronous tasks. SIMULA 67 is well documented and has been adapted to a variety of computers. A product of the Norwegian University Computing Center in Oslo, SIMULA 67 is an outstanding achievement. The SIMULA 67 coroutine structure, and the *class* construct used to represent it, have had a profound influence on other language designers, for example, Brinch Hansen (1975) with the language CONCURRENT PASCAL, Griswold and Hanson (1977) [and Hanson and Griswold (1978)] with the language SL5, and Goldberg and Kay (1976) with the language SMALL TALK.

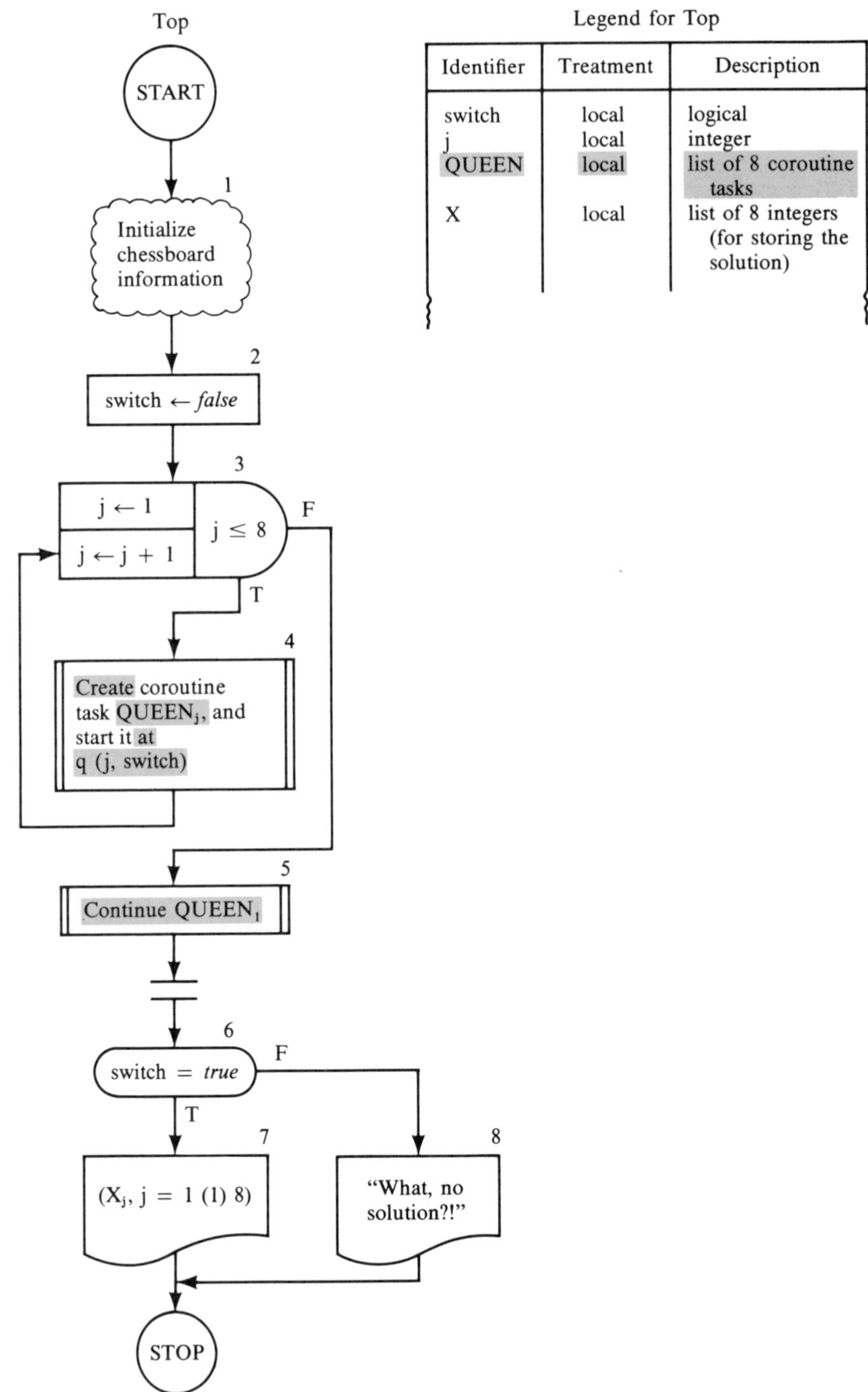

Legend for Top

Identifier	Treatment	Description
switch	local	logical
j	local	integer
QUEEN	local	list of 8 coroutine tasks
X	local	list of 8 integers (for storing the solution)

Figure 9-16a. **One solution to the eight Queens problem using coroutines.**

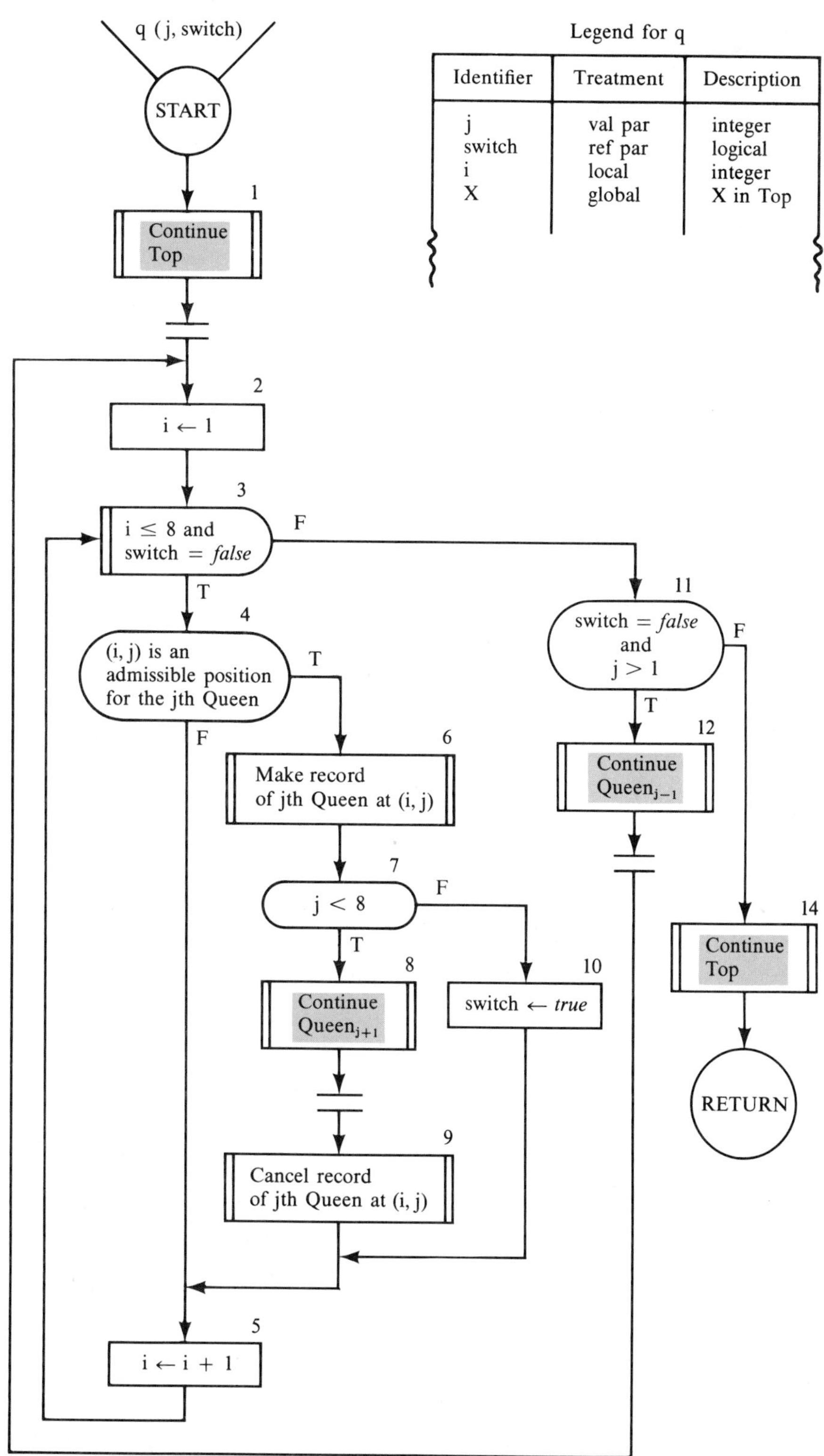

Identifier	Treatment	Description
j	val par	integer
switch	ref par	logical
i	local	integer
X	global	X in Top

Figure 9-16b

10 PASCAL

10-1 INTRODUCTION

Pascal, one of the most popular offshoots of Algol, was designed and developed by Niklaus Wirth in the early 1970s. Previously Wirth had contributed a series of augmentations to ALGOL 60, leading up to his most recent design. Pascal is widely used, primarily in university computer science departments. Just as Burroughs ALGOL is important for its development of multisequencing primitives (see Chapter 9), Pascal is interesting for its powerful data structure facilities.

We are well aware that the expressive power of a language derives largely from its data types, its data structuring declaratives, and its primitive operations on data structures. The first high-level languages were comparatively weak in such facilities. The early emphasis was to provide powerful control structures such as procedures and various parameter mechanisms, block structuring, and later coroutines and asynchronous tasks. As storage costs dropped, allowing programs random access to an ever larger work space, the importance of good data structure facilities grew apace.

Pascal belongs to a new class of languages reflecting the importance of data management in the expressive power provided, enabling the programmer to deal more efficiently and precisely with the processing and management of data. In this regard Pascal utilizes certain ideas and features of Cobol and PL/I, ALGOL W, and ALGOL 68. Cobol, still the most widely used high-level language, was the first to provide data structure declarations. Not only did PL/I provide similar declarative facilities, but it also incorporated a richer set of primitives to manipulate components of data structures. Pascal incorporates most of the data facilities of Cobol and PL/I, but offers a new richness of expression set in an Algol-like framework.

Because Pascal programs have the syntax and semantic structure of an Algol-like language, we should be able to appreciate Pascal quickly and easily, provided we take advantage of our earlier study of Algol. Since the two languages in both syntax and semantics are more alike than they are different, we shall concentrate on the differences first.

The principal differences lie in

a. primitive data types (Section 10-2)
b. data structures (defined types) formed from the primitive types (Section 10-3)
c. program structure (Section 10-4)
d. constructs of structured programming (Section 10-5)
e. parameter treatment (Section 10-6)
f. input/output (Section 10-7)

Each of these differences will be discussed in brief and informal terms in the indicated section of this chapter. As is the case for all the languages treated in this book, a more complete description of the language Pascal is to be found elsewhere, as may be noted from the references cited at the end of this chapter.*

10-2 PRIMITIVE DATA TYPES

A primitive data type is a finite, ordered set of values. Not only do primitive types include the familiar Boolean, integer, and real, from Algol, as well as type char (for *character*), but other primitive types can be defined just by enumerating the values belonging to the type.† For example:

(2.1) **var** *A, B* : *integer*;
(2.2) **var** *P, r, s* : *Boolean*;
(2.3) **var** *T*: *real*; *name, address*: *char*;
(2.4) **type** *card_suit* = (*Clubs, Diamonds, Hearts, Spades*);
(2.5) **type** *color* = (*blue, yellow, red*);
(2.6) **type** *day_of_year* = *1..365*;
(2.6a) **var** *pile_1, pile_2, pile_3, pile_4*: *card_suit*;
hue1, hue2: *color*;
day_number: *day_of_year*;

Examples 2.1–2.3 correspond to the familiar declarations of Algol. Examples 2.4 and 2.5 illustrate defining a type by enumerating all the values belonging to the

*In the descriptions that follow, we have taken two minor "liberties" with the syntax out of a desire to make our illustrations more readable and more consistent with the dialect of Pascal that was available to the authors.

1. A Pascal identifier may not include connective underscore characters, but we shall use them. Thus we shall permit ourselves to write *day_of_year* in place of *dayofyear.*
2. We shall show program comments delimited with double quote marks, as "this is a comment," whereas Pascal requires the use of curley brackets, as {this is a comment.}.

†In Algol the number of primitive data types is fixed, and so for increased legibility these identifiers (**Boolean, integer,** and **real**) are printed in boldface along with other reserved words such as **if, for, begin,** and **end.** In Pascal the situation is different. Here the number of primitive data types and the choice of identifiers is essentially open ended and varies from program to program. The rule, therefore, in Pascal is that primitive data types are treated as ordinary identifiers. They are printed in italics.

type as an ordered sequence. Example 2.6 illustrates *subrange* notation, a shorthand for enumeration; the expression 1..365 is recognized by the Pascal compiler as the sequence 1, 2, 3, . . . , 364, 365 (a subset of the integers). Example 2.6a declares certain variables of type *card_suit*, *color*, and *day_of_year*, respectively. Thus the variables *pile_1*, *pile_2*, etc., are instances of type *card_suit*; *hue1* and *hue2* are instances of type *color*, etc.

Subrange notation is not confined to type integer, Boolean, or real, as can be seen from the following:

(2.7) **type** *day_of_week* = (*Sunday, Monday, Tuesday, Wednesday, Thursday, Friday, Saturday*);

(2.8) **type** *weekday* = *Monday..Friday*;

In (2.8) the type *weekday* is enumerated indirectly in subrange notation because the identifiers *Monday* and *Friday* have previously appeared in the enumeration of type *day_of_week*.

Constant Definitions

Pascal programs are easier to read and to modify because of a definition facility that permits the association of constants with meaningful identifiers. The prefix **const** precedes any sequence of constant definitions. For example

(2.9)

```
const pi = 3.1416;
      teachers = 'Mark_Rich_Elliott'; "the current ones"
      maxarg = 12;
      idlength = 10;
      pagelength = 256;
      printlimit = 18;
      reallength = 2; "BYTES"
      setlength = 16; "BYTES"
      max_string_length = 80; "CHARS"
      version_date = 'Feb.25,1976'; "date of this version"
```


Once a constant has been given a name, that name may be used anywhere in the program instead of the constant. When and if we decide to change this constant, we need to modify only the constant definition declaration even though the constant name may appear throughout the program.

The strings of characters bounded by double quote marks are comments.* A comment may appear anywhere in a Pascal program where a blank (not part of a character string) may be placed.

*See the first footnote on the preceding page.

10-3 STRUCTURED DATA TYPES

One can declare a data type whose structure is a composite of primitive (and structured) data types. Structured data types fall into certain major categories. Three of these are*

record   array   set

Records

Record types are used to describe treelike data structures where each node of the tree is named by a distinct selector name. (Students familiar with Cobol may recognize a certain similarity here.)

```
(3.1)    type  Date = record    day : 1..31;
                              month : 1..12;
                               year : 1000..2000
                    end
```

In (3.1) we declare that a record of type *Date* is a three-component structure whose individual components may be referred to by the selector names: *day, month,* and *year.* For example,

```
(3.2)    var  x, y, z: Date;
         .
         .
         .
           x.day := 7;
(3.3)    x.month := 5;
          x.year := 1976
```

Here the identifiers x, y, and z are declared as variables of type *Date.* Later, for example, the *month* component of x is assigned the value *5.* Note that the syntactic construction

x.month

uses the period to connect an identifier with its *field* selector. The identifier x is a variable of type *Date* by virtue of (3.2), and hence there is a three-compartment storage cell allocated for it, whereas the identifier *month* is not a variable but merely selects or *specifies* the compartment of a *Date* variable to which one wishes to refer.

In (3.4) below we have a more complex example of record structure. Here some of the individual components (or fields of the record) are themselves structure types. Thus *name* and *firstname* are of type *alfa,* an array of characters.

*A fourth one, files, is omitted from discussion in this chapter.

(We shall soon see how to define array types.) *Birthdate* is of type *Date,* whose structure has already been discussed, and *sex* and *marstatus* are primitive types.

```
(3.4)    type Person = record     name : alfa;
                              firstname : alfa;
                              birthdate : Date;
                                    sex : (male, female);
                              marstatus : (single, married,
                                           widowed, divorced)
                   end
```

A variable of type *Person* can have the following value:

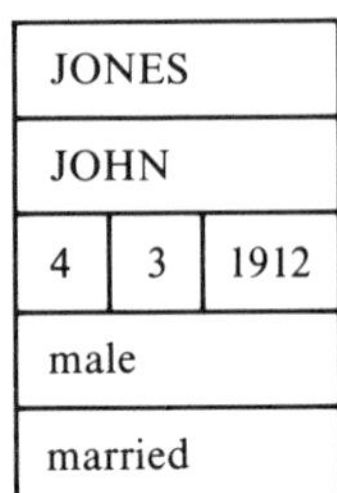

To assign a record value to a variable of type *Person,* we may write

```
(3.5)    var student: Person;
         .
         .
         .
(3.6)    student := Person ('JONES', 'JOHN', Date (4, 3, 1912),
                    male, married);
```

Of course, it is also possible to compose a record by writing out a sequence of assignments, for example,

```
(3.6')             student.name := 'JONES';
              student.firstname := 'JOHN';
          student.birthdate.day := 4;
        student.birthdate.month := 3;
         student.birthdate.year := 1912;
                    student.sex := male;
              student.marstatus := married;
```

To reduce the wordiness of (3.6'), Pascal provides the so-called **with** statement, which has the form

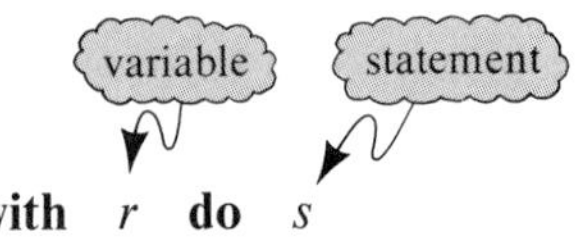

with *r* **do** *s*

Such a statement allows selector names for the variable *r* to be used without prefix within the statement *s.* These selectors are understood to refer to the variable *r*. Thus we may now rewrite (3.6') as

(3.6'')
```
with student do
   begin
            name := 'JONES';
       firstname := 'JOHN';
    birthdate.day := 4;
  birthdate.month := 3;
   birthdate.year := 1912;
              sex := male;
        marstatus := married
   end
```

or, since **with** statements may be nested, we may write

(3.6''')
```
with student do
   begin
         name := 'JONES';
    firstname := 'JOHN';
   with birthdate do
     begin
          day := 4;
        month := 3;
         year := 1912
     end;
          sex := male;
    marstatus := married
   end
```

Record Structure Variants

Variants in the substructure of a record may be declared using a **case** structure syntax. That is, it may be natural to define a record structure such that some fields are common to every record of the type, while other fields are present or not present according to some secondary criterion. For example, a record of type *Ship* may include fields that are common to every record of type *Ship,* such as *name, date commissioned, displacement tonnage, fuel capacity, crew size, speed,* and *flag,* independent of the ship's class and, in addition, may contain some fields that pertain only according to the class of the ship described. (There are passenger ships, cargo ships, tankers, etc.) In this instance *ship_class* is the secondary criterion that determines the *variant* parts of the record. Thus, for a record of a passenger ship, we may want to define a group of subfields such as

(*num_passengers*, *num_suites*, *num_cabins*, *num_restaurants*: *integer*;
first_class, *second_class*, *tourist*: *Boolean*);

while for a cargo ship we may want to define another group, such as

```
(materials_carried: (liquids, solids, mixed);
num_bulkheads: integer;
loading_days: real);
```

For example,

(3.7)
```
Type Ship = record
        name: alfa;
        commissioned: Date;
        tonnage, fuel_capacity,
          crew_size, knots: integer;
        flag: (Liberia, Panama, U.S., Greece,
          Finland, Norway, Taiwan, England,
          Germany, France);
        homeport: (New_York, Bergen, Hamburg,
          Liverpool, Athens, le_Havre, Helsinki);
        case ship_class: (passenger, cargo) of
          passenger: (num_passengers,
            num_suites,
            num_cabins,
            num_restaurants: integer;
            first_class,
            second_class,
            tourist: Boolean);
          cargo: (materials: (liquids, solids, mixed);
            num_bulkheads: integer;
            loading_days: real)
        end
      end
```

common part

variant part

Of course, there could be similar groups of fields for tankers, container ships, and other ship classes, if these were needed. For example,

(3.8)
```
case  ship_class: (passenger, cargo, tanker, container) of
      passenger: (⟨fields pertaining to passenger ships⟩);
          cargo: (⟨fields pertaining to cargo ships⟩);
         tanker: (⟨fields pertaining to tankers⟩);
      container: (⟨fields pertaining to container ships⟩;
end
```

An actual instance of this **case** structure begins with a field containing the ship_class value for this record, for example, cargo, and is followed by the fields pertaining to cargo ships.

The identifiers *passenger* and *cargo* are called *case selectors.* In general, a **case** structure allows us to distinguish among two or more variants using two or more case selectors. A related syntactical form is used for multiway branching, which is described in Section 10-5.

If we have declared *y* to be a variable of type *ship* as in (3.7), then we can refer to *y*'s component parts using the names

y.name
y.commissioned
y.tonnage
y.flag
y.homeport

and, if *y* is a passenger ship,

y.num_passengers,
y.num_suites,
etc.

or if *y* is a cargo ship,

y.materials
y.num_bulkheads,
etc.

Note that if *y.ship_class* contains the value *passenger,* it would be a logical error to fetch or store from/to *y.materials.* A similar error would arise if a reference is made to *y.num_suites* when *y.ship_class* contains the value *cargo.* (A Pascal compiler cannot catch this error, and so it must be caught, if at all, during run-time testing.) Of course, the *ship_class* field in each record of type *Ship* should contain the information that determines the applicable variant. So, when referencing the record *y,* we can predetermine which variant fields to access by executing a suitable **if** statement, for example,

if *y.ship_class* = *passenger* **then**. . . .

All the common fields of a record definition must appear *before* the fields of the variant part, and this rule was followed in (3.7), but there need not be any common part in a record definition. For example,

tag field
enumerated list of constituent types

```
(3.9)    type  Coordinate = record
                        case kind: (Cartesian, polar) of
                            Cartesian : (x, y: real);
                                polar : (r:real; phi:angle)
                   end
```

Here the set of values denoted by type *Coordinate is* really the *union* of the two types referred to as *Cartesian* and *polar.* Given an instance of a record of type *Coordinate,* we can determine whether it represents a *Cartesian* or *polar* pair by examining the current value of the *y.kind* field.

Arrays

Variables may be specified as arrays in declarations similar to Algol **array** declarations. For example,

(3.10) **var** *b*: **array** [*0..12*] **of** *integer*;

which denotes that *b* is a linear array of 13 components, which may be indexed by values in the subrange 0..12.

The code fragment in (3.11) declares that *M* and *N* are 10×5 matrices whose components are of type *real,* and later assigns the value of a particular element of *N* to a particular element of *M*.

```
(3.11)    var  M, N : array [1..10, 1..5] of real;
               .
               .
               .
               M [i, j] := N [j, i + 1];
```

But note that array types may be declared, leading to a more powerful array structuring than was available in ALGOL:

```
(3.12)    type  alfa  = array [1..12] of char;
(3.13)    type  Row   = array [1..10] of real;
(3.14)    type  sales = array [weekday] of integer;
(3.15)    var   Q, R:  array [1..17] of Row;
                street : alfa;
```

In (3.12) type *alfa,* a structure consisting of a linear array of 12 characters is declared, and then in (3.15) the variable *street* is declared to be of type *alfa.* In (3.13) type *Row* is declared as an array of type *real* and in (3.14) type *sales* is declared as an array of type *integer.* In (3.15) variables *Q* and *R* are declared to be arrays of 17 elements, each of which is of type *Row;* hence *Q* and *R* are also 17×10 matrices, whose elements can be addressed either as entire rows, or as individual matrix elements, for example,

```
(3.16)    Q [3]      := R [4];
(3.17)    R [i] [j]  := Q [j] [i + 1];
```

where (3.16) assigns the fourth row of *R* to the third row of *Q,* while (3.17) assigns a particular element of *Q*'s *j*th row to a particular element of *R*'s *i*th row.

Finally, note that the type *sales* in (3.14) is a structure consisting of an array of integers whose elements are indexed by values of type *weekday.* Thus, if type *weekday* is defined as in (2.8), then the valid indices for an array of type *sales* are *Monday* through *Friday.*

Set Structures

Sets of variables may be declared. If a variable *x* is declared as a set of type *T,* then the domain of values of *x* is the set of all subsets of *T,* which means that any subset of the elements of set *T,* including the empty set, is a valid value of *x*.

Examples

(3.18) **type** *integer_set* = **set of** *0..30*;

⋮

(3.19) **var** *x, y*: *integer_set*;

Line (3.19) states that *x* and *y* are of type *integer_set*. A value of type *integer_set* is any subset of the values 0 through 30.

(3.20) **type** *attributes* = (*corner_lot, near_car_line, close_in, shade_trees, nearby_shops*);
(3.21) **type** *property_description* = **set of** *attributes*;
(3.22) **var** *prop_list*: *array* [*1..12*] **of** *property_description*;

Line (3.22) states that *prop_list* is an array of 12 elements, each of type *property_description*. An element of type *property_description* is a subset of the attributes enumerated on line (3.20).

Some possible assignments to *x, y,* and *prop_list* are illustrated below:

(3.23) *x* := [*1, 4, 16*];
(3.24) *y* := [ ];
(3.25) *prop_list* [*2*] := [*corner_lot, nearby_shops*];
(3.26) *prop_list* [*7*] := [*near_car_line*];
(3.27) *prop_list* [*12*] := [*corner_lot..nearby_shops*];

Here line (3.23) assigns to *x* the subset of integer values 1, 4, 16. Line (3.24) assigns to *y* the empty set. Line (3.25) assigns to *prop_list* [*2*] the *property_description* consisting of the set of two attributes, namely, *corner_lot* and *nearby_shops*. Line (3.27) assigns to *prop_list* [*12*] the entire set of *property_description* attributes.

Operators associated with set types are

Symbol	Meaning	Relative precedence
*	set intersection	highest
+	set union	next highest
−	set difference	next highest
<=	is a subset of	lowest
>=	is a superset of	lowest
in	is a member of	lowest

If *X* and *Y* are sets of integers, and if *j* is an integer, then the following are valid expressions whose types are given on the right:

X * *Y*	**set of** integer
X + *Y*	**set of** integer
X − *Y*	**set of** integer
X <= *Y*	Boolean
X >= *Y*	Boolean
j **in** *X*	Boolean

In the computer store, sets can be represented by bit strings. For example, each element of *prop_list* above may be represented by a string of five bits, each bit indicating the presence or absence of one of the five attributes enumerated on line (3.20). Thus the value assigned to *prop_list* [*2*], as indicated on line (3.25), would be represented as

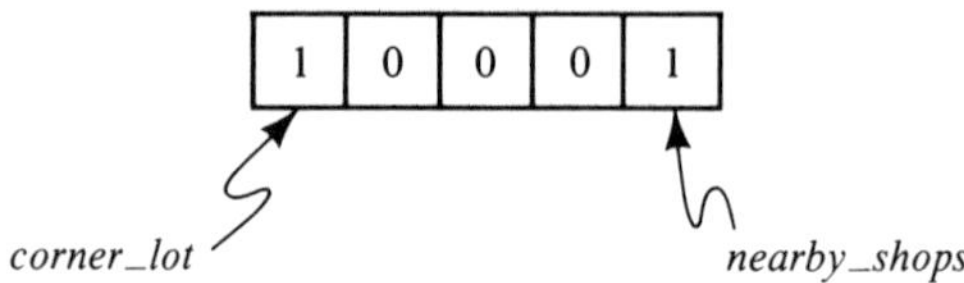

With this type of representation the set operations can be implemented by logical and masking operations, which are available as primitive operation codes in most computers. Thus, to determine the set union indicated by the expression

prop_list [*2*] + *prop_list* [*7*]

the computer need only apply the logical operation *OR* to the two 5-bit fields as follows:

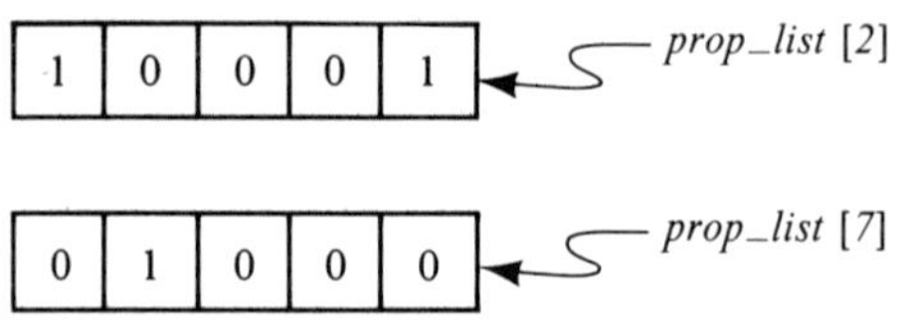

to obtain

1	1	0	0	1	← set union of above

Pointer Types

It is possible to explicitly declare a variable to be a pointer to a particular type of data. For example,

(3.28) **type** *int_ptr* = ↑ *integer*
(3.29) **var** *q*, *r*, *s*: *int_ptr*; *i*:*integer*; *t*, *u*:*Boolean*;

Here the variables *q*, *r*, and *s* are declared to be of type *int_ptr*, which in turn is a type consisting of pointer values restricted to point to variables of type *integer*. This restriction is enforced by the computer and prevents a programmer from using pointers indiscriminantly. Thus, the assignment,

(3.30) *q* := *s*;

would be considered valid by the Pascal compiler, but the assignment

(3.31) *r* := *i*;

would be invalid since the value of *i* is not a pointer to an integer. On the other hand, the assignment

(3.32) *i* := *r* ↑;

will be accepted, since it states that the integer variable *i* is assigned the (integer) value that *r* points to. (The notation $p\uparrow$, where *p* is of type *pointer*, means *the value that p points to.*) Note that at run time, neither (3.30) nor (3.32) will make sense unless *s* and *r*, respectively, have been previously assigned meaningful pointer values.

A value for a type pointer variable is generated whenever a data item is dynamically allocated (from the "heap"). To allocate from the heap, one makes an explicit call on the built-in procedure called *new*. For example,

```
(3.33)   type trans_ptr   = ↑ transaction;
(3.34)   type transaction = record
                              name: alfa;
                              acct_no: integer;
                              purchase_date: Date;
                              purchase_amt: integer;
                              next_trans: trans_ptr
                           end

(3.35)   var  p, q, r: trans_ptr;
           .
           .
           .
(3.36)   new (p); new (q); new (r);
```

Here each call on *new* in (3.36) allocates a record of type *transaction* from the heap. A pointer to the first of these records is assigned to *p*, a pointer to the second to *q*, and a pointer to the third to *r*. Note also that a record of type *transaction* has the component named *next_trans* declared as of type *trans_ptr*, a pointer to a *transaction*, so that *transaction* records can be linked together in a chain (as a "one-way linked list"), using statements such as

```
(3.37)   p ↑ .next_trans := q;
         q ↑ .next_trans := r;
         r ↑ .next_trans := nil;
```

Executing this sequence will yield the structure

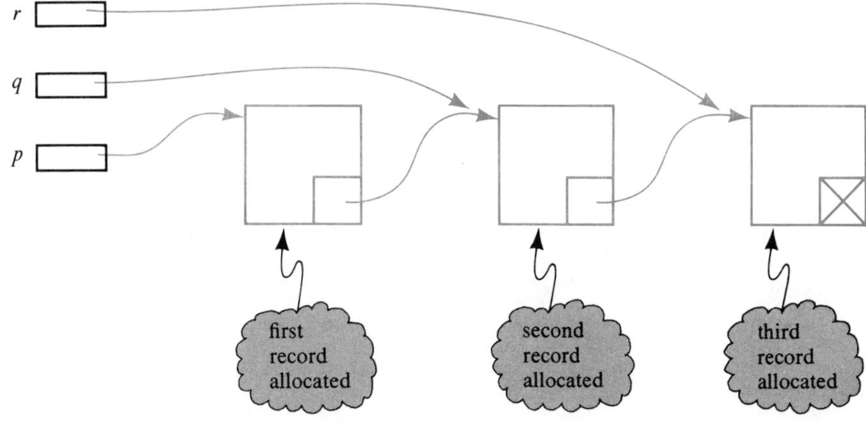

Note here that **nil** is a special key word in Pascal meaning *a pointer to nothing at all.*

Several other remarks are worth noting about pointers.

1. The only operation defined on pointers is equality (and inequality) and so the assignments

(3.38) $t := q = r;$ $\qquad u := q <> s;$

make sense. That is, the Boolean variables t and u are assigned values *true* or *false*, according to the truth or falsity of $q = r$ and $q <> s$, respectively.

2. The ability to reference a value pointed to by a variable of type *pointer* can be exploited in various useful ways. We have already noted the technique for linking records into a structure. Arbitrary graphs can also be represented using this technique; the pointer fields of a node N represent edges emanating from N and the remaining fields represent the properties of N. Other illustrations of the ↑ accessing are

(3.39)
```
with p ↑ .purchase_date do
  begin
      day := 3;
    month := 2;
     year := 1929
  end
```

Also, assuming the linked list achieved by executing the steps of (3.37), comparisons can be made of like fields in pairs of records. Thus expressions like

(3.40) *q* ↑ *.purchase_amt* ≤ *r* ↑ *.purchase_amt*;

or, equivalently,

(3.41) *q* ↑ *.purchase_amt* ≤ *q* ↑ *.next_trans* ↑ *.purchase_amt*;

could be used to compare transactions according to amounts purchased.

10-4 PROGRAM STRUCTURE

A Pascal program has a structure similar to an Algol procedure. It begins with a program heading, is followed by a block, and is terminated with a period. A program heading is similar to the procedure heading of Algol, for example,

⟨program heading⟩ ::= **program** ⟨program name⟩⟨parameter list⟩;

except that the word **program** is used instead of **procedure.** The block that follows the program heading consists of all the declarations in a required partial ordering followed by a compound statement. The declarations must be ordered into three groups, one after the other, as follows:

1. constant declarations and type declarations,
2. variable declarations,
3. procedure and function declarations.

The ordering within any one group is immaterial. Syntax charts that summarize what we have just said are given in Figure 10-1. Items in rectangles denote non-terminal elements defined in other syntax charts, while items in circles or ovals denote terminal elements of the Pascal language.

Figure 10-2 shows a very simple Pascal program to illustrate the top-level structure of a program. The example program determines the first term of the

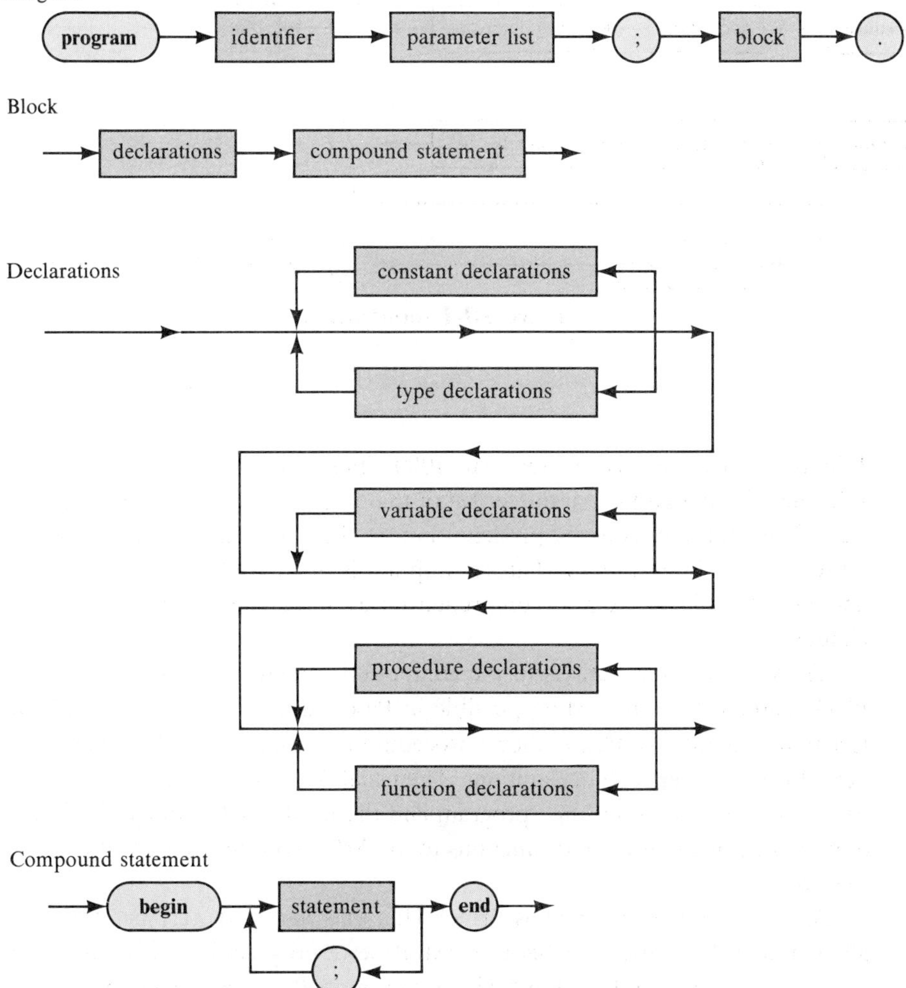

Figure 10-1. **Partial syntax of a Pascal program.**

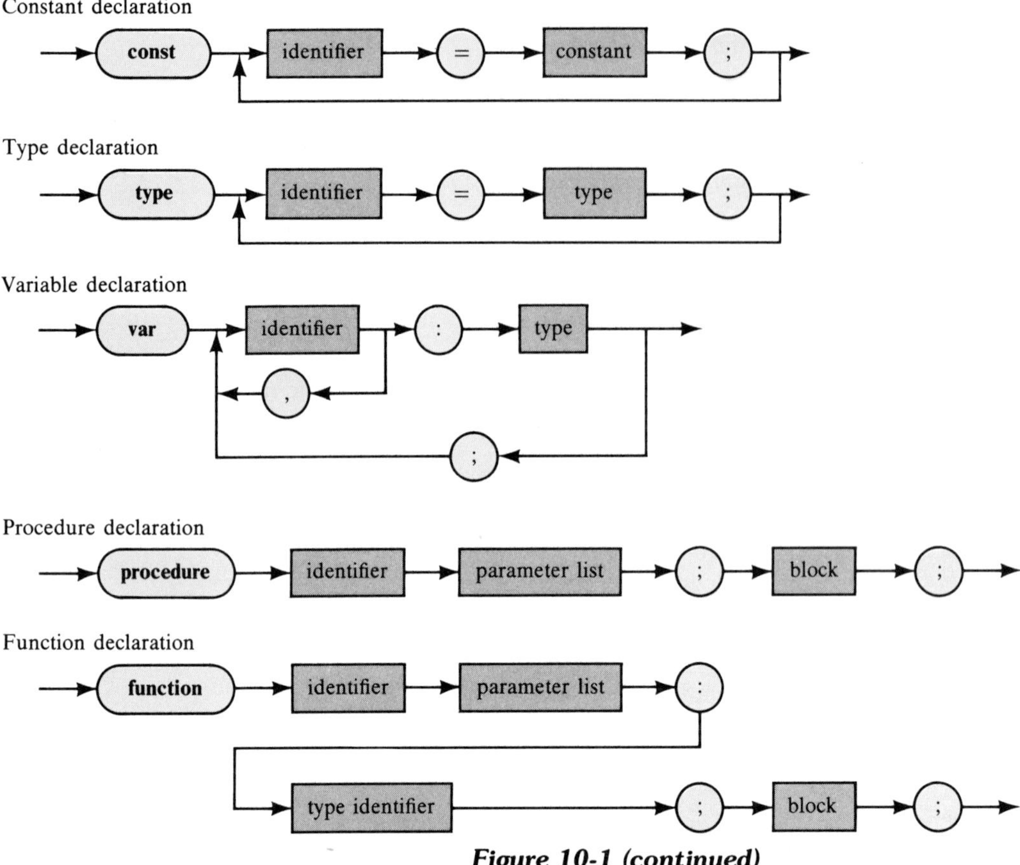

Figure 10-1 (continued)

Fibonacci series that is greater than 1000. (Please refer to Figure 1-1 for a refresher.) Note that the parameter list of the program heading is empty in this case. The program assumes predefinition of the procedure *write_int,* which writes out one integer value. This assumption is made to defer details of input and output until later. A more comprehensive example appears at the end of this chapter.

There are no declarations in the compound statement portion of a Pascal block, and so the only nesting possible in Pascal is within the procedure and function declarations. Pascal allows procedure and function declarations to be nested within other such declarations. The usual Algol scope rules apply to the nesting of procedures within a program and these rules determine accessibility of variables, procedures, and functions to the MC executing at a given point in the program.

Some Pascal dialects such as Brinch Hansen's SEQUENTIAL PASCAL do not allow nested declarations. A SEQUENTIAL PASCAL program has a *flat* structure, and each procedure or function declaration is globally accessible everywhere in the program. That is, every declared procedure or function in such an imple-

```
program fibonacci;
  var next_latest, latest, sum:integer;
  begin "initialize"
    begin next_latest := 0;
               latest := 1;
               sum := 0
    end;
    while sum ≤ 1000 do
      begin
           sum := latest + next_latest;
           next_latest := latest;
           latest := sum
      end;
    write_int (sum)
end.
```

Figure 10-2. **A very simple Pascal program.**

mentation can be called from the main program or from any other procedure or function.

Suppose, for such a dialect, the compiler is designed to scan the text only once. Then there are complications. For example, if a procedure or function *P* refers to another procedure or function *Q* whose declaration has not yet been encountered (as would be the case if the body of *P* calls *Q*, which in turn calls *P*, giving mutually recursive procedures), it is necessary to supply a dummy declaration for the routine whose declaration has not yet been encountered. A dummy declaration usually contains the key word **forward** in place of the block, as suggested in Figure 10-3. A program structure involving mutually recursive procedures *P* and *Q* would then contain three declarations. For example,

procedure *Q* ⟨parameter list⟩; **forward**;
procedure *P* ⟨parameter list⟩; ⟨block of procedure *P*⟩;
procedure *Q*; ⟨block of procedure *Q*⟩;

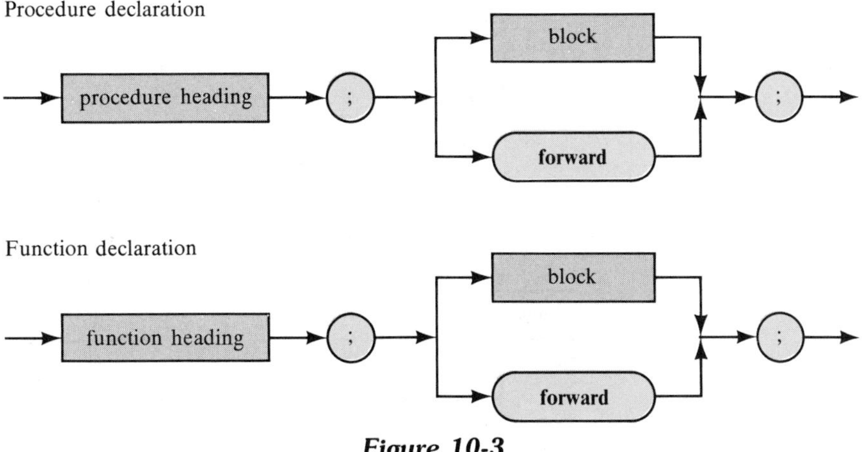

Figure 10-3

10-5 CONSTRUCTS FOR STRUCTURED PROGRAMMING

Pascal was designed to encourage programmers to use good structure. Thus in some dialects, such as SEQUENTIAL PASCAL, there are no **go to** statements and hence no statement labels, either. (Pascal itself has both **go to**'s and labels, as in Algol.) The compound statement portion of a Pascal block has the same structure as the compound statement of Algol:

```
begin
   statement 1;
   statement 2;
      .
      .
      .
   statement n
end
```

that is, a sequence of statements executed in order, from top to bottom. Execution of the last statement constitutes termination of the program or a return from the procedure or function, as the case may be. Hence, as in Algol, there is no need for a stop or return statement in Pascal, and none exists.

Of course, a statement may be a simple imperative statement, a selection statement, a loop structure, or any sequence of these, that is, a compound statement.

(1) *Simple imperative statements* include assignment and procedure call statements, which include calls to procedures for input and output.

(2) *Selection statements* include **if then, if then else** constructs for one- or two-way selection, and **case** statements for one-, two-, three-, or higher-way selection.

A **case** statement has the form shown in Figure 10-4. The ⟨expression⟩ to be evaluated must be identical to the value of one of the component selectors Cl,

Figure 10-4

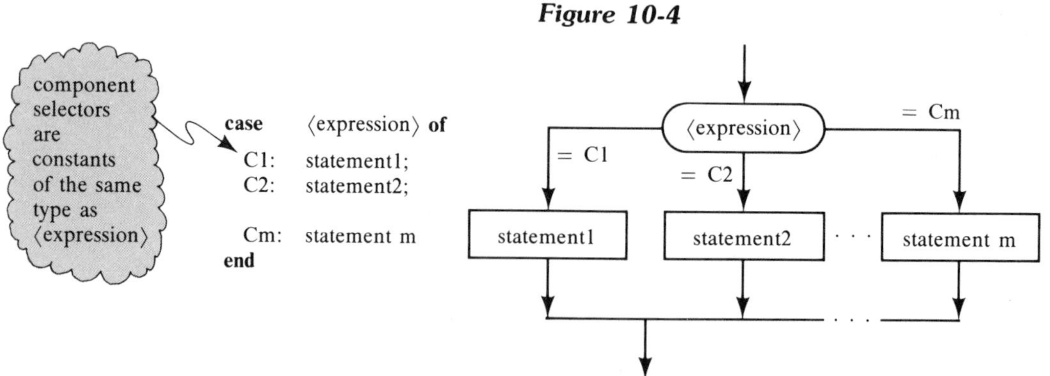

C2, . . . , Cm. If the value of ⟨expression⟩ equals Ci, then statement i is executed. Any selected statement may be a compound statement.

(3) *Loop structures* for definite and indefinite iteration use a **for** statement similar to the one in Algol and **while** and **repeat until** statements. The Pascal **for** statement is confined to step sizes of 1 or -1, and so the step size never appears explicitly. For example,

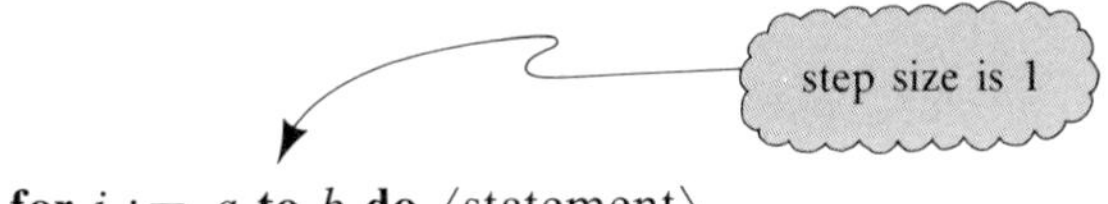

for *i* := *a* **to** *b* **do** ⟨statement⟩

or

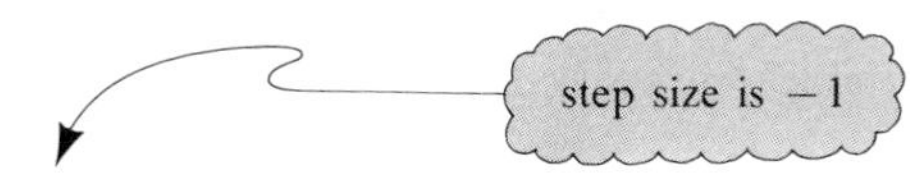

for *i* := *a* **downto** *b* **do** ⟨statement⟩

Indefinite iteration is achieved with either a **while** or a **repeat until** statement, for example,

while ⟨Boolean expression⟩ **do** ⟨statement⟩

or

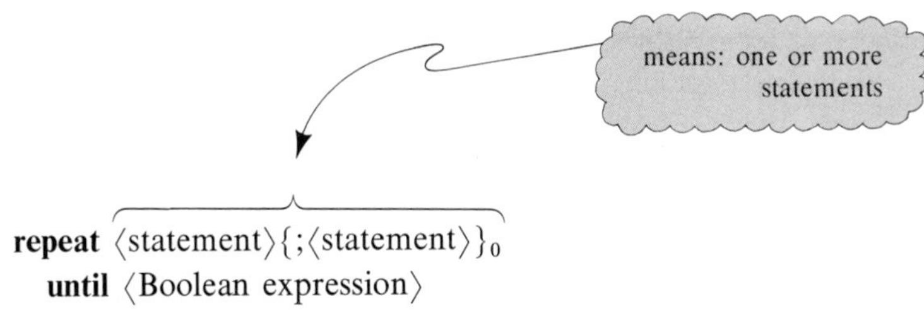

repeat ⟨statement⟩$\{$;⟨statement⟩$\}_0$
until ⟨Boolean expression⟩

Escape from a **while** statement can only occur when ⟨Boolean expression⟩ is *false*, whereas escape from a **repeat until** statement can only occur when ⟨Boolean expression⟩ is *true*.

Statements are separated by the semicolon or by grouping marks such as **begin end,** or **repeat until** pairs.

10-6 PARAMETER SPECIFICATION AND TREATMENT

The treatment of each parameter of a procedure or function is established by its specification as an element in the parameter list. Parameters are specified either as reference or value. A reference parameter must be preceded by the key word **var** to denote a variable parameter, that is, a parameter whose matching argument value can be assigned a new value during execution of the procedure. Functions may not have variable parameters, thus guaranteeing that the invocation of a function can have no side effects except those caused by assigning values to global variables.

Examples are

(6.1) **procedure** *get_token* (**var** *id* : *alfa*; *line* : *integer*);

(6.2) **function** *cons* (*l*, *r* : *e_ptr*) : *e_ptr*;

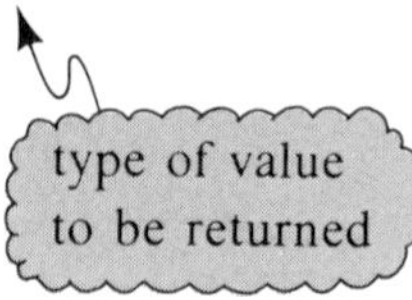

Line (6.1) is a heading for the procedure named *get_token*. It has two parameters, *id* and *line*. The first parameter is to be called by reference, by virtue of the prefix **var,** while the second parameter, *line*, is to be called by value. The parameter *id* is of type *alfa* and parameter *line* is of type *integer*. Line (6.2) is a heading for a value-returning function named *cons*, which has two parameters, *l* and *r*, each of type *e_ptr*. A function heading also specifies the type of the value to be returned, in this case a value of type *e_ptr*. (Readers may wish to consider how such a function may be defined to simulate the action of the Lisp CONS function.)

Pascal is known as a language with *strong typing*. The compiler checks each call on a function or procedure to see if the type of each argument properly matches the specified type of its corresponding parameter.* Failure to match in this way leads to a fatal error. In some dialects, such as in SEQUENTIAL PASCAL, one can relax this compatibility constraint to a certain extent. For example, prefixing a specified parameter type with the key word **univ,** for example,

(6.3) **procedure** *get_token* (**var** *id* : **univ** *alfa*; *line* : *integer*);

would indicate that the parameter *id* may match any corresponding argument whose storage structure is compatible with a value of type *alfa*. A **univ** prefix would allow a match, for example, between an argument of type *real* and a parameter of type *integer*, so long as the amount of storage allocated for each type is the same.†

The syntax charts defining procedure heading and parameter list are given in Figure 10-5. The charts in this figure show the following:

1. A parameter list may be empty.
2. A parameter may represent a variable argument (if so it may be called by reference using the prefix **var**).

*A subtle but important exception is discussed at the end of this section.

†In SEQUENTIAL PASCAL the **univ** prefix may not, however, be applied to a parameter when it or its matching argument is a data item that contains a pointer type as a component. Generally speaking an inexperienced programmer should avoid the use of the **univ** prefix, since its advantage is mainly one of efficiency.

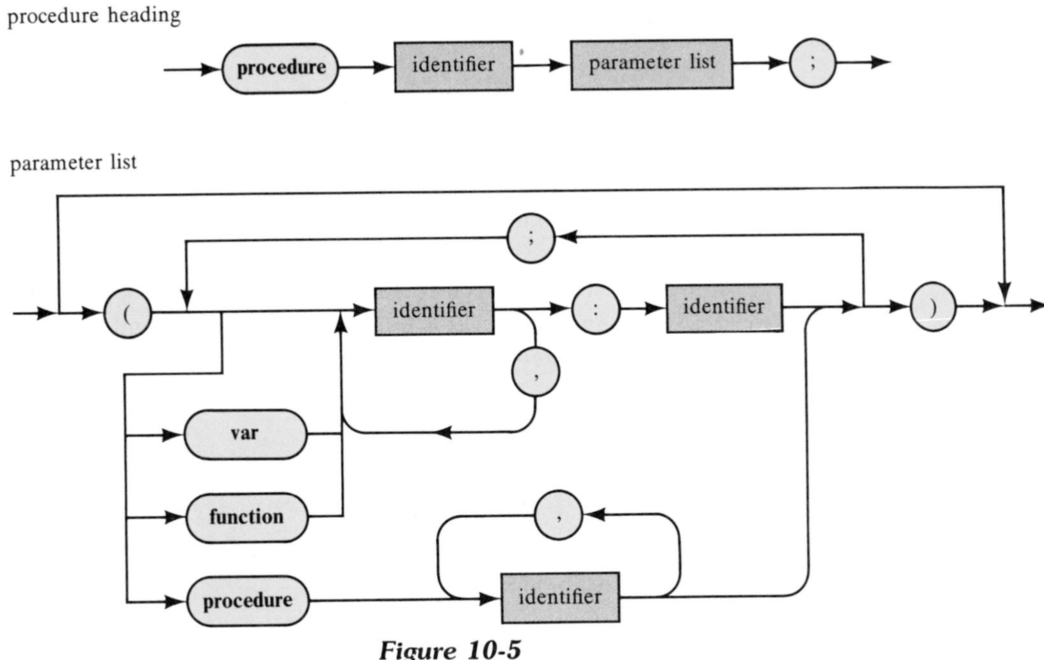

Figure 10-5

3. A parameter may also be an identifier intended to match a function or procedure argument. Such a parameter must be prefixed by the word **function** or **procedure.** Moreover, a function parameter must be followed by its type. For example,

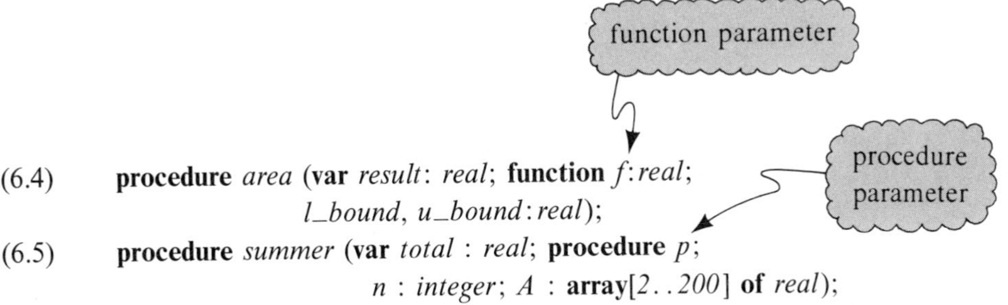

(6.4) **procedure** *area* (**var** *result*: *real*; **function** *f*:*real*;
l_bound, *u_bound*:*real*);

(6.5) **procedure** *summer* (**var** *total* : *real*; **procedure** *p*;
n : *integer*; *A* : **array**[*2..200*] **of** *real*);

Note, however, that neither a function parameter nor a procedure parameter is followed by the types of its respective parameters. As a result an important kind of type checking cannot be done by a Pascal compiler but must be done at run time: Consider a call on procedure *Q* from procedure *P*, with a function (or procedure) argument *F* that is matched to the function (or procedure) parameter *FF* in *Q*. A Pascal compiler cannot check that the arguments used in calls on *FF* in the body of *Q* properly match the declared parameters of *F*. [The only language in (reasonably) wide use today designed to permit the compiler to make a complete type check is ALGOL 68.]

10-7 INPUT/OUTPUT

The facilities for input and output in Pascal are left in the hands of the system implementer. In this section we discuss and illustrate the approach taken in SEQUENTIAL PASCAL, whose input/output facilities are quite primitive; all fancier facilities must be provided by users in the form of procedures and functions defined for particular needs.

There are two built-in procedures; one for input, called *read*, which reads the next character from the input stream (for example, card reader), and one for output called *write*, which writes one character to the output stream (for example, line printer).

The procedure heading for *read* is

procedure *read* (**var** *C* : *char*);

The procedure heading for *write* is

procedure *write* (*C* : *char*);

The best way to see what *read* and *write* are good for is to compose some more useful input output procedures that make use of *read* and *write*. We do this in the examples that follow.

Examples

1 We shall define a procedure *read_card* that transfers an 80-column card image into a buffer array of characters:

```
type cardbuffer = array [1..80] of char;
procedure read_card (var card : cardbuffer);
  var i : integer;
  begin for i := 1 to 80 do read (card [i]) end;
```

2 To write a line on the printer we need to specify that the printer should skip to a new line and reset its buffer pointer to print position 1. This is done simply by calling *write* with the special newline identifier *NL*, which is a predefined constant that provides the proper signal to the operating system's output routines, that is,

write (*NL*);

NL is a control code of type *char*.

Now, to fill the system's output buffer (with up to 132 characters for the line), it is necessary only to issue up to 132 calls on *write* and then issue another newline signal. This can be done using a procedure that we may wish to define ourselves. For example, the procedure *writetext* (Figure 10-6) may be defined to take as its argument an array of up to 132 characters and transfer these one at a time to the system's output buffer via calls to *write*. In case we wish to print fewer than 132 characters from the array argument, an unprintable character may be used. The symbol for this sentinel,

```
type line = array [1 . . 132] of char;
procedure writetext (text: line);
  var i : integer;
    begin i := 1;
      while (text [i] <> NUL) & (i ≤ 132) do
        begin
          write (text [i]);
          i := i + 1
        end;
      write (NL)
end;
```

Figure 10-6

NUL, is also predefined. [In this dialect of Pascal the ampersand symbol (&) is used in place of the logical operator **and.**] To illustrate use of this procedure, Figure 10-7 shows a sample piece of code to print a 12-character line having the form

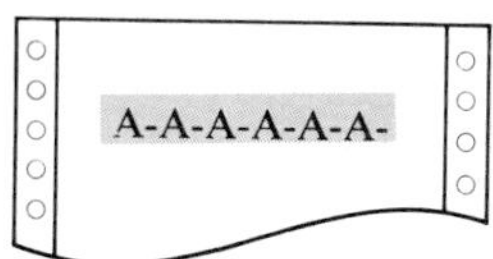

The procedure *writetext* is also useful for printing string constants directly. A string constant, that is, any string of m characters bounded by single quote marks, is regarded by the Pascal compiler as a one-dimensional array of m characters. Thus we may also call *writetext* by

writetext ('*A-A-A-A-A-A-*');

if we wish, but there is one problem here. We need to be able to force the *NUL* character, which is unprintable, to be the thirteenth character of the string, to force the line printer to reset for a new line after printing the printable characters of the current line.

```
var l : line ; j : integer ;
for j := 1 to 6 do
  begin
    l[2 * j - 1] := 'A' ; l[2 * j] := '-'
  end
  l[13] := NUL;
writetext(l)
```

Figure 10-7

The Sequential Pascal convention for representing unprintable characters is quite primitive (and nasty!). An unprintable character is represented by its integer equivalent bounded on the left by (: and on the right by :). Thus the NUL character, whose integer code is zero, may be represented as the character constant

'(:*0*:)'

Now, to guarantee printing only the string constant we wish and no more, we merely add this "phony" character to the end of our string constant, for example,

writetext ('*A-A-A-A-A-A*-(:*0*:) ');

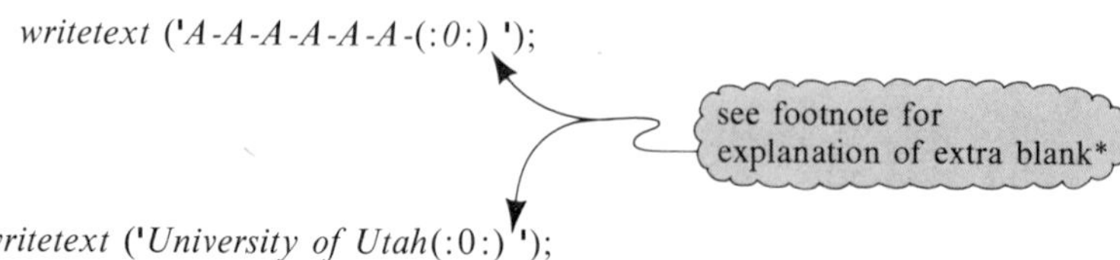

or

writetext ('*University of Utah*(:0:) ');

Since the Sequential Pascal procedures *read* and *write* operate only on single-character arguments, from and to the input and output streams, other user-defined procedures will be required to convert a value of type *char* to an integer and vice versa. Table 10-1 shows the integer codes used by Sequential Pascal for the ASCII character set. To assist users in this task, two built-in functions have been defined:

function *ord* (*ch* : *char*) : *integer*;

and

function *chr* (*x* : *integer*) : *char*;

The function *ord* returns the *integer code equivalent* to the given character *ch*, and the function *chr* returns the character value of the given integer *x*. For example, the function reference

ord ('%')

returns the integer value 37 (See Table 10-1). The function reference

chr (*47*)

returns the character '/' as its value.

Ord will prove useful in converting input strings consisting of decimal characters to values of type *integer*. *Chr* will prove useful in the reverse operation of converting values of type *integer* to strings of decimal characters for output.

*Another special requirement of Sequential Pascal is observed in the above. For this implementation string constants must be of even length since the system is designed for a machine that packs two characters per word.

TABLE 10-1
ASCII Character Set

0	nul	32		64	@	96	
1	soh	33	!	65	A	97	a
2	stx	34	"	66	B	98	b
3	etx	35	#	67	C	99	c
4	eot	36	$	68	D	100	d
5	enq	37	%	69	E	101	e
6	ack	38	&	70	F	102	f
7	bel	39	'	71	G	103	g
8	bs	40	(	72	H	104	h
9	ht	41	)	73	I	105	i
10	lf	42	*	74	J	106	j
11	vt	43	+	75	K	107	k
12	ff	44	,	76	L	108	l
13	cr	45	−	77	M	109	m
14	so	46	.	78	N	110	n
15	si	47	/	79	O	111	o
16	dle	48	0	80	P	112	p
17	dc1	49	1	81	Q	113	q
18	dc2	50	2	82	R	114	r
19	dc3	51	3	83	S	115	s
20	dc4	52	4	84	T	116	t
21	nak	53	5	85	U	117	u
22	syn	54	6	86	V	118	v
23	etb	55	7	87	W	119	w
24	can	56	8	88	X	120	x
25	em	57	9	89	Y	121	y
26	sub	58	:	90	Z	122	z
27	esc	59	;	91	[	123	{
28	fs	60	<	92	\	124	|
29	gs	61	=	93	]	125	}
30	rs	62	>	94	^	126	¬
31	us	63	?	95	–	127	del

SEQUENTIAL PASCAL Summary

Table 10-2 is a condensed version of the foregoing highlights of Pascal as captured by the SEQUENTIAL PASCAL implementation. A few of the details reflect the particular implementation, but most of it faithfully represents the spirit and form of Pascal proper.

TABLE 10-2
Syntactic Summary for SEQUENTIAL PASCAL

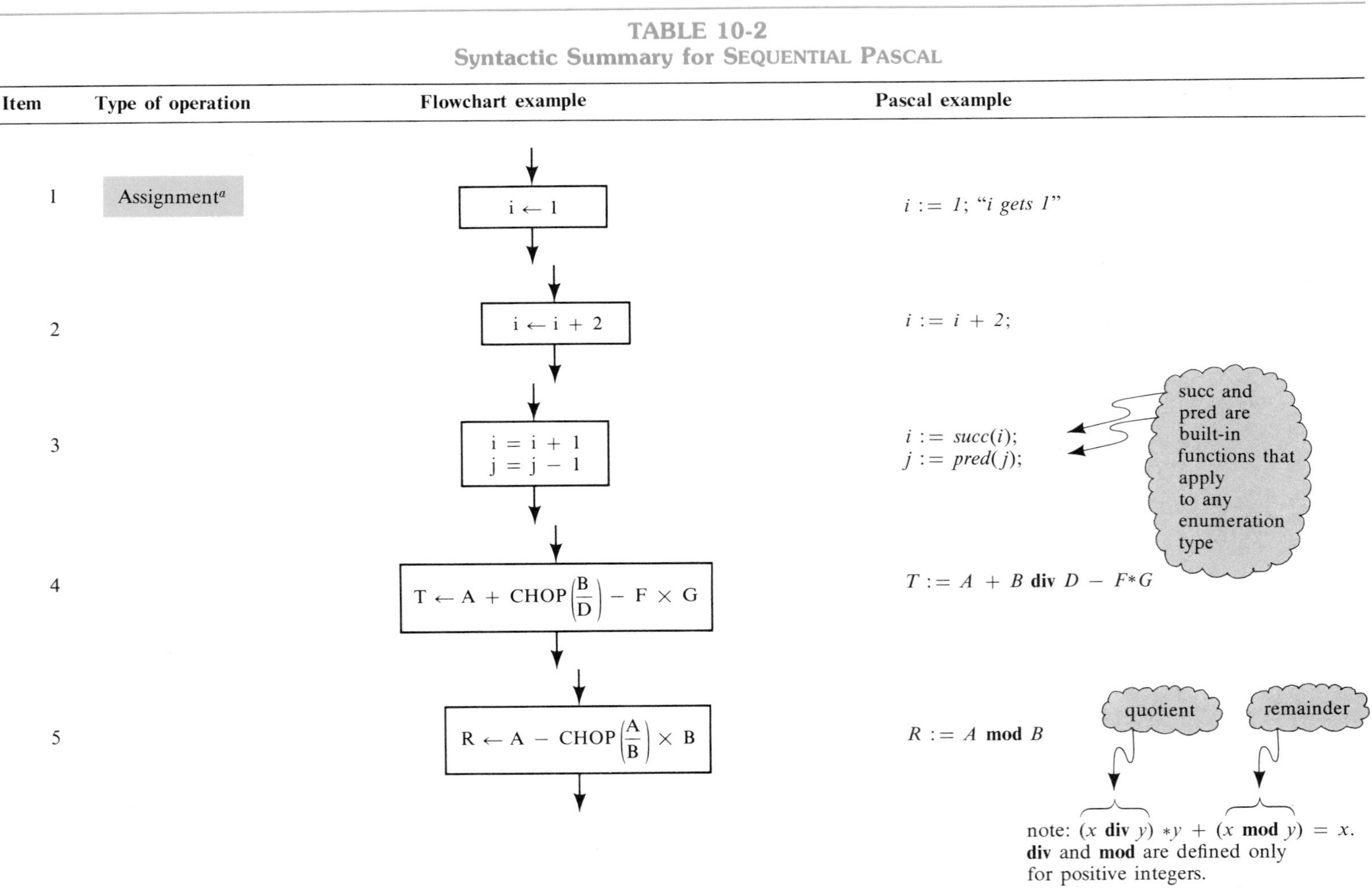

Item	Type of operation	Flowchart example	Pascal example
1	Assignment[a]	i ← 1	*i := 1; "i gets 1"*
2		i ← i + 2	*i := i + 2;*
3		i = i + 1 j = j − 1	*i := succ(i);* *j := pred(j);*
4		T ← A + CHOP$\left(\frac{B}{D}\right)$ − F × G	*T := A + B* **div** *D − F***G*
5		R ← A − CHOP$\left(\frac{A}{B}\right)$ × B	*R := A* **mod** *B*

note: (*x* **div** *y*) **y* + (*x* **mod** *y*) = *x*. **div** and **mod** are defined only for positive integers.

[a]Notes:
(1) *Comments* (any string of characters bounded by double quote marks) may appear anywhere in the program. See Item 1, for example.
(2) The functions *succ* and *pred* are built into SEQUENTIAL PASCAL. They are not *key words*. If we have the declarations

type *fruit* = (*apple*, *pear*, *peach*, *orange*);
var *x*, *y* : *fruit*;

then if we execute the assignments
x := *pear*;   *y* := *orange*;

then

x := *succ*(*x*);

causes *x* to be assigned *peach*, and

y := *pred*(*y*);

causes *y* to be assigned *peach*, whereas

y := *succ*(*y*);

causes a bounds error at run time.

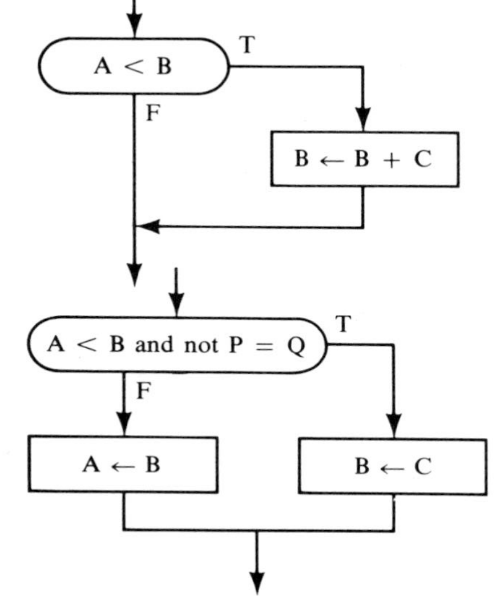

6	Path selection (two-way)[b]	**if** *A* < *B* **then** *B* := *B* + *C*;
7		**if** (*A* < *B*) & (*NOT P* = *Q*) **then** *B* := *C* **else** *A* := *B*;

TABLE 10-2 (*continued*)

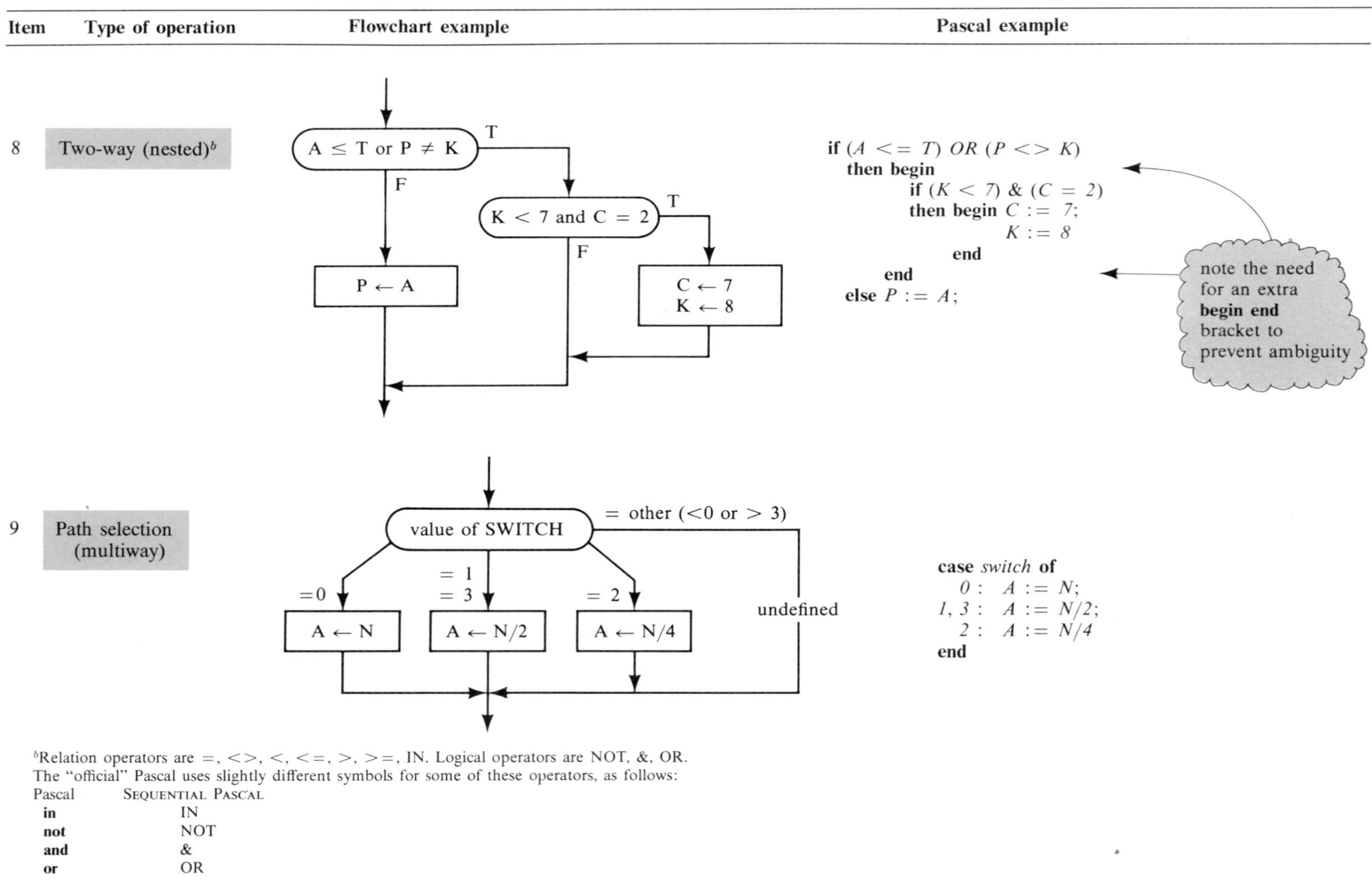

Item	Type of operation	Flowchart example	Pascal example
8	Two-way (nested)[b]		**if** (*A* <= *T*) *OR* (*P* <> *K*) **then begin** **if** (*K* < *7*) & (*C* = *2*) **then begin** *C* := *7*; *K* := *8* **end** **end** **else** *P* := *A*;
9	Path selection (multiway)		**case** *switch* **of** *0* : *A* := *N*; *1, 3* : *A* := *N/2*; *2* : *A* := *N/4* **end**

[b]Relation operators are =, <>, <, <=, >, >=, IN. Logical operators are NOT, &, OR. The "official" Pascal uses slightly different symbols for some of these operators, as follows:

Pascal	Sequential Pascal
in	IN
not	NOT
and	&
or	OR

14

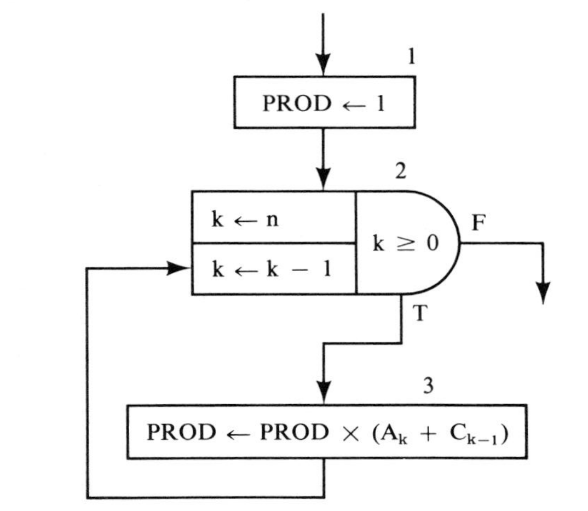


```
PROD := 1;
for k := n downto 0 do
PROD := PROD*(A[k] + C[k - 1]);
```

15 indefinite iteration

(while loop)

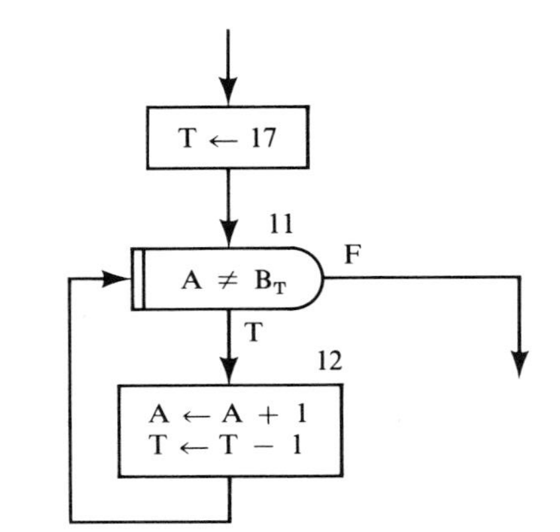


```
T := 17;
while A <> B[T] do
  begin
    A := succ(A);
    T := pred(T)
  end;
```

TABLE 10-2 *(continued)*

Item	Type of operation	Flowchart example	Pascal example

16	repeat until loop	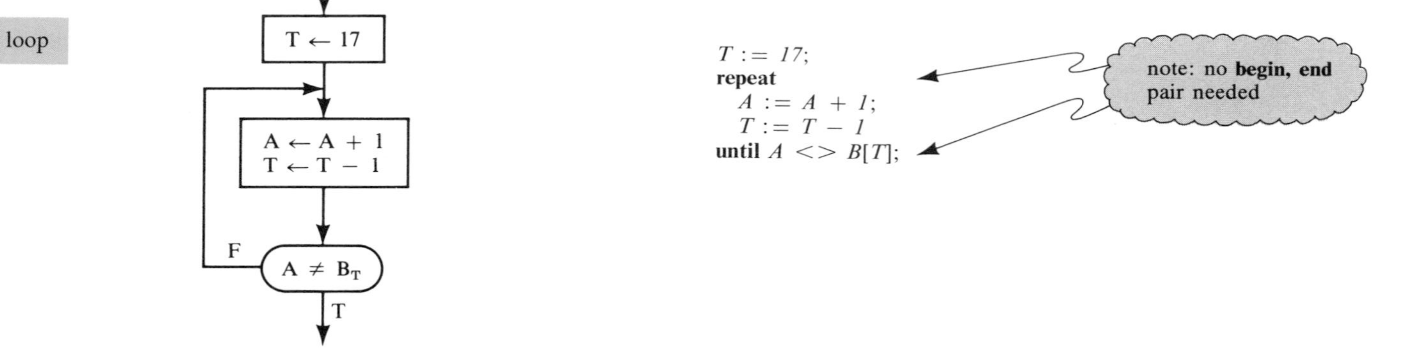	*T* := *17*;
			repeat
			  A := *A* + *1*;
			  T := *T* − *1*
			until *A* <> *B*[*T*];
			
			note: no **begin, end** pair needed

17 nested iteration

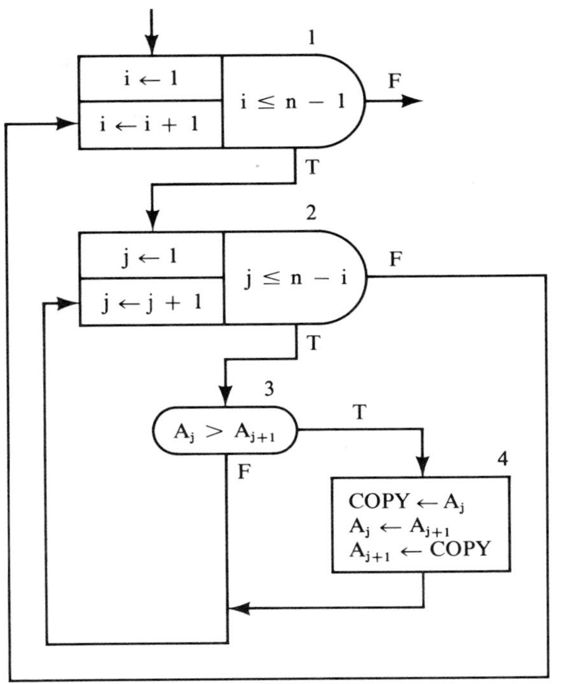


```
for i := 1 to n - 1 do
  for j := 1 to n - i do
    if A[j] > A[j + 1]
      then begin COPY := A[j];
                 A[j] := A[j + 1];
               A[j + 1] := COPY
           end;
```

TABLE 10-2 (*continued*)

Item	Type of operation	Flowchart example		Pascal example
18	Input	A	where A is of type char	*read*(*A*);
19		B	where B is an array of characters of length m	**for** *i* := *1* **to** *m* **do** *read*(*B*);
20		a	where a is an integer	*get_next_int*(*a*);
				user must define this procedure, which must call on the built-in function read either directly or indirectly (see Figure 10-15)
21		a, b, c	where a, b, and c are integers	*get_next_int* (*a*); *get_next_int* (*b*); *get_next_int* (*c*);

22		$(d_i, = 1\ (1)\ n)$	where d is a list of integers	**for** *i* := *1* **to** *n* **do** *read_integer* (*d*[*i*]);

23		$(d_i, e_i, i = 1\ (2)\ n)$	where d and e are list of integers	**for** *i* := *1* **to** (*n* + *1*) **div** *2* **do**
				begin
				get_next_int (*d*[*2***i* − *1*]);
				get_next_int (*e*[*2***i* − *1*])
				end
				(see Figure 10-6)

24	Output	"Results are:" A, B	where A and B are arrays of char of lengths m and n, respectively	*writetext* ('*Results are:*'); **for** *i* := *1* **to** *m* **do** *write* (*A*[*i*]); **for** *i* := *1* **to** *n* **do** *write* (*A*[*i*]); *write*(*NL*);
25	Procedure call	update (A, B, C + 2)		*update*(*A*, *B*, *C* + *2*);
26	Function call	T ← MAX (A, n)		*T* := *MAX* (*A*, *n*);

TABLE 10-2 (*continued*)

Item	Type of operation	Flowchart example	Pascal example
27	Procedure declaration	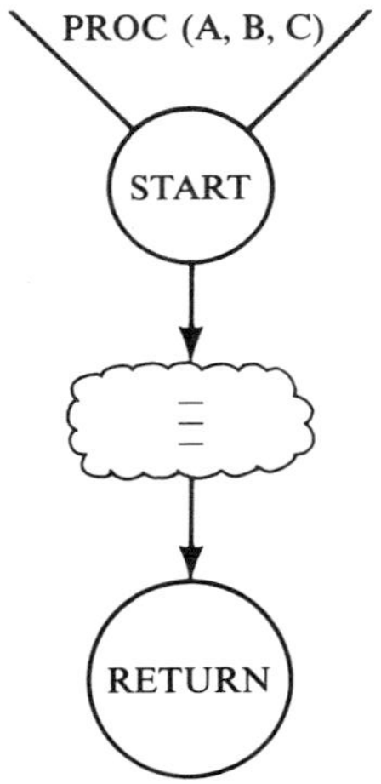 PROC (A, B, C) START RETURN	**type** *string* = **array**[*1..m*] **of** *char*; **type** *list* = **array**[*1..n*] **of** *integer*; ⋮ **procedure** *proc* (**var** *A*, *B* : *string*; *C* : *list*); **var** *i*, *j* : *integer*; **begin** ⋮ **end**:

Legend for PROC

Identifier	Treatment	Description
A, B	ref par	string
C	val par	list of integers
i, j	local	integer

28 Value-returning function declaration

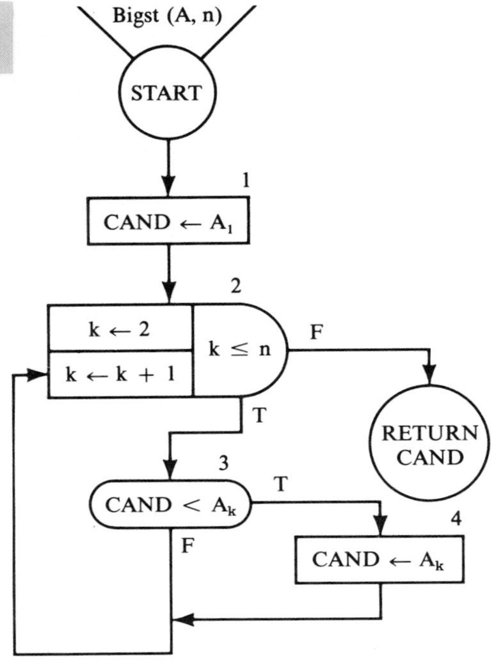

Legend for Bigst

Identifier	Treatment	Description
A	ref par	list of n integers
n	val par	integer
k, CAND	local	integer

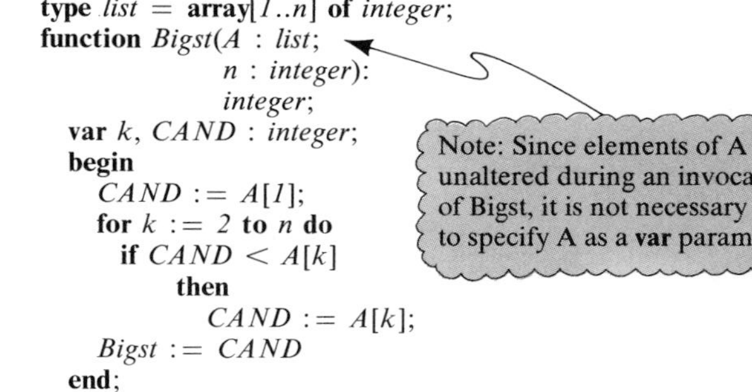

```
type list = array[1..n] of integer;
function Bigst(A : list;
               n : integer):
               integer;
  var k, CAND : integer;
  begin
    CAND := A[1];
    for k := 2 to n do
      if CAND < A[k]
         then
            CAND := A[k];
    Bigst := CAND
  end;
```

TABLE 10-2 (*continued*)

Item	Type of operation	Flowchart example	Pascal example

29 Declarations

Flowchart example:

A structure of the shape:

P T R (U W under T)

where component R is an array

Legend

Identifier	Treatment	Description
i, j	local	integer
P	local	string of 30 characters
X	local	*list* of 50 integers
Q	local	*list* of 20 strings, each of length 10
S	local	*tree* with 3 offspring: P, an integer; T, a subtree of two offspring: U, an integer, and W, a string of length 2; R, a list of 12 strings, each of length 8.

Pascal example:

```
var i, j: integer;
        P: array[1..30] of char;
        X: array[1..50] of integer;
        Q: array[1..20] of array [1..10] of char;

type tree2 = record
            U: integer;
            W: array[1..2] of char
          end;
type tree3 = record
            P: integer;
            T: tree2;
            R: array[1..12] of
                array[1..8] of char
          end;
var S: tree3;
```

30

Flowchart example:

An array each of whose elements is a structure with shape

B C (B1 B2 B3 under B)

Legend

Identifier	Treatment	Description
A	local	list of 70 elements. Each element is a structure of two components, B and C. B is a structure of three components: B1, set of the integers, 0 thru 36; B2, array of three Booleans; B3, set of the colors red, yellow, and blue; C is a string of 1 character.

Pascal example:

```
type subelement = record
                    B1: set of 0..36;
                    B2: array [1..3]
                          of Boolean;
                    B3: set of (red,
                          yellow, blue)
                  end;
type element = record
                  B : subelement;
                  C : char
                end;
var A : array [1..70] of element:
```

10-8 CASE STUDY: THE FOUR-COLOR PROBLEM

We choose one case study to exhibit most of the Pascal language features discussed in this chapter. The problem, determining whether a given map can be colored in four or fewer colors, is taken from our favorite elementary computer science text [Forsythe *et al.* (1975)]. The algorithm discussed here does not solve the famous four-color problem, which is to decide whether *any* map can be colored in four or fewer colors. That problem was recently solved by Kolata [1976]. Instead, for a *particular map* whose coloring topology (which countries have common borders with which) is expressed as a connection matrix, we develop an algorithm to decide how many colors are required to color the map so that no two countries with a common border are painted with the same color.

As an example, consider the map given in Figure 10-8 or its stylized version in Figure 10-9. Input data for a coloring algorithm can, in principle, be reduced to just the information included in the "reduced connection table" given in Figure 10-10. For each country this table shows the neighbors that will already have been colored, provided all countries are colored in sequence, from lowest country number to highest. With access to the colors chosen for neighbor countries, the algorithm consults the data of this table to decide, for each country, what color choices remain.

The strategy of the algorithm is a tree search. For each map there exists a coloring tree, such that segments along each path from the root node to a terminal represent color choices. Segments emanating from the root node represent color choices for country 1. Segments emanating from the next node in the path represent color choices for country number 2. In general, the nth segment along a path from the root represents a coloring choice for country n. Figure 10-11 shows the full coloring tree for the 12-country map in Figure 10-9. Colors are coded 1, 2, 3, and 4. Assuming the colors chosen for the first three

***Figure 10-8.* A 12-country map.**

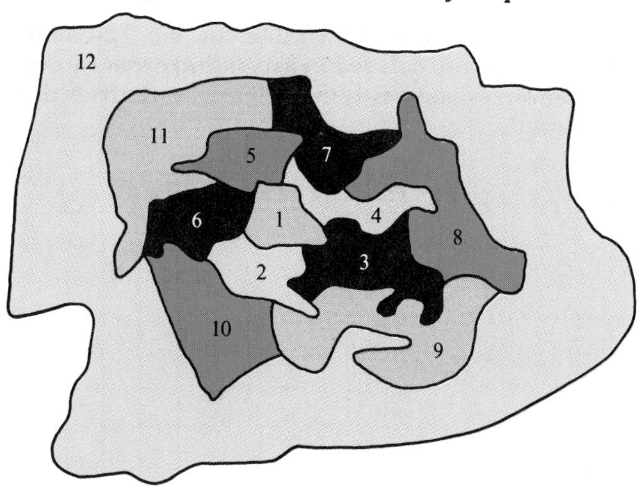

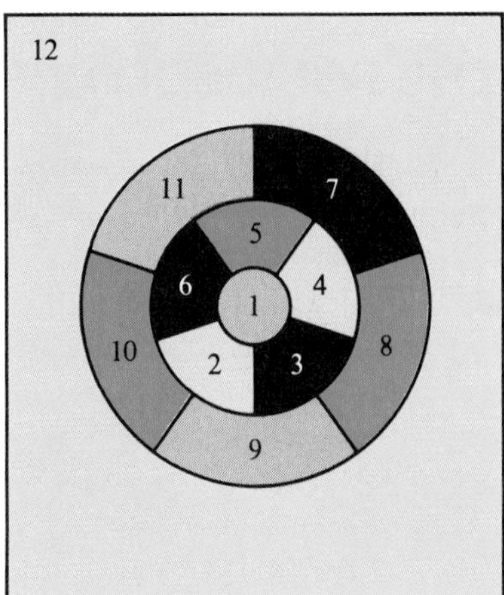

Figure 10-9. **Stylized version of the 12-country map given in Figure 10-8.**

countries are selected arbitrarily as colors 1, 2, and 3, respectively, then the remaining choices lead to ten distinct successful four-colorings of this map. These ten possibilities are represented by the ten paths that descend to level 12 and terminate in a success (S) node. Other choice sequences lead to failures (F). These are decision sequences that would require the use of more than four colors. The particular coloring choices shown in Figure 10-9 correspond to the colored path in the tree of Figure 10-11.

Figure 10-12 shows the flowchart algorithm. The accompanying legends appear in Figure 10-13. Study these figures until you are convinced you understand the algorithm they represent. The mapping of the flowcharts and legends to a Pascal program, in particular to a SEQUENTIAL PASCAL program, is straightforward, except for the not-so-trivial step of inputting the data. (We use the input/output conventions of SEQUENTIAL PASCAL throughout.)

Figure 10-10. **Reduced connection table for the 12-country map in Figure 10-9. If countries are colored in ascending order by country number, then row i shows, for country i, the neighbor countries that will have already been colored.**

Country number	Previously colored neighbor countries				
1					
2	1				
3	1	2			
4	1	3			
5	1	4			
6	1	2	5		
7	4	5			
8	3	4	7		
9	2	3	8		
10	2	6	9		
11	5	6	7	10	
12	7	8	9	10	11

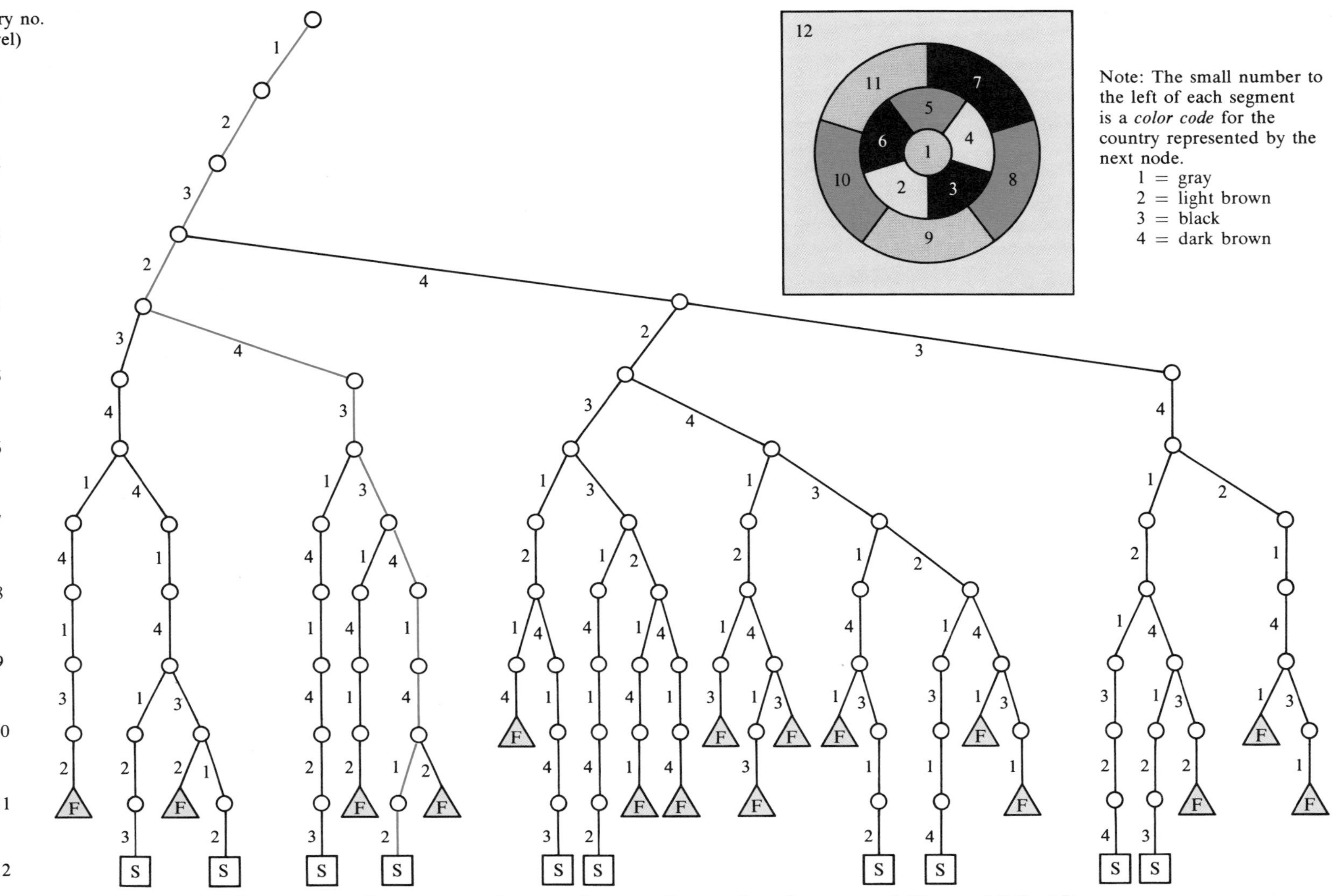

Figure 10-11. **An entire coloring tree showing how to four-color the map of Figure 10-9. 10 successes, marked by terminal nodes (S); 16 failures, marked by terminal nodes (F).**

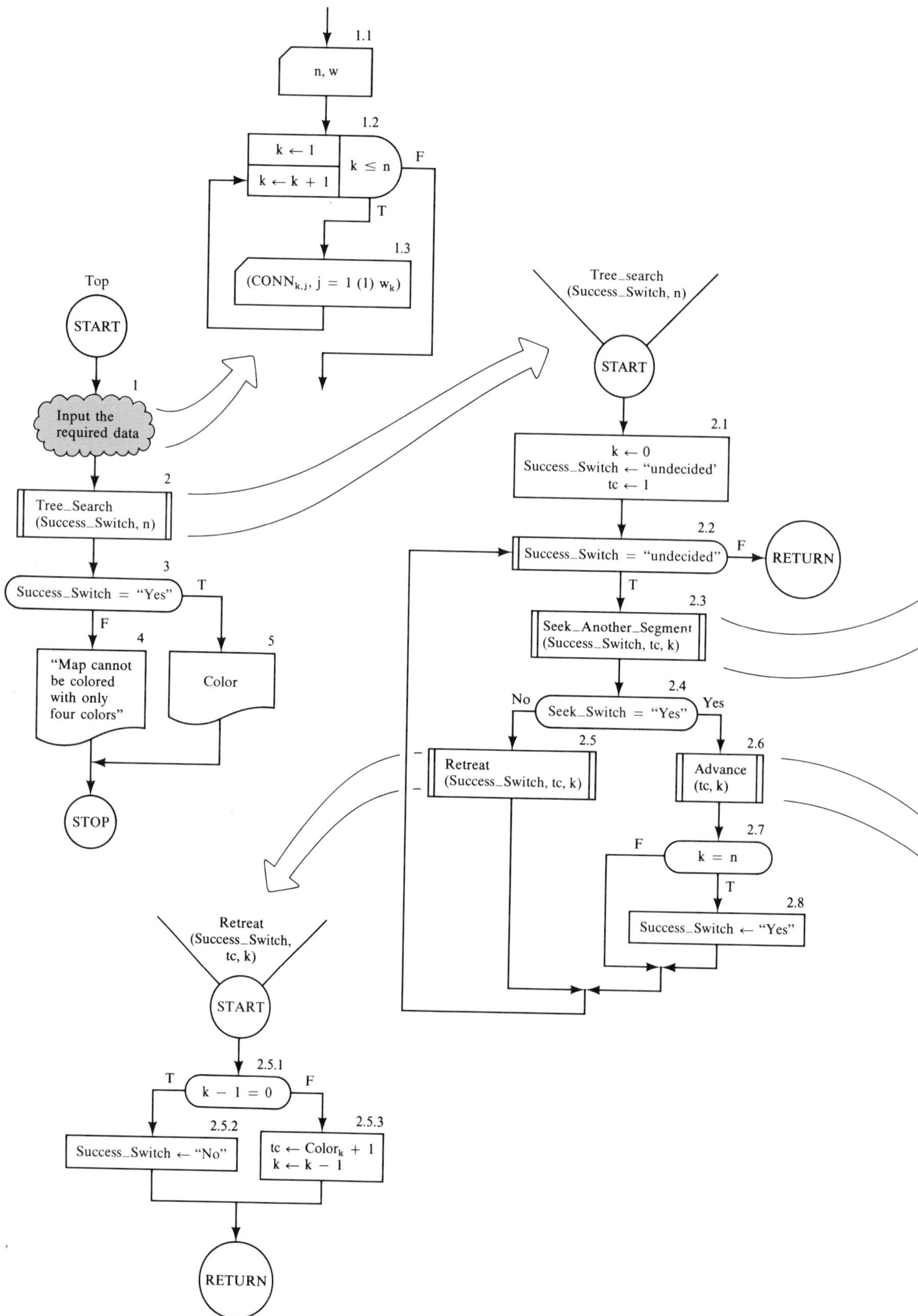

Figure 10-12. **Four-coloring algorithm flowchart. For companion legends, see Figure 10-13.**

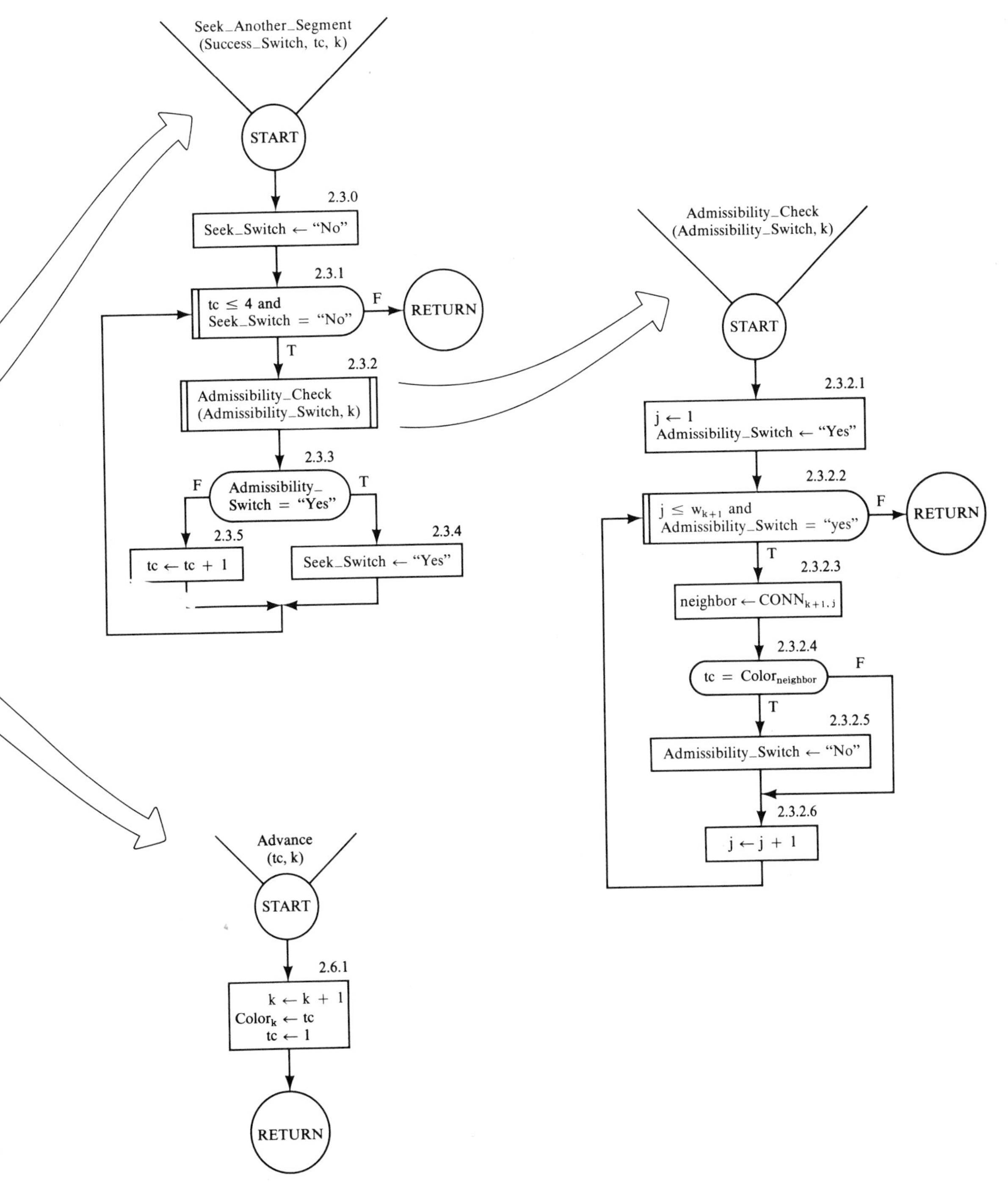

Seek_Another_Segment
(Success_Switch, tc, k)
START
2.3.0
Seek_Switch ← "No"
2.3.1
tc ≤ 4 and
Seek_Switch = "No"
F
RETURN
T
2.3.2
Admissibility_Check
(Admissibility_Switch, k)
2.3.3
F
Admissibility_
Switch = "Yes"
T
2.3.5
tc ← tc + 1
2.3.4
Seek_Switch ← "Yes"
Admissibility_Check
(Admissibility_Switch, k)
START
2.3.2.1
j ← 1
Admissibility_Switch ← "Yes"
2.3.2.2
j ≤ w_{k+1} and
Admissibility_Switch = "yes"
F
RETURN
T
2.3.2.3
neighbor ← CONN_{k+1, j}
2.3.2.4
tc = Color_{neighbor}
F
T
2.3.2.5
Admissibility_Switch ← "No"
2.3.2.6
j ← j + 1
Advance
(tc, k)
START
2.6.1
k ← k + 1
Color_k ← tc
tc ← 1
RETURN

Legend for Top

Identifier	Treatment	Description
n	local	number of countries
k	local	loop counter
Success_Switch	local	string
w	local	list of n integers
Color	local	list of colorcodes
CONN	local	array of integers having n rows. The kth row has w_k columns

Legend for Tree_Search

Identifier	Treatment	Description
Success_Switch	ref par	string
n	val par	integer
k	local	level counter, i.e., number of countries colored so far
tc	local	tentative color for next country to be colored
Seek_Switch	local	Boolean

Legend for Seek_Another_Segment

Identifier	Treatment	Description
Seek_Switch	ref par	Boolean
tc	ref par	tentative color
k	val par	integer
Admissibility_Switch	local	Boolean

Legend for Advance

Identifier	Treatment	Description
tc	ref par	tentative color
k	ref par	integer
Color	global	Color in Top

Legend for Retreat

Identifier	Treatment	Description
Success_Switch	ref par	string
tc	ref par	tentative color
k	ref par	integer
Color	global	Color in Top

Legend for Admissibility_Check

Identifier	Treatment	Description
Admissibility_Switch	ref par	Boolean
k	val par	integer
j	local	loop counter
neighbor	local	integer
w	global	w in Top
CONN	global	CONN in Top

Figure 10-13. **Legends for flowcharts in Figure 10-12.**

The program is actually shown in pieces, in the order in which they might appear as one big program. Figure 10-14 shows the program heading and declarations. Figure 10-15 shows utility procedures *get_next_int*, *write_int*, and *initialize*. Figure 10-16 gives the procedure *input*. Figure 10-17 provides the procedures used in the main part of the four-color algorithm:

advance and *retreat* (10-17a)
admissibility_check and *seek_another_segment* (10-17b)
tree_search (10-17c)

Finally, the compound statement that forms the "body" of the main program is given in Figure 10-18. By deliberately not nesting the procedure declarations, for example, *advance* and *retreat* within *tree_search*, we believe the program as a whole is easier to read.

The utility procedures especially coded for this illustration are normally available as *library procedures* in most Pascal systems. The cloud marked "input the required data" in Figure 10-12 is treated in Figure 10-18 as the procedure call:

input (*end_of_file_switch*);

which performs the input if a complete data set is provided. If the Boolean *end_of_file_switch* is set *false*, as a result of invoking *input* (Figure 10-16), an error message is printed using the *writetext* procedure, previously displayed in Figure 10-6.

***Figure 10-14.* Program heading and declarations for the four-color algorithm.**

```
program four_color_algorithm;
  "from the flowcharts and legends
  of Figures 10-12 and 10-13."
  const nmax = 40 "max no. of countries";
        wmax = 10 "max no. of neighbors per country";
  type switch3 = (yes, no, undecided);
       colors_4 = (red, yellow, blue, green);
       colors_5 = (red, yellow, blue, green, no_good);
  var w: array [1..nmax] of 1..wmax "list of no. of neighbors";
      n: integer "no. of countries in this data set";
      digits: set of char; "see procedure initialize"
      color: array [1..nmax] of colors_4
             "list of colors selected for countries of
             the map";
      k: 1..nmax "level counter";
      tc: colors_5 "tentative color code";
      CONN: array [1..nmax, 1..wmax] of 1..nmax
             "connection matrix for a map having
             nmax countries, each country having
             up to wmax neighbors";
      success_switch: switch3;
      end_of_file_switch: Boolean;
```

```
procedure get_next_int (var val:integer; var switch: Boolean);
  const eof = '(:25:)'; "end of file marker"
  var ch:char; "digits set defined globally"
  begin
    val := 0;
    switch := true;
    "find first digit of next integer"
    repeat read (ch) until (ch in digits ) OR ch = eof;
    if ch = eof
      then
        switch := false;
      else
        begin
          while (ch in digits) & switch do
            begin
              val := val*10 + (ord (ch) - ord (0));
                "augment val by next decimal digit"
              read (ch)
            end;
          if ch = eof then switch := false
        end
  end;
```



```
procedure write_int (n : integer);
  var Q, R : integer;
  begin
    R := n mod 10; "assign lowest-order (rightmost) digit of n to R"
    Q := n div 10; "assign high-order digits of n to Q"
    if Q <> 0 then write_int (Q);
    write (chr (R + ord (0)))
  end;
```



```
procedure initialize; "initializes the set of digit characters"
  begin
    digits := ['0', '1', '2', '3', '4', '5', '6', '7',
               '8', '9'] "digits is globally defined"
  end;
```

***Figure 10-15.* The utility procedures *get_next_int*, *write_int*, and *initialize*.**

The procedure *input*, in turn, calls on the procedure *get_next_int* (Figure 10-15), which scans the input stream for the next string of characters that can be interpreted as an unsigned integer and converts that string to an integer.

Another utility procedure needed in this program is

write_int

which converts a given nonnegative integer to a string of characters and writes it out. This procedure is recursively defined (See Figure 10-15). Finally, another procedure, *initialize*, initializes the set variable, *digits*. This variable, a set of the decimal characters '*0*', '*1*', through '*9*', is very useful in the input procedure.

```
procedure input (var switch : Boolean); "Inputs the data set."
    "Note. If the end of file marker eof is encountered during any activation
    of get_next_int, the second argument (switch)
    will be set to false."
  var i, j : integer:
  begin
    get_next_int (n, switch); "n is global."
    i := 1;
    while (i <= n) & switch do
      begin
        get_next_int (w [i], switch);
        i := i + 1
      end
    i := 1;
    while (i <= n) & switch do
      begin
        j := 1;
        while (j <= w [i]) & switch do "w is global"
          begin
              get_next_int (CONN [i, j]); "CONN is global"
            j := j + 1
          end;
        i := i + 1
    end
  end;
```

***Figure 10-16.* The utility procedure *input*.**

***Figure 10-17a.* The procedures *advance* and *retreat*.**

```
procedure advance (var tc: colors_5; var k: integer);
  begin
    k := k + 1;
    color [k] := tc;
    tc := red
  end;


procedure retreat (var success_switch: switch3; var tc: color_5; var k: integer);
  begin
    if k - 1 = 0 then success_switch := no
                      else begin
                             tc := succ (COLOR [k]);
                             k := k - 1
                           end
  end;
```

It is instructive to draw contour diagram snapshots at key points in the execution of the SEQUENTIAL PASCAL four-color program. We show only one such snapshot and leave as an exercise for the reader the task of drawing others. For

```
procedure admissibility_check (var admissibility_switch: Boolean; k: integer);
  var j: integer; neighbor: 1..nmax;
    begin
      j := 1;
      admissibility_switch := true;
      while (j <= w [k + 1]) & admissibility_switch do
        begin
          neighbor := CONN [k + 1, j];
          if tc = color [neighbor]
            then admissibility_switch := false;
          j := j + 1
        end
    end;

procedure seek_another_segment (var seek_switch: Boolean; var tc: colors_5; k: integer);
  var admissibility_switch: Boolean;
    begin
      seek_switch := false;
      while (tc <> no_good) & NOT seek_switch do
        begin
          admissibility_check (admissibility_switch, k);
          if admissibility_switch
            then seek_switch := true
            else tc := red
        end
    end;
```

Figure 10-17b.* The procedures *admissibility_check* and *seek_another_segment.

Figure 10-17c.* The procedure *tree_search.

```
procedure tree_search (var success_switch: switch3; n: integer);
  var seek_switch: Boolean;
    begin
      k := 0;
      success_switch := undecided;
      tc := red;
      while success_switch = undecided do
        begin
          seek-another-segment (seek_switch, tc, k);
          if seek_switch
            then begin advance (tc, k);
                       if k = n then success_switch := true
                     end
            else retreat (success_switch, tc, k);
        end
    end;
```

the snapshot to be presented, we consider the case where the data set refers to the map shown in Figure 10-19a. The related coloring tree is shown in Figure 10-19b, and the arrow indicates the spot in the computation where we wish to take our snapshot. This is the point where country number 5 has just been colored for the second time (but before country 6 has been colored). Figure 10-19c shows the data values for the list w and the array *CONN* representing the reduced connection matrix of the map shown in Figure 10-19a.

The snapshot shown in Figure 10-20 is taken just before executing the return step in the seventh invocation of *advance.* (We presume here that the two

```
begin
  initialize;
  input (end_of_file switch);
  if end_of_file_switch
    then
      begin
        tree_search (success_switch, n);
        if success_switch
          then for i := 1 to n do write_int (color [i])
            "display the color array"
          else write_text ('map cannot be colored with 4 colors')
      end
    else write_text ('incomplete data set.')
end.
```

Figure 10-18. **Compound statement for the *top level* of the four-color program.**

Figure 10-19. **Data for a six-country map with four-coloring tree.**

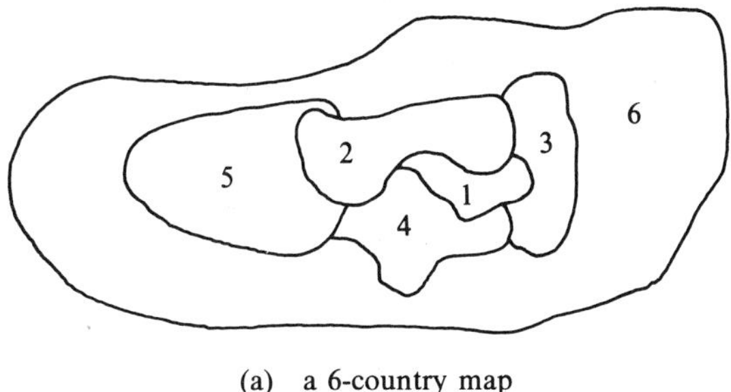

(a) a 6-country map

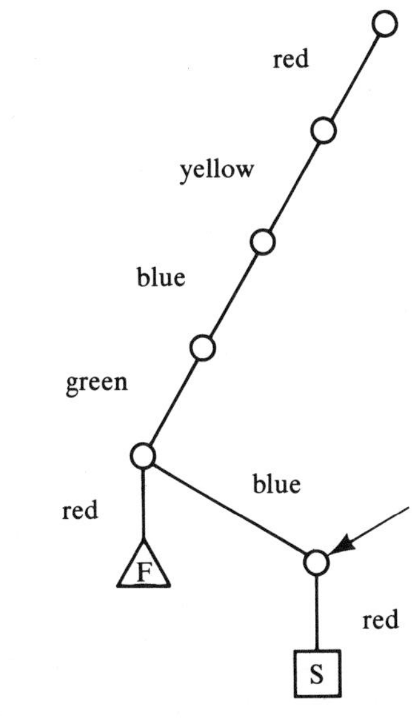

(b) coloring tree

	w	CONN
1	0	–
2	1	1
3	2	1 2
4	4	1 2 3
5	2	2 4
6	4	2 3 4 5

(c) reduced connection matrix

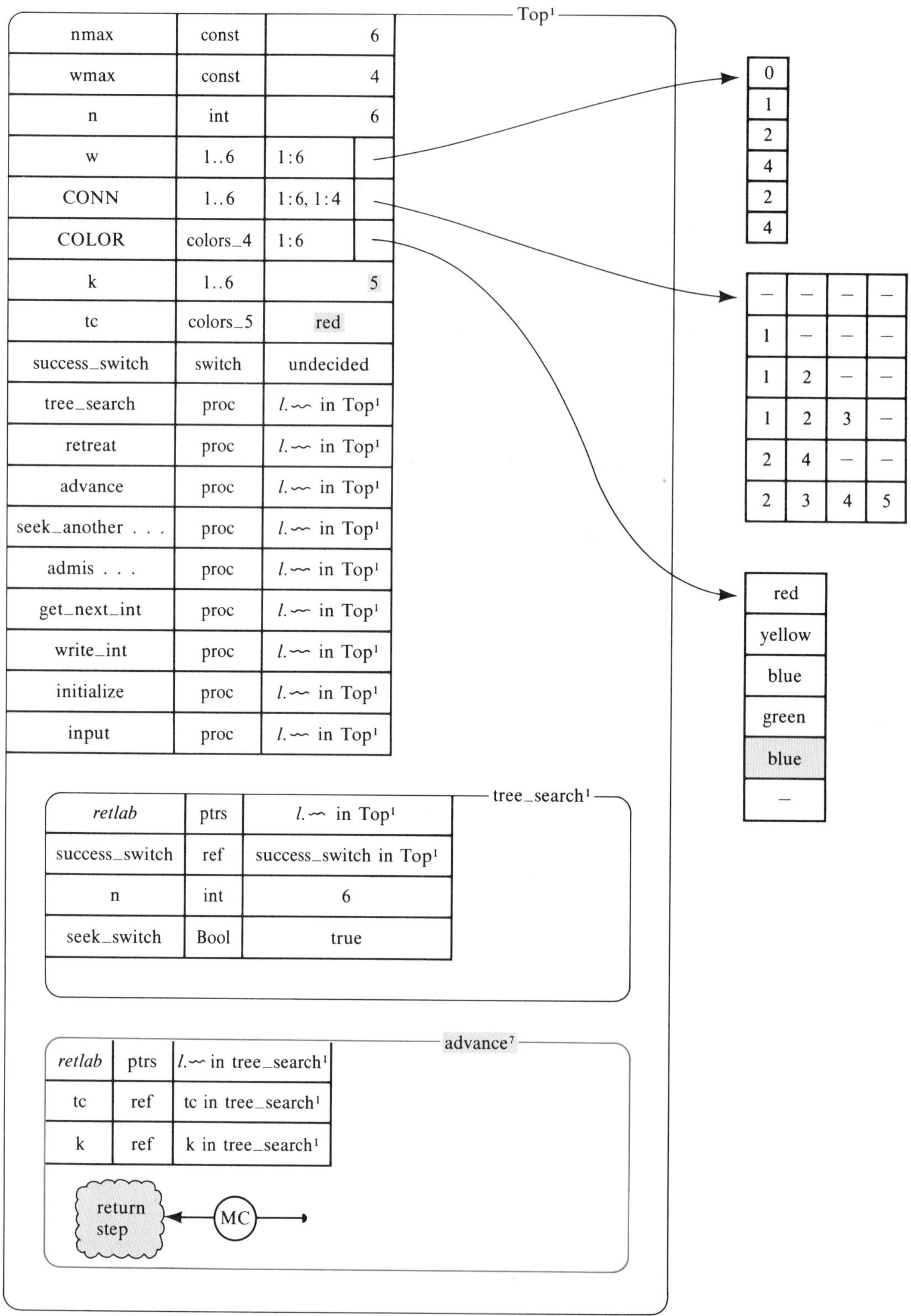

Figure 10-20. **Snapshot of the SEQUENTIAL PASCAL four-color program taken at a point where control is about to return from the seventh invocation of advance.**

global constants *nmax* and *wmax* have been redefined as 6 and 4, respectively. This allows us to show smaller arrays in the snapshot.) In the seventh invocation of *advance*, the level counter *k* has been incremented to 5, the fifth country has been colored blue in the *COLOR* list, and the tentative color red has been selected as a candidate color for country number 6.

Exercises 10-8, Set A

Design a ten-country map that appears interesting to you, and determine for that map the appropriate set of input data for the four-color program. Now construct a snapshot showing the state of the computation either just before the first return from *retreat* or just before the return from the invocation of *advance* that colors country number 8, whichever occurs first.

Exercises 10-8, Set B

Consult Exercise 3 at the end of Chapter 9, which discusses the well-known eight Queens problem. As indicated in that discussion, the better-known solutions usually involve a recursive procedure, or an iterative procedure that simulates the type of recursion (tree walk) thought to be needed. (This type of recursion is frequently referred to as *backtracking.*) Note that our solution of the four-color problem (Figure 10-12) is in essence an iterative simulation of a recursive solution.

1 Study Figure 10-21, which gives flowcharts for a recursive solution analogous to the the coroutine solution of Figure 9-16. (The arrays X, A, B and C in Figure 10-21 correspond to arrays rowofcol, onrow, onSWdiag, and onSEdiag, respectively, that were discussed on p. 556.) Convert the solution shown in Figure 10-21 to a Pascal program.

2 Develop a snapshot of the execution taken the first time control is about to execute box 9 of the procedure *Eight_Q* in Figure 10-21. This point of progress corresponds with the one used in the snapshot asked for in Exercise 3 at the end of Chapter 9. If you have worked that exercise, compare the two snapshots and comment on their relative clarity.

3 Revise the solution in Figure 10-21 to eliminate recursion. Your iterative solution should have a structure similar to that of Figure 10-12.

4 Write a Pascal program corresponding to the flowcharts you prepared in response to Exercise 3. In preparing your Pascal solution it is not necessary to observe the constraints of SEQUENTIAL PASCAL, prohibiting the nesting of procedure declarations. These constraints were observed by the authors in preparing the program exhibited in Figures 10-14 through 10-18.

10-9 REFERENCES AND SUGGESTIONS FOR FURTHER READING

The Pascal language is frequently studied not only as a replacement for Algol but also as a system design and specification language. The best text and reference book is Wirth and Jensen (1975). Other fine texts such as Wirth (1973, 1976) introduce programming concepts and reveal the wide applicability of Pascal. Brinch Hansen (1973) used Pascal as a base for an entire text on operating systems principles. More dialects and subsets of Pascal, such as given in Brinch Hansen (1975) and Brinch Hansen and Hartmann (1975), will no doubt develop as programmers begin to use the language in more specialized contexts.

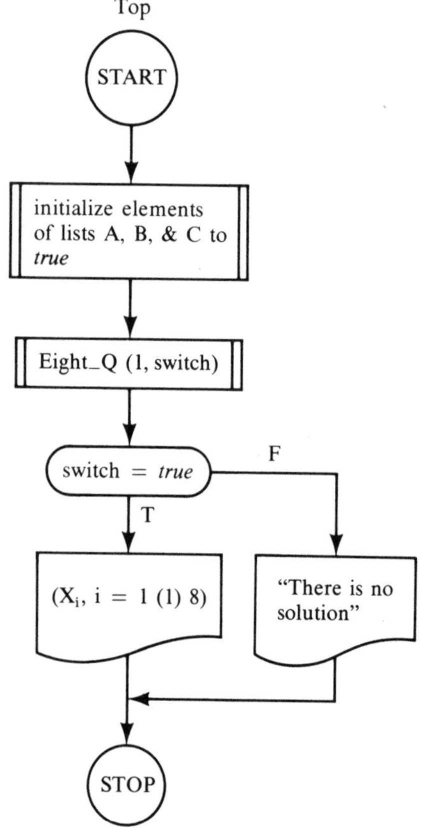

Legend for Top

Identifier	Treatment	Description
switch	local	logical
i	local	integer
X	local	list of 8 integers
A	local	list of 8 logicals
B	local	list of 15 logicals indexed 2 to 16
C	local	list of 15 logicals indexed −7 to 7

Legend for Eight_Q

Identifier	Treatment	Description
i	val par	integer
switch	ref par	logical (indicates success)
j, k	local	integer
X	global	X in Top
A	global	A in Top
B	global	B in Top
C	global	C in Top

Figure 10-21

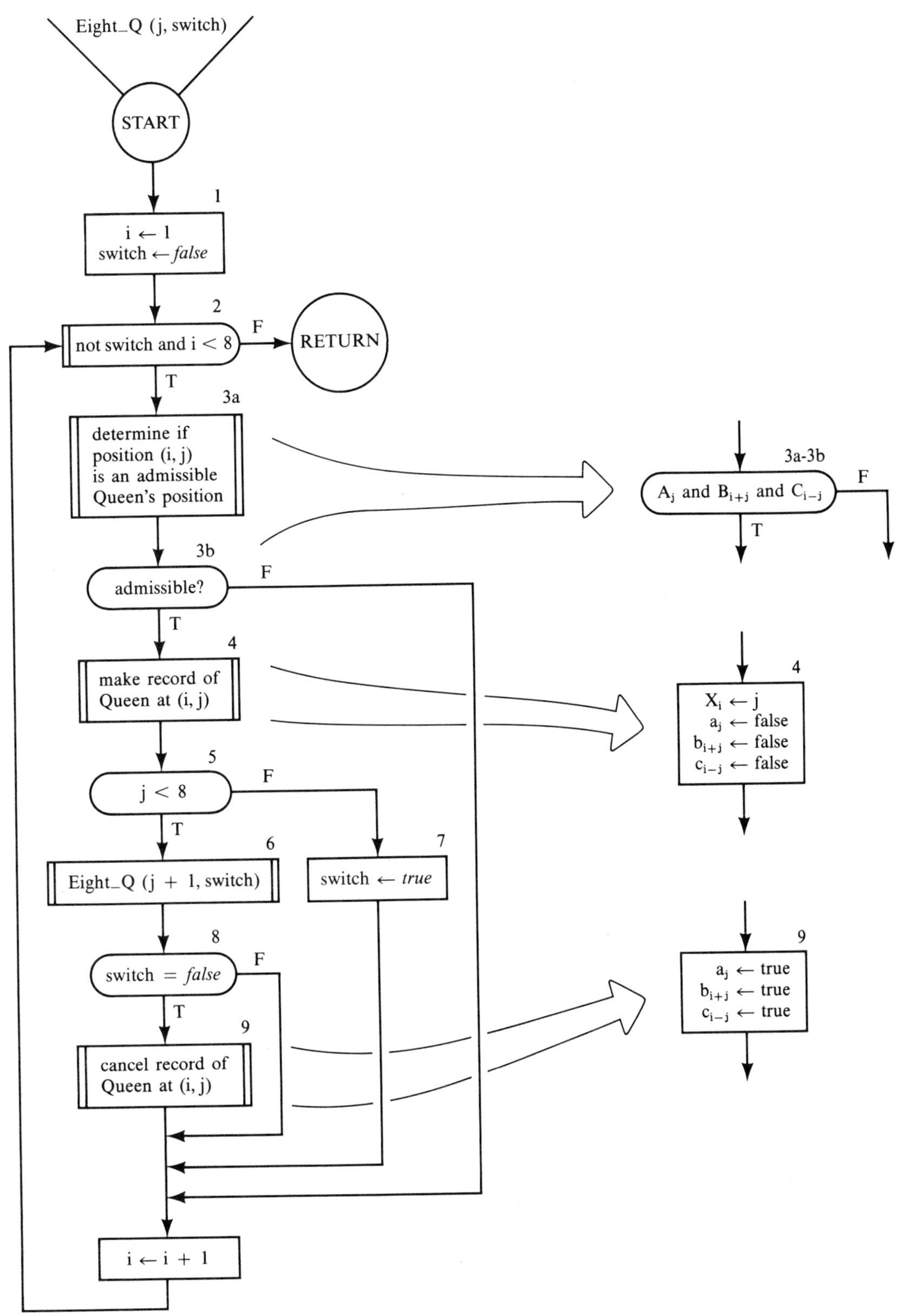
Eight_Q (j, switch)
START
1
i ← 1
switch ← false
2
not switch and i < 8
F
RETURN
T
3a
determine if position (i, j) is an admissible Queen's position
3a-3b
A_j and B_{i+j} and C_{i-j}
F
T
3b
admissible?
F
T
4
make record of Queen at (i, j)
4
$X_i \leftarrow j$
$a_j \leftarrow$ false
$b_{i+j} \leftarrow$ false
$c_{i-j} \leftarrow$ false
5
j < 8
F
T
6
Eight_Q (j + 1, switch)
7
switch ← true
8
switch = false
F
T
9
cancel record of Queen at (i, j)
9
$a_j \leftarrow$ true
$b_{i+j} \leftarrow$ true
$c_{i-j} \leftarrow$ true
i ← i + 1

APPENDIX

ALGOL 60 SYNTAX

The following syntax for ALGOL 60 is taken from Naur [1963]. All but the first section of the report is reproduced here. That first section describes BNF (Backus–Naur Form), a formalism used to describe syntax. (See Chapter 4 of this book.) The only formula or definition found in Section 1 of the report is the following:

⟨empty⟩ ::=

where the right-hand side represents the null string of symbols.

2 Basic Symbols, Identifiers, Numbers, and Strings. Basic Concepts

⟨basic symbol⟩ ::= ⟨letter⟩ | ⟨digit⟩ | ⟨logical value⟩ | ⟨delimiter⟩

2.1. LETTERS

⟨letter⟩ ::= *a* | *b* | *c* | *d* | *e* | *f* | *g* | *h* | *i* | *j* | *k* | *l* | *m* | *n* | *o* | *p* | *q* | *r* | *s* | *t* | *u* | *v* | *w* | *x* | *y* | *z* |
A | *B* | *C* | *D* | *E* | *F* | *G* | *H* | *I* | *J* | *K* | *L* | *M* | *N* | *O* | *P* | *Q* | *R* | *S* | *T* | *U* | *V* | *W* | *X* | *Y* | *Z*

2.2.1. Digits

⟨digit⟩ ::= *0* | *1* | *2* | *3* | *4* | *5* | *6* | *7* | *8* | *9*

2.2.2. Logical Values

⟨logical value⟩ ::= **true** | **false**

2.3. DELIMITERS

⟨delimiter⟩ ::= ⟨operator⟩ | ⟨separator⟩ | ⟨bracket⟩ | ⟨declarator⟩ | ⟨specificator⟩
⟨operator⟩ ::= ⟨arithmetic operator⟩ | ⟨relational operator⟩ |
⟨logical operator⟩ | ⟨sequential operator⟩
⟨arithmetic operator⟩ ::= $+ \mid - \mid \times \mid / \mid \div \mid \uparrow$
⟨relational operator⟩ ::= $< \mid \leq \mid = \mid \geq \mid > \mid \neq$
⟨logical operator⟩ ::= $\equiv \mid \supset \mid \vee \mid \wedge \mid \neg$

⟨sequential operator⟩ ::= **go to** | **if** | **then** | **else** | **for** | **do**
⟨separator⟩ ::= , | . | $_{10}$ | : | ; | := | ␣ | **step** | **while** | **comment**
⟨bracket⟩ ::= (|) | [|] | ‘ | ’ | **begin** | **end**
⟨declarator⟩ ::= **own** | **Boolean** | **integer** | **real** | **array** | **switch** | **procedure**
⟨specificator⟩ ::= **string** | **label** | **value**

2.4. IDENTIFIERS

⟨identifier⟩ ::= ⟨letter⟩ | ⟨identifier⟩⟨letter⟩ | ⟨identifier⟩⟨digit⟩

2.5. NUMBERS

⟨unsigned integer⟩ ::= ⟨digit⟩ | ⟨unsigned integer⟩⟨digit⟩
⟨integer⟩ ::= ⟨unsigned integer⟩ | + ⟨unsigned integer⟩ | − ⟨unsigned integer⟩
⟨decimal fraction⟩ ::= . ⟨unsigned integer⟩
⟨exponent part⟩ ::= $_{10}$ ⟨integer⟩
⟨decimal number⟩ ::= ⟨unsigned integer⟩ | ⟨decimal fraction⟩ |
  ⟨unsigned integer⟩⟨decimal fraction⟩
⟨unsigned number⟩ ::= ⟨decimal number⟩ | ⟨exponent part⟩ |
  ⟨decimal number⟩⟨exponent part⟩
⟨number⟩ ::= ⟨unsigned number⟩ | + ⟨unsigned number⟩ |
  − ⟨unsigned number⟩

2.6. STRINGS

⟨proper string⟩ ::= ⟨any sequence of basic symbols not containing ‘ or ’⟩ | ⟨empty⟩
⟨open string⟩ ::= ⟨proper string⟩ | ‘ ⟨open string⟩ ’ |
  ⟨open string⟩⟨open string⟩
⟨string⟩ ::= ‘ ⟨open string⟩ ’

3
Expressions

⟨expression⟩ ::= ⟨arithmetic expression⟩ | ⟨Boolean expression⟩ |
  ⟨designational expression⟩

3.1. VARIABLES

⟨variable identifier⟩ ::= ⟨identifier⟩
⟨simple variable⟩ ::= ⟨variable identifier⟩
⟨subscript expression⟩ ::= ⟨arithmetic expression⟩
⟨subscript list⟩ ::= ⟨subscript expression⟩ |
  ⟨subscript list⟩, ⟨subscript expression⟩
⟨array identifier⟩ ::= ⟨identifier⟩
⟨subscripted variable⟩ ::= ⟨array identifier⟩[⟨subscript list⟩]
⟨variable⟩ ::= ⟨simple variable⟩ | ⟨subscripted variable⟩

3.2. FUNCTION DESIGNATORS

⟨procedure identifier⟩ ::= ⟨identifier⟩

⟨actual parameter⟩ ::= ⟨string⟩ | ⟨expression⟩ | ⟨array identifier⟩ | ⟨switch identifier⟩ | ⟨procedure identifier⟩

⟨letter string⟩ ::= ⟨letter⟩ | ⟨letter string⟩⟨letter⟩

⟨parameter delimiter⟩ ::= , |)⟨letter string⟩ : (

⟨actual parameter list⟩ ::= ⟨actual parameter⟩ | ⟨actual parameter list⟩⟨parameter delimiter⟩⟨actual parameter⟩

⟨actual parameter part⟩ ::= ⟨empty⟩ | (⟨actual parameter list⟩)

⟨function designator⟩ ::= ⟨procedure identifier⟩⟨actual parameter part⟩

3.3. ARITHMETIC EXPRESSIONS

⟨adding operator⟩ ::= + | −

⟨multiplying operator⟩ ::= × | / | ÷

⟨primary⟩ ::= ⟨unsigned number⟩ | ⟨variable⟩ | ⟨function designator⟩ | (⟨arithmetic expression⟩)

⟨factor⟩ ::= ⟨primary⟩ | ⟨factor⟩ ↑ ⟨primary⟩

⟨term⟩ ::= ⟨factor⟩ | ⟨term⟩⟨multiplying operator⟩⟨factor⟩

⟨simple arithmetic expression⟩ ::= ⟨term⟩ | ⟨adding operator⟩⟨term⟩ | ⟨simple arithmetic expression⟩⟨adding operator⟩⟨term⟩

⟨if clause⟩ ::= **if** ⟨Boolean expression⟩ **then**

⟨arithmetic expression⟩ ::= ⟨simple arithmetic expression⟩ | ⟨if clause⟩⟨simple arithmetic expression⟩ **else** ⟨arithmetic expression⟩

3.4. BOOLEAN EXPRESSIONS

⟨relational operator⟩ ::= < | ≤ | = | ≥ | > | ≠

⟨relation⟩ ::= ⟨simple arithmetic expression⟩⟨relational operator⟩ ⟨simple arithmetic expression⟩

⟨Boolean primary⟩ ::= ⟨logical value⟩ | ⟨variable ⟩ | ⟨function designator⟩ | ⟨relation⟩ | (⟨Boolean expression⟩)

⟨Boolean secondary⟩ ::= ⟨Boolean primary⟩ | ¬ ⟨Boolean primary⟩

⟨Boolean factor⟩ ::= ⟨Boolean secondary⟩ | ⟨Boolean factor⟩ ∧ ⟨Boolean secondary⟩

⟨Boolean term⟩ ::= ⟨Boolean factor⟩ | ⟨Boolean term⟩ ∨ ⟨Boolean factor⟩

⟨implication⟩ ::= ⟨Boolean term⟩ | ⟨implication⟩ ⊃ ⟨Boolean term⟩

⟨simple Boolean⟩ ::= ⟨implication⟩ | ⟨simple Boolean⟩ ≡ ⟨implication⟩

⟨Boolean expression⟩ ::= ⟨simple Boolean⟩ | ⟨if clause⟩⟨simple Boolean⟩ **else** ⟨Boolean expression⟩

3.5. DESIGNATIONAL EXPRESSIONS

⟨label⟩ ::= ⟨identifier⟩ | ⟨unsigned integer⟩

⟨switch identifier⟩ ::= ⟨identifier⟩

⟨switch designator⟩ ::= ⟨switch identifier⟩[⟨subscript expression⟩]

⟨simple designational expression⟩ ::= ⟨label⟩ | ⟨switch designator⟩ | (⟨designational expression⟩)

⟨designational expression⟩ ::= ⟨simple designational expression⟩ | ⟨if clause⟩⟨simple designational expression⟩ **else** ⟨designational expression⟩

4 Statements

4.1. COMPOUND STATEMENTS AND BLOCKS

⟨unlabelled basic statement⟩ ::= ⟨assignment statement⟩ | ⟨go to statement⟩ | ⟨dummy statement⟩ | ⟨procedure statement⟩

⟨basic statement⟩ ::= ⟨unlabelled basic statement⟩ | ⟨label⟩ : ⟨basic statement⟩

⟨unconditional statement⟩ ::= ⟨basic statement⟩ | ⟨compound statement⟩ | ⟨block⟩

⟨statement⟩ ::= ⟨unconditional statement⟩ | ⟨conditional statement⟩ | ⟨for statement⟩

⟨compound tail⟩ ::= ⟨statement⟩ **end** | ⟨statement⟩ ; ⟨compound tail⟩

⟨block head⟩ ::= **begin** ⟨declaration⟩ | ⟨block head⟩ ; ⟨declaration⟩

⟨unlabelled compound⟩ ::= **begin** ⟨compound tail⟩

⟨unlabelled block⟩ ::= ⟨block head⟩ ; ⟨compound tail⟩

⟨compound statement⟩ ::= ⟨unlabelled compound⟩ | ⟨label⟩ : ⟨compound statement⟩

⟨block⟩ ::= ⟨unlabelled block⟩ | ⟨label⟩ : ⟨block⟩

⟨program⟩ ::= ⟨block⟩ | ⟨compound statement⟩

4.2. ASSIGNMENT STATEMENTS

⟨left part⟩ ::= ⟨variable⟩ := | ⟨procedure identifier⟩ :=

⟨left part list⟩ ::= ⟨left part⟩ | ⟨left part list⟩⟨left part⟩

⟨assignment statement⟩ ::= ⟨left part list⟩⟨arithmetic expression⟩ | ⟨left part list⟩⟨Boolean expression⟩

4.3. GO TO STATEMENTS

⟨go to statement⟩ ::= **go to** ⟨designational expression⟩

4.4. DUMMY STATEMENTS

⟨dummy statement⟩ ::= ⟨empty⟩

4.5. CONDITIONAL STATEMENTS

⟨if clause⟩ ::= **if** ⟨Boolean expression⟩ **then**

⟨unconditional statement⟩ ::= ⟨basic statement⟩ | ⟨compound statement⟩ | ⟨block⟩

⟨if statement⟩ ::= ⟨if clause⟩⟨unconditional statement⟩

⟨conditional statement⟩ ::= ⟨if statement⟩ | ⟨if statement⟩ **else** ⟨statement⟩ | ⟨if clause⟩⟨for statement⟩ | ⟨label⟩ : ⟨conditional statement⟩

4.6. FOR STATEMENTS

⟨for list element⟩ ::= ⟨arithmetic expression⟩|
⟨arithmetic expression⟩ **step** ⟨arithmetic expression⟩ **until**
⟨arithmetic expression⟩|
⟨arithmetic expression⟩ **while** ⟨Boolean expression⟩
⟨for list⟩ ::= ⟨for list element⟩|⟨for list⟩,⟨for list element⟩
⟨for clause⟩ ::= **for** ⟨variable⟩ := ⟨for list⟩ **do**
⟨for statement⟩ ::= ⟨for clause⟩⟨statement⟩|⟨label⟩ : ⟨for statement⟩

4.7. PROCEDURE STATEMENTS

⟨actual parameter⟩ ::= ⟨string⟩|⟨expression⟩|⟨array identifier⟩|
⟨switch identifier⟨|⟨procedure identifier⟩
⟨letter string⟩ ::= ⟨letter⟩|⟨letter string⟩⟨letter⟩
⟨parameter delimiter⟩ ::= ,|) ⟨letter string⟩ :(
⟨actual parameter list⟩ ::= ⟨actual parameter⟩|
⟨actual parameter list⟩⟨parameter delimiter⟩⟨actual parameter⟩
⟨actual parameter part⟩ ::= ⟨empty⟩|(⟨actual parameter list⟩)
⟨procedure statement⟩ ::= ⟨procedure identifier⟩⟨actual parameter part⟩

5
Declarations

⟨declaration⟩ ::= ⟨type declaration⟩|⟨array declaration⟩|
⟨switch declaration⟩|⟨procedure declaration⟩

5.1. TYPE DECLARATIONS

⟨type list⟩ ::= ⟨simple variable⟩|⟨simple variable⟩,⟨type list⟩
⟨type⟩ ::= **real**|**integer**|**Boolean**
⟨local or own type⟩ ::= ⟨type⟩|**own** ⟨type⟩
⟨type declaration⟩ ::= ⟨local or own type⟩⟨type list⟩

5.2. ARRAY DECLARATIONS

⟨lower bound⟩ ::= ⟨arithmetic expression⟩
⟨upper bound⟩ ::= ⟨arithmetic expression⟩
⟨bound pair⟩ ::= ⟨lower bound⟩ : ⟨upper bound⟩
⟨bound pair list⟩ ::= ⟨bound pair⟩|⟨bound pair list⟩,⟨bound pair⟩
⟨array segment⟩ ::= ⟨array identifier⟩[⟨bound pair list⟩]|
⟨array identifier⟩,⟨array segment⟩
⟨array list⟩ ::= ⟨array segment⟩|⟨array list⟩,⟨array segment⟩
⟨array declaration⟩ ::= **array** ⟨array list⟩|
⟨local or own type⟩ **array** ⟨array list⟩

5.3. SWITCH DECLARATIONS

⟨switch list⟩ ::= ⟨designational expression⟩ |
  ⟨switch list⟩, ⟨designational expression⟩
⟨switch declaration⟩ ::= **switch** ⟨switch identifier⟩ := ⟨switch list⟩

5.4. PROCEDURE DECLARATIONS

⟨formal parameter⟩ ::= ⟨identifier⟩
⟨formal parameter list⟩ ::= ⟨formal parameter⟩ |
  ⟨formal parameter list⟩⟨parameter delimiter⟩⟨formal parameter⟩
⟨formal parameter part⟩ ::= ⟨empty⟩ | (⟨formal parameter list⟩)
⟨identifier list⟩ ::= ⟨identifier⟩ | ⟨identifier list⟩, ⟨identifier⟩
⟨value part⟩ ::= **value** ⟨identifier list⟩ ; | ⟨empty⟩
⟨specifier⟩ ::= **string** | ⟨type⟩ | **array** | ⟨type⟩ **array** | **label** | **switch** |
  procedure | ⟨type⟩ **procedure**
⟨specification part⟩ ::= ⟨empty⟩ | ⟨specifier⟩⟨identifier list⟩; |
  ⟨specification part⟩⟨specifier⟩⟨identifier list⟩ ;
⟨procedure heading⟩ ::= ⟨procedure identifier⟩⟨formal parameter part⟩;
  ⟨value part⟩⟨specification part⟩
⟨procedure body⟩ ::= ⟨statement⟩ | ⟨code⟩
⟨procedure declaration⟩ ::=
  procedure ⟨procedure heading⟩⟨procedure body⟩ |
  ⟨type⟩ **procedure** ⟨procedure heading⟩⟨procedure body⟩

BIBLIOGRAPHY

ACM (1964). "FORTRAN vs. Basic FORTRAN." *Comm. ACM* 7 (no. 10), 591–625.

ACM (1971). "Clarification of FORTRAN standards-second report." *Comm. ACM* 14 (no. 10), 628–642.

Aho, A. V., and Johnson, S. C. (1974). "LR Parsing." *Computing Surveys,* vol. 6, no. 2, pp. 99–124. ACM, New York.

Aho, A. V., and Ullman, J. D. (1972). *"Theory of Parsing, Translation and Compiling."* vol. 1, *Parsing;* vol. 2, *Compiling.* Prentice-Hall, Englewood Cliffs, New Jersey.

ANSI (1966). *American National Standard Fortran* (ANS X3.9-1966). American National Standards Institute, New York.

Barron, D. W. (1968). *Recursive Programming Techniques.* American Elsevier, New York.

Baumann, R., Feliciano, M., Bauer, F. L., and Samelson, K. (1964). *Introduction to ALGOL.* Prentice-Hall, Englewood Cliffs, New Jersey.

Beech, D. (1970). "A Structural View of PL/I." *Computing Surveys,* vol. 2, no. 1, pp. 33–64. ACM, New York.

Berkeley, E. C., and Bobrow, O. G., eds. (1964). *The Programming Language LISP: Its Operation and Applications,* 382 pp. Information International Inc., Cambridge, Massachusetts.

Berry, D. M. (1971). "Introduction to Oregano." *SIGPLAN Notices,* vol. 6, no. 2, pp. 171–190. ACM, New York.

Birtwistle, G. M., Dahl, O.-J., Myhrhaug. B., and Nygaard, K. (1973). *Simula Begin.* Auerbach, Philadelphia.

Brainerd, W. S. *et al.* (1978). "Fortran 77." *Comm. ACM* vol 21 (to be published).

Brinch Hansen, P. (1973). *Operating System Principles.* Prentice-Hall, Englewood Cliffs, New Jersey.

Brinch Hansen, P. (1975). "The Programming Language Concurrent Pascal." *IEEE Trans. Software Eng.* SE-1 (no. 2), 199–207.

Brinch Hansen, P., and Hartmann, A. C. (1975). *Sequential Pascal Report.* Information Science, Calif. Institute of Technology, Pasadena, California, July.

Burkhardt, W. H. (1968). "Metalanguage and Syntax Specification." *Comm. ACM* 8 (no. 5), 304–305.

Burroughs (1971). "Extended Algol Reference Manual." The Burroughs Corp., Detroit (form no. 5000128).

Computing Surveys (1974). *Special Issue: Programming,* vol. 6, no. 4. ACM, New York.

Cress, P., Dirksen, P., and Graham, W. J. (1970). *Fortan IV with WATFOR and WATFIV.* Prentice-Hall, Englewood Cliffs, New Jersey.

Dahl, O.-J., Dijkstra, E. W., and Hoare, C. A. R. (1972). *Structured Programming.* Academic Press, New York.

Elson, M. (1973). *Concepts of Programming Languages.* Science Research Associates, Chicago.

Feldman, J., *et al.* (1972). "Recent Developments in SAIL—An ALGOL-based language for artificial intelligence." *AFIPS Conference Proceedings,* vol. 41, part II, pp. 1193–1202. AFIPS. Montvale, New Jersey.

Forsythe, A. I., *et al.* (1975a). *Computer Science: A First Course,* 2nd ed. Wiley, New York.

Forsythe, A. I., *et al.* (1975b). *Computer Science: Programming in FORTRAN IV with WATFOR and WATFIV.* Wiley, New York.

FOR-WORD (1975–). *Fortran Development Newsletter.* SIGPLAN, ACM, New York.

Friedman, D. P. (1974). *The Little Lisper.* Science Research Associates, Chicago.

Gear, C. W. (1973). *Introduction to Computer Science.* Science Research Associates, Chicago.

Goldberg, A., and Kay, A., eds. (1976). "Small Talk-72 Instruction Manual. Xerox Palo Alto Research Center, Palo Alto, California.

Gries, D. (1971). *Compiler Construction for Digital Computers.* Wiley, New York.

Griswold, R. E. (1972). *The Macro Implementation of SNOBOL4.* Freeman, San Francisco.

Griswold, R. E. (1975). *String and List Processing in SNOBOL4.* Prentice-Hall, Englewood Cliffs, New Jersey.

Griswold, R. E., and Griswold, M. T. (1973). *A SNOBOL4 Primer.* Prentice-Hall, Englewood Cliffs, New Jersey.

Griswold, R. E., and Hanson, D. R. (1977). "Overview of SL5." *SIGPLAN Notices* 12 (no. 4), 40–50.

Griswold, R. E., Poage, J., and Polonsky, I. (1971). *The SNOBOL4 Programming Language,* 2nd ed. Prentice-Hall, Englewood Cliffs, New Jersey.

Hanson, D. R. (1976). "The Procedure Mechanism for Backtrack Programming," *National Conference Proceedings,* pp. 401–405, ACM, New York.

Hanson, D. R., and Griswold, R. E. (1978). "The SL5 Procedure Mechanism." *Comm. ACM,* 21 (no. 5).

Hearn, A. C. (1968). "REDUCE—A User Oriented Interactive System for Algebraic Simplification," in *Interactive Systems for Experimental Applied Mathematics,* pp. 79–90. Academic Press, New York.

Hearn, A. C. (1971). "A Program and Language for Algebraic Manipulation." *Proceedings of the Second Symposium on Symbolic and Algebraic Manipulation,* pp. 128–133. ACM, New York.

Hearn, A. C. (1973). "REDUCE 2 User's Manual." University of Utah Report no. UCP-19, March.

Hearn, A. C. (1974). "REDUCE 2 Symbolic Mode Primer." University of Utah Report no. UCP-5.1, October.

Hull, T. E., and Day, D. D. F. (1970). *Computers and Problem Solving* Addison-Wesley, Reading, Massachusetts.

Johnston, J. B. (1971). "The Contour Model of Block Structured Processes." *SIGPLAN Notices,* vol. 6, no. 2, pp. 55–82. ACM, New York.

Kernighan, B. W., and Plauger, P. J. (1974). *The Elements of Programming Style.* McGraw-Hill, New York.

Knuth, D. E., *et al.* (1964). "A Proposal for Input-Output Conventions in ALGOL 60." *Comm. ACM* 7 (no. 5), 273–283.

Kolata, G. B. (1976). "The Four-Color Conjecture: A Computer-Aided Proof." *Science, Research News Section* 193 (13 August), 564–565.

Landin, P. J. (1964). "The mechanical evaluation of expressions." *The Computer Journal* 6 (no. 4, January), 308–320.

Ledgard, H. F. (1975). *Programming Proverbs.* Hayden, Rochelle Park, New Jersey.

McCarthy, J., *et al.* (1962). *LISP 1.5 Programmer's Manual,* 2nd ed. M.I.T. Press, Cambridge, Massachusetts.

McGowan, C. L., and Kelly, J. R. (1975). *Top-Down Structured Programming Techniques.* Petrocelli/Charter, New York.

Moses, J. (1970). "The Function of FUNCTION in LISP." *SIGSAM Bulletin* (July) pp. 13–27. ACM, New York.

Naur, P. ed (1963). "Revised Report on the Algorithmic Language ALGOL 60." *Comm. ACM,* Vol. 6, No. 1. pp. 1–17.

Nicholls, J. E. (1975). *The Structure and Design of Programming Languages.* Addison-Wesley, Reading, Massachusetts.

Nolan, R. L. (1971). *Fortran IV Computing and Applications.* Addison-Wesley, Reading, Massachusetts.

Organick, E. I. (1973). *Computer System Organization: The B5700/B6700 Series.* Academic Press, New York.

Organick, E. I., and Meissner, L. P. (1974). *FORTRAN IV,* 2nd ed. Addison-Wesley, Reading, Massachusetts.

Perlis, A. J. (1975). *Introduction to Computer Science.* Harper and Row, New York.

Petersen, W. W. (1974). *Introduction to Programming Languages.* Prentice-Hall, Englewood Cliffs, New Jersey.

Pratt, T. W. (1975). *Programming Languages: Design and Implementation.* Prentice-Hall, Englewood Cliffs, New Jersey.

Randell, B. and Russell, L. (1964). *ALGOL 60 Implementation.* Academic Press, New York.

Rice, J. K., and Rice, J. R. (1969). *Introduction to Computing.* Holt, Rinehart and Winston, New York.

Rosen, S. (1967). *Programming Systems and Languages.* McGraw-Hill, New York.

Sammet, J. E. (1969). *Programming Languages: History and Fundamentals.* Prentice-Hall, Englewood Cliffs, New Jersey.

SIGPLAN (1976). "Draft Proposed ANS FORTRAN." *SIGPLAN Notices,* vol. 11, no. 3. ACM, New York.

Stevens, W. P., Myers, G. P., and Constantine, L. L. (1974). "Structured Design." *IBM Systems Journal* 13 (no. 2), 115–139.

Strachey, C. (1965). "A General Purpose Macrogenerator." *The Computer Journal* 8, 225–241.

Tannenbaum, A. S. (1976). "A Tutorial on ALGOL 68." *Computing Surveys,* vol. 8, no. 2, pp. 155–190. ACM, New York.

Ullman, J. D. (1976). *Fundamental Concepts of Programming Systems.* Addison-Wesley, Reading, Massachusetts.

Wegner, P., (1968). *Programming Languages Information Structures and Machine Organization.* McGraw-Hill, New York.

Wegner, P. (1971). "Data Structure Models for Programming Languages." *SIGPLAN Notices,* vol. 6, no. 2, pp. 1–54. ACM, New York.

Weissman, C. (1967). *LISP 1.5 PRIMER.* Dickenson, Belmont, California.

Wirth, N. (1973). *Systematic Programming: An Introduction.* Prentice-Hall, Englewood Cliffs, New Jersey.

Wirth, N. (1976). *Algorithms + Data Structures = Programs.* Prentice-Hall, Englewood Cliffs, New Jersey.

Wirth, N., and Hoare, C. A. R. (1966). "A Contribution to the Development of ALGOL." *Comm. ACM* 9 (no. 6), 413–431.

Wirth, N., and Jensen, K. (1975). *PASCAL User Manual and Report.* Springer–Verlag. New York.

Wirth, N., and Weber, H. (1966). "EULER: A Generalization of ALGOL and Its Formal Definition." Part I, *Comm. ACM* 9 (no. 1), 13–23; Part II, *Comm. ACM* 9 (no. 2), 89–99.

ANSWERS TO SELECTED PROBLEMS

Chapter 1

Exercises 1–4

3.

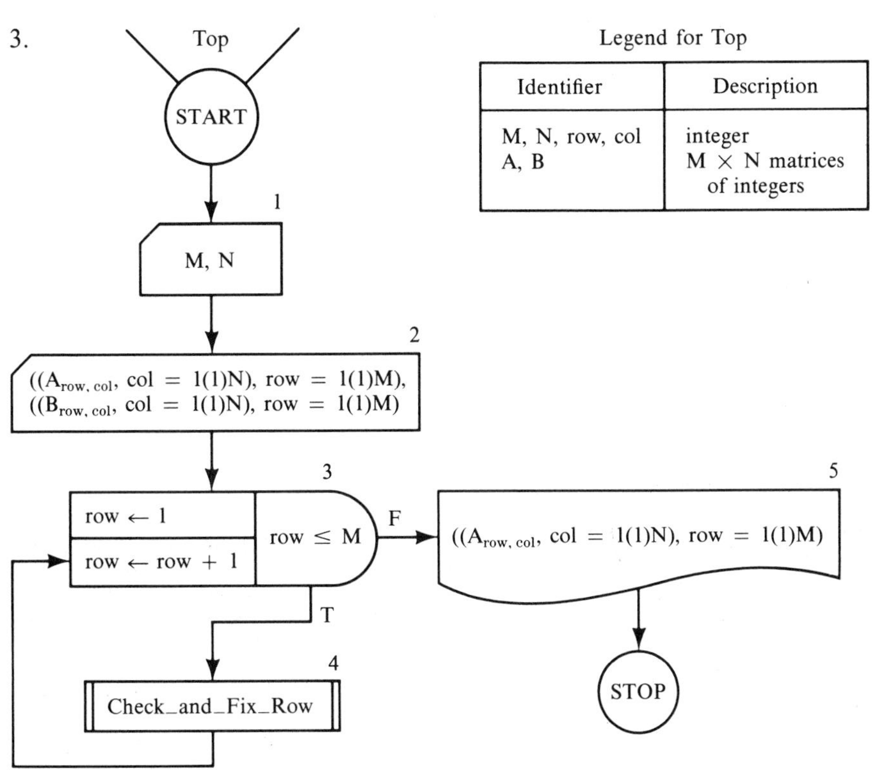

Legend for Top

Identifier	Description
M, N, row, col A, B	integer M × N matrices of integers

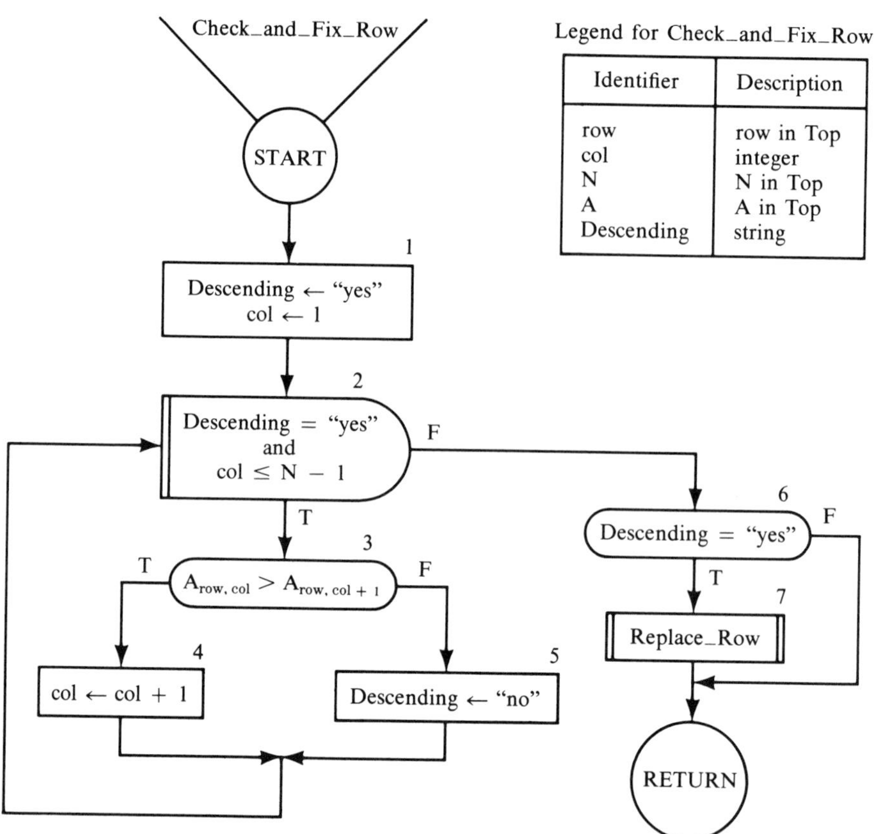

Legend for Check_and_Fix_Row

Identifier	Description
row	row in Top
col	integer
N	N in Top
A	A in Top
Descending	string

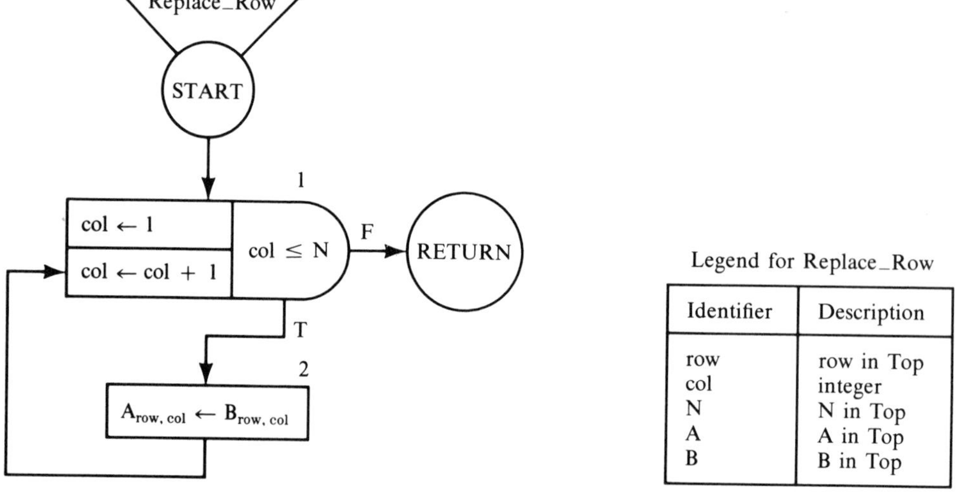

Legend for Replace_Row

Identifier	Description
row	row in Top
col	integer
N	N in Top
A	A in Top
B	B in Top

Exercises 1–5

3.

(a)

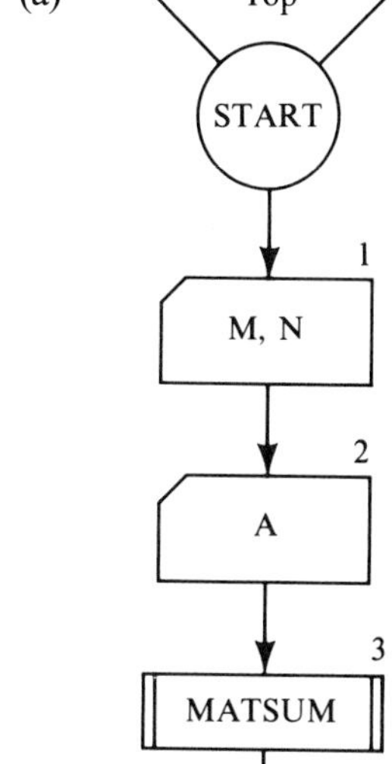

(b)

Legend for Top

Identifier	Treatment	Description
M, N	local	integer
A	local	matrix of $M \times N$ reals
TOTAL	local	real

Legend for MATSUM

Identifier	Treatment	Description
TOTAL	global	Total in Top
i	local	integer
M	global	M in Top
SUM	local	real

Legend for ROWSUM

Identifier	Treatment	Description
SUM	global	SUM in MATSUM
j	local	integer
N	global	N in Top
A	global	A in Top

(c)

MATSUM^1

retlab	box 4 in Top^1
TOTAL	TOTAL in Top^1
i	2
M	M in Top^1
SUM	7

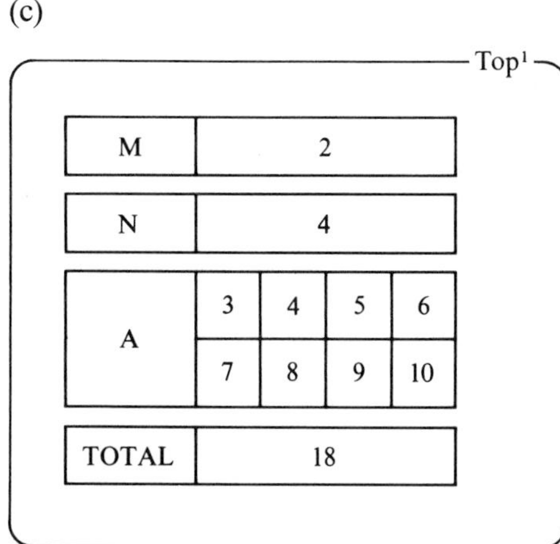

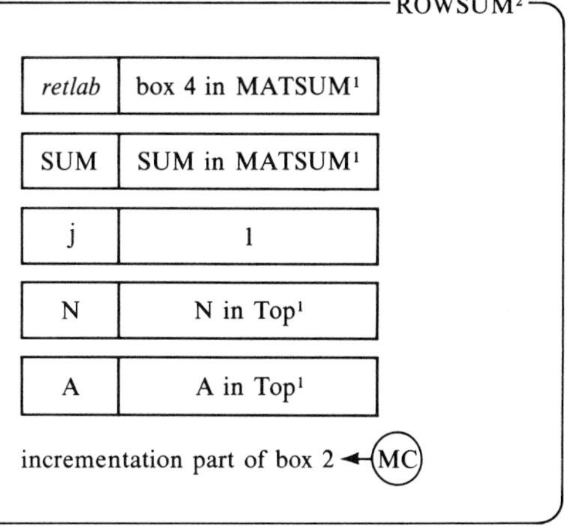

Chapter 2

Exercises 2–4

1.

(a)

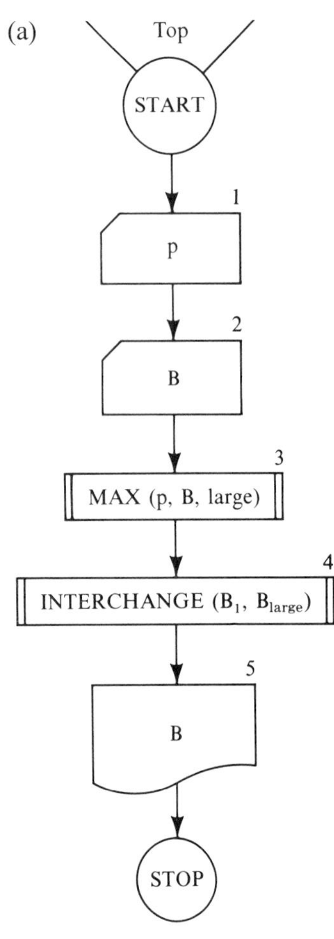

Legend for Top

Identifier	Treatment	Description
p	local	integer
B	local	list of p reals
large	local	integer

In the legend for MAX, the treatment for k must be ref par; the treatment for n and A may be val par or ref par.
In the legend for INTERCHANGE, the treatment for A and B must be ref par.

(b)

i. No. INTERCHANGE must be able to have an effect on storage cells in the contour from which it is called. If A and B were value parameters, the interchange would be local to INTERCHANGE.
ii. MAX would not communicate its result back to its caller.
iii. Yes, since it is not the job of MAX to change any of the values of the list that is its second argument.

3.

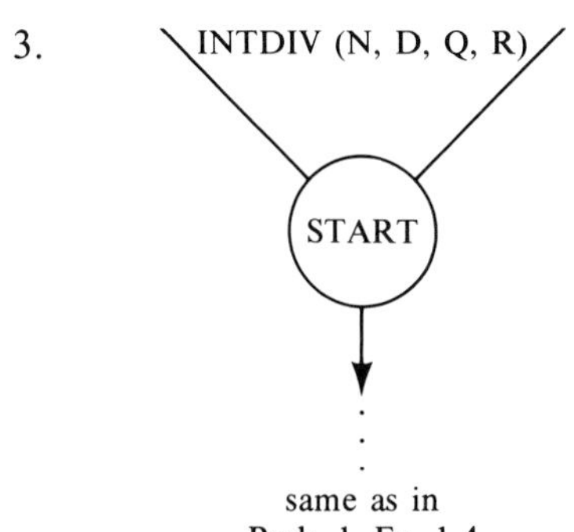

Legend for INTDIV

Identifier	Treatment	Description
N, D Q, R	val par ref par	integer integer

5. (a)

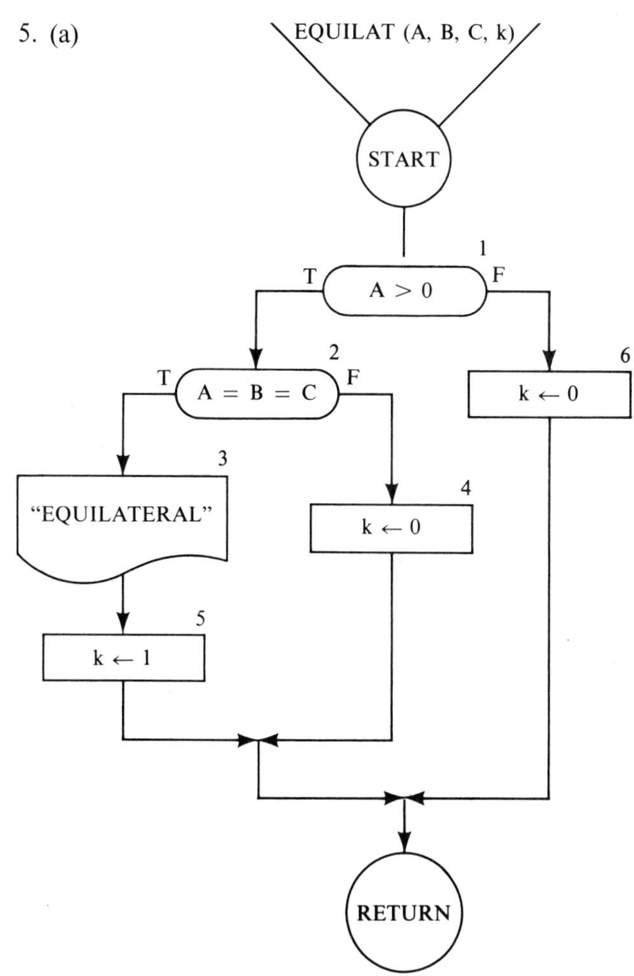

Legend for EQUILAT

Identifier	Treatment	Description
A, B, C k	val par ref par	integer integer

(b) A, B, and C could be value or reference parameters, but value was chosen since EQUILAT should not change the value of A, B, or C. k must be a reference parameter since it is used to send the result of EQUILAT back to the caller.

(c)

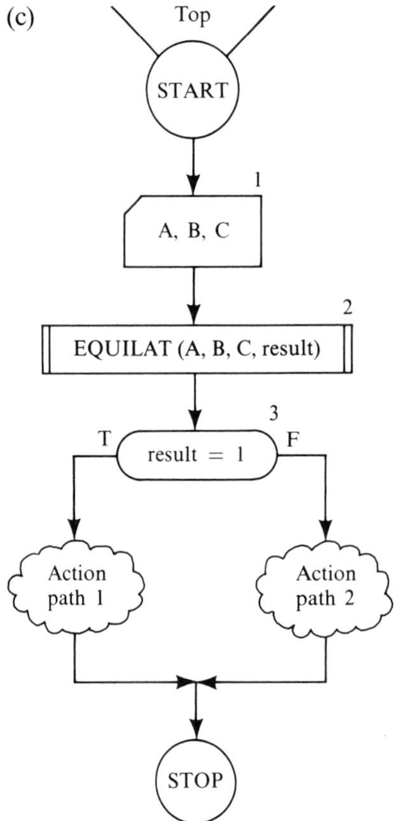

Legend for Top

Identifier	Treatment	Description
A, B, C, result	local	integer

8.

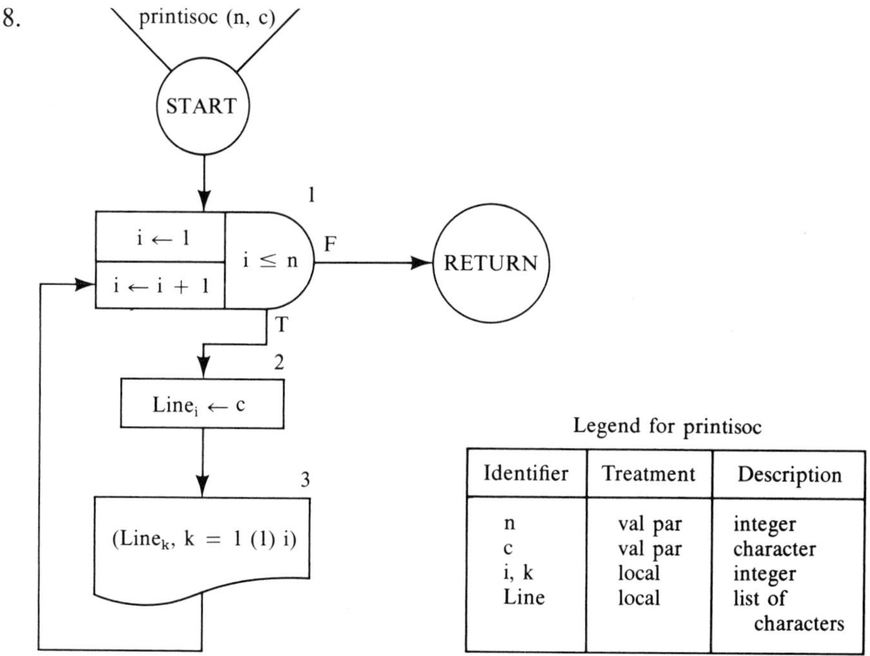

Legend for printisoc

Identifier	Treatment	Description
n	val par	integer
c	val par	character
i, k	local	integer
Line	local	list of characters

Exercises 2–6

1.

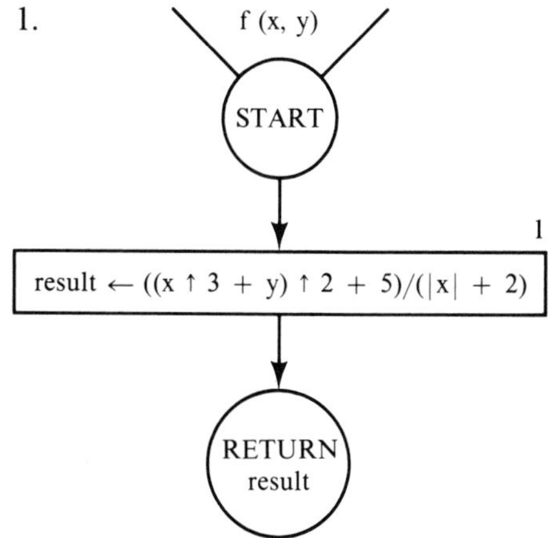

Legend for f

Identifier	Treatment	Description
x, y	val par	real
result	local	real

2. (a)

Legend for RIGHT

Identifier	Treatment	Description
a, b, c result	val par local	integer integer

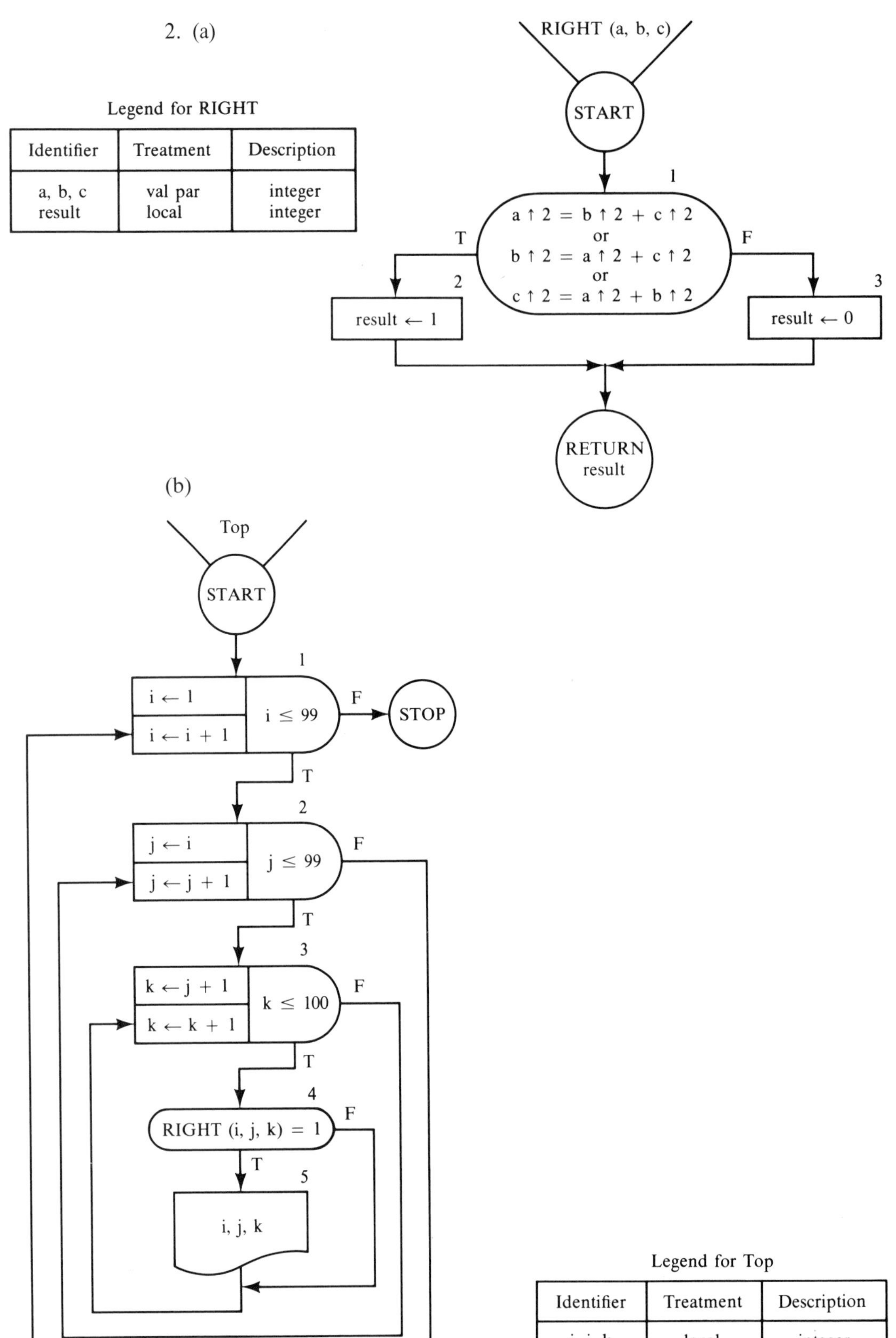

Legend for Top

Identifier	Treatment	Description
i, j, k	local	integer

5.

(a) The 2nd and 3rd calls of GCF do not have the original list B as their second argument, since B has been modified by previous execution(s) of box 3 of Top.

(b)

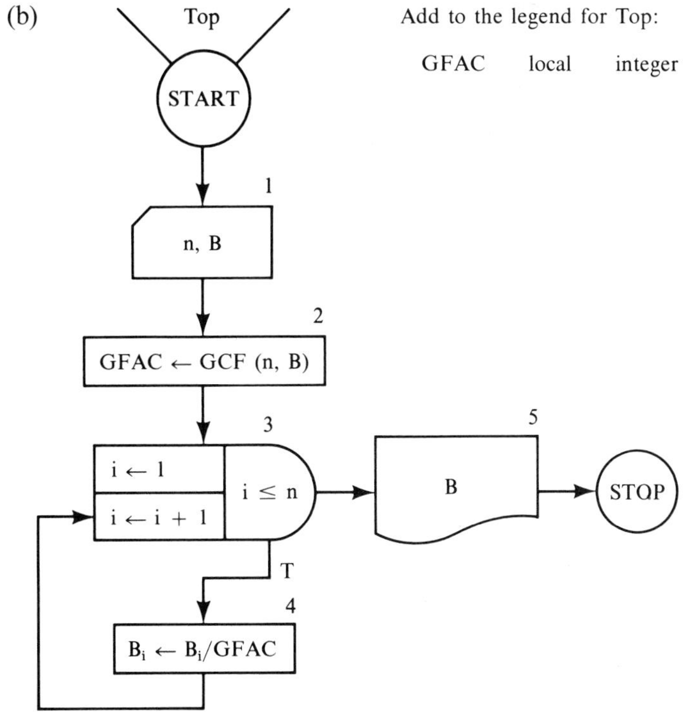

Add to the legend for Top:

GFAC	local	integer

Exercises 2–8 Set B

3.

(a)

Top^1

POINT1	real	0.0
POINT2	real	6.0
TOLERANCE	real	2.0
ZERO	real	–
G	proc	G in packet

box 2 ← MC

(b)

Top^1

POINT1	real	0.0
POINT2	real	6.0
TOLERANCE	real	2.0
ZERO	real	1.5
G	proc	G in packet

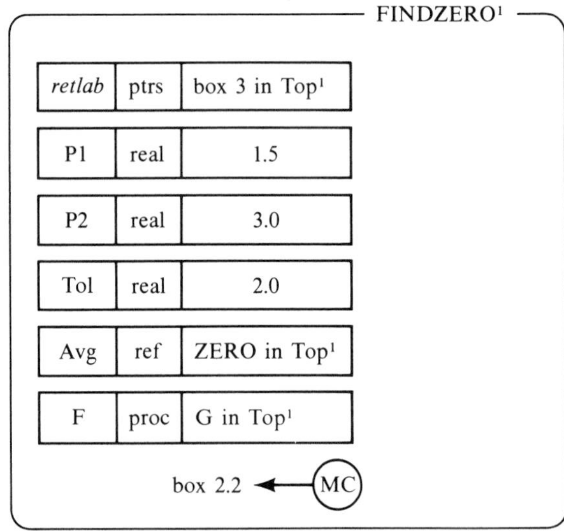

(c) AN APPROXIMATE ROOT OF G(X) IS 1.5

(d) The cell for Avg in FINDZERO^1 would be

Avg	form	"ZERO" in Top^1

The printed result would be the same.

4.

(a) F was called from P, as shown by the value in the *retlab* cell in F^1.

(b)

variable	value used
M	2
I	8
N	4
L	1

(c) The assignment changes the value of X in Top^1 to 15.

(d)

variable	value used
A	13
V	5
B	3
I	6
R	3

(e) The assignment changes the value of Y in Top^1 to 27.

(f) 1st box: 4 is assigned to I in Top^1.
2nd box: 14 is assigned to X in Top^1.

Chapter 3

Exercises 3–1, Set B

1. (a) The path from box 1 to box 5.
   (b) Box 5. Box 4 can't be reached until the return takes place from the final recursive call of GCDR. That return is through box 5.
   (c) The MC places the value returned (the value of M) on his stack and moves back to box 3 in the environment of the caller (the previous call of GCDR). The value on the stack is then assigned to K. In box 4, the value of K is placed on the stack and another RETURN is executed.
   (d) In terms of the final result—yes, it is equivalent. Slightly different actions are performed by the MC since he moves from box 4 directly to the previous box 4 (RETURN box), without temporarily storing the value returned in K.

(e)

Call	M	N	K	R	value returned
1	65	35	5	30	5
2	35	30	5	5	5
3	30	5	5	0	5
4	5	0	—	—	5

6. Data sets

n	B	Purpose
4	2, 3, 0, 1, 2	These data sets represent "normal" calls on Evaluate.
1	2, 3	
0	2	This set checks for correct operation in the "special case" where n = 0.
0	5	These data sets all contain errors. Appropriate messages should be printed.
3	1, −2, 3	
2	4, 2, 3	
−1	2	
−2	−1, 0, 5	
2	0, 0, 0	Another special case: each element of **B** is 0.

Each pathway through the flowchart is used at least once when the algorithm is tested with these data sets. Potentially troublesome data sets are included, as are data sets with errors.

Exercises 3–3

3. (a) U(4) = 88

(b)

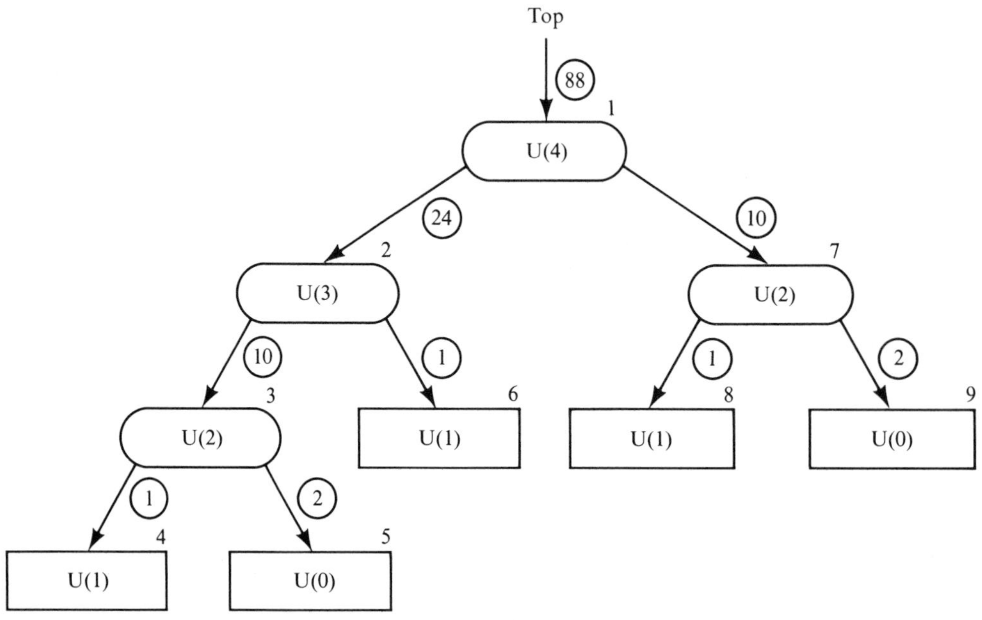

(c)

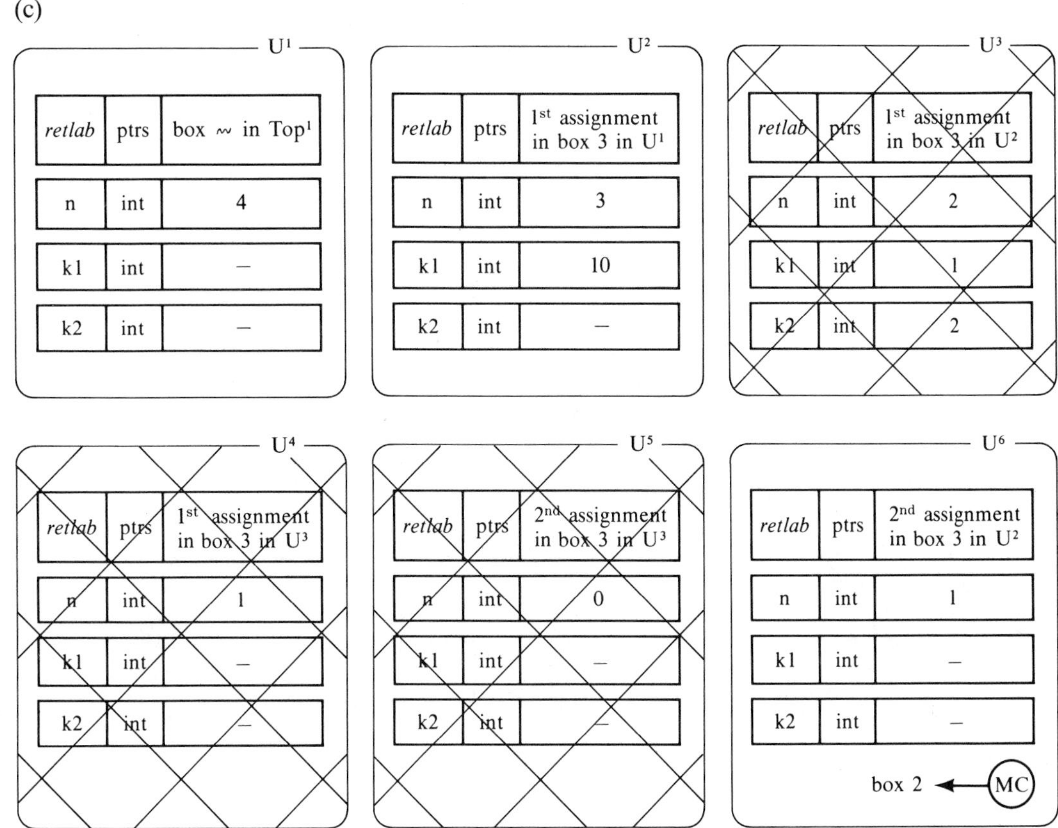

Cross–hatching shows inaccessible contours.

Exercises 3–5

1.

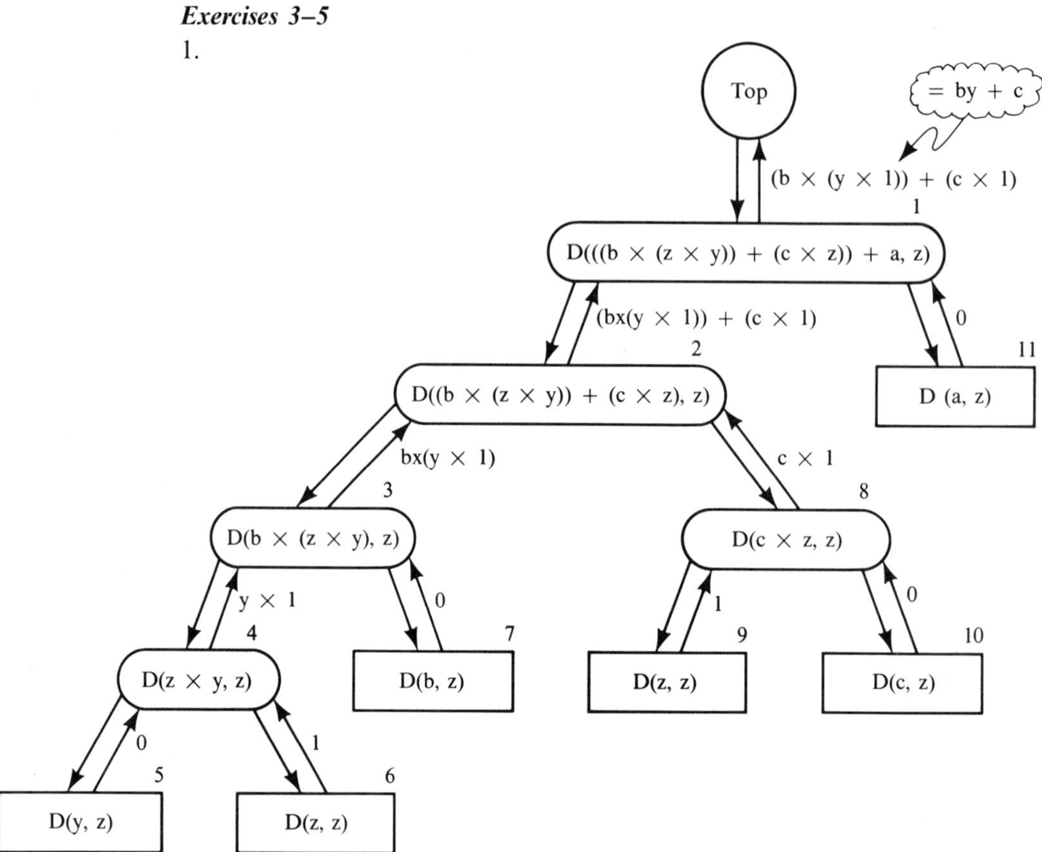

To improve readability, simplifications have been made in the value returned by some calls on D. For example, the value of the 4th call is shown as y × 1 rather than (z × 0) + (y × 1). In a later chapter, we discuss an algorithm that performs such simplifications.

Exercises 3–6

2. Shown below is a snapshot taken when the nut has just been found.

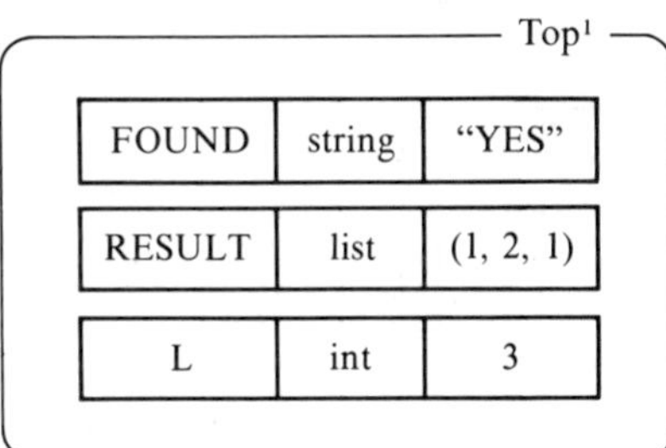

Top^1

FOUND	string	"YES"
RESULT	list	(1, 2, 1)
L	int	3

TS^1

retlab	ptrs	box 12 in Top^1
path	list	( )
length	int	0
FOUND	ref	FOUND in Top^1
Nut	ref	RESULT in Top^1
Nutlen	ref	L in Top^1
k	int	1
max	int	2
newpath	list	(1)

TS^2

retlab	ptrs	box 6 in TS^1
path	list	(1)
length	int	1
FOUND	ref	FOUND in TS^1
Nut	ref	Nut in TS^1
Nutlen	ref	Nutlen in TS^1
k	int	2
max	int	2
newpath	list	(1, 2)

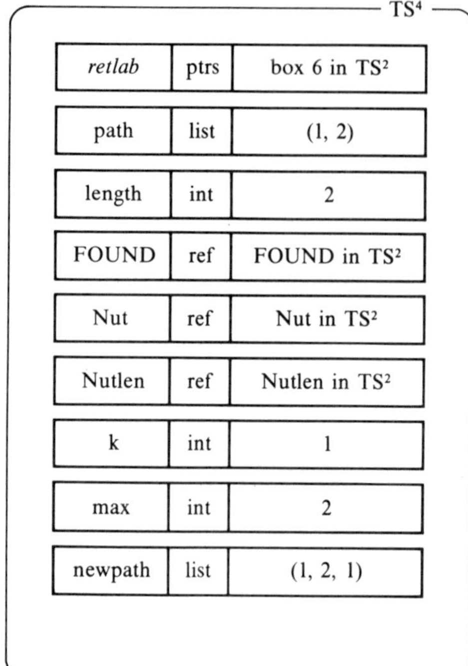

TS^4

retlab	ptrs	box 6 in TS^2
path	list	(1, 2)
length	int	2
FOUND	ref	FOUND in TS^2
Nut	ref	Nut in TS^2
Nutlen	ref	Nutlen in TS^2
k	int	1
max	int	2
newpath	list	(1, 2, 1)

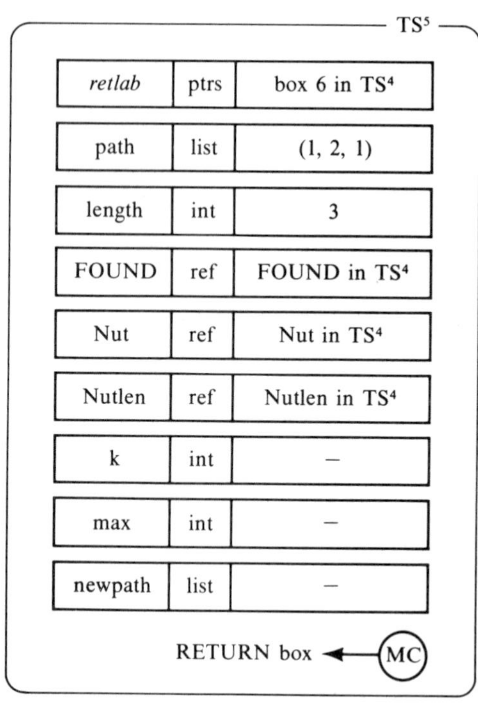

TS^5

retlab	ptrs	box 6 in TS^4
path	list	(1, 2, 1)
length	int	3
FOUND	ref	FOUND in TS^4
Nut	ref	Nut in TS^4
Nutlen	ref	Nutlen in TS^4
k	int	–
max	int	–
newpath	list	–

The TS^3 environment is no longer accessible and is not shown.

4. The variables RESULT and L of Top could be used globally in Treesearch. (This could also be done with FOUND.)

Chapter 4

(no exercises)

Chapter 5

Exercises 5–3

```
      begin
         D1;
         procedure P2(par1):
            D21;
            D22;
            begin
               D31;
P2             procedure P4(par1):
            P4    D41;
         B3       S42;
               S31;
               S32
            end;
         S1;
B1       S2;
         begin
            D51;
            procedure P6(par1):
      P6       D61;
               D62;
   B5          S61;
            S51;
            begin
      B7       D71;
               S72
            end
         end
      end
```

Note: P2 here is P2 with a bar over it ($\overline{P2}$), and likewise $\overline{P4}$ and $\overline{P6}$. The numbers after D and S are subscripts: D_1, D_{21}, D_{22}, D_{31}, D_{41}, S_{42}, S_{31}, S_{32}, S_1, S_2, D_{51}, D_{61}, D_{62}, S_{61}, S_{51}, D_{71}, S_{72}.

Exercises 5–7

2. (a) Shown below is snapshot 5 for each of the Algol programs (just before the return from lrgst).

For the program in Figure 5-25:

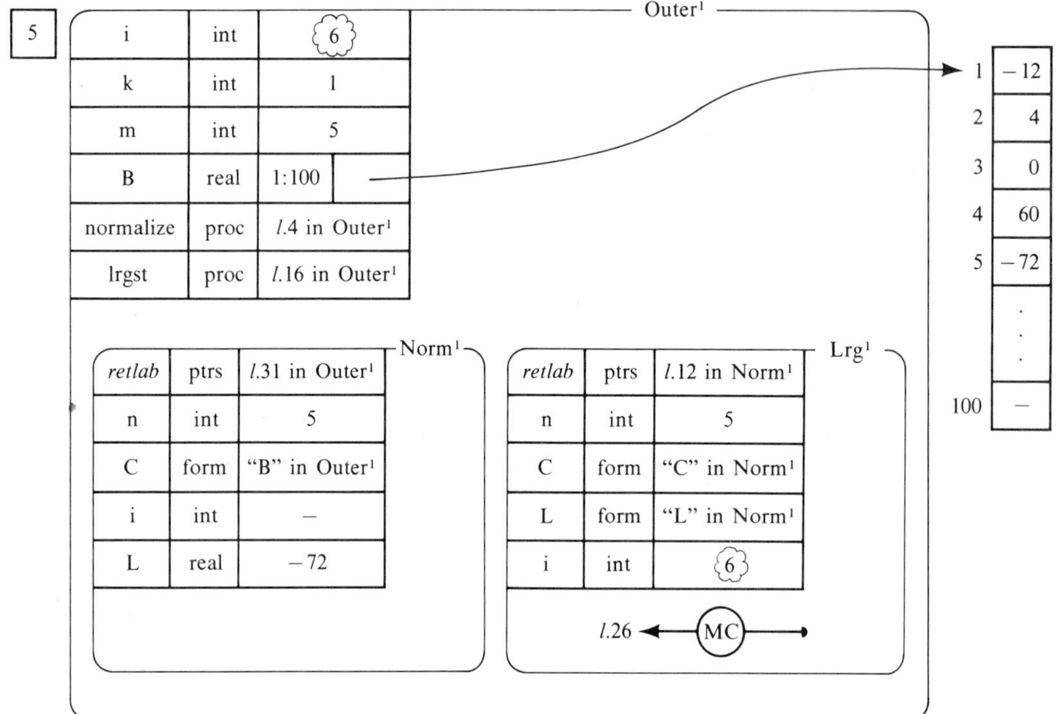

For the program in Figure 5-26:

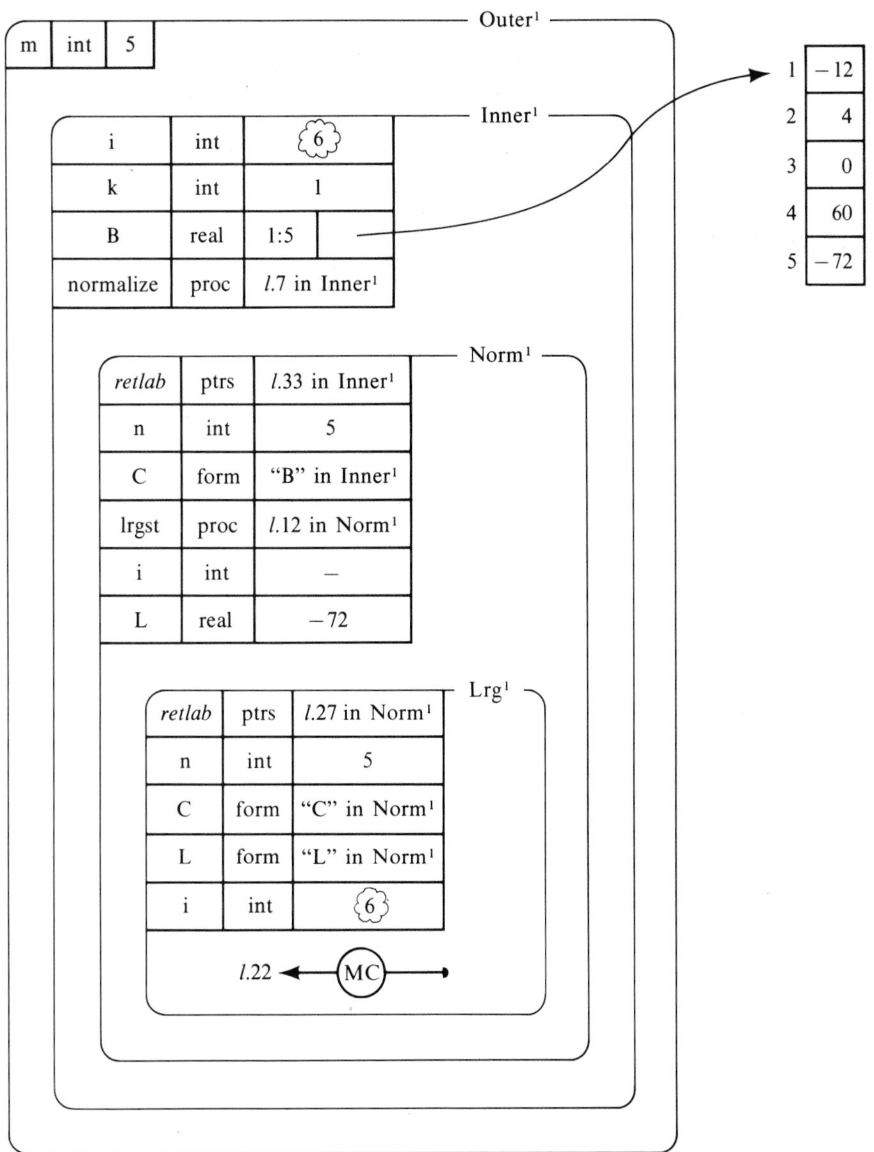

(b) Use the technique shown in Figure 5-23.

Exercises 5–9

1. The same values would be printed. The important point in the operation of procedure SUM is that assignments to i affect the same storage cell that is used in the evaluation of the name parameter u (whose value is a formula involving i). The cell for i in $Outer^1$ will be used for both purposes if i is global to SUM *or* if i is a name parameter to SUM.

Chapter 6

Exercises 6–3

2. True. In Fortran, the only globals are cells in $Prog^1$. Thus no globals can be local to a procedure. In Algol, cells local to procedure A are global to procedure B if B is declared inside A (and the names of the cells are not reused in declarations inside B).

Exercises 6–7, Set A

1.

```
C     * TOP STARTS HERE ***
      INTEGER B, N, I, K
      COMMON N, B (50)
   20 READ, N
      READ, (B(I), I = 1, N)
      CALL EVLIST (N, B)
      GO TO 20
      END

C     * EVLIST STARTS HERE ***
      SUBROUTINE EVLIST
      INTEGER C, M, K, E (50), I, EVEN
      COMMON M, C (50)
      COMMON /IBLOCK/I
      K = 0
      DO 45 I = 1, M
         IF (EVEN .NE.1) GO TO 45
           K = K + 1
           E (K) = C (I)
   45 CONTINUE
      IF (K .EQ. 0) GO TO 6
      PRINT, (E (I), I = 1, K)
      GO TO 8
    6 PRINT, 'NONE'
    8 RETURN
      END

C     * EVEN STARTS HERE ***
      INTEGER FUNCTION EVEN
      INTEGER DUMMY, C, I, R
      COMMON DUMMY, C (50)
      COMMON /IBLOCK/I
      IF (C (I) .EQ. INT
     *   (C (I)/2) 2) GO TO 2
      R = 0
      GO TO 4
    2 R = 1
    4 EVEN = R
      RETURN
      END
```

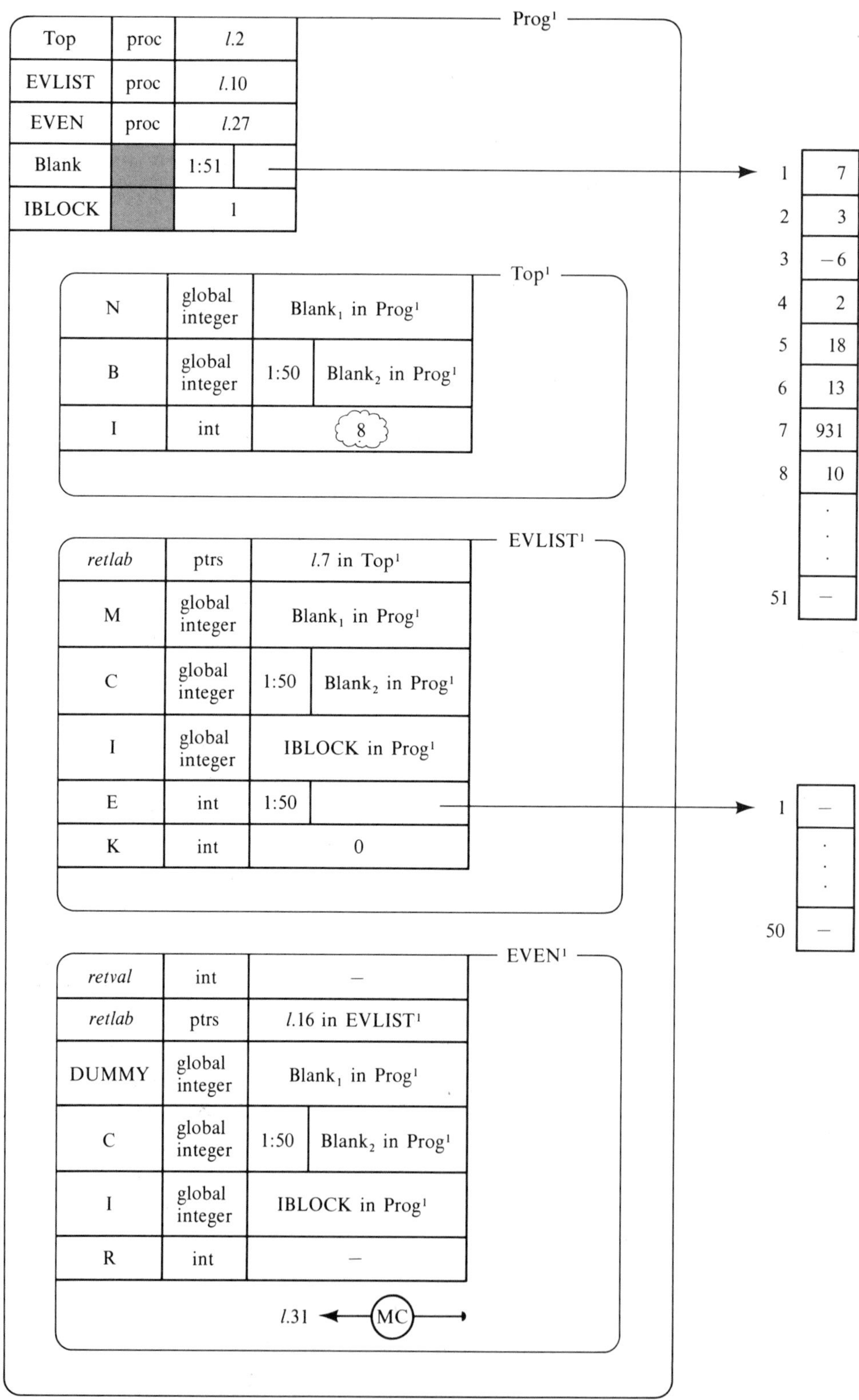
Prog[1]
Top proc l.2
EVLIST proc l.10
EVEN proc l.27
Blank 1:51
IBLOCK 1
Top[1]
N global integer Blank$_1$ in Prog[1]
B global integer 1:50 Blank$_2$ in Prog[1]
I int 8
EVLIST[1]
retlab ptrs l.7 in Top[1]
M global integer Blank$_1$ in Prog[1]
C global integer 1:50 Blank$_2$ in Prog[1]
I global integer IBLOCK in Prog[1]
E int 1:50
K int 0
EVEN[1]
retval int —
retlab ptrs l.16 in EVLIST[1]
DUMMY global integer Blank$_1$ in Prog[1]
C global integer 1:50 Blank$_2$ in Prog[1]
I global integer IBLOCK in Prog[1]
R int —
l.31
MC
1 7
2 3
3 −6
4 2
5 18
6 13
7 931
8 10
51 —
1 —
50 —

Chapter 7

Exercises 7–4, Set A

1. (a) ((A . B) . C)
   (b) ((A . B) . (X . Y))
   (e) (((A . B) . C) . D)
   (g) ((A)(B)(C))
2. (a) CAAR(Z)
   (c) CADR(Z)
   (e) CDAAR(Z)
   (g) CAADDR(Z)

Exercises 7–8

1. In RLISP:

```
LISP PROCEDURE COPATOMLIST(X);
  IF NULL(X) THEN NIL
      ELSE CONS(CAR(X), COPATOMLIST(CDR(X)));
```

In LISP:

```
(DEFINE '(
  (COPATOMLIST (LAMBDA (X) (COND ((NULL X) NIL)
                      (T (CONS (CAR X) (COPATOMLIST (CDR X))))))
  ))
```

Exercises 7–9

1. In RLISP:

```
LISP PROCEDURE EQATLISTS(X,Y);
  IF NULL (X) THEN T
    ELSE AND(EQ(CAR(X),CAR(Y)),EQATLISTS(CDR(X),CDR(Y)));
```

An alternative definition:

```
LISP PROCEDURE EQATLISTS (X, Y);
  IF NULL (X) THEN T
    ELSE IF NOT(EQ(CAR(X), CAR(Y))) THEN NIL
    ELSE EQATLISTS (CDR(X), CDR(Y));
```

In LISP:

```
(DEFINE '(
  (EQATLISTS (LAMBDA (X Y) (COND ((NULL X) T)
    (T (AND (EQ (CAR X) (CAR Y))
      (EQATLISTS (CDR X) (CDR Y)))))))
))
```

or

```
(DEFINE '(
  (EQATLISTS (LAMBDA (X Y) (COND ((NULL X) T)
    ((NOT(EQ (CAR X) (CAR Y))) NIL)
    (T (EQATLISTS (CDR X) (CDR Y))))))
))
```

Exercises 7–11

1. The following snapshot shows the "deepest" point of the recursion:

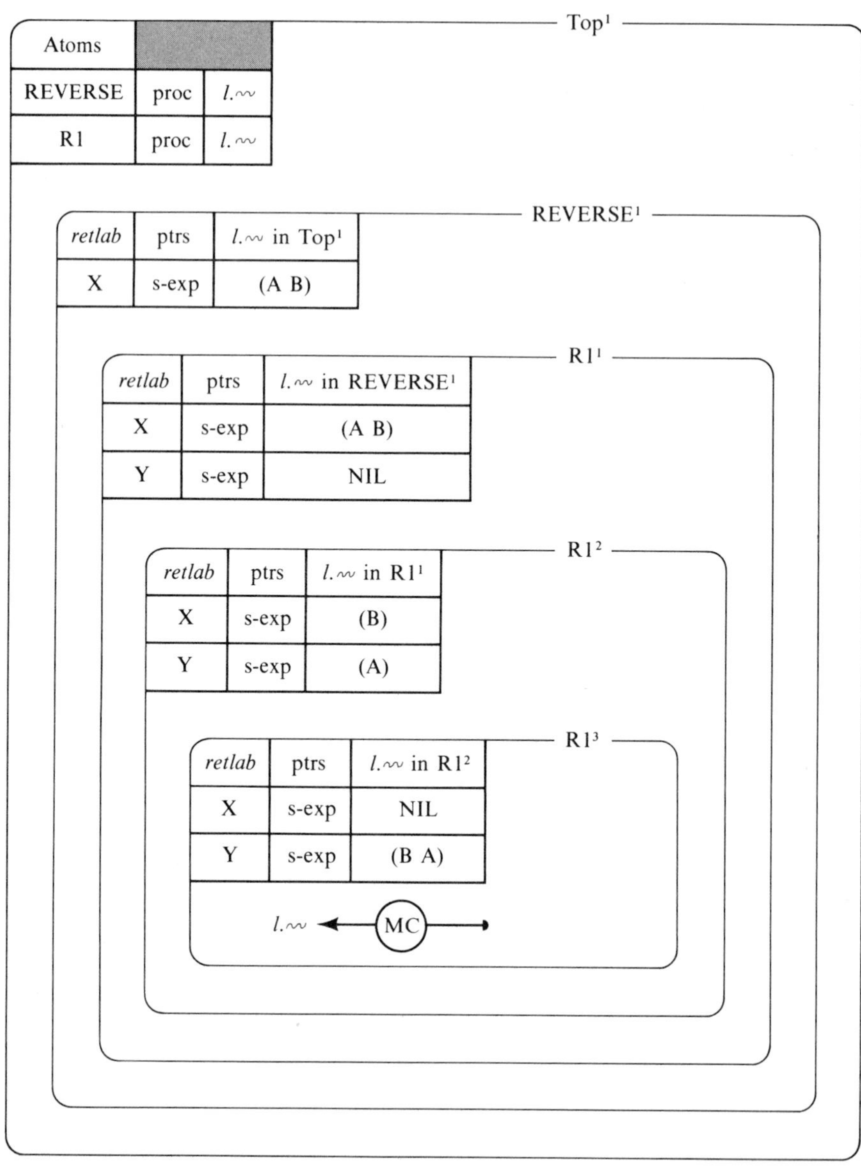

Chapter 8

Exercises 8–8

Ten lines of input are read, trimmed, and concatenated as the value of LINE.

Exercises 8–10

1.

```
          DEFINE('REVERSE(L)', 'REVSTART')
             .
             .
             .
REVSTART  IDENT(L, 'NIL') : F(NOTEMPTY)
          REVERSE = 'NIL' : (RETURN)
NOTEMPTY  REVERSE = APPEND(REVERSE(CDR(L)),
                    CONS(CAR(L), 'NIL')) : (RETURN)
```

Chapter 9

Exercises 9–4

1. (a) The program "deadlocks" with all MC's asleep. Top and task TB are waiting on eventA, and task TA is waiting on eventB. Snapshot of the final state:

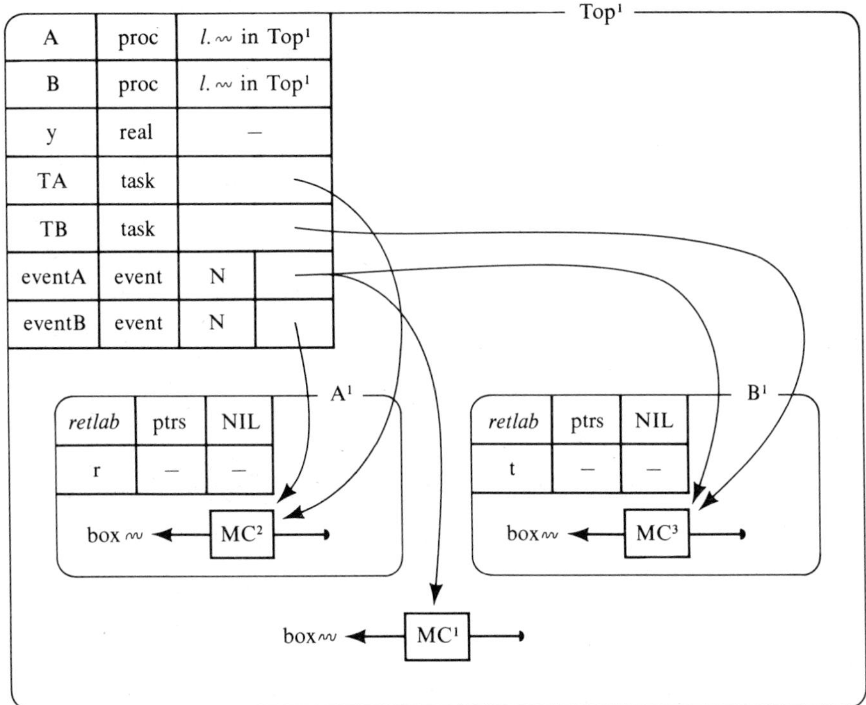

2. All possible transitions:

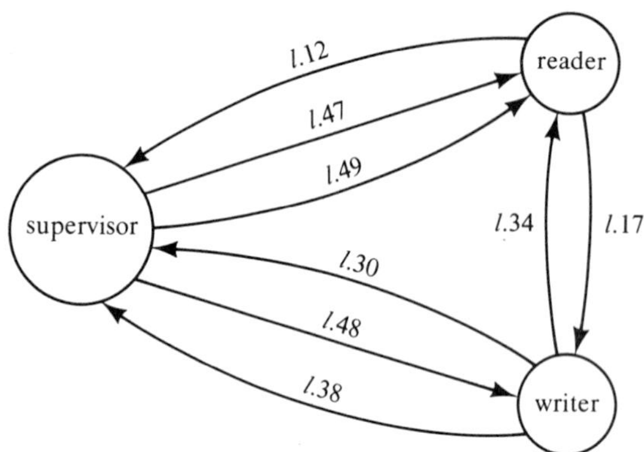

Chapter 10

Exercises 10–8, Set A

Map

Reduced Connection Table

Country No.	Previously colored neighbor countries
1	–
2	1
3	1 2
4	2 3
5	1 3
6	1 2 5
7	2 6
8	2 4 7
9	3 4 5 8
10	5 6 9

Snapshot taken just before the return from advance[8].

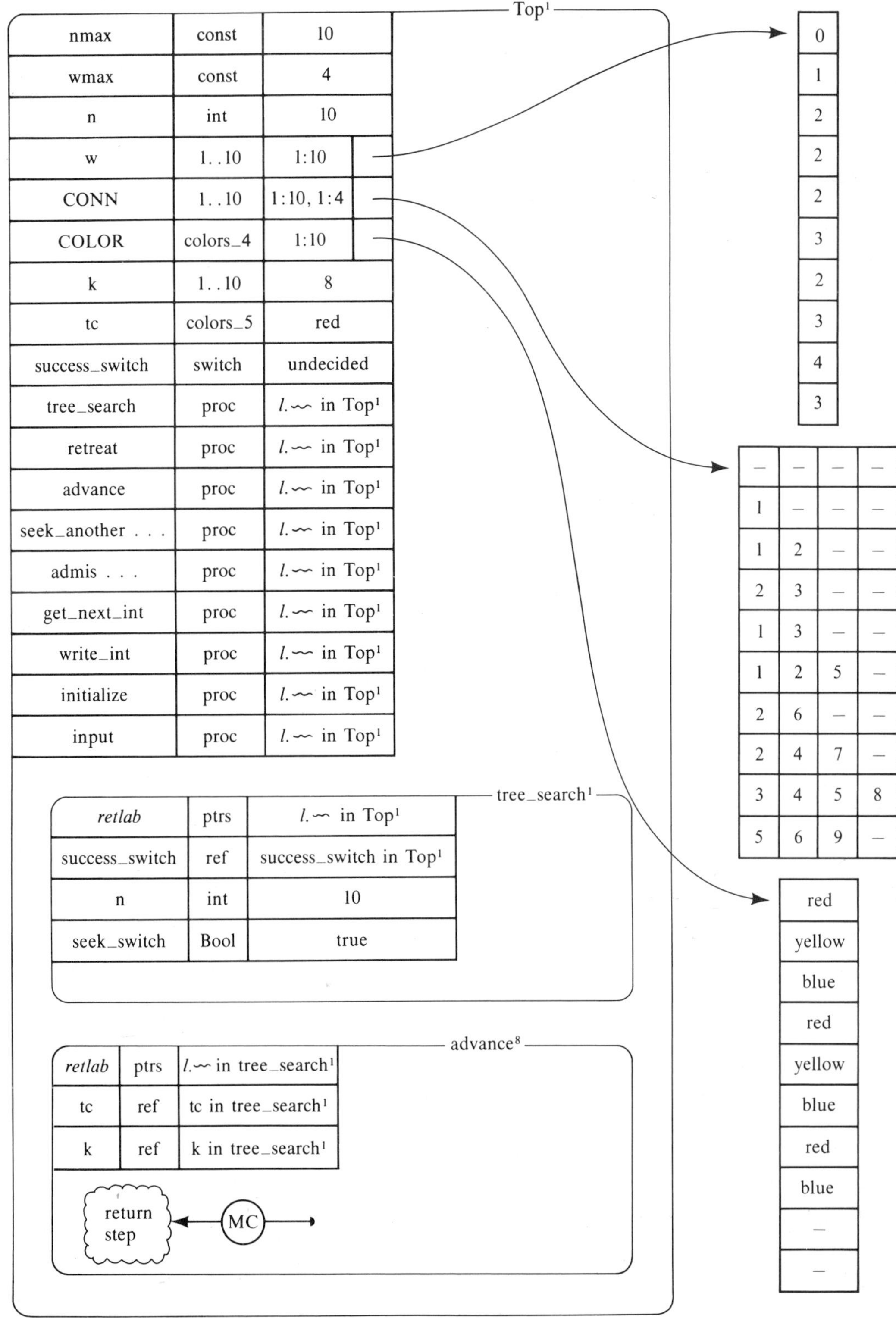

INDEX

Abstract machine model, 193
Action sequences,
concurrent action, 519
initiation, termination and coordination of, 520
ALGOL 60, 3, 195, 308 (*Same as* ALGOL)

Addressing environment, 233
Block
begin, end pair, 202
body, 195
entry, 216
exit, 219
head, 195
nesting, 196
static, 199
structure, 195, 370
Burroughs (EXTENDED) ALGOL, 3, 520
Asleep state of a task, 526
Asynchronous task, 522
coordination, 523
example program, 525, 535
experimental results, 534, 535–538
snapshot sequence for, 527–533
in operating systems, 549
invocation, 525
NIL return pointer for, 532
relative rate of progress, 530
sending a message to a, 525
termination, 523
Awake state of a task, 526
Buffer storage cell, 519
call statement for creation of coroutines, 543
cause procedure, 531, 533
awakening mechanism, 531
continue command, 540, 544
specified, 544, 546
unspecified, 545, 546
Coroutine tasks
communication between, 540
computation structures, 540
contour, initiator cell, 546
contour diagrams for, 520
control structure, 547
as a state transition graph, 548
Eight Queens problem solved using, 555, 556, 558, 559
environments, snapshots for, 546, 547
outer block supervisor, 546
execution by taking turns, 540
model of resource sharing, 540
reader and writer, 548
retained environments for, 540
structure, 542
water sharing case study, 541
event
parameter, 526
type, 526
variable, 526
dummy, 527
happened and not happened values of, 526
initial value of, 526
Literature, 557
Mailbox, 548
Process keyword, 526
Producer and consumer algorithm, 519
coroutine solution, 548
flowcharts and legend, 550, 551
program, 552
Programs, 525, 535, 545, 552
task
array, 556
state, 526
type, 526
variable, 526
value of a, 526
wait and *cause*
library routines, 526
mechanism for sending and receiving messages, 526
task synchronization procedures, 533
wait procedure, 526, 533
Waiting, for an event to occur, 523
Water-sharing problem, illustration of coroutines, 541
program, 545
snapshot, 547
BNF
definitions for terminal symbols, 208
syntax definitions, 206, 612–617

ALGOL (*continued*)

Case studies, 226
case 1, squeezing zeros out of a list, 227
flowcharts and legends, 228
program, 230, 231
snapshot sequence, 230–236
case 2, finding even values in a list, 235
flowcharts and legends, 236
program, 237
snapshot sequence, 239–245
case 3, factorial, 249
flowcharts and legends, 250
program, 250
snapshot sequence, 249–256
case 4, binomial coefficient, 256
call tree, 258
flowcharts and legends, 257
programs, 257, 265
snapshot sequences, 258–265, 267–272
case 5, name parameter (as a marching rule), 276
flowcharts and legends, 277
program, 278
snapshot sequence, 278–286
case 6, procedure parameter (as a marching rule), 288
flowcharts and legends, 289
program, 290
snapshot sequence, 291–295
Comparison with Fortran, 370
Compound statement, 200, 373
Comments, 209
Declarations, 195, 208
for sharing of globals, 213
function procedure, 214, 215
procedure, 213
syntax, 206, 208–215, 612–618
type, 212
Dynamic,
declaration of arrays, 370
storage allocation, 227, 370
Exercises,
block structure and recursion, 296–303
factorial, 256
normalize a list, 245–248
tree traversal, 304, 305
Input/output, 373
List cell, 232, 239
pointer, 232, 239
Name parameter, 224
own identifier, 305, 311
relationship with block structure, 306
problems with **own** arrays, 307
Parameters, 202
analogous legend entries, 202
formal, 233
name matched to expressions, 272
procedure, 288
dummy name, 291
simple, 202
specifiers, 202
Procedure
Boolean, 238
declaration, 199
definition, 202
entry, 221
heading, 202
specification part, 202
value part, 202
return, 223
Processing of nonnumeric data, 375
Program, 196
schematic, 202, 204
scoping lines, 202
tree structure, 196, 205, 221
depth, 200
Return value cell (*retval*), 240
Scoping lines, 202
Semantics
block
entry, 216
exit, 219
contour
creation, 218
deallocation, 219
diagram of environments, 218
for-loop counter value after normal exit, 232
for–while, 282, 283
name parameters, 224
cell structure for, 225, 226
contour diagram, 226
nested environments, 217
precedence of locals over globals, 217
procedure, declaration, 220
entry, 221
snapshots, 222
invocation, 220
return, 223
snapshots, 223
value-returning procedures, 235
Stack
notation, 266
of returned results, 266
of the MC, 241
Statement syntax, 206, 208–215, 615–616
assignment, 209
compound, 200, 373
conditional, 211, 374
for, 212
go to, 245
if then, 211
if then else, 211, 212
input/output, 210
iteration, 212
Static binding, 220
Storage allocation
dynamic, 229, 370
utilization, 235, 370
Syntax, 208
arrays and subscript bounds, 209
assignment symbol :=, 208
BNF, 206, 208, 612–618
character strings, 214
comments, 209
conditional statement, 209
for statement, 209
keywords, 208
separator (semicolon), 215
summary, with comparison to flowchart syntax, 209–215
Translation of flowcharts to code, 227

Variables
declaration of global, 372
explicit declaration of, 372
Variations and extensions, 195

Algol W, 560
Algol 68, 111, 520, 560
type checking, 579
Algorithm
development, bottom up and top down, 16
flowchart representation, 12
multisequence, 519
performed by two or more controllers, 519
specification, 4
Allocation, of a new MC, 521
Allocator, 22
APL language, 3
Argument(s), 56
-parameter matching, 63
with protection, 79
postponed evaluation of, 101
regarded as a formula, 101
that are expressions, 89
Artificial intelligence, 376
ASCII character set, 583

Backus–Naur Form, 184, *see also* BNF
Basic, 3
Binary tree, 162
traversal, 167
Binomial coefficient, 150, 256
Blank character, 17, 42
symbol "□", 17
BNF
notation, 206
syntax, Algol, 206, 612–618
Fortran, 316
Lisp, 398, 410, 411
Snobol, 473
B6700-type computer, 533

Call
chain, 149
tree, 149
for symbolic differentiation, 172
Case study, 3
Chain, of references, 67
Chessboard, printing, algorithm, 57
Chess Queen, scope, 7
Cobol, 3, 560, 563
Complexity, managing of programs, 77
Computer model, 21
contour, 24
control unit, 22
environment, 23
master computer, 22, *see also* MC
program, 22
snapshot, 24
storage, 24
Concurrent Pascal language, 520
Contour, 24
diagram, 520
origin, 121
procedure, 36
name
qualified with a superscript, 33
Control
of repetition, 11
sequence, 11
Coroutine
relationship, 521
suspension and resumption, 523

Deadlock, 553
Decision step, 11
Declaration, 4
Definite iteration, 10, 18
Differentiation
recursive process, 444
rules, 444

Eight Queens problem, 555, 610–611
Empty string, 186
Englishlike language for describing an algorithm, 4, 6
Enumerated
array notation, 20
list notation, 18
Environment, 24
calling, 56
of a procedure, 34
of a subprogram, 30
pointer, 35, 50
ep, *see* environment pointer
Escape hatch concept in recursion, 124, 378
Expression
argument in a procedure call, 89
matched to a reference parameter, 90
infix, 52
postfix, 52

Fibonacci series algorithm, 4
Find zero procedure
exercise, 117
flowchart, 119
Flowchart(s), 4
choosing between, and textual forms, 6
conventions, 7
ensembles, 30
language summary, 17–19
postponing details, 6
representation of an algorithm, 12
top-level, 22
Flowchart/legend, 6
Formal differentiation, 170, *see also* symbolic differentiation

Fortran, 308
Arrays
declaration of, 370
in the 1977 Standard, 341
Allocation
of storage, 351, 370
strategy
for array space, 338
BNF syntax definitions, 319
of terminal symbols, 320
Case studies
case 1, squeezing zeros out of a list, 336
flowcharts and legends, 336
program, 337, 342
snapshot sequence, 338–340
case 2, finding even values in a list, 342
flowcharts and legends, 343
program, 344, 345
snapshot sequence, 346–351
case 3, procedure parameter (as a marching rule), 352
flowcharts and legends, 354
program, 355, 356
snapshot sequence, 358–364
CHARACTER data type, 340
Comments, 320, 321
COMMON
blocks, 314
blank, 317
labeled, 317, 357
named, 317
declarations, 313
Comparison with Algol, 370
Concatenation operator (//), 340
Continuation
code, 320
line, 321
Contour(s)
accessibility of leftover values, 311
allocation, 310
static, 312
deallocation, 311
preallocation, 312
reuse of, 339
Data initialization declaration, 322
Declarations
COMMON, 328
DATA initialization, 322
DIMENSION, 328
EQUIVALENCE, 322, 334, 371
FUNCTION subprogram, 330, 331
SUBROUTINE subprogram, 329
type, 328
DO statement, 322, 326, 327
implied, 338, 350
loop semantics, 326, 337, 340
in the 1977 Standard, 340, 341
value of counter after normal exit, 338
Early development, 308
END statement
of a program 320
of a subprogram, 329–331
EQUIVALENCE declaration, 322, 334, 371
Exercises
normalize a list, 352, 353
simulating recursive calls, 365
using FORMAT statements, 370
Field
descriptors, 367
Hollerith, 368
width in format codes, 368
Format, 367–370
fields, 367–369
field descriptors, 367–369
specification, 369
statement, 367, 369
Function reference, 332
Goal of, designers, 309
Global variables, 312
accessing structure, 313
blank array, 314
declaration, 313, *see also* COMMON
sharing of, 328
GOTO statement, 320, 322
computed, 322, 325
Identifier
for temporary, without conflict with a programmer-written name, 357
rules of formation, 334
synonym, 334, *see also* EQUIVALENCE declaration, 334
IF statement, 187–189, 324, 374
Indefinite iteration, 325
Input/output, 366, 373
for pretty print, 366
machine dependence, 373
simplified, 323, 324, 341, 366
unit numbers, 369
Keywords, 322
Labels, 320
Library and predefined functions
COS, 332
equivalence of CHOP and INT, 333
FLOAT, 333
IFIX, 333
INT, 333
Lifetime of variables, 371
Linking program, 373
Parameters, reference type, 312
Preallocation of workspace, 312
Preprocessor, 374
Procedure, parameter, 352
reference, 332, *see also* CALL statement
Procedures, 312
separate compilability of, 372
Processing of nonnumeric data, 375
Program
structure, 309, 310
units, 309, 373
linking and relinking of, 373
Program examples
1966 Fortran, 321, 337, 344, 353, 355
1977 Fortran, 342, 345, 356
PRINT statement, 366
Recursive procedures
prohibition, 312
simulation, 312, 365
Reference parameters, 336
copying of references technique, 347

Semantics, 310
  contour diagrams for, 310
Separate compilability feature, 372
Statement(s)
  assignment, 323
  CALL, 332
  compound, 373
  conditional, 324, 341, 373
  CONTINUE, 326
  DO, 326, 327
  FORMAT, 367
  format free input/output, 323, 324, 341, 366
  GOTO, 320, 373
  IF, 324, 327
  IF THEN ELSE, 341
  input, 323
  labels, 320
  line layout, 320
    comment column, 320, 321
    continuation field, 320, 321
  mapped from flowchart counterparts, 321
  n-way branch, 325
  numbers, 320
  output, 324
  PRINT, 366
  RETURN, 329–331
  SAVE, 341
Storage
  allocation of, 338, 351, 370
  utilization, 370
Subprogram examples, 329–331
Subscripts, allowable range for, 322, 341
Syntax, 319
  BNF definitions, 319
    of terminal symbols, 320
    summary for 1966 Fortran, 323–334
Terminal symbols, 320
Type, specification, 320
  explicit versus implicit, 320, 372
  integer, 320
  real, 320
Types, default, 372
Variable names, 334, *see also* identifier
Variable(s)
  global, 312
    declaration, 313
  lifetimes, 371
  temporary, with special names, 357
  type, 320
1966 Standard, 308
  function procedure constraint, 353
  syntax summary, 323–334
1977 Standard, 309, 340, 341
Four coloring
  algorithm, 180
    input data, 597
    connection matrix and table, 597
    as a tree search, 597
Four color problem, 597
Function
  exercise for converting from a procedure, 99
  procedures, 93
  value returned, 113
  values, 56

Global variable, 42
Greatest common
  divisor, GCD exercise, 83
  factor, GCF exercise, 85

High-level language, 2

Indefinite iteration, 9, 18
Infix expression, 52, 53
Information sharing, 56
Input, output, 18, 19, 20
Instruction pointer, ip, 35, 50
ip. *see* instruction pointer
(ip, ep) pair, 35
Integer division exercise, 39, 77
Iteration
  box, 10
  definite, 10, 18
  indefinite, 9, 18
  variable, 11
Iterative algorithm for
  factorial, 124
  Fibonacci series, 165

Language preprocessors, 464
  similarities and differences, 2
  syntax
    Backus–Naur Form, 184
    charts, 189
    formal definition, 184
Least common multiple, LCM, exercise, 81
  using GCD procedure, 94
  using gcd function, 95
Legend, 16
  entry, 6
    corresponding declaration, 7
  for a flowchart, 4, 5, 12
  for a subflowchart, 30
  form, and corresponding contour cell form, 112
Legend entries for different types of parameters, 80
Library procedures, 22
Lisp, 3, 376
  AND predicate, 414, 454
  APPEND function, 415, 417
  Arguments
    evaluation before application, 392
    postponing evaluation with QUOTE, 392
  Arithmetic functions and predicates, 416
  Arithmetic operations, 416

Lisp (*continued*)
- Atom, 377
  - literal, 377
  - NIL, 378
  - numeric, 377, 389
  - table, 381
- Atomic symbol, 377
- ATOM predicate, 389, 414
- Basic functions, 385
  - ATOM, 389, 414
  - EQ, 389, 413, 414
  - CAR, 387, 414
  - CDR, 387, 414
  - CONS, 385, 414
- CAAR, 404, *see also* CAR and CDR chains, 387
- CAR, 387, 414
- CAR and CDR chains, 387
  - abbreviations for, 388
- CDAR, 404, *see also* CAR and CDR chains, 387
- CDR, 387, 414
- Case studies
  - case 1, APPEND
    - flowchart, 418
    - LISP program, 418
    - RLISP program, 418
    - snapshot sequence, 419–422
  - case 2, REVERSE
    - computer display in RLISP, 430
    - LISP program, 423
    - RLISP program, 423
    - snapshot sequence, 424–429
  - case 3, use of funargs
    - Part 1, MAPCAR, 434
      - RLISP program, 434
      - snapshot sequence, 435–410
    - Part 2, USEY, 441
      - RLISP program, 441
      - snapshot sequence, 442, 443
  - case 4, symbolic differentiation
    - flowcharts
      - collect, 458
      - differentiate, 444
      - simplify, 453
        - plus, 455
        - times, 457
    - LISP program, 446
    - RLISP program, 447, 454, 456, 457, 459
    - sample input and output, 447, 448, 449, 451
    - simplification rules, 448
      - by pattern match, 450, 452
- Command, 394
- Conditional expression, 400, 411
- COND, 411
- CONS, 385, 414
  - applied to quoted atoms, 393
- Contour cell for a procedure parameter, 431
- Contour cells, shorthand notation, 407
- Contours, nesting of, 397
- Data objects, 377
- Dotted pair, 377
- Empty list symbol, 378
- EQ predicate, 389, 413, 414
- EQUAL predicate, 413, 414, 453
- EVAL function, 457
  - use of a second argument for, 463
- Exercises
  - copy a list of atoms, 412
  - determine if two lists of atoms are equal, 413
  - determine equality of two S-expressions, 413
  - determine membership in a list of atoms, 413
  - form a list of pairs, 412
  - processing character strings with pattern match, 461
  - remove an atom from a list, 413
  - reverse a list (REVERSE), 429
  - reverse a list (SUPERREVERSE), 429
- FIRST, 387, *see also* CAR
- Funarg, 431
  - placement of its contour, 432
    - case where, is critical, 441
  - use of, 433
- Function applied to argument, 392
- Function arguments, 431, *see also* funarg
- FUNCTION function, 431
  - proper use of, 434
- Garbage collection, 384
- HEAD, 387, *see also* CAR
- HEAP, 381
  - cell, 381
  - treelike arrangement of, cells, 382
- Interaction, 395
- Interactive run, 395
- Interpreter, 394
- LENGTH function, 417, 434
- LISP, 398
  - BNF syntax, 410, 412
  - COND, 411
  - conditional expression, 411
  - DEFINE function, 411
  - procedure definition, 411, 412
    - lambda expressions for, 411
  - program examples, *see* Lisp case studies
- LISP 1.5, 410, *see also* LISP, 398
- Lists, 378
  - empty, symbol, 378
  - convention for mapping, into S-expressions, 378
  - correspondence, with dotted pair notation, 379
  - generalized, 398, 399
  - linked, 381
- LIST function, 414, 423
- MEMBER predicate, 415
- Name parameter simulation, 461
- NIL
  - as a list terminator, 378
  - atom, 378
  - S-expression, 378
- NULL predicate, 399, 414
- Number representation, 417
- NUMBERP predicate, 416, 453
- Numeric atoms, 377, 389, 454
- Pattern match with replacement, 460
- PLUS function, 416, 459
- Pointer to an S-expression, 384

Predefined functions, 414
Predicate, 388
  ATOM, 389
  EQ, 389
Prefix form of algebraic expressions, 444, 445
  equivalent S-expressions, 444
Prefix notation, 378
Primitive operations, 385
Procedure
  definitions, 396
    at one level, 397
  parameters, 431
  types of cells contained in, contours, 397
Program, 394
  environment for, 396
  schematic of, with BNF syntax, 396
QUOTE, 392
REST, 387, *see also* CDR
retval cell, nonnecessity for, 407
RETURN semantics, 406, 407
REVERSE function, 414
  case study, 422
  use in case study 3, 435
RLISP, 398
  BNF syntax, 398
  conditional expressions, 411
  procedure definition, 398, 411
  program examples, *see also* Lisp case studies
    LENGTH, 417
    LOOK, 401
      snapshot sequence, 402–406, 408–410
Spaces, 377
Storage
  allocation for S-expressions, 384
  management, 384
  structures, for lists, 381
Symbolic expression, 377, *see also* S-expression
S-expression, 381
  allocation of storage for, 384
  correspondence with binary trees, 379, 382
  multiple occurrences of same, in the HEAP, 390
  pointer to, 384
  storage structures for, 381
    two-compartment HEAP cells for, 381
Table look-up using LOOK procedure, 399
TAIL, 387, *see also* CDR
TIMES function, 416, 459
Top level, 406
Value parameters, 397
Variables, 384, 393
  sharing of structures in the HEAP for, 384
List
  sorting, exercise, 46, 73
  variable, 23
Local variable, 42
Loop body, 11

Manipulation of algebraic formulas, 376
Master computer, MC, 22
  state of, 50
Match of parameter and argument, 62, 63
Matrix sum, exercise, 74
MC, *see also* master computer
  rate of progress, 530
Multisequence algorithms, 519
Multisequencing
  asynchronous tasks, 520
  commands, 520
  coroutines, 520
  languages with, features, 520
  linguistic features to specify, 520
  semantic basis for, 520
  semantics explained with contour diagrams, 520

Name parameter, 101
  cell structure, 102
  contrasted with reference parameter, 106
  matched to expressions, 272
  matched to simple arguments, 104
Natural order tree search, 153
Null string, *see* empty string

Operating systems, 549

Parameter, 56, 59
  distinction between name and reference, 106
  mechanism, 56
  name, 101
  reference type, 62, 63
    achieving effect of, in actual computers, 67, 69
  standing for a procedure or function, 107
  value, 80
Parameter-argument
  matching, 62
    mechanisms, 66
Parameters in preference to globals, 67
Pascal's triangle, 151
Pascal, 3, 560
  Array type, 568
    subscript range specification, 568
  Assignment statement, 576, 584
  Block, 576
    compound statement form of, 576
  Case
    statement, 576, 586–587
    structure, 565
      selectors, 566
      tag field, 567
  Constant (**const**) definitions, 562
  Data
    management, 560
    structure declarations, 560
    structured, types, 563
  Declaration
    function, 595
    procedure, 594
    var, 561, 596

Pascal (*continued*)
Definitions
const, 562
type, 561, 596
Enumeration shorthand, 562
file type, 563
for statement, 577, 588–589, 591
forward keyword, 575
Function
call, 593
declaration, 595
if then and **if then else** statements, 576, 585, 586
Input/output, 580, 592–593
Linked lists, construction of, 571
Loop structures, 577, 588–591
new function, 571
nil keyword, 572
Parameter
function, 579
list syntax, 578–579
procedure, 579
specification, 577
variable (**var**), 577
Pointer
for use in representation of arbitrary graphs, 572
operations defined on pointers, 572
type, 570
↑ symbol for, 570
values, 570
automatic creation of, 571
pred function, 584
Primitive data types, 561
Principal difference from Algol, 561
Procedure
call, 576, 593
declaration, 594
heading syntax, 578–579
Program examples
Fibonacci series, 575
four-coloring algorithm, 597
flowcharts and legends, 600–602
program (in SEQUENTIAL PASCAL code), 603–607
snapshot, 608
Program structure, 572
nesting of procedure and function declarations, 574
syntax charts for description of, 573–574
Record structure, 563
common part of, 566
field selectors, 563
variant part of, 565
case structure for, 565
record type, 563
Reference parameter, 577
repeat until statement, 577, 590
Scope rules, 574
SEQUENTIAL PASCAL, 574
absence of goto's and labels, 576
chr and *ord* functions, 582
input/output, 580, 592–593
built-in procedures, 580
convention for representing unprintable characters, 582
new-line identifier, NL, 580
nesting restrictions, 574
syntactic summary, 584–596
univ prefix, 578
set type, 568
notation for empty set, 569
notation for subset, 569
operators, 569
Structured programming constructs, 576
Subrange, notation, 562
succ function, 584
Syntax, liberties taken by authors of this book, 561
Type
checking limitation, 579
conversion from/to char and integer, 582
type definition, 561
Typing
of a function, 578
strong, 578
Variable (**var**) declaration, 561
while statement, 577, 589
with statement, 564
nesting, 565
write-int procedure, 574
PL/I language, 3, 520, 560
Pointer
environment, ep, 35
instruction, ip, 35
Postfix
expression, 52, 53
exercise, 169
machines, 52
Prefix expression, 167
Prime factorization (exercise), 92, 93
Primitive actions of an underlying machine, 10
Private storage of the MC, 51
Procedure(s)
box, 19
call box, 27
call step, 27
explicit declaration of, 111
identifier, 26
interchangeability, 74
interfacing, 56
invocation, 35
parameter, 107
contour diagrams for, 109
flowchart illustrations, 108
matching argument for, 112
storage cell, 109
return step, 27
side effect, 74
Proc par, *see* procedure parameter
Protection of arguments, 77

Question-answering system, 376

Reader/Assigner, 22
Recursion, 122, 149
as a conceptual tool, 122

Recursive
  algorithm
    binomial coefficient, 150, 152
      snapshot sequences, 154–163
    climbing stairs, 122
    design of, 145
    determining membership, 147
    factorial, 124
      procedure definition, 125
      snapshot sequence, 129–136
    Fibonacci series, 165
    function procedure, 126
    prime factorization (exercise), 140–143
    summing elements of a list, 146
    symbolic differentiation, 170
      flowchart, 171
      rules for, 170
    tree, search, 177
      walk, 176
  definition of
    binary tree, 163
    strings, 163
    syntactical forms, 186
  function, GCDR (exercise), 139
    flowchart, 140
  process of differentiation, 170, 444
  structure of tree traversal, 175
Reference parameter, 62
  access to matching argument, 63
  mechanism
    chain of references, 67
    copy method, 67
    value/result, 71
ref par, *see* reference parameter
retlab, 54
  cell, 66
Return
  label, 35
    cell, 54, *see also retlab*
  step, 30
  value cell, *see also retval,* 240

Scratch pad of the MC, 51
Search, *see* tree search
Semantics, 2, 193, *see also entries under individual languages*
  mathematical vs. operational, 193
  of multisequencing, 520
Sequence, *see also* task
  spawned, 521
  spawner, 521
  spawning, as an act of resource allocation, 521
Sequences
  asynchronous relationship for, 522
  coroutine relationship for, 522
  creation of, 520
  hierarchical structure of, 521
  initiation and termination of, 521
Side effect prevention, 75–77
Simple variable, 23
SIMULA 67, language, 520, 541
SL5 language, 520, 541
Snapshot, 24, 36
Snobol, 464
  Alternation operator (|), 475
  ARB pattern component, 474
  Arithmetic operations, 472
  ARRAY
    data type, 513
    function, 512
      second argument for, 513
  Arrays, 512
    allocation and initialization, 513
  Assignment
    conditional, 480
    operator, =, 473
    statement, 473
      input and output as, 474
    success or failure of, 480
  ATOM predicate, 507
  BAL (balanced pattern component), 492, 496
  Blank character, symbol "□", 465
    in column 1, 472
    permissible, 472
  Capture
    clause, 477
    of unknowns, 477
    variable, 468
  CODE data type, 503
  Comment line, 476
  Constants, 472
  Continuation field, 471
  Control field, 471, 472
    for transferring to data of type CODE, 503, 504
      syntax for, 503
  Conversion between strings and numbers, 472
  CONVERT function, 502–504
  DATA function, 505
  Data type(s)
    conversion, 502
      from STRING to CODE, 503, 504
    creating instances of new, 505
    defining and using new, 505
    TABLE, 464
    user-defined, 464
  DATATYPE function, 503, 505
  DEFINE function, 483
  Distinctive features, 464
  EQL predicate, 507
  EVAL function, 501
  Exercises
    Fortran preprocessor, 517, 518
    simulating a Lisp interpreter, 509–512
  Expressions, 472
  Fields of a statement, 471
  FRETURN pseudolabel, 482
  Function call as a means of controlling a branch, 480
  HEAP, 480, 481
    cell, 480
  IDENT function, 479

Snobol (*continued*)
Label, 471
  END, 471, 476
  field, 471
Labels, distinctness requirement for, 489
LEN function, 474
Pattern
  list element unknown, component, 468
  with unknown components, 468
Pattern component, 469
  balanced unknown, 492, 496, *see also* BAL
  unknown, of length n, 469, 474
    of arbitrary length, 469, 474
Pattern match, 464, 466, 474
  box, 466
  success and failure of, 474
  with capture of unknowns, 477
  with replacement, 466, 467
  with unknowns of arbitrary length, 468
Period as continuation indicator, 471
Pointer, to a HEAP cell, 480
Predefined functions, 479
Procedure
  call, 479
    semantics, 482
    success or failure of, 479
    syntax, 482
  contours, placement of, 488
  declaration, 482
    placement of, body, 483
    skeleton, 482
    syntax, 482
  entry, 485
  return, 486
    success or failure signals, 486
Program examples
  palindrome tester, 484, 487
  symbolic differentiation, 495, 496
  text processing, 478
Program structure, 471
Pseudolabel, 482
Reference parameters, simulation of, 499
  indirect, operator, $, 500
Replacement, arrow, ⇐, 466
  operator, 474
RETURN pseudolabel, 482
Semantics of procedure call and return,
    similarity with Lisp, 489
Simulating Lisp, 507
SNOBOL 4 version, 464
Spaces, 479, *see also* blank character symbol
  significance of, 479
Statement field, 471, 472
  assignment, 473
  pattern match, 474
  procedure call, 479
Storage structures, 480
String(s)
  concatenation, 465, 472
  empty or null, 465
  expression, fully parenthesized, 489
  uniqueness in storage, 480
String processing, 464
  flowcharts for, 465
Symbolic differentiation case study, 489
  call tree, 497
  flowcharts and legends, 490, 492–495
  input and output, 491, 496, 498
  program, 495, 496
  rules, 490
  use of TRACE, 491
Syntax, 471
  absence of variable declarations, 471
  BNF, 473
Table(s), 512
  access by pattern matching, 512
  represented as arrays, 515
    retrieving from, 515
  represented as strings, 513
    retrieving from, 514
TABLE, data type, 514
  function, 516
TRACE function, 491
Variable
  cells, allocation of, as needed, 471
  dynamic association of type for a, 482
  null string initial value of, 475
  storage structures for, 480
$ Symbol for indirect referencing, 500
Stack, 51
  computers, 52
  empty, 54
  end marker, 54
  notation, 266
  of the MC, 53
State of the MC, 50
  transition diagram, 548
Stepwise decomposition, 16
Storage cells
  invented names for, 90, 357
  recycling, 30
Storage environments, 30
String, 145, 146
  array declaration, 549
  definition, 163
  empty, 145
  processing, *see* Snobol string
Structured programming, 7
Subalgorithm, 26
Subflowchart, 27
Subprogram, 26
Subroutine, 26
Subtree, 16
SUPERREVERSE procedure, 429, 434
Symbolic
  computation, 376
  data, 376
  differentiation, 170, 444, 464, 489
Syntax, *see also* entries under individual
    languages
  and semantics, 193
  BNF, 206
  charts, 189–191
  definitions of familiar forms, 186–189
  rule, 184

Task
  allocation, 523
  coordination, 523
  deletion of a spawned, 523
  relative speed of a, 523
Time-sharing, 521
Towers of Hanoi (exercise), 183
Trace
  of an algorithm, 21
  of a computation, 54
Tree, 16
  binary, 162
  of calls, *see* call tree
  root node, 16
  search
    natural order, 153
    notation and methods, 153
    of a tree with arbitrary structure, 173
    procedure, 177
  terminal node, 16
  traversal, algorithm converted to a tree search algorithm, 175
    natural order, 153, 169
    procedures for, 173–176
    recursive structure, 175
Treewalk (exercise), 179–181
Val par, *see* value parameter
Value parameter
  specification mechanism, 80
  treatment, 80
Variables, 12, 22, *see also* entries under individual languages
  dummy, 59
  global, 40
    and local in a procedure environment, 56
  globally accessible, 42
  list, 23
  local, 40, 42
    and global, summary, 45
    to a procedure, 43
  simple, 23
Virtual
  MC, 521
  processor, 521

While box, 9

A
B 8
C 9
D 0
E 1
F 2
G 3
H 4
I 5
J 6